A History of Western Society

Ninth Edition

A History of Western Society

Since 1300

John P. McKay
University of Illinois at Urbana-Champaign

Bennett D. Hill
Late of Georgetown University

John Buckler
University of Illinois at Urbana-Champaign

Clare Haru Crowston
University of Illinois at Urbana-Champaign

Merry E. Wiesner-Hanks
University of Wisconsin–Milwaukee

HOUGHTON MIFFLIN COMPANY
Boston   New York

Publisher: Suzanne Jeans
Senior Sponsoring Editor: Nancy Blaine
Senior Marketing Manager: Katherine Bates
Development Editor: Melissa Mashburn
Senior Project Editor: Christina Horn
Art and Design Manager: Jill Haber
Cover Design Director: Tony Saizon
Senior Photo Editor: Jennifer Meyer Dare
Composition Buyer: Chuck Dutton
Editorial Associate: Adrienne Zicht
Marketing Assistant: Lauren Bussard
Editorial Assistant: Carrie Parker

Since 1300 cover image: *Juan de Pareja,* 1650, by Diego Velázquez (1599–1660). The Metropolitan Museum of Art/Bridgeman Art Library.

Copyright © 2008 by Houghton Mifflin Company. All rights reserved.

No part of this work may be reproduced or transmitted in any form or by any means, electronic or mechanical, including photocopying and recording, or by any information storage or retrieval system without the prior written permission of Houghton Mifflin Company unless such copying is expressly permitted by federal copyright law. Address inquiries to College Permissions, Houghton Mifflin Company, 222 Berkeley Street, Boston, MA 02116-3764.

Printed in the U.S.A.

Library of Congress Control Number: 2007927730

ISBN-13: 978-0-618-94607-5
ISBN-10: 0-618-94607-1

123456789-VH-11 10 09 08 07

In Memoriam

Bennett David Hill
1934 – 2005

Bennett Hill, who authored many of the chapters in earlier editions of this book, was born in Baltimore, Maryland, the son of African American Catholics. When Bennett was ten, the family moved north to Philadelphia, where his father worked for the U.S. Postal Service and his mother for the Veterans Administration. Bennett attended public schools, and his intellectual prowess was soon evident. He won a scholarship to Princeton University, where he received an excellent education that he always treasured. Majoring in history and graduating cum laude, Bennett was a trailblazer—one of the first African Americans to receive an undergraduate degree from Princeton. He subsequently earned a doctorate in European history at Princeton, joined the history department of the University of Illinois at Urbana-Champaign, and later served as department chair. Bennett was a popular but demanding teacher with a passion for medieval social history. His colleagues at Illinois remember especially his keen intellect, elegant taste, literary flair, and quick, sometimes mischievous wit. (He once persuaded some of his students that he followed medieval tradition and trimmed his front lawn with sheep rather than a lawn mower.) Establishing a scholarly reputation as a leading expert on medieval monasticism, Bennett heeded a spiritual call in midlife and became a Benedictine monk and ordained priest at St. Anselm's Abbey in Washington, D.C. He often served Mass at the parish church of his grandparents in Baltimore. Yet Bennett never lost his passion for European and world history, teaching regularly as a visiting professor at Georgetown University. An indefatigable worker with insatiable curiosity, he viewed each new edition as an exciting learning opportunity. At the time of his sudden and unexpected death in February 2005 he was working on a world history of slavery, which grew out of his research and reflected his proud heritage and intensely ethical concerns. A complex and many-sided individual, Bennett was a wonderful conversationalist, an inspiring human being, and the beloved brother and uncle of a large extended family. His sudden passing has been a wrenching loss for all who knew him.

About the Authors

John P. McKay Born in St. Louis, John P. McKay received his B.A. from Wesleyan University (1961), his M.A. from the Fletcher School of Law and Diplomacy (1962), and his Ph.D. from the University of California, Berkeley (1968). He began teaching history at the University of Illinois in 1966 and became a Professor there in 1976. John won the Herbert Baxter Adams Prize for his book *Pioneers for Profit: Foreign Entrepreneurship and Russian Industrialization, 1885–1913* (1970). He has also written *Tramways and Trolleys: The Rise of Urban Mass Transport in Europe* (1976) and has translated Jules Michelet's *The People* (1973). His research has been supported by fellowships from the Ford Foundation, the Guggenheim Foundation, the National Endowment for the Humanities, and IREX. He has written well over a hundred articles, book chapters, and reviews, which have appeared in numerous publications, including *The American Historical Review, Business History Review, The Journal of Economic History,* and *Slavic Review.* He contributed extensively to C. Stewart and P. Fritzsche, eds., *Imagining the Twentieth Century* (1997).

Bennett D. Hill A native of Philadelphia, Bennett D. Hill earned an A.B. from Princeton (1956) and advanced degrees from Harvard (A.M., 1958) and Princeton (Ph.D., 1963). He taught history at the University of Illinois, where he was department chair from 1978 to 1981. He published *English Cistercian Monasteries and Their Patrons in the Twelfth Century* (1968), *Church and State in the Middle Ages* (1970), and articles in *Analecta Cisterciensia, The New Catholic Encyclopaedia, The American Benedictine Review,* and *The Dictionary of the Middle Ages.* His reviews appeared in *The American Historical Review, Speculum, The Historian,* the *Journal of World History,* and *Library Journal.* He was one of the contributing editors to *The Encyclopedia of World History* (2001). He was a Fellow of the American Council of Learned Societies and served on the editorial board of *The American Benedictine Review,* on committees of the National Endowment for the Humanities, and as vice president of the American Catholic Historical Association (1995–1996). A Benedictine monk of St. Anselm's Abbey in Washington, D.C., he was also a Visiting Professor at Georgetown University.

John Buckler Born in Louisville, Kentucky, John Buckler received his Ph.D. from Harvard University in 1973. In 1980 Harvard University Press published his *Theban Hegemony, 371–362 B.C.* He published *Philip II and the Sacred War* (Leiden, 1989) and also edited *BOIOTIKA: Vorträge vom 5. Internationalen Böotien-Kolloquium* (Munich, 1989). In 2003 he published *Aegean Greece in the Fourth Century B.C.* In the following year appeared his editions of W. M. Leake, *Travels in the Morea* (three volumes), and Leake's *Peloponnesiaca.* Cambridge University Press published his *Central Greece and the Politics of Power in the Fourth Century*, edited by Hans Beck, in 2007.

Clare Haru Crowston Born in Cambridge, Massachusetts, and raised in Toronto, Clare Haru Crowston received her B.A. in 1985 from McGill University and her Ph.D. in 1996 from Cornell University. Since 1996, she has taught at the University of Illinois, where she has served as associate chair and Director of Graduate Studies, and is currently Associate Professor of history. She is the author of *Fabricating Women: The Seamstresses of Old Regime France, 1675–1791* (Duke University Press, 2001), which won two awards, the Berkshire Prize and the Hagley Prize. She edited two special issues of the *Journal of Women's History* (vol. 18, nos. 3 and 4) and has published numerous articles and reviews in journals such as *Annales: Histoire, Sciences Sociales, French Historical Studies, Gender and History,* and the *Journal of Economic History.* Her research has been supported with grants from the National Endowment for the Humanities, the Mellon Foundation, and the Bourse Châteaubriand of the French government. She is a past president of the Society for French Historical Studies and a former chair of the Pinkney Prize Committee.

Merry E. Wiesner-Hanks Having grown up in Minneapolis, Merry E. Wiesner-Hanks received her B.A. from Grinnell College in 1973 (as well as an honorary doctorate some years later), and her Ph.D. from the University of Wisconsin–Madison in 1979. She taught first at Augustana College in Illinois, and since 1985 at the University of Wisconsin–Milwaukee, where she is currently UWM Distinguished Professor in the department of history. She is the co-editor of the *Sixteenth Century Journal* and the author or editor of nineteen books and many articles that have appeared in English, German, Italian, Spanish, and Chinese. These include *Early Modern Europe, 1450–1789* (Cambridge, 2006), *Women and Gender in Early Modern Europe* (Cambridge, 3d ed., 2008), and *Gender in History* (Blackwell, 2001). She currently serves as the Chief Reader for Advanced Placement World History and has also written a number of source books for use in the college classroom, including *Discovering the Western Past* (Houghton Mifflin, 6th ed., 2007) and *Discovering the Global Past* (Houghton Mifflin, 3d ed., 2006), and a book for young adults, *An Age of Voyages, 1350–1600* (Oxford, 2005).

Brief Contents

Chapter 12	The Crisis of the Later Middle Ages, 1300–1450	371
Chapter 13	European Society in the Age of the Renaissance, 1350–1550	407
Chapter 14	Reformations and Religious Wars, 1500–1600	445
Chapter 15	European Exploration and Conquest, 1450–1650	483
Chapter 16	Absolutism and Constitutionalism in Western Europe, ca 1589–1715	523
Chapter 17	Absolutism in Central and Eastern Europe to 1740	559
Chapter 18	Toward a New Worldview, 1540–1789	589
Chapter 19	The Expansion of Europe in the Eighteenth Century	621
Chapter 20	The Changing Life of the People	653
Chapter 21	The Revolution in Politics, 1775–1815	683
Chapter 22	The Revolution in Energy and Industry, ca 1780–1860	717
Chapter 23	Ideologies and Upheavals, 1815–1850	747
Chapter 24	Life in the Emerging Urban Society in the Nineteenth Century	779
Chapter 25	The Age of Nationalism, 1850–1914	815
Chapter 26	The West and the World, 1815–1914	847
Chapter 27	The Great Break: War and Revolution, 1914–1919	879
Chapter 28	The Age of Anxiety, ca 1900–1940	913
Chapter 29	Dictatorships and the Second World War, 1919–1945	945
Chapter 30	Cold War Conflicts and Social Transformations, 1945–1985	981
Chapter 31	Revolution, Rebuilding, and New Challenges: 1985 to the Present	1019

Contents

Maps	xvii
Listening to the Past	xviii
Preface	xix

Chapter 12
The Crisis of the Later Middle Ages, 1300–1450 — 371

Prelude to Disaster	**371**
Climate Change and Famine	371
Government Ineptitude	373
The Black Death	**374**
Pathology	374
Spread of the Disease	375
Mapping the Past Map 12.1: The Course of the Black Death in Fourteenth-Century Europe	376
Care	377
Social, Economic, and Cultural Consequences	378
The Hundred Years' War	**381**
Causes	381
The Popular Response	382
The Course of the War to 1419	383
Joan of Arc and France's Victory	385
Costs and Consequences	385
Challenges to the Church	**387**
The Babylonian Captivity and Great Schism	387
The Conciliar Movement	388
Lay Piety and Mysticism	389
INDIVIDUALS IN SOCIETY Jan Hus	391
Economic and Social Change	**390**
Peasant Revolts	390
Urban Conflicts	392
Sex in the City	393
Fur-Collar Crime	396
Ethnic Tensions and Restrictions	397
Literacy and Vernacular Literature	399
Chapter Summary	401
Key Terms	402
Suggested Reading	402
Notes	403
LISTENING TO THE PAST Christine de Pizan	404

Chapter 13
European Society in the Age of the Renaissance, 1350–1550 — 407

Economic and Political Developments	**408**
Commercial Developments	408
Communes and Republics	409
The Balance of Power Among the Italian City-States	410
Intellectual Change	**412**
Humanism	412
Education	414
Political Thought	415
Secular Spirit	416
Christian Humanism	416
The Printed Word	418
Mapping the Past Map 13.2: The Growth of Printing in Europe	420
Art and the Artist	**421**
Art and Power	421
Subjects and Style	422
Patronage and Creativity	425
INDIVIDUALS IN SOCIETY Leonardo da Vinci	427
Social Hierarchies	**428**
Race	429
Class	431
Gender	432
Politics and the State in the Renaissance (ca 1450–1521)	**434**
France	434
England	435
Spain	436
Chapter Summary	439
Key Terms	440

Suggested Reading	440
Notes	441
LISTENING TO THE PAST *An Age of Gold*	442

Chapter 14
Reformations and Religious Wars, 1500–1600 — 445

The Early Reformation	445
The Christian Church in the Early Sixteenth Century	446
Martin Luther	446
Protestant Thought	449
The Appeal of Protestant Ideas	450
The Radical Reformation	451
The German Peasants' War	454
The Reformation and Marriage	455
• **Images in Society** *Art in the Reformation*	452
The Reformation and German Politics	457
The Rise of the Habsburg Dynasty	457
The Political Impact of the Protestant Reformation	458
The Spread of the Protestant Reformation	459
The Reformation in England and Ireland	461
Calvinism	463
The Establishment of the Church of Scotland	465
The Reformation in Eastern Europe	465
The Catholic Reformation	466
Mapping the Past *Map 14.2: Religious Divisions in Europe*	468
The Reformed Papacy	467
The Council of Trent	467
New Religious Orders	469
INDIVIDUALS IN SOCIETY *Teresa of Ávila*	471
Religious Violence	472
French Religious Wars	472
The Netherlands Under Charles V	473
The Great European Witch-Hunt	475
Chapter Summary	478
Key Terms	479
Suggested Reading	479
Notes	479
LISTENING TO THE PAST *Martin Luther, On Christian Liberty*	480

Chapter 15
European Exploration and Conquest, 1450–1650 — 483

World Contacts Before Columbus	483
The Trading World of the Indian Ocean	484
Africa	485
The Ottoman and Persian Empires	488
Genoese and Venetian Middlemen	490
The European Voyages of Discovery	492
Causes of European Expansion	492
Technological Stimuli to Exploration	493
The Portuguese Overseas Empire	495
Mapping the Past *Map 15.2: Overseas Exploration and Conquest, Fifteenth and Sixteenth Centuries*	496
The Problem of Christopher Columbus	498
Later Explorers	500
New World Conquest	501
Europe and the World After Columbus	504
Spanish Settlement and Indigenous Population Decline	504
Sugar and Slavery	505
The Columbian Exchange	508
Silver and the Economic Effects of Spain's Discoveries	509
The Birth of the Global Economy	510
Spain's Global Empire	511
INDIVIDUALS IN SOCIETY *Juan de Pareja*	507
Changing Attitudes and Beliefs	513
New Ideas About Race	513
Michel de Montaigne and Cultural Curiosity	514
Elizabethan and Jacobean Literature	514
Chapter Summary	516
Key Terms	517
Suggested Reading	517
Notes	520
LISTENING TO THE PAST *Columbus Describes His First Voyage*	518

Chapter 16
Absolutism and Constitutionalism in Western Europe, ca 1589–1715 — 523

Seventeenth-Century Crisis and Rebuilding	523
Economic and Demographic Crisis	524

Seventeenth-Century State-Building:
Common Obstacles and Achievements 525
Warfare and the Growth of Army Size 526
Popular Political Action 527

Absolutism in France and Spain 528
The Foundations of Absolutism: Henry IV,
Sully, and Richelieu 528
Louis XIV and Absolutism 530
Financial and Economic Management
Under Louis XIV: Colbert 532
Louis XIV's Wars 533
The Decline of Absolutist Spain in the
Seventeenth Century 534

Mapping the Past   Map 16.2: Europe in 1715 536
Colonial Administration 538

The Culture of Absolutism 539
Baroque Art and Music 539
Court Culture 540
French Classicism 541

Constitutionalism 542
Absolutist Claims in England (1603–1649) 543
Religious Divides 544
Puritanical Absolutism in England:
Cromwell and the Protectorate 546
The Restoration of the English Monarchy 547
The Triumph of England's Parliament:
Constitutional Monarchy and Cabinet
Government 548
The Dutch Republic in the Seventeenth
Century 549

INDIVIDUALS IN SOCIETY   Glückel of Hameln 551
Chapter Summary 553
Key Terms 554
Suggested Reading 554
Notes 555

LISTENING TO THE PAST   The Court at Versailles 556

Chapter 17
Absolutism in Central and Eastern Europe to 1740 559

Warfare and Social Change in Central and Eastern Europe 559
Origins of Serfdom 560
The Consolidation of Serfdom 560
The Thirty Years' War 562
Consequences of the Thirty Years' War 563

The Rise of Austria and Prussia 565
The Austrian Habsburgs 565
Austrian Rule in Hungary 566
Prussia in the Seventeenth Century 567
The Consolidation of Prussian Absolutism 571

• **Images in Society**   Absolutist Palace Building 568

The Development of Russia and the Ottoman Empire 572
The Mongol Yoke and the Rise of Moscow 572

Mapping the Past   Map 17.3: The Expansion of Russia to 1725 573
Tsar and People to 1689 574
The Reforms of Peter the Great 576
The Growth of St. Petersburg 578
The Growth of the Ottoman Empire 580
Religious Diversity in the Ottoman Empire 584

INDIVIDUALS IN SOCIETY   Hürrem 583

Chapter Summary 584
Key Terms 585
Suggested Reading 585
Notes 585

LISTENING TO THE PAST   A Foreign Traveler in Russia 586

Chapter 18
Toward a New Worldview, 1540–1789 589

The Scientific Revolution 590
Scientific Thought in 1500 590
The Copernican Hypothesis 591
From Brahe to Galileo 592
Newton's Synthesis 594
Causes of the Scientific Revolution 595
Science and Society 597

The Enlightenment 598
The Emergence of the Enlightenment 598
The Philosophes and the Public 600
The Enlightenment Outside of France 603
Urban Culture and the Public Sphere 603
Late Enlightenment 607
Race and the Enlightenment 608

The Enlightenment and Absolutism 609
Frederick the Great of Prussia 609
Catherine the Great of Russia 610
The Austrian Habsburgs 613

Mapping the Past *Map 18.1: The Partition of Poland and Russia's Expansion, 1772–1795* 614
    Evaluating "Enlightened Absolutism" 615

INDIVIDUALS IN SOCIETY *Moses Mendelssohn and the Jewish Enlightenment* 611

Chapter Summary 616
Key Terms 617
Suggested Reading 617
Notes 617

LISTENING TO THE PAST *Voltaire on Religion* 618

Chapter 19
The Expansion of Europe in the Eighteenth Century 621

Agriculture and the Land 622
    The Open-Field System 622
    The Agricultural Revolution 622
    The Leadership of the Low Countries and England 624

The Beginning of the Population Explosion 625
    Limitations on Population Growth 626
    The New Pattern of the Eighteenth Century 627

Cottage Industry and Urban Guilds 628
    The Putting-Out System 629

Mapping the Past *Map 19.1: Industry and Population in Eighteenth-Century Europe* 630
    The Textile Industry 631
    Urban Guilds 631
    The Industrious Revolution 633

Building the Global Economy 634
    Mercantilism and Colonial Wars 634
    Land and Labor in British America 640
    The Atlantic Slave Trade 641
    Revival in Colonial Latin America 643
    Trade and Empire in Asia 644
    Adam Smith and Economic Liberalism 647

• **Images in Society** *London: The Remaking of a Great City* 638

INDIVIDUALS IN SOCIETY *Olaudah Equiano* 645

Chapter Summary 648
Key Terms 649
Suggested Reading 649
Notes 649

LISTENING TO THE PAST *The Debate over the Guilds* 650

Chapter 20
The Changing Life of the People 653

Marriage and the Family 653
    Late Marriage and Nuclear Families 653
    Work Away from Home 654
    Premarital Sex and Community Controls 656
    New Patterns of Marriage and Illegitimacy 656

Children and Education 658
    Child Care and Nursing 658
    Foundlings and Infanticide 659
    Attitudes Toward Children 660
    Schools and Popular Literature 661

Mapping the Past *Map 20.1: Literacy in France on the Eve of the French Revolution* 662

Food, Medicine, and New Consumption Habits 663
    Diets and Nutrition 664
    Toward a Consumer Society 665
    Medical Practitioners 667

INDIVIDUALS IN SOCIETY *Madame du Coudray, the Nation's Midwife* 669

Religion and Popular Culture 671
    The Institutional Church 671
    Protestant Revival 672
    Catholic Piety 674
    Leisure and Recreation 675

Chapter Summary 676
Key Terms 677
Suggested Reading 677
Notes 680

LISTENING TO THE PAST *A Day in the Life of Paris* 678

Chapter 21
The Revolution in Politics, 1775–1815 683

Background to Revolution 683
    Legal Orders and Social Change 684
    The Crisis of Political Legitimacy 685
    The Impact of the American Revolution 687
    Financial Crisis 688

Revolution in Metropole and Colony, 1789–1791 689
    The Formation of the National Assembly 689

Contents

The Revolt of the Poor and the Oppressed	690
A Limited Monarchy	691
Revolutionary Aspirations in Saint-Domingue	693

World War and Republican France, 1791–1799 — 694
- Foreign Reactions and the Beginning of War — 694
- The Second Revolution — 696
- Total War and the Terror — 697
- Revolution in Saint-Domingue — 700
- The Thermidorian Reaction and the Directory, 1794–1799 — 702

The Napoleonic Era, 1799–1815 — 703
- Napoleon's Rule of France — 703
- Napoleon's Expansion in Europe — 705
- The War of Haitian Independence — 707
- The Grand Empire and Its End — 708

INDIVIDUALS IN SOCIETY *Toussaint L'Ouverture* — 709

Mapping the Past *Map 21.2: Napoleonic Europe in 1810* — 710

Chapter Summary — 712
Key Terms — 713
Suggested Reading — 713
Notes — 713

LISTENING TO THE PAST *Revolution and Women's Rights* — 714

Chapter 22
The Revolution in Energy and Industry, ca 1780–1860 — 717

The Industrial Revolution in Britain — 718
- Eighteenth-Century Origins — 718
- The First Factories — 719
- The Problem of Energy — 721
- The Steam Engine Breakthrough — 721
- The Coming of the Railroads — 723
- Industry and Population — 725

Industrialization in Continental Europe — 727
- National Variations — 727
- The Challenge of Industrialization — 728

Mapping the Past *Map 22.3: Continental Industrialization, ca 1850* — 729
- Agents of Industrialization — 730
- Government Support and Corporate Banking — 730

Relations Between Capital and Labor — 732
- The New Class of Factory Owners — 732
- The New Factory Workers — 734
- Conditions of Work — 736
- The Sexual Division of Labor — 738
- The Early Labor Movement in Britain — 740

INDIVIDUALS IN SOCIETY *The Strutt Family* — 735

Chapter Summary — 741
Key Terms — 742
Suggested Reading — 742
Notes — 742

LISTENING TO THE PAST *The Testimony of Young Mine Workers* — 744

Chapter 23
Ideologies and Upheavals, 1815–1850 — 747

Mapping the Past *Map 23.1: Europe in 1815* — 748

The Peace Settlement — 749
- The European Balance of Power — 749
- Intervention and Repression — 751
- Metternich and Conservatism — 751

Radical Ideas and Early Socialism — 753
- Liberalism — 753
- Nationalism — 754
- French Utopian Socialism — 756
- The Birth of Marxian Socialism — 757

The Romantic Movement — 758
- Romanticism's Tenets — 758
- Literature — 758
- Art and Music — 760

Reforms and Revolutions — 761
- National Liberation in Greece — 761
- Liberal Reform in Great Britain — 763
- Ireland and the Great Famine — 766
- The Revolution of 1830 in France — 767

The Revolutions of 1848 — 768
- A Democratic Republic in France — 770
- The Austrian Empire in 1848 — 772
- Prussia and the Frankfurt Assembly — 773

INDIVIDUALS IN SOCIETY *Jules Michelet* — 769

Chapter Summary — 774
Key Terms — 775
Suggested Reading — 775
Notes — 775

LISTENING TO THE PAST *Speaking for the Czech Nation*	776

Chapter 24
Life in the Emerging Urban Society in the Nineteenth Century — 779

Taming the City	779
Industry and the Growth of Cities	780

Mapping the Past Map 24.1: European Cities of 100,000 or More, 1800 and 1900	780
Public Health and the Bacterial Revolution	781
Urban Planning and Public Transportation	784

Rich and Poor and Those in Between	786
Social Structure	786
The Middle Classes	788
Middle-Class Culture	789
The Working Classes	790
Working-Class Leisure and Religion	795

• Images in Society *Class and Gender Boundaries in Women's Fashion, 1850–1914*	792

The Changing Family	797
Premarital Sex and Marriage	797
Prostitution	798
Kinship Ties	799
Gender Roles and Family Life	799
Child Rearing	802

INDIVIDUALS IN SOCIETY *Franziska Tiburtius*	801

Science and Thought	804
The Triumph of Science	804
Social Science and Evolution	805
Realism in Literature	807
Chapter Summary	810
Key Terms	810
Suggested Reading	810
Notes	811

LISTENING TO THE PAST *Middle-Class Youth and Sexuality*	812

Chapter 25
The Age of Nationalism, 1850–1914 — 815

Napoleon III in France	815
The Second Republic and Louis Napoleon	816
Napoleon III's Second Empire	817

Nation Building in Italy and Germany	818
Italy to 1850	818
Cavour and Garibaldi in Italy	818
Germany Before Bismarck	821
Bismarck and the Austro-Prussian War, 1866	821
The Taming of the Parliament	822

Mapping the Past Map 25.2: The Unification of Germany, 1866–1871	823
The Franco-Prussian War, 1870–1871	824

Nation Building in the United States	825

The Modernization of Russia and the Ottoman Empire	826
The "Great Reforms"	827
The Revolution of 1905	828
Decline and Reform in the Ottoman Empire	829

The Responsive National State, 1871–1914	831
General Trends	831
The German Empire	832
Republican France	833
Great Britain and Ireland	835
The Austro-Hungarian Empire	836
Jewish Emancipation and Modern Anti-Semitism	837

Marxism and the Socialist Movement	838
The Socialist International	838
Unions and Revisionism	840

INDIVIDUALS IN SOCIETY *Theodor Herzl*	839
Chapter Summary	842
Key Terms	843
Suggested Reading	843
Notes	843

LISTENING TO THE PAST *The Making of a Socialist*	844

Chapter 26
The West and the World, 1815–1914 — 847

Industrialization and the World Economy	847
The Rise of Global Inequality	848
The World Market	849
The Opening of China and Japan	850
Western Penetration of Egypt	853

The Great Migration	854
The Pressure of Population	855
European Migrants	856
Asian Migrants	858

Western Imperialism, 1880–1914	859
The Scramble for Africa	859

Mapping the Past   *Map 26.2: The Partition of Africa*   860

Imperialism in Asia	865
Causes of the New Imperialism	865
A "Civilizing Mission"	867
Critics of Imperialism	867

INDIVIDUALS IN SOCIETY   *Cecil Rhodes*   863

Responding to Western Imperialism	868
The Pattern of Response	868
Empire in India	868
The Example of Japan	870
Toward Revolution in China	872
Chapter Summary	*874*
Key Terms	*874*
Suggested Reading	*874*
Notes	*875*

LISTENING TO THE PAST   *A British Woman in India*   876

Chapter 27
The Great Break: War and Revolution, 1914–1919   879

The First World War	879
The Bismarckian System of Alliances	880
The Rival Blocs	881
The Outbreak of War	883
Reflections on the Origins of the War	884
Stalemate and Slaughter	887
The Widening War	888
The Home Front	890
Mobilizing for Total War	890
The Social Impact	892
Growing Political Tensions	894

INDIVIDUALS IN SOCIETY   *Vera Brittain*   893

The Russian Revolution	895
The Fall of Imperial Russia	895
The Provisional Government	896
Lenin and the Bolshevik Revolution	896
Trotsky and the Seizure of Power	898
Dictatorship and Civil War	899
The Peace Settlement	901
The End of the War	901
Revolution in Germany	901
The Treaty of Versailles	902
The Peace Settlement in the Middle East	903

Mapping the Past   *Map 27.4: Shattered Empires and Territorial Changes After World War I*   904

American Rejection of the Versailles Treaty	907
Chapter Summary	*908*
Key Terms	*909*
Suggested Reading	*909*
Notes	*909*

LISTENING TO THE PAST   *Arab Political Aspirations in 1919*   910

Chapter 28
The Age of Anxiety, ca 1900–1940   913

Uncertainty in Modern Thought	913
The "Cruelly Injured Mind"	913
Modern Philosophy	915
The Revival of Christianity	917
The New Physics	917
Freudian Psychology	919
Twentieth-Century Literature	920
Modern Art and Music	921
Architecture and Design	921
Modern Painting	922
Modern Music	926

• **Images in Society**   *Pablo Picasso and Modern Art*   924

Movies and Radio	926
The Search for Peace and Political Stability	928
Germany and the Western Powers	928
Hope in Foreign Affairs, 1924–1929	930
Hope in Democratic Government	930

INDIVIDUALS IN SOCIETY   *Gustav Stresemann*   931

The Great Depression, 1929–1939	933
The Economic Crisis	933

Mapping the Past   *Map 28.1: The Great Depression in the United States, Britain, and Europe*   934

Mass Unemployment	935
The New Deal in the United States	936
The Scandinavian Response to the Depression	937
Recovery and Reform in Britain and France	938

Chapter Summary	940
Key Terms	940
Suggested Reading	940
Notes	941

LISTENING TO THE PAST *Life on the Dole in Great Britain* — 942

Chapter 29
Dictatorships and the Second World War, 1919–1945 — 945

Authoritarian States	946
Conservative Authoritarianism	946
Radical Totalitarian Dictatorships	946
Stalin's Soviet Union	949
From Lenin to Stalin	949
The Five-Year Plans	950
Life and Culture in Soviet Society	952
Stalinist Terror and the Great Purges	954
Mussolini and Fascism in Italy	955
The Seizure of Power	955
The Regime in Action	956
Hitler and Nazism in Germany	957
The Roots of Nazism	957
Hitler's Road to Power	958
The Nazi State and Society	960
Hitler's Popularity	961
Aggression and Appeasement, 1933–1939	962
The Second World War	966
Hitler's Empire, 1939–1942	966
The Holocaust	967

Mapping the Past *Map 29.2: World War II in Europe* — 968

Japan's Empire in Asia	970
The Grand Alliance	972
The War in Europe, 1942–1945	973
The War in the Pacific, 1942–1945	974

INDIVIDUALS IN SOCIETY *Primo Levi* — 971

Chapter Summary	975
Key Terms	976
Suggested Reading	976
Notes	977

LISTENING TO THE PAST *Stalin Justifies the Five-Year Plan* — 978

Chapter 30
Cold War Conflicts and Social Transformations, 1945–1985 — 981

The Division of Europe	981
The Origins of the Cold War	982
West Versus East	983
The Western Renaissance, 1945–1968	985
The Postwar Challenge	985

Mapping the Past *Map 30.2: European Alliance Systems, 1949–1989* — 988

Toward European Unity	989
Decolonization in East Asia	989
Decolonization in the Middle East and Africa	992
America's Civil Rights Revolution	994
Soviet Eastern Europe, 1945–1968	995
Stalin's Last Years, 1945–1953	995
Reform and De-Stalinization, 1953–1964	996
The End of Reform	997
The Soviet Union to 1985	998
Postwar Social Transformations, 1945–1968	999
Science and Technology	999
The Changing Class Structure	1000
New Roles for Women	1002
Youth and the Counterculture	1004
Conflict and Challenge in the Late Cold War, 1968–1985	1006
The United States and Vietnam	1006
Détente or Cold War?	1008
The Women's Movement	1009
The Troubled Economy	1010
Society in a Time of Economic Uncertainty	1011

INDIVIDUALS IN SOCIETY *Margaret Thatcher* — 1013

Chapter Summary	1014
Key Terms	1015
Suggested Reading	1015
Notes	1015

LISTENING TO THE PAST *A Feminist Critique of Marriage* — 1016

Chapter 31
Revolution, Rebuilding, and New Challenges: 1985 to the Present — 1019

The Decline of Communism in Eastern Europe	1020

Solidarity in Poland	1020
Gorbachev's Reforms in the Soviet Union	1022

The Revolutions of 1989   1024

The Collapse of Communism in Eastern Europe	1025
The Disintegration of the Soviet Union	1026
German Unification and the End of the Cold War	1028
The Gulf War of 1991	1030

Building a New Europe in the 1990s   1030

Common Patterns and Problems	1031
Recasting Russia	1033
Progress in Eastern Europe	1035

Mapping the Past   *Map 31.3: Contemporary Europe*   *1036*

Tragedy in Yugoslavia	1037
Unity and Identity in Western Europe	1039

New Challenges in the Twenty-first Century   1041

The Prospect of Population Decline	1041
The Growth of Immigration	1042
Promoting Human Rights	1044

The West and the Islamic World   1045

The al-Qaeda Attack of September 11, 2001	1045
The War in Iraq	1047
The West and Its Muslim Citizens	1048

INDIVIDUALS IN SOCIETY   *Tariq Ramadan*   *1051*

The Future in Perspective   1050

Chapter Summary	*1053*
Key Terms	*1053*
Suggested Reading	*1053*
Notes	*1056*

LISTENING TO THE PAST   *The French Riots: Will They Change Anything?*   *1054*

Index   I-1

Maps

• Mapping the Past

12.1 •	The Course of the Black Death in Fourteenth-Century Europe	376
12.2	English Holdings in France During the Hundred Years' War	384
12.3	Fourteenth-Century Peasant Revolts	392
13.1	The Italian City-States, ca 1494	411
13.2 •	The Growth of Printing in Europe	420
13.3	Spain in 1492	437
14.1	The Global Empire of Charles V	460
14.2 •	Religious Divisions in Europe	468
14.3	The Netherlands, 1559–1609	474
15.1	The Afro-Eurasian Trading World Before Columbus	486
15.2 •	Overseas Exploration and Conquest, Fifteenth and Sixteenth Centuries	496
15.3	Seaborne Trading Empires in the Sixteenth and Seventeenth Centuries	506
16.1	The Acquisitions of Louis XIV, 1668–1713	533
16.2 •	Europe in 1715	536
16.3	Seventeenth-Century Dutch Commerce	552
17.1	Europe After the Thirty Years' War	564
17.2	The Growth of Austria and Brandenburg-Prussia to 1748	570
17.3 •	The Expansion of Russia to 1725	573
17.4	The Ottoman Empire at Its Height, 1566	581
18.1 •	The Partition of Poland and Russia's Expansion, 1772–1795	614
19.1 •	Industry and Population in Eighteenth-Century Europe	630
19.2	The Atlantic Economy in 1701	636
19.3	European Claims in North America Before and After the Seven Years' War	637
20.1 •	Literacy in France on the Eve of the French Revolution	662
21.1	The Haitian Revolution	701
21.2 •	Napoleonic Europe in 1810	710
22.1	Cottage Industry and Transportation in Eighteenth-Century England	718
22.2	The Industrial Revolution in England, ca 1850	725
22.3 •	Continental Industrialization, ca 1850	729
23.1 •	Europe in 1815	748
23.2	Peoples of the Habsburg Monarchy, 1815	752
24.1 •	European Cities of 100,000 or More, 1800 and 1900	780
24.2	The Modernization of Paris, ca 1850–1870	784
25.1	The Unification of Italy, 1859–1870	819
25.2 •	The Unification of Germany, 1866–1871	823
25.3	Slavery in the United States, 1860	826
26.1	European Investment to 1914	851
26.2 •	The Partition of Africa	860
26.3	Asia in 1914	864
27.1	The Balkans After the Congress of Berlin, 1878	884
27.2	The Balkans in 1914	884
27.3	The First World War in Europe	886
27.4 •	Shattered Empires and Territorial Changes After World War I	904
27.5	The Partition of the Ottoman Empire, 1914–1923	906
28.1 •	The Great Depression in the United States, Britain, and Europe	934
29.1	The Growth of Nazi Germany, 1933–1939	963
29.2 •	World War II in Europe	968
29.3	World War II in the Pacific	972
30.1	The Results of World War II in Europe	986
30.2 •	European Alliance Systems, 1949–1989	988
30.3	The New States in Africa and Asia	990
31.1	Democratic Movements in Eastern Europe, 1989	1024
31.2	Russia and the Successor States	1029
31.3 •	Contemporary Europe	1036
31.4	The Ethnic Composition of Yugoslavia, 1991	1038

Listening to the Past

Chapter 12	Christine de Pizan	404
Chapter 13	An Age of Gold	442
Chapter 14	Martin Luther, *On Christian Liberty*	480
Chapter 15	Columbus Describes His First Voyage	518
Chapter 16	The Court at Versailles	556
Chapter 17	A Foreign Traveler in Russia	586
Chapter 18	Voltaire on Religion	618
Chapter 19	The Debate over the Guilds	650
Chapter 20	A Day in the Life of Paris	678
Chapter 21	Revolution and Women's Rights	714
Chapter 22	The Testimony of Young Mine Workers	744
Chapter 23	Speaking for the Czech Nation	776
Chapter 24	Middle-Class Youth and Sexuality	812
Chapter 25	The Making of a Socialist	844
Chapter 26	A British Woman in India	876
Chapter 27	Arab Political Aspirations in 1919	910
Chapter 28	Life on the Dole in Great Britain	942
Chapter 29	Stalin Justifies the Five-Year Plan	978
Chapter 30	A Feminist Critique of Marriage	1016
Chapter 31	The French Riots: Will They Change Anything?	1054

Preface

A History of Western Society grew out of the authors' desire to infuse new life into the study of Western Civilization. We knew that historians were using imaginative questions and innovative research to open up vast new areas of historical interest and knowledge. We also recognized that these advances had dramatically affected the subject of European economic, intellectual, and, especially, social history, while new research and fresh interpretations were also revitalizing the study of the traditional mainstream of political, diplomatic, and religious developments. Despite history's vitality as a discipline, however, it seemed to us at the time that both the broad public and the intelligentsia were generally losing interest in the past. That, fortunately for us all, has not proven the case.

It was our conviction, based on considerable experience introducing large numbers of students to the broad sweep of Western Civilization, that a book in which social history was the core element could excite readers and inspire a renewed interest in history. Our strategy was thus twofold. First, we incorporated recent research by social historians as we sought to re-create the life of ordinary people in appealing human terms. At the same time, we were determined to give great economic, political, cultural, and intellectual developments the attention they unquestionably deserve. We wanted to give individual readers and instructors a balanced, integrated perspective so that they could pursue—on their own or in the classroom—those themes and questions that they found particularly exciting and significant. In an effort to realize fully the potential of our fresh yet balanced approach, we made many changes, large and small, in the editions that followed.

Changes in the Ninth Edition

In preparing the Ninth Edition we have worked hard to keep our book up-to-date by including as much valuable and relevant new scholarship as possible. We have also strengthened our distinctive yet balanced approach to a wide range of topics. In addition, we have revised the layout of the chapters somewhat to foreground the historical questions posed and answered in each chapter, and added a new map feature. This edition includes the best of previous editions, while blending in the most important recent findings.

Conceptual and Content Revisions

Several main lines of revision have guided our many changes. In particular, we have approached the history of the West as part of the history of the world and have devoted more space to Europe's interactions with the rest of the world. This has meant that some parts of the book have been completely reconceptualized and reorganized, as have many of the sections within chapters. Chapter 15 is now entirely devoted to European exploration, discovery, and conquest and also includes coverage of world contacts before Columbus. Chapter 7 includes fuller discussion of Central Asian steppe peoples; Chapter 19 includes discussion of European trade with Asia; and Chapter 20 incorporates extended coverage of the impact of colonial products, including sugar, tea, coffee, and tobacco. Chapter 21 has considerable new material on the Haitian revolution; Chapter 29 includes more on World War II outside of Europe; and Chapter 30 has more on decolonization in the Middle East and Africa.

A second major change is updated discussion of gender throughout the text. The development of women's and gender history has been a central part of the expansion of historical knowledge over the last several decades, and this edition includes even fuller discussion of the role of gender in shaping human experience than did previous editions. Some of this new material focuses on women, including expanded discussion of women in medieval monasticism (Chapter 10), women's role in the court culture of early modern Europe (Chapter 16), and women's work in the Industrial Revolution (Chapter 22). Some new text focuses explicitly on norms and patterns of masculinity, including those of classical Athens and Sparta (Chapter 3) and medieval knightly culture (Chapter 10). Other sections ask readers to consider the ways in which gender is related to other social hierarchies, such as social status and race (Chapters 1, 13, and 30), or ways in which religious or intellectual concepts are gendered (Chapters 2 and 16). New scholarship on gender has meant revisions in other sections as well, including discussion of the Roman family, the Reformation, the witch-hunts, the scientific revolution, nineteenth-century cities, and cold war Europe. The discussion of gender is accompanied by updates to the material on sexuality in many chapters, as this is a field of scholarship growing very rapidly.

These two major lines of revision are accompanied by continued enhancement of content that began in earlier editions. The social history focus that has been the core element of this book since its first edition continues, with more material on Roman family life (Chapter 5), popular religious practices (Chapters 10, 11, and 20), and the consumer revolution (Chapter 20), to cite just a few examples. In addition to more material on Europe in a global perspective, we have continued to incorporate more discussion of groups and regions that are frequently shortchanged in the general histories of Europe and Western Civilization. This expanded scope reflects the renewed awareness within the profession of Europe's enormous historical diversity, as well as the efforts of contemporary Europeans to understand the ambivalent and contested meanings of their national, regional, ethnic, and pan-European identities. Examples of this enlarged scope include more discussion of the Celts and Huns (Chapter 7), more on the Vikings and Magyars in eastern Europe (Chapter 8), and more material on Scandinavia in several chapters. Chapter 10 has been reconceptualized from a unit that focuses solely on Christians to one that explores Muslim and Jewish as well as Christian popular religion, and it includes discussions of similarities and differences among these three groups. The history of Jews in Europe is incorporated into a number of chapters as well. Several chapters examine notions of race during times of significant cultural change, including the Renaissance (Chapter 13), the first wave of colonization (Chapter 15), the Enlightenment (Chapter 18), and nineteenth-century urban society (Chapter 24).

An important part of this continued broader focus is material on Islam. Chapter 8 now begins with the development of Islam and includes comprehensive discussion of Muslim Spain. Chapter 9 maintains the discussion of the Arab influence in medieval Sicily highlighted in previous editions. Chapters 17, 25, and 27 all include significant new material on the Ottoman Empire. Several of the new features focus on Muslims living in Europe, as well as issues involving Christian-Muslim relations.

We believe that including examples of problems of historical interpretations in our text helps our readers develop the critical-thinking skills that are among the most precious benefits of studying history. Examples of this more open-ended, interpretive approach include a discussion of the importance of the Lost Gospels (Chapter 6), disagreements about the pathology of the Black Death (Chapter 12), debates about the impact of Enlightenment thought (Chapter 18), and renewed debate on personal and collective responsibility for the Holocaust (Chapter 29).

Concern with terminology is key to new ways in which history is being studied, researched, and presented, and among the historiographical issues we present are some that ask readers to consider the implications of words they (and historians) use regularly without thinking much about them. This includes a consideration of what we mean by "the West" (Chapter 1), discussion of the terms "Middle Ages" (Chapter 8), "Renaissance," and "modern" (Chapter 13), and disputes about who was and was not part of "the nation" (Chapter 25) or included in understandings of "Europe" (Chapter 31).

This edition includes several major changes in the organization of chapters. Chapter 7 now focuses explicitly on late antiquity, taking into account the exciting new scholarship on this period of transition. Chapter 9 brings together material on political developments in the High Middle Ages previously in several chapters, and Chapter 11 focuses on medieval urban life and culture. Chapter 14 now includes material on the Reformations, religious wars, and witch-hunts, while, as noted above, Chapter 15 now focuses on exploration and overseas expansion.

New Pedagogical Features

To help focus and guide the reader, we pose specific historical questions keyed to the main chapter headings at the beginning of each chapter. These questions are then answered in the course of each chapter and repeated in an end-of-chapter summary that concisely reiterates the chapter's findings. For this edition, many of the questions have been reframed, and the chapter summaries rewritten, to maximize the usefulness of this popular pedagogical device. Dates have been added to most chapter titles.

This edition also adds a new feature, "Mapping the Past." Historians have long relied on maps to help explain the stories that they tell, but we have found that students often do not pay as much attention to the maps as they should. Thus in the new "Mapping the Past" feature, one map in each chapter includes questions for discussion. Some of these questions refer only to a single map, while others encourage students to compare different maps in order to trace processes over time.

Distinctive Features

In addition to the new "Mapping the Past" feature, this edition continues to include distinctive features from earlier editions that guide the reader in the process of historical understanding.

Individuals in Society

Included in each chapter is the feature "Individuals in Society," which offers a brief study of a woman, man, or group, informing us about the societies in which they lived. Each study or biographical sketch has been carefully integrated into the body of the text. The "Individuals in Society" feature grew out of our long-standing focus on people's lives and the varieties of historical experience, and we believe that readers will empathize with these human beings as they themselves seek to define their own identities. The spotlighting of individuals, both famous and obscure, perpetuates the greater attention to cultural and intellectual developments that we used to invigorate our social history in earlier editions, and it reflects changing interests within the historical profession as well as the development of "micro-history."

The range of men and women we consider is broad. For this edition, and sometimes at readers' suggestion, we have dropped some individuals and replaced them with others who add their own contributions to history. Chapter 4 now focuses on the Greek mathematician Archimedes and the practical application of science. Chapter 10 looks at the German abbess and mystic Hildegard of Bingen and Chapter 11 at the Italian merchant Francesco Datini. In keeping with this edition's increasing attention to individuals from outside western Europe who had an impact on European developments, Chapter 17 looks at Hürrem, first the concubine and then the wife of Suleiman the Magnificent, and Chapter 21 at Toussaint L'Ouverture, leader of the revolution in the French colony of Saint-Domingue. Chapter 23 focuses on the French historian Jules Michelet, who viewed nationalism as a means of lessening social tensions, and Chapter 30 on Margaret Thatcher, the first woman to become prime minister in Britain. Chapter 31 focuses on Tariq Ramadan, the controversial European-Muslim intellectual. In addition to these new individuals, in some cases, such as Nefertiti (Chapter 1), Theodora (Chapter 7), and Leonardo da Vinci (Chapter 13), we have kept the same individuals, but completely rewritten the feature to bring it in line with current scholarship.

Listening to the Past

A two-page feature called "Listening to the Past" extends and illuminates a major historical issue considered in each of the text's chapters through the presentation of a source or small group of sources. In the new edition we have reviewed our selections and made judicious substitutions. Chapter 5 now focuses on a complex magic charm used during the Roman Empire and perhaps earlier to attract a lover. Chapter 11 again takes up the theme of love, exploring the courtly love tradition in medieval literature. Chapter 20 focuses on Louis Sebastien Mercier's comments on everyday life in eighteenth-century Paris, and Chapter 23 on the reflections of a Czech historian writing during the revolution of 1848. Chapter 27 features Arab protests regarding the establishment of the League of Nations mandates in the former Ottoman Empire and the establishment of a Jewish homeland in Palestine. Chapter 31 examines riots in the suburbs of Paris by French people of Arab descent in late 2005. As in the "Individuals in Society" feature, in addition to these brand-new sources, sources that appeared in previous editions have often been contextualized in new ways reflective of current scholarship.

Each primary source opens with a problem-setting introduction and closes with "Questions for Analysis" that invite students to evaluate the evidence as historians would. Drawn from a range of writings addressing a variety of social, cultural, political, and intellectual issues, these sources promote active involvement and critical interpretation. Selected for their interest and importance and carefully fitted into their historical context, these sources do indeed allow the student to "listen to the past" and to observe how history has been shaped by individual men and women, some of them great aristocrats, others ordinary folk.

Images in Society

This edition continues to include the photo essay "Images in Society." The complete text now contains eight essays, each consisting of a short narrative with questions, accompanied by several pictures. The goal of the feature is to encourage students to think critically: to view and compare visual illustrations and draw conclusions about the societies and cultures that produced those objects. Thus, in Chapter 1 appears the discovery of the "Iceman," the frozen remains of an unknown herdsman. "The Roman Villa at Chedworth" in Britain mirrors Roman provincial culture (Chapter 6). The essay "From Romanesque to Gothic" treats the architectural shift in medieval church building and aims to show how the Gothic cathedral reflected the ideals and values of medieval society (Chapter 11). "Art in the Reformation" (Chapter 14) examines both the Protestant and Catholic views of religious art. Chapter 17 presents the way monarchs displayed their authority visually in "Absolutist Palace Building." Moving to modern times, the focus in Chapter 19 changes to "London: The Remaking of a Great City," which depicts how Londoners rebuilt their city after a great catastrophe. "Class and Gender Boundaries in Women's Fashion, 1850–1914" studies women's clothing in relationship to women's evolving position in society and gender relations (Chapter 24). "Pablo Picasso and Modern Art" looks at some of Picasso's greatest paintings to gain insight into his principles and the modernist revolution in art (Chapter 28).

Additional Features

The illustrative component of our work has been carefully revised. We have added many new illustrations to our extensive art program, which includes more than four hundred color reproductions, letting great art and important events come alive. As in earlier editions, all illustrations have been carefully selected to complement the text, and all carry informative captions, based on thorough research, that enhance their value and have been revised for the current edition. Artwork remains an integral part of our book; the past can speak in pictures as well as in words. The use of full color serves to clarify the maps and graphs and to enrich the textual material. The maps and map captions have been updated to correlate directly to the text, and new maps, as well as the "Mapping the Past" feature, have been added.

Each chapter includes a chronology feature that lists major developments in the period discussed in the chapter. In addition, topic-specific timelines appear at key points throughout the book. Once again we provide a unified timeline at the end of the text. Comprehensive and easy to locate, this useful timeline allows students to compare developments over the centuries.

A list of Key Terms concludes each chapter. These terms are highlighted in boldface in the text. The student may use these terms to test his or her understanding of the chapter's material.

In addition to posing chapter-opening questions and presenting more problems in historical interpretation, we have quoted extensively from a wide variety of primary sources in the narrative, demonstrating in our use of these quotations how historians evaluate evidence. Thus primary sources are examined as an integral part of the narrative as well as presented in extended form in the "Listening to the Past" chapter feature. We believe that such an extensive program of both integrated and separate primary source excerpts will help readers learn to interpret and think critically.

Each chapter concludes with a carefully selected list of suggestions for further reading, revised and updated to keep them current with the vast amount of new work being done in many fields. These bibliographies are shorter than those in previous editions, as readers may now find more extensive suggestions for further reading on the website **college.hmco.com/history/west/mckay/western_society/9e/student_home.html**.

Throughout the text, icons direct students to online interactive maps and primary sources corresponding to discussions in the text and to the student and instructor websites.

Flexible Format

Western Civilization courses differ widely in chronological structure from one campus to another. To accommodate the various divisions of historical time into intervals for a two-quarter, three-quarter, or two-semester period, *A History of Western Society* is published in four versions, three of which embrace the complete work:

- One-volume hardcover edition
- Two-volume paperback: *Volume I: From Antiquity to the Enlightenment* (Chapters 1–17); *Volume II: From Absolutism to the Present* (Chapters 16–31)
- Three-volume paperback: *Volume A: From Antiquity to 1500* (Chapters 1–13); *Volume B: From the Renaissance to 1815* (Chapters 12–21); *Volume C: From the Revolutionary Era to the Present* (Chapters 21–31)
- *Since 1300* (Chapters 12–31), paperback for courses on Europe since the Renaissance

Note that overlapping chapters in both the two- and the three-volume sets permit still wider flexibility in matching the appropriate volume with the opening and closing dates of a course term.

Ancillaries

A wide array of supplements accompany this text to help students better master the material and to help instructors in teaching from the book:

- Student Website
- Instructor Website
- Online Instructor's Resource Manual
- HM Testing CD-ROM (powered by Diploma)
- Online Study Guide (powered by eCommerce)
- PowerPoint maps, images, and lecture outlines
- PowerPoint questions for personal response systems
- Blackboard™ and WebCT™ course cartridges
- Eduspace™ (powered by Blackboard™)
- Interactive ebook
- HistoryFinder

The *Student Website,* prepared by Leslie Kauffman, is a companion website for students that includes a wide range of material correlated to each book chapter such as learning objectives, chapter outlines, pre-class quizzes, interactive flashcards, chronological ordering exercises, primary sources, interactive map exercises, and ACE self-tests. Students can also find general text resources such as an online glossary, audio mp3 files of chapter summaries, and material on how to study more effectively. Throughout the text, icons direct students to relevant exercises and self-testing material located on the student website. Access the student website for this text by visiting **college.hmco.com/history/west/mckay/western_society/9e/student_home.html**.

The *Instructor Website* is a companion website for instructors. It features all of the material on the student website plus additional password-protected resources that help instructors teach the course, such as an electronic version of the *Instructor's Resource Manual* and *PowerPoint* slides. Access the instructor website for this text by visiting **college.hmco.com/history/west/mckay/western_society/9e/instructor_home.html**.

The *Instructor's Resource Manual,* prepared by John Reisbord, contains instructional objectives, chapter outlines, lecture suggestions, guidelines for using primary sources, classroom activities, map activities, audiovisual bibliographies, Internet resources, and suggested readings.

HM Testing (powered by *Diploma*) offers instructors a flexible and powerful tool for test generation and test management. Now supported by the Brownstone Research Group's market-leading *Diploma* software, this new version of *HM Testing* significantly improves on functionality and ease of use by offering all the tools needed to create, author, deliver, and customize multiple types of tests. *Diploma* is currently in use at thousands of college and university campuses throughout the United States and Canada. The *HM Testing* content for this text was developed by John Reisbord and offers key term identification, essay questions (with guidelines for how to effectively write the essay), multiple-choice questions (with page references to the correct responses), and map questions that refer to maps in the text, as well as a final exam.

The *Online Study Guide* (powered by *eCommerce*) offers students additional materials to aid their study and mastery of the text. The *Study Guide* content was developed by Carla Falkner of Northeast Mississippi Community College and offers learning objectives, chapter key points, review questions, major political ideas exercises, issues for essay and discussion, geography questions, map feature questions, and primary source analysis.

We are pleased to offer a collection of Western Civilization *PowerPoint* lecture outlines, maps, and images for use in classroom presentations. Detailed lecture outlines correspond to the book's chapters and make it easier for instructors to cover the major topics in class. The art collection includes all of the photos and maps in the text, as well as numerous other images from our Western Civilization titles. *PowerPoint* questions and answers for use with personal response system software are also offered to adopters free of charge.

A variety of assignable homework and testing material has been developed to work with the *Blackboard*™ and *WebCT*™ course management systems, as well as with *Eduspace*™: Houghton Mifflin's Online Learning Tool (powered by *Blackboard*™). *Eduspace*™ is a web-based online learning environment that provides instructors with a gradebook and communication capabilities, such as synchronous and asynchronous chats and announcement postings. It offers access to assignments such as over 650 gradable homework exercises, writing assignments, interactive maps with questions, primary sources, discussion questions for online discussion boards, and tests, which all come ready to use. Instructors can choose to use the content as is, modify it, or even add their own. *Eduspace*™ also contains an interactive ebook, which contains in-text links to interactive maps, primary sources, and audio pronunciation files, as well as review and self-testing material for students.

HistoryFinder, a new Houghton Mifflin technology initiative, helps instructors create rich and exciting classroom presentations. This online tool offers thousands of online resources, including art, photographs, maps, primary sources, multimedia content, Associated Press interactive modules, and ready-made *PowerPoint* slides. *HistoryFinder*'s assets can easily be searched by keyword, or browsed from pull-down menus of topic, media type, or by textbook. Instructors can then browse, preview, and download resources straight from the website.

Acknowledgments

It is a pleasure to thank the many instructors who read and critiqued the manuscript through its development:

Hugh Agnew
George Washington University

Melanie Bailey
Centenary College of Louisiana

Rachael Ball
Ohio State University

Eugene Boia
Cleveland State University

Robert Brown
State University of New York, Finger Lakes Community College

Richard Eichman
Sauk Valley Community College

David Fisher
Texas Technical University

Wayne Hanley
West Chester University of Pennsylvania

Michael Leggiere
Louisiana State University, Shreveport

John Mauer
Tri-County Technical College

Nick Miller
Boise State University

Wyatt Moulds
Jones County Junior College

Elsa Rapp
Montgomery County Community College

Anne Rodrick
Wofford College

Sonia Sorrell
Pepperdine University

Lee Shai Weissbach
University of Louisville

Special thanks also go to Dr. Todd A. Beach, Advanced Placement History teacher at Eastview High School in Apple Valley, Minnesota, for his work on the DBQ appendix of the Advanced Placement Edition of this text.

It is also a pleasure to thank our many editors at Houghton Mifflin for their efforts over many years. To Christina Horn, who guided production, and to Tonya Lobato and Melissa Mashburn, our development editors, we express our special appreciation. And we thank Carole Frohlich for her contributions in photo research and selection.

Many of our colleagues at the University of Illinois and the University of Wisconsin–Milwaukee continue to provide information and stimulation, often without even knowing it. We thank them for it. John Buckler thanks Professor Jack Cargill for his advice on topics in Chapter 2. He also wishes to thank Professor Nicholas Yalouris, former General Inspector of Antiquities, for his kind permission to publish the mosaic from Elis, Greece, in Chapter 3. He is likewise grateful to Dr. Amy C. Smith, Curator of the Ure Museum of Archaeology of the University of Reading, for her permission to publish the vase on page 64. Sincerest thanks go also to Professor Paul Cartledge of Clare College, Cambridge University, for his kind permission to publish his photograph of the statue of Leonidas in Chapter 3. John McKay expresses his deep appreciation to Jo Ann McKay for her sharp-eyed editorial support and unfailing encouragement. For their invaluable comments and suggestions, Clare Crowston thanks the following individuals: Martin Bruegel, Antoinette Burton, Don Crummey, Max Edelson, Tara Fallon, Masumi Iriye, Craig Koslofsky, Janine Lanza, John Lynn, M. J. Maynes, Kathryn Oberdeck, Dana Rabin, and John Randolph. Merry Wiesner-Hanks would like to thank the many students over the years with whom she has used earlier editions of this book. Their reactions and opinions helped shape her revisions to this edition, and she hopes it remains worthy of the ultimate praise that they bestowed on it, that it's "not boring like most textbooks." She would, as always, also like to thank her husband, Neil, without whom work on this project would not be possible.

Each of us has benefited from the criticism of his or her coauthors, although each of us assumes responsibility for what he or she has written. John Buckler has written the first six chapters; Bennett Hill continued the narrative through Chapter 16; and John McKay has written Chapters 17 through 31. Beginning with this edition, Merry Wiesner-Hanks assumed primary responsibility for Chapters 7 through 14 and Clare Crowston assumed primary responsibility for Chapters 15 through 21. Finally, we continue to welcome the many comments and suggestions that have come from our readers, for they have helped us greatly in this ongoing endeavor.

J. P. M.   B. D. H.   J. B.   C. H. C.   M. E. W.

A History of Western Society

In this lavishly illustrated French chronicle, Wat Tyler, the leader of the English Peasant's Revolt, is stabbed during a meeting with the king. Tyler died soon afterward, and the revolt was ruthlessly crushed. *(Bibliothèque nationale de France)*

chapter 12

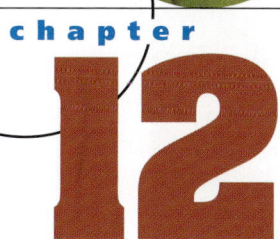

THE CRISIS OF THE LATER MIDDLE AGES, 1300–1450

chapter preview

Prelude to Disaster
• *What were the demographic and economic consequences of climate change?*

The Black Death
• *How did the spread of the plague shape European society?*

The Hundred Years' War
• *What were the causes of the Hundred Years' War, and how did the war affect European politics, economics, and cultural life?*

Challenges to the Church
• *What challenges faced the Christian church in the fourteenth century, and how did church leaders, intellectuals, and ordinary people respond?*

Economic and Social Change
• *How did economic and social tensions contribute to revolts, crime, violence, and a growing sense of ethnic and national distinctions?*

During the later Middle Ages, the last book of the New Testament, the Book of Revelation, inspired thousands of sermons and hundreds of religious tracts. The Book of Revelation deals with visions of the end of the world, with disease, war, famine, and death. It is no wonder this part of the Bible was so popular. Between 1300 and 1450 Europeans experienced a frightful series of shocks: climate change, economic dislocation, plague, war, social upheaval, and increased crime and violence. Death and preoccupation with death make the fourteenth century one of the most wrenching periods of Western civilization. Yet, in spite of the pessimism and crises, important institutions and cultural forms, including representative assemblies and national literatures, emerged. Even institutions that experienced severe crisis, such as the Christian church, saw new types of vitality.

Prelude to Disaster

In the first half of the fourteenth century, Europe experienced a series of climate changes that led to lower levels of food production, which had dramatic and disastrous ripple effects. Political leaders attempted to find solutions, but were unable to deal with the economic and social problems that resulted.

• *What were the demographic and economic consequences of climate change?*

Climate Change and Famine

The period from about 1000 to about 1300 saw warmer than usual climate in Europe, which underlay all the changes and vitality of the High Middle Ages. About 1300 the climate changed, becoming colder and wetter. Historical geographers refer to the period from 1300 to 1450 as a "little ice age," which they can trace through both natural and human records.

Online Study Center
This icon will direct you to interactive activities and study materials on the website **college.hmco.com/pic/mckaywest9e**

Death from Famine In this fifteenth-century painting, dead bodies lie in the middle of a path, while a funeral procession at the right includes a man with an adult's coffin and a woman with the coffin of an infant under her arm. People did not simply allow the dead to lie in the street in medieval Europe, though during famines and epidemics it was sometimes difficult to maintain normal burial procedures. *(Erich Lessing/Art Resource, NY)*

Evidence from nature emerges through the study of Alpine and polar glaciers, tree rings, and pollen left in bogs. Human-produced sources include written reports of rivers freezing and crops never ripening, as well as archaeological evidence such as the abandoned villages of Greenland, where ice floes cut off contact with the rest of the world and the harshening climate meant that the few hardy crops grown earlier could no longer survive. The Viking colony on Greenland died out completely, though Inuit people who relied on hunting sea mammals continued to live in the far north, as they had before the arrival of Viking colonists.

An unusual number of storms brought torrential rains, ruining the wheat, oat, and hay crops on which people and animals almost everywhere depended. Since long-distance transportation of food was expensive and difficult, most urban areas depended for bread and meat on areas no more than a day's journey away. Poor harvests—and one in four was likely to be poor—led to scarcity and starvation. Almost all of northern Europe suffered a "Great Famine" in the years 1315–1322, which contemporaries interpreted as a recurrence of the biblical "seven lean years" (Genesis 42). Even in non-famine years, the cost of grain, livestock, and dairy products rose sharply.

Reduced caloric intake meant increased susceptibility to disease, especially for infants, children, and the elderly. Workers on reduced diets had less energy, which in turn meant lower productivity, lower output, and higher grain prices. The Great Famine proved to be a demographic disaster in France; in Burgundy perhaps one-third of the population died. The many religious houses of Flanders experienced a high loss of monks, nuns, and priests. In Scandinavia and the Baltic countries, low cereal harvests, declines in meat and dairy production, economic recessions, and the lack of salt, used for preserving herring, resulted in terrible food shortages.

Hardly had western Europe begun to recover from this disaster when another struck: an epidemic of typhoid fever carried away thousands. In 1316, 10 percent of the population of the city of Ypres may have died between

May and October alone. Then in 1318 disease hit cattle and sheep, drastically reducing the herds and flocks. Another bad harvest in 1321 brought famine and death.

The province of Languedoc in France presents a classic example of agrarian crisis. For more than 150 years Languedoc had enjoyed continual land reclamation, steady agricultural expansion, and enormous population growth. Then the fourteenth century opened with four years of bad harvests. Torrential rains in 1310 ruined the harvest and brought on terrible famine. Harvests failed again in 1322 and 1329. In 1332 desperate peasants survived the winter on raw herbs. In the half century from 1302 to 1348, poor harvests occurred twenty times. These catastrophes had grave social consequences. Poor harvests and famine led to the abandonment of homesteads. In parts of the Low Countries and in the Scottish-English borderlands, entire villages were abandoned. This meant a great increase in the number of vagabonds, what we call "homeless people." In Flanders and East Anglia (eastern England), where aspects of the famine have been carefully analyzed, some peasants were forced to mortgage, sublease, or sell their holdings to get money to buy food. Rich farmers bought out their poorer neighbors. When conditions improved, debtors tried to get their lands back, leading to a very volatile land market. To reduce the labor supply and the mouths to feed in the countryside, young men and women sought work in the towns. Poor harvests probably meant that marriage had to be postponed. Later marriages and the deaths caused by famine and disease meant a reduction in population. Meanwhile, the international character of trade and commerce meant that a disaster in one country had serious implications elsewhere. For example, the infection that attacked English sheep in 1318 caused a sharp decline in wool exports in the following years. Without wool, Flemish weavers could not work, and thousands were laid off. Without woolen cloth, the businesses of Flemish, Hanseatic, and Italian merchants suffered. Unemployment encouraged people to turn to crime.

Government Ineptitude

To none of these problems did governments have effective solutions. The three sons of Philip the Fair who sat on the French throne between 1314 and 1328 condemned speculators, who held stocks of grain back until conditions were desperate and prices high; forbade the sale of grain abroad; and published legislation prohibiting fishing with traps that took large catches. These measures had few positive results. As the subsistence crisis deepened, popular discontent and paranoia increased.

Chronology

1309–1376	Babylonian Captivity; papacy in Avignon
1310–1320	Dante, *Divine Comedy*
1315–1322	Famine in northern Europe
1324	Marsiglio of Padua, *Defensor Pacis*
1337–1453	Hundred Years' War
1348	Black Death arrives in mainland Europe
1358	Jacquerie peasant uprising in France
1378	Ciompi revolt in Florence
1378–1417	Great Schism
1381	Peasants' Revolt in England
1387–1400	Chaucer, *Canterbury Tales*
1415	English smash the French at Agincourt
1429	French victory at Orléans; Charles VII crowned king
1431	Joan of Arc declared a heretic and burned at the stake

Starving people focused their anger on the rich, speculators, and the Jews, who were targeted as creditors fleecing the poor through pawnbroking. (Expelled from France in 1306, Jews were readmitted in 1315 and were granted the privilege of lending at high interest rates.) Rumors spread of a plot by Jews and their agents, the lepers, to kill Christians by poisoning the wells. Based on "evidence" collected by torture, many lepers and Jews were killed, beaten, or hit with heavy fines.

In England Edward I's incompetent son, Edward II (r. 1307–1327), used Parliament to set price controls, first on the sale of livestock after disease and poor lambing had driven prices up, and then on ale, which was made from barley (the severe rains of 1315 had contributed to molds and mildews, sharply reducing the crop). Baronial conflicts and wars with the Scots dominated Edward II's reign. Fearing food riots and violence, Edward condemned speculators, which proved easier than enforcing price controls. He did try to buy grain abroad, but yields in the Baltic were low; the French crown, as we have seen, forbade exports; and the grain shipped from Castile in northern Spain was grabbed by Scottish, English, and rogue Hanseatic pirates on the high seas. Such grain as reached southern English ports was stolen by looters and sold on the black market. The Crown's efforts at famine relief failed.

The Black Death

Royal attempts to provide food from abroad were unsuccessful, but they indicate the extent of long-distance shipping by the beginning of the fourteenth century. In 1291 Genoese sailors had opened the Strait of Gibraltar to Italian shipping by defeating the Moroccans. Then, shortly after 1300, important advances were made in the design of Italian merchant ships. A square rig was added to the mainmast, and ships began to carry three masts instead of just one. Additional sails better utilized wind power to propel the ship. The improved design permitted year-round shipping for the first time, and Venetian and Genoese merchant ships could sail the dangerous Atlantic coast even in the winter months.

Ships continually at sea carried all types of cargo, and they also carried vermin of all types, especially insects and rats, which often harbored disease pathogens. Rats, fleas, and cockroaches could live for months on the cargo carried along the coasts, disembarking at ports with the grain, cloth, or other merchandise. Just as modern air travel has allowed diseases such as AIDS and SARS to spread quickly over very long distances, medieval shipping did the same. The most frightful of these diseases first emerged in western Europe in 1347, carried on Genoese ships, a disease that was later called the **Black Death.**

- *How did the spread of the plague shape European society?*

Pathology

Most historians and almost all microbiologists identify the disease that spread in the fourteenth century as the bubonic plague, caused by the bacillus *Yersinia pestis.* The disease normally afflicts rats. Fleas living on the infected rats drink their blood; the bacteria that cause the plague multiply in the flea's gut; and the flea passes them on to the next rat it bites by throwing up into the bite. Usually the disease is limited to rats and other rodents, but at certain points in history—perhaps when most rats have been killed off—the fleas have jumped from their rodent hosts to humans and other animals. One of these times appears to have been in the Eastern Roman Empire in the sixth century, when a plague killed millions of people. Another was in China and India in the 1890s, when millions died. Doctors and epidemiologists closely studied this outbreak, identified the bacillus as bubonic plague, and learned about the exact cycle of infection for the first time.

The fourteenth-century outbreak showed many similarities to the nineteenth-century outbreak, but also some differences. There are no reports of massive rat die-offs in fourteenth-century records. The plague was often transmitted directly from one person to another through coughing and sneezing (what epidemiologists term *pneumonic* transmission) as well as through flea bites. The fourteenth-century outbreak spread much faster than the nineteenth-century outbreak and was much more deadly, killing as much as one-third of the population when it first spread to an area. These differences have led some historians to question whether the fourteenth-century disease was actually bubonic plague or whether it was some other disease, perhaps something like the Ebola virus. In the late 1990s French paleomicrobiologists studying the tooth pulp from bodies in two plague cemeteries found DNA from *Y. pestis,* a finding that has been viewed as convincing by most medical historians, though similar studies of English plague cemeteries have not yielded the same results.

These debates fuel continued study of medical aspects of the plague. Some scholars suggest that the type of fleas that normally live on humans might have also been agents in plague transmission in the fourteenth century (which would account for the lack of a rat die-off), or that the fourteenth-century strain of the disease might have been particularly deadly, or that improvements in sanitation and public health by the nineteenth century—even in poor countries such as India—might have limited the mortality rate significantly.

Though there is some disagreement about exactly what kind of disease the plague was, there is no dispute about its dreadful effects on the body. The classic symptom of the bubonic plague was a growth the size of a nut or an apple in the armpit, in the groin, or on the neck. This was the boil, or **bubo,** that gave the disease its name and caused agonizing pain. If the bubo was lanced and the pus thoroughly drained, the victim had a chance of recovery. The next stage was the appearance of black spots or blotches caused by bleeding under the skin. (This syndrome did not give the disease its common name; contemporaries did not call the plague the Black Death. Sometime in the fifteenth century, the Latin phrase *atra mors,* meaning "dreadful death," was translated as "black death," and the phrase stuck.) Finally, the victim began to cough violently and spit blood. This stage, indicating the presence of millions of bacilli in the

Procession of Saint Gregory According to the *Golden Legend*, a thirteenth-century collection of saints' lives, the bubonic plague ravaged Rome when Gregory I was elected pope (590–604). This fourteenth-century painting, produced at a time when plague was again striking Europe, shows Gregory leading a procession around the city as new victims fall (*center*). The artist shows everyone in fourteenth-century clothing and may have seen similar plague processions in his own city. *(Musée Condé, Chantilly/Art Resource, NY)*

bloodstream, signaled the end, and death followed in two or three days.

Spread of the Disease

Plague symptoms were first described in 1331 in southwestern China, part of the Mongol Empire. Plague-infested rats accompanied Mongol armies and merchant caravans carrying silk, spices, and gold across Central Asia in the 1330s. Then they stowed away on ships, carrying the disease to the ports of the Black Sea by the 1340s. Later stories told of more dramatic means of spreading the disease as well, reporting that Mongol armies besieging the city of Kaffa on the shores of the Black Sea catapulted plague-infected corpses over the walls to infect those inside. The city's residents dumped the corpses into the sea as fast as they could, but they were already infected.

In October 1347 Genoese ships brought the plague from Kaffa to Messina, from which it spread across Sicily. Venice and Genoa were hit in January 1348, and from the port of Pisa the disease spread south to Rome and east to Florence and all of Tuscany. By late spring southern Germany was attacked. Frightened French authorities chased a galley bearing the disease away from the port of Marseilles, but not before plague had infected the city, from which it spread to Languedoc and Spain. In June 1348 two ships entered the Bristol Channel and introduced it into England. All Europe felt the scourge of this horrible disease (see Map 12.1).

Although urban authorities from London to Paris to Rome had begun to try to achieve a primitive level of sanitation by the fourteenth century, urban conditions remained ideal for the spread of disease. Narrow streets filled with refuse and human excrement were as much cesspools as thoroughfares. Dead animals and sore-covered

Mapping the Past

MAP 12.1 The Course of the Black Death in Fourteenth-Century Europe Use the map and the information in the text to answer the following questions: ❶ How did the expansion of trade that resulted from the commercial revolution contribute to the spread of the Black Death? ❷ When did the plague reach Paris? Why do you think it got to Paris before it spread to the rest of northern France or to southern Germany? ❸ Which cities were spared? What might account for this? ❹ Which regions were spared? Would the reasons for this be the same as those for cities, or might other causes have been operating in rural areas?

Online Study Center **Improve Your Grade** Interactive Map: Bubonic Plague and Social Upheaval in Fourteenth-Century Europe

---

beggars greeted the traveler. Houses whose upper stories projected over the lower ones blocked light and air. And extreme overcrowding was commonplace. When all members of an aristocratic family lived and slept in one room, it should not be surprising that six or eight persons in a middle-class or poor household slept in one bed—if they had one. Closeness, after all, provided warmth. Houses were beginning to be constructed of brick, but many wood, clay, and mud houses remained. A determined rat had little trouble entering such a house.

Standards of personal hygiene remained frightfully low. True, most large cities had public bathhouses, but we have no way of knowing how frequently ordinary people used them. Lack of personal cleanliness, combined with any number of temporary ailments such as diarrhea and the common cold, weakened the body's resistance to serious disease. Fleas and body lice were universal afflictions: everyone from peasants to archbishops had them. One more bite did not cause much alarm. But if that nibble came from a bacillus-bearing flea, an entire household or area was doomed.

Mortality rates cannot be specified because population figures for the period before the arrival of the plague do not exist for most countries and cities. The largest amount of material survives for England, but it is difficult to use; after enormous scholarly controversy, only educated guesses can be made. Of a total English population of perhaps 4.2 million, probably 1.4 million died of the Black Death in its several visits. Densely populated Italian cities endured incredible losses. Florence lost between one-half and two-thirds of its 1347 population of 85,000 when the plague visited in 1348. The most widely accepted estimate for western Europe is that the plague killed about one-third of the population in the first wave of infection.

Nor did central and eastern Europe escape the ravages of the disease. Moving northward from the Balkans, eastward from France, and southward from the Baltic, the plague swept through the German Empire. In the Rhineland in 1349, Cologne and Mainz endured heavy losses. In 1348 it swept through Bavaria, entered the Moselle Valley, and pushed into northern Germany. One chronicler records that, in the summer and autumn of 1349, between five hundred and six hundred died every day in Vienna. Styria, in what today is central Austria, was very hard hit, with cattle straying unattended in the fields.

As the Black Death took its toll on the German Empire, waves of emigrants fled to Poland, Bohemia, and Hungary. The situation there was better, though disease was not completely absent. The plague seems to have entered Poland through the Baltic seaports and spread from there. Still, population losses were lower than elsewhere in Europe. The plague spread from Poland to Russia, reaching Pskov, Novgorod, and Moscow. No estimates have been made of population losses there or in the Balkans. In Serbia, though, the plague left vast tracts of land unattended, which prompted an increase in Albanian immigration to meet the labor shortage.

Across Europe the Black Death recurred intermittently from the 1360s to 1400. It reappeared with reduced virulence from time to time over the following centuries, making its last appearance in the French port city of Marseilles in 1721. Survivors became more prudent. Because periods of famine had caused malnutrition, making people vulnerable to disease, Europeans controlled population growth so that population did not outstrip food supply. Western Europeans improved navigation techniques and increased long-distance trade, which permitted the importation of grain from sparsely populated Baltic regions. They strictly enforced quarantine measures. They worked on the development of vaccines. But it was only in 1947, six centuries after the arrival of the plague in the West, that the American microbiologist Selman Waksman discovered an effective vaccine, streptomycin. Plague continues to infect rodent and human populations sporadically today.

Care

Fourteenth-century medical literature indicates that physicians could sometimes ease the pain, but they had no cure. Medical doctors observed that crowded cities had high death rates, especially when the weather was warm and moist. We understand that warm, moist conditions make it easier for germs, viruses, and bacteria to grow and spread, but fourteenth-century people—lay, scholarly, and medical—thought in terms of "poisons" in the air or "corrupted air" rather than germs. This "corrupted air" came from swamps, unburied animal or human corpses, too much rain, the position of planets or stars, or perhaps other causes. The poisons caused illness, which doctors thought of as an imbalance in the fluids in the body, especially blood. Certain symptoms of the plague, especially bleeding and vomiting, were believed to be the body's natural reaction to too much fluid. These were often symptoms of other illnesses as well, and doctors frequently prescribed bloodletting, that is, taking blood from the body by applying leeches or making small cuts in veins, as standard treatment.

If the plague came from poisoned air, people reasoned, then strong-smelling herbs or other substances, like rosemary, juniper, or sulfur, held in front of the nose or burned as incense might stop it. Perhaps loud sounds like ringing church bells or firing the newly invented cannon might help. Medicines made from plants that were bumpy or that oozed liquid might work, keeping the more dangerous swelling and oozing of the plague away. Because the plague seemed to strike randomly, perhaps wearing jewelry with random number and letter combinations, or drinking water in which ink used to write these magical combinations had been dissolved, would help. Such letter and number combinations, called *cryptograms,* were especially popular in Muslim areas. They were often the first letters of words in prayers or religious sayings, and they gave people a sense of order when faced with the randomness with which the plague seemed to strike.

The Italian writer Giovanni Boccaccio (1313–1375), describing the course of the disease in Florence in the preface to his book of tales, *The Decameron,* identified what many knew—that the disease passed from person to person:

> Moreover, the virulence of the pest was the greater by reason that intercourse was apt to convey it from the sick to the whole, just as fire devours things dry or greasy when they are brought close to it. Nay, the evil went yet further, for not merely by speech or association with the sick was the malady communicated to the healthy with consequent peril of common death, but any that touched the clothes of the sick or aught else that had been touched or used by them, seemed thereby to contract the disease.[1]

Online Study Center Improve Your Grade
Primary Source: The Plague Hits Florence

Wealthier people often fled cities for the countryside, though sometimes this simply spread the plague faster. Some cities tried shutting their gates to prevent infected people and animals from coming in, which worked in a few cities. They also walled up houses in which there was plague, trying to isolate those who were still healthy from the sick. When the disease struck the town of Salé in Morocco, Ibu Abu Madyan shut in the members of his household with sufficient food and water and allowed no one to enter or leave until the plague had passed. Abu Madyan was entirely successful.

Along with looking for medical causes and cures, people also searched for scapegoats, and savage cruelty sometimes resulted. Many people believed that the Jews had poisoned the wells of Christian communities and thereby infected the drinking water. This charge led to the murder of thousands of Jews across Europe. According to one chronicler, sixteen thousand were killed at the imperial city of Strasbourg alone in 1349. Though sixteen thousand is probably a typical medieval numerical exaggeration, the horror of the massacre is not lessened. Scholars have yet to explain the economic impact that the loss of so many productive people had on Strasbourg and other cities.

If medical science had no effective treatment, could victims' suffering be eased? Perhaps it could, in hospitals. What was the geographical distribution of hospitals, and, although our estimates of medieval populations remain rough, what was the hospital-to-population ratio? How many patients could a hospital serve? Whereas earlier the feudal lord had made philanthropic foundations, beginning in the thirteenth century individual merchants—out of compassion, generosity, and the custom of giving to parish collections, and in the belief that the sick would be prayerful intercessors with God for the donors' sins—endowed hospitals. Business people established hospitals in the towns of northern France and Flanders; Milan, Genoa, and Venice were well served, and the thirty hospitals in Florence provided a thousand beds in 1339. Sixty hospitals served Paris in 1328—but probably not enough for its population of two hundred thousand. The many hospitals in the Iberian Peninsula continued the Muslim tradition of care for the poor and ill. Merchants in the larger towns of the German Empire, in Poland, and in Hungary also founded hospitals in the fourteenth century, generally later than those in western Europe. Sailors, long viewed as potential carriers of disease, benefited from hospitals reserved for them; in 1300 the Venetian government paid a surgeon to care for sick sailors. At the time the plague erupted, therefore, most towns and cities had hospital facilities.

When trying to determine the number of people a hospital could accommodate, the modern researcher considers the number of beds, the size of the staff, and the building's physical layout. Since each medieval hospital bed might serve two or more patients, we cannot calculate the number of patients on the basis of the beds alone. We do know that rural hospices usually had twelve to fifteen beds, and city hospitals, as at Lisbon, Narbonne, and Genoa, had on average twenty-five to thirty beds, but these figures do not tell us how many patients were accommodated. Only the very rare document listing the number of wrapping sheets and coffins for the dead purchased in a given period provides the modern scholar with information on the number of patients a hospital had. Hospitals could offer only shelter, compassion, and care for the dying.

Many people did not see the plague as a medical issue, but instead interpreted it as the result of something within themselves. God must be punishing them for terrible sins, they thought, so the best remedies were religious ones: asking for forgiveness, praying, trusting in God, making donations to churches, and trying to live better lives. In Muslim areas, religious leaders urged virtuous living in the face of death: give to the poor, reconcile with your enemies, free your slaves, and say a proper goodbye to your friends and family.

Social, Economic, and Cultural Consequences

It is noteworthy that, in an age of mounting criticism of clerical wealth, the behavior of the clergy during the

Patients in a Hospital Ward, Fifteenth Century In many cities hospitals could not cope with the large numbers of plague victims. The practice of putting two or more adults in the same bed, as shown here, contributed to the spread of the disease. At the Hôtel-Dieu in Paris, nurses complained of being forced to put eight to ten children in a single bed in which a patient had recently died. *(Giraudon/The Bridgeman Art Library)*

plague was often exemplary. Priests, monks, and nuns cared for the sick and buried the dead. In places like Venice, from which even physicians fled, priests remained to give what ministrations they could. Consequently, their mortality rate was phenomenally high. The German clergy especially suffered a severe decline in personnel in the years after 1350.

In taking their pastoral responsibilities seriously, some clergy did things that the church in a later age would vigorously condemn. The institutional church has traditionally opposed letting laymen and, especially, laywomen administer the sacraments. But the shortage of priests was so great that in 1349 Ralph, bishop of Bath and Wells in England (1329–1363), advised his people that "if they are on the point of death and cannot secure the services of a priest, then they should make confession to each other, as is permitted in the teaching of the Apostles, whether to a layman or, if no man is present, even to a woman."[2]

Economic historians and demographers sharply dispute the impact of the plague on the economy in the late fourteenth century. The traditional view that the plague had a disastrous effect has been greatly modified. The clearest evidence comes from England, where the agrarian economy showed remarkable resilience. While the severity of the disease varied from region to region, it appears that by about 1375 most landlords enjoyed revenues near those of the pre-plague years. By the early fifteenth century seigneurial prosperity reached a medieval peak. Why? The answer appears to lie in the fact that England and many parts of Europe suffered from overpopulation in the early fourteenth century. Population losses caused by the Black Death led to increased productivity by restoring a more efficient balance between labor, land, and capital.

What impact did visits of the plague have on urban populations? The rich evidence from a census of the city of Florence and its surrounding territory taken between

1427 and 1430 is fascinating. The region had suffered repeated epidemics since 1347. In a total population of 260,000 persons, 15 percent were age sixty or over (a very high proportion), suggesting that the plague took the young rather than the mature. Children and youths up to age nineteen constituted 44 percent of the people. Adults between the ages of twenty and fifty-nine, the most economically productive group, represented 41 percent of Florentine society.

The high mortality rate of craftsmen led Florentine guilds to recruit many new members. For example, between 1328 and 1347 the silk merchants guild accepted 730 members, and between 1408 and 1427 it admitted 784. It appears that economic organizations tried to keep their numbers constant, even though the size of the population and its pool of potential guild members was shrinking. Moreover, in contrast to the pre-1348 period, many new members of the guilds were not related to existing members. Thus the post-plague years represent an age of "new men."

The Black Death brought on a general European inflation. High mortality produced a fall in production, shortages of goods, and a general rise in prices. The shortage of labor and workers' demands for higher wages put guild masters on the defensive. They retaliated with measures such as the Statute of Laborers (1351), an attempt by the English Parliament to freeze the wages of English workers at pre-1347 levels. Such statutes could not be enforced and thus were unsuccessful. The price of wheat in most of Europe increased, as did the costs of meat, sausage, and cheese. This inflation continued to the end of the fourteenth century. But wages in the towns rose faster, and the broad mass of people enjoyed a higher standard of living. Population decline meant a sharp increase in per capita wealth. The greater demand for labor meant greater mobility for peasants in rural areas and for industrial workers in the towns and cities. Labor shortages caused by the Black Death throughout the Mediterranean region, from Constantinople to Spain, presented aggressive businessmen with a golden opportunity, and the price of slaves rose sharply.

Even more significant than the social effects were the psychological consequences. The knowledge that the disease meant almost certain death provoked the most profound pessimism. Imagine an entire society in the grip of the belief that it was at the mercy of a frightful affliction

Flagellants In this manuscript illumination from 1349, shirtless flagellants scourge themselves with whips as they walk through the streets of the Flemish city of Tournai. The text notes that they are asking for God's grace to return to the city after it had been struck with the "most grave" illness. *(HIP/Art Resource, NY)*

about which nothing could be done, a disgusting disease from which family and friends would flee, leaving one to die alone and in agony. It is not surprising that some sought release in wild living, while others turned to the severest forms of asceticism and frenzied religious fervor. Some extremists joined groups of **flagellants,** who whipped and scourged themselves as penance for their and society's sins in the belief that the Black Death was God's punishment for humanity's wickedness. Groups of flagellants traveled from town to town, often provoking hysteria against Jews and growing into unruly mobs. Officials worried that they would provoke violence and riots, and ordered groups of them to disband or forbade them to enter cities.

Plague ripped apart the social fabric. In the thirteenth century, funerals, traditionally occasions for the mutual consolation of the living as much as memorial services for the dead, grew increasingly elaborate, with large cortages and many mourners. In the fourteenth century, public horror at the suffering of the afflicted and at the dead reduced the size of mourning processions and eventually resulted in failure even to perform the customary death rites. Fear of infection led to the dead being buried hastily, sometimes in mass graves.

People often used pilgrimages to holy places as justification for their flight from cities. Suspected of being carriers of plague, travelers, pilgrims, and the homeless aroused deep hostility. All European port cities followed the example of Ragusa (modern Dubrovnik in southwestern Croatia on the Dalmatian coast) and quarantined arriving ships, crews, passengers, and cargoes to determine whether they brought the plague. Deriving from a Venetian word, the English term *quarantine* originally meant forty days' isolation.

Popular endowments of educational institutions multiplied. The years of the Black Death witnessed the foundation of new colleges at old universities, such as Corpus Christi and Clare Colleges at Cambridge and New College at Oxford, and of entirely new universities. The beginnings of Charles University in Prague (1348) and the Universities of Florence (1350), Vienna (1364), Cracow (1364), and Heidelberg (1385) were all associated with the plague: their foundation charters specifically mention the shortage of priests and the decay of learning. Whereas universities such as those at Bologna and Paris had international student bodies, new institutions established in the wake of the Black Death had more national or local constituencies. Thus the international character of medieval culture weakened. The decline of cultural cohesion paved the way for schism in the Catholic Church even before the Reformation.

The literature and art of the fourteenth century reveal a terribly morbid concern with death. One highly popular artistic motif, the Dance of Death, depicted a dancing skeleton leading away a living person.

The Hundred Years' War

The plague ravaged populations in Asia, North Africa, and Europe; in western Europe a long international war added further misery to the frightful disasters of the plague. England and France had engaged in sporadic military hostilities from the time of the Norman Conquest in 1066, and in the middle of the fourteenth century these became more intense. From 1337 to 1453, the two countries intermittently fought one another in what was the longest war in European history, ultimately dubbed the Hundred Years' War though it actually lasted 116 years.

- *What were the causes of the Hundred Years' War, and how did the war affect European politics, economics, and cultural life?*

Causes

The Hundred Years' War had both distant and immediate causes. In 1259 France and England signed the Treaty of Paris, in which the English king agreed to become—for himself and his successors—vassal of the French crown for the duchy of Aquitaine. The English claimed Aquitaine as an ancient inheritance. French policy, however, was strongly expansionist, and the French kings resolved to absorb the duchy into the kingdom of France.

In January 1327 Queen Isabella of England, her lover Mortimer, and a group of barons, having deposed and murdered Isabella's incompetent husband, King Edward II, proclaimed his fifteen-year-old son king as Edward III. Isabella and Mortimer, however, held real power until 1330, when Edward seized the reins of government. In 1328 Charles IV of France, the last surviving son of Philip the Fair, died childless. With him ended the Capetian dynasty. An assembly of French barons, meaning to exclude Isabella—who was Charles's sister and the daughter of Philip the Fair—and her son Edward III from the French throne, proclaimed that "no woman nor her son could succeed to the [French] monarchy." French lawyers defended the position with the claim that the exclusion of women from ruling or passing down the right to rule was part of Salic Law, a sixth-century Germanic law code (see page 216), and that Salic Law itself

English Merchants in Flanders In this 1387 illustration, an English merchant requests concessions from the count of Flanders to trade English wool at a favorable price. Flanders was officially on the French side during the Hundred Years' War, but Flemish cities depended heavily on English wool for their textile manufacturing. Hence the count of Flanders agreed to the establishment of the Merchant Staple, an English trading company with a monopoly on trade in wool. *(British Library)*

was part of the fundamental law of France. They used this invented tradition to argue that Edward should be barred from the French throne. (This notion became part of French legal tradition until the end of the monarchy in 1789.) The barons passed the crown to Philip VI of Valois (r. 1328–1350), a nephew of Philip the Fair.

In 1329 Edward III paid homage to Philip VI for Aquitaine. In 1337 Philip, eager to exercise full French jurisdiction in Aquitaine, confiscated the duchy. Edward III interpreted this action as a gross violation of the treaty of 1259 and as a cause for war. Moreover, Edward argued, as the eldest directly surviving male descendant of Philip the Fair, he must assume the title of king of France in order to wield his rightful authority in Aquitaine. In short, Edward rejected the decision of the French barons excluding him from the throne. Edward III's dynastic argument upset the feudal order in France: to increase their independent power, French vassals of Philip VI used the excuse that they had to transfer their loyalty to a more legitimate overlord, Edward III. One reason the war lasted so long was that it became a French civil war, with some French barons supporting English monarchs in order to thwart the centralizing goals of the French crown.

Economic factors involving the wool trade and the control of Flemish towns had served as justifications for war between France and England for centuries. The wool trade between England and Flanders served as the cornerstone of both countries' economies; they were closely interdependent. Flanders was a fief of the French crown, and the Flemish aristocracy was highly sympathetic to the monarchy in Paris. But the wealth of Flemish merchants and cloth manufacturers depended on English wool, and Flemish burghers strongly supported the claims of Edward III. The disruption of commerce with England threatened their prosperity.

The Popular Response

The governments of both England and France manipulated public opinion to support the war. Whatever significance modern scholars ascribe to the economic factor, public opinion in fourteenth-century England held that the war was waged for one reason: to secure for King Edward the French crown he had been unjustly denied. Edward III issued letters to the sheriffs describing the evil deeds of the French in graphic terms and listing royal needs. Kings in both countries instructed the clergy to deliver sermons filled with patriotic sentiment. The royal courts sensationalized the wickedness of the other side and stressed the great fortunes to be made from the war. Philip VI sent agents to warn communities about the dangers of invasion and to stress the French crown's revenue needs to meet the attack.

The royal campaign to rally public opinion was highly successful, at least in the early stage of the war. Edward III gained widespread support in the 1340s and 1350s. The English developed a deep hatred of the French and feared that King Philip intended "to have seized and slaughtered the entire realm of England." When England was successful in the field, pride in the country's military proficiency increased.

Most important of all, the Hundred Years' War was popular because it presented unusual opportunities for wealth and advancement. Poor knights and knights who were unemployed were promised regular wages. Criminals who enlisted were granted pardons. The great nobles expected to be rewarded with estates. Royal exhortations to the troops before battles repeatedly stressed that, if victorious, the men might keep whatever they seized. The French chronicler Jean Froissart wrote that, at the time of Edward III's expedition of 1359, men of all ranks flocked to the English king's banner. Some came to acquire honor, but many came "to loot and pillage the fair and plenteous land of France."³

Online Study Center **Improve Your Grade**
Primary Source: Warfare Without Chivalry: The Sack of Limoges

The Course of the War to 1419

The war was fought almost entirely in France and the Low Countries (see Map 12.2). It consisted mainly of a series of random sieges and cavalry raids. In 1335 the French began supporting Scottish incursions into northern England, ravaging the countryside in Aquitaine, and sacking and burning English coastal towns, such as Southampton. Such tactics lent weight to Edward III's propaganda campaign. In fact, royal propaganda on both sides fostered a kind of early nationalism.

During the war's early stages, England was highly successful. At Crécy in northern France in 1346, English longbowmen scored a great victory over French knights and crossbowmen. Although the aim of the longbow was not very accurate, it allowed for rapid reloading, and an English archer could send off three arrows to the French crossbowman's one. The result was a blinding shower of arrows that unhorsed the French knights and caused mass confusion. The ring of cannon—probably the first use of artillery in the West—created further panic. Thereupon the English horsemen charged and butchered the French.

This was not war according to the chivalric rules that Edward III would have preferred. Nevertheless, his son, Edward the Black Prince, used the same tactics ten years

Siege of the Castle of Mortagne Near Bordeaux (1377) Medieval warfare usually consisted of small skirmishes and attacks on castles. This miniature shows the French besieging an English-held castle, which held out for six months. Most of the soldiers use longbows, although at the left two men shoot primitive muskets above a pair of cannon. Painted in the late fifteenth century, the scene reflects military technology available at the time it was painted, not the time of the actual siege. *(British Library)*

MAP 12.2 English Holdings in France During the Hundred Years' War The year 1429 marked the greatest extent of English holdings in France.

later to smash the French at Poitiers, where he captured the French king and held him for ransom. Again, at **Agincourt** near Arras in 1415, the chivalric English soldier-king Henry V (r. 1413–1422) gained the field over vastly superior numbers. Henry followed up his triumph at Agincourt with the reconquest of Normandy. By 1419 the English had advanced to the walls of Paris (see Map 12.2). But the French cause was not lost. Though England had scored the initial victories, France won the war.

Joan of Arc and France's Victory

The ultimate French success rests heavily on the actions of an obscure French peasant girl, **Joan of Arc,** whose vision and work revived French fortunes and led to victory. A great deal of pious and popular legend surrounds Joan the Maid because of her peculiar appearance on the scene, her astonishing success, her martyrdom, and her canonization by the Catholic Church. The historical fact is that she saved the French monarchy, which was the embodiment of France.

Born in 1412 to well-to-do peasants in the village of Domrémy in Champagne, Joan of Arc grew up in a religious household. During adolescence she began to hear voices, which she later said belonged to Saint Michael, Saint Catherine, and Saint Margaret. In 1428 these voices spoke to her with great urgency, telling her that the dauphin (the uncrowned King Charles VII) had to be crowned and the English expelled from France. Joan went to the French court, persuaded the king to reject the rumor that he was illegitimate, and secured his support for her relief of the besieged city of Orléans.

The astonishing thing is not that Joan the Maid overcame serious obstacles to see the dauphin, and not even that Charles and his advisers listened to her. What is amazing is the swiftness with which they were convinced. French fortunes had been so low for so long that the court believed that only a miracle could save the country. Because Joan cut her hair short and dressed like a man, she scandalized the court. But hoping she would provide the miracle, Charles allowed her to accompany the army that was preparing to raise the English siege of Orléans.

In the meantime Joan, herself illiterate, dictated this letter calling on the English to withdraw:

King of England . . . , do right in the King of Heaven's sight. Surrender to The Maid *sent hither by God the King of Heaven, the keys of all the good towns you have taken and laid waste in France. She comes in God's name to establish the Blood Royal, ready to make peace if you agree to abandon France and repay what you have taken. And you,* archers, comrades in arms, gentles and others, who are before the town of Orléans, retire in God's name to your own country.[4]

Joan arrived before Orléans on April 28, 1429. Seventeen years old, she knew little of warfare and believed that if she could keep the French troops from swearing and frequenting brothels, victory would be theirs. On May 8 the English, weakened by disease and lack of supplies, withdrew from Orléans. Ten days later Charles VII was crowned king at Reims. These two events marked the turning point in the war.

Online Study Center **Improve Your Grade**
Primary Source: The Trial of Joan of Arc

Joan's presence at Orléans, her strong belief in her mission, and the fact that she was wounded enhanced her reputation and strengthened the morale of the army. In 1430 England's allies, the Burgundians, captured Joan and sold her to the English. When the English handed her over to the ecclesiastical authorities for trial, the French court did not intervene. While the English wanted Joan eliminated for obvious political reasons, sorcery (witchcraft) was the ostensible charge at her trial. Witch persecution was increasing in the fifteenth century, and Joan's wearing of men's clothes appeared not only aberrant but indicative of contact with the Devil. In 1431 the court condemned her as a heretic—her claim of direct inspiration from God, thereby denying the authority of church officials, constituted heresy—and burned her at the stake in the marketplace at Rouen. A new trial in 1456 rehabilitated her name. In 1920 she was canonized and declared a holy maiden, and today she is revered as the second patron saint of France, along with King Louis IX. The nineteenth-century French historian Jules Michelet extolled Joan of Arc as a symbol of the vitality and strength of the French peasant classes.

The relief of Orléans stimulated French pride and rallied French resources. As the war dragged on, loss of life mounted, and money appeared to be flowing into a bottomless pit, demands for an end increased in England. The clergy and intellectuals pressed for peace. Parliamentary opposition to additional war grants stiffened. Slowly the French reconquered Normandy and, finally, ejected the English from Aquitaine. At the war's end in 1453, only the town of Calais remained in English hands.

Costs and Consequences

In France the English had slaughtered thousands of soldiers and civilians. In the years after the sweep of the

Black Death, this additional killing meant a grave loss of population. The English had laid waste to hundreds of thousands of acres of rich farmland, leaving the rural economy of many parts of France a shambles. The war had disrupted trade and the great fairs, resulting in the drastic reduction of French participation in international commerce. Defeat in battle and heavy taxation contributed to widespread dissatisfaction and aggravated peasant grievances.

In England only the southern coastal ports experienced much destruction, and the demographic effects of the Black Death actually worked to restore the land-labor balance (see page 379). The costs of the war, however, were tremendous. England spent over £5 million on the war effort, a huge sum at the time. Manpower losses had greater social consequences. The knights who ordinarily handled the work of local government as sheriffs, coroners, jurymen, and justices of the peace were abroad, and their absence contributed to the breakdown of order at the local level. The English government attempted to finance the war effort by raising taxes on the wool crop. Because of steadily increasing costs, Flemish and Italian buyers could not afford English wool. Consequently, raw wool exports slumped drastically between 1350 and 1450.

Many men of all social classes had volunteered for service in France in the hope of acquiring booty and becoming rich. The chronicler Walsingham, describing the period of Crécy, wrote: "For the woman was of no account who did not possess something from the spoils of . . . cities overseas in clothing, furs, quilts, and utensils . . . tablecloths and jewels, bowls of murra [semiprecious stone] and silver, linen and linen cloths."[5] Walsingham is referring to 1348, in the first generation of war. As time went on, most fortunes seem to have been squandered as fast as they were made.

If English troops returned with cash, they did not invest it in land. In the fifteenth century returning soldiers were commonly described as beggars and vagabonds, roaming about making mischief. Even the large sums of money received from the ransom of the great—such as the £250,000 paid to Edward III for the freedom of King John of France—and the money paid as indemnities by captured towns and castles did not begin to equal the more than £5 million spent. England suffered a serious net loss.

The war stimulated technological experimentation, especially with artillery. Cannon revolutionized warfare, making the stone castle no longer impregnable. Because only central governments, not private nobles, could afford cannon, they strengthened the military power of national states.

The long war also had a profound impact on the political and cultural lives of the two countries. Most notably, it stimulated the development of the English Parliament. Between 1250 and 1450, **representative assemblies** flourished in many European countries. In the English Parliament, German diets, and Spanish cortes, deliberative practices developed that laid the foundations for the representative institutions of modern liberal-democratic nations. While representative assemblies declined in most countries after the fifteenth century, the English Parliament endured. Edward III's constant need for money to pay for the war compelled him to summon not only the great barons and bishops, but knights of the shires and burgesses from the towns as well. Parliament met in thirty-seven of the fifty years of Edward's reign.[6]

The frequency of the meetings is significant. Representative assemblies were becoming a habit. Knights and wealthy urban residents—or the "Commons," as they came to be called—recognized their mutual interests and began to meet apart from the great lords. The Commons gradually realized that they held the country's purse strings, and a parliamentary statute of 1341 required that all nonfeudal levies have parliamentary approval. By signing the law, Edward III acknowledged that the king of England could not tax without Parliament's consent. During the course of the war, money grants were increasingly tied to royal redress of grievances: to raise money, the government had to correct the wrongs its subjects protested.

In England, theoretical consent to taxation and legislation was given in one assembly for the entire country. France had no such single assembly; instead, there were many regional or provincial assemblies. Why did a national representative assembly fail to develop in France? The initiative for convening assemblies rested with the king, who needed revenue almost as much as the English ruler. But the French monarchy found the idea of representative assemblies thoroughly distasteful. Large gatherings of the nobility potentially or actually threatened the king's power. The advice of a counselor to King Charles VI (r. 1380–1422), "above all things be sure that no great assemblies of nobles or of *communes* take place in your kingdom," was accepted.[7] Charles VII (r. 1422–1461) even threatened to punish those proposing a national assembly.

No one in France wanted a national assembly. Linguistic, geographical, economic, legal, and political differences were very strong. People tended to think of themselves as Breton, Norman, Burgundian, or whatever, rather than French. Through much of the fourteenth and early fifteenth centuries, weak monarchs lacked the power to call a national assembly. Provincial assemblies, highly jealous of their independence, did not want a national assembly. The costs of sending delegates to it would be high, and the result was likely to be increased taxation.

In both countries, however, the war did promote the growth of **nationalism**—the feeling of unity and identity that binds together a people. After victories, each country experienced a surge of pride in its military strength. Just as English patriotism ran strong after Crécy and Poitiers, so French national confidence rose after Orléans. French national feeling demanded the expulsion of the enemy not merely from Normandy and Aquitaine but from all French soil. Perhaps no one expressed this national consciousness better than Joan of Arc when she exulted that the enemy had been "driven out of *France*."

Challenges to the Church

In times of crisis or disaster, people of all faiths have sought the consolation of religion. In the fourteenth century, however, the official Christian church offered little solace. In fact, the leaders of the church added to the sorrow and misery of the times. In response to this lack of leadership, members of the clergy challenged the power of the pope, and laypeople challenged the authority of the church itself. Women and men increasingly relied on direct approaches to God, often through mystical encounters, rather than on the institutional church.

- *What challenges faced the Christian church in the fourteenth century, and how did church leaders, intellectuals, and ordinary people respond?*

The Babylonian Captivity and Great Schism

In order to control the church and its policies, Philip the Fair of France pressured Pope Clement V to settle permanently in Avignon in southeastern France, where the popes already had their summer residence (see Map 11.3 on page 346). Clement, critically ill with cancer, lacked the will to resist Philip. The popes lived in Avignon from 1309 to 1376, a period in church history often called the **Babylonian Captivity** (referring to the seventy years the ancient Hebrews were held captive in Mesopotamian Babylon).

The Babylonian Captivity badly damaged papal prestige. The Avignon papacy reformed its financial administration and centralized its government. But the seven popes at Avignon concentrated on bureaucratic matters to the exclusion of spiritual objectives. Though some of the popes led austere lives, the general atmosphere was one of luxury and extravagance. (See the feature "Individuals in Society: Francesco Datini" in Chapter 11 on page 343.) The leadership of the church was cut off from its historic roots and the source of its ancient authority, the city of Rome. In the absence of the papacy, the Papal States in Italy lacked stability and good government. The economy of Rome had been based on the presence of the papal court and the rich tourist trade the papacy attracted. The Babylonian Captivity left Rome poverty-stricken.

In 1377 Pope Gregory XI brought the papal court back to Rome. Unfortunately, he died shortly after the return. At Gregory's death, Roman citizens demanded an Italian pope who would remain in Rome. Between the time of Gregory's death and the opening of the conclave, great pressure was put on the cardinals to elect an Italian. At the time, none of them protested this pressure, and they chose a distinguished administrator, the archbishop of Bari, Bartolomeo Prignano, who took the name Urban VI.

Urban VI (1378–1389) had excellent intentions for church reform, but he went about this in a tactless and bullheaded manner. He attacked clerical luxury, denouncing individual cardinals by name, and even threatened to excommunicate certain cardinals.

The cardinals slipped away from Rome and met at Anagni. They declared Urban's election invalid because it had come about under threats from the Roman mob, and they asserted that Urban himself was excommunicated. The cardinals then elected Cardinal Robert of Geneva, the cousin of King Charles V of France, as pope. Cardinal Robert took the name Clement VII. There were thus two popes—Urban at Rome and Clement VII (1378–1394), who set himself up at Avignon in opposition to Urban. So began the **Great Schism**, which divided Western Christendom until 1417.

The powers of Europe aligned themselves with Urban or Clement along strictly political lines. France naturally recognized the French pope, Clement. England, France's historic enemy, recognized the Italian pope, Urban. Scotland, whose attacks on England were subsidized by France, followed the French and supported Clement. Aragon, Castile, and Portugal hesitated before deciding for Clement at Avignon. The emperor, who bore ancient hostility to France, recognized Urban. At first the Italian city-states recognized Urban; when he alienated them, they opted for Clement.

John of Spoleto, a professor at the law school at Bologna, eloquently summed up intellectual opinion of the schism, or division: "The longer this schism lasts, the more it appears to be costing, and the more harm it does; scandal, massacres, ruination, agitations, troubles and disturbances."[8] The common people, wracked by inflation, wars, and plague, were thoroughly confused about which pope was legitimate. The schism weakened the religious faith of many Christians and brought church leadership into serious disrepute. The schism also brought to the fore conciliar ideas about church government.

The Conciliar Movement

Theories about the nature of the Christian church and its government originated in the very early church, but the years of the Great Schism witnessed their maturity. **Conciliarists** believed that reform of the church could best be achieved through periodic assemblies, or general councils, representing all the Christian people. While acknowledging that the pope was head of the church, conciliarists held that the pope derived his authority from the entire Christian community, whose well-being he existed to promote. Conciliarists favored a balanced or constitutional form of church government, with papal authority shared with a general council, in contrast to the monarchical one that prevailed.

A half century before the Great Schism, in 1324, Marsiglio of Padua, then rector of the University of Paris, had published *Defensor Pacis* (The Defender of the Peace). Marsiglio argued that the state was the great unifying power in society and that the church was subordinate to the state. He put forth the revolutionary ideas that the church had no inherent jurisdiction and should own no property. Authority in the Christian church, according to Marsiglio, should rest in a general council made up of laymen as well as priests, and the council should be superior to the pope. These ideas directly contradicted the medieval notion of a society governed by the church and the state, with the church supreme. *Defensor Pacis* was condemned by the pope, and Marsiglio was excommunicated.

Even more earthshaking than the theories of Marsiglio of Padua were the ideas of the English scholar and theologian John Wyclif (ca 1330–1384). Wyclif wrote that papal claims of temporal power had no foundation in the Scriptures and that the Scriptures alone should be the standard of Christian belief and practice. He urged the abolition of such practices as the veneration of saints, pilgrimages, pluralism, and absenteeism. Sincere Christians, according to Wyclif, should read the Bible for themselves. In response to that idea, the first English translation of the Bible was produced and circulated. Wyclif's views had broad social and economic significance. He urged that the church be stripped of its property. His idea that every Christian free of mortal sin possessed lordship was seized on by peasants in England during a revolt in 1381 and used to justify their goals.

In advancing these views, Wyclif struck at the roots of medieval church structure. Consequently, he has been hailed as the precursor of the Protestant Reformation of the sixteenth century. Although Wyclif's ideas were vigorously condemned by ecclesiastical authorities, they were widely disseminated by humble clerics and enjoyed great popularity in the early fifteenth century. Wyclif's followers were called "Lollards." The term, which means "mumblers of prayers and psalms," refers to what they criticized. Lollard teaching allowed women to preach. Women, some well educated, played a significant role in the movement. After Anne, sister of Wenceslaus, king of Germany and Bohemia, married Richard II of England, members of her household carried Lollard books back to Bohemia.

In response to continued calls throughout Europe for a council, the two colleges of cardinals—one at Rome, the other at Avignon—summoned a council at Pisa in 1409. That gathering of prelates and theologians deposed both popes and selected another. Neither the Avignon pope nor the Roman pope would resign, however, and the appalling result was the creation of a threefold schism.

Finally, because of the pressure of the German emperor Sigismund, a great council met at the imperial city of Constance (1414–1418). It had three objectives: to end the schism, to reform the church "in head and members" (from top to bottom), and to wipe out heresy. The council condemned the Czech reformer Jan Hus (see the feature "Individuals in Society: Jan Hus"), and he was burned at the stake. The council eventually deposed both the Roman pope and the successor of the pope chosen at Pisa, and it isolated the Avignon antipope. A conclave elected a new leader, the Roman cardinal Colonna, who took the name Martin V (1417–1431).

Martin proceeded to dissolve the council. Nothing was done about reform. The schism was over, and though councils subsequently met at Basel and at Ferrara-Florence, in 1450 the papacy held a jubilee celebrating its triumph over the conciliar movement. In the later fifteenth century the papacy concentrated on Italian problems to the exclusion of universal Christian interests. But the schism and the conciliar movement had exposed the crying need for ecclesiastical reform, thus laying the foundation for the great reform efforts of the sixteenth century.

Spoon with Fox Preaching to Geese (southern Netherlands, ca 1430) Taking as his text a contemporary proverb, "When the fox preaches, beware your geese," the artist shows, in the bowl of a spoon, a fox dressed as a monk or friar, preaching with three dead geese in his hood, while another fox grabs one of the congregation. The preaching fox reads from a scroll bearing the word *pax* (peace), implying the perceived hypocrisy of the clergy. The object suggests the widespread criticism of churchmen in the later Middle Ages. *(Painted enamel and gilding on silver; 17.6 cm [6 ⅞ in]. Museum of Fine Arts, Boston, Helen and Alice Coburn Fund, 51.2472)*

Lay Piety and Mysticism

During the fourteenth and fifteenth centuries the laity began to exercise increasing control over parish affairs. The constant quarrels of the mendicant orders (the Franciscans and Dominicans), the mercenary and grasping attitude of the parish clergy, the scandal of the Great Schism, and a divided Christendom all did much to weaken the spiritual mystique of the clergy in the popular mind. The laity steadily took responsibility for the management of parish lands and secured jurisdiction over the structure of the church building and its vestments, books, and furnishings. Lay Christian men and women often formed **confraternities,** voluntary lay groups organized by occupation, devotional preference, neighborhood, or charitable activity. Confraternities expanded rapidly in larger cities and many villages with the growth of the mendicant orders in the thirteenth century. Some confraternities specialized in praying for souls in purgatory, either for specific individuals or for the anonymous mass of all souls. In England they were generally associated with a parish, so are called parish guilds, parish fraternities, or lights; by the late Middle Ages they held dances, church ales, and collections to raise money to clean and repair church buildings and to supply the church with candles and other liturgical objects. Like craft guilds, most confraternities were groups of men, but separate women's confraternities were formed in some towns, often to oversee the production of vestments, altar cloths, and other items made of fabric.

In Holland, beginning in the late fourteenth century, a group of pious laypeople called the Brethren and Sisters of the Common Life lived in stark simplicity while daily carrying out the Gospel teaching of feeding the hungry, clothing the naked, and visiting the sick. The Brethren also taught in local schools with the goal of preparing devout candidates for the priesthood. They sought to make religion a personal inner experience. The spirituality of the Brethren and Sisters of the Common Life found its finest expression in the classic ***The Imitation of Christ*** by Thomas à Kempis, which gained wide appeal among laypeople. It urges Christians to take Christ as their model, seek perfection in a simple way of life, and look to the Scriptures for guidance in living a spiritual life. In the mid-fifteenth century the movement had founded houses in the Netherlands, in central Germany, and in the Rhineland.

Online Study Center Improve Your Grade
Primary Source: *The Imitation of Christ: On True Charity*

Most of this lay piety centered on prayer, pious actions, and charitable giving, but for some individuals, religious devotion included mystical experiences. Bridget of Sweden (1303–1373) was a noblewoman who journeyed to Rome after her husband's death. She began to see visions and gave advice based on these visions to both laypeople and church officials. Because she could not speak Latin, she dictated her visions in Swedish; these were later translated and eventually published in Latin. At the end of her life, Bridget made a pilgrimage to Jerusalem, where she saw visions of the Virgin Mary, who described to her exactly how she was standing "with my knees bent" when she gave birth to Jesus, and how she "showed to the shepherds the nature and male sex of the child."⁹ Bridget's visions convey her deep familiarity with biblical texts taught to her through sermons or stories, as there was no Bible available in Swedish. They also provide evidence of the ways in which laypeople used their own experiences to enhance their religious understanding;

Bridget's own experiences of childbirth shaped the way she viewed the birth of Jesus, and she related to the Virgin Mary in part as one mother to another.

Economic and Social Change

In the fourteenth century economic and political difficulties, disease, and war profoundly affected the lives of European peoples. Decades of slaughter and destruction, punctuated by the decimating visits of the Black Death, made a grave economic situation virtually disastrous. In many parts of France and the Low Countries, fields lay in ruin or untilled for lack of labor power. In England, as taxes increased, criticisms of government policy and mismanagement multiplied. Crime and new forms of business organization aggravated economic troubles, and throughout Europe the frustrations of the common people erupted into widespread revolts.

- **How did economic and social tensions contribute to revolts, crime, violence, and a growing sense of ethnic and national distinctions?**

Peasant Revolts

Nobles, clergy, and city dwellers lived on the produce of peasant labor. Early in the thirteenth century the French preacher Jacques de Vitry asked rhetorically, "How many serfs have killed their lords or burnt their castles?"[10] And in the fourteenth and fifteenth centuries social and economic conditions caused a great increase in peasant uprisings (see Map 12.3). They were very common and provide most of the evidence of peasants' long suffering and exploitation.

We will never be able fully to answer Jacques de Vitry's questions, for peasants were not literate and, apart from their explosive uprisings, left no record of their aspirations. The clerical writers who mentioned the rebellions viewed the peasants with aristocratic disdain and hostility. Recent research provides some insight into **peasant revolts** in Flanders in the 1320s. Long-existing conflicts along the Flemish-French border came to a head at Courtrai in July 1302 when Flemish infantry smashed a French army, killing many knights and nobles (their golden spurs retrieved from the battlefield gave the battle its name, the Battle of the Spurs). The Flemish victory failed to resolve disputes over the French crown's claim to fiscal rights over the county of Flanders. Moreover, the peace agreements imposed heavy indemnities on Flemish peasants, who in 1323 began to revolt in protest of officials' demands for taxes and of the misappropriation of the money collected. Also, monasteries pressed peasants for fees higher than the customary tithes. In retaliation, peasants subjected castles and aristocratic country houses to arson and pillage. A French army intervened and on August 23, 1328, near the town of Cassel in southwestern Flanders, crushed peasant forces. Savage repression and the confiscation of peasant property followed in the 1330s.

In 1358, when French taxation for the Hundred Years' War fell heavily on the poor, the frustrations of the French peasantry exploded in a massive uprising called the **Jacquerie,** after a mythical agricultural laborer, Jacques Bonhomme (Good Fellow). Two years earlier the English had captured the French king John and many nobles and held them for ransom. The peasants resented paying for their lords' release. Recently hit by plague, experiencing famine in some areas, and harassed by nobles, peasants in Picardy, Champagne, and the Île-de-France erupted in anger and frustration. Crowds swept through the countryside, slashing the throats of nobles, burning their castles, raping their wives and daughters, and killing or maiming their horses and cattle. Peasants blamed the nobility for oppressive taxes, for the criminal brigandage of the countryside, for defeat in war, and for the general misery. Artisans, small merchants, and parish priests joined the peasants. Urban and rural groups committed terrible destruction, and for several weeks the nobles were on the defensive. Then the upper class united to repress the revolt with merciless ferocity. Thousands of the "Jacques," innocent as well as guilty, were cut down. That forcible suppression of social rebellion, without any effort to alleviate its underlying causes, served to drive protest underground.

The Peasants' Revolt in England in 1381 involved thousands of people (see Map 12.3). Its causes were complex and varied from place to place. In general, though, the thirteenth century had witnessed the steady commutation of labor services for cash rents, and the Black Death had drastically cut the labor supply. As a result, peasants demanded higher wages and fewer manorial obligations. The parliamentary Statute of Laborers of 1351 (see page 380) had declared:

Whereas to curb the malice of servants who after the pestilence were idle and unwilling to serve without securing excessive wages, it was recently ordained . . . that such servants, both men and women, shall be bound to serve in return for salaries and wages that were customary . . . five or six years earlier.[11]

Individuals in Society

Jan Hus

In May 1990 the Czech Republic's parliament declared July 6, the date of Jan Hus's execution in 1415, a Czech national holiday. The son of free farmers, Hus (ca 1369–1415) was born in Husinec in southern Bohemia, an area of heavy German settlement, and grew up conscious of the ethnic differences between Czechs and Germans. Most of his professors at Charles University in Prague were Germans. In 1396 he received a master's degree, and just before his ordination as a priest in 1400 he wrote that he would not be a "clerical careerist," implying that ambition for church offices motivated many of his peers.

The young priest lectured at the university and preached at the private Bethlehem Chapel. During his twelve years there Hus preached only in Czech. He denounced superstition, the sale of indulgences, and other abuses, but his remarks were thoroughly orthodox. He attracted attention among artisans and the small Czech middle class, but not Germans. His austere life and lack of ambition enhanced his reputation.

Around 1400, Czech students returning from study at Oxford introduced into Bohemia the reforming ideas of the English theologian John Wyclif. When German professors condemned Wyclif's ideas as heretical, Hus and the Czechs argued "academic freedom," the right to read and teach Wyclif's works regardless of their particular merits. When popular demonstrations against ecclesiastical abuses and German influence at the university erupted, King Vaclav IV (1378–1419) placed control of the university in Czech hands. Hus was elected rector, the top administrative official.

The people of Prague, with perhaps the largest urban population in central Europe, 40 percent of it living below the poverty line and entirely dependent on casual labor, found Hus's denunciations of an overendowed church appealing. Hus considered the issues theological; his listeners saw them as socioeconomic.

Church officials in Prague were split about Hus's ideas, and popular unrest grew. The king forced Hus to leave the city, but he continued to preach and write. He disputed papal authority, denounced abuses, and argued that everyone should receive both bread and wine in the Eucharist. (By this time, in standard Western Christian practice, the laity received only the bread; the priest received the wine *for* the laity, a mark of his distinctiveness.) Hus also defended transubstantiation (see page 449); insisted that church authority rested on Scripture, conscience, and tradition (in contrast to sixteenth-century Protestant reformers, who placed authority in Scripture alone); and made it clear that he had no intention of leaving the church or inciting a popular movement.

In 1413 the emperor Sigismund urged the calling of a general council to end the schism. Hus was invited, and, given the emperor's safe conduct (protection from attack or arrest), agreed to go. What he found was an atmosphere of inquisition. The safe conduct was disregarded, and Hus was arrested. Under questioning about his acceptance of Wyclif's ideas, Hus repeatedly replied, "I have not held; I do not hold." Council members were more interested in proving Hus a Wyclite than in his responses. They took away his priesthood, banned his teachings, burned his books, and burned Hus himself at the stake. He then belonged to the ages.

The execution of Jan Hus.
(University of Prague/The Art Archive)

The ages have made good use of him. His death aggravated the divisions between the bishops at Constance and the Czech clerics and people. In September 1415, 452 nobles from all parts of Bohemia signed a letter saying that Hus had been unjustly executed and rejecting council rulings. This event marks the first time that an ecclesiastical decision was publicly defied. Revolution swept through Bohemia, with Hussites—Czech nobles and people—insisting on clerical poverty and both the bread and wine at the Eucharist, and with German citizens remaining loyal to the Roman church. In the sixteenth century reformers hailed Hus as the forerunner of Protestantism. In the eighteenth century Enlightenment philosophes evoked Hus as a defender of freedom of expression. In the nineteenth century central European nationalists used Hus's name to defend national sentiment against Habsburg rule. And in the twentieth century Hus's name was used against German fascist and Russian communist tyranny.

Questions for Analysis

1. Since Jan Hus lived and died insisting that his religious teaching was thoroughly orthodox, why has he been hailed as a reformer?
2. What political and cultural interests did the martyred Hus serve?

Online Study Center **Improve Your Grade**
Going Beyond Individuals in Society

MAP 12.3 Fourteenth-Century Peasant Revolts In the later Middle Ages, peasant and urban uprisings were endemic, as common as factory strikes in the industrial world. The threat of insurrection served to check unlimited exploitation.

Online Study Center Improve Your Grade
Interactive Map: Fourteenth-Century Peasant Revolts

But this attempt to freeze wages and social mobility could not be enforced. Some scholars believe that in most places the peasantry was better off in the period 1350 to 1450 than it had been for centuries before or was to be for four centuries after.

Why then was the outburst in England in 1381 so serious? It was provoked by a crisis of rising expectations. The relative prosperity of the laboring classes led to demands that the upper classes were unwilling to grant. Unable to climb higher, the peasants sought release for their economic frustrations in revolt. Economic grievances combined with other factors. The south of England, where the revolt broke out, had been subjected to destructive French raids. The English government did little to protect the south, and villagers grew increasingly frightened and insecure. Moreover, decades of aristocratic violence against the weak peasantry had bred hostility and bitterness. Social and religious agitation by the popular preacher John Ball fanned the embers of discontent. Ball's famous couplet "When Adam delved and Eve span; Who was then the gentleman?" reflected real revolutionary sentiment.

The straw that broke the camel's back in England was the reimposition of a head tax on all adult males. Despite widespread opposition to the tax in 1380, the royal council ordered the sheriffs to collect it again in 1381 on penalty of a huge fine. Beginning with assaults on the tax collectors, the uprising in England followed a course similar to that of the Jacquerie in France. Castles and manors were sacked. Manorial records were destroyed. Many nobles, including the archbishop of Canterbury, who had ordered the collection of the tax, were murdered.

The center of the revolt lay in the highly populated and economically advanced south and east, but sections of the north and the Midlands also witnessed rebellions. Violence took different forms in different places. Urban discontent merged with rural violence. In English towns where skilled Flemish craftsmen were employed, fear of competition led to their being attacked and murdered. Apprentices and journeymen, frustrated because the highest positions in the guilds were closed to them, rioted.

The boy-king Richard II (r. 1377–1399) met Wat Tyler and other leaders of the revolt, agreed to charters ensuring peasants' freedom, tricked them with false promises, and then crushed the uprising with terrible ferocity. The nobility tried to restore ancient duties of serfdom, but nearly a century of freedom had elapsed, and the commutation of manorial services continued. Rural serfdom disappeared in England by 1550.

Urban Conflicts

In Flanders, France, and England, peasant revolts often blended with conflicts involving workers in cities. Unrest also occurred in other cities. In Florence in 1378 the *ciompi*, the poor propertyless workers, revolted. Serious social trouble occurred in Lübeck, Brunswick, and other German cities. In Spain in 1391 aristocratic attempts to impose new forms of serfdom, combined with demands for tax relief, led to massive working-class and peasant uprisings in Seville and Barcelona.

These revolts often occurred in cities where the conditions of work were changing for many people. In the thirteenth century craft guilds had organized production of most goods, with masters, journeymen, and apprentices working side by side. Beginning in the fourteenth century in a few areas of Europe such as Florence and Flanders, individuals who had made money in trade and banking invested in production. They wanted to make products on a larger scale than guilds would allow, so they hired many households, with each household performing only one step of the process. Craft guilds sometimes protested these changes, but in other cities more enterprising or wealthier masters recognized the benefits of this new system and began to hire other households to work for them. This promoted a greater division within guilds between wealthier masters and the poorer masters and journeymen they hired. Some masters became so wealthy that they no longer had to work in a shop themselves, nor did their wives and family members. Instead of being artisans, they became capitalist investors, though they still generally belonged to the craft guild.

While capitalism provided opportunities for some artisans to become investors and entrepreneurs, especially in cloth production, for many it led to a decrease in income and status. Guilds often responded to competition by limiting membership to existing guild families, which meant that journeymen who were not master's sons or who could not find a master's widow or daughter to marry could never become masters themselves. They remained journeymen their entire lives, losing their sense of solidarity with the masters of their craft and in some cities forming separate journeymen's guilds. These journeymen's guilds tried to prevent anyone who was not a member of the guild from working in any craft shop, enforcing their aims with boycotts, strikes, and riots. Such actions often led cities to prohibit journeymen's guilds, but they were still set up illegally, and their secrecy made them stronger. Journeymen developed elaborate initiation rituals and secret ceremonies to enhance group solidarity, and they carried their organizations with them when they traveled in search of work.

Urban uprisings were most often touched off by economic issues, as low- and middle-class workers deeply resented the widening economic and social gap separating them from mercantile elites, but they were also sparked by issues involving honor, such as employers' requiring workers to do tasks they regarded as beneath them. As their actual status and economic prospects declined and their work became basically wage labor, journeymen and poorer masters emphasized skill and honor as qualities that set them apart from less-skilled workers.

The sense of honor developed by craft and journeymen's guilds was a gendered one. When urban economies were expanding in the High Middle Ages, the master's wife and daughters worked alongside him, and the journeymen and apprentices and female domestic servants also carried out productive tasks. (See the feature "Listening to the Past: Christine de Pizan" on pages 404–405.) Women and girls served as a labor reservoir to be utilized when guild needs required. Masters' widows ran shops after the death of their husbands and were expected to pay all guild fees, though they could not participate in running the guild. This informal participation began to change in the fourteenth century, as guilds increasingly came to view the honor of their work as tied to an all-male workplace. First, masters' widows were limited in the amount of time they could keep operating a shop or were prohibited from hiring journeymen; then female domestic servants were excluded from any productive tasks; then the number of his daughters a master craftsman could employ was limited. The timing of these restrictions varied from craft to craft, town to town, and country to country, but because women's participation in guild shops was generally not guaranteed by guild regulations and because widows had no political voice in running the guilds, women as a group were not able to protect their right to work. A few might be allowed to work, but this was on an individual basis and was viewed as a substitute for charity. The separate journeymen's guilds were even more hostile to women's work and never allowed female members. Their secret rituals offered opportunities for men to bond with one another and to express their resentment of economic change through hostility toward women's work as well as toward merchants' privileges.

Sex in the City

Peasant and urban revolts and riots had clear economic bases, but some historians have suggested that late medieval marital patterns may have also played a role in unrest. At what age did people usually marry? The largest amount of evidence on age at first marriage survives from Italy. For girls, population surveys at Prato place the age at 16.3 years in 1372 and at 21.1 years in 1470. Noble and wealthy urban women in cities elsewhere in Europe also generally married while in their late teens, but peasant and poorer urban women, especially in northwestern Europe—including the British Isles, Scandinavia, France, and Germany—waited until their mid- or late twenties to marry. The northwestern European marriage pattern resulted largely from the idea that couples should be economically independent before they married, so both spouses spent long periods as servants or workers in other households saving money and learning skills, or they waited until their own parents had died and the family property was distributed.

The most unusual feature of this pattern was the late age of marriage for women. Women entered marriage as adults and took charge of running a household immediately. They were thus not as dependent on their husbands or their mothers-in-law as were women who married at younger ages. They had fewer pregnancies than women who married earlier, though not necessarily fewer surviving children.

Men of all social groups were older when they married. An Italian chronicler writing about 1354 says that men did not marry before the age of thirty. At Prato in 1371 the average age of men at first marriage was twenty-four years, very young for Italian men, but these data may signal an attempt to regain population losses due to the recent attack of the plague. In general, men were in their middle or late twenties at first marriage, with wealthier urban merchants often much older. Journeymen and apprentices were often explicitly prohibited from marrying, as were the students at universities, as they were understood to be in "minor orders" and thus like clergy, even if they were not intending on careers in the church.

The prohibitions on marriage for certain groups of men and the late age of marriage for most men meant that cities and villages were filled with large numbers of young adult men with no family responsibilities who often formed the core of riots and unrest. Not surprisingly, this situation also contributed to a steady market for sexual services outside of marriage, what in later centuries was termed *prostitution*. Research on the southern French province of Languedoc in the fourteenth and fifteenth centuries has revealed the establishment of legal houses of prostitution in many cities. Municipal authorities in Toulouse, Montpellier, Albi, and other towns set up houses or red-light districts either outside the city walls or away from respectable neighborhoods. For example, authorities in Montpellier set aside Hot Street for prostitution, required public women to live there, and forbade anyone to molest them. Prostitution thus passed from being a private concern to a social matter requiring public supervision. The towns of Languedoc were not unique. Public authorities in Amiens, Dijon, Paris, Venice, Genoa, London, Florence, Rome, most of the larger German towns, and the English port of Sandwich set up brothels.

Many cities set down rules for the women and their customers, and they justified the existence of municipal brothels with the comment that such women protected honorable girls and women from the uncontrollable lust of young men, an argument at least as old as Saint Augustine. In a few cities such as Florence, authorities also noted that brothels might keep young men from homosexual relations, another, far worse alternative in their eyes. Visiting brothels was associated with achieving manhood in the eyes of young men, though for the women themselves their activities were work. Indeed, in some cases the women had no choice, for they had been traded to the brothel manager by their parents or other people in payment for debt, or had quickly become indebted to him (or, more rarely, her) for the clothes and other finery regarded as essential to their occupation. Poor women—and men—also sold sex illegally outside of city brothels, combining this with other sorts of part-time work such as laundering or sewing. Prostitution was an urban phenomenon because only populous towns had large numbers of unmarried young men, communities of transient merchants, and a culture accustomed to a cash exchange.

Though selling sex for money was legal in the Middle Ages, the position of women who did so was always marginal. In the late fifteenth century cities began to limit brothel residents' freedom of movement and choice of clothing, requiring them to wear distinctive head coverings or bands on their clothing so that they would not be mistaken for "honorable" women. The cities also began to impose harsher penalties on women who did not live in the designated house or section of town. A few prostitutes did earn enough to donate money to charity or buy property, but most were very poor.

Along with buying sex, young men also took it by force. Unmarried women often found it difficult to avoid sexual contacts. Many of them worked as domestic servants, where their employers or employers' sons or male relatives could easily coerce them, or they worked in proximity to men. Female servants were sent on errands alone or with men or worked by themselves in fields far from other people. Notions of female honor kept upper-class women secluded in their homes, particularly in southern and eastern Europe, but there was little attempt anywhere to keep female servants or day laborers from the risk of seduction or rape. Rape was a capital crime in many parts of Europe, but the actual sentences handed out were more likely to be fines and brief imprisonment,

Prostitute Invites a Traveling Merchant Poverty drove women into prostitution, which, though denounced by moralists, was accepted as a normal part of the medieval social fabric. In the cities and larger towns where prostitution flourished, public officials passed laws requiring prostitutes to wear a special mark on their clothing, regulated hours of business, forbade women to drag men into their houses, and denied business to women with the "burning sickness," gonorrhea. *(Bodleian Library, MS. Bodl. 264, fol. 245V)*

with the severity of the sentence dependent on the social status of the victim and the perpetrator. According to a study of the legal evidence from Venice in the years 1338 to 1358, rape was not considered a particularly serious crime against either the victim or society. Noble youths committed a higher percentage of rapes than their small numbers in Venetian society would imply. The rape of a young girl of marriageable age or a child under twelve was considered a graver crime than the rape of a married woman. Nevertheless, the punishment for rape of a noble marriageable girl was only a fine or about six months' imprisonment. In an age when theft and robbery could be punished by mutilation and forgery and sodomy by burning, this penalty was mild indeed. When an upper-class youth was convicted of the rape of a non-noble girl, his punishment was even lighter. By contrast, the sexual assault of a noblewoman by a working-class man, which was extraordinarily rare, resulted in severe penalization because the crime had social and political overtones.

According to laws regarding rape in most parts of Europe, the victim had to prove that she had cried out and had attempted to repel the attacker, and she had to bring the charge within a short period of time after the attack had happened. Women bringing rape charges were often more interested in getting their own honorable reputations back than in punishing the perpetrators, and for this reason they sometimes asked the judge to force their rapists to marry them.

Same-sex relations—what in the late nineteenth century would be termed *homosexuality*—were another feature of medieval urban life (and of village life, though there are very few sources relating to sexual relations of any type in the rural context). Same-sex relations were of relatively little concern to church or state authorities in the early Middle Ages, but this attitude changed beginning in the late twelfth century. By 1300 most areas had defined such actions as "crimes against nature," with authorities seeing them as particularly reprehensible because they thought they did not occur anywhere else in creation. Same-sex relations, usually termed *sodomy*, became a capital crime in most of Europe, with adult offenders threatened with execution by fire. The Italian cities of Venice, Florence, and Lucca created special courts to deal with sodomy, which saw thousands of investigations.

How prevalent was homosexuality? This is difficult to answer, even in modern society, but Florence provides a provocative case study. The city of Florence passed legislation against sodomy in 1415 and 1418, and in 1432 it set up a special magistracy, the Office of the Night, to "root out . . . the abominable vice of sodomy." This board of professional men at least forty-five years of age and married was elected annually and charged with pursuing and punishing sodomitical activity between males.[12] The name of the magistracy derived from the nocturnal activities of most male encounters, especially in the spring and summer months and on feast days and

Sundays. Between 1432 and the abolition of the magistracy in 1502, about seventeen thousand men came to its attention, which, even over a seventy-year period, represents a great number in a population of about forty thousand. Moreover, careful statistical analysis of judicial records shows that all classes of society engaged in it—men in the textile trade, in commerce, in education, and in the food industry, especially butchers, as well as construction workers, tavern keepers, artists, and innkeepers. Sodomy was not a marginal practice, which may account for the fact that, despite harsh laws and special courts, actual executions for sodomy were rare in Italy. They were also uncommon in England, where despite harsh laws there were only six trials for sodomy during the entire long reign of Queen Elizabeth I (1564–1603). Trials were more common in the Iberian Peninsula, where those charged with sodomy were sometimes tortured to reveal other names, so that sodomy accusations often occurred in waves.

Almost all cases heard by the Florentine court and courts in other cities involved an adult man and an adolescent boy and ranged from sex exchanged for money or gifts to long-term affectionate relationships. Florentines believed in a generational model in which different roles were appropriate to different stages in life. In a socially and sexually hierarchical world, the boy in the passive role was identified as subordinate, dependent, and mercenary, words usually applied to women. Florentines, however, never described the dominant partner in feminine terms, for he had not compromised his masculine identity or violated a gender ideal; in fact, the adult partner might be married or have female sexual partners as well as male. Only if an adult male assumed the passive role was his masculinity jeopardized. Such cases were extremely rare. Same-sex relations often developed within the context of all-male environments, such as the army, the craft shop, and the artistic workshop, and were part of the collective male experience. Homoerotic relationships played important roles in defining stages of life, expressing distinctions of status, and shaping masculine gender identity.

Same-sex relations involving women almost never came to the attention of legal authorities, so it is difficult to find out much about them. Most commentators about sexual relations were male clergy who viewed sex between women as categorically different than sex between men, if they regarded it as sex at all. Female-female desire is expressed in songs, plays, and stories, as is male-male desire. Such literary sources can be used as evidence of the way people understood same-sex relations, though not how common such relations were.

Same-Sex Relations This illustration, from a thirteenth-century French book of morals, interprets female and male same-sex relations as the work of devils, who hover over the couples. This illustration was painted at the time that religious and political authorities were increasingly criminalizing same-sex relations. *(Austrian National Library, Vienna, Cod. 2554, fol. 2r)*

Fur-Collar Crime

The Hundred Years' War had provided employment and opportunity for thousands of idle and fortune-seeking knights. But during periods of truce and after the war finally ended, many nobles once again had little to do. Inflation hurt them. Although many were living on fixed incomes, their chivalric code demanded lavish generosity and an aristocratic lifestyle. Many nobles turned to crime as a way of raising money. The fourteenth and fifteenth centuries witnessed a great deal of "fur-collar crime," so called for the miniver fur nobles alone were allowed to wear on their collars.

Fur-collar crime rarely involved such felonies as homicide, robbery, rape, and arson. Instead, nobles used their superior social status to rob and extort from the weak and then to corrupt the judicial process. Groups of noble brigands roamed the English countryside stealing from both rich and poor. Sir John de Colseby and Sir William Bussy led a gang of thirty-eight knights who stole goods worth £3,000 in various robberies. Operating like modern urban racketeers, knightly gangs demanded that peasants pay "protection money" or else have their hovels burned and their fields destroyed.

Attacks on the rich often took the form of kidnapping and extortion. Wealthy travelers were seized on the highways and held for ransom. In northern England a gang of gentry led by Sir Gilbert de Middleton abducted Sir Henry Beaumont; his brother, the bishop-elect of Durham; and two Roman cardinals in England on a peacemaking visit. Only after ransom was paid were the victims released.

Fur-collar criminals were terrorists, but like some modern-day white-collar criminals who commit nonviolent crimes, medieval aristocratic criminals got away with their outrages. When accused of wrongdoing, fur-collar criminals intimidated witnesses. They threatened jurors. They used "pull" or cash to bribe judges. As a fourteenth-century English judge wrote to a young nobleman, "For the love of your father I have hindered charges being brought against you and have prevented execution of indictment actually made."[13] Criminal activity by nobles continued decade after decade because governments were too weak to stop it.

The ballads of Robin Hood, a collection of folk legends from late medieval England, describe the adventures of the outlaw hero and his band of followers who lived in Sherwood Forest and attacked and punished those who violated the social system and the law. Most of the villains in these simple tales are fur-collar criminals—grasping landlords, wicked sheriffs such as the famous sheriff of Nottingham, and mercenary churchmen. Robin and his merry men performed a sort of retributive justice. Robin Hood was a popular figure because he symbolized the deep resentment of aristocratic corruption and abuse; he represented the struggle against tyranny and oppression.

Ethnic Tensions and Restrictions

Large numbers of people in the twelfth and thirteenth centuries migrated from one part of Europe to another: the English into Scotland and Ireland; Germans, French, and Flemings into Poland, Bohemia, and Hungary; the French into Spain. The colonization of frontier regions meant that peoples of different ethnic backgrounds lived side by side. Everywhere in Europe, towns recruited people from the countryside (see pages 333). In frontier regions, townspeople were usually long-distance immigrants and, in eastern Europe, Ireland, and Scotland, ethnically different from the surrounding rural population. In eastern Europe, German was the language of the towns; in Irish towns, French, the tongue of Norman or English settlers, predominated.

In the early periods of conquest and colonization, and in all regions with extensive migrations, a legal dualism existed: native peoples remained subject to their traditional laws; newcomers brought and were subject to the laws of the countries from which they came. On the Prussian and Polish frontier, for example, the law was that "men who come there . . . should be judged on account of any crime or contract engaged in there according to Polish custom if they are Poles and according to German custom if they are Germans."[14] Likewise, in Spain Mudéjars, Muslim subjects of Christian kings, received guarantees of separate but equal judicial rights. King Alfonso I of Aragon's charter to the Muslims of Toledo states, "They shall be in lawsuits and pleas under their (Muslim) qadi (judges) . . . as it was in the times of the Moors."[15] Thus conquered peoples, whether Muslims in Spain or minority immigrant groups such as Germans in eastern Europe, had legal protection and lived in their own juridical enclaves. Subject peoples experienced some disabilities, but the broad trend was toward legal pluralism.

The great exception to this broad pattern was Ireland. From the start, the English practiced an extreme form of discrimination toward the native Irish. The English distinguished between the free and the unfree, and the entire Irish population, simply by the fact of Irish birth, was unfree. In 1210 King John declared that "English law and custom be established there (in Ireland)." Accordingly, a legal structure modeled on that of England, with county courts, itinerant justices, and the common law (see pages 271–274), was set up. But the Irish had no access to the common-law courts. In civil (property) disputes, an English defendant need not respond to his Irish plaintiff; no Irish person could make a will. In criminal procedures, the murder of an Irishman was not considered a felony. In 1317–1318 Irish princes sent a Remonstrance to the pope complaining that "any non-Irishman is allowed to bring legal action against an Irishman, but an Irishman . . . except any prelate (bishop or abbot) is barred from every action by that fact alone." An English defendant in the criminal matter would claim "that he is not held to answer . . . since he [the plaintiff] is Irish and not of free blood."[16] Naturally, this emphasis on blood descent provoked bitterness.

Other than in Ireland, although native peoples commonly held humbler positions, both immigrant and native townspeople prospered during the expanding economy of the thirteenth century. When economic recession hit during the fourteenth century, ethnic tensions multiplied.

The later Middle Ages witnessed a movement away from legal pluralism or dualism and toward legal homogeneity and an emphasis on blood descent. Competition for ecclesiastical offices and the cultural divisions between town and country people became arenas for ethnic tension. Since bishoprics and abbacies carried religious authority, spiritual charisma, and often rights of appointment to subordinate positions, they were natural objects of ambition. When prelates of a language or "nationality" different from those of the local people gained church positions, the latter felt a loss of influence. Bishops were supposed to be pastors. Their pastoral work involved preaching, teaching, and comforting, duties that could be performed effectively only when the bishop (or priest) could communicate with the people. Ideally, in a pluralistic society, he should be bilingual; often he was not.

In the late thirteenth century, as waves of Germans migrated into Danzig on the Baltic, into Silesia, and into the Polish countryside and towns, they encountered Jakub Swinka, archbishop of Gniezno (1283–1314), whose jurisdiction included these areas of settlement. The bishop hated Germans and referred to them as "dog heads." His German contemporary, Bishop John of Cracow, detested the Poles, wanted to expel all Polish people, and refused to appoint Poles to any church office. In Ireland, English colonists and the native Irish competed for ecclesiastical offices until 1217, when the English government in London decreed:

Since the election of Irishmen in our land of Ireland has often disturbed the peace of that land, we command you . . . that henceforth you allow no Irishman to be elected . . . or preferred in any cathedral . . . (and) you should seek by all means to procure election and promotion to vacant bishoprics of . . . honest Englishmen.[17]

Although criticized by the pope and not totally enforceable, this law remained in effect in many dioceses for centuries.

Likewise, the arrival of Cistercians and mendicants (Franciscans and Dominicans) from France and Germany in Baltic and Slavic lands provoked ethnic hostilities. Slavic prelates and princes saw the German mendicants as "instruments of cultural colonization," and Slavs were strongly discouraged from becoming friars. In 1333, when John of Drazic, bishop of Prague, founded a friary at Roudnice (Raudnitz), he specified that "we shall admit no one to this convent or monastery of any nation except a Bohemian [Czech], born of two Czech-speaking parents."[18] In the fourteenth-century *Dalimil Chronicle,* a survey of Bohemian history written in Czech and pervaded with Czech hostility toward Germans, one anti-German prince offered 100 marks of silver "to anyone who brought him one hundred noses cut off from the Germans."[19] Urban residents, who were German, countered with their own restrictions. Cobblers in fourteenth-century Beeskow, a town close to the large Slavic population of Lausitz in Silesia, required that "an apprentice who comes to learn his craft should be brought before the master and guild members. . . . We forbid the sons of barbers, linen workers, shepherds, Slavs." The bakers of the same town decreed: "Whoever wishes to be a member must bring proof to the councillors and guildsmen that he is born of legitimate, upright, German folk. . . . No one of Wendish (Slavic) race may be in the guild."[20]

Ethnic purity can be maintained across generations only by prohibiting marriage among groups, and laws did just this. Intermarriage was forbidden in many places, such as Riga on the Baltic (now the capital of Latvia), where legislation for the bakers guild stipulated that "whoever wishes to have the privilege of membership in our company shall not take as a wife any woman who is ill-famed . . . or non-German; if he does marry such a woman, he must leave the company and office." Not only the guilds but also eligibility for public office depended on ethnic purity, as at the German burgher settlement of Pest in Hungary, where a town judge had to have four German grandparents.

The most extensive attempt to prevent intermarriage and protect ethnic purity is embodied in Ireland's **Statute of Kilkenny** (1366), which states that "there were to be no marriages between those of immigrant and native stock; that the English inhabitants of Ireland must employ the English language and bear English names; that they must ride in the English way (that is, with saddles) and have English apparel; that no Irishmen were to be granted ecclesiastical benefices or admitted to monasteries in the English parts of Ireland."[21] Rulers of the Christian kingdoms of Spain drew up comparable legislation discriminating against the Mudéjars.

Late medieval chroniclers used words such as *gens* (race or clan) and *natio* (species, stock, or kind) to refer to different groups. They held that peoples differed according to language, traditions, customs, and laws. None of these were unchangeable, however, and commentators increasingly also described ethnic differences in terms of "blood"—"German blood," "English blood," and so on—which made ethnicity heritable. Religious beliefs also came to be conceptualized as blood, with people re-

Opening Page from the *Dalimil Chronicle* This history of Bohemia (now part of the Czech Republic) was the first book to be written in the Czech language, and was an important tool in the creation of a Czech national identity. The section reproduced here includes references to "our people" and "our land." The book remains an important part of Czech identity; in 2005 the National Library of the Czech Republic purchased a fragment of an illustrated fourteenth-century Latin translation for nearly half a million dollars. Similar historical chronicles were written in the vernacular languages of many parts of Europe in the fifteenth century and contributed to a growing sense of ethnic and national distinctions. (*Austrian National Library, Vienna*)

garded as having Jewish blood, Muslim blood, or Christian blood. The most dramatic expression of this was in Spain, where "purity of the blood"—having no Muslim or Jewish ancestors—became an obsession. Blood was also used as a way to talk about social differences, especially for nobles. Just as Irish and English were prohibited from marrying each other, those of "noble blood" were prohibited from marrying commoners in many parts of Europe. As Europeans increasingly came into contact with people from Africa and Asia, and particularly as they developed colonial empires, these notions of blood also became a way of conceptualizing racial categories (see page 429).

Literacy and Vernacular Literature

The development of ethnic identities had many negative consequences, but a more positive effect was the increasing use of national languages. In the High Middle Ages most official documents and works of literature were written in Latin. Beginning in the fourteenth century, however, national languages—the **vernacular**—came into widespread use not only in verbal communication but in literature as well. Two masterpieces of European culture, Dante's *Divine Comedy* (1310–1320) and Chaucer's *Canterbury Tales* (1387–1400), brilliantly manifest this new national pride.

Dante Alighieri (1265–1321) descended from a landowning family in Florence, where he held several positions in the city government. Dante called his work a "comedy" because he wrote it in Italian and in a different style from the "tragic" Latin; a later generation added the adjective *divine,* referring both to its sacred subject and to Dante's artistry. The *Divine Comedy* is an allegorical trilogy of one hundred cantos (verses), each of whose three equal parts (1 + 33 + 33 + 33) describes one of the realms of the next world: Hell, Purgatory, and Paradise. The Roman poet Virgil, representing reason, leads Dante through Hell, where he observes the torments of the damned and denounces the disorders of his own time, especially ecclesiastical ambition and corruption. Passing up into Purgatory, Virgil shows the poet how souls are purified of their disordered inclinations. From Purgatory, Beatrice, a woman

Schoolmaster and Schoolmistress Teaching Ambrosius Holbein, elder brother of the more famous Hans Holbein, produced this signboard for the Swiss educator Myconius; it is an excellent example of what we would call commercial art—art used to advertise, in this case Myconius's profession. The German script above promised that all who enrolled, girls and boys, would learn to read and write. Most schools were for boys only, but a few offered instruction for girls as well. By modern standards the classroom seems bleak: the windows have glass panes but they don't admit much light, and the schoolmaster is prepared to use the sticks if the boy makes a mistake. *(Kunstmuseum Basel/Martin Buhler, photographer)*

Dante once loved and the symbol of divine revelation in the poem, leads him to Paradise. In Paradise, home of the angels and saints, Saint Bernard—representing mystic contemplation—leads Dante to the Virgin Mary. Through her intercession, he at last attains a vision of God.

The *Divine Comedy* portrays contemporary and historical figures, comments on secular and ecclesiastical affairs, and draws on Scholastic philosophy. Within the framework of a symbolic pilgrimage to the City of God, the *Divine Comedy* embodies the psychological tensions of the age. A profoundly Christian poem, it also contains bitter criticism of some church authorities. In its symmetrical structure and use of figures from the ancient world, such as Virgil, the poem perpetuates the classical tradition, but as the first major work of literature in the Italian vernacular, it is distinctly modern.

Geoffrey Chaucer (1342–1400), the son of a London wine merchant, was an official in the administrations of the English kings Edward III and Richard II and wrote poetry as an avocation. Chaucer's *Canterbury Tales* is a collection of stories in lengthy rhymed narrative. On a pilgrimage to the shrine of Saint Thomas Becket at Canterbury (see page 271), thirty people of various social backgrounds tell tales. The Prologue sets the scene and describes the pilgrims, whose characters are further revealed in the story each one tells. For example, the gross Miller tells a vulgar story about a deceived husband; the earthy Wife of Bath, who has buried five husbands, sketches a fable about the selection of a spouse; and the elegant Prioress, who violates her vows by wearing jewelry, delivers a homily on the Virgin. In depicting the interests and behavior of all types of people, Chaucer presents a rich panorama of English social life in the fourteenth century. Like the *Divine Comedy*, *Canterbury Tales* reflects the cultural tensions of the times. Ostensibly Christian, many of the pilgrims are also materialistic, sensual, and worldly, suggesting the ambivalence of the broader society's concern for the next world and frank enjoyment of this one.

Beginning in the fourteenth century, a variety of evidence attests to the increasing literacy of laypeople. Wills and inventories reveal that many people, not just nobles, possessed books—mainly devotional, but also romances, manuals on manners and etiquette, histories, and sometimes legal and philosophical texts. In England the number of schools in the diocese of York quadrupled between 1350 and 1500. Information from Flemish and German towns is similar: children were sent to schools and were taught the fundamentals of reading, writing, and arithmetic. Laymen increasingly served as managers or stewards of estates and as clerks to guilds and town governments; such positions obviously required that they be able to keep administrative and financial records.

The penetration of laymen into the higher positions of governmental administration, long the preserve of clerics, also illustrates rising lay literacy. For example, in 1400 beneficed clerics held most of the posts in the English Exchequer; by 1430 clerics were the exception. With growing frequency, the upper classes sent their daughters to convent schools, where, in addition to instruction in singing, religion, needlework, deportment, and household management, girls gained the rudiments of reading and sometimes writing. Reading and writing were taught separately, and many young people, especially girls, were taught to read but not to write.

The spread of literacy represents a response to the needs of an increasingly complex society. Trade, commerce, and expanding government bureaucracies required more and more literate people. Late medieval culture remained an oral culture in which most people received information by word of mouth. But by the mid-fifteenth century, even before the printing press was turning out large quantities of reading materials, the evolution toward a literary culture was already perceptible.

Chapter Summary

 Online Study Center ACE the Test

- *What were the demographic and economic consequences of climate change?*
- *How did the spread of the plague shape European society?*
- *What were the causes of the Hundred Years' War, and how did the war affect European politics, economics, and cultural life?*
- *What challenges faced the Christian church in the fourteenth century, and how did church leaders, intellectuals, and ordinary people respond?*
- *How did economic and social tensions contribute to revolts, crime, violence, and a growing sense of ethnic and national distinctions?*

The crises of the fourteenth and fifteenth centuries were acids that burned deeply into the fabric of traditional medieval society. Bad weather brought poor harvests, which contributed to widespread famine and disease and an international economic depression. Political leaders attempted to find solutions, but were unable to deal with the economic and social problems that resulted.

In 1348 a new disease, most likely the bubonic plague, came to mainland Europe, carried from the Black Sea by ships. It spread quickly by land and sea and within two years may have killed as much as one-third of the European population. Contemporary medical explanations for the plague linked it to poisoned air or water, and treatments were ineffective. Many people regarded the plague as a divine punishment and sought remedies in religious practices such as prayer, pilgrimages, or donations to churches. Population losses caused by the Black Death led to inflation but in the long run may have contributed to more opportunities for the peasants and urban workers who survived the disease.

The miseries of the plague were enhanced in England and France by the Hundred Years' War, which was fought intermittently in France from 1337 to 1453. The war began as a dispute over the succession to the French crown, and royal propaganda on both sides fostered a kind of early nationalism. The English won most of the battles and in 1419 advanced to the walls of Paris. The appearance of Joan of Arc rallied the French cause, and French troops eventually pushed English forces out of all of France except the port of Calais. The war served as a catalyst for the development of representative government in England. In France, on the other hand, the war stiffened opposition to national assemblies.

Religious beliefs offered people solace through these difficult times, but the Western Christian church was going through a particularly difficult period in the fourteenth and early fifteenth centuries. The Avignon papacy and the Great Schism weakened the prestige of the church and people's faith in papal authority. The conciliar movement, by denying the church's universal sovereignty, strengthened the claims of secular governments to jurisdiction over all their peoples. As members of the clergy challenged the power of the pope, laypeople challenged the authority of the church itself. Women and men increasingly relied on direct approaches to God, often through mystical encounters, rather than on the institutional church. Some, including John Wyclif and Jan Hus, questioned basic church doctrines.

The plague and the war both led to higher taxes and economic dislocations, which sparked peasant revolts in Flanders, France, and England. Peasant revolts often blended with conflicts involving workers in cities, where working conditions were changing to create a greater gap between wealthy merchant-producers and poor propertyless workers. Unrest in the countryside and cities may have been further exacerbated by marriage patterns that left large numbers of young men unmarried and rootless. The pattern of late marriage for men contributed to a growth in prostitution, which was an accepted feature of medieval urban society. Along with peasant revolts and urban crime and unrest, violence perpetrated by nobles was a common part of late medieval life. The economic and demographic crises of the fourteenth century also contributed to increasing ethnic tensions in the many parts of Europe where migration had brought different population groups together. A growing sense of ethnic and national identity led to restrictions and occasionally to violence, but also to the increasing use of national languages for works of literature. The increasing number of schools that led to the growth of lay literacy represents another positive achievement of the later Middle Ages.

Key Terms

- Great Famine
- Black Death
- bubo
- flagellants
- Agincourt
- Joan of Arc
- representative assemblies
- nationalism
- Babylonian Captivity
- Great Schism
- conciliarists
- confraternities
- *The Imitation of Christ*
- peasant revolts
- Jacquerie
- Statute of Kilkenny
- vernacular

Online Study Center Improve Your Grade Flashcards

Suggested Reading

Allmand, Christopher. *The Hundred Years War: England and France at War, ca 1300–1450,* rev. ed. 2005. Designed for students; examines the war from political, military, social, and economic perspectives and compares the way England and France reacted to the conflict.

Boswell, John. *Christianity, Social Tolerance, and Homosexuality: Gay People in Western Europe from the Beginning of the Christian Era to the Fourteenth Century.* 1981. Remains an important broad analysis of attitudes toward same-sex relations throughout the Middle Ages.

Dunn, Alastair. *The Peasants' Revolt: England's Failed Revolution of 1381.* 2004. Offers new interpretations of the causes and consequence of the English Peasants' Revolt.

Dyer, Christopher. *Standards of Living in the Later Middle Ages.* 1989. Examines economic realities and social conditions more generally.

Herlihy, David. *The Black Death and the Transformation of the West,* 2d ed. 1997. A fine treatment of the causes and cultural consequences of the disease that remains the best starting point for study of the great epidemic.

Holt, James Clarke. *Robin Hood.* 1982. A soundly researched and highly readable study of the famous outlaw.

Jordan, William Chester. *The Great Famine: Northern Europe in the Early Fourteenth Century.* 1996. Discusses catastrophic weather, soil exhaustion, and other factors that led to the Great Famine and the impact of the famine on community life.

Karras, Ruth M. *Sexuality in Medieval Europe: Doing onto Others.* 2005. A brief overview designed for undergraduates that incorporates the newest scholarship.

Kieckhefer, Richard. *Unquiet Souls: Fourteenth-Century Saints and Their Religious Milieu.* 1984. Sets the ideas of the mystics in their social and intellectual contexts.

Koch, H. W. *Medieval Warfare.* 1978. A beautifully illustrated book covering strategy, tactics, armaments, and costumes of war.

Lehfeldt, Elizabeth, ed. *The Black Death.* 2005. Includes excerpts from debates about many aspects of the Black Death.

Oakley, Frances. *The Western Church in the Later Middle Ages.* 1979. An excellent broad survey.

Robertson, D. W., Jr. *Chaucer's London.* 1968. Evokes the social setting of *Canterbury Tales* brilliantly.

Swanson, R. N. *Religion and Devotion in Europe, c. 1215–c. 1515.* 2004. Explores many aspects of spirituality.

Tuchman, Barbara. *A Distant Mirror: The Calamitous Fourteenth Century.* 1978. Written for a general audience, this remains a vivid description of this tumultuous time.

Notes

1. J. M. Rigg, trans., *The Decameron of Giovanni Boccaccio* (London: J. M. Dent & Sons, 1903), p. 6.
2. Quoted in D. Herlihy, *The Black Death and the Transformation of the West* (Cambridge, Mass.: Harvard University Press, 1997), p. 42.
3. Quoted in J. Barnie, *War in Medieval English Society: Social Values and the Hundred Years' War* (Ithaca, N.Y.: Cornell University Press, 1974), p. 34.
4. W. P. Barrett, trans., *The Trial of Jeanne d'Arc* (London: George Routledge, 1931), pp. 165–166.
5. Quoted in Barnie, *War in Medieval English Society,* pp. 36–37.
6. See G. O. Sayles, *The King's Parliament of England* (New York: W. W. Norton, 1974), app., pp. 137–141.
7. Quoted in P. S. Lewis, "The Failure of the Medieval French Estates," *Past and Present* 23 (November 1962): 6.
8. Quoted in J. H. Smith, *The Great Schism, 1378: The Disintegration of the Medieval Papacy* (New York: Weybright & Talley, 1970), p. 15.
9. Quoted in Katharina M. Wilson, ed., *Medieval Women Writers* (Athens: University of Georgia Press, 1984), p. 245.
10. Quoted in M. Bloch, *French Rural History,* trans. J. Sondeimer (Berkeley: University of California Press, 1966), p. 169.
11. C. Stephenson and G. Marcham, eds., *Sources of English Constitutional History,* rev. ed. (New York: Harper & Row, 1972), p. 225.
12. M. Rocke, *Forbidden Friendships: Homosexuality and Male Culture in Renaissance Florence* (New York: Oxford University Press, 1996), p. 45.
13. Quoted in B. A. Hanawalt, "Fur Collar Crime: The Pattern of Crime Among the Fourteenth-Century English Nobility," *Journal of Social History* 8 (Spring 1975): 7.
14. Quoted in R. Bartlett, *The Making of Europe: Conquest, Colonization and Cultural Change, 950–1350* (Princeton, N.J.: Princeton University Press, 1993), p. 205.
15. Quoted ibid., p. 208.
16. Quoted ibid., p. 215.
17. Quoted ibid., p. 224.
18. Quoted ibid., p. 228.
19. Quoted ibid., p. 236.
20. Quoted ibid., p. 238.
21. Quoted ibid., p. 239.

Listening to the Past

Christine de Pizan

Christine de Pizan (1364?–1430; earlier spelled "Pisan") was the daughter and wife of highly educated men who held positions at the court of the king of France. She was widowed at twenty-five with young children and an elderly mother to support. Christine, who herself had received an excellent education, decided to support her family through writing, an unusual choice for anyone in this era before the printing press and unheard of for a woman. She began to write prose works and poetry, sending them to wealthy individuals in the hope of receiving their support. Her works were well received, and Christine gained commissions to write specific works, including a biography of the French king Charles V, several histories, a long poem celebrating Joan of Arc's victory, and a book of military tactics. She became the first woman in Europe to make her living as a writer.

Among Christine's many works were several in which she considered women's nature and proper role in society, which had been a topic of debate since ancient times. The best known of these was The City of Ladies *(1404)*, in which she ponders why so many men have a negative view of women and provides examples of virtuous women to counter this view. Immediately afterward she wrote The Treasure of the City of Ladies *(1405, also called* The Book of Three Virtues*)*, which provides moral suggestions and practical advice on behavior and household management for women of all social classes. Most of the book is directed toward princesses and court ladies (who would have been able to read it), but she also includes shorter sections for the wives of merchants and artisans, serving-women, female peasants, and even prostitutes. This is her advice to the wives of artisans, whose husbands were generally members of urban craft guilds, such as blacksmiths, bakers, or shoemakers.

All wives of artisans should be very painstaking and diligent if they wish to have the necessities of life. They should encourage their husbands or their workmen to get to work early in the morning and work until late, for mark our words, there is no trade so good that if you neglect your work you will not have difficulty putting bread on the table. And besides encouraging the others, the wife herself should be involved in the work to the extent that she knows all about it, so that she may know how to oversee his workers if her husband is absent, and to reprove them if they do not do well. She ought to oversee them to keep them from idleness, for through careless workers the master is sometimes ruined. And when customers come to her husband and try to drive a hard bargain, she ought to warn him solicitously to take care that he does not make a bad deal. She should advise him to be chary of giving too much credit if he does not know precisely where and to whom it is going, for in this way many come to poverty, although sometimes the greed to earn more or to accept a tempting proposition makes them do it.

In addition, she ought to keep her husband's love as much as she can, to this end: that he will stay at home more willingly and that he may not have any reason to join the foolish crowds of other young men in taverns and indulge in unnecessary and extravagant expense, as many tradesmen do, especially in Paris. By treating him kindly she should protect him as well as she can from this. It is said that three things drive a man from his home: a quarrelsome wife, a smoking fireplace and a leaking roof. She too ought to stay at home gladly and not go every day traipsing hither and yon gossiping with the neighbours and visiting her chums to find out what everyone is doing. That is done by slovenly housewives roaming about the town in groups. Nor should

Several manuscripts of Christine's works included illustrations showing her writing, which would have increased their appeal to the wealthy individuals who purchased them. *(British Library)*

she go off on these pilgrimages got up for no good reason and involving a lot of needless expense. Furthermore, she ought to remind her husband that they should live so frugally that their expenditure does not exceed their income, so that at the end of the year they do not find themselves in debt.

If she has children, she should have them instructed and taught first at school by educated people so that they may know how better to serve God. Afterwards they may be put to some trade by which they may earn a living, for whoever gives a trade or business training to her child gives a great possession. The children should be kept from wantonness and from voluptuousness above all else, for truly it is something that most shames the children of good towns and is a great sin of mothers and fathers, who ought to be the cause of the virtue and good behavior of their children, but they are sometimes the reason (because of bringing them up to be finicky and indulging them too much) for their wickedness and ruin.

Questions for Analysis

1. How would you describe Christine's view of the ideal artisan's wife?

2. The regulations of craft guilds often required that masters who ran workshops be married. What evidence does Christine's advice provide for why guilds would have stipulated this?

3. How are economic and moral virtues linked for Christine?

Source: Christine de Pisan, *The Treasure of the City of Ladies,* translated with an introduction by Sarah Lawson (Peguin Classics, 1985). This translation copyright © 1985 by Sarah Lawson. Reprinted by permission of Penguin Books Ltd. For more on Christine, see C. C. Willard, *Christine de Pisan: Her Life and Works* (1984), and S. Bell, *The Lost Tapestries of the City of Ladies: Christine de Pizan's Renaissance Legacy* (2004).

Michelangelo's frescoes in the Sistine Chapel in the Vatican, commissioned by the pope. The huge ceiling includes biblical scenes, and the far wall, painted much later, shows a dramatic and violent Last Judgment. *(Vatican Museum)*

chapter 13

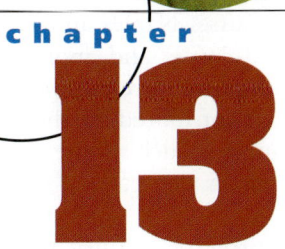

European Society in the Age of the Renaissance, 1350–1550

chapter preview

Economic and Political Developments
- *What economic and political developments in Italy provided the setting for the Renaissance?*

Intellectual Change
- *What were the key ideas of the Renaissance, and how were they different for men and women and for southern and northern Europeans?*

Art and the Artist
- *How did changes in art both reflect and shape new ideas?*

Social Hierarchies
- *What were the key social hierarchies in Renaissance Europe, and how did ideas about hierarchy shape people's lives?*

Politics and the State in the Renaissance (ca 1450–1521)
- *How did the nation-states of western Europe evolve in this period?*

While the Four Horsemen of the Apocalypse seemed to be carrying war, plague, famine, and death across northern Europe, a new culture was emerging in southern Europe. The fourteenth century witnessed the beginnings of remarkable changes in many aspects of Italian intellectual, artistic, and cultural life. Artists and writers thought that they were living in a new golden age, but not until the sixteenth century was this change given the label we use today—the **Renaissance,** from the French version of a word meaning "rebirth." That word was first used by the artist and art historian Giorgio Vasari (1511–1574) to describe the art of "rare men of genius" such as his contemporary Michelangelo. Through their works, Vasari judged, the glory of the classical past had been reborn—or perhaps even surpassed—after centuries of darkness. Vasari used *Renaissance* to describe painting, sculpture, and architecture, what he termed the "Major Arts." Gradually, however, the word was used to refer to many aspects of life at this time, first in Italy and then in the rest of Europe. This new attitude had a slow diffusion out of Italy, with the result that the Renaissance "happened" at different times in different parts of Europe: Italian art of the fourteenth through the early sixteenth century is described as "Renaissance," and so is English literature of the late sixteenth century, including Shakespeare's plays and poetry.

About a century after Vasari coined the word *Renaissance*, scholars began to use the words *Middle Ages* to refer to the millennium between the ancient world and the Renaissance. They increasingly saw the cultural and political changes of the Renaissance, along with the religious changes of the Reformation (see Chapter 14) and the European voyages of exploration (see Chapter 15), as ushering in the "modern" world. Since then, some historians have chosen to view the Renaissance as a bridge between the medieval and modern eras because it corresponded chronologically with the late medieval period and because there were many continuities along with the changes. Others have questioned whether the word *Renaissance* should be used at all to describe an era in which many social groups saw decline rather than advance. These debates remind us that these labels—medieval, Renaissance, modern—are

Online Study Center
This icon will direct you to interactive activities and study materials on the website **college.hmco.com/pic/mckaywest9e**

intellectual constructs, devised after the fact. They all contain value judgments, just as do other chronological designations, such as the "golden age" of Athens and the "Roaring Twenties."

Economic and Political Developments

The cultural achievements of the Renaissance rest on the economic and political developments of earlier centuries. Economic growth laid the material basis for the Italian Renaissance, and ambitious merchants gained political power to match their economic power. They then used their money and power to buy luxuries and hire talent.

- **What economic and political developments in Italy provided the setting for the Renaissance?**

Commercial Developments

In the great commercial revival of the eleventh century, northern Italian cities led the way. By the middle of the twelfth century Venice, supported by a huge merchant marine, had grown enormously rich through overseas trade. Genoa and Milan also enjoyed the benefits of a large volume of trade with the Middle East and northern Europe. These cities fully exploited their geographical positions as natural crossroads for mercantile exchange between the East and the West. Furthermore, in the early fourteenth century Genoa and Venice made important strides in shipbuilding that for the first time allowed their ships to sail all year long. Advances in ship construction greatly increased the volume of goods that could be transported; improvements in the mechanics of sailing accelerated speed.

Scholars tend to agree that the first artistic and literary manifestations of the Italian Renaissance appeared in Florence, which possessed enormous wealth despite geographical constraints: it was an inland city without easy access to sea transportation. But toward the end of the thirteenth century, Florentine merchants and bankers acquired control of papal banking. From their position as tax collectors for the papacy, Florentine mercantile families began to dominate European banking on both sides of the Alps. These families had offices in Paris, London, Bruges, Barcelona, Marseilles, Tunis and other North African ports, and, of course, Naples and Rome. The profits from loans, investments, and money exchanges that poured back to Florence were pumped into urban industries. Such profits contributed to the city's economic vitality. Banking families, such as the Medici in Florence, controlled the politics and culture of their cities.

By the first quarter of the fourteenth century, the economic foundations of Florence were so strong that even severe crises could not destroy the city. In 1344 King Edward III of England repudiated his huge debts to Florentine bankers and forced some of them into bankruptcy. Florence suffered frightfully from the Black Death, losing at least half its population. Serious labor unrest, such as the *ciompi* revolts of 1378 (see page 392), shook the political establishment. Nevertheless, the basic Florentine economic structure remained stable. Driving enterprise, technical know-how, and competitive spirit saw Florence through the difficult economic period of the late fourteenth century.

A Bank Scene, Florence Originally a "bank" was just a counter; moneychangers who sat behind the counter became "bankers," exchanging different currencies and holding deposits for merchants and business people. In this scene from fifteenth-century Florence, the bank is covered with an imported Ottoman geometric rug, one of many imported luxury items handled by Florentine merchants. *(Prato, San Francesco/Scala/Art Resource, NY)*

Communes and Republics

The northern Italian cities were **communes,** sworn associations of free men seeking complete political and economic independence from local nobles. The merchant guilds that formed the communes built and maintained the city walls, regulated trade, raised taxes, and kept civil order. In the course of the twelfth century, communes at Milan, Florence, Genoa, Siena, and Pisa fought for and won their independence from surrounding feudal nobles. The nobles, attracted by the opportunities of long-distance and maritime trade, the rising value of urban real estate, the new public offices available in the expanding communes, and the chances for advantageous marriages into rich commercial families, frequently settled in the cities. Marriage vows often sealed business contracts between the rural nobility and wealthy merchants, with the large dowries of brides providing cash for their new husbands' businesses. This merger of the northern Italian feudal nobility and the commercial elite created a powerful **oligarchy,** or small group that ruled a city and its surrounding countryside. The ruling oligarchy in any city was tied together by blood, economic interests, and social connections, but was also often divided by hostilities of kinship groups toward one another. Such hostilities sometimes erupted in violence, and Italian communes were often politically unstable.

Conflict between families within the ruling oligarchy was exacerbated by unrest coming from below. Merchant elites made citizenship in the communes dependent on a property qualification, years of residence within the city, and social connections. Only a tiny percentage of the male population possessed these qualifications and thus could hold office in the commune's political councils. The common people, called the **popolo,** were disenfranchised and heavily taxed, and they bitterly resented their exclusion from power. The popolo wanted places in the communal government and equality of taxation. Throughout most of the thirteenth century, in city after city, the popolo used armed force and violence to take over the city governments. Republican governments—in which political power theoretically resides in the people and is exercised by their chosen representatives—were established in Bologna, Siena, Parma, Florence, Genoa, and other cities. The victory of the popolo proved temporary, however, because they could not establish civil order within their cities. Merchant oligarchies reasserted their power and sometimes brought in powerful military leaders to establish order. These military leaders, called **condottieri** (singular, condottiero), had their own mercenary armies, and in many cities they took over political power as well. The military leader often invented a long noble lineage to justify his takeover of power, pretending he descended from a Germanic king or Roman leader. There was not much that merchant oligarchies could do to retain their power, and many cities in Italy became **signori,** in which one man ruled and handed down the right to rule to his son. Some signori (the word is plural in Italian and is used for both persons and forms of government) kept the institutions of communal government in place, but these had no actual power.

For the next two centuries the Italian city-states were ruled by signori or by merchant oligarchies. Oligarchic regimes possessed constitutions and often boasted about how much more democratic their form of government was than the government in neighboring signori. In actuality, there wasn't much difference. In oligarchies, a small, restricted class of wealthy merchants exercised the judicial, executive, and legislative functions of government. Thus, in 1422 Venice had a population of eighty-four thousand, but two hundred men held all the power; Florence had about forty thousand people, but only six hundred men were part of the government. Even this number is an illusion, for real power in Florence for most of the fifteenth century was actually held by the Medici family. Oligarchic regimes maintained only a façade of republican government. The Renaissance nostalgia for the Roman form of government, combined with calculating shrewdness, prompted the leaders of Venice, Milan, and Florence to use the old forms.

Chronology

1350–1353	Boccaccio, *The Decameron*
1434–1494	Medici family in power in Florence
1440s	Invention of movable metal type
1469	Marriage of Isabella of Castile and Ferdinand of Aragon
1486	Pico della Mirandola, *On the Dignity of Man*
1494	Invasion of Italy by Charles VIII of France
1508–1512	Michelangelo paints ceiling of Sistine Chapel
1513	Machiavelli, *The Prince*
1516	More, *Utopia*
1528	Castiglione, *The Courtier*

In the fifteenth century the signori in many cities and the most powerful merchant oligarchs in others transformed their households into **courts.** They built magnificent palaces in the centers of cities and required all political business be done there. They hired architects to design and build these palaces, artists to fill them with paintings and sculptures, and musicians and composers to fill them with music. They supported writers and philosophers, flaunting their patronage of learning and the arts. They used ceremonies connected with family births, baptisms, marriages, funerals, or triumphant entrances into the city as occasions for magnificent pageantry and elaborate ritual. Courtly culture afforded signori and oligarchs the opportunity to display and assert their wealth and power. The courts of the rulers of Milan, Florence, and other cities were models for those developed later by rulers of nation-states.

The Balance of Power Among the Italian City-States

Renaissance Italians had a passionate attachment to their individual city-states: political loyalty and feeling centered on the local city. This intensity of local feeling perpetuated the dozens of small states and hindered the development of one unified state.

In the fifteenth century five powers dominated the Italian peninsula: Venice, Milan, Florence, the Papal States, and the kingdom of Naples (see Map 13.1). The rulers of the city-states—whether signori in Milan, patrician elitists in Florence, or oligarchs in Venice—governed as monarchs. They crushed urban revolts, levied taxes, killed their enemies, and used massive building programs to employ, and the arts to overawe, the masses.

Venice, with its enormous trade and vast colonial empire, ranked as an international power. Though Venice had a sophisticated constitution and was a **republic** in name, an oligarchy of merchant aristocrats actually ran the city. Milan was also called a republic, but the condottieri-turned-signori of the Sforza family ruled harshly and dominated the smaller cities of the north. Likewise, in Florence the form of government was republican, with authority vested in several councils of state. In reality, between 1434 and 1494, power in Florence was held by the great Medici banking family. Though not public officers, Cosimo (1434–1464) and Lorenzo (1469–1492) ruled from behind the scenes.

Central Italy consisted mainly of the Papal States, which during the Babylonian Captivity had come under the sway of important Roman families. Pope Alexander VI (1492–1503), aided militarily and politically by his son Cesare Borgia, reasserted papal authority in the papal lands. Cesare Borgia became the hero of Machiavelli's *The Prince* (see page 415) because he began the work of uniting the peninsula by ruthlessly conquering and exacting total obedience from the principalities making up the Papal States.

South of the Papal States was the kingdom of Naples, consisting of virtually all of southern Italy and, at times, Sicily. The kingdom of Naples had long been disputed by the Aragonese and by the French. In 1435 it passed to Aragon.

The major Italian city-states controlled the smaller ones, such as Siena, Mantua, Ferrara, and Modena, and competed furiously among themselves for territory. The large cities used diplomacy, spies, paid informers, and any other available means to get information that could be used to advance their ambitions. While the states of northern Europe were moving toward centralization and consolidation, the world of Italian politics resembled a jungle where the powerful dominated the weak.

In one significant respect, however, the Italian city-states anticipated future relations among competing European states after 1500. Whenever one Italian state appeared to gain a predominant position within the peninsula, other states combined to establish a *balance of power* against the major threat. In the formation of these alliances, Renaissance Italians invented the machinery of modern diplomacy: permanent embassies with resident ambassadors in capitals where political relations and commercial ties needed continual monitoring. The resident ambassador was one of the great achievements of the Italian Renaissance.

At the end of the fifteenth century Venice, Florence, Milan, and the papacy possessed great wealth and represented high cultural achievement. However, their imperialistic ambitions at one another's expense and their resulting inability to form a common alliance against potential foreign enemies made Italy an inviting target for invasion. When Florence and Naples entered into an agreement to acquire Milanese territories, Milan called on France for support.

At Florence the French invasion had been predicted by Dominican friar Girolamo Savonarola (1452–1498). In a number of fiery sermons between 1491 and 1494, Savonarola attacked what he called the paganism and moral vice of the city, the undemocratic government of Lorenzo de' Medici, and the corruption of Pope Alexander VI. For a time Savonarola enjoyed popular support among the ordinary people; he became the religious

Economic and Political Developments • 411

MAP 13.1 The Italian City-States, ca 1494 In the fifteenth century the Italian city-states represented great wealth and cultural sophistication. The political divisions of the peninsula invited foreign intervention.

leader of Florence and as such contributed to the fall of the Medici dynasty. Eventually, however, people tired of his moral denunciations, and he was excommunicated by the pope and executed. Savonarola stands as proof that the common people did not share the worldly outlook of the commercial and intellectual elite. His career also illustrates the internal instability of Italian cities such as Florence, an instability that invited foreign invasion.

The invasion of Italy in 1494 by the French king Charles VIII (r. 1483–1498) inaugurated a new period in Italian and European power politics. Italy became the focus of international ambitions and the battleground of foreign armies, particularly those of France and the Holy Roman Empire in a series of conflicts called the Habsburg-Valois Wars (named for the German and French dynasties). The Italian cities suffered severely from

Uccello: Battle of San Romano Fascinated by perspective—the representation of spatial depth or distance on a flat surface—the Florentine artist Paolo Uccello (1397–1475) celebrated the Florentine victory over Siena (1432) in a painting with three scenes. Though a minor battle, it started Florence on the road to domination over smaller nearby states. The painting hung in Lorenzo de' Medici's bedroom. *(National Gallery, London/Erich Lessing/Art Resource, NY)*

continual warfare, especially in the frightful sack of Rome in 1527 by imperial forces under the emperor Charles V. Thus the failure of the city-states to form some federal system, to consolidate, or at least to establish a common foreign policy led to centuries of subjection by outside invaders. Italy was not to achieve unification until 1870.

Intellectual Change

The Renaissance was characterized by self-conscious awareness among fourteenth- and fifteenth-century Italians that they were living in a new era. The realization that something new and unique was happening first came to men of letters in the fourteenth century, especially to the poet and humanist Francesco Petrarch (1304–1374). Petrarch thought that he was living at the start of a new age, a period of light following a long night of Gothic gloom.

Medieval people had believed that they were continuing the glories that had been ancient Rome and had recognized no cultural division between the world of the emperors and their own times. But for Petrarch, the Germanic migrations had caused a sharp cultural break with the glories of Rome and inaugurated what he called the "Dark Ages." Along with many of his contemporaries, Petrarch believed that he was witnessing a new golden age of intellectual achievement.

• **What were the key ideas of the Renaissance, and how were they different for men and women and for southern and northern Europeans?**

Humanism

Petrarch and other poets, writers, and artists showed a deep interest in the ancient past, in both the physical remains of the Roman Empire and classical Latin texts. The study of Latin classics became known as the *studia humanitates,* usually translated as "liberal studies" or the "liberal arts." Like all programs of study, they contained an implicit philosophy, generally known as **humanism,** a term devised by the Florentine rhetorician and historian Leonardo Bruni (1370–1444). The words *humanism* and *humanist* derive ultimately from the Latin *humanitas,* which the ancient Roman writer Cicero had used to mean the literary culture needed by anyone who would be considered educated and civilized. Humanists studied the Latin classics to learn what they reveal about human nature. Humanism emphasized human beings and their achievements, interests, and capabilities.

Appreciation for the literary culture of the Romans had never died in the West, but medieval writers had studied the ancients in order to come to know God. Medieval scholars had interpreted the classics in a Christian sense and had invested the ancients' poems and histories with Christian meaning.

Renaissance humanists approached the classics differently. Whereas medieval writers looked to the classics to reveal God, Renaissance humanists studied the classics to understand human nature. They viewed humanity from a strongly Christian perspective, however: men (and women, though to a lesser degree) were made in the image and likeness of God. For example, in a remarkable essay, *On the Dignity of Man* (1486), the Florentine writer Giovanni Pico della Mirandola (1463–1494) stressed that man possesses great dignity because he was made as Adam in the image of God before the Fall and as Christ after the Resurrection. According to Pico, man's place in the universe is somewhere between the beasts and the angels, but because of the divine image planted in him, there are no limits to what he can accomplish. Humanists generally rejected classical ideas that were opposed to Christianity, or they sought through reinterpretation an underlying harmony between the pagan and secular and the Christian faith.

Interest in human achievement led humanists to emphasize the importance of the individual. Groups such as families, guilds, and religious organizations continued to provide strong support for the individual and to exercise great social influence. Yet in the Renaissance, intellectuals, unlike their counterparts in the Middle Ages, prized their own uniqueness.

The Renaissance witnessed the emergence of many distinctive personalities who gloried in their individuality; they had enormous confidence in their ability to achieve great things. Leon Battista Alberti (1404–1472), a writer, architect, and mathematician, remarked, "Men can do all things if they will."[1] Florentine goldsmith and

Benvenuto Cellini: Saltcellar of Francis I (ca 1540) In gold and enamel, Cellini depicts the Roman sea god, Neptune (with trident, or three-pronged spear), sitting beside a small boat-shaped container holding salt from the sea. Opposite him, a female figure personifying Earth guards pepper, which derives from a plant. Portrayed on the base are the four seasons and the times of day, symbolizing seasonal festivities and daily meal schedules. Classical figures portrayed with grace, poise, and elegance were common subjects in Renaissance art. *(Kunsthistorisches Museum, Vienna/The Bridgeman Art Library)*

sculptor Benvenuto Cellini (1500–1574) prefaced his *Autobiography* with a declaration:

My cruel fate hath warr'd with me in vain:
Life, glory, worth, and all unmeasur'd skill,
Beauty and grace, themselves in me fulfil
That many I surpass, and to the best attain.[2]

Cellini, certain of his genius, wrote so that the whole world might appreciate it.

This attitude of **individualism** stressed personality, uniqueness, genius, and full development of one's capabilities and talents. Thirst for fame, the quest for glory, a driving ambition, and a burning desire for success drove people such as Alberti and Cellini.

The fourteenth- and fifteenth-century humanists loved the language of the classics and considered it superior to the corrupt Latin of the medieval schoolmen. The leading humanists of the early Renaissance were rhetoricians, seeking effective and eloquent oral and written communication. Literary humanists of the fourteenth century wrote each other highly stylized letters imitating ancient authors, and they held witty philosophical dialogues in conscious imitation of the Platonic Academy of the fourth century B.C. They eventually became concerned about form more than about content, however, and more about the way an idea was expressed than about the significance and validity of the idea.

Education

One of the central preoccupations of the humanists was education and moral behavior. Humanists poured out treatises, often in the form of letters, on the structure and goals of education and the training of rulers. They taught that a life active in the world should be the aim of all educated individuals and that education was not simply for private or religious purposes, but benefited the public good. In one of the earliest systematic programs for the young, Peter Paul Vergerio (1370–1444) wrote Ubertinus, the ruler of Carrara:

For the education of children is a matter of more than private interest; it concerns the State, which indeed regards the right training of the young as, in certain aspects, within its proper sphere....

We call those studies liberal which are worthy of a free man; those studies by which we attain and practice virtue and wisdom; that education which calls forth, trains, and develops those highest gifts of body and mind which ennoble men, and which are rightly judged to rank next in dignity to virtue only.[3]

Part of Vergerio's treatise specifies subjects for the instruction of young men in public life: history teaches virtue by examples from the past, ethics focuses on virtue itself, and rhetoric or public speaking trains for eloquence.

Humanists did not simply talk about education, but also put their ideas into practice. They opened schools and academies in Italian cities and courts in which pupils began with Latin grammar and rhetoric, went on to study Roman history and political philosophy, and then learned Greek in order to study Greek literature and philosophy. These classics, humanists taught, would provide models of how to write clearly, argue effectively, and speak persuasively, important skills for future diplomats, lawyers, military leaders, businessmen, and politicians. Merchants and bankers sent their sons to humanist schools, and ambitious young men from outside Italy flocked to these schools or to schools that opened later in their own cities. Humanist teachers and their ideas spread out from Florence across the Alps and eventually to northern European cities like London and Paris. Gradually humanist education became the basis for intermediate and advanced education for a large share of middle- and upper-class males.

Their emphasis on the public role and reputation of the educated individual made humanists ambivalent in their attitudes about education for women. If the best models of moral behavior and clear thought were to be found in classical authors, why should women be denied access to these? Should the new virtues of self-confidence and individualism be extended to include women? Most humanists thought that a program of study that emphasized eloquence and action was not proper for women, for women were not to engage in public activities. They agreed with Leonard Bruni that "rhetoric in all its forms lies absolutely outside the province of women" and that the "field of religion and morals" should be the primary focus of women's education.[4] The Italian humanist and polymath Leon Battista Alberti (1404–1472), discussing morality in his *On the Family,* stressed that a wife's role should be restricted to the orderliness of the household, food and the serving of meals, the education of children, and the supervision of servants. (Alberti never married, so he never put his ideas into practice in his own household.) Humanists never established schools for girls, though a few women of very high social status did gain a humanist education from private tutors. The ideal Renaissance woman looked a great deal more like her medieval counterpart than did the Renaissance man, leading the historian Joan Kelly to ask, in a now-famous essay, "Did women have a Renaissance?" (Her answer was no.)

No book on education had broader influence than Baldassare Castiglione's *The Courtier* (1528). This treatise sought to train, discipline, and fashion the young man into the courtly ideal, the gentleman. According to Castiglione, who himself was a courtier serving several different rulers, the educated man of the upper class should have a broad background in many academic subjects, and his spiritual and physical as well as intellectual capabilities should be trained. The courtier should have easy familiarity with dance, music, and the arts. Castiglione envisioned a man who could compose a sonnet, wrestle, sing a song and accompany himself on an instrument, ride expertly, solve difficult mathematical problems, and, above all, speak and write eloquently. Castiglione also included discussion of the perfect court lady, who, like the courtier, was to be well-educated and able to play a musical instrument, to paint, and to dance. Physical beauty, delicacy, affability, and modesty were also important qualities for court ladies, however, though these were not expected of gentlemen.

Raphael: Portrait of Castiglione In this portrait by Raphael, the most sought-after portrait painter of the Renaissance, Castiglione is shown dressed exactly as he advised courtiers to dress, in elegant, but subdued, clothing that would enhance the splendor of the court, but never outshine the ruler. (Scala/Art Resource, NY)

In the sixteenth and seventeenth centuries, *The Courtier* was translated into every European language and widely read. It influenced the social mores and patterns of conduct of elite groups in Renaissance and early modern Europe. Echoes of its ideal for women have perhaps had an even longer life.

Political Thought

No Renaissance book on any topic has been more widely read and studied in all the centuries since its publication (1513) than the short political treatise **The Prince** by Niccolò Machiavelli (1469–1527). The subject of *The Prince* is political power: how the ruler should gain, maintain, and increase it. Machiavelli implicitly addresses the question of the citizen's relationship to the state. As a good humanist, he explores the problems of human nature and concludes that human beings are selfish and out to advance their own interests. This pessimistic view of humanity led him to maintain that the prince might have to manipulate the people in any way he finds necessary:

For a man who, in all respects, will carry out only his professions of good, will be apt to be ruined amongst so many who are evil. A prince therefore who desires to maintain himself must learn to be not always good, but to be so or not as necessity may require.[5]

The prince should combine the cunning of a fox with the ferocity of a lion to achieve his goals. Asking rhetorically whether it is better for a ruler to be loved or feared, Machiavelli writes, "It will naturally be answered that it would be desirable to be both the one and the other; but as it is difficult to be both at the same time, it is much more safe to be feared than to be loved, when you have to choose between the two."[6]

Online Study Center Improve Your Grade
Primary Source: *The Prince:* Power Politics During the Italian Renaissance

Medieval political theory had derived ultimately from Saint Augustine's view that the state arose as a consequence of Adam's fall and people's propensity to sin. The test of good government was whether it provided justice, law, and order. Political theorists and theologians from Alcuin to Marsiglio of Padua had stressed the way government *ought* to be; they had set high moral and Christian standards for the ruler's conduct.

Machiavelli maintained that the ruler should be concerned not with the way things ought to be but with the way things actually are. The sole test of a "good" government is whether it is effective, whether the ruler increases his power. Machiavelli did not advocate amoral behavior, but he believed that political action cannot be restricted by moral considerations. While amoral action might be the most effective approach in a given situation, he did not argue for generally amoral, rather than moral, behavior. Nevertheless, on the basis of a crude interpretation of *The Prince*, the word *Machiavellian* entered the language as a synonym for the politically devious, corrupt, and crafty, indicating actions in which the end justifies the means. The ultimate significance of Machiavelli rests on two ideas: first, that one permanent social order reflecting God's will cannot be established, and second, that politics has its own laws, based on expediency, not morality.

Secular Spirit

Machiavelli's *The Prince* is often seen as a prime example of another aspect of the Renaissance, secularism. **Secularism** involves a basic concern with the material world instead of with the eternal world of spirit. A secular way of thinking tends to find the ultimate explanation of everything and the final end of human beings within the limits of what the senses can discover. Even though medieval business people ruthlessly pursued profits and medieval monks fought fiercely over property, the dominant ideals focused on the otherworldly, on life after death. Renaissance people often had strong and deep spiritual interests, but in their increasingly secular society, attention was concentrated on the here and now. Wealth allowed greater material pleasures, a more comfortable life, and the leisure time to appreciate and patronize the arts. The rich, social-climbing residents of Venice, Florence, Genoa, and Rome came to see life more as an opportunity to be enjoyed than as a painful pilgrimage to the City of God.

In *On Pleasure,* humanist Lorenzo Valla (1406–1457) defends the pleasures of the senses as the highest good. Scholars praise Valla as a father of modern historical criticism. His study *On the False Donation of Constantine* (1444) demonstrates by careful textual examination that an anonymous eighth-century document supposedly giving the papacy jurisdiction over vast territories in western Europe was a forgery. Medieval people had accepted the Donation of Constantine as a reality, and the proof that it was an invention weakened the foundations of papal claims to temporal authority. Lorenzo Valla's work exemplifies the application of critical scholarship to old and almost sacred writings as well as the new secular spirit of the Renaissance.

The tales in *The Decameron* (1350–1353) by the Florentine Giovanni Boccaccio (1313–1375), which describe ambitious merchants, lecherous friars, and cuckolded husbands, portray a frankly acquisitive, sensual, and worldly society. Although Boccaccio's figures were stock literary characters, *The Decameron* contains none of the "contempt of the world" theme so pervasive in medieval literature. Renaissance writers justified the accumulation and enjoyment of wealth with references to ancient authors.

Nor did church leaders do much to combat the new secular spirit. In the fifteenth and early sixteenth centuries, the papal court and the households of the cardinals were just as worldly as those of great urban patricians. Of course, most of the popes and higher church officials had come from the bourgeois aristocracy. Renaissance popes beautified the city of Rome, patronized artists and men of letters, and expended enormous enthusiasm and huge sums of money. Pope Julius II (1503–1513) tore down the old Saint Peter's Basilica and began work on the present structure in 1506. Michelangelo's dome for Saint Peter's is still considered his greatest work. Papal interests, which were far removed from spiritual concerns, fostered, rather than discouraged, the new worldly attitude.

Despite their interest in secular matters, however, few people (including Machiavelli) questioned the basic tenets of the Christian religion. Italian humanists and their aristocratic patrons were anti-ascetic, but they were not agnostics or skeptics. The thousands of pious paintings, sculptures, processions, and pilgrimages of the Renaissance period prove that strong religious feeling persisted.

Christian Humanism

The blend of religious and secular concerns of the Italian humanists is even more pronounced among humanists from northern Europe. In the last quarter of the fifteenth century, students from the Low Countries, France, Germany, and England flocked to Italy, imbibed the "new learning," and carried it back to their countries. Northern humanists, often called **Christian humanists,** interpreted Italian ideas about and attitudes toward classical antiquity, individualism, and humanism in terms of their own traditions. They developed a program for broad social reform based on Christian ideals.

Christian humanists were interested in an ethical way of life. To achieve it, they believed that the best elements of classical and Christian cultures should be combined. For example, the classical ideals of calmness, stoical patience, and broad-mindedness should be joined in human conduct with the Christian virtues of love, faith, and hope. Northern humanists also stressed the use of reason, rather than acceptance of dogma, as the foundation for an ethical way of life. Like the Italians, they were impatient with Scholastic philosophy. Christian humanists had profound faith in the power of human intellect to bring about moral and institutional reform. They believed that, although human nature had been corrupted by sin, it was fundamentally good and capable of improvement through education.

The Englishman Thomas More (1478–1535) towered above other figures in sixteenth-century English social and intellectual history. Trained as a lawyer, More lived as a student in the London Charterhouse, a Carthusian monastery. He subsequently married and practiced law but became deeply interested in the classics. His household served as a model of warm Christian family life and as a mecca for foreign and English humanists, who were

Bennozzo Gozzoli: Procession of the Magi, 1461 This segment of a huge fresco covering three walls of a chapel in the Medici Palace in Florence shows members of the Medici family and other contemporary individuals in a procession accompanying the biblical three wise men (*magi* in Italian) as they brought gifts to the infant Jesus. The painting was ordered by Cosimo and Piero de' Medici, who had just finished building the family palace in the center of the city. Reflecting the self-confidence of his patrons, Gozzoli places the elderly Cosimo and Piero at the head of the procession, accompanied by their grooms. The group behind them includes Pope Pius II (in the last row in a red hat that ties under the chin) and the artist (in the second to the last row in a red hat with gold lettering). *(Scala/Art Resource, NY)*

particularly impressed with the linguistic skills of More's daughters, whom he had trained in Latin and Greek. In the career pattern of such Italian humanists as Petrarch, More entered government service under Henry VIII and was sent as ambassador to Flanders. There More found the time to write *Utopia* (1516), which presents a revolutionary view of society.

Utopia, which means "nowhere," describes an ideal socialistic community on an island somewhere off the mainland of the New World. All children receive a good education, primarily in the Greco-Roman classics, and learning does not cease with maturity, for the goal of all education is to develop rational faculties. Adults divide their days between manual labor or business pursuits and intellectual activities.

Because profits from business and property are held in common, there is absolute social equality. The Utopians use gold and silver to make chamber pots and to prevent wars by buying off their enemies. By this casual use of precious metals, More meant to suggest that the basic problems in society are caused by greed. Citizens of Utopia lead an ideal, nearly perfect existence because they live by reason; their institutions are perfect. More punned on the word *utopia*, which he termed "a good place. A good place which is no place."

More's ideas were profoundly original in the sixteenth century. Contrary to the long-prevailing view that vice and violence existed because people were basically corrupt, More maintained that acquisitiveness and private property promoted all sorts of vices and civil disorders. Since society protected private property, society's flawed institutions were responsible for corruption and war. According to More, the key to improvement and reform of the individual was reform of the social institutions that molded the individual. Today this view is so much taken for granted that it is difficult to appreciate how radical More's approach was in the sixteenth century.

Online Study Center **Improve Your Grade**
Primary Source: *Utopia:* A Question over Diplomatic Advice

Better known by contemporaries than Thomas More was the Dutch humanist Desiderius Erasmus (1466?–1536) of Rotterdam. Orphaned as a small boy, Erasmus was forced to enter a monastery. Although he hated the monastic life, he developed an excellent knowledge of the Latin language and a deep appreciation for the Latin classics. During a visit to England in 1499, Erasmus met the scholar John Colet, who decisively influenced his life's work: the application of the best humanistic learning to the study and explanation of the Bible. As a mature scholar with an international reputation stretching from Cracow to London, a fame that rested largely on his exceptional knowledge of Greek, Erasmus could boast with truth, "I brought it about that humanism, which among the Italians . . . savored of nothing but pure paganism, began nobly to celebrate Christ."[7]

Erasmus's long list of publications includes *The Education of a Christian Prince* (1504), a book combining idealistic and practical suggestions for the formation of a ruler's character through the careful study of Plutarch, Aristotle, Cicero, and Plato; *The Praise of Folly* (1509), a satire of worldly wisdom and a plea for the simple and spontaneous Christian faith of children; and, most important, a critical edition of the Greek New Testament (1516). In the preface to the New Testament, Erasmus explained the purpose of his great work:

For I utterly dissent from those who are unwilling that the sacred Scriptures should be read by the unlearned translated into their vulgar tongue, as though Christ had taught such subtleties that they can scarcely be understood even by a few theologians. . . . Christ wished his mysteries to be published as openly as possible. I wish that even the weakest woman should read the Gospel—should read the epistles of Paul. And I wish these were translated into all languages, so that they might be read and understood, not only by Scots and Irishmen, but also by Turks and Saracens.[8]

Two fundamental themes run through all of Erasmus's work. First, education is the means to reform, the key to moral and intellectual improvement. The core of education ought to be study of the Bible and the classics. (See the feature "Listening to the Past: An Age of Gold" on pages 442–443.) Second, the essence of Erasmus's thought is, in his own phrase, "the philosophy of Christ." By this Erasmus meant that Christianity is an inner attitude of the heart or spirit. Christianity is not formalism, special ceremonies, or law; Christianity is Christ—his life and what he said and did, not what theologians have written. The Sermon on the Mount, for Erasmus, expresses the heart of the Christian message.

The Printed Word

The fourteenth-century humanist Petrarch and the sixteenth-century humanist Erasmus had similar ideas about many things, but the immediate impact of their ideas was very different because of one thing: the printing press with movable metal type. The ideas of Petrarch were spread the same way that ideas had been for centuries, from person to person by hand copying. The ideas of Erasmus were spread through print, in which hundreds or thousands of identical copies could be made in a short time. Erasmus actually spent his later years living with printer friends, checking his own and others' work for errors as well as translating and writing. Print shops were gathering places for those interested in new ideas. Though printers were trained through apprenticeships just like blacksmiths or butchers, they had connections to the world of politics, art, and scholarship that other craftsmen did not.

Printing with movable metal type developed in Germany in the middle of the fifteenth century as a combination of existing technologies. Several metal-smiths, most prominently Johan Gutenberg, recognized that the metal stamps used to mark signs on jewelry could be covered with ink and used to mark symbols onto a surface, in the same way that other craftsmen were using carved wood stamps. These craftsmen carved a whole page in wood, inked it, and pressed it on paper, and then assembled the paper into a book called a *block-book*. Block printing had been used in China and Korea since at least the eighth century and had spread to Europe by the thirteenth. The carvings could be used only a few dozen times before they became ink-soaked and unreadable, however; and since each word, phrase, or picture was on a separate block, this method of reproduction was extraordinarily expensive and time-consuming.

Using molds as smiths did for tableware or other metal items, Gutenberg and his assistants made stamps—later called *type*—for every letter of the alphabet and built racks that held the type in rows. This type could be rearranged for every page and so used over and over; it could also be melted down and remade once it became flattened through repeated use. They experimented with different types of ink, settling on a type of artists' ink, and with different types of presses, adapting the presses used to press grapes for wine, stamp patterns on fabric, or make block-books.

Books were printed on paper, and by the middle of the fifteenth century, acquiring paper was no problem. The knowledge of paper manufacture had originated in China, and the Arabs introduced it to the West in the twelfth century. Europeans quickly learned that durable paper was far less expensive than the vellum (calfskin) and parchment (sheepskin) on which medieval scribes had relied for centuries. By the fifteenth century the increase in urban literacy, the development of primary schools, and the opening of more universities had created an expanding market for reading materials of all types (see pages 400–401). When Gutenberg developed what he saw at first as a faster way to copy, professional copyists writing by hand

The Print Shop This sixteenth-century engraving captures the busy world of a print shop. On the left, men set pieces of type, and an individual wearing glasses checks a copy. At the rear, another applies ink to the type, while a man carries in fresh paper on his head. At the right, the master printer operates the press, while a boy removes the printed pages and sets them to dry. The well-dressed figure in the right foreground may be the patron checking to see whether his job is done. *(Giraudon/Art Resource, NY)*

and block-book makers, along with monks and nuns in monasteries, were already churning out reading materials on paper as fast as they could for the growing number of people who could read.

Gutenberg's invention involved no special secret technology or materials, and he was not the only one to recognize the huge market for books. Other craftsmen made their own type, built their own presses, and bought their own paper, setting themselves up in business in the cities of Germany, Switzerland, and the Netherlands, and then in Italy, England, and France. By 1480 about 110 cities in Europe had presses, with Venice employing the most and producing about one-eighth of all printed books in Europe. Printing continued to spread to Spain and Scandinavia, and by 1500, roughly fifty years after the first printed books, more than 200 cities and towns in Europe had presses (see Map 13.2). Historians estimate that somewhere between 8 million and 20 million books were printed in Europe before 1500, many more than the number of books produced in all of Western history up to that point.

The effects of the invention of movable-type printing were not felt overnight. Nevertheless, within a half century of the publication of Gutenberg's Bible of 1456, movable type had brought about radical changes. Printing transformed both the private and the public lives of Europeans. It gave hundreds or even thousands of people identical books, so that they could more easily discuss the ideas that the books contained with one another in person or through letters. Printed materials reached an invisible public, allowing silent individuals to join causes and groups of individuals widely separated by geography to form a common identity; this new group consciousness could compete with older, localized loyalties.

Government and church leaders both used and worried about printing. They printed laws, declarations of war, battle accounts, and propaganda, and they also attempted to censor books and authors whose ideas they thought were wrong. Officials developed lists of prohibited books and authors, enforcing their prohibitions by confiscating books, arresting printers and booksellers, or destroying the presses of printers who disobeyed. None of this was very effective, and books were printed secretly, with fake title pages, authors, and places of publication, and smuggled all over Europe.

Printing also stimulated the literacy of laypeople and eventually came to have a deep effect on their private lives. Although most of the earliest books and pamphlets dealt with religious subjects, students, merchants, and upper- and middle-class people sought books on all subjects, and printers produced anything that would sell. They produced law codes bound in fancy leather bindings

Mapping the Past

MAP 13.2 The Growth of Printing in Europe The speed with which artisans spread printing technology across Europe provides strong evidence for the existing market in reading material. Presses in the Ottoman Empire were first established by Jewish immigrants who printed works in Hebrew, Greek, and Spanish. Use this map and those in other chapters to answer the following questions: ❶ What part of Europe had the greatest number of printing presses by 1550? Why might this be? ❷ Printing was developed in response to a market for reading materials. Use Maps 11.2 and 11.3 (pages 340 and 346) to help explain why printing spread the way it did. ❸ Many historians also see printing as an important factor in the spread of the Protestant Reformation. Use Map 14.2 (page 468) to test this assertion.

Online Study Center **Improve Your Grade** Interactive Map: The Growth of Printing in matching sets for lawyers; medical manuals and guides to healing herbs for doctors, surgeons, pharmacists, and midwives; grammars and dictionaries for students, often in small sizes with paper covers so that they were cheap and could be carried to class; and books of prayers and sermons for members of the clergy. They printed historical romances, biographies, and how-to manuals, such as cookbooks and books of home remedies. They discovered that illustrations increased a book's sales, so published both history and pornography full of woodcuts and engravings. Single-page broadsides and flysheets allowed great public festivals, religious ceremonies, political events, and "wonders" such as comets or two-headed calves to be experienced vicariously by the stay-at-home. Since books and other printed materials were read aloud to illiterate listeners, print bridged the gap between the written and oral cultures.

Art and the Artist

No feature of the Renaissance evokes greater admiration than its artistic masterpieces. The 1400s (*quattrocento*) and 1500s (*cinquecento*) bore witness to dazzling creativity in painting, architecture, and sculpture. In all the arts, the city of Florence led the way. According to Vasari, the painter Perugino once asked why it was in Florence and not elsewhere that men achieved perfection in the arts. The first answer he received was, "There were so many good critics there, for the air of the city makes men quick and perceptive and impatient of mediocrity."[9] But Florence was not the only artistic center, for Rome and Venice also became important, and northern Europeans perfected their own styles.

- *How did changes in art both reflect and shape new ideas?*

Art and Power

In early Renaissance Italy, art manifested corporate power. Powerful urban groups such as guilds or religious confraternities commissioned works of art. The Florentine cloth merchants, for example, delegated Filippo Brunelleschi to build the magnificent dome on the cathedral of Florence and selected Lorenzo Ghiberti to design the bronze doors of the Baptistery. These works represented the merchants' dominant influence in the community. Corporate patronage was also reflected in the Florentine government's decision to hire Michelangelo to create the sculpture of David, the great Hebrew hero and king. The subject matter of art through the early fifteenth century, as in the Middle Ages, remained overwhelmingly religious. Religious themes appeared in all media—woodcarvings, painted frescoes, stone sculptures, paintings. As in the Middle Ages, art served an educational purpose. A religious picture or statue was intended to spread a particular doctrine, act as a profession of faith, or recall sinners to a moral way of living.

Increasingly in the later fifteenth century, individuals and oligarchs, rather than corporate groups, sponsored works of art. Patrician merchants and bankers and popes and princes supported the arts as a means of glorifying themselves and their families, becoming artistic **patrons.** Vast sums were spent on family chapels, frescoes, religious panels, and tombs. Writing about 1470, Florentine oligarch Lorenzo de' Medici declared that his family had spent the astronomical sum of 663,755 gold florins for artistic and architectural commissions over the previous thirty-five years. Yet "I think it casts a brilliant light on our estate [public reputation] and it seems to me that the monies were well spent and I am very pleased with this."[10] Powerful men wanted to exalt themselves, their families, and their offices. A magnificent style of living enriched by works of art served to prove the greatness and the power of the despot or oligarch.

In addition to power, art reveals changing patterns of consumption in Renaissance Italy. In the rural world of the Middle Ages, society had been organized for war. Men of wealth spent their money on military gear—swords, armor, horses, crenelated castles, towers, family compounds—all of which represent offensive or defensive warfare. As Italian nobles settled in towns (see page 333), they adjusted to an urban culture. Rather than employing knights for warfare, cities hired mercenaries. Expenditure on military hardware declined. For the rich merchant or the noble recently arrived from the countryside, the urban palace represented the greatest outlay of cash. It was his chief luxury, and although a private dwelling, the palace implied grandeur. Within the palace, the merchant-prince's chamber, or bedroom, where he slept and received his intimate guests, was the most important room. In the fourteenth and fifteenth centuries a large, intricately carved wooden bed, a chest, and perhaps a bench served as its sole decorations. The chest held the master's most precious goods—silver, tapestries, jewelry, clothing. Other rooms, even in palaces of fifteen to twenty rooms, were sparsely furnished. As the fifteenth century advanced and wealth increased, the other rooms were gradually furnished with carved chests, tables,

Botticelli: Primavera, or Spring (ca 1482) Framed by a grove of orange trees, Venus, goddess of love, is flanked on her left by Flora, goddess of flowers and fertility, and on her right by the Three Graces, goddesses of banquets, dance, and social occasions. Above, Venus's son Cupid, the god of love, shoots darts of desire, while at the far right the wind god Zephyrus chases the nymph Chloris. The entire scene rests on classical mythology, though some art historians claim that Venus is an allegory for the Virgin Mary. Botticelli captured the ideal for female beauty in the Renaissance: slender, with pale skin, a high forehead, red-blond hair, and sloping shoulders. *(Digital image © The Museum of Modern Art/Licensed by Scala/Art Resource, NY)*

benches, chairs, tapestries for the walls, paintings (an innovation), and sculptural decorations, and a private chapel was added. Wealthy individuals and families ordered gold dishes, embroidered tablecloths, and paintings of all sizes as art became a means of displaying wealth. By the late sixteenth century the Strozzi banking family of Florence spent more on household goods than on anything else except food; the value of those furnishings was three times that of their silver and jewelry.

After the palace itself, the private chapel within the palace symbolized the largest expenditure. Equipped with the ecclesiastical furniture—tabernacles, chalices, thuribles, and other liturgical utensils—and decorated with religious scenes, the chapel served as the center of the household's religious life and its cult of remembrance of the dead. In fifteenth-century Florence, only the Medici had a private chapel, but by the late sixteenth century most wealthy Florentine families had private chapels.

Subjects and Style

The content and style of Renaissance art were often different from those of the Middle Ages. The individual portrait emerged as a distinct artistic genre. In the fifteenth century members of the newly rich middle class often had themselves painted in scenes of romantic chivalry or courtly society. Rather than reflecting a spiritual ideal, as medieval painting and sculpture tended to do, Renaissance portraits showed human ideals, often portrayed in a more realistic style. The Florentine painter Giotto (1276–1337) led the way in the use of realism; his treatment of the human body and face replaced the formal stiffness and artificiality that had long characterized representation of the human body. Piero della Francesca (1420–1492) and Andrea Mantegna (1430/31–1506) seem to have pioneered *perspective* in painting, the linear representation of distance and space on a flat surface.

As the fifteenth century advanced, the subject matter of art in Italy became steadily more secular. The study of classical texts brought deeper understanding of ancient ideas. Classical themes and motifs, such as the lives and loves of pagan gods and goddesses, figured increasingly in painting and sculpture. Religious topics, such as the Annunciation of the Virgin and the Nativity, remained popular among both patrons and artists, but frequently the patron had himself and his family portrayed. People were conscious of their physical uniqueness and wanted their individuality immortalized.

The sculptor Donatello (1386–1466) probably exerted the greatest influence of any Florentine artist before Michelangelo. His many statues express an appreciation of the incredible variety of human nature. Whereas medieval artists had depicted the nude human body in a spiritualized and moralizing context only, Donatello revived the classical figure, with its balance and self-awareness. The short-lived Florentine Masaccio (1401–1428), sometimes called the father of modern painting, inspired a new style characterized by great realism, narrative power, and remarkably effective use of light and dark. *The Last Supper* by Leonardo da Vinci (1452–1519), with its stress on the tension between Christ and the disciples, is an incredibly subtle psychological interpretation.

Andrea Mantegna: Adoration of the Magi (ca 1495–1505) Applying his study of ancient Roman relief sculpture, Mantegna painted for the private devotion of the Gonzaga family of Mantua this scene of the three wise men coming to visit the infant Christ. The three wise men, depicted as kings, represent the entire world—that is, the three continents known to medieval Europeans: Europe, Asia, and Africa. They also symbolize the three stages of life: youth, maturity, and old age. Here Melchior, the oldest, his large cranium symbolizing wisdom, personifies Europe. He offers gold in a Chinese porcelain cup from the Ming Dynasty. Balthazar, with an olive complexion and dark beard, stands for Asia and maturity. He presents frankincense in a stunning vessel of Turkish tombac ware. Caspar, representing Africa and youth, gives myrrh in an urn of striped marble. The three wise men were a common subject in Renaissance art (compare the illustration on page 417), as they allowed artists to show exotic figures and sumptuous clothing. (*© The J. Paul Getty Museum, Los Angeles. Mantegna, Andrea,* Adoration of the Magi, *ca 1495–1505, distemper on linen, 54.6 × 70.7 cm [85.PA.417]*)

As humanists looked to the classical past for inspiration in their writing, so did architects in constructing buildings. The Florentine architect Filippo Brunelleschi (1377–1446) designed a new hospital for orphans and foundlings set up by the silk-workers' guild in Florence, in which all proportions—of the windows, height, floor plan, and covered walkway with a series of rounded arches—were carefully thought out to achieve a sense of balance and harmony. Brunelleschi later turned his talents to designing and constructing a dome for the Florence Cathedral, based to some degree on Roman domes, but higher and more graceful.

Art produced in northern Europe in the fourteenth and fifteenth centuries tended to be more religious in orientation than that produced in Italy. Some Flemish painters, notably Rogier van der Weyden (1399/1400–1464) and Jan van Eyck (1366–1441), were considered the artistic equals of Italian painters and were much admired in Italy. Van Eyck, one of the earliest artists to use oil-based paints successfully, shows the Flemish love for detail in paintings such as *Ghent Altarpiece* and the portrait *Giovanni Arnolfini and His Bride;* the effect is great realism and remarkable attention to human personality. Northern architecture was little influenced by the classical revival so obvious in Renaissance Italy.

In the fifteenth century Florence was the center of the new art in Italy, but in the early sixteenth century this shifted to Rome, where wealthy cardinals and popes wanted visual expression of the church's and their own families' power and piety. Michelangelo, a Florentine who had spent his young adulthood at the court of Lorenzo de' Medici, went to Rome about 1500 and began the series of statues, paintings, and architectural projects from which he gained an international reputation: the Pieta, Moses, the redesigning of the Capitoline Hill in central Rome, and, most famously, the ceiling and altar wall of the Sistine Chapel. Pope Julius II, who commissioned the Sistine Chapel, demanded that Michelangelo work as fast as he could and frequently visited the artist at his work with suggestions and criticisms. Michelangelo complained in person and by letter about the pope's meddling, but his reputation did not match the

Rogier van der Weyden: Deposition Taking as his subject the suffering and death of Jesus, a popular theme of Netherlandish piety, van der Weyden describes (in an inverted T) Christ's descent from the cross, surrounded by nine sorrowing figures. An appreciation of human anatomy, the rich fabrics of the clothes, and the pierced and bloody hands of Jesus were all intended to touch the viewers' emotions. *(Museo del Prado/Scala/Art Resource, NY)*

power of the pope, and he kept working. Raphael Sanzio (1483–1520), another Florentine, got the commission for frescoes in the papal apartments, and in his relatively short life he painted hundreds of portraits and devotional images, becoming the most sought-after artist in Europe. Raphael also oversaw a large workshop with many collaborators and apprentices—who assisted on the less difficult sections of some paintings—and wrote treatises on his philosophy of art in which he emphasized the importance of imitating nature and developing an orderly sequence of design and proportion.

Venice became another artistic center in the sixteenth century. Titian (1490–1576) produced portraits, religious subjects, and mythological scenes, developing techniques of painting in oil without doing elaborate drawings first, which speeded up the process and pleased patrons eager to display their acquisition. Titian and other sixteenth-century painters developed an artistic style known in English as "mannerism" (from *maniera* or "style" in Italian) in which artists sometimes distorted figures, exaggerated musculature, and heightened color to express emotion and drama more intently. (This is the style in which Michelangelo painted the Last Judgment in the Sistine Chapel, shown in the frontispiece to this chapter.) Until the twentieth century, "mannerism" was a negative term; critics and art historians preferred the more naturalistic and elegant style of Botticelli and Raphael, but modern critics and artists have appreciated its sense of movement, vivid colors, and passionate expressions.

Patronage and Creativity

Artists in the Renaissance did not produce unsolicited pictures or statues for the general public, but usually worked on commission from patrons. A patron could be an individual, a group such as a guild, a convent, a ruler, or a city council. Patrons varied in their level of involvement as a work progressed; some simply ordered a specific subject or scene, while others oversaw the work of the artist or architect very closely, suggesting themes and styles and demanding changes while the work was in progress.

The right patrons rewarded certain artists very well. Lorenzo Ghiberti's salary of 200 florins a year compared favorably with that of the head of the city government, who earned 500 florins. Moreover, at a time when a person could live in a princely fashion on 300 ducats a year, Leonardo da Vinci was making 2,000 ducats annually.

Renaissance society respected the distinguished artist. In 1537 the prolific letter writer, humanist, and satirizer of princes Pietro Aretino (1492–1556) wrote to Michelangelo while he was painting *The Last Judgment* behind the altar in the Sistine Chapel:

To the Divine Michelangelo: Sir, just as it is disgraceful and sinful to be unmindful of God so it is reprehensible and dishonourable for any man of discerning judgment not to honour you as a brilliant and venerable artist whom the very stars use as a target at which to shoot the rival arrows of their favour. . . . It is surely my duty to honour you with this salutation, since the world has many kings but only one Michelangelo.[11]

Aretino was not alone in addressing Michelangelo as "divine," for the word was widely applied to him, and to a few other artists as well. (See the feature "Individuals in Society: Leonardo da Vinci.") Vasari described a number of painters, sculptors, and architects, in fact, as "rare men of genius." This adulation of the artist has led many historians to view the Renaissance as the beginning of the concept of the artist as genius. In the Middle Ages people believed that only God created, albeit through individuals; the medieval conception recognized no particular value in artistic originality. Renaissance artists and humanists came to think that a work of art was the deliberate creation of a unique personality who transcended traditions, rules, and theories. A genius had a peculiar gift, which ordinary laws should not inhibit.

Renaissance artists were not only aware of their creative power, but they also boasted about it. Describing his victory over five others, including Brunelleschi, in the competition to design the bronze doors of Florence's Baptistery, Ghiberti exulted, "The palm of victory was conceded to me by all the experts and by all my fellow-competitors. By universal consent and without a single exception the glory was conceded to me."[12] Some medieval painters and sculptors had signed their works; Renaissance artists almost universally did so, and many of them incorporated self-portraits, usually as bystanders, in their paintings.

It is important not to overemphasize the Renaissance notion of genius. As certain artists became popular and well-known, they could assert their own artistic styles and pay less attention to the wishes of patrons, but even major artists like Raphael generally worked according to the patron's specific guidelines. Whether in Italy or northern Europe, most Renaissance artists trained in the workshops of older artists; Botticelli, Raphael, Titian, and at times even Michelangelo were known for their large, well-run, and prolific workshops. Though they might be "men of genius," artists were still expected to

Gentile and Giovanni Bellini: Saint Mark Preaching in Alexandria (1504–1507) The Venetian artists Gentile and Giovanni Bellini combine figures and architecture in this painting of Saint Mark, the patron saint of Venice. Saint Mark (on the platform) is wearing ancient Roman dress. Behind him are male citizens of Venice in sixteenth-century Italian garb. In front of him are Ottoman Muslim men in turbans, Muslim women in veils, and various other figures. The buildings in the background are not those of first-century Alexandria (where Saint Mark is reported to have preached) but of Venice and Constantinople in the sixteenth century. The setting is made even more fanciful with a camel and a giraffe in the background. The painting glorifies cosmopolitan Venice's patron saint, a more important feature for the Venetian patron who ordered it than was historical accuracy. Its clear colors and effective perspective and the individuality of the many faces make this a fine example of Renaissance art. (Scala/Art Resource, NY)

be well-trained in proper artistic techniques and stylistic conventions, for the notion that artistic genius could show up in the work of an untrained artist did not emerge until the twentieth century. Beginning artists spent years copying drawings and paintings, learning how to prepare paint and other artistic materials, and, by the sixteenth century, reading books about design and composition. Younger artists gathered together in the evenings for further drawing practice; by the later sixteenth century some of these informal groups had turned into more formal artistic "academies," the first of which was begun in 1563 in Florence by Vasari under the patronage of the Medicis.

As Vasari's phrase indicates, the notion of artistic genius that developed in the Renaissance was gendered. All the most famous and most prolific Renaissance artists were male; there are no female architects whose names are known and only one female sculptor. The types of art in which more women were active, such as textiles, needlework, and painting on porcelain, were not regarded as "major arts," but only as "minor" or "decorative" arts. (The division between "major" and "minor" arts begun in the Renaissance continues to influence the way museums and collections are organized today.) Like painting, embroidery changed in the Renaissance to become more classical in its subject matter, naturalistic, and visually complex. Embroiderers were not trained to view their work as products of individual genius, however, so they rarely included their names on their works, and there is no way to discover who they were.

Several women did become well-known as painters in their day. Stylistically, their works are different from one another, but their careers show many similarities. The majority of female painters were the daughters of painters or of minor noblemen with ties to artistic circles. Many were eldest daughters or came from families in which there were no sons, so their fathers took unusual interest in their careers. Many women began their careers before they were twenty and produced far fewer paintings after they married, or stopped painting entirely. Women were

Individuals in Society

Leonardo da Vinci

What makes a genius? An infinite capacity for taking pains? A deep curiosity about an extensive variety of subjects? A divine spark as manifested by talents that far exceed the norm? Or is it just "one percent inspiration and ninety-nine percent perspiration," as Thomas Edison said? To most observers, Leonardo da Vinci was one of the greatest geniuses in the history of the Western world. In fact, Leonardo was one of the individuals that the Renaissance label "genius" was designed to describe: a special kind of human being with exceptional creative powers.

Leonardo (who, despite the title of a recent best-seller, is always called by his first name) was born in Vinci, near Florence, the illegitimate son of Caterina, a local peasant girl, and Ser Piero da Vinci, a notary public. Caterina later married another native of Vinci. When Ser Piero's marriage to Donna Albrussia produced no children, he and his wife took in Leonardo. Ser Piero secured Leonardo's apprenticeship with the painter and sculptor Andrea del Verrocchio in Florence. In 1472, when Leonardo was just twenty years old, he was listed as a master in Florence's "Company of Artists."

Leonardo's most famous portrait, *Mona Lisa*, shows a woman with an enigmatic smile that Giorgio Vasari described as "so pleasing that it seemed divine rather than human." The portrait, probably of the young wife of a rich Florentine merchant (her exact identity is hotly debated), may actually be the best-known painting in the history of art. One of its competitors in that designation would be another work of Leonardo's, *The Last Supper,* which has been called "the most revered painting in the world."

Leonardo's reputation as a genius does not rest simply on his paintings, however, which are actually few in number, but rather on the breadth of his abilities and interests. In these, he is often understood to be the first "Renaissance man," a phrase we still use for a multi-talented individual. He wanted to reproduce what the eye can see, and he drew everything he saw around him, including executed criminals hanging on gallows as well as the beauties of nature. Trying to understand how the human body worked, Leonardo studied live and dead bodies, doing autopsies and dissections to investigate muscles and circulation. He carefully analyzed the effects of light, and he experimented with perspective.

Leonardo used his drawings as the basis for his paintings and also as a tool of scientific investigation. He drew plans for hundreds of inventions, many of which would become reality centuries later, such as the helicopter, tank, machine gun, and parachute. He was hired by one of the powerful new rulers in Italy, Duke Ludovico Sforza of Milan, to design weapons, fortresses, and water systems, as well as to produce works of art. Leonardo left Milan when Sforza was overthrown in war and spent the last years of his life painting, drawing, and designing for the pope and the French king.

Leonardo da Vinci, Lady with an Ermine. *The enigmatic smile and smoky quality of this portrait can be found in many of Leonardo's works.*
(Czartoryski Museum, Krakow/The Bridgeman Art Library)

Leonardo experimented with new materials for painting and sculpture, some of which worked and some of which did not. The experimental method he used to paint *The Last Supper* caused the picture to deteriorate rapidly, and it began to flake off the wall as soon as it was finished. Leonardo actually regarded it as never quite completed, for he could not find a model for the face of Christ that would evoke the spiritual depth he felt it deserved. His gigantic equestrian statue in honor of Ludovico's father, Duke Francesco Sforza, was never made and the clay model collapsed. He planned to write books on many subjects but never finished any of them, leaving only notebooks. Leonardo once said that "a painter is not admirable unless he is universal." The patrons who supported him—and he was supported very well—perhaps wished that his inspirations would have been a bit less universal in scope, or at least accompanied by more perspiration.

Questions for Analysis

1. In what ways do the notion of a "genius" and of a "Renaissance man" both support and contradict one another? Which better fits Leonardo?
2. Has the idea of artistic genius changed since the Renaissance? How?

Sources: Giorgio Vasari, *Lives of the Artists,* vol. 1, trans. G. Bull (London: Penguin Books, 1965); S. B. Nuland, *Leonardo da Vinci* (New York: Lipper/Viking, 2000).

Online Study Center Improve Your Grade
Going Beyond Individuals in Society

Artemisia Gentileschi: Esther Before Ahasuerus (ca 1630) In this oil painting, Gentileschi shows an Old Testament scene of the Jewish woman Esther who saved her people from being killed by her husband, King Ahasuerus. This deliverance is celebrated in the Jewish holiday of Purim. Both figures are in the elaborate dress worn in Renaissance courts. Typical of a female painter, Artemisia Gentileschi was trained by her father. She mastered the dramatic style favored in the early seventeenth century and became known especially for her portraits of strong biblical and mythological heroines. *(Image copyright © The Metropolitan Museum of Art/Art Resource, NY)*

not allowed to study the male nude, which was viewed as essential if one wanted to paint large history paintings with many figures. Women could also not learn the technique of fresco, in which colors are applied directly to wet plaster walls, because such works had to be done out in public, which was judged inappropriate for women. Joining a group of male artists for informal practice was also seen as improper, and the artistic academies that were established were for men only. Like universities, humanist academies, and most craft guild shops, artistic workshops were male-only settings in which men of different ages came together for training and created bonds of friendship, influence, patronage, and sometimes intimacy.

Women were not alone in being excluded from the institutions of Renaissance culture. Though a few "rare men of genius" such as Leonardo or Michelangelo emerged from artisanal backgrounds, most scholars and artists came from families with at least some money. Renaissance culture did not influence the lives of most people in cities and did not affect life in the villages at all. A small, highly educated minority of literary humanists and artists created the culture of and for an exclusive elite. The Renaissance maintained, or indeed enhanced, a gulf between the learned minority and the uneducated multitude that has survived for many centuries.

Social Hierarchies

The division between educated and uneducated people was only one of many social hierarchies evident in the Renaissance. Every society has social hierarchies; in ancient Rome, for example, there were patricians and plebeians (see page 128). Such hierarchies are to some degree descriptions of social reality, but they are also idealizations—that is, they describe how people *imagined* their society to be, without all the messy reality of social-climbing plebeians or groups that did not fit the standard categories. Social hierarchies in the Renaissance built on those of the Middle Ages but also developed new features that contributed to modern social hierarchies.

- **What were the key social hierarchies in Renaissance Europe, and how did ideas about hierarchy shape people's lives?**

Race

Renaissance ideas about what we would term "race" were closely linked with those about ethnicity and "blood" discussed in Chapter 12 (see page 399). In law codes, histories, and other writings, ethnic and religious groups were referred to as *gens* or *natio*, words generally translated as "people" or "nation": the German nation, the Irish people, the Jewish people, and so on. What exactly *made* them German or Irish or Jewish was viewed as a mixture of language, traditions, and customs, but these were also conceptualized as "blood," and people were described as having French blood or Jewish blood. The word *race* was also used in several European languages in the Renaissance to describe such groupings—the French race, the Spanish race—or other social groups, such as "the race of learned gentlemen" or "the race of mankind." It was also used to refer to family line, kindred, or lineage. With all these words—nation, people, blood, race—people did not clearly distinguish between things that we would regard as biologically heritable, such as hair color, and as socially constructed, such as being well-dressed. (The boundaries between these two are not always clear today, of course, as arguments about certain groups being "naturally" gifted musicians or mathematicians demonstrate.)

The contemporary meaning of *race* as a system dividing people into very large groups by skin color and other physical characteristics originated in the eighteenth century, when European natural scientists sought to develop one single system that would explain human differences. They first differentiated "races" by continent of origin—Americanus, Europaeus, Asiaticus, and Africanus—and then by somewhat different geographical areas. The word *Caucasian* was first used by the German anatomist and naturalist Johann Friedrich Blumenbach (1752–1840) to describe light-skinned people of Europe and western Asia because he thought that the Caucasus Mountains on the border between Russia and Georgia were most likely their original home. He thought that they were the first humans, and the most attractive. (His judgment about Caucasian attractiveness came through studying a large collection of skulls and measuring all other skulls against one from Georgia that he judged to be "the most beautiful form of the skull.") This meaning of *race* has had a long life, though biologists and anthropologists today do not use it, as it has no scientific meaning or explanatory value. Renaissance people thus did not use *race* the way we do, but they did make distinctions based on skin color. These distinctions were interwoven with ethnic, national, and religious distinctions, and they provide some of the background for later conceptualizations of race.

Ever since the time of the Roman republic, a few black Africans had lived in western Europe. They had come, along with white slaves, as the spoils of war. Even after the collapse of the Roman Empire, Muslim and Christian merchants continued to import them. Unstable political conditions in many parts of Africa enabled enterprising merchants to seize people and sell them into slavery. Local authorities afforded them no protection. Long tradition, moreover, sanctioned the practice of slavery. The evidence of medieval art attests to the continued presence of Africans in Europe throughout the Middle Ages and to Europeans' awareness of them.

Beginning in the fifteenth century sizable numbers of black slaves entered Europe. Portuguese explorers imported perhaps a thousand a year and sold them at the markets of Seville, Barcelona, Marseilles, and Genoa. In the late fifteenth century this flow increased, with thousands of people leaving the West African coast. By 1530 between four thousand and five thousand were being sold to the Portuguese each year. By the mid-sixteenth century blacks, slave and free, constituted about 10 percent of the population of the Portuguese cities of Lisbon and Évora; other cities had smaller percentages. In all, blacks made up roughly 3 percent of the Portuguese population. In the Iberian Peninsula, African slaves intermingled with the people they lived among and sometimes intermarried. Cities such as Lisbon had significant numbers of people of mixed African and European descent.

Although blacks were concentrated in the Iberian Peninsula, there must have been some Africans in northern Europe as well. In the 1580s, for example, Queen Elizabeth I of England complained that there were too many "blackamoores" competing with needy English people for places as domestic servants.[13] Black servants were much sought after; the medieval interest in curiosities, the exotic, and the marvelous continued in the

Carpaccio: Black Laborers on the Venetian Docks (detail) Enslaved and free blacks, besides working as gondoliers on the Venetian canals, served on the docks: here, seven black men careen—clean, caulk, and repair—a ship. Carpaccio's reputation as one of Venice's outstanding painters rests on his eye for details of everyday life. *(Gallerie dell'Accademia, Venice/Scala/Art Resource, NY)*

Renaissance. Italian aristocrats had their portraits painted with their black pageboys to indicate their wealth (see the illustration on page 417, in which Gozzoli's depiction of Cosimo de' Medici shows him with a black groom). Blacks were so greatly in demand at the Renaissance courts of northern Italy, in fact, that the Venetians defied papal threats of excommunication to secure them. In the late fifteenth century Isabella, the wife of Gian Galazzo Sforza, took pride in the fact that she owned ten blacks, seven of them females. A black lady's maid was both a curiosity and a symbol of wealth. In 1491 Isabella of Este, duchess of Mantua, instructed her agent to secure a black girl between four and eight years old, "shapely and as black as possible." The duchess saw the child as a source of entertainment: "We shall make her very happy and shall have great fun with her." She hoped the girl would become "the best buffoon in the world,"[14] as the cruel ancient practice of a noble household's retaining a professional "fool" for the family's amusement persisted through the Renaissance—and down to the twentieth century. Tradition, stretching back at least as far as the thirteenth century, connected blacks with music and dance. In Renaissance Spain and Italy, blacks performed as dancers, as actors and actresses in courtly dramas, and as musicians, sometimes making up full orchestras.

Africans were not simply amusements at court. Adult black slaves served as maids, valets, and domestic servants in Spanish and Italian cities. The Venetians employed blacks—slave and free—as gondoliers and stevedores on the docks. In Portugal, kings, nobles, laborers, monasteries and convents, and prostitutes owned slaves. Slaves supplemented the labor force in virtually all occupations—as agricultural laborers, as craftsmen, and as seamen on ships going to Lisbon and Africa. Agriculture in Europe did not involve large plantations, so large-scale agricultural slavery did not develop there; African slaves formed the primary workforce on the sugar plantations set up by Europeans on the Atlantic islands in the late fifteenth century, however (see page 505).

Until the voyages down the African coast in the late fifteenth century, Europeans had little concrete knowledge of Africans and their cultures. What Europeans did know was based on biblical accounts. The European attitude toward Africans was ambivalent. On the one hand, Europeans perceived Africa as a remote place, the home of strange people isolated by heresy and Islam from superior European civilization. Africans' contact, even as slaves, with Christian Europeans could only "improve" the blacks. Theologians taught that God was light and linked black skin color with the hostile forces of the underworld: evil, sin, and the Devil. Thus the Devil was commonly represented as a black man in medieval and early Renaissance art (see the illustration on page 396). On the other hand, blackness possessed certain positive qualities. It symbolized the emptiness of worldly goods and the humility of the monastic way of life. Black clothes permitted a conservative and discreet display of wealth. Black vestments and funeral trappings indicated grief, and Christ had said that those who mourn are blessed. Negative preconceptions about blackness largely outweighed positive ones, however, and the expanding slave trade only reinforced these.

Class

Just as *race* did not develop its current meaning until after the Renaissance, neither did *class*. The notion of class—working class, middle class, upper class—was developed by nineteenth-century social theorists, most prominently Karl Marx. Looking at their own industrial societies, they decided that the most basic social division was between men who owned the "means of production," that is, factories and equipment, and those who did not and worked for wages. The former were the "bourgeoisie" (the middle class) and the latter the "proletariat" (the working class). (How women fit into this division was not clear. Married women in the nineteenth century could not own property and had no right to their wages, which belonged to their husbands.) This was a system of social differentiation based primarily on wealth.

By contrast, the medieval system of social differentiation was based on function—or least theoretical function—in society. Medieval Europeans conceptualized society in three basic groups: those who pray, or the clergy; those who fight, or the nobility; and those who work, or everyone else (see page 295). These groups were termed **"orders"** or "estates," and many medieval representative assemblies, including those of France and the Low Countries, were organized into three houses by estate. The society of orders worked fairly well in setting out sociolegal categories for membership in representative bodies. It also highlighted the most important social distinction in both medieval and Renaissance Europe, that between noble and commoner. Status as a noble generally brought freedom from direct taxation and rights of jurisdiction over a piece of property and the people who lived on it.

By the thirteenth century, however, and even more so by the fifteenth, the more fixed and inherited hierarchy of orders was interwoven with a more changeable hierarchy based on wealth, what would later come to be termed "social class." This was particularly true in towns. Most residents of towns were technically members of the "third estate," that is, not nobles or clergy, but they included wealthy merchants who oversaw vast trading empires and lived in splendor that rivaled the richest nobles. As we saw above, in many cities these merchants had gained political power to match their economic might, becoming merchant oligarchs who ruled through city councils.

The development of a hierarchy of wealth did not mean an end to the hierarchy of orders, however. Those in the first estate were far more likely to be wealthy than those in the third, but even if they were poorer, they had higher status. If this had not been the case, wealthy Italian merchants would not have bothered to buy noble titles and country villas as they began doing in the fifteenth century, nor would wealthy English or Spanish merchants have been eager to marry their daughters and sons into often impoverished noble families. The nobility maintained its status in most parts of Europe not by maintaining rigid boundaries, but by taking in and integrating the new social elite of wealth. Wealth allowed some male commoners to buy or gain noble titles and female commoners to marry into noble families.

Along with being tied to the hierarchy of orders, social status was also linked with considerations of honor. Among the nobility, for example, certain weapons and battle tactics were favored because they were viewed as more honorable. Among urban dwellers, certain occupations, such as city executioner or manager of the municipal brothel, might be well paid but were understood to be "dishonorable" and so of low status.

Cities were where the hierarchy of orders met the hierarchy of wealth most dramatically. In many cities, a number of urban merchants and bankers were wealthier than all but the highest level of the nobility. Some of these men climbed into the nobility through marriage, service to a monarch, or purchase of a title. More of them heightened social and political distinctions within cities, trying to set themselves off as a privileged social group. Wealthy merchants often dominated city councils, and they made it increasingly difficult for new residents to become citizens. They passed sumptuary laws, essentially urban dress codes that created easily visible distinctions between social groups (see page 338). Nobles and wealthy urban residents could wear fine silk clothing, jewelry, and bright colors and guild masters and artisans

Italian City Scene In this detail from a fresco of the life of Saint Barbara by the Italian painter Lorenzo Lotto, the artist captures the mixing of social groups in a Renaissance Italian city. The crowd of men in the right foreground surrounding the biblical figures includes wealthy merchants in elaborate hats and colorful coats. Two mercenary soldiers (carrying a sword and a pike), probably in hire to a condottiero, wear short doublets and tight hose stylishly slit to reveal colored undergarments, while boys play with toy weapons at their feet. Clothing like that of the soldiers, which emphasized the masculine form, was frequently the target of sumptuary laws for both its expense and its "indecency." At the left, women sell vegetables and bread, which would have been a common sight at any city marketplace. At the very rear, men judge the female saint, who was thought to have been martyred for her faith in the third century. *(Scala/Art Resource, NY)*

linen garments, while servants were restricted to rough, dark clothes and aprons. Individuals tried to evade these laws by wearing the clothing restricted to the group above them, though there were fines for doing so. Sumptuary laws also regulated spending on celebrations such as weddings or baptisms according to social class, and they were justified as a way to limit frivolous spending on luxuries and promote local production, for many laws restricted the purchase of imported clothing or foodstuffs. Along with setting out a hierarchy of wealth, sumptuary laws marked certain groups as outside the social order: Jews were obliged to wear specific symbols on their clothes or hats of a specific color (often yellow) so that they would be easily recognizable, and prostitutes might also be ordered to sew stripes of yellow or red on their clothing, wear a specific type or color of cloak, or keep their hair uncovered so people would not mistake them for "honorable" women.

Gender

While "race" is an eighteenth-century concept and "class" a nineteenth-century concept, "gender" is a concept that grew out of the women's movement that began in the 1970s. Advocates of women's rights increasingly distinguished between "sex," by which they meant physical and anatomical differences (what are often called "biological differences") and "gender," by which they meant a culturally constructed and historically changing system of differences. The boundaries between "sex" and "gender" are debated (are men "biologically" better at math, and women "biologically" more peaceful, or do such differences simply come from their upbringing?), and the recently emerged transgender movement has questioned whether a model with two sexes or two genders is adequate. The word *gender* is becoming increasingly common, however, even on government forms.

Renaissance people would have understood the word *gender* to refer to categories of nouns in many European languages, not categories of people, but they would have easily grasped the concept. Toward the end of the fourteenth century, learned men (and a few women) began what was termed the **"debate about women"** (*querelle des femmes*), a debate about women's character and nature that would last for centuries. Misogynist critiques of women from both clerical and secular authors denounced females as devious, domineering, and demanding. In answer, several authors, including Giovanni Boccaccio and Christine de Pizan, compiled long lists of famous and praiseworthy women exemplary for their loyalty, bravery, and morality. (See the feature "Listening to the Past: Christine de Pizan" in Chapter 12 on pages

404–405.) Boccaccio's tribute is somewhat ambiguous, for the highest praise he can bestow on a woman is that she is like a man: "What can we think except that it was an error of nature to give female sex to a body which had been endowed by God with a magnificent virile spirit?"[15] Christine de Pizan and several other writers were interested not only in defending women, but also in exploring the reasons behind women's secondary status—that is, why the great philosophers, statesmen, and poets had generally been men. In this they were anticipating recent discussions about the "social construction of gender" by six hundred years.

Online Study Center Improve Your Grade
Primary Source: *The Book of the City of Ladies: Advice for a "Wise Princess"*

Some authors who wrote defenses of women also wrote attacks, or, like Baldassare Castiglione in *The Courtier*, included both sides of the argument in a single work, so that it is difficult to gauge their actual opinions. The debate was clearly more than a literary game among intellectuals, however. With the development of the printing press, popular interest in the debate about women grew, and works were translated, reprinted, and shared around Europe. The debate about women also found visual expression, particularly in single-sheet prints that were hung in taverns or people's homes. Prints that juxtaposed female virtues and vices were very popular, with the virtuous women depicted as those of the classical or biblical past and the vice-ridden dressed in contemporary clothes. The favorite metaphor for the virtuous wife was either the snail or the tortoise, both animals that never leave their "houses" and are totally silent, although such images were never as widespread as those depicting wives beating their husbands or hiding their lovers from them.

Beginning in the sixteenth century, the debate about women also became one about female rulers, sparked primarily by dynastic accidents in many countries, including Spain, England, France, and Scotland, which led to women serving as advisers to child kings or ruling in their own right (see pages 436 and 463). The questions vigorously and at times viciously disputed directly concerned the social construction of gender: could a woman's being born into a royal family and educated to rule allow her to overcome the limitations of her sex? Should it? Or stated another way: which was (or should be) the stronger determinant of character and social role, gender or rank? There were no successful rebellions against female rulers simply because they were women, but in part this was because female rulers, especially Queen Elizabeth I of England, emphasized qualities regarded as masculine—physical bravery, stamina, wisdom, duty—whenever they appeared in public. Machiavelli also linked rule and masculinity, using "effeminate" to describe the worst kind of ruler. (*Effeminate* in the Renaissance carried different connotations than it does today, however; strong heterosexual passion was not a sign of manliness, but could make one "effeminate," that is, dominated by as well as similar to a woman.) Male rulers also made sure that they appeared and were portrayed on horseback with armor, weapons, and other symbols of masculinity. The ideal Renaissance king or courtier may have been able to sing and dance, but he was also careful to have people see him as a warrior.

Renaissance Wedding Chest (Tuscany, late fifteenth century) Well-to-do brides provided huge dowries to their husbands in Renaissance Italy, and grooms often gave smaller gifts in return, such as this wedding chest. Appreciated more for their decorative value than for practical storage purposes, such chests were prominently displayed in people's homes. This 37-inch by 47-inch by 28-inch chest is carved with a scene from classical mythology in which Ceres, the goddess of agriculture, is searching for her daughter Proserpina (also known as Persephone), who has been abducted by Pluto, the god of the underworld. The subject may have been a commentary on Renaissance marriage, in which young women often married much older men and went to live in their houses. (*Philadelphia Museum of Art. Purchased with the Bloomfield Moore Fund and with Museum Funds, 1944 [1944-15-7]*)

Ideas about women's and men's proper roles shaped the actions of the most powerful Renaissance monarchs and determined those of ordinary men and women even more forcefully. The dominant notion of the "true" man was that of the married head of household, so men whose class and age would have normally conferred political power but who remained unmarried did not participate on the same level as their married brothers. Unmarried men in Venice, for example, could not be part of the ruling council. Women were also understood as "married or to be married," even if the actual marriage patterns in Europe left many women (and men) unmarried until quite late in life (see page 394). This meant that women's work was not viewed as supporting a family—even if it did—and was valued less than men's. If they worked for wages, and many women did, women earned about half to two-thirds of what men did even for the same work, and they received less food (and much less ale or wine) if wages included food.

The maintenance of appropriate power relationships between men and women, with men dominant and women subordinate, served as a symbol of the proper functioning of society as a whole. Disorder in the proper gender hierarchy was linked with other types of social upheaval and was viewed as the most threatening way in which the world could be turned upside down. Carnival plays, woodcuts, and stories frequently portrayed domineering wives in pants and henpecked husbands washing diapers alongside professors in dunce caps and peasants riding princes. Men and women involved in relationships in which the women were thought to have power—an older woman who married a younger man, or a woman who scolded her husband—were often subjected to public ridicule, with bands of neighbors shouting insults and banging sticks and pans in disapproval. Of all the ways in which Renaissance society was hierarchically arranged—class, age, level of education, rank, race, occupation—gender was regarded as the most "natural" and therefore the most important to defend.

Politics and the State in the Renaissance (ca 1450–1521)

The High Middle Ages had witnessed the origins of many of the basic institutions of the modern state. Sheriffs, inquests, juries, circuit judges, professional bureaucracies, and representative assemblies all trace their origins to the twelfth and thirteenth centuries (see pages 259–273). The linchpin for the development of states, however, was strong monarchy, and during the period of the Hundred Years' War, no ruler in western Europe was able to provide effective leadership. The resurgent power of feudal nobilities weakened the centralizing work begun earlier.

Beginning in the fifteenth century, rulers utilized the aggressive methods implied by Renaissance political ideas to rebuild their governments. First in Italy, then in France, England, and Spain, rulers began the work of reducing violence, curbing unruly nobles, and establishing domestic order. They emphasized royal majesty and royal sovereignty and insisted on the respect and loyalty of all subjects. These monarchs ruthlessly suppressed opposition and rebellion, especially from the nobility. They loved the business of kingship and worked hard at it.

- **How did the nation-states of western Europe evolve in this period?**

France

The Hundred Years' War left France drastically depopulated, commercially ruined, and agriculturally weak. Nonetheless, the ruler whom Joan of Arc had seen crowned at Reims, Charles VII (r. 1422–1461), revived the monarchy and France. He seemed an unlikely person to do so. Frail, indecisive, and burdened with questions about his paternity (his father had been deranged; his mother, notoriously promiscuous), Charles VII nevertheless began France's long recovery.

Charles reconciled the Burgundians and Armagnacs, who had been waging civil war for thirty years. By 1453 French armies had expelled the English from French soil except in Calais. Charles reorganized the royal council, giving increased influence to middle-class men, and strengthened royal finances through such taxes as the **gabelle** (on salt) and the *taille* (land tax). These taxes remained the Crown's chief sources of income until the Revolution of 1789.

By establishing regular companies of cavalry and archers—recruited, paid, and inspected by the state—Charles created the first permanent royal army. In 1438 Charles published the **Pragmatic Sanction of Bourges,** asserting the superiority of a general council over the papacy, giving the French crown major control over the appointment of bishops, and depriving the pope of French ecclesiastical revenues. The Pragmatic Sanction established Gallican (or French) liberties because it affirmed the special rights of the French crown over the French church. Greater control over the church and the army helped consolidate the authority of the French crown.

Charles's son Louis XI (r. 1461–1483), called the "Spider King" because of his treacherous character, was very much a Renaissance prince. Facing the perpetual French problem of reduction of feudal disorder, he saw money as the answer. Louis promoted new industries, such as silk weaving at Lyons and Tours. He welcomed foreign craftsmen and entered into commercial treaties with England, Portugal, and the towns of the Hanseatic League (see page 341). He used the revenues raised through these economic activities and severe taxation to improve the army. With the army, Louis stopped aristocratic brigandage and slowly cut into urban independence.

Luck favored his goal of expanding royal authority and unifying the kingdom. On the timely death of Charles the Bold, duke of Burgundy, in 1477, Louis invaded Burgundy and gained some territories. Three years later, the extinction of the house of Anjou brought Louis the counties of Anjou, Bar, Maine, and Provence.

Two further developments strengthened the French monarchy. The marriage of Louis XII (r. 1498–1515) and Anne of Brittany added the large western duchy of Brittany to the state. Then the French king Francis I and Pope Leo X reached a mutually satisfactory agreement in 1516. The new treaty, the Concordat of Bologna, rescinded the Pragmatic Sanction's assertion of the superiority of a general council over the papacy and approved the pope's right to receive the first year's income of new bishops and abbots. In return, Leo X recognized the French ruler's right to select French bishops and abbots. French kings thereafter effectively controlled the appointment and thus the policies of church officials in the kingdom.

England

English society suffered severely from the disorders of the fifteenth century. The aristocracy dominated the government of Henry IV (r. 1399–1413) and indulged in mischievous violence at the local level. Population, decimated by the Black Death, continued to decline. Between 1455 and 1471 adherents of the ducal houses of York and Lancaster waged civil war, commonly called the **Wars of the Roses** because the symbol of the Yorkists was a white rose and that of the Lancastrians a red one. The chronic disorder hurt trade, agriculture, and domestic industry. Under the pious but mentally disturbed Henry VI (r. 1422–1461), the authority of the monarchy sank lower than it had been in centuries.

The Yorkist Edward IV (r. 1461–1483) began establishing domestic tranquillity. He succeeded in defeating the Lancastrian forces and after 1471 began to reconstruct the monarchy. Edward, his brother Richard III (r. 1483–1485), and Henry VII (r. 1485–1509) of the Welsh house of Tudor worked to restore royal prestige, to crush the power of the nobility, and to establish order and law at the local level. All three rulers used methods that Machiavelli himself would have praised—ruthlessness, efficiency, and secrecy.

The Hundred Years' War had been financed by Parliament. Dominated by baronial factions, Parliament had been the arena in which the nobility exerted its power. As long as the monarchy was dependent on the Lords and the Commons for revenue, the king had to call Parliament. Edward IV and subsequently the Tudors, excepting Henry VIII, conducted foreign policy on the basis of diplomacy, avoiding expensive wars. Thus the English monarchy did not depend on Parliament for money, and the Crown undercut that source of aristocratic influence.

Henry VII did summon several meetings of Parliament in the early years of his reign, primarily to confirm laws, but the center of royal authority was the **royal council,** which governed at the national level. There Henry VII revealed his distrust of the nobility: though not completely excluded, very few great lords were among the king's closest advisers. Regular representatives on the council numbered between twelve and fifteen men, and while many gained high ecclesiastical rank (the means, as it happened, by which the Crown paid them), their origins were in the lesser landowning class, and their education was in law. They were, in a sense, middle class.

The royal council handled any business the king put before it—executive, legislative, and judicial. For example, the council conducted negotiations with foreign governments and secured international recognition of the Tudor dynasty through the marriage in 1501 of Henry VII's eldest son Arthur to Catherine of Aragon, the daughter of Ferdinand and Isabella of Spain. The council dealt with real or potential aristocratic threats through a judicial offshoot, the **court of Star Chamber,** so called because of the stars painted on the ceiling of the room. The court applied principles of Roman law, and its methods were sometimes terrifying: accused persons were not entitled to see evidence against them; sessions were secret; torture could be applied to extract confessions; and juries were not called. These procedures ran directly counter to English common-law precedents, but they effectively reduced aristocratic troublemaking.

Unlike the continental countries of Spain and France, England had no standing army or professional civil service bureaucracy. The Tudors relied on the support of unpaid local officials, the **justices of the peace.** These influential landowners in the shires handled all the work of local government. They apprehended and punished criminals, enforced parliamentary statutes, fixed wages and prices, maintained proper standards of weights and measures, and even checked up on moral behavior.

The Tudors won the support of the influential upper middle class because the Crown linked government policy with the interests of that class. A commercial or agricultural upper class fears and dislikes few things more than disorder and violence. The Tudors promoted peace and social order, and the gentry did not object to arbitrary methods, like those of the court of Star Chamber, because the government had halted the long period of anarchy.

Secretive, cautious, and thrifty, Henry VII rebuilt the monarchy. He encouraged the cloth industry and built up the English merchant marine. English exports of wool and the royal export tax on that wool steadily increased. Henry crushed an invasion from Ireland and secured peace with Scotland through the marriage of his daughter Margaret to the Scottish king. When Henry VII died in 1509, he left a country at peace both domestically and internationally, a substantially augmented treasury, and the dignity and role of the royal majesty much enhanced.

Spain

While England and France laid the foundations of unified nation-states during the Renaissance, Spain remained a conglomerate of independent kingdoms. Castile and León formed a single political organization, but Aragon consisted of the principalities of Aragon, Valencia, Majorca, Sicily, Cardeña, and Naples, each tied to the crown of Aragon in a different way. On the one hand, the legacy of Hispanic, Roman, Visigothic, Jewish, and Muslim peoples made for rich cultural diversity; on the other hand, the Iberian Peninsula lacked a common cultural tradition.

The centuries-long reconquista—the wars of the northern Christian kingdoms to control the entire peninsula (see pages 265–267)—had military and religious objectives: conversion or expulsion of the Muslims and Jews and political control of the south. By the middle of the fifteenth century, the kingdoms of Castile and Aragon dominated the weaker Navarre, Portugal, and Granada, and the Iberian Peninsula, with the exception of Granada, had been won for Christianity. But even the wedding in 1469 of the dynamic and aggressive Isabella of Castile and the crafty and persistent Ferdinand of Aragon did not bring about administrative unity. Rather, their marriage constituted a dynastic union of two royal houses, not the political union of two peoples. Although Ferdinand and Isabella (r. 1474–1516) pursued a common foreign policy, until about 1700 Spain existed as a loose confederation of separate kingdoms (see Map 13.3), each maintaining its own *cortes* (parliament), laws, courts, and systems of coinage and taxation.

To curb the rebellious and warring aristocracy, Ferdinand and Isabella revived an old medieval institution: the **hermandades,** or "brotherhoods," which were popular groups in the towns given authority to act as local police forces and judicial tribunals. The hermandades repressed violence with such savage punishments that by 1498 they could be disbanded.

The decisive step Ferdinand and Isabella took to curb aristocratic power was the restructuring of the royal council. Aristocrats and great territorial magnates were rigorously excluded; thus the influence of the nobility on state policy was greatly reduced. Ferdinand and Isabella intended the council to be the cornerstone of their government system, with full executive, judicial, and legislative powers under the monarchy. The council was also to be responsible for the supervision of local authorities. The king and queen therefore appointed only people of middle-class background to the council. The council and various government boards recruited men trained in Roman law, which exalted the power of the Crown as the embodiment of the state.

In the extension of royal authority and the consolidation of the territories of Spain, the church was the linchpin. If the Spanish crown could select the higher clergy, the monarchy could influence ecclesiastical policy, wealth, and military resources. Through a diplomatic alliance with the Spanish pope Alexander VI, the Spanish monarchs secured the right to appoint bishops in Spain and in the Hispanic territories in America. This power enabled the "Catholic Kings of Spain," a title granted Ferdinand and Isabella by the papacy, to establish, in effect, a national church.

Revenues from ecclesiastical estates provided the means to raise an army to continue the reconquista. The victorious entry of Ferdinand and Isabella into Granada on January 6, 1492, signaled the culmination of eight centuries of Spanish struggle against the Arabs in southern Spain and the conclusion of the reconquista (see Map 9.3 on page 266). Granada in the south was incorporated into the Spanish kingdom, and in 1512 Ferdinand conquered Navarre in the north.

There still remained a sizable and, in the view of the majority of the Spanish people, potentially dangerous minority, the Jews. During the long centuries of the reconquista, Christian kings had renewed Jewish rights and privileges; in fact, Jewish industry, intelligence, and money had supported royal power. While Christians of

MAP 13.3 Spain in 1492 The marriage of Ferdinand of Aragon and Isabella of Castile in 1469 represented a dynastic union of two houses, not a political union of two peoples. Some principalities, such as León (part of Castile) and Catalonia (part of Aragon), had their own cultures, languages, and legal systems. Barcelona, the port city of Catalonia, controlled a commercial empire throughout the Mediterranean. Most of the people in Granada were Muslims, and Muslims and Jews lived in other areas as well.

all classes borrowed from Jewish moneylenders and while all who could afford them sought Jewish physicians, a strong undercurrent of resentment of Jewish influence and wealth festered. When the kings of France and England had expelled the Jews from their kingdoms (see page 310), many had sought refuge in Spain. In the fourteenth century Jews formed an integral and indispensable part of Spanish life. With vast numbers of Muslims, Jews, and Moorish Christians, medieval Spain represented the most diverse and cosmopolitan country in Europe. Diversity and cosmopolitanism, however, were not medieval social ideals.

Since ancient times, governments had seldom tolerated religious pluralism; religious faiths that differed from the official state religion were considered politically dangerous. But in the fourteenth century anti-Semitism in Spain rose more from popular sentiment than from royal policies. Rising anti-Semitic feeling was aggravated by fiery anti-Jewish preaching, by economic dislocation, and by the search for a scapegoat during the Black Death. In 1331 a mob attacked the Jewish community of Gerona in Catalonia. In 1355 royal troops massacred Jews in Toledo. On June 4, 1391, inflamed by "religious" preaching, mobs sacked and burned the Jewish community in Seville and compelled the Jews who survived to accept baptism. From Seville anti-Semitic pogroms swept the towns of Valencia, Barcelona, Burgos, Madrid, and Segovia. One scholar estimates that 40 percent of the Jewish population of Spain was killed or forced to convert.[16] Those converted were called *conversos* or **New Christians.**

Conversos were often well-educated and successful. In the administration of Castile, New Christians held the royal secretaryship, controlled the royal treasury, and composed a third of the royal council. In the church,

Felipe Bigarny: Ferdinand and Isabella In these wooden sculptures, the Burgundian artist Felipe Bigarny portrays Ferdinand and Isabella as paragons of Christian piety, kneeling at prayer. Ferdinand is shown in armor, a symbol of his military accomplishments and masculinity. Isabella wears a simple white head-covering rather than something more elaborate to indicate her modesty, a key virtue for women, though her actions and writings indicate that she was more determined and forceful than Ferdinand. *(Capilla Real, Granada/Laurie Platt Winfrey, Inc.)*

they held high positions as archbishops, bishops, and abbots. In the administration of the towns, conversos often held the highest public offices; in Toledo they controlled the collection of royal revenues. They included some of the leading merchants and business people. They also served great magnates, and by intermarrying with the nobility they gained political leverage. In the professions of medicine and law, New Christians held the most prominent positions. Numbering perhaps two hundred thousand in a total Spanish population of about 7.5 million, New Christians and Jews exercised influence disproportionate to their numbers.

Such successes bred resentment. Aristocratic grandees resented their financial dependence; the poor hated the converso tax collectors; and churchmen doubted the sincerity of their conversions. Queen Isabella shared these suspicions, and she and Ferdinand sought permission to set up an Inquisition in Spain. Pope Sixtus IV's bull authorizing the Inquisition reached Spain in November 1478, and on September 28, 1480, Ferdinand and Isabella ordered the establishment of tribunals to "search out and punish converts from Judaism who had transgressed against Christianity by secretly adhering to Jewish beliefs and performing rites of the Jews."[17] Investigations and trials began immediately, as officials of the Inquisition looked for conversos who showed any sign of incomplete conversion, such as not eating pork.

Recent scholarship has carefully analyzed documents of the Inquisition. Most conversos identified themselves as Christians. They insisted that they were happy to be Christians and failed to see why they should be labeled New Christians: many came from families that had received baptism generations before.

In response, officials of the Inquisition developed a new type of anti-Semitism. A person's status as a Jew, they argued, could not be changed by religious conversion, but was in the person's nature as a human being. Judaism was in their blood and was heritable, so Jews could never be true Christians. In what were known as "purity of the blood" laws, having pure Christian blood became a requirement for noble status. Intermarriage between Old and New Christians had been common for centuries, but now many families sought to hide their ancestors. Ideas about Jews developed in Spain were important components in European concepts of race, and discussions of "Jewish blood" later expanded into notions of the "Jewish race."

This new racially based anti-Semitism emerged at the very time a Spanish national feeling was emerging, a national sentiment that looked to the building of a single nation. Whereas earlier anti-Semitism, such as that during the time of the Black Death, alleged Jewish schemes to kill off entire Christian populations—by poisoning the wells, for example, from which Jews derived no profit—fifteenth-century theories held that Jews or New Christians planned to take over all public offices in Spain. Jews, therefore, represented a grave threat to national unity.

Although the Inquisition was a religious institution established to ensure the Catholic faith, it was controlled by the Crown and served primarily as a politically unifying tool. Because the Spanish Inquisition commonly applied torture to extract confessions, first from conversos, then from Muslims, and later from Protestants, it gained a notorious reputation. Thus the word *inquisition,* meaning "any judicial inquiry conducted with ruthless severity," came into the English language. The methods of the Spanish Inquisition were cruel, though not as cruel as the investigative methods of some twentieth-century governments.

Shortly after the conquest of the Moorish stronghold at Granada in 1492, Isabella and Ferdinand issued an edict expelling all practicing Jews from Spain. Of the community of perhaps 200,000 Jews, 150,000 fled. (Efforts were made, through last-minute conversions, to retain good Jewish physicians.) Many Muslims in Granada were forcibly baptized and became another type of New Christian investigated by the Inquisition. Absolute religious orthodoxy and purity of blood ("untainted" by Jews or Muslims) served as the theoretical foundation of the Spanish national state.

The diplomacy of the Catholic rulers of Spain achieved a success they never anticipated. Partly out of hatred for the French and partly out of a desire to gain international recognition for their new dynasty, in 1496 Ferdinand and Isabella married their second daughter Joanna, heiress to Castile, to the archduke Philip, heir through his mother to the Burgundian Netherlands and through his father to the Holy Roman Empire. Philip and Joanna's son, Charles V (r. 1519–1556), thus succeeded to a vast patrimony. When Charles's son Philip II joined Portugal to the Spanish crown in 1580, the Iberian Peninsula was at last politically united. The various kingdoms, however, were administered separately.

Chapter Summary

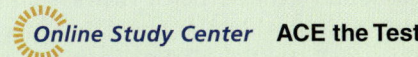 Online Study Center ACE the Test

- **What economic and political developments in Italy provided the setting for the Renaissance?**
- **What were the key ideas of the Renaissance, and how were they different for men and women and for southern and northern Europeans?**
- **How did changes in art both reflect and shape new ideas?**
- **What were the key social hierarchies in Renaissance Europe, and how did ideas about hierarchy shape people's lives?**
- **How did the nation-states of western Europe evolve in this period?**

The Italian Renaissance rested on the phenomenal economic growth of the High Middle Ages. In the period from about 1050 to 1300, a new economy emerged based on Venetian and Genoese shipping and long-distance trade and on Florentine banking and cloth manufacture. These commercial activities, combined with the struggle of urban communes for political independence from surrounding feudal lords, led to the appearance of a new ruling group in Italian cities—merchant oligarchs. Unrest in some cities led to their being taken over by single rulers, but however Italian cities were governed, they jockeyed for power with one another and prevented the establishment of a single Italian nation-state.

The Renaissance was characterized by self-conscious awareness among fourteenth- and fifteenth-century Italians, particularly scholars and writers known as humanists, that they were living in a new era. Key to this attitude was a serious interest in the Latin classics, a belief in individual potential, and a more secular attitude toward life. All these are evident in political theory developed in the Renaissance, particularly that of Machiavelli. Humanists opened schools for boys and young men to train them for an active life of public service, but they had doubts about whether humanist education was appropriate for women. As humanism spread to northern Europe, religious concerns became more pronounced, and Christian humanists set out plans for the reform of church and society. Their ideas were spread to a much wider audience than those of early humanists because of the development of the printing press with movable metal type, which revolutionized communication.

Interest in the classical past and in the individual also shaped Renaissance art in terms of style and subject matter. Painting became more naturalistic, and the individual portrait emerged as a distinct artistic genre. Wealthy merchants, cultured rulers, and powerful popes all hired painters, sculptors, and architects to design and ornament public and private buildings. Art in Italy became more secular and classical, while that in northern Europe retained a more religious tone. Artists began to understand themselves as having a special creative genius, though they continued to produce works on order for patrons, who often determined the content and form.

Social hierarchies in the Renaissance built on those of the Middle Ages, but also developed new features that contributed to the modern social hierarchies of race, class, and gender. Black Africans entered Europe in sizable numbers for the first time since the collapse of the Roman Empire, and Europeans fit them into changing understandings of ethnicity and race. The medieval hierarchy of orders based on function in society intermingled with a new hierarchy based on wealth, with new types of elites becoming more powerful. The Renaissance debate about women led many to discuss women's nature and proper role in society, a discussion sharpened by the presence of a number of ruling queens in this era.

With taxes provided by business people, kings in western Europe established greater peace and order, both essential for trade. Feudal monarchies gradually evolved in the direction of nation-states. In Spain, France, and England, rulers also emphasized royal dignity and authority, and they utilized Machiavellian ideas to ensure the preservation and continuation of their governments. Like the merchant oligarchs and signori of Italian city-states, Renaissance monarchs manipulated culture to enhance their power.

Key Terms

- Renaissance
- communes
- oligarchy
- popolo
- condottieri
- signori
- courts
- republic
- humanism
- individualism
- *The Prince*
- secularism
- Christian humanists
- patrons
- orders
- debate about women
- gabelle
- Pragmatic Sanction of Bourges
- Wars of the Roses
- royal council
- court of Star Chamber
- justices of the peace
- hermandades
- New Christians

Online Study Center — **Improve Your Grade** Flashcards

Suggested Reading

Clark, Samuel. *State and Status: The Rise of the State and Aristocratic Power.* 1995. Discusses the relationship between centralizing states and the nobility.

Earle, T. F., and K. J. P. Lowe, eds. *Black Africans in Renaissance Europe.* 2005. Includes essays discussing many aspects of ideas about race and the experience of Africans in Europe.

Eisenstein, Elizabeth. *The Printing Press as an Agent of Change: Communications and Cultural Transformations in Early Modern Europe.* 1979. The definitive study of the impact of printing.

Ertman, Thomas. *The Birth of Leviathan: Building States and Regimes in Medieval and Early Modern Europe.* 1997. A good introduction to the creation of nation-states.

Grafton, Anthony, and Lisa Jardine. *From Humanism to the Humanities: Education and the Liberal Arts in Fifteenth and Sixteenth Century Europe.* 1986. Discusses humanist education and other developments in Renaissance learning.

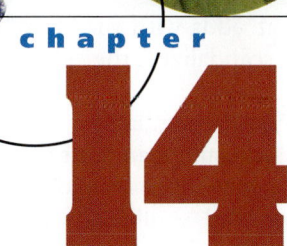

chapter 14

Reformations and Religious Wars, 1500–1600

chapter preview

The Early Reformation
- What were the central ideas of the reformers, and why were they appealing to different social groups?

The Reformation and German Politics
- How did the political situation in Germany shape the course of the Reformation?

The Spread of the Protestant Reformation
- How did Protestant ideas and institutions spread beyond German-speaking lands?

The Catholic Reformation
- How did the Catholic Church respond to the new religious situation?

Religious Violence
- What were the causes and consequences of religious violence, including riots, wars, and witch-hunts?

Calls for reform of the Christian church began very early in its history. When Christianity became the official religion of the Roman Empire in the fourth century, many believers thought that the church had abandoned its original mission, and they called for a return to a church that was not linked to the state. Throughout the Middle Ages individuals and groups argued that the church had become too wealthy and powerful and urged monasteries, convents, bishoprics, and the papacy to give up their property and focus on service to the poor. Some asserted that basic teachings of the church were not truly Christian and that changes were needed in theology as well as in institutional structures and practices. The Christian humanists of the late fifteenth and early sixteenth centuries urged reform, primarily through educational and social change.

Sixteenth-century cries for reformation were hardly new. Throughout the centuries, men and women believed that the early Christian church represented a golden age, akin to the golden age of the classical past celebrated by Renaissance humanists. What was new was the breadth of acceptance and the ultimate impact of the calls for reform. In 1500 there was one Christian church in western Europe to which all Christians at least nominally belonged. Fifty years later there were many, a situation that continues today.

Along with the Renaissance, the Reformation is often seen as a key element in the creation of the "modern" world. This radical change contained many elements of continuity, however. Sixteenth-century reformers looked back to the early Christian church for their inspiration, and many of their reforming ideas had been advocated for centuries.

The Early Reformation

Calls for reform in the church came from many quarters in early-sixteenth-century Europe—from educated laypeople such as Christian humanists and urban residents, from villagers and artisans, and from church officials themselves. This dissatisfaction helps explain why the

Online Study Center
This icon will direct you to interactive activities and study materials on the website **college.hmco.com/pic/mckaywest9e**

445

ideas of an obscure professor from a new and not very prestigious German university found a ready audience. Within a decade of his first publishing his ideas (using the new technology of the printing press), much of central Europe and Scandinavia had broken with the Catholic Church and even more radical concepts of the Christian message were being developed and linked to calls for social change.

- *What were the central ideas of the reformers, and why were they appealing to different social groups?*

The Christian Church in the Early Sixteenth Century

If external religious observances are a measure of depth of heartfelt conviction, Europeans in the early sixteenth century were deeply pious and remained loyal to the Roman Catholic Church. Villagers participated in processions honoring the local saints. Middle-class people made pilgrimages to the great shrines, such as Saint Peter's in Rome. The upper classes continued to remember the church in their wills. People of all social classes devoted an enormous amount of their time and income to religious causes and foundations.

Despite—or perhaps because of—the depth of their piety, many people were also highly critical of the Roman Catholic Church and its clergy. The papal conflict with the German emperor Frederick II in the thirteenth century, followed by the Babylonian Captivity and then the Great Schism, badly damaged the prestige of church leaders. Humanists denounced corruption in the church. In *The Praise of Folly,* Erasmus condemned the superstitions of the parish clergy and the excessive rituals of the monks (see page 325). Many ordinary people agreed. Court records, bishop's visitations of parishes, and even popular songs and printed images show widespread **anticlericalism,** or opposition to the clergy.

Online Study Center **Improve Your Grade**
Primary Source: *The Praise of Folly:* Erasmus on Popular Religious Practice

In the early sixteenth century critics of the church concentrated their attacks on three disorders—clerical immorality, clerical ignorance, and clerical pluralism, with the related problem of absenteeism. Many priests, particularly those ministering to country people, had concubines, and reports of neglect of the rule of celibacy were common. Clerical drunkenness, gambling, and indulgence in fancy dress were also frequent charges. Because such conduct was completely at odds with the church's rules and moral standards, it scandalized the educated faithful.

The bishops only casually enforced regulations regarding the education of priests. As a result, standards for ordination were shockingly low. Many priests could barely read and write, and critics laughed at illiterate priests mumbling Latin words of the Mass that they could not understand. In northern Europe—in England, for example—recent research shows an improvement in clerical educational standards in the early sixteenth century. Nevertheless, parish priests throughout Europe were not as educated as the educated laity, who condemned the irregularity and poor quality of sermons.

In regard to absenteeism and **pluralism,** many clerics, especially higher ecclesiastics, held several *benefices* (or offices) simultaneously but seldom visited the benefices, let alone performed the spiritual responsibilities those offices entailed. Instead, they collected revenues from all of them and hired a poor priest, paying him just a fraction of the income to fulfill the spiritual duties of a particular local church. Many Italian officials in the papal curia held benefices in England, Spain, and Germany. Revenues from those countries paid the Italian priests' salaries, provoking not only charges of absenteeism but also nationalistic resentment.

There was also local resentment of clerical privileges and immunities. Priests, monks, and nuns were exempt from civic responsibilities, such as defending the city and paying taxes. Yet religious orders frequently held large amounts of urban property, in some cities as much as one-third. City governments were increasingly determined to integrate the clergy into civic life by reducing their privileges and giving them public responsibilities. This brought city leaders into opposition with bishops and the papacy, which for centuries had stressed the independence of the church from lay control and the distinction between members of the clergy and laypeople.

Martin Luther

By itself, widespread criticism of the church did not lead to the dramatic changes of the sixteenth century. Those resulted from the personal religious struggle of a German university professor, Martin Luther (1483–1546), who was also an Augustinian friar. The Augustinian friars were a mendicant order, like the Dominicans and Franciscans, whose members often preached, taught, and assisted the poor. Martin Luther was born at Eisleben in Saxony and was the second son of a copper miner and, later, mine owner. At considerable sacrifice, his father sent him to school and then to the University of Erfurt, where he earned a master's degree with distinction at the young age of twenty-one. Hans Luther intended his son to proceed to the study of law and a legal career, which for centuries had been the steppingstone to public office and material success. Badly frightened during a thunderstorm, however, Martin Luther vowed to become a friar. Much to his father's dismay, he entered the monastery of the Augustinian friars at Erfurt in 1505. Luther was ordained a priest in 1507 and after additional study earned a doctorate of theology. From 1512 until his death in 1546, he served as professor of the Scriptures at the new University of Wittenberg. Luther was deadly serious when he said, years later, "I would not take all the world's goods for my doctorate." His doctorate led to his professorship, and his professorship conferred on him the authority to teach: throughout his life, he frequently cited his professorship as justification for his reforming work.

Martin Luther was a very conscientious friar. His scrupulous observance of the religious routine, frequent confessions, and fasting, however, gave him only temporary relief from anxieties about sin and his ability to meet God's demands. These apprehensions in turn led him to doubt the value of the monastic life itself. Since the medieval church had long held that the monastic life was a sure and certain road to salvation, Luther's confusion and anxieties increased.

Luther's wise and kindly confessor, John Staupitz, directed him to study Saint Paul's letters in the New Testament. Gradually Luther arrived at a new understanding of the Pauline letters and of all Christian doctrine. His understanding is often summarized as "faith alone, grace alone, Scripture alone" (*sola fide, sola gratia, sola Scriptura*). For Christians, salvation and justification come through faith, not good works, though true faith leads to love and to the active expression of faith in helping others. Faith is a free gift of God, not the result of human effort. God's word is revealed only in Scripture, not in the traditions of the church.

At the same time Luther was engaged in scholarly reflections and professorial lecturing, Archbishop Albert of Mainz, who controlled the area in which Wittenberg was located, sought to become the bishop of several other territories as well. He borrowed money from the Fuggers, a wealthy banking family of Augsburg, to pay for the papal dispensation of the rules regarding pluralism. Meanwhile, Pope Leo X, a member of the Medici family, was constructing family chapels and tombs (for which he hired Michelangelo) and continuing the building of St. Peter's Basilica in Rome. He authorized a special St. Peter's indulgence and allowed Albert to keep a portion of the revenue collected in the territories over which he was bishop to pay back the Fuggers.

Albert hired a friar from the Dominican order, Johann Tetzel, to run the indulgence sale. Tetzel mounted an advertising blitz. He was a very effective salesman, hawking indulgences—printed on the newly developed printing press—in a way that promised full forgiveness for sins or the end of time in purgatory for one's friends and relatives. One of his slogans—"As soon as coin in coffer rings, the soul from purgatory springs"—brought phenomenal success. Tetzel even drew up a chart with prices for the forgiveness of particular sins.

Chronology

1477	Union of Burgundian and Habsburg dynasties
1517	Martin Luther, "Ninety-five Theses on the Power of Indulgences"
1521	Diet of Worms
1521–1559	Habsburg-Valois Wars
1525	Peasants' War in Germany
1526	Turkish victory at Mohács, which allows spread of Protestantism in Hungary
1536	John Calvin, *The Institutes of the Christian Religion*
1540	Papal approval of Society of Jesus (Jesuits)
1542	Sacred Congregation of the Holy Office and Roman Inquisition
1545–1563	Council of Trent
1553–1558	Reign of Mary Tudor and temporary restoration of Catholicism in England
1555	Peace of Augsburg, official recognition of Lutheranism
1558–1603	Reign of Elizabeth and the "Elizabethan Settlement" in England
1559	Treaty of Cateau-Cambrésis
1560–1660	Height of the European witch-hunt
1568–1578	Civil war in the Netherlands
1572	Saint Bartholomew's Day massacre
1598	Edict of Nantes

The Folly of Indulgences In this woodcut from the early Reformation, the church's sale of indulgences is viciously satirized. With one claw in holy water, another resting on the coins paid for indulgences, and a third stretched out for offerings, the church, in the form of a rapacious bird, writes out an indulgence with excrement. The creature's head and gaping mouth represent Hell, with foolish Christians inside, others being cooked in a pot above, and a demon delivering the pope in a three-tiered crown and holding the keys to Heaven, a symbol of papal authority. Illustrations such as this, often printed as single-sheet broadsides and sold very cheaply, clearly conveyed criticism of the church to people who could not read. *(Kunstsammlungen der Veste Coburg)*

What exactly was an **indulgence?** According to Catholic theology, individuals who sin alienate themselves from God. To be reconciled to God, the sinner must confess his or her sins to a priest and do an assigned **penance,** a religious act such as praying or fasting. Sometimes earthly penance is not enough, and beginning in the twelfth century learned theologians increasingly emphasized the idea of **purgatory,** a place where souls on their way to Heaven after death went to make amends for their earthly sins. (Those on their way to Hell went straight there.) When it was first discussed, purgatory was a rather neutral place, unpleasant largely because one was separated from God, but by the fifteenth century it had acquired the fire and brimstone of Hell. Time in purgatory could be shortened by actions of the living, however, such as arranging for memorial masses or saying prayers for the dead.

According to Catholic theology, the church has the authority to grant sinners the remission of the penalties for sin by drawing on what was termed the "treasury of merits." This was a collection of all the virtuous acts that Christ, the apostles, and the saints had done during their lives; their virtue was infinite, and so was the treasury of merit. People thought of it as a sort of strongbox, like those in which merchants carried coins. An indulgence was a piece of parchment (and later paper), signed by the pope or another church official, that substituted a virtuous act from the treasury of merit for penance. The papacy and bishops had given Crusaders such indulgences, and by the later Middle Ages they were offered for making pilgrimages or other pious activities and also sold outright. People widely believed that indulgences secured total remission of penalties for sin and could substitute for both penance and time in purgatory. They ensured swift entry into Heaven and, like prayers for the dead, were effective on behalf of relatives or friends already dead.

Luther was severely troubled that ignorant people believed that they had no further need for repentance once they had purchased indulgences. He wrote a letter to Archbishop Albert on the subject and enclosed in Latin "Ninety-five Theses on the Power of Indulgences." His argument was that indulgences undermined the seriousness of the sacrament of penance, competed with the preaching of the Gospel, and downplayed the importance of charity in Christian life. After Luther's death, biographies reported that the theses were also posted on the door of the church at Wittenberg Castle on October 31, 1517. Such an act would have been very strange— they were in Latin and written for those learned in theology, not for normal churchgoers—but it has become a standard part of Luther lore. In any case, Luther intended the theses for academic debate, but by December 1517 they had been translated into German and were read throughout the Roman Empire.

Online Study Center **Improve Your Grade**
Primary Source: "Ninety-five Theses on the Power and Efficacy of Indulgences"

Luther was ordered to come to Rome, which he was able to avoid because of the political situation in the empire, but he did engage in formal scholarly debate with a representative of the church, Johann Eck, at Leipzig in 1519. He denied both the authority of the pope and the infallibility of a general council. The Council of Constance, he said, had erred when it had condemned Jan Hus (see page 391).

The papacy responded with a letter condemning some of Luther's propositions, ordering that his books be burned, and giving him two months to recant or be excommunicated. Luther retaliated by publicly burning the letter. By January 3, 1521, when the excommunication was supposed to become final, the controversy involved more than theological issues. The papal legate wrote, "All Germany is in revolution. Nine-tenths shout 'Luther' as their war cry; and the other tenth cares nothing about Luther, and cries 'Death to the court of Rome.'"[1]

In this highly charged atmosphere, the twenty-one-year-old emperor Charles V held his first diet (assembly of the Estates of the empire) in the German city of Worms. Charles summoned Luther to appear before the **Diet of Worms.** When ordered to recant, Luther replied in language that rang all over Europe:

Unless I am convinced by the evidence of Scripture or by plain reason—for I do not accept the authority of the Pope or the councils alone, since it is established that they have often erred and contradicted themselves—I am bound by the Scriptures I have cited and my conscience is captive to the Word of God. I cannot and will not recant anything, for it is neither safe nor right to go against conscience. God help me. Amen.[2]

Protestant Thought

As he developed his ideas, Luther gathered followers, who came to be called Protestants. The word **Protestant** derives from the protest drawn up by a small group of reforming German princes at the Diet of Speyer in 1529. The princes "protested" the decisions of the Catholic majority. At first Protestant meant "Lutheran," but with the appearance of many protesting sects, it became a general term applied to all non-Catholic western European Christians.

The most important early reformer other than Luther was the Swiss humanist, priest, and admirer of Erasmus, Ulrich Zwingli (1484–1531). In Zurich, Zwingli announced in 1519 that he would preach not from the church's prescribed readings but, relying on Erasmus's New Testament, go right through the New Testament "from A to Z," that is, from Matthew to Revelation.

Zwingli was convinced that Christian life rested on the Scriptures, which were the pure words of God and the sole basis of religious truth. He went on to attack indulgences, the Mass, the institution of monasticism, and clerical celibacy. In his gradual reform of the church in Zurich, where he remained the rest of his life, he had the strong support of the city authorities, who had long resented the privileges of the clergy.

Luther, Zwingli, and other Protestants agreed on many things. First, how is a person to be saved? Traditional Catholic teaching held that salvation is achieved by both faith and good works. Protestants held that salvation comes by faith alone. Women and men are saved by the arbitrary decision of God, irrespective of good works or the sacraments. God, not people, initiates salvation. (See the feature "Listening to the Past: Martin Luther, *On Christian Liberty*" on pages 480–481.) Second, where does religious authority reside? Christian doctrine had long maintained that authority rests both in the Bible and in the traditional teaching of the church. For Protestants, authority rests in the Word of God as revealed in the Bible alone and as interpreted by an individual's conscience. For a doctrine or issue to be valid, it had to have a scriptural basis. Because of this, most Protestants rejected Catholic teachings about the sacraments (see page 308), holding that only baptism and the Eucharist have scriptural support.

Third, what is the church? Protestants held that the church is a spiritual *priesthood of all believers,* an invisible fellowship not fixed in any place or person, which differed markedly from the Roman Catholic practice of a clerical, hierarchical institution headed by the pope in Rome. Luther re-emphasized the Catholic teaching that the church consists of the entire community of Christian believers. Medieval churchmen, in contrast, had tended to identify the church with the clergy. Fourth, what is the highest form of Christian life? The medieval church had stressed the superiority of the monastic and religious life over the secular. Luther argued that all vocations, whether ecclesiastical or secular, have equal merit and that every person should serve God in his or her individual calling. Celibacy was not superior to marriage, and vows of celibacy went against both human nature and God's commandment.

Protestants did not agree on everything. One important area of dispute was the ritual of the Eucharist (also called communion, or the Lord's Supper). Catholics hold the dogma of **transubstantiation:** by the consecrating words of the priest during the Mass, the bread and wine become the actual body and blood of Christ, who is then fully present in the bread and wine. In opposition,

Lucas Cranach the Elder: The Ten Commandments, 1516 Cranach, who was the court painter for the elector of Saxony from 1505 to 1553, painted this giant illustration of the Ten Commandments (more than 5 feet by 11 feet) for the city hall in Wittenberg just at the point that Luther was beginning to question Catholic doctrine. Cranach became an early supporter of Luther, and many of his later works depict the reformer and his ideas. This close association, and the fact that the painting captures the Protestant emphasis on biblical texts very well, led it to be moved to the Luther House in Wittenberg, the largest museum of the Protestant Reformation in the world. Paintings were used by both Protestants and Catholics to teach religious ideas. *(Lutherhalle, Wittenberg/The Bridgeman Art Library)*

Luther believed that Christ is really present in the consecrated bread and wine, but this is the result of God's mystery, not the actions of a priest. Zwingli understood the Lord's Supper as a *memorial*, in which Christ was present in spirit among the faithful, but not in the bread and wine. The Colloquy of Marburg, summoned in 1529 to unite Protestants, failed to resolve these differences, though Protestants reached agreement on almost everything else.

The Appeal of Protestant Ideas

Every encounter Luther had with ecclesiastical or political authorities attracted attention. Pulpits and printing presses spread his message all over Germany. By the time of his death, people of all social classes had become Lutheran. What was the immense appeal of Luther's religious ideas and those of other Protestants?

Educated people and humanists were much attracted by Luther's words. He advocated a simpler personal religion based on faith, a return to the spirit of the early church, the centrality of the Scriptures in the liturgy and in Christian life, and the abolition of elaborate ceremonies—precisely the reforms the Christian humanists had been calling for. His insistence that everyone should read and reflect on the Scriptures attracted the literate and thoughtful middle classes partly because Luther appealed to their intelligence. This included many priests and monks, who became clergy in the new Protestant churches. There was no official position for women in Protestant churches, but Protestant literature was smuggled into convents. Some nuns (most famously Katharina von Bora, who became Luther's wife) accepted Luther's idea that celibacy was not especially worthy and left their convents, while others remained in their convents but otherwise accepted Protestant teachings.

As we saw above, many townspeople envied the church's wealth, disapproved of the luxurious lifestyle of some churchmen, and resented tithes and ecclesiastical taxation. Protestant doctrines of the priesthood of all believers not only raised the religious status of laypeople, but also provided greater income for city treasuries. After

Zurich became Protestant, the city council taxed the clergy and placed them under the jurisdiction of civil courts.

Hymns, psalms, and Luther's two catechisms (1529), compendiums of basic religious knowledge, show the power of language in spreading the ideals of the Reformation. Such hymns as the famous "A Mighty Fortress Is Our God" (which Luther wrote) expressed deep human feelings, were easily remembered, and imprinted central points of doctrine on the mind. Luther's *Larger Catechism* contained brief sermons on the main articles of faith, whereas the *Shorter Catechism* gave concise explanations of doctrine in question-and-answer form. Both catechisms stressed the importance of the Ten Commandments, the Lord's Prayer, the Apostle's Creed, and the sacraments for the believing Christian. Although originally intended for the instruction of pastors, these catechisms became powerful techniques for the indoctrination of men and women of all ages, especially the young.

Scholars in many disciplines have attributed Luther's fame and success to the invention of the printing press, which rapidly reproduced and made known his ideas. Many printed works included woodcuts and other illustrations, so that even those who could not read could grasp the main ideas. (See the feature "Images in Society: Art in the Reformation" on pages 452–453.) Equally important was Luther's incredible skill with language. Luther's linguistic skill, together with his translation of the New Testament into German in 1523, led to the acceptance of his dialect of German as the standard version of German.

Both Luther and Zwingli recognized that if reforms were going to be permanent, political authorities as well as concerned individuals and religious leaders would have to accept them. Zwingli worked closely with the city council of Zurich, and in other cities and towns of Switzerland and south Germany city councils similarly took the lead. They appointed pastors that they knew had accepted Protestant ideas, required them to swear an oath of loyalty to the council, and oversaw their preaching and teaching.

Luther lived in a territory ruled by a noble—the elector of Saxony—and he also worked closely with political authorities, viewing them as fully justified in asserting control over the church in their territories. Indeed, in his 1520 *Address to the Christian Nobility of the German Nation* he demanded that German rulers reform the papacy and ecclesiastical institutions, and in *On Secular Government* he instructed all Christians to obey their secular rulers, whom he saw as divinely ordained to maintain order. In terms of the process of the Reformation, Luther's hopes were largely fulfilled. Individuals may have been convinced of the truth of Protestant teachings by hearing sermons, listening to hymns, or reading pamphlets, but a territory became Protestant when its ruler, whether a noble or a city council, brought in a reformer or to re-educate the territory's clergy, sponsored public sermons, and confiscated church property. This happened in many of the states of the empire during the 1520s. In every area that became Protestant, there was a slightly differ-ent balance between popular religious ideas and the aims of the political authorities. In some areas certain groups, such as clergy or journeymen, pushed for reforms, while in others the ruler or city council forced religious change on a population that was disinterested or hostile.

The first area outside the empire to officially accept the Reformation was the kingdom of Denmark-Norway under King Christian III (r. 1536–1559). Danish scholars studied at the University of Wittenberg, and Lutheran ideas spread into Denmark very quickly. In the 1530s the king officially broke with the Catholic Church, and most clergy followed. The process went smoothly in Denmark, but in northern Norway and Iceland (which Christian also ruled) there were violent reactions, and Lutheranism was only gradually imposed on a largely unwilling populace. In Sweden, Gustavus Vasa (r. 1523–1560), who came to the throne during a civil war with Denmark, also took over control of church personnel and income, and Protestant ideas spread, though the Swedish church did not officially accept Lutheran theology until later in the century.

The Radical Reformation

Some individuals and groups rejected the idea that church and state needed to be united, and sought to create a voluntary community of believers as they understood it to have existed in New Testament times. In terms of theology and spiritual practices, these individuals and groups varied widely, though they are generally termed "radicals" for their insistence on a more extensive break with the past. Many of them repudiated infant baptism, for they wanted only members who had intentionally chosen to belong. Some adopted the baptism of believers—for which they were given the title of "Anabaptists" or rebaptizers by their enemies—while others saw all outward sacraments or rituals as misguided and concentrated on inner spiritual transformation. Some groups attempted to follow Christ's commandments in the Gospels literally, while others reinterpreted the nature

Images in Society

Art in the Reformation

In the Reformation era, controversy raged over the purpose and function of art. Protestants and Catholics disagreed, and Protestant groups disagreed with one another. The Bible specifically prohibits making images of anything "in the heavens above or the earth below or the waters beneath the earth" (Exodus 20:4–6 and Deuteronomy 5:8–10). Based on this, some Protestant leaders, including Ulrich Zwingli, stressed that "the Word of God" should be the only instrument used in the work of evangelization. Martin Luther disagreed, saying he was not "of the opinion that the Gospel should blight and destroy all the arts." Luther believed that painting and sculpture had value in spreading the Gospel message because "children and simple folk are more apt to retain the divine stories when taught by pictures and parables than merely by words or instruction." Similar debates involved music, with Luther supporting and even writing hymns, and Swiss Protestants removing organs from their churches.

Lucas Cranach the Elder (1472–1553), a close friend of Luther's, is the finest representative of Protestant Reformation artists. He and Luther collaborated on the production of woodcuts and paintings, such as *The Ten Commandments* (see page 450), that spread the new evangelical theology. Each square in Cranach's painting represents one of the Ten Commandments.

Lucas Cranach the Younger (1515–1586) continued his father's work of spreading Luther's message. His woodcut *The True and False Churches* (Image 1) contains blatant and more subtle messages. At the center Luther stands in a pulpit, preaching the word of God from an open Bible. At the right, a flaming open mouth symbolizing the jaws of Hell engulfs the pope, cardinals, and friars, one kind of "false church." The scene at the left actually suggests another kind of "false church," however. Cranach shows a crucified Christ emerging out of the "lamb of God" on the altar as people are receiving communion. This image represents the Lutheran understanding of the Lord's Supper, in which Christ is really present in the bread and wine, in contrast to other Protestants who saw the ceremony as a memorial (see page 450). The woodcut thus could be understood on different levels by different viewers, which is true of much effective religious art.

For John Calvin, the utter transcendence of God made impossible any attempt to bring God down to human level through visual portraiture; to domesticate or to humanize God would deprive him of his glory. In houses of worship Calvin emphasized the centrality of the divine word, allowing wall inscriptions from the Bible. In later life, Calvin tolerated narrative biblical scenes as long as they did not include pictures of God or Jesus Christ. In the Netherlands, which adopted a Calvinist version of Protestantism, many formerly Catholic churches were stripped of all statues, images, and decoration and were redesigned with a stark, bare simplicity that mirrored the Calvinist ideal. Notice the interior of the church of Saint Bavo in Haarlem (Image 2).

The Catholic Church officially addressed the subject of art at the Council of Trent in December 1563. The church declared that honor and veneration should be given to likenesses of Christ, the Virgin Mary, and the

Image 1 Lucas Cranach the Younger: The True and False Churches
(Staatliche Kunstsammlungen Dresden)

Image 2 Church of Saint Bavo, Haarlem *(Pieter Jansz, Saenredam, S. Bavo in Haarlem. John G. Johnson Collection, Philadelphia Museum of Art [J 599])*

Image 3 Jesuit Priest Distributing Holy Pictures *(From Pierre Chenu,* The Reformation *[New York: St. Martin's Press, 1986])*

Image 4 Ceiling of the Gesù *(Scala/Art Resource, NY)*

saints; that images would remind people of the saints' virtues, which should be imitated; and that pictorial art would promote piety and the love of God. Examine the painting *Jesuit Priest Distributing Holy Pictures* (Image 3). Such pictures and images of saints were often given to children to help educate them on matters of doctrine. How do these pictures serve the same function as the Protestant *Ten Commandments*?

Both Protestants and Catholics used religious art for propaganda purposes, to oppose religious heterodoxy, and to arouse piety in laypeople. Catholic Reformation art came into full flowering with the style later known as baroque (see page 539). Baroque art originated in Rome and reflected the dynamic and proselytizing spirit of the Counter-Reformation. The church encouraged artists to appeal to the senses, to touch the souls and kindle the faith of ordinary people while proclaiming the power and confidence of the reformed Catholic Church.

In addition to this underlying religious emotionalism, the baroque drew from the Catholic Reformation a sense of drama, motion, and ceaseless striving. The interior of the Jesuit Church of Jesus—the Gesù—combined all these characteristics in its lavish, shimmering, wildly active decorations and frescoes (Image 4). This triumphant, elaborate, and flamboyant church celebrates both the Catholic baroque and Rome as the artistic capital of Europe. How would you compare the Gesù with the Saint Bavo Church (Image 2)?

Online Study Center Improve Your Grade
Going Beyond Images in Society

Domestic Scene The Protestant notion that the best form of Christian life was marriage and a family helps explain its appeal to middle-class urban men and women, such as those shown in this domestic scene. The engraving, titled "Concordia" (harmony), includes the biblical inscription of what Jesus called the greatest commandment—"You shall love the Lord your God with all your heart and all your soul and your neighbor as yourself" (Deuteronomy 6; Matthew 22)—on tablets at the back. The father presides as his son says grace; the mother passes bread; the older daughters seem to have begun eating; and small children and animals complete the scene. The large covered bed at the back was both a standard piece of furniture in urban homes and a symbol of proper marital sexual relations. *(Mary Evans Picture Library)*

of Christ. Radicals were often pacifists and refused to hold office or swear oaths, which were required of nearly everyone with any position of authority, including city midwives and toll collectors, as well as anyone involved in court proceedings. Some groups attempted communal ownership of property, living very simply and rejecting anything they thought unbiblical. Different groups blended these practices in different ways and often reacted harshly to a member who deviated, banning the person from the group and requiring other group members—sometimes including the spouse—to shun, or have no contact with, the offending member until he or she changed behavior and asked for forgiveness. Others, however, argued for complete religious toleration and individualism.

Ideas such as absolute pacifism and the distinction between the Christian community and the state brought down on these unfortunate people fanatical hatred and bitter persecution. Protestants and Catholics all saw—quite correctly—the separation of church and state as leading ultimately to the secularization of society. The powerful rulers of Swiss and German society immediately saw the connection between religious heresy and economic dislocation. Civil authorities feared that the combination of religious differences and economic grievances would lead to civil disturbances. In Saxony, in Strasbourg, and in the Swiss cities, radicals were either banished or cruelly executed by burning, beating, or drowning. Their community spirit and the edifying example of their lives, however, contributed to the survival of radical ideas. Later, the Quakers, with their gentle pacifism; the Baptists, with their emphasis on inner spiritual light; the Congregationalists, with their democratic church organization; and in 1787 the authors of the U.S. Constitution, with their opposition to the "establishment of religion" (state churches), would all trace their origins, in part, to the radicals of the sixteenth century.

The German Peasants' War

The radicals represent one way that the ideas of early reformers were pushed farther; as we have seen, many of their ideas had social, economic, and political implications, which is in part why they were seen as so dangerous. Groups that linked Protestant ideas directly to various political and social programs were also threatening. The most far-reaching of these was the German Peasants' War of 1525.

Peasant revolts had erupted in many parts of Europe in the fourteenth and fifteenth centuries (see page 390). In the early sixteenth century the economic condition of the peasantry varied from place to place but was generally worse than it had been in the fifteenth century and was deteriorating. Crop failures in 1523 and 1524 aggravated an explosive situation. In 1525 representatives of the Swabian peasants met at the city of Memmingen and drew up the Twelve Articles expressing their grievances. The Twelve Articles condemned lay and ecclesiastical lords and summarized the agrarian crisis of the early sixteenth century. They complained that nobles had seized village common lands, which traditionally had been used by all; that they had imposed new rents on manorial properties and new services on the peasants working those properties; and that they had forced the poor to pay unjust death duties in the form of the peasants' best horses or cows. Wealthy, socially mobile peasants especially resented these burdens, which they emphasized as new. The peasants believed that their demands conformed to the Scriptures and cited Luther as a theologian who could prove that they did.

Luther wanted to prevent rebellion. Initially he sided with the peasants, and he blasted the lords in his tract *An Admonition to Peace* (1525):

We have no one on earth to thank for this mischievous rebellion, except you lords and princes, especially you blind bishops and mad priests and monks. . . . In your government you do nothing but flay and rob your subjects in order that you may lead a life of splendor and pride, until the poor common folk can bear it no longer.[3]

But, he warned, nothing justified the use of armed force: "The fact that rulers are unjust and wicked does not excuse tumult and rebellion; to punish wickedness does not belong to everybody, but to the worldly rulers who bear the sword." As for biblical support for the peasants' demands, he maintained that Scripture had nothing to do with earthly justice or material gain, a position that Zwingli supported.[4]

Massive revolts first broke out near the Swiss frontier and then swept through Swabia, Thuringia, the Rhineland, and Saxony. The crowds' slogans came directly from Protestant writings. "God's righteousness" and the "Word of God" were invoked in an effort to secure social and economic justice. The peasants who expected Luther's support were soon disillusioned. Freedom for Luther meant independence from the authority of the Roman church; it did *not* mean opposition to legally established secular powers. Firmly convinced that rebellion would hasten the end of civilized society, he wrote the tract *Against the Murderous, Thieving Hordes of the Peasants:* "Let everyone who can smite, slay, and stab [the peasants], secretly and openly, remembering that nothing can be more poisonous, hurtful or devilish than a rebel."[5] The nobility ferociously crushed the revolt. Historians estimate that more than seventy-five thousand peasants were killed in 1525.

The German Peasants' War of 1525 greatly strengthened the authority of lay rulers. Not surprisingly, the Reformation lost much of its popular appeal after 1525, though peasants and urban rebels sometimes found a place for their social and religious ideas in radical groups. Peasants' economic conditions did moderately improve, however. For example, in many parts of Germany, enclosed fields, meadows, and forests were returned to common use.

The Reformation and Marriage

At the same time they were reacting so harshly to radicals and peasants, Luther and Zwingli decided to marry, Luther to a former nun, Katharina von Bora (1499–1532), and Zwingli to a Zurich widow, Anna Reinhart (1491–1538). Both women quickly had several children. Most other Protestant reformers also married, and their wives had to create a new and respectable role for themselves—pastor's wife—to overcome being viewed as simply a new type of priest's concubine. They were living demonstrations of their husband's convictions about the superiority of marriage to celibacy, and they were expected to be models of wifely obedience and Christian charity.

Though they denied that marriage was a sacrament, many Protestant reformers praised marriage in formal treatises, commentaries on the Book of Genesis, household guides, and—most importantly—wedding sermons. They stressed that it had been ordained by God when he presented Eve to Adam, served as a "remedy" for the unavoidable sin of lust, provided a site for the pious rearing of the next generation of God-fearing Christians, and offered husbands and wives companionship and consolation. A proper marriage was one that reflected both the spiritual equality of men and women and the proper social hierarchy of husbandly authority and wifely obedience.

Protestants did not break with medieval scholastic theologians in their idea that women were to be subject to men, a subjection rooted in their original nature and made more pronounced by Eve's primary responsibility for the Fall. Women were advised to be cheerful rather than grudging in their obedience, for in doing so they

Martin Luther and Katharina von Bora, by Lucas Cranach the Elder Cranach painted this double marriage portrait to celebrate Luther's wedding in 1525 to Katharina von Bora, a former nun. The artist was one of the witnesses at the wedding and, in fact, had presented Luther's marriage proposal to Katharina. Using a go-between for proposals was very common, as was having a double wedding portrait painted. This particular couple quickly became a model of the ideal marriage, and many churches wanted their portraits. More than sixty similar paintings, with slight variations, were produced by Cranach's workshop and hung in churches and wealthy homes. *(Uffizi, Florence/Scala/Art Resource, NY)*

demonstrated their willingness to follow God's plan. Men were urged to treat their wives kindly and considerately, but also to enforce their authority, through physical coercion if necessary. Both continental and English marriage manuals use the metaphor of breaking a horse for teaching a wife obedience, though laws did set limits on the husband's power to do so. A few women took Luther's idea about the priesthood of all believers to heart and wrote religious pamphlets and hymns, but no sixteenth-century Protestants officially allowed women to hold positions of religious authority, though monarchs such as Elizabeth I of England and female territorial rulers of the states of the Holy Roman Empire did determine religious policies.

Catholics viewed marriage as a sacramental union that, if validly entered into, could not be dissolved. Protestants saw marriage as a contract in which each partner promised the other support, companionship, and the sharing of mutual goods. Because, in Protestant eyes, marriage was created by God as a remedy for human weakness, marriages in which spouses did not comfort or support one another physically, materially, or emotionally endangered their own souls and the surrounding community. The only solution might be divorce and remarriage, which most Protestants came to allow. Protestant marital courts in Germany, Switzerland, Scandinavia, and later Scotland and France allowed divorce for adultery and impotence, and sometimes for contracting a contagious disease, "malicious" desertion (meaning intentional desertion, as opposed to unintentional desertion such as extended army service), conviction for a capital crime, or deadly assault. Some of them allowed both parties to marry again, and some only the innocent.

This was a dramatic change in marital law, as Catholic canon law had allowed only separation from bed and board with no remarriage, but it had a less than dramatic impact. Because marriage was the cornerstone of society socially and economically, divorce was a desperate last resort. In many Protestant jurisdictions the annual divorce rate hovered around 0.02 to 0.06 per thousand people. (By contrast, in 2000 the U.S. divorce rate was 4.1 per thousand people.)

Marriage was the proper remedy for lust, and Protestants uniformly condemned prostitution. The licensed brothels that were a common feature of late medieval urban life (see page 394) were closed in Protestant cities, and harsh punishments were set for prostitution. Selling sex was couched in moral rather than economic terms, as simply one type of "whoredom," a term that also included premarital sex, adultery, and other unacceptable sexual activities. Religious reformers such as Luther described women who sold sex in very negative terms and also regarded "whore" as the worst epithet they could hurl at their theological opponents.

Closing the official brothels did not end the exchange of sex for money, of course, but simply reshaped it. Smaller illegal brothels were established, or women moved to areas right outside city walls. Police and other authorities were influenced or bribed to overlook such activities. For Italian city authorities, this fluid situation was more worrisome, and they tended to favor regulation over suppression. They also viewed selling sex as a significant source of municipal income. From 1559 until the mid-eighteenth century in Florence, for example, all women registered as prostitutes were required to contribute an annual tax based on their income, which went to support a convent for women who wished to give up prostitution. Payment of extra taxes would allow a woman to live where she wished in the city and wear any type of clothes she chose, rather than having to follow the sumptuary laws requiring prostitutes to dress a certain way (see page 394).

The Protestant Reformation clearly had a positive impact on marriage, but its impact on women was more mixed. Many nuns had lacked a religious vocation, but convents nevertheless provided women of the upper classes with scope for their literary, artistic, medical, or administrative talents if they could not or would not marry. The Reformation generally brought the closing of monasteries and convents, and marriage became virtually the only occupation for upper-class Protestant women. Women in some convents recognized this and fought the Reformation, or argued that they could still be pious Protestants within convent walls. Most nuns left, however, and we do not know what happened to them. The Protestant emphasis on marriage made unmarried women (and men) suspect, for they did not belong to the type of household regarded as the cornerstone of a proper, godly society.

The Reformation and German Politics

Criticism of the church was widespread in Europe in the early sixteenth century, and calls for reform came from many areas. It was no accident, however, that the reformer whose ideas had the most impact lived in the politically divided Holy Roman Empire. Unlike Spain, France, and England, the Holy Roman Empire lacked a strong central power. The emperor was elected in a process established by the Golden Bull of 1356, a decree issued by the Holy Roman emperor Charles IV (and named after the golden seal attached to it). There were only seven electors—the archbishops of Mainz, Trier, and Cologne, the margrave of Brandenburg, the duke of Saxony, the count palatine of the Rhine, and the king of Bohemia. All these individuals were powerful, but so were many other nobles and church officials who ruled the hundreds of largely independent states in the empire.

Against this background of decentralization and strong local power, Martin Luther had launched a movement to reform the church. Two years after Luther published the Ninety-five Theses, the electors chose as emperor a nineteen-year-old Habsburg prince who ruled as Charles V. The course of the Reformation was shaped by this election and by the political relationships surrounding it.

- **How did the political situation in Germany shape the course of the Reformation?**

The Rise of the Habsburg Dynasty

War and diplomacy were important ways that states increased their power in sixteenth-century Europe, but so was marriage. Because almost all of Europe was ruled by hereditary dynasties—the Papal States and a few cities being the exceptions—claiming and holding resources involved shrewd marital strategies, for it was far cheaper to gain land by inheritance than by war. Royal and noble sons and daughters were important tools of state policy. Even popes and city leaders were often part of such marital strategies; papal nieces, nephews, and sometimes children were coveted marriage partners, as were the wealthy daughters of urban elites. Wealthy urban families, especially in Italy, also transformed themselves into hereditary dynasties through coups and alliances during this period, and they cemented their position through marriages with more established ruling houses.

The benefits of an advantageous marriage, particularly if the wife had no brothers and thus inherited territory, stretched across generations, a process that can be seen most dramatically with the Habsburgs. The Holy Roman emperor Frederick III, a Habsburg who was the ruler of most of Austria, acquired only a small amount of territory—but a great deal of money—with his marriage to Princess Eleonore of Portugal in 1452. He arranged for his son Maximilian to marry Europe's most prominent heiress, Mary of Burgundy, in 1477; she inherited the Netherlands, Luxembourg, and the County of Burgundy in what is now eastern France. Through this union with the rich and powerful duchy of Burgundy, the Austrian house of Habsburg, already the strongest ruling family in the empire, became an international power. The marriage of Maximilian and Mary angered the French, however, who considered Burgundy French territory, and inaugurated centuries of conflict between the Austrian house of Habsburg and the kings of France.

"Other nations wage war; you, happy Austria, marry." Historians dispute the origins of this adage, but no one questions its accuracy, at least in terms of marriage. (The frequency with which the Habsburgs went to war make the saying somewhat ironic.) Maximilian learned the lesson of marital politics well, marrying his son and daughter to the children of Ferdinand and Isabella, the rulers of Spain, much of southern Italy, and eventually the Spanish New World empire. His grandson Charles V (1500–1558) fell heir to a vast conglomeration of territories. Through a series of accidents and unexpected deaths, Charles inherited Spain from his mother, her New World possessions, and the Spanish dominions in Italy, Sicily, and Sardinia. From his father he inherited the Habsburg lands in Austria, southern Germany, the Low Countries, and Franche-Comté in east-central France. Charles would eventually rule about half of Europe.

Charles's inheritance was an incredibly diverse collection of states and peoples, each governed in a different manner and held together only by the person of the emperor (see Map 14.1 on page 460). Charles's Italian adviser, the grand chancellor Gattinara, told the young ruler, "God has set you on the path toward world monarchy." Charles not only believed this but also was convinced that it was his duty to maintain the political and religious unity of Western Christendom.

The Political Impact of the Protestant Reformation

In the sixteenth century the practice of religion remained a public matter. Everyone participated in the religious life of the community, just as almost everyone shared in the local agricultural work. Whatever spiritual convictions individuals held in the privacy of their consciences, the emperor, king, prince, magistrate, or other civil authority determined the official form of religious practice in his (or occasionally her) jurisdiction. Almost everyone believed that the presence of a faith different from that of the majority represented a political threat to the security of the state. Only a tiny minority, and certainly none of the rulers, believed in religious liberty.

Against this background, the religious storm launched by Martin Luther swept across Germany. Anticlericalism blended with hostility to the papacy, which was increasingly seen as Italian rather than international. Papal tax collectors had long been more active in the empire than they were in the more unified nation-states such as France, where royal power restricted them. Luther and other reformers highlighted papal financial exploitation of Germany in their sermons and pamphlets. Though Germany was not a nation, people did have an understanding of being German because of their language and traditions. Luther frequently used the phrase "we Germans" in his attacks on the papacy. Luther's appeal to German patriotism gained him strong support, and national feeling influenced many rulers otherwise confused by or indifferent to the complexities of the religious issues. Some German rulers were sincerely attracted to Lutheran ideas, but material considerations swayed many others to embrace the new faith. The rejection of Roman Catholicism and adoption of Protestantism would mean the legal confiscation of lush farmlands, rich monasteries, and wealthy shrines. A steady stream of duchies, margraviates, free cities, and bishoprics secularized church property, accepted Lutheran theological doctrines, and adopted simpler services conducted in German. Thus many political authorities in the empire used the religious issue to extend their financial and political power and to enhance their independence from the emperor.

Charles V was a vigorous defender of Catholicism, however, so it is not surprising that the Reformation led to religious wars. The first battleground was Switzerland, which was officially part of the Holy Roman Empire, though it was really a loose confederation of thirteen largely autonomous territories called "cantons." Some cantons remained Catholic, and some became Protestant, and in the late 1520s the two sides went to war. Zwingli was killed on the battlefield in 1531, and both sides quickly decided that a treaty was preferable to further fighting. The treaty basically allowed each canton to determine its own religion and ordered each side to give up its foreign alliances, a policy of neutrality that has been characteristic of modern Switzerland.

Trying to halt the spread of religious division, Charles V called an Imperial Diet in 1530, to meet at Augsburg. The Lutherans developed a statement of faith, later called the Augsburg Confession, and the Protestant princes presented this to the emperor. (The Augsburg Confession remained an authoritative statement of belief for many Lutheran churches for centuries.) Charles refused to accept it and ordered all Protestants to return to the Catholic Church and give up any confiscated church property. This threat backfired, and Protestant territories in the empire—mostly north German princes and south German cities—formed a military alliance. The emperor could not respond militarily, as he was in the midst of a

Giorgio Vasari: Fresco of Pope Clement VII and the Emperor Charles V In this double portrait, Vasari uses matching hand gestures to indicate agreement between the pope and the emperor, though the pope's red hat and cape make him the dominant figure. Charles V remained loyal to Catholicism, though the political situation and religious wars in Germany eventually required him to compromise with Protestants. *(Palazzo Vecchio, Florence/Scala/Art Resource, NY)*

series of wars with the French: the Habsburg-Valois Wars, fought in Italy along the eastern and southern borders of France and eventually in Germany. The Turks had also taken much of Hungary and in 1529 were besieging Vienna.

The 1530s and early 1540s saw complicated political maneuvering among many of the powers of Europe. The emperor, the pope, France, England, Protestant and Catholic princes and cities in Germany, Scotland, Sweden, Denmark, and even the Turks made and broke alliances, and the Habsburg-Valois rivalry continued to be played out militarily. Various attempts were made to heal the religious split with a church council, but intransigence on both sides made it increasingly clear that this would not be possible and that war was inevitable. Charles V realized that he was fighting not only for religious unity, but also for a more unified state against territorial rulers who wanted to maintain their independence. He was thus defending both church and empire.

Fighting began in 1546, and initially the emperor was very successful. This success alarmed both France and the pope, however, who did not want Charles to become even more powerful. The pope withdrew papal troops, and the Catholic king of France sent money and troops to the Lutheran princes. Finally, in 1555 Charles agreed to the Peace of Augsburg, which, in accepting the status quo, officially recognized Lutheranism. The political authority in each territory was permitted to decide whether the territory would be Catholic or Lutheran. Most of northern and central Germany became Lutheran, while the south remained Roman Catholic. There was no freedom of religion, however. Princes or town councils established state churches to which all subjects of the area had to belong. Dissidents had to convert or leave.

Online Study Center Improve Your Grade
Primary Source: The Religious Peace of Augsburg

There were limitations and problems in the Peace of Augsburg that would become clear by the late sixteenth century, but it accomplished what its makers hoped it would. It ended religious war in Germany for many decades, and it put political, religious, and economic life clearly in the hands of the territorial rulers. It was immediately evident that this agreement ended Charles V's hope of creating a united empire with a single church. He abdicated in 1556 and moved to a monastery, transferring power over his Spanish and Netherlandish holdings to his son Philip and his imperial power to his brother Ferdinand.

The Spread of the Protestant Reformation

States within the empire and the kingdom of Denmark-Norway were the earliest territories to accept the Protestant Reformation, but by the later 1520s Protestant ideas and dynastic considerations combined to bring religious

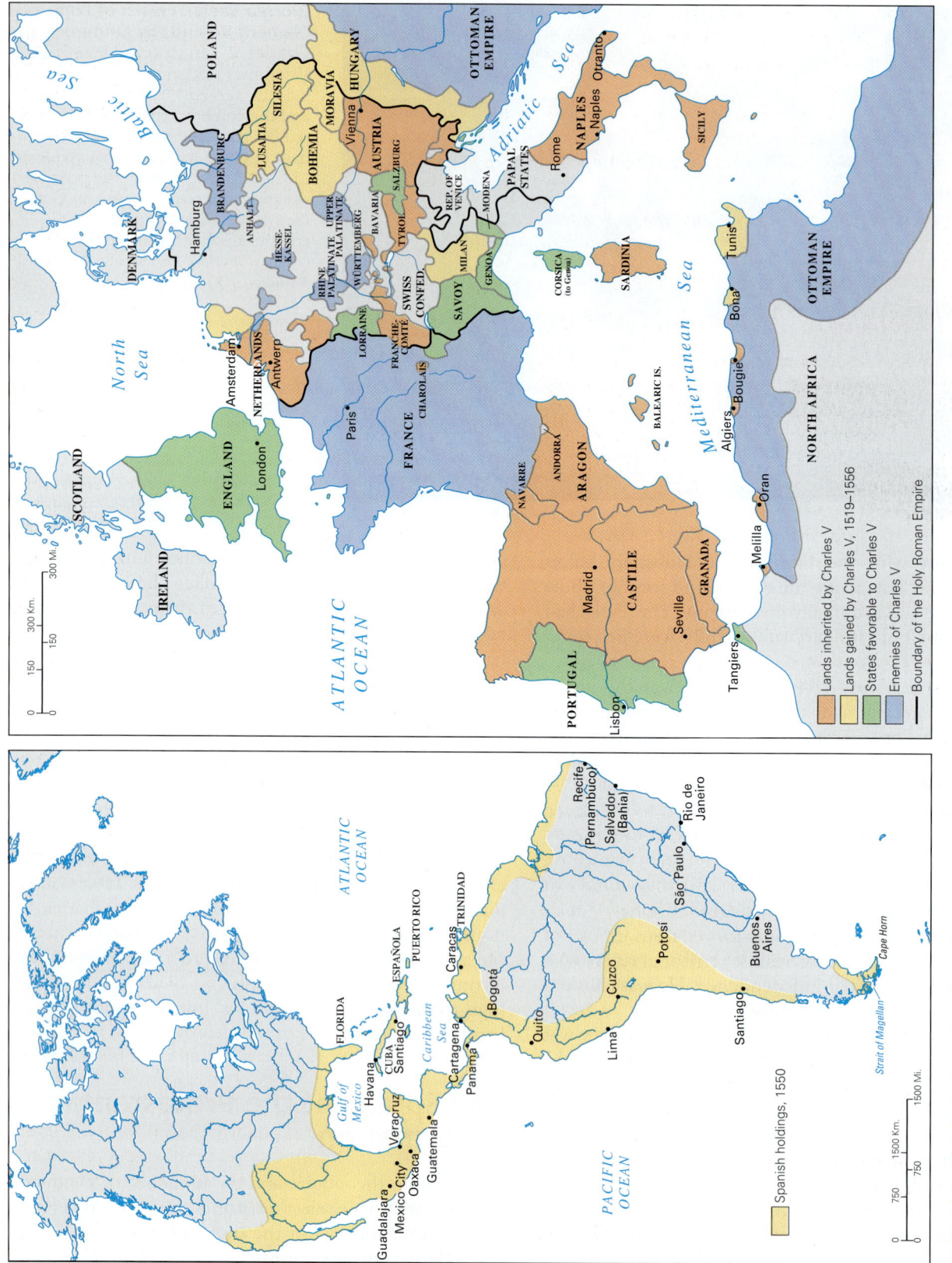

MAP 14.1 The Global Empire of Charles V Charles V exercised theoretical jurisdiction over more European territory than anyone since Charlemagne. He also claimed authority over large parts of North and South America, though actual Spanish control was weak in much of this area.

change to England. Protestant ideas also spread into France and eastern Europe. In all these areas, a second generation of reformers built on Lutheran and Zwinglian ideas to develop their own theology and plans for institutional change. The most important of the second-generation reformers was John Calvin, whose ideas would come to shape Christianity over a much wider area than did Luther's.

- **How did Protestant ideas and institutions spread beyond German-speaking lands?**

The Reformation in England and Ireland

As on the continent, the Reformation in England had economic as well as religious causes. When the personal matter of the divorce of King Henry VIII (r. 1509–1547) became enmeshed with political issues, a complete break with Rome resulted.

Henry was married to Catherine of Aragon, the daughter of Ferdinand and Isabella. Catherine had originally been married to his older brother Arthur, who had died as a youth. Marriage to a brother's widow went against canon law, and Henry had been required to obtain a special papal dispensation to marry Catherine. The marriage was about average for royal marriages—they neither especially hated nor loved one another—but it had produced only one living heir, a daughter, Mary. By 1527 Henry decided that God was showing his displeasure with the marriage by denying him a son, and he appealed to the pope to have the marriage annulled. He was also in love with a court lady-in-waiting, Anne Boleyn, and assumed that she would give him the son he wanted. Normally an annulment would not have been a problem, but the troops of Emperor Charles V were in Rome at that point, and Pope Clement VII was essentially their prisoner. Charles V was the nephew of Catherine of Aragon and thus was vigorously opposed to an annulment, which would have declared his aunt a fornicator and his cousin Mary a bastard. (An annulment declares that there never was a marriage, making children of such a union illegitimate.) The military situation in Rome, added to the fact that an annulment would have called into question the pope's right to grant a dispensation from something proscribed by the Bible, led the pope to stall.

Since Rome appeared to be thwarting Henry's matrimonial plans, he decided to remove the English church from papal jurisdiction. Henry used Parliament to legalize the Reformation in England. The Act in Restraint of Appeals (1533) declared the king to be the supreme sovereign in England and forbade judicial appeals to the papacy, thus establishing the Crown as the highest legal authority in the land. The Supremacy Act (1534) declared the king the supreme head of the Church of England. Both the Act in Restraint of Appeals and the Supremacy Act led to heated debate in the House of Commons. Some opposed the king. John Fisher, the bishop of Rochester, a distinguished scholar and a humanist, lashed the clergy with scorn for its cowardice in abjectly bending to the king's will. Another humanist, Thomas More, resigned the chancellorship: he could not take the oath required by the Supremacy Act because it rejected papal authority and made the king head of the English church. Fisher, More, and other dissenters were beheaded.

When Anne Boleyn failed twice to produce a male child, Henry VIII charged her with adulterous incest and in 1536 had her beheaded. Parliament promptly proclaimed Anne's daughter, the princess Elizabeth, illegitimate and, with the royal succession thoroughly confused, left the throne to whomever Henry chose. His third wife, Jane Seymour, gave Henry the desired son, Edward, but died in childbirth. Henry went on to three more wives. Before he died in 1547, he got Parliament to reverse the decision of 1536, relegitimating Mary and Elizabeth and fixing the succession first in his son and then in his daughters.

Between 1535 and 1539, under the influence of his chief minister, Thomas Cromwell, Henry decided to dissolve the English monasteries because he wanted their wealth. The king ended nine hundred years of English monastic life, dispersing the monks and nuns and confiscating their lands. Hundreds of properties were sold to the middle and upper classes and the proceeds spent on war. The dissolution of the monasteries did not achieve a more equitable distribution of land and wealth. Rather, the redistribution of land strengthened the upper classes and tied them to the Tudor dynasty.

Henry's motives combined personal, political, social, and economic elements. Theologically he retained such traditional Catholic practices and doctrines as confession, clerical celibacy, and transubstantiation. Meanwhile, Protestant literature circulated, and Henry approved the selection of men of Protestant sympathies as tutors for his son.

Did the religious changes accompanying this political upheaval have broad popular support? Some people were certainly dissatisfied with the church in England, but traditional Catholicism exerted an enormously strong and vigorous hold over the imagination and loyalty of the people. The surviving evidence does not allow us to gauge the degree of opposition to (or support for) Henry's

Allegory of the Tudor Dynasty The unknown creator of this work intended to glorify the virtues of the Protestant succession; the painting has no historical reality. Enthroned Henry VIII (r. 1509–1547) hands the sword of justice to his Protestant son Edward VI (r. 1547–1553). The Catholic Queen Mary (r. 1553–1558) and her husband Philip of Spain are followed by Mars, god of war, signifying violence and civil disorder. At right the figures of Peace and Plenty accompany the Protestant Elizabeth I (r. 1558–1603), symbolizing England's happy fate under her rule. *(Yale Center for British Art, Paul Mellon Collection/The Bridgeman Art Library)*

break with Rome. Most clergy and officials accepted Henry's moves, but all did not quietly acquiesce. In 1536 popular opposition in the north to the religious changes led to the Pilgrimage of Grace, a massive multi-class rebellion that proved the largest in English history. The "pilgrims" accepted a truce, but their leaders were arrested, tried, and executed. Recent scholarship points out that people rarely "converted" from Catholicism to Protestantism overnight, particularly where changes were piecemeal and the religious policies of the Crown itself varied, as in England. People responded to an action of the Crown that was played out in their own neighborhood—the closing of a monastery, the ending of Masses for the dead—with a combination of resistance, acceptance, cooperation, and collaboration.

Loyalty to the Catholic Church was particularly strong in Ireland. Ireland had been claimed by English kings since the twelfth century, but in reality the English had firm control of only the area around Dublin, known as the Pale. In 1536, on orders from London, the Irish parliament, which represented only the English landlords and the people of the Pale, approved the English laws severing the church from Rome. The Church of Ireland was established on the English pattern, and the (English) ruling class adopted the new reformed faith. Most of the Irish people remained Roman Catholic, thus adding religious antagonism to the ethnic hostility that had been a feature of English policy toward Ireland for centuries (see page 397). Irish armed opposition to the Reformation led to harsh repression by the English. Catholic property was confiscated and sold, and the profits were shipped to England. With the Roman church driven underground, Catholic clergy acted as national as well as religious leaders.

The nationalization of the church and the dissolution of the monasteries led to important changes in government administration in both England and Ireland. Vast tracts of formerly monastic land came temporarily under the Crown's jurisdiction, and new bureaucratic machinery had to be developed to manage those properties. Cromwell reformed and centralized the king's household, the council, the secretariats, and the Exchequer. New departments of state were set up. Surplus funds from all departments went into a liquid fund to be applied to areas where there were deficits. This balancing resulted in greater efficiency and economy. Henry VIII's reign saw the growth of the modern centralized bureaucratic state.

In the short reign of Henry's sickly son, Edward VI (r. 1547–1553), strongly Protestant ideas exerted a significant influence on the religious life of the country. Archbishop Thomas Cranmer simplified the liturgy, invited Protestant theologians to England, and prepared the first **Book of Common Prayer** (1549). In stately and dignified English, the *Book of Common Prayer* included, together with the Psalter, the order for all services of the Church of England.

The equally brief reign of Mary Tudor (r. 1553–1558) witnessed a sharp move back to Catholicism. The devoutly Catholic daughter of Catherine of Aragon, Mary rescinded the Reformation legislation of her father's reign and restored Roman Catholicism. Mary's marriage to her cousin Philip of Spain, son of the emperor Charles V, proved highly unpopular in England, and her execution of several hundred Protestants further alienated her subjects. During her reign, many Protestants fled to the continent. Mary's death raised to the throne her sister Elizabeth (r. 1558–1603) and inaugurated the beginnings of religious stability.

Elizabeth had been raised a Protestant, but at the start of her reign sharp differences existed in England. On the one hand, Catholics wanted a Roman Catholic ruler. On the other hand, a vocal number of returning exiles wanted all Catholic elements in the Church of England eliminated. The latter, because they wanted to "purify" the church, were called "Puritans." Probably one of the shrewdest politicians in English history, Elizabeth chose a middle course between Catholic and Puritan extremes. She insisted on dignity in church services and political order in the land. She required her subjects to attend church or risk a fine, but did not care what they actually believed as long as they kept quiet about it. She required officials, clergy, and nobles to swear allegiance to her as the "supreme governor of the Church of England." She initially chose the word *governor* rather than *head* to provide a loophole for English Catholics to remain loyal to her without denying the primacy of the pope. She also realized that *head* might be viewed as inappropriate for a woman, for treatises about the family and proper gender relations always referred to men as the "head."

The parliamentary legislation of the early years of Elizabeth's reign—laws sometimes labeled the **Elizabethan Settlement**—required outward conformity to the Church of England and uniformity in all ceremonies. In 1563 a convocation of bishops approved the Thirty-nine Articles, a summary in thirty-nine short statements of the basic tenets of the Church of England. During Elizabeth's reign, the Anglican church (from the Latin *Ecclesia Anglicana*), as the Church of England was called, moved in a moderately Protestant direction. Services were conducted in English, monasteries were not reestablished, and clergymen were (grudgingly) allowed to marry. But the episcopate was not abolished, and the bishops remained as church officials; apart from language, the services were quite traditional.

Calvinism

In 1509, while Luther was studying for a doctorate at Wittenberg, John Calvin (1509–1564) was born in Noyon in northwestern France. Luther inadvertently launched the Protestant Reformation. Calvin, however, had the greater impact on future generations. His theological writings profoundly influenced the social thought and attitudes of Europeans and English-speaking peoples all over the world, especially in Canada and the United States. Although he had originally intended to have an ecclesiastical career, Calvin studied law, which had a decisive impact on his mind and later thought. In 1533 he experienced a religious crisis, as a result of which he converted to Protestantism.

Convinced that God selects certain people to do his work, Calvin believed that God had specifically called him to reform the church. Accordingly, he accepted an invitation to assist in the reformation of the city of Geneva. There, beginning in 1541, Calvin worked assiduously to establish a Christian society ruled by God through civil magistrates and reformed ministers. Geneva, "a city that was a church," became the model of a Christian community for sixteenth-century Protestant reformers.

To understand Calvin's Geneva, it is necessary to understand Calvin's ideas. These he embodied in **The Institutes of the Christian Religion,** first published in 1536 and definitively issued in 1559. The cornerstone of Calvin's theology was his belief in the absolute sovereignty and omnipotence of God and the total weakness of humanity. Before the infinite power of God, he asserted, men and women are as insignificant as grains of sand.

Calvin did not ascribe free will to human beings because that would detract from the sovereignty of God. Men and women cannot actively work to achieve salvation; rather, God in his infinite wisdom decided at the beginning of time who would be saved and who damned. This viewpoint constitutes the theological principle called **predestination:**

Predestination we call the eternal decree of God, by which he has determined in himself, what he would have become of every individual. . . . For they are not all created with a similar destiny; but eternal life is foreordained for some, and eternal damnation for others. . . . In conformity, therefore, to the clear doctrine of the Scripture, we assert, that by an eternal and immutable counsel, God has once for all determined, both whom he would admit to salvation, and whom he would condemn to destruction. . . . To those whom he devotes to condemnation, the gate of life is closed by a just and irreprehensible, but incomprehensible, judgment. How exceedingly presumptuous it is only to inquire into the causes of the Divine will; which is in fact, and is justly entitled to be, the cause of everything that exists. . . . For the will of God is the highest justice; so that what he wills must be considered just, for this very reason, because he wills it.[6]

Many people consider the doctrine of predestination, which dates back to Saint Augustine and Saint Paul, to be a pessimistic view of the nature of God, who, they feel, revealed himself in the Old and New Testaments as merciful as well as just. But "this terrible decree," as even Calvin called it, did not lead to pessimism or fatalism. Rather, the Calvinist believed in the redemptive work of Christ and was confident that God had elected (saved) him or her. Predestination served as an energizing dynamic, forcing a person to undergo hardships in the constant struggle against evil.

Calvin aroused Genevans to a high standard of morality. He had two remarkable assets: complete mastery of the Scriptures and exceptional eloquence. Through his sermons and a program of religious education, God's laws and man's were enforced in Geneva. Calvin's powerful sermons delivered the Word of God and thereby monopolized the strongest contemporary means of communication: preaching. Through his *Genevan Catechism,* published in 1541, children and adults memorized set questions and answers and acquired a summary of their faith and a guide for daily living. Calvin's sermons and his *Catechism* gave a whole generation of Genevans thorough instruction in the reformed religion.[7]

Young John Calvin Even in youth, Calvin's face showed the strength and determination that were later to characterize his religious zeal. *(Bibliothèque de Genève, Département iconographique)*

In the reformation of the city, the Genevan Consistory also exercised a powerful role. This body consisted of twelve laymen plus the Company of Pastors, of which Calvin was the permanent moderator (presider). The duties of the Consistory were "to keep watch over every man's life [and] to admonish amiably those whom they see leading a disorderly life." Even though Calvin emphasized that the Consistory's activities should be thorough and "its eyes may be everywhere," corrections were considered only "medicine to turn sinners to the Lord."[8]

Although all municipal governments in early modern Europe regulated citizens' conduct, none did so with the severity of Geneva's Consistory under Calvin's leadership. Nor did it make any distinction between what we would consider crimes against society and simple un-Christian conduct. Absence from sermons, criticism of ministers, dancing, card playing, family quarrels, and heavy drinking were all investigated and punished by the

Consistory. Serious crimes and heresy were handled by the civil authorities, which, with the Consistory's approval, sometimes used torture to extract confessions. Between 1542 and 1546 alone seventy-six persons were banished from Geneva and fifty-eight executed for heresy, adultery, blasphemy, and witchcraft.

Calvin reserved his harshest condemnation for religious dissenters, declaring them "dogs and swine":

God makes plain that the false prophet is to be stoned without mercy. We are to crush beneath our heel all affections of nature when His honor is concerned. The father should not spare his child, . . . nor husband his own wife or the friend who is dearer to him than life. No human relationship is more than animal unless it be grounded in God.[9]

In the 1550s Spanish humanist Michael Servetus had gained international notoriety for his publications denying the Christian dogma of the Trinity. Servetus had been arrested by the Inquisition but escaped to Geneva, where he was promptly rearrested. At his trial, he not only held to his belief that there is no scriptural basis for the Trinity but also rejected child baptism and insisted that a person under twenty cannot commit a mortal sin. The city fathers considered this last idea dangerous to public morality, "especially in these days when the young are so corrupted." Though Servetus begged that he be punished by banishment, Calvin and the town council maintained that the denial of child baptism and the Trinity amounted to a threat to all society. Servetus was burned at the stake.

Online Study Center Improve Your Grade
Primary Source: The Trial of Michael Servetus in Calvin's Geneva

To many sixteenth-century Europeans Calvin's Geneva seemed "the most perfect school of Christ since the days of the Apostles." Religious refugees from France, England, Spain, Scotland, and Italy visited the city. Subsequently, the Reformed church of Calvin served as the model for the Presbyterian church in Scotland, the Huguenot church in France, and the Puritan churches in England and New England.

Calvinism became the compelling force in international Protestantism. The Calvinist ethic of the "calling" dignified all work with a religious aspect. Hard work, well done, was pleasing to God. This doctrine encouraged an aggressive, vigorous activism. These factors, together with the social and economic applications of Calvin's theology, made Calvinism the most dynamic force in sixteenth- and seventeenth-century Protestantism.

The Establishment of the Church of Scotland

Calvinism found a ready audience in Scotland. There as elsewhere, political authority was the decisive influence in reform. The monarchy was weak, and factions of virtually independent nobles competed for power. King James V and his daughter Mary, Queen of Scots (r. 1560–1567), staunch Catholics and close allies of Catholic France, opposed reform. The Scottish nobles supported it. One man, John Knox (1505?–1572), dominated the movement for reform in Scotland.

In 1559 Knox, a dour, single-minded, and fearless man with a reputation as a passionate preacher, set to work reforming the church. He was determined to structure the Scottish church after the model of Geneva, where he had studied and worked with Calvin. In 1560 Knox persuaded the Scottish parliament, which was dominated by reform-minded barons, to enact legislation ending papal authority. The Mass was abolished. Knox then established the Presbyterian Church of Scotland, so named because *presbyters*, or ministers, not bishops, governed it. The Church of Scotland was strictly Calvinist in doctrine, adopted a simple and dignified service of worship, and laid great emphasis on preaching. Knox's *Book of Common Order* (1564) became the liturgical directory for the church. The Presbyterian Church of Scotland was a national, or state, church, and many of its members maintained close relations with English Puritans.

The Reformation in Eastern Europe

While political and economic issues determined the course of the Reformation in western and northern Europe, ethnic factors often proved decisive in eastern Europe. In the later Middle Ages, the migration of diverse peoples into Bohemia, Poland, and Hungary meant that those countries had heterogeneous populations in the sixteenth century. Ethnic background tended to resolve religious matters.

In Bohemia in the fifteenth century, the ethnic grievances of the Czech majority against German economic and ecclesiastical domination (see page 391) fused with Czech resentment at the corruption of the Roman church. By 1500 most Czechs had adopted the ideas of Jan Hus, and the emperor had been forced to recognize a separate Hussite church. Lutheranism spread rapidly among Germans in Bohemia in the 1520s and 1530s; many Germans lived near the border of Luther's Saxony. Moreover, the nobility's identification of Lutheranism with opposition to the Habsburgs contributed, as in Germany, to the growth of Protestantism. The forces of the Catholic Reformation promoted a Catholic spiritual revival in Bohemia, and some areas reconverted. This complicated situation would be one of the causes of the Thirty Years' War (see pages 562–565).

By 1500 Poland and the Grand Duchy of Lithuania were united in a dynastic union. A king, senate, and diet (parliament) governed, but the two territories retained separate officials, judicial systems, armies, and forms of citizenship. In the fifteenth century rulers had granted the Polish *szlachta* (nobility) extensive rights; though hereditary, the monarchy was weak and had to cooperate with the szlachta. The combined realms covered about 440,150 square miles, making Poland-Lithuania the largest European polity. A population of only about 7.5 million people was very thinly scattered over that land.

In comparison with western Europe, Poland-Lithuania was overwhelmingly rural; its largest cities—Gdansk (30,000) and Cracow (15,000)—were very small in population by Italian or French standards. Yet with Germans, Italians, Tartars, and Jews, Poland-Lithuania represented great diversity. Such peoples had come as merchants, invited by medieval rulers because of their wealth or to make agricultural improvements. Each group spoke its native language, though all educated people spoke Latin. In the late fifteenth century Italian Renaissance humanism influenced Polish art, architecture, literature, and historical writing.

Luther's ideas spread first to the German-speaking Baltic towns, then to the University of Cracow, where his works were translated. His ideas met two major obstacles: King Sigismund I (r. 1506–1548) banned Luther's teachings in Poland, and strong anti-German feeling among Poles meant that Lutheranism would have limited success outside Germanized towns.

The Reformed tradition of John Calvin, with its stress on the power of church elders, appealed to the Polish szlachta, however. The fact that Calvinism originated in France, not in Germany, also made it more attractive than Lutheranism. Several Polish magnates, including Jan Laski (1499–1560), converted to Calvinism, and Calvinist nobles dominated the important diet of 1555. But doctrinal differences among Calvinists, Lutherans, and other groups prevented united opposition to Catholicism.

Under Stanislaus Hosius (1505–1579), who attended the Council of Trent, a systematic Counter-Reformation gained momentum. Hosius pressed for reform within the Catholic Church, held provincial synods, and published a comprehensive and clear statement of Roman Catholic faith and morals. The Jesuits (see page 469) complemented his work by establishing schools for the sons of the szlachta. By 1650 the identification of Poland and Roman Catholicism was well established.

Merchants from Poland carried the first news about Martin Luther to Hungary in 1521. Hungarian students flocked to Wittenberg; they became the major agents for the spread of Lutheranism in Hungary, and sympathy for it developed at the royal court at Buda. But concern about "the German heresy" by the Catholic hierarchy and among the magnates found expression in a decree of the Hungarian diet in 1523 that "all Lutherans and those favoring them . . . should have their property confiscated and themselves punished with death as heretics."[10]

A military event on August 26, 1526, had profound consequences for both the Hungarian state and the Protestant Reformation there. On the plain of Mohács in southern Hungary, the Ottoman sultan Suleiman the Magnificent (see page 566) inflicted a crushing defeat on the Hungarians, killing King Louis II, many of the magnates, and more than sixteen thousand ordinary soldiers. Rival factions elected different kings, and the Hungarian kingdom was divided into three parts: the Ottoman Turks absorbed the great plains, including the capital, Buda; the Habsburgs ruled the north and west; and Ottoman-supported Janos Zapolya held eastern Hungary and Transylvania. The Turks were indifferent to the religious conflicts of the infidels.

Mohács led to a great advance of Protestantism. Many Magyar (Hungarian) magnates accepted Lutheranism; Lutheran schools and parishes headed by men educated at Wittenberg multiplied; and peasants welcomed the new faith. In spite of the foundation of Jesuit colleges, in 1585 the papal nuncio noted that 85 percent of the population was Protestant, 10 percent remained Greek Orthodox, and just 5 percent (concentrated in Croatia) stayed Catholic. Hungary seemed lost to Catholicism. Then, in the late seventeenth century, Hungarian nobles' recognition of Habsburg (Catholic) rule and Ottoman Turkish withdrawal in 1699 led to Catholic restoration.

The Catholic Reformation

Between 1517 and 1547 Protestantism made remarkable advances. Nevertheless, the Roman Catholic Church made a significant comeback. After about 1540 no new large areas of Europe, other than the Netherlands, accepted Protestant beliefs (see Map 14.2). Many historians see the developments within the Catholic Church after the Protestant Reformation as two interrelated movements: one a drive for internal reform linked to earlier reform efforts, and the other a Counter-Reformation that opposed Protestants intellectually, politically, militarily, and institutionally. In both movements, the papacy, new religious orders, and the Council of Trent that met from 1545 to 1563 were important agents.

- **How did the Catholic Church respond to the new religious situation?**

The Reformed Papacy

The Renaissance princes who sat on the throne of Saint Peter were not blind to the evils that existed. Modest reform efforts were undertaken, but the idea of reform was closely linked to the idea of a general council representing the entire church. Remembering fifteenth-century conciliar attempts to limit papal authority, early sixteenth-century popes resisted calls for a council. The papal bureaucrats who were the popes' intimates warned the popes against a council, fearing loss of power, revenue, and prestige.

This changed beginning with Pope Paul III (1534–1549), and the papal court became the center of the reform movement rather than its chief opponent. Paul appointed reform-minded cardinals, abbots, and bishops who improved education for the clergy, tried to enforce moral standards among them, and worked on correcting the most glaring abuses. Reform measures that had been suggested since the late Middle Ages, such as prohibiting pluralism and absenteeism, were gradually adopted during the sixteenth century. Paul III and his successors supported the establishment of new religious orders that preached to the common people, the opening of seminaries for training priests, the end of the selling of church offices, and stricter control of clerical life. Their own lives were models of decorum and piety, in contrast to Renaissance popes who had concentrated on building and decorating churches and palaces and on enhancing the power of their own families.

In 1542 Pope Paul III established the Sacred Congregation of the **Holy Office,** with jurisdiction over the Roman Inquisition, a powerful instrument of the Catholic Reformation. The Inquisition was a committee of six cardinals with judicial authority over all Catholics and the power to arrest, imprison, and execute. Under the fervent Cardinal Caraffa, it vigorously attacked heresy.

The Roman Inquisition operated under the principles of Roman law. It accepted hearsay evidence, was not obliged to inform the accused of charges against them, and sometimes applied torture. Echoing one of Calvin's remarks about heresy, Cardinal Caraffa wrote, "No man is to lower himself by showing toleration towards any sort of heretic, least of all a Calvinist."[11] The Holy Office published the *Index of Prohibited Books,* a catalogue of forbidden reading.

Within the Papal States, the Inquisition effectively destroyed heresy (and some heretics). Outside the papal territories, however, its influence was slight. In Venice, a major publishing center, the *Index* had no influence on scholarly research in nonreligious areas such as law, classical literature, and mathematics.

The Council of Trent

Pope Paul III also called an ecumenical council, which met intermittently from 1545 to 1563 at Trent, an imperial city close to Italy. It was called not only to reform the church but also to secure reconciliation with the Protestants. Lutherans and Calvinists were invited to participate, but their insistence that the Scriptures be the sole basis for discussion made reconciliation impossible. International politics repeatedly cast a shadow over the theological debates. Charles V opposed discussions on any matter that might further alienate his Lutheran subjects, fearing the loss of additional imperial territory to Lutheran princes. Meanwhile, the French kings worked against the reconciliation of Roman Catholicism and Lutheranism. As long as religious issues divided the German states, the empire would be weakened, and a weak and divided empire meant a stronger France. Portugal, Poland, Hungary, and Ireland sent representatives, but very few German bishops attended.

In spite of the obstacles, the achievements of the Council of Trent were impressive. The council dealt with both doctrinal and disciplinary matters. It gave equal validity to the Scriptures and to tradition as sources of religious truth and authority. It reaffirmed the seven sacraments and the traditional Catholic teaching on transubstantiation. Thus it rejected Lutheran and Calvinist positions.

The council tackled the problems arising from ancient abuses by strengthening ecclesiastical discipline. Tridentine (from *Tridentum,* the Latin word for Trent) decrees required bishops to reside in their own dioceses, suppressed pluralism and simony, and forbade the sale of indulgences. Clerics who kept concubines were to give them up. The jurisdiction of bishops over all the clergy of their dioceses was made almost absolute, and bishops were ordered to visit every religious house within the diocese at least once every two years. In a highly original decree, the council required every diocese to establish a

seminary for the education and training of the clergy; the council even prescribed the curriculum and insisted that preference for admission be given to sons of the poor. Seminary professors were to determine whether candidates for ordination had *vocations,* genuine callings as determined by purity of life, detachment from the broader secular culture, and a steady inclination toward the priesthood. This was a novel idea, since from the time of the early church, parents had determined their sons' (and daughters') religious careers. Finally, great emphasis was laid on preaching and instructing the laity, especially the uneducated.

One decision had especially important social consequences for laypeople. Since the time of the Roman Empire, many couples had treated marriage as a completely personal matter, had exchanged vows privately without witnesses, and had thus formed what were called clandestine (secret) unions. This widespread practice frequently led later to denials by one party, conflicts over property, and disputes in the ecclesiastical courts that had jurisdiction over marriage once it became a sacrament (which occurred in the twelfth century). The Tridentine decree Tametsi (November 1563) stipulated that for a marriage to be valid, consent (the essence of marriage) as given in the vows had to be made publicly before witnesses, one of whom had to be the parish priest. Trent thereby ended secret marriages in Catholic countries. (They remained a problem for civil and church courts in England until the Hardwicke Act of 1753 abolished them.)

The Council of Trent did not meet everyone's expectations. Reconciliation with Protestantism was not achieved, nor was reform brought about immediately. Nevertheless, the Tridentine decrees laid a solid basis for the spiritual renewal of the church and for the enforcement of correction. For four centuries the doctrinal and disciplinary legislation of Trent served as the basis for Roman Catholic faith, organization, and practice.

New Religious Orders

The establishment of new religious orders within the church reveals a central feature of the Catholic Reformation. Most of these new orders developed in response to one crying need: to raise the moral and intellectual level of the clergy and people. (See the feature "Individuals in Society: Teresa of Ávila.") Education was a major goal of the two most famous orders.

The Ursuline order of nuns, founded by Angela Merici (1474–1540), attained enormous prestige for the education of women. The daughter of a country gentleman, Angela Merici worked for many years among the poor, sick, and uneducated around her native Brescia in northern Italy. In 1535 she established the Ursuline order to combat heresy through Christian education. The first women's religious order concentrating exclusively on teaching young girls, the Ursulines sought to re-Christianize society by training future wives and mothers. Because the Council of Trent placed great stress on the *claustration* (strict enclosure) of religious women and called for the end of all active ministries for women, Angela had great difficulty gaining papal approval. Official recognition finally came in 1565, and the Ursulines rapidly spread to France and the New World. Their schools in North America, stretching from Quebec to New Orleans, provided superior education for young women and inculcated the spiritual ideals of the Catholic Reformation.

The Society of Jesus, or **Jesuits,** founded by Ignatius Loyola (1491–1556), a former Spanish soldier, played a powerful international role in resisting the spread of Protestantism, converting Asians and Latin American Indians to Catholicism, and spreading Christian education all over Europe. While recuperating from a severe battle wound in his legs, Loyola studied a life of Christ and other religious books and decided to give up his military career and become a soldier of Christ. During a year spent in seclusion, prayer, and personal mortification, he gained insights that went into his great classic, *Spiritual Exercises* (1548). This work, intended for study during a four-week period of retreat, directed the individual imagination and will to the reform of life and a new spiritual piety.

Mapping the Past

MAP 14.2 Religious Divisions in Europe The Reformations shattered the religious unity of Western Christendom. The situation was even more complicated than a map of this scale can show. Many cities within the Holy Roman Empire, for example, accepted a different faith than the surrounding countryside; Augsburg, Basel, and Strasbourg were all Protestant, though surrounded by territory ruled by Catholic nobles. Use the map and the information in the book to answer the following questions: ❶ Why was the Holy Roman Empire the first arena of religious conflict in sixteenth-century Europe? ❷ Are there similarities in regions where a particular branch of the Christian faith was maintained or took root? ❸ To what degree can nonreligious factors be used as an explanation for the religious divisions in sixteenth-century Europe?

Online Study Center **Improve Your Grade** Interactive Map: Protestant and Catholic Reformations

School of Titian: The Council of Trent Since the early sessions were sparsely attended, this well-attended meeting seems to be a later session or an idealization. The seated figures in the tall white hats are bishops, while the dark-clothed figures around the edges are church lawyers and officials. The guards in the foreground are members of the Swiss guards, founded by Pope Julius II in 1505 to defend the papacy and still serving in that role (and in similar uniforms) today. In the sixteenth century Switzerland was a poor country, as its mountainous terrain was not good for agriculture, and mercenary soldiers were one of its chief "exports." *(Louvre/Réunion des Musées Nationaux/Art Resource, NY)*

Loyola was a man of considerable personal magnetism. After study at universities in Salamanca and Paris, he gathered a group of six companions and in 1540 secured papal approval of the new Society of Jesus. The first Jesuits, recruited primarily from the wealthy merchant and professional classes, saw the Reformation as a pastoral problem, its causes and cures related not to doctrinal issues but to people's spiritual condition. Reform of the church, as Luther and Calvin understood that term, played no role in the future the Jesuits planned for themselves. Their goal was "to help souls." Loyola also possessed a gift for leadership that consisted in spotting talent and in seeing "how at a given juncture change is more consistent with one's scope than staying the course."[12]

The Society of Jesus developed into a highly centralized, tightly knit organization. Candidates underwent a two-year novitiate, in contrast to the usual one-year probation. In addition to the traditional vows of poverty, chastity, and obedience, professed members vowed "special obedience to the sovereign pontiff regarding missions."[13] Thus as stability—the promise to live his life in the monastery—was what made a monk, so mobility—the commitment to go anywhere for the help of souls—was the defining characteristic of a Jesuit. Flexibility and the willingness to respond to the needs of time and circumstance formed the Jesuit tradition. In this respect, Jesuits were very modern, and they attracted many recruits. They achieved phenomenal success for the papacy and the reformed Catholic Church. Jesuit schools adopted

Individuals in Society

Teresa of Ávila

Her family derived from Toledo, center of the Moorish, Jewish, and Christian cultures in medieval Spain. Her grandfather, Juan Sanchez, made a fortune in the cloth trade. A "New Christian" (see pages 437–439), he was accused of secretly practicing Judaism. Although he endured the humiliation of a public repentance, he moved his family south to Ávila. Beginning again, he recouped his wealth and, aspiring to the prestige of an "Old Christian," bought noble status. Juan's son Alzonzo Sanchez de Cepeda married a woman of thoroughly Christian background, giving his family an aura of impeccable orthodoxy. The third of their nine children, Teresa, became a saint and in 1970 was the first woman declared a Doctor of the Church, a title given to a theologian of outstanding merit.

At age twenty, inspired more by the fear of Hell than the love of God, Teresa (1515–1582) entered the Carmelite Convent of the Incarnation in Ávila. Most of the nuns were daughters of Ávila's leading citizens; they had entered the convent because of a family decision about which daughters would marry and which would become nuns. Their lives were much like those of female family members outside the convent walls, with good food, comfortable surroundings, and frequent visits from family and friends. Teresa was frequently ill, but she lived quietly in the convent for many years. In her late thirties, she began to read devotional literature intensely and had profound mystical experiences—visions and voices in which Christ chastised her for her frivolous life and friends. She described one such experience in 1560:

It pleased the Lord that I should see an angel. . . . Short, and very beautiful, his face was so aflame that he appeared to be one of the highest types of angels. . . . In his hands I saw a long golden spear and at the end of an iron tip I seemed to see a point of fire. With this he seemed to pierce my heart several times so that it penetrated to my entrails. When he drew it out . . . he left me completely afire with the great love of God.*

Teresa responded with a new sense of purpose: although she encountered stiff opposition, she resolved to found a reformed house. Four basic principles were to guide the new convent. First, poverty was to be fully observed, symbolized by the nuns' being barefoot, hence *discalced*. Charity and the nuns' own work must support the community. Second, the convent must keep strict enclosure; the visits of powerful benefactors with material demands were forbidden. Third, Teresa intended an egalitarian atmosphere in which class distinctions were forbidden. She had always rejected the emphasis on "purity of blood," a distinctive and racist feature of Spanish society that was especially out of place in the cloister. All sisters, including those of aristocratic background, must share the manual chores. Finally, like Ignatius Loyola and the Jesuits, Teresa placed great emphasis on obedience, especially to one's confessor.

Seventeenth-century cloisonné enamelwork illustrating Teresa of Ávila's famous vision of an angel piercing her heart. (By gracious permission of Catherine Hamilton Kappauf)

Between 1562 and Teresa's death in 1582, she founded or reformed fourteen other houses of nuns, traveling widely to do so. Though Teresa did not advocate institutionalized roles for women outside the convent, she did chafe at the restrictions placed on her because of her sex, and she thought of the new religious houses she founded as answers to the Protestant takeover of Catholic churches elsewhere in Europe. From her brother, who had obtained wealth in the Spanish colonies, Teresa learned about conditions in Peru and instructed her nuns "to pray unceasingly for the missionaries working among the heathens." Through prayer, Teresa wrote, her nuns could share in the exciting tasks of evangelization and missionary work otherwise closed to women. Her books, along with her five hundred extant letters, show her as a practical and down-to-earth woman as well as a mystic and a creative theologian.

Questions for Analysis

1. How did sixteenth-century convent life reflect the values of Spanish society?
2. How is the life of Teresa of Ávila typical of developments in the Catholic Reformation? How is her life unusual?

**The Autobiography of St. Teresa of Ávila*, trans. and ed. E. A. Peers (New York: Doubleday, 1960), pp. 273–274.

Online Study Center Improve Your Grade
Going Beyond Individuals in Society

Juan de Valdes Leal: Pope Paul III Approves the Jesuit Constitutions This painting by a Spanish artist celebrates the founding of the Jesuits by his fellow countryman Ignatius Loyola. When the Jesuit constitutions were read to him, Paul III supposedly murmured, "There is the finger of God." Judging by other portraits, the depiction of Loyola here is a reasonable likeness, that of the pope an idealization: in 1540 he was a very old man. *(Institut Amatller d'Art Hispanic)*

the modern humanist curricula and methods, and though they first concentrated on the children of the poor, they were soon educating the sons of the nobility. As confessors and spiritual directors to kings, Jesuits exerted great political influence. Operating on the principle that the end sometimes justifies the means, they were not above spying. Indifferent to physical comfort and personal safety, they carried Christianity to India and Japan before 1550 and to Brazil, North America, and the Congo in the seventeenth century. Within Europe the Jesuits brought southern Germany and much of eastern Europe back to Catholicism.

Religious Violence

In 1559 France and Spain signed the Treaty of Cateau-Cambrésis, which ended the long conflict known as the Habsburg-Valois Wars. Spain was the victor. France, exhausted by the struggle, had to acknowledge Spanish dominance in Italy, where much of the fighting had taken place. The Treaty of Cateau-Cambrésis did not bring peace, however. Instead, over the next century religious differences led to riots, civil wars, and international conflicts. Especially in France and the Netherlands, Protestants and Catholics used violent actions as well as preaching and teaching against each other, for each side regarded the other as a poison in the community that would provoke the wrath of God. Catholics continued to believe that Calvinists and Lutherans could be reconverted; Protestants persisted in thinking that the Roman church should be destroyed. Catholics and Protestants alike feared people of other faiths, who they often saw as agents of Satan. Even more, they feared those who were explicitly identified with Satan: witches living in their midst. The era of religious wars was also the time of the most virulent witch persecutions in European history, as both Protestants and Catholics tried to make their cities and states more godly.

- *What were the causes and consequences of religious violence, including riots, wars, and witch-hunts?*

French Religious Wars

The Habsburg-Valois Wars, waged intermittently through the first half of the sixteenth century, cost more than the French government could afford. In addition to the time-honored practices of increasing taxes and engaging in heavy borrowing, King Francis I (r. 1515–1547) tried two new devices to raise revenue: the sale of public offices and a treaty with the papacy. The former proved to be only a temporary source of money. The offices sold tended to become hereditary within a family, and once a man bought an office he and his heirs were exempt from taxation.

The treaty with the papacy was the Concordat of Bologna (see page 435), in which Francis agreed to recognize the supremacy of the papacy over a universal council. In return, the French crown gained the right to appoint all French bishops and abbots. This understanding gave the monarchy a rich supplement of money and offices and a power over the church that lasted until the Revolution of 1789. The Concordat of Bologna helps explain why France did not later become Protestant: in effect, it established Catholicism as the state religion. Because French rulers possessed control over appointments and had a vested financial interest in Catholicism, they had no need to revolt against Rome.

Luther's tracts first appeared in France in 1518, and his ideas attracted some attention. After the publication of Calvin's *Institutes* in 1536, sizable numbers of French people were attracted to the "reformed religion," as Calvinism was called. Because Calvin wrote in French rather than Latin, his ideas gained wide circulation. Initially, Calvinism drew converts from among reform-minded members of the Catholic clergy, the industrious middle classes, and artisan groups. Most French Calvinists (called **Huguenots**) lived in major cities, such as Paris, Lyons, and Rouen. When Henry II died in 1559, perhaps one-tenth of the population had become Calvinist.

The feebleness of the French monarchy was the seed from which the weeds of civil violence sprang. The three weak sons of Henry II who occupied the throne could not provide the necessary leadership, and they were often dominated by their mother, Catherine de' Medici. The French nobility took advantage of this monarchical weakness. In the second half of the sixteenth century between two-fifths and one-half of the nobility at one time or another became Calvinist. Just as German princes in the Holy Roman Empire had adopted Lutheranism as a means of opposition to Emperor Charles V, so French nobles frequently adopted the reformed religion as a religious cloak for their independence. Armed clashes between Catholic royalist lords and Calvinist antimonarchical lords occurred in many parts of France. Both Calvinists and Catholics believed that the others' books, services, and ministers polluted the community. Preachers incited violence, and ceremonies such as baptisms, marriages, and funerals triggered it.

Protestant teachings called the power of sacred images into question, and mobs in many cities took down and smashed statues, stained-glass windows, and paintings. They ridiculed and tested religious images, throwing them into latrines, using them as cooking fuel or building material, or giving them as toys or masks for children. Though it was often inspired by fiery Protestant sermons, this **iconoclasm** is an example of men and women carrying out the Reformation themselves, rethinking the church's system of meaning and the relationship between the unseen and the seen. Catholic mobs responded by defending images, and crowds on both sides killed their opponents, often in gruesome ways.

A savage Catholic attack on Calvinists in Paris on August 24, 1572 (Saint Bartholomew's Day), followed the usual pattern. The occasion was a religious ceremony, the marriage of the king's sister Margaret of Valois to the Protestant Henry of Navarre, which was intended to help reconcile Catholics and Huguenots. Instead Huguenot wedding guests in Paris were massacred, and other Protestants were slaughtered by mobs. Religious violence spread to the provinces, where thousands were killed. This **Saint Bartholomew's Day massacre** led to a civil war that dragged on for fifteen years. Agriculture in many areas was destroyed; commercial life declined severely; and starvation and death haunted the land.

What ultimately saved France was a small group of moderates of both faiths called **politiques** who believed that only the restoration of strong monarchy could reverse the trend toward collapse. No religious creed was worth the incessant disorder and destruction. Therefore, the politiques favored accepting the Huguenots as an officially recognized and organized pressure group. (But religious toleration, the full acceptance of peoples of different religious persuasions within a pluralistic society, with minorities having the same civil liberties as the majority, developed only in the eighteenth century.) The death of Catherine de' Medici, followed by the assassination of King Henry III, paved the way for the accession of Henry of Navarre (the unfortunate bridegroom of the Saint Bartholomew's Day massacre), a politique who became Henry IV (r. 1589–1610).

Henry knew that the majority of the French were Roman Catholics. Allegedly saying "Paris is worth a Mass," Henry knelt before the archbishop of Bourges and was received into the Roman Catholic Church. Henry's willingness to sacrifice religious principles to political necessity saved France. The **Edict of Nantes,** which Henry published in 1598, granted liberty of conscience and liberty of public worship to Huguenots in 150 fortified towns, such as La Rochelle. The reign of Henry IV and the Edict of Nantes prepared the way for French absolutism in the seventeenth century by helping restore internal peace in France.

The Netherlands Under Charles V

Hostility to a monarch was also part of religious wars in the Netherlands. What began as a movement for the reformation of the church developed into a struggle for Dutch independence.

Emperor Charles V (r. 1519–1556) had inherited the seventeen provinces that compose present-day Belgium and the Netherlands (see page 458). Each of the seventeen provinces of the Netherlands possessed historical liberties: each was self-governing and enjoyed the right to make its own laws and collect its own taxes. In addition to important economic connections, only the recognition of a common ruler in the person of Emperor Charles V united the provinces. The cities of the Netherlands made their living by trade and industry.

In the Low Countries as elsewhere, corruption in the Roman church and the critical spirit of the Renaissance provoked pressure for reform, and Lutheran ideas spread. Charles V had grown up in the Netherlands, however, and he was able to limit their impact. In 1556 Charles V abdicated, dividing his territories between his brother Ferdinand, who received Austria and the Holy Roman Empire, and his son Philip, who inherited Spain, the Low Countries, Milan and the kingdom of Sicily, and the Spanish possessions in the Americas. Philip had grown up in Spain and did not understand the Netherlands.

By the 1560s Protestants in the Netherlands were primarily Calvinists, not Lutherans, and were more militant in their beliefs. Calvinism appealed to the middle classes because of its intellectual seriousness, moral gravity, and emphasis on any form of labor well done. It took deep root among the merchants and financiers in Amsterdam and the northern provinces. Working-class people were also converted. Whereas Lutherans taught respect for the powers that be, Calvinism tended to encourage opposition to "illegal" civil authorities.

In the 1560s Spanish authorities attempted to suppress Calvinist worship and raised taxes, which sparked riots. Thirty churches in Antwerp were sacked and the religious images in them destroyed in a wave of iconoclasm. From Antwerp the destruction spread to Brussels and Ghent and north to the provinces of Holland and Zeeland. From Madrid Philip II sent twenty thousand Spanish troops under the duke of Alva to pacify the Low Countries. Alva interpreted "pacification" to mean the ruthless extermination of religious and political dissidents. On top of the Inquisition, he opened his own tribunal, soon called the "Council of Blood." On March 3, 1568, fifteen hundred men were executed.

For ten years, between 1568 and 1578, civil war raged in the Netherlands between Catholics and Protestants and between the seventeen provinces and Spain. Eventually the ten southern provinces, the Spanish Netherlands (the future Belgium), came under the control of the Spanish Habsburg forces. The seven northern provinces, led by Holland, formed the **Union of Utrecht** and in

MAP 14.3 The Netherlands, 1559–1609 This map shows the division of the seventeen provinces as a result of the religious wars. Some provinces were overwhelmingly agricultural; some were involved in manufacturing; and others were heavily commercial.

1581 declared their independence from Spain. The north was Protestant; the south remained Catholic (see Map 14.3). Philip did not accept this, and war continued, with the Dutch troops gaining victories under the leadership of a local nobleman, William of Nassau, prince of Orange (1533–1584), known as William the Silent. William was shot by a French assassin loyal to Philip (the first known assassination of a political leader by a handgun), and the leaders of the United Provinces looked beyond their borders to other Protestant areas for assistance against the Spanish.

They particularly appealed to the Protestant queen of England, Elizabeth, for assistance. Fearing that the next step would be a Spanish invasion of England, Elizabeth reluctantly sent money and troops. Philip responded by planning and launching an invasion of England, but the Spanish fleet scattered in the English Channel and only half the ships made it back to Spain (see pages 512–513).

Fighting continued off and on in the Netherlands, but the borders set by the Union of Utrecht gradually became permanent, and in 1609 Spain agreed to a truce that recognized the independence of the United Provinces.

The Great European Witch-Hunt

The relationship between the Reformation and the upsurge in trials for witchcraft that occurred at roughly the same time is complex. Increasing persecution for witchcraft actually began before the Reformation in the 1480s, but it became especially common about 1560. Religious reformers' extreme notions of the Devil's powers and the insecurity created by the religious wars contributed to this increase. Both Protestants and Catholics tried and executed witches, with church officials and secular authorities acting together. They regarded both their religious opponents and witches as deluded by the Devil but made a clear distinction between them; heretics might merit burning, but they were only rarely accused of witchcraft. Witches were a special kind of heretic, but their primary crime was a pact with the Devil, not incorrect doctrine.

The heightened sense of God's power and divine wrath in the Reformation era was an important factor in the witch-hunts, but other factors were also significant. One of these was a change in the idea of what a witch was. Nearly all premodern societies believe in witchcraft and make some attempts to control witches, who are understood to be people who use magical forces to do evil deeds. Witches themselves often believe in their own powers, which they can use to earn a living or gain influence over their neighbors. In the later Middle Ages, however, many educated Christian theologians, canon lawyers, and officials added a demonological component to this notion of what a witch was. For them, the essence of witchcraft was making a pact with the Devil that required the witch to do the Devil's bidding. Witches were no longer simply people who used magical power to get what they wanted, but rather people used by the Devil to do what *he* wanted. This demonological or Satanic idea of witchcraft was fleshed out, and witches were thought to engage in wild sexual orgies with the Devil, fly through the night to meetings called sabbats, which parodied the Mass, and steal communion wafers and unbaptized babies to use in their rituals. Some demonological theorists also claimed that witches were organized in an international conspiracy to overthrow Christianity, with a hierarchy similar to the hierarchy of angels and archangels that Christian philosophers had invented. Witchcraft was

Iconoclasm in the Netherlands Calvinist men and women break stained-glass windows, remove statues, and carry off devotional altarpieces. Iconoclasm, or the destruction of religious images, is often described as a "riot," but here the participants seem very purposeful. Calvinist Protestants regarded pictures and statues as sacrilegious and saw removing them as a way to purify the church. *(The Fotomas Index/The Bridgeman Art Library)*

thus spiritualized, and witches became the ultimate heretics, enemies of God.

Trials involving this new notion of witchcraft as diabolical heresy began in Switzerland and southern Germany in the late fifteenth century, became less numerous in the early decades of the Reformation when Protestants and Catholics were busy fighting each other, and then picked up again about 1560. Because so many records have been lost or destroyed, it is difficult to make an estimate for all of Europe, but most scholars agree that during the sixteenth and seventeenth centuries somewhere between 100,000 and 200,000 people were officially tried for witchcraft and between 40,000 and 60,000 were executed.

Though the gender balance varied widely in different parts of Europe, between 75 and 85 percent of those tried and executed were women. Ideas about women, and the roles women actually played in society, were thus important factors shaping the witch-hunts. Some demonologists expressed virulent **misogyny,** or hatred of women, and particularly emphasized women's powerful sexual desire, which could be satisfied only by a demonic lover. Most people viewed women as weaker and so more likely to give in to any kind of offer by the Devil, including better food or nicer clothing. Women were associated with nature, disorder, and the body, all of which were linked with the demonic. Women's actual lack of power in society and gender norms about the use of violence meant that they were more likely to use scolding and cursing to get what they wanted instead of taking people to court or beating them up. Curses were generally expressed (as they often are today) in religious terms; "go to Hell" was calling on the powers of Satan. Women also had more contact with areas of life in which bad things happened unexpectedly, such as preparing food or caring for new mothers, children, and animals.

Learned ideas about the diabolical nature of witchcraft gradually filtered down to common people. Illustrated pamphlets and broadsides portrayed witches riding on pitchforks to sabbats where they engaged in anti-Christian acts such as spitting on the communion host and having sexual relations with demons. Though witch trials were secret, executions were not; they were public spectacles witnessed by huge crowds, with the list of charges read out for all to hear. By the late sixteenth century popular accusations of witchcraft in many parts of Europe involved at least some parts of the demonic conception of witchcraft.

Legal changes also played a role in causing, or at least allowing for, massive witch trials. One of these was a change from an accusatorial legal procedure to an inquisitorial procedure. In the former, a suspect knew the accusers and the charges they had brought, and an accuser could in turn be liable for trial if the charges were not proven; in the latter, legal authorities themselves brought the case. This change made people much more willing to accuse others, for they never had to take personal responsibility for the accusation or face the accused's relatives. Inquisitorial procedure involved intense questioning of the suspect, often with torture; areas in Europe that did not make this change saw very few trials. Torture was also used to get the names of additional suspects, as most lawyers firmly believed that no witch could act alone.

The use of inquisitorial procedure did not always lead to witch-hunts, however. The most famous inquisitions in early modern Europe, those in Spain, Portugal, and Italy, were in fact very lenient in their treatment of people accused of witchcraft: the Inquisition in Spain executed only a handful of witches, the Portuguese Inquisition only one, and the Roman Inquisition none, though in each of these areas there were hundreds of cases. Inquisitors certainly believed in the power of the Devil and were no less misogynist than other judges, but they doubted very much whether the people accused of witchcraft had actually made pacts with the Devil that gave them special powers. They viewed such people not as diabolical Devil-worshipers but as superstitious and ignorant peasants who should be educated rather than executed. Thus most people brought up before the Inquisition for witchcraft were sent home with a warning and a penance.

Most witch trials began with a single accusation in a village or town. Individuals accused someone they knew of using magic to spoil food, make children ill, kill animals, raise a hailstorm, or do other types of harm. Tensions within families, households, and neighborhoods often played a role in these accusations. Women number very prominently among accusers and witnesses as well as among those accused of witchcraft because the actions witches were initially charged with, such as harming children or curdling milk, were generally part of women's sphere. A woman also gained economic and social security by conforming to the standard of the good wife and mother and by confronting women who deviated from it.

Once a charge was made, judges began to question other neighbors and acquaintances, building up a list of suspicious incidents that might have taken place over decades. Historians have pointed out that one of the reasons those accused of witchcraft were often older was that it took years to build up a reputation as a witch. At this point, the suspect was brought in for questioning by legal authorities. Judges and inquisitors sought the exact details of a witch's demonic contacts, including sexual ones. Suspects were generally stripped and shaved in a search for a "witch's mark," or "pricked" to find a spot insensitive to pain, and then tortured.

Detailed records of witch trials survive for many parts of Europe. They have been used by historians to study many aspects of witchcraft, but they cannot directly answer what seems to us an important question: did people really practice witchcraft and think they were witches? They certainly

Religious Violence

Hans Baldung Grien: Witches' Sabbat (1510) In this woodcut, Grien combines learned and popular beliefs about witches: they traveled at night, met at sabbats (or assemblies), feasted on infants (in dish held high), concocted strange potions, and had animal "familiars" that were really demons (here a cat). Grien also highlights the sexual nature of witchcraft by portraying the women naked and showing them with goats, which were common symbols of sexuality. *(Germanisches Nationalmuseum Nürnberg)*

confessed to evil deeds and demonic practices, sometimes without torture, but where would we draw the line between reality and fantasy? Clearly people were not riding through the air on pitchforks, but did they think they did? Did they actually invoke the Devil when they were angry at a neighbor, or was this simply in the mind of their accusers? Trial records cannot tell us, and historians have answered these questions very differently, often using insights from psychoanalysis or the study of more recent victims of torture in their explanations.

Once the initial suspect had been questioned, and particularly if he or she had been tortured, the people who had been implicated were brought in for questioning. This might lead to a small hunt, involving from five to ten victims, and it sometimes grew into a much larger hunt, what historians have called a "witch panic." Panics were most common in the part of Europe that saw the most witch accusations in general—the Holy Roman Empire, Switzerland, and parts of France. Most of this area consisted of very small governmental units, which were jealous of each other and after the Reformation were divided by religion. The rulers of these small territories often felt more threatened than did the monarchs of western Europe, and they saw persecuting witches as a way to demonstrate their piety and concern for order.

Sometimes witch panics were the result of legal authorities' rounding up a group of suspects together. Such panics often occurred after some type of climatic disaster, such as an unusually cold and wet summer, and they came in waves. In large-scale panics a wider variety of suspects were taken in—wealthier people, children, a greater proportion of men. Mass panics tended to end when it became clear to legal authorities, or to the community itself, that the people being questioned or executed were not what they understood witches to be, or that the scope of accusations was beyond belief. Some from their community might be in league with Satan, they thought, but not this type of person and not as many as this.

Similar skepticism led to the gradual end of witch-hunts in Europe. Even in the sixteenth century a few individuals questioned whether witches could ever do harm, make a pact with the Devil, or engage in the wild activities attributed to them. Doubts about whether secret denunciations were valid or torture would ever yield a truthful confession gradually spread among the same type of religious and legal authorities who had so vigorously persecuted witches. Prosecutions for witchcraft became less common and were gradually outlawed. Sporadic trials continued into the eighteenth century, but by then people who thought themselves witches were more likely to be regarded as deluded or mentally defective, meriting pity rather than persecution, even by people who still firmly believed in the Devil. Belief in the power of witches continued among uneducated people, but educated people now sneered at this as superstition. People ceased to bring formal accusations when they knew they would simply be dismissed, and witch trials ended. The last official execution for witchcraft in England was in 1682, though the last one in the Holy Roman Empire was not until 1775.

Chapter Summary

- What were the central ideas of the reformers, and why were they appealing to different social groups?
- How did the political situation in Germany shape the course of the Reformation?
- How did Protestant ideas and institutions spread beyond German-speaking lands?
- How did the Catholic Church respond to the new religious situation?
- What were the causes and consequences of religious violence, including riots, wars, and witch-hunts?

Online Study Center **ACE the Test**

The Catholic Church in the early sixteenth century had serious problems, and many individuals and groups had long called for reform. This background of discontent helps explain why Martin Luther's ideas found such a ready audience. Luther and other Protestants developed a new understanding of Christian doctrine that emphasized faith, the power of God's grace, and the centrality of the Bible. Protestant ideas were attractive to educated people and urban residents, and they spread rapidly through preaching, hymns, and the printing press. By 1530 many parts of the Holy Roman Empire and Scandinavia had broken with the Catholic Church. Some reformers developed more radical ideas about infant baptism, the ownership of property, and separation between church and state. Both Protestants and Catholics regarded these as dangerous, and radicals were banished or executed. The German Peasants' War, in which Luther's ideas were linked to calls for social and economic reform, was similarly put down harshly. The Protestant reformers did not break with medieval ideas about the proper gender hierarchy, though they did elevate the status of marriage and viewed orderly households as the key building blocks of society.

The progress of the Reformation was shaped by the political situation in the Holy Roman Empire. The Habsburg emperor, Charles V, ruled almost half of Europe along with Spain's overseas colonies. Within the empire his authority was limited, however, and local princes, nobles, and cities actually held most power. This decentralization allowed the Reformation to spread. Charles remained firmly Catholic, and in the 1530s religious wars began in Germany. These were brought to an end with the Peace of Augsburg in 1555, which allowed rulers to choose whether their territory would be Catholic or Lutheran.

In England the political issue of the royal succession triggered the break with Rome, and a Protestant church was established. Protestant ideas also spread into France and eastern Europe. In all these areas, a second generation of reformers built on Lutheran and Zwinglian ideas to develop their own theology and plans for institutional change. The most important of the second-generation reformers was John Calvin, whose ideas would come to shape Christianity over a much wider area than did Luther's.

The Roman Catholic Church responded slowly to the Protestant challenge, but by the 1530s the papacy was leading a movement for reform within the church instead of blocking it. Catholic doctrine was reaffirmed at the Council of Trent, and reform measures such as the opening of seminaries for priests and a ban on holding multiple church offices were introduced. New religious orders such as the Jesuits and the Ursulines spread Catholic ideas through teaching, and in the case of the Jesuits through missionary work.

Religious differences led to riots, civil wars, and international conflicts in the later sixteenth century. In France and the Netherlands, Calvinist Protestants and Catholics used violent actions against one another, and religious differences mixed with political and economic grievances. Long civil wars resulted, which in the case of the Netherlands became an international conflict. War ended in France with the Edict of Nantes in which Protestants were given some civil rights, and in the Netherlands with a division of the country into a Protestant north and Catholic south. The era of religious wars was also the time of the most extensive witch persecutions in European history, as both Protestants and Catholics tried to rid their cities and states of people they regarded as linked to the Devil.

Key Terms

- anticlericalism
- pluralism
- indulgence
- penance
- purgatory
- *Diet of Worms*
- Protestant
- transubstantiation
- *Book of Common Prayer*
- Elizabethan Settlement
- *The Institutes of the Christian Religion*
- predestination
- Holy Office
- Jesuits
- Huguenots
- iconoclasm
- Saint Bartholomew's Day massacre
- politiques
- Edict of Nantes
- Union of Utrecht
- misogyny

 Improve Your Grade Flashcards

Suggested Reading

Bossy, John. *Christianity in the West, 1500–1700*. 1985. A lively brief overview.

Bouwsma, William J. *John Calvin: A Sixteenth-Century Portrait*. 1988. An authoritative study that situates Calvin within Renaissance culture.

Elton, Geoffrey R. *Reform and Reformation: England, 1509–1558*. 1977. Combines religious, political, and social history.

Holt, Mack P. *The French Wars of Religion, 1562–1629*. 1995. A thorough survey designed for students.

Hsia, R. Po-Chia. *The World of Catholic Renewal, 1540–1770*. 1998. Situates the Catholic Reformation in a global context and provides coverage of colonial Catholicism.

Levack, Brian. *The Witchhunt in Early Modern Europe*, 3d ed. 2007. A good introduction to and helpful bibliographies of the vast literature on witchcraft.

Levi, Anthony. *Renaissance and Reformation: The Intellectual Genesis*. 2002. Surveys the ideas of major Reformation figures against the background of important political issues.

Lindbergh, Carter. *The European Reformations*. 1996. A thorough discussion of the Protestant Reformation and some discussion of Catholic issues.

Monter, William E. *Calvin's Geneva*. 1967. Shows the effect of Calvin's reforms on the social life of the Swiss city.

Oberman, Heiko. *Luther: Man Between God and the Devil*. 1989. Provides a thorough grounding in his thought.

O'Malley, John W. *Trent and All That: Renaming Catholicism in the Early Modern Era*. 2000. Provides an excellent historiographical review of the literature and explains why and how early modern Catholicism influenced early modern European history.

Roper, Lyndal. *The Holy Household: Women and Morals in Reformation Augsburg*. 1991. An important study in local religious history as well as the history of gender and the family.

Shagan, Ethan. *Popular Politics and the English Reformation*. 2003. Analyzes the process of the Reformation in local areas.

Wheatcroft, Andrew. *The Habsburgs: Embodying Empire*. 1995. A solid study of political developments surrounding the Reformation.

Notes

1. Quoted in O. Chadwick, *The Reformation* (Baltimore: Penguin Books, 1976), p. 55.
2. Quoted in E. H. Harbison, *The Age of Reformation* (Ithaca, N.Y.: Cornell University Press, 1963), p. 52.
3. Quoted in S. E. Ozment, *The Age of Reform, 1250–1550: An Intellectual and Religious History of Late Medieval and Reformation Europe* (New Haven, Conn.: Yale University Press, 1980), p. 280.
4. Quoted ibid., p. 281.
5. Quoted ibid., p. 284.
6. J. Allen, trans., *John Calvin: The Institutes of the Christian Religion* (Philadelphia: Westminster Press, 1930), bk. 3, chap. 21, paras. 5, 7.
7. E. W. Monter, *Calvin's Geneva* (New York: John Wiley & Sons, 1967), pp. 98–108.
8. Ibid., p. 137.
9. Quoted in R. H. Bainton, *Women of the Reformation in Germany and Italy* (Minneapolis: Augsburg, 1971), pp. 69–70.
10. Quoted in D. P. Daniel, "Hungary," in *The Oxford Encyclopedia of the Reformation*, vol. 2, ed. H. J. Hillerbrand (New York: Oxford University Press, 1996), p. 273.
11. Quoted in Chadwick, *The Reformation*, p. 270.
12. See J. W. O'Malley, *The First Jesuits* (Cambridge, Mass.: Harvard University Press, 1993), p. 376.
13. Ibid., p. 298.

Listening to the Past

Martin Luther, *On Christian Liberty*

The idea of liberty or freedom has played a powerful role in the history of Western society and culture, but the meaning and understanding of liberty has undergone continual change and interpretation. In the Roman world, where slavery was a basic institution, liberty meant the condition of being a free man, independent of obligations to a master. In the Middle Ages possessing liberty meant having special privileges or rights that other persons or institutions did not have. A lord or a monastery, for example, might speak of his or its liberties, and citizens in London were said to possess the "freedom of the city," which allowed them to practice trades and own property without interference. Likewise, the first chapter of Magna Carta (1215), often called the "Charter of Liberties," states: "Holy Church shall be free and have its rights entire and its liberties inviolate," meaning that the English church was independent of the authority of the king.

The idea of liberty also has a religious dimension, and the reformer Martin Luther formulated a classic interpretation of liberty in his treatise On Christian Liberty *(sometimes translated* On the Freedom of a Christian*), arguably his finest piece. Written in Latin for the pope but translated immediately into German and published widely, it contains the main themes of Luther's theology: the importance of faith, the relationship of Christian faith and good works, the dual nature of human beings, and the fundamental importance of Scripture. Luther writes that Christians were freed from sin and death through Christ, not through their own actions.*

Christian faith has appeared to many an easy thing; nay, not a few even reckon it among the social virtues, as it were; and this they do because they have not made proof of it experimentally, and have never tasted of what efficacy it is. For it is not possible for any man to write well about it, or to understand well what is rightly written, who has not at some time tasted of its spirit, under the pressure of tribulation; while he who has tasted of it, even to a very small extent, can never write, speak, think, or hear about it sufficiently. . . .

I hope that . . . I have attained some little drop of faith, and that I can speak of this matter, if not with more elegance, certainly with more solidity. . . .

A Christian man is the most free lord of all, and subject to none; a Christian man is the most dutiful servant of all, and subject to everyone.

Although these statements appear contradictory, yet, when they are found to agree together, they will do excellently for my purpose. They are both the statements of Paul himself, who says, "Though I be free from all men, yet have I made myself a servant unto all" (I Cor. 9:19), and "Owe no man anything but to love one another" (Rom. 13:8). Now love is by its own nature dutiful and obedient to the beloved object. Thus even Christ, though Lord of all things, was yet made of a woman; made under the law; at once free and a servant; at once in the form of God and in the form of a servant.

Let us examine the subject on a deeper and less simple principle. Man is composed of a twofold nature, a spiritual and a bodily. As regards the spiritual nature, which they name the soul, he is called the spiritual, inward, new man; as regards the bodily nature, which they name the flesh, he is called the fleshly, outward, old man. The Apostle speaks of this: "Though our outward man perish, yet the inward man is renewed day by day" (II Cor. 4:16). The result of this diversity is that in the Scriptures opposing statements are made concerning the same man, the fact being that in the same man these two men are opposed to one another; the flesh lusting against the spirit, and the spirit against the flesh (Gal. 5:17).

We first approach the subject of the inward man, that we may see by what means a man becomes justified, free, and a true Christian; that is, a spiritual, new, and inward man. It is certain that absolutely none among outward things, under whatever name they may be reckoned, has any influence in producing Christian righteousness or liberty, nor, on the other hand, unrighteousness or slavery. This can be shown by an easy argument.

What can it profit to the soul that the body should be in good condition, free, and full of life, that it should eat, drink, and act according to its pleasure, when even the most impious slaves of every kind of vice are prosperous in these matters? Again, what harm can ill health, bondage, hunger, thirst, or any other outward evil, do to the soul, when even the most pious of men, and the freest in the purity of their conscience, are harassed by these things? Neither of these states of things has to do with the liberty or the slavery of the soul.

And so it will profit nothing that the body should be adorned with sacred vestment, or dwell in holy places, or be occupied in sacred offices, or pray, fast, and abstain from certain meats, or do whatever works can be done through the body and in the body. Something widely different will be necessary for the justification and liberty of the soul, since the things I have spoken of can be done by an impious person, and only hypocrites are produced by devotion to these things. On the other hand, it will not at all injure the soul that the body should be clothed in profane raiment, should dwell in profane places, should eat and drink in the ordinary fashion, should not pray aloud, and should leave undone all the things above mentioned, which may be done by hypocrites.

. . . One thing, and one alone, is necessary for life, justification, and Christian liberty; and that is the most Holy Word of God, the Gospel of Christ, as He says, "I am the resurrection and the life; he that believeth in me shall not die eternally" (John 9:25), and also, "If the Son shall make you free, ye shall be free indeed" (John 8:36), and "Man shall not live by bread alone, but by every word that proceedeth out of the mouth of God" (Matt. 4:4).

Let us therefore hold it for certain and firmly established that the soul can do without everything except the Word of God, without which none at all of its wants is provided for. But, having the Word, it is rich and wants for nothing, since that is the Word of life, of truth, of light, of peace, of justification, of salvation, of joy, of liberty, of wisdom, of virtue, of grace, of glory, and of every good thing. . . .

But you will ask, "What is this Word, and by what means is it to be used, since there are so many words of God?" I answer, "The Apostle Paul (Rom. 1) explains what it is, namely the Gospel of God, concerning His Son, incarnate, suffering, risen, and glorified through the Spirit, the Sanctifier." To preach Christ is to feed the soul, to justify it, to set it free, and to save it, if it believes the preaching. For faith alone, and the efficacious use of the Word of

On effective preaching, especially to the uneducated, Luther urged the minister "to keep it simple for the simple." *(Church of St. Marien, Wittenberg/The Bridgeman Art Library)*

God, bring salvation. "If thou shalt confess with thy mouth the Lord Jesus, and shalt believe in thine heart that God hath raised Him from the dead, thou shalt be saved" (Rom. 9:9); . . . and "The just shall live by faith" (Rom. 1:17). . . .

But this faith cannot consist of all with works; that is, if you imagine that you can be justified by those works, whatever they are, along with it. . . . Therefore, when you begin to believe, you learn at the same time that all that is in you is utterly guilty, sinful, and damnable, according to that saying, "All have sinned, and come short of the glory of God" (Rom. 3:23). . . . When you have learned this, you will know that Christ is necessary for you, since He has suffered and risen again for you, that, believing on Him, you might by this faith become another man, all your sins being remitted, and you being justified by the merits of another, namely Christ alone.

. . . [A]nd since it [faith] alone justifies, it is evident that by no outward work or labour can the inward man be at all justified, made free, and saved; and that no works whatever have any relation to him. . . . Therefore the first care of every Christian ought to be to lay aside all reliance on works, and strengthen his faith alone more and more, and by it grow in knowledge, not of works, but of Christ Jesus, who has suffered and risen again for him, as Peter teaches (I Peter 5).

Questions for Analysis

1. What did Luther mean by liberty?
2. Why, for Luther, was Scripture basic to Christian life?

Source: Luther's Primary Works, ed. H. Wace and C. A. Buchheim (London: Holder and Stoughton, 1896). Reprinted in *The Portable Renaissance Reader*, ed. James Bruce Ross and Mary Martin McLaughlin (New York: Penguin Books, 1981), pp. 721–726.

A detail from an early-seventeenth-century Flemish painting depicting maps, illustrated travel books, a globe, a compass, and an astrolabe. *(Reproduced by courtesy of the Trustees, The National Gallery, London)*

chapter 15

European Exploration and Conquest, 1450–1650

chapter preview

World Contacts Before Columbus
- What was the Afro-Eurasian trading world before Columbus?

The European Voyages of Discovery
- How and why did Europeans undertake ambitious voyages of expansion that would usher in a new era of global contact?

Europe and the World After Columbus
- What effect did overseas expansion have on the conquered societies, on enslaved Africans, and on world trade?

Changing Attitudes and Beliefs
- How did culture and art in this period respond to social and cultural transformation?

Prior to 1400 Europeans were relatively marginal players in a centuries-old trading system that linked Africa, Asia, and Europe. Elite classes everywhere prized Chinese porcelains and silks, while wealthy members of the Celestial Kingdom, as China called itself, wanted ivory and black slaves from East Africa, and exotic goods and peacocks from India. African people wanted textiles from India and cowrie shells from the Maldive Islands. Europeans craved spices and silks, but they had few desirable goods to offer their trading partners.

Within little more than a century, European nations had embarked on a remarkably ambitious project to dominate this trading system. The European search for Southeast Asian spices led to a new overseas empire in the Indian Ocean and the accidental discovery of the Western Hemisphere. Within a short time, South and North America had joined a worldwide economic and imperial web. The results were trading networks and political empires of truly global proportions. The era of "globalization" had begun.

European states' intrusions into Indian Ocean trade and into new economies in the New World gave them wealth and power. Over time the old Asian-dominated trading world gave way to a new European-dominated one that encompassed the vast territories of the Americas and the Pacific Ocean. Global contacts created new forms of cultural exchange, assimilation, conversion, and resistance. Europeans sought to impose their cultural values on the people they encountered and struggled to comprehend the peoples and societies they found. New forms of racial prejudice emerged in this period, but so did new openness and curiosity about different ways of life. Together with the developments of the Renaissance and the Reformation, the Age of Discovery laid the foundations for the modern world as we know it today.

World Contacts Before Columbus

Columbus did not sail west on a whim. To understand his voyages—and the European explorations that preceded and succeeded them—we must

Online Study Center
This icon will direct you to interactive activities and study materials on the website **college.hmco.com/pic/mckaywest9e**

first understand late medieval trade networks. Historians now recognize important ties between Europe and other parts of the world prior to Columbus's voyages, arguing that a type of "world economy" linked the products and people of Europe, Asia, and Africa in the fifteenth century. The West was not the dominant player in 1492, and the European voyages derived from the possibilities and constraints of this system. The global impact of the discoveries in the New World must be viewed in the context of this world trading system, which it would in turn revolutionize.

- **What was the Afro-Eurasian trading world before Columbus?**

The Trading World of the Indian Ocean

The center of the pre-Columbian world trade network was the Indian Ocean, the globe's third-largest waterway (after the Atlantic and Pacific). To the west its arms reach into the Red and Arabian Seas, through the former to the Mediterranean Sea, and through the latter into the Persian Gulf and southwestern Asia. To the north the Indian Ocean joins the Bay of Bengal; to the east the Pacific; and to the south the west coast of Australia (see Map 15.1). The monsoon winds blow from the west or south between April and August, and from the northwest or northeast between December and March. These seasonal climate patterns determined the rhythms of trade.

The location of the Indian Ocean made it a crossroads for commercial and cultural exchange. Since Han and Roman times, seaborne trade between China (always the biggest market for Southeast Asian goods), India, the Middle East, Africa, and Europe had flowed across the Indian Ocean. From the seventh through the thirteenth centuries, the volume of this trade steadily increased. After a period of decline resulting from the Black Death, demand for Southeast Asian goods accelerated once more in the late fourteenth century.

Merchants congregated in a series of port cities strung around the ocean that harbored a bewildering array of peoples and cultures. The most developed area of this commercial web lay to the east on the South China Sea. In the fifteenth century the port of **Malacca** became a great commercial **entrepôt**, to which goods were shipped for temporary storage while awaiting redistribution to other places. To Malacca came Chinese porcelains, silks, and camphor (used in the manufacture of many medications, including those to reduce fevers); pepper, cloves, nutmeg, and raw materials such as sappanwood and sandalwood from the Moluccas; sugar from the Philippines; and Indian printed cotton and woven tapestries, copper weapons, incense, dyes, and opium. Merchants at Malacca stockpiled goods in fortified warehouses while waiting for the next monsoon. With its many mosques and elegant homes, Malacca enjoyed the reputation of being a sophisticated city, full of "music, ballads, and poetry."[1]

Women in Southeast Asia enjoyed relatively high autonomy. Their important role in planting and harvesting rice, the traditional agricultural crop, gave them authority and economic power. In contrast to Europe, the more daughters a Southeast Asian man had, the richer he was. At marriage the groom paid the bride (or sometimes her family) a sum of money, called bride wealth, which remained under her control. This practice was in sharp contrast to the European dowry, which was provided by the wife's family and came under the husband's control. Married couples usually resided in the wife's village and administered property jointly. All children, regardless of gender, inherited equally, and even after Islam took root in parts of the region, the rule that sons receive double the inheritance of daughters was never implemented.

This respect for women's capacity to handle financial affairs carried over to the commercial sphere. Women participated in business as independent entrepreneurs or partners in family businesses, even undertaking long sea voyages to accompany their wares. When Portuguese and Dutch men settled in the region and married local women, their wives continued to play an important role in trade and commerce.

China played a key role in the fifteenth-century revival of Indian Ocean trade. Given its size and its sophisticated artisanal production, China was an economic powerhouse. Historians agree that medieval China had the most advanced economy in the world; one scholar's controversial theory is that its economic superiority to the West continued to 1800.[2]

The Mongol emperors opened the doors of China to the West, encouraging European traders like Marco Polo to do business there. Marco Polo's tales of his travels from 1271 to 1295 and his encounter with the Great Khan fueled Western fantasies about the exotic "Orient." Unbeknownst to the West, the Mongols fell to the new Ming Dynasty in 1368. During the Ming Dynasty (1368–1644), China entered a period of agricultural and commercial expansion, population growth, and urbanization. By the end of the dynasty, the Chinese population had doubled to perhaps 100 million people. The city of Nanjing had one million inhabitants, making it the largest city in the world, while the new capital, Beijing, had more than six hundred thousand inhabitants.

Population growth was one reason for the Chinese desire for more goods. Another was the celebrated naval expeditions led by **Admiral Zheng He.** Between 1405 and 1433 Zheng He led seven voyages to achieve the emperor Yongle's diplomatic, political, geographical, and commercial goals. Yongle wanted to secure China's hegemony over tributary states and form new tribute-paying relations with profitable trade centers. Zheng He's first fleet was composed of 317 ships—including junks, supply ships, water tankers, warships, transports for horses, and patrol boats—carrying twenty-eight thousand sailors and soldiers. Because it bore tons of beautiful porcelains, elegant silks, lacquer ware, and exquisite artifacts to be exchanged for goods abroad, the Chinese called it the "treasure fleet." Sailing as far west as Egypt, the expeditions brought back spices, books, hardwood, and a giraffe from the kingdom of Mali for the imperial zoo. Zheng He may have been appointed commander because as a Muslim he could more easily negotiate with Muslim merchants on the Indian Ocean.

Court conflicts and the need to defend against renewed Mongol encroachment led to the abandonment of the expeditions and shipbuilding after the deaths of Zheng He and the emperor. Despite the Chinese decision not to pursue overseas voyages, trade continued in the South China Sea. A vast immigration of Chinese people to Southeast Asia, sometimes called the Chinese diaspora, followed the expeditions. Immigrants carried with them Chinese culture, including social customs, diet, and practical objects of Chinese technology—calendars, books, scales for weights and measures, and musical instruments.

Another center of trade in the Indian Ocean was India, the crucial link between the Persian Gulf and the Southeast Asian and East Asian trade networks. The subcontinent had ancient links with its neighbors to the northwest: trade between South Asia and Mesopotamia dates back to the origins of civilization. Fashionable women of the Roman Empire were addicted to Indian cotton; and until the decline of Rome exotic animals, ivory, and Chinese silk also made their way to Europe through India. Trade with the Indian Ocean was revived by Arab merchants who circumnavigated India on their way to trade in the South China Sea. The need for stopovers led to the establishment of trading posts at Gujarat and on the Malabar coast, where the cities of Calicut and Quilon became thriving commercial centers.

The inhabitants of India's southeast, Coromandel Coast, traditionally looked east to Southeast Asia, where they had ancient trading and cultural ties. Hinduism and Buddhism arrived in Southeast Asia from India during the Middle Ages, and a brisk trade between Southeast Asian and Coromandel port cities persisted through the early modern period. India itself was an important contributor of goods to the world trading system. Most of the world's pepper was grown in India, and Indian cotton and silk textiles, mainly from the Gujarat region, were also highly prized.

The Indian Ocean trading system was characterized by ancient and active trade conducted from multicultural, cosmopolitan port cities, most of which had some form of autonomous self-government. When the Portuguese arrived, they found a rich commercial world in which mutual self-interest had largely limited violence and attempts to monopolize trade. As one historian stated, "before the arrival of the Portuguese . . . in 1498 there had been no organised attempt by any political power to control the sea-lanes and the long-distance trade of Asia. . . . The Indian Ocean as a whole and its different seas were not dominated by any particular nations or empires."[3]

Africa

Often neglected by historians, Africa played an important role in the world trade system before Columbus. Around 1450 Africa had a few large and developed empires along with hundreds of smaller polities. From 1250 until its defeat by the Ottomans in the sixteenth century, the Mameluke Egyptian empire was one of the most

Chronology

1443	Portuguese establish first African trading post at Arguim
1450–1650	Age of Discovery
1492	Columbus lands on San Salvador
1511	Portuguese capture Malacca from Muslims
1518	Atlantic slave trade begins
1519–1522	Magellan's expedition circumnavigates the world
1520	Spaniards defeat Aztec army
1532	Pizarro arrives in Peru and defeats Inca Empire
1547	Oviedo, *General History of the Indies*
1570–1630	Worldwide commercial boom
1602	Dutch East India Company established

MAP 15.1 The Afro-Eurasian Trading World Before Columbus The Indian Ocean was the center of the Afro-Eurasian trading world. After a period of decline following the Black Death and the Mongol invasions, trade revived in the fifteenth century. Muslim merchants dominated trade, linking ports in East Africa and the Red Sea with those in India and the Malay Archipelago. The Chinese Admiral Zheng He's voyages (1405–1433) followed the most important Indian Ocean trade routes, hoping to impose Ming dominance of trade and tribute. (Source: Some data from The Times Atlas of World History, 3d ed., page 146.)

The Port of Banten in Western Java Influenced by Muslim traders and emerging in the early sixteenth century as a Muslim kingdom, Banten evolved into a thriving entrepôt. The city stood on the trade route to China and, as this Dutch engraving suggests, in the seventeenth century the Dutch East India Company used Banten as an important collection point for spices purchased for sale in Europe. *(Archives Charmet/The Bridgeman Art Library)*

powerful on the continent. Its capital, Cairo, was a center of Islamic learning and religious authority as well as a hub for Indian Ocean trade goods, which the Mamelukes helped to re-orient through the Red Sea. Sharing in the newfound Red Sea prosperity was the African highland state of Ethiopia, which in 1270, saw the rise of a new dynasty claiming descent from the biblical King Solomon and the Queen of Sheba. On the east coast of Africa Swahili-speaking city-states engaged in the Indian Ocean trade, exchanging ivory, rhinoceros horn, tortoise shells, copra, and slaves for textiles, spices, cowrie shells, porcelain, and other goods. The most important cities were Mogadishu, Mombasa, and Kilwa, which had converted to Islam by the eleventh century. Peopled by confident and urbane merchants, they were known for their prosperity and culture.

Another important African contribution to world trade was gold. In the fifteenth century most of the gold that reached Europe came from Sudan in West Africa and from the Akan peoples living near present-day Ghana. After the introduction of camels around A.D. 300, trade routes crisscrossed the Sahara. In exchange for Saharan salt, Arab and African traders brought gold from the cities of Niani and Timbuktu to be sold in the Mediterranean ports of Fez, Marrakesh, Tunis, and Tripoli. Other trading routes led to the Egyptian cities of Alexandria and Cairo, where the Venetians held commercial privileges.

Nations in the inland savannah that sat astride the north-south caravan routes grew wealthy from this trade. In the mid-thirteenth century Sundiata Keita founded the powerful kingdom of Mali. African merchants carried not only goods, but also ideas, helping spread Islam to West Africa. The celebrated pilgrimage of Keita's successor, **Mansa Musa,** to Mecca in 1324 underscores the links between West Africa and the Muslim world in this period. On his way to Mecca, Musa arrived in Cairo with a caravan that included sixty thousand people and eighty camels, with more than two tons of gold for gifts. Word of this spectacular caravan spread across Europe. The famous Spanish world map of 1375, known as the Catalan atlas, depicts Musa as the king of Africa with scepter in one hand and gold nugget in another. He reportedly even discussed sending vessels to explore the Atlantic Ocean, suggesting that not only Europeans envisaged westward naval exploration.

Mansa Musa used his wealth to invest in new mosques and religious schools, making Timbuktu a renowned center of culture and learning. The Muslim traveler Ibn Battuta visited the city and remarked on the rigorous discipline in its religious schools and also on the "extraordinary" state of affairs between men and women. Not only did families trace descent through the mother's line, but the "women show no bashfulness before men and do not veil themselves, though they are assiduous in attending the prayers."[4] Both husbands and wives, he reported, could have "friends" and "companions" of the opposite sex without provoking dishonor or jealousy. By the time the Portuguese arrived, however, the Malian empire was fading, to be replaced by the Songhay, who themselves fell to Moroccan invasion at the end of the sixteenth century. The Portuguese diversion of gold away from the trans-Sahara routes weakened this area politically and economically, and led to its decline as a center of Islamic scholarship.

Gold was one important object of trade; slaves were another. Slavery was practiced in Africa, as virtually everywhere else in the world, before the arrival of Europeans. Arabic and African merchants crossed the Sahara in both directions with slaves. They took West African slaves to the Mediterranean to be sold in European, Egyptian, or Mideastern markets and also brought eastern Europeans—a major element of European slavery—to West Africa as slaves. In addition, Indian and Arabic merchants traded slaves in the coastal regions of East Africa. European contact would revolutionize the magnitude and character of African slavery (see page 508).

Africa—or legends about Africa—played an important role in Europeans' imagination of the outside world. They long cherished the belief in a Christian nation in Africa ruled by a mythical king, Prester John, thought to be a descendant of one of the three kings who visited Jesus after his birth. In 1165 a letter purportedly written by Prester John to the Byzantine emperor describing the king's vast wealth and the fantastic subjects over whom he ruled appeared in Europe. The letter also promised friendship and solidarity with Christian Europe against Islam. Portuguese explorers carried letters of introduction to Prester John on their voyages along the African coast and were convinced they had found him when, in 1520, a Portuguese embassy reached the Christian Ethiopian court.

The Ottoman and Persian Empires

The Middle East was crucial to the late medieval world trade system, serving as an intermediary for trade from all points of the compass. It was situated at the crossroads between the Baltic States, Central Asia, and Russia to the north; Arabia, Egypt, and East Africa to the south; the Mediterranean, Europe, and West and North Africa to the west; and Southeast and East Asia to the east. In addition to serving as a conduit to trade, the Middle East was an important supplier of goods for foreign exchange, especially silk and cotton.

The most famous trade route leading through the Middle East was the ancient Silk Road that linked the West to the Far East. After its collapse in the aftermath of Mongol rule in the fourteenth century, merchants turned to a northern overland route, which led from the Baltic Sea to Russia, Central Asia, and China. Along this route traveled slaves, fur and timber to the east, and Asian luxury goods to the west. Even more important were the two southern sea routes that brought products from the Indian Ocean trading system. The first came across the Arabian Sea and then up the Red Sea past Aden to Cairo. The second led past Hormuz up the Persian Gulf and on to Baghdad. Standing at the mouths of two seas, Aden and Hormuz had vital economic and strategic importance. From the magnificent capitals of Cairo and Baghdad, goods were sent to bustling trading posts on the eastern Mediterranean coast, such as Alexandria, Damascus, Beirut, and Aleppo.

Two great rival Islamic empires, the Turkish Ottomans and the Persian Safavids, dominated this region. The Ottomans combined excellent military strategy with efficient administration of their conquered territories. Under Sultan Mohammed II (r. 1451–1481), the Ottomans captured **Constantinople** in May 1453, sending shock waves through Europe. Renamed Istanbul, the city became the capital of the Ottoman Empire. With a population of 600,000 to 750,000, it was by far the largest city in Europe and the Middle East and rivaled the great Chinese cities in size.

Online Study Center **Improve Your Grade**
Primary Source: The Fall of Constantinople to the Ottomans: A Lamentation

Having completed the conquest of Anatolia in 1461, the emperor Suleiman I (1494–1566) pressed northwest into the Balkans and by the early sixteenth century controlled the sea trade on the eastern Mediterranean. In 1516 the sultan's forces took Syria and Palestine, followed by Egypt in 1517 and the rest of northern Africa. After defeating the Hungarian king in 1526 and bringing portions of his kingdom into the empire, Suleiman turned to the Habsburg state ruled by Ferdinand I, brother to Habsburg emperor Charles V. In 1529 the Turks besieged the Habsburg capital of Vienna. After a siege of several weeks and high casualties on both sides, the Turks retreated, leaving Vienna as the westward limit of Ottoman expansion into Europe.

Ottoman expansion had political, economic, and religious goals. The Ottomans wished to control the Balkans and the Mediterranean so as to monopolize trade routes with the West and spread Islamic rule. The Balkans themselves were a precious source of timber, dye, and silver. With the defeat of the Mameluke empire, expansion into Egypt gave the Ottomans new access to sources of African gold and control over Red Sea shipping. Similarly, conquest of Baghdad brought control of shipping west out of the Persian Gulf.

Turkish expansion badly frightened Europeans. Ottoman armies seemed nearly invincible and the empire's desire for expansion limitless. In France in the sixteenth century, twice as many books were printed about the Turkish threat as about the American discoveries. The strength of the Ottomans helps explain some of the missionary fervor Christians brought to new territories. It also raised economic concerns. With trade routes to the east in the hands of the Ottomans, Europeans were convinced that they needed new trade routes.

Europeans were not alone in opposing Ottoman ambitions. In the early sixteenth century the Persian Safavid Empire became a powerful Muslim state, reaching its height under Shah Abbas I (r. 1587–1629). Like the Ottomans, the Persians were important intermediary figures in the Afro-Eurasian trading system. Persian merchants could be found throughout this trading world in diaspora communities they formed as far away as the Indian Ocean. Persia was also a major producer and exporter of silk.

The Safavids had complex, often hostile relations with their Ottoman neighbors. Although both were Muslim states, the Ottomans' Sunni faith clashed with the Persians' adherence to Shi'ism. Economically, the two competed for control over trade routes to the east. These conflicts led to the Ottoman-Safavid war of 1615–1618 and to periodic confrontations in the following years.

The Taking of Constantinople by the Turks, April 22, 1453 The Ottoman conquest of the capital of the Byzantine Empire in 1453 sent waves of shock and despair through Europe. Capitalizing on the city's strategic and commercial importance, the Ottomans made it the center of their empire. *(Bibliothèque nationale de France)*

However, the two empires also relied on each other economically; for example, the Ottoman silk industry depended on raw silk imported from Iran.[5]

Despite the fear generated by the Ottomans and the military clashes between Ottoman and European forces, it is important to emphasize that no "iron curtain" separated Christian Europe from the Muslim Middle East. Despite explicit religious laws dividing the world into Muslims and infidels, in practice the Ottoman state tolerated religious differences, protecting Christian and Jewish lives and property. Foreign merchants, travelers, and pilgrims were permitted to enter, and the cities of the empire had established settlements of Christian merchants (see Chapter 17).

It is also important to emphasize the disunities within each world. "Muslims" could be Mameluke Egyptians, Ottomans, Persians, Indians, Africans, or Southeast Asians. In many ways Islam helped foster commerce by offering a common Islamic commercial law and culture; however, there were also many divisions among Muslims. Rivalries among European powers as well as among Muslim states like the Sunni Ottomans and the Shi'ite Persians encouraged a shifting pattern of pragmatic and self-interested alliances that breached the borders supposedly dividing East and West. Eventually the Turks formed a loose alliance with the Portuguese against the Persians, which helped both sides ameliorate their trading positions. For his part, Shah Abbas I sent emissaries to Europe seeking alliances against the Ottomans. He offered trade concessions to the English for their help in eliminating the Portuguese from Hormuz. Before then the Safavids had purchased arms from the Portuguese (acquired from India) to use in combat with the Ottomans.

Genoese and Venetian Middlemen

Europe was the western terminus of the world trading system. Before the Portuguese and Spanish voyages, the Italian city-states of Venice and Genoa controlled the European luxury trade with the East. Centuries-old rivals for this trade, Venice and Genoa both lost importance with the rise of Ottoman power in the eastern Mediterranean and with Portuguese, then Dutch, intrusion into the **spice trade** at its source. After a brilliant period during the late Middle Ages, they entered a long period of decline. However, Italian experience in colonial administration, slaving, and international trade and finance served as crucial models for the Iberian states as they pushed European expansion to new heights. Mariners, merchants, and financiers from Venice and Genoa—most notably Christopher Columbus—played a crucial role in bringing the fruits of this experience to the Iberian Peninsula.

Venice grew in importance with the creation of the Crusader kingdoms, gaining territory and special trading concessions in return for aiding the Crusader armies. The Venetian fleet sacked Constantinople in 1204, placing a new emperor on the throne and gaining exclusive trading rights. When the political situation reversed and they lost those privileges, the Venetians turned their attention south. In 1304 the city established formal relations with the sultan of Mameluke Egypt, opening permanent offices in Cairo, the gateway to trade from India, Southeast Asia, and China.

Venice specialized in expensive luxury goods like spices, silks, and carpets. Venetian traders did not, as later Europeans did, explore new routes to get to the sources of supply of these goods. Instead, they obtained them from middlemen in the eastern Mediterranean and Asia Minor. A little went a long way. Venetians purchased no more than five hundred tons of spices a year around 1400, but with a profit of around 40 percent. The most important by far was pepper, grown in India and Indonesia, which composed 60 percent of the spices they purchased in 1400. In all, one historian has estimated that 70 percent of the Western trade in spices belonged to the Venetians.[6] Other imported goods included grain and sugar from Egypt and silk and cotton from Syria. Venetian merchants redistributed these goods throughout Europe.

Another major element of Venetian trade was slavery. Venetian merchants purchased slaves, many of whom were fellow Christians, in the Balkans. The men went to Egypt for the sultan's army or to work as agricultural laborers on Venetian possessions in the Mediterranean. Young girls, who made up the majority of the trade, were sold in western Mediterranean ports as servants or concubines.

The Venetians exchanged Eastern luxury goods for European products they could trade abroad, including Spanish and English wool, German metal goods, Flemish textiles, and silk cloth made in their own manufactures with imported raw materials. The demand for such goods in the East, however, was low. To make up the difference, the Venetians earned currency in the shipping industry and through trade in firearms and slaves. At least half of what they traded with the East took the form of precious metal, much of it acquired in Egypt and North Africa. When the Portuguese arrived in Asia, they found Venetian coins everywhere.

The spice trade brought riches and power to Venice. After the catastrophe of the Black Death, Venice reached the height of its glory in the 1400s. By 1500 the city's population was 120,000, making it one of the largest in Europe. From its origins as a small fishing village in the sixth century A.D., Venice had created a sizable empire. It controlled an expansive region on the Italian peninsula and had trading posts in North Africa, the Levant, and northern Europe in addition to outright colonies on the west coast of the Adriatic. The islands of Crete and later Cyprus were also controlled by Venice.

Merchant wealth endowed the city with beautiful buildings, art, and a rich and vibrant culture, whose legacy can

Bellini: Procession in the Piazza San Marco The Piazza San Marco was, and remains, the principal square of Venice. Located on the Grand Canal, it is home to Saint Mark's Basilica and the palace of the doge, the officer elected for life by the city's aristocracy to rule the city. Many Venetian festivals, like this procession recorded in 1496 by the great artist Gentile Bellini, took place in the square. *(Erich Lessing/Art Resource, NY)*

still be appreciated today. The Venetian city-state organized international trade meticulously; its impressive fleet of state-sponsored ships was one of the finest naval forces in Europe.

French invasions in the 1490s distracted and weakened the city, as did the new claims on the spice trade made by the Portuguese in the early 1500s, which the Venetians' Egyptian allies were unable to counter. The Ottoman conquest of Egypt in 1516 raised Venice's hopes briefly. Eager to improve Red Sea trade and to oppose Portuguese attempts to monopolize the spice trade, the Ottomans encouraged traders to bypass Portuguese ports. Spices began to flow again through the Red Sea to Venetian merchants in Cairo. By the 1600s, however, the Dutch had succeeded in monopolizing this trade, ending Venice's centuries-old role as the main European entrepôt for Asian spices. Venice also lost its eastern Mediterranean colonies to Ottoman conquest, leading to a loss of supplies of slaves and other trade goods.

Venice's ancient rival was Genoa. As was the case with Venice, Genoa's fortunes rose with its participation in the Crusades. Having undone Venetian control of Constantinople, Genoa dominated the northern route to Asia through the Black Sea. Expansion in the thirteenth and fourteenth centuries took the Genoese as far as Persia and the Far East. In 1291 they sponsored an expedition into the Atlantic in search of "parts of India" by the Vivaldi brothers. The ships were lost, and their exact destination and motivations remain unknown. However, the voyage underlines the long history of Genoese aspirations for Atlantic exploration.

In the fifteenth century Genoa made a bold change of direction. With Venice claiming victory over the spice trade, the Genoese shifted focus from trade to finance and from the Black Sea to the western Mediterranean. Given its location on the northwestern coast of Italy, Genoa had always been active in the western Mediterranean, trading with North African ports, southern France, Spain, and even England and Flanders through the Strait of Gibraltar. When new voyages took place in the western Atlantic, Genoese merchants, navigators, and financiers provided their skills to the Iberian monarchs, whose own subjects had much less commercial experience. The Genoese, for example, ran many of the sugar plantations established on the Atlantic islands colonized by the Portuguese. From their settlement in Seville, Genoese merchants financed Spanish colonization of the New World and conducted profitable trade with its colonies.

The Genoese were also enthusiastic slavers. Like the Venetians, they supplied slaves for agricultural labor on their colonial possessions and as slave soldiers to Mameluke Egypt. Once more, the majority of the slaves were young women sent to serve in southern Europe or Genoa. It was a brutal trade:

In a ship sailing from the Crimea to Chios in 1455 30 per cent of the slaves on board died. Genoese law accepted that a master could beat his slave to death, whilst for the rape of a female the punishment was merely a modest fine combined with the obligation to compensate her owner for the damage to his property.[7]

After the loss of the Black Sea—and thus the source of slaves—to the Ottomans, the Genoese sought new supplies in the West, taking the Guanches (indigenous peoples from the Canary Islands), Muslim prisoners and Jewish refugees from Spain, and by the early 1500s both black and Berber Africans. With the growth of Spanish colonies in the New World, Genoese merchants became important players in the Atlantic slave trade.

The European Voyages of Discovery

As we have seen, Europe was by no means isolated before the voyages of exploration and the "discovery" of the New World; the Europeans were aware of and in contact with the riches of the Indian Ocean trading world. From the time of the Crusades, Italian merchants brought the products of the East to luxury markets in Europe eager for silks, spices, porcelain, and other fine goods. But because they did not produce many products desired by Eastern elites, Europeans were relatively modest players in the Afro-Eurasian trading world. Their limited role was reduced even further in the mid-fourteenth century, when the Black Death, combined with the ravages of the Mongol warlord Tamerlane, led to a collapse in trade routes and commercial markets.

From these lows, however, Europeans would soon undertake new and unprecedented expansion. As population and trade recovered, new European players entered the scene, eager to spread Christianity and to undo Italian dominance of trade with the East. A century after the plague, Iberian explorers began the overseas voyages that helped create the modern world, with staggering consequences for their own continent and the rest of the planet.

- *How and why did Europeans undertake ambitious voyages of expansion that would usher in a new era of global contact?*

Causes of European Expansion

European expansion had multiple causes. By the middle of the fifteenth century, Europe was experiencing a revival of population and economic activity after the lows of the Black Death. While this revival was not sufficient to create population pressure in Europe, it did create new demands for luxury goods from the East and for spices in particular. The fall of Constantinople in 1453 and subsequent Ottoman control of trade routes created obstacles to fulfilling these desires. Europeans needed to find new sources of precious metal to trade with the Ottomans or sources of supply for themselves and thereby eliminate Ottoman interference.

Why were spices so desirable? Introduced into western Europe by the Crusaders in the twelfth century, pepper, nutmeg, ginger, mace, cinnamon, and cloves added flavor and variety to the monotonous diet of Europeans. Spices evoked the scent of the Garden of Eden; they seemed a marvel and a mystery. It is also important to remember that the term *spices* referred not only to flavorings added to food but also to perfumes, medicines, drugs, and dyes. Take, for example, cloves, for which Europeans found many uses. If picked green and sugared, the buds could be transformed into conserve (a kind of jam); if salted and pickled, cloves became a flavoring for vinegar. Cloves sweetened the breath. When added to food or drink, cloves were thought to stimulate the appetite and clear the intestines and bladder. When crushed and powdered, they were a medicine rubbed on the forehead to relieve head colds and applied to the eyes to strengthen vision. Taken with milk, cloves were believed to enhance the pleasures of sexual intercourse.

Apart from a desire for trade goods, religious fervor was another important catalyst for expansion. The passion and energy ignited by the Iberian reconquista encouraged the Portuguese and Spanish to continue the Christian crusade. Just seven months separated Isabella and Ferdinand's entry into Granada on January 2 and Columbus's departure westward on August 3, 1492. Overseas exploration was in some ways a transfer of their religious zeal, enthusiasm for conquest and expansion, and certainty of God's blessing on their ventures from the European continent to new non-Christian territories.

Since organized Muslim polities such as the Ottoman Empire were too strong to defeat, Iberians turned their attention to non-Christian peoples elsewhere.

Combined with eagerness for profits and to spread Christianity was the desire for glory and the urge to chart new waters. Scholars have frequently described the European discoveries as a manifestation of Renaissance curiosity about the physical universe—the desire to know more about the geography and peoples of the world. The detailed journals kept by such voyagers as Christopher Columbus and Antonio Pigafetta (a survivor of Magellan's world circumnavigation) attest to their wonder and fascination with the new peoples and places they visited.

Individual explorers combined these motivations in unique ways. Christopher Columbus was a devout Christian who was increasingly haunted by messianic obsessions in the last years of his life. As Bartholomew Diaz put it, his own motives were "to serve God and His Majesty, to give light to those who were in darkness and to grow rich as all men desire to do." When Vasco da Gama reached the port of Calicut, India, in 1498 and a native asked what the Portuguese wanted, he replied, "Christians and spices."[8] The bluntest of the Spanish conquistadors, Hernando Cortés, announced as he prepared to conquer Mexico, "I have come to win gold, not to plow the fields like a peasant."[9]

Eagerness for exploration could be heightened by a lack of opportunity at home. After the reconquista, enterprising young men of the Spanish upper classes found their economic and political opportunities greatly limited. As a study of the Castilian city of Ciudad Real shows, the ancient aristocracy controlled the best agricultural land and monopolized urban administrative posts. Great merchants and a few nobles (surprisingly, since Spanish law forbade participation by nobles in commercial ventures) dominated the textile and leather-glove manufacturing industries. Consequently, many ambitious men turned to the Americas to seek their fortunes.[10]

Whatever the motivations, the voyages were made possible by the growth of government power. Mariners and explorers did not possess the massive sums needed to explore mysterious oceans and control remote continents. Reassertion of monarchical authority and state centralization in the fifteenth century provided rulers with such resources. In the fifteenth century Isabella and Ferdinand had consolidated their several kingdoms to achieve a more united Spain and had revamped the Spanish bureaucracy. The Spanish monarchy was stronger than before and in a position to support foreign ventures. In Portugal the steadfast financial and moral support of **Prince Henry the Navigator** led to Portugal's phenomenal success in the spice trade. Like voyagers, monarchs shared a mix of motivations, from desire to please God to desire to win glory and profit from trade.

For ordinary sailors, life at sea was dangerous, overcrowded, unbearably stench-ridden, filled with hunger, and ill-paid. For months at a time, 100 to 120 people lived and worked in a space of between 150 and 180 square meters, with no available water except a small amount for drinking. Each person had an average of 1.5 meters of space, with more going to officers and wealthy passengers.[11] A lucky sailor would find enough space on deck to unroll his sleeping mat. This is not to mention the horses, cows, pigs, chickens, rats, and lice that accompanied the voyages. As one scholar concluded, "traveling on a ship must have been one of the most uncomfortable and oppressive experiences in the world."[12]

Why did men choose to go to sea? They did so to escape poverty at home, to continue a family trade, to win a few crumbs of the great riches of empire, or to find a better life as illegal immigrants in the colonies. Moreover, many orphans and poor boys were placed on board as young pages and had little say in the decision. Women also paid a price for the voyages of exploration. Left alone for months or years at a time, and frequently widowed, sailors' wives struggled to feed their families. The widow of a sailor lost on Magellan's 1519 voyage had to wait until 1547 to collect her husband's salary from the Crown.[13]

The people who stayed at home had a powerful impact on the process. Court coteries and factions influenced a monarch's decisions and could lavishly reward individuals or cut them out of the spoils of empire. Then there was the public: the small number of people who could read were a rapt audience for tales of fantastic places and unknown peoples. Cosmography, natural history, and geography aroused enormous interest among educated people in the fifteenth and sixteenth centuries. Just as science fiction and speculation about life on other planets excite readers today, quasi-scientific literature about Africa, Asia, and the Americas captured the imaginations of literate Europeans. Gonzalo Fernández de Oviedo's **General History of the Indies** (1547), a detailed eyewitness account of plants, animals, and peoples, was widely read. Indeed, the elite's desire for the exotic goods brought by overseas trade helped propel the whole process of expansion.

Technological Stimuli to Exploration

Technological developments in shipbuilding, weaponry, and navigation provided another impetus for European expansion. Since ancient times, most seagoing vessels had been narrow, open boats called *galleys,* propelled largely by manpower. Slaves or convicts who had been sentenced to the galleys manned the oars of the ships that sailed the Mediterranean, and both cargo ships and warships carried soldiers for defense. Though well suited to the placid and thoroughly explored waters of the Mediterranean, galleys could not withstand the rough winds and uncharted shoals of the Atlantic. The need for sturdier craft, as well as population losses caused by the Black Death, forced the development of a new style of ship that would not require soldiers for defense or much manpower to sail.

In the course of the fifteenth century, the Portuguese developed the **caravel,** a small, light, three-masted sailing ship. Though somewhat slower than the galley, the caravel held more cargo. Its triangular lateen sails and sternpost rudder also made the caravel a much more maneuverable vessel. When fitted with cannon, it could dominate larger vessels, such as the round ships commonly used as merchantmen.

By 1350 *cannon*—iron or bronze guns that fired iron or stone balls—had been fully developed. These pieces of artillery emitted frightening noises and great flashes of fire and could batter down fortresses and even city walls. Early cannon posed serious technical difficulties. Iron cannon were cheaper than bronze to construct, but they were difficult to cast effectively and were liable to crack and injure artillerymen. Bronze guns, made of copper and tin, were less subject than iron to corrosion, but they were very expensive. All cannon were extraordinarily difficult to move, required considerable time for reloading, and were highly inaccurate. They thus proved inefficient for land warfare. However, they could be used at sea.

Great strides in cartography and navigational aids were also made in this period. Around 1410 Arab scholars reintroduced Europeans to **Ptolemy's *Geography.*** Written in the second century A.D. by a Hellenized Egyptian, the work was a formidable synthesis of the geographical knowledge of the classical world. Its republication provided significant improvements over medieval cartography, showing the world as round and introducing the idea of latitude and longitude to plot position accurately. Ptolemy's work also contained crucial errors. Ignorant of the existence of the Americas, he showed the world as much smaller than it is, so that Asia appeared not very distant from Europe to the west. Based on this work, cartographers fashioned new maps that combined classical knowledge with the latest information from mariners.

Ptolemy's *Geography* The recovery of Ptolemy's *Geography* in the early fifteenth century gave Europeans new access to ancient geographical knowledge. This 1486 world map, based on Ptolemy, is a great advance over medieval maps but contains errors with significant consequences for future exploration. It shows the world watered by a single ocean, with land covering three-quarters of the world's surface and with Europe, Africa, and Asia as the only continents. Africa and Asia are joined, making the Indian Ocean a landlocked sea and rendering the circumnavigation of Africa impossible. The continent of Asia is stretched far to the east, greatly shortening the distance from Europe to Asia. *(Giraudon/Art Resource, NY)*

First the Genoese and Venetians, and then the Portuguese and Spanish, took the lead in these advances.[14]

The magnetic compass enabled sailors to determine their direction and position at sea. The astrolabe, an instrument invented by the ancient Greeks and perfected by Muslim navigators, was used to determine the altitude of the sun and other celestial bodies. It permitted mariners to plot their latitude, or position north or south of the equator.

Many scholars have argued that it was superior European weaponry, shipbuilding, and navigational skill that allowed them to undertake such astonishing voyages and to overcome the resistance of numerically far superior forces. As in the Industrial Revolution, they have argued, the key to European success over others was its openness to new technology and its interest in developing and adopting the most advanced technologies.

These arguments have encountered criticism in recent years. Some scholars have emphasized the extent to which European technology was borrowed from the East. For example, gunpowder, the compass, and the sternpost rudder were all Chinese inventions. The lateen sail, which allowed European ships to tack against the wind, was a product of the Indian Ocean trading world and was brought to the Mediterranean on Arab ships. Navigational aids, such as the astrolabe, were also acquired from others, and advances in cartography drew on the rich tradition of Judeo-Arabic mathematical and astronomical learning in Iberia. This assistance sometimes assumed human form. It was not his own seafaring abilities but assistance from a local guide that helped Vasco da Gama find a sea route from the East African coast to India. In exploring new territories, European sailors thus called on techniques and knowledge developed over centuries in China and the trading world of the Indian Ocean.

Other historians have argued that technological advances were in themselves not that important. Not only were cannon inaccurate and unreliable, but in the tropical conditions of Africa, India, and South America gunpowder got wet and cannon did not fire. Native populations quickly acquired firepower from Europeans who were eager to profit from the weapons trade. These historians have concluded that technological developments arose to meet the needs of exploration, rather than being a necessary precursor to them. To support this case, one scholar points out that the first Portuguese voyages took place in whatever boats were available and with crews unable to make use of a compass or a sea chart. Columbus himself relied on dead reckoning—at which he proved extremely adept—rather than on new navigational devices. As this

Nocturnal An instrument for determining the hour of night at sea by finding the progress of certain stars around the polestar (center aperture). *(National Maritime Museum, London)*

historian concludes, "Neither in Asia nor anywhere else was empire the inevitable corollary of technological superiority."[15]

The Portuguese Overseas Empire

At the end of the fourteenth century Portugal was a small and poor nation on the margins of European life whose principal activities were fishing and subsistence farming. It would have been hard for a European to predict Portugal's phenomenal success overseas in the next two centuries. Yet Portugal had a long history of seafaring and navigation. Blocked from access to western Europe by Spain, the Portuguese turned to the Atlantic and North Africa, whose waters they knew better than almost any other Europeans. Nature favored the Portuguese: winds blowing along their coast offered passage to Africa, its Atlantic islands, and, ultimately, Brazil.

In the early phases of Portuguese exploration, Prince Henry (1394–1460), a younger son of the king, played a leading role. A nineteenth-century scholar dubbed Henry "the Navigator" because of his support for the study of geography and navigation and for the annual expeditions he sponsored down the western coast of Africa. Although he never personally participated in voyages of exploration, Henry's enthusiasm for discovery and his financial support

ensured that Portugal did not abandon the effort despite early disappointments.

The objectives of Portuguese policy included aristocratic desires for martial glory, the historic Iberian crusade to Christianize Muslims, and the quest to find gold, slaves, an overseas route to the spice markets of India, and the mythical king Prester John. Portugal's conquest of Ceuta, an Arab city in northern Morocco, in 1415 marked the beginning of European exploration and control of overseas territory. In the late 1420s, under Henry's direction, the Portuguese began to settle the Atlantic islands of Madeira (ca 1420) and the Azores (1427). In 1443 the Portuguese founded their first African commercial settlement at Arguim in present-day Mauritania. By the time of Henry's death in 1460, his support for exploration was vindicated by thriving plantations on the Atlantic islands and new access to gold.

Under King John II (r. 1481–1495) the Portuguese established trading posts and forts on the gold-rich Guinea coast and penetrated into the African continent all the way to Timbuktu (see Map 15.2). Portuguese ships transported gold to Lisbon, and by 1500 Portugal controlled the flow of African gold to Europe. The golden century of Portuguese prosperity had begun.

Still the Portuguese pushed farther south down the west coast of Africa. In 1487 Bartholomew Diaz rounded the Cape of Good Hope at the southern tip, but storms and a threatened mutiny forced him to turn back. On a later expedition in 1497 **Vasco da Gama** commanded a fleet of four ships in search of a sea route to the Indian Ocean trade. Da Gama's ships rounded the Cape and sailed up the east coast of Africa. With the help of an Indian guide, da Gama sailed across the Arabian Sea to the port of Calicut in India. Overcoming local hostility, he returned to Lisbon loaded with spices and samples of In-

The Portuguese Fleet Embarked for the Indies This image shows a Portuguese trading fleet in the late fifteenth century, bound for the riches of the Indies. Between 1500 and 1635, over nine hundred ships sailed from Portugal to ports on the Indian Ocean, in annual fleets composed of five to ten ships. *(British Museum/HarperCollins Publishers/The Art Archive)*

Mapping the Past

MAP 15.2 Overseas Exploration and Conquest, Fifteenth and Sixteenth Centuries The voyages of discovery marked a dramatic new phase in the centuries-old migrations of European peoples. This map depicts the voyages of Ferdinand Magellan, Christopher Columbus, and Vasco da Gama. ❶ What was the contemporary significance of each of these voyages? ❷ Was the importance of the voyages primarily economic, political, or cultural? ❸ Which voyage had the most impact, and why?

Online Study Center **Improve Your Grade** Interactive Map: World Exploration, 1492–1535

dian cloth. He had failed to forge any trading alliances with local powers, and Portuguese arrogance ensured the future hostility of Muslim merchants who dominated the trading system. Nonetheless, he had proved the possibility of lucrative trade with the East via the Cape route.

King Manuel (r. 1495–1521) promptly dispatched thirteen ships under the command of Pedro Alvares Cabral, assisted by Diaz, to set up trading posts in India. On April 22, 1500, Cabral's fleet sighted the coast of Brazil in South America and claimed it for the Crown of Portugal. Cabral then proceeded south and east around the Cape of Good Hope and reached India. Half the fleet was lost on the return voyage, but the six spice-laden vessels that dropped anchor in Lisbon harbor in July 1501 more than paid for the entire expedition. Thereafter, a Portuguese convoy set out for passage around the Cape every March. Lisbon became the entrance port for Asian goods into Europe—but this was not accomplished without a fight.

For centuries, port city-states had controlled the rich spice trade of the Indian Ocean, and they did not surrender it willingly. Portuguese commercial activities were accompanied by the destruction or seizure of strategic coastal forts, which later served Portugal as both trading posts and military bases. Alfonso de Albuquerque, whom the Portuguese crown appointed as governor of India (1509–1515), decided that these bases, not inland territories, should control the Indian Ocean. Accordingly, his cannon blasted open the ports of Malacca, Calicut, Ormuz, and Goa, the vital centers of Muslim domination of South Asian trade. This bombardment laid the foundation for Portuguese imperialism in the sixteenth and seventeenth centuries—a strange way to bring Christianity to "those who were in darkness." As one scholar wrote about the opening of China to the West, "while Buddha came to China on white elephants, Christ was borne on cannon balls."[16]

In March 1493, between the voyages of Diaz and da Gama, Spanish ships under a triumphant Genoese mariner named **Christopher Columbus** (1451–1506), in the service of the Spanish crown, entered Lisbon harbor. Spain also had begun the quest for an empire.

The Problem of Christopher Columbus

The year 1992, which marked the quincentenary of Columbus's first voyages to the Americas, spawned an enormous amount of discussion about the significance of his voyages. Journalists, scholars, amateurs, and polemicists debated Columbus's accomplishments and failures. Until the 1980s most writers would have generally agreed with Harvard historian Samuel Eliot Morison in his 1942 biography of the explorer:

The whole history of the Americas stems from the Four Voyages of Columbus; today a score of independent nations and dominions unite in homage to Columbus, the stout-hearted son of Genoa, who carried Christian civilization across the Ocean Sea.[17]

In 1942, the Western Powers believed they were engaged in a life-and-death struggle to defend "Christian civilization" against the evil of fascism.

In contrast to this lavish praise, Columbus has recently been severely criticized. He enslaved and sometimes killed the Indians he encountered. He was a cruel and ineffective governor of Spain's Caribbean colony. Moreover, he did not discover the Americas: Native Americans had occupied the New World for millennia before Columbus, and other Europeans, including the Vikings, had been there before him. Not only did he not discover the continents, but he also misunderstood what he found. Other writers have faulted Columbus as an opportunistic adventurer who originated European exploitation of the non-European world.

Rather than judging Columbus by debates and standards of our time, it is more important to put him into the context of his own time. First, what kind of man was Columbus, and what forces or influences shaped him? Second, in sailing westward from Europe, what were his goals? Third, did he achieve his goals, and what did he make of his discoveries?

Columbus grew up in Genoa and thus drew on the centuries-old tradition of Genoese participation in international trade. In his dream of a westward passage to the Indies, he embodied a long-standing Genoese ambition to circumvent Venetian domination of eastward trade, which was now being claimed by the Portuguese. Columbus was also very knowledgeable about the sea. He had worked as a mapmaker, and he was familiar with such fifteenth-century Portuguese navigational developments as *portolans*—written descriptions of the courses along which ships sailed, showing bays, coves, capes, ports, and the distances between these places—and the use of the magnetic needle as a nautical instrument. As he implied in his *Journal,* he had acquired not only theoretical but also practical experience: "I have spent twenty-three years at sea and have not left it for any length of time worth mentioning, and I have seen everything from east to west [meaning he had been to England] and I have been to Guinea [north and west Africa]."[18] Although some of Columbus's geographical information, such as his measurement of the distance from Portugal to Japan as 2,760 miles when it is actually 12,000, proved inaccurate, his successful thirty-three-day voyage to the Caribbean owed a great deal to his seamanship.

Columbus was also a deeply religious man. He began the *Journal* of his voyage to the Americas in the form of a letter to Ferdinand and Isabella of Spain:

On 2 January in the year 1492, when your Highnesses had concluded their war with the Moors who reigned in Europe, I saw your Highnesses' banners victoriously raised on the towers of the Alhambra, the citadel of the city, and the Moor-

ish king come out of the city gates and kiss the hands of your Highnesses and the prince, My Lord. And later in that same month, on the grounds of information I had given your Highnesses concerning the lands of India . . . your Highnesses decided to send me, Christopher Columbus, to see these parts of India and the princes and peoples of those lands and consider the best means for their conversion.[19]

Columbus had witnessed the Spanish reconquest of Granada and shared fully in the religious and nationalistic fervor surrounding that event. Like the Spanish rulers and most Europeans of his age, Columbus understood Christianity as a missionary religion that should be carried to places and peoples where it did not exist. Although Columbus certainly had material and secular goals, first and foremost, as he wrote in 1498, he believed he was a divine agent: "God made me the messenger of the new heaven and the new earth of which he spoke in the Apocalypse of St. John . . . and he showed me the post where to find it."[20]

What was the object of this first voyage? Columbus gave the answer in the very title of the expedition, "The Enterprise of the Indies." He wanted to find a direct ocean trading route to Asia. Rejected by the Portuguese in 1483 and by Ferdinand and Isabella in 1486, the project finally won the backing of the Spanish monarchy in 1492. The **Santa Fe capitulations** named Columbus viceroy over any territory he might discover and gave him one-tenth of the material rewards of the journey. Inspired by the stories of Marco Polo, Columbus dreamed of reaching the court of the Great Khan (not realizing that the Ming Dynasty had overthrown the Mongols in 1368). Based on Ptolemy's *Geography* and other texts, he expected to pass the islands of Japan and then land on the east coast of China. He carried letters from Ferdinand and Isabella to the khan and an Arabic interpreter, for he assumed that the Great Khan must be in dialogue with Arabic-speaking powers.

How did Columbus interpret what he had found, and in his mind did he achieve what he had set out to do? Columbus's small fleet left the seaport of Palos on August 3 bound for a first stop at the Canary Islands, the westernmost outpost of European civilization. He landed in the Bahamas on October 12, which he christened San Salvador. Columbus believed he had found some small islands off the east coast of Cipangu (Japan). On encountering natives of the islands, he gave them some beads and "many other trifles of small value," pronouncing them delighted with these gifts and eager to trade. In a letter he wrote to Ferdinand and Isabella on his return to Spain, Columbus described the natives as handsome, peaceful, and primitive people whose body painting reminded him of the Canary Islands natives. He concluded that they would make good slaves and could quickly be converted to Christianity. (See the feature "Listening to the Past: Columbus Describes His First Voyage" on pages 518–519.)

Columbus received reassuring reports—via hand gestures and mime—of the presence of gold and of a great king in the vicinity. From San Salvador, Columbus sailed southwest, believing that this course would take him to Japan or the coast of China. He landed on Cuba on October 28. Deciding that he must be on the mainland near the coastal city of Quinsay (Hangzhou), he sent a small embassy inland with letters from Ferdinand and Isabella and instructions to locate the grand city.

The landing party, however, found only sparsely populated villages. In response to this disappointment, Columbus set a course that is still controversial among historians. Instead of continuing north, he turned southwest, apparently giving up on his aim to meet the Great Khan in preference to trying to find gold among the peoples he had discovered. In January, having failed to find the source of gold but having made contact with natives seemingly apt for Christianization and confident of the existence of gold somewhere in the vicinity, he headed back to Spain.

Over the next decades, Columbus's change of course was reconfirmed as the Spanish adopted the model of conquest and colonization they had already introduced in the Canary Islands rather than one of exchange with equals (as envisaged for the Mongol khan). On his second voyage, Columbus forcibly subjugated the island of Hispaniola, enslaved its indigenous peoples, and laid the basis for a system of land grants tied to their labor service. Columbus himself, however, had little interest in or capacity for governing. Revolt soon broke out against him and his brother on Hispaniola. A royal expedition sent to investigate returned the brothers to Spain in chains. Columbus was quickly cleared of wrongdoing, but he did not recover his authority over the territories. Instead, they came under royal control.

Columbus was very much a man of his times. To the end of his life in 1506, he believed that he had found small islands off the coast of Asia. He never realized the scope of his achievement: to have found a vast continent unknown to Europeans, except for a fleeting Viking presence centuries earlier. He could not know that the scale of his discoveries would revolutionize world power, raising issues of trade, settlement, government bureaucracy, and the rights of native and African peoples.

Later Explorers

News of Columbus's first voyage rapidly spread across Europe. On April 1, 1493, a printer in Barcelona published Columbus's letter to Ferdinand and Isabella describing what he had found. By the end of that month the letter had been translated into Latin and published in Rome. Within a year printers in Paris, Basel, Antwerp, and Venice had brought out six more Latin editions, which were soon followed by translations into other European languages. In a 1503 letter Florentine navigator Amerigo Vespucci (1454–1512) wrote about his discoveries on the coast of modern-day Venezuela, stating: "Those new regions which we found and explored with the fleet . . . we may rightly call a New World." This letter, titled *Mundus Novus* (The New World), was the first document to describe America as a continent separate from Asia. In recognition of Amerigo's bold claim, the continent was named for him. (When later cartographers realized that Columbus had made the discovery first, it was too late to change the maps.)

To settle competing claims to the Atlantic discoveries, Spain and Portugal turned to Pope Alexander VI. The **Treaty of Tordesillas** (1494) gave Spain everything to the west of an imaginary line drawn down the Atlantic and Portugal everything to the east. This arbitrary division worked in Portugal's favor when in 1500 an expedition led by Pedro Alvares Cabral landed on the coast of Brazil, which Cabral claimed as Portuguese territory. The country's name derives from the brazilwood trees found there, an important source of red dye (from the word *brasa*, or the reddish color of burning coals).

The search for profits determined the direction of Spanish exploration and expansion into South America. When it became apparent that placer mining (in which ore is separated from soil by panning) in the Caribbean islands was unrewarding and that the Portuguese were reaping enormous riches in Asian trade, new routes to the East and new sources of gold and silver were sought. In 1519 the Spanish ruler Charles V commissioned the Portuguese mariner **Ferdinand Magellan** (1480–1521) to find a direct route to the spices of the Moluccas off the southeast coast of Asia. Magellan sailed southwest across the Atlantic to Brazil, and after a long search along the coast he located the treacherous straits that now bear his name (see Map 15.2). The new ocean he sailed into after a rough passage through the straits seemed so peaceful that Magellan dubbed it the Pacific. He was soon to realize his mistake. His fleet sailed north up the west coast of South America and then headed west into the immense expanse of the Pacific toward the Malay Archipelago. (Some of these islands were conquered in the 1560s and named the "Philippines" for Philip II of Spain.)

Terrible storms, disease, starvation, and violence haunted the expedition. Magellan had set out with a fleet of five ships and around 270 men. Sailors on two of the

World Map of Diogo Ribeiro, 1529 This map integrates the wealth of new information provided by European explorers in the decades after Columbus's 1492 voyage. Working on commission for the Spanish king Charles V, the mapmaker incorporated new details on Africa, South America, India, the Malay Archipelago, and China. Note the inaccuracy in his placement of the Moluccas, or Spice Islands, which are much too far east. This "mistake" was intended to serve Spain's interests in trade negotiations with the Portuguese. (*Biblioteca Apostolica Vaticana*)

ships attempted mutiny on the South American coast; one ship was lost, and another ship deserted and returned to Spain before even traversing the straits. The trip across the Pacific took ninety-eight days, and the men survived on rats and sawdust. Magellan himself was killed in a skirmish in the Philippines. The expedition had enough survivors to man only two ships, and one of them was captured by the Portuguese. One ship with eighteen men returned to Spain from the east by way of the Indian Ocean, the Cape of Good Hope, and the Atlantic in 1522. The voyage had taken almost exactly three years.

Despite the losses, this voyage revolutionized Europeans' understanding of the world by demonstrating the vastness of the Pacific. The earth was clearly much larger than Columbus had believed. The voyage actually made a small profit in spices, but Magellan had proved the westward passage to the Indies to be too long and dangerous for commercial purposes. Turning to its New World colonies, Spain abandoned the attempt to oust Portugal from the Eastern spice trade.

Resounding success in this arena belonged to the Dutch. By the end of the sixteenth century Amsterdam had overtaken Antwerp as the financial capital of Europe. The Dutch had also embarked on foreign exploration and conquest. The Dutch East India Company, founded in 1602, became the major organ of Dutch imperialism and within a few decades expelled the Portuguese from Ceylon and other East Indian islands. By 1650 the Dutch West India Company had successfully intruded on the Spanish possessions in the Americas, in the process gaining control of much of the African and American trade.

English and French explorations lacked the immediate, sensational results of those of the Spanish and Portuguese. In 1497 John Cabot, a Genoese merchant living in London, sailed for Brazil but discovered Newfoundland. The next year he returned and explored the New England coast, perhaps going as far south as Delaware. Since these expeditions found no spices or gold, Henry VII lost interest in exploration. Between 1534 and 1541 Frenchman Jacques Cartier made several voyages and explored the St. Lawrence region of Canada. The first permanent French settlement, at Quebec, was founded in 1608.

New World Conquest

In the West Indies the slow recovery of gold, the shortage of a healthy labor force, and sheer restlessness sped up Spain's search for wealth. In 1519, the year Magellan departed on his worldwide expedition, a brash and determined Spanish adventurer named **Hernando Cortés** (1485–1547) crossed from Hispaniola to mainland Mexico with six hundred men, seventeen horses, and ten cannon. The conquest of Aztec Mexico had begun.

Cortés landed at Vera Cruz in February 1519. In November he entered **Tenochtitlán** (now Mexico City), capital of the sophisticated Aztec Empire ruled by Montezuma II (r. 1502–1520). Larger than any European city of the time, the capital was the heart of a civilization with advanced mathematics, astronomy, and engineering, with a complex social system, and with oral poetry and historical traditions. In less than two years Cortés had destroyed the monarchy, gained complete control of the capital city, and extended his jurisdiction over much of the Aztec Empire. Why did a strong people defending its own territory succumb to a handful of Spaniards fighting in dangerous and unfamiliar circumstances? Scholars continue to debate this question. The best answer is that, at the time of the Spanish arrival, the Aztec Empire faced internal weaknesses brought on by the resentment of recently subjugated tribes and by the Aztecs' own psychology and attitudes toward war.

Online Study Center Improve Your Grade
Primary Source: Cortés on the Aztecs: Two Letters to Charles V

The Spaniards arrived in late summer, when the Aztecs were preoccupied with harvesting their crops and not thinking of war. From the Spaniards' perspective, the timing was ideal. A series of natural phenomena, signs, and portents seemed to augur disaster for the Aztecs. A comet was seen in daytime, and two temples were suddenly destroyed, one by lightning unaccompanied by thunder. These and other apparently inexplicable events had an unnerving and demoralizing effect on the Aztecs.

Even more important was the alienation of newly conquered tribes and the Aztecs' failure to provide an effective military resistance. The Aztec state religion, the sacred cult of Huitzilopochtli, necessitated constant warfare against neighboring peoples to secure captives for religious sacrifice and laborers for agricultural and infrastructural work. When Cortés landed, recently defeated tribes were not yet fully integrated into the empire. Increases in tribute provoked revolt, which led to reconquest, retribution, and demands for higher tribute, which in turn sparked greater resentment and fresh revolt. When the Spaniards appeared, the Totonacs greeted them as liberators, and other subject peoples joined them against the Aztecs.[21]

Montezuma himself refrained from attacking the Spaniards as they advanced toward his capital and welcomed Cortés and his men into Tenochtitlán. Historians have

The Aztec Capital of Tenochtitlán Occupying a large island, Tenochtitlán was laid out in concentric circles. The administrative and religious buildings were at the heart of the city, which was surrounded by residential quarters. Cortés himself marveled at the city in his letters: "It has four approaches by means of artificial causeways. . . . The city is as large as Seville or Cordoba. . . . There are bridges, very large, strong, and well constructed, so that, over many, ten horsemen can ride abreast. . . . The city has many squares where markets are held. . . . There is one square, twice as large as that of Salamanca, all surrounded by arcades, where there are daily more than sixty thousand souls, buying and selling. In the service and manners of its people, their fashion of living was almost the same as in Spain, with just as much harmony and order." *(The Newberry Library)*

often condemned the Aztec ruler for vacillation and weakness. But he relied on the advice of his state council, itself divided, and on the dubious loyalty of tributary communities. When Cortés—with incredible boldness— took Montezuma hostage, the emperor's influence over his people crumbled.

Forced to leave Tenochtitlán to settle a conflict elsewhere, Cortés placed his lieutenant, Alvarado, in charge. Alvarado's harsh rule drove the Aztecs to revolt, and they almost succeeded in destroying the Spanish garrison. When Cortés returned just in time, the Aztecs allowed his reinforcements to join Alvarado's besieged force. No threatened European or Asian state would have conceived of doing such a thing: dividing an enemy's army and destroying the separate parts was basic to their military tactics. But for the Aztecs warfare was a ceremonial act in which "divide and conquer" had no place.

Having allowed the Spanish forces to reunite, the entire population of Tenochtitlán attacked the invaders and killed many Spaniards. In retaliation, the Spaniards executed Montezuma. The Spaniards escaped from the city and inflicted a crushing defeat on the Aztec army at Otumba near Lake Texcoco on July 7, 1520. Aztec weapons proved no match for the terrifyingly noisy and lethal Spanish cannon, muskets, crossbows, and steel swords. After this victory Cortés began the systematic conquest of Mexico.

More amazing than the defeat of the Aztecs was the Spanish victory over the remote Inca Empire perched at 9,800 to 13,000 feet above sea level. Like the Aztecs, the

Incas had created a civilization that rivaled the Europeans in population and complexity. The borders of this vast empire were well fortified and were threatened by no foreign invaders. Like the Romans, the Incas had built an extensive network of roads linking all parts of the empire, which permitted the operation of a highly efficient postal service. The imperial government taxed, fed, and protected its subjects. Grain was plentiful. Apart from an outbreak of smallpox in a distant province—introduced by the Spaniards—no natural disaster upset the general peace. An army of fifty thousand loyal troops stood at the ruler's disposal.

The Incas were totally isolated. They had no contact with other Amerindian cultures and knew nothing of Aztec civilization or its collapse in 1520. Since about 1500 Inca scouts had reported "floating houses" on the seas manned by white men with beards, and tradesmen told of strange large animals with feet of silver (the appearance of horseshoes in the brilliant sunshine). The Spanish told the Incas that they were sent by God—whom Incans may have associated with their creator-god **Virocha**—and the Incas initially believed these claims of good faith.

From 1493 to 1525 the Inca Huayna Capac ruled as a benevolent despot (the word *Inca* refers both to the ruler of the Andeans who lived in the valleys of the Andes in present-day Peru and to the people themselves). His millions of subjects considered him a link between the earth and the sun-god. In 1525 Huascar succeeded his father as Inca and was crowned at Cuzco, the Incas' capital city, with the fringed headband symbolizing his imperial office. However, his rule was threatened by the claims of his half-brother Atauhualpa. Civil war ensued, and Atauhualpa emerged victorious.[22] The five-year struggle may have exhausted him and damaged his judgment.

Francisco Pizarro (ca 1475–1541), a conquistador of modest Spanish origins, landed on the northern coast of Peru on May 13, 1532, the very day Atauhualpa won the decisive battle. The Spaniard soon learned about the war and its outcome. As Pizarro advanced across the steep Andes toward Cuzco, Atauhualpa was proceeding to the capital for his coronation. Like Montezuma in Mexico, Atauhualpa was kept fully informed of the Spaniards' movements, and he stopped at the provincial town of Cajamarca. His plan was to lure the Spaniards into a trap, seize their horses and ablest men for his army, and execute

Doña Marina Translating for Hernando Cortés During His Meeting with Montezuma In April 1519 Doña Marina (or La Malinche as she is known in Mexico) was among twenty women given to the Spanish as slaves. Fluent in Nahuatl and Yucatec Mayan (spoken by a Spanish priest accompanying Cortés), she acted as an interpreter and diplomatic guide for the Spanish. She had a close personal relationship with Cortés and bore his son Don Martín Cortés in 1522. Doña Marina has been seen as a traitor to her people, as a victim of Spanish conquest, and as the founder of the Mexican people. She highlights the complex interaction between native peoples and the Spanish and the particular role women often played as cultural mediators between the two sides. *(American Museum of Natural History, Image VC #31)*

the rest. What had the Inca, surrounded by his thousands of troops, to fear? Atauhualpa thus accepted Pizarro's invitation to meet in the central plaza of Cajamarca with his bodyguards "unarmed so as not to give offense." The Spaniards captured him and collected an enormous ransom in gold. Instead of freeing the new emperor, however, they killed him.

Decades of violence ensued, marked by Incan resistance and internal struggles among Spanish forces for the spoils of empire. By the 1570s the Spanish crown had succeeded in imposing control. With Spanish conquest, a new chapter opened in European relations with the New World.

Europe and the World After Columbus

Europeans had maintained commercial relations with Asia and sub-Saharan Africa since Roman times. In the Carolingian era the slave trade had linked northern Europe and the Islamic Middle East. The High Middle Ages had witnessed a great expansion of trade with Africa and Asia. But with the American discoveries, for the first time commercial and other relations became worldwide, involving all the continents except Australia. European involvement in the Americas led to the acceleration of global contacts. In time, these contacts had a profound influence on European society and culture.

- **What effect did overseas expansion have on the conquered societies, on enslaved Africans, and on world trade?**

Spanish Settlement and Indigenous Population Decline

In the sixteenth century perhaps two hundred thousand Spaniards immigrated to the New World. Mostly soldiers demobilized from the Spanish and Italian campaigns and adventurers and drifters unable to find employment in Spain, they did not come to work. After assisting in the conquest of the Aztecs and the subjugation of the Incas, these drifters wanted to settle down and become a ruling class. They carved out vast estates in temperate grazing areas and imported Spanish sheep, cattle, and horses for the kinds of ranching with which they were familiar. In coastal tropic areas unsuited for grazing the Spanish erected huge sugar plantations. Columbus had introduced sugar into the West Indies; Cortés had introduced it into Mexico. Sugar was a great luxury in Europe, and demand was high. Around 1550 the discovery of silver at Zacatecas and Guanajuato in Mexico and Potosí in present-day Bolivia stimulated silver rushes. How were the cattle ranches, sugar plantations, and silver mines to be worked? Obviously, by the Amerindians.

The Spanish quickly established the **encomienda system.** The Crown granted the conquerors the right to employ groups of Amerindians as agricultural or mining laborers or as tribute payers. Theoretically, the Spanish were forbidden to enslave the natives; in actuality, the encomiendas were a legalized form of slavery. The European demand for sugar, tobacco, and silver prompted the colonists to exploit the Amerindians mercilessly. Unaccustomed to forced labor, especially in the blistering heat of tropical cane fields or in the dark, dank, and dangerous mines, they died in staggering numbers.

Students of the history of medicine have suggested another crucial explanation for indigenous population losses: disease. Contact with disease builds up bodily resistance; peoples isolated from other societies are not exposed to some diseases and thus do not build resistance. At the beginning of the sixteenth century Amerindians probably had the unfortunate distinction of longer isolation from the rest of humankind than any other people on earth. Crowded concentrations of laborers in the mining camps bred infection, which the miners carried to their home villages. Having little or no resistance to diseases brought from the Old World, the inhabitants of the highlands of Mexico and Peru, especially, fell victim to smallpox, typhus, influenza, and other diseases. According to one expert, smallpox caused "in all likelihood the most severe single loss of aboriginal population that ever occurred."[23] (The old belief that syphilis was a New World disease imported to Europe by Columbus's sailors has been discredited by the discovery of pre-Columbian skeletons in Europe bearing signs of the disease.)

Although disease was the most important cause of indigenous population decline, there were many others. With the native population diverted from traditional agricultural work, cultivation of crops suffered, leading to malnutrition, reduced fertility rates, and starvation. Women forced to work were separated from their infants, leading to high infant mortality rates in a population with no livestock to supply alternatives to breast milk. Malnutrition and hunger in turn reduced resistance to disease.

Many indigenous peoples died through outright violence.[24] According to the Franciscan missionary Bartolomé de Las Casas (1474–1566), the Spanish maliciously murdered thousands:

This infinite multitude of people [the Indians] was . . . without fraud, without subtilty or malice . . . toward the Spaniards whom they serve, patient, meek and peaceful. . . .

To these quiet Lambs . . . came the Spaniards like most c(r)uel Tygres, Wolves and Lions, enrag'd with a sharp and tedious hunger; for these forty years past, minding nothing else but the slaughter of these unfortunate wretches, whom with divers kinds of torments neither seen nor heard of before, they have so cruelly and inhumanely butchered, that of three millions of people which Hispaniola itself did contain, there are left remaining alive scarce three hundred persons.[25]

Las Casas's remarks concentrate on the tropical lowlands, but the death rate in the highlands was also overwhelming.

The Franciscan, Dominican, and Jesuit missionaries who accompanied the conquistadors and settlers played an important role in converting the Amerindians to Christianity, teaching them European methods of agriculture, and inculcating loyalty to the Spanish crown. In terms of numbers of people baptized, missionaries enjoyed phenomenal success, though the depth of the Amerindians' understanding of Christianity remains debatable. Missionaries, especially Las Casas, asserted that the Amerindians had human rights, and through Las Casas's persistent pressure the emperor Charles V abolished the worst abuses of the encomienda system in 1531.

For colonial administrators the main problem posed by the astronomically high death rate was the loss of a subjugated labor force. As early as 1511 King Ferdinand of Spain observed that the Amerindians seemed to be "very frail" and that "one black could do the work of four Indians."[26] Thus was born an absurd myth and the new tragedy of the Atlantic slave trade.

Sugar and Slavery

Throughout the Middle Ages slavery was deeply entrenched in the Mediterranean. The bubonic plague, famines, and other epidemics created a severe shortage of agricultural and domestic workers throughout Europe, encouraging Italian merchants to buy slaves from the Balkans, Thrace, southern Russia, and central Anatolia. During the Renaissance the slave trade represented an important aspect of Italian business enterprise: where profits were high, papal threats of excommunication failed to stop slave traders. The Genoese set up colonial stations in the Crimea and along the Black Sea, and according to an international authority on slavery, these outposts were "virtual laboratories" for the development of slave plantation agriculture in the New World.[27] This form of slavery had nothing to do with race; almost all slaves were white. How, then, did black African slavery enter the European picture and take root in South and then North America?

In 1453 the Ottoman capture of Constantinople halted the flow of white slaves from the Black Sea region and the Balkans. Mediterranean Europe, cut off from its traditional source of slaves, then turned to sub-Saharan Africa, which had a long history of slave trading. The centuries-old trans-Saharan trade was greatly stimulated by the existence of a ready market for slaves in the vineyards and sugar plantations of Sicily and Majorca. (See the feature "Individuals in Society: Juan de Pareja.")

Native to the South Pacific, **sugar** was taken in ancient times to India, where farmers learned to preserve cane juice as granules that could be stored and shipped. From there, sugar traveled to China and the Mediterranean, where islands like Crete, Sicily, and Cyprus had the necessary warm and wet climate. When Genoese and other Italians colonized the Canary Islands and the Portuguese settled on the Madeira Islands, sugar plantations came to the Atlantic. In this stage of European expansion, "the history of slavery became inextricably tied up with the history of sugar."[28] Originally sugar was an expensive luxury that only the very affluent could afford, but population increases and monetary expansion in the fifteenth century led to an increasing demand for it.

Resourceful Italians provided the capital, cane, and technology for sugar cultivation on plantations in southern Portugal, Madeira, and the Canary Islands. Meanwhile, in the period 1490 to 1530, Portuguese traders brought between three hundred and two thousand black slaves to Lisbon each year (see Map 15.3), where they performed most of the manual labor and constituted 10 percent of the city's population. From there slaves were transported to the sugar plantations of Madeira, the Azores, and the Cape Verde Islands. Sugar and the small Atlantic islands gave New World slavery its distinctive shape. Columbus himself, who spent a decade in Madeira, brought sugar plants on his voyages to "the Indies."

Online Study Center Improve Your Grade
Primary Source: Fifteenth-Century Slave Trade: The Portuguese in West Africa

As already discussed, European expansion across the Atlantic led to the economic exploitation of the Americas. In the New World, the major problem settlers faced was a shortage of labor. As early as 1495 the Spanish solved the problem by enslaving the native Indians. In

MAP 15.3 Seaborne Trading Empires in the Sixteenth and Seventeenth Centuries By the mid-seventeenth century, trade linked all parts of the world, except for Australia. Notice that trade in slaves was not confined to the Atlantic but involved almost all parts of the world.

Online Study Center Improve Your Grade Interactive Map: Worldwide Slave Trade

Individuals in Society

Juan de Pareja

A marginal person is one who lives outside the mainstream of the dominant society, who is not fully assimilated into or accepted by that society. Apart from revealing little known aspects of past cultures, marginalized people teach us much about the values and ideals of the dominant society. Such a person was the Spanish religious and portrait painter Juan de Pareja.

Pareja was born in Antequera, an agricultural region and the old center of Muslim culture near Seville in southern Spain. Of his parents we know nothing. Because a rare surviving document calls him a "mulatto," one of his parents must have been white and the other must have had some African blood. The Spanish word *mulatto* derives from the Arabic *muwallad*, a person of mixed race, and some scholars, using religion to describe ethnic category, speak of Pareja's "Muslim descent." The region from which he came makes that possible, but we do not know whether he actually believed in or practiced Islam.

In 1630 Pareja applied to the mayor of Seville for permission to travel to Madrid to visit his brother and "to perfect his art." The document lists his occupation as "a painter in Seville." Since it mentions no other name, it is reasonable to assume that Pareja arrived in Madrid a free man. Sometime between 1630 and 1648, however, he came into the possession of the artist Diego Velázquez (1599–1660); Pareja became a slave.

In the twelfth century Muslim slaves helped build the cathedral of Saint James at Santiago de Compostela, one of the great shrines of medieval Christendom. During the long wars of the reconquista, Muslims and Christians captured each other in battle and used the defeated as slaves. The fifteenth and sixteenth centuries had seen a steady flow of sub-Saharan Africans into the Iberian Peninsula. Thus early modern Spain was a slaveholding society.

How did Velázquez acquire Pareja? By purchase? As a gift? Had Pareja fallen into debt or committed some crime and thereby lost his freedom? We do not know. Velázquez, the greatest Spanish painter of the seventeenth century, had a large studio with many assistants. Pareja was set to grinding powders to make colors and to preparing canvases. He must have demonstrated ability because, when Velázquez went to Rome in 1648, he chose Pareja to accompany him.

In 1650, as practice for a portrait of Pope Innocent X, Velázquez painted Pareja. That same year, Velázquez signed the document that gave Pareja his freedom, to become effective in 1654. From 1654 until his death Pareja worked in Madrid as an independent painter. Although he received recognition for his work, only one painting survives: *The Calling of Saint Matthew*, signed and dated 1661 (see page 540). Modern art historians dispute its merit. Some believe it shows a forceful baroque energy and considerable originality; others consider it derivative of Velázquez.

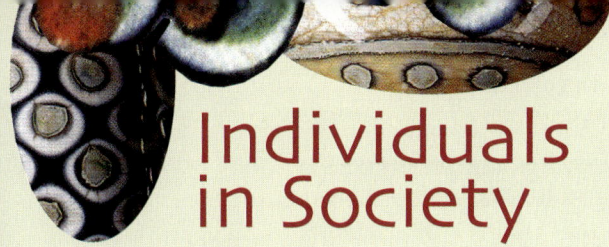

Velázquez, Juan de Pareja *(1650).* (The Metropolitan Museum of Art, Fletcher Fund, Rogers Fund, and Bequest of Miss Adelaide Milton de Groot (1876–1967), by exchange, supplemented by gifts from friends of the Museum, 1971. [1971.86]. Photograph © 1986 The Metropolitan Museum of Art)

What does the public career of this seventeenth-century marginal person tell us about the man and his world? After living in Seville and Madrid, he traveled widely, visiting Genoa, Venice, Rome, and Naples. Travel may have broadened him, producing a cosmopolitan man. Pareja's career suggests that a person of talent and ability could rise in Spanish society despite the social and religious barriers that existed at the time. Jonathan Brown, the leading authority on Velázquez, describes Pareja's appearance in Velázquez's portrait as "self-confident." A more enthusiastic student writes, "The Metropolitan is probably the greatest museum in the world . . . and this [Velázquez's portrait of Pareja] is its greatest painting. . . . The man was technically a slave. . . . However, we can see from Velázquez's painting that the two were undeniably equals. That steady look of self-controlled power can even make us wonder which of the two had a higher opinion of himself."

Questions for Analysis

1. Since slavery was an established institution in Spain, speculate on Velázquez's possible reasons for giving Pareja his freedom.
2. What issues of cultural diversity might Pareja have faced in seventeenth-century Spain?

Sources: Jonathan Brown, *Velázquez: Painter and Courtier* (New Haven, Conn.: Yale University Press, 1986); *Grove Dictionary of Art* (New York: Macmillan, 2000); *Sister Wendy Beckett's 1000 Masterpieces* (New York: Dorling Kindersley Inc., 1999).

Online Study Center Improve Your Grade
Going Beyond Individuals in Society

A New World Sugar Refinery, Brazil Sugar was the most important and most profitable plantation crop in the New World. This image shows the processing and refinement of sugar on a Brazilian plantation. Sugar cane was grown, harvested, and processed by African slaves who labored under brutal and ruthless conditions to generate enormous profits for plantation owners. *(The Bridgeman Art Library/Getty Images)*

the next two centuries the Portuguese, Dutch, and English followed suit. The horrifyingly rapid decline of the Amerindian population, however, led to the search for new forms of labor.

In Africa, where slavery was entrenched (as it was in the Islamic world, southern Europe, and China), African kings and dealers sold black slaves to European merchants who participated in the transatlantic trade. The Portuguese brought the first slaves to Brazil; by 1600 four thousand were being imported annually. After its founding in 1621, the Dutch West India Company, with the full support of the government of the United Provinces, transported thousands of Africans to Brazil and the Caribbean. In the late seventeenth century, with the chartering of the Royal African Company, the English got involved. Altogether, traders from all these countries brought an estimated ten million African slaves to the Americas from 1650 to 1870.

European sailors found the Atlantic passage cramped and uncomfortable, but conditions for African slaves were lethal. Before 1700, when slavers decided it was better business to improve conditions, some 20 percent of slaves died on the voyage.[29] The most common cause of death was from dysentery induced by poor-quality food and water, intense crowding, and lack of sanitation. Men were often kept in irons during the passage, while women and girls were fair game for sailors. To increase profits, slave traders packed several hundred captives on each ship. One slaver explained that he removed his boots before entering the slave hold because he had to crawl over their packed bodies.[30]

The eighteenth century witnessed the peak of the Atlantic slave trade. In 1790 there were 757,181 blacks in a total U.S. population of 3,929,625. When the first census was taken in Brazil in 1798, blacks numbered about 2 million in a total population of 3.25 million.

The Columbian Exchange

An important historical study asserts that the most significant changes brought about by the Columbian voyages were biosocial. The Age of Discovery led to the migration of peoples, which in turn led to an exchange of fauna and flora—of animals, plants, and disease, a complex process known as the **Columbian Exchange.** Spanish and Portuguese immigrants to the Americas wanted the lifestyle and diet with which they were familiar. Foods that Iberian settlers considered essential—wheat for bread, grapes for wine, olive oil for both culinary and sacramental purposes—were not grown in America. So the migrants sought to turn the New World into the Old: they searched for climatic zones favorable to those crops. Everywhere they settled they raised wheat—in the highlands of Mexico, the Rio de la Plata, New Granada (in northern South America), and Chile. By 1535 Mexico was exporting wheat. Grapes did well in parts of Peru and Chile. It took the Spanish longer to discover areas where suitable soil and adequate rainfall would nourish olive trees, but by the 1560s the coastal valleys of Peru and Chile were dotted with olive groves. Columbus had brought sugar plants on his second voyage; Spaniards also introduced rice and bananas from the Canary Islands, and the Portuguese carried these items to Brazil. All nonindigenous plants and trees had to be brought from Europe, but not all plants arrived intentionally. In clumps of mud on shoes and in the folds of textiles came immigrant grasses such as Kentucky bluegrass, daisies, and the common dandelion.

Apart from wild turkeys and game, Native Americans had no animals for food; apart from alpacas and llamas, they had no animals for travel or to use as beasts of burden. (Human power had moved the huge stones needed to build the monumental Aztec temples.) On his second voyage in 1493 Columbus introduced horses, cattle, sheep, dogs, pigs, chickens, and goats. The multiplication of these animals proved spectacular. By the 1550s, when the Spaniards explored, they brought along herds of swine. The horse enabled the Spanish conquerors and the Amerindians to travel faster and farther and to transport heavy loads.

In return, the Spanish and Portuguese took back to Europe the main American cereal, maize (corn), from Mexico; white potatoes from Peru; and many varieties of beans, squash, pumpkins, avocados, and tomatoes (which Europeans distrusted, fearing that they were sexually stimulating). Maize was the great gift of the Amerindians to all the peoples of the world as food for humans and livestock. Because maize grows in climates too dry for rice and too wet for wheat, gives a high yield per unit of land, and has a short growing season, it proved an especially important crop for Europeans. Initially they looked on the white potato with contempt, but they gradually recognized its nutritional value. Its cultivation slowly spread from west to east—to Ireland, England, and France in the seventeenth century; and to Germany, Poland, Hungary, and Russia in the eighteenth. Ironically, the white potato reached New England from old England in 1718.

Silver and the Economic Effects of Spain's Discoveries

The sixteenth century has often been called Spain's golden century, but silver was far more important than gold. The influence of Spanish armies, Spanish Catholicism, and Spanish wealth was felt all over Europe. This greatness rested largely on the influx of silver from the Americas.

In 1545, at an altitude of fifteen thousand feet where nothing grew because of the cold, and after a two-and-a-half-month journey by pack animal from Lima, Peru, the Spanish discovered an incredible source of silver at Potosí (in present-day Bolivia) in territory conquered from the Inca Empire. The place had no population. By 1600, 160,000 people lived there, making it about the size of the city of London. In the second half of the sixteenth century Potosí yielded perhaps 60 percent of all the silver mined in the world. From Potosí and the mines at Zacatecas and Guanajuato in Mexico, huge quantities of precious metals poured forth. To protect this treasure from French and English pirates, armed convoys transported it to Spain each year. Between 1503 and 1650, 16 million kilograms of silver and 185,000 kilograms of gold entered Seville's port. Spanish predominance, however, proved temporary.

In the sixteenth century Spain experienced a steady population increase, creating a sharp rise in the demand for food and goods. Spanish colonies in the Americas also represented a demand for products. Since Spain had expelled some of its best farmers and businessmen—the Muslims and Jews—in the fifteenth century, the Spanish economy was suffering and could not meet the new demands, and prices rose. Because the cost of manufacturing cloth and other goods increased, Spanish products could not compete with cheaper products made elsewhere in the international market. The textile industry was badly hurt. Prices spiraled upward faster than the government could levy taxes to dampen the economy. (Higher taxes would have cut the public's buying power; with fewer goods sold, prices would have come down.)

Did the flood of silver bullion from America cause the inflation? Prices rose most steeply before 1565, but bullion imports reached their peak between 1580 and 1620. Thus there is no direct correlation between silver imports and the inflation rate. Did the substantial population growth accelerate the inflation rate? It may have done so. After 1600, when population pressure declined, prices gradually stabilized. One fact is certain: the **price revolution** severely strained government budgets. Several times between 1557 and 1647, Spain's King Philip II and his successors repudiated the state debt, thereby undermining confidence in the government and leaving the economy in shambles.

As Philip II paid his armies and foreign debts with silver bullion, Spanish inflation was transmitted to the rest of Europe. Between 1560 and 1600 much of Europe experienced large price increases. Prices doubled and in some cases quadrupled. Spain suffered most severely, but all European countries were affected. Because money bought less, people who lived on fixed incomes, such as the continental nobles, were badly hurt. Those who owed fixed sums of money, such as the middle class, prospered: in a time of rising prices, debts had less value each year. Food costs rose most sharply, and the poor fared worst of all.

In many ways, it was not Spain but China that controlled the world trade in silver. The Chinese demanded silver for its products and for the payment of imperial taxes. China was thus the main buyer of world silver, serving as a "sink" for half the world's production of silver. Just as China was the heart of world trade, so was it, not Europe, the center of the early modern bullion trade. The silver market drove world trade, with the Americas and Japan being mainstays on the supply side and China dominating the demand side.

The Birth of the Global Economy

With the Europeans' discovery of the Americas and their exploration of the Pacific, the entire world was linked for the first time in history by seaborne trade. That trade brought into being three successive commercial empires: the Portuguese, the Spanish, and the Dutch.

In the sixteenth century naval power and shipborne artillery gave Portugal hegemony over the sea route to India. To Lisbon the Portuguese fleet brought spices, which the Portuguese paid for with textiles produced at Gujarat and Coromandel in India and with gold and ivory from East Africa (see Map 15.3). From their fortified bases at Goa on the Arabian Sea and at Malacca on the Malay Peninsula, ships of Malabar teak carried goods to the Portuguese settlement at Macao in the South China Sea. From Macao Portuguese ships loaded with Chinese silks and porcelains sailed to the Japanese port of Nagasaki and to the Philippine port of Manila, where Chinese goods were exchanged for Spanish (that is, Latin American) silver. Throughout Asia the Portuguese traded in slaves—black Africans, Chinese, and Japanese. The Portuguese exported to India horses from Mesopotamia and copper from Arabia; from India they exported hawks and peacocks for the Chinese and Japanese markets.

Across the Atlantic Portuguese Brazil provided most of the sugar consumed in Europe in the sixteenth and early seventeenth centuries. African slave labor produced the sugar on the plantations of Brazil, and Portuguese merchants controlled both the slave trade between West Africa and Brazil and the commerce in sugar between Brazil and Portugal. The Portuguese were the first worldwide traders, and Portuguese was the language of the Asian maritime trade.

Spanish possessions in the New World constituted basically a land empire, and in the sixteenth century the Spaniards devised a method of governing that empire (see page 538). But across the Pacific the Spaniards also built a seaborne empire centered at Manila in the Philippines, which had been "discovered" by Ferdinand Magellan in 1521. Between 1564 and 1571 the Spanish navigator Miguel Lopez de Legazpi sailed from Mexico and through a swift and almost bloodless conquest took over the Philippine Islands. The city of Manila henceforth served as the transpacific bridge between Spanish America and the extreme Eastern trade.

Chinese silk, sold by the Portuguese in Manila for American silver, was transported to Acapulco in Mexico, and from there it was carried overland to Vera Cruz for re-export to Spain. Because hostile Pacific winds prohibited direct passage from the Philippines to Peru, large shipments of silk also went south from Acapulco to Peru (see Map 15.3). Spanish merchants could never satisfy the European demand for silk, so huge amounts of bullion went from Acapulco to Manila. In 1597, for example, 12 million pesos of silver, almost the total value of the transatlantic trade, crossed the Pacific. After about 1640 the Spanish silk trade declined because it could not compete with Dutch imports.

Stimulated by a large demand for goods in Europe, India, China, and Japan, a worldwide commercial boom occurred from about 1570 to 1630. Many people throughout the world profited: capitalists who advanced money for voyages, captains and crews of ships, and port officials. As spices moved westward or northward, as silks and porcelains moved southward and westward, and as cloth moved eastward and westward, these various goods grew more valuable in the boom of long-distance trade.[31]

In the latter half of the seventeenth century the worldwide Dutch seaborne trade predominated. The Dutch Empire was built on spices. In 1599 a Dutch fleet recrative spice trade. The seaborne empires of Portugal, Spain, and Holland paved the way for the eighteenth-century mercantilist empires of France and Great Britain.

Spain's Global Empire

Spanish expansion into the New World and Asia are even more amazing when considered in light of Spanish expansion within Europe itself. As discussed in Chapter 14, Charles V combined vast and scattered territories across Europe under his rule. From his father's side, he inherited in 1506 the Burgundian lands, which included the Low Countries and Flanders, and in 1519 the Habsburg domains in Austria. As the grandson of Ferdinand and Isabella, in 1516 he became the first monarch to rule a united Spain. In 1530 he capped off this list by being named Holy Roman emperor. Under his reign, Spanish conquistadors brought new territories to Spain's colonial empire. Charles ruled over a vast and multiethnic array of territories (see Map 14.1 on page 460) and thus ruled the first global empire in history.

By 1556 Charles was exhausted by decades of administering this great empire. He had warred with France and the Ottoman Empire throughout his reign. He had also devoted enormous energy to a futile attempt to stamp out the burgeoning Protestant Reformation. (It was he who summoned Martin Luther to the Diet of Worms.) Charles abdicated the Spanish crown and the Netherlands to his son Philip II of Spain and Austria, and other territories in central Europe and the title of Holy Roman emperor to his brother Ferdinand.

Philip inherited his father's overseas Spanish Empire as well as the cascade of silver now flowing from the Americas. In today's world we might view the birth of globalization as a monumental turning point; Philip, however, was more concerned with religious rivalries in Europe. Traditional scholarship has depicted Philip as morose and melancholic, a religious bigot determined to re-impose Roman Catholicism on northern Europe. Recent research portrays him as a more complicated figure. In his youth, "he had visited northern Italy, the Alps, southern Germany, the Rhineland, the Netherlands, parts of France, and southern England."[32] He had walked the streets of Antwerp, Augsburg, Brussels, Cologne, London, and Trent. With the exception of his father, no other European ruler of the time had traveled or seen so much or had accumulated so much political experience in international relations.

Chinese Porcelain This porcelain from a seventeenth-century Chinese ship's cargo, recovered from the sea, was intended for European luxury markets. *(Christie's Images)*

turned to Amsterdam carrying 600,000 pounds of pepper and 250,000 pounds of cloves and nutmeg. Those who had invested in the expedition received a 100 percent profit. The voyage led to the establishment in 1602 of the Dutch East India Company, founded with the stated intention of capturing the spice trade from the Portuguese.

The Dutch fleet, sailing from the Cape of Good Hope and avoiding the Portuguese forts in India, steered directly for the Sunda Strait in Indonesia (see Map 15.3). The Dutch wanted direct access to and control of the Indonesian sources of spices. In return for assisting Indonesian princes in local squabbles and disputes with the Portuguese, the Dutch won broad commercial concessions. Through agreements, seizures, and outright war, they gained control of the western access to the Indonesian archipelago. Gradually, they acquired political domination over the archipelago itself. Exchanging European manufactured goods—armor, firearms, linens, and toys—the Dutch soon had a monopoly on the very lu-

Philip II, ca 1533 This portrait of Philip II as a young man and crown prince of Spain is by the celebrated artist Titian, who was court painter to Philip's father, Charles V. After taking the throne, Philip became another great patron of the artist. *(Scala/Art Resource, NY)*

After Philip buried his fourth wife, Anna of Austria, to whom he had been deeply devoted, contemporaries noticed a more marked devotion to religion. He relied more and more on God for political help. On the issues of the Inquisition and religious toleration, Philip was completely inflexible. He identified toleration with the growth of heresy, civil disorder, violence, and bloodshed: "Had there been no inquisition (in Spain) there would have been more heretics, and the country would be in a lamentable state like others (the Netherlands) where there is no inquisition as we have in Spain."[33] In this respect, Philip II differed little from the Protestant reformers Luther and Calvin, who initially called for individual liberty of conscience and then insisted on the right of church and civil powers to extirpate heresy within their jurisdictions. Philip was a man of his times, and the times did not favor religious toleration.

With his determination to crush heresy in the Low Countries and with the enormous wealth of American silver enabling him to hire the mercenary armies he needed, why did Philip II have such trouble achieving his goal? Philip was preoccupied with other parts of his vast empire, especially the advance of the Ottoman Turks into the western Mediterranean. This issue—combined with the death of his son and heir Don Carlos and then a revolt of the Moriscos (Muslims) in Granada—made it impossible to concentrate on the Netherlands. At one point in 1566 he complained, "I have so much on my mind that I rarely know what I am doing or saying." Only after Philip learned of the death of Suleiman the Magnificent did he feel able to focus on the Netherlands.[34]

But the Netherlands could not be separated in Philip's mind from what he perceived as the "British problem." In 1586 Mary, Queen of Scots, cousin and heir of Elizabeth of England, became implicated in a plot to assassinate Elizabeth. Hoping to reunite England with Catholic Europe through Mary, Philip gave the conspiracy his full backing. Mary was discovered and beheaded on February 18, 1587. News of her execution reached Philip in mid-April. When Pope Sixtus V (1585–1590) learned of Mary's death on March 24 (the dates suggest the slowness of communication in the late sixteenth century), he promised to pay Philip one million gold ducats the moment Spanish troops landed in England. Conquering England promised the additional benefit of cutting off financial support to the Dutch rebels.

As plans for a naval expedition to attack England proceeded in 1587, two serious difficulties burdened the king. First, he was so badly crippled by gout that he could not sign documents and needed a cane to walk, painfully. Second, official reports indicated that the Ottoman Turks might seize the moment of preoccupation with the Netherlands and England to attack Spain from the Mediterranean. Philip prepared a vast fleet to sail from Lisbon to Flanders, fight off Elizabeth's navy if it attacked, rendezvous with the duke of Parma, commander of Spanish forces in the Netherlands, and escort barges carrying Parma's troops across the English Channel. On May 9, 1588, *la felícissima armada*—"the most fortunate fleet," as it was ironically called in official documents—sailed from Lisbon harbor composed of more than 130 vessels. The **Spanish Armada** met an English fleet in the Channel. The English ships were smaller, faster, and more maneuverable, and many of them had greater firing power than their Spanish counterparts. A combination of storms and squalls, spoiled food and rank water, inadequate Spanish ammunition, and, to a lesser extent, English fire ships that caused the Spanish to scatter gave England the victory. The Armada was defeated before it even reached the Netherlands. On the journey home many Spanish ships went down around Ireland; perhaps 65 managed to reach home ports.

The battle in the Channel has frequently been described as one of the decisive battles in world history. In fact, it had mixed consequences. Spain soon rebuilt its navy, and after 1588 the quality of the Spanish fleet improved. The destruction of the Spanish Armada did not halt the flow of silver from the New World. More silver reached Spain between 1588 and 1603 than in any other fifteen-year period. The war between England and Spain dragged on for years.

The defeat of the Spanish Armada was decisive, however, in the sense that it prevented Philip II from reimposing religious unity on western Europe by force. He did not conquer England, and Elizabeth continued her financial and military support of the Dutch. In the Netherlands neither side gained significant territory. The borders of 1581 tended to become permanent. In 1609 Philip III of Spain (r. 1598–1621) agreed to a truce, in effect recognizing the independence of the United Provinces. In seventeenth-century Spain memory of the loss of the Spanish Armada contributed to a spirit of defeatism. In England the victory contributed to a David and Goliath legend that enhanced English national sentiment.

Changing Attitudes and Beliefs

The age of religious wars and overseas expansion was characterized by an extraordinary degree of intellectual and artistic ferment. This effervescence can be seen in the development of the essay as a distinct literary genre, in other prose, in poetry, in drama, in art, and in music. In many ways, literature, the visual arts, music, and the drama of the period mirrored the social and cultural conditions that gave rise to them. An important theme running through the culture of this time was the encounter with radically new places and peoples.

- **How did culture and art in this period respond to social and cultural transformation?**

New Ideas About Race

Ancient Greeks and Romans were in close contact with Africa and they also practiced slavery, but they did not associate one with the other. Slavery, which was endemic in the ancient world, stemmed from either capture in war or debt. Although generations could be born in captivity, no particular ethnic or racial associations were involved (see page 137). How did slavery come to be so closely associated with race in the Age of Discovery?

Settlers brought to the Americas the racial attitudes they had absorbed in Europe. Their beliefs and attitudes toward Africans derived from Christian theological speculation and Arab ideas. In the sixteenth and seventeenth centuries the English, for example, were extremely curious about Africans' lives and customs, and slavers' accounts were extraordinarily popular. Travel literature depicted Africans as savages because of their eating habits, morals, clothing, and social customs; as barbarians because of their language and methods of war; and as heathens because they were not Christian (nearly the identical language with which the English described the Irish—see page 398). Africans were believed to possess a potent sexuality; African women were considered sexually aggressive, with a "temper hot and lascivious."[35]

"At the time when Columbus sailed to the New World, Islam was the largest world religion, and the only world religion that showed itself capable of expanding rapidly in areas as far apart and as different from each other as Senegal [in northwest Africa], Bosnia [in the Balkans], Java, and the Philippines."[36] Medieval Arabic literature spoke of blacks' physical repulsiveness, mental inferiority, and primitivism. In contrast to civilized peoples from the Mediterranean to China, some Arab writers absurdly claimed, sub-Saharan blacks were the only peoples who had produced no sciences or stable states. Though black kings, the Muslim historian Ibn Khaldun alleged, sold their subjects without even a pretext of crime or war, the victims bore no resentment because they gave no thought to the future and had "by nature few cares and worries; dancing and rhythm are for them inborn."[37]

Medieval Christians and Arabs therefore had similar notions of blacks as primitive people ideally suited to enslavement. The racial biases that the Portuguese, Spanish, Dutch, and English brought to the New World, however, derived primarily from Christian theological speculation. As Europeans turned to Africa for new sources of slaves, they used ideas about Africans' primitiveness and barbarity to defend slavery and even argue that enslavement benefited Africans by bringing the light of Christianity to heathen peoples. Thus, the institution of slavery contributed to the dissemination of more rigid notions of racial inferiority. From rather vague assumptions and prejudices, Europeans developed more elaborate ideological notions of racial superiority and inferiority to safeguard the ever-increasing profits gained from plantation slavery.

Michel de Montaigne and Cultural Curiosity

Racism was not the only possible reaction to the new worlds emerging in the sixteenth century. Decades of religious fanaticism, bringing civil anarchy and war, led both Catholics and Protestants to doubt that any one faith contained absolute truth. Added to these doubts was the discovery of peoples in the New World who had radically different ways of life. These shocks helped produce ideas of **skepticism** and cultural relativism in the sixteenth and seventeenth centuries. Skepticism is a school of thought founded on doubt that total certainty or definitive knowledge is ever attainable. The skeptic is cautious and critical and suspends judgment. Cultural relativism suggests that one culture is not necessarily superior to another, just different. Both notions found expression in the work of Frenchman Michel de Montaigne (1533–1592).

Montaigne descended from a bourgeois family that had made a fortune selling salted herring and wine and in 1477 had purchased the title and property of Montaigne in Gascony. His mother came from a Jewish family that had been forced to flee Spain. Montaigne received a classical education, studied law, and secured a judicial appointment in 1554. He condemned the ancient nobility for being more concerned with war and sports than with the cultivation of the mind.

At the age of thirty-eight Montaigne resigned his judicial post, retired to his estate, and devoted the rest of his life to study, contemplation, and an effort to understand himself. His wealth provided him with the leisure time to do so. A humanist, he believed that the object of life was to "know thyself," for self-knowledge teaches men and women how to live in accordance with nature and God. Montaigne developed a new literary genre, the essay—from the French *essayer*, meaning "to test or try"—to express his thoughts and ideas.

Montaigne's *Essays* provides insight into the mind of a remarkably civilized man. From the ancient authors, especially the Roman Stoic Seneca, Montaigne acquired a sense of calm, patience, tolerance, and broad-mindedness. Montaigne had grown up during the French civil wars, perhaps the worst kind of war. Religious ideology had set family against family, even brother against brother. He wrote:

In this controversy . . . France is at present agitated by civil wars, the best and soundest side is undoubtedly that which maintains both the old religion and the old government of the country. However, among the good men who follow that side . . . we see many whom passion drives outside the bounds of reason, and makes them sometimes adopt unjust, violent, and even reckless courses.[38]

Though he remained a Catholic, Montaigne possessed detachment, independence, openness of mind, and the willingness to look at all sides of a question. As he wrote, "other people's reasons can serve to support me, but seldom to change my course. I listen to them all favorably and decently; but so far as I can remember, I have never up to this moment followed any but my own. I set little value on my own opinion, but I set just as little on those of others."[39]

Montaigne's essay "On Cannibals" reveals the impact of overseas discoveries on one European's consciousness. His tolerant mind rejected the notion that one culture is superior to another:

I long had a man in my house that lived ten or twelve years in the New World, discovered in these latter days, and in that part of it where Villegaignon landed [Brazil]. . . .

I find that there is nothing barbarous and savage in [that] nation, . . . excepting, that every one gives the title of barbarism to everything that is not in use in his own country. As, indeed, we have no other level of truth and reason, than the example and idea of the opinions and customs of the place wherein we live.[40]

Montaigne's rejection of dogmatism, his secularism, and his skepticism thus represented a basic change. In his own time and throughout the seventeenth century, few would have agreed with him. The publication of his ideas, however, anticipated a basic shift in attitudes. Montaigne inaugurated an era of doubt. "Wonder," he said, "is the foundation of all philosophy, research is the means of all learning, and ignorance is the end."[41]

Online Study Center Improve Your Grade
Primary Source: Michel de Montaigne on the Fallibility of Human Understanding

Elizabethan and Jacobean Literature

In addition to the essay as a literary genre, the period fostered remarkable creativity in other branches of literature. England, especially in the latter part of Elizabeth's reign and in the first years of her successor, James I (r. 1603–1625), witnessed remarkable literary expression. The terms *Elizabethan* and *Jacobean* (referring to the reign of James) are used to designate the English music, poetry, prose, and drama of this period. The poetry of Sir Philip Sidney (1554–1586), such as *Astrophel and Stella*, strongly influenced later poetic writing. *The Faerie Queene* of Edmund Spenser (1552–1599) endures as one of the greatest moral epics in any language. The rare poetic beauty of the plays of Christopher Marlowe (1564–1593), such as *Tamburlaine* and *The Jew of Malta*, paved the way for the work of Shakespeare. Above all, the immortal dramas of William Shakespeare (1564–1616) and the stately prose of the Authorized, or King James, Bible marked the Elizabethan and Jacobean periods as the golden age of English literature.

William Shakespeare, the son of a successful glove manufacturer in Stratford-on-Avon, chose a career on the London stage. By 1592 he had gained recognition as an actor and playwright. He performed in the Lord Chamberlain's Company and became co-owner of the Globe Theatre, which after 1603 presented his plays. Shakespeare's genius lay in the originality of his characterizations, the diversity of his plots, his understanding of human psychology, and his unexcelled gift for language. Shakespeare was a Renaissance man in his deep appreciation of classical culture, individualism, and humanism. Such plays as *Julius Caesar, Pericles,* and *Antony and Cleopatra* deal with classical subjects and figures. Several of his comedies have Italian Renaissance settings. The nine history plays, including *Richard II, Richard III,* and *Henry IV,* enjoyed the greatest popularity among Shakespeare's contemporaries. Written during the decade after the defeat of the Spanish Armada, the history plays express English national consciousness.

Shakespeare's later tragedies, including *Hamlet, Othello,* and *Macbeth,* explore an enormous range of human problems and are open to an almost infinite variety of interpretations. *Othello* portrays an honorable man destroyed by a flaw in his own character and the satanic evil of his supposed friend Iago. *Macbeth*'s central theme is

Titus Andronicus With classical allusions, fifteen murders and executions, a Gothic queen who takes a black lover, and incredible violence, this early Shakespearean tragedy (1594) was a melodramatic thriller that enjoyed enormous popularity with the London audience. Modern critics believe that it foreshadowed *King Lear* with its emphasis on suffering and madness. *(Reproduced by permission of the Marquess of Bath, Longleat House, Warminster, Wilts)*

exorbitant ambition. Shakespeare analyzes the psychology of sin in the figures of Macbeth and Lady Macbeth, whose mutual love under the pressure of ambition leads to their destruction. The central figure in *Hamlet,* a play suffused with individuality, wrestles with moral problems connected with revenge and with the human being's relationship to life and death.

Shakespeare's last play, *The Tempest*, is now viewed by critics as one of his best. The sorcerer-prince Prospero and his daughter Miranda are stranded on an island by Prospero's treacherous brother. There Prospero finds and raises Caliban, whom he instructs in his own language and religion. After Caliban's attempted rape of Miranda, Prospero enslaves him, earning the rage and resentment of his erstwhile pupil. Modern scholars often note the echoes between this play and the realities of imperial conquest and settlement in Shakespeare's day. It is no accident, they argue, that the poet portrayed Caliban as a monstrous, dark-skinned island native whose natural condition is servitude. The author himself borrows words from Montaigne's essay "On Cannibals," suggesting that his portrayal may have implied criticism of superior colonial attitudes rather than an unqualified endorsement.

Another great masterpiece of the Jacobean period was the Authorized Bible. At a theological conference in 1604, a group of Puritans urged James I to support a new translation of the Bible. The king assigned the task to a committee of scholars, and their version was published in 1611. Divided into chapters and verses, the Authorized Version is actually more a revision of earlier Bibles than an original work. Yet it provides a superb expression of the mature English vernacular of the early seventeenth century. Consider Psalm 37:

Fret not thy selfe because of evill doers, neither bee thou envious against the workers of iniquitie.
For they shall soone be cut downe like the grasse; and wither as the greene herbe.
Trust in the Lord, and do good, so shalt thou dwell in the land, and verely thou shalt be fed.

The Authorized Version, so called because it was produced under royal sponsorship (it had no official ecclesiastical endorsement), represented the Anglican and Puritan desire to encourage laypeople to read the Scriptures. It quickly achieved great popularity and displaced all earlier versions. British settlers carried this Bible to the North American colonies, where it became known as the King James Bible. For centuries the King James Bible has had a profound influence on the language and lives of English-speaking peoples.

Chapter Summary

 Online Study Center   ACE the Test

- What was the Afro-Eurasian trading world before Columbus?
- How and why did Europeans undertake ambitious voyages of expansion that would usher in a new era of global contact?
- What effect did overseas expansion have on the conquered societies, on enslaved Africans, and on world trade?
- How did culture and art in this period respond to social and cultural transformation?

Prior to Columbus's voyages, well-developed trade routes linked the peoples and products of Africa, Asia, and Europe. The Indian Ocean was the center of the Afro-Eurasian trade world, ringed by cosmopolitan commercial cities such as Mombasa, Malacca, and Macao. Venetian and Genoese merchants brought sophisticated luxury goods, like silks and spices, into western Europe from the East. Overall, though, Europeans played a minor role in the Afro-Eurasian trading world, since they did not produce many products desired by Eastern elites.

In the sixteenth and seventeenth centuries Europeans gained access to large parts of the globe for the first time. European peoples had the intellectual curiosity, driving ambition, and material incentive to challenge their marginal role in the pre-existing trade world. The revived monarchies of the sixteenth century now possessed sufficient resources to back ambitious seafarers like Christopher Columbus and Vasco da Gama. Exploration and exploitation contributed to a more sophisticated standard of living, in the form of spices and Asian luxury goods, and to a terrible international inflation resulting from the influx of South American silver and gold. Governments, the upper classes, and the peasantry were badly hurt by the resulting inflation. Meanwhile, the middle class of bankers, shippers, financiers, and manufacturers prospered for much of the seventeenth century.

Other consequences of European expansion had global proportions. Indian Ocean trade, long dominated by Muslim merchants operating from autonomous city-ports, increasingly fell under the control of Portuguese merchants sponsored by their Crown. In the New World Europeans discovered territories wholly unknown to them and forcibly established new colonies. The resulting Columbian exchange decimated native populations and fostered exchange of a myriad of plant, animal, and viral species. The slave trade took on new proportions of scale and intensity, as many millions of Africans were transported to labor in horrific conditions in the mines and plantations of the New World.

Cultural attitudes were challenged as well. While most Europeans did not question the superiority of Western traditions and beliefs, new currents of religious skepticism and new ideas about race were harbingers of developments to come. The essays of Montaigne, the plays of Shakespeare, and the King James Bible remain classic achievements of the Western cultural heritage. They both reflected dominant cultural values and projected new ideas into the future.

Key Terms

- Malacca
- entrepôt
- Admiral Zheng He
- Mansa Musa
- Constantinople
- spice trade
- Prince Henry the Navigator
- *General History of the Indies*
- caravel
- Ptolemy's *Geography*
- Vasco da Gama
- Christopher Columbus
- Santa Fe capitulations
- Treaty of Tordesillas
- Ferdinand Magellan
- Hernando Cortés
- Tenochtitlán
- Virocha
- Francisco Pizarro
- encomienda system
- sugar
- Columbian exchange
- price revolution
- Spanish Armada
- skepticism

Online Study Center Improve Your Grade Flashcards

Suggested Reading

Crosby, Alfred W. *The Columbian Exchange and Cultural Consequences of 1492*, 30th anniversary ed. 2003. An innovative and highly influential account of the environmental impact of Columbus's voyages.

Davis, David B. *Slavery and Human Progress*. 1984. A moving and authoritative account of New World slavery.

Fernández-Armesto, Felip. *Columbus*. 1992. An excellent biography of Christopher Columbus.

Frederickson, George M. *The Arrogance of Race: Historical Perspectives on Slavery, Racism, and Social Inequality*. 1988. Analyzes the social and economic circumstances associated with the rise of plantation slavery.

Greenblatt, Stephen. *Marvelous Possessions: The Wonder of the New World*. 1991. Describes the cultural impact of New World discoveries on Europeans.

Northrup, David, ed. *The Atlantic Slave Trade*. 1994. Collected essays by leading scholars on many different aspects of the slave trade.

Pérez-Mallaína, Pablo E. *Spain's Men of the Sea: Daily Life on the Indies Fleet in the Sixteenth Century*. 1998. A description of recruitment, daily life, and career paths for ordinary sailors and officers in the Spanish fleet.

Pomeranz, Kenneth, and Steven Topik. *The World That Trade Created: Society, Culture and the World Economy, 1400 to the Present*. 1999. The creation of a world market presented through rich and vivid stories of merchants, miners, slaves, and farmers.

Restall, Matthew. *Seven Myths of Spanish Conquest*. 2003. A re-examination of common ideas about why and how the Spanish conquered native civilizations in the New World.

Scammell, Geoffrey V. *The World Encompassed: The First European Maritime Empires, c. 800–1650*. 1981. A detailed overview of the first European empires, including the Italian city-states, Portugal, and Spain.

Schwarz, Stuart B., ed. *Implicit Understandings: Observing, Reporting and Reflecting on the Encounters Between Europeans and Other Peoples in the Early Modern Era*. 1994. A collection of articles examining the cultural and intellectual impact of encounters between Europeans and non-Europeans during the Age of Discovery.

Subrahamanyam, Sanjay. *The Career and Legend of Vasco da Gama*. 1998. A probing biography that places Vasco da Gama in the context of Portuguese politics and society.

(continued on page 520)

Listening to the Past

Columbus Describes His First Voyage

On his return voyage to Spain in January 1493, Christopher Columbus composed a letter intended for wide circulation and had copies of it sent ahead to Isabella and Ferdinand and others when the ship docked at Lisbon. Because the letter sums up Columbus's understanding of his achievements, it is considered the most important document of his first voyage. Remember that his knowledge of Asia rested heavily on Marco Polo's Travels, *published around 1298.*

Since I know that you will be pleased at the great success with which the Lord has crowned my voyage, I write to inform you how in thirty-three days I crossed from the Canary Islands to the Indies, with the fleet which our most illustrious sovereigns gave me. I found very many islands with large populations and took possession of them all for their Highnesses; this I did by proclamation and unfurled the royal standard. No opposition was offered.

I named the first island that I found "San Salvador," in honour of our Lord and Saviour who has granted me this miracle. . . . When I reached Cuba, I followed its north coast westwards, and found it so extensive that I thought this must be the mainland, the province of Cathay.* . . . From there I saw another island eighteen leagues eastwards which I then named "Hispaniola."†

Hispaniola is a wonder. The mountains and hills, the plains and meadow lands are both fertile and beautiful. They are most suitable for planting crops and for raising cattle of all kinds, and there are good sites for building towns and villages. The harbours are incredibly fine and there are many great rivers with broad channels and the majority contain gold.‡ The trees, fruits and plants are very different from those of Cuba. In Hispaniola there are many spices and large mines of gold and other metals. . . .§

The inhabitants of this island, and all the rest that I discovered or heard of, go naked, as their mothers bore them, men and women alike. A few of the women, however, cover a single place with a leaf of a plant or piece of cotton which they weave for the purpose. They have no iron or steel or arms and are not capable of using them, not because they are not strong and well built but because they are amazingly timid. All the weapons they have are canes cut at seeding time, at the end of which they fix a sharpened stick, but they have not the courage to make use of these, for very often when I have sent two or three men to a village to have conversation with them a great number of them have come out. But as soon as they saw my men all fled immediately, a father not even waiting for his son. And this is not because we have harmed any of them; on the contrary, wherever I have gone and been able to have conversation with them, I have given them some of the various things I had, a cloth and other articles, and received nothing in exchange. But they have still remained incurably timid. True, when they have been reassured and lost their fear, they are so ingenuous and so liberal with all their possessions that no one who has not seen them would believe it. If one asks for anything they have they never say no. On the

---

*Cathay is the old name for China. In the log-book and later in this letter Columbus accepts the native story that Cuba is an island that they can circumnavigate in something more than twenty-one days, yet he insists here and later, during the second voyage, that it is in fact part of the Asiatic mainland.

†Hispaniola is the second largest island of the West Indies; Haiti occupies the western third of the island, the Dominican Republic the rest.

‡This did not prove to be true.

§These statements are also inaccurate.

contrary, they offer a share to anyone with demonstrations of heartfelt affection, and they are immediately content with any small thing, valuable or valueless, that is given them. I forbade the men to give them bits of broken crockery, fragments of glass or tags of laces, though if they could get them they fancied them the finest jewels in the world.

I hoped to win them to the love and service of their Highnesses and of the whole Spanish nation and to persuade them to collect and give us of the things which they possessed in abundance and which we needed. They have no religion and are not idolaters; but all believe that power and goodness dwell in the sky and they are firmly convinced that I have come from the sky with these ships and people. In this belief they gave me a good reception everywhere, once they had overcome their fear; and this is not because they are stupid—far from it, they are men of great intelligence, for they navigate all those seas, and give a marvellously good account of everything—but because they have never before seen men clothed or ships like these. . . .

In all these islands the men are seemingly content with one woman, but their chief or king is allowed more than twenty. The women appear to work more than the men and I have not been able to find out if they have private property. As far as I could see whatever a man had was shared among all the rest and this particularly applies to food. . . . In another island, which I am told is larger than Hispaniola, the people have no hair. Here there is a vast quantity of gold, and from here and the other islands I bring Indians as evidence.

In conclusion, to speak only of the results of this very hasty voyage, their Highnesses can see that I will give them as much gold as they require, if they will render me some very slight assistance; also I will give them all the spices and cotton they want. . . . I will also bring them as much aloes as they ask and as many slaves, who will be taken from the idolaters. I believe also that I have found rhubarb and cinnamon and there will be countless other things in addition. . . .

So all Christendom will be delighted that our Redeemer has given victory to our most illustrious King and Queen and their renowned kingdoms, in this great matter. They should hold great celebrations and render solemn thanks to the Holy Trinity with many solemn prayers, for the great triumph which they will have, by the conversion of so many peoples to our holy faith and for the temporal benefits which will follow, for not only Spain, but all Christendom will receive encouragement and profit.

This is a brief account of the facts. Written in the caravel off the Canary Islands.||
15 February 1493

At your orders
THE ADMIRAL

Christopher Columbus, by Ridolpho Ghirlandio. Friend of Raphael and teacher of Michelangelo, Ghirlandio (1483–1561) enjoyed distinction as a portrait painter, and so we can assume that this is a good likeness of the older Columbus. *(Scala/Art Resource, NY)*

Questions for Analysis

1. How did Columbus explain the success of his voyage?
2. What was Columbus's view of the Native Americans he met?
3. Evaluate his statements that the Caribbean islands possessed gold, cotton, and spices.
4. Why did Columbus cling to the idea that he had reached Asia?

||Actually, Columbus was off Santa Maria in the Azores.

Source: *The Four Voyages of Christopher Columbus* (Penguin Classics, 1958), pp. 115–123. Copyright © J. M. Cohen, 1958. Reproduced by permission of Penguin Books Ltd.

Notes

1. A. Reid, *Southeast Asia in the Age of Commerce, 1450–1680,*. vol. 2: *Expansion and Crisis* (New Haven, Conn.: Yale University Press, 1993), Chaps. 1 and 2, pp. 1–131.
2. Andre Gunder Frank, *Re-Orient: Global Economy in the Asian Age* (Berkeley: University of California Press, 1998).
3. K. N. Chaudhuri, *Trade and Civilisation in the Indian Ocean: An Economic History from the Rise of Islam to 1750* (Cambridge: Cambridge University Press, 1985), p. 14.
4. Quoted in Erik Gilbert and Jonathan T. Reynolds, *Africa in World History: From Prehistory to the Present* (Upper Saddle River, N.J.: Pearson, 2004), p. 93.
5. Halil Inalcik and Donald Quataert, eds., *An Economic and Social History of the Ottoman Empire, 1300–1914* (Cambridge: Cambridge University Press, 1994), p. 219.
6. G. V. Scammell, *The World Encompassed: The First European Maritime Empires, c. 800–1650* (Berkeley: University of California Press, 1981), pp. 101, 104.
7. Ibid., p. 174.
8. Quoted in C. M. Cipolla, *Guns, Sails, and Empires: Technological Innovation and the Early Phases of European Expansion, 1400–1700* (New York: Minerva Press, 1965), p. 132.
9. Quoted in F. H. Littell, *The Macmillan Atlas: History of Christianity* (New York: Macmillan, 1976), p. 75.
10. See C. R. Phillips, *Ciudad Real, 1500–1750: Growth, Crisis, and Readjustment in the Spanish Economy* (Cambridge, Mass.: Harvard University Press, 1979), pp. 103–104, 115.
11. Pablo E. Pérez-Mallaína, *Spain's Men of the Sea: Daily Life on the Indies Fleet in the Sixteenth Century* (Baltimore: Johns Hopkins University Press, 1998), p. 130.
12. Ibid., p. 133.
13. Ibid., p. 19.
14. Scammell, *The World Encompassed,* p. 207.
15. Ibid., p. 265.
16. Quoted in Cipolla, *Guns, Sails, and Empires,* pp. 115–116.
17. S. E. Morison, *Admiral of the Ocean Sea: A Life of Christopher Columbus* (Boston: Little, Brown, 1942), p. 339.
18. Quoted in F. Maddison, "Tradition and Innovation: Columbus' First Voyage and Portuguese Navigation in the Fifteenth Century," in *Circa 1492: Art in the Age of Exploration,* ed. J. A. Levenson (Washington, D.C.: National Gallery of Art, 1991), p. 69.
19. J. M. Cohen, ed. and trans., *The Four Voyages of Christopher Columbus* (New York: Penguin Books, 1969), p. 37.
20. Quoted in R. L. Kagan, "The Spain of Ferdinand and Isabella," in *Circa 1492: Art in the Age of Exploration,* ed. J. A. Levenson (Washington, D.C.: National Gallery of Art, 1991), p. 60.
21. G. W. Conrad and A. A. Demarest, *Religion and Empire: The Dynamics of Aztec and Inca Expansionism* (New York: Cambridge University Press, 1993), pp. 67–69.
22. Ibid., pp. 135–139.
23. Quoted in Crosby, *The Columbian Exchange: Biological and Cultural Consequences of 1492* (Westport, Conn.: Greenwood, 1972), p. 39.
24. Ibid., pp. 35–59.
25. Quoted in C. Gibson, ed., *The Black Legend: Anti-Spanish Attitudes in the Old World and the New* (New York: Knopf, 1971), pp. 74–75.
26. Quoted in L. B. Rout, Jr., *The African Experience in Spanish America* (New York: Cambridge University Press, 1976), p. 23.
27. C. Verlinden, *The Beginnings of Modern Colonization,* trans. Y. Freccero (Ithaca, N.Y.: Cornell University Press, 1970), pp. 5–6, 80–97.
28. This section leans heavily on D. B. Davis, *Slavery and Human Progress* (New York: Oxford University Press, 1984), pp. 54–62; the quotation is on p. 58.
29. Herbert S. Klein, "Profits and the Causes of Mortality," in David Northrup, ed., *The Atlantic Slave Trade* (Lexington, Mass.: D. C. Heath and Co., 1994), p. 116.
30. Malcolm Cowley and Daniel P. Mannix, "The Middle Passage," in David Northrup, ed., *The Atlantic Slave Trade* (Lexington, Mass.: D. C. Heath and Co., 1994), p. 101.
31. Reid, *Southeast Asia,* vol. 2, pp. 10–26.
32. H. Kamen, *Philip of Spain* (New Haven: Yale University Press, 1997), p. 77.
33. Quoted in ibid., p. 235.
34. Parker, *Grand Strategy of Philip II* (New Haven, Conn.: Yale University Press, 2000), pp. 115–122; the quotation is on p. 119.
35. Quoted in D. P. Mannix, with M. Cowley, *Black Cargoes: A History of the Atlantic Slave Trade* (New York: Viking Press, 1968), p. 19.
36. See P. Brown, "Understanding Islam," *New York Review of Books,* February 22, 1979, pp. 30–33.
37. Quoted in Davis, *Slavery and Human Progress,* pp. 43–44.
38. D. M. Frame, trans., *The Complete Works of Montaigne* (Stanford, Calif.: Stanford University Press, 1958), pp. 175–176.
39. Ibid., p. 618.
40. C. Cotton, trans., *The Essays of Michel de Montaigne* (New York: A. L. Burt, 1893), pp. 207, 210.
41. Ibid., p. 523.

Hyacinthe Rigaud, *Louis XIV, King of France and Navarre* (1701). Louis XIV is surrounded by the symbols of his power: the sword of justice, the scepter of power, and the crown. The vigor and strength of the king's stocking-covered legs contrast with the age and wisdom of his lined face. *(Scala/Art Resource, NY)*

chapter 16
Absolutism and Constitutionalism in Western Europe, ca 1589–1715

chapter preview

Seventeenth-Century Crisis and Rebuilding
• What were the common crises and achievements of seventeenth-century states?

Absolutism in France and Spain
• To what extent did French and Spanish monarchs succeed in creating absolute monarchies?

The Culture of Absolutism
• What cultural forms flourished under absolutist governments?

Constitutionalism
• What is constitutionalism, and how did this form of government emerge in England and the Dutch Republic?

The seventeenth century was a period of crisis and transformation. Agricultural and manufacturing slumps meant that many people struggled to feed themselves and their families. After a long period of growth, population rates stagnated or even fell. Religious and dynastic conflicts led to almost constant war, visiting violence and destruction on ordinary people.

The demands of war reshaped European states. Armies grew larger than they had been since the time of the Roman Empire. To pay for these armies, governments greatly increased taxes. They also created new bureaucracies to collect the taxes and to foster economic activity that might increase state revenue. Despite numerous obstacles, European states succeeded in gathering more power during this period. What one historian described as the long European "struggle for stability" that originated with the Reformation in the early sixteenth century was largely resolved by 1680.[1]

Important differences existed, however, in terms of *which* authority within the state possessed sovereignty—the Crown or privileged groups. Between roughly 1589 and 1715 two basic patterns of government emerged in Europe: absolute monarchy and the constitutional state. Almost all subsequent European governments have been modeled on one of these patterns.

Seventeenth-Century Crisis and Rebuilding

Historians often refer to the seventeenth century as an "age of crisis." After the economic and demographic growth of the sixteenth century, Europe faltered into stagnation and retrenchment. This was partially due to climate changes beyond anyone's control, but it also resulted from the bitterness of religious divides, the increased pressures exerted by governments, and the violence and dislocation of war. Overburdened peasants and city-dwellers took action to defend themselves, sometimes profiting

Online Study Center
This icon will direct you to interactive activities and study materials on the website **college.hmco.com/pic/mckaywest9e**

from elite conflicts to obtain redress of their grievances. In the long run, however, governments proved increasingly able to impose their will on the populace. This period witnessed a spectacular growth in army size as well as new forms of taxation, government bureaucracies, and increased state sovereignty.

- **What were the common crises and achievements of seventeenth-century states?**

Economic and Demographic Crisis

In the seventeenth century the vast majority of western Europeans lived in the countryside. The hub of the rural world was the small peasant village centered on a church and a manor. Life was in many ways circumscribed by the village, although we should not underestimate the mobility induced by war, food shortage, fortune-seeking, and religious pilgrimage.

A small number of peasants in each village owned enough land to feed themselves and the livestock and ploughs necessary to work their land. These independent farmers were leaders of the peasant village. They employed the landless poor, rented out livestock and tools, and served as agents for the noble lord. Below them were small landowners and tenant farmers who did not have enough land to be self-sufficient. These families sold their best produce on the market to earn cash for taxes, rent, and food. At the bottom were the rural proletariat who worked as dependent laborers and servants.

Rich or poor, bread was the primary element of the diet. Ignoring our modern health concerns, the richest ate a white loaf, leaving brown bread to those who could not afford better. Peasants paid stiff fees to the local miller for grinding grain into flour and sometimes to the lord for the right to bake bread in his oven. Bread was most often accompanied with a soup made of roots, herbs, beans, and perhaps a small piece of salt pork. One of the biggest

An English Food Riot Nothing infuriated ordinary women and men more than the idea that merchants and landowners were withholding grain from the market in order to push high prices even higher. In this cartoon an angry crowd hands out rough justice to a rich farmer accused of hoarding. *(Courtesy of the Trustees of the British Museum)*

annual festivals in the rural village was the killing of the family pig. The whole family gathered to help, sharing a rare abundance of meat with neighbors and carefully salting the extra and putting down the lard. In some areas, menstruating women were careful to stay away from the kitchen for fear they might cause the lard to spoil.

Rural society lived on the edge of subsistence. A bad harvest, an illness, or a drop in prices could lead to debt and the loss of one's land. Because of the crude technology and low crop yield, peasants were constantly threatened by scarcity and famine. The fear of hunger marked popular culture, and death was a familiar presence.

The seventeenth century put new stresses on this fragile balance. A colder and wetter climate meant a shorter farming season. Conditions were so bad that scholars refer to this period as a "little ice age." A bad harvest created dearth; a series of bad harvests could lead to famine. Recurrent famines had a significant effect on the population levels of early modern Europe. Using parish registers, historians have traced the correspondence between high prices on the one hand and burials and low birth and marriage rates on the other. Most people did not die of outright starvation, but rather of diseases brought on by malnutrition and exhaustion. Facilitated by the weakened population, outbreaks of bubonic plague continued in Europe until the 1720s.

Industry also suffered. While the evidence does not permit broad generalizations, it appears that the output of woolen textiles, one of the most important European manufactures, declined sharply in the first half of the century. Food prices were high, wages stagnated, and unemployment soared. This economic crisis was not universal: it struck various regions at different times and to different degrees. In the middle decades of the century, Spain, France, Germany, and England all experienced great economic difficulties; but these years were the golden age of the Netherlands.

Peasants and the urban poor were the first to suffer from bad harvests and economic depression. When the price of bread rose beyond their capacity to pay, they frequently took action. In towns they invaded the bakers' shop to seize bread and resell it at a "just price." In rural areas groups of peasants attacked convoys taking grain away to the cities and also redistributed it for what they considered a fair price. Women often took the lead in these actions, since their role as mothers with children to feed gave them some impunity in authorities' eyes. Historians have labeled this vision of a world in which community needs predominate over competition and profit a **moral economy.**

Chronology

1589–1610	Henry IV in France
1598	Edict of Nantes
1602	Dutch East India Company founded
1605–1715	Food riots common across Europe
1635	Birth of French Academy
1640–1680	Golden age of Dutch art (Vermeer, Van Steen, Rembrandt)
1642–1649	English civil war ends with execution of Charles I
1643–1715	Louis XIV in France
1648–1653	The Fronde
1653–1658	Military rule in England under Oliver Cromwell
1659	Treaty of the Pyrenees marks end of Spanish imperial dominance
1660	Restoration of English monarchy under Charles II
1665–1683	Jean-Baptiste Colbert applies mercantilism to France
1685	Edict of Nantes revoked
1688–1689	Glorious Revolution in England
1701–1713	War of the Spanish Succession
1713	Peace of Utrecht

Seventeenth-Century State-Building: Common Obstacles and Achievements

In this context of economic and demographic depression, monarchs began to make new demands on their people. Traditionally, historians have distinguished sharply between the "absolutist" governments of France, Spain, central Europe, and Russia and the constitutionally limited governments of England and the Dutch Republic. Whereas absolutist monarchs gathered all power under their personal control, Dutch and English rulers were obliged to respect laws passed by representative institutions. More recently, historians have emphasized commonalities among these powers. Despite their political differences, absolutist and constitutional monarchs shared common projects of protecting and expanding their frontiers, raising new taxes, and consolidating state control.

Rulers who wished to increase their authority encountered formidable obstacles. Some were purely material. Without paved roads, telephones, or other modern technology, it took weeks to convey orders from the central government to the provinces. States like France and Spain were vast, especially if we take their overseas empires into account. Rulers also suffered from a lack of information about their realms, due to the limited size of their bureaucracies. Without accurate knowledge of the number of inhabitants and the wealth they possessed, it was impossible to police and tax the population effectively. Cultural and linguistic differences presented their own obstacles. Seventeenth-century Basques, Bretons, Languedocians, and Alsatians spoke not French but their own languages. These differences decreased even further their willingness to obey a distant monarch's commands.

A more concrete obstacle was the array of privileged groups who shared in authority and its spoils. The traditional enemy of monarchical power was the nobility. Across Europe, nobles retained great legal, military, political, and financial powers, not to mention the traditional social prestige they commanded. Nobles were not alone in opposing monarchs' new claims. Other competitors included the church, the legislative corps, town councils, guilds, and other bodies that had acquired autonomy over the course of the Middle Ages. In some countries whole provinces held separate privileges and exemptions granted when they entered the kingdom. This special status reinforced local power structures and identities.

A long historical consensus held that absolutist monarchs succeeded in breaking the power of these institutions, with Louis XIV of France serving as the model for absolutist power across Europe. By contrast, mighty kings were humbled in England and the Dutch Republic and were forced to concede political power to elected representatives. Today, historians paint a more nuanced picture of this divide. On the one hand, they emphasize the extent to which absolutist monarchs had to compromise with existing power structures. Louis XIV succeeded because he co-opted and convinced nobles, rather than by crushing their power. On the other hand, historians also recognize that traditional elites retained power in England and the Netherlands. Constitutional limits did not mean democracy, the rule of the people.

If we take a step back from the political differences, we see that these states all succeeded—albeit to varying degrees—in overcoming the obstacles and achieving new levels of central control. Four achievements stand out in particular: greater taxation, growth in armed forces, larger and more efficient bureaucracies, and the increased ability to compel obedience from their subjects.

Increasing the size and power of the state required new sources of revenue. Medieval kings frequently found temporary financial support through bargains with the nobility: the nobility agreed to an ad hoc grant of money in return for freedom from future taxation. Over the course of the seventeenth century, rulers succeeded in generating new levels of income by either forcing direct taxes ever higher or devising alternative methods of raising money.

Taxation both permitted and required a larger government apparatus. This period witnessed the expansion of government bureaucracies and the creation of administrative techniques to improve communication and efficiency. Bureaucracies were now composed of career officials appointed by and solely accountable to the king. The backgrounds of these civil servants varied. They sometimes came from the middle classes, as in France, the Netherlands, and England. In Spain and eastern Europe, monarchs utilized members of the nobility instead (see Chapter 17).

Over time, government power added up to something close to **sovereignty**. A state may be termed sovereign when it possesses a monopoly over the instruments of justice and the use of force within clearly defined boundaries. In a sovereign state, no system of courts, such as ecclesiastical tribunals, competes with state courts in the dispensation of justice; and private armies, such as those of feudal lords, present no threat to central authority because the state's army is stronger. State law touches all persons in the country. While seventeenth-century states did not acquire total sovereignty, they made important strides toward that goal.

Warfare and the Growth of Army Size

The driving force of seventeenth-century state-building was warfare, characterized by dramatic changes in the size and style of armies. Medieval armies had been raised by feudal lords for particular wars or campaigns, after which the troops were disbanded. In the seventeenth century monarchs took command of recruiting and maintaining armies—in peacetime as well as wartime. Kings deployed their troops both inside and outside the country in the interests of the monarchy. Instead of serving their own interests, army officers were required to be loyal and obedient to the monarchs who commanded them. New techniques for training and deploying soldiers meant a rise in the professional standards of the army.

Along with professionalization came an explosive growth in army size. The French took the lead, with the army growing from roughly 125,000 men in the Thirty Years' War (1630–1648) to 250,000 during the Dutch War (1672–1678) and 340,000 during the War of the League of Augsburg (1688–1697).[2] This growth was caused in part by changes in the style of armies. Mustering a royal army took longer than simply hiring a mercenary band, giving enemies time to form coalitions. The large coalitions Louis XIV confronted required him to fight on multiple fronts with huge armies. In turn, the relative size and wealth of France among European nations allowed Louis to field enormous armies and thereby to pursue the ambitious foreign policies that caused his alarmed neighbors to form coalitions against him.

The death toll was startlingly high for noble officers, who personally led their men in battle. The paramount value of honor for noblemen outshone concerns for safety or material benefit. Nobles had to purchase their positions in the army and supply horses, food, uniforms, and weapons for themselves and their troops. Royal stipends did not begin to cover these expenses, and an officer's position could not be sold if he died in battle. The only legacy an officer's widow received was the debt incurred to fund her husbands' military career. It was not until the 1760s that the French government assumed the costs of equipping troops.

Other European powers were quick to follow the French example. The rise of absolutism in central and eastern Europe was similarly marked by a vast expansion in the size of armies (see Chapter 17). Great Britain followed a similar, albeit distinctive pattern. Instead of building a land army, the British focused on naval forces and eventually built the largest navy in the world.

Many historians believe that the new loyalty, professionalism, and size of the French army is the best case for the success of absolutism under Louis XIV. Whatever his compromises elsewhere, the French monarch had firm control of his armed forces. As in so many other matters, Louis's model was followed across Europe.

Popular Political Action

In the seventeenth century increased pressures of taxation and warfare turned bread riots into armed uprisings. **Popular revolts** were extremely common in England, France, Spain, Portugal, and Italy in the mid-seventeenth century.[3] In 1640 Philip IV of Spain faced revolt in Catalonia, the economic center of his realm. This was the same time he was struggling to put down an uprising in Portugal and the revolt of the northern provinces of the Netherlands. In 1647 the city of Palermo, in Spanish-occupied Sicily, exploded in protest over food shortages caused by a series of bad harvests. Fearing public unrest, the city government subsidized the price of bread, attracting even more starving peasants from the countryside. When Madrid ordered an end to

The Spider and the Fly In reference to the insect symbolism (*upper left*), the caption on the lower left side of this illustration states, "The noble is the spider, the peasant the fly." The other caption (*upper right*) notes, "The more people have, the more they want. The poor man brings everything—wheat, fruit, money, vegetables. The greedy lord sitting there ready to take everything will not even give him the favor of a glance." This satirical print summarizes peasant grievances. *(The New York Public Library/Art Resource, NY)* subsidies, municipal leaders decided to lighten the loaf rather than raise prices. Not fooled by this change, local women led a bread riot, shouting "Long live the king and down with the taxes and the bad government!" The uprising spread to the rest of the island and eventually to Naples on the mainland. Apart from affordable food, rebels demanded the suppression of extraordinary taxes and participation in municipal government. Some dreamed of a republic in which noble tax exemptions would be abolished. Despite initial successes, the revolt lacked unity and strong leadership and could not withstand the forces of aristocratic reaction.[4]

In France urban disorders became so frequent an aspect of the social and political landscape as to be "a distinctive feature of life."[5] Major insurrections occurred at Dijon in 1630 and 1668, at Bordeaux in 1635 and 1675, at Montpellier in 1645, at Lyons in 1667–1668 and 1692, and at Amiens in 1685, 1695, 1704, and 1711. All were characterized by deep popular anger, a vocabulary of violence, and what a recent historian calls "the culture of retribution"—that is, the punishment of royal "outsiders," officials who attempted to announce or collect taxes.[6] These officials were sometimes seized, beaten, and hacked to death. For example, in 1673 Louis XIV's imposition of new taxes on legal transactions, tobacco, and pewter ware provoked an uprising in Bordeaux.

Municipal and royal authorities often struggled to overcome popular revolt. They feared that stern repressive measures, such as sending in troops to fire on crowds, would create martyrs and further inflame the situation, while forcible full-scale military occupation of a city would be very expensive. The limitations of royal authority gave some leverage to rebels. Royal edicts were sometimes suspended, prisoners released, and discussions initiated.

By the end of the seventeenth century, this leverage had largely disappeared. Municipal governments were better integrated into the national structure, and local authorities had prompt military support from the central government. People who publicly opposed royal policies and taxes received swift and severe punishment.[7]

Absolutism in France and Spain

In the Middle Ages jurists held that as a consequence of monarchs' coronation and anointment with sacred oil, they ruled "by the grace of God." Law was given by God; kings discovered or "found" the law and acknowledged that they must respect and obey it. In the absolutist state, kings amplified these claims, asserting that, as they were chosen by God, they were responsible to God alone. They claimed exclusive power to make and enforce laws, denying any other institution or group the authority to check their power.

In 1651 in *Leviathan,* the English philosopher Thomas Hobbes provided a theoretical justification for absolute monarchical authority, arguing that any limits on or divisions of government power would lead only to paralysis or civil war. At the court of Louis XIV the theologian Bossuet proclaimed that the king was the "image" of God on earth and that it was a sacred duty to obey him: "The prince need render account of his acts to no one. . . . Without this absolute authority the king could neither do good nor repress evil. It is necessary that his power be such that no one can hope to escape him, and, finally, the only protection of individuals against the public authority should be their innocence." Historians have been debating since his reign how successfully Louis XIV and other absolutist monarchs realized these claims.

- **To what extent did French and Spanish monarchs succeed in creating absolute monarchies?**

The Foundations of Absolutism: Henry IV, Sully, and Richelieu

Louis XIV's absolutism had long roots. In 1589 his grandfather Henry IV (r. 1589–1610), the founder of the Bourbon dynasty, acquired a devastated country. Civil wars had wracked France since 1561. Catastrophically poor harvests meant that peasants across France lived on the verge of starvation. Commercial activity had fallen to one-third its 1580 level. Nobles, officials, merchants, and peasants wanted peace, order, and stability. "Henri le Grand" (Henry the Great), as the king was called, promised "a chicken in every pot" and inaugurated a remarkable recovery. He was beloved because of the belief that he cared about the people; he was the only king whose statue the Paris crowd did not tear down in the Revolution of 1789.

Aside from a short war in 1601, Henry kept France at peace. Maintaining that "if we are without compassion for the people, they must succumb and we all perish with them," Henry sharply lowered taxes on the overburdened peasants. In compensation for lost revenues, in 1602–1604 he introduced the *paulette,* an annual fee paid by royal officials to guarantee heredity in their offices. (Although effective at the time, the long-term effect of this tax was to reduce royal control over officeholders.)

Along with his able chief minister, the Protestant Maximilien de Béthune, duke of Sully, Henry IV laid the foundations for the growth of state power. He combined the indirect taxes on salt, sales, and transit and leased their collection to financiers. Although the number of taxes declined, revenues increased because of the revival of trade.[8] Henry improved the infrastructure of the country, building new roads and canals and repairing the ravages of years of civil war. In only twelve years he restored public order in France.

As a divinely appointed leader of his people, Henry sought to heal the religious divisions that had torn France apart. In 1598 he issued the **Edict of Nantes** as a compromise between Catholics and Huguenots. The edict allowed Protestants the right to worship in 150 traditionally Protestant towns throughout France; the king gave the towns 180,000 écus to support the maintenance of their military garrisons. This was too much for some devout Catholics. Henry was murdered in 1610 by François Ravaillac, a Catholic zealot, setting off national crisis.

Online Study Center Improve Your Grade
Primary Source: Henry IV's Edict of Nantes Grants Limited Toleration to the Huguenots

After the death of Henry IV his wife, the queen-regent Marie de' Medici, headed the government for the child-king Louis XIII (r. 1610–1643). In 1624 Marie de' Medici secured the appointment of Armand Jean du Plessis—Cardinal Richelieu (1585–1642)—to the council of ministers. It was a remarkable appointment. The next year Richelieu became president of the council, and after 1628 he was first minister of the French crown. Richelieu used his strong influence over King Louis XIII to exalt the French monarchy as the embodiment of the French state. One of the greatest servants of that state, Richelieu struggled through the turmoil of the Thirty Years' War to maintain the monarchy's position within Europe and within its own borders.

Richelieu's goal was to subordinate competing groups and institutions to the French monarchy. The nobility constituted the foremost threat. Nobles ran the army, controlled large provinces of France, sat in royal councils, and were immune from direct taxation. Richelieu sought to curb their power. In 1624 he succeeded in reshuffling the royal council, eliminating potential power brokers. Thereafter Richelieu dominated the council in an unprecedented way.

The constructive genius of Cardinal Richelieu is best reflected in the administrative system he established to strengthen royal control. He extended the use of the royal commissioners called **intendants.** France was divided into thirty-two *généralités* (districts), in each of which after 1634 a royal intendant held a commission to perform specific tasks, often financial but also judicial and policing. Intendants painstakingly collected information from local communities for Paris and delivered royal orders from the capital to their districts. Almost always recruited from the newer judicial nobility, the **noblesse de robe** or robe nobility, intendants were appointed directly by the monarch, to whom they were solely responsible. They could not be natives of the districts where they held authority; thus they had no vested interest in their localities. The intendants recruited men for the army, supervised the collection of taxes, presided over the administration of local law, checked up on the local nobility, and regulated economic activities—commerce, trade, the guilds, marketplaces—in their districts. They were to use their power for three related purposes: to inform the central government about their généralités, to enforce royal orders, and to undermine the influence of the regional nobility. As the intendants' power increased under Richelieu, so did the power of the centralized French state.

Under Richelieu the French monarchy also reasserted the principle of one people united by one faith. In 1627 Louis XIII decided to end Protestant military and political independence because, he said, it constituted "a state within a state." According to Louis, Huguenots demanded freedom of conscience but did not allow Catholics to worship in their cities. He interpreted this inequity as *political* disobedience.[9] Attention focused on La Rochelle, fourth largest of the French Atlantic ports and a major commercial center with strong ties to the northern Protestant states of Holland and England. Louis personally supervised the siege of La Rochelle. After the city fell in October 1628, its municipal government was suppressed and its walled fortifications were destroyed. Although Protestants retained the right of public worship, the king reinstated the Catholic liturgy, and Cardinal Richelieu himself celebrated the first Mass. The fall of La Rochelle weakened the influence of aristocratic Huguenots and was one step in the removal of Protestantism as a strong force in French life.

The elimination of potential dissidents at home did not mean hostility to Protestants abroad. Foreign policy under Richelieu aimed primarily at the destruction of the fence of Habsburg territories that surrounded France. Consequently, Richelieu supported the Habsburgs' enemies, including Protestants. In 1631 he signed a treaty with the Lutheran king Gustavus Adolphus promising French support against the Catholic Habsburgs in what has been called the Swedish phase of the Thirty Years' War (see page 562). French influence became an important factor in the political future of the German Empire. Richelieu acquired for France extensive rights in Alsace in the east and Arras in the north.

In building the French state, Richelieu knew that his approach sometimes seemed to contradict traditional Christian teaching. As a priest and bishop, how did he justify his policies? He developed his own *raison d'état* (reason of state): "Where the interests of the state are concerned, God absolves actions which, if privately committed, would be a crime."[10]

Richelieu's successor as chief minister for the boy-king Louis XIV was Cardinal Jules Mazarin (1602–1661). Along with the regent, Queen Mother Anne of Austria, Mazarin continued Richelieu's centralizing policies. His struggle to increase royal revenues to meet the costs of war with Spain led to the uprisings of 1648–1653 known as the **Fronde**. The word *fronde* means "slingshot" or "catapult," and a *frondeur* was originally a street urchin who threw mud at the passing carriages of the rich. The word came to be applied to the many individuals and groups who opposed the policies of the government. The Fronde began among the robe nobility when the judges of the Parisian high law court (the *Parlement*) rejected Anne and Mazarin's proposal to raise new revenues by rescinding judicial salaries. The arrest of several magistrates sparked a popular riot in the capital, whose inhabitants had suffered to meet the costs of war. With the boy-king, Anne of Austria fled the capital for safety. Essentially traditional and conservative, the magistrates agreed to a compromise with the government that largely favored their demands.

The second stage of the Fronde saw the conflict extend to the **noblesse d'épée** or sword nobility, who were also angered by the increasing powers of the central government. The Prince de Condé, one of the highest nobles in France, entered open warfare against the Crown, followed by other nobles and their followers. Popular rebellions led by aristocratic factions broke out in the provinces and spread to Paris.[11] As rebellion continued, civil order broke down completely. In 1651 Anne's regency ended with the declaration of Louis as king in his own right. Much of the rebellion died away, and its leaders came to terms with the government.

The conflicts of the Fronde had significant results for the future. First, it became apparent that compromise between the king and the sword and robe nobility was necessary. Neither side was strong enough to subjugate the other; only violence and disorder could come from a refusal to negotiate. This meant, in some ways, a victory for the forces opposing the king, who were guaranteed the preservation of their traditional privileges. However, the Fronde also quelled—and in some cases killed—the most vociferous opponents of the Crown. The twin evils of noble factionalism and popular riots left the French wishing for peace and for a strong monarch to re-impose order. This was the legacy that Louis XIV inherited when he assumed personal rule in 1661. Humiliated by his flight from Paris, he was determined to avoid any recurrence of rebellion.

Louis XIV and Absolutism

In the reign of Louis XIV (r. 1643–1715), the longest in European history, the French monarchy reached the peak of absolutist development. In the magnificence of his court, in the brilliance of the culture that he presided over and that permeated all of Europe, and in his remarkably long life, the "Sun King" dominated his age.

The boy-king received an education appropriate for his position. He learned to speak Italian and Spanish fluently, spoke and wrote elegant French, and knew some French history and a great deal of European geography. Louis also imbibed the devout Catholicism of his mother, Anne of Austria, and throughout his long life scrupulously performed his religious duties. Religion, Anne, and Mazarin all taught Louis the doctrine of the **divine right of kings:** God had established kings as his rulers on earth, and they were answerable ultimately to God alone. Though kings were divinely anointed and shared in the sacred nature of divinity, they could not simply do as they pleased. They had to obey God's laws and rule for the good of the people.

Louis worked very hard at the business of governing. He ruled his realm through several councils of state, which he personally attended, and through the intendants who acted for the councils in the provinces. A stream of questions and instructions flowed between local districts and Versailles, helping centralize and standardize a hopelessly complex administration. Louis insisted on taking a personal role in many of the decisions issued by the councils.

Councilors of state came from the recently ennobled or the upper middle class. Royal service provided a means of social mobility. These professional bureaucrats served the state in the person of the king, but they did not share power with him. Louis stated that he chose bourgeois officials because he wanted "people to know by the rank of the men who served him that he had no intention of

Rubens: The Death of Henry IV and the Proclamation of the Regency (1622–1625) In 1622 the regent Marie de' Medici commissioned Peter Paul Rubens to paint a cycle of paintings depicting her life. This one portrays two distinct moments: the assassination of Henry IV (shown on the left ascending to Heaven), and Marie's subsequent proclamation as regent. The queen is seated on a throne in mourning clothes, with the goddess Athena on her right (representing Prudence), a woman in the air holding a rudder (symbolizing regency), and the personification of France kneeling before her offering an orb (symbolizing government). The other twenty-three canvasses in the cycle similarly glorify Marie, a tricky undertaking given her unhappy marriage to Henry IV and her tumultuous relationship with her son Louis XIII, who removed her from the regency in 1617. As in this image, Rubens frequently resorted to allegory and classical imagery to elevate the events of Marie's life. *(Réunion des Musées Nationaux/Art Resource, NY)*

sharing power with them."[12] If great ones were the king's advisers, they would seem to share the royal authority; professional administrators from the middle class would not.

Despite increasing financial problems, Louis never called a meeting of the Estates General. The nobility therefore had no means of united expression or action. Nor did Louis have a first minister; he kept himself free from worry about the inordinate power of a Richelieu. Louis also used spying and terror—a secret police force, a system of informers, and the practice of opening private letters—to eliminate potential threats.

Religion was also a tool of national unity under Louis, who continued Richelieu's persecution of Protestants. In 1685 Louis revoked the Edict of Nantes, by which his grandfather Henry IV had granted liberty of conscience to French Huguenots. The new law ordered the destruction of Huguenot churches, the closing of schools, the Catholic baptism of Huguenots, and the exile of Huguenot pastors who refused to renounce their faith. The result was the departure of some of his most loyal and industrially skilled subjects.

There had been so many mass conversions of Protestants in France that the king's second wife, Madame de Maintenon, could say that "nearly all the Huguenots were converted." Moreover, Richelieu had already deprived French Calvinists of political rights. Why, then, did Louis XIV undertake such an apparently unnecessary, cruel, and self-destructive measure? First, Louis considered religion primarily a political question. Although he was personally tolerant, he hated division within the realm and insisted that religious unity was essential to his royal dignity and to the security of the state. As he put it, his goal was "one king, one law, one faith." Second, while France in the early years of Louis's reign permitted religious liberty, it was not a popular policy. Aristocrats had long petitioned Louis to crack down on Protestants. His decision to do so won him enormous praise: "If the flood of congratulation means anything, it . . . was probably the one act of his reign that, at the time, was popular with the majority of his subjects."13

Louis's personal hold on power, his exclusion of great nobles from his councils, and his ruthless pursuit of religious unity persuaded many earlier historians that his reign witnessed the creation of an **absolute monarchy**. Louis supposedly crushed the political pretensions of the nobility, leaving them with social grandeur and court posing but no real power. A later generation of historians has revised that view, showing the multiple constraints on Louis's power and his need to cooperate with the nobles. Louis may have declared his absolute power, but in practice he governed through collaboration with nobles, who maintained tremendous prestige and authority in their ancestral lands. Scholars also underline the traditional nature of Louis's motivations. Like his predecessors, Louis XIV sought to enhance the glory of his dynasty and his country, mostly through war. The creation of a new state apparatus was a means to that goal, not an end in itself.

Financial and Economic Management Under Louis XIV: Colbert

France's ability to build armies and fight wars depended on a strong economy. The king named Jean-Baptiste Colbert (1619–1683), the son of a wealthy merchant-financier of Reims, as controller general of finances. Colbert came to manage the entire royal administration and proved himself a financial genius. His central principle was that the wealth and the economy of France should serve the state. He did not invent the system called "mercantilism," but he rigorously applied it to France.

Mercantilism is a collection of governmental policies for the regulation of economic activities, especially commercial activities, by and for the state. In seventeenth- and eighteenth-century economic theory, a nation's international power was thought to be based on its wealth, specifically its gold supply. Because resources were limited, mercantilist theory held, state intervention was needed to secure the largest part of a limited resource. To accumulate gold, a country always had to sell more goods abroad than it bought. Colbert thus insisted that France should be self-sufficient, able to produce within its borders everything French subjects needed. Consequently, the outflow of gold would be halted; debtor states would pay in bullion; unemployment and poverty would greatly diminish; and with the wealth of the nation increased, its power and prestige would be enhanced.

Colbert attempted to accomplish self-sufficiency by supporting old industries and creating new ones, especially in textiles, the most important sector of the economy. To ensure high-quality finished products, Colbert reinforced the system of state inspection and regulation and formed guilds in many industries. Colbert encouraged foreign craftsmen to immigrate to France, and he gave them special privileges. He also took measures to bring more female workers into the labor force. To protect French goods, he abolished many domestic tariffs and enacted high foreign tariffs, which prevented foreign products from competing with French ones.

One of Colbert's most ambitious projects was the creation of a merchant marine to transport French goods. He gave bonuses to French shipowners and shipbuilders and established a method of maritime conscription, arsenals, and academies for training sailors. In 1661 France possessed 18 unseaworthy vessels; by 1681 it had 276 frigates, galleys, and ships of the line. In 1664 Colbert founded the Company of the East Indies with (unfulfilled) hopes of competing with the Dutch for Asian trade.

Online Study Center **Improve Your Grade**
Primary Source: Colbert Promotes "The Advantages of Overseas Trade"

Colbert also hoped to make Canada—rich in untapped minerals and some of the best agricultural land in the world—part of a vast French empire. He gathered four thousand peasants from western France and shipped them to Canada, where they peopled the province of Quebec. (In 1608, one year after the English arrived at Jamestown, Virginia, Sully had established the city of Quebec, which became the capital of French Canada.) Subsequently, the Jesuit Jacques Marquette and the merchant Louis Joliet sailed down the Mississippi River and took possession of the land on both sides as far south as present-day Arkansas. In 1684 the French explorer Robert La Salle continued down the Mississippi to its mouth and claimed vast territories and the rich delta for Louis XIV. The area was called, naturally, "Louisiana."

Colbert's most pressing concern was tax collection. Extensive military reform, war, an expanding professional bureaucracy, and the court at Versailles cost a great deal of money. Yet there were many difficulties in raising taxes. English kings relied on one national assembly, Parliament, for consent to taxation for the entire country. The French system was both more complicated and more inequitable. In some provinces, provincial **estates** (representative bodies of clergy, nobles, and commoners) held the authority to negotiate with the Crown over taxes. In provinces without estates, the king held direct control over taxation through his intendants. Throughout France the nobility and clergy enjoyed exemption from the direct property tax, or *taille*; even bourgeois city-dwellers often gained exemption from it. This meant that the tax burden fell most heavily on those with the least wealth. Finally, the practice of subcontracting tax collection to financiers, known as tax-farmers, meant that a good portion of state money fell into private hands.

Despite these difficulties, Colbert managed to raise revenues significantly by cracking down on inefficiencies and corruption. During Colbert's tenure as controller general, Louis was able to pursue his goals without massive tax increases and without creating a stream of new offices. The constant pressure of warfare after Colbert's death, however, undid many of his economic achievements.

MAP 16.1 The Acquisitions of Louis XIV, 1668–1713
The desire for dynastic glory and the weakness of his German neighbors encouraged Louis's wars, but his country paid a high price for his acquisitions.

Louis XIV's Wars

Louis XIV wrote that "the character of a conqueror is regarded as the noblest and highest of titles." In pursuit of the title of conqueror, he kept France at war for thirty-three of the fifty-four years of his personal rule. In 1666 Louis appointed François le Tellier (later, marquis de Louvois) as secretary of state for war. Under the king's watchful eye, Louvois created a professional army that was modern in the sense that the French state, rather than private nobles, employed the soldiers. Louvois utilized several methods in recruiting troops: dragooning, in which press gangs seized men off the streets; conscription; and, after 1688, lottery. With these techniques, the French army grew to some 340,000 men at its height, enormous by the standards of the day. Louvois also imposed new levels of professionalization. Uniforms and weapons were standardized and a rational system of training and promotion devised. This new military machine gave one state the potential to dominate the affairs of the continent for the first time in European history.

Louis's supreme goal was to expand France to what he considered its "natural" borders and to secure those lands from any threat of outside invasion. A defensive policy in his eyes, it appeared frighteningly aggressive to onlookers. In 1667, using a dynastic excuse, he invaded Flanders, part of the Spanish Netherlands, and Franche-Comté in the east. In consequence, he acquired twelve towns, including the important commercial centers of Lille and Tournai (see Map 16.1). Five years later Louis personally led an army of over one hundred thousand men into Holland, and the Dutch ultimately saved themselves only by opening the dikes and flooding the countryside. The Dutch war lasted six years and eventually involved the Holy Roman Empire and Spain. At the Treaty of Nijmegen (1678), Louis gained additional Flemish towns and all of Franche-Comté. In 1681 Louis seized the city of Strasbourg, and three years later he sent his armies into the province of Lorraine. At that moment the king seemed invincible. In fact, Louis had reached the limit of his expansion. The wars of the 1680s and 1690s brought no additional territories.

Louis understood his wars largely as defensive undertakings, but his enemies naturally viewed French expansion with great alarm. Louis's wars inspired the formation of Europe-wide coalitions against him. As a result, he was obliged to support a huge army in several different theaters of war. This task placed unbearable strains on French resources, especially given the inequitable system of taxation.

Claude Le Peletier, Colbert's successor as minister of finance, resorted to the devaluation of the currency and the old device of selling offices and tax exemptions. Colbert's successors also created new income taxes in 1695 and 1710, which nobles and clergymen had to pay for the first time. In exchange for this money, the king reaffirmed the traditional social hierarchies by granting honors, pensions, and titles to the nobility. Moreover, he did not lessen the burden on commoners, who had to pay the new taxes as well as the old ones.

A series of bad harvests between 1688 and 1694 added social to fiscal catastrophe. The price of wheat skyrocketed. The result was widespread starvation, and in many provinces the death rate rose to several times the normal figure. Parish registers reveal that France buried at least one-tenth of its population in those years, perhaps 2 million in 1693 and 1694 alone. Rising grain prices, new taxes for war, a slump in manufacturing, and the constant nuisance of pillaging troops all meant great suffering for the French people. France wanted peace at any price and won a respite for five years, which was shattered by the War of the Spanish Succession (1701–1713).

In 1700 the childless Spanish king Charles II (r. 1665–1700) died, opening a struggle for control of Spain and its colonies. His will bequeathed the Spanish crown and its empire to Philip of Anjou, Louis XIV's grandson (Louis's wife, Maria-Theresa, had been Charles's sister). This testament violated a prior treaty by which the European powers had agreed to divide the Spanish possessions between the king of France and the Holy Roman emperor, both brothers-in-law of Charles II. Claiming that he was following both Spanish national interests and French dynastic and national interests, Louis broke with the treaty and accepted the will.

In 1701 the English, Dutch, Austrians, and Prussians formed the Grand Alliance against Louis XIV. The allied powers united to prevent France from becoming too strong in Europe and to check France's expanding commercial power in North America, Asia, and Africa. The war dragged on until 1713. The **Peace of Utrecht,** which ended the war, applied the principle of partition. Louis's grandson Philip remained the first Bourbon king of Spain on the understanding that the French and Spanish crowns would never be united. France surrendered Newfoundland, Nova Scotia, and the Hudson Bay territory to England, which also acquired Gibraltar, Minorca, and control of the African slave trade from Spain. The Dutch gained little because Austria received the former Spanish Netherlands (see Map 16.2).

The Peace of Utrecht had important international consequences. It represented the balance-of-power principle in operation, setting limits on the extent to which any one power—in this case, France—could expand. The treaty completed the decline of Spain as a great power. It vastly expanded the British Empire, and it gave European powers experience in international cooperation. The Peace of Utrecht also marked the end of French expansion. Thirty-five years of war had brought rights to all of Alsace and the gain of important cities in the north such as Lille, as well as Strasbourg. But at what price? In 1714 an exhausted France hovered on the brink of bankruptcy. It is no wonder that when Louis XIV died on September 1, 1715, many subjects felt as much relief as they did sorrow.

The Decline of Absolutist Spain in the Seventeenth Century

Spanish absolutism and greatness had preceded those of the French. In the sixteenth century Spain (or, more precisely, the kingdom of Castile) had developed the standard features of absolutist monarchy: a permanent bureaucracy staffed by professionals employed in the various councils of state, a standing army, and national taxes, the *servicios,* which fell most heavily on the poor. France depended on financial and administrative unification within its borders; Spain had developed an international absolutism on the basis of silver bullion from Peru. Spanish gold and silver, armies, and glory had dominated the continent for most of the sixteenth century. In 1580 the Spanish crown annexed Portugal, putting an end to earlier conflicts over the boundaries of their overseas empires.

The Inquisition continued to ensure a dogmatic Catholic orthodoxy in Spain. Converted Jews and Muslims were always under suspicion and subject to imprisonment and even execution. In 1609 Philip III expelled all converted Muslims, known as Moriscos, from Spain. Some three hundred thousand individuals left the country, many going to the Ottoman Empire and North Africa. This measure satisfied the king's Catholic conscience and his fears of potential insurrection, but it was destructive for Spanish society, which lost precious skilled workers and merchants.

Tiepolo: The Triumph of Spain This painting is from the ceiling of the Royal Palace in Madrid. Arguably the greatest Italian painter of the eighteenth century, Giovanni Tiepolo depicted the Spanish Empire as the self-assured champion of Christian cultural values in Europe and America. *(Palacio Real de Madrid/The Bridgeman Art Library)*

By the early seventeenth century the seeds of disaster were sprouting. By 1715 agricultural crisis and population decline, the loss of artisans and merchants, failure to invest in productive enterprises, and intellectual isolation and psychological malaise all combined to reduce Spain to a second-rate power. The fabulous and seemingly inexhaustible flow of silver from Mexico and Peru, together with the sale of cloth, grain, oil, and wine to the colonies, had greatly enriched Spain. In the early seventeenth century, however, the Dutch and English began to trade with the Spanish colonies, cutting into the revenues that had gone to Spain. Mexico and Peru themselves developed local industries, further lessening their need to buy from Spain. Between 1610 and 1650 Spanish trade with the colonies fell 60 percent. At the same time, the native Indians and African slaves who toiled in the South American silver mines suffered frightful epidemics of disease. Ultimately, the lodes started to run dry, and the quantity of metal produced steadily declined.

In Madrid, however, royal expenditures constantly exceeded income. To meet mountainous state debt and declining revenues, the Crown repeatedly devalued the coinage and declared bankruptcy. In 1596, 1607, 1627, 1647, and 1680, Spanish kings found no solution to the problem of an empty treasury other than to cancel the national debt. Given the frequency of cancellation, national credit plummeted.

In contrast to the other countries of western Europe, Spain had only a tiny middle class. Public opinion, taking its cue from the aristocracy, condemned moneymaking

as vulgar and undignified. Those with influence or connections sought titles of nobility and social prestige. Thousands entered economically unproductive professions: there were said to be nine thousand monasteries in the province of Castile alone. The flood of gold and silver had produced severe inflation, pushing the costs of production in the textile industry to the point that Castilian cloth could not compete in colonial and international markets. Many businessmen found so many obstacles in the way of profitable enterprise that they simply gave up.[14]

Spanish aristocrats, attempting to maintain an extravagant lifestyle they could no longer afford, increased the rents on their estates. High rents and heavy taxes in turn drove the peasants from the land. Agricultural production suffered, and peasants departed for the large cities, where they swelled the ranks of unemployed beggars.

Their most Catholic majesties, the kings of Spain, had no solutions to these dire problems. If one can discern personality from pictures, the portraits of Philip III (r. 1598–1622), Philip IV (r. 1622–1665), and Charles II (r. 1665–1700) hanging in the Prado, the Spanish national museum in Madrid, reflect the increasing weakness of the dynasty. Philip III, a pallid, melancholy, and deeply pious man handed the government over to the duke of Lerma, who used it to advance his personal and familial wealth. Philip IV left the management of his several kingdoms to Gaspar de Guzmán, count-duke of Olivares.

Olivares was an able administrator who has often been compared to Richelieu. He did not lack energy and ideas, and he succeeded in devising new sources of revenue. But he clung to the grandiose belief that the solution to Spain's difficulties rested in a return to the imperial tradition. Unfortunately, the imperial tradition demanded the revival of war with the Dutch at the expiration of a twelve-year truce in 1622 and a long war with France over Mantua (1628–1659). Spain thus became embroiled in the Thirty Years' War. These conflicts, on top of an empty treasury, brought disaster.

In 1640 Spain faced serious revolts in Catalonia and Portugal. The Portuguese succeeded in regaining independence from Habsburg rule under their new king, John IV (r. 1640–1656). In 1643 the French inflicted a crushing defeat on a Spanish army at Rocroi in what is now Belgium. By the Treaty of the Pyrenees of 1659, which ended the French-Spanish conflict, Spain was compelled to surrender extensive territories to France. This treaty marked the decline of Spain as a great power. Spain's long conflict with France ended with the bequeathing of the Spanish crown to a French prince, igniting the War of the Spanish Succession.

Seventeenth-century Spain was the victim of its past. It could not forget the grandeur of the sixteenth century and look to the future. The bureaucratic councils of state continued to function as symbols of the absolute Spanish monarchy. But because those councils were staffed by aristocrats, it was the aristocracy that held real power. Spanish absolutism had been built largely on slave-produced gold and silver. When the supply of bullion decreased, the power and standing of the Spanish state declined.

The most cherished Spanish ideals were military glory and strong Roman Catholic faith. In the seventeenth century Spain lacked the finances and the manpower to fight the expensive wars in which it got involved. Spain also ignored the new mercantile ideas and scientific methods because they came from heretical nations, Holland and England. The incredible wealth of South America destroyed what remained of the Spanish middle class and created contempt for business and manual labor.

The decadence of the Habsburg dynasty and the lack of effective royal councilors also contributed to Spanish failure. Spanish leaders seemed to lack the will to reform. Pessimism and fatalism permeated national life. In the reign of Philip IV, a royal council was appointed to plan the construction of a canal linking the Tagus and Manzanares Rivers in Spain. After interminable debate, the committee decided that "if God had intended the rivers to be navigable, He would have made them so."

In the brilliant novel **Don Quixote,** Spanish writer Miguel de Cervantes (1547–1616) produced one of the

Mapping the Past

MAP 16.2 Europe in 1715 The series of treaties commonly called the Peace of Utrecht (April 1713–November 1715) ended the War of the Spanish Succession and redrew the map of Europe. A French Bourbon king succeeded to the Spanish throne. France surrendered to Austria the Spanish Netherlands (later Belgium), then in French hands, and France recognized the Hohenzollern rulers of Prussia. Spain ceded Gibraltar to Great Britain, for which it has been a strategic naval station ever since. Spain also granted to Britain the *asiento,* the contract for supplying African slaves to America. ❶ Identify the areas on the map that changed hands as a result of the Peace of Utrecht. How did these changes affect the balance of power in Europe? ❷ How and why did so many European countries possess scattered or discontiguous territories? What does this suggest about European politics in this period? ❸ Does this map suggest potential for future conflict?

Peeter Snayers: Spanish Troops (detail) The long wars that Spain fought over Dutch independence, in support of Habsburg interests in Germany, and against France left the country militarily exhausted and financially drained by the mid-1600s. Here Spanish troops—thin, emaciated, and probably unpaid—straggle away from battle. *(Museo Nacional del Prado, Madrid. Photo: José Baztan y Alberto Otero)*

great masterpieces of world literature. *Don Quixote* delineates the whole fabric of sixteenth-century Spanish society. The main character, Don Quixote, lives in a world of dreams, traveling about the countryside seeking military glory. From the title of the book, the English language has borrowed the word *quixotic*. Meaning "idealistic but impractical," the term characterizes seventeenth-century Spain. As a leading scholar has written, "The Spaniard convinced himself that reality was what he felt, believed, imagined. He filled the world with heroic reverberations. Don Quixote was born and grew."[15]

Colonial Administration

Whatever its problems within Europe, Spain continued to rule a vast empire in the Americas. Columbus, Cortés, and Pizarro had claimed the lands they had "discovered" for the Crown of Spain. How were these lands governed? According to the Spanish theory of absolutism, the Crown was entitled to exercise full authority over all imperial lands. In the sixteenth century the Crown divided its New World territories into four **viceroyalties,** or administrative divisions: New Spain, which consisted of Mexico, Central America, and present-day California, Arizona, New Mexico, and Texas, with the capital at Mexico City; Peru, originally all the lands in continental South America, later reduced to the territory of modern Peru, Chile, Bolivia, and Ecuador, with the viceregal seat at Lima; New Granada, including present-day Venezuela, Colombia, Panama, and, after 1739, Ecuador, with Bogotá as its administrative center; and La Plata, consisting of Argentina, Uruguay, and Paraguay, with Buenos Aires as the capital.

Within each territory, the viceroy, or imperial governor, exercised broad military and civil authority as the direct representative of the sovereign in Madrid. The viceroy presided over the *audiencia,* a board of twelve to fifteen judges that served as his advisory council and the highest judicial body. The reform-minded Spanish king Charles III (r. 1759–1788) introduced the system of *in-*

tendants, pioneered by the Bourbon kings of France, to the New World territories. These royal officials possessed broad military, administrative, and financial authority within their intendancies and were responsible not to the viceroy but to the monarchy in Madrid.

From the early sixteenth century to the beginning of the nineteenth century, the Spanish monarchy acted on the mercantilist principle that the colonies existed for the financial benefit of the home country. The mining of gold and silver was always the most important industry in the colonies. The Crown claimed the **quinto,** one-fifth of all precious metals mined in South America. Gold and silver yielded the Spanish monarchy 25 percent of its total income. In return, it shipped manufactured goods to the Americas and discouraged the development of native industries.

The Portuguese governed their colony of Brazil in a similar manner. After the union of the Crowns of Portugal and Spain in 1580, Spanish administrative forms were introduced. Local officials called *corregidores* held judicial and military powers. Mercantilist policies placed severe restrictions on Brazilian industries that might compete with those of Portugal. In the seventeenth century the use of black slave labor made possible the cultivation of coffee and cotton, and in the eighteenth century Brazil led the world in the production of sugar. The unique feature of colonial Brazil's culture and society was its thoroughgoing intermixture of Indians, whites, and blacks.

The Culture of Absolutism

Under absolutist monarchs, culture became an instrument of state power. The baroque style in art and music flourished in the context of the Catholic Reformation. Baroque masters like Rubens painted portraits celebrating the glory of European monarchs. The baroque was particularly popular in Spain, Italy, and central Europe. Along with art, architecture became an important tool for absolutist monarchs. Louis XIV made the magnificent palace of Versailles the center of his kingdom, inspiring imitators across Europe (see Chapter 17). Even language reflected the growing power of the Crown. Within France Richelieu established an academy to oversee French literature and language. Outside its borders French became the common language of the European elite.

- **What cultural forms flourished under absolutist governments?**

Baroque Art and Music

Throughout European history, the cultural tastes of one age have often seemed unsatisfactory to the next. So it was with the baroque. The term **baroque** itself may have come from the Portuguese word for an "odd-shaped, imperfect pearl" and was commonly used by late-eighteenth-century art critics as an expression of scorn for what they considered an overblown, unbalanced style. These critics also scorned the Gothic style of medieval cathedrals in favor of a classicism inspired by antiquity and the Renaissance. Specialists now agree that the baroque style marked one of the high points in the history of Western culture.

Rome and the revitalized Catholic Church of the later sixteenth century played an important role in the early development of the baroque. The papacy and the Jesuits encouraged the growth of an intensely emotional, exuberant art. These patrons wanted artists to go beyond the Renaissance focus on pleasing a small, wealthy cultural elite. They wanted artists to appeal to the senses and thereby touch the souls and kindle the faith of ordinary churchgoers while proclaiming the power and confidence of the reformed Catholic Church. In addition to this underlying religious emotionalism, the baroque drew its sense of drama, motion, and ceaseless striving from the Catholic Reformation. The interior of the famous Jesuit Church of Jesus in Rome—the Gesù—combined all these characteristics in its lavish, shimmering, wildly active decorations and frescoes.

Taking definite shape in Italy after 1600, the baroque style in the visual arts developed with exceptional vigor in Catholic countries—in Spain and Latin America, Austria, southern Germany, and Poland. Yet baroque art was more than just "Catholic art" in the seventeenth century and the first half of the eighteenth. True, neither Protestant England nor the Netherlands ever came fully under the spell of the baroque, but neither did Catholic France. And Protestants accounted for some of the finest examples of baroque style, especially in music. The baroque style spread partly because its tension and bombast spoke to an agitated age that was experiencing great violence and controversy in politics and religion.

In painting, the baroque reached maturity early with Peter Paul Rubens (1577–1640), the most outstanding and most representative of baroque painters. Studying in his native Flanders and in Italy, where he was influenced by masters of the High Renaissance such as Michelangelo, Rubens developed his own rich, sensuous, colorful style, which was characterized by animated figures, melodramatic contrasts, and monumental size. Rubens excelled

Juan de Pareja: The Calling of Saint Matthew Using rich but subdued colors, Pareja depicts the biblical text (Mark 2:13–17), with Jesus in traditional first-century dress and the other figures, arranged around a table covered with an Oriental carpet, in seventeenth-century apparel. Matthew, at Jesus' right hand, seems surprised by the "call." Pareja, following a long tradition, includes himself (*standing, rear center*). *(Museo Nacional del Prado, Madrid/The Bridgeman Art Library)*

in glorifying monarchs such as Queen Mother Marie de' Medici of France (see the painting on page 531). He was also a devout Catholic; nearly half of his pictures treat Christian subjects. Yet one of Rubens's trademarks was fleshy, sensual nudes who populate his canvases as Roman goddesses, water nymphs, and remarkably voluptuous saints and angels.

Rubens was enormously successful. To meet the demand for his work, he established a large studio and hired many assistants to execute his rough sketches and gigantic murals. Sometimes the master artist added only the finishing touches. Rubens's wealth and position—on occasion he was given special diplomatic assignments by the Habsburgs—affirmed that distinguished artists continued to enjoy the high social status they had won in the Renaissance.

In music, the baroque style reached its culmination almost a century later in the dynamic, soaring lines of the endlessly inventive Johann Sebastian Bach (1685–1750).

Organist and choirmaster of several Lutheran churches across Germany, Bach was equally at home writing secular concertos and sublime religious cantatas. Bach's organ music combined the baroque spirit of invention, tension, and emotion in an unforgettable striving toward the infinite. Unlike Rubens, Bach was not fully appreciated in his lifetime, but since the early nineteenth century his reputation has grown steadily.

Court Culture

For much of the seventeenth century, the courts of Europe looked to France, and to the palace of Versailles, for cultural as well as political inspiration. (See the feature "Listening to the Past: The Court at Versailles" on pages 556–557.) Versailles began as a modest hunting lodge. Under Louis XIV's orders, his architects, Le Nôtre and Le Vau, turned what the duke of Saint-Simon called "the most dismal and thankless of sights" into a magnificent palace. Everywhere, the viewer had a sense of grandeur, vastness, and elegance. Enormous staterooms became display galleries for inlaid tables, Italian marble statuary, tapestries woven at the royal factory in Paris, and beautiful furniture. In the gigantic Hall of Mirrors, hundreds of candles illuminated the domed ceiling, where allegorical paintings celebrated the king's victories. The formal gardens celebrated the rationality and order imposed by the Sun King; its classical sculptures depicted Louis as Apollo, king of the gods.

In 1682 Louis formally established his court at Versailles, which became the center of the kingdom: a model of rational order and the perfect symbol of the king's power. The art and architecture of Versailles were tools of Louis's policy, used to overawe his subjects and foreign visitors. The Russian tsar Peter the Great imitated Versailles in the construction of his palace, Peterhof, as did the Prussian emperor Frederick the Great in his palace at Potsdam outside Berlin and the Habsburgs at Schonbrunn outside Vienna. (See the feature "Images in Society: Absolutist Palace Building" on pages 568–569.)

The palace was the summit of political, social, and cultural life. The king required all great nobles to spend at least part of the year in attendance on him at Versailles. Between three thousand and ten thousand people occupied the palace each day. Given the demand for space, even high nobles had to make do with cramped and uncomfortable living quarters. The palace gardens, and the palace itself on some occasions, were open to the public, allowing even local peasants a glimpse of their sovereign. More than a royal residence or administrative center, Versailles was a mirror of French greatness to the world.

Much has been made of the "domestication" of the nobility at Versailles. Elaborate rituals attended every moment of Louis's day, from waking up and dressing in the morning to removing his clothing and retiring at night. Nobles had to follow a tortuous system of court etiquette, and they vied for the honor of serving the monarch, with the highest in rank claiming the privilege to hand the king his shirt. Endless squabbles broke out over what type of chair one could sit on at court and the order in which great nobles entered and were seated in the chapel for Mass.

These rituals were far from meaningless or trivial. The king controlled immense resources and privileges; access to him meant favored treatment for pensions, military and religious posts, honorary titles, and a host of other benefits. Courtiers sought these rewards for themselves and for their family members and followers. As in ancient Rome, patron-client relations—in which a higher-ranked individual protected a lower-ranked one in return for loyalty and services—dominated political life. **Patronage** flowed from the court to the provinces; it was the mechanism through which Louis gained cooperation from social elites.

One family demonstrates the interplay between the state's rationalizing impulses and its reliance on very traditional patterns of nepotism and patronage. Long credited as the "modernizer" of the French army, the minister Louvois acquired his position through family ties, not merit. His father, Michel LeTellier was secretary of war from 1643 to 1677; Louvois succeeded his father in this position from 1677 to his death in 1691 and was succeeded in turn by his own son Barbézieux from 1691 to 1701. The Louvois family not only had powerful connections within the French bureaucracy, but also bought court offices for younger family members to ensure their influence at Versailles.

Although they were denied public offices and posts, women played a central role in the patronage system. At court, the king's wife, mistresses, and other female relatives used their high rank to establish their own patronage relations. They recommended individuals for honors, advocated policy decisions, and brokered alliances between noble factions. Noblewomen played a similar role, bringing their family connections to marriage to form powerful social networks. Onlookers sometimes resented the influence of powerful women at court. The Duke of Saint-Simon said of Madame de Maintenon, Louis XIV's mistress and secret second wife:

The power of Madame de Maintenon was, as may be imagined, immense. She had everybody in her hands, from the highest and most favored ministers to the meanest subject of the realm. Many people have been ruined by her, without having been able to discover the author of the ruin, search as they might.

French Classicism

To this day, culture is a central element of French national pride and identity. French emphasis on culture dates back to Cardinal Richelieu, whose efforts at state centralization embraced cultural activities. In 1635 he gave official recognition to a group of scholars interested in grammar and rhetoric. Thus was born the French Academy. With Richelieu's encouragement, the French Academy began the preparation of a dictionary to standardize the French language; the dictionary was completed in 1694 and has been updated in many successive editions. The Academy survives today as a prestigious society, and retains authority over correct usage in the French language.

Scholars characterize the art and literature of the age of Louis XIV as **French classicism.** By this they mean that the artists and writers of the late seventeenth century imitated the subject matter and style of classical antiquity, that their work resembled that of Renaissance Italy, and that French art possessed the classical qualities of discipline, balance, and restraint. This was a movement away from the perceived excesses of baroque style.

Louis XIV danced gracefully at court ballets in his youth and was an enthusiastic patron of the arts. Music and theater frequently served as backdrops for court ceremonials. Louis favored Jean-Baptiste Lully (1632–1687), whose orchestral works combined lively animation with the restrained austerity typical of French classicism. Lully also composed court ballets, and his operatic productions were a powerful influence throughout Europe. Louis supported François Couperin (1668–1733), whose harpsichord and organ works possessed the regal grandeur the king loved, and Marc-Antoine Charpentier (1634–1704), whose solemn religious music entertained him at meals. Charpentier received a pension for the *Te Deums,* hymns of thanksgiving, he composed to celebrate French military victories.

Louis XIV loved the stage, and in the plays of Molière and Racine his court witnessed the finest achievements in the history of the French theater. When Jean-Baptiste Poquelin (1622–1673), the son of a prosperous tapestry maker, refused to join his father's business and entered the theater, he took the stage name "Molière." As playwright, stage manager, director, and actor, Molière produced comedies that exposed the hypocrisies and follies of society through brilliant caricature. *Tartuffe* satirized the religious hypocrite; *Le Bourgeois Gentilhomme* (The Bourgeois Gentleman) attacked the social parvenu; and *Les Précieuses ridicules* (The Pretentious Young Ladies) mocked the pretensions of the *précieuses,* elite women who ran intellectual salons and wrote and spoke in an elegant and pretentious manner. In structure Molière's plays followed classical models, but they were based on careful social observation. Molière made the bourgeoisie the butt of his ridicule; he stopped short of criticizing the high nobility, reflecting the policy of his royal patron.

Online Study Center **Improve Your Grade**
Primary Source: Molière's Bourgeois Gentlewoman, Mme. Jourdain, Rejects a Noble Son-in-Law

While Molière dissected social mores, his contemporary Jean Racine (1639–1699) based his tragic dramas on Greek and Roman legends. His persistent theme was the conflict of good and evil. Several plays—*Andromaque, Bérénice, Iphigénie,* and *Phèdre*—bear the names of women and deal with the power of female passion. Louis preferred *Mithridate* and *Britannicus* because of the "grandeur" of their themes. For simplicity of language, symmetrical structure, and calm restraint, the plays of Racine represent the finest examples of French classicism. His tragedies and Molière's comedies are still produced today.

With Versailles as the center of European politics, French culture grew in international prestige. Beginning in the reign of Louis XIV, French became the language of polite society and international diplomacy. French also gradually replaced Latin as the language of scholarship and learning. The royal courts of Sweden, Russia, Poland, and Germany all spoke French. In the eighteenth century the great Russian aristocrats were more fluent in French than in Russian. In England the first Hanoverian king, George I, spoke fluent French and only halting English. France inspired a cosmopolitan European culture in the late seventeenth century, which looked to Versailles as its center.

Constitutionalism

While France and later Prussia, Russia, and Austria solved the question of sovereignty with the absolutist state, England and Holland evolved toward the constitutional state. **Constitutionalism** is the limitation of government by law. Constitutionalism also implies a balance between the authority and power of the government, on the one hand, and the rights and liberties of the subjects, on the other.

A nation's constitution may be written or unwritten. It may be embodied in one basic document, occasionally revised by amendment, like the Constitution of the United States. Or it may be only partly formalized and include parliamentary statutes, judicial decisions, and a body of traditional procedures and practices, like the English and Dutch constitutions. Whether written or unwritten, a constitution gets its binding force from the government's acknowledgment that it must respect that constitution—that is, that the state must govern according to the laws. In a constitutional monarchy, a king or queen serves as the head of state and possesses some residual political authority, but the ultimate, or sovereign, power rests in the electorate.

A constitutional government is not the same as a democratic government. In a complete democracy, *all* the people have the right to participate either directly or indirectly (through their elected representatives) in the government of the state. Most men could not vote in Europe until the late nineteenth century, and women gained the franchise only in the twentieth century.

- **What is constitutionalism, and how did this form of government emerge in England and the Dutch Republic?**

Absolutist Claims in England (1603–1649)

In 1588 Queen Elizabeth I of England exercised very great personal power; by 1689 the English monarchy was severely circumscribed. Change in England was anything but orderly. Seventeenth-century England executed one king and experienced a bloody civil war; experimented with military dictatorship, then restored the son of the murdered king; and finally, after a bloodless revolution, established constitutional monarchy. Political stability came only in the 1690s. After such a violent and tumultuous century, how did England produce a constitutional monarchy? What combination of political, socioeconomic, and religious factors brought on a civil war in 1642–1649 and then the constitutional settlement of 1688–1689?

The extraordinary success of Elizabeth I rested on her political shrewdness and flexibility, her careful management of finances, her wise selection of ministers, her clever manipulation of Parliament, and her sense of royal dignity and devotion to hard work. A rare female monarch, Elizabeth imposed her authority in part by refusing to marry. If she had married, proper wifely submission to her husband would have made it difficult to assert royal authority over her subjects. The problem with this strategy was that it left the queen with no immediate heir to continue her legacy.

In 1603 Elizabeth's Scottish cousin James Stuart succeeded her as James I (r. 1603–1625). King James was well educated, learned, and, with thirty-five years' experience as king of Scotland, politically shrewd. But he was not as interested in displaying the majesty of monarchy as Elizabeth had been. Urged to wave at the crowds who waited to greet their new ruler, James complained that he was tired and threatened to drop his breeches "so they can cheer at my arse." The new king failed to live up to the role expected of him in England. Moreover, in contrast to Elizabeth, James was a poor judge of character, and in a society already hostile to the Scots, James's Scottish accent was a disadvantage.[16]

James's greatest problems, however, arose in resistance to his claims for monarchical authority. Like his French counterpart, James was devoted to the theory of the divine right of kings. He expressed his ideas in his essay "The Trew Law of Free Monarchy." According to James I, a monarch has a divine (or God-given) right to his authority and is responsible only to God. Rebellion is the worst of political crimes. If a king orders something evil, the subject should respond with passive disobedience but should be prepared to accept any penalty for noncompliance. James went so far as to lecture the House of Commons: "There are no privileges and immunities which can stand against a divinely appointed King." This notion, implying total royal jurisdiction over the liberties, persons, and properties of English men and women, formed the basis of the Stuart concept of absolutism. Such a view ran directly counter to the long-standing English idea that a person's property could not be taken away without due process of law. James's expression of such views before the English House of Commons was a grave political mistake.

The House of Commons guarded the state's pocketbook, and James and later Stuart kings badly needed to open that pocketbook. Elizabeth had left James a sizable royal debt. Elizabeth had managed to escape public disapprobation for the debt, but James was left to face the consequences. Elizabeth had also left her Stuart successors a House of Commons that appreciated its own financial strength and intended to use that strength to acquire a greater say in the government of the state. The knights and burgesses who sat at Westminster in the late sixteenth and early seventeenth centuries wanted a voice in royal expenditures, religious reform, and foreign affairs. Essentially, the Commons wanted a measure of sovereignty.

Profound social changes had occurred since the sixteenth century. The English House of Commons during the reigns of James I and his son Charles I (r. 1625–1649) was very different from the assembly Henry VIII had manipulated into passing his Reformation legislation. The dissolution of the monasteries and the sale of monastic land had enriched many people. Enclosure of the common lands and new agricultural techniques had also enriched landowners, while many people invested successfully in commercial ventures, such as the expanding cloth industry. These developments led to a great deal of social mobility. Both in commerce and in agriculture, the English in the late sixteenth and early seventeenth centuries were capitalists, investing their profits to make more money.

The typical pattern was for the commercially successful to set themselves up as country gentry, thus creating an elite group that possessed a far greater proportion of land and of the national wealth in 1640 than had been the case in 1540. Small wonder that in 1640 someone could declare in the House of Commons that "We could buy

Van Dyck: Charles I (ca 1635) Anthony Van Dyck was the greatest of Rubens's many students. In 1633 he became court painter to Charles I. His portrait of Charles just dismounted from a horse emphasizes the aristocratic bearing, elegance, and innate authority of the king. This monarch seemingly needs no pomp or magnificence to display his sovereignty. Van Dyck's success led to innumerable commissions by members of the court and aristocratic society. He had a profound influence on English portraiture and was revered, for example, by Gainsborough. Some scholars believe that this portrait influenced Rigaud's 1701 portrait of Louis XIV (see page 522). *(Scala/Art Resource, NY)*

the House of Lords three times over." Increased wealth had also produced a better-educated and more articulate House of Commons. Many members had acquired at least a smattering of legal knowledge, which they used to search for medieval precedents from which to argue against the king.

In England, unlike France, there was no social stigma attached to paying taxes. Members of the House of Commons were willing to assess and pay taxes provided they had some say in the expenditure of those taxes and in the formulation of state policies. The Stuart kings, however, considered such ambitions intolerable and a threat to their divine-right prerogative. Consequently, at every Parliament between 1603 and 1640, bitter squabbles erupted between the Crown and the articulate and legally minded Commons. Charles I's attempt to govern without Parliament (1629–1640) and to finance his government by arbitrary nonparliamentary levies, brought the country to a crisis.

Religious Divides

Religious issues also embittered relations between the king and the House of Commons. In the early seventeenth century increasing numbers of English people felt dissatisfied with the Church of England established by Henry VIII and reformed by Elizabeth. Many **Puritans** (see page 463) believed that the Reformation had not gone far enough. They wanted to "purify" the Anglican church of Roman Catholic elements—elaborate vestments and ceremonials, bishops, and even the giving and wearing of wedding rings.

It is difficult to establish what proportion of the English population was Puritan. According to present scholarly consensus, the dominant religious groups in the early seventeenth century were Calvinist; their more zealous members were Puritans. It also seems clear that many English people were attracted by the socioeconomic implications of John Calvin's theology. Calvinism emphasized hard work, sobriety, thrift, competition, and postponement of pleasure, and it tended to link poverty with weakness and moral corruption. These values, which have frequently been called the "Protestant ethic" or "capitalist ethic," fit in precisely with the economic approaches and practices of many successful business people and farmers. While it is hazardous to identify capitalism with Protestantism—there were many successful Catholic capitalists, for example—the "Protestant virtues" represented the prevailing values of members of the House of Commons.

Puritans wanted to abolish bishops in the Church of England, and when James I said, "No bishop, no king," he meant that the bishops were among the chief supporters of the throne. His son Charles I gave the impression of being sympathetic to Roman Catholicism. First, Charles married the French Catholic princess Henrietta Maria, a daughter of Henry IV. Charles also supported the policies of William Laud (1573–1645), archbishop of Canterbury, who tried to impose elaborate ritual on all churches. Laud insisted on complete uniformity of church services and enforced that uniformity through an ecclesiastical court called the "Court of High Commission." People believed that the country was being led back to Roman Catholicism.

In 1637 Laud attempted to impose two new elements on church organization in Scotland: a new prayer book, modeled on the Anglican *Book of Common Prayer*, and bishoprics, which the Presbyterian Scots firmly rejected. The Scots therefore revolted. To finance an army to put down the Scots, King Charles was compelled to summon Parliament in November 1640.

Charles I was an intelligent man, but contemporaries found him deceitful, dishonest, and treacherous. After quarreling with Parliament over his right to collect customs duties on wine and wool and over what the Commons perceived as religious innovations, Charles had dissolved Parliament in 1629. From 1629 to 1640, he ruled without Parliament, financing his government through extraordinary stopgap levies considered illegal by most English people. For example, the king revived a medieval law requiring coastal districts to help pay the cost of ships for defense, but he levied the tax, called "ship money," on inland as well as coastal counties. Most members of Parliament believed that such taxation without consent amounted to despotism. Consequently, they were not willing to trust the king with an army. Moreover, many supported the Scots' resistance to Charles's religious innovations and had little wish for military action against them. Accordingly, this Parliament, called the "Long Parliament" because it sat from 1640 to 1660, enacted legislation that limited the power of the monarch and made arbitrary government impossible.

In 1641 the Commons passed the Triennial Act, which compelled the king to summon Parliament every three years. The Commons impeached Archbishop Laud and abolished the Court of High Commission, then went further and threatened to abolish bishops. King Charles, fearful of a Scottish invasion—the original reason for summoning Parliament—accepted these measures. Understanding and peace were not achieved, however, partly because radical members of the Commons pushed increasingly revolutionary propositions, and partly because Charles maneuvered to rescind those he had already approved.

The next act in the conflict was precipitated by the outbreak of rebellion in Ireland. Ever since Henry II had conquered Ireland in 1171, English governors had mercilessly ruled the land, and English landlords had ruthlessly exploited the Irish people. The English Reformation had made a bad situation worse: because the Irish remained Catholic, religious differences united with economic and political oppression. In 1641 the Catholic gentry led an uprising in response to a feared invasion by anti-Catholic forces of the Long Parliament.

Puritan Occupations These twelve engravings depict typical Puritan occupations and show that the Puritans came primarily from the artisan and lower middle classes. The governing classes and peasants adhered to the traditions of the Church of England. *(Visual Connection Archive)*

Without an army, Charles I could neither come to terms with the Scots nor respond to the Irish rebellion, and the Long Parliament remained unwilling to place an army under a king it did not trust. After a failed attempt to arrest parliamentary leaders, Charles left London for the north of England. There, he recruited an army drawn from the nobility and its cavalry staff, the rural gentry, and mercenaries. The parliamentary army was composed of the militia of the city of London, country squires with business connections, and men with a firm belief in the spiritual duty of serving.

The English civil war (1642–1649) tested whether sovereignty in England was to reside in the king or in Parliament. In 1645 Parliament reorganized its forces into the **New Model Army** under the leadership of Sir Thomas Fairfax and Oliver Cromwell, a member of the House of Commons who had emerged as a military leader during the war. After three years of inconclusive fighting, parliamentary forces finally defeated the king's armies at the Battles of Naseby and Langport in the summer of 1645. To all appearances, the war was over and the parliamentary side had prevailed. The only remaining issue was to obtain formal recognition from Charles on restrictions on royal authority and church reform. Charles, though, refused to concede defeat. Both sides jockeyed for position, waiting for a decisive event. This arrived in the form of the army. In 1647 Cromwell's forces captured the king and dismissed members of the Parliament who opposed his actions. In 1649 the remaining representatives, known as the "Rump Parliament," put Charles on trial for high treason, a severe blow to the theory of divine-right monarchy. Charles was found guilty and beheaded on January 30, 1649, an act that sent shockwaves around Europe.

Puritanical Absolutism in England: Cromwell and the Protectorate

With the execution of Charles, kingship was abolished. A *commonwealth,* or republican government, was proclaimed. Theoretically, legislative power rested in the surviving members of Parliament, and executive power was lodged in a council of state. In fact, the army that had defeated the king controlled the government, and Oliver Cromwell controlled the army. Though called the **Protectorate,** the rule of Cromwell (1653–1658) constituted military dictatorship.

The army prepared a constitution, the Instrument of Government (1653), that invested executive power in a lord protector (Cromwell) and a council of state. The instrument provided for triennial parliaments and gave Par-

Cartoon of 1649: "The Royall Oake of Brittayne" Chopping down this tree signifies the end of royal authority, stability, Magna Carta (see page 272), and the rule of law. As pigs graze (representing the unconcerned common people), being fattened for slaughter, Oliver Cromwell, with his feet in Hell, quotes Scripture. This is a royalist view of the collapse of Charles I's government and the rule of Cromwell. *(Courtesy of the Trustees of the British Museum)*

liament the sole power to raise taxes. But after repeated disputes, Cromwell tore the document up. He continued the standing army and proclaimed quasi-martial law. He divided England into twelve military districts, each governed by a major general. The state rigorously censored the press, forbade sports, and kept the theaters closed in England. On the issue of religion, Cromwell favored some degree of toleration, and the Instrument of Government gave all Christians except Roman Catholics the right to practice their faith. As for Irish Catholicism, Cromwell identified it with sedition and heresy. In September 1649 his army crushed a rebellion at Drogheda and massacred the garrison. Another massacre followed in October. These brutal acts left a legacy of Irish hatred for England that has not yet subsided. Cromwell defended his actions by claiming to have acted only against soldiers in arms and said that a strong deterrent would prevent future bloodshed. After Cromwell's departure for England, the atrocities worsened. Sir William Petty, who served the English government in Ireland, estimated that over six hundred thousand people, or one-third of Ireland's population, died or were exiled as a result of the civil wars. The English banned Catholicism in Ireland, executed priests, and confiscated land from Catholics for English and Scottish settlers.

In England, Cromwell's regulation of the nation's economy had features typical of seventeenth-century absolutism. The lord protector's policies were mercantilist, similar to those Colbert established in France. Cromwell enforced a Navigation Act (1651), requiring that English goods be transported on English ships. The Navigation Act was a great boost to the development of an English merchant marine and brought about a short but successful war with the commercially threatened Dutch. Cromwell also welcomed the immigration of Jews because of their skills, and they began to return to England after four centuries of absence.

Military government collapsed when Cromwell died in 1658 and his ineffectual son succeeded him. Fed up with military rule, the English longed for a return to civilian government, restoration of the common law, and social stability. Government by military dictatorship was an experiment that the English never forgot or repeated. By 1660 they were ready to restore the monarchy.

The Restoration of the English Monarchy

The Restoration of 1660 re-established the monarchy in the person of Charles II (r. 1660–1685), eldest son of Charles I, who returned from exile on the continent to take the throne. At the same time, both houses of Parliament were restored, together with the established Anglican church, the courts of law, and the system of local government through justices of the peace. The Restoration failed to resolve two serious problems, however. What was to be the attitude of the state toward Puritans, Catholics, and dissenters from the established church? And what was to be the relationship between the king and Parliament?

About the first of these issues, Charles II, an easygoing and sensual man, was basically indifferent. He was not interested in doctrinal issues. Members of Parliament were, and they enacted a body of laws that sought to compel religious uniformity. Those who refused to receive the Eucharist of the Church of England could not vote, hold public office, preach, teach, attend the universities, or even assemble for meetings, according to the **Test Act** of 1673. But these restrictions could not be enforced. When the Quaker William Penn held a meeting of his Friends and was arrested, the jury refused to convict him.

In politics Charles II was determined "not to set out in his travels again," which meant that he intended to get along with Parliament. Generally good rapport existed between the king and the strongly royalist Parliament that had restored him. This rapport was due largely to the king's appointment of a council of five men who served both as his major advisers and as members of Parliament, thus acting as liaison agents between the executive and the legislature. This body—known as the "Cabal" from the names of its five members (Clifford, Arlington, Buckingham, Ashley-Cooper, and Lauderdale)—was an ancestor of the later cabinet system. Although its members sometimes disagreed and intrigued among themselves, it gradually came to be accepted that the Cabal was answerable in Parliament for the decisions of the king. This development gave rise to the concept of ministerial responsibility: royal ministers must answer to the Commons.

Harmony between the Crown and Parliament rested on the understanding that Charles would summon frequent Parliaments and that Parliament would vote him sufficient revenues. But Parliament did not grant him an adequate income. Accordingly, in 1670 Charles entered into a secret agreement with his cousin Louis XIV (Charles's mother Henrietta-Maria was the daughter of Henry IV, Louis' grandfather). The French king would give Charles two hundred thousand pounds annually, and in return Charles would relax the laws against Catholics, gradually re-Catholicize England, support French policy against the Dutch, and convert to Catholicism himself. When the details of this treaty leaked out, a great wave of anti-Catholic fear swept England. This fear was compounded by a crucial fact: with no legitimate heir, Charles would be succeeded by his Catholic brother, James, duke of York. A combination of hatred for French absolutism and hostility to Catholicism produced virtual hysteria. The Commons passed an exclusion bill denying the succession to a Roman Catholic, but Charles quickly dissolved Parliament, and the bill never became law.

When James II (r. 1685–1688) succeeded his brother, the worst English anti-Catholic fears, already aroused by Louis XIV's revocation of the Edict of Nantes, were realized. In violation of the Test Act, James appointed Roman Catholics to positions in the army, the universities, and local government. When these actions were challenged in the courts, the judges, whom James had appointed, decided for the king. The king was suspending the law at will and appeared to be reviving the absolutism of his father and grandfather. He went further. Attempting to broaden his base of support with Protestant dissenters and nonconformists, James issued a declaration of indulgence granting religious freedom to all.

Two events gave the signals for revolution. First, seven bishops of the Church of England petitioned the king that they not be forced to read the declaration of indulgence because of their belief that it was an illegal act. They were imprisoned in the Tower of London but subsequently acquitted amid great public enthusiasm. Second, in June 1688 James's second wife produced a male heir. A Catholic dynasty seemed ensured. The fear of a Roman Catholic monarchy supported by France and ruling outside the law prompted a group of eminent persons to offer the English throne to James's Protestant daughter Mary and her Dutch husband, Prince William of Orange. In December 1688 James II, his queen, and their infant son fled to France and became pensioners of Louis XIV. Early in 1689 William and Mary were crowned king and queen of England.

The Triumph of England's Parliament: Constitutional Monarchy and Cabinet Government

The English call the events of 1688 and 1689 the "Glorious Revolution" because it replaced one king with another with a minimum of bloodshed. It also represented the destruction, once and for all, of the idea of divine-right monarchy. William and Mary accepted the English throne from Parliament and in so doing explicitly recognized the supremacy of Parliament. The revolution of 1688 established the principle that sovereignty, the ultimate power in the state, was divided between king and Parliament and that the king ruled with the consent of the governed.

The men who brought about the revolution quickly framed their intentions in the Bill of Rights, the cornerstone of the modern British constitution. The principles of the Bill of Rights were formulated in direct response to Stuart absolutism. Law was to be made in Parliament; once made, it could not be suspended by the Crown. Parliament had to be called at least once every three years. Both elections to and debate in Parliament were to be free in the sense that the Crown was not to interfere in them (this aspect of the bill was widely disregarded in the eighteenth century). The independence of the judiciary was established. No longer could the Crown get the judicial decisions it wanted by threats of removal. There was to be no standing army in peacetime—a limitation designed to prevent the repetition of Cromwellian military government. The Bill of Rights granted "that the subjects which are Protestants may have arms for their defense suitable to their conditions and as allowed by law,"[17] meaning that Catholics could not possess arms because the Protestant majority feared them. Additional legislation granted freedom of worship to Protestant dissenters and nonconformists and required that the English monarch always be Protestant.

The Glorious Revolution found its best defense in political philosopher John Locke's **Second Treatise of Civil Government** (1690). Locke (1632–1704) maintained that people set up civil governments to protect life, liberty, and property. A government that oversteps its proper function—protecting the natural rights of life, liberty, and property—becomes a tyranny. (By "natural" rights Locke meant rights basic to all men because all have the ability to reason.) Under a tyrannical government, the people have the natural right to rebellion. Such rebellion can be avoided if the government carefully respects the rights of citizens and if people zealously defend their liberty. Arguing for a close relationship between economic and political freedom, Locke linked economic liberty and private property with political freedom. On the basis of this link, he justified limiting the vote to property owners. Locke served as the great spokesman for the liberal English revolution of 1688 and 1689 and for representative government. His idea that there are natural or universal rights equally valid for all peoples and societies was especially popular in colonial America. (Colonists also appreciated his arguments that Native Americans had no property rights since they did not cultivate the land and, by extension, no political rights because they possessed no property.)

Online Study Center **Improve Your Grade**
Primary Source: John Locke's Vindication for the Glorious Revolution: The Social Contract

The events of 1688 and 1689 did not constitute a *democratic* revolution. The revolution placed sovereignty in Parliament, and Parliament represented the upper classes. The great majority of English people acquired no say in their government. The English revolution established a constitutional monarchy; it also inaugurated an age of aristocratic government that lasted at least until 1832 and in many ways until 1928, when women received full voting rights.

The Dutch Republic in the Seventeenth Century

In the late sixteenth century the seven northern provinces of the Netherlands fought for and won their independence from Spain as the Republic of United Provinces of the Netherlands—an independence that was confirmed by the Peace of Westphalia ending the Thirty Years' War in 1648 (see page 563). The seventeenth century witnessed an unparalleled flowering of Dutch scientific, artistic, and literary achievement. In this period, often called the "golden age of the Netherlands," Dutch ideas and attitudes played a profound role in shaping a new and modern worldview. At the same time, the United Provinces was another model of the development of the modern constitutional state.

Within each province, an oligarchy of wealthy merchants called "regents" handled domestic affairs in the local Estates. The provincial Estates held virtually all the power. A federal assembly, or **States General,** handled matters of foreign affairs, such as war. But the States General did not possess sovereign authority; all issues had to be referred back to the local Estates for approval. The States General appointed a representative, the **stadholder,** in each province. As the highest executive there, the stadholder carried out ceremonial functions and was responsible for defense and good order. Maurice and

Jan Steen: The Christening Feast As the mother, surrounded by midwives, rests in bed (*rear left*) and the father proudly displays the swaddled child, thirteen other people, united by gestures and gazes, prepare the celebratory meal. Very prolific, Steen was a master of warm-hearted domestic scenes. In contrast to the order and cleanliness of many seventeenth-century Dutch genre paintings, Steen's more disorderly portrayals gave rise to the epithet "a Jan Steen household," meaning an untidy house. *(Wallace Collection, London/The Bridgeman Art Library)*

Room from Het Scheepje (The Little Ship) A retired sea captain who became a successful brewer in Haarlem owned the house (adjacent to his brewery) that included this room. The brass chandelier, plates, tiles, Turkish rug on the table (probably from Transylvania in the Ottoman Empire), oak mantelpiece, and paneling make this a superb example of a Dutch domestic interior during the golden age. A bed built into the wall paneling was warmed at night by coals in the pan hanging by the fireplace. *(Room from Het Scheepje, Haarlem, The Netherlands, early 17th century. Philadelphia Museum of Art, Gift of Edward W. Bok. 1928-66-1)*

William Louis, the sons of William the Silent, held the office of stadholder in all seven provinces. As members of the House of Orange, they were closely identified with Dutch patriotism. The regents in each province jealously guarded local independence and resisted efforts at centralization. Nevertheless, Holland, which had the largest navy and the most wealth, dominated the republic and the States General. Significantly, the Estates assembled at Holland's capital, The Hague.

The government of the United Provinces had none of the standard categories of seventeenth-century political organization. The Dutch were not monarchical but rather fiercely republican. The government was controlled by wealthy merchants and financiers. Though they were rich, their values were strongly middle class, not aristocratic. The Dutch republic was not a strong federation but a confederation—that is, a weak union of strong provinces. The provinces were a temptation to powerful neighbors, yet the Dutch resisted the long Spanish effort at reconquest and withstood both French and English attacks in the second half of the century.

The political success of the Dutch rested on the phenomenal commercial prosperity of the Netherlands. The moral and ethical bases of that commercial wealth were thrift, frugality, and religious toleration. John Calvin had written, "From where do the merchant's profits come except from his own diligence and industry?" This attitude encouraged a sturdy people who had waged a centuries-old struggle against the sea.

Alone of all European peoples in the seventeenth century, the Dutch practiced religious toleration. Peoples of all faiths were welcome within their borders. Although there is scattered evidence of anti-Semitism, Jews enjoyed a level of acceptance and assimilation in Dutch business and general culture unique in early modern Europe. (See the feature "Individuals in Society: Glückel of Hameln.") For example, Benedict Spinoza (1632–1677), a descendant of Spanish Jews who fled the Inquisition, passed his entire life in Amsterdam, supporting himself as a lens grinder while producing important philosophical treatises. The urbanity of Dutch society allowed a rare degree of religious freedom. As long as business people conducted their religion in private, the government did not interfere with them.

In the Dutch Republic, toleration paid off: it attracted a great deal of foreign capital and investment. Deposits at the Bank of Amsterdam were guaranteed by the city council, and in the middle years of the century the bank became Europe's best source of cheap credit and commercial intelligence and the main clearing-house for bills of exchange. People of all races and creeds traded in Amsterdam, at whose docks on the Amstel River five thousand ships were berthed. Joost van den Vondel, the poet of Dutch imperialism, exulted:

Individuals in Society

Glückel of Hameln

In 1690 a Jewish widow in the small German town of Hameln* in Lower Saxony sat down to write her autobiography. She wanted to distract her mind from the terrible grief she felt over the death of her husband and to provide her twelve children with a record "so you will know from what sort of people you have sprung, lest today or tomorrow your beloved children or grandchildren came and know naught of their family." Out of her pain and heightened consciousness, Glückel (1646–1724) produced an invaluable source for scholars.

She was born in Hamburg two years before the end of the Thirty Years' War. In 1649 the merchants of Hamburg expelled the Jews, who moved to nearby Altona, then under Danish rule. When the Swedes overran Altona in 1657–1658, the Jews returned to Hamburg "purely at the mercy of the Town Council." Glückel's narrative proceeds against a background of the constant harassment to which Jews were subjected—special papers, permits, bribes—and in Hameln she wrote, "And so it has been to this day and, I fear, will continue in like fashion."

When Glückel was "barely twelve," her father betrothed her to Chayim Hameln. She married at age fourteen. She describes him as "the perfect pattern of the pious Jew," a man who stopped his work every day for study and prayer, fasted, and was scrupulously honest in his business dealings. Only a few years older than Glückel, Chayim earned his living dealing in precious metals and in making small loans on pledges (articles held on security). This work required his constant travel to larger cities, markets, and fairs, often in bad weather, always over dangerous roads. Chayim consulted his wife about all his business dealings. As he lay dying, a friend asked if he had any last wishes. "None," he replied. "My wife knows everything. She shall do as she has always done." For thirty years Glückel had been his friend, full business partner, and wife. They had thirteen children, twelve of whom survived their father, eight then unmarried. As Chayim had foretold, Glückel succeeded in launching the boys in careers and in providing dowries for the girls.

Glückel's world was her family, the Jewish community of Hameln, and the Jewish communities into which her children married. Social and business activities took her to Amsterdam, Baiersdorf, Bamberg, Berlin, Cleves, Danzig, Metz, and Vienna, so her world was not narrow or provincial. She took great pride that Prince Frederick of Cleves, later king of Prussia, danced at the wedding of her eldest daughter. The rising prosperity of Chayim's businesses allowed the couple to maintain up to six servants.

Glückel was deeply religious, and her culture was steeped in Jewish literature, legends, and mystical and secular works. Above all, she relied on the Bible. Her language, heavily sprinkled with scriptural references, testifies to a rare familiarity with the basic book of Western civilization. The Scriptures were her consolation, the source of her great strength in a hostile world.

Students who would learn about business practices, the importance of the dowry in marriage, childbirth, the ceremony of bris, birthrates, family celebrations, and even the meaning of life can gain a good deal from the memoirs of this extraordinary woman who was, in the words of one of her descendants, the poet Heinrich Heine, "the gift of a world to me."

Gentleness and deep mutual devotion seem to pervade Rembrandt's The Jewish Bride. (Rijksmuseum-Stichting Amsterdam)

Questions for Analysis

1. Consider the ways in which Glückel of Hameln was both an ordinary and an extraordinary woman of her times. Would you call her a marginal or a central person in her society?
2. How was Glückel's life affected by the broad events and issues of the seventeenth century?

* A town immortalized by the Brothers Grimm. In 1284 the town contracted with the Pied Piper to rid it of rats and mice; he lured them away by playing his flute. When the citizens refused to pay, he charmed away their children in revenge.

Source: *The Memoirs of Glückel of Hameln*, (New York: Schocken Books, 1977).

Online Study Center Improve Your Grade
Going Beyond Individuals in Society

MAP 16.3 Seventeenth-Century Dutch Commerce Dutch wealth rested on commerce, and commerce depended on the huge Dutch merchant marine, manned by perhaps forty-eight thousand sailors. The fleet carried goods from all parts of the globe to the port of Amsterdam.

> *God, God, the Lord of Amstel cried, hold every conscience free;*
> *And Liberty ride, on Holland's tide, with billowing sails to sea,*
> *And run our Amstel out and in; let freedom gird the bold,*
> *And merchant in his counting house stand elbow deep in gold.*[18]

The fishing industry was the original cornerstone of the Dutch economy. For half the year, from June to December, fishing fleets combed the dangerous English coast and the North Sea and raked in tiny herring. Profits from herring stimulated shipbuilding, and even before 1600 the Dutch were offering the lowest shipping rates in Europe. The Dutch merchant marine was the largest in Europe. In 1650 contemporaries estimated that the Dutch had sixteen thousand merchant ships, half the European total. All the wood for these ships had to be imported: the Dutch bought whole forests from Norway. They also bought entire vineyards from French growers before the grapes were harvested. They controlled the Baltic grain trade, buying entire wheat and rye crops in Poland, east Prussia, and Swedish Pomerania. Because the Dutch dealt in bulk, nobody could undersell them. Foreign merchants coming to Amsterdam could buy anything from precision lenses for the microscope (recently invented by Dutchman Anton van Leeuwenhoek) to muskets for an army of five thousand. Although Dutch cities became famous for their exports—diamonds and linens from Haarlem, pottery from Delft—Dutch wealth depended less on exports than on transport.

In 1602 a group of the regents of Holland formed the **Dutch East India Company,** a joint stock company. The investors each received a percentage of the profits proportional to the amount of money they had put in. Within half a century the Dutch East India Company had cut heavily into Portuguese trading in East Asia. The Dutch seized the Cape of Good Hope, Ceylon, and Malacca and established trading posts in each place. In the 1630s the Dutch East India Company was paying its investors about a 35 percent annual return on their investments. The Dutch West India Company, founded in 1621, traded extensively with Latin America and Africa (see Map 16.3).

Trade and commerce brought the Dutch prodigious wealth. In the seventeenth century the Dutch enjoyed the highest standard of living in Europe, perhaps in the world. Amsterdam and Rotterdam built massive granaries where the surplus of one year could be stored against possible shortages the next. Thus, except in the 1650s, when bad harvests reduced supplies, food prices fluctuated very little. By the standards of Cologne, Paris, or London, salaries were high for all workers—except women, but even women's wages were high when compared with those of women in other parts of Europe. All classes of society, including unskilled laborers, ate well. The low price of bread meant that, compared to other places in Europe, a higher percentage of the worker's income could be spent on fish, cheese, butter, vegetables, and even meat. A scholar has described the Netherlands as "an island of plenty in a sea of want." Consequently, the Netherlands experienced very few of the food riots that characterized the rest of Europe.[19]

Although the initial purpose of the Dutch East and West India Companies was commercial—the import of spices and silks to Europe—the Dutch found themselves involved in the imperialist exploitation of parts of East Asia and Latin America, with great success. In 1652 the Dutch founded Cape Town on the southern tip of Africa as a fueling station for ships planning to cross the Pacific. But war with France and England in the 1670s hurt the United Provinces. The long War of the Spanish Succession—in which the Dutch prince William of Orange, who was King William III of England, utilized English wealth in the Dutch fight against Louis XIV—was a costly drain on Dutch labor and financial resources. The peace signed in 1713 to end the war marked the beginning of Dutch economic decline.

Chapter Summary

- What were the common crises and achievements of seventeenth-century states?
- To what extent did French and Spanish monarchs succeed in creating absolute monarchies?
- What cultural forms flourished under absolutist governments?
- What is constitutionalism, and how did this form of government emerge in England and the Dutch Republic?

Most parts of Europe experienced the seventeenth century as a period of severe economic, social, and military crisis. Across the continent, rulers faced popular rebellions from their desperate subjects, who were pushed to the brink by poor harvests, high taxes, and decades of war. Many forces, including powerful noblemen, the church, and regional and local loyalties, constrained the state's authority. Despite these obstacles, most European states emerged from the seventeenth century with increased powers and more centralized control. Whether they ruled through monarchical fiat or parliamentary negotiation, European governments strengthened their bureaucracies, raised more taxes, and significantly expanded their armies.

According to Thomas Hobbes, the central drive in every human is "a perpetual and restless desire of Power, after Power, that ceaseth only in Death." The seventeenth century solved the problem of sovereign power in two fundamental ways: absolutism and constitutionalism. Under Louis XIV France witnessed the high point of absolutist ambition in western Europe. The king saw himself as the representative of God on earth, and it has been said that "to the seventeenth century imagination God was a sort of image of Louis XIV."[20] Under Louis's rule, France developed a centralized bureaucracy, a professional army, and a state-directed economy, all of which he personally supervised.

Despite his claims to absolute power, historians now agree that Louis XIV ruled, in practice, by securing the collaboration of high nobles. In exchange for confirmation of their ancient privileges, the nobles were willing to cooperate with the expansion of state power. This was a common pattern in attempts at absolutism across Europe. In Spain, where monarchs made similar claims to absolute power, the seventeenth century witnessed economic catastrophe and a decline in royal capacities. Spanish rule continued in the colonies and foreshadowed a revival of Spanish fortunes in the eighteenth century.

France's dominant political role in Europe elevated its cultural influence as well. French became the common language of the European elite, as all heads turned to Versailles and the radiant aristocratic culture emanating from it. Within France, the Bourbon monarchy pursued culture as one more aspect of absolutist policy, creating cultural academies, sponsoring playwrights and musicians, and repressing Protestantism with a bloody hand.

As Louis XIV personified absolutist ambitions, so Stuart England exemplified the evolution of the constitutional state. The conflicts between Parliament and the first two Stuart rulers, James I and Charles I, tested where sovereign power would reside. The resulting civil war did not solve the problem. The Instrument of Government provided for a balance of government authority and recognition of popular rights; as such, the Instrument has been called the first modern constitution. Unfortunately, it lacked public support. James II's absolutist tendencies brought on the Glorious Revolution of 1688 and 1689, and the people who made that revolution settled three basic issues: sovereign power was divided between king and Parliament, with Parliament enjoying the greater share; government was to be based on the rule of law; and the liberties of English people were made explicit in written form in the Bill of Rights.

Having won independence from Spain, the United Provinces of the Netherlands provided another model of constitutional government, one dominated by wealthy urban merchants rather than the landed gentry who controlled the English system. The federal constitution of the Netherlands invested power in the Estates General, but diluted their authority by giving veto power to provincial assemblies. Dominated by Holland, the Netherlands provided a shining example of industriousness, prosperity, and relative tolerance for the rest of Europe.

Key Terms

moral economy
sovereignty
popular revolts
Edict of Nantes
intendants
noblesse de robe (robe nobility)
Fronde
noblesse d'épée (sword nobility)
divine right of kings
absolute monarchy
mercantilism
estates
Peace of Utrecht
Don Quixote
viceroyalties
quinto
baroque
patronage
French classicism
constitutionalism
Puritans
New Model Army
Protectorate
Test Act
Second Treatise of Civil Government
States General
stadholder
Dutch East India Company

Online Study Center   **Improve Your Grade** Flashcards

Suggested Reading

Beik, William. *Urban Protest in Seventeenth-Century France*. 1997. Explores urban violence in France during harsh years of economic and social crisis.

Benedict, Philip, and Myron P. Gutmann, eds. *Early Modern Europe: From Crisis to Stability*. 2005. A helpful introduction to the many facets of the seventeenth-century crisis.

Burke, Peter. *The Fabrication of Louis XIV*. 1992. Explains the use of architecture, art, medals, and other symbols to promote the king's image.

Collins, James B. *The State in Early Modern France*. 1995. A detailed and well-argued survey of French administration from Louis XIII to Louis XVI.

Elliott, John H. *Richelieu and Olivares*. 1984. A comparison of the chief ministers of France and Spain that also reveals differences and similarities in the countries they led.

Gaunt, Peter, ed. *The English Civil War: The Essential Readings*. 2000. A collection showcasing leading historians' interpretations of the civil war.

Hutton, Ronald. *Charles II: King of England, Scotland and Ireland*. 1989. A reliable and highly readable biography of King Charles II.

Israel, Jonathan. *The Dutch Republic: Its Rise, Greatness and Fall, 1477–1806*. 1995. A thorough study of the political history of the republic.

Kettering, Sharon. *Patronage in Sixteenth- and Seventeenth-Century France*. 2002. A collection of essays exploring the role of patronage in politics and noble life, including women's role in patronage networks.

Lynn, John A. *Giant of the Grand Siècle: The French Army, 1610–1715*. 1997. Examines the tremendous growth and professionalization of the French army under Louis XIV.

Pagden, Anthony. *Spanish Imperialism and the Political Imagination*. 1990. Explores Spanish ideas of empire, primarily in Italy and the Americas.

Schama, Simon. *The Embarrassment of Riches: An Interpretation of Dutch Culture in the Golden Age*. 1987. A lengthy but vivid and highly readable account of Dutch culture in the seventeenth century, including a chapter on the mania for speculation on the tulip market.

Te Brake, Wayne. *Shaping History: Ordinary People in European Politics, 1500–1700*. 1998. Examines the political activities of the non-elite in early modern Europe.

Underdown, David. *Revel, Riot, and Rebellion*. 1985. Discusses ordinary people's roles in the English civil war.

Wrightson, Keith. *English Society, 1580–1680*. 1982. Good coverage of English political and social issues of the seventeenth century.

Young, John, ed. *Celtic Dimensions of the British Civil Wars*. 1997. Explores Scotland and Ireland and their involvement in the civil wars in Great Britain.

Notes

1. The classic study Theodore K. Rabb, *The Struggle for Stability in Early Modern Europe* (Oxford: Oxford University Press, 1975).
2. John A. Lynn, "Recalculating French Army Growth," in *The Military Revolution Debate: Readings on the Military Transformation of Early Modern Europe*, ed. Clifford J. Rogers (Boulder, Colo.: Westview Press, 1995), p. 125.
3. G. Parker and L. M. Smith, "Introduction," and N. Steensgaard, "The Seventeenth Century Crisis," in *The General Crisis of the Seventeenth Century*, ed. G. Parker and L. M. Smith (London: Routledge & Kegan Paul, 1985), pp. 1–53, esp. p. 12.
4. H. G. Koenigsberger, "The Revolt of Palermo in 1647," *Cambridge Historical Journal* 8 (1944–1946): 129–144.
5. See W. Beik, *Urban Protest in Seventeenth-Century France: The Culture of Retribution* (New York: Cambridge University Press, 1997), p. 1.
6. Ibid.
7. See ibid., chaps. 1, 2, 3, and 11.
8. Ibid., pp. 22–26.
9. See M. Turchetti, "The Edict of Nantes," in *The Oxford Encyclopedia of the Reformation*, ed. H. J. Hillerbrand, vol. 3 (New York: Oxford University Press, 1996), pp. 126–128.
10. Quoted in J. H. Elliott, *Richelieu and Olivares* (Cambridge: Cambridge University Press, 1984), p. 135; and in W. F. Church, *Richelieu and Reason of State* (Princeton, N.J.: Princeton University Press, 1972), p. 507.
11. James B. Collins, *The State in Early Modern France* (Cambridge: Cambridge University Press, 1995), pp. 65–78.
12. Quoted in J. Wolf, *Louis XIV* (New York: W. W. Norton, 1968), p. 146.
13. Ibid.
14. J. H. Elliott, *Imperial Spain, 1469–1716* (New York: Mentor Books, 1963), pp. 306–308.
15. B. Bennassar, *The Spanish Character: Attitudes and Mentalities from the Sixteenth to the Nineteenth Century*, trans. B. Keen (Berkeley: University of California Press, 1979), p. 125.
16. For a revisionist interpretation, see J. Wormald, "James VI and I: Two Kings or One?" *History* 62 (June 1983): 187–209.
17. C. Stephenson and G. F. Marcham, *Sources of English Constitutional History* (New York: Harper & Row, 1937), p. 601.
18. Quoted in D. Maland, *Europe in the Seventeenth Century* (New York: Macmillan, 1967), pp. 198–199. Copyright © 1967 by A & C Black Ltd.
19. S. Schama, *The Embarrassment of Riches: An Interpretation of Dutch Culture in the Golden Age* (New York: Alfred A. Knopf, 1987), pp. 165–170; quotation is on p. 167.
20. C. J. Friedrich and C. Blitzer, *The Age of Power* (Ithaca, N.Y.: Cornell University Press, 1957), p. 112.

Listening to the Past

The Court at Versailles

Although the duke of Saint-Simon (1675–1755) was a soldier, courtier, and diplomat, his enduring reputation rests on The Memoirs (1788), his eyewitness account of the personality and court of Louis XIV. A nobleman of extremely high status, Saint-Simon resented Louis's high-handed treatment of the ancient nobility and his promotion of newer nobles and the bourgeoisie. The Memoirs, excerpted here, remains a monument of French literature and an indispensable historical source, partly for its portrait of the court at Versailles.

Very early in the reign of Louis XIV the Court was removed from Paris, never to return. The troubles of the minority had given him a dislike to that city; his enforced and surreptitious flight from it still rankled in his memory; he did not consider himself safe there, and thought cabals would be more easily detected if the Court was in the country, where the movements and temporary absences of any of its members would be more easily noticed. . . . No doubt that he was also influenced by the feeling that he would be regarded with greater awe and veneration when no longer exposed every day to the gaze of the multitude.

His love-affair with Mademoiselle de la Vallière, which at first was covered as far as possible with a veil of mystery, was the cause of frequent excursions to Versailles. . . . The visits of Louis XIV becoming more frequent, he enlarged the *château* by degrees till its immense buildings afforded better accommodation for the Court than was to be found at St. Germain, where most of the courtiers had to put up with uncomfortable lodgings in the town. The Court was therefore removed to Versailles in 1682, not long before the Queen's death. The new building contained an infinite number of rooms for courtiers, and the King liked the grant of these rooms to be regarded as a coveted privilege.

He availed himself of the frequent festivities at Versailles, and his excursions to other places, as a means of making the courtiers assiduous in their attendance and anxious to please him; for he nominated beforehand those who were to take part in them, and could thus gratify some and inflict a snub on others. He was conscious that the substantial favours he had to bestow were not nearly sufficient to produce a continual effect; he had therefore to invent imaginary ones, and no one was so clever in devising petty distinctions and preferences which aroused jealousy and emulation. The visits to Marly later on were very useful to him in this way; also those to Trianon [Marly and Trianon were small country houses], where certain ladies, chosen beforehand, were admitted to his table. It was another distinction to hold his candlestick at his *coucher;* as soon as he had finished his prayers he used to name the courtier to whom it was to be handed, always choosing one of the highest rank among those present. . . .

Not only did he expect all persons of distinction to be in continual attendance at Court, but he was quick to notice the absence of those of inferior degree; at his *lever* [formal rising from bed in the morning], his *coucher* [preparations for going to bed], his meals, in the gardens of Versailles (the only place where the courtiers in general were allowed to follow him), he used to cast his eyes to right and left; nothing escaped him, he saw everybody. If any one habitually living at Court absented himself he insisted on knowing the reason; those who came there only for flying visits had also to give a satisfactory explanation; any one who seldom or never appeared there was certain to incur his displeasure. If asked to bestow a favour on such persons he would reply haughtily: "I do not know him"; of such as rarely presented themselves he would say, "He is a man I never see"; and from these judgements there was no appeal.

He always took great pains to find out what was going on in public places, in society, in private houses, even family secrets, and maintained an immense number of spies and tale-bearers. These were of all sorts; some did not know that their reports were carried to him; others did know it; there were others, again, who used to write to him directly, through channels which he prescribed; others who were admitted by the backstairs and saw him in his private room. Many a man in all ranks of life was ruined by these methods, often very unjustly, without ever being able to discover the reason; and when the King had once taken a prejudice against a man, he hardly ever got over it. . . .

No one understood better than Louis XIV the art of enhancing the value of a favour by his manner of bestowing it; he knew how to make the most of a word, a smile, even of a glance. If he addressed any one, were it but to ask a trifling question or make some commonplace remark, all eyes were turned on the person so honored; it was a mark of favour which always gave rise to comment. . . .

He loved splendour, magnificence, and profusion in all things, and encouraged similar tastes in his Court; to spend money freely on equipages [the king's horse carriages] and buildings, on feasting and at cards, was a sure way to gain his favour, perhaps to obtain the honour of a word from him. Motives of policy had something to do with this; by making expensive habits the fashion, and, for people in a certain position, a necessity, he compelled his courtiers to live beyond their income, and gradually reduced them to depend on his bounty for the means of subsistence. This was a plague which, once introduced, became a scourge to the whole country, for it did not take long to spread to Paris, and thence to the armies and the provinces; so that a man of any position is now estimated entirely according to his expenditure on his table and other luxuries. This folly, sustained by pride and ostentation, has already produced widespread confusion; it threatens to end in nothing short of ruin and a general overthrow.

Louis XIV was extremely proud of the gardens at Versailles and personally led ambassadors and other highly ranked visitors on tours of the extensive palace grounds. *(Erich Lessing/Art Resource, NY)*

Questions for Analysis

1. What was the role of etiquette and ceremony at the court of Versailles? How could Louis XIV use them in everyday life at court to influence and control nobles?

2. How important do you think Louis's individual character and personality were to his style of governing? What challenges might this present to his successors?

3. Consider the role of ceremony in some modern governments, such as the U.S. government. How does it compare to Louis XIV's use of ceremony as portrayed by Saint-Simon?

4. Do you think Saint-Simon is an objective and trustworthy recorder of life at court? Why?

Source: F. Arkwright, ed., *The Memoirs of the Duke de Saint-Simon,* vol. 5 (New York: Brentano's, n.d.), pp. 271–274, 276–278.

Peter the Great's magnificent new crown, created for his joint coronation in 1682 with his half-brother Ivan. *(State Museum of the Kremlin, Moscow)*

chapter 17

ABSOLUTISM IN CENTRAL AND EASTERN EUROPE TO 1740

chapter preview

Warfare and Social Change in Central and Eastern Europe
• What social and economic changes affected central and eastern Europe from 1400 to 1650?

The Rise of Austria and Prussia
• How and why did the rulers of Austria and Prussia, each in different political and social environments, manage to build powerful absolute monarchies that proved more durable than that of Louis XIV?

The Development of Russia and the Ottoman Empire
• What were the distinctive features of Russian and Ottoman absolutism in this period?

The crises of the seventeenth century—religious division, economic depression, and war—were not limited to the West. Central and eastern Europe experienced even more catastrophic dislocation, with German lands serving as the battleground of the Thirty Years' War and borders constantly vulnerable to attack from the east. In Prussia and Habsburg Austria absolutist states emerged in the aftermath of this conflict.

Russia and the Ottoman Turks also developed absolutist governments. These empires seemed foreign and exotic to western Europeans, who saw them as the antithesis of their political, religious, and cultural values. To Western eyes, their monarchs respected law—either divine or constitutional—while Eastern despots ruled with an iron fist. The Ottoman Muslim state was home to fanaticism and heresy, and even Russian Orthodoxy had rituals and traditions, if not core beliefs, that differed sharply from either Catholicism or Protestantism. Beneath the surface, however, these Eastern governments shared many similarities with Western ones.

The most successful Eastern empires lasted until 1918, far longer than monarchical rule endured in France, the model of absolutism under Louis XIV. Eastern monarchs had a powerful impact on architecture and the arts, encouraging new monumental construction to reflect their glory. Questions about the relationship between East and West remain potent today, when Turkey's bid for membership in the European Union is controversial both at home and abroad.

Warfare and Social Change in Central and Eastern Europe

When absolute monarchy emerged in the seventeenth century, it built on social and economic foundations laid between roughly 1400 and 1650. In those years the elites of eastern Europe—with the major exception of the Ottoman rulers in the Balkans—rolled back the gains made by the peasantry during the High Middle Ages and re-imposed a harsh serfdom on the rural masses. The nobility also reduced the importance of the

Online Study Center
This icon will direct you to interactive activities and study materials on the website **college.hmco.com/pic/mckaywest9e**

towns and the middle classes. This process differed from developments in western Europe, where peasants won greater freedom and the urban middle class continued its rise. The Thirty Years' War represented the culmination of these changes. Decades of war in central Europe led to depopulation and economic depression, which allowed lords to impose ever-harsher controls on the peasantry.

- *What social and economic changes affected central and eastern Europe from 1400 to 1650?*

Origins of Serfdom

The period from 1050 to 1300 was a time of general economic expansion in eastern Europe characterized by the growth of trade, towns, and population. This meant clearing the forests and colonizing the frontier beyond the Elbe River. Eager to attract settlers to sparsely populated lands, the rulers of eastern Europe offered newcomers economic and legal incentives, providing land on excellent terms and granting greater personal freedom. These benefits were also gradually extended to the local Slavic populations, even those of central Russia. Thus, by 1300 **serfdom** had all but disappeared in eastern Europe. Peasants bargained freely with their landlords and moved about as they pleased. Opportunities and improvements in the East had a positive impact on the West, where the weight of serfdom was also reduced between 1100 and 1300. Thus fundamental social and economic developments moved in tandem across Europe in the High Middle Ages.

After about 1300, however, as Europe's population and economy declined grievously, mostly as a result of the Black Death, East and West parted paths. Across Europe, lords sought to solve their economic problems by more heavily exploiting the peasantry. This reaction generally failed in the West, where by 1500 almost all peasants were free or had their serf obligations greatly reduced. East of the Elbe, however, the landlords won.

Eastern landlords successfully used their political and police power against the peasantry in two ways. First, they restricted or eliminated the peasants' time-honored right of freedom of movement. Thus a peasant could no longer leave the land without his lord's permission, and the lord had no reason to make such concessions. In Prussian territories by 1500 the law required that runaway peasants be hunted down and returned to their lords. Until the mid-fifteenth century, medieval Russian peasants were free to move wherever they wished. Thereafter this freedom was gradually curtailed, so that by 1497 a Russian peasant had the right to move only during a two-week period after the fall harvest. Eastern peasants were losing their status as free and independent men and women.

Second, lords steadily took more of their peasants' land and imposed heavier labor obligations. Instead of being independent farmers paying freely negotiated rents, peasants became forced laborers on the lords' estates. By the early 1500s, lords in many territories could command their peasants to work without pay as many as six days a week.

The gradual erosion of the peasantry's economic position was bound up with manipulation of the legal system. The local lord was also the local prosecutor, judge, and jailer. There were no independent royal officials to provide justice or uphold the common law, allowing lords to rule in their own favor in disputes with peasants.

The Consolidation of Serfdom

Between 1500 and 1650 the social, legal, and economic conditions of peasants in eastern Europe continued to decline, and free peasants became serfs. In Poland nobles gained complete control over their peasants in 1574, after which they could legally inflict the death penalty whenever they wished. In Prussia in 1653 peasants were assumed to be tied to their lords in **hereditary subjugation**—bound to their lords and the land from one generation to the next. In Russia peasants' right to move from an estate was permanently abolished in 1603. In 1649 the tsar lifted the nine-year time limit on the recovery of runaways and eliminated all limits on lords' authority over their peasants. Although political development in the various Eastern states differed, the legal re-establishment of permanent hereditary serfdom was the common fate of Eastern peasants by the mid-seventeenth century.

The consolidation of serfdom accompanied the growth of estate agriculture, particularly in Poland and eastern Germany. In the sixteenth century European economic expansion and population growth resumed after the great declines of the late Middle Ages. Prices for agricultural commodities also rose sharply as gold and silver flowed in from the New World. Thus Polish and German lords had powerful economic incentives to increase the production of their estates. And they did. Lords seized more peasant land for their own estates and then demanded more unpaid labor on those enlarged estates. Though the estates were generally inefficient and technically backward, the great Polish nobles and middle-rank German lords squeezed sizable profits from their impoverished peasants. Surpluses in wheat and timber were sold to foreign merchants, who exported them to the growing cities of the West. Thus the poor East helped feed the wealthier West.

The re-emergence of serfdom in eastern Europe cannot be explained by economic factors alone. Western Europe experienced similar agricultural and population decline in the fourteenth and fifteenth centuries, but its peasants won better rather than harsher conditions. It seems likely that political, rather than economic, factors were crucial. Eastern lords enjoyed much greater political power than did their Western counterparts. In the late Middle Ages central and eastern Europe experienced innumerable wars and general political chaos, which allowed noble landlords to increase their political power. There were, for example, many disputed royal successions, so that weak kings were forced to grant political

Chronology

ca 1400–1650	Re-emergence of serfdom in eastern Europe
1462–1505	Reign of Ivan III in Russia
1533–1584	Reign of Ivan the Terrible in Russia
1620	Habsburgs crush Protestantism in Bohemia
1620–1740	Growth of absolutism in Austria and Prussia
1640–1688	Reign of Frederick William in Prussia
1652	Nikon reforms Russian Orthodox Church
1670–1671	Cossack revolt led by Razin
ca 1680–1750	Construction of palaces by absolutist rulers
1683–1718	Habsburgs defend Vienna, win war with Ottoman Turks
1702	Peter the Great founds St. Petersburg
1713–1740	Growth of Prussian military

Estonia in the 1660s The Estonians were conquered by German military nobility in the Middle Ages and reduced to serfdom. The German-speaking nobles ruled the Estonian peasants with an iron hand, and Peter the Great reaffirmed their domination when Russia annexed Estonia (see Map 17.3 on page 573). *(Mansell Collection/Time Life Pictures/Getty Images)*

favors to win the nobility's support. Thus while strong monarchs and effective central government were rising in Spain, France, and England, kings were generally losing power in the East and could not resist the demands of lords regarding peasants.

Moreover, most Eastern monarchs did not oppose the growth of serfdom. The typical king was only first among noble equals. He, too, wanted to squeeze his peasants. The Western concept of sovereignty, as embodied in a king who protected the interests of all his people, was not well developed in eastern Europe before 1650.

It was not only the peasants who suffered. Also with the approval of kings, landlords systematically undermined the medieval privileges of the towns and the power of the urban classes. Instead of selling products to local merchants, landlords sold directly to foreigners. For example, Dutch ships sailed up the rivers of Poland and eastern Germany to the loading docks of the great estates, completely bypassing the local towns. Moreover, "town air" no longer "made people free," for the Eastern towns had lost their medieval right of refuge and were now compelled to return runaways to their lords. The population of the towns and the importance of the urban middle classes declined greatly.

The Thirty Years' War

The Holy Roman Empire was a confederation of hundreds of principalities, independent cities, duchies, and other polities loosely united under an elected emperor. An uneasy truce had prevailed in the Holy Roman Empire since the Peace of Augsburg of 1555 (see page 459). According to the settlement, the faith of the prince determined the religion of his subjects. Later in the century, however, Catholics grew alarmed because Lutherans, in violation of the Peace of Augsburg, were steadily acquiring German bishoprics. The spread of Calvinism further confused the issue: the Augsburg settlement had pertained only to Lutheranism and Catholicism, so Calvinists ignored it and converted several princes. Also, the militantly active Jesuits had reconverted several Lutheran princes to Catholicism. Lutherans feared that the Augsburg principles would be undermined by Catholic and Calvinist gains. Lutheran princes felt compelled to form the **Protestant Union** (1608), and Catholics retaliated with the Catholic League (1609). Each alliance was determined that the other should make no religious or territorial advance. Dynastic interests were also involved; the Spanish Habsburgs strongly supported the goals of their Austrian relatives—the unity of the empire and the preservation of Catholicism within it.

Violence erupted in 1617 when Ferdinand of Styria, the new Catholic king in Bohemia, closed some Protestant churches. On May 23, 1618, Protestants hurled two of Ferdinand's officials from a castle window in Prague. They fell seventy feet but survived: Catholics claimed that angels had caught them; Protestants said that the officials had fallen on a heap of soft horse manure. Called the "defenestration of Prague," this event marked the beginning of the Thirty Years' War (1618–1648).

The war is traditionally divided into four phases. The first, or Bohemian, phase (1618–1625) was characterized by civil war in Bohemia between the Catholic League, led by Ferdinand, and the Protestant Union, headed by Frederick, the elector of the Palatinate. The Bohemians fought for religious liberty and independence from Habsburg rule. In 1620 Catholic forces defeated Frederick at the Battle of the White Mountain. Ferdinand, who had recently been elected Holy Roman emperor as Ferdinand II, followed up his victories by wiping out Protestantism in Bohemia through forcible conversions and Jesuit missionary work. Within ten years Bohemia was completely Catholic.

The second, or Danish, phase of the war (1625–1629)—so called because of the leadership of the Protestant king Christian IV of Denmark (r. 1588–1648)—witnessed additional Catholic victories. The Catholic imperial army led by Albert of Wallenstein swept through Silesia, north to the Baltic, and east into Pomerania, scoring smashing victories. Wallenstein, an unscrupulous opportunist who used his vast riches to build an army loyal only to himself, seemed interested more in carving out his own empire than in aiding the Catholic cause. He quarreled with the Catholic League, and soon the Catholic forces were divided. Religion was eclipsed as a basic issue of the war.

Habsburg power peaked in 1629. The emperor issued the Edict of Restitution, whereby all Catholic properties lost to Protestantism since 1552 were restored, and only Catholics and Lutherans were allowed to practice their faiths. When Wallenstein began ruthless enforcement, Protestants throughout Europe feared the collapse of the balance of power in north-central Europe.

The third, or Swedish, phase of the war (1630–1635) began with the arrival in Germany of the Swedish king Gustavus Adolphus (r. 1594–1632). The ablest administrator of his day and a devout Lutheran, he intervened to support the empire's oppressed Protestants. Cardinal Richelieu, chief minister of King Louis XIII of France (r. 1610–1643), subsidized the Swedes, hoping to weaken Habsburg power in Europe. In 1631, with a small but well-disciplined army equipped with superior muskets, Gustavus Adolphus won a brilliant victory at Breitenfeld. Again in 1632 he was victorious at Lützen, though he was fatally wounded in the battle.

The participation of the Swedes in the Thirty Years' War proved decisive for the future of Protestantism and German history. When Gustavus Adolphus landed on German soil, he headed a Baltic empire under Swedish influence. The Swedish victories ended the Habsburg ambition to unite the German states under imperial authority.

Gustavus Adolphus's death in 1632, followed by the Swedes' defeat at the Battle of Nördlingen in 1634, prompted the French to enter the war on the Protestant side, beginning the French, or international, phase of the Thirty Years' War (1635–1648). For almost a century French foreign policy was based on opposition to the Habsburgs because a weak empire enhanced France's international stature. In 1635 Cardinal Richelieu declared war on Spain and again sent financial and military assistance to the Swedes and the German Protestant princes. The war dragged on. The French, Dutch, and Swedes, supported by Scots, Finns, and German mercenaries, burned, looted, and destroyed German agriculture and commerce. The Thirty Years' War lasted so long because neither side had the resources to win a quick, decisive victory. Finally, in October 1648 peace was achieved.

Soldiers Pillage a Farmhouse Billeting troops among civilian populations caused untold hardships. In this late-seventeenth-century Dutch illustration, brawling soldiers take over a peasant's home, eat his food, steal his possessions, and insult his family. Peasant retaliation sometimes proved swift and bloody. *(Rijksmuseum-Stichting Amsterdam)*

Consequences of the Thirty Years' War

The 1648 **Peace of Westphalia** that ended the Thirty Years' War marked a turning point in European history. Conflicts fought over religious faith ended. The treaties recognized the sovereign, independent authority of more than three hundred German princes (see Map 17.1). Since the time of Holy Roman Emperor Frederick II (1194–1250), Germany had followed a pattern of state-building different from that of France and England: the emperor shared authority with the princes. After the Peace of Westphalia, the emperors' power continued to be severely limited, and the Holy Roman Empire remained a loosely knit federation.

The peace agreement acknowledged the independence of the United Provinces of the Netherlands. France acquired the province of Alsace along with the advantages of the weakened status of the empire. Sweden received a large cash indemnity and jurisdiction over German territories along the Baltic Sea, leaving it as a major threat to the future kingdom of Brandenburg-Prussia. The agreement also denied the papacy the right to participate in central European religious affairs—a restriction symbolizing the reduced political role of the church. In religion, the Peace of Westphalia made the Augsburg agreement of 1555 permanent, with the sole modification that Calvinism, along with Catholicism and Lutheranism, would be a legally permissible creed. The north German states remained Protestant, the south German states Catholic.

The Thirty Years' War was probably the most destructive event for the central European economy and society prior to the twentieth century. Perhaps one-third of urban residents and two-fifths of the rural population died. Entire areas were depopulated by warfare, by the flight of refugees, and by disease. Typhus, dysentery, bubonic plague, and syphilis accompanied the movements of armies.

Because the Thirty Years' War was fought on German soil, the empire experienced untold losses in agricultural land, livestock, trade, and commerce. The trade of south-

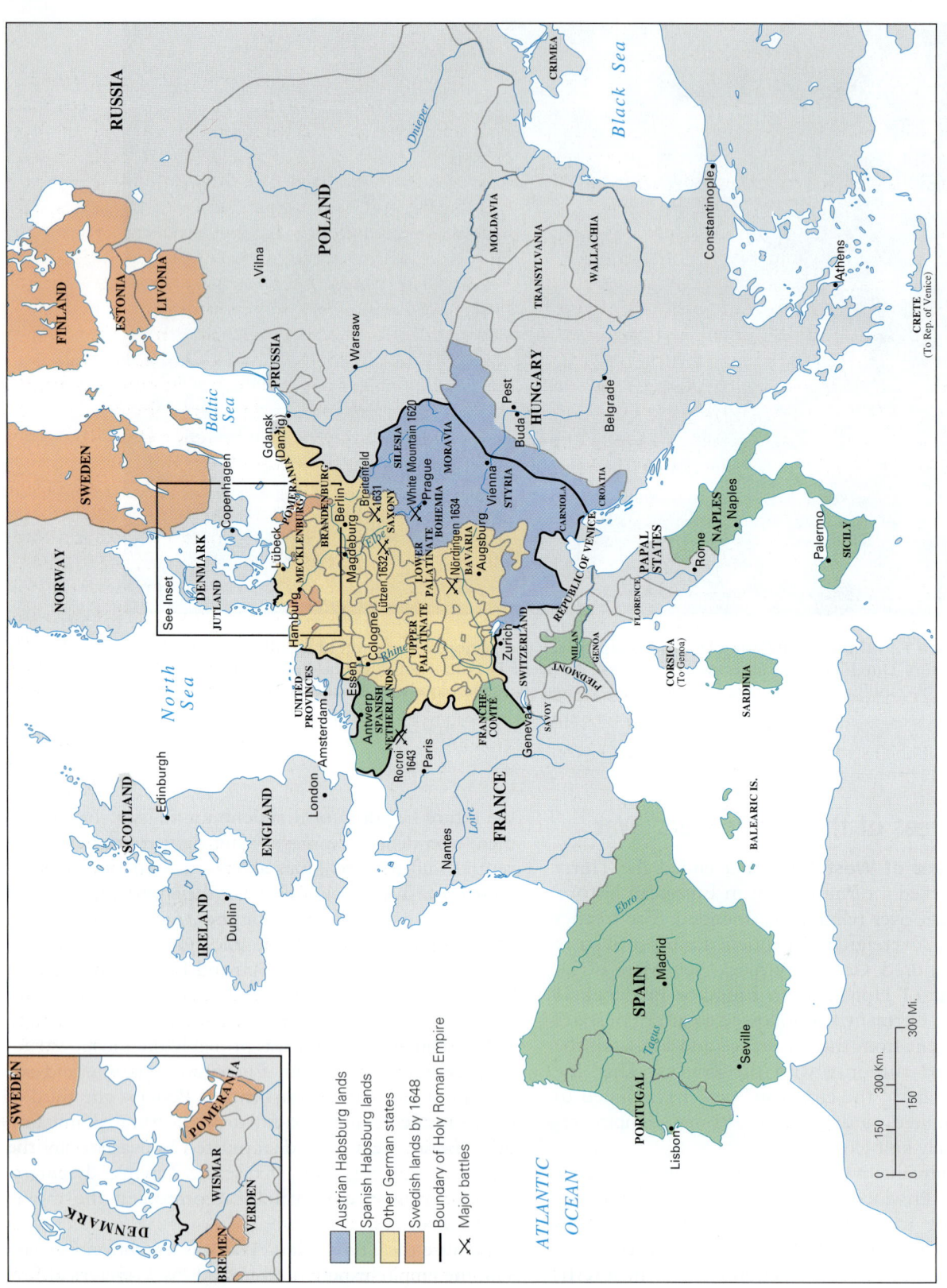

MAP 17.1 Europe After the Thirty Years' War Which country emerged from the Thirty Years' War as the strongest European power? What dynastic house was that country's major rival in the early modern period?

Improve Your Grade Interactive Map: Europe During Thirty Years' War ern cities such as Augsburg, already hard hit by the shift in transportation routes from the Mediterranean to the Atlantic, was virtually destroyed. All of Europe was experiencing severe inflation due to the influx of Spanish silver, but the destruction of land and foodstuffs made the price rise worse in central Europe than anywhere else. Agricultural areas suffered catastrophically. Many small farmers lacked the revenue to rework their holdings and had to become day laborers. In parts of central Europe, especially in areas east of the Elbe River, loss of land contributed to the consolidation of serfdom.[1]

Although the Thirty Years' War contributed to the legal and economic decline of the majority of the population, some people prospered. Nobles and landlords bought the land of failed small farmers, thereby acquiring even greater estates. Northern towns such as Lübeck, Hamburg, and Bremen as well as Essen in the Ruhr area also prospered because of the many refugees they attracted.

The Rise of Austria and Prussia

Serfdom and the Thirty Years' War aided Eastern rulers greatly in their attempts to build absolute monarchies. These rulers not only fought one another but also battled with armies of invaders from Asia. In this atmosphere of continual wartime emergency, monarchs were able to increase the powers of the central state. In exchange for leaving nobles the unchallenged masters of their peasants, the would-be absolutist monarchs of central and eastern Europe gradually gained political power in three key areas. First, they imposed permanent taxes without consent. Second, they maintained permanent standing armies to police the country and fight abroad. Third, they conducted relations with other states as they pleased.

As with all general historical developments, there were important variations on the absolutist theme in eastern Europe. Royal **absolutism** in Prussia was stronger and more effective than in Austria. This would give Prussia a thin edge in the struggle for power in east-central Europe in the eighteenth century. Prussian-style absolutism had great long-term political significance, for it was a rising Prussia that unified the German people in the nineteenth century and imposed on them a militaristic stamp.

- *How and why did the rulers of Austria and Prussia, each in different political and social environments, manage to build powerful absolute monarchies that proved more durable than that of Louis XIV?*

The Austrian Habsburgs

The Austrian Habsburgs controlled a scattered group of territories in central and eastern Europe. By 1618 the Habsburg realm included the German-speaking provinces of Austria, Tyrol, and Styria; the Czech-speaking kingdom of Bohemia; and parts of the kingdom of Hungary. Habsburg lands encompassed different languages, ethnicities, and religious affiliations; some lay within the Holy Roman Empire and some beyond its borders.

Like all of central Europe, the Habsburgs emerged from the Thirty Years' War impoverished and exhausted. Their efforts to destroy Protestantism in the German lands and to turn the weak Holy Roman Empire into a real state had failed. Although the Habsburgs remained the hereditary emperors, real power lay in the hands of a bewildering variety of separate political jurisdictions, including independent cities, small principalities, medium-size states such as Bavaria and Saxony, and some of the territories of Prussia and the Habsburgs.

Defeat in central Europe encouraged the Habsburgs to turn away from a quest for imperial dominance and to focus inward and eastward in an attempt to unify their diverse holdings. An important step in this direction had occurred in Bohemia during the Thirty Years' War. Protestantism had been strong among the Czechs in Bohemia. The lesser Czech nobility was largely Protestant in 1600 and had considerable political power because it dominated the **Bohemian Estates**—the representative body of the different estates, or legal orders. The Habsburgs believed that religious diversity fatally weakened royal power. If they could not impose Catholicism in the empire, at least they could do so in their own domains.

In 1618 the Bohemian Estates rose up in defense of Protestant rights. The Habsburgs crushed the revolt in 1620 at the Battle of the White Mountain. The victorious king, Ferdinand II (r. 1619–1637), drastically reduced the power of the Bohemian Estates. He also confiscated the landholdings of many Protestant nobles and gave them to a few loyal Catholic nobles and to the foreign aristocratic mercenaries who led his armies. After 1650 a large portion of the Bohemian nobility was of recent origin and owed everything to the Habsburgs.

With the help of this new nobility, the Habsburgs established direct rule over Bohemia. The condition of the enserfed peasantry worsened substantially: three days per week of unpaid labor—the *robot*—became the norm, and a quarter of the serfs worked for their lords every day but Sundays and religious holidays. Protestantism was also stamped out. The reorganization of Bohemia was a giant

The Battle of Mohács, 1526 The *Süleymanname* (Book of Suleiman), a biography, contains these fascinating illustrations of the great Ottoman victory at Mohács, which enabled the Turks to add Hungary to their expanding empire. In the right panel, Suleiman in a white turban sits on a black horse surrounded by his personal guard, while his janissary soldiers fire their muskets and cannon at the enemy. In the left panel, the Europeans are in disarray, in contrast to the Turks' discipline and order. *(Topkapi Saray Museum)*

step toward creating absolutist rule. As in France in the same years, the pursuit of religious unity was an essential element of absolutism.

After the Thirty Years' War, Ferdinand III (r. 1637–1657) continued to build state power. He centralized the government in the hereditary German-speaking provinces, which formed the core Habsburg holdings. For the first time, a permanent standing army was ready to put down any internal opposition.

Austrian Rule in Hungary

The Habsburg monarchy then turned toward the plains of Hungary. After the **Battle of Mohács** in 1526, the kingdom of Hungary was divided between the Ottomans and the Habsburgs. Transylvania in the east became an Ottoman dependent, while the Habsburgs ruled the west and north. In the 1540s the Ottomans organized their Hungarian territories into provinces of the empire. Warfare between the Ottomans and the Habsburgs devastated Hungary during the sixteenth century. Between 1683 and 1699 the Habsburgs pushed the Ottomans from most of Hungary and Transylvania. The recovery of all of the former kingdom of Hungary was completed in 1718.

The Hungarian nobility, despite its reduced strength, effectively thwarted the full development of Habsburg absolutism. Throughout the seventeenth century Hungarian nobles—the most numerous in Europe—rose in revolt against attempts to impose absolute rule. They never triumphed decisively, but neither were they crushed the way the Czech nobility had been in 1620.

The Hungarians resisted because many of them remained Protestants, especially in areas formerly ruled by the Turks. Ottoman rule had been relatively light-handed compared to the harsh reconversion efforts of the Habsburgs. Until the end of the seventeenth century the Ottomans still ruled parts of Hungary, providing a powerful military ally to nobles in areas recovered by the Habsburgs. Finally, the Hungarian nobility, and even part of the peasantry, became attached to a national ideal long before most of the other peoples of eastern Europe. Hungarian nobles were determined to maintain as much independence and local control as possible. In 1703, with the Habsburgs bogged down in the War of the Spanish Succession (see page 534), the Hungarians rose in one last patriotic rebellion under Prince Francis Rákóczy.

Rákóczy and his forces were eventually defeated, but the Habsburgs had to accept a compromise. Charles VI restored many of the traditional privileges of the aristocracy in return for Hungarian acceptance of hereditary Habsburg rule. Thus Hungary, unlike Austria and Bohemia, was never fully integrated into a centralized, absolute Habsburg state.

Despite checks on their ambitions in Hungary, the Habsburgs made significant achievements in state-building by forging consensus with the church and the nobility. A sense of common identity and loyalty to the monarchy grew among elites in Habsburg lands, even to a certain extent in Hungary. The best evidence for this consensus is the spectacular sums approved by the estates for the growth of the army. By the end of the seventeenth century Emperor Leopold commanded a standing army of a hundred thousand men funded by contributions from the provincial estates. German became the language of the common culture and, with ongoing Protestant conversion and emigration, zealous Catholicism also helped fuse a collective identity. Vienna became the political and cultural center of the empire. By 1700 it was a thriving city with a population of one hundred thousand, with its own version of Versailles, the royal palace of Schönbrunn. (See the feature "Images in Society: Absolutist Palace Building" on pages 568–569.)

Empowered by the imperial government, the landed nobility took charge of economic recovery. The nobles increased the burdens of serfdom and profited from the war's population losses to take over vast tracts of land. With technical and commercial innovations, they created a new form of capitalist, market-oriented agriculture, which allowed them to increase their holdings even more at the expense of smaller landowners.

In 1713 Charles VI (r. 1711–1740) proclaimed the so-called **Pragmatic Sanction,** which stated that Habsburg possessions were never to be divided, even if it meant allowing a woman to take the throne. Lacking a male heir, Charles spent much of his reign trying to get this principle accepted within and beyond his realm. His success resulted in the crowning of his daughter Maria Theresa upon Charles's death in 1740.

Prussia in the Seventeenth Century

After 1400 a revitalized landed nobility became the undisputed ruling class in eastern Germany. The Hohenzollern family, which ruled through its senior and junior branches as the imperial electors of Brandenburg and the dukes of Prussia, had little real power. Nothing suggested that this family and its territories would ever play an important role in European or even regional affairs. The **elector of Brandenburg** had the right to help choose the Holy Roman emperor, which bestowed prestige, but the elector had no military strength of his own. Moreover, Brandenburg, the area around Berlin and the elector's power base, was a land-locked combination of sand and swamp (see Map 17.2) that lacked defensible natural frontiers. Contemporaries contemptuously called it the "sand-box of the Holy Roman Empire."[2]

The territory of the elector's cousin, the duke of Prussia, was completely separated from Brandenburg and was part of the kingdom of Poland. By 1600 Prussia's German-speaking peasants had much in common with Polish peasants, for both ethnic groups had seen most of their freedoms reduced or revoked by their noble landlords. (Poland's numerous lesser nobles dominated the Polish state, which was actually a constitutional republic headed by an elected king who had little real power.) In 1618 the junior branch of the Hohenzollern family died out, and Prussia reverted to the elector of Brandenburg.

The elector of Brandenburg was a helpless spectator in the Thirty Years' War, his territories alternately ravaged by Swedish and Habsburg armies. Population fell drastically, and many villages disappeared. Yet this devastation paved the way for Hohenzollern absolutism because foreign armies dramatically weakened the political power of the estates, which helped the very young elector Frederick William (r. 1640–1688), later known as the "Great Elector," to ride roughshod over traditional representative rights and to take a giant step toward royal absolutism. This constitutional struggle was the most crucial in Prussian history until that of the 1860s.

Images in Society

Absolutist Palace Building

By 1700 palace building had become a veritable obsession for the rulers of central and eastern Europe. Their dramatic palaces symbolized the age of absolutist power, just as soaring Gothic cathedrals had expressed the idealized spirit of the High Middle Ages. With its classically harmonious, symmetrical, and geometric design, Versailles, shown in Image 1, served as the model for the wave of palace building that began in the last decade of the seventeenth century.

Located ten miles southwest of Paris, Versailles began as a modest hunting lodge built by Louis XIII in 1623. His son, Louis XIV, loved the site so much that he spent decades enlarging and decorating the original chateau. Between 1668 and 1670, his architect Louis Le Vau enveloped the old building within a much larger second structure that still exists today. In 1682 the new palace became the official residence of the Sun King and his court, although construction continued until 1710, when the royal chapel was completed. At any one time, several thousand people lived in the bustling and crowded palace. The awesome splendor of the eighty-yard Hall of Mirrors, replete with floor-to-ceiling mirrors and ceiling murals illustrating the king's triumphs, contrasted with the strong odors from the courtiers who commonly relieved themselves in discreet corners. Royal palaces like Versailles were intended to overawe the people and proclaim their owners' authority and power.

In 1693 Charles XI of Sweden, having reduced the power of the aristocracy, ordered the construction of his Royal Palace, which dominates the center of Stockholm to this day. Another such palace was Schönbrunn, an enormous Viennese Versailles begun in 1695 by Emperor Leopold to celebrate Austrian military victories and Habsburg might. Image 2 shows architect Joseph Bernhard Fischer von Erlach's ambitious plan for Schönbrunn palace. Erlach's plan emphasizes the palace's vast size and its role as a site for military demonstrations. Ultimately financial constraints resulted in a more modest building.

Petty German princes contributed mightily to the palace-building mania. Frederick the Great of Prussia noted that every descendant of a princely family "imagines himself to be something like Louis XIV. He builds his Versailles, has his mistresses, and maintains his army."* The elector-archbishop of Mainz, the ruling prince of that city, confessed apologetically that "building is a craze which costs much, but every fool likes his own hat."†

In central and eastern Europe, the favorite noble servants of royalty became extremely rich and powerful, and they too built grandiose palaces in the capital cities. These palaces were in part an extension of the monarch, for they surpassed the buildings of less-favored nobles and showed all the high road to fame and fortune. Take, for example, the palaces of Prince Eugene of Savoy, a French nobleman who became Austria's most famous military hero. It was Eugene who led the Austrian army, smashed the Turks, fought Louis XIV to a standstill, and generally guided the triumph of absolutism in Austria. Rewarded with great wealth by his grateful king, Eugene called on the leading architects of the day, J. B. Fischer von Erlach and

Image 1 Pierre-Denis Martin: View of the Chateau de Versailles, 1722 *(Châteaux de Versailles et de Trianon, Versailles/Réunion des Musées Nationaux/Art Resource, NY)*

Image 2 Project for the Palace at Schönbrunn (ca 1700)
(Austrian National Library, Vienna)

Image 4 View of the Petit Parc at Versailles from the Canal *(Bibliothèque nationale de France)*

Image 3 Prince Eugene's Summer Palace, Vienna *(Erich Lessing/Art Resource, NY)*

Johann Lukas von Hildebrandt, to consecrate his glory in stone and fresco. Fischer built Eugene's Winter (or Town) Palace in Vienna, and he and Hildebrandt collaborated on the prince's Summer Palace on the city's outskirts, shown in Image 3. The prince's summer residence featured two baroque gems, the Lower Belvedere and the lovely Upper Belvedere, completed in 1722 and shown here. The building's interior is equally stunning, with crouching giants serving as pillars and a magnificent great staircase.

Palace gardens were an extension of the architecture. The rational orderliness and symmetry of a garden showed that the ruler's force extended even to nature, which offered its subjugated pleasures to the delight of sovereign and courtiers. The terraces and waterworks of these gardens served as showcases for the latest techniques in military and civil engineering. Exotic plants and elaborate designs testified to the sovereign's global trading networks and elevated taste.

The gardens at Versailles, shown in Image 4, exemplify absolutist palace gardens. In the foreground of this image we see a mock naval campaign being enacted on the canal for the edification of courtiers. For diplomatic occasions, Louis XIV himself wrote lengthy guides for viewing the gardens of Versailles. Modern visitors can still follow his itineraries. The themes of the sculptures in the Versailles gardens also hailed Louis's power, with images of Apollo, the sun-god, and Neptune, the sea-god, making frequent appearances.

Compare the image of Prince Eugene's summer palace with the plans for Schönbrunn and the palace of Versailles. What did concrete objects and the manipulation of space accomplish for these rulers that mere words could not? What disadvantages might stem from using architecture in this way? Is the use of space and monumental construction still a political tool in today's world?

*Quoted in R. Ergang, *The Potsdam Fuhrer: Frederick William I, Father of Prussian Militarism* (New York: Octagon Books, 1972), p. 13.
†Quoted in J. Summerson, in *The Eighteenth Century: Europe in the Age of Enlightenment,* ed. A. Cobban (New York: McGraw-Hill, 1969), p. 80.

Online Study Center Improve Your Grade
Going Beyond Images in Society

MAP 17.2 The Growth of Austria and Brandenburg-Prussia to 1748 Austria expanded to the southwest into Hungary and Transylvania at the expense of the Ottoman Empire. It was unable to hold the rich German province of Silesia, however, which was conquered by Brandenburg-Prussia.

When he came to power in 1640, the twenty-year-old Great Elector was determined to unify his three provinces and enlarge them by diplomacy and war. These provinces were Brandenburg; Prussia, inherited in 1618; and scattered holdings along the Rhine, inherited in 1614 (see Map 17.2). Each was inhabited by German-speakers, but each had its own estates. Although the estates had not met regularly during the chaotic Thirty Years' War, taxes could not be levied without their consent. The estates of Brandenburg and Prussia were dominated by the nobility and the landowning classes, known as the **Junkers.** But this was also the case in most European countries that had representative bodies, including the English Parliament before and after the civil war. Had the estates successfully resisted the absolutist demands of the Great Elector, they too might have evolved toward more broadly based constitutionalism.

The struggle between the Great Elector and the provincial estates was long and intense. After the Thirty Years' War, noble representatives zealously reasserted the estates' control over taxes. Yet first in Brandenburg in 1653 and then in Prussia between 1661 and 1663, the Great Elector eventually had his way.

To pay for the permanent standing army he first established in 1660, Frederick William forced the estates to accept the introduction of permanent taxation without consent. The estates' power declined rapidly thereafter, for the Great Elector had both financial independence and superior force. The state's total revenue tripled during his reign, and the size of the army leaped by ten. In 1688 a population of one million was supporting a peacetime standing army of thirty thousand.

Two factors were central to the Great Elector's triumph. First, as in the formation of every absolutist state, war was a decisive factor. The ongoing struggle between Sweden and Poland for control of the Baltic after 1648 and the wars of Louis XIV in western Europe created an atmosphere of permanent crisis. The nomadic Tatars of the Crimea in southern Russia swept through Prussia in the winter of 1656–1657, killing and carrying off thousands as slaves. This invasion softened up the estates and strengthened the urgency of the Great Elector's demands for more military funding.

Second, the nobility proved willing to accept Frederick William's new claims in exchange for reconfirmation of their own privileges. The Junkers had long dominated the government through the estates, but they refused to join representatives of the towns in a common front. Instead, they accepted a compromise with the state whereby the bulk of the new taxes fell on towns and the Junkers received legal confirmation of their authority over the serfs. The elector used naked force to break the liberties of the towns; the main leader of urban opposition in the key city of Königsberg, for example, was arrested and imprisoned for life without trial.

Like Louis XIV, the Great Elector built his absolutist state on collaboration with traditional elites, reaffirming their privileges in return for loyal service and revenue. He also created a larger centralized government bureaucracy to oversee his realm and to collect the new taxes. Pre-existing representative institutions were bypassed. The Diet of Brandenburg did not meet again after 1652. In 1701 the elector's son, Frederick I, received the elevated title of king of Prussia (instead of elector) as a reward for aiding the Holy Roman emperor in the War of the Spanish Succession.

The Consolidation of Prussian Absolutism

Frederick William I, "the Soldiers' King" (r. 1713–1740), completed his grandfather's work. Though crude and ruthless, Frederick William I was the most talented reformer produced by the Hohenzollern family. Under his rule, Prussia built the best army in Europe for its size and transformed into a model military state. It was he who truly established Prussian absolutism and gave it its unique character. In the words of a famous historian of Prussia:

For a whole generation, the Hohenzollern subjects were victimized by a royal bully, imbued with an obsessive bent for military organization and military scales of value. This left a deep mark upon the institutions of Prussiandom and upon the molding of the "Prussian spirit."[3]

Frederick William was intensely attached to military life. He had, for example, an extreme fondness for tall soldiers, whom he credited with superior strength and endurance. Profoundly militaristic in temperament, Frederick William always wore an army uniform, and he lived the highly disciplined life of the professional soldier. He began his work by five or six in the morning; at ten he almost always went to the parade ground to drill or inspect his troops. His love of the army was based on a hard-headed conception of the struggle for power. Years later he summed up his life's philosophy in his instructions to his son: "A formidable army and a war chest large enough to make this army mobile in times of need can create great respect for you in the world, so that you can speak a word like the other powers."[4] This unshakable belief that the welfare of king and state depended on the army above all else reinforced Frederick William's passion for the soldier's life.

The cult of military power provided the rationale for a great expansion of absolutism in Prussia. As the king put it: "I must be served with life and limb, with house and wealth, with honour and conscience, everything must be committed except eternal salvation—that belongs to God, but all else is mine."[5] To achieve these extraordinary demands, Frederick William created a strong centralized bureaucracy and eliminated the last traces of the parliamentary estates and local self-government.

The king's power grab brought him into considerable conflict with the Junkers. In his early years he even threatened to destroy them; yet, in the end, the Prussian nobility was not destroyed but enlisted—into the army. Responding to a combination of threats and opportunities, the Junkers became the officer caste. A new compromise was worked out whereby the proud nobility imperiously commanded the peasantry in the army as well as on the estates.

Penny-pinching and hard-working, Frederick William achieved results. Above all, he built a first-rate army with third-rate resources. The standing army increased from thirty-eight thousand to eighty-three thousand during his reign. Prussia, twelfth in Europe in population, had the fourth largest army by 1740. Moreover, soldier for soldier, the Prussian army was the best in Europe, astonishing foreign observers with its precision, skill, and discipline. For the next two hundred years Prussia and then Prussianized Germany would win many crucial military battles.

Frederick William and his ministers also built an exceptionally honest and conscientious bureaucracy to administer the country and foster economic development. Like the miser he was known to be, the king loved his "blue boys" so much that he hated to "spend" them. This most militaristic of kings was, paradoxically, almost always at peace.

Nevertheless, Prussians paid a heavy and lasting price for the obsessions of their royal drillmaster. Civil society became rigid and highly disciplined, and Prussia became the "Sparta of the North"; unquestioning obedience was the highest virtue. As a Prussian minister later summed up, "To keep quiet is the first civic duty."[6] Thus the policies of Frederick William I combined with harsh peasant bondage and Junker tyranny to lay the foundations for a highly militaristic country.

The Development of Russia and the Ottoman Empire

A favorite parlor game of nineteenth-century intellectuals was debating whether Russia was a Western (European) or non-Western (Asian) society. This question was particularly fascinating because it was unanswerable. To this day Russia differs fundamentally from the West in some basic ways, though its history has paralleled that of the West in other aspects.

There was no question in the mind of Europeans, however, that the Ottomans were outsiders. Even absolutist rulers disdained Ottoman sultans as cruel and tyrannical despots. Despite stereotypes, the Ottomans were in many ways more tolerant than the West, providing protection and security to other religions while steadfastly maintaining their Muslim faith. The Ottoman state combined the Byzantine heritage of the territory they conquered with Persian and Arab traditions. Flexibility and openness to other ideas and practices were sources of strength for the empire.

- *What were the distinctive features of Russian and Ottoman absolutism in this period?*

The Mongol Yoke and the Rise of Moscow

The eastern Slavs might have emerged from the Middle Ages weak and politically divided had it not been for the Mongol conquest of the Kievan principality. The Mongols were nomadic tribes from present-day Mongolia who had been temporarily unified in the thirteenth century by Chinggis Khan (1162–1227). In five years his armies subdued all of China. His successors then turned westward, smashing everything in their path and reaching the plains of Hungary before pulling back in 1242. The Mongol army—the Golden Horde—used terror to reduce con-

A Prussian Giant Grenadier Frederick William I wanted tall, handsome soldiers. He dressed them in tight bright uniforms to distinguish them from the peasant population from which most soldiers came. He also ordered several portraits of his favorites from his court painter, J. C. Merk. Grenadiers wore the miter cap instead of an ordinary hat so that they could hurl their heavy grenades unimpeded by a broad brim. *(The Royal Collection © 2007, Her Majesty Queen Elizabeth II)*

MAP 17.3 The Expansion of Russia to 1725 After the disintegration of the Kievan state and the Mongol conquest, the princes of Moscow and their descendants gradually extended their rule over an enormous territory. ❶ Compare this map with Map 17.4, which shows Ottoman expansion from 1300. What explains the fantastic success of both the Russians and the Ottomans in expanding their territories? Why was the sixteenth century such an important period for expansion? ❷ How do you explain the geographical direction that expansion followed in each case? ❸ What happened after the periods shown on these maps? Did the territorial development of the two states diverge from each other or follow the same trajectory?

Online Study Center Improve Your Grade Interactive Map: Expansion of Russia to 1725

quered peoples to submission. As a show of force, the army would destroy an entire city, slaughtering the whole population before burning the city to the ground.

The Mongols ruled the eastern Slavs for more than two hundred years, the period of the so-called **Mongol Yoke.** They built their capital of Saray on the lower Volga (see Map 17.3) and forced the rival Slavic princes to submit to their rule and to give them tribute and slaves. If conquered peoples rebelled, the Mongols used ruthless violence to re-impose control. The Mongol khan was acknowledged by all the eastern Slavs as the supreme ruler.

Online Study Center Improve Your Grade
Primary Source: Russia's Conquest by the Mongols: A Song to Lost Lands

Unification transformed the internal political situation. Although the Mongols conquered, they were quite willing to use local princes as obedient servants and tax collectors. Thus, they did not abolish the title of "great prince," bestowing it instead on the prince who served them best and paid them most handsomely. Beginning with Alexander Nevsky in 1252, the princes of Moscow became particularly adept at serving the Mongols. They loyally put down popular uprisings and collected the khan's taxes. As reward, the princes of Moscow emerged as hereditary great princes. Eventually the Muscovite princes were able to destroy their princely rivals. Ivan III (r. 1462–1505) consolidated power around Moscow and won Novgorod, almost reaching the Baltic Sea (see Map 17.3).

By about 1480 Ivan III felt strong enough to stop acknowledging the khan as his supreme ruler. To legitimize their new authority, the princes of Moscow drew on two sources of authority. First, they declared themselves *autocrats*, meaning that, like the khans, they were the sole source of power. In addition to political authority, Moscow also took over Mongol tribute relations and borrowed institutions like the tax system, postal routes, and the census.

The second source of legitimacy lay in Moscow's claim to the political and religious inheritance of the Byzantine Empire. The title **tsar** is a contraction of *caesar*. After the fall of Constantinople to the Turks in 1453, the princes of Moscow saw themselves as the heirs of both the caesars and Orthodox Christianity, the one true faith. All the other kings of Europe were heretics; only the tsars were rightful and holy rulers. The idea was promoted by Orthodox churchmen, who spoke of "holy Russia" as the "Third Rome." Ivan's marriage to the daughter of the last Byzantine emperor further enhanced the aura of Moscow's imperial inheritance.

Historians long took at face value the tsars' claims to unlimited autocratic power over their people, from the peasants to the highest-ranking nobles or **boyars.** More recently they have begun to emphasize the considerable consensus that existed between the nobility and the self-styled *autocrat*. Along with Mongol tribute relations, Moscow inherited a tradition of ruling in cooperation with local elites. The tsars' success in combining grandiose claims to power with an extremely limited government apparatus is explained through their collaboration with boyars in Moscow and with the provincial gentry. The Russian Orthodox Church helped cement this consensus. Since the national borders of Russia corresponded to the borders of the church, religion was a source of patriotic nationalism and loyalty to the Crown.

The tsars ensured the loyalty of the elite in part by creating new nobles personally loyal to them. These new nobles made up the **service nobility,** whose members held the tsar's land on the explicit condition that they serve in his army.

Tsar and People to 1689

Developments in Russia took a chaotic turn with the reign of Ivan IV (r. 1533–1584), the famous "Ivan the Terrible," who ascended the throne at age three. His mother died, possibly poisoned, when he was eight, leaving Ivan to suffer insults and neglect from the boyars at court. At age sixteen he suddenly pushed aside his hated advisers, and in an awe-inspiring ceremony, complete

Ivan the Terrible Ivan IV, the first to take the title tsar of Russia, executed many Muscovite boyars and their peasants and servants. His ownership of all the land, trade, and industry restricted economic development. *(National Museum, Copenhagen, Denmark)*

with gold coins pouring down on his head, Ivan majestically crowned himself, taking the august title of tsar for the first time.

Selecting the beautiful and kind Anastasia of the Romanov family as his queen, the young tsar soon declared war on the remnants of Mongol power. He defeated the khanates of Kazan and Astrakhan between 1552 and 1556, adding vast new territories to the realm and laying the foundations for the huge, multiethnic Russian empire. In the course of these wars, Ivan virtually abolished the old distinction between hereditary boyar private property and land temporarily granted for service. All nobles, old and new, had to serve the tsar in order to hold land.

In 1557 Ivan turned westward, and for the next twenty-five years he waged an exhausting, unsuccessful war primarily against the large Polish-Lithuanian state. Quarreling with the boyars over the war and suspecting them of a role in the sudden death of his beloved Anastasia in 1560, the increasingly demented Ivan struck down all who stood in his way. A reign of terror ensued in which Ivan jailed and executed anyone he suspected of opposing him. He created a special corps of black-clad soldiers to execute his alleged enemies, along with their families, friends, servants, and peasants. Many victims were intimates of the court from the leading boyar families of Moscow. Their large estates were broken up and reapportioned. Ivan gave about half of the land acquired through such purges to the lower service nobility; the rest he maintained as a personal domain.

Ivan also took strides toward making all commoners servants of the tsar. His endless wars and violent purges depopulated much of central Russia. As the service nobles demanded more from the remaining peasants, growing numbers fled toward wild, recently conquered territories to the east and south. There they formed free groups and outlaw armies known as **Cossacks** and maintained a precarious independence. The solution to the problem of peasant flight was to tie peasants ever more firmly to the land and to the noble landholders, who in turn served the tsar.

Simultaneously, urban traders and artisans were also bound to their towns and jobs so that the tsar could tax them more heavily. Ivan assumed that the tsar owned Russia's trade and industry, just as he owned all the land. The urban classes had no security in their work or property, and even the wealthiest merchants were dependent agents of the tsar. Royal monopolization and service obligations checked the growth of the Russian middle classes and stood in sharp contrast to developments in western Europe, where the middle classes were gaining security in their private property.

As so often in Russia, the death of an iron-fisted tyrant—in this case, Ivan the Terrible in 1584—opened an era of violent struggles for power. Ivan's son, Theodore, died in 1598 without an heir, ushering in the "Time of Troubles" (1598–1613). The close relatives of the deceased tsar intrigued against and murdered one another, alternately fighting and welcoming the invading Swedes

Saint Basil's Cathedral, Moscow With its sloping roofs and colorful onion-shaped domes, Saint Basil's is a striking example of powerful Byzantine influences on Russian culture. According to tradition, an enchanted Ivan the Terrible blinded the cathedral's architects to ensure that they would never duplicate their fantastic achievement, which still dazzles the beholder in today's Red Square. *(George Holton/Photo Researchers)*

and Poles. Cossack bands, led by a former slave named Ivan Bolotnikov, marched northward, rallying peasants and slaughtering nobles and officials. Cossacks and peasants called for the "true tsar," who would restore their freedom of movement, reduce their heavy taxes, and lighten the yoke imposed by the landlords.

This social explosion from below brought the nobles, big and small, to their senses. They put aside their quarrels and finally crushed the Cossack rebellion at the gates of Moscow. In 1613 the nobles elected Ivan the Terrible's sixteen-year-old grandnephew, Michael Romanov, the new hereditary tsar (r. 1613–1645). Michael's election was represented as a restoration of tsarist autocracy. (See the feature "Listening to the Past: A Foreign Traveler in Russia" on pages 586–587.)

Although the new tsar successfully reconsolidated central authority, social and religious uprisings continued through the seventeenth century. In 1652 the patriarch Nikon determined to bring "corrupted" Russian practices of worship into line with the Greek Orthodox model. The self-serving church hierarchy quickly went along, but the intensely religious common people resisted. They saw Nikon as the Antichrist who was stripping them of the only thing they had—the true religion of "holy Russia." Great numbers left the church and formed communities of "Old Believers," who were hunted down and persecuted. As many as twenty thousand people burned themselves alive, singing the "hallelujah" in their chants three times rather than twice, as Nikon had demanded. After the Great Schism, the Russian masses were alienated from the established church, which became dependent on the state for its authority.

The Cossacks revolted once more against a state that was doggedly trying to reduce them to serfdom. Under Stenka Razin they moved up the Volga River in 1670 and 1671, attracting a great army of urban poor and peasants, killing landlords and government officials, and proclaiming freedom from oppression. Eventually this rebellion was defeated.

The normal obstacles to state-building were exacerbated in Russia's case by the huge size of its territory, its thinly spread population, and the economic devastation wrought by the Time of Troubles. Nevertheless, Romanov tsars made several important achievements during the second half of the seventeenth century. After a long war, Russia gained a large mass of Ukraine from weak and decentralized Poland in 1667 (see Map 17.3) and completed the conquest of Siberia by the end of the century. Territorial expansion was accompanied by growth of the bureaucracy and the army. Russian tsars turned to imported foreign experts to help build and reform the Russian army. The great profits from Siberia's natural resources, especially furs, funded the Romanov's bid for great power status.

The Reforms of Peter the Great

Heir to the first efforts at state-building, Peter the Great (r. 1682–1725) embarked on a tremendous campaign to accelerate and complete these processes. A giant for his time, at six feet seven inches, and possessing enormous energy and willpower, Peter was determined to build and improve the army. He was equally determined to continue the tsarist tradition of territorial expansion. After 1689 Peter ruled independently for thirty-six years, only one of which was peaceful.

Fascinated by weapons and foreign technology, the tsar led a group of 250 Russian officials and young nobles on an eighteen-month tour of western European capitals. Traveling unofficially to avoid lengthy diplomatic ceremonies, Peter worked with his hands at various crafts and met with foreign kings and experts. He was particularly impressed with the growing power of the Dutch and the English, and he considered how Russia could profit from their example.

Returning to Russia, Peter entered into a secret alliance with Denmark and Poland to wage a sudden war of aggression against Sweden. Despite the country's small population and limited agricultural resources, Swedish rulers in the seventeenth century had developed a strong absolutist state and had built an excellent standing army. Like other absolutist rulers, Charles XI of Sweden built a beautiful palace in his capital, modeled after Louis XIV's Versailles. Expanding beyond its borders, Sweden held substantial territory in northern Germany, Finland, and Estonia. Yet these possessions were scattered and appeared vulnerable. Above all, Peter and his allies believed that their combined forces could win easy victories because Sweden was in the hands of a new and inexperienced king.

Eighteen-year-old Charles XII (1697–1718) surprised Peter. He defeated Denmark quickly in 1700, then turned on Russia. In a blinding snowstorm, his well-trained professional army attacked and routed unsuspecting Russians besieging the Swedish fortress of Narva on the Baltic coast. Peter and the survivors fled in panic to Moscow. It was, for the Russians, a grim beginning to the long and brutal Great Northern War, which lasted from 1700 to 1721.

Suffering defeat and faced with a military crisis, the energetic Peter responded with a long series of practical but far-reaching measures designed to increase state power,

Gustaf Cederstrom: The Swedish Victory at Narva (1701) This poignant re-creation focuses on the contrast between the Swedish officers in handsome dress uniforms and the battered Russian soldiers laying down their standards in surrender. Charles XII of Sweden scored brilliant, rapid-fire victories over Denmark, Saxony, and Russia, but he failed to make peace with Peter while he was ahead and eventually lost Sweden's holdings on the Baltic coast. *(The National Museum of Fine Arts, Stockholm)*

strengthen his armies, and gain victory. Tightening up Muscovy's old service system, he required every nobleman, great or small, to serve in the army or in the civil administration—for life. Since a more modern army and government required skilled technicians and experts, Peter created schools and universities to produce them. One of his most hated reforms was requiring a five-year education away from home for every young nobleman. Peter established an interlocking military-civilian bureaucracy with fourteen ranks, and he decreed that all had to start at the bottom and work toward the top. Some people of non-noble origins rose to high positions in this embryonic meritocracy. Drawing on his experience abroad, Peter searched out talented foreigners and placed them in his service. These measures gradually combined to make the army and government more powerful and efficient.

Peter also greatly increased the service requirements of commoners. In the wake of the Narva disaster, he established a regular standing army of more than two hundred thousand peasant-soldiers commanded by officers from the nobility. In addition, special forces of Cossacks and foreigners numbered more than one hundred thousand. The departure of a drafted peasant boy was celebrated by his family and village almost like a funeral, since the recruit was drafted for life. The peasantry also served with its taxes, which increased threefold during Peter's reign. Serfs were arbitrarily assigned to work in the growing

Peter the Great in 1723 This compelling portrait by Grigory Musikiysky captures the strength and determination of the warrior-tsar after more than three decades of personal rule. In his hand Peter holds the scepter, symbol of royal sovereignty, and across his breastplate is draped an ermine fur, a mark of honor. In the background are the battleships of Russia's new Baltic fleet and the famous St. Peter and St. Paul Fortress that Peter built in St. Petersburg. *(Kremlin Museums, Moscow/The Bridgeman Art Library)*

number of factories and mines. Most of these industrial enterprises were directly or indirectly owned by the state, and they were worked almost exclusively for the military.

The constant warfare of Peter's reign consumed 80 to 85 percent of all revenues and brought only modest territorial expansion. Yet the Great Northern War with Sweden was crowned in the end by Russian victory. Peter's new war machine crushed the smaller army of Sweden in Ukraine at Poltava in 1709, one of the most significant battles in Russian history. The war dragged on until 1721, but Sweden never regained the offensive. Estonia and present-day Latvia (see Map 17.3) came under Russian rule for the first time. Russia became the dominant power on the Baltic Sea and very much a European Great Power. If victory or defeat is the ultimate historical criterion, Peter's reforms were a success.

There were other important consequences of Peter's reign. Because of his feverish desire to use modern technology to strengthen the army, many Westerners and Western ideas flowed into Russia for the first time. For Peter, modernization meant westernization. He thus required nobles to shave their heavy beards and wear Western clothing, previously banned in Russia. He required them to attend parties where young men and women would mix together and freely choose their own spouses. He forced a warrior elite to accept administrative service as an honorable occupation. From these efforts a new class of Western-oriented Russians began to emerge.

Online Study Center Improve Your Grade
Primary Source: Peter the Great Imposes Western Styles on the Russians

At the same time, vast numbers of Russians hated Peter's massive changes. For nobles, one of Peter's most detested reforms was the imposition of unigeniture—inheritance of land by one son alone—cutting daughters and other sons from family property. For peasants, the reign of the reforming tsar saw a significant increase in the bonds of serfdom. The gulf between the enserfed peasantry and the educated nobility widened more, even though all were caught up in the demands of the sovereign.

Thus Peter built on the service obligations of old Muscovy. His monarchical absolutism was truly the culmination of the long development of a unique Russian civilization. Yet the creation of a more modern army and state introduced much that was new and Western to Russia. This development paved the way for Russia to move somewhat closer to the European mainstream in its thought and institutions during the Enlightenment, especially under Catherine the Great.

The Growth of St. Petersburg

Nothing exemplifies the scope of Peter's reforms like his creation of St. Petersburg. In 1700, when the Great Northern War began, the city did not exist; there was only a small Swedish fortress on one of the waterlogged islands at the mouth of the Neva River, where it flows into the Baltic Sea. In 1702 Peter the Great's armies seized this desolate outpost. Within a year the reforming tsar decided to build a new city there and to make it, rather than ancient Moscow, his capital.

To secure the Baltic coast, military construction was the main concern for the next eight years. A mighty fortress was built on the newly named Peter Island, and a port and shipyards were built across the river on the mainland as a Russian navy came into being. From the inhospitable northern marshland Peter would create a future metropolis gloriously bearing his name.

After the decisive Russian victory at Poltava in 1709 greatly reduced the threat of Swedish armies, Peter moved into high gear. In one imperious decree after another, he ordered his people to build a city equal to any in the world. Such a city had to be Western and modern, just as Peter's army had to be Western and permanent. From such a "window on Europe," Peter believed, it would be easier to reform the country militarily and administratively.

These general political goals matched Peter's architectural ideas, which had been influenced by his travels in western Europe. First, Peter wanted a comfortable, "modern" city. Modernity meant broad, straight, stone-paved avenues; houses built in a uniform line and not haphazardly set back from the street; large parks; canals for drainage; stone bridges; and street lighting. Second, all buildings had to conform to detailed architectural regulations set down by the government. Finally, each social group—the nobility, the merchants, the artisans, and so on—was to live in a certain section of town. In short, the city and its population were to conform to a carefully defined urban plan.

Peter used the traditional methods of Russian autocracy to build his modern capital. Its creation was just one

St. Petersburg, ca 1760 Rastrelli's remodeled Winter Palace, which housed the royal family until the Russian Revolution of 1917, stands on the left along the Neva River. The Navy Office with its famous golden spire and other government office buildings are nearby and across the river. Russia became a naval power and St. Petersburg a great port. *(Michael Holford)*

of the heavy obligations he dictatorially imposed on all of Russian society. The peasants bore the heaviest burdens. Just as the government drafted peasants for the army, it also drafted twenty-five thousand to forty thousand men each summer to labor in St. Petersburg for three months without pay. Every ten to fifteen peasant households had to furnish one worker each summer and then pay a special tax in order to feed him in St. Petersburg.

Peasants hated this forced labor, and each year one-fourth to one-third of those sent risked brutal punishment to run away. Many peasant construction workers died from hunger, sickness, and accidents. Thus beautiful St. Petersburg was built by the shoveling, carting, and paving of a mass of conscripted serfs.

Peter also drafted more privileged groups to his city. Nobles were summarily ordered to build costly stone houses and palaces in St. Petersburg and to live in them most of the year. The more serfs a noble possessed, the bigger his dwelling had to be. Merchants and artisans were also commanded to settle and build in St. Petersburg. These nobles and merchants were then required to pay for the city's avenues, parks, canals, embankments, and bridges, all of which were costly in money and lives because they were built on a swamp. The building of St. Petersburg was, in truth, an enormous direct tax levied on the wealthy, which in turn forced the peasantry to do most of the work.

By the time of Peter's death in 1725, there were at least six thousand houses and numerous impressive government buildings in St. Petersburg. The city blossomed in the eighteenth century, at least in its wealthy showpiece sections. Peter's youngest daughter, Elizabeth (r. 1741–1762), named as her chief architect Bartolomeo Rastrelli, who came to Russia from Italy as a boy of fifteen in 1715. Combining Italian and Russian traditions into a unique, wildly colorful St. Petersburg style, Rastrelli built many palaces for the nobility and all the larger government buildings erected during Elizabeth's reign. He also rebuilt the Winter Palace as an enormous, aqua-colored royal residence, now the Hermitage Museum. All the while St. Petersburg grew rapidly, and its almost three hundred thousand inhabitants in 1782 made it one of the world's largest cities. Peter and his successors created a magnificent royal city from nothing, which unmistakably proclaimed the power of Russia's rulers and the creative potential of the absolutist state.

The Growth of the Ottoman Empire

Most Christian Europeans perceived the Ottomans as the antithesis of their own values and traditions and viewed the empire as driven by an insatiable lust for warfare and conquest. In their view the fall of Constantinople was a catastrophe and the taking of the Balkans a despotic imprisonment of those territories. The Ottoman Empire seemed the epitome of Eastern exoticism, religious fanaticism, and tyranny. From the perspective of the Ottomans, the world looked very different. The siege of Constantinople liberated a glorious city from its long decline under the Byzantines. Rather than being a despoiled captive, the Balkans became a haven for refugees fleeing the growing intolerance of Western Christian powers. The Ottoman Empire provided Jews, Muslims, and even some Christians safety from the Inquisition and religious war: the Iberian powers tried to impose Christianity through conversion or exile, but Islam and Judaism remained part of the conversation of post-Reformation Europe because of the presence of the Ottoman Empire at Europe's gate.

The Ottomans came out of Central Asia as conquering warriors, settled in Anatolia (present-day Turkey), and created one of history's greatest empires (see pages 466 and 566). At their peak in the mid-sixteenth century under Sultan Suleiman the Magnificent (r. 1520–1566), they ruled the most powerful empire in the world. Their possessions stretched from western Persia across North Africa and into the heart of central Europe (see Map 17.4). In 1690 a Turkish visitor to Versailles wrote in his travel diary: "The King of France is the Sultan Suleiman of our time."

Ottoman expansion borrowed from the peoples they conquered. They were heirs to the Byzantine Empire and, through it, of Rome and its vision of universal empire. From the Byzantines, they adopted the tax structure and the use of religion to bind together a diverse empire. From the Persians, the Ottomans borrowed political and financial practices, and from the Arabs, religion and spirituality. This openness and adaptability—missing from most Western accounts of the Ottomans—was largely responsible for the empire's longevity.

When the Ottomans captured Constantinople in 1453, they fulfilled a long-held Islamic dream. They also shattered a bulwark of Christian identity. Founded by the emperor who introduced the Christian church to mighty Rome, for a millennium Constantinople had stood as a symbol of Christianity and its links to imperial power. Though the Byzantine Empire gradually shrank, the city itself had withstood numerous sieges. The loss of Constantinople was not just symbolic but strategic as well. The city stands at the natural gateway between the Black and Mediterranean Seas, between Europe and the Balkans. With the capture of Constantinople—renamed

MAP 17.4 The Ottoman Empire at Its Height, 1566 The Ottomans, like their great rivals the Habsburgs, rose to rule a vast dynastic empire encompassing many different peoples and ethnic groups. The army and the bureaucracy served to unite the disparate territories into a single state under an absolutist ruler.

Istanbul—the Ottomans and Islam occupied a permanent place in the European landscape. By 1600 Istanbul was one of the largest cities in the world, with a population of seven hundred thousand.

Ottoman expansion continued to the south as well. The Ottomans first conquered Syria and Iraq, and in 1517 Sultan Selim I (r. 1512–1520) invaded the Egyptian Mameluke empire and quickly captured Egypt, North Africa, and the Arabian peninsula. His successor, Suleiman the Magnificent, turned north, capturing Bosnia, Croatia, Romania, Ukraine, and part of Hungary at the Battle of Mohács in 1526. For the next hundred and fifty years, the Ottomans ruled the many different ethnic groups living in southeastern Europe and the eastern Mediterranean. In 1529 their European expansion was halted with a failed siege of the Habsburg capital, Vienna. The Ottoman loss at the Battle of Lepanto in 1571, against the Christian Holy League, confirmed the limits of their ambitions in Europe.

The Ottoman Empire was originally built on a unique model of state and society. There was an almost complete absence of private landed property. Agricultural land was the personal hereditary property of the **sultan,** and peasants paid taxes to use the land. There was therefore no security of landholding and no hereditary nobility, two key features of western European society.

The Ottomans also employed a distinctive form of government administration. The top ranks of the bureaucracy were staffed by the sultan's slave corps. Because Muslim law prohibited enslaving other Muslims, the sultan's agents purchased slaves along the borders of the empire. Within the realm, the sultan levied a "tax" of one thousand to three thousand male children on the conquered Christian populations in the Balkans every year. Young slaves were raised in Turkey as Muslims and were trained to fight and to administer. The most talented rose to the top of the bureaucracy, where they might acquire wealth and power; the less fortunate formed the brave and skillful core of the sultan's army, the janissary corps. Lurid accounts of weeping Christian boys being carried off into Ottoman slavery did much to foster the idea of the brutal, fanatical Turk in the European mind.

After 1453 Istanbul became the capital of the empire and, with the transfer of the caliphate from Cairo, the religious center of Sunni Islam. The "old palace" was for the sultan's female family members, who lived in isolation under the care of eunuchs. The newly constructed Topkapi Palace was where officials worked and young slaves trained for future administrative or military careers. To prevent wives from bringing foreign influence into government—a constant concern in the West—sultans procreated only with their concubines and not with official wives. They also adopted a policy of allowing each concubine to produce only one male heir. At a young age, each son went to govern a province of the empire under his mother's supervision. These practices were intended to stabilize power and prevent a recurrence of the civil wars of the late fourteenth and early fifteenth centuries.

Sultan Suleiman undid these policies when he boldly married his concubine and had several children with her. He established a wing in the Topkapi Palace for his own female family members and his brothers' families. Starting with Suleiman, imperial wives began to take on more power. Marriages were arranged between sultans' daughters and high-ranking servants, creating powerful new members of the imperial household. Over time, the sultan's exclusive authority waned in favor of a more bureaucratic administration. These changes brought the Ottoman court closer to the European model of factionalism, intrigue, and informal female power. (See the feature "Individuals in Society: Hürrem.")

In this period the Ottoman Empire experienced the same economic and social crises that affected the rest of Europe. In the 1580s and 1590s rebellions broke out among many different groups in the vast empire: frustrated students, underpaid janissaries, and ambitious provincial governors. Revolts continued during the sev-

The Sultan's Harem at Topkapi Palace, Istanbul Sultan Suleiman I created separate quarters at the Topkapi Palace for his wife Hürrem and her ladies-in-waiting. His successors transferred all of their wives, concubines, and female family members to the harem at Topkapi, carefully situated out of sight of the staterooms and courtyards where public affairs took place. The harem was the object of intense curiosity and fascination in the West. (*Vanni/Art Resource, NY*)

enteenth century as the janissaries formed alliances with court factions that resulted in the overthrow or execution of several Ottoman sultans.

In the late seventeenth century the Ottomans succeeded in marshaling their forces for one last attack on the Habsburgs, and a huge Turkish army laid siege to Vienna in 1683. After holding out against great odds for two months, the city was relieved at the last minute by reinforcements, and the Ottomans were forced to retreat. Soon the retreat became a rout. As Russian and Venetian allies attacked on other fronts, the Habsburgs conquered almost all of Hungary and Transylvania by 1699 (see Map 17.4). The Habsburgs completed their victory in 1718, with the Treaty of Passarowitz. These defeats might have led to reform of Ottoman political, military, and economic structures. They did not, and the empire's strength slowly eroded and with it Western fears of the Ottoman threat.

Individuals in Society

Hürrem

In Muslim culture *harem* means a sacred place or a sanctuary, which is forbidden to profane outsiders. The term was applied to the part of the household occupied by women and children and forbidden to men outside the family. The most famous member of the Ottoman sultan's harem was Hürrem, wife of Suleiman the Magnificent.

Hürrem (1505?–1558) came to the harem as a slave-concubine. Like many of the sultan's concubines, Hürrem was of foreign birth. Tradition holds that she was born Aleksandra Lisowska in what was the kingdom of Poland and today is Ukraine. She was captured during a Tatar raid and enslaved. Between 1517 and 1520, when she was about fifteen years old, she entered the imperial harem. Venetian reports insist that she was not outstandingly beautiful but was possessed of wonderful grace, charm, and good humor. These qualities gained her the Turkish nickname Hürrem, or "joyful one." After her arrival in the harem, Hürrem quickly became the imperial favorite.

Suleiman's love for Hürrem led him to break all precedents for the role of a concubine, including the rule that concubines must cease having children once they give birth to a male heir. By 1531 Hürrem had given birth to one daughter and five sons. In 1533 or 1534 Suleiman entered formal marriage with his consort—an unprecedented honor for a concubine. He reportedly gave his exclusive attention to his wife and also defied convention by allowing Hürrem to remain in the palace throughout her life instead of accompanying her son to a provincial governorship as other concubines had done.

Contemporaries were shocked by Hürrem's influence over the sultan and resentful of the apparent role she played in politics and diplomacy. The Venetian ambassador Bassano wrote that "the Janissaries and the entire court hate her and her children likewise, but because the Sultan loves her, no one dares to speak."* She was suspected of using witchcraft to control the sultan and accused of ordering the death of the sultan's first-born son (with another mother) in 1553. These stories were based on court gossip and rumor. The correspondence between Suleiman and Hürrem, unavailable until the nineteenth century, along with Suleiman's own diaries, confirms her status as the sultan's most trusted confidant and adviser. During his frequent absences, the pair exchanged passionate love letters. Hürrem included information about the political situation and warnings about any potential uprisings. She also intervened in affairs between the empire and her former home. She wrote to Polish king Sigismund Augustus and seems to have helped Poland attain its privileged diplomatic status. She brought a particularly feminine touch to diplomatic relations, sending the Persian shah and the Polish king personally embroidered articles.

Hürrem used her enormous pension to contribute a mosque, two schools, a hospital, a fountain, and two public baths to Istanbul. In Jerusalem, Mecca, and Istanbul, she provided soup kitchens and hospices for pilgrims and the poor. She died in 1558, eight years before her husband. Her son Selim II (r. 1566–1574) inherited the throne.

Hürrem and her ladies in the harem.
(Bibliothèque nationale de France)

Drawing from reports of contemporary Western observers, historians depicted Hürrem as a manipulative and power-hungry social climber. They saw her career as the beginning of a "sultanate of women" in which strong imperial leadership gave way to court intrigue and dissipation. More recent historians have emphasized the intelligence and courage Hürrem demonstrated in navigating the ruthlessly competitive world of the harem.

Hürrem's journey from Ukrainian maiden to harem slave girl to sultan's wife captured enormous public attention. She is the subject of numerous paintings, plays, and novels as well as of an opera, a ballet, and a symphony by the composer Haydn. Interest in and suspicion of Hürrem continues. In 2003 a Turkish miniseries once more depicted her as a scheming intriguer.

Questions for Analysis

1. Compare Hürrem to other powerful early modern women such as Isabella of Castile, Elizabeth I of England, and Catherine de' Medici of France.
2. What can an exceptional woman like Hürrem reveal about the broader political and social world in which she lived?

*Cited in Galina Yermolenko, "Roxolana: The Greatest Empress of the East," in *The Muslim World* 95 (2005): 2.

Source: Leslie P. Pierce, *The Imperial Harem: Women and Sovereignty in the Ottoman Empire* (New York: Oxford University Press, 1993).

Online Study Center Improve Your Grade
Going Beyond Individuals in Society

Religious Diversity in the Ottoman Empire

Despite Western perceptions, the Ottomans were more tolerant of religious differences than were the Europeans. They recognized Christians and Jews as "peoples of the Book" who followed the same biblical tradition as Islam. Building on the practices of the great Middle Eastern empires, the Ottomans divided their subjects into religious communities, and each *millet,* or "nation," enjoyed autonomous self-government under its religious leaders. (The Ottoman Empire recognized Orthodox Christians, Jews, Armenian Christians, and Muslims as distinct millets.) The **millet system** created a powerful bond between the Ottoman ruling class and the different religious leaders, who supported the sultan's rule in return for extensive authority over their own communities. Each millet collected taxes for the state, regulated group behavior, and maintained law courts, schools, synagogues, and hospitals for its people. Individuals outside the ruling elite had status only through their millet membership.

Supported and reassured by religious toleration and cultural autonomy, non-Muslim minorities coexisted and commingled with the Muslim majority. Greek, Jewish, and Armenian merchants moved easily to and from Europe, drawing Ottomans and Europeans closer together despite recurring war and conflict. Armenian merchants excelled as international silk merchants, Jews as textile manufacturers and financiers, and Greeks as mariners and shipowners, although all three groups participated in all Ottoman occupations in the sixteenth and seventeenth centuries.[7] Religious diversity was mostly a source of strength for the Ottomans, allowing them to integrate many different ethnicities into the empire and to profit from the skills and networks of each group.

Despite its tolerance, the Ottoman Empire was an explicitly Islamic state. Members of the Muslim religious elite were educated at religious schools (*medreses*) attached to mosques. *Muftis* supervised mosques and religious schools and wrote interpretations of Islamic law, and state-appointed *kadis* administered the law. Whereas non-Muslims had their own courts for dealings among themselves, any conflict involving a Muslim was regulated by a kadi in an Islamic court. Wariness of the Islamic courts encouraged non-Muslims to deal with their own as much as possible. However, the Ottomans showed the same openness in law as in empire building. They adopted the most flexible of Muslim law traditions, and they accepted provincial law codes that respected pre-existing local laws. Under Suleiman the Magnificent and his successors, a process of legal centralization began; provincial laws were codified and standardized. The sultan's claim to be caliph—the guide for the community of all Muslims—helped legitimize this process of legal centralization. The legal reforms won Suleiman the title "the Lawgiver" from his subjects.

Chapter Summary

- What social and economic changes affected central and eastern Europe from 1400 to 1650?
- How and why did the rulers of Austria and Prussia, each in different political and social environments, manage to build powerful absolute monarchies that proved more durable than that of Louis XIV?
- What were the distinctive features of Russian and Ottoman absolutism in this period?

From about 1400 to 1650 social and economic developments in eastern Europe diverged from those in western Europe. In the East, after enjoying relative freedom in the Middle Ages, peasants and townspeople lost freedom and fell under the economic, social, and legal authority of the nobles, who increased their power and prestige.

Within this framework of resurgent serfdom and entrenched nobility, Austrian and Prussian monarchs fashioned absolutist states in the seventeenth and early eighteenth centuries. These monarchs won absolutist control over standing armies, taxation, and representative bodies, but they did not question underlying social and economic relationships. Indeed, they enhanced the privileges of the nobles, who filled enlarged armies and growing state bureaucracies. In exchange for entrenched privileges over their peasants, nobles thus cooperated with the growth of state power.

In Russia the social and economic trends were similar, but the timing of political absolutism was different. Mongol conquest and rule were a crucial experience, and a harsh indigenous tsarist autocracy was firmly in place by the reign of Ivan the Terrible in the sixteenth century. More than a century later Peter the Great succeeded in modernizing Russia's traditional absolutism by reforming the army and the bureaucracy. Farther to the east, the Ottoman sultans developed a distinctive political and economic system in which all land theoretically belonged to the sultan, who was served by a slave corps of administrators and soldiers. The Ottoman Empire was relatively tolerant on religious matters and served as a haven for Jews and other marginalized religious groups.

Triumphant absolutism interacted spectacularly with the arts. Central and eastern European rulers built grandiose palaces, and even whole cities, like St. Petersburg, to glorify their power and majesty.

Key Terms

serfdom
hereditary subjugation
Protestant Union
Peace of Westphalia
absolutism
Bohemian Estates
Battle of Mohács
Pragmatic Sanction
elector of Brandenburg
Junkers
Mongol Yoke
tsar
boyars
service nobility
Cossacks
sultan
millet system

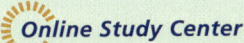 Online Study Center **Improve** Your Grade Flashcards

Suggested Reading

Bushkovitch, Paul. *Peter the Great: The Struggle for Power, 1671–1725.* 2001. An outstanding biography of the Russian tsar.

Engel, Barbara A. *Women in Russia, 1700–2000.* 2004. An excellent account of the role of women in Russian society over three centuries.

Goffman, Daniel. *The Ottoman Empire and Early Modern Europe.* 2002. An original and valuable study of Ottoman relations with the European world.

Hagen, William W. *Ordinary Prussians: Brandenburg Junkers and Villagers, 1500–1840.* 2002. Provides a fascinating encounter with the people of a Prussian estate.

Hughes, Lindsey, ed. *Peter the Great and the West: New Perspectives.* 2001. Essays by leading scholars on the reign of Peter the Great and his opening of Russia to the West.

Ingrao, Charles W. *The Habsburg Monarchy,* 2d ed. 2000. An excellent synthesis of the social development of the Habsburg empire in the early modern period.

Kappeler, Adreas. *The Russian Empire: Ethnicity and Nationalism.* 2001. Explains the rise of a multiethnic empire in Russia from the seventeenth century on.

Kollmann, N. Shields. *By Honor Bound: State and Society in Early Modern Russia.* 1999. An excellent study of politics and values among the Russian elite.

Lincoln, W. Bruce. *Sunlight at Midnight: St. Petersburg and the Rise of Modern Russia.* 2001. Captures the spirit of Peter the Great's new northern capital.

McKay, Derek. *The Great Elector: Frederick William of Brandenburg-Prussia.* 2001. Examines the formative years of Prussian power.

Murphey, Rhoads. *Ottoman Warfare, 1500–1700.* 1999. A good introduction to Ottoman military history, including warfare between the Ottomans and European states.

Ogilvie, Sheilagh, and Bob Scribner, eds. *Germany: A New Economic and Social History, 1450–1800,* 2 vols. 1996. A broad overview of life in central Europe in the early modern period.

Parker, Geoffrey. *The Thirty Years War,* 2d ed. 1997. The standard account of the Thirty Years' War.

Quataert, Donald. *The Ottoman Empire, 1700–1922.* 2000. A recent synthesis of Ottoman history by a leading historian.

Riasanovsky, Nicholas V., and Mark Steinberg. *A History of Russia to 1855.* 2004. An excellent starting place for students interested in Russian history.

Notes

1. H. Kamen, "The Economic and Social Consequences of the Thirty Years' War," *Past and Present* 39 (April 1968): 44–61.
2. Quoted in F. L. Carsten, *The Origins of Prussia* (Oxford: Clarendon Press, 1954), p. 175.
3. H. Rosenberg, *Bureaucracy, Aristocracy, and Autocracy: The Prussian Experience, 1660–1815* (Boston: Beacon Press, 1966), p. 38.
4. Ibid., p. 43.
5. Quoted in R. A. Dorwart, *The Administrative Reforms of Frederick William I of Prussia* (Cambridge, Mass.: Harvard University Press, 1953), p. 226.
6. Quoted in Rosenberg, *Bureaucracy, Aristocracy, and Autocracy,* p. 40.
7. D. Goffman, *The Ottoman Empire and Early Modern Europe* (Cambridge: Cambridge University Press, 2002), pp. 9–18, 83–91.

Listening to the Past

A Foreign Traveler in Russia

Seventeenth-century Russia remained a remote and mysterious land for western and even central Europeans, who had few direct contacts with the tsar's dominion. Developing their ideas of refined society and gradual progress (see Chapter 18), Westerners portrayed eastern Europe as more "barbaric" and less "civilized" than their homelands. Thus they expanded eastern Europe's undeniably harsher social and economic conditions to encompass a very debatable cultural and moral inferiority.

Knowledge of Russia came mainly from occasional travelers who had visited Muscovy and sometimes wrote accounts of what they saw. The most famous of these accounts was by the German Adam Olearius (ca 1599–1671), who was sent to Moscow by the duke of Holstein on three diplomatic missions in the 1630s. These missions ultimately proved unsuccessful, but they provided Olearius with a rich store of information for his *Travels in Muscovy*, from which the following excerpts are taken. Published in German in 1647 and soon translated into several languages (but not Russian), Olearius's unflattering but well-informed study played a major role in shaping European ideas about Russia.

The government of the Russians is what political theorists call a "dominating and despotic monarchy," where the sovereign, that is, the tsar or the grand prince who has obtained the crown by right of succession, rules the entire land alone, and all the people are his subjects, and where the nobles and princes no less than the common folk—townspeople and peasants—are his serfs and slaves, whom he rules and treats as a master treats his servants. . . .

If the Russians be considered in respect to their character, customs, and way of life, they are justly to be counted among the barbarians. . . . The vice of drunkenness is so common in this nation, among people of every station, clergy and laity, high and low, men and women, old and young, that when they are seen now and then lying about in the streets, wallowing in the mud, no attention is paid to it, as something habitual. If a cart driver comes upon such a drunken pig whom he happens to know, he shoves him onto his cart and drives him home, where he is paid his fare. No one ever refuses an opportunity to drink and to get drunk, at any time and in any place, and usually it is done with vodka. . . .

The Russians being naturally tough and born, as it were, for slavery, they must be kept under a harsh and strict yoke and must be driven to do their work with clubs and whips, which they suffer without impatience, because such is their station, and they are accustomed to it. Young and half-grown fellows sometimes come together on certain days and train themselves in fisticuffs, to accustom themselves to receiving blows, and, since habit is second nature, this makes blows given as punishment easier to bear. Each and all, they are slaves and serfs. . . .

Because of slavery and their rough and hard life, the Russians accept war readily and are well suited to it. On certain occasions, if need be, they reveal themselves as courageous and daring soldiers. . . .

Although the Russians, especially the common populace, living as slaves under a harsh yoke, can bear and endure a great deal out of love for their masters, yet if the pressure is beyond measure, then it can be said of them: "Patience, often wounded, finally turned into fury." A dangerous indignation results, turned not so much against their sovereign as against the lower authorities, especially if the people have been much oppressed by them and by their supporters and have not been protected by the higher authorities. And once they are aroused and enraged, it is not easy to appease them. Then, disregarding all dangers that may ensue, they resort to every kind of

The brutality of serfdom is shown in this illustration from Olearius's *Travels in Muscovy.* *(University of Illinois Library, Champaign)*

violence and behave like madmen. . . . They own little; most of them have no feather beds; they lie on cushions, straw, mats, or their clothes; they sleep on benches and, in winter, like the non-Germans [natives] in Livonia, upon the oven, which serves them for cooking and is flat on the top; here husband, wife, children, servants, and maids huddle together. In some houses in the countryside we saw chickens and pigs under the benches and the ovens. . . . Russians are not used to delicate food and dainties; their daily food consists of porridge, turnips, cabbage, and cucumbers, fresh and pickled, and in Moscow mostly of big salt fish which stink badly, because of the thrifty use of salt, yet are eaten with relish. . . .

The Russians can endure extreme heat. In the bathhouse they stretch out on benches and let themselves be beaten and rubbed with bunches of birch twigs and wisps of bast (which I could not stand); and when they are hot and red all over and so exhausted that they can bear it no longer in the bathhouse, men and women rush outdoors naked and pour cold water over their bodies; in winter they even wallow in the snow and rub their skin with it as if it were soap; then they go back into the hot bathhouse. And since bathhouses are usually near rivers and brooks, they can throw themselves straight from the hot into the cold bath. . . .

Generally noble families, even the small nobility, rear their daughters in secluded chambers, keeping them hidden from outsiders; and a bridegroom is not allowed to have a look at his bride until he receives her in the bridal chamber. Therefore some happen to be deceived, being given a misshapen and sickly one instead of a fair one, and sometimes a kinswoman or even a maidservant instead of a daughter; of which there have been examples even among the highborn. No wonder therefore that often they live together like cats and dogs and that wife-beating is so common among Russians. . . .

In the Kremlin and in the city there are a great many churches, chapels, and monasteries, both within and without the city walls, over two thousand in all. This is so because every nobleman who has some fortune has a chapel built for himself, and most of them are of stone. The stone churches are round and vaulted inside. . . . They allow neither organs nor any other musical instruments in their churches, saying: Instruments that have neither souls nor life cannot praise God. . . .

In their churches there hang many bells, sometimes five or six, the largest not over two hundredweights. They ring these bells to summon people to church, and also when the priest during mass raises the chalice. In Moscow, because of the multitude of churches and chapels, there are several thousand bells, which during the divine service create such a clang and din that one unaccustomed to it listens in amazement.

Questions for Analysis

1. In what ways were all social groups in Russia similar, according to Olearius?
2. How did Olearius characterize the Russians in general? What supporting evidence did he offer for his judgment?
3. Does Olearius's account help explain Stenka Razin's rebellion? In what ways?
4. On the basis of these representative passages, why do you think Olearius's book was so popular and influential in central and western Europe?

Source: G. Vernadsky and R. T. Fisher, Jr., eds., *A Source Book for Russian History from Early Times to 1917,* vol. 1 (New Haven: Yale University Press, 1972), pp. 249–251. Copyright © 1972 by Yale University Press. Reprinted by permission of Yale University Press.

Voltaire, the renowned Enlightenment thinker, leans forward on the left to exchange ideas and witty conversation with Frederick the Great, king of Prussia. *(Bildarchiv Preussischer Kulturbesitz/ Art Resource, NY)*

chapter 18

TOWARD A NEW WORLDVIEW, 1540–1789

chapter preview

The Scientific Revolution
- What was revolutionary in new attitudes toward the natural world?

The Enlightenment
- How did the new worldview affect the way people thought about society and human relations?

The Enlightenment and Absolutism
- What impact did this new way of thinking have on political developments and monarchical absolutism?

The intellectual developments of the seventeenth and eighteenth centuries created the modern worldview that the West continues to hold—and debate—to this day. In the seventeenth century fundamentally new ways of understanding the natural world emerged. Those leading the changes saw themselves as philosophers and referred to their field of study as "natural philosophy." In the nineteenth century scholars hailed their achievements as a "scientific revolution" that produced modern science as we know it. The new "science" created in the seventeenth century entailed the search for precise knowledge of the physical world based on the union of experimental observations with sophisticated mathematics. Whereas medieval scholars looked to authoritative texts like the Bible or the classics, seventeenth-century natural philosophers performed experiments and relied on increasingly complex mathematical calculations. The resulting conception of the universe and its laws remained in force until Einstein's discoveries in the first half of the twentieth century.

In the eighteenth century philosophers extended the use of reason from nature to human society. They sought to bring the light of reason to bear on the darkness of prejudice, outmoded traditions, and ignorance. Self-proclaimed members of an "Enlightenment" movement, they wished to bring the same progress to human affairs as their predecessors had brought to the understanding of the natural world. While the scientific revolution ushered in modern science, the Enlightenment created concepts of human rights, equality, progress, universalism, and tolerance that still guide Western societies today.

While many view the scientific revolution and the Enlightenment as bedrocks of the achievement of Western civilization, others have seen a darker side. For these critics, the mastery over nature permitted by the scientific revolution threatens to overwhelm the earth's fragile equilibrium, and the belief in the universal application of "reason" can lead to arrogance and intolerance, particularly intolerance of other people's spiritual values. Such vivid debates about the legacy of these intellectual and cultural developments testify to their continuing importance in today's world.

Online Study Center

This icon will direct you to interactive activities and study materials on the website **college.hmco.com/pic/mckaywest9e**

The Scientific Revolution

The emergence of modern science was a development of tremendous long-term significance. A noted historian has even said that the scientific revolution of the late sixteenth and seventeenth centuries "outshines everything since the rise of Christianity and reduces the Renaissance and Reformation to the rank of mere episodes, mere internal displacements, within the system of medieval Christendom." The scientific revolution was "the real origin both of the modern world and the modern mentality."[1] This statement is an exaggeration, but not much of one. Of all the great civilizations, only that of the West developed modern science. With the scientific revolution Western society began to acquire its most distinctive traits.

- **What was revolutionary in new attitudes toward the natural world?**

Scientific Thought in 1500

Since developments in astronomy and physics were at the heart of the scientific revolution, one must begin with the traditional European conception of the universe. It is important to remember that the practitioners of the scientific revolution did not consider their field *science* but rather **natural philosophy.** Their intention was not to create modern science but to ask fundamental questions about the nature of the universe, its purpose, and how it functioned. They did not set supernatural questions aside, as do modern scientists, but incorporated them in their speculations, which made reference not only to Christian theology but often to magic, alchemy, and astrology as well. The dividing line between matter and spirit, or reason and faith, was much less rigid for participants in the scientific revolution than it is for scientists today.

In the early 1500s natural philosophy was still based primarily on the ideas of Aristotle, the great Greek philosopher of the fourth century B.C. These ideas had gradually been recovered during the Middle Ages. Medieval theologians such as Thomas Aquinas brought Aristotelian philosophy into harmony with Christian doctrines. According to this revised Aristotelian view, a motionless earth was fixed at the center of the universe. Around it moved ten separate transparent crystal spheres. In the first eight spheres were embedded, in turn, the moon, the sun, the five known planets, and the fixed stars. Then followed two spheres added during the Middle Ages to account for slight changes in the positions of the stars over the centuries. Beyond the tenth sphere was Heaven, with the throne of God and the souls of the saved. Angels kept the spheres moving in perfect circles.

Aristotle's views, suitably revised by medieval philosophers, also dominated thinking about physics and motion on earth. Aristotle had distinguished sharply between the world of the celestial spheres and that of the earth—the sublunar world. The spheres consisted of a perfect, incorruptible "quintessence," or fifth essence. The sublunar world, however, was made up of four imperfect, changeable elements. The "light" elements (air and fire) naturally moved upward, while the "heavy" elements (water and earth) naturally moved downward. These nat-

The Aristotelian Universe as Imagined in the Sixteenth Century A round earth is at the center, surrounded by spheres of water, air, and fire. Beyond this small nucleus, the moon, the sun, and the five planets were embedded in their own rotating crystal spheres, with the stars sharing the surface of one enormous sphere. Beyond, the heavens were composed of unchanging ether. (*Image Select/Art Resource, NY*)

ural directions of motion did not always prevail, however, for elements were often mixed together and could be affected by an outside force such as a human being. Aristotle and his followers also believed that a uniform force moved an object at a constant speed and that the object would stop as soon as that force was removed.

Aristotle's ideas about astronomy and physics were accepted with minor revisions for two thousand years, and with good reason. First, they offered an understandable, commonsense explanation for what the eye actually saw. Second, Aristotle's science as interpreted by Christian theologians fit neatly with Christian doctrines. It established a home for God and a place for Christian souls. It put human beings at the center of the universe and made them the critical link in a "great chain of being" that stretched from the throne of God to the most lowly insect on earth. Thus examination of the natural world was primarily a branch of theology, and it reinforced religious thought.

The Copernican Hypothesis

The desire to explain and thereby glorify God's handiwork led to the first great departure from the medieval system. This departure was the work of the Polish clergyman and astronomer Nicolaus Copernicus (1473–1543). As a young man Copernicus studied church law and astronomy in various European universities. He saw how professional astronomers still depended for their most accurate calculations on the second century B.C. work of Ptolemy. Author of a geographical synthesis that profoundly influenced European voyages of exploration (see page 494), Ptolemy was also a great astronomer. His achievement had been to work out complicated rules to explain the minor irregularities in the movement of the planets. These rules enabled stargazers and astrologers to track the planets with greater precision. Many people then (and now) believed that the changing relationships between planets and stars influenced events on earth.

The young Copernicus was uninterested in astrology and felt that Ptolemy's cumbersome and occasionally inaccurate rules detracted from the majesty of a perfect Creator. He preferred an old Greek idea being discussed in Renaissance Italy: that the sun, rather than the earth, was at the center of the universe. Finishing his university studies and returning to a church position in East Prussia, Copernicus worked on his hypothesis from 1506 to 1530. Never questioning the Aristotelian belief in crystal spheres or the idea that circular motion was most perfect and divine, Copernicus theorized that the stars and planets, including the earth, revolved around a fixed sun.

Chronology

ca 1540–1690	Scientific revolution
1543	Copernicus, *On the Revolutions of the Heavenly Spheres*
1564–1642	Life of Galileo
1571–1630	Life of Kepler
1662	Royal Society of London founded
1687	Newton, *Principia* and law of universal gravitation
1690	Locke, *Essay Concerning Human Understanding*
ca 1690–1780	Enlightenment
1694–1778	Life of Voltaire
1700–1789	Growth of book publishing
1720–1780	Rococo style in art and decoration
ca 1740–1780	Salons led by elite women
1740–1786	Reign of Frederick the Great of Prussia
ca 1750–1790	Enlightened absolutists
1751–1765	Diderot and d'Alembert, *Encyclopedia*
1762	Rousseau, *The Social Contract*
1762–1796	Reign of Catherine the Great of Russia
1780–1790	Reign of Joseph II of Austria

Yet Copernicus was a cautious man. Fearing the ridicule of other astronomers, he did not publish his *On the Revolutions of the Heavenly Spheres* until 1543, the year of his death.

The **Copernican hypothesis** had enormous scientific and religious implications, many of which the conservative Copernicus did not anticipate. First, it put the stars at rest, their apparent nightly movement simply a result of the earth's rotation. Thus it destroyed the main reason for believing in crystal spheres capable of moving the stars around the earth. Second, Copernicus's theory suggested a universe of staggering size. If in the course of a year the earth moved around the sun and yet the stars appeared to remain in the same place, then the universe was unthinkably large. Finally, by characterizing the earth as just another planet, Copernicus destroyed the basic idea of Aristotelian physics—that the earthly world was quite different from the heavenly one. Where, then, was the realm of perfection? Where were Heaven and the throne of God?

Online Study Center Improve Your Grade
Primary Source: Commentariolus: Copernicus Outlines His Thesis

The Copernican hypothesis brought sharp attacks from religious leaders, especially Protestants. Martin Luther spoke of him as the "new astrologer who wants to prove that the earth moves and goes round. . . . The fool wants to turn the whole art of astronomy upside down." Luther noted that "as the Holy Scripture tells us, so did Joshua bid the sun stand still and not the earth."[2] John Calvin also condemned Copernicus. Catholic reaction was milder at first. The Catholic Church had never held to literal interpretations of the Bible, and not until 1616 did it officially declare the Copernican hypothesis false.

This slow reaction also reflected the slow progress of Copernicus's theory for many years. Other events were almost as influential in creating doubts about traditional astronomical ideas. In 1572 a new star appeared and shone very brightly for almost two years. The new star, which was actually a distant exploding star, made an enormous impression on people. It seemed to contradict the idea that the heavenly spheres were unchanging and therefore perfect. In 1577 a new comet suddenly moved through the sky, cutting a straight path across the supposedly impenetrable crystal spheres. It was time, as a typical scientific writer put it, for "the radical renovation of astronomy."[3]

From Brahe to Galileo

One astronomer who agreed was Tycho Brahe (1546–1601). Born into a prominent Danish noble family, Brahe was tremendously impressed by a partial eclipse of the sun at an early age. Completing his studies abroad and returning to Denmark, he established himself as Europe's leading astronomer with his detailed observations of the new star of 1572. Aided by generous grants from the king of Denmark, Brahe built the most sophisticated observatory of his day. For twenty years he meticulously observed the stars and planets with the naked eye. An imposing man who had lost a piece of his nose in a duel and replaced it with a special bridge of gold and silver alloy, a noble who exploited his peasants arrogantly and approached the heavens humbly, Brahe contributed a great mass of data. His limited understanding of mathematics prevented him, however, from making much sense out of his data. Part Ptolemaic, part Copernican, he believed that all the planets revolved around the sun and that the entire group of sun and planets revolved in turn around the earth-moon system.

It was left to Brahe's brilliant young assistant, Johannes Kepler (1571–1630), to go much further. Kepler was a medieval figure in many ways. Coming from a minor German noble family and trained for the Lutheran ministry, he long believed that the universe was built on mystical mathematical relationships and a musical harmony of the heavenly bodies. Working and reworking Brahe's mountain of observations in a staggering effort after the Dane's death, this brilliant mathematician eventually went beyond mystical intuitions.

Kepler formulated three famous laws of planetary motion. First, building on Copernican theory, he demonstrated in 1609 that the orbits of the planets around the sun are elliptical rather than circular. Second, he demonstrated that the planets do not move at a uniform speed in their orbits. Third, in 1619 he showed that the time a planet takes to make its complete orbit is precisely related to its distance from the sun. Kepler's contribution was monumental. Whereas Copernicus had speculated, Kepler proved mathematically the precise relations of a sun-centered (solar) system. His work demolished the old system of Aristotle and Ptolemy, and in his third law he came close to formulating the idea of universal gravitation.

While Kepler was unraveling planetary motion, a young Florentine named Galileo Galilei (1564–1642) was challenging all the old ideas about motion. Like so many early scientists, Galileo was a poor nobleman first marked for a religious career. However, he soon became fascinated by mathematics. A brilliant student, in 1589 Galileo became a professor of mathematics at age twenty-five. He proceeded to examine motion and mechanics in a new way. Indeed, his great achievement was the elaboration and consolidation of the **experimental method**. That is, rather than speculate about what might or should happen, Galileo conducted controlled experiments to find out what actually *did* happen. In his famous acceleration experiment, he showed that a uniform force—in this case, gravity—produced a uniform acceleration. Here is how Galileo described his pathbreaking method and conclusion in his *Two New Sciences*:

A piece of wooden moulding . . . was taken; on its edge was cut a channel a little more than one finger in breadth. Having made this groove very straight, smooth and polished, and having lined it with parchment, also as smooth and polished as possible, we rolled along it a hard, smooth and very round bronze ball. . . . Noting . . . the time required to make the descent . . . we now rolled the ball only one-quarter the length of the channel; and having measured the time of its descent, we found it precisely one-half of the former.... In such experiments [over many distances], repeated a full hundred times, we always found that the spaces traversed were to each other as the squares of the times, and that this was true for all inclinations of the plane.[4]

With this and other experiments, Galileo formulated the law of inertia. Rest was not the natural state of objects. Rather, an object continues in motion forever unless stopped by some external force. Aristotelian physics was in shambles.

In the tradition of Brahe, Galileo also applied the experimental method to astronomy. On hearing details about the invention of the telescope in Holland, Galileo made one for himself and trained it on the heavens. He quickly discovered the first four moons of Jupiter, which clearly suggested that Jupiter could not possibly be embedded in any impenetrable crystal sphere. This discovery provided new evidence for the Copernican theory, in which Galileo already believed. Galileo then pointed his telescope at the moon. He wrote in 1610 in *Siderus Nuncius:*

I feel sure that the moon is not perfectly smooth, free from inequalities, and exactly spherical, as a large school of philosophers considers with regard to the moon and the other heavenly bodies. On the contrary, it is full of inequalities, uneven, full of hollows and protuberances, just like the surface of the earth itself, which is varied.... The next object which I have observed is the essence or substance of the Milky Way. By the aid of a telescope anyone may behold this in a manner which so distinctly appeals to the senses that all the disputes which have tormented philosophers through so many ages are exploded by the irrefutable evidence of our eyes, and we are freed from wordy disputes upon the subject. For the galaxy is nothing else but a mass of innumerable stars planted together in clusters.[5]

Reading these famous lines, one feels a crucial corner in Western civilization being turned. The traditional religious worldview, which rested on determining and accepting the proper established authority, was beginning to give way to a new method. This new method of learning and investigating was the greatest accomplishment of the entire scientific revolution, for it proved capable of great extension. A historian investigating documents of

Galileo's Paintings of the Moon When Galileo published the results of his telescopic observations of the moon, he added these paintings to illustrate the marvels he had seen. Galileo made two telescopes, which are shown here. The larger one magnifies fourteen times, the smaller one twenty times. *(Biblioteca Nazionale Centrale, Florence/Art Resource, NY; Museum of Science, Florence/Art Resource, NY)*

the past, for example, is not so different from a Galileo studying stars and rolling balls.

Galileo was employed in Florence by the Medici grand dukes of Tuscany, and his work eventually aroused the ire of some theologians. The issue was presented in 1624 to Pope Urban VIII, who permitted Galileo to write about different possible systems of the world as long as he did not presume to judge which one actually existed. After the publication in Italian of his widely read *Dialogue on the Two Chief Systems of the World* in 1632, which openly lampooned the traditional views of Aristotle and Ptolemy and defended those of Copernicus, Galileo was tried for heresy by the papal Inquisition. Imprisoned and threatened with torture, the aging Galileo recanted, "renouncing and cursing" his Copernican errors.

Newton's Synthesis

The accomplishments of Kepler, Galileo, and other scientists had taken effect by about 1640. The old astronomy and physics were in ruins, and several fundamental breakthroughs had been made. The new findings had not, however, been fused together in a new synthesis, a single explanatory system that would comprehend motion both on earth and in the skies. That synthesis, which prevailed until the twentieth century, was the work of Isaac Newton (1642–1727).

Newton was born into lower English gentry and attended Cambridge University. A genius who spectacularly united the experimental and theoretical-mathematical sides of modern science, Newton was also fascinated by alchemy. He sought the elixir of life and a way to change base metals into gold and silver. Newton was also intensely religious. He was far from being the perfect rationalist so endlessly eulogized by writers in the eighteenth and nineteenth centuries.

Of his intellectual genius and incredible powers of concentration there can be no doubt. Arriving at some of his most basic ideas about physics in 1666 at age twenty-four, but unable to prove these theories mathematically, he attained a professorship and studied optics for many years. In 1684 Newton returned to physics for eighteen extraordinarily intensive months. For weeks on end he seldom left his room except to read his lectures. His meals were sent up, but he usually forgot to eat them, his mind fastened like a vise on the laws of the universe. He opened the third book of his immortal *Mathematical Principles of Natural Philosophy*, published in Latin in 1687 and generally known as the *Principia*, with these lines:

Isaac Newton This portrait suggests the depth and complexity of the great genius. Is the powerful mind behind those piercing eyes thinking of science or of religion, or perhaps of both? *(Scala/Art Resource, NY)*

In the preceding books I have laid down the principles of philosophy [that is, science]. . . . These principles are the laws of certain motions, and powers or forces, which chiefly have respect to philosophy. . . . It remains that from the same principles I now demonstrate the frame of the System of the World.

Newton made good his grandiose claim. His towering accomplishment was to integrate in a single explanatory system the astronomy of Copernicus, as corrected by Kepler's laws, with the physics of Galileo and his predecessors. Newton did this by means of a set of mathematical laws that explain motion and mechanics. These laws of dynamics are complex, and it took scientists and engineers two hundred years to work out all their implications. Nevertheless, the key feature of the Newtonian synthesis was the **law of universal gravitation.** According to this law, every body in the universe attracts every other body in the universe in a precise mathematical relationship, whereby the force of attraction is proportional to the quantity of matter of the objects and inversely proportional to the square of the distance between them. The whole universe—from Kepler's elliptical orbits to Galileo's rolling balls—was unified in one majestic system.

Causes of the Scientific Revolution

The scientific revolution drew on long-term developments in European culture. The first was the development of the medieval university. By the thirteenth century permanent universities with professors and large student bodies had been established in western Europe to train the lawyers, doctors, and church leaders society required. By 1300 philosophy had taken its place alongside law, medicine, and theology. Medieval philosophers developed a limited but real independence from theologians and a sense of free inquiry. They nobly pursued a body of knowledge and tried to arrange it meaningfully by means of abstract theories.

Within this framework what we now think of as science was able to emerge as a minor but distinct branch of philosophy. In the fourteenth and fifteenth centuries leading universities established new professorships of mathematics, astronomy, and physics (natural philosophy) within their faculties of philosophy. Although the prestige of the new fields was low, critical thinking was now applied to scientific problems by a permanent community of scholars. And an outlet existed for the talents of a Galileo or a Newton: all the great pathfinders either studied or taught at universities.

Second, the Renaissance also stimulated scientific progress. The recovery of the finest works of Greek mathematics—a byproduct of Renaissance humanism's ceaseless search for the knowledge of antiquity—greatly improved European mathematics. The recovery of more texts also showed that classical mathematicians had their differences; Europeans were thus forced to try to resolve these ancient controversies by means of their own efforts. Finally, Renaissance patrons, especially in Italy, often supported scientists as well as artists and writers. Various rulers and wealthy business people funded scientific investigations, as the Medicis of Florence did for Galileo.

The navigational problems of long sea voyages in the age of overseas expansion were a third factor in the scientific revolution. Ship captains on distant shores needed to be able to chart their positions as accurately as possible so that reliable maps could be drawn and the risks of international trade reduced. As early as 1484 the king of Portugal appointed a commission of mathematicians to perfect tables to help seamen find their latitude. This resulted in the first European navigation manual. Navigational problems were also critical in the development of many new scientific instruments, such as the telescope, barometer, thermometer, pendulum clock, microscope, and air pump. Better instruments, which permitted more accurate observations, often led to important new knowledge. Galileo with his telescope was by no means unique.

Better instruments were part of a fourth factor in the scientific revolution: the development of better ways of obtaining knowledge about the world. Two important thinkers, Francis Bacon (1561–1626) and René Descartes (1596–1650), represented key aspects of this improvement in scientific methodology.

The English politician and writer Francis Bacon was the greatest early propagandist for the new experimental method. Rejecting the Aristotelian and medieval method of using speculative reasoning to build general theories, Bacon argued that new knowledge had to be pursued through empirical experimental research. The researcher who wants to learn more about leaves or rocks should not speculate about the subject but should rather collect a multitude of specimens and then compare and analyze them, he said. General principles will then emerge. Bacon's contribution was to formalize the empirical method, which had already been used by Brahe and Galileo, into the general theory of inductive reasoning known as **empiricism.**

Online Study Center **Improve Your Grade**
Primary Source: Francis Bacon Rejects Superstition and Extols the Virtue of Science

The French philosopher René Descartes was a true genius who made his first great discovery in mathematics. As a twenty-three-year-old soldier serving in the Thirty Years' War, he experienced a life-changing intellectual vision on a single night in 1619. Descartes saw that there was a perfect correspondence between geometry and algebra and that geometrical, spatial figures could be expressed as algebraic equations and vice versa. A major step forward in the history of mathematics, Descartes's discovery of analytic geometry provided scientists with an important new tool.

Descartes's greatest achievement was to develop his initial vision into a whole philosophy of knowledge and science. He decided it was necessary to doubt everything that could reasonably be doubted and then, as in geometry, to use deductive reasoning from self-evident principles to ascertain scientific laws. Descartes's reasoning ultimately reduced all substances to "matter" and

The Observatory at Nuremberg The quest for scientific knowledge in the seventeenth century was already an expensive undertaking that required teamwork and government support, as this encyclopedic illustration suggests. Nuremberg was a historic center of commerce and culture in southern Germany, and its observatory played a pioneering role in early astronomical advances. *(Kunstsammlungen der Veste Coburg)*

"mind"—that is, to the physical and the spiritual. His view of the world as consisting of two fundamental entities is known as **Cartesian dualism.** Descartes was a profoundly original and extremely influential thinker.

Bacon's inductive experimentalism and Descartes's deductive, mathematical reasoning are combined in the modern scientific method, which began to crystallize in the late seventeenth century. Neither man's extreme approach was sufficient by itself. Bacon's inability to appreciate the importance of mathematics and his obsession with practical results clearly showed the limitations of antitheoretical empiricism. Likewise, some of Descartes's positions—he believed, for example, that it was possible to deduce the whole science of medicine from first principles—demonstrated the inadequacy of rigid, dogmatic rationalism. Thus the modern scientific method has joined precise observations and experimentalism with the search for general laws that may be expressed in rigorously logical, mathematical language.

Finally, there is the question of the role of religion in the development of science. Just as some historians have argued that Protestantism led to the rise of capitalism, others have concluded that Protestantism was a fundamental factor in the rise of modern science. Protestantism, particularly in its Calvinist varieties, supposedly made scientific inquiry a question of individual conscience and not of religious doctrine. The Catholic Church, in contrast, supposedly suppressed scientific theories that conflicted with its teachings and thus discouraged scientific progress. The truth is more complicated. *All* Western religious authorities—Catholic, Protestant, and Jewish—opposed the Copernican system to a greater or lesser extent until about 1630, by which time the scientific revolution was definitely in progress. The Catholic Church was initially less hostile than Protestant and Jewish religious leaders, and Italian scientists played a crucial role in scientific progress right up to the trial of Galileo in 1633. Thereafter, the Counter-Reformation church became more hostile to science, a change that helped account for the decline of science in Italy (but not in Catholic France) after 1640. At the same time, Protestant countries such as the Netherlands and Denmark became quite "pro-science," especially countries that lacked a strong religious authority capable of imposing religious orthodoxy on scientific questions.

This was certainly the case with Protestant England after 1630. English religious conflicts became so intense that the authorities could not impose religious unity on anything, including science. Significantly, the forerunners of the Royal Society agreed to discuss only "neutral" scientific questions so as not to come to blows over closely related religious and political disputes. The work of Bacon's many followers during Oliver Cromwell's commonwealth helped solidify the neutrality and independence of science. Bacon advocated the experimental approach precisely because it was open-minded and independent of preconceived religious and philosophical ideas. Neutral and useful, science became an accepted part of life and developed rapidly in England after about 1640.

Science and Society

The rise of modern science had many consequences, some of which are still unfolding. First, it went hand in hand with the rise of a new and expanding social group—the international **scientific community.** Members of this community were linked together by common interests and shared values as well as by journals and the learned scientific societies founded in many countries in the later seventeenth and eighteenth centuries. Expansion of knowledge was the primary goal of this community, and scientists' material and psychological rewards depended on their success in this endeavor. Thus science became competitive, and even more scientific advance was inevitable. Second, as governments intervened to support and sometimes direct research, the new scientific community became closely tied to the state and its agendas. National academies of science were created under state sponsorship in London in 1662, Paris in 1666, Berlin in 1700, and later across Europe.

Third, the scientific revolution introduced not only new knowledge about nature but also a new and revolutionary way of obtaining such knowledge—the modern scientific method. In addition to being both theoretical and experimental, this method was highly critical. It refused to base its conclusions on tradition and established sources, on ancient authorities and sacred texts. This critical attitude to established authority would inspire thinkers to question traditions in other domains as well.

Some things did not change in the scientific revolution. New "rational" methods for approaching nature did not question traditional inequalities between the sexes—and may have worsened them in some ways. When Renaissance courts served as centers of learning, talented noblewomen could find niches in study and research. The rise of a professional scientific community raised barriers for women because the new academies that furnished professional credentials did not accept female members. (This continued for a long time. Marie Curie, the first person to win two Nobel prizes, was rejected by the French Academy of Science in 1911 because she was a woman.[6])

There were, however, a number of noteworthy exceptions. In Italy, universities and academies did offer posts to women, attracting some foreigners spurned by their own countries. In addition, some sectors of accomplishment were more accessible to women, with fine arts being the most important. Women excelled as makers of wax anatomical models and as botanical and zoological illustrators. Because the new scientific method relied on precise observation, illustration became a highly valued skill. Women were also very much involved in informal scientific communities, attending salons, participating in scientific experiments, and writing learned treatises. Some female intellectuals were recognized as full-fledged members of the philosophical dialogue. In England, Margaret Cavendish, Anne Conway, and Mary Astell all con-

Metamorphoses of the Caterpillar and Moth Maria Sibylla Merian (1647–1717), the stepdaughter of a Dutch painter, became a celebrated scientific illustrator in her own right. Her finely observed pictures of insects in the South American colony of Surinam introduced many new species, shown in their various stages of development. For Merian, science was intimately tied with art: she not only painted but also bred caterpillars and performed experiments on them. Her two-year stay in Surinam, accompanied by a teenage daughter, was a daring feat for a seventeenth-century woman. *(Bildarchiv Preussischer Kulturbesitz/Art Resource, NY)*

tributed to debates about Descartes's mind-body dualism, among other issues. Descartes himself conducted an intellectual correspondence with the princess Elizabeth of Bohemia, of whom he stated: "I attach more weight to her judgement than to those messieurs the Doctors, who take for a rule of truth the opinions of Aristotle rather than the evidence of reason."[7]

If women themselves played a limited role in scientific discovery, scholars have recently emphasized the importance of representations of femininity and masculinity in the scientific revolution. Nature was often depicted as a female, whose veil of secrecy needed to be stripped away and penetrated by male experts. In the same time period, the Americas were similarly depicted as a female terrain whose potentially fertile lands needed to be controlled and impregnated by male colonists.

The scientific revolution had few consequences for economic life and the living standards of the masses until the late eighteenth century. True, improvements in the techniques of navigation facilitated overseas trade and helped enrich states and merchant companies. But science had relatively few practical economic applications. Thus the scientific revolution of the seventeenth century was first and foremost an intellectual revolution. For more than a hundred years its greatest impact was on how people thought and believed.

The Enlightenment

The scientific revolution was the single most important factor in the creation of the new worldview of the eighteenth-century **Enlightenment**. This worldview, which has played a large role in shaping the modern mind, grew out of a rich mix of diverse and often conflicting ideas. For the talented (and not-so-talented) writers who espoused them, these ideas competed vigorously for the attention of a growing public of well-educated but fickle readers, who remained a minority of the population. Despite the diversity, three central concepts stand at the core of Enlightenment thinking. The most important and original idea was that the methods of natural science could and should be used to examine and understand all aspects of life. This was what intellectuals meant by *reason*, a favorite word of Enlightenment thinkers. Nothing was to be accepted on faith. Everything was to be submitted to **rationalism**, a secular, critical way of thinking. A second important Enlightenment concept was that the scientific method was capable of discovering the laws of human society as well as those of nature. Thus was social science born. Its birth led to the third key idea, that of **progress**. Armed with the proper method of discovering the laws of human existence, Enlightenment thinkers believed that it was at least possible for human beings to create better societies and better people. Their belief was strengthened by some modest improvements in economic and social life during the eighteenth century.

- *How did the new worldview affect the way people thought about society and human relations?*

The Emergence of the Enlightenment

Loosely united by certain key ideas, the European Enlightenment was a broad intellectual and cultural movement that gained strength gradually and did not reach its maturity until about 1750. Yet it was the generation that came of age between the publication of Newton's *Principia* in 1687 and the death of Louis XIV in 1715 that tied the crucial knot between the scientific revolution and a new outlook on life. Talented writers of that generation popularized hard-to-understand scientific achievements for the educated elite.

The most famous and influential popularizer was a versatile French man of letters, Bernard de Fontenelle (1657–1757), who set out to make science witty and entertaining—as easy to read as a novel—for a broad nonscientific audience. This was a tall order, but Fontenelle largely succeeded. His most famous work, *Conversations on the Plurality of Worlds* (1686), begins with two elegant figures walking in the gathering shadows of a large park. One is a woman, a sophisticated aristocrat, and the other is her friend, perhaps even her lover. They gaze at the stars, and their talk turns to a passionate discussion of . . . astronomy! The man confides that "each star may well be a different world," then gently stresses how error is giving way to truth. At one point he explains:

> There came on the scene . . . one Copernicus, who made short work of all those various circles, all those solid skies, which the ancients had pictured to themselves. . . . Fired with the noble zeal of a true astronomer, he took the earth and spun it very far away from the center of the universe, where it had been installed, and in that center he put the sun, which had a far better title to the honor.[8]

Rather than despair at this dismissal of traditional understanding, Fontenelle's lady rejoices in the knowledge that the human mind is capable of making great progress.

This concept of progress was essentially a creation of the later seventeenth century. Medieval and Reformation thinkers had been concerned primarily with sin and salvation. The humanists of the Renaissance had emphasized worldly matters, but they had looked backward. They had believed it might be possible to equal the magnificent accomplishments of the ancients, but they did not ask for more. Fontenelle and like-minded writers had come to believe that, at least in science and mathematics, their era had gone far beyond antiquity. Progress, at least intellectual progress, was very possible.

Fontenelle and other writers of his generation were also instrumental in bringing science into conflict with religion. This was a major innovation because many seventeenth-century scientists, both Catholic and Protestant, did not draw antireligious implications from their scientific findings and believed that their work exalted God. The greatest scientist of them all, Isaac Newton, was a devout, if unorthodox, Christian who saw all his studies as directed toward explaining God's message. Fontenelle, in contrast, was skeptical about absolute truth and cynical about the claims of organized religion. Since such unorthodox views could not be stated openly in an absolute monarchy like Louis XIV's France, Fontenelle made his point through subtle editorializing about science. His depiction of the cautious Copernicus as a self-conscious revolutionary was typical. In *Eulogies of Scientists,* Fontenelle exploited with endless variations the fundamental theme of rational, progressive scientists versus prejudiced, reactionary priests.

The progressive and antireligious implications that writers such as Fontenelle drew from the scientific revolution reflected a very real crisis in European thought at the end of the seventeenth century. This crisis had its roots in several intellectual uncertainties and dissatisfactions, of which the demolition of Aristotelian-medieval science was only one.

A second uncertainty involved the whole question of religious truth. The destructive wars of religion that culminated in the Thirty Years' War (1618–1648) had been fought, in part, because religious freedom was an intolerable idea in Europe in the early seventeenth century. Both Catholics and Protestants had believed that religious truth was absolute and therefore worth fighting and dying for. Most Catholics and Protestants also believed that a strong state required unity in religious faith. Yet the disastrous results of the many attempts to impose such religious unity, such as Louis XIV's brutal expulsion of the French Huguenots in 1685, led some people to ask whether ideological conformity in religious matters was really necessary. Others skeptically asked if religious truth could ever be known with absolute certainty and concluded that it could not.

The most famous of these skeptics was Pierre Bayle (1647–1706), a French Huguenot who despised Louis

Popularizing Science The frontispiece illustration of Fontenelle's *Conversations on the Plurality of Worlds* invites the reader to share the pleasures of astronomy with an elegant lady and an entertaining teacher. The drawing shows the planets revolving around the sun. *(By permission of the Syndics of Cambridge University Library)*

XIV and found refuge in the Netherlands. A teacher by profession and a crusading journalist by inclination, Bayle took full advantage of the toleration and intellectual freedom of his adopted land. He critically examined the religious beliefs and persecutions of the past in his *Historical and Critical Dictionary,* written in French and published in the Netherlands in 1697. Demonstrating that human beliefs had been extremely varied and very often mistaken, Bayle concluded that nothing can ever be known beyond all doubt. In religion as in philosophy, humanity's best hope was open-minded toleration. Bayle's **skepticism** was very influential. Reprinted frequently in the Netherlands and in England, his four-volume *Dictionary* was found in more private libraries of eighteenth-century France than was any other book.

The rapidly growing travel literature on non-European lands and cultures was a third cause of uncertainty. In the wake of the great discoveries, Europeans were learning that the peoples of China, India, Africa, and the Americas all had their own very different beliefs and customs. Europeans shaved their faces and let their hair grow. Turks shaved their heads and let their beards grow. In Europe a man bowed before a woman to show respect. In Siam a man turned his back on a woman when he met her because it was disrespectful to look directly at her. Countless similar examples discussed in the travel accounts helped change the perspective of educated Europeans. They began to look at truth and morality in relative, rather than absolute, terms. If anything was possible, who could say what was right or wrong?

A fourth cause and manifestation of European intellectual turmoil was John Locke's epoch-making *Essay Concerning Human Understanding*. Published in 1690—the same year Locke published his famous *Second Treatise of Civil Government* (see page 548)—Locke's essay brilliantly set forth a new theory about how human beings learn and form their ideas. In doing so, he rejected the prevailing view of Descartes, who had held that all people are born with certain basic ideas and ways of thinking. Locke insisted that all ideas are derived from experience. The human mind at birth is like a blank tablet, or **tabula rasa**, on which the environment writes the individual's understanding and beliefs. Human development is therefore determined by education and social institutions, for good or for evil. Locke's *Essay Concerning Human Understanding* passed through many editions and translations. Along with Newton's *Principia,* it was one of the dominant intellectual inspirations of the Enlightenment.

The Philosophes and the Public

By the time Louis XIV died in 1715, many of the ideas that would soon coalesce into the new worldview had been assembled. Yet Christian Europe was still strongly attached to its traditional beliefs, as witnessed by the powerful revival of religious orthodoxy in the first half of the eighteenth century (see pages 672–673). By the outbreak of the American Revolution in 1775, however, a large portion of western Europe's educated elite had embraced many of the new ideas. This acceptance was the work of one of history's most influential groups of intellectuals, the **philosophes.** It was the philosophes who proudly proclaimed that they, at long last, were bringing the light of knowledge to their ignorant fellow creatures in an Age of Enlightenment.

Philosophe is the French word for "philosopher," and it was in France that the Enlightenment reached its highest development. There were at least three reasons for this. First, French was the international language of the educated classes in the eighteenth century, and the education of the rich and the powerful across Europe often lay in the hands of French tutors espousing Enlightenment ideas. France's cultural leadership was reinforced by the fact that it was still the wealthiest and most populous country in Europe.

Second, after the death of Louis XIV, French absolutism and religious orthodoxy remained strong, but not too strong. Critical books were often banned by the censors, and their authors were sometimes jailed or exiled—but they were not tortured or burned. Intellectual radicals battled against powerful opposition in France, but they did not face the overwhelming restraints generally found in eastern and east-central Europe.

Third, the French philosophes were indeed philosophers, asking fundamental philosophical questions about the meaning of life, God, human nature, good and evil, and cause and effect. But in the tradition of Bayle and Fontenelle, they were not content with abstract arguments or ivory-tower speculations. They were determined to reach and influence all the French (and European) economic and social elites, many of which were joined together in the eighteenth-century concept of the "republic of letters," an imaginary, transnational realm constituted by all members of the educated or enlightened public.

Suspicious of the people but intensely committed to reason, reform, and slow, difficult progress, the great philosophes and their imitators were not free to write as they wished, since it was illegal in France to openly criticize either church or state. Their most radical works had to circulate in manuscript form. Knowing that direct attacks would probably be banned or burned, the philosophes wrote novels and plays, histories and philosophies, dictionaries and encyclopedias, all filled with satire and double meanings to spread their message to the public. One of the greatest philosophes, the baron de Montesquieu (1689–1755), brilliantly pioneered this approach in *The Persian Letters,* an extremely influential social satire published in 1721. This work consisted of amusing letters supposedly written by two Persian travelers, Usbek and Rica, who see European customs in unique ways and thereby allow Montesquieu to cleverly criticize existing practices and beliefs.

Like many Enlightenment philosophes, Montesquieu saw relations between men and women as particularly representative of overall social and political systems. He used the oppression of women in the Persian harem, described in letters from Usbek's wives, to symbolize Eastern political tyranny. At the end of the book, the rebellion of Usbek's harem against the cruel eunuchs he left in charge of them demonstrates that despotism must ultimately fail. Montesquieu also uses the Persians' observations of habitual infidelity among French wives and the strength of female power behind the throne to poke fun at European social and political customs. As Rica remarks:

The thing is that, for every man who has any post at court, in Paris, or in the country, there is a woman through whose hands pass all the favours and sometimes the injustices that he does. These women are all in touch with one another, and compose a sort of commonwealth whose members are always busy giving each other mutual help and support.

Montesquieu was exaggerating, but he echoed other critics of the informal power women gained in an absolutist system, where royal mistresses and female courtiers could have more access to the king than government ministers. Having gained fame by using wit as a weapon against cruelty and superstition, Montesquieu settled down on his family estate to study history and politics. His interest was partly personal, for, like many members of the French robe nobility, he was disturbed by the growth in royal absolutism under Louis XIV. But Montesquieu was also inspired by the example of the physical sciences, and he set out to apply the critical method to the problem of government in *The Spirit of Laws* (1748). The result was a complex comparative study of republics, monarchies, and despotisms—a great pioneering inquiry in the emerging social sciences.

Showing that forms of government were shaped by history, geography, and customs, Montesquieu focused on the conditions that would promote liberty and prevent tyranny. He argued that despotism could be avoided if there was a **separation of powers,** with political power divided and shared by a variety of classes and legal estates holding unequal rights and privileges. A strong, independent upper class was especially important, according to Montesquieu, because in order to prevent the abuse of power "it is necessary that by the arrangement of things, power checks power." Admiring greatly the English balance of power among the king, the houses of Parliament, and the independent courts, Montesquieu believed that in France the thirteen high courts—the *parlements*—were frontline defenders of liberty against royal despotism. Apprehensive about the uneducated poor, Montesquieu was clearly no democrat, but his theory of separation of powers had a great impact on France's wealthy, well-educated elite. The constitutions of the young United States in 1789 and of France in 1791 were based in large part on this theory.

Online Study Center Improve Your Grade
Primary Source: Montesquieu Identifies the Necessity for the Separation of Governmental Powers

The most famous and in many ways most representative philosophe was François Marie Arouet, who was known by the pen name Voltaire (1694–1778). In his long career, this son of a comfortable middle-class family wrote more than seventy witty volumes, hobnobbed with kings and queens, and died a millionaire because of shrewd business speculations. His early career, however, was turbulent. In 1717 Voltaire was imprisoned for eleven months in the Bastille in Paris for insulting the regent of France. In 1726 a barb from his sharp tongue led a great French nobleman to have him beaten and arrested. This experience made a deep impression on Voltaire. All his life he struggled against legal injustice and unequal treatment before the law. Released from prison after promising to leave the country, Voltaire lived in England for three years and came to share Montesquieu's enthusiasm for English institutions.

Returning to France and soon threatened again with prison in Paris, Voltaire had the great fortune of meeting Gabrielle-Emilie Le Tonnelier de Breteuil, marquise du Châtelet (1706–1749), an intellectually gifted woman from the high aristocracy with a passion for science. Inviting Voltaire to live in her country house at Cirey in Lorraine and becoming his long-time companion (under the eyes of her tolerant husband), Madame du Châtelet studied physics and mathematics and published scientific articles and translations.

Perhaps the finest representative of a small number of elite Frenchwomen and their intellectual accomplishments during the Enlightenment, Madame du Châtelet suffered nonetheless because of her gender. Excluded on principle from the Royal Academy of Sciences, she depended on private tutors for instruction and became uncertain of her ability to make important scientific discoveries. Madame du Châtelet therefore concentrated on spreading the ideas of others, and her translation with an accompanying commentary of Newton's *Principia* into French for the first (and only) time was her greatest work. But she, who had patiently explained Newton's

Madame du Châtelet The marquise du Châtelet was fascinated by the new world system of Isaac Newton. She helped spread Newton's ideas in France by translating his *Principia* and by influencing Voltaire, her companion for fifteen years until her death. *(Giraudon/Art Resource, NY)*

complex mathematical proofs to Europe's foremost philosophe, had no doubt that women's limited scientific contributions in the past were due to limited and unequal education. She once wrote that if she were a ruler, "I would reform an abuse which cuts off, so to speak, half the human race. I would make women participate in all the rights of humankind, and above all in those of the intellect."⁹

While living at Cirey, Voltaire wrote various works praising England and popularizing English scientific progress. Newton, he wrote, was history's greatest man, for he had used his genius for the benefit of humanity. "It is," wrote Voltaire, "the man who sways our minds by the prevalence of reason and the native force of truth, not they who reduce mankind to a state of slavery by force and downright violence . . . that claims our reverence and admiration."¹⁰ In the true style of the Enlightenment, Voltaire mixed the glorification of science and reason with an appeal for better individuals and institutions.

Yet like almost all of the philosophes, Voltaire was a reformer, not a revolutionary, in social and political matters. He was eventually appointed royal historian in 1743, and his *Age of Louis XIV* portrayed Louis as the dignified leader of his age. Voltaire also began a long correspondence with Frederick the Great and, after the death of his beloved Emilie, accepted Frederick's invitation to come brighten up the Prussian court in Berlin. The two men later quarreled, but Voltaire always admired Frederick as a free thinker and an enlightened monarch.

Unlike Montesquieu, Voltaire pessimistically concluded that the best one could hope for in the way of government was a good monarch, since human beings "are very rarely worthy to govern themselves." Nor did he believe in social and economic equality in human affairs. The idea of making servants equal to their masters was "absurd and impossible." The only realizable equality, Voltaire thought, was that "by which the citizen only depends on the laws which protect the freedom of the feeble against the ambitions of the strong."¹¹

Voltaire's philosophical and religious positions were much more radical. In the tradition of Bayle, his voluminous writings challenged, often indirectly, the Catholic Church and Christian theology at almost every point. Though he was considered by many devout Christians to be a shallow blasphemer, Voltaire's religious views were ambiguous and quite typical of the complex attitudes toward religion held by Enlightenment thinkers. Voltaire clearly believed in God, but his was a distant, deistic God, the great Clockmaker who built an orderly universe and then stepped aside and let it run. Above all, Voltaire and most of the philosophes hated all forms of religious intolerance, which they believed often led to fanaticism and savage, inhuman action. Simple piety and human kindness—as embodied in Christ's great commandments to "love God and your neighbor as yourself"—were religion enough, as may be seen in Voltaire's famous essay on religion. (See the feature "Listening to the Past: Voltaire on Religion" on pages 618–619.)

The ultimate strength of the French philosophes lay in their number, dedication, and organization. The philosophes felt keenly that they were engaged in a common undertaking that transcended individuals. Their greatest and most representative intellectual achievement was, quite fittingly, a group effort—the seventeen-volume *Encyclopedia: The Rational Dictionary of the Sciences, the Arts, and the Crafts*, edited by Denis Diderot (1713–1784) and Jean le Rond d'Alembert (1717–1783). They were a curious pair. Diderot began his career as a hack writer, first attracting attention with a skeptical tract on religion that was quickly burned by the judges of Paris.

D'Alembert was one of Europe's leading scientists and mathematicians, the orphaned and illegitimate son of celebrated aristocrats. From different circles and with different interests, the two men set out to find coauthors who would examine the rapidly expanding whole of human knowledge. Even more fundamentally, they set out to teach people how to think critically and objectively about all matters. As Diderot said, he wanted the *Encyclopedia* to "change the general way of thinking."¹²

The editors of the *Encyclopedia* had to conquer innumerable obstacles. After the appearance in 1751 of the first volume, which dealt with such controversial subjects as atheism, the soul, and blind people (all words beginning with *a* in French), the government temporarily banned publication. The pope later placed the work on the Catholic Church's index of forbidden works and pronounced excommunication on all who read or bought it. In an attempt to appease the authorities, the timid publisher watered down some of the articles in the last ten volumes without the editors' consent. Yet Diderot's unwavering belief in the importance of his mission held the encyclopedists together for fifteen years, and the enormous work was completed in 1765. Hundreds of thousands of articles by leading scientists, famous writers, skilled workers, and progressive priests treated every aspect of life and knowledge.

Not every article was daring or original, but the overall effect was little short of revolutionary. Science and the industrial arts were exalted, religion and immortality questioned. Intolerance, legal injustice, and out-of-date social institutions were openly criticized. More generally, the writers of the *Encyclopedia* showed that human beings could use the process of reasoning to expand human knowledge. The encyclopedists were convinced that greater knowledge would result in greater human happiness, for knowledge was useful and made possible economic, social, and political progress. The *Encyclopedia* was widely read, especially in less-expensive reprint editions published in Switzerland, and it was extremely influential in France and throughout western Europe as well. It summed up the new worldview of the Enlightenment.

The Enlightenment Outside of France

For all the importance of Paris as a center of Enlightenment thought, historians now recognize the existence of important strands of Enlightenment thought in other areas of Europe. They have identified distinctive Enlightenment movements in eighteenth-century Italy, Greece, the Balkans, Poland, Hungary, and Russia.

Different areas followed different strands of Enlightenment thinking. In England and Germany, scholars have described a more conservative Enlightenment that tried to integrate the findings of the scientific revolution with religious faith and practices. After the Act of Union with England and Ireland in 1707, Scotland was freed from political crisis to experience a vigorous period of intellectual growth. The Scottish Enlightenment, centered in Edinburgh, was marked by an emphasis on pragmatic and scientific reasoning. Intellectual revival was stimulated by the creation of the first public educational system in Europe. The most important figure in Edinburgh was David Hume (1711–1776), whose carefully argued religious skepticism had a powerful impact at home and abroad.

Building on Locke's teachings on learning, Hume argued that the human mind is really nothing but a bundle of impressions. These impressions originate only in sense experiences and our habits of joining these experiences together. Since our ideas ultimately reflect only our sense experiences, our reason cannot tell us anything about questions that cannot be verified by sense experience (in the form of controlled experiments or mathematics), such as the origin of the universe or the existence of God. Paradoxically, Hume's rationalistic inquiry ended up undermining the Enlightenment's faith in the power of reason.

Urban Culture and the Public Sphere

Enlightenment ideas did not float on air. A series of new institutions and practices emerged in the late seventeenth and eighteenth centuries to facilitate the spread of Enlightenment ideas. First, the European production and consumption of books grew dramatically in the eighteenth century. In Germany the number of new titles appearing annually grew substantially, from roughly six hundred new titles in 1700 to about eleven hundred in 1764 and about twenty-six hundred in 1780. France also witnessed an explosive growth in book consumption. The number of books in the hands of elite readers increased eightfold to tenfold between the 1690s and the 1780s, when the private library of the typical noble contained more than three hundred volumes.

Moreover, the types of books people read changed dramatically. The proportion of religious and devotional books published in Paris declined precipitously, from one-half of the total in the 1690s to one-tenth of the total in the 1780s. History and law held constant, while the proportion of published books treating the arts and sciences surged.

Even these figures understate the shift in French taste because France's unpredictable but pervasive censorship

Illustrating the *Encyclopedia*: "The Print Shop" Diderot wanted to present all valid knowledge—that is, knowledge based on reason and the senses and not on tradition and authority. This plate, one of 3,000 detailed illustrations accompanying the 70,000 essays in the *Encyclopedia*, shows (*from left to right*) compositors setting type, arranging lines, and blocking down completed forms. Printed sheets dry above. *(Division of Rare & Manuscript Collections, Cornell University Library)*

caused many books to be printed abroad and smuggled back into the country for "under-the-cloak" sale. Experts believe that perhaps the majority of French books produced between 1750 and 1789 came from publishing companies outside of France. These publishers, located primarily in the Netherlands and Switzerland but also in England and a few small west German principalities, also smuggled forbidden books in French and other languages into the absolutist states of central, southern, and eastern Europe.

The illegal book trade in France also featured an astonishing growth of scandalmongering denunciations of high political figures and frankly pornographic works. These literary forms frequently came together in scathing pornographic accounts of the moral and sexual depravity of the French court, allegedly mired in luxury, perversion, and adultery. Echoing Montesquieu, a favorite theme was the way that some beautiful but immoral aristocratic women used their sexual charms to gain power over weak rulers and high officials, thereby corrupting the process of government. These tracts included graphic accounts and images of sexual debauchery among aristocrats and even by the queen herself. Spurred by repeated royal directives, the French police did their best to stamp out this underground literature, but new slanders kept cropping up, with corrosive effects on public confidence in the monarchy.

Reading more books on many more subjects, the educated public in France and throughout Europe increasingly approached reading in a new way. The result was what some scholars have called a **reading revolution.** The old style of reading in Europe had been centered on sacred texts, full of authority, inspiring reverence and teaching earthly duty and obedience to God. Reading had been patriarchal and communal, with the father of the family slowly reading the text aloud and the audience savoring each word. Now reading involved many texts, which were constantly changing and commanded no special respect. Reading became individual, silent, and rapid. The well-educated classes were reading insatiably, skeptically, and carelessly. Subtle but profound, the reading revolution ushered in new ways of relating to the written word.

Conversation, discussion, and debate also played a critical role in the Enlightenment. Paris set the example, and other French and European cities followed. In Paris a number of talented, wealthy women presided over regular social gatherings of the great and near-great in their elegant private drawing rooms, or **salons.** There they encouraged a d'Alembert and a Fontenelle to exchange witty, uncensored observations on literature, science, and philosophy with great aristocrats, wealthy middle-class financiers, high-ranking officials, and noteworthy foreigners. (D'Alembert himself was the illegitimate son of a well-known salon hostess, Madame de Tencin, who abandoned him on the steps of a Parisian church.) Talented hostesses, or *salonnières,* brought the various French elites together and mediated the public's freewheeling examination of Enlightenment thought.

Elite women also exercised an unprecedented feminine influence on artistic taste. Soft pastels, ornate interiors, sentimental portraits, and starry-eyed lovers protected by hovering cupids were all hallmarks of the style they favored. This style, known as **rococo,** was popular throughout Europe in the eighteenth century. It has been argued that feminine influence in the drawing room went hand in hand with the emergence of polite society and the general attempt to civilize a rough military nobility. Similarly, some philosophes championed greater rights and expanded education for women, claiming that the

Selling Books, Promoting Ideas This appealing bookshop with its intriguing ads for the latest works offers to put customers "Under the Protection of Minerva," the Roman goddess of wisdom. Large packets of books sit ready for shipment to foreign countries. Book consumption surged in the eighteenth century. *(Musée des Beaux-Arts, Dijon/Art Resource, NY)*

Enlightenment Culture An actor performs the first reading of a new play by Voltaire at the salon of Madame Geoffrin. Voltaire, then in exile, is represented by a bust statue. (Réunion des Musées Nationaux/Art Resource, NY)

position and treatment of women were the best indicators of a society's level of civilization and decency.[13] To be sure, for these male philosophes greater rights for women did not mean equal rights, and the philosophes were not particularly disturbed by the fact that elite women remained legally subordinate to men in economic and political affairs. Elite women lacked many rights, but so did most men.

One of the most famous salons was that of Madame Geoffrin, the unofficial godmother of the *Encyclopedia*. Having lost her parents at an early age, she was married at fifteen by her well-meaning grandmother to a rich and boring businessman of forty-eight. After dutifully raising her children, Madame Geoffrin broke out of her gilded cage. With the aid of an aristocratic neighbor and in spite of her husband's loud protests, she developed a twice-weekly salon that counted Fontenelle and Montesquieu among its regular guests. Inheriting a large fortune after her husband's death, Madame Geoffrin gave the encyclopedists generous financial aid and helped save their enterprise from collapse. Corresponding with the king of Sweden and Catherine the Great of Russia, Madame Geoffrin remained her own woman, a practicing Christian who would not tolerate attacks on the church in her house.

The salon also provided an informal apprenticeship for younger women who aspired to lead salons of their own. One such woman was Julie de Lespinasse. Eventually forming her own highly informal salon and attracting the keenest minds in France and Europe, Lespinasse epitomized the skills of the Enlightenment hostess. As one philosophe wrote:

She could unite the different types, even the most antagonistic, sustaining the conversation by a well-aimed phrase, animating and guiding it at will. . . . Politics, religion, philosophy, news: nothing was excluded. Her circle met daily from five to nine. There one found men of all ranks in the State, the Church, and the Court, soldiers and foreigners, and the leading writers of the day.[14]

As this passage suggests, the salons created a cultural realm free from religious dogma and political censorship. There a diverse but educated public could debate issues and form its own ideas. Through their invitation lists, salon hostesses brought together members of the intellectual, economic, and social elites. In such an atmosphere, the philosophes, the French nobility, and the prosperous middle classes intermingled and influenced one another. Thinking critically about almost any question became fashionable and flourished alongside hopes for human progress through greater knowledge and enlightened public opinion.

Membership at the salons was restricted to the well-born, the well-connected, and the exceptionally talented. A number of institutions emerged for those who aspired to follow, rather than lead, the Enlightenment. Lending libraries served an important function for people who could not afford to buy their own books. The coffeehouses that first appeared in the late seventeenth century became meccas of philosophical discussion. Then, as now, one could linger for hours to read or debate for the price of a cup of coffee. In addition to these institutions, book clubs, Masonic lodges, and journals all played roles in the creation of a new **public sphere** that celebrated open debate informed by critical reason. The public sphere was an idealized space where members of society came together as individuals to discuss issues relevant to the society, economics, and politics of the day.

What of the common people? Did they participate in the Enlightenment? Enlightenment philosophes did not direct their message to peasants or urban laborers. Whether of middling or noble origin, intellectuals sought patronage from the wealthy and powerful. They believed that the masses had no time or talent for philosophical speculation and that elevating them would be a long, slow, potentially dangerous process. Deluded by superstitions and driven by violent passions, they thought, the people were like little children in need of firm parental guidance. French philosophe d'Alembert characteristically made a sharp distinction between "the truly enlightened public" and "the blind and noisy multitude."[15]

There is some evidence, however, that the people were not immune to the words of the philosophes. At a time of rising literacy, book prices were dropping in cities and towns, and many philosophical ideas were popularized in cheap pamphlets. Moreover, even illiterate people had access to written material, through the practice of public reading. The Parisian glass-worker Jacques-Louis Ménétra, whose education consisted of a few years of schooling and his trade apprenticeship, claimed in his autobiography to have cultivated a friendship with Jean-Jacques Rousseau and to have enjoyed a game of chess and a philosophical discussion with the writer. Although they were barred from salons and academies, ordinary people were not immune to the new ideas in circulation.

Late Enlightenment

After about 1770 a number of thinkers and writers began to attack the Enlightenment's faith in reason, progress, and moderation. The most famous of these was the Swiss Jean-Jacques Rousseau (1712–1778), a brilliant and difficult thinker and an appealing but neurotic individual. Born into a poor family of watchmakers in Geneva, Rousseau went to Paris and was greatly influenced by Diderot and Voltaire. Always extraordinarily sensitive and suspicious, he came to believe that his philosophe friends and the women of the Parisian salons were plotting against him. In the mid-1750s he broke with them personally and intellectually, living thereafter as a lonely outsider with his uneducated common-law wife and going in his own highly original direction.

Like other Enlightenment thinkers, Rousseau was passionately committed to individual freedom. Unlike them, however, he attacked rationalism and civilization as destroying, rather than liberating, the individual. Warm, spontaneous feeling had to complement and correct cold intellect. Moreover, the basic goodness of the individual and the unspoiled child had to be protected from the cruel refinements of civilization. Rousseau's ideals greatly influenced the early romantic movement (see pages 660–661), which rebelled against the culture of the Enlightenment in the late eighteenth century.

Reconfirming Montesquieu's critique of women's influence in public affairs, Rousseau called for a rigid division of gender roles. According to Rousseau, women and men were radically different beings. Destined by nature to assume a passive role in sexual relations, women should also be passive in social life. A woman's role was to care for her children at home and to please her husband with good housekeeping, a modest demeanor, and a fresh, natural appearance. Women's passion for fashion, attending salons, and pulling the strings of power was unnatural and had a corrupting effect on both politics and society. Rousseau thus rejected the sophisticated way of life of elite Parisian women. Against them, he rearticulated conventional stereotypes as a form of natural law, against which debate was impossible. These views had a strong impact on both men and women in the late eighteenth century, contributing to calls for privileged women to abandon their stylish corsets and to breast-feed their children.

Rousseau's contribution to political theory in *The Social Contract* (1762) was equally significant. His contribution was based on two fundamental concepts: the general will and popular sovereignty. According to Rousseau, the general will is sacred and absolute, reflecting the common interests of all the people, who have displaced the monarch as the holder of sovereign power. The general will is not necessarily the will of the majority, however. At times the general will may be the authentic, long-term needs of the people as correctly interpreted by a farseeing minority. Little noticed before the French Revolution, Rousseau's concept of the general will appealed greatly to democrats and nationalists after 1789. (The concept has since been used by many dictators who have claimed that they, rather than some momentary majority of the voters, represent the general will.) Rousseau was both one of the most influential voices of the Enlightenment and, in his rejection of rationalism and social discourse, a harbinger of reaction against Enlightenment ideas.

Online Study Center Improve Your Grade
Primary Source: Rousseau Espouses Popular Sovereignty and the General Will

As the reading public developed, it joined forces with the philosophes to call for the autonomy of the printed word. Immanuel Kant (1724–1804), a professor in East Prussia and the greatest German philosopher of his day, posed the question of the age when he published a pamphlet in 1784 entitled *What Is Enlightenment?* Kant answered, "*Sapere Aude!* [dare to know] Have courage to use your own understanding!—that is the motto of enlightenment." He argued that if serious thinkers were granted the freedom to exercise their reason publicly in print, enlightenment would almost surely follow. Kant was no revolutionary; he also insisted that in their private lives, individuals must obey all laws, no matter how unreasonable, and should be punished for "impertinent" criticism. Kant thus tried to reconcile absolute monarchical authority with a critical public sphere. This balancing act characterized experiments with "enlightened absolutism" in the eighteenth century.

Race and the Enlightenment

In addition to criticizing their own societies and political systems, Enlightenment thinkers wrote about society and human nature outside their borders. In recent years, historians have found in the scientific revolution and the Enlightenment a crucial turning point in European ideas about race. Many of the most important thinkers of the Enlightenment devoted substantial attention to comparisons of European and non-European cultures, deriving their understanding of people at home from differences with people abroad. The result was the formation of highly influential new understandings of racial difference. As with other strands of Enlightenment thought, the new scientific method, and its apparently neutral, rational thinking, provided intellectual legitimacy for their findings.

A primary catalyst for new ideas about race was the urge to classify nature unleashed by the scientific revolution's insistence on careful empirical observation. In *The System of Nature* (1735) Swedish botanist Carl von Linné argued that nature was organized into a God-given hierarchy, which mankind must uncover and chart meticulously. As scientists developed more elaborate taxonomies of plant and animal species, they also began to classify humans into hierarchically ordered "races" and to investigate the origins of race. The Comte de Buffon argued that humans originated with one species that then developed into distinct races due largely to climactic conditions. In *A Natural History* he describes experiments conducted on African bodies to determine the cause of their "blackness," which was assumed to be an acquired variation from humans' originally white skin.

Using the word *race* to designate biologically distinct groups of humans, akin to distinct animal species, was new. Previously, Europeans grouped other peoples into "nations" based on their historical, political, and cultural affiliations, rather than on supposedly innate physical differences. Unsurprisingly, when European thinkers drew up a hierarchical classification of human species, their own "race" was placed at the top. Europeans had long believed they were culturally superior to "barbaric" peoples in Africa and, since 1492, the New World. Now emerging ideas about racial difference taught them they were biologically superior as well.

Enlightenment thinkers such as David Hume and Immanuel Kant helped popularize these ideas. In *Of Natural Characters* (1748), Hume wrote:

I am apt to suspect the negroes and in general all other species of men (for there are four or five different kinds) to be naturally inferior to the whites. There never was a civilized nation of any other complexion than white, nor even any individual eminent amongst them, no arts, no sciences. . . . Such a uniform and constant difference could not happen, in so many countries and ages if nature had not made an original distinction between these breeds of men.[16]

The Prussian philosopher Immanuel Kant taught and wrote as much about "anthropology" and "geography" as he did about standard philosophical themes such as logic, metaphysics, and moral philosophy. He shared and elaborated Hume's views about race in *On the Different Races of Man* (1775), claiming that there were four human races, each of which had derived from an original race of "white brunette" people. According to Kant, the closest descendants of the original race were the white inhabitants of northern Germany. In deriving new physical characteristics, the other races had degenerated both physically and culturally from this origin.

These ideas did not go unchallenged. James Beattie responded directly to Hume's claims of white superiority by pointing out that Europeans had started out as savage as nonwhites and that many non-European peoples in the Americas, Asia, and Africa had achieved high levels of civilization. Johann von Herder criticized Kant, arguing that humans could not be classified into races based on skin color and that each culture was as intrinsically worthy as any other. These challenges to emerging scientific notions of racial inequality, however, were in the minority. Many other Enlightenment voices agreeing with Kant and Hume—Thomas Jefferson among them—may be found.

Scholars are only at the beginning of efforts to understand links between Enlightenment ideas about race and its notions of equality, progress, and reason. There are clear parallels, though, between the use of science to propagate racial hierarchies and its use to defend social inequalities between men and women. As Rousseau used women's "natural" passivity to argue for their passive role in society, so a Hume and a Kant used non-Europeans' "natural" inferiority to defend slavery and colonial domination. The new powers of science and reason were thus marshaled to imbue traditional stereotypes with the force of natural law.

The Enlightenment and Absolutism

How did the Enlightenment influence political developments? To this important question there is no easy answer. Most Enlightenment thinkers outside of England and the Netherlands believed that political change could best come from above—from the ruler—rather than from below, especially in central and eastern Europe. Royal absolutism was a fact of life, and the kings and queens of Europe's leading states clearly had no intention of giving up their great power. Therefore, the philosophes and their sympathizers realistically concluded that a benevolent absolutism offered the best opportunities for improving society. Critical thinking was turning the art of good government into an exact science. It was necessary to educate and "enlighten" the monarch, who could then make good laws and promote human happiness.

The philosophes' influence was heightened by the fact that many government officials were attracted to and interested in philosophical ideas. They were among the best-educated and best-informed members of society, and their daily involvement in complex affairs of state made them naturally interested in ideas for improving or reforming human society. Encouraged and instructed by these officials, some absolutist rulers of the later eighteenth century tried to govern in an "enlightened" manner. Yet the actual programs and accomplishments of these rulers varied greatly. It is necessary to examine the evolution of monarchical absolutism at close range before trying to judge the Enlightenment's effect and the meaning of what historians have often called the **enlightened absolutism** of the later eighteenth century.

Enlightenment teachings inspired European rulers in small as well as large states in the second half of the eighteenth century. Absolutist princes and monarchs in several west German and Italian states, as well as in Scandinavia, Spain, and Portugal, proclaimed themselves more enlightened. A few smaller states were actually the most successful in making reforms, perhaps because their rulers were not overwhelmed by the size and complexity of their realms. Denmark, for example, carried out extensive and progressive land reform in the 1780s that practically abolished serfdom and gave Danish peasants secure tenure on their farms. Yet by far the most influential of the new-style monarchs were in Prussia, Russia, and Austria, and they deserve primary attention.

• *What impact did this new way of thinking have on political developments and monarchical absolutism?*

Frederick the Great of Prussia

Frederick II (r. 1740–1786), commonly known as Frederick the Great, built masterfully on the work of his father, Frederick William I (see page 571). This was somewhat surprising, for, like many children with tyrannical parents, he rebelled against his family's wishes in his early years. Rejecting the crude life of the barracks, Frederick embraced culture and literature, even writing poetry and fine prose in French, a language his father detested. After trying unsuccessfully to run away in 1730 at age eighteen, he was virtually imprisoned and compelled to watch as his companion in flight was beheaded at his father's command. Yet like many other rebellious youths, Frederick eventually reconciled with his father, and by the time he came to the throne ten years later Frederick was determined to use the splendid army that his father had left him.

Therefore, when the ruler of Austria, Charles VI, also died in 1740 and his young and charismatic daughter Maria Theresa inherited the Habsburg dominions, Frederick suddenly and without warning invaded her rich, mainly German province of Silesia. This action defied solemn Prussian promises to respect the Pragmatic Sanction, which guaranteed Maria Theresa's succession. Maria Theresa's disunited army was no match for Prussian precision; in 1742, as other greedy powers were falling on her lands in the general European War of the Austrian Succession (1740–1748), she was forced to cede almost all of Silesia to Prussia (see Map 17.2 on page 570). In one stroke Prussia had doubled its population to six million people. Now Prussia unquestionably towered above all the other German states and stood as a European Great Power.

Though successful in 1742, Frederick had to spend much of his reign fighting against great odds to save Prussia from total destruction. Maria Theresa was determined to regain Silesia, and when the ongoing competition between Britain and France for colonial empire brought another great conflict in 1756 (see page 635), Austria fashioned an aggressive alliance with France and Russia. During the Seven Years' War (1756–1763), the aim of the alliance was to conquer Prussia and divide up its territory. Frederick led his army brilliantly, striking repeatedly at vastly superior forces invading from all sides. At times he believed all was lost, but he fought on with stoic courage. In the end he was miraculously saved: Peter III came to the Russian throne in 1762 and called off the attack against Frederick, whom he greatly admired.

In the early years of his reign Frederick II had kept his enthusiasm for Enlightenment culture strictly separated from a brutal concept of international politics. He wrote:

Of all States, from the smallest to the biggest, one can safely say that the fundamental rule of government is the principle of extending their territories. . . . The passions of rulers have no other curb but the limits of their power. Those are the fixed laws of European politics to which every politician submits.[17]

But the terrible struggle of the Seven Years' War tempered Frederick and brought him to consider how more humane policies for his subjects might also strengthen the state. Thus Frederick went beyond a superficial commitment to Enlightenment culture for himself and his circle. He tolerantly allowed his subjects to believe as they wished in religious and philosophical matters. He promoted the advancement of knowledge, improving his country's schools and permitting scholars to publish their findings. Moreover, Frederick tried to improve the lives of his subjects more directly. As he wrote his friend Voltaire, "I must enlighten my people, cultivate their manners and morals, and make them as happy as human beings can be, or as happy as the means at my disposal permit."

The legal system and the bureaucracy were Frederick's primary tools. Prussia's laws were simplified, torture of prisoners was abolished, and judges decided cases quickly and impartially. Prussian officials became famous for their hard work and honesty. After the Seven Years' War ended in 1763, Frederick's government energetically promoted the reconstruction of agriculture and industry in his war-torn country. Frederick himself set a good example. He worked hard and lived modestly, claiming that he was "only the first servant of the state." Thus Frederick justified monarchy in terms of practical results and said nothing of the divine right of kings.

Frederick's dedication to high-minded government went only so far, however. He never tried to change Prussia's existing social structure. True, he condemned serfdom in the abstract, but he accepted it in practice and did not even free the serfs on his own estates. He accepted and extended the privileges of the nobility, which he saw as his primary ally in the defense and extension of his realm. The Junker nobility remained the backbone of the army and the entire Prussian state.

Nor did Frederick listen to thinkers like Moses Mendelssohn (1729–1786), who urged that Jews be given freedom and civil rights. (See the feature "Individuals in Society: Moses Mendelssohn and the Jewish Enlightenment.") As in other German states, Jews in Prussia remained an oppressed group. The vast majority were confined to tiny, overcrowded ghettos, were excluded by law from most business and professional activities, and could be ordered out of the kingdom at a moment's notice. A very few Jews in Prussia did manage to succeed and to obtain the right of permanent settlement, usually by performing some special service for the state. But they were the exception, and Frederick firmly opposed any general emancipation for the Jews, as he did for the serfs.

Catherine the Great of Russia

Catherine the Great of Russia (r. 1762–1796) was one of the most remarkable rulers of her age, and the French philosophes adored her. Catherine was a German princess from Anhalt-Zerbst, a totally insignificant principality sandwiched between Prussia and Saxony. Her father commanded a regiment of the Prussian army, but

Individuals in Society

Moses Mendelssohn and the Jewish Enlightenment

In 1743 a small, humpbacked Jewish boy with a stammer left his poor parents in Dessau in central Germany and walked eighty miles to Berlin, the capital of Frederick the Great's Prussia. According to one story, when the boy reached the Rosenthaler Gate, the only one through which Jews could pass, he told the inquiring watchman that his name was Moses and that he had come to Berlin "to learn." The watchman laughed and waved him through. "Go Moses, the sea has opened before you."* Embracing the Enlightenment and seeking a revitalization of Jewish religious thought, Moses Mendelssohn did point his people in a new and uncharted direction.

Turning in Berlin to a learned rabbi he had previously known in Dessau, the young Mendelssohn studied Jewish law and eked out a living copying Hebrew manuscripts in a beautiful hand. But he was soon fascinated by an intellectual world that had been closed to him in the Dessau ghetto. There, like most Jews throughout central Europe, he had spoken Yiddish—a mixture of German, Polish, and Hebrew. Now, working mainly on his own, he mastered German; learned Latin, Greek, French, and English; and studied mathematics and Enlightenment philosophy. Word of his exceptional abilities spread in Berlin's Jewish community (1,500 of the city's 100,000 inhabitants). He began tutoring the children of a wealthy Jewish silk merchant, and he soon became the merchant's clerk and later his partner. But his great passion remained the life of the mind and the spirit, which he avidly pursued in his off hours.

Gentle and unassuming in his personal life, Mendelssohn was a bold thinker. Reading eagerly in Western philosophy since antiquity, he was, as a pious Jew, soon convinced that Enlightenment teachings need not be opposed to Jewish thought and religion. Indeed, he concluded that reason could complement and strengthen religion, although each would retain its integrity as a separate sphere.† Developing this idea in his first great work, "On the Immortality of the Soul" (1767), Mendelssohn used the neutral setting of a philosophical dialogue between Socrates and his followers in ancient Greece to argue that the human soul lived forever. In refusing to bring religion and critical thinking into conflict, he was strongly influenced by contemporary German philosophers who argued similarly on behalf of Christianity. He reflected the way the German Enlightenment generally supported established religion, in contrast to the French Enlightenment, which attacked it. This was the most important difference in Enlightenment thinking between the two countries.

Mendelssohn's treatise on the human soul captivated the educated German public, which marveled that a Jew could have written a philosophical masterpiece. In the excitement, a Christian zealot named Lavater challenged Mendelssohn in a pamphlet to accept Christianity or to demonstrate how the Christian faith was not "reasonable." Replying politely but passionately, the Jewish philosopher affirmed that all his studies had only strengthened him in the faith of his fathers, although he certainly did not seek to convert anyone not born into Judaism. Rather, he urged toleration in religious matters. He spoke up courageously for his fellow Jews and decried the oppression they endured, and he continued to do so for the rest of his life.

Orthodox Jew and German philosophe, Moses Mendelssohn serenely combined two very different worlds. He built a bridge from the ghetto to the dominant culture over which many Jews would pass, including his novelist daughter Dorothea and his famous grandson, the composer Felix Mendelssohn.

Lavater (right) *attempts to convert Mendelssohn, in a painting by Moritz Oppenheim of an imaginary encounter.*
(Collection of the Judah L. Magnes Museum, Berkeley)

Questions for Analysis

1. How did Mendelssohn seek to influence Jewish religious thought in his time?
2. How do Mendelssohn's ideas compare with those of the French Enlightenment?

---

*H. Kupferberg, *The Mendelssohns: Three Generations of Genius* (New York: Charles Scribner's Sons, 1972), p. 3.

†D. Sorkin, *Moses Mendelssohn and the Religious Enlightenment* (Berkeley: University of California Press, 1996), pp. 8 ff.

Online Study Center **Improve Your Grade**
Going Beyond Individuals in Society

Catherine the Great as Equestrian and Miniature of Count Grigory Grigoryevich Orlov
Catherine conspired with her lover Count Orlov to overthrow her husband Peter III and became empress of Russia. Strongly influenced by the Enlightenment, she cultivated the French philosophes and instituted moderate reforms, only to reverse them in the aftermath of Pugachev's rebellion. This equestrian portrait now hangs above her throne in the palace throne room.
(left: Musée des Beaux-Arts, Chartres/The Bridgeman Art Library; right: © The State Hermitage Museum, St. Petersburg)

her mother was related to the Romanovs of Russia, and that proved to be Catherine's chance.

Peter the Great had abolished the hereditary succession of tsars so that he could name his successor and thus preserve his policies. This move opened a period of palace intrigue and a rapid turnover of rulers until Peter's youngest daughter, Elizabeth, came to the Russian throne in 1741. A shrewd but crude woman, Elizabeth named her nephew Peter heir to the throne and chose Catherine to be his wife in 1744. It was a mismatch from the beginning. The fifteen-year-old Catherine was intelligent and attractive; her husband shared neither of these qualities. Ignored by her husband, Catherine carefully studied Russian, endlessly read writers such as Bayle and Voltaire, and made friends at court. Soon she knew what she wanted: "I did not care about Peter," she wrote in her *Memoirs*, "but I did care about the crown."[18]

As the old empress Elizabeth approached death, Catherine plotted against her unpopular husband. She selected as her new lover a dashing young officer named Grigory Orlov, who with his four officer brothers commanded considerable support among the soldiers stationed in St. Petersburg. When Peter came to the throne in 1762, his decision to withdraw Russian troops from the coalition against Prussia alienated the army. At the end of six months Catherine and her conspirators deposed Peter III in a palace revolution, and the Orlov brothers murdered him. The German princess became empress of Russia.

Catherine had drunk deeply at the Enlightenment well. Never questioning the common assumption that absolute monarchy was the best form of government, she set out to rule in an enlightened manner. She had three main goals. First, she worked hard to continue Peter the Great's effort to bring the culture of western Europe to backward Russia. To do so, she imported Western architects, sculptors, musicians, and intellectuals. She bought masterpieces of Western art in wholesale lots and patronized the philosophes. An enthusiastic letter writer, she corresponded extensively with Voltaire and praised him as the "champion of the human race." When the French government banned the *Encyclopedia*, she offered to publish it in St. Petersburg, and she sent money to Diderot when he needed it. With these and countless similar actions, Catherine won good press in the West for herself and for her country. Moreover, this intellectual ruler, who wrote plays and loved good talk, set the tone for the entire Russian nobility. Peter the Great westernized Russian armies, but it was Catherine who westernized the imagination of the Russian nobility.

Catherine's second goal was domestic reform, and she began her reign with sincere and ambitious projects. Better laws were a major concern. In 1767 she appointed a special legislative commission to prepare a new law code. No new unified code was ever produced, but Catherine did restrict the practice of torture and allowed limited religious toleration. She also tried to improve education and strengthen local government. The philosophes applauded these measures and hoped more would follow.

Online Study Center Improve Your Grade
Primary Source: Catherine the Great's Grand Instruction to the Legislative Commission

Such was not the case. In 1773 a common Cossack soldier named Emelian Pugachev sparked a gigantic uprising of serfs, very much as Stenka Razin had done a century earlier (see page 576). Proclaiming himself the true tsar, Pugachev issued "decrees" abolishing serfdom, taxes, and army service. Thousands joined his cause, slaughtering landlords and officials over a vast area of southwestern Russia. Pugachev's untrained forces eventually proved no match for Catherine's noble-led regular army. Betrayed by his own company, Pugachev was captured and savagely executed.

Pugachev's rebellion was a decisive turning point in Catherine's domestic policy. On coming to the throne, she had condemned serfdom in theory, but Pugachev's rebellion put an end to any intentions she might have had about reforming the system. The peasants were clearly dangerous, and her empire rested on the support of the nobility. After 1775 Catherine gave the nobles absolute control of their serfs. She extended serfdom into new areas, such as Ukraine. In 1785 she formalized the nobility's privileged position, freeing nobles forever from taxes and state service. Under Catherine the Russian nobility attained its most exalted position, and serfdom entered its most oppressive phase.

Catherine's third goal was territorial expansion, and in this respect she was extremely successful. Her armies subjugated the last descendants of the Mongols, the Crimean Tatars, and began the conquest of the Caucasus. Her greatest coup by far was the partition of Poland (see Map 18.1). By 1700 Poland had become a weak and decentralized republic with an elected king (see page 567), and Poland's fate in the late eighteenth century demonstrated the dangers of failing to build a strong absolutist state. All important decisions continued to require the unanimous agreement of all nobles elected to the Polish Diet, which meant that nothing could ever be done to strengthen the state. When, between 1768 and 1772, Catherine's armies scored unprecedented victories against the Turks and thereby threatened to disturb the balance of power between Russia and Austria in eastern Europe, Frederick of Prussia obligingly came forward with a deal. He proposed that Turkey be let off easily and that Prussia, Austria, and Russia each compensate itself by taking a gigantic slice of Polish territory. Catherine jumped at the chance. The first partition of Poland took place in 1772. Two more partitions, in 1793 and 1795, gave all three powers more Polish territory, and the ancient republic of Poland vanished from the map.

Expansion helped Catherine keep the nobility happy, for it provided her with vast new lands to give to her faithful servants. Until the end this remarkable woman—who always believed that, in spite of her domestic setbacks, she was slowly civilizing Russia—kept her zest for life. Fascinated by a new twenty-two-year-old flame when she was a grandmother in her sixties, she happily reported her good fortune to a favorite former lover: "I have come back to life like a frozen fly; I am gay and well."[19]

The Austrian Habsburgs

In Austria two talented rulers did manage to introduce major reforms, although traditional power politics was more important than Enlightenment teachings. One was Joseph II (r. 1780–1790), a fascinating individual. For an earlier generation of historians, he was the "revolutionary emperor," a tragic hero whose lofty reforms were undone by the landowning nobility he dared to challenge. More recent scholarship has revised this romantic interpretation and has stressed how Joseph II continued the state-building work of his mother, the empress Maria Theresa (1740–1780), a remarkable but old-fashioned absolutist.

Mapping the Past

MAP 18.1 The Partition of Poland and Russia's Expansion, 1772–1795 During the sixteenth century the Polish nobility confirmed its right to elect the kings of Poland. The parliament could be blocked by the veto of a single member. In the seventeenth century warfare with Sweden and Russian Cossacks resulted in Poland's loss of the Baltic areas and Ukraine. In 1772 war threatened between Russia and Austria over Russian gains from the Ottoman Empire. To satisfy desires for expansion without fighting, Prussia's Frederick the Great proposed that parts of Poland be divided among Austria, Prussia, and Russia. In 1793 and 1795 the three powers partitioned the remainder, and the ancient republic of Poland vanished from the map. ❶ Why was Poland vulnerable to partition in the latter half of the eighteenth century? What does it say about European politics at the time that a country could simply cease to exist on the map? Could that happen today? ❷ Of the three powers that divided the kingdom of Poland, which benefited the most? How did the partition affect the geographical boundaries of each state, and what was the significance? ❸ What border with the former Poland remained unchanged? Why do you think this was the case?

Emerging from the long War of the Austrian Succession in 1748 with the serious loss of Silesia, Maria Theresa and her closest ministers were determined to introduce reforms that would make the state stronger and more efficient. Three aspects of these reforms were most important. First, Maria Theresa introduced measures aimed at limiting the papacy's political influence in her realm. Second, a whole series of administrative reforms strengthened the central bureaucracy, smoothed out some provincial differences, and revamped the tax system, taxing even the lands of nobles without special exemptions. Third, the government sought to improve the lot of the agricultural population, cautiously reducing the power of lords over their hereditary serfs and their partially free peasant tenants.

Maria Theresa The empress and her husband pose with eleven of their sixteen children at Schönbrunn palace in this family portrait by court painter Martin Meytens (1695–1770). Joseph, the heir to the throne, stands at the center of the star pattern. Wealthy women often had very large families, in part because they, unlike poor women, seldom nursed their babies. (*Réunion des Musées Nationaux/Art Resource, NY*)

Coregent with his mother from 1765 onward and a strong supporter of change, Joseph II moved forward rapidly when he came to the throne in 1780. He controlled the established Catholic Church even more closely in an attempt to ensure that it produced better citizens. He granted religious toleration and civic rights to Protestants and Jews—a radical innovation that impressed his contemporaries. In even more spectacular peasant reforms, Joseph abolished serfdom in 1781, and in 1789 he decreed that all peasant labor obligations be converted into cash payments. This measure was violently rejected not only by the nobility but also by the peasants it was intended to help since their primitive barter economy was woefully lacking in money. When a disillusioned Joseph died prematurely at forty-nine, the entire Habsburg empire was in turmoil. His brother Leopold II (r. 1790–1792) canceled Joseph's radical edicts in order to re-establish order. Peasants once again were required to do forced labor for their lords.

Evaluating "Enlightened Absolutism"

Despite differences, the leading eastern European monarchs of the later eighteenth century all claimed that they were acting on the principles of the Enlightenment. The philosophes generally agreed with this assessment and cheered them on. Beginning in the mid-nineteenth century historians developed the idea of a common "enlightened despotism" or "enlightened absolutism," and they canonized Frederick, Catherine, and Joseph as its most outstanding examples. More recent research has raised doubts about this old interpretation and has led to a fundamental revaluation.

There is general agreement that these absolutists, especially Catherine and Frederick, did encourage and spread the cultural values of the Enlightenment. Perhaps this was their greatest achievement. Skeptical in religion and intensely secular in basic orientation, they unabashedly accepted the here and now and sought their happiness in the enjoyment of it. At the same time, they were proud of their intellectual accomplishments and good taste, and they supported knowledge, education, and the arts. No wonder the philosophes felt that these monarchs were kindred spirits.

Historians also agree that the absolutists believed in change from above and tried to enact needed reforms. Yet the results of these efforts brought only very modest improvements, and the life of the peasantry remained very hard in the eighteenth century. Thus some historians have concluded that these monarchs were not really sincere in their reform efforts. Others disagree, arguing that powerful nobilities blocked the absolutists' genuine commitment to reform. (The old interpretation of Joseph II as the tragic revolutionary emperor forms part of this argument.)

The emerging answer to this controversy is that the later Eastern absolutists were indeed committed to reform but that humanitarian objectives were of secondary importance. Above all, the absolutists wanted reforms that would strengthen the state and allow them to compete militarily with their neighbors. Modern scholarship has therefore stressed how Catherine, Frederick, and Joseph were in many ways simply continuing the state-building of their predecessors, reorganizing armies and expanding bureaucracies to raise more taxes and troops. The reason for this continuation was simple. The international political struggle was brutal, and the stakes were high. First Austria under Maria Theresa and then Prussia under Frederick the Great had to engage in bitter fighting to escape dismemberment, while decentralized Poland was coldly divided and eventually liquidated.

Yet in this drive for more state power, the later absolutists were also innovators, and the idea of an era of enlightened absolutism retains a certain validity. Sharing the Enlightenment faith in critical thinking and believing that knowledge meant power, these absolutists really were more enlightened than their predecessors because they put state-building reforms in a new, broader perspective. Above all, the later absolutists considered how more humane laws and practices could help their populations become more productive and satisfied and thus able to contribute more substantially to the welfare of the state. It was from this perspective that they introduced many of their most progressive reforms, tolerating religious minorities, simplifying legal codes, and promoting practical education.

The primacy of state over individual interests also helps explain some puzzling variations in social policies. For example, Catherine the Great took measures that worsened the peasants' condition because she looked increasingly to the nobility as her natural ally and sought to strengthen it. Frederick the Great basically favored the status quo, limiting only the counterproductive excesses of his trusted nobility against its peasants. Joseph II believed that greater freedom for peasants was the means to strengthen his realm, and he acted accordingly. Each enlightened absolutist sought greater state power, but each believed that a different policy would attain it.

The eastern European absolutists of the later eighteenth century combined old-fashioned state-building with the culture and critical thinking of the Enlightenment. In doing so, they succeeded in expanding the role of the state in the life of society. They perfected bureaucratic machines that were to prove surprisingly adaptive and capable of enduring into the twentieth century. Their failure to implement policies we would recognize as humane and enlightened—such as abolishing serfdom—may reveal inherent limitations in Enlightenment thinking about equality and social justice, rather than in their execution of an Enlightenment program. The fact that leading philosophes supported rather than criticized Eastern rulers' policies suggests some of the blinders of the era.

Chapter Summary

- What was revolutionary in new attitudes toward the natural world?
- How did the new worldview affect the way people thought about society and human relations?
- What impact did this new way of thinking have on political developments and monarchical absolutism?

Decisive breakthroughs in astronomy and physics in the seventeenth century demolished the imposing medieval synthesis of Aristotelian philosophy and Christian theology. These developments had only limited practical consequences at the time, but the impact of new scientific knowledge on intellectual life was enormous. The emergence of modern science was a distinctive characteristic of Western civilization and became a key element of Western identity. During the eighteenth century scientific thought fostered new ideas about racial differences and provided justifications for belief in Western superiority.

Interpreting scientific findings and Newtonian laws in a manner that was both antitradition and antireligion, Enlightenment philosophes extolled the superiority of rational, critical thinking. This new method, they believed, promised not just increased knowledge but even the discovery of the fundamental laws of human society. Although they reached different conclusions when they turned to social and political realities, they did stimulate absolute monarchs to apply reason to statecraft and the search for useful reforms. Above all, the philosophes succeeded in shaping an emerging public opinion and spreading their radically new worldview.

The ideas of the Enlightenment were an inspiration for monarchs, particularly absolutist rulers in central and eastern Europe who saw in them important tools for reforming and rationalizing their governments. Their primary goal was to strengthen their states and increase the efficiency of their bureaucracies and armies. Enlightened absolutists believed that these reforms would ultimately improve the lot of ordinary people, but this was not their chief concern. With few exceptions, they did not question the institution of serfdom. The fact that leading philosophes supported rather than criticized Eastern rulers' policies suggests some of the limitations of the era.

Key Terms

natural philosophy
Copernican hypothesis
experimental method
law of inertia
law of universal gravitation
empiricism
Cartesian dualism
scientific community
Enlightenment
rationalism
progress
skepticism
tabula rasa
philosophes
separation of powers
reading revolution
salons
rococo
public sphere
general will
racial difference
enlightened absolutism

 Online Study Center **Improve Your Grade** Flashcards

Suggested Reading

Alexander, John T. *Catherine the Great: Life and Legend*. 1989. The best biography of the famous Russian tsarina.
Beales, Derek. *Joseph II*. 1987. A fine biography of the reforming Habsburg ruler.
Chartier, Roger. *The Cultural Origins of the French Revolution*. 1991. An imaginative analysis of the changing attitudes of the educated public.
Eze, E. Chukwudi, ed. *Race and the Enlightenment: A Reader*. 1997. A pioneering source on the origins of modern racial thinking in the Enlightenment.
Goodman, Dena. *The Republic of Letters: A Cultural History of the Enlightenment*. 1994. An innovative study of the role of salons and salon hostesses in the rise of the Enlightenment.
MacDonogh, Giles. *Frederick the Great*. 2001. An outstanding biography of the Prussian king.
Munck, Thomas. *The Enlightenment: A Comparative History*. 2000. Compares developments in Enlightenment thought in different countries.

Muthu, Sankar. *Enlightenment Against* [...] ines Enlightenment figures' opposit[...]
Outram, Dorinda. *The Enlightenment*, [...] standing and accessible introduction to En[...] bates that emphasizes the Enlightenment's soc[...] and global reach.
Schiebinger, Londa. *The Mind Has No Sex? Women in the Origins of Modern Science*. 1998. Discusses how the new science excluded women.
Shapin, Steven. *The Scientific Revolution*. 2001. A concise and well-informed general introduction to the scientific revolution.
Sorkin, David. *Moses Mendelssohn and the Religious Enlightenment*. 1996. A brilliant study of the Jewish philosopher and of the role of religion in the Enlightenment.

Notes

1. H. Butterfield, *The Origins of Modern Science* (New York: Macmillan, 1951), p. viii.
2. Quoted in A. G. R. Smith, *Science and Society in the Sixteenth and Seventeenth Centuries* (New York: Harcourt Brace Jovanovich, 1972), p. 97.
3. Quoted in Butterfield, *The Origins of Modern Science,* p. 47.
4. Ibid., pp. 115–116.
5. Ibid., p. 120.
6. L. Schiebinger, *The Mind Has No Sex? Women in the Origins of Modern Science* (Cambridge, Mass.: Harvard University Press, 1989), p. 2.
7. Jacqueline Broad, *Women Philosophers of the Seventeenth Century* (Cambridge: Cambridge University Press, 2003), p. 17.
8. Quoted in P. Hazard, *The European Mind, 1680–1715* (Cleveland: Meridian Books, 1963), pp. 304–305.
9. Schiebinger, *The Mind Has No Sex?* p. 64.
10. Quoted in L. M. Marsak, ed., *The Enlightenment* (New York: John Wiley & Sons, 1972), p. 56.
11. Quoted in G. L. Mosse et al., eds., *Europe in Review* (Chicago: Rand McNally, 1964), p. 156.
12. Quoted in P. Gay, "The Unity of the Enlightenment," *History* 3 (1960): 25.
13. See E. Fox-Genovese, "Women in the Enlightenment," in *Becoming Visible: Women in European History,* 2d ed., ed. R. Bridenthal, C. Koonz, and S. Stuard (Boston: Houghton Mifflin, 1987), esp. pp. 252–259, 263–265.
14. Quoted in G. P. Gooch, *Catherine the Great and Other Studies* (Hamden, Conn.: Archon Books, 1966), p. 149.
15. Jean Le Rond d'Alembert, *Eloges lus dans les séances publiques de l'Académie française* (Paris, 1779), p. ix, quoted in Mona Ozouf, "'Public Opinion' at the End of the Old Regime," *The Journal of Modern History* 60, Supplement: Rethinking French Politics in 1788 (September 1988), p. S9.
16. Quoted in Emmanuel Chukwudi Eze, ed., *Race and the Enlightenment: A Reader* (Oxford: Blackwell, 1997), p. 33. This section draws heavily on this reader.
17. Quoted in L. Krieger, *Kings and Philosophers, 1689–1789* (New York: W. W. Norton, 1970), p. 257.
18. Quoted in Gooch, *Catherine the Great,* p. 15.
19. Ibid., p. 53.

Listening to the Past

Voltaire on Religion

Voltaire was the most renowned and probably the most influential of the French *philosophes*. His biting satirical novel *Candide* (1759) is still widely assigned in college courses, and his witty yet serious *Philosophical Dictionary* remains a source of pleasure and stimulation. The *Dictionary* consists of a series of essays on topics ranging from Adam to Zoroaster, from certainty to circumcision. The following passage is taken from the essay on religion.

Voltaire began writing the *Philosophical Dictionary* in 1752, at the age of fifty-eight, after arriving at the Prussian court in Berlin. Frederick the Great applauded Voltaire's efforts, but Voltaire put the project aside after leaving Berlin, and the first of several revised editions was published anonymously in 1764. It was an immediate and controversial success. Snapped up by an "enlightened" public, it was denounced by religious leaders as a threat to the Christian community and was burned in Geneva and Paris.

I meditated last night; I was absorbed in the contemplation of nature; I admired the immensity, the course, the harmony of those infinite globes which the vulgar do not know how to admire.

I admired still more the intelligence which directs these vast forces. I said to myself: "One must be blind not to be dazzled by this spectacle; one must be stupid not to recognize its author; one must be mad not to worship the Supreme Being. What tribute of worship should I render Him? Should not this tribute be the same in the whole of space, since it is the same Supreme Power which reigns equally in all space?

"Should not a thinking being who dwells on a star in the Milky Way offer Him the same homage as a thinking being on this little globe of ours? Light is the same for the star Sirius as for us; moral philosophy must also be the same. If a feeling, thinking animal on Sirius is born of a tender father and mother who have been occupied with his happiness, he owes them as much love and care as we owe to our parents. If someone in the Milky Way sees a needy cripple, and if he can aid him and does not do so, then he is guilty toward all the globes.

"Everywhere the heart has the same duties: on the steps of the throne of God, if He has a throne; and in the depths of the abyss, if there is an abyss."

I was deep in these ideas when one of those genii who fill the spaces between the worlds came down to me. I recognized the same aerial creature who had appeared to me on another occasion to teach me that the judgments of God are different from our own, and how a good action is preferable to a controversy.

The genie transported me into a desert all covered with piles of bones. . . . He began with the first pile. "These," he said, "are the twenty-three thousand Jews who danced before a calf, together with the twenty-four thousand who were killed while fornicating with Midianitish women. The number of those massacred for such errors and offences amounts to nearly three hundred thousand.

"In the other piles are the bones of the Christians slaughtered by each other because of metaphysical disputes. They are divided into several heaps of four centuries each. One heap would have mounted right to the sky; they had to be divided."

"What!" I cried, "brothers have treated their brothers like this, and I have the misfortune to be of this brotherhood!"

"Here," said the spirit, "are the twelve million native Americans killed in their own land because they had not been baptized."

"My God! . . . Why assemble here all these abominable monuments to barbarism and fanaticism?"

An impish Voltaire, by the French sculptor Houdon. (Courtesy of Board of Trustees of the Victoria & Albert Museum)

"To instruct you. . . . Follow me now." [The genie takes Voltaire to the "heroes of humanity, who tried to banish violence and plunder from the world," and tells Voltaire to question them.]

[At last] I saw a man with a gentle, simple face, who seemed to me to be about thirty-five years old. From afar he looked with compassion upon those piles of whitened bones, through which I had been led to reach the sage's dwelling place. I was astonished to find his feet swollen and bleeding, his hands likewise, his side pierced, and his ribs laid bare by the cut of the lash. "Good God!" I said to him, "is it possible for a just man, a sage, to be in this state? I have just seen one who was treated in a very hateful way, but there is no comparison between his torture and yours. Wicked priests and wicked judges poisoned him; is it by priests and judges that you were so cruelly assassinated?"

With great courtesy he answered, "Yes."

"And who were these monsters?"

"They were hypocrites."

"Ah! that says everything; I understand by that one word that they would have condemned you to the cruelest punishment. Had you then proved to them, as Socrates did, that the Moon was not a goddess, and that Mercury was not a god?"

"No, it was not a question of planets. My countrymen did not even know what a planet was; they were all arrant ignoramuses. Their superstitions were quite different from those of the Greeks."

"Then you wanted to teach them a new religion?"

"Not at all; I told them simply: 'Love God with all your heart and your neighbor as yourself, for that is the whole of mankind's duty.' Judge yourself if this precept is not as old as the universe; judge yourself if I brought them a new religion." . . .

"But did you say nothing, do nothing that could serve them as a pretext?"

"To the wicked everything serves as pretext."

"Did you not say once that you were come not to bring peace, but a sword?"

"It was a scribe's error; I told them that I brought peace and not a sword. I never wrote anything; what I can't have been changed without evil intention."

"You did not then contribute in any way by your teaching, either badly reported or badly interpreted, to those frightful piles of bones which I saw on my way to consult with you?"

"I have only looked with horror upon those who have made themselves guilty of all these murders."

. . . [Finally] I asked him to tell me in what true religion consisted.

"Have I not already told you? Love God and your neighbor as yourself."

"Is it necessary for me to take sides either for the Greek Orthodox Church or the Roman Catholic?"

"When I was in the world I never made any difference between the Jew and the Samaritan."

"Well, if that is so, I take you for my only master." Then he made a sign with his head that filled me with peace. The vision disappeared, and I was left with a clear conscience.

Questions for Analysis

1. Why did Voltaire believe in a Supreme Being? Does this passage reflect the influence of Isaac Newton's scientific system? If so, how?
2. Was Voltaire trying to entertain, teach, or do both? Was he effective? Why?
3. If Voltaire was trying to convey serious ideas about religion and morality, what were those ideas? What was he attacking?
4. If a person today thought and wrote like Voltaire, would that person be called a defender or a destroyer of Christianity? Why?

Source: F. M. Arouet de Voltaire, *Oeuvres complètes,* vol. 8, trans. J. McKay (Paris: Firmin-Didot, 1875), pp. 188–190.

The East India Dock, London (detail), by Samuel Scott, a painting infused with the spirit of maritime expansion. *(© Board of Trustees of the Victoria & Albert Museum)*

chapter 19

THE EXPANSION OF EUROPE IN THE EIGHTEENTH CENTURY

chapter preview

Agriculture and the Land
- What were the causes and effects of the agricultural revolution, and what nations led the way in these developments?

The Beginning of the Population Explosion
- Why did European population rise dramatically in the eighteenth century?

Cottage Industry and Urban Guilds
- How and why did economic production intensify in the eighteenth century, particularly in the countryside?

Building the Global Economy
- How did colonial markets boost Europe's economic and social development, and what conflicts and adversity did world trade entail?

The world of absolutism and aristocracy, a combination of raw power and elegant refinement, was a world apart from that of the common people. For most people in the eighteenth century, life remained a struggle with poverty and uncertainty, with the landlord and the tax collector. In 1700 peasants on the land and artisans in their shops lived little better than had their ancestors in the Middle Ages. Only in science and thought, and there only among intellectual elites and their followers, had Western society succeeded in going beyond the great achievements of the High Middle Ages, achievements that in turn owed much to Greece and Rome.

Everyday life was a struggle because European societies still could not produce very much by modern standards. Ordinary men and women might work like their beasts in the fields, but there was seldom enough good food, warm clothing, and decent housing. Life went on; history went on. The wars of religion ravaged Germany in the seventeenth century; Russia rose to become a Great Power; the state of Poland disappeared; monarchs and nobles continually jockeyed for power and wealth. In 1700 the idea of progress, of substantial improvement in the lives of great numbers of people, was still the dream of only a small elite in fashionable salons.

Yet the economic basis of European life was beginning to change. In the course of the eighteenth century the European economy emerged from the long crisis of the seventeenth century, responded to challenges, and began to expand once again. Population resumed its growth, while colonial empires developed and colonial elites prospered. Some areas were more fortunate than others. The rising Atlantic powers—Holland, France, and above all England—and their colonies led the way. The expansion of agriculture, industry, trade, and population marked the beginning of a surge comparable to that of the eleventh- and twelfth-century springtime of European civilization. But this time, broadly based expansion was not cut short. This time the response to new challenges led toward one of the most influential developments in human history, the Industrial Revolution, considered in Chapter 22.

Online Study Center
This icon will direct you to interactive activities and study materials on the website **college.hmco.com/pic/mckaywest9e**

Agriculture and the Land

At the end of the seventeenth century the economy of Europe was agrarian. With the possible exception of Holland, at least 80 percent of the people of all western European countries drew their livelihoods from agriculture. In eastern Europe the percentage was considerably higher. Men and women lavished their attention on the land, plowing fields and sowing seed, reaping harvests and storing grain. Yet even in a rich agricultural region such as the Po Valley in northern Italy, every bushel of wheat sown yielded on average only five or six bushels of grain at harvest during the seventeenth century. By modern standards output was distressingly low.

In most regions of Europe in the sixteenth and seventeenth centuries, climatic conditions produced poor or disastrous harvests every eight or nine years. Unbalanced and inadequate food in famine years made people extremely susceptible to illness. Eating material unfit for human consumption, such as bark or grass, resulted in intestinal ailments of many kinds. Influenza and smallpox preyed on populations weakened by famine. In famine years the number of deaths soared far above normal. A third of a village's population might disappear in a year or two. But new developments in agricultural technology and methods gradually brought an end to the ravages of hunger in western Europe.

- **What were the causes and effects of the agricultural revolution, and what nations led the way in these developments?**

The Open-Field System

These new developments drew on long roots. The great accomplishment of medieval agriculture was the **open-field system** of village farming. That system divided the land to be cultivated by the peasants of a given village into several large fields, which were in turn cut up into long, narrow strips. The fields were open, and the strips were not enclosed into small plots by fences or hedges. Each family followed the same pattern of plowing, sowing, and harvesting in accordance with tradition and the village leaders.

The ever-present problem was soil exhaustion. Wheat planted year after year in a field will deplete the nitrogen in the soil. Since the supply of manure for fertilizer was limited, the only way for the land to recover was to lie fallow for a period of time. In the early Middle Ages a year of fallow was alternated with a year of cropping; then three-year rotations were introduced, especially on more fertile lands. This system permitted a year of wheat or rye to be followed by a year of oats or beans and only then by a year of fallow. Significant gains in agricultural production resulted.

Traditional village rights reinforced communal patterns of farming. In addition to rotating field crops in a uniform way, villages maintained open meadows for hay and natural pasture. These lands were **common lands,** set aside primarily for draft horses and oxen, but open to the cows and pigs of the community as well. After the harvest villagers also pastured their animals on the wheat or rye stubble. In many places such pasturing followed a brief period, also established by tradition, for the gleaning of grain. Poor women would go through the fields picking up the few single grains that had fallen to the ground in the course of the harvest.

In the age of absolutism and nobility, the state and landlords continued to levy heavy taxes and high rents, thereby stripping peasants of much of their meager earnings. The level of exploitation varied. Generally speaking, the peasants of eastern Europe were worst off. As we saw in Chapter 17, they were serfs bound to their lords in hereditary service. In much of eastern Europe, five or six days of unpaid work per week on the lord's land were not uncommon. Well into the nineteenth century individual Russian serfs and serf families were regularly sold with and without land.

Social conditions were better in western Europe, where peasants were generally free from serfdom. In France, western Germany, England, and the Low Countries, they owned land and could pass it on to their children. Yet life in the village was unquestionably hard, and poverty was the great reality for most people. The privileges of Europe's ruling elites weighed heavily on the people of the land.

The Agricultural Revolution

One way for European peasants to improve their difficult position was to take land from those who owned it but did no labor. Yet the social and political conditions that sustained the ruling elites were ancient and deeply rooted, and powerful forces stood ready to crush protest. Only with the coming of the French Revolution were European peasants, mainly in France, able to improve their position by means of radical mass action.

Technological progress offered another possibility. If peasants (and their noble landlords) could replace the idle fallow with crops, they could greatly increase the land under cultivation. So remarkable were the possibilities and the results that historians have often spoken of the progressive elimination of the fallow, which occurred gradually throughout Europe from the mid-seventeenth century on, as an **agricultural revolution.** This revolution, which took longer than historians used to believe, was a great milestone in human development.

Because grain crops exhaust the soil and make fallowing necessary, the secret to eliminating the fallow lies in alternating grain with nitrogen-storing crops. The most important of these land-reviving crops are peas and beans, root crops such as turnips and potatoes, and clovers and grasses. As the eighteenth century went on, the number of crops that were systematically rotated grew. New patterns of organization allowed some farmers to develop increasingly sophisticated patterns of **crop rotation** to suit different kinds of soils. For example, farmers in French Flanders near Lille in the late eighteenth century used a ten-year rotation, alternating a number of grain, root, and hay crops in a given field on a ten-year schedule. Continual experimentation led to more scientific farming.

Improvements in farming had multiple effects. The new crops made ideal feed for animals, and because peasants and larger farmers had more fodder, hay, and root crops for the winter months, they could build up their herds of cattle and sheep. More animals meant more meat and better diets. More animals also meant more manure for fertilizer and therefore more grain for bread and porridge.

Advocates of the new crop rotations, who included an emerging group of experimental scientists, some government officials, and a few big landowners, believed that new methods were scarcely possible within the traditional framework of open fields and common rights. A farmer who wanted to experiment with new methods would have to get all the landholders in a village to agree to the plan. Advocates of improvement argued that innovating agriculturalists needed to enclose and consolidate their scattered holdings into compact, fenced-in fields in order to farm more effectively. In doing so, the innovators also needed to enclose their individual shares of the natural pasture, the common. According to proponents of this movement, known as **enclosure,** a revolution in village life and organization was the necessary price of technical progress.

That price seemed too high to many poor rural people who had small, inadequate holdings or very little land at all. Traditional rights were precious to these poor peasants. They used commonly held pastureland to graze livestock, and marshlands or moorlands outside the village as a source for firewood, berries, and other foraged goods that could make the difference between survival and famine in harsh times. Thus when the small landholders and the village poor could effectively oppose the enclosure of the open fields and the common lands, they did so. Moreover, in many countries they found allies among the larger, predominately noble landowners who were also wary of enclosure because it required large investments and posed risks for them as well.

The old system of unenclosed open fields and the new system of continuous rotation coexisted in Europe for a long time. Open fields could be found in much of France and Germany in the early years of the nineteenth century because peasants there had successfully opposed efforts to introduce the new techniques in the late eighteenth century. Until the end of the eighteenth century, the new system was extensively adopted only in the Low Countries and England.

Chronology

ca 1650–1790	Growth of Atlantic economy
ca 1650–1850	Agricultural improvement and revolution
1651–1663	British Navigation Acts
1652–1674	Anglo-Dutch wars; rise of British mercantilism
ca 1690–1780	Enlightenment
1700–1790	Height of Atlantic slave trade; expansion of rural industry in Europe
1701–1713	War of the Spanish Succession
1701–1763	Mercantilist wars of empire
1720–1722	Last of bubonic plague in Europe
1720–1789	Growth of European population
1740–1748	War of the Austrian Succession
1750–1790	Rise of economic liberalism
1756–1763	Seven Years' War
1759	Fall of Quebec
1760–1815	Height of parliamentary enclosure in England
1776	Smith, *Wealth of Nations*
1807	British slave trade abolished

Hendrick Sorgh: Vegetable Market (1662) The wealth and well-being of the industrious, capitalistic Dutch shine forth in this winsome market scene. The market woman's baskets are filled with delicious fresh produce that ordinary citizens can afford—eloquent testimony to the responsive, enterprising character of Dutch agriculture. *(Rijksmuseum, Amsterdam)*

The Leadership of the Low Countries and England

The new methods of the agricultural revolution originated in the Low Countries. Seventeenth-century republican Holland, already the most advanced country in Europe in many areas of human endeavor (see pages 549–553), led the way. By the middle of the seventeenth century intensive farming was well established, and the innovations of enclosed fields, continuous rotation, heavy manuring, and a wide variety of crops were all present. Agriculture was highly specialized and commercialized.

One reason for early Dutch leadership in farming was that the area was one of the most densely populated in Europe. In order to feed themselves and provide employment, the Dutch were forced at an early date to seek maximum yields from their land and to increase the cultivated area through the steady draining of marshes and swamps.

The pressure of population was connected with the second cause: the growth of towns and cities. Stimulated by commerce and overseas trade, Amsterdam grew from thirty thousand to two hundred thousand inhabitants in its golden seventeenth century. The growing urban population provided Dutch peasants with markets for all they could produce and allowed each region to specialize in what it did best. Thus the Dutch could develop their potential, and the Low Countries became "the Mecca of foreign agricultural experts who came . . . to see Flemish agriculture with their own eyes, to write about it and to propagate its methods in their home lands."[1]

The English were the best students. Drainage and water control were one subject in which they received instruction. Large parts of seventeenth-century Holland had once been sea and sea marsh, and the efforts of centuries had made the Dutch the world's leaders in the skills of drainage. In the first half of the seventeenth century Dutch experts made a great contribution to draining the extensive marshes, or fens, of wet and rainy England. The most famous of these Dutch engineers, Cornelius Vermuyden, directed one large drainage project in Yorkshire and another in Cambridgeshire. In the Cambridge fens, Vermuyden and his Dutch workers eventually reclaimed forty thousand acres, which were then farmed intensively in the Dutch manner. Swampy wilderness was converted into thousands of acres of some of the best land in England.

Jethro Tull (1674–1741), part crank and part genius, was an important English innovator. A true son of the early Enlightenment, Tull adopted a critical attitude toward accepted ideas about farming and tried to develop better methods through empirical research. He was especially enthusiastic about using horses, rather than slower-moving oxen, for plowing. He also advocated sowing seed with drilling equipment rather than scattering it by hand. Drilling distributed seed in an even manner and at the proper depth. There were also improvements in livestock, inspired in part by the earlier successes of English country gentlemen in breeding ever-faster horses for the races and fox hunts that were their passions. Selective breeding of ordinary livestock was a marked improvement over the haphazard old pattern.

By the mid-eighteenth century English agriculture was in the process of a long but radical transformation. The eventual result was that by 1870 English farmers were producing 300 percent more food than they had produced in 1700, although the number of people working the land had increased by only 14 percent. This great surge of agricultural production provided food for England's rapidly growing urban population.

Growth in production was achieved in part by land enclosures. About half the farmland in England was enclosed through private initiatives prior to 1700; in the eighteenth century Parliament completed this work. From the 1760s through the Napoleonic wars of the early nineteenth century, a series of acts of Parliament enclosed most of the remaining common land.

By eliminating common rights and greatly reducing the access of poor men and women to the land, the eighteenth-century enclosure movement marked the completion of two major historical developments in England—the rise of market-oriented estate agriculture and the emergence of a landless rural proletariat. By 1815 a tiny minority of wealthy English (and Scottish) landowners held most of the land and pursued profits aggressively, leasing their holdings through agents at competitive prices to middle-size farmers, who relied on landless laborers for their workforce. These landless la-

Enclosure in Streatley, Berkshire County, England This map shows the results of enclosure in early-nineteenth-century Streatley, a village ten miles west of Reading on the River Thames. The area marked in yellow was the enclosed territory, appropriated mostly by a few large landowners and the city of Reading. The legend provides a detailed list of land ownership, including references to "old inclosures." *(Courtesy, Berkshire Record Office, Ref # Streatley (1817), MRI 256)*

borers worked very long hours, usually following a dawn-to-dusk schedule six days a week all year long. Moreover, landless laborers had lost that bit of independence and self-respect that common rights had provided and were completely dependent on cash wages. In no other European country had this **proletarianization**—this transformation of large numbers of small peasant farmers into landless rural wage earners—gone so far. And England's village poor found the cost of change heavy and unjust.

The Beginning of the Population Explosion

Another factor that affected the existing order of life and forced economic changes in the eighteenth century was the beginning of the "population explosion." Explosive growth continued in Europe until the twentieth century, by which time it was affecting nonwestern areas of the globe. What caused the growth of population, and what did the challenge of more mouths to feed and more hands to employ do to the European economy?

- **Why did European population rise dramatically in the eighteenth century?**

Limitations on Population Growth

Many commonly held ideas about population in the past are wrong. One such mistaken idea is the belief that population was always growing too fast. On the contrary, until 1700 the total population of Europe grew slowly much of the time, and it followed an irregular cyclical pattern (see Figure 19.1). This cyclical pattern had a great influence on many aspects of social and economic life. The terrible ravages of the Black Death caused a sharp drop in population and prices after 1350 and also created a labor shortage throughout Europe. Some economic historians calculate that for those common people in western Europe who managed to steer clear of warfare and of power struggles within the ruling class, the later Middle Ages was an era of exceptional well-being.

But this well-being eroded in the course of the sixteenth century. The second great surge of population growth (see Figure 19.1) outstripped the growth of agricultural production after about 1500. There was less food per person, and food prices rose more rapidly than wages, a development intensified by the inflow of precious metals from the Americas and a general, if uneven, European price revolution. The result was a substantial decline in living standards throughout Europe. By 1600 the pressure of population on resources was severe in much of Europe, and widespread poverty was an undeniable reality.

For this reason, population growth slowed and stopped in seventeenth-century Europe. Births and deaths, fertility and mortality, were in a crude but effective balance. The population grew modestly in normal years at a rate of perhaps 0.5 to 1 percent, or enough to double the population in 70 to 140 years. This is, of course, a generalization encompassing many different patterns. In areas such as Russia and colonial New England, where there was a great deal of frontier to be settled, the annual rate of natural increase, not counting in-migration, might well have exceeded 1 percent. In a country such as France, where the land had long been densely settled, the rate of increase might have been less than 0.5 percent.

FIGURE 19.1 The Growth of Population in England, 1000–1800 England is a good example of both the uneven increase of European population before 1700 and the third great surge of growth, which began in the eighteenth century. *(Source: E. A. Wrigley,* Population and History. *Copyright © 1969 by McGraw-Hill. Reprinted by permission of The McGraw-Hill Companies.)*

Although population growth of even 1 percent per year seems fairly modest, it will produce a very large increase over a long period: in three hundred years it will result in sixteen times as many people. Such gigantic increases simply did not occur in agrarian Europe. In certain abnormal years and tragic periods—the Black Death was only the most extreme example—many more people died than were born. Total population fell sharply, even catastrophically. A number of years of modest growth would then be necessary to make up for those who had died in an abnormal year. Such savage increases in deaths occurred periodically in the seventeenth century on a local and regional scale, and these demographic crises combined to check the growth of population until after 1700.

The grim reapers of demographic crisis were famine, epidemic disease, and war. Famine, the inevitable result of low yields and periodic crop failures, was particularly murderous because it was accompanied by disease. With a brutal one-two punch, famine stunned and weakened a population, and disease finished it off. War was another scourge, and its indirect effects were even more harmful than the organized killing. Soldiers and camp followers passed all manner of contagious diseases throughout the countryside. Armies also requisitioned scarce food supplies and disrupted the agricultural cycle. The Thirty Years' War witnessed all possible combinations of distress. In the German states, the number of inhabitants declined by more than *two-thirds* in some large areas and by at least one-third almost everywhere else.

The Plague at Marseilles in 1720 The last great wave of bubonic plague in Europe occurred at Marseilles in 1720, when a merchant ship from Syria arrived at the Mediterranean port city with infected passengers. The plague spread quickly, killing half the inhabitants of the city. A wall was erected to quarantine the city, but it did not prevent the spread of disease to the surrounding region. Altogether, about a hundred thousand people died before the epidemic ended in 1722. *(Giraudon/Art Resource, NY)*

The New Pattern of the Eighteenth Century

In the eighteenth century the population of Europe began to grow markedly. This increase in numbers occurred in all areas of Europe, western and eastern, northern and southern, dynamic and stagnant. Growth was especially dramatic after about 1750 (see Figure 19.2).

What caused this population growth? In some areas women had more babies than before because new opportunities for employment in rural industry allowed them to marry at an earlier age. But the basic cause for Europe as a whole was a decline in mortality—fewer deaths.

The bubonic plague mysteriously disappeared. Following the Black Death in the fourteenth century, plagues had remained part of the European experience, striking again and again with savage force, particularly in towns. As late as 1720 a ship from Syria and the Levant brought the disease to Marseilles, killing up to one hundred thousand in the city and surrounding region. By 1722 the epidemic had passed, and that was the last time plague fell on western and central Europe. Exactly why plague disappeared is unknown. Stricter measures of quarantine in Mediterranean ports and along the Austrian border with Turkey helped by carefully isolating human carriers of plague. Chance and plain good luck were probably just as important.

Advances in medical knowledge did not contribute much to reducing the death rate in the eighteenth century. The most important advance in preventive medicine in this period was inoculation against smallpox, and this great improvement was long confined mainly to England, probably doing little to reduce deaths throughout Europe until the latter part of the century. However,

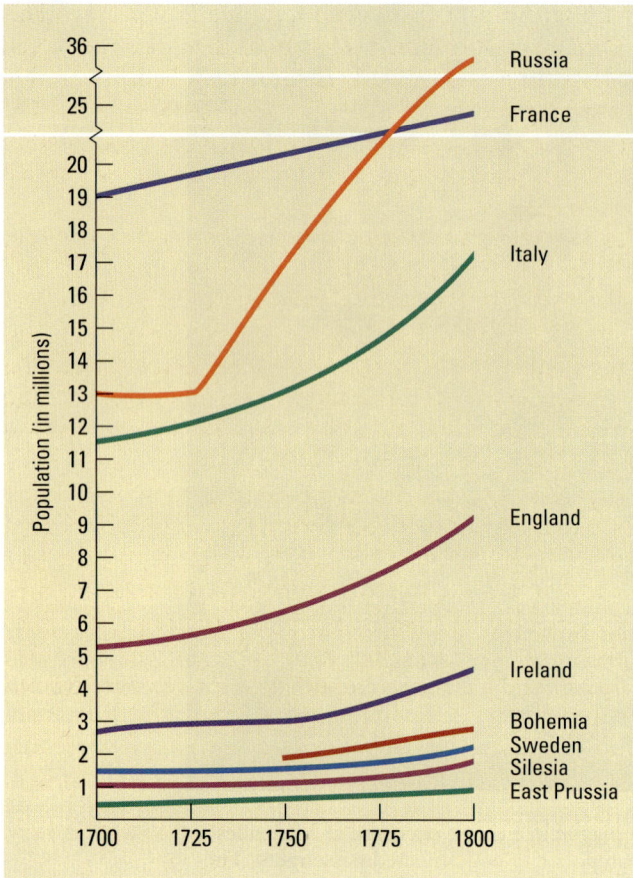

FIGURE 19.2 The Increase of Population in Europe in the Eighteenth Century France's large population continued to support French political and intellectual leadership. Russia emerged as Europe's most populous state because natural increase was complemented by growth from territorial expansion.

improvements in the water supply and sewerage, which were frequently promoted by strong absolutist monarchies, resulted in somewhat better public health and helped reduce such diseases as typhoid and typhus in some urban areas of western Europe. Improvements in water supply and the drainage of swamps also reduced Europe's large insect population. Flies and mosquitoes played a major role in spreading diseases, especially those striking children and young adults. Thus early public health measures helped the decline in mortality that began with the disappearance of plague and continued into the early nineteenth century.

Human beings also became more successful in their efforts to safeguard the supply of food. The eighteenth century was a time of considerable canal and road building in western Europe. These advances in transportation, which were also among the more positive aspects of strong absolutist states, lessened the impact of local crop failure and famine. Emergency supplies could be brought in, and localized starvation became less frequent. Wars became more gentlemanly and less destructive than in the seventeenth century and spread fewer epidemics. New foods, particularly the potato from South America, were introduced. In short, population grew in the eighteenth century primarily because years of abnormal death rates were less catastrophic. Famines, epidemics, and wars continued to occur, but their severity moderated.

Cottage Industry and Urban Guilds

The growth of population increased the number of rural workers with little or no land, and this in turn contributed to the development of industry in rural areas. The poor in the countryside increasingly needed to supplement their agricultural earnings with other types of work, and urban capitalists were eager to employ them, often at lower wages than urban workers were paid. **Cottage industry,** which consisted of manufacturing with hand tools in peasant cottages and work sheds, grew markedly in the eighteenth century and became a crucial feature of the European economy.

To be sure, peasant communities had always made clothing, processed food, and constructed housing for their own use. But medieval peasants did not produce manufactured goods on a large scale for sale in a market. By the eighteenth century, however, the pressures of rural poverty and the need to employ landless proletarians were overwhelming the efforts of urban artisans to maintain their traditional monopoly over industrial production.

Guilds continued to dominate production in towns and cities, providing their masters with economic privileges as well as a fixed social identity. Those excluded from guild membership—women, day laborers, Jews, and foreigners—worked on the margins of the urban economy. Critics attacked the guilds in the second half of the eighteenth century as outmoded institutions that obstructed technical progress and innovation. Until recently, most historians repeated that view. An ongoing re-assessment of guilds now emphasizes their ability to adapt to changing economic circumstances.

• *How and why did economic production intensify in the eighteenth century, particularly in the countryside?*

The Putting-Out System

Cottage industry was often organized through the **putting-out system.** The two main participants in the putting-out system were the merchant capitalist and the rural worker. The merchant loaned, or "put out," raw materials to cottage workers who processed the raw materials in their own homes and returned the finished products to the merchant. There were endless variations on this basic relationship. Sometimes rural workers bought their own raw materials and worked as independent producers before they sold to the merchant. Sometimes whole families were involved in domestic industry; at other times the tasks were closely associated with one gender. Sometimes several workers toiled together to perform a complicated process in a workshop outside the home. The relative importance of earnings from the land and from industry varied greatly for handicraft workers, although industrial wages usually became more important for a given family with time.

As industries grew in scale and complexity, production was often broken into many stages. For example, a merchant would provide raw wool to one group of workers for spinning into thread. He would then pass the thread to another group of workers to be bleached, to another for dying, and to another for weaving into cloth. The merchant paid outworkers by the piece and proceeded to sell the finished product to regional, national, or international markets.

The putting-out system grew because it had competitive advantages. Underemployed labor was abundant, and poor peasants and landless laborers would work for low wages. Since production in the countryside was unregulated, workers and merchants could change procedures and experiment as they saw fit. Because they did not need to meet rigid guild standards, cottage industry became capable of producing many kinds of goods. Textiles; all manner of knives, forks, and housewares; buttons and gloves; and clocks could be produced quite satisfactorily in the countryside. Luxury goods for the rich, such as exquisite tapestries and fine porcelain, demanded special training, close supervision, and centralized workshops. Yet such goods were as exceptional as those who used them. The skills of rural industry were sufficient for everyday articles.

The Weaver's Repose
This painting by Decker Cornelis Gerritz (1594–1637) captures the pleasure of release from long hours of toil in cottage industry. The loom realistically dominates the cramped living space and the family's modest possessions. *(Musées Royaux des Beaux-Arts, Brussels. Copyright A.C.I.)*

Mapping the Past

MAP 19.1 Industry and Population in Eighteenth-Century Europe The growth of cottage manufacturing in rural areas helped country people increase their income and contributed to population growth. The putting-out system began in England, and much of the work was in the textile industry. Cottage industry was also strong in the Low Countries—modern-day Belgium and Holland. ❶ What types of textiles were produced in Europe? How would you account for the distribution of each type of cloth across Europe? ❷ What was the relationship between population density and the growth of textile production? Was this a fixed or variable relationship? What geographical characteristics seem to have played a role in encouraging this industry? ❸ Did metal production draw on different demographic and geographical conditions? Why do you think this was the case?

Online Study Center **Improve Your Grade** Interactive Map: Population and Production in Eighteenth-Century Europe

Rural manufacturing did not spread across Europe at an even rate. It developed most successfully in England, particularly for the spinning and weaving of woolen cloth. By 1500 half of England's textiles were being produced in the countryside. By 1700 English industry was generally more rural than urban and heavily reliant on the putting-out system. Most continental countries, with the exception of Flanders and the Netherlands, developed rural industry more slowly. The latter part of the eighteenth century witnessed a remarkable expansion of rural industry in certain densely populated regions of continental Europe (see Map 19.1).

The Textile Industry

Until the nineteenth century, the industry that employed the most people in Europe was textiles. The making of linen, woolen, and eventually cotton cloth was the typical activity of cottage workers engaged in the putting-out system. A look inside the cottage of the English weaver illustrates a way of life as well as an economic system.

The rural worker lived in a small cottage with tiny windows and little space. Indeed, the worker's cottage was often a single room that served as workshop, kitchen, and bedroom. There were only a few pieces of furniture, of which the weaver's loom was by far the largest and most important. That loom had changed somewhat in the early eighteenth century when John Kay's invention of the flying shuttle enabled the weaver to throw the shuttle back and forth between the threads with one hand. Aside from that improvement, however, the loom was as it had been for much of history and as it would remain until the arrival of mechanized looms in the first decades of the nineteenth century.

Handloom weaving was a family enterprise. All members of the family helped in the work, so that "every person from seven to eighty (who retained their sight and who could move their hands) could earn their bread," as one eighteenth-century English observer put it.[2] Operating the loom was considered a man's job, reserved for the male head of the family. Women and children worked at auxiliary tasks; they prepared the warp (vertical) threads and mounted them on the loom, wound threads on bobbins for the weft (horizontal) threads, and sometimes operated the warp frame while the father passed the shuttle.

There was always a serious imbalance in textile manufacture before mechanization: the work of four or five spinners was needed to keep one weaver steadily employed. Since the weaver's family usually could not produce enough thread, alternate sources of labor were needed. Merchants turned to the wives and daughters of agricultural workers, who took on spinning work in their spare time. Many widows and single women also became "spinsters," so many in fact that the word became a synonym for an unmarried woman. (In other parts of Europe, such as the Rhineland, spinning employed whole families and was not reserved for women.) As the industry expanded and merchants covered ever greater distances in search of workers, they sometimes turned to local shopkeepers to manage the spinners in their villages.

Relations between workers and employers were often marked by sharp conflict. An English popular song written about 1700, called "The Clothier's Delight, or the Rich Men's Joy and the Poor Men's Sorrow," has the merchant boasting of the countless tricks he uses to "beat down wages":

We heapeth up riches and treasure great store
Which we get by griping and grinding the poor.
And this is a way for to fill up our purse
Although we do get it with many a curse.[3]

There were constant disputes over the weights of materials and the quality of finished work. Merchants accused workers of stealing raw materials, and weavers complained that merchants delivered underweight bales. Suspicion abounded.

Conditions were particularly hard for female workers. While men could earn decent wages through long hours of arduous labor, women's wages were always terribly low. In the Yorkshire wool industry, a male wool comber earned a good wage of twelve shillings or more a week, while a spinner could hope for only three-and-a-half shillings.[4] A single or widowed spinner faced a desperate struggle with poverty. Any period of illness or unemployment could spell disaster for her and any dependent children.

There was another problem, at least from the merchant capitalist's point of view. Rural labor was cheap, scattered, and poorly organized. For these reasons it was hard to control. Moreover, the pace of work depended on the agricultural calendar. In spring and late summer planting and haymaking occupied all hands in the rural village, leading to shortages in the supply of thread. Merchants, whose livelihood depended on their ability to meet orders on time, bitterly resented their lack of control over rural labor. They accused workers—especially female spinners—of laziness, intemperance, and immorality. If workers failed to produce enough thread, they reasoned, it must be because their wages were too high and they had little incentive to work. Merchants thus insisted on maintaining the lowest possible wages to force the "idle" poor into productive labor. They also successfully lobbied for, and obtained, new police powers over workers. Imprisonment and public whipping became common punishments for pilfering small amounts of yarn or cloth. For poor workers, their right to hold on to the bits and pieces left over in the production process was akin to the traditional peasant right of gleaning in common lands.

Urban Guilds

The high point of the **guild system** in most of Europe occurred in the seventeenth and eighteenth centuries,

Guild Procession in Seventeenth-Century Brussels Guilds played an important role in the civic life of the early modern city. They collected taxes from their members, imposed quality standards and order on the trades, and represented the interests of commerce and industry to the government. In return, they claimed exclusive monopolies over their trades and the right to govern their own affairs. Guilds marched in processions at important moments in the life of the city, proudly displaying their corporate insignia. *(Victoria & Albert Museum, London/Art Resource, NY)*

rather than in the High Middle Ages as previously believed. Guilds grew in number in cities and towns across Europe during this period. In Louis XIV's France, for example, finance minister Jean-Baptiste Colbert revived the urban guilds and used them to encourage high-quality production and to collect taxes. The number of guilds in the city of Paris grew from 60 in 1672 to 129 in 1691.

Guild masters occupied the summit of the world of work. Each guild received a detailed set of privileges from the Crown, including exclusive rights to produce and sell certain goods, access to restricted markets in raw materials, and the rights to train apprentices, hire workers, and open shops. Any individual who violated these monopolies could be prosecuted. Guilds also served social and religious functions, providing a locus of sociability and group identity to the middling classes of European cities.

To ensure there was enough work to go around, guilds jealously restricted their membership to local men who were good Christians, had several years of work experience, paid stiff membership fees, and completed a masterpiece. They also favored family connections. Masters' sons enjoyed automatic access to their fathers' guilds, while outsiders were often barred from entering. In the 1720s Parisian guild masters numbered only about thirty-five thousand in a population of five hundred thousand. Most men and women worked in non-guild trades, as domestic servants, as manual laborers, and as vendors of food and other small goods.

The guilds' ability to enforce their rigid barriers varied a great deal across Europe. In England, national regulations superseded guild regulations, sapping their importance. In France, the Crown developed an ambiguous attitude toward guilds, relying on them for taxes and enforcement of quality standards, yet allowing non-guild production to flourish in the countryside after 1762, and even in some urban neighborhoods. The Faubourg Saint-

Antoine, an eastern suburb of Paris, maintained freedom from guild privileges through an old legal loophole, acting as a haven for the "false-workers" bitterly denounced by masters. The German guilds were perhaps the most powerful in Europe, and the most conservative. Journeymen in German cities, with their masters' support, violently protested the encroachment of non-guild workers. Whereas French guilds were washed away by the Revolution's attack on royal privilege, guilds persisted in parts of Germany until the second half of the nineteenth century.

Critics of guilds in France derided them as outmoded and exclusionary institutions that obstructed technical innovation and progress. (See the feature "Listening to the Past: The Debate over the Guilds" on pages 650–651.) Many historians have repeated that charge. More recent scholarship, however, has emphasized the flexibility and adaptability of the guild system and its vitality through the eighteenth century. Guild masters adopted new technologies and found creative ways to circumvent impractical rules. For many merchants and artisans, economic regulation did not hinder commerce but instead fostered the confidence necessary to stimulate it. In an economy where buyers' and sellers' access to information was so limited, regulation helped each side trust in the other's good faith.

Online Study Center Improve Your Grade
Primary Source: Turgot Abolishes the French Guilds

Over the eighteenth century some guilds grew more accessible to women. This was particularly the case in dressmaking; given the great increase in textile production, more hands were needed to fashion clothing for urban elites. In 1675 Colbert granted seamstresses a new all-female guild in Paris, and soon seamstresses joined tailors' guilds in parts of France, England, and the Netherlands. In the late seventeenth century new vocational training programs were established for poor girls in many European cities, mostly in needlework. There is also evidence that more women were hired as skilled workers by male guilds, often in defiance of official statutes. Like their rural counterparts, urban girls and women were entering the paid labor market in greater numbers. When French guilds received new statutes in 1777, all were formally opened to women. The guilds' final abolition in 1791 makes it impossible to know how this experiment in sexual equality would have fared.

While many artisans welcomed the economic liberalization that followed the Revolution, some continued to espouse the ideals of the guilds. Because they had always been semi-clandestine, journeymen's associations frequently survived into the nineteenth century. They espoused the values of hand craftsmanship and limited competition, in contrast to the proletarianization and loss of skills they endured in mechanized production. Nevertheless, by the middle of the nineteenth century economic deregulation was championed by most European governments and elites.

The Industrious Revolution

One scholar has used the term **industrious revolution** to describe the social and economic changes taking place in Europe in the late seventeenth and early eighteenth centuries.[5] This occurred as households in northwestern Europe reduced leisure time, stepped up the pace of work, and, most importantly, redirected the labor of women and children away from the production of goods for household consumption and toward wage work. By working harder and increasing the number of wageworkers, households could purchase more goods, even in a time of stagnant or falling real wages.

The effect of these changes is still debated. While some scholars lament the encroachment of longer work hours and stricter discipline, others insist that poor families made decisions based on their own self-interests. With more finished goods becoming available at lower prices, households sought cash income to participate in a nascent consumer economy. The role of women and girls in this new economy is particularly controversial. When women entered the labor market, they almost always worked at menial, tedious jobs for very low wages. The fantastic rise of the British textile industry in the eighteenth century was built on the exhausted fingers and blighted eyesight of untold numbers of female cottage workers. Yet when women earned their own wages, they also seem to have taken on a proportionately greater role in household decision making. Most of their scant earnings went for household necessities, items they could no longer produce now that they worked full-time, but there were sometimes a few shillings left for a few ribbons or a new pair of stockings. Women's control over their surplus income thus helped spur the rapid growth of the textile industries in which they labored so hard.

New sources and patterns of labor established important foundations for the Industrial Revolution of the late eighteenth and nineteenth centuries. They created households in which all members worked for wages rather than in a united family business and in which consumption relied on market-produced rather than homemade goods. It was not until the mid-nineteenth century, with rising industrial wages, that a new model emerged in which the male "breadwinner" was expected to earn

The Linen Industry in Ireland Many steps went into making textiles. Here the women are beating away the woody part of the flax plant so that the man can comb out the soft part. The combed fibers will then be spun into thread and woven into cloth by this family enterprise. The increased labor of women and girls from the late seventeenth century helped produce an "industrious revolution." *(Victoria and Albert Museum London/Eileen Tweedy/The Art Archive)*

enough to support the whole family and women and children were relegated back to the domestic sphere. With 77 percent of U.S. women between ages twenty-five and fifty-four in the workforce in the year 2000, today's world is experiencing a second industrious revolution in a similar climate of stagnant wages and increased demand for consumer goods.

Building the Global Economy

In addition to agricultural improvement, population pressure, and growing cottage industry, the expansion of Europe in the eighteenth century was characterized by the growth of world trade. Spain and Portugal revitalized their empires and began drawing more wealth from renewed development. Yet once again the countries of northwestern Europe—the Netherlands, France, and above all Great Britain—benefited most. Great Britain, which was formed in 1707 by the union of England and Scotland into a single kingdom, gradually became the leading maritime power. Thus the British played the critical role in building a fairly unified Atlantic economy that provided remarkable opportunities for them and their colonists. They also conducted ruthless competition with France and the Netherlands for trade and territory in Asia.

• How did colonial markets boost Europe's economic and social development, and what conflicts and adversity did world trade entail?

Mercantilism and Colonial Wars

Britain's commercial leadership in the eighteenth century had its origins in the mercantilism of the seventeenth century (see page 532). European **mercantilism** was a system of economic regulations aimed at increasing the power of the state. As practiced by a leading advocate such as Colbert under Louis XIV, mercantilism aimed particularly at creating a favorable balance of foreign trade in order to increase a country's stock of gold. A country's gold holdings served as an all-important treasure chest that could be opened periodically to pay for war in a violent age. Early English mercantilists shared these views.

The result of the English desire to increase both military power and private wealth was the mercantile system of the **Navigation Acts.** Oliver Cromwell established the first of these laws in 1651, and the restored monarchy of Charles II extended them in 1660 and 1663; these Navigation Acts were not seriously modified until 1786. The acts required that most goods imported from Europe into England and Scotland be carried on British-owned ships with British crews or on ships of the country producing the article. Moreover, these laws gave British merchants and shipowners a virtual monopoly on trade with British colonies. The colonists were required to ship their products on British (or American) ships and to buy almost all European goods from Britain. It was believed that these economic regulations would help British merchants and workers as well as colonial plantation owners and farmers; and the emerging British Empire would develop a shipping industry with a large number of experienced seamen who could serve when necessary in the Royal Navy.

The Navigation Acts were a form of economic warfare. Their initial target was the Dutch, who were far ahead of the English in shipping and foreign trade in the mid-seventeenth century (see page 553). In conjunction with three Anglo-Dutch wars between 1652 and 1674, the Navigation Acts seriously damaged Dutch shipping and commerce. The British seized the thriving Dutch colony of New Amsterdam in 1664 and renamed it "New York." By the late seventeenth century the Netherlands was falling behind England in shipping, trade, and colonies.

Thereafter France stood clearly as England's most serious rival in the competition for overseas empire. Rich in natural resources, with a population three or four times that of England, and allied with Spain, continental Europe's leading military power was already building a powerful fleet and a worldwide system of rigidly monopolized colonial trade. Thus from 1701 to 1763 Britain and France were locked in a series of wars to decide, in part, which nation would become the leading maritime power and claim the profits of Europe's overseas expansion (see Map 19.2).

The first round was the War of the Spanish Succession (see page 534), which started when Louis XIV accepted the Spanish crown willed to his grandson. Besides upsetting the continental balance of power, a union of France and Spain threatened to encircle and destroy the British colonies in North America (see Map 19.2). Defeated by a great coalition of states after twelve years of fighting, Louis XIV was forced in the Peace of Utrecht (1713) to cede Newfoundland, Nova Scotia, and the Hudson Bay territory to Britain. Spain was compelled to give Britain control of its West African slave trade—the so-called *asiento*—and to let Britain send one ship of merchandise into the Spanish colonies annually through Porto Bello on the Isthmus of Panama.

France was still a mighty competitor. The War of the Austrian Succession (1740–1748), which started when Frederick the Great of Prussia seized Silesia from Austria's Maria Theresa (see page 610), gradually became a world war that included Anglo-French conflicts in India and North America. The war ended with no change in the territorial situation in North America.

This inconclusive standoff helped set the stage for the Seven Years' War (1756–1763). In central Europe, Austria's Maria Theresa sought to win back Silesia and crush Prussia, thereby re-establishing the Habsburgs' traditional leadership in German affairs. She almost succeeded in her goals, but Prussia survived with its boundaries intact.

Inconclusive in Europe, the Seven Years' War was the decisive round in the Franco-British competition for colonial empire. The fighting began in North America. The population of New France was centered in Quebec and along the St. Lawrence River, but French soldiers and Canadian fur traders had also built forts and trading posts along the Great Lakes, through the Ohio country, and down the Mississippi to New Orleans (see Map 19.3). Allied with many Native American tribes, the French built more forts in 1753 in what is now western Pennsylvania to protect their claims. The following year a Virginia force attacked a small group of French soldiers, and soon the war to conquer Canada was on.

Although the inhabitants of New France were greatly outnumbered—Canada counted fifty-five thousand inhabitants, as opposed to 1.2 million in the thirteen English colonies—French and Canadian forces under the experienced marquis de Montcalm fought well and scored major victories until 1758. Then, led by their new chief minister, William Pitt, whose grandfather had made a fortune in India, the British diverted men and money from the war in Europe, using superior sea power to destroy the French fleet and choke off French commerce around the world. In 1759 a combined British naval and land force laid siege to Quebec for four long months, defeating Montcalm's army in a dramatic battle that sealed the fate of France in North America.

British victory on all colonial fronts was ratified in the **Treaty of Paris** (1763). France lost its possessions on mainland North America. Canada and all French territory east of the Mississippi River passed to Britain, and France

MAP 19.2 The Atlantic Economy in 1701 The growth of trade encouraged both economic development and military conflict in the Atlantic basin. Four continents were linked together by the exchange of goods and slaves.

MAP 19.3 European Claims in North America Before and After the Seven Years' War (1756–1763) France lost its vast territories in North America, though the British government then prohibited colonists from settling west of the Appalachian Mountains in 1763. The British had raised taxes on themselves and the colonists to pay for the war, and they wanted to avoid costly conflicts with Native Americans living in the newly conquered territory. One of the few remaining French colonies in the Americas, Saint Domingue (on the island of Hispaniola) was the most profitable plantation colony in the New World.

Online Study Center **Improve Your Grade** Interactive Map: European Claims in North America Before and After the Seven Years' War

ceded Louisiana to Spain as compensation for Spain's loss of Florida to Britain. France also gave up most of its holdings in India, opening the way to British dominance on the subcontinent. By 1763 British naval power, built in large part on the rapid growth of the British shipping industry after the passage of the Navigation Acts, had triumphed decisively: Britain had realized its goal of monopolizing a vast trading and colonial empire.

In the eighteenth century, stimulated by trade and empire building, London grew into the West's largest and richest city. (See the feature "Images in Society: London: The Remaking of a Great City" on pages 638–639.) Above all, the rapidly growing and increasingly wealthy agricultural populations of the mainland colonies provided an expanding market for English manufactured goods. This situation was extremely fortunate, for England in the eighteenth century was gradually losing, or only slowly expanding, its sales to many of its traditional European markets.

As trade with Europe stagnated, protected colonial markets came to the rescue (see Figure 19.3). English exports of manufactured goods to the Atlantic economy—

Images in Society

London: The Remaking of a Great City

The imperial capital and intercontinental trade center of London dominated Britain and astonished the visitor. Equal in population to Paris with four hundred thousand inhabitants in 1650, the super city of the West grew to nine hundred thousand in 1801, while second-place Paris had six hundred thousand. And as London grew, its citizens created a new urban landscape and style of living.

Image 1 shows the "true profile" of London and its built environment as viewed from the south before the Great Fire of 1666, which raged for four days and destroyed about 80 percent of the old, predominately wooden central city. With the River Thames flowing eastward toward the sea, one sees from left to right pre-Fire St. Paul's Cathedral, London Bridge crowded with houses, ships at the wharves, and the medieval Tower of London. Clearly visible in the distance are the open fields of the large estates surrounding London, while beyond view on the left are the royal palace and adjacent government buildings. Also missing is the famous London smog, the combination of fog and smoke from coal-burning fireplaces that already polluted the metropolis. How would you characterize pre-Fire London?

Reconstruction proceeded quickly after the Great Fire so that people could regain shelter and employment. Brick construction was made mandatory to prevent fire, but only a few streets were straightened or widened. Thus social classes remained packed together in the rebuilt city. The rich merchant family in a first-class city residence (Image 2), built in the 1670s and still standing in 1939, shared a tiny courtyard and constantly rubbed shoulders with poor and middling people in everyday life.

As London rebuilt and kept growing, big noble landowners followed two earlier examples and sought to increase their incomes by setting up residential developments on their estates west of the city. A landowner would lay out a square with streets and building lots, which he or she would lease to speculative builders who put up fine houses for sale or rent. Soho Square, first laid out in the 1670s and shown in Image 3 as it appeared in 1731, was fairly typical. The spacious square with its gated park is surrounded by three-story row houses set on deep, narrow lots. Set in the country but close to the city, a square like Soho was a kind of elegant "village" with restrictive building codes that catered to aristocrats, officials, and successful professionals who were served by artisans and shopkeepers living in alleys and side streets. Do you see a difference between the houses on the square and on the street behind? How would you compare Soho

Image 1 London Before the Great Fire *(Hulton Archive/Getty Images)*

Image 2 Merchant Family's Residence (built 1670–1680) *(English Heritage/NMR)*

Image 3 Soho Square, 1731 *(Private Collection/The Stapleton Collection/ The Bridgeman Art Library)*

Square with the hills in the distance and with the old London of Images 1 and 2? The classy, new area, known as the West End, contrasted sharply with the shoddy rentals and makeshift shacks of laborers and sailors in the mushrooming East End, which artists rarely painted. Thus residential segregation by income level increased substantially in eighteenth-century London.

As the suburban villages grew and gradually merged together, the West End increasingly attracted the well-to-do from all over England. Rural landowners and provincial notables came for the social season from October to May. Operating out of comfortable second homes purchased or rented in the West End, they played the national market for mortgages, marriages, and recreation. Image 4, showing classy Bloomsbury Square in 1787 and the original country mansion of the enterprising noble developer, provides a glimpse into this well-born culture. How does Image 4 complement Image 3? What message is the artist conveying with the milkmaid and her cows? Some historians believe that London's West End was an important social innovation. Reconsidering these images, do you agree?

Image 4 Bloomsbury Square, 1787 *(HarperCollins Publishers)*

Online Study Center **Improve Your Grade**
Going Beyond Images in Society

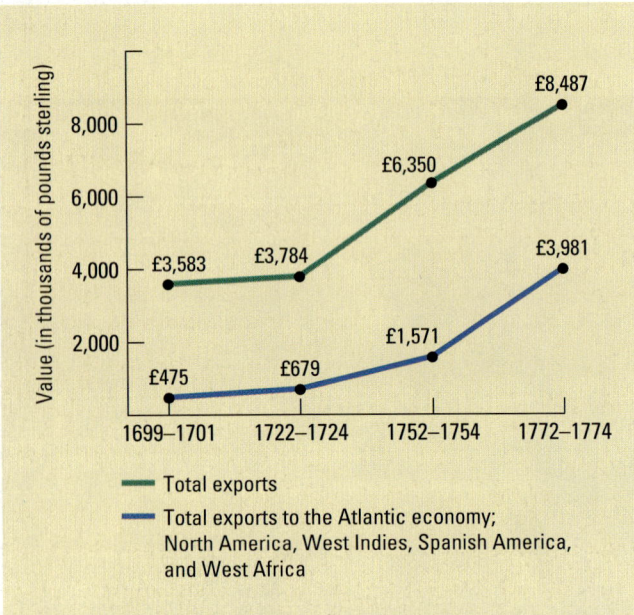

FIGURE 19.3 Exports of English Manufactured Goods, 1700–1774 While trade between England and Europe stagnated after 1700, English exports to Africa and the Americas boomed and greatly stimulated English economic development. (Source: R. Davis, "English Foreign Trade, 1700–1774," Economic History Review, 2d ser., 15 (1962): 302–303.)

primarily the mainland colonies of North America and the West Indian sugar islands, with an important assist from West Africa and Latin America—soared from £500,000 to £4.0 million. Sales to other colonies—Ireland and India—also rose substantially in the eighteenth century.

English exports also became more balanced and diversified. To America and Africa went large quantities of metal items—axes to frontier settlers, firearms and chains to slave owners. There were also clocks and coaches, buttons and saddles, china and furniture, musical instruments and scientific equipment, and a host of other things. Foreign trade became the bread and butter of some industries; for example, by 1750 half the nails made in England were going to the colonies. Thus, the mercantilist system achieved remarkable success for England in the eighteenth century, and by the 1770s England stood on the threshold of the epoch-making industrial changes that are described in Chapter 22.

Although they lost many possessions to the English, the French still profited enormously from colonial trade. The colonies of Saint Domingue (modern-day Haiti) and Martinique and Guadeloupe (which remain French departments today) provided immense fortunes in sugar plantations, coffee, and slave trading during the second half of the eighteenth century. By 1789 the population of Saint Domingue included five hundred thousand slaves whose labor had allowed the colony to become the world's leading producer of coffee and sugar. It was the most profitable plantation colony in the New World and the one that consumed the greatest number of slaves.[6] The wealth generated from colonial trade fostered the confidence of the merchant classes in Paris, Bordeaux, and other large cities, and merchants soon joined other elite groups clamoring for more political responsibility.

Land and Labor in British America

As Britain built its empire in North America, it secured an important outlet for surplus population, so that migration abroad limited poverty at home. The settlers also benefited, for they enjoyed privileged access to virtually free and unlimited land. The situation in the American colonies contrasted sharply with that in the British Isles, where land was already highly concentrated in the hands of the nobility and gentry in 1700. White settlers who came to the colonies as free men and women could obtain their own farms on easy terms, and those who came as indentured servants pledged to work seven years for their passage or as convicts could do so as soon as they had their personal freedom. Unlike the great majority of European peasants, American farmers kept most of what they produced.

Cheap land and the tremendous demand for scarce labor also fostered the growth of slavery in the British colonies. The Spanish and the Portuguese had introduced slavery into the Americas in the sixteenth century. Because Native Americans died in large numbers when enslaved, the Spanish and Portuguese began importing most slaves from Africa. In the seventeenth century the Dutch aggressively followed their example and transported some two hundred thousand Africans to the Americas. There slaves worked on sugar plantations that normally earned large profits for plantation owners and European traders.

As England adopted mercantilist policies after 1650, big investors established valuable sugar plantations in the Caribbean and brought slave laborers from Africa to work them. The small white farmers, who had settled the islands and grew tobacco, generally sold out and migrated to the mainland colonies. Black slaves then became the overwhelming majority of the population, as they were in other European colonies in the Caribbean. By 1700 the pattern of plantations based on slave exploitation had spread to the Virginia lowlands, and by

A Slave Ship and Its Victims This 1827 lithograph of slaves in the hold of a ship bound for Brazil depicts the "scene of horror almost inconceivable" that Equiano encountered in crossing the Atlantic. Inhuman overcrowding of slaves resulted in shocking death rates. The man on the right will be thrown overboard. *(Houghton Library, Harvard University)*

1730 the large plantations there were worked entirely by black slaves. The harsh exploitation of slave labor permitted an astonishing tenfold increase in tobacco production between 1700 and 1774 and created a wealthy planter class in Maryland and Virginia. In 1790, when the U.S. population was approaching 4 million, slaves accounted for almost 20 percent of the total.

Slavery was uncommon in New England and the middle colonies, and in the course of the eighteenth century these areas began to export foodstuffs to the West Indies to feed the slaves. The plantation owners, whether they grew tobacco in Virginia and Maryland or sugar in the West Indies, had the exclusive privilege of supplying the British Isles with their products. Thus white colonists, too, had their place in the protective mercantile system of the Navigation Acts.

The abundance of almost free land resulted in a rapid increase in the colonial population. In a mere three-quarters of a century after 1700, the white population of the mainland colonies multiplied ten times as immigrants arrived and colonial couples raised large families. Rapid population growth did not reduce the white settlers to poverty. On the contrary, agricultural development resulted in fairly high standards of living, and on the eve of the American Revolution white men and women in the mainland British colonies had one of the highest living standards in the world.[7]

The Atlantic Slave Trade

Although the trade in African people was a worldwide phenomenon, the **Atlantic slave trade** became its most significant portion. In the words of a leading historian, by 1700 "it was impossible to imagine the Atlantic system without slavery and the slave trade."[8]

The forced migration of millions of Africans—cruel, unjust, and tragic—remained a key element in the Atlantic system and western European economic expansion

Slaves Harvesting Sugar Cane In this 1828 print a long line of hard-working slaves systematically harvests the ripe cane on the island of Antigua, while on the right more slaves load cut cane into wagons for refining at the plantation's central crushing mill. The manager on horseback may be ordering the overseer to quicken the work pace, always brutal and unrelenting at harvest time. Slave labor made high-intensity capitalist production of sugar possible in the Americas. *(John Carter Brown Library at Brown University)*

throughout the eighteenth century. Indeed, the brutal trade intensified dramatically after 1700 and especially after 1750. According to one authoritative estimate, European traders purchased and shipped 6.13 million African slaves across the Atlantic between 1701 and 1800—fully 52 percent of the estimated total of 11.7 million Africans transported between 1450 and 1900, not including an additional 10 to 15 percent who died in procurement and transit.[9] By the peak decade of the 1780s, shipments averaged about eighty thousand individuals per year in an attempt to satisfy the constantly rising demand for labor power—and slave owners' profits—in the Americas.

Taken to the Americas in chains, Africans made a decisive contribution to the development of the Atlantic economy. Above all, the labor of enslaved Africans made possible large-scale production of valuable commodities for sale in Europe, for Africans transported to the Americas could not go off and farm for themselves as white settlers did. Indeed, an important recent study concludes that in the years from 1761 to 1800 Africans and their descendants in Brazil, Spanish America, the Caribbean, and Britain's mainland slave colonies accounted for more than *four-fifths* of all the commodities produced in the Americas for sale in the Atlantic economy.[10] It was this flood of ever-cheaper sugar, coffee, tobacco, rice, and (in the nineteenth century) cotton that generated hard cash in the Americas—cash that paid for manufactured goods and services from Britain and Europe as well as for more slaves from Africa.

Intensification of the slave trade resulted in fundamental changes in its organization. Before 1700 European states waged costly wars with one another through monopolist trading companies in the hope of controlling slave exports. European agents in fortified trading posts tapped into traditional African networks for slaves, who were mainly captives taken in battles between African states, plus some Africans punished with slavery by local societies or secured through small-scale raiding. After

1700, as Britain became the undisputed leader in the slave trade, European governments and ship captains cut back on fighting among themselves and concentrated on commerce. They generally adopted the shore method of trading, which was less expensive. Thus European ships sent boats ashore or invited African dealers to bring traders and slaves out to their ships. This method allowed ships to move easily along the coast from market to market and to depart more quickly for the Americas.

Increasing demand resulted in rising prices for African slaves in the eighteenth century. Some African merchants and rulers who controlled exports profited, and some Africans secured foreign products that they found appealing because of price or quality. But generally such economic returns did not spread very far, and the negative consequences of the expanding slave trade predominated. Wars between Africans to obtain salable captives increased, and leaders purchased more arms and bought relatively fewer textiles and consumer goods.

The kingdom of Dahomey, which entered the slave trade in the eighteenth century and made it a royal monopoly, built up its army, attacked far into the interior, and profited greatly as a major supplier of slaves. More common perhaps was the experience of the kingdom of the Congo in central Africa, where the perpetual Portuguese search for slaves undermined the monarchy, destroyed political unity, and led to constant disorder. All along Africa's western coast small-scale slave raiding also spread far into the interior. There kidnappers seized and enslaved men and women like Olaudah Equiano and his sister, whose tragic separation, exile, and exploitation personified the full horror of the Atlantic slave trade. (See the feature "Individuals in Society: Olaudah Equiano.") Africans who committed crimes had traditionally paid fines, but because of the urgent demand for slaves many misdemeanors became punishable by sale to slave dealers. Finally, while the population of Europe (and Asia) grew substantially in the eighteenth century, that of Africa stagnated or possibly declined.

Online Study Center Improve Your Grade
Primary Source: An Eyewitness Describes the Slave Trade in Guinea

Until 1700, and perhaps even 1750, almost all Europeans considered the African slave trade a legitimate business. But shiploads of African slaves never landed in northwestern Europe, partly because cheap labor abounded there. Blacks did arrive in Europe as personal slaves, but if a slave ran away, the courts and the poor often supported the slave, not the slave owner. Runaways merged into London's growing population of free and escaped blacks; unions between blacks and whites were not uncommon. In 1772 a high court ruling, though limited in scope, "clearly doomed the slave status in England."[11]

After 1775 a much broader campaign to abolish slavery developed in Britain, and between 1788 and 1792, according to some recent scholarship, it grew into the first peaceful mass political movement based on the mobilization of public opinion in British history. British women played a critical role in this mass movement, denouncing the immorality of human bondage and stressing the cruel and sadistic treatment of female slaves and slave families. These attacks put the defenders of slavery on the defensive. In 1807 Parliament abolished the British slave trade, although slavery continued in British colonies and the Americas for years.

Revival in Colonial Latin America

When the last Spanish Habsburg, Charles II, died in 1700 (see page 534), Spain's vast empire lay ready for dismemberment. Yet in one of those striking reversals with which history is replete, Spain revived. The empire held together and even prospered, while a European-oriented landowning aristocracy enhanced its position in colonial society. Spain recovered in part because of better leadership. Louis XIV's grandson, who took the throne as Philip V (r. 1700–1746), brought new men and fresh ideas with him from France and rallied the Spanish people to his Bourbon dynasty in the long War of the Spanish Succession. When peace was restored, a series of reforming ministers reasserted royal authority, overhauling state finances and strengthening defense.

Revitalization in Madrid had positive results in the colonies, which defended themselves from numerous British attacks and even increased in size. Spain won Louisiana from France in 1763, and missionaries and ranchers extended Spanish influence all the way to northern California. Political success was matched by economic improvement. After declining markedly in the seventeenth century, silver mining recovered greatly, and in 1800 Spanish America accounted for half the world's silver production. Silver mining also stimulated food production for the mining camps and gave the **Creoles**—people of Spanish blood born in America—the means to purchase more and more European luxuries and manufactured goods. A class of wealthy Creole merchants arose to handle this flourishing trade, which often relied on smuggled goods from Great Britain.

Rivaling officials dispatched from Spain, Creole estate owners controlled much of the land and strove to be-

Forming the Mexican People A new genre of paintings, called "casta paintings" in English, appeared in eighteenth-century New Spain (Mexico). These paintings, which focused on race and racial mixing, were usually painted as a series of sixteen, each with a mother, a father, and a child representing a different racial category. This painting, by an unknown eighteenth-century artist, shows the union of a Spanish man and a Native American woman that has produced a racially mixed mestizo child on the left, and a group that features a mestizo woman and a Spaniard with their little daughter on the right. Casta paintings reflect contemporary fascination with the spectrum of racial difference produced in the colonies. *(Private Collection, Mexico)*

come a genuine European aristocracy. Estate owners believed that field work was the proper occupation of poor peasants, and the defenseless Native Americans suited their needs. As the indigenous population recovered in numbers, slavery and forced labor gave way to widespread **debt peonage** from 1600 on. Under this system, a planter or rancher would keep the estate's Christianized, increasingly Hispanicized Indians in perpetual debt bondage by advancing food, shelter, and a little money. Debt peonage was a form of serfdom.

The large middle group in Spanish colonies consisted of racially mixed **mestizos,** the offspring of Spanish men and Indian women. The most talented mestizos aspired to join the Creoles, for enough wealth and power could classify one as white. Thus by the end of the colonial era roughly 20 percent of the population was classified as white and about 30 percent as mestizo. Pure-blooded Indians accounted for most of the remainder, but some black slaves were also found in every part of Spanish America. Great numbers of slaves worked the enormous sugar plantations of Portuguese Brazil, and about half the Brazilian population in the early nineteenth century was of African origin. South America occupied an important place in the expanding Atlantic economy.

Trade and Empire in Asia

As the Atlantic economy took shape, Europeans continued to vie for dominance in the Asian trade. Between 1500 and 1600 the Portuguese had become major play-

Individuals in Society

Olaudah Equiano

The slave trade was a mass migration involving millions of human beings. It was also the sum of individual lives spent partly or entirely in slavery. Although most of those lives remain hidden to us, Olaudah Equiano (1745–1797) is an important exception.

Equiano was born in Benin (modern Nigeria) of Ibo ethnicity. His father, one of the village elders (or chieftains), presided over a large household that included "many slaves," prisoners captured in local wars. All people, slave and free, shared in the cultivation of family lands. One day, when all the adults were in the fields, two strange men and a woman broke into the family compound, kidnapped the eleven-year-old boy and his sister, tied them up, and dragged them into the woods. Brother and sister were separated, and Olaudah was sold several times to various dealers before reaching the coast. As it took six months to walk there, his home must have been far inland.

The slave ship and the strange appearance of the white crew terrified the boy. Much worse was the long voyage from Benin to Barbados in the Caribbean, as Equiano later recounted. "The stench of the [ship's] hold . . . became absolutely pestilential . . . [and] brought on a sickness among the slaves, of which many died. . . . The shrieks of the women and the groans of the dying rendered the whole a scene of horror almost inconceivable." Placed on deck with the sick and dying, Equiano saw two and then three of his "enchained countrymen" escape somehow through the nettings and jump into the sea, "preferring death to such a life of misery."*

Equiano's new owner, an officer in the Royal Navy, took him to England and saw that the lad received some education. Engaged in bloody action in Europe for almost four years as a captain's boy in the Seven Years' War, Equiano hoped that his loyal service and Christian baptism would help secure his freedom. He also knew that slavery was generally illegal in England. But his master deceived him. Docking in London, he and his accomplices forced a protesting and heartbroken Equiano onto a ship bound for the Caribbean.

There he was sold to Robert King, a Quaker merchant from Philadelphia who dealt in sugar and rum. Equiano developed his mathematical skills, worked hard to please as a clerk in King's warehouse, and became first mate on one of King's ships. Allowed to trade on the side for his own profit, Equiano amassed capital, repaid King his original purchase price, and received his deed of manumission at the age of twenty-one. King urged his talented former slave to stay on as a business partner, but Equiano hated the limitations and dangers of black freedom in the colonies—he was almost kidnapped back into slavery while loading a ship in Georgia—and could think only of England. Settling in London, Equiano studied, worked as a hairdresser, and went to sea periodically as a merchant seaman. He developed his ardent Christian faith and became a leading member of London's sizable black community.

Olaudah Equiano, in an engraving from his autobiography. (National Portrait Gallery, Smithsonian Institution/Art Resource, NY)

Equiano loathed the brutal slavery and the vicious exploitation that he saw in the West Indies and Britain's mainland colonies. A complex and sophisticated man, he also respected the integrity of Robert King and admired British navigational and industrial technologies. He encountered white oppressors and made white friends. He once described himself as "almost an Englishman." In the 1780s he joined with white and black activists in the antislavery campaign and wrote *The Interesting Narrative of the Life of Olaudah Equiano Written by Himself*, a well-documented autobiographical indictment of slavery. Above all, he urged Christians to live by the principles they professed and to treat Africans equally as free human beings and children of God. With the success of his widely read book, he carried his message to large audiences across Britain and Ireland and inspired the growing movement to abolish slavery.

Questions for Analysis

1. What aspects of Olaudah Equiano's life as a slave were typical? What aspects were atypical?
2. Describe Equiano's culture and personality. What aspects are most striking? Why?

*Olaudah Equiano, *The Interesting Narrative of the Life of Olaudah Equiano Written by Himself*, ed. with an introduction by Robert J. Allison (Boston: Bedford Books, 1995), pp. 56–57. Recent scholarship has re-examined Equiano's life and thrown some details of his identity into question.

Online Study Center   Improve Your Grade
Going Beyond Individuals in Society

ers in the Indian Ocean trading world, eliminating Venice as Europe's chief supplier of spices and other Asian luxury goods. The Portuguese dominated but did not fundamentally alter the age-old pattern of Indian Ocean trade, which involved merchants from many areas as more or less autonomous players. This situation changed radically with the intervention of the Dutch and then the English.

In the 1590s Dutch fleets sailed from the Cape of Good Hope and, avoiding Portuguese forts in India, steered directly for Indonesia and its wealth of spices. The voyages were a rousing success. In 1599 a Dutch fleet returned to Amsterdam carrying 600,000 pounds of pepper and 250,000 pounds of cloves and nutmeg. Those who had invested in the expedition received a 100 percent profit. In 1602 the Dutch East India Company was founded with the explicit intention of capturing the spice trade from the Portuguese. In addition to financial assistance, the States General granted the company political sovereignty over the territories it acquired.

The British in India (ca 1785)   This Indian miniature shows the wife (*center*) of a British officer attended by many Indian servants. A British merchant (*left*) awaits her attention. The picture reflects the luxurious lifestyle of the British elite in India, many members of which returned home with colossal fortunes. *(Scala/Art Resource, NY)*

In return for assisting Indonesian princes in local conflicts and disputes with the Portuguese, the Dutch won broad commercial concessions. Gradually they gained control of western access to the Indonesian archipelago and eventually of the archipelago itself. In 1619 company forces seized the port of Jakarta in Java. Renamed Batavia, the port became the center of Dutch operations in the Indian Ocean. Exchanging European manufactured goods—armor, firearms, linens, and toys—the Dutch soon captured a monopoly on the lucrative spice trade. Within a few decades they had expelled the Portuguese from Ceylon and other East Indian islands. Unlike the Portuguese, the Dutch transformed the Indian Ocean trading world, turning formerly autonomous business partners into dependents (see Map 16.3 on page 552).

The Dutch hold in Asia faltered in the eighteenth century because of the company's failure to diversify to meet changing consumption patterns. Spices continued to comprise much of its shipping, despite their declining importance in the European diet. Fierce competition from its main rival, the English East India Company (est. 1600), also severely undercut Dutch trade.

Britain initially struggled for a foothold in Asia. With the Dutch monopolizing the Indian Ocean, the British focused on India, where they were minor players throughout the seventeenth century. The English East India Company relied on trade concessions from the powerful Mughal emperor, who granted only piecemeal access to the subcontinent. Finally, in 1716 the Mughals conceded empire-wide trading privileges. To further their economic interests, East India Company agents increasingly intervened in local affairs and made alliances or waged war against Indian princes.

Britain's great rival for influence in India was France. Warfare in Europe in the 1740s spread to British and French forces in India, who supported opposing rulers in local power struggles. Their rivalry was finally resolved by the Treaty of Paris that ended the Seven Years' War in 1763. Among French losses in this war were all of its possessions in India.

With the elimination of the French, British ascendancy in India accelerated. In 1764 company forces defeated the Mughal emperor, leaving him on the throne as a ruler in title only. Robert Clive, a company agent who had led its forces in battle, became the first British governor general of Bengal, in northeast India, with direct authority over the province. By the early 1800s the British had overcome vigorous Indian resistance to gain economic and political dominance of much of the subcontinent, and India was lauded as the "jewel" in the British Empire in the nineteenth century.

Adam Smith and Economic Liberalism

Although mercantilist policies strengthened European colonial empires in the eighteenth century, a strong reaction against mercantilism ultimately set in. Creole merchants chafed at regulations imposed from Madrid. Small English merchants complained loudly about the injustice of handing over exclusive trading rights to great combines such as the East India Company. Wanting a bigger position in overseas commerce, independent merchants in many countries began campaigning against "monopolies" and calling for "free trade."

The general idea of freedom of enterprise in foreign trade was developed by Adam Smith (1723–1790), a professor of philosophy and a leading figure of the Scottish Enlightenment. Smith, whose *Inquiry into the Nature and Causes of the Wealth of Nations* (1776) established the basis for modern economics, was highly critical of eighteenth-century mercantilism. Mercantilism, he said, meant a combination of stifling government regulations and unfair privileges for state-approved monopolies and government favorites. Far preferable was free competition, which would best protect consumers from price gouging and give all citizens a fair and equal right to do what they did best. In keeping with his deep-seated fear of political oppression and with the "system of natural liberty" that he advocated, Smith argued that government should limit itself to "only three duties": it should provide a defense against foreign invasion, maintain civil order with courts and police protection, and sponsor certain indispensable public works and institutions that could never adequately profit private investors.

Smith saw the pursuit of self-interest in a competitive market as the source of an underlying and previously unrecognized harmony that he believed would result in gradual progress. According to Smith:

[Every individual generally] neither intends to promote the public interest, nor knows how much he is promoting it.... He is in this case, as in many cases, led by an invisible hand to promote an end which was no part of his intention. Nor is it always the worse for society that it was not part of it. I have never known much good done by those who affected to trade for the public good.[12]

In the nineteenth and twentieth centuries Smith was often seen as an advocate of unbridled capitalism, but his ideas were considerably more complex. In his own mind, spoke for truth, not for special interests. Unlike many disgruntled merchant capitalists, he applauded the modest rise in real wages of British workers in the eighteenth century and went on to say that "No society can surely be flourishing and happy, of which the far greater part of the members are poor and miserable." Quite realistically, Smith concluded that employers were "always and everywhere in a sort of tacit, but constant and uniform combination, not to raise the wages of labour above their actual rate" and sometimes entered "into particular combinations to sink the wages even below this rate."[13] He also deplored the deadening effects of the division of labor and called for government intervention to raise workers' living standards.

Primary Source: *The Wealth of Nations:* A Natural Law of Economy

Smith's provocative work had a great international impact, going through eight editions in English and being translated into several languages within twenty years. It quickly emerged as the classic argument for **economic liberalism**.

Chapter Summary

- What were the causes and effects of the agricultural revolution, and what nations led the way in these developments?
- Why did European population rise dramatically in the eighteenth century?
- How and why did economic production intensify in the eighteenth century, particularly in the countryside?
- How did colonial markets boost Europe's economic and social development, and what conflicts and adversity did world trade entail?

While the European educated elite was developing a new view of the world in the eighteenth century, Europe as a whole was experiencing a gradual but far-reaching expansion. As agriculture began showing signs of modest improvement across the continent, first the Low Countries and then England launched changes that gradually revolutionized it. New crops and intensified crop rotation created new food sources for both people and livestock. Enclosure of common land allowed landowners to reap the fruits of agricultural innovation at the cost of excluding poor peasants from their traditional access to the land. The gap between wealthy landowner and landless poor stretched wider in this period.

For reasons historians do not yet understand, the recurring curse of bubonic plague disappeared. Less vulnerable to food shortages and free from the plague, the populations of all European countries grew significantly. During the eighteenth century the European population recovered from the stagnation and losses of the previous century to reach unprecedented new levels.

Population growth encouraged the growth of wage labor, cottage industry, and merchant capitalism. To escape the constraints of urban guilds, merchants transported production to the countryside. Peasant households set up industrial production within their cottages, allocating family members' labor during the slack seasons of agriculture or, in some cases, abandoning farming altogether for a new life of weaving or spinning. The spread of cottage industry was one sign of an "industrious revolution" that helped pave the path of the Industrial Revolution of the late eighteenth century. Women's labor was crucial to the spread of cottage industry and the renewed vitality of the urban trades.

The products of peasant industry were exported across Europe and even across the world. During the eighteenth century Europeans continued their overseas expansion, fighting for empire and profit and, in particular, consolidating their hold on the Americas. A revived Spain and its Latin American colonies participated fully in this expansion. As in agriculture and cottage industry, however, England and its empire proved most successful. The English concentrated much of the growing Atlantic trade in their hands, a development that challenged and enriched

English industry and intensified interest in new methods of production and in an emerging economic liberalism. Thus, by the 1770s England was approaching an economic breakthrough as fully significant as the great political upheaval destined to develop shortly in neighboring France.

Key Terms

- open-field system
- common lands
- agricultural revolution
- crop rotation
- enclosure
- proletarianization
- cottage industry
- putting-out system
- guild system
- industrious revolution
- mercantilism
- Navigation Acts
- Treaty of Paris
- Atlantic slave trade
- Creoles
- debt peonage
- mestizos
- economic liberalism

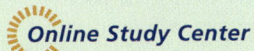 **Improve Your Grade** Flashcards

Suggested Reading

Allen, Robert, et al., eds. *Living Standards in the Past: New Perspectives on Well-Being in Asia and Europe.* 2004. Offers rich comparative perspectives on demographic trends and living standards among common people.

De Vries, Jan, and Ad van der Woude. *The First Modern Economy: Success, Failure, and Perseverance of the Dutch Economy, 1500–1815.* 1997. Examines the early success of the Dutch economy and the challenges it faced in the eighteenth century.

Farr, James R. *Artisans in Europe, 1300–1914.* 2000. Provides an overview of guilds and artisanal labor.

Gullickson, Gary L. *Spinners and Weavers of Auffay: Rural Industry and the Sexual Division of Labor in a French Village, 1750–1850.* 1986. Examines women's labor in cottage industry in northern France.

Harms, Robert W. *The Diligent: A Voyage Through the Worlds of the Slave Trade.* 2002. A deeply moving account of a French slave ship and its victims.

Klein, Herbert S. *The Atlantic Slave Trade.* 1999. An excellent short synthesis on slavery in the Atlantic world.

Liebersohn, Harry. *The Traveler's World: Europe to the Pacific.* 2006. Imaginatively recounts European explorations and imaginations of the Pacific.

Ormrod, David. *The Rise of Commercial Empires: England and the Netherlands in the Age of Mercantilism, 1650–1770.* 2003. Examines the battle for commercial and maritime supremacy in the North Sea.

Overton, Mark. *Agricultural Revolution in England.* 1996. Charts the path of agricultural progress in England.

Porter, Roy. *London: A Social History.* 1994. A sparkling combination of fine scholarship and exciting popular history.

Prak, Maarten, ed. *Early Modern Capitalism: Economic and Social Change in Europe, 1400–1800.* 2001. Collected essays on economic and social developments in early modern Europe.

Rothschild, Emma. *Economic Sentiments: Adam Smith, Condorcet, and the Enlightenment.* 2001. A fascinating reconsideration of Smith and early liberalism.

Notes

1. B. H. Slicher van Bath, *The Agrarian History of Western Europe, A.D. 500–1850* (New York: St. Martin's Press, 1963), p. 240.
2. Quoted in I. Pinchbeck, *Women Workers and the Industrial Revolution, 1750–1850* (New York: F. S. Crofts, 1930), p. 113.
3. Quoted in P. Mantoux, *The Industrial Revolution in the Eighteenth Century* (New York: Harper & Row, 1961), p. 75.
4. Richard J. Soderlund, "'Intended as a Terror to the Idle and Profligate': Embezzlement and the Origins of Policing in the Yorkshire Worsted Industry, c. 1750–1777," *Journal of Social History* 31 (Spring 1998): 658.
5. Ibid. In addition, Jan de Vries, "The Industrial Revolution and the Industrious Revolution," *The Journal of Economic History* 54, 2 (June 1994): 249–270, discusses the second industrious revolution of the second half of the twentieth century.
6. Laurent Dubois and John D. Garrigus, *Slave Revolution in the Carribean, 1789–1904* (New York: Palgrave, 2006), p. 8.
7. G. Taylor, "America's Growth Before 1840," *Journal of Economic History* 24 (December 1970): 427–444.
8. Seymour Drescher, "Free Labor vs. Slave Labor: The British and Caribbean Cases," in *Terms of Labor: Slavery, Serfdom, and Free Labor,* ed. Stanley L. Engerman (Stanford, Calif.: Stanford University Press, 1999), pp. 52–53.
9. P. E. Lovejoy, *Transformations in Slavery: A History of Slavery in Africa* (Cambridge: Cambridge University Press, 1983), p. 19.
10. J. Inikori, *Africans and the Industrial Revolution in England: A Study in International Trade and Economic Development* (Cambridge: Cambridge University Press, 2002), pp. 481–482.
11. Seymour Drescher, *Capitalism and Antislavery: British Mobilization in Comparative Perspective* (London: Macmillan, 1986), p. 38.
12. Ibid., p. 265.
13. R. Heilbroner, ed., *The Essential Adam Smith* (New York: W. W. Norton, 1986), p. 196.

Listening to the Past

The Debate over the Guilds

Guilds, also known as trade corporations, claimed that their rules guaranteed fair wages, high-quality goods, and community values. However, both French philosophes and enlightened government officials increasingly disagreed. The first excerpt, from a 1776 law abolishing French guilds by the reform minister Jacques Turgot, is an important example of the liberal critique in action. A vociferous response from the guilds led to the law's repeal only six months later. New guild regulations responded to some of the critiques, for example, by allowing women to join all guilds. In 1791 French revolutionaries definitively abolished the guild system. The second excerpt, from a letter by a Prussian official, explains what it meant "to work free" and testifies to the growth of the putting-out system alongside the guilds in the German states.

Edict Abolishing the Guilds in France

In nearly all the towns of our Kingdom the practice of different arts and crafts is concentrated in the hands of a small number of masters, united in a corporation, who alone have the exclusive right to manufacture and sell particular articles; so that those of our subjects who, through wish or necessity intend to practise in these fields, must have attained the mastership, to which they are admitted only after very long tests which are as difficult as they are useless, and after having satisfied rules or manifold exactions, which absorb part of the funds they need to set up in business or even to exist. . . .

God, in giving man needs, by making work necessary, has made the right to work a universal prerogative, and this is the first, the most sacred and the most indefeasible of all rights.

We regard it as one of the first duties of our law, and one of the acts most worthy of our charity, to free our subjects from all attacks against the inalienable right of mankind. Consequently, we wish to abolish these arbitrary institutions, which do not allow the poor man to earn his living; which reject a sex whose weakness has given it more needs and fewer resources, and which seem, in condemning it to an inevitable misery, to support seduction and debauchery; which destroy emulation and industry and nullify the talents of those whose circumstances have excluded them from membership of a corporation; which deprive the State and the arts of all the knowledge brought to them by foreigners; which retard the progress of these arts through the innumerable difficulties encountered by inventors with whom different corporations dispute the right to exploit their discoveries . . . which, by the huge expenses artisans are obliged to sustain to obtain the right to work, by their various exactions and frequent fines for alleged illegalities, by all kinds of expenditure, waste and interminable law suits, resulting from the respective claims of all these corporations on the extent of their exclusive privileges, burden industry with an oppressive tax, which bears heavily on the people, and is without benefit to the State; which finally, by the facility they provide for members of corporations to combine to force the poorest members to submit to the laws of the rich, become an instrument of privilege and encourage developments, the effect of which is to raise above their natural level the price of those goods which are most essential for the people.

Breakdown of the Guilds in Germany

Following the repeated complaint of the woollen and worsted weaver named Ast, calling himself a manufacturer of woollen materials, about the runaway apprentice Leder, Your Majesty demanded on 10th and 21st inst. to be informed what the term "to work free" means. It is well known that the [free] woollen and worsted

A German brush maker and guild member shows a customer his wares. *(The Fotomas Index/The Bridgeman Art Library)*

weavers in Germany and abroad are without a guild, that is to say, do not belong to a company which is governed by certain rules or privileges, but follow their trade as woollen and worsted weavers without regulation. For in an organized trade with its own Charter within which it has to operate and which has an assessor appointed whose task it is to see that it is observed, no apprentice may be taken on, unless he first proves by his birth certificate or patent of legitimacy that he was born in wedlock, or legitimized by royal patent. Further, according to the rules of apprenticeship, no apprentice may be given his freedom until his years of apprenticeship are ended according to the registry, and his master declares before the assembled trade when his indenture as journeyman is made out that he has an adequate knowledge of his craft. Similarly, no one can achieve the rights of mastership without having completed two years as journeyman as laid down, and produced the appropriate masterpiece.

All these regulations are omitted in the case of free weavers. For there are really no masters, journeymen and apprentices among them; but if a weaver is able and has resources to set up looms, he sets on workers, usually lads or those who have some knowledge of the trade, who may call themselves apprentices or journeymen, but are not recognized and esteemed as such by those within the guild, since the employer has not produced a masterpiece, the journeymen and apprentices have no indentures or birth certificates, they have no privileges, no assessor, and thus live without a regulation. Such a woollen or worsted weaver will then be called a "free worker." . . .

If such woollen weavers, who have mostly been attracted into the country by the large manufacturers, want to set up here on their own, although they have not been properly brought up within their company, and cannot be accepted as masters, they can receive permission, for themselves only, "to work free." Many of the weavers working "free" have felt the disadvantages of exclusion from their guild, so that some years ago, after some long-drawn-out disputes between the organized and unorganized weavers, they were granted the concession, on certain prescribed conditions, to be accepted as members of their guilds, whereby the number of unorganized ones has been much reduced, except for the large manufacturers and their workers, who are largely still unorganized.

Such outsiders as have risen to the level of manufacturers, by which it is meant that they man several, perhaps many, looms with unorganized workers, have never been granted this concession, but have, as the term goes, "worked free"; and since they cannot become masters and therefore are not allowed to use the term of master, have termed themselves woollen manufacturers, in order to distinguish themselves from the other excluded, but minor, weavers.

Questions for Analysis

1. How did Turgot justify the abolition of French guilds? Do you think his reasons are valid? How might the guilds respond?
2. How were woolen weavers and their employers organized in Prussia?
3. Do guilds—and modern-day unions—help or hurt workers? Defend your position.

Source: S. Pollard and C. Holmes, eds., *Documents of European Economic History*, vol. 1: *The Process of Industrialization, 1750–1870* (New York: St. Martin's Press, 1968), pp. 53, 55–56. Copyright © S. Pollard and C. Holmes. Reprinted with permission of Palgrave.

A quack doctor uses a snake and a dog to sell a miraculous cure-all in an Italian village market, in a painting (detail) by Michele Graneri (1736–1778). *(Dagli Orti/Private Collection/The Art Archive)*

chapter 20

The Changing Life of the People

chapter preview

Marriage and the Family
• What changes occurred in marriage and the family in the course of the eighteenth century?

Children and Education
• What was life like for children, and how did attitudes toward childhood evolve?

Food, Medicine, and New Consumption Habits
• How did new patterns of consumption and changing medical care affect people's lives?

Religion and Popular Culture
• What were the patterns of popular religion and culture, and how did they interact with the worldview of the educated public and the Enlightenment?

The discussion of agriculture and industry in the last chapter showed the common people at work, straining to make ends meet within the larger context of population growth, gradual economic expansion, and ferocious political competition. The world of work was embedded in a rich complex of family organization, community practices, everyday experiences, and collective attitudes.

In recent years, historians have intensively studied all these aspects of popular life. The challenge has been formidable because regional variations abounded and the common people left few written records. Yet imaginative research has resulted in major findings and much greater knowledge. It is now possible to follow the common people into their homes, workshops, churches, and taverns and to ask, "What were the everyday experiences of ordinary people?"

Marriage and the Family

The basic unit of social organization is the family. It is within the structure of the family that human beings love, mate, and reproduce. It is primarily the family that teaches the child, imparting values and customs that condition an individual's behavior for a lifetime. The family is also an institution woven into the web of history. It evolves and changes, assuming different forms in different times and places.

• **What changes occurred in marriage and the family in the course of the eighteenth century?**

Late Marriage and Nuclear Families

In the previous chapter, we noted the common misconception that populations of the past always grew quickly. Another popular error is that before the modern era people married at a young age and settled in large multigenerational households. In recent years historians have used previ-

Online Study Center
This icon will direct you to interactive activities and study materials on the website **college.hmco.com/pic/mckaywest9e**

ously neglected parish registers of births, deaths, and marriages to uncover details of European family life before the nineteenth century. It is now clear that the extended, three-generation family was a rarity in western and central Europe by 1700. Indeed, the extended family may never have been common in Europe, although it is hard to know about the early Middle Ages because very few records survive. When young European couples married, they normally established their own households and lived apart from their parents. If a three-generation household came into existence, it was usually because a widowed parent moved into the home of a married child.

Moreover, most people did not marry young in the seventeenth and eighteenth centuries. The average person who was neither rich nor aristocratic married surprisingly late, many years after reaching adulthood and many more after beginning to work. In one well-studied, apparently typical English village in the seventeenth and eighteenth centuries, both men and women married for the first time at an average age of twenty-seven or older. A similar pattern existed in eighteenth-century France, where women married around age twenty-five and men around age twenty-seven. A substantial portion of men and women never married at all.

The custom of late marriage combined with a nuclear-family household distinguished European society from other areas of the world. It seems likely that the aggressive dynamism that has characterized European society derived in large part from this marriage pattern. Late marriage joined a mature man and a mature woman—two adults who had already accumulated social and economic capital and could transmit self-reliance and skills to the next generation.

Why was marriage delayed? The main reason was that couples normally did not marry until they could support themselves economically. Peasants often needed to wait until the father's death to inherit land and marry. In the towns, men and women worked to accumulate enough savings to start a small business and establish a household. Most youths began apprenticeships in their mid-teens; given average marriage ages, we may deduce that it took about ten more years of work to earn enough for marriage.

Ten years was a long time for sexually mature young people to wait. Laws and community controls sought to temper impetuous love and physical attraction. In some areas couples needed the legal permission or tacit approval of the local lord or landowner in order to marry. Austria and Germany had legal restrictions on marriage, and well into the nineteenth century poor couples had particular difficulty securing the approval of local offi-

Boucher: The Pretty Cook Increased migration to urban areas in the eighteenth century contributed to a loosening of traditional morals and soaring illegitimacy rates. Young women who worked as servants or shop girls could not be supervised as closely as those who lived at home. The themes of seduction, fallen virtue, and familial conflict were popular in eighteenth-century art, such as this painting by François Boucher (1703–1770), master of the rococo. *(Réunion des Musées Nationaux/Art Resource, NY)*

cials. The officials believed that freedom to marry for the lower classes would mean more landless paupers, more abandoned children, and more money for welfare. Village elders often agreed. Thus prudence, law, and custom combined to postpone the march to the altar. This pattern helped society maintain some kind of balance between the number of people and the available economic resources.

Work Away from Home

Many young people worked within their families until they could start their own households. Boys plowed and wove; girls spun and tended the cows. Many others left home to work elsewhere. In the towns a lad would begin apprenticeship around age fifteen and finish in his late teens or early twenties. During that time he would not be permitted to marry. In most trades he earned little and worked hard, but if he was lucky, he might eventually be admitted to a guild and establish his economic independence. Many poor families could not afford apprenticeship, leaving their sons without the skills and status of guild journeymen. These youths drifted from one tough job to another: hired hand for a small farmer, wage laborer on a new road, carrier of water in a nearby town. They were always subject to economic fluctuations, and unemployment was a constant threat.

Many girls also left their families to work in adolescence. The range of opportunities open to them was more limited, however. Apprenticeship was available in some cities, usually with mistresses in traditionally female occupations like seamstresses, linen drapers, or midwives. With the growth in production of finished goods for the emerging consumer economy during the eighteenth century, demand rose for skilled female labor. Even male guildsmen hired girls and women, despite guild restrictions.

Service in another family's household was by far the most common job for girls, and even middle-class families often sent their daughters into service. The legions of young servant girls worked hard but had little independence. Sometimes the employer paid the girl's wages directly to her parents. Constantly under the eye of her mistress, the servant girl had many tasks—cleaning, shopping, cooking, caring for the baby. Often the work was endless, for there were few laws to limit exploitation. Court records are full of servant girls' complaints of physical mistreatment by their mistresses. There were many like the fifteen-year-old English girl in the early eighteenth century who told the judge that her mistress had not only called her "very opprobrious names, as Bitch, Whore and the like," but also "beat her without provocation and beyond measure."[1]

Male apprentices told similar tales of verbal and physical abuse at their masters' hands. Boys were far less vulnerable, though, to the sexual harassment and assault that threatened female servants. In theory, domestic service offered a young girl protection and security in a new family. But in practice she was often the easy prey of a lecherous master or his sons or friends. Indeed, "the evidence suggests that in all European countries, from Britain to Russia, the upper classes felt perfectly free to exploit sexually girls who were at their mercy."[2] If the girl became pregnant, she could be quickly fired and thrown out in disgrace to make her own way. Prostitution and petty thievery were often the harsh consequences of unwanted pregnancy. "What are we?" exclaimed a bitter Parisian prostitute. "Most of us are unfortunate women, without origins, without education, servants and maids for the most part."[3]

Prostitutes encountered increasingly harsh and repressive laws in the sixteenth and early seventeenth centuries, as officials across Europe began to close licensed brothels and declare prostitution illegal. Despite this repression, prostitution flourished in European cities and towns in the eighteenth century. Most prostitutes were working women who turned to the sex trade when confronted with unemployment or seasonal shortages of work. Such women did not become social pariahs, but retained ties with the communities of laboring poor to which they belonged. If caught by the police, however, they were liable to imprisonment or banishment. Venereal disease was also a constant threat. Farther up the social scale were courtesans whose wealthy protectors provided apartments, servants, beautiful clothing, and cash allowances. After a brilliant, but brief, career, such a woman could descend once more to streetwalking.

Chronology

1717	Elementary school attendance mandatory in Prussia
1720–1780	Government-run foundling homes established
1740–1780	Reign of Maria Theresa in Austria
1740–1786	Reign of Frederick the Great in Prussia
1750–1790	Wesley preaches revival in England
1750–1850	Illegitimacy explosion
1757	Madame du Coudray, *Manual on the Art of Childbirth*
1762	Rousseau advocates more attentive child care in *Emile*
1763	Louis XV orders Jesuits out of France
1775–1783	American Revolution
1789–1799	French Revolution
1796	Jenner performs first smallpox vaccination
1799–1815	Napoleonic era

Premarital Sex and Community Controls

Did the plight of some former servant girls mean that late marriage in preindustrial Europe went hand in hand with premarital sex and many illegitimate children? For most of western and central Europe until at least 1750, the answer is no. English parish registers seldom listed more than one illegitimate child out of every twenty children baptized. Some French parishes in the seventeenth century had extraordinarily low rates of illegitimacy, with less than 1 percent of the babies born out of wedlock. Illegitimate babies were apparently a rarity, at least as far as the official church records are concerned.

Many unmarried couples satisfied their sexual desires with fondling and petting. Others went further and engaged in premarital intercourse. In one well-studied English village, 33 percent of all first children were conceived before the couple was married, and many were born within three months of the marriage ceremony. In the mid-eighteenth century 20 percent of the women in the French village of Auffay in Normandy were pregnant when they got married, although only 2 percent of all babies in the village were born to unwed mothers. No doubt many of these French and English couples were already betrothed, or at least "going steady," before they entered into intimate relationships, and pregnancy simply set the marriage date once and for all.

The combination of very low rates of illegitimate birth with large numbers of pregnant brides reflects the powerful **community controls** of the traditional village, particularly the open-field village, with its pattern of cooperation and common action. That spirit of common action was rapidly mobilized by the prospect of an unwed (and therefore poor) mother with an illegitimate child, a condition inevitably viewed as a grave threat to the economic, social, and moral stability of the closely knit community. Irate parents, anxious village elders, indignant priests, and stern landlords all combined to pressure young people who wavered about marriage in the face of unexpected pregnancies. In the countryside these controls meant that premarital sex was not entered into lightly and that it was generally limited to those contemplating marriage.

The concerns of the village and the family weighed heavily on most aspects of a couple's life both before and after marriage. Whereas uninvolved individuals today are inclined to stay out of the domestic disputes and marital scandals of their neighbors, the people in peasant communities gave such affairs loud and unfavorable publicity either at the time of the event or during the Carnival season (see page 675). Relying on degrading public rituals, the young men of the village would typically gang up on the person they wanted to punish and force him or her to sit astride a donkey facing backward and holding up the donkey's tail. They would parade the overly brutal spouse-beating husband (or wife), or the couple whose adultery had been discovered, all around the village, loudly proclaiming the offender's misdeeds with scorn and ridicule. The donkey ride and other colorful humiliations ranging from rotten vegetables splattered on the doorstep to obscene and insulting midnight serenades were common punishments throughout much of Europe. They epitomized the community's far-reaching effort to police personal behavior and maintain community standards.

Community controls did not extend to family planning, however. Once a man and a woman married, they generally had several children. Birth control within marriage was not unknown in western and central Europe before the nineteenth century, but it was primitive and quite undependable. The most common method was *coitus interruptus*—withdrawal by the male before ejaculation. The French, who were apparently early leaders in contraception, were using this method extensively to limit family size by the end of the eighteenth century. Mechanical and other means of contraception were also used in the eighteenth century, but mainly by certain sectors of the urban population. The "fast set" of London used the "sheath" regularly, although primarily to protect against venereal disease, not against pregnancy. Prostitutes used various contraceptive techniques to prevent pregnancy, and such information was available in large towns if a person really sought it.

New Patterns of Marriage and Illegitimacy

In the second half of the eighteenth century, the pattern of late marriage and few births out of wedlock began to break down. The number of illegitimate births soared between about 1750 and 1850 as much of Europe experienced an **illegitimacy explosion.** In Frankfurt, Germany, for example, illegitimate births rose steadily from about 2 percent of all births in the early 1700s to a peak of about 25 percent around 1850. In Bordeaux, France, 36 percent of all babies were being born out of wedlock by 1840. Small towns and villages experienced less startling climbs, but between 1750 and 1850 increases from a range of 1 to 3 percent initially to 10 to 20 percent were commonplace. Fewer young people were abstaining from premarital intercourse, and, more important, fewer

David Allan: The Penny Wedding (1795) The spirited merrymaking of a peasant wedding was a popular theme of European artists. In rural Scotland "penny weddings" like this one were common: guests provided cash gifts; any money left after paying for the wedding went to the newlyweds to help them get started. Dancing, feasting, and drinking characterized these community parties, which led the Presbyterian church to oppose them and hasten their decline. *(National Galleries of Scotland)*

young men were marrying the women they got pregnant. Thus a profound sexual and cultural transformation took place.

Historians are still debating the meaning of this transformation, but two interrelated ideas dominate most interpretations. First, the growth of cottage industry created new opportunities for earning a living, opportunities not tied to the land. Cottage industry tended to develop in areas where the land was poor in quality and divided into small, inadequate holdings. As cottage industry took hold in such areas, population grew rapidly because young people attained greater independence and did not have to wait to inherit a farm in order to get married. A scrap of ground for a garden and a cottage for the loom and spinning wheel could be quite enough for a modest living. A contemporary observer of an area of rapidly growing cottage industry in Switzerland at the end of the eighteenth century described these changes:

The increased and sure income offered by the combination of cottage manufacture with farming hastened and multiplied marriages and encouraged the division of landholdings, while enhancing their value; it also promoted the expansion and embellishment of houses and villages.[4]

Cottage workers married not only at an earlier age but also for different reasons. Nothing could be so businesslike as peasant marriages that were often dictated by the needs of the couples' families. After 1750, however, courtship became more extensive and freer as cottage industry grew. It was easier to yield to the attraction of the opposite sex and fall in love. Members of the older generation were often highly critical of the lack of responsibility they saw in the union of "people with only two spinning wheels and not even a bed." But such scolding did not stop cottage workers from marrying for love rather than for economic considerations as they blazed a path that factory workers would follow in the nineteenth century.

Second, the needs of a growing population sent many young villagers to towns and cities in search of employment. Mobility in turn encouraged new sexual and marital relationships that were less subject to village tradition and more likely to produce illegitimate births. Most young women in urban areas found work only as servants or textile workers. Poorly paid, insecure, and with little possibility of truly independent lives, they looked to marriage and family life as an escape from the vulnerabilities of the single life.

Promises of marriage from a man of the working girl's own class often led to sex, which was viewed as part of serious courtship. In one medium-size French city in 1787–1788, the great majority of unwed mothers stated that sexual intimacy had followed promises of marriage. Their sisters in rural Normandy reported again and again that they had been "seduced in anticipation of marriage."[5] Many soldiers, day laborers, and male servants were no doubt sincere in their proposals. But their lives were also insecure, and many hesitated to take on the burden of a wife and child.

Thus it became increasingly difficult for a woman to convert pregnancy into marriage, and in a growing number of cases the intended marriage did not take place. The romantic, yet practical dreams and aspirations of many young people were frustrated by low wages, inequality, and changing economic and social conditions. Old patterns of marriage and family were breaking down. Only in the late nineteenth century would more stable patterns reappear.

Children and Education

In the traditional framework of agrarian Europe, women married late but then began bearing children rapidly. If a woman married before she was thirty, and if both she and her husband lived to fifty, she would most likely give birth to six or more children. The newborn child entered a dangerous world. Newborns were vulnerable to infectious diseases of the chest and stomach, and many babies died of dehydration brought about by bad bouts of ordinary diarrhea. Of those who survived infancy, many more died in childhood. Even in rich families little could be done for an ailing child. Childbirth could also be dangerous. Women who bore six children faced a cumulative risk of dying in childbirth of 5 to 10 percent, a thousand times as great as the risk in Europe today.[6]

Schools and formal education played only a modest role in the lives of ordinary children, and many boys and many more girls never learned to read. Nevertheless, basic literacy was growing among the popular classes, whose reading habits have been intensively studied in recent years. Attempting to peer into the collective attitudes of the common people and compare them with those of the book-hungry cultivated public, historians have produced some fascinating insights.

- **What was life like for children, and how did attitudes toward childhood evolve?**

Child Care and Nursing

In the countryside, women of the lower classes generally breast-fed their infants for two years or more. Breast-feeding decreases the likelihood of pregnancy for the average woman by delaying the resumption of ovulation. By nursing their babies, women limited their fertility and spaced their children from two to three years apart. If a newborn baby died, nursing stopped, and a new life could be created. Nursing also saved lives: the breast-fed infant received precious immunity-producing substances with its mother's milk and was more likely to survive than when it was given other food.

Women of the aristocracy and upper middle class seldom nursed their own children. The upper-class woman felt that breast-feeding was crude and undignified. Instead, she hired a live-in wet nurse to suckle her child (which usually meant sending the nurse's own infant away to be nursed). Urban mothers of more modest means also relied on wet nurses because they were needed for full-time work. Unable to afford live-in wet nurses, they often turned to the cheaper services of women in the countryside. Rural **wet-nursing** was a widespread business in the eighteenth century, conducted within the framework of the putting-out system. The traffic was in babies rather than in yarn or cloth, and two or three years often passed before the wet-nurse worker in the countryside finished her task. The wet nurse generally had little contact with the family that hired her, and she was expected to privilege the newcomer at the expense of her own nursing child.

Wet-nursing was particularly common in northern France. Whereas the trend was toward more maternal nursing in other parts of Europe, wet-nursing grew substantially in Paris and other northern cities over the eighteenth century. Toward the end of the century roughly twenty thousand babies were born in Paris each year. Almost half were placed with rural wet nurses through a government-supervised distribution network; 20 to 25 percent were placed with Parisian nurses personally selected by their parents; and another 20 to 25 percent were abandoned to foundling hospitals, which would send them to wet nurses in the countryside. The remainder (perhaps 10 percent) were nursed at home by their mothers or live-in nurses.[7]

Reliance on wet nurses contributed to high levels of infant mortality. A study of parish registers in northern France during the late seventeenth and early eighteenth centuries reveals that 35 percent of babies died before their first birthdays, and another 20 percent before age ten.[8] In England, where more mothers nursed, only some 30 percent of children did not reach their tenth birthdays. Frenchwomen also gave birth to more children since nursing tends to slow down the return of fertility after childbirth.

Arrival of the Wet Nurses Wet-nursing was big business in eighteenth-century France, particularly in Paris and the north. Here, rural wet nurses bring their charges back to the city to be reunited with their families after around two years of care. These children were lucky survivors of a system that produced high mortality rates. *(Réunion des Musées Nationaux/Art Resource, NY)*

Why did Frenchwomen send their babies to wet-nurse, given these high mortality rates? Historians have offered several explanations, including parental indifference to the babies' survival. The likeliest explanation appears to be a combination of cultural, socioeconomic, and biological factors. Wet-nursing was a centuries-old tradition in France, so families were merely following well-established patterns. Moreover, in this period migration to the cities, high prices, and stagnant wages pushed more women into the workforce, often into jobs outside the home where it was impossible to nurse their babies. A third factor was that few alternatives existed to breast milk. In an era before germ theory and sterilization, artificial feeding methods were known to be dangerous to the newborn. By turning to wet nurses, mothers who could not nurse sought the safest affordable alternative.

In the second half of the eighteenth century critics mounted a harsh attack against wet-nursing. Upper-class women responded positively to the new mindset, but poor urban women continued to rely on wet nurses until the late-nineteenth-century introduction of sterilized cows' milk and artificial nipples.

Foundlings and Infanticide

The young woman who could not provide for a child had few choices, especially if she had no prospect of marriage. Abortions were illegal, dangerous, and apparently rare. In desperation, some women, particularly in the countryside, hid unwanted pregnancies, delivered in secret, and smothered their newborn infants. If discovered, **infanticide** was punishable by death.

Women in cities had more choices to dispose of babies they could not keep. Foundling homes first took hold in Italy, Spain, and France, spreading to northern and central Europe after 1700. In eighteenth-century England, for example, the government acted on a petition calling for a foundling hospital "to prevent the frequent murders of poor, miserable infants at birth" and "to suppress the inhuman custom of exposing newborn children to perish in the streets." As new homes were established and old ones expanded in the eighteenth century, the number of foundlings being cared for surged. By the end of the century European foundling hospitals were admitting annually about one hundred thousand abandoned children, nearly all of them infants. In the early nineteenth century the foundling home in St. Petersburg had twenty-five thousand children in its care and was receiving five thousand new babies a year. Still, demand always exceeded the supply of places.

Across Europe, foundling homes emerged as a favorite charity of the rich and powerful. At their best eighteenth-century foundling homes were a good example of Christian charity and social concern in an age of great poverty and inequality. Yet the foundling home was no panacea. By the 1770s, one-third of all babies born in Paris were being immediately abandoned to foundling homes by their mothers. Moreover, fully one-third of all those foundlings were abandoned by married couples, a powerful commentary on the standard of living among the working poor, for whom an additional mouth to feed often meant tragedy. The tremendous increase in foundlings resulted not only from a growth in unwanted illegitimate children, but also from the growing tendency of desperately poor parents to abandon children to foundling homes.[9]

Great numbers of babies entered foundling homes, but few left. Even in the best of these homes, 50 percent of the babies normally died within a year. In the worst, fully 90 percent did not survive.[10] They succumbed to long journeys over rough roads, intentional and unintentional neglect by their wet nurses, and customary childhood illnesses. So great were the losses that some contemporaries called the foundling hospitals "legalized infanticide."

Attitudes Toward Children

What were the typical circumstances of children's lives? The topic of parental attitudes toward children in the early modern period remains controversial. Some scholars have claimed that parents did not risk forming emotional attachments to young children because of high mortality rates. With a reasonable expectation that a child might die, some scholars believe, parents maintained an attitude of indifference, if not downright negligence.

Online Study Center Improve Your Grade
Primary Source: Births and Deaths in an English Gentry Family

Certainly, contemporaries were well aware of the dangers of childhood and of the high mortality rates. The great eighteenth-century English historian Edward Gibbon (1737–1794) wrote, with some exaggeration, that "the death of a new born child before that of its parents may seem unnatural but it is a strictly probable event, since of any given number the greater part are extinguished before the ninth year, before they possess the faculties of the mind and the body." Gibbon's father named all his boys Edward after himself, hoping that at least one of them would survive to carry his name. His prudence was not misplaced. Edward the future historian and eldest survived. Five brothers and sisters who followed him all died in infancy.

Emotional prudence could lead to emotional distance. The French essayist, Michel de Montaigne, who lost five of his six daughters in infancy, wrote, "I cannot abide that passion for caressing new-born children, which have neither mental activities nor recognisable bodily shape by which to make themselves loveable and I have never willingly suffered them to be fed in my presence."[11]

In contrast to this harsh picture, however, historians have drawn ample evidence from diaries, letters, and family portraits that many parents did cherish their children and suffered greatly when they died. The English poet Ben Jonson wrote movingly of the death of his six-year-old son Benjamin, which occurred during a London plague outbreak in 1603:

On My First Son
Farewell, thou child of my right hand, and joy;
My sin was too much hope of thee, loved boy.
Seven years thou wert lent to me, and I thee pay,
Exacted by thy fate, on the just day.

In a society characterized by violence and brutality, discipline of children was often severe. The novelist Daniel Defoe (1659–1731), who was always delighted when he saw young children working hard in cottage industry, coined the axiom "Spare the rod and spoil the child." He meant it. So did Susannah Wesley (1669–1742), mother of John Wesley, the founder of Methodism. According to her, the first task of a parent toward her children was "to conquer the will, and bring them to an obedient temper." She reported that her babies were "taught to fear

Cultivating the Joy of Discovery This English painting by Joseph Wright of Derby (1734–1797) reflects new attitudes toward child development and education, which advocated greater freedom and direct experience. The children rapturously watch a planetarium, which illustrates the movements and positions of the planets in the solar system. Wise teachers stand by, letting the children learn at their own pace. *(Derby Museum & Art Gallery/The Bridgeman Art Library)*

the rod, and to cry softly; by which means they escaped the abundance of correction they might otherwise have had, and that most odious noise of the crying of children was rarely heard in the house."[12]

The Enlightenment produced an enthusiastic new discourse about childhood and child rearing. Starting around 1760, critics called for greater tenderness toward children and proposed imaginative new teaching methods. In addition to supporting foundling homes and urging women to nurse their babies, these new voices ridiculed the practice of swaddling babies and using rigid whale-boned corsets to form children's bodies properly by "straightening them out." Instead of dressing children in miniature versions of adult clothing, critics called for simpler and more comfortable clothing to allow freedom of movement. These voices belonged to the overall Enlightenment celebration of nature and the natural laws that should guide human behavior. For Enlightenment critics, the best hopes for creating a new society, untrammeled by the prejudices of the past, lay in a radical revision of child-rearing techniques.

One of the century's most influential works on child rearing was Jean-Jacques Rousseau's *Emile*, which fervently advocated breast-feeding and natural dress. Rousseau argued that boys' education should include plenty of fresh air and exercise and that they should be taught practical craft skills in addition to book learning. Reacting to what he perceived as the vanity and frivolity of upper-class Parisian women, Rousseau insisted girls' education focus on their future domestic responsibilities. For Rousseau, women's "nature" destined them solely for a life of marriage and child rearing. The ideas of Rousseau and other reformers were enthusiastically adopted by elite women, who did not adopt universal nursing but did at least begin to supervise their wet nurses more carefully.

For all his influence, Rousseau also reveals the occasional hypocrisy of Enlightenment thinkers. With regard to the child-rearing techniques he believed would create a better society, Rousseau had extremely high expectations; when it came to the five children he fathered with his common-law wife, however, he abandoned them all in foundling hospitals despite their mother's protests. None are known to have survived. For Rousseau, the idea of creating a natural man was more important than was raising real children.

Schools and Popular Literature

The availability of formal education outside the home increased during the eighteenth century. The aristocracy and the rich led the way in the sixteenth century with special colleges, often run by Jesuits. Schools charged specifically with elementary education of the children of the common people usually did not appear until the

Mapping the Past

MAP 20.1 Literacy in France on the Eve of the French Revolution Literacy rates increased but still varied widely between and within states in eighteenth-century Europe. ❶ What trends in French literacy rates does this map reveal? Which regions seem to be ahead? How would you account for the regional variations? ❷ The map is based on the percentage of bridegrooms able to sign their names at marriage. Who is missing from the map? How do you think literacy rates may have varied for people not covered by this source? ❸ Note the areas marked "unknown." Why do you think historians do not know the literacy rates for those areas? What alternate methods might they use to find this information?

Prussia led the way in the development of universal education, inspired by the Protestant idea that every believer should be able to read the Bible and by the new idea of a population capable of effectively serving the state. As early as 1717 Prussia made attendance at elementary schools compulsory, and more Protestant German states, such as Saxony and Württemberg, followed in the eighteenth century. Religious motives were also extremely important elsewhere. From the middle of the seventeenth century, Presbyterian Scotland was convinced that the path to salvation lay in careful study of the Scriptures, and it established an effective network of parish schools for rich and poor alike. The Church of England and the dissenting congregations established "charity schools" to instruct poor children, and in 1682 France began setting up Christian schools to teach the catechism and prayers as well as reading and writing. France did less well than the Habsburg state, the only Catholic land to promote elementary education enthusiastically in the eighteenth century. Some elementary education was becoming a reality, and schools were of growing significance in the life of the child.

The result of these efforts was a remarkable growth in basic literacy between 1600 and 1800. Whereas in 1600 only one male in six was barely literate in France and Scotland, and one in four in England, by 1800 almost nine out of ten Scottish males, two out of three French males (see Map 20.1), and more than half of English males were literate. In all three countries, the bulk of the jump occurred in the eighteenth century. Women were also increasingly literate, although they lagged behind men.

The growth in literacy promoted a growth in reading, and historians have carefully examined what the common people read in an attempt to discern what they were thinking. While the Bible remained the overwhelming favorite, especially in Protestant countries, short pamphlets known as chapbooks were the staple of popular literature. Printed on the cheapest paper available, many chapbooks dealt with religious subjects. They featured Bible stories, prayers, devotions, and the lives of saints and exemplary Christians. Promising happiness after death, devotional literature was also intensely practical. It gave the believer moral teachings and a confidence in God that helped in daily living.

Entertaining, often humorous stories formed a second element of popular literature. Fairy tales, medieval romances, true crime stories, and fantastic adventures were some of the delights that filled the peddler's pack as he approached a village. These tales presented a world of danger and magic, of supernatural powers, fairy godmothers, and evil trolls. The significance of these enter-

seventeenth century. Such schools specialized in teaching seven- to twelve-year-old boys and girls basic literacy, religion, and perhaps some arithmetic for the boys and needlework for the girls.

The religious struggle unleashed by the Protestant and Catholic Reformations promoted popular literacy between 1500 and 1800. Both Protestant and Catholic reformers encouraged reading as a means of instilling their teachings more effectively. Thus literacy was often highest in border areas, such as eastern France, that were open to outside influences and to competition for believers from different churches. The growth of popular education quickened in the eighteenth century, but there was no revolutionary acceleration, and many common people received no formal education.

an almanac."¹³ In this way, elites still shared some elements of a common culture with the masses.

While it is safe to say that the vast majority of ordinary people—particularly peasants in isolated villages—did not read the great works of the Enlightenment, that does not mean they were immune to its ideas. Urban working people were exposed to new ideas through the rumor and gossip that spread across city streets, workshops, markets, cafés, taverns, and public gardens. They also had access to cheap broadsides, pamphlets, and newspapers that helped translate Enlightenment critiques into ordinary language. Servants, who usually came from rural areas and traveled home periodically, were well placed to receive ideas from educated employers and disseminate them to the village.

Certainly some ordinary people did assimilate Enlightenment ideals. Thomas Paine, author of some of the most influential texts of the American Revolution, was an English corsetmaker's son who left school at age twelve and carried on his father's trade before emigrating to the colonies. His 1776 pamphlet *Common Sense* attacked the weight of custom and the evils of government against the natural society of men. This text, which sold six hundred thousand copies, is vivid proof of working people's ability to receive Enlightenment ideas; Paine's stirring mastery of them was unique, but his access to them was surely not.

Food, Medicine, and New Consumption Habits

One of the most important developments in European society in the eighteenth century was the emergence of a fledgling consumer culture. Much of the expansion took place in the upper and upper-middle classes, but a boom in cheap reproductions of luxury items also permitted people of modest means to purchase more objects. From food to ribbons and from coal stoves to umbrellas, the material worlds of city dwellers grew richer and more diverse. These developments created new expectations for comfort and hygiene in daily life. Medical practitioners greatly increased in number, although their techniques did not differ much from those of previous generations.

The possibility of picking and choosing among a new variety of consumer goods and provisioners encouraged the development of new notions of individuality and self-expression. A shop girl could stand out from her peers by her choice of a striped jacket, a colored parasol, or simply a new ribbon for her hair. New attitudes about privacy and intimate life also emerged. Whereas families

Raoux: Young Woman Reading a Letter Literacy rates for men and women rose substantially during the eighteenth century. The novel also emerged as a new literary genre in this period. With its focus on emotions, love, and family melodrama, the novel was seen as a particularly feminine genre, and it allowed women writers more access to publication. Writing and reading letters were also associated with women. Some contemporaries worried that women's growing access to reading and writing would excite their imagination and desires, leading to moral dissolution. *(Réunion des Musées Nationaux/Art Resource, NY)*

taining stories for the peasant reader is debated. Many scholars see them reflecting a desire for pure escapism and a temporary flight from harsh everyday reality. Others see the tales reflecting ancient folk wisdom and counseling prudence in a world full of danger and injustice, where wolves dress up like grandmothers and eat Little Red Riding Hoods.

Finally, some popular literature was highly practical, dealing with rural crafts, household repairs, useful plants, and similar matters. Much lore was stored in almanacs, where calendars listing secular, religious, and astrological events were mixed with agricultural schedules, arcane facts, and jokes. The almanac was universal, was not controversial, and was highly appreciated even by many in the comfortable classes. "Anyone who could would read previously shared common living spaces, in the eighteenth century they erected new partitions within their homes to create private nooks. Alongside an upturn in economic production, this "consumer revolution," as it has been called, dramatically changed European life in the eighteenth century. As in other developments, England led the way.

• **How did new patterns of consumption and changing medical care affect people's lives?**

Diets and Nutrition

At the beginning of the eighteenth century, ordinary men and women depended on grain as fully as they had in the past. Bread was quite literally the staff of life. Peasants in the Beauvais region of France ate two pounds of bread a day, washing it down with water, wine, or beer. Their dark bread was made from roughly ground wheat and rye—the standard flour of the common people. The poor also ate grains in soup and gruel. Even peasants normally needed to buy some grain for food, and, in full accord with landless laborers and urban workers, they believed in the moral economy and the idea of the **just price.** That is, they believed that prices should be "fair," protecting both consumers and producers, and that just prices should be imposed by government decree if necessary. When prices rose above this level, they often took action (see page 525).

The rural poor also ate a fair quantity of vegetables. Peas and beans were probably the most common; grown as field crops in much of Europe since the Middle Ages, they were eaten fresh in late spring and summer. Dried, they became the basic ingredients in the soups and stews of the long winter months. In most regions other vegetables appeared in season on the tables of the poor, primarily cabbages, carrots, and wild greens. Fruit was uncommon and limited to the summer months. Milk was used primarily to make cheese and butter, which peasants sold in the market to earn cash for taxes and land rents.

The common people of Europe loved meat and eggs but seldom ate their fill. Indeed, the poor ate less meat in 1700 than in 1500 because their general standard of living had declined as the population surged in the sixteenth century (see page 626) and meat became more expensive. Moreover, harsh game laws in most European countries deprived the poor of the right to hunt and eat game such as rabbits, deer, and partridges. Only nobles and large landowners could legally kill game. Few laws were more bitterly resented—or more frequently broken—by ordinary people than those governing hunting.

The diet of small traders and master craftsmen—the people of the towns and cities—was less monotonous than that of the peasantry. The markets, stocked by market gardens on the outskirts, provided a substantial variety of meats, vegetables, and fruits, although bread and beans still formed the bulk of such families' diets.

The diet of the rich was traditionally quite different from that of the poor. The upper classes were rapacious carnivores, and a truly elegant dinner consisted of an abundance of rich meat and fish dishes, laced with piquant sauces and complemented with sweets, cheeses, and nuts of all kinds. During such dinners, it was common to spend five or more hours at table. There was also an enormous amount of overdrinking. The English squire, for example, who loved to hunt with his hounds loved to drink with a similar passion. Sometimes he ended the evening under the table in a drunken stupor, but very often he did not. Wine and meat were consumed together in long hours of sustained excess, permitting the gentleman and his guests to drink enormous quantities without getting stupefyingly drunk. Gout was a common affliction of the rich. No wonder they were often caricatured as dragging their flabby limbs and bulging bellies to the table to stuff their swollen cheeks and poison their livers.

There were also regional dietary differences in 1700. Generally speaking, northern, Atlantic Europe ate better than southern, Mediterranean Europe. The poor of England and the Netherlands probably ate best of all. Contemporaries on both sides of the Channel often contrasted the English citizen's consumption of meat with the French peasant's greater dependence on bread and vegetables.

Patterns of food consumption changed markedly as the century progressed. There was a general growth of market gardening, and a greater variety of vegetables appeared in towns and cities. This was particularly the case in the Low Countries and England, which pioneered new methods of farming. Introduced into Europe from the Americas—along with corn, squash, tomatoes, and many other useful plants—the humble potato provided an excellent new food source. Containing a good supply of carbohydrates, calories, and vitamins A and C, the potato offset the lack of vitamins from green vegetables in the poor person's diet, and it provided a much higher caloric yield than grain for a given piece of land. After initial resistance, the potato became an important dietary supplement in much of Europe by the end of the century. In the course of the eighteenth century the large towns and cities of maritime Europe also began to receive semitropical fruits, such as oranges and lemons, from Portugal and the West Indies, but they remained expensive.

Royal Interest in the Potato Frederick the Great of Prussia, shown here supervising cultivation of the potato, used his influence and position to promote the new food on his estates and throughout Prussia. Peasants could grow potatoes with the simplest hand tools, but it was backbreaking labor, as this painting by R. Warthmüller suggests. *(Private Collection, Hamburg/akg-images)*

The most remarkable dietary change in the eighteenth century was in the consumption of sugar and tea. No other commodities grew so quickly in consumption. Previously expensive and rare luxury items, they became dietary staples for people of all social classes. This was possible because of the steady drop in prices created by the expansion of colonial production and slave labor. Other colonial goods also became important items of daily consumption in this period, including coffee, tobacco, and chocolate. Part of the motivation for consuming these products was a desire to emulate the habits of "respectable" people. The accelerating pace of work in the eighteenth century also seems to have created new needs for stimulants among working people. (See the feature "Listening to the Past: A Day in the Life of Paris" on pages 678–679.) Whereas the gentry took tea as a leisurely and genteel ritual, the lower classes usually drank tea at work. With the widespread adoption of these products (which turned out to be mildly to extremely addictive), working people in Europe became increasingly dependent on faraway colonial economies. Their understanding of daily necessities and how to procure those necessities shifted definitively, linking them into a globalized capitalism far beyond their ability to shape or control.

Toward a Consumer Society

Along with foodstuffs, all manner of other goods increased in variety and number in the eighteenth century. This proliferation led to a growth in consumption and new attitudes toward consumer goods so wide-ranging that some historians have referred to an eighteenth-century "consumer revolution." The result of this revolution was the birth of a new type of society, in which people had greater access to finished goods and derived their self-identity as much from their consuming practices as from their working lives and place in the production process. The full emergence of a **consumer society** did not take place until much later, but its roots lie in the developments of the eighteenth century.

Increased demand for consumer goods was not merely an innate response to increased supply. Eighteenth-century merchants cleverly pioneered new techniques

The Fashion Merchant's Shop Shopping in fancy boutiques became a favorite leisure pastime of the rich in the eighteenth century. Whereas shops had previously been dark, cramped spaces, now they were filled with light from large plate-glass windows, staffed by finely dressed attendants, and equipped with chairs and large mirrors for a comfortable shopping experience. Fashion merchants (or milliners) sold hats, shawls, parasols, and an infinite variety of accessories and decorations. (Courtesy, University of Illinois Library)

to incite demand: they initiated marketing campaigns, opened fancy boutiques with large windows, and advertised the patronage of royal princes and princesses. By diversifying their product lines and greatly accelerating the turnover of styles, they seized the reins of fashion from the courtiers who had earlier controlled it. Instead of setting new styles, duchesses and marquises now bowed to the dictates of fashion merchants. Fashion also extended beyond court circles to touch many more items and social groups.

Clothing was one of the chief indicators of nascent consumerism. The wiles of entrepreneurs made fashionable clothing seem more desirable, while legions of women entering the textile and needle trades made it ever cheaper. As a result, eighteenth-century western Europe witnessed a dramatic rise in the consumption of clothing, particularly in large cities. One historian has documented an enormous growth in the size and value of Parisians' wardrobes from 1700 to 1789, as well as a new level of diversity in garments and accessories, colors, and fabrics. Colonial economies played an important role, supplying new materials, such as cotton and vegetable dyes, at low cost. Cheaper copies of elite styles made it possible for working people to aspire to follow fashion for the first time.[14] Elite onlookers were bemused by the sight of lower-class people in fashionable dress. In 1784 Mrs. Fanny Cradock described encountering her milkman during an evening stroll "dressed in a fashionable suit, with an embroidered waistcoat, silk knee-breeches and lace cuffs."[15]

Mrs. Cradock's milkman notwithstanding, this was primarily a female phenomenon. Parisian women significantly out-consumed men, acquiring larger and more expensive wardrobes than those of their husbands, brothers, and fathers. This was true across the social spectrum; in ribbons, shoes, gloves, and lace, French working women reaped in the consumer revolution what they had sown in the industrious revolution (see pages 633–634). There were also new gender distinctions in dress. Previously, noblemen vied with noblewomen in the magnificence and ostentation of their dress; by the end of the eighteenth century men had renounced brilliant colors and voluptuous fabrics to don early versions of the plain dark suit that remains standard male formalwear in the West. This was one more aspect of the increasingly rigid opposition drawn between appropriate male and female behavior.

Changes in outward appearances were reflected in inner spaces. Historians have used the probate inventories drawn up by notaries after people's death to peer into ordinary people's homes. In 1700 the cramped home of a modest family consisted of a few rooms, each of which had multiple functions. The same room was used for sleeping, receiving friends, and producing artisanal goods. In the eighteenth century rents rose sharply, making it impossible to gain more space, but families began attributing specific functions to specific rooms. They also began to erect inner barriers within the home to provide small niches in which individuals could seek privacy.

New levels of comfort and convenience accompanied this trend toward more individualized ways of life. In 1700 a meal might be served in a common dish, with each person dipping his or her spoon into the pot. By the end of the eighteenth century even humble households contained a much greater variety of cutlery and dishes, making it possible for each person to eat from his or her own plate. More books and prints, which also proliferated at lower prices, decorated the walls. Improvements in glass-making provided more transparent glass, which allowed daylight to penetrate into gloomy rooms. Cold and smoky hearths were increasingly replaced by more efficient and cleaner coal stoves, which also eliminated the backache of cooking over an open fire. Rooms were warmer, better lit, more comfortable, and more personalized.

The scope of the new consumer economy should not be exaggerated. These developments were concentrated in large cities in northwestern Europe and North America. Even in these centers the elite benefited the most from new modes of life. This was not yet the society of mass consumption that emerged toward the end of the nineteenth century with the full expansion of the Industrial Revolution. The eighteenth century did, however, lay the foundations for one of the most distinctive features of modern Western life: societies based on the consumption of goods and services obtained through the market in which individuals form their identities and self-worth through the goods they consume.

Medical Practitioners

With these advances in daily life, how did the care of sickness, pain, and disease evolve? Medical science continued to struggle in vain against these scourges. Yet the Enlightenment's growing focus on discovering the laws of nature and on human problems did give rise to a great deal of research and experimentation. The century also saw a remarkable rise in the number of medical practitioners. Therefore, when significant breakthroughs in knowledge came in the middle and late nineteenth century, they could be rapidly evaluated and diffused.

Care of the sick in the eighteenth century was the domain of several competing groups: faith healers, apothecaries (or pharmacists), physicians, surgeons, and midwives. Both men and women were prominent in the healing arts, as had been the case since the Middle Ages. But by 1700 the range of medical activities open to women was severely restricted because women were generally denied admission to medical colleges and lacked the diplomas necessary to practice. In the course of the eighteenth century, the position of women as midwives and healers further eroded.

Faith healers remained active. They and their patients believed that demons and evil spirits caused disease by lodging in people and that the proper treatment was to exorcise, or drive out, the offending devil. This demonic view of disease was strongest in the countryside, where popular belief placed great faith in the healing power of religious relics, prayer, and the laying on of hands.

In the larger towns and cities, apothecaries sold a vast number of herbs, drugs, and patent medicines for every conceivable "temperament and distemper." Their prescriptions were incredibly complex—a hundred or more drugs might be included in a single prescription—and often very expensive. Some of the drugs and herbs undoubtedly worked. For example, strong laxatives were given to the rich for their constipated bowels, and regular **purging** of the bowels was considered essential for good health and the treatment of illness. Like all varieties of medical practitioners, apothecaries advertised their wares, their high-class customers, and their miraculous cures in newspapers and commercial circulars. Medicine, like food and fashionable clothing, thus joined the era's new commercial culture.

Physicians, who were invariably men, were apprenticed in their teens to practicing physicians for several years of on-the-job training. This training was then rounded out with hospital work or some university courses. Because such prolonged training was expensive, physicians came mainly from prosperous families, and they usually concentrated on urban patients from similar social backgrounds. They had little contact with urban workers and less with peasants.

Physicians in the eighteenth century were increasingly willing to experiment with new methods, but time-honored practices lay heavily on them. Like apothecaries, they laid great stress on purging, and bloodletting was still considered a medical cure-all. It was the way "bad blood," the cause of illness, was removed and the balance of humors necessary for good health was restored.

Surgeons, in contrast to physicians, made considerable medical and social progress in the eighteenth century. Long considered to be ordinary male artisans comparable to butchers and barbers, surgeons began studying

An Eighteenth-Century Pharmacy In this lively painting a woman consults an apothecary (in the elegant red suit) while his assistants assemble drugs for new prescriptions. By 1700 apothecaries had emerged as a separate group of state-licensed medical professionals. They drew on published lists and books describing the properties and dosages of their concoctions, but there were many different "recipes" and trade secrets. *(Civico Museo Bibliograco Musicale, Bologna, Italy/ The Bridgeman Art Library)*

anatomy seriously and improved their art. With endless opportunities to practice, army surgeons on gory battlefields led the way. They learned that a soldier with an extensive wound, such as a shattered leg or arm, could perhaps be saved if the surgeon could obtain a flat surface above the wound that could be cauterized with fire. Thus if a soldier (or a civilian) had a broken limb and the bone stuck out, the surgeon amputated so that the remaining stump could be cauterized and the likelihood of death reduced.

The eighteenth-century surgeon (and patient) labored in the face of incredible difficulties. Almost all operations were performed without painkillers, for the anesthesias of the day were hard to control and were believed too dangerous for general use. Many patients died from the agony and shock of such operations. Surgery was also performed in utterly unsanitary conditions, for there was no knowledge of bacteriology and the nature of infection. The simplest wound treated by a surgeon could fester and lead to death.

Midwives continued to deliver the overwhelming majority of babies throughout the eighteenth century. Trained initially by another woman practitioner—and regulated by a guild in many cities—the midwife primarily assisted in labor and delivering babies. She also treated female problems, such as irregular menstrual cycles, breast-feeding difficulties, infertility, and venereal disease, and ministered to small children.

The midwife orchestrated labor and birth in a woman's world, where friends and relatives offered the pregnant woman assistance and encouragement in the familiar surroundings of her own home. Excluded by tradition and modesty, the male surgeon (and the husband) rarely entered this world, because most births, then as now, were normal and spontaneous. Following the invention of the forceps, which might have helped in exceptionally difficult births, surgeon-physicians used their monopoly over this and other instruments to seek lucrative new business. Attacking midwives as ignorant and dangerous, they persuaded growing numbers of wealthy women of the superiority of their services and sought to undermine faith in midwives.

Recent research suggests that women practitioners successfully defended much but not all of their practice in the eighteenth century. In France one enterprising Parisian midwife secured royal financing for her campaign to teach better birthing techniques to village midwives, which reinforced the position of women practitioners. (See the feature "Individuals in Society: Madame du Coudray, the Nation's Midwife.") In northern Italy state

Individuals in Society

Madame du Coudray, the Nation's Midwife

Plate from Madame du Coudray's manual, illustrating "another incorrect method of delivery." (Rare Books Division, Countway [Francis A.] Library of Medicine)

In 1751 a highly esteemed Parisian midwife left the capital for a market town in central France. Having accepted an invitation to instruct local women in the skills of childbirth, Madame Angelique Marguerite Le Boursier du Coudray soon demonstrated a marvelous ability to teach students and win their respect. The thirty-six-year-old midwife found her mission: she would become the nation's midwife.

For eight years Madame du Coudray taught young women from the impoverished villages of Auvergne. In doing so, she entered into the world of unschooled midwives who typically were solid matrons with several children who relied on traditional birthing practices and folk superstitions. Trained in Paris through a rigorous three-year apprenticeship and imbued with an Enlightenment faith in the power of knowledge, du Coudray had little sympathy for these village midwives. Many peasant mothers told her about their difficult deliveries and their many uterine "infirmities," which they attributed to "the ignorance of the women to whom they had recourse, or to that of some inexperienced village [male] surgeons."* Du Coudray agreed. Botched deliveries by incompetents resulted in horrible deformities and unnecessary deaths.

Determined to raise standards, Madame du Coudray saw that her unlettered pupils learned through the senses, not through books. Thus she made, possibly for the first time in history, a life-size obstetrical model—a "machine"—out of fabric and stuffing for use in her classes. "I had . . . the students maneuver in front of me on a machine . . . which represented the pelvis of a woman, the womb, its opening, its ligaments, the conduit called the vagina, the bladder, and *rectum intestine*. I added an [artificial] child of natural size, whose joints were flexible enough to be able to be put in different positions." Now du Coudray could demonstrate the problems of childbirth, and each student could practice on the model in the "lab session."

As her reputation grew, Madame du Coudray sought to reach a national audience. In 1757 she published the first of several editions of her *Manual on the Art of Childbirth*. Handsomely and effectively illustrated (see the image above), the *Manual* incorporated her hands-on teaching method and served as a text and reference for students and graduates. In 1759 the government authorized Madame du Coudray to carry her instruction "throughout the realm" and promised financial support. Her reception was not always warm, for she was a self-assured and demanding woman who could anger old midwives, male surgeons, and skeptical officials. But aided by servants, a niece, and her husband, this inspired and indefatigable woman took her course from town to town until her retirement in 1784. Typically her students were young peasant women on tiny stipends who came into town from surrounding villages for two to three months of instruction. Classes met mornings and afternoons six days a week, with ample time to practice on the mannequin. After a recuperative break, Madame du Coudray and her entourage moved on.

Teaching thousands of fledgling midwives, Madame du Coudray may well have contributed to the decline in infant mortality and to the increase in population occurring in France in the eighteenth century—an increase she and her royal supporters fervently desired. Certainly she spread better knowledge about childbirth from the educated elite to the common people.

Questions for Analysis

1. How do you account for Madame du Coudray's remarkable success?
2. Does Madame du Coudray's career reflect tensions between educated elites and the common people? If so, how?

*Quotes are from Nina Gelbart, *The King's Midwife: A History and Mystery of Madame du Coudray* (Berkeley: University of California Press, 1998), pp. 60–61. This definitive biography is excellent.

Online Study Center Improve Your Grade
Going Beyond Individuals in Society

and church pressures led to major changes in midwife training and certification, but women remained dominant in the birthing trade. It appears that midwives generally lost no more babies than did male doctors, who were still summoned to treat non-elite women only when life-threatening situations required surgery.

Experimentation and the intensified search for solutions to human problems led to some real advances in medicine after 1750. The eighteenth century's greatest medical triumph was the conquest of smallpox. With the progressive decline of bubonic plague, smallpox became the most terrible of the infectious diseases, and it is estimated that 60 million Europeans died of it in the eighteenth century. Fully 80 percent of the population was stricken at some point in life.

The first step in the conquest of this killer in Europe came in the early eighteenth century. An English aristocrat whose beauty had been marred by the pox, Lady Mary Wortley Montagu, learned about the long-established practice of **smallpox inoculation** in the Muslim lands of western Asia while her husband was serving as British ambassador to the Ottoman Empire. She had her own son successfully inoculated with the pus from a smallpox victim and was instrumental in spreading the practice in England after her return in 1722. But inoculation was risky and was widely condemned because about one person in fifty died from it. In addition, people who had been inoculated were infectious and often spread the disease.

Subsequent success in reducing the risks of inoculation and in finding cheaper methods led to something approaching mass inoculation in England in the 1760s. On the continent, the well-to-do were also inoculated, beginning with royal families and then spreading to the middle classes. By the later years of the century smallpox inoculation was playing some part in the decline of the death rate and the general increase in European population.

The final breakthrough against smallpox came at the end of the century. Edward Jenner (1749–1823), a talented country doctor, noted that there was a long-standing belief in the English countryside that dairy maids who had contracted cowpox did not get smallpox. Cowpox produces sores that resemble those of smallpox on the cow's udder and on the hands of the milker, but the disease is mild and is not contagious.

Hospital Life Patients crowded into hospitals like this one in Hamburg in 1746 had little chance of recovery. A priest by the window administers last rites, while in the center a surgeon coolly saws off the leg of a man who has received no anesthesia. *(Germanisches Nationalmuseum, Nuremberg)*

For eighteen years Jenner practiced a kind of Baconian science, carefully collecting data on protection against smallpox by cowpox. Finally, in 1796 he performed his first vaccination on a young boy using matter taken from a milkmaid with cowpox. After performing more successful vaccinations, Jenner published his findings in 1798. The new method of treatment spread rapidly, and smallpox soon declined to the point of disappearance in Europe and then throughout the world. Jenner eventually received prizes totaling £30,000 from the British government for his great discovery, a fitting recompense for a man who helped lay the foundation for the science of immunology.

Religion and Popular Culture

Though the critical spirit of the Enlightenment made great inroads in the eighteenth century, the majority of ordinary men and women, especially those in rural areas, remained committed Christians. Religious faith promised salvation and eternal life, and it gave comfort and courage in the face of sorrow and death. Religion also remained strong because it was usually embedded in local traditions, everyday social experience, and popular culture.

Yet the popular religion of village Europe was everywhere enmeshed in a larger world of church hierarchies and state power. These powerful outside forces sought to regulate religious life at the local level. Their efforts created tensions that helped set the scene for a vigorous religious revival in Germany and England. Similar tensions arose in Catholic countries, where powerful elites criticized and attacked popular religious practices that their increasingly rationalistic minds deemed foolish and superstitious.

- **What were the patterns of popular religion and culture, and how did they interact with the worldview of the educated public and the Enlightenment?**

The Institutional Church

As in the Middle Ages, the local parish church remained the basic religious unit all across Europe. Still largely coinciding with the agricultural village, the parish fulfilled many needs. The parish church was the focal point of religious devotion, which went far beyond sermons and Holy Communion. It organized colorful processions and pilgrimages to local shrines. Even in Protestant countries, where such activities were severely restricted, congregations gossiped and swapped stories after services, and neighbors came together in church for baptisms, marriages, funerals, and special events. Thus the parish church was woven into the very fabric of community life.

Moreover, the local church had important administrative tasks. Priests and parsons were truly the bookkeepers of agrarian Europe, and it is because parish registers were so complete that historians have learned so much about population and family life. Parishes also normally distributed charity to the destitute, looked after orphans, and provided whatever primary education was available for the common people.

The many tasks of the local church were usually the responsibility of a resident priest or pastor, a full-time professional working with assistants and lay volunteers. All clerics—whether Roman Catholic, Protestant, Greek Orthodox, or Russian Orthodox—also shared the fate of middlemen in a complicated institutional system. Charged most often with ministering to poor peasants, the priest or parson was the last link in a powerful church-state hierarchy that was everywhere determined to control religion down to the grassroots. However, the regulatory framework of belief, which went back at least to the fourth century when Christianity became the official religion of the Roman Empire, had undergone important changes since 1500. The Protestant Reformation had burst forth as a culmination of medieval religiosity and a desire to purify Christian belief. Martin Luther, the most influential of the early reformers, preached that all men and women were saved from their sins and God's damnation only by personal faith in Jesus Christ. The individual could reach God directly, without need of priestly intermediaries.

As the Reformation gathered force, with peasant upheaval and doctrinal competition, German princes and monarchs in northern Europe put themselves at the head of official churches in their territories. Protestant authorities, with generous assistance from state-certified theologians like Luther, then proceeded to regulate their "territorial churches" strictly, selecting personnel and imposing detailed rules. They joined with Catholics to crush the Anabaptists, who, with their belief in freedom of conscience and separation of church and state, had become the real revolutionaries. Thus the Reformation, initially so radical in its rejection of Rome and its stress on individual religious experience, eventually resulted in a bureaucratization of the church and local religious life in Protestant Europe.

The Reformation era also increased the practical power of Catholic rulers over "their" churches, but it was only in the eighteenth century that some Catholic monarchs began to impose striking reforms. These reforms, which had counterparts in Orthodox Russia, had a very "Protestant" aspect. They increased state control over the Catholic Church, making it less subject to papal influence. Spain, a deeply Catholic country with devout rulers, took firm control of ecclesiastical appointments. Papal proclamations could not even be read in Spanish churches without prior approval from the government. Spain also asserted state control over the Spanish Inquisition, which pursued heresy as an independent agency under Rome's direction and went far toward creating a "national" Catholic Church, as France had done earlier.

A more striking indication of state power and papal weakness was the fate of the Society of Jesus, or **Jesuits.** The well-educated Jesuits were extraordinary teachers, missionaries, and agents of the papacy. In many Catholic countries, they exercised tremendous political influence, since individual members held high government positions and Jesuit colleges formed the minds of Europe's Catholic nobility. Yet by playing politics so effectively, the Jesuits eventually elicited a broad coalition of enemies. Bitter controversies led Louis XV to order the Jesuits out of France in 1763 and to confiscate their property. France and Spain then pressured Rome to dissolve the Jesuits completely. In 1773 a reluctant pope caved in, although the order was revived after the French Revolution.

Some Catholic rulers also believed that the clergy in monasteries and convents should make a more practical contribution to social and religious life. Austria, a leader in controlling the church (see page 615) and promoting primary education, showed how far the process could go. Maria Theresa began by sharply restricting entry into "unproductive" orders. In his Edict on Idle Institutions, her successor Joseph II abolished contemplative orders, henceforth permitting only orders that were engaged in teaching, nursing, or other practical work. The state also expropriated the dissolved monasteries and used their wealth for charitable purposes and higher salaries for ordinary priests. These measures recalled the radical transformation of the Protestant Reformation.

Protestant Revival

In their attempt to recapture the vital core of the Christian religion, Protestant reformers had rigorously suppressed medieval practices they considered nonessential or erroneous. For example, they had taken seriously the commandment "Thou shalt not make any graven image" (Exodus 20:4), and their radical reforms had reordered church interiors. Relics and crucifixes were removed, and stained-glass windows were smashed and walls and murals whitewashed. Processions and pilgrimages, saints and shrines—all such practices were eliminated because they had no Scriptural basis. Such revolutionary changes often troubled ordinary churchgoers, but by the late seventeenth century the vast reforms of the Reformation were complete and routinized in most Protestant churches.

Indeed, many official Protestant churches had settled into a smug complacency. In the Reformation heartland, one concerned German minister wrote that the Lutheran church "had become paralyzed in forms of dead doctrinal conformity" and badly needed a return to its original inspiration.[16] His voice was one of many that prepared and then guided a powerful Protestant revival that succeeded because it answered the intense but increasingly unsatisfied needs of common people.

The Protestant revival began in Germany. It was known as **Pietism,** and three aspects helped explain its powerful appeal. First, Pietism called for a warm, emotional religion that everyone could experience. Enthusiasm—in prayer, in worship, in preaching, in life itself—was the key concept. "Just as a drunkard becomes full of wine, so must the congregation become filled with spirit," declared one exuberant writer. Another said simply, "The heart must burn."[17]

Second, Pietism reasserted the earlier radical stress on the priesthood of all believers, thereby reducing the gulf between official clergy and Lutheran laity. Bible reading and study were enthusiastically extended to all classes, and this provided a powerful spur for popular education as well as individual religious development (see page 662). Finally, Pietists believed in the practical power of Christian rebirth in everyday affairs. Reborn Christians were expected to lead good, moral lives and to come from all social classes.

Pietism had a major impact on John Wesley (1703–1791), who served as the catalyst for popular religious revival in England. Wesley came from a long line of ministers, and when he went to Oxford University to prepare for the clergy, he mapped a fanatically earnest "scheme of religion." Like some students during final exams, he organized every waking moment. After becoming a teaching fellow at Oxford, Wesley organized a Holy Club for similarly minded students, who were soon known contemptuously as **Methodists** because they were so methodical in their devotion. Yet like the young Luther, Wesley remained intensely troubled about his own salvation even after his ordination as an Anglican priest in 1728.

Wesley's anxieties related to grave problems of the faith in England. The government shamelessly used the

Hogarth's Satirical View of the Church
William Hogarth (1697–1764) was one of the foremost satirical artists of his day. This image mocks a London Methodist meeting, where the congregation swoons in enthusiasm over the preacher's sermon. The woman in the foreground giving birth to rabbits refers to a hoax perpetrated in 1726 by a servant named Mary Tofts; the credulousness of those who believed Tofts is likened to that of the Methodist congregation. *(HIP/Art Resource, NY)*

Church of England to provide favorites with high-paying jobs. Building of churches practically stopped while the population grew, and in many parishes there was a shortage of pews. Services and sermons had settled into an uninspiring routine. The separation of religion from local customs and social life was symbolized by church doors that were customarily locked on weekdays. Moreover, Enlightenment skepticism was making inroads among the educated classes, and deism was becoming popular. Some bishops and church leaders seemed to believe that doctrines such as the Virgin Birth were little more than elegant superstitions.

Spiritual counseling from a sympathetic Pietist minister from Germany prepared Wesley for a mystical, emotional "conversion" in 1738. He described this critical turning point in his *Journal*:

> *In the evening I went to a [Christian] society in Aldersgate Street where one was reading Luther's preface to the Epistle to the Romans. About a quarter before nine, while he was describing the change which God works in the heart through faith in Christ, I felt my heart strangely warmed. I felt I did trust in Christ, Christ alone for salvation; and an assurance was given me that he had taken away my sins, even mine, and saved me from the law of sin and death.*[18]

Wesley's emotional experience resolved his intellectual doubts. Moreover, he was convinced that any person, no matter how poor or uneducated, might have a similarly heartfelt conversion and gain the same blessed assurance.

Wesley took the good news to the people, traveling some 225,000 miles by horseback and preaching more than forty thousand sermons in fifty years. Since existing churches were often overcrowded and the church-state establishment was hostile, Wesley preached in open fields. People came in large numbers. Of critical importance was Wesley's rejection of Calvinist predestination—the doctrine of salvation granted to only a select few. Instead, he preached that *all* men and women who earnestly sought salvation might be saved. It was a message of hope and joy, of free will and universal salvation.

Online Study Center Improve Your Grade
Primary Source: Wesley Lays Down the Ground Rules for Methodism

Wesley's ministry won converts, formed Methodist cells, and eventually resulted in a new denomination. And as Wesley had been inspired by the Pietist revival in Germany, so evangelicals in the Church of England and the old dissenting groups now followed Wesley's example, giving impetus to an even broader awakening among the lower classes. In Protestant countries, religion remained a vital force in the lives of the people.

Procession of Nuns at Port-Royal des Champs The convent of Port-Royal, located twenty miles southwest of Paris, was a center of Jansenist activity throughout the seventeenth century. Angered by the nuns' defiance, Louis XIV ordered them forcibly relocated in 1709. To generate support, the artist Magdelaine Horthemels painted a series of images depicting the pious and placid religious life at the convent. The convent was nonetheless destroyed by Louis's forces in 1710. This image is one of many copies of Horthemels' work made by Jansenists in the eighteenth century. *(Réunion des Musées Nationaux/Art Resource, NY)*

Catholic Piety

Religion also flourished in Catholic Europe around 1700, but there were important differences from Protestant practice. First, the visual contrast was striking; baroque art had lavished rich and emotionally exhilarating figures and images on Catholic churches, just as Protestants had removed theirs. People in Catholic Europe also remained intensely religious. More than 95 percent of the population probably attended church for Easter Communion, the climax of the Catholic year.

The tremendous popular strength of religion in Catholic countries reflected religion's integral role in community life and popular culture. Thus, although Catholics reluctantly confessed their sins to priests, they enthusiastically joined together in religious festivals to celebrate the passage of the liturgical year. In addition to the great processional days—such as Palm Sunday, the joyful reenactment of Jesus' triumphal entry into Jerusalem—each parish had its own saints' days, processions, and pilgrimages. Led by its priest, a congregation might march around the village or across the countryside to a local shrine. Before each procession or feast day, the priest explained its religious significance to kindle group piety. But processions were also folklore and tradition, an escape from work, and a form of recreation. A holiday atmosphere sometimes reigned on longer processions, with drinking and dancing and couples disappearing into the woods.

Catholicism did have its own version of the Pietist revivals that shook Protestant Europe. **Jansenism** has been described by one historian as the "illegitimate off-spring of the Protestant Reformation and the Catholic Counter-Reformation."[19] It originated with the Flemish theologian Cornelius Jansen (1585–1638), who called for a return to the austere early Christianity of Saint Augustine. In contrast to the worldly Jesuits, Jansen emphasized the heavy weight of original sin and accepted the doctrine of predestination. Although outlawed by papal and royal edicts as Calvinist heresy, Jansenism attracted Catholic followers eager for religious renewal, particularly in France. Many members of elite French society, especially judicial nobles and some parish priests, became known for their Jansenist piety and spiritual devotion. Such stern religious values encouraged the judiciary's increasing opposition to the monarchy in the second half of the eighteenth century. Among the poor, a different strain of Jansenism took hold. Prayer meetings brought men and women together in ecstatic worship, and some participants fell into convulsions and spoke in tongues.

Jansenism was an urban phenomenon. In the countryside, many peasants in Catholic countries held religious beliefs that were marginal to the Christian faith altogether, often of obscure or even pagan origin. On the Feast of Saint Anthony, for example, priests were expected to bless salt and bread for farm animals to protect them from disease. One saint's relics could help cure a child of fear, and there were healing springs for many ailments. The ordinary person combined strong Christian faith with a wealth of time-honored superstitions.

Inspired initially by the fervor of the Catholic Counter-Reformation and then to some extent by the critical rationalism of the Enlightenment, parish priests and Catholic hierarchies sought increasingly to "purify" popular religious practice. Thus one parish priest in France lashed out at his parishioners, claiming that they were "more superstitious than devout . . . and sometimes appear as baptized idolators."[20] French priests particularly denounced the "various remnants of paganism" found in popular bonfire ceremonies during Lent, in which young men, "yelling and screaming like madmen," tried to jump over the bonfires in order to help the crops grow and protect themselves from illness. One priest saw rational Christians regressing into pagan animals—"the triumph of Hell and the shame of Christianity."[21]

In contrast with Protestant reformers, many Catholic priests and hierarchies preferred a compromise between theological purity and the people's piety. Thus the severity of the attack on popular Catholicism varied widely by country and region. Where authorities pursued purification vigorously, as in Austria under Joseph II, pious peasants saw only an incomprehensible attack on the true faith and drew back in anger.

Leisure and Recreation

The combination of religious celebration and popular recreation seen in festivals and processions was most strikingly displayed at **Carnival,** a time of reveling and excess in Catholic and Mediterranean Europe. Carnival preceded Lent—the forty days of fasting and penitence before Easter—and for a few exceptional days in February or March, a wild release of drinking, masquerading, and dancing reigned. Moreover, a combination of plays, processions, and rowdy spectacles turned the established order upside down. Peasants dressed up as nobles and men as women, and rich masters waited on their servants at the table. This annual holiday gave people a much-appreciated chance to release their pent-up frustrations and aggressions before life returned to the usual pattern of hierarchy and hard work.

Despite the spread of literacy, the culture of the common people was largely oral rather than written. In the cold, dark winter months, families gathered around the fireplace to talk, sing, tell stories, do craftwork, and keep warm. In some parts of Europe, women would gather together in groups in someone's cottage to chat, sew, spin, and laugh. Sometimes a few young men would be invited so that the daughters (and mothers) could size up potential suitors in a supervised atmosphere. A favorite recreation of men was drinking and talking with buddies in public places, and it was a sorry village that had no tavern. In addition to old favorites such as beer and wine, the common people turned with gusto toward cheap and potent hard liquor, which fell in price because of improved techniques for distilling grain in the eighteenth century.

Towns and cities offered a wide range of amusements. Many of these had to be paid for because the eighteenth century saw a sharp increase in the commercialization of leisure-time activities. Urban fairs featured prepared foods, acrobats, freak shows, open-air performances, optical illusions, and the like. Such entertainments attracted a variety of social classes. So did the growing number of commercial, profit-oriented spectator sports. These ranged from traveling circuses and horse races to boxing matches and bullfights. Modern sports heroes, such as brain-bashing heavyweight champions and haughty matadors, made their appearance on the historical scene.

Blood sports, such as bullbaiting and cockfighting, remained popular with the masses. In bullbaiting the bull, usually staked on a chain in the courtyard of an inn, was attacked by ferocious dogs for the amusement of the innkeeper's clients. Eventually the maimed and tortured animal was slaughtered by a butcher and sold as meat. In cockfighting two roosters, carefully trained by their owners and armed with razor-sharp steel spurs, slashed and clawed each other in a small ring until the victor won—and the loser died. An added attraction of cockfighting was that the screaming spectators could bet on the lightning-fast combat and its uncertain outcome.

Cockfighting in England This engraving by William Hogarth (see also the illustration on page 673) satirizes the popular taste for blood sports, which Hogarth despised and lampooned in his famous *Four Stages of Cruelty*. The central figure in the wildly excited gathering is a blind nobleman who actually existed and seldom missed a fight. Note the steel spurs on the birds' legs. *(Courtesy of the Trustees of the British Museum)*

In trying to place the vibrant popular culture of the common people in broad perspective, historians have stressed the growing criticism levied against it by the educated elites in the second half of the eighteenth century. These elites, which had previously shared the popular enthusiasm for religious festivals, Carnival, drinking in taverns, blood sports, and the like, now tended to see superstition, sin, disorder, and vulgarity.[22] The resulting attack on popular culture, which had its more distant origins in the Protestant clergy's efforts to eliminate frivolity and superstition, was intensified as an educated public embraced the critical worldview of the Enlightenment.

Chapter Summary

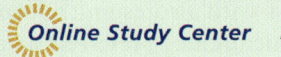

- What changes occurred in marriage and the family in the course of the eighteenth century?
- What was life like for children, and how did attitudes toward childhood evolve?
- How did new patterns of consumption and changing medical care affect people's lives?
- What were the patterns of popular religion and culture, and how did they interact with the worldview of the educated public and the Enlightenment?

In the current generation, imaginative research has greatly increased our understanding of ordinary life and social patterns of the past. In the eighteenth century the life of the people remained primarily rural and oriented toward the local community. Tradition, routine, and well-established codes of behavior framed much of the everyday experience. Thus just as the three-field agricultural cycle and its pattern of communal rights had determined traditional patterns of grain production, so did community values in the countryside strongly encourage a late marriage age and a low rate of illegitimate births. Yet powerful forces also worked for change. Many came from outside and above, from the aggressive capitalists, educated elites, and government officials discussed in the last two chapters. Closely knit villages began to lose control over families and marital practices, as could be seen in the earlier marriages of cottage workers and in the beginning of the explosion in illegitimate births.

Infancy and childhood were highly vulnerable stages of life. In some parts of Europe fewer than half of all children reached the age of ten. Infant mortality was high in areas, like France, in which wet-nursing was commonly practiced. Treatment of children could be harsh in an early modern society that was characterized by much higher levels of violence and brutality than are Western societies today. The second half of the eighteenth century witnessed a new concern with methods of child raising inspired by Enlightenment efforts to reform human society. Schools for middling and poor children spread across Europe, leading to a growth in literacy rates.

The urban populace benefited from the surge in agricultural and industrial production. People found a greater variety of food products at the market, including new stimulants produced in the colonies that soon became staples of elite and popular consumption. Within homes, standards of comfort and hygiene increased, and the emerging consumer society offered new possibilities for self-expression and individuality. Medical techniques continued to follow traditional patterns, but the number of practitioners grew, and great strides were made against smallpox.

In the background of these changes, patterns of recreation and leisure, from churchgoing and religious festivals to sewing and drinking in groups within an oral culture, reflected and reinforced community ties and values. Many long-standing ideas and beliefs, ranging from obscure religious customs to support for fair prices, remained strong forces and sustained continuity in popular life. A wave of religious revival counteracted the secular tendencies of the Enlightenment, ensuring that religion continued to have a strong hold over the popular classes. The next great wave of change would be inaugurated by revolution in politics.

Key Terms

- community controls
- illegitimacy explosion
- wet-nursing
- infanticide
- just price
- consumer society
- purging
- smallpox inoculation
- Jesuits
- Pietism
- Methodists
- Jansenism
- Carnival
- blood sports

Online Study Center   **Improve Your Grade** Flashcards

Suggested Reading

Brewer, John, and Roy Porter, eds. *Consumption and the World of Goods.* 1993. Pioneering essays from leading scholars on the consumer revolution of eighteenth-century Europe.

Bridenthal, Renate, Susan Mosher Stuard, and Merry Wiesner, eds. *Becoming Visible: Women in European History,* 3d ed. 1998. A valuable starting point for the history of women and gender.

Burke, Peter. *Popular Culture in Early Modern Europe.* 1978. A classic introduction to everyday life, mentalities, and leisure pursuits.

Carrell, Jennifer. *The Speckled Monster: A Historical Tale of Battling Smallpox.* 2003. A lively popular account of the spread of inoculation.

Gelbart, Nina. *The King's Midwife: A History and Mystery of Madame Du Coudray.* 2002. A vivid and accessible biography of the most famous midwife of eighteenth-century France.

Hartman, Mary S. *The Household and the Making of History.* 2004. A bold study of the economic and social ramifications of the European pattern of early marriage.

Kertzer, David I., and Marzio Barbagli, eds. *Family Life in Early Modern Times, 1500–1789.* 2001. A rich collection of essays on the history of the family, women, and children in early modern Europe.

Mintz, Sidney W. *Sweetness and Power: The Place of Sugar in Modern History.* 1985. A fascinating exploration of the shifting cultural significance of sugar and its transformation from elite luxury good to everyday staple.

(continued on page 680)

Listening to the Past

A Day in the Life of Paris

Louis-Sébastien Mercier (1740–1814) was the best chronicler of everyday life in eighteenth-century Paris. His masterpiece was the Tableau de Paris (1781–1788), a multivolume work composed of 1,049 chapters that covered subjects ranging from convents to cafés, bankruptcy to booksellers, the latest fashions to royal laws. As this excerpt demonstrates, he aimed to convey the infinite diversity of people, places, and things he saw around him, and in so doing he left future generations a precious record of the changing dynamics of Parisian society in the second half of the eighteenth century.

Mercier's family belonged to the respectable artisan classes. This middling position ideally suited Mercier for observing the extremes of wealth and poverty around him. Although these volumes contain many wonderful glimpses of daily life, they should not be taken for an objective account. Mercier brought his own moral and political sensibilities, influenced by Jean-Jacques Rousseau, to the task.

Chapter 39: How the Day Goes

It is curious to see how, amid what seems perpetual life and movement, certain hours keep their own characteristics, whether of bustle or of leisure. Every round of the clock-hand sets another scene in motion, each different from the last, though all about equal in length.

Seven o'clock in the morning sees all the gardeners, mounted on their nags and with their baskets empty, heading back out of town again. No carriages are about, and not a presentable soul, except a few neat clerks hurrying to their offices.

Nine o'clock sets all the barbers in motion, covered from head to foot with flour—hence their soubriquet of "whitings"—wig in one hand, tongs in the other. Waiters from the lemonade-shops are busy with trays of coffee and rolls, breakfast for those who live in furnished rooms. . . .

An hour later the Law comes into action; a black cloud of legal practitioners and hangers-on descend upon the Châtelet,* and the other courts; a procession of wigs and gowns and brief-bags, with plaintiffs and defendants at their heels.

Midday is the stockbrokers' hour, and the idlers'; the former hurry off to the Exchange, the latter to the Palais-Royal.† The Saint-Honoré‡ quarter, where all the financiers live, is at its busiest now, its streets are crowded with the customers and clients of the great.

At two o'clock those who have invitations to dine set out, dressed in their best, powdered, adjusted, and walking on tiptoe not to soil their stockings. All the cabs are engaged, not one is to be found on the rank; there is a good deal of competition for these vehicles, and you may see two would-be passengers jumping into a cab together from different sides, and furiously disputing which was first; on which the cabman whips up and drives them both off to the Commissary of Police, who takes the burden of decision off his shoulders.

Three o'clock and the streets are not so full; everyone is at dinner; there is a momentary calm, soon to be broken, for at five fifteen the din is as though the gates of hell were opened, the streets are impassable with traffic going all ways at once, towards the playhouses or the public gardens. Cafés are at their busiest.

Towards seven the din dies down, everywhere and all at once. You can hear the cab-horses' hoofs pawing the stones as they wait—in vain. It is as though the whole town were gagged and bound, suddenly, by an invisible hand. This is the most dangerous time of the whole day for thieves and such, especially towards autumn when the days begin to draw in; for the watch is not yet about, and violence takes its opportunity.

*The main criminal court of Paris.
†The garden surrounded by arcades with shops and cafés constructed by the Duke of Orléans.
‡The neighborhood around the rue Saint-Honoré, between the Palais-Royal and the Place Vendôme; a fashionable quarter for the wealthy.

A page from Mercier's original manuscript. (*Bibliothèque nationale de France*)

Night falls; and, while scene-shifters set to work at the play-houses, swarms of other workmen, carpenters, masons and the like, make their way towards the poorer quarters. They leave white footprints from the plaster on their shoes, a trail that any eye can follow. They are off home, and to bed, at the hour which finds elegant ladies sitting down to their dressing-tables to prepare for the business of the night.

At nine this begins; they all set off for the play. Houses tremble as the coaches rattle by, but soon the noise ceases; all the fine ladies are making their evening visits, short ones, before supper. Now the prostitutes begin their night parade, breasts uncovered, heads tossing, colour high on their cheeks, and eyes as bold as their hands. These creatures, careless of the light from shop-windows and street lamps, follow and accost you, trailing through the mud in their silk stockings and low shoes, with words and gestures well matched for obscenity. . . .

By eleven, renewed silence. People are at supper, private people, that is; for the cafés begin at this hour to turn out their patrons, and to send the various idlers and workless and poets back to their garrets for the night. A few prostitutes still linger, but they have to use more circumspection, for the watch is about, patrolling the streets, and this is the hour when they "gather em in"; that is the traditional expression.

A quarter after midnight, a few carriages make their way home, taking the non–card players back to bed. These lend the town a sort of transitory life; the tradesman wakes out of his first sleep at the sound of them, and turns to his wife, by no means unwilling. More than one young Parisian must owe his existence to this sudden passing rattle of wheels. Thunder sends up the birth-rate here too, as it does everywhere else.

At one in the morning six thousand peasants arrive, bringing the town's provision of vegetables and fruits and flowers, and make straight for the Halles;§ their beasts have come eighteen leagues perhaps, and are weary. As for the market itself, it never sleeps. Morpheus never shakes his poppy-seed there. Perpetual noise, perpetual motion, the curtain never rings down on the enormous stage; first come the fishmongers, and after these the egg-dealers, and after these the retail buyers; for the Halles keep all the other markets of Paris going; they are the warehouses whence these draw their supplies. The food of the whole city is shifted and sorted in high-piled baskets; you may see eggs, pyramids of eggs, moved here and there, up steps and down, in and out of the throngs, miraculous; not one is ever broken. . . .

This impenetrable din contrasts oddly with the sleeping streets, for at that hour none but thieves and poets are awake.

Twice a week, at six, those distributors of the staff of life, the bakers of Gonesse,** bring in an enormous quantity of loaves to the town, and may take none back through the barriers. And at this same hour workmen take up their tools, and trudge off to their day's labour. Coffee with milk is, unbelievably, the favoured drink among these stalwarts nowadays.

At street-corners, where the pale light from a street lamp falls, the coffee women stand, carrying their tin urns on their backs; they sell their coffee in earthenware cups, two sous a cup, one penny, and not too well sugared at that; but our workmen find it very much to their taste. . . .

So coffee-drinking has become a habit, and one so deep-rooted that the working classes will start the day on nothing else. It is not costly, and has more flavour to it, and more nourishment too, than anything else they can afford to drink; so they consume immense quantities, and say that if a man can only have coffee for breakfast it will keep him going till nightfall. They take only two meals in the twenty-four hours; that at midday and the evening snack of supper, what they call the *persillade*.

§The city's central wholesale food market.

Questions for Analysis

1. What different social groups does Mercier describe in Paris? On what basis does he categorize people?
2. What is Mercier's attitude toward the poor and the rich? Does he approve or disapprove of Parisian society as he describes it?
3. How does the division of the day in 1780s Paris compare to your lifestyle today?

**A suburb of Paris, famous for the excellent bread baked there.

Source: Panorama of Paris: Selections from "Le Tableau de Paris," Louis-Sébastien Mercier, based on the translation by Helen Simpson, edited and with a new preface and translations by Jeremy D. Popkin. Copyright © 1999 The Pennsylvania State University. Reprinted by permission of Penn State Press.

Ramsey, Matthew. *Professional and Popular Medicine in France, 1770–1830: The Social World of Medical Practice.* 1988. A good introduction to the medical profession.

Sussman, George D. *Selling Mother's Milk: The Wet-Nursing Business in France, 1715–1914.* 1982. An engrossing account of the large-scale organization of wet-nursing in eighteenth-century France.

Wrightson, Keith. *Earthly Necessities: Economic Lives in Early Modern Britain.* 2000. Examines the economics of everyday life.

Notes

1. Quoted in J. M. Beattie, "The Criminality of Women in Eighteenth-Century England," *Journal of Social History* 8 (Summer 1975): 86.
2. W. L. Langer, "Infanticide: A Historical Survey," *History of Childhood Quarterly* 1 (Winter 1974): 357.
3. Quoted in R. Cobb, *The Police and the People: French Popular Protest, 1789–1820* (Oxford: Clarendon Press, 1970), p. 238.
4. Quoted in D. S. Landes, ed., *The Rise of Capitalism* (New York: Macmillan, 1966), pp. 56–57.
5. G. Gullickson, *Spinners and Weavers of Auffay: Rural Industry and the Sexual Division of Labor in a French Village, 1750–1850* (Cambridge: Cambridge University Press, 1986), p. 186. See also L. A. Tilly, J. W. Scott, and M. Cohen, "Women's Work and European Fertility Patterns," *Journal of Interdisciplinary History* 6 (Winter 1976): 447–476.
6. Pier Paolo Viazzo, "Mortality, Fertility, and Family," in *Family Life in Early Modern Times, 1500–1789,* ed. David I. Kertzer and Marzio Barbagli (New Haven: Yale University Press, 2001), p. 180.
7. George Sussman, *Selling Mothers' Milk: The Wet-Nursing Business in France, 1715–1914* (Urbana: University of Illinois Press, 1982), p. 22.
8. Robert Woods, "Did Montaigne Love His Children? Demography and the Hypothesis of Parental Indifference," *Journal of Interdisciplinary History* 33, 3 (2003): 426.
9. P. Viazzo, "Mortality, Fertility, and Family," in *The History of the European Family,* vol. 1, ed. D. Kertzer and M. Barbagli (New Haven: Yale University Press, 2001), pp. 176–178.
10. Alysa Levene, "The Estimation of Mortality at the London Foundling Hospital, 1741–99," *Population Studies* 59, 1 (2005): 87–97.
11. Cited in Woods, "Did Montaigne Love His Children?," p. 421.
12. Ibid., pp. 13, 16.
13. E. Kennedy, *A Cultural History of the French Revolution* (New Haven: Yale University Press, 1989), p. 47.
14. Daniel Roche, *The Culture of Clothing: Dress and Fashion in the Ancien Regime.* Translated by Jean Birrell (Cambridge: Cambridge University Press, 1996).
15. Quoted in Cissie Fairchilds, "The Production and Marketing of Populuxe Goods in Eighteenth-Century Paris," in *Consumption and the World of Goods*, ed. John Brewer and Roy Porter (London: Routledge, 1993), p. 228.
16. Quoted in K. Pinson, *Pietism as a Factor in the Rise of German Nationalism* (New York: Columbia University Press, 1934), p. 13.
17. Ibid., pp. 43–44.
18. Quoted in S. Andrews, *Methodism and Society* (London: Longmans, Green, 1970), p. 327.
19. Dale Van Kley, "The Rejuvenation and Rejection of Jansenism in History and Historiography," *French Historical Studies* 29 (Fall 2006): 649–684.
20. Quoted in I. Woloch, *Eighteenth-Century Europe: Tradition and Progress, 1715–1789* (New York: W. W. Norton, 1982), p. 292.
21. Quoted in T. Tackett, *Priest and Parish in Eighteenth-Century France* (Princeton, N.J.: Princeton University Press, 1977), p. 214.
22. Woloch, *Eighteenth-Century Europe,* pp. 220–221; see also pp. 214–220 for this section.

In this painting by the female artist Nanine Vallain, the figure of Liberty bears a copy of the Declaration of the Rights of Man and of the Citizen in one hand and a pike to defend them in the other. The painting hung in the Jacobin club until its fall from power. *(Musée de la Revolution Française, Vizille/The Bridgeman Art Library)*

chapter 21

THE REVOLUTION IN POLITICS, 1775–1815

chapter preview

Background to Revolution
- What social, political, and economic factors formed the background to the French Revolution?

Revolution in Metropole and Colony, 1789–1791
- What were the immediate events that sparked the Revolution, and how did they result in the formation of a constitutional monarchy in France? How did the ideals and events of the early Revolution raise new aspirations in the colonies?

World War and Republican France, 1791–1799
- How and why did the Revolution take a radical turn at home and in the colonies?

The Napoleonic Era, 1799–1815
- Why did Napoleon Bonaparte assume control of France, and what factors led to his downfall? How did the new republic of Haiti gain independence from France?

The last years of the eighteenth century were a time of great upheaval. A series of revolutions and revolutionary wars challenged the old order of monarchs and aristocrats. The ideas of freedom and equality, ideas that have not stopped shaping the world since that era, flourished and spread. The revolutionary era began in North America in 1775. Then in 1789 France, the most influential country in Europe, became the leading revolutionary nation. It established first a constitutional monarchy, then a radical republic, and finally a new empire under Napoleon. Inspired by both the ideals of the Revolution and internal colonial conditions, the slaves of Saint-Domingue rose up in 1791. Their rebellion led to the creation of the new independent nation of Haiti in 1805.

The armies of France violently exported revolution beyond the nation's borders in an effort to establish new governments throughout much of Europe. The world of modern domestic and international politics was born.

Background to Revolution

Since July 1789 the origins of the French Revolution have been one of the most debated topics in history. Historians long explained the Revolution as a clash between the rising bourgeoisie and the entrenched nobility in which the former asserted its right to political power commensurate with its new economic strength. It is now apparent that such a simplistic explanation cannot account for the complexity of an event that spanned several decades and involved millions of people and numerous nations. In uncovering the path to revolution, numerous interrelated factors must be taken into account. These include deep social changes in France, a long-term political crisis that eroded monarchical legitimacy, the impact of new political ideas derived from the Enlightenment, the emergence of a "public sphere" in which such opinions were formed and shared, and, perhaps most importantly, a financial crisis created by France's participation in expensive overseas wars.

Online Study Center
This icon will direct you to interactive activities and study materials on the website **college.hmco.com/pic/mckaywest9e**

While these developments built a fundamental thirst for fundamental political reform, there was nothing inevitable in the unfolding of the Revolution. As in many historical events, chance played a significant role in leading the French to revolution and in the course of events after its outbreak. Examining the background of institutions, events, and ideas helps explain how the fascinating and complex phenomenon known as the French Revolution came into being.

- **What social, political, and economic factors formed the background to the French Revolution?**

Legal Orders and Social Change

As in the Middle Ages, France's 25 million inhabitants were still legally divided into three orders, or **estates**—the clergy, the nobility, and everyone else. As the nation's first estate, the clergy numbered about one hundred thousand and had important privileges. It owned about 10 percent of the land and paid only a "voluntary gift," rather than regular taxes, to the government every five years. Moreover, the church levied a tax (the tithe) on landowners, which averaged somewhat less than 10 percent.

The second estate consisted of some four hundred thousand nobles, the descendants of "those who fought" in the Middle Ages. Nobles owned about 25 percent of the land in France outright, and they too were lightly taxed. Moreover, nobles continued to enjoy certain **manorial rights**, or privileges of lordship, that dated back to medieval times. These included exclusive rights to hunt and fish, village monopolies on baking bread and pressing grapes for wine, fees for justice, and a host of other "useful privileges." In addition, nobles had "honorific privileges" such as the right to precedence on public occasions and the right to wear swords. These rights conspicuously proclaimed the nobility's legal superiority and exalted social position.

Everyone else was a commoner, legally a member of the third estate. A few commoners—prosperous merchants, lawyers, and officials—were well educated and rich, and they might even have purchased manorial rights as a way of obtaining profit and social honor. The vast majority of the third estate consisted of peasants and agricultural workers in the countryside and urban artisans and unskilled day laborers. Thus the third estate was a conglomeration of very different social groups united only by their shared legal status as distinct from the nobility and clergy.

The Three Estates In this political cartoon from 1789 a peasant of the third estate struggles under the crushing burden of a happy clergyman and a plumed nobleman. The caption—"Let's hope this game ends soon"—sets forth a program of reform that any peasant could understand. (*Réunion des Musées Nationaux/Art Resource, NY*)

In discussing the origins of the French Revolution, historians long focused on growing tensions between the nobility and the comfortable members of the third estate, the *bourgeoisie* or upper middle class. Increasing in size, wealth, culture, and self-confidence, this rising bourgeoisie became progressively exasperated by archaic "feudal" laws restraining the economy and by the pretensions of a reactionary nobility that was closing ranks against middle-class aspirations. As a result, the French bourgeoisie eventually rose up to lead the entire third estate in a great social revolution that destroyed feudal privileges and established a capitalist order based on individualism and a market economy.

In recent years, a flood of new research has challenged these accepted views. Above all, revisionist historians have questioned the existence of growing social conflict between a progressive capitalistic bourgeoisie and a reactionary feudal nobility in eighteenth-century France. Instead, they see both bourgeoisie and nobility as highly fragmented, riddled with internal rivalries. The ancient sword nobility, for example, was profoundly separated from the newer robe nobility by differences in wealth, education, and worldview. Differences within the bourgeoisie—between wealthy financiers and local lawyers, for example—were no less profound. Rather than standing as unified blocs against each other, nobility and bourgeoisie formed two parallel social ladders increasingly linked together at the top by wealth, marriage, and Enlightenment culture.

Revisionist historians stress three developments in particular. First, the nobility remained a fluid and relatively open order. Throughout the eighteenth century substantial numbers of successful commoners continued to seek and obtain noble status through government service and purchase of expensive positions conferring nobility. Second, key sections of the nobility were no less liberal than the middle class, and until revolution actually began, both groups generally supported the judicial opposition to the government led by the Parlement of Paris. Third, the nobility and the bourgeoisie were not really at odds in the economic sphere. Investment in land and government service were the preferred activities of both groups, and the ideal of the merchant capitalist was to gain enough wealth to retire from trade, purchase an estate, and live nobly as a large landowner. At the same time, wealthy nobles often acted as aggressive capitalists, investing especially in mining, metallurgy, and foreign trade.

Revisionists have clearly shaken the belief that the bourgeoisie and the nobility were inevitably locked in growing conflict before the Revolution. But in stressing the similarities between the two groups, especially at the top, revisionists have also reinforced the view that the Old Regime had ceased to correspond with social reality by the 1780s. Legally, society was still based on rigid orders inherited from the Middle Ages. In reality, France had already moved far toward being a society based on wealth and education in which an emerging elite that included both aristocratic and bourgeois notables was frustrated by a bureaucratic monarchy that continued to claim the right to absolute power.

Chronology

1773	Boston Tea Party
1775	Paine, *Common Sense*
1775–1783	American Revolution
1786–1789	Financial crisis in France
1789	Feudalism abolished in France; ratification of U.S. Constitution; storming of the Bastille
1789–1799	French Revolution
1790	Burke, *Reflections on the Revolution in France*
1791	Slave insurrection in Saint-Domingue
1792	Wollstonecraft, *A Vindication of the Rights of Woman*
1793	Execution of Louis XVI
1793–1794	Economic controls to help poor in France; Robespierre's Reign of Terror
1794	Robespierre deposed and executed
1794–1799	Thermidorian reaction
1799–1815	Napoleonic era
1805	Haitian republic declares independence
1812	Napoleon invades Russia
1814–1815	Napoleon defeated and exiled

The Crisis of Political Legitimacy

Overlaying these social changes was a century-long political and fiscal struggle between the monarchy and its opponents that was primarily enacted in the law courts. When Louis XIV finally died in 1715 and was succeeded by his five-year-old great-grandson, Louis XV (r. 1715–1774), the Sun King's elaborate system of absolutist rule was challenged. Favored by the duke of Orléans (1674–1723), who governed as regent until 1723, a number of institutions retrieved powers they had lost under Louis XIV. Instead of assuming personal rule, the regent reinstated councils of state to aid in decision making.

Most important, in 1715 the duke restored to the high courts of France—the parlements—the ancient right to evaluate royal decrees publicly in writing before they were registered and given the force of law. The restoration of this right, which had been suspended under Louis XIV, was a fateful step. The magistrates of the parlements were leaders of the robe nobility. In 1604 Henry IV had created the paulette (see page 528) on royal offices as a way to raise desperately needed revenue. The unintended consequence of this act was to transform royal offices, including judicial positions, into a form of private property passed down from father to son. By allowing a well-entrenched and highly articulate branch of the nobility to evaluate the king's decrees before they became law, the duke of Orléans sanctioned a counterweight to absolute power.

These implications became clear when the heavy expenses of the War of the Austrian Succession plunged France into financial crisis. In 1748 Louis XV appointed a finance minister who decreed a 5 percent income tax on every individual regardless of social status. Exemption from most taxation had long been a hallowed privilege of the nobility, and other important groups—the clergy, the large towns, and some wealthy bourgeoisie—had also gained special tax advantages over time. The result was a vigorous protest from many sides led by the influential Parlement of Paris. The monarchy retreated; the new tax was dropped.

Following the disastrously expensive Seven Years' War (see pages 635–637), the conflict re-emerged. The government tried to maintain emergency taxes after the war ended; the Parlement of Paris protested and even challenged the basis of royal authority, claiming that the king's power had to be limited to protect liberty. Once again the government caved in and withdrew the taxes. The judicial opposition then asserted that the king could not levy taxes without the consent of the Parlement of Paris, which was acting as the representative of the entire nation.

After years of attempting to compromise with the parlements, Louis XV roused himself for a determined defense of his absolutist inheritance. "The magistrates," he angrily told the Parlement of Paris in a famous face-to-face confrontation, "are my officers. . . . In my person only does the sovereign power rest."[1] In 1768 Louis appointed a tough career official named René de Maupeou as chancellor and ordered him to crush the judicial opposition.

Maupeou abolished the existing parlements and exiled the vociferous members of the Parlement of Paris to the provinces. He created a new and docile parlement of royal officials, known as the **Maupeou parlements,** and he began once again to tax the privileged groups. A few philosophes applauded these measures: the sovereign was using his power to introduce badly needed reforms that had been blocked by a self-serving aristocratic elite. Most philosophes, and public opinion as a whole, sided with the old parlements, however, and there was widespread criticism of "royal despotism."

Learned dissent was accompanied by scandalous libels. Known as Louis *le bien-aimé* (beloved Louis) in his youth, the king found his people turning against him for moral as well as political reasons. Kings had always maintained mistresses who were invariably chosen from the court nobility. Louis XV broke that pattern with Madame de Pompadour, daughter of a disgraced bourgeois financier. As favorite from 1745 to 1750, Pompadour exercised tremendous influence over literature, art, and the decorative arts, using her patronage to support Voltaire and promote the rococo style. Even after their love affair ended, Pompadour wielded considerable influence over the king, helping bring about the alliance with Austria that resulted in the Seven Years' War. Pompadour's low birth and hidden political influence generated a stream of resentful pamphleteering.

After Pompadour, the king appeared to sink ever lower in licentiousness; his last favorite, Madame du Barry, was derided as a common streetwalker, and the king was accused of maintaining a brothel of teenage girls at Versailles to serve his lusts. The illegal stream of scandal-mongering became a torrent. Lurid and pornographic depictions of the court ate away at the foundations of royal authority, especially among the common people in turbulent Paris. The king was being stripped of the sacred aura of God's anointed on earth and was being reinvented in the popular imagination as a degenerate.

Despite this progressive **desacralization** of the monarchy, its power was still great enough to ride over the opposition, and Louis XV would probably have prevailed if he had lived to a ripe old age, but he died in 1774. The new king, Louis XVI (r. 1774–1792), was a shy twenty-year-old with good intentions. Taking the throne, he is reported to have said, "What I should like most is to be loved."[2] The eager-to-please monarch yielded in the face of vehement opposition from France's educated elite. He dismissed chancellor Maupeou and repudiated the strong-willed minister's work. Louis also waffled on the economy, dismissing controller-general Turgot when his attempts to liberalize the economy drew fire. A weakened but unreformed monarchy now faced a judicial opposition that claimed to speak for the entire French nation. Increasingly locked in stalemate, the country was drifting toward renewed financial crisis and political upheaval.

The Impact of the American Revolution

Coinciding with the first years of Louis XVI's reign, the American Revolution had an enormous impact on France both in practical and ideological terms. French expenses to support the colonists bankrupted the Crown, while the ideals of liberty and equality provided heady inspiration for political reform.

Like the French Revolution, the American Revolution had its immediate origins in struggles over increased taxes. The high cost of the Seven Years' War—fought with little financial contribution from the colonies—doubled the British national debt. When the government tried to recoup some of the losses in increased taxes on the colonies in 1765, the colonists reacted with anger.

The key questions were political rather than economic. To what extent could the home government assert its power while limiting the authority of colonial legislatures and their elected representatives? Accordingly, who should represent the colonies, and who had the right to make laws for Americans? The British government replied that Americans were represented in Parliament, albeit indirectly (like most British people themselves), and that the absolute supremacy of Parliament throughout the empire could not be questioned. Many Americans felt otherwise.

In 1773 the dispute over taxes and representation flared up again after the British government awarded a monopoly on Chinese tea to the East India Company, suddenly excluding colonial merchants from a lucrative business. In response, Boston men disguised as Indians held a rowdy "tea party" and threw the company's tea into the harbor. This led to extreme measures. The so-called Coercive Acts closed the port of Boston, curtailed local elections, and greatly expanded the royal governor's power. County conventions in Massachusetts protested vehemently and urged that the acts be "rejected as the attempts of a wicked administration to enslave America." Other colonial assemblies joined in the denunciations. In September 1774 the First Continental Congress met in Philadelphia, where the more radical members argued successfully against concessions to the Crown. Compromise was also rejected by the British Parliament, and in April 1775 fighting began at Lexington and Concord.

The fighting spread, and the colonists moved slowly but inevitably toward open rebellion and a declaration of independence. The uncompromising attitude of the British government and its use of German mercenaries dissolved long-standing loyalties to the home country and rivalries among the separate colonies. Some colonists

Toward Revolution in Boston The Boston Tea Party was only one of many angry confrontations between British officials and Boston patriots. On January 27, 1774, an angry crowd seized a British customs collector and tarred and feathered him. This French engraving of 1784 commemorates the defiant and provocative action. *(The Granger Collection, New York)*

remained loyal to the Crown; large numbers of these Loyalists emigrated to the northern colonies of Canada.

On July 4, 1776, the Second Continental Congress adopted the Declaration of Independence. Written by Thomas Jefferson, it boldly listed the tyrannical acts committed by George III (r. 1760–1820) and confidently proclaimed the natural rights of mankind and the **sovereignty** of the American states. Sometimes called the world's greatest political editorial, the Declaration of Independence in effect universalized the traditional rights of English people and made them the rights of all mankind. It stated that "all men are created equal. . . . They are endowed by their Creator with certain unalienable rights. . . . Among these are life, liberty, and the pursuit of happiness."

On the international scene, the French wanted revenge for the humiliating defeats of the Seven Years' War.

They sympathized with the rebels and supplied guns and gunpowder from the beginning. By 1777 French volunteers were arriving in Virginia, and a dashing young nobleman, the marquis de Lafayette (1757–1834), quickly became one of George Washington's most trusted generals. In 1778 the French government offered a formal alliance to the American ambassador in Paris, Benjamin Franklin, and in 1779 and 1780 the Spanish and Dutch declared war on Britain. Catherine the Great of Russia helped organize the League of Armed Neutrality in order to protect neutral shipping rights, which Britain refused to recognize.

Thus by 1780 Great Britain was engaged in an imperial war against most of Europe as well as against the thirteen colonies. In these circumstances, and in the face of severe reverses, a new British government decided to cut its losses and offered peace on extremely generous terms. By the Treaty of Paris of 1783, Britain recognized the independence of the thirteen colonies and ceded all its territory between the Allegheny Mountains and the Mississippi River to the Americans. Out of the bitter rivalries of the Old World, the Americans snatched dominion over a vast territory.

Europeans who dreamed of a new era were fascinated by the political lessons of the American Revolution. The Americans had begun with a revolutionary defense against tyrannical oppression, and they had been victorious. They had then shown how rational beings could assemble together to exercise sovereignty and write a permanent constitution—a new social contract. All this gave greater reality to the concepts of individual liberty and representative government and reinforced one of the primary ideas of the Enlightenment: that a better world was possible.

No country felt the consequences of the American Revolution more directly than France. Hundreds of French officers served in America and were inspired by the experience, the marquis de Lafayette chief among them. French intellectuals and publicists engaged in passionate analysis of the new federal Constitution as well as the constitutions of the various states of the new United States. Perhaps more importantly, the expenses of supporting the revolutionary forces provided the last nail in the coffin for the French treasury.

Financial Crisis

The French Revolution thus had its immediate origins in the financial difficulties of the government. The efforts of Louis XV's ministers to raise taxes had been thwarted by the high courts, led by the Parlement of Paris, which was strengthened in its opposition by widespread popular support. When renewed efforts to reform the tax system met a similar fate in 1776, the government was forced to finance all of its enormous expenditures during the American war with borrowed money. As a result, the national debt and the annual budget deficit soared.

By the 1780s, fully 50 percent of France's annual budget went for interest payments on the debt. Another 25 percent went to maintain the military, while 6 percent was absorbed by the king and his court at Versailles. Less than 20 percent of the entire national budget was available for the productive functions of the state, such as transportation and general administration. This was an impossible financial situation.

One way out would have been for the government to declare partial bankruptcy, forcing its creditors to accept greatly reduced payments on the debt. The Spanish monarchy had regularly repudiated large portions of its debt in earlier times, and France had done likewise after an attempt to establish a national bank ended in financial disaster in 1720. Yet by the 1780s the French debt was being held by an army of aristocratic and bourgeois creditors, and the French monarchy, though absolute in theory, had become too weak for such a drastic and unpopular action.

Nor could the king and his ministers print money and create inflation to cover their deficits. Unlike England and Holland, which had far larger national debts relative to their populations, France had no central bank, no paper currency, and no means of creating credit. French money was good gold coin. Therefore, when a depressed economy and public distrust made it increasingly difficult for the government to obtain new gold loans in 1786, it had no alternative but to try to increase taxes. Since France's tax system was unfair and out-of-date, increased revenues were possible only through fundamental reform. Such reforms, which would affect all groups in France's complex and fragmented society, opened a Pandora's box of social and political demands.

The Revolution was looming by 1787, though no one could have realized what was to follow. Spurred by a depressed economy and falling tax receipts, Louis XVI's minister of finance revived old proposals to impose a general tax on all landed property as well as to form provincial assemblies to help administer the tax, and he convinced the king to call an **Assembly of Notables** to gain support for the idea. The notables, who were mainly important noblemen and high-ranking clergy, opposed the new tax. In exchange for their support, they demanded that control over all government spending be given to the provincial assemblies. When the government refused, the notables responded that such sweeping tax changes required the approval of the Estates General, the representative body of all three estates, which had not met since 1614.

Facing imminent bankruptcy, the king tried to reassert his authority. He dismissed the notables and established new taxes by decree. In stirring language, the judges of the Parlement of Paris promptly declared the royal initiative null and void. When the king tried to exile the judges, a tremendous wave of protest swept the country. Frightened investors also refused to advance more loans to the state. Finally, in July 1788, Louis XVI bowed to public opinion and called for a spring session of the Estates General.

Revolution in Metropole and Colony, 1789–1791

Although inspired by the ideals of the American Revolution, the French Revolution did not mirror the American example. It was more radical and more complex, more influential and more controversial, more loved and more hated. For Europeans and most of the rest of the world, it was the great revolution of the eighteenth century, *the* revolution that opened the modern era in politics. In turn, the slave insurrection in Saint-Domingue—which ultimately resulted in the second independent republic of the Americas—inspired liberation movements across the world.

- What were the immediate events that sparked the Revolution, and how did they result in the formation of a constitutional monarchy in France? How did the ideals and events of the early Revolution raise new aspirations in the colonies?

The Formation of the National Assembly

Once Louis had agreed to hold the **Estates General,** following precedent, he set elections for the three orders. As at previous meetings of the Estates General, local assemblies were to prepare a list of grievances for their representatives to bring to the next electoral level. This request, as traditional as it was, set off a flood of debate, criticism, and demands throughout France. All across the country, clergy, nobles, and commoners came together in their respective orders to draft petitions for change and to elect delegates to the Estates General. These documents reveal the main complaints French subjects had on the eve of revolution. The local assemblies of the clergy showed considerable dissatisfaction with the church hierarchy. The nobles were politically divided. A conservative majority was drawn from the poorer and more numerous provincial nobility, but fully one-third of the nobility's representatives were liberals committed to major changes.

As for the third estate, there was great popular participation in the elections. Almost all male commoners twenty-five years of age and older had the right to vote. However, most of the representatives selected by the third estate were well-educated, prosperous members of the middle class. Most were not businessmen but rather lawyers and government officials. Social status and prestige were matters of particular concern to this economic elite. No delegates from the great mass of laboring poor—the peasants and urban artisans—were elected.

The petitions for change coming from the three estates showed a surprising degree of consensus. There was general agreement that royal absolutism should give way to a constitutional monarchy in which laws and taxes would require the consent of the Estates General in regular meetings. All agreed that individual liberties would have to be guaranteed by law and that economic regulations should be loosened. The striking similarities in the grievance petitions of the clergy, nobility, and third estate reflected a shared commitment to a basic reform platform among the educated elite.

Online Study Center Improve Your Grade
Primary Source: The Third Estate Speaks: The Cahier de Doleances of the Carcassonne

Yet an increasingly bitter quarrel undermined this consensus during the intense electoral campaign: *how* would the Estates General vote, and precisely *who* would lead in the political reorganization that was generally desired? The Estates General of 1614 had sat as three separate houses. Each house held one vote, despite the enormous numerical discrepancies between the estates in the general population. Given the close ties between them, the nobility and clergy would control all decisions. As soon as the estates were called, the aristocratic Parlement of Paris, mainly out of respect for tradition but partly out of a desire to enhance the nobility's political position, ruled that the Estates General should once again sit separately. The ruling was quickly denounced by some intellectuals, who demanded instead a single assembly dominated by the third estate to ensure fundamental reforms. In his famous 1789 pamphlet *What Is the Third Estate?* the abbé Emmanuel Joseph Sieyès argued that the nobility was a tiny, overprivileged minority and that the neglected third estate constituted the true strength of the French nation. When the government agreed that the third estate should have as many delegates as the clergy and the nobility combined but then rendered this act meaningless by upholding voting by separate order, reform-minded critics saw fresh evidence of an aristocratic conspiracy.

In May 1789 the twelve hundred delegates of the three estates paraded in medieval pageantry through the streets of Versailles to an opening session resplendent with feudal magnificence. The estates were almost immediately deadlocked. Delegates of the third estate refused to transact any business until the king ordered the clergy and nobility to sit with them in a single body. Finally, after a six-week war of nerves, a few parish priests began to go over to the third estate, which on June 17 voted to call itself the **National Assembly**. On June 20 the delegates of the third estate, excluded from their hall because of "repairs," moved to a large indoor tennis court. There they swore the famous Oath of the Tennis Court, pledging not to disband until they had written a new constitution.

The king's response was ambivalent. On June 23 he made a conciliatory speech urging reforms to a joint session, and four days later he ordered the three estates to meet together. At the same time, the vacillating and indecisive monarch apparently followed the advice of relatives and court nobles who urged him to dissolve the Estates General by force. The king called an army of eighteen thousand troops toward Versailles, and on July 11 he dismissed his finance minister and his other more liberal ministers. As Louis XVI belatedly reasserted his "divine right" to rule, middle-class delegates and their allies from the liberal nobility resigned themselves to being disbanded at bayonet point. One third-estate delegate reassured a worried colleague, "You won't hang—you'll only have to go back home."³

The Revolt of the Poor and the Oppressed

While delegates of the third estate pressed for political rights, economic hardship gripped the common people. Grain was the basis of the diet of ordinary people in the eighteenth century, and in 1788 the harvest had been extremely poor. The price of bread began to soar. In Paris, where bread was regularly subsidized by the government in an attempt to prevent popular unrest, the price rose to 4 sous. The poor could scarcely afford to pay 2 sous per pound, for even at that price a laborer with a wife and three children had to spend half his wages on the family's bread.

Harvest failure and high bread prices unleashed a classic economic depression of the preindustrial age. With food so expensive and with so much uncertainty, the demand for manufactured goods collapsed. Thousands of artisans and small traders were thrown out of work. By the end of 1789 almost half of the French people would be in need of relief. One person in eight was a pauper living in extreme want. In Paris perhaps 150,000 of the city's 600,000 people were without work in July 1789.

Against this background of poverty and ongoing political crisis, the people of Paris entered decisively onto the revolutionary stage. They believed in a general, though ill-defined, way that the economic distress had human causes. They believed that they should have steady work and enough bread at fair prices to survive. Specifically, they feared that the dismissal of the king's moderate finance minister would put them at the mercy of aristocratic landowners and grain speculators. Rumors that the king's troops would sack the city began to fill the air. Angry crowds formed, and passionate voices urged action. On July 13 the people began to seize arms for the defense of the city as the king's armies moved toward Paris, and on July 14 several hundred people marched to the Bastille to search for weapons and gunpowder.

A medieval fortress with walls ten feet thick and eight great towers each one hundred feet high, the Bastille had long been used as a royal prison. It was guarded by eighty retired soldiers and thirty Swiss mercenaries. The governor of the fortress-prison refused to hand over the powder, panicked, and ordered his men to resist, killing ninety-eight people attempting to enter. Cannon were brought to batter the main gate, and fighting continued until the prison surrendered. The governor of the prison was later hacked to death, and his head was stuck on a pike and paraded through the streets. The next day a committee of citizens appointed the marquis de Lafayette commander of the city's armed forces. Paris was lost to the king, who was forced to recall the finance minister and disperse his troops. The popular uprising had broken the power monopoly of the royal army and thereby saved the National Assembly.

Online Study Center Improve Your Grade
Primary Source: The Taking of the Bastille and Its Aftermath: An English Perspective

As the delegates resumed their inconclusive debates at Versailles, the countryside sent them a radical and unmistakable message. Throughout France peasants began to rise in insurrection against their lords, ransacking manor houses and burning feudal documents that recorded their obligations. In some areas peasants reinstated traditional village practices, undoing recent enclosures and re-occupying old common lands. They seized forests, and taxes went unpaid. Fear of vagabonds and outlaws—called the **Great Fear** by contemporaries—seized the countryside and fanned the flames of rebellion. The long-suffering peasants were doing their best to free themselves from manorial rights and exploitation.

Faced with chaos, yet afraid to call on the king to restore order, some liberal nobles and middle-class delegates at Versailles responded to peasant demands with a surprise maneuver on the night of August 4, 1789. The duke of Aiguillon, also notably one of France's greatest noble landowners, declared that

> in several provinces the whole people forms a kind of league for the destruction of the manor houses, the ravaging of the lands, and especially for the seizure of the archives where the title deeds to feudal properties are kept. It seeks to throw off at last a yoke that has for many centuries weighted it down.[4]

He urged equality in taxation and the elimination of feudal dues. In the end, all the old noble privileges—peasant serfdom where it still existed, exclusive hunting rights, fees for justice, village monopolies, the right to make peasants work on the roads, and a host of other dues—were abolished. Thus the French peasantry, which already owned about 30 percent of all the land, achieved an unprecedented victory in the early days of revolutionary upheaval. Henceforth, French peasants would seek mainly to protect and consolidate their triumph. As the Great Fear subsided in the countryside, they became a force for order and stability.

A Limited Monarchy

The National Assembly moved forward. On August 27, 1789, it issued the Declaration of the Rights of Man and of the Citizen, which stated, "Men are born and remain free and equal in rights." The declaration also maintained that mankind's natural rights are "liberty, property, security, and resistance to oppression" and that "every man is presumed innocent until he is proven guilty." As for law, "it is an expression of the general will; all citizens have the right to concur personally or through their representatives in its formation. . . . Free expression of thoughts and opinions is one of the most precious rights of mankind: every citizen may therefore speak, write, and publish freely." In short, this clarion call of the liberal revolutionary ideal guaranteed equality before the law, representative government for a sovereign people, and individual freedom. This revolutionary credo, only two pages long, was disseminated throughout France and Europe and around the world.

Online Study Center Improve Your Grade
Primary Source: The Declaration of the Rights of Man and of the Citizen

Moving beyond general principles to draft a constitution proved difficult. The questions of how much power the king should retain and whether he could permanently veto legislation led to another deadlock. Once again the decisive answer came from the poor—in this instance, the poor women of Paris.

Women customarily bought the food and managed the poor family's slender resources. In Paris great numbers of women also worked for wages, making garments and luxury items destined for an aristocratic and international clientele. Immediately after the fall of the Bastille, many of France's great court nobles began to leave Versailles for foreign lands, so that a plummeting demand for luxuries intensified the general economic crisis. International markets also declined. The church was no longer able to give its traditional grants of food and money to the poor. Increasing unemployment and hunger put tremendous pressure on household managers, and the result was another popular explosion.

On October 5 some seven thousand desperate women marched the twelve miles from Paris to Versailles to demand action. A middle-class deputy looking out from the Assembly saw "multitudes arriving from Paris including fishwives and bullies from the market, and these people wanted nothing but bread." This great crowd invaded the Assembly, "armed with scythes, sticks and pikes." One tough old woman defiantly shouted into the debate, "Who's that talking down there? Make the chatterbox shut up. That's not the point: the point is that we want bread."[5] Hers was the genuine voice of the people, essential to any understanding of the French Revolution.

The women invaded the royal apartments, slaughtered some of the royal bodyguards, and furiously searched for the queen, Marie Antoinette, who was widely despised for her frivolous and supposedly immoral behavior. "We are going to cut off her head, tear out her heart, fry her liver, and that won't be the end of it," they shouted, surging through the palace in a frenzy. It seems likely that only the intervention of Lafayette and the National Guard saved the royal family. But the only way to calm the disorder was for the king to live in Paris, as the crowd demanded.

The next day the royal family left for Paris in the midst of a strange procession. The heads of two aristocrats, stuck on pikes, led the way. They were followed by the

The Women of Paris March to Versailles On October 5, 1789, a large group of Parisian market women marched to Versailles to protest the price of bread. For the people of Paris, the king was the baker of last resort, responsible for feeding his people during times of scarcity. The crowd forced the royal family to return with them and to live in Paris, rather than remain isolated from their subjects at court. *(Erich Lessing/Art Resource, NY)*

remaining members of the royal bodyguard, unarmed and mocked by fierce men holding sabers and pikes. A mixed and victorious multitude surrounded the carriage of the captured royal family, hurling crude insults at the queen. There was drinking and eating among the women, who had emerged as a major element in the Parisian revolutionary crowd.[6]

The National Assembly followed the king to Paris, and the next two years, until September 1791, saw the consolidation of the liberal revolution. Under middle-class leadership, the National Assembly abolished the French nobility as a legal order and pushed forward with the creation of a **constitutional monarchy,** which Louis XVI reluctantly agreed to accept in July 1790. In the final constitution, the king remained the head of state, but all lawmaking power was placed in the hands of the National Assembly, elected by the economic upper half of French males.

New laws broadened women's rights to seek divorce, to inherit property, and to obtain financial support for illegitimate children from fathers. But women were not allowed to vote or hold political office for at least two reasons. First, the great majority of comfortable, well-educated males in the National Assembly believed that women should be limited to child rearing and domestic duties and should leave politics and most public activities to men, as Rousseau had advocated in his influential writings (see page 607). Second, the delegates to the National Assembly were convinced that political life in absolutist France had been profoundly corrupt and that a prime example of this corruption was the way that some talented but immoral aristocratic women had used their sexual charms to manipulate weak rulers and their ministers. Thus delegates argued that excluding women from politics would help create the civic virtue that had been missing: pure, home-focused wives would raise the high-minded sons needed to govern the nation.

The National Assembly replaced the complicated patchwork of historic provinces with eighty-three departments of approximately equal size. The jumble of weights and measures that varied from province to province was reformed, leading to the introduction of the metric system in 1793. Monopolies, guilds, and workers' associations were prohibited, and barriers to trade within France were abolished in the name of economic liberty. Thus the National Assembly applied the critical spirit of the Enlightenment in a thorough reform of France's laws and institutions.

The Assembly also imposed a radical reorganization on the country's religious life. It granted religious freedom to the small minority of French Jews and Protestants. Of greater impact, it then nationalized the Catholic Church's property and abolished monasteries as useless relics of a distant past. The government used all former church property as collateral to guarantee a new paper currency, the assignats, and then sold the property in an attempt to put the state's finances on a solid footing. Although the church's land was sold in large blocks, peasants eventually purchased much when it was subdivided. These purchases strengthened their attachment to the new revolutionary order in the countryside.

The religious reorganization of France brought the new government into conflict with the Catholic Church and many sincere Christians, especially in the countryside. Imbued with the rationalism and skepticism of the eighteenth-century philosophes, many delegates distrusted popular piety and "superstitious religion." Thus they established a national church, with priests chosen by voters. The National Assembly then forced the Catholic clergy to take a loyalty oath to the new government. The pope formally condemned this attempt to subjugate the church, and only half the priests of France swore the oath. The result was a deep religious divide within the country and the clergy. The attempt to remake the Catholic Church, like the Assembly's abolition of guilds and workers associations, sharpened the conflict between the educated classes and the common people that had been emerging in the eighteenth century. This policy toward the church was the revolutionary government's first important failure.

Revolutionary Aspirations in Saint-Domingue

The French Revolution radically transformed not only the territorial nation of France but its overseas colonies as well. On the eve of the Revolution, Saint-Domingue—the most profitable of all Caribbean colonies—was even more rife with social tensions than France itself. In addition to distinctions between noble and commoner or rich and poor, Saint-Domingue harbored divisions between free and unfree and a racial spectrum that included black, mixed race, and white people.

The colony's slave population was at least five hundred thousand, in comparison to a white population of approximately forty thousand. Because the brutal conditions created very high death rates among slaves, traders brought a constant stream of new arrivals from Africa. In 1789 up to two-thirds of slaves in Saint-Domingue had been born in Africa, most in the west-central region of the continent. Many were veterans of wars in Africa.

The free population was divided by color and by wealth. The European population included French colonial officials, wealthy planters and merchants, and poor immigrants. A sizable population of free people of African and mixed African European descent also existed, who referred to themselves as "free coloreds" or **free people of color.** They varied from modest artisans, to plantation managers and clerks, to wealthy established planters who owned slaves themselves. Failing to achieve their dreams of a colonial fortune, poor whites bitterly resented the privileges of the others, especially the free-colored elite. The white elite harbored its own grudges against France's monopoly on colonial trade and the royal government's attempts in the 1780s to impose legislation requiring humane treatment of slaves.

The 1685 *Code noir* (Black Code) that set the parameters of slavery had granted free people of color the same legal status as whites: they could own property, live where they wished, and pursue any education or career they desired. From the 1760s on, however, colonial administrators began rescinding these rights, and by the time of the Revolution, myriad aspects of free coloreds' lives—from the professions they could practice, to the names they could adopt, to the clothes they could wear—were ruled by discriminatory laws. White planters eagerly welcomed these laws, convinced that the best defense of slavery was a rigid color line.

The political and intellectual turmoil of the 1780s, with its growing rhetoric of liberty, equality, and fraternity, raised new challenges and possibilities for each of these groups. For slaves, news of abolitionist movements in France, and the royal government's own attempts to rein in the worst abuses of slavery, led to hopes that the mother country might grant them freedom. Free people of color found in such rhetoric the principles on which to base a defense of their legal and political rights. They looked to political reforms in Paris as a means of gaining political enfranchisement and reasserting equal status with whites. The white elite, not surprisingly, saw matters very differently. Infuriated by talk of abolition and determined to protect their way of life, they looked to revolutionary ideals of representative government for the chance to gain control of their own affairs, as had the American colonists before them. The meeting of the Estates General and the Declaration of the Rights of Man raised these conflicting colonial aspirations.

The Assembly, however, frustrated the hopes of both groups. Cowed by colonial representatives who claimed that support for free coloreds would result in slave insurrection and independence, the Assembly refused to extend French constitutional safeguards to the colonies. Instead, it ruled that each colony would draft its own constitution, with free rein over decisions on slavery and the enfranchisement of free people of color. After dealing this blow to the aspirations of slaves and free coloreds, the committee also reaffirmed French monopolies over colonial trade, thereby angering planters as well.

In July 1790 Vincent Ogé, a free man of color, returned to Saint-Domingue from Paris determined to redress these issues. He raised an army of several hundred, occupied the town of Grande-Rivière, and sent letters to the new Provincial Assembly of Saint-Domingue demanding political rights for all free citizens, a statute already passed in France. After initial victories, his army was defeated, and Ogé himself was tortured and executed. In an attempt to forge compromise, in May 1791 the National Assembly granted political rights to free people of color born to two free parents who possessed sufficient property. When news of this legislation arrived in Saint-Domingue, the white elite was furious and the colonial governor refused to enact it. Violence now erupted between groups of whites and free coloreds in parts of the colony. The liberal revolution had failed to satisfy the contradictory ambitions in the colonies.

World War and Republican France, 1791–1799

When Louis XVI accepted the final version of the National Assembly's constitution in September 1791, a young and still obscure provincial lawyer and delegate named Maximilien Robespierre (1758–1794) concluded, "The Revolution is over." Robespierre was both right and wrong. He was right in the sense that the most constructive and lasting reforms were in place. Nothing substantial in the way of liberty and fundamental reform would be gained in the next generation. He was wrong in the sense that a much more radical stage lay ahead. New heroes and new ideologies were to emerge in revolutionary wars and international conflict in which Robespierre himself would play a central role.

- *How and why did the Revolution take a radical turn at home and in the colonies?*

Foreign Reactions and the Beginning of War

The outbreak and progress of revolution in France produced great excitement and a sharp division of opinion in Europe and the United States. Liberals and radicals saw a mighty triumph of liberty over despotism. In Great Britain especially, they hoped that the French example would lead to a fundamental reordering of Parliament, which was in the hands of the aristocracy and a few wealthy merchants. After the French Revolution began, conservative leaders such as Edmund Burke (1729–1797) were deeply troubled by the aroused spirit of reform. In 1790 Burke published *Reflections on the Revolution in France,* one of the great defenses of European conservatism. He defended inherited privileges in general and those of the English monarchy and aristocracy. He glorified the unrepresentative Parliament and predicted that thoroughgoing reform like that occurring in France would lead only to chaos and tyranny. Burke's work sparked much debate.

One passionate rebuttal came from a young writer in London, Mary Wollstonecraft (1759–1797). Born into the middle class, Wollstonecraft was schooled in adversity by a mean-spirited father who beat his wife and squandered his inherited fortune. Determined to be independent in a society that expected women of her class to become obedient wives, she struggled for years to earn her living as a governess and a teacher—practically the only acceptable careers for single, educated women—before attaining success as a translator and author. Incensed by Burke's book, Wollstonecraft immediately wrote a blistering, widely read attack, *A Vindication of the Rights of Man* (1790).

Then she made a daring intellectual leap, developing for the first time the logical implications of natural-law philosophy in her masterpiece, *A Vindication of the Rights of Woman* (1792). To fulfill the still-unrealized potential of the French Revolution and to eliminate the sexual inequality she had felt so keenly, she demanded that

> the Rights of Women be respected . . . [and] JUSTICE for one-half of the human race. . . . It is time to effect a revolution in female manners, time to restore to them their lost dignity, and make them, as part of the human species, labor, by reforming themselves, to reform the world.

Setting high standards for women—"I wish to persuade women to endeavor to acquire strength, both of mind and body"—Wollstonecraft broke with those who had a low opinion of women's intellectual potential. She advocated rigorous coeducation, which would make women better wives and mothers, good citizens, and economically independent. Women could manage businesses and enter politics if only men would give them the chance. Men themselves would benefit from women's rights, for Wollstonecraft believed that "the two sexes mutually corrupt and improve each other."[7] Wollstonecraft's analysis testified to the power of the Revolution to excite and inspire outside of France. Paralleling ideas put forth independently in France by Olympe de Gouges (1748–1793), a self-taught writer and woman of the people (see the feature "Listening to the Past: Revolution and Women's Rights" on pages 714–715), Wollstonecraft's work marked the birth of the modern women's movement for equal rights, and it was ultimately very influential.

Online Study Center **Improve Your Grade**
Primary Source: A Feminist Analysis of Natural Law and the Rights of Women

The kings and nobles of continental Europe, who had at first welcomed the revolution in France as weakening a competing power, began to feel no less threatened than did Burke and his supporters. In June 1791, Louis XVI and Marie Antoinette were arrested and returned to Paris after trying unsuccessfully to slip out of France. The shock of this arrest led the monarchs of Austria and Prussia to issue the Declaration of Pillnitz in August 1791. This carefully worded statement declared their willingness to intervene in France in certain circumstances and was expected to have a sobering effect on revolutionary France without causing war.

But the crowned heads of Europe misjudged the revolutionary spirit in France. When the National Assembly disbanded, it sought popular support by decreeing that none of its members would be eligible for election to the new Legislative Assembly. This meant that when the new representative body convened in October 1791, it had a different character. The great majority of the legislators were still prosperous, well-educated middle-class men, but they were younger and less cautious than their predecessors. Many of the deputies belonged to a political club called the **Jacobin club,** after the name of the former monastery in which they held their meetings. Such clubs had proliferated in Parisian neighborhoods since the beginning of the Revolution, drawing men and women to debate the burning political questions of the day.

The Capture of Louis XVI, June 1791 This painting commemorates a dramatic turning point in the French Revolution, the midnight arrest of Louis XVI and the royal family as they tried to flee France in disguise and reach counter-revolutionaries in the Austrian Netherlands. Recognized and stopped at Varennes, just forty miles from the border, the king still nearly succeeded, telling municipal officers that dangerous mobs controlled Paris and securing promises of safe passage. But within hours the local leaders reversed themselves, and by morning Louis XVI was headed back to Paris. (*Bibliothèque nationale de France*)

The new representatives to the Assembly were passionately committed to the Revolution and distrustful of monarchy after Louis's attempted flight. They increasingly lumped "useless aristocrats" and "despotic monarchs" together, and they whipped themselves into a patriotic fury with bombastic oratory. If the courts of Europe were attempting to incite a war of kings against France, then "we will incite a war of people against kings.... Ten million Frenchmen, kindled by the fire of liberty, armed with the sword, with reason, with eloquence would be able to change the face of the world and make the tyrants tremble on their thrones."[8] Only Robespierre and a very few others argued that people would not welcome liberation at the point of a gun. Such warnings were brushed aside. France would "rise to the full height of her mission," as one deputy urged. In April 1792 France declared war on Francis II, the Habsburg monarch.

France's crusade against tyranny went poorly at first. Prussia joined Austria in the Austrian Netherlands (present-day Belgium), and French forces broke and fled at their first encounter with armies of this First Coalition. The road to Paris lay open, and it is possible that only conflict between the Eastern monarchs over the division of Poland saved France from defeat.

Military reversals and patriotic fervor led the Legislative Assembly to declare the country in danger. Volunteer armies from the provinces streamed through Paris, fraternizing with the people and singing patriotic songs like the stirring "Marseillaise," later the French national anthem. In this supercharged wartime atmosphere, rumors of treason by the king and queen spread in Paris. On August 10, 1792, a revolutionary crowd attacked the royal palace at the Tuileries, capturing it after heavy fighting with the Swiss Guards. The king and his family fled for their lives to the nearby Legislative Assembly, which suspended the king from all his functions, imprisoned him, and called for a new National Convention to be elected by universal male suffrage. Monarchy in France was on its deathbed, mortally wounded by war and popular upheaval.

The Second Revolution

The fall of the monarchy marked a rapid radicalization of the Revolution, a phase that historians often call the **second revolution.** Louis's imprisonment was followed by the September Massacres. Wild stories that imprisoned counter-revolutionary aristocrats and priests were plotting with the allied invaders seized the city. As a result, angry crowds invaded the prisons of Paris and slaughtered half the men and women they found. In late September 1792 the new, popularly elected National Convention proclaimed France a republic.

The republic sought to create a new popular culture, fashioning compelling symbols that broke with the past and glorified the new order. It adopted a brand-new revolutionary calendar, which eliminated saints' days and renamed the days and the months after the seasons of the year. The republic energetically promoted broad, open-air, democratic festivals. These spectacles brought the entire population together and sought to redirect the people's traditional enthusiasm for Catholic religious celebrations to secular holidays instilling republican virtue and a love of nation. These spectacles were less successful in villages than in cities, where popular interest in politics was greater and Catholicism was weaker.

All the members of the National Convention were republicans, and at the beginning almost all belonged to the Jacobin club of Paris. But the Jacobins themselves were increasingly divided into two bitterly competitive groups—the **Girondists,** named after a department in southwestern France that was home to several of their leaders, and **the Mountain,** led by Robespierre and another young lawyer, Georges Jacques Danton. The Mountain was so called because its members sat on the uppermost benches on the left side of the assembly hall. A majority of the indecisive Convention members, seated in the "Plain" below, floated back and forth between the rival factions.

This division emerged clearly after the National Convention overwhelmingly convicted Louis XVI of treason. The Girondists accepted his guilt but did not wish to put the king to death. By a narrow majority, the Mountain carried the day, and Louis was executed on January 21, 1793, on the newly invented guillotine. One of his last statements was "I am innocent and shall die without fear. I would that my death might bring happiness to the French, and ward off the dangers which I foresee."[9]

Both the Girondists and the Mountain were determined to continue the "war against tyranny." The Prussians had been stopped at the Battle of Valmy on September 20, 1792, one day before the republic was proclaimed. French armies then invaded Savoy and captured Nice, moved into the German Rhineland, and by November 1792 were occupying the entire Austrian Netherlands. Everywhere they went French armies of occupation chased the princes, "abolished feudalism," and found support among some peasants and middle-class people.

But the French armies also lived off the land, requisitioning food and supplies and plundering local treasures. The liberators looked increasingly like foreign invaders.

International tensions mounted. In February 1793 the National Convention, at war with Austria and Prussia, declared war on Britain, Holland, and Spain as well. Republican France was now at war with almost all of Europe, a great war that would last almost without interruption until 1815.

As the forces of the First Coalition drove the French from the Austrian Netherlands, peasants in western France revolted against being drafted into the army. They were supported and encouraged in their resistance by devout Catholics, royalists, and foreign agents. In Paris the National Convention was locked in a life-and-death political struggle between the Girondists and the Mountain. Both groups were sincere republicans, hating privilege and wanting to temper economic liberalism with social concern. Yet personal hatreds ran deep. The Girondists feared a bloody dictatorship by the Mountain, and the Mountain was no less convinced that the more moderate Girondists would turn to conservatives and even royalists in order to retain power.

With the middle-class delegates so bitterly divided, the laboring poor of Paris emerged as the decisive political factor. The laboring men and women of Paris always constituted—along with the peasantry in the summer of 1789—the elemental force that drove the Revolution forward. It was the artisans, day laborers, market women, and garment workers who had stormed the Bastille, marched on Versailles, driven the king from the Tuileries, and carried out the September Massacres. The laboring poor and the petty traders were often known as the **sans-culottes,** "without breeches," because sans-culottes men wore trousers instead of the knee breeches of the aristocracy and the solid middle class. The immediate interests of the sans-culottes were mainly economic, and in spring 1793 rapid inflation, unemployment, and food shortages were again weighing heavily on poor families.

Moreover, by spring 1793 the sans-culottes had become keenly interested in politics. Encouraged by the so-called angry men, such as the passionate young ex-priest and journalist Jacques Roux, sans-culottes men and women were demanding radical political action to guarantee them their daily bread. At first the Mountain joined the Girondists in rejecting these demands. But in the face of military defeat, peasant revolt, and hatred of the Girondists, the Mountain and especially Robespierre became more sympathetic. The Mountain joined with sans-culottes activists in the city government to engineer a popular uprising that forced the Convention to arrest thirty-one Girondist deputies for treason on June 2. All power passed to the Mountain.

Robespierre and others from the Mountain joined the recently formed Committee of Public Safety, to which the Convention had given dictatorial power to deal with the national emergency. These developments in Paris triggered revolt in leading provincial cities, such as Lyons and Marseilles, where moderates denounced Paris and demanded a decentralized government. The peasant revolt spread, and the republic's armies were driven back on all fronts. By July 1793 only the areas around Paris and on the eastern frontier were firmly held by the central government. Defeat seemed imminent.

Total War and the Terror

A year later, in July 1794, the Austrian Netherlands and the Rhineland were once again in the hands of conquering French armies, and the First Coalition was falling apart. This remarkable change of fortune was due to the revolutionary government's success in harnessing, for perhaps the first time in history, the explosive forces of a planned economy, revolutionary terror, and modern nationalism in a total war effort.

Robespierre and the Committee of Public Safety advanced with implacable resolution on several fronts in 1793 and 1794. First, they collaborated with the fiercely patriotic and democratic sans-culottes, who retained the common people's traditional faith in fair prices and a moral economic order and who distrusted most wealthy capitalists and all aristocrats. Thus Robespierre and his coworkers established, as best they could, a **planned economy** with egalitarian social overtones. Rather than let supply and demand determine prices, the government set maximum allowable prices for key products. Though the state was too weak to enforce all its price regulations, it did fix the price of bread in Paris at levels the poor could afford. Rationing was introduced, and bakers were permitted to make only the "bread of equality"—a brown bread made of a mixture of all available flours. White bread and pastries were outlawed as luxuries. The poor of Paris may not have eaten well, but at least they ate.

They also worked, mainly to produce arms and munitions for the war effort. The government told craftsmen what to produce, nationalized many small workshops, and requisitioned raw materials and grain. Sometimes planning and control did not go beyond orders to meet the latest emergency. But failures to control and coordinate were failures of means and not of desire. The second revolution and the ascendancy of the sans-culottes had produced an embryonic emergency socialism, which thoroughly frightened Europe's propertied classes and

Contrasting Visions of the Sans-Culottes The woman on the left, with her playful cat and calm simplicity, suggests how the French sans-culottes saw themselves as democrats and virtuous citizens. The ferocious sans-culotte harpy on the right, a creation of wartime England's vivid counter-revolutionary imagination, screams for more blood, more death: "I am the Goddess of Liberty! Long live the guillotine!" *(Bibliothèque nationale de France)*

had great influence on the subsequent development of socialist ideology.

Second, while radical economic measures supplied the poor with bread and the armies with weapons, the **Reign of Terror** (1793–1794) used revolutionary terror to solidify the home front. Special revolutionary courts responsible only to Robespierre's Committee of Public Safety tried rebels and "enemies of the nation" for political crimes. Drawing on popular support centered in the local Jacobin clubs, these local courts ignored normal legal procedures and judged severely. Some forty thousand French men and women were executed or died in prison. Another three hundred thousand suspects were arrested.

Robespierre's Reign of Terror is one of the most controversial phases of the French Revolution. Most historians now believe that the Reign of Terror was not directed against any single class. Rather, it was a political weapon directed impartially against all who might oppose the revolutionary government. For many Europeans of the time, however, the Reign of Terror represented a frightening perversion of the generous ideals of 1789, strengthening the belief that France had foolishly replaced a weak king with a bloody dictatorship.

The third and perhaps most decisive element in the French republic's victory over the First Coalition was its ability to draw on the explosive power of patriotic dedication to a national state and a national mission. An essential part of modern **nationalism**, this commitment was something new in history. With a common language and a common tradition newly reinforced by the ideas of popular sovereignty and democracy, large numbers of French people were stirred by a common loyalty. They developed an intense emotional commitment to the defense of the nation, and they imagined the nation as a great loving family that included all right-thinking patriots. In such circumstances war was no longer the gentlemanly game of the eighteenth century, but rather total war, a life-and-death struggle between good and evil.

The French Revolution

May 5, 1789	Estates General convene at Versailles.
June 17, 1789	Third estate declares itself the National Assembly.
June 20, 1789	Oath of the Tennis Court is sworn.
July 14, 1789	Storming of the Bastille occurs.
July–August 1789	Great Fear ravages the countryside.
August 4, 1789	National Assembly abolishes feudal privileges.
August 27, 1789	National Assembly issues Declaration of the Rights of Man and of the Citizen.
October 5, 1789	Women march on Versailles and force royal family to return to Paris.
November 1789	National Assembly confiscates church lands.
July 1790	Civil Constitution of the Clergy establishes a national church. Louis XVI reluctantly agrees to accept a constitutional monarchy.
June 1791	Royal family is arrested while attempting to flee France.
August 1791	Austria and Prussia issue the Declaration of Pillnitz. Slave insurrections break out in Saint-Domingue.
April 1792	France declares war on Austria. Legislative Assembly enfranchises free people of color.
August 1792	Parisian mob attacks the palace and takes Louis XVI prisoner.
September 1792	September Massacres occur. National Convention declares France a republic and abolishes monarchy.
January 1793	Louis XVI is executed.
February 1793	France declares war on Britain, Holland, and Spain. Revolts take place in some provincial cities.
March 1793	Bitter struggle occurs in the National Convention between Girondists and the Mountain.
April–June 1793	Robespierre and the Mountain organize the Committee of Public Safety and arrest Girondist leaders.
September 1793	Price controls are instituted to aid the sans-culottes and mobilize the war effort. British troops invade Saint-Domingue.
1793–1794	Reign of Terror darkens Paris and the provinces.
February 1794	National Convention abolishes slavery in all French territories.
Spring 1794	French armies are victorious on all fronts.
July 1794	Robespierre is executed. Thermidorian reaction begins.
1795–1799	The Directory rules.
1795	Economic controls are abolished, and suppression of the sans-culottes begins. Toussaint L'Ouverture named brigadier general.
1797	Napoleon defeats Austrian armies in Italy and returns triumphant to Paris.
1798	Austria, Great Britain, and Russia form the Second Coalition against France.
1799	Napoleon overthrows the Directory and seizes power.

Everyone had to participate in the national effort. According to a famous decree of August 23, 1793:

The young men shall go to battle and the married men shall forge arms. The women shall make tents and clothes, and shall serve in the hospitals; children shall tear rags into lint. The old men will be guided to the public places of the cities to kindle the courage of the young warriors and to preach the unity of the Republic and the hatred of kings.

The all-out mobilization of French resources under the Terror combined with the fervor of modern nationalism to create an awesome fighting machine. After August 1793 all unmarried young men were subject to the draft, and by January 1794 the French had about eight hundred thousand soldiers on active duty in fourteen armies. A force of this size was unprecedented in the history of European warfare, and recent research concludes that the French armed forces outnumbered their enemies almost four to one.[10] Well trained, well equipped, and constantly indoctrinated, the enormous armies of the republic were led by young, impetuous generals. These generals often had risen from the ranks, and they personified the opportunities the Revolution offered gifted sons of the people. Following orders from Paris to attack relentlessly, French generals used mass assaults at bayonet point to overwhelm the enemy. "No maneuvering, nothing elaborate," declared the fearless General Hoche. "Just cold steel, passion and patriotism."[11] By spring 1794 French armies were victorious on all fronts. The republic was saved.

Revolution in Saint-Domingue

The second stage of revolution in Saint-Domingue also resulted from decisive action from below. In August 1791 slaves, previously fettered witnesses to the confrontation between whites and free coloreds, took events into their own hands. Groups of slaves held a series of nighttime meetings to plan a mass insurrection. These meetings reportedly included religious ceremonies in

Slave Revolt on Saint-Domingue Starting in August 1791 the slaves of Saint-Domingue rose in revolt. *(Giraudon/Art Resource, NY)*

MAP 21.1 **The Haitian Revolution** Neighbored by the Spanish colony of Santo Domingo, Saint-Domingue was the most profitable European colony in the Caribbean. In 1770 the French transferred the capital from Le Cap to Port-au-Prince, which became capital of the newly independent Haiti in 1804. Slave revolts erupted in the north, near Le Cap, in 1791.

which participants made ritual offerings and swore a sacred oath of secrecy and revenge. The rituals belonged to the religious practices, later known as "voodoo," that slaves had created on Saint-Domingue plantations from a combination of Catholicism and African cults. French soldiers later reported that religious incantations and African songs accompanied rebel slaves into combat. African culture thus played an important role in the Saint-Domingue revolution, alongside Enlightenment ideals of freedom and equality.

Revolts began on a few plantations on the night of August 22; within a few days the uprising had swept much of the northern plain, creating a slave army estimated at around 2,000 individuals. By August 27 it was "10,000 strong, divided into 3 armies, of whom 700 or 800 are on horseback, and tolerably well-armed."[12] During the next month slaves attacked and destroyed hundreds of sugar and coffee plantations.

On April 4, 1792, as war loomed with the European states, the National Assembly issued a new decree enfranchising all free blacks and free people of color, but not slaves. The loyalty of free men of color, the Paris government reasoned, was crucial to defeating the slave rebellion and stabilizing the colony.

Warfare in Europe soon spread to Saint-Domingue (see Map 21.1), adding another complicating factor to its racial and political conflicts. Since the beginning of the slave insurrection, the Spanish in neighboring Santo Domingo had supported rebel slaves, and in early 1793 they began to bring slave leaders and their soldiers into the Spanish army. Toussaint L'Ouverture, a freed slave who had joined the slave revolt, was named a Spanish officer. The British navy also blockaded the colony, and invading British troops captured French territory on the island. For the Spanish and British, revolutionary chaos provided a tempting opportunity to capture a profitable colony.

Desperate for forces to oppose France's enemies, the commissioners sent by the newly elected National Convention turned to slaves. They began by promising freedom to those who fought for France. By October 1793 they had abolished slavery throughout the colony. On February 4, 1794, the Convention ratified the **abolition of slavery** and extended it to all French territories, including the Caribbean colonies of Martinique and Guadeloupe. The new constitution of 1795 reaffirmed abolition and the principle that the same laws would apply in the colonies as in metropolitan France. In just four years insurgent slaves had ended centuries of bondage in the French Caribbean and won full political rights.

For the future, the problem loomed of how these rights would be applied. The most immediate question, however, was whether France would be able to retain the colony, which was still under attack by Spanish and British forces. The tide began to turn when Toussaint L'Ouverture switched sides, bringing his military and political skills, along with four thousand well-trained soldiers, to support the French war effort.

By 1796 the French had gradually regained control of the colony, and L'Ouverture had emerged as the key leader of the combined slave and free colored forces. In May 1796 he was named commander of the western province of Saint-Domingue (see Map 21.1). The increasingly conservative nature of the French government during the Thermidorian reaction, however, threatened to undo the gains made by former slaves and free people of color. As exiled planters gained a stronger voice in French policymaking, L'Ouverture and other local leaders grew ever more wary of what the future might hold.

Online Study Center **Improve Your Grade**
Primary Source: A Black Revolutionary Leader in Haiti: Toussaint L'Ouverture

The Thermidorian Reaction and the Directory, 1794–1799

The success of the French armies led Robespierre and the Committee of Public Safety to relax the emergency economic controls, but they extended the political Reign of Terror. In March 1794, to the horror of many sans-culottes, Robespierre's Terror wiped out many of the angry men who had been criticizing Robespierre for being soft on the wealthy and who were led by the radical social democrat Jacques Hébert. Two weeks later, Robespierre sent many of his long-standing collaborators, including the famous orator Danton, up the steps to the guillotine. A strange assortment of radicals and moderates in the Convention, knowing that they might be next, organized a conspiracy. They howled down Robespierre when he tried to speak to the National Convention on 9 Thermidor (July 27, 1794). The next day it was Robespierre's turn to be shaved by the revolutionary razor.

As Robespierre's closest supporters followed their leader to the guillotine, France unexpectedly experienced a thorough reaction to the despotism of the Reign of Terror. In a general way, this **Thermidorian reaction** recalled the early days of the Revolution. The respectable middle-class lawyers and professionals who had led the liberal revolution of 1789 reasserted their authority, drawing support from their own class, the provincial

The Execution of Robespierre The guillotine was painted red and was completely wooden except for the heavy iron blade. Large crowds witnessed the executions in a majestic public square in central Paris, then known as the Place de la Revolution and now called the Place de la Concorde (Harmony Square). *(Snark/Art Resource, NY)*

cities, and the better-off peasants. The National Convention abolished many economic controls, let prices rise sharply, and severely restricted the local political organizations in which the sans-culottes had their strength.

The collapse of economic controls, coupled with runaway inflation, hit the working poor very hard. The sans-culottes accepted private property, but they believed passionately in small business, decent wages, and economic justice. Increasingly disorganized after Robespierre purged radical leaders, the common people of Paris finally revolted against the emerging new order in early 1795. The Convention quickly used the army to suppress these insurrections and made no concessions to the poor. In the face of all these reversals, the revolutionary fervor of the laboring poor in Paris finally subsided. Excluded and disillusioned, the urban poor would have little interest in and influence on politics until 1830.

In villages and small towns there arose a great cry for peace and a turning toward religion, especially from women, who had seldom experienced the political radicalization of sans-culottes women in the big cities. Instead, these women had tenaciously defended their culture and religious beliefs against the often heavy-handed attacks of antireligious revolutionary officials after 1789. As the government began to retreat on the religious question from 1796 to 1801, the women of rural France brought back the Catholic Church and the open worship of God.

As for the middle-class members of the National Convention, in 1795 they wrote yet another constitution that they believed would guarantee their economic position and political supremacy. As in previous elections, the mass of the population voted only for electors, whose number was cut back to men of substantial means. Electors then elected the members of a reorganized legislative assembly as well as key officials throughout France. The new assembly also chose a five-man executive—the Directory.

The Directory continued to support French military expansion abroad. War was no longer so much a crusade as a means to meet ever-present, ever-unsolved economic problems. Large, victorious French armies reduced unemployment at home and were able to live off the territories they conquered and plundered.

The unprincipled action of the Directory reinforced widespread disgust with war and starvation. This general dissatisfaction revealed itself clearly in the national elections of 1797, which returned a large number of conservative and even monarchist deputies who favored peace at almost any price. The members of the Directory, fearing for their skins, used the army to nullify the elections and began to govern dictatorially. Two years later Napoleon Bonaparte ended the Directory in a coup d'état and substituted a strong dictatorship for a weak one. The effort to establish stable representative government had failed.

The Napoleonic Era, 1799–1815

For almost fifteen years, from 1799 to 1814, France was in the hands of a keen-minded military dictator of exceptional ability. One of history's most fascinating leaders, Napoleon Bonaparte (1769–1821) realized the need to put an end to civil strife in France in order to create unity and consolidate his rule. And he did. But Napoleon saw himself as a man of destiny, and the glory of war and the dream of universal empire proved irresistible. For years he spiraled from victory to victory, but in the end he was destroyed by a mighty coalition united in fear of his restless ambition.

- *Why did Napoleon Bonaparte assume control of France, and what factors led to his downfall? How did the new republic of Haiti gain independence from France?*

Napoleon's Rule of France

In 1799 when he seized power, young General Napoleon Bonaparte was a national hero. Born in Corsica into an impoverished noble family in 1769, Napoleon left home and became a lieutenant in the French artillery in 1785. After a brief and unsuccessful adventure fighting for Corsican independence in 1789, he returned to France as a French patriot and a dedicated revolutionary. Rising rapidly in the new army, Napoleon was placed in command of French forces in Italy and won brilliant victories there in 1796 and 1797. His next campaign, in Egypt, was a failure, but Napoleon returned to France before the fiasco was generally known, and his reputation remained intact.

Napoleon soon learned that some prominent members of the legislature were plotting against the Directory. The dissatisfaction of these plotters stemmed not so much from the fact that the Directory was a dictatorship as from the fact that it was a weak dictatorship. Ten years of upheaval and uncertainty had made firm rule much more appealing than liberty and popular politics to these disillusioned revolutionaries. The abbé Sieyès personified this evolution in thinking. In 1789 he had written that the nobility was grossly overprivileged and that the entire people should rule the French nation. Now Sieyès's

The Napoleonic Era

November 1799	Napoleon overthrows the Directory.
December 1799	French voters overwhelmingly approve Napoleon's new constitution.
1800	Napoleon founds the Bank of France.
1801	France defeats Austria and acquires Italian and German territories in the Treaty of Lunéville.
	Napoleon signs the Concordat with the pope.
1802	France signs the Treaty of Amiens with Britain.
	French forces arrive in Saint-Domingue.
April 1803	Toussaint L'Ouverture dies in France.
January 1804	Jean Jacques Dessalines declares Haitian independence.
March 1804	Napoleonic Code comes into force.
December 1804	Napoleon crowns himself emperor.
May 1805	First Haitian constitution promulgated.
October 1805	Britain defeats the French and Spanish fleet at the Battle of Trafalgar.
December 1805	Napoleon defeats Austria and Russia at the Battle of Austerlitz.
1807	Napoleon redraws the map of Europe in the treaties of Tilsit.
1810	The Grand Empire is at its height.
June 1812	Napoleon invades Russia with 600,000 men.
Fall–Winter 1812	Napoleon makes a disastrous retreat from Russia.
March 1814	Russia, Prussia, Austria, and Britain sign the Treaty of Chaumont, pledging alliance to defeat Napoleon.
April 1814	Napoleon abdicates and is exiled to Elba.
February–June 1815	Napoleon escapes from Elba and rules France until he is defeated at the Battle of Waterloo.

motto was "Confidence from below, authority from above."

Like the other members of his group, Sieyès wanted a strong military ruler. The flamboyant thirty-year-old Napoleon was ideal. Thus the conspirators and Napoleon organized a takeover. On November 9, 1799, they ousted the Directors, and the following day soldiers disbanded the legislature at bayonet point. Napoleon was named first consul of the republic, and a new constitution consolidating his position was overwhelmingly approved in a plebiscite in December 1799. Republican appearances were maintained, but Napoleon was already the real ruler of France.

The essence of Napoleon's domestic policy was to use his great and highly personal powers to maintain order and end civil strife. He did so by working out unwritten agreements with powerful groups in France whereby the groups received favors in return for loyal service. Napoleon's bargain with the solid middle class was codified in the famous Civil Code of 1804, which reasserted two of the fundamental principles of the liberal and essentially moderate revolution of 1789: equality of all male citizens before the law and absolute security of wealth and private property. Napoleon and the leading bankers of Paris established the privately owned Bank of France, which loyally served the interests of both the state and the financial oligarchy. Napoleon's defense of the new economic order also appealed successfully to peasants, who had gained both land and status from the revolutionary changes. Thus Napoleon reconfirmed the gains of the peasantry and reassured the solid middle class, which had lost a large number of its revolutionary illusions in the face of social upheaval.

At the same time Napoleon accepted and strengthened the position of the French bureaucracy. Building on the solid foundations that revolutionary governments had inherited from the Old Regime, he perfected a thoroughly centralized state. As recent scholarship shows, Napoleon consolidated his rule by recruiting disillusioned revolutionaries for the network of ministers, prefects, and centrally appointed mayors that depended on him and came to serve him well. Only former revolutionaries who leaned too far to the left or to the right were pushed to the sidelines.[13] Nor were members of the old nobility slighted. In 1800 and again in 1802 Napoleon granted amnesty to one hundred thousand émigrés on the condition that they return to France and take a loyalty oath. Members of this returning elite soon ably occupied many high posts in the expanding centralized state. Only one thousand die-hard monarchists were exempted and remained abroad. Napoleon also created a new imperial nobility in order to reward his most talented generals and officials.

Napoleon's skill in gaining support from important and potentially hostile groups is illustrated by his treatment of the Catholic Church in France. In 1800 the French clergy was still divided into two groups: those who had taken an oath of allegiance to the revolutionary government and those in exile or hiding who had refused to do so. Personally uninterested in religion, Napoleon wanted to heal the religious division so that a united Catholic Church could serve as a bulwark of order and social peace in France. After arduous negotiations, Napoleon and Pope Pius VII (1800–1823) signed the Concordat of 1801. The pope gained the precious right for French Catholics to practice their religion freely, but Napoleon gained political power: his government now nominated bishops, paid the clergy, and exerted great influence over the church in France.

The domestic reforms of Napoleon's early years were his greatest achievement. Much of his legal and administrative reorganization has survived in France to this day. More generally, Napoleon's domestic initiatives gave the great majority of French people a welcome sense of stability and national unity.

Order and unity had a price: Napoleon's authoritarian rule. Women, who had often participated in revolutionary politics without having legal equality, lost many of the gains they had made in the 1790s. Under the law of the new Napoleonic Code, women were dependents of either their fathers or their husbands, and they could not make contracts or even have bank accounts in their own names. Indeed, Napoleon and his advisers aimed at re-establishing a family monarchy, where the power of the husband and father was as absolute over the wife and the children as that of Napoleon was over his subjects.

Free speech and freedom of the press were continually violated. By 1811 only four newspapers were left, and they were little more than organs of government propaganda. The occasional elections were a farce. Later laws prescribed harsh penalties for political offenses. These changes in the law were part of the creation of a police state in France. Since Napoleon was usually busy making war, this task was largely left to Joseph Fouché, an unscrupulous opportunist who had earned a reputation for brutality during the Reign of Terror. As minister of police, Fouché organized a ruthlessly efficient spy system that kept thousands of citizens under continual police surveillance. People suspected of subversive activities were arbitrarily detained, placed under house arrest, or consigned to insane asylums. After 1810 political suspects were held in state prisons, as they had been during the Terror. There were about twenty-five hundred such political prisoners in 1814.

Napoleon's Expansion in Europe

Napoleon was above all a military man, and a great one. After coming to power in 1799 he sent peace feelers to Austria and Great Britain, the two remaining members of the Second Coalition that had been formed against France in 1798. When these overtures were rejected, French armies led by Napoleon decisively defeated the Austrians. In the Treaty of Lunéville (1801) Austria accepted the loss of almost all its Italian possessions, and German territory on the west bank of the Rhine was incorporated into France. Once more, as in 1797, the British were alone, and war-weary, like the French.

Still seeking to consolidate his regime domestically, Napoleon concluded the Treaty of Amiens with Great Britain in 1802. France remained in control of Holland, the Austrian Netherlands, the west bank of the Rhine, and most of the Italian peninsula. The Treaty of Amiens was clearly a diplomatic triumph for Napoleon, and peace with honor and profit increased his popularity at home.

In 1802 Napoleon was secure but unsatisfied. Ever a romantic gambler as well as a brilliant administrator, he could not contain his power drive. Aggressively redrawing the map of Germany so as to weaken Austria and encourage the secondary states of southwestern Germany to side with France, Napoleon tried to restrict British trade with all of Europe. After deciding to renew war

The Coronation of Napoleon, 1804 (detail) In this grandiose painting by Jacques-Louis David, Napoleon prepares to crown his wife, Josephine, in an elaborate ceremony in Notre Dame Cathedral. Napoleon, the ultimate upstart, also crowned himself. Pope Pius VII, seated glumly behind the emperor, is reduced to being a spectator. *(Louvre/Réunion des Musées Nationaux/Art Resource, NY)*

with Britain in May 1803, Napoleon concentrated his armies in the French ports on the Channel in the fall and began making preparations to invade England. Great Britain remained dominant on the seas, and when Napoleon tried to bring his Mediterranean fleet around Gibraltar to northern France, a combined French and Spanish fleet was virtually annihilated by Lord Nelson at the Battle of Trafalgar on October 21, 1805. Invasion of England was henceforth impossible. Renewed fighting had its advantages, however, for the first consul used the wartime atmosphere to have himself proclaimed emperor in late 1804.

Austria, Russia, and Sweden joined with Britain to form the Third Coalition against France shortly before the Battle of Trafalgar. Actions such as Napoleon's assumption of the Italian crown had convinced both Alexander I of Russia and Francis II of Austria that Napoleon was a threat to their interests and to the European balance of power. Yet the Austrians and the Russians were no match for Napoleon, who scored a brilliant victory over them at the Battle of Austerlitz in December 1805. Alexander I decided to pull back, and Austria accepted large territorial losses in return for peace as the Third Coalition collapsed.

Napoleon then proceeded to reorganize the German states to his liking. In 1806 he abolished many of the tiny German states as well as the ancient Holy Roman Empire and established by decree the German Confederation of the Rhine, a union of fifteen German states minus Austria, Prussia, and Saxony. Naming himself "protector" of the confederation, Napoleon firmly controlled western Germany.

Napoleon's intervention in German affairs alarmed the Prussians, who mobilized their armies after more than a decade of peace with France. Napoleon attacked and won two more brilliant victories in October 1806 at Jena and Auerstädt, where the Prussians were outnumbered two to one. The war with Prussia, now joined by Russia, continued into the following spring, and after Napoleon's larger armies won another victory, Alexander I of Russia wanted peace.

For several days in June 1807 the young tsar and the French emperor negotiated face to face on a raft anchored in the middle of the Niemen River. All the while, the helpless Frederick William III of Prussia rode back and forth on the shore anxiously awaiting the results. As the German poet Heinrich Heine said later, Napoleon had but to whistle and Prussia would have ceased to exist. In the subsequent treaties of Tilsit, Prussia lost half of its population, while Russia accepted Napoleon's reorganization of western and central Europe and promised to enforce Napoleon's economic blockade against British goods.

The War of Haitian Independence

In the midst of these victories, Napoleon was forced to accept defeat overseas. With Toussaint L'Ouverture acting increasingly as an independent ruler of the western province of Saint-Domingue, another general, André Rigaud, set up his own government in the southern peninsula, which had long been more isolated from France than the rest of the colony. Both leaders maintained policies, initially established by the French, of requiring former slaves to continue to work on their plantations. They believed that reconstructing the plantation economy was crucial to maintaining their military and political victories, and they harshly suppressed resistance from former slaves.

Tensions mounted, however, between L'Ouverture and Rigaud. While L'Ouverture was a freed slave of African descent, Rigaud belonged to the free colored elite. This elite resented the growing power of former slaves like L'Ouverture, who in turn accused them of adopting the racism of white settlers. Civil war broke out between the two sides in 1799, when L'Ouverture's forces, led by his lieutenant Jean Jacques Dessalines, invaded the south. Victory over Rigaud gave Toussaint control of the entire colony. (See the feature "Individuals in Society: Toussaint L'Ouverture.")

This victory was soon challenged by Napoleon's arrival in power. Napoleon intended to reinvigorate the Caribbean plantation economy as a basis for expanding French power. His new constitution of 1799 opened the way for a re-establishment of slavery much feared in the colony. When the colonial assembly of Saint-Domingue, under L'Ouverture's direction, drafted its own constitution—which reaffirmed the abolition of slavery and granted L'Ouverture governorship for life—Napoleon viewed it as a seditious act. He ordered his brother-in-law General Charles-Victor-Emmanuel Leclerc to lead an expedition to the island to crush the new regime. Napoleon placed a high premium on bringing the colony to heel, writing to Leclerc: "Once the blacks have been disarmed and the principal generals sent to France, you will have done more for the commerce and civilization of Europe than we have done in our most brilliant campaigns." An officer sent to serve in the colony had a more cynical interpretation, writing that he was being sent to "fight with the Negroes for their own sugar."[14]

In 1802 Leclerc landed in Saint-Domingue. Although Toussaint L'Ouverture cooperated with the French and turned his army over to them, Leclerc had him arrested and deported to France, along with his family, where he died in 1803. After arresting L'Ouverture, Leclerc moved to defuse the threat posed by former slaves by taking away their arms. This effort aroused armed resistance on the plantations and led to the defection of the remnants of L'Ouverture's army. Jean Jacques Dessalines united the resistance under his command and led them to a crushing victory over the French forces. Of the fifty-eight thousand French soldiers, fifty thousand were lost in combat and to disease. On January 1, 1804, Dessalines formally declared the independence of Saint-Domingue and the creation of the new sovereign nation of Haiti, the name used by the pre-Columbian inhabitants of the island. (The remaining French Caribbean colonies—Guadeloupe, Martinique, and French Guiana—remained part of France. Slavery was re-established and remained in force until 1848.)

Haiti, the second independent state in the Americas and the first in Latin America, was thus born from the first successful large-scale slave revolt in history. Fearing the spread of slave rebellion to the United States, President Thomas Jefferson refused to recognize Haiti. Both the American and the French Revolutions thus exposed their limits by acting to protect economic interests at the expense of revolutionary ideals of freedom and equality. Yet, Haitian independence had fundamental repercussions for world history. As one recent historian of the Haitian revolution commented:

The slave insurrection of Saint-Domingue led to the expansion of citizenship beyond racial barriers despite the massive political and economic investment in the slave system at the time. If we live in a world in which democracy is meant to exclude no one, it is in no small part because of the actions of those slaves in Saint-Domingue who insisted that human rights were theirs too.[15]

The Grand Empire and Its End

Napoleon resigned himself to the loss of Saint-Domingue, but he still maintained imperial ambitions in Europe. Increasingly, he saw himself as the emperor of Europe and not just of France. The so-called **Grand Empire** he built had three parts. The core, or first part, was an ever-expanding France, which by 1810 included Belgium, Holland, parts of northern Italy, and much German territory on the east bank of the Rhine. Beyond French borders Napoleon established the second part: a number of dependent satellite kingdoms, on the thrones of which he placed (and replaced) the members of his large family. The third part comprised the independent but allied states of Austria, Prussia, and Russia. After 1806 both satellites and allies were expected to support Napoleon's continental system and to cease trade with Britain.

The impact of the Grand Empire on the peoples of Europe was considerable. In the areas incorporated into France and in the satellites (see Map 21.2), Napoleon introduced many French laws, abolishing feudal dues and serfdom where French revolutionary armies had not already done so. Some of the peasants and middle class benefited from these reforms. Yet Napoleon had to put the prosperity and special interests of France first in order to safeguard his power base. Levying heavy taxes in money and men for his armies, he came to be regarded more as a conquering tyrant than as an enlightened liberator. Thus French rule sparked patriotic upheavals and encouraged the growth of reactive nationalism, for individuals in different lands learned to identify emotionally with their own embattled national families as the French had done earlier.

Online Study Center **Improve Your Grade**
Interactive Map: Napoleonic Europe, 1810

The first great revolt occurred in Spain. In 1808 a coalition of Catholics, monarchists, and patriots rebelled against Napoleon's attempts to make Spain a French satellite with a Bonaparte as its king. French armies occupied Madrid, but the foes of Napoleon fled to the hills and waged uncompromising guerrilla warfare. Spain was a clear warning: resistance to French imperialism was growing.

Yet Napoleon pushed on, determined to hold his complex and far-flung empire together. In 1810, when the Grand Empire was at its height, Britain still remained at war with France, helping the guerrillas in Spain and Portugal. The continental system, organized to exclude British goods from the continent and force that "nation of shopkeepers" to its knees, was a failure. Instead, it was France that suffered from Britain's counter-blockade, which created hard times for French artisans and the middle class. Perhaps looking for a scapegoat, Napoleon turned on Alexander I of Russia, who in 1811 openly repudiated Napoleon's war of prohibitions against British goods.

Napoleon's invasion of Russia began in June 1812 with a force that eventually numbered 600,000, probably the largest force yet assembled in a single army. Only one-third of this Great Army was French, however; nationals of all the satellites and allies were drafted into the operation. Originally planning to winter in the Russian city of Smolensk if Alexander did not sue for peace, Napoleon reached Smolensk and recklessly pressed on toward Moscow. The great Battle of Borodino that followed was a draw, and the Russians retreated in good order. Alexander ordered the evacuation of Moscow, which then burned in part, and he refused to negotiate. Finally, after five weeks in the abandoned city, Napoleon ordered a retreat. That retreat was one of the greatest military disasters in history. The Russian army, the Russian winter, and starvation cut Napoleon's army to pieces. When the frozen remnants staggered into Poland and Prussia in December, 370,000 men had died and another 200,000 had been taken prisoner.[16]

Leaving his troops to their fate, Napoleon raced to Paris to raise yet another army. Possibly he might still have saved his throne if he had been willing to accept a France reduced to its historical size—the proposal offered by Austria's foreign minister, Prince Klemens von Metternich. But Napoleon refused. Austria and Prussia deserted Napoleon and joined Russia and Great Britain in the Treaty of Chaumont in March 1814, by which the four powers pledged allegiance to defeat the French emperor. All across Europe patriots called for a "war of liberation" against Napoleon's oppression, and the well-disciplined regular armies of Napoleon's enemies closed in for the kill. Less than a month later, on April 4, 1814, a defeated Napoleon abdicated his throne. After this unconditional abdication, the victorious allies granted Napoleon the island of Elba off the coast of Italy as his own tiny state. Napoleon was even allowed to keep his imperial title, and France was required to pay him a yearly income of 2 million francs.

The allies also agreed to the restoration of the Bourbon dynasty, in part because demonstrations led by a few

Individuals in Society

Toussaint L'Ouverture

Little is known of the early life of the brilliant military and political leader Toussaint L'Ouverture. He was born in 1743 on a plantation outside Le Cap owned by the Count de Bréda. According to tradition, Toussaint was the eldest son of a captured African prince from modern-day Benin. Toussaint Bréda, as he was then called, occupied a privileged position among slaves. Instead of performing backbreaking labor in the fields, he served his master as a coachman and livestock keeper. He also learned to read and write French and some Latin, but he was always more comfortable with the Creole dialect.

During the 1770s the plantation manager emancipated Toussaint, who subsequently leased his own small coffee plantation, worked by slaves. He married Suzanne Simone, who already had one son, and the couple had another son during their marriage.

Toussaint L'Ouverture entered history in 1791 when he joined the slave uprisings that swept Saint-Domingue. (At some point he took on the cryptic *nom de guerre* "l'ouverture" meaning "the opening.") Toussaint rose to prominence among rebel slaves allied with Spain and by early 1794 controlled his own army. In 1794 he defected to the French side and led his troops to a series of victories against the Spanish. In 1795 the National Convention promoted L'Ouverture to brigadier general.

Over the next three years L'Ouverture successively eliminated rivals for authority on the island. First he freed himself of the French commissioners sent to govern the colony. With a firm grip on power in the northern province, Toussaint defeated General André Rigaud in 1800 to gain control in the south. His army then marched on the capital of Spanish Santo Domingo on the eastern half of the island, meeting little resistance. The entire island of Hispaniola was now under his command.

As one historian has described him, L'Ouverture was a "small, wiry man, very black, with mobile, penetrating eyes; he greatly impressed most who met him, even those who thought him ugly. He had lost his upper set of front teeth in battle and his ears were deformed by wearing heavy gold earrings, but his presence was commanding and suggested enormous self-control."* A devout Catholic who led a frugal and ascetic life, L'Ouverture impressed others with his enormous physical energy, intellectual acumen, and air of mystery.

With control of Saint-Domingue in his hands, L'Ouverture was confronted with the challenge of building a post-emancipation society, the first of its kind. The task was made even more difficult by the chaos wreaked by war, the destruction of plantations, and bitter social and racial tensions. For L'Ouverture the most pressing concern was to re-establish the plantation economy. Without revenue to pay his army, the gains of the rebellion could be lost. He therefore encouraged white planters to return and reclaim their property. He also adopted harsh policies toward former slaves, forcing them back to their plantations and restricting their ability to acquire land. When they resisted, he sent troops across the island to enforce submission.

In 1801 L'Ouverture convened a colonial assembly to draft a new constitution that reaffirmed his draconian labor policies. The constitution named L'Ouverture governor for life, leaving Saint-Domingue as a colony in name alone. When news of the constitution arrived in France, an angry Napoleon dispatched General Leclerc to re-establish French control. In June 1802 Leclerc's forces arrested L'Ouverture and took him to France. He was jailed at Fort de Joux in the Jura Mountains near the Swiss border, where he died of pneumonia on April 7, 1803. It was left to his lieutenant, Jean Jacques Dessalines, to win independence for the new Haitian nation.

Equestrian portrait of Toussaint L'Ouverture. (Réunion des Musées Nationaux/Art Resource, NY)

Questions for Analysis

1. Toussaint L'Ouverture was both slave and slave owner. How did each experience shape his life and actions?
2. Despite their differences, what did Toussaint L'Ouverture and Napoleon Bonaparte have in common? Why did they share a common fate?

*David Patrick Geggus, *Haitian Revolutionary Studies* (Bloomington: Indiana University Press, 2002), p. 22.

Online Study Center **Improve Your Grade**
Going Beyond Individuals in Society

The Napoleonic Era, 1799–1815

The War in Spain This unforgettable etching by the Spanish painter Francisco Goya (1746–1828) comes from his famous collection "The Disasters of the War." A French firing squad executes captured Spanish rebels almost as soon as they are captured, an everyday event in a war of atrocities on both sides. Do you think these rebels are "terrorists" or "freedom fighters"? *(Foto Marburg/Art Resource, NY)*

Mapping the Past

MAP 21.2 Napoleonic Europe in 1810 Only Great Britain remained at war with Napoleon at the height of the Grand Empire. Many British goods were smuggled through Helgoland, a tiny but strategic British possession off the German coast. Compare this map with Map 16.2, which shows the division of Europe in 1715. ❶ How had the balance of power shifted in Europe from 1715 to 1810? What changed, and what remained the same? ❷ Why did Napoleon succeed in achieving vast territorial gains where Louis XIV did not? ❸ In comparing Map 16.2 with this map, what was the impact of Napoleon's wars on Germany and the Italian peninsula? What significance do you think this had for these regions in the nineteenth century?

Online Study Center **Improve Your Grade** Interactive Map: Napoleonic Europe, 1810

dedicated French monarchists indicated some support among the French people for that course of action. The new monarch, Louis XVIII (r. 1814–1824), tried to consolidate that support by issuing the Constitutional Charter, which accepted many of France's revolutionary changes and guaranteed civil liberties. Indeed, the charter gave France a constitutional monarchy roughly similar to that established in 1791, although far fewer people had the right to vote for representatives to the resurrected Chamber of Deputies. Moreover, in an attempt to strengthen popular support for Louis XVIII's new government, France was treated leniently by the allies, which agreed to meet in Vienna to work out a general peace settlement.

Yet Louis XVIII—old, ugly, and crippled by gout—totally lacked the glory and magic of Napoleon. Hearing of political unrest in France and diplomatic tensions in Vienna, Napoleon staged a daring escape from Elba in February 1815. Landing in France, he issued appeals for support and marched on Paris with a small band of followers. French officers and soldiers who had fought so long for their emperor responded to the call. Louis XVIII fled, and once more Napoleon took command. But Napoleon's gamble was a desperate long shot, for the allies were united against him. At the end of a frantic period known as the Hundred Days, they crushed his forces at Waterloo on June 18, 1815, and imprisoned him on the rocky island of St. Helena, far off the western coast of Africa. Louis XVIII returned again and recommenced his reign. The allies now dealt more harshly with the apparently incorrigible French. As for Napoleon, he took revenge by writing his memoirs, skillfully nurturing the myth that he had been Europe's revolutionary liberator, a romantic hero whose lofty work had been undone by oppressive reactionaries. An era had ended.

Chapter Summary

- What social, political, and economic factors formed the background to the French Revolution?
- What were the immediate events that sparked the Revolution, and how did they result in the formation of a constitutional monarchy in France? How did the ideals and events of the early Revolution raise new aspirations in the colonies?
- How and why did the Revolution take a radical turn at home and in the colonies?
- Why did Napoleon Bonaparte assume control of France, and what factors led to his downfall? How did the new republic of Haiti gain independence from France?

The French Revolution was forged by multiple and complex factors. Whereas an earlier generation of historians was convinced that the origins of the Revolution lay in class struggle between the entrenched nobility and the rising bourgeoisie, it is now clear that many other factors were involved. Certainly, French society had undergone significant transformations during the eighteenth century, which dissolved many economic and social differences among elites without removing the legal distinction between them. These changes were accompanied by political struggles between the monarchy and its officers, particularly in the high law courts. Emerging public opinion focused on the shortcomings of monarchical rule, and a rising torrent of political theory, cheap pamphlets, gossip, and innuendo offered scathing and even pornographic depictions of the king and his court. With their sacred royal aura severely tarnished, Louis XV and his successor Louis XVI found themselves unable to respond to the financial crises generated by French involvement in the Seven Years' War and the American Revolution. Louis XVI's half-hearted efforts to redress the situation were quickly overwhelmed by elite and popular demands for fundamental reform.

Forced to call a meeting of the Estates General for the first time in almost two centuries, Louis XVI fell back on the traditional formula of one vote for each of the three orders of society. Debate over the composition of the assembly called forth a bold new paradigm: that the Third Estate in itself constituted the French nation. By 1791 the National Assembly had eliminated Old Regime privileges and had established a constitutional monarchy. Talk in France of liberty, equality, and fraternity raised new and contradictory aspirations in the colony of Saint-Domingue. White planters lobbied for increased colonial autonomy; free people of color sought the return of legal equality; slaves of African birth or descent took direct action on revolutionary ideals by rising in rebellion against their masters.

With the execution of the royal couple and the declaration of terror as the order of the day, the French Revolution took an increasingly radical turn from the end of 1792. Popular fears of counter-revolutionary conspiracy combined with the outbreak of war against a mighty alliance of European monarchs convinced many that the Revolution was vulnerable and must be defended against its multiple enemies. In a spiraling cycle of accusations and executions, the Jacobins eliminated political opponents and then factions within its own party. The Directory government that took power after the fall of Robespierre restored political equilibrium at the cost of the radical platform of social equality he had pursued.

Wearied by the weaknesses of the Directory, a group of conspirators gave Napoleon Bonaparte control of France. His brilliant reputation as a military leader and his charisma and determination made him seem ideal to lead France to victory over its enemies. As is so often the case in history, Napoleon's relentless ambitions ultimately led to his downfall. His story is paralleled by that of Toussaint L'Ouverture, another soldier who emerged to the political limelight from the chaos of revolution only to endure exile and defeat.

As complex as its origins are the legacies of the French Revolution. These include liberalism, assertive nationalism, radical democratic republicanism, embryonic socialism, self-conscious conservatism, abolitionism, decolonization, and movements for racial and sexual equality. The Revolution also left a rich and turbulent history of electoral competition, legislative assemblies, and even mass politics. Thus the French Revolution and conflicting interpretations of its significance presented a whole range of political options and alternative visions of the future. For this reason, it was truly the revolution in modern European politics.

Key Terms

- estates
- manorial rights
- Maupeou parlements
- desacralization
- sovereignty
- Assembly of Notables
- Estates General
- National Assembly
- Great Fear
- constitutional monarchy
- free people of color
- Jacobin club
- second revolution
- Girondists
- the Mountain
- sans-culottes
- planned economy
- Reign of Terror
- nationalism
- abolition of slavery
- Thermidorian reaction
- Grand Empire

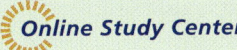 **Improve Your Grade** Flashcards

Suggested Reading

Bell, David A. *The Cult of the Nation in France: Inventing Nationalism, 1680–1800.* 2001. Traces early French nationalism through its revolutionary culmination.

Blanning, T. C. W. *The French Revolutionary Wars (1787–1802).* 1996. A masterful account of the revolutionary wars that also places the French Revolution in its European context.

Broers, Michael. *Europe Under Napoleon.* 2002. Probes Napoleon's impact on the territories he conquered.

Connelly, Owen. *The French Revolution and Napoleonic Era.* 1991. An excellent introduction to the French Revolution and Napoleon.

Desan, Suzanne. *The Family on Trial in Revolutionary France.* 2004. Studies the effects of revolutionary law on the family, including the legalization of divorce.

Dubois, Laurent. *Avengers of the New World: The Story of the Haitian Revolution.* 2004. An excellent and highly readable account of the revolution that transformed the French colony of Saint-Domingue into the independent state of Haiti.

Englund, Steven. *Napoleon: A Political Life.* 2004. A good biography of the French emperor.

Hunt, Lynn. *Politics, Culture and Class in the French Revolution,* 2d ed. 2004. A pioneering examination of the French Revolution as a cultural phenomenon that generated new festivals, clothing, and songs and even a new calendar.

Landes, John B. *Visualizing the Nation: Gender, Representation, and Revolution in Eighteenth-Century France.* 2001. Analyzes images of gender and the body in revolutionary politics.

Schechter, Ronald. *Obstinate Hebrews: Representations of Jews in France, 1715–1815.* 2003. An illuminating study of Jews and attitudes toward them in France from Enlightenment to emancipation.

Sutherland, Donald. *France, 1789–1815.* 1986. An overview of the French Revolution that emphasizes its many opponents, as well as its supporters.

Tackett, Timothy. *When the King Took Flight.* 2003. An exciting re-creation of the royal family's doomed effort to escape from Paris.

Notes

1. Quoted in R. R. Palmer, *The Age of Democratic Revolution,* vol. 1 (Princeton, N.J.: Princeton University Press, 1959), pp. 95–96.
2. Quoted in G. Wright, *France in Modern Times,* 4th ed. (New York: W. W. Norton, 1987), p. 34.
3. G. Lefebvre, *The Coming of the French Revolution* (New York: Vintage Books, 1947), p. 81.
4. P. H. Beik, ed., *The French Revolution* (New York: Walker, 1970), p. 89.
5. G. Pernoud and S. Flaisser, eds., *The French Revolution* (Greenwich, Conn.: Fawcett, 1960), p. 61.
6. O. Hufton, *Women and the Limits of Citizenship in the French Revolution* (Toronto: University of Toronto Press, 1992), pp. 3–22.
7. Quotations from Wollstonecraft are drawn from E. W. Sunstein, *A Different Face: The Life of Mary Wollstonecraft* (New York: Harper & Row, 1975), pp. 208, 211; and H. R. James, *Mary Wollstonecraft: A Sketch* (London: Oxford University Press, 1932), pp. 60, 62, 69.
8. Quoted in L. Gershoy, *The Era of the French Revolution, 1789–1799* (New York: Van Nostrand, 1957), p. 150.
9. Pernoud and Flaisser, *The French Revolution,* pp. 193–194.
10. T. Blanning, *The French Revolutionary Wars, 1787–1802* (London: Arnold, 1996), pp. 116–128.
11. Quoted ibid., p. 123.
12. Quoted in Laurent Dubois, *Avengers of the New World: The Story of the Haitian Revolution* (Cambridge: Harvard University Press, 2004), p. 97.
13. I. Woloch, *Napoleon and His Collaborators: The Making of a Dictatorship* (New York: W. W. Norton, 2001), pp. 36–65.
14. Quoted in Dubois, *Avengers of the New World,* pp. 255–256.
15. Ibid., p. 3.
16. D. Sutherland, *France, 1789–1815: Revolution and Counterrevolution* (New York: Oxford University Press, 1986), p. 420.

Listening to the Past

Revolution and Women's Rights

The 1789 Declaration of the Rights of Man and of the Citizen was a revolutionary call for legal equality, representative government, and individual freedom. But the new rights were strictly limited to men; Napoleon tightened further the subordination of French women. Among those who saw the contradiction in granting supposedly universal rights to only half the population was Marie Gouze (1748–1793), known to history as Olympe de Gouges. The daughter of a provincial butcher and peddler, she pursued a literary career in Paris after the death of her husband. Between 1790 and 1793 she wrote more than two dozen political pamphlets under her new name. De Gouges's great work was her "Declaration of the Rights of Woman" (1791). Excerpted here, de Gouges's manifesto went beyond the 1789 Rights of Man. It called on males to end their oppression of women and to give women equal rights. A radical on women's issues, de Gouges sympathized with the monarchy and criticized Robespierre in print. Convicted of sedition, she was guillotined in November 1793.

. . . Man, are you capable of being just? . . . Tell me, what gives you sovereign empire to oppress my sex? Your strength? Your talents? Observe the Creator in his wisdom . . . and give me, if you dare, an example of this tyrannical empire. Go back to animals, consult the elements, study plants . . . and distinguish, if you can, the sexes in the administration of nature. Everywhere you will find them mingled; everywhere they cooperate in harmonious togetherness in this immortal masterpiece.

Man alone has raised his exceptional circumstances to a principle. . . . [H]e wants to command as a despot a sex which is in full possession of its intellectual faculties; he pretends to enjoy the Revolution and to claim his rights to equality in order to say nothing more about it.

DECLARATION OF THE RIGHTS OF WOMAN AND THE FEMALE CITIZEN

For the National Assembly to decree in its last sessions, or in those of the next legislature:

Preamble

Mothers, daughters, sisters and representatives of the nation demand to be constituted into a national assembly. Believing that ignorance, omission, or scorn for the rights of woman are the only causes of public misfortunes and of the corruption of governments, [the women] have resolved to set forth in a solemn declaration the natural, inalienable, and sacred rights of woman. . . .

. . . the sex that is as superior in beauty as it is in courage during the sufferings of maternity recognizes and declares in the presence and under the auspices of the Supreme Being, the following Rights of Woman and of Female Citizens:

I. Woman is born free and lives equal to man in her rights. Social distinctions can be based only on the common utility.

II. The purpose of any political association is the conservation of the natural and imprescriptible rights of woman and man; these rights are liberty, property, security, and especially resistance to oppression.

III. The principle of all sovereignty rests essentially with the nation, which is nothing but the union of woman and man. . . .

IV. Liberty and justice consist of restoring all that belongs to others; thus, the only limits on the exercise of the natural rights of woman are perpetual male tyranny; these limits are to be reformed by the laws of nature and reason.

V. Laws of nature and reason proscribe all acts harmful to society. . . .

VI. The law must be the expression of the general will; all female and male citizens must contribute either personally or through their representatives to its formation; it must be the same for all: male and female citizens, being equal in the eyes of the law, must be equally admitted to all honors, positions, and public employment according to their capacity and without other distinctions besides those of their virtues and talents.

VII. No woman is an exception; she is accused, arrested, and detained in cases determined by law. Women, like men, obey this rigorous law.

VIII. The law must establish only those penalties that are strictly and obviously necessary. . . .

IX. Once any woman is declared guilty, complete rigor is [to be] exercised by the law.

X. No one is to be disquieted for his very basic opinions; woman has the right to mount the scaffold; she must equally have the right to mount the rostrum, provided that her demonstrations do not disturb the legally established public order.

XI. The free communication of thoughts and opinions is one of the most precious rights of woman, since that liberty assures the recognition of children by their fathers. Any female citizen thus may say freely, I am the mother of a child which belongs to you, without being forced by a barbarous prejudice to hide the truth. . . .

XIII. For the support of the public force and the expenses of administration, the contributions of woman and man are equal; she shares all the duties . . . and all the painful tasks; therefore, she must have the same share in the distribution of positions, employment, offices, honors, and jobs. . . .

XIV. Female and male citizens have the right to verify, either by themselves or through their representatives, the necessity of the public contribution. This can only apply to women if they are granted an equal share, not only of wealth, but also of public administration. . . .

XV. The collectivity of women, joined for tax purposes to the aggregate of men, has the right to demand an accounting of his administration from any public agent.

XVI. No society has a constitution without the guarantee of rights and the separation of powers; the constitution is null if the majority of individuals comprising the nation have not cooperated in drafting it.

XVII. Property belongs to both sexes whether united or separate; for each it is an inviolable and sacred right. . . .

Postscript

Women, wake up. . . . Discover your rights. . . . Oh, women, women! When will you cease to be

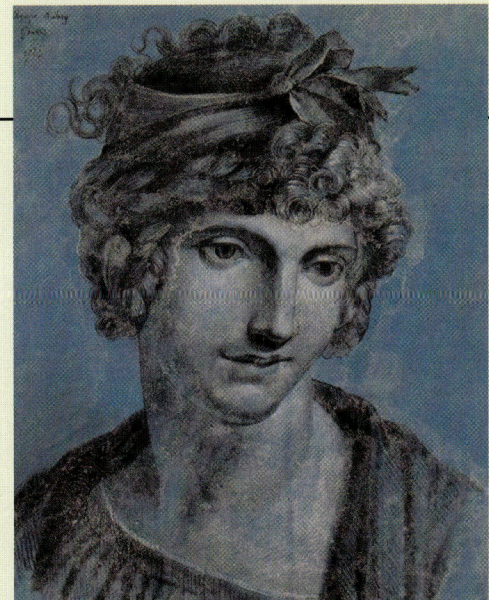

Olympe de Gouges in 1784; aquatint by Madame Aubry (1748–1793). *(Musée de la Ville de Paris, Musée Carnavalet, Paris, France/The Bridgeman Art Library)*

blind? What advantage have you received from the Revolution? A more pronounced scorn, a more marked disdain. . . . [If men persist in contradicting their revolutionary principles,] courageously oppose the force of reason to the empty pretensions of superiority . . . and you will soon see these haughty men, not groveling at your feet as servile adorers, but proud to share with you the treasure of the Supreme Being. Regardless of what barriers confront you; it is in your power to free yourselves; you have only to want to. . . .

Questions for Analysis

1. On what basis did de Gouges argue for gender equality? Did she believe in natural law?
2. What consequences did "scorn for the rights of woman" have for France, according to de Gouges?
3. Did de Gouges stress political rights at the expense of social and economic rights? If so, why?

Source: Olympe de Gouges, "Declaration of the Rights of Woman," in Darline G. Levy, Harriet B. Applewhite, and Mary D. Johnson, eds., *Women in Revolutionary Paris, 1789–1795* (Urbana: University of Illinois Press, 1979), pp. 87–96. Copyright © 1979 by the Board of Trustees, University of Illinois. Used with permission.

A colorful timetable poster lists the trains from London to Folkstone, the English Channel's gateway port to the European continent, and proudly proclaims the speed of the journey. *(Private Collection/The Bridgeman Art Library)*

chapter 22

THE REVOLUTION IN ENERGY AND INDUSTRY, CA 1780–1860

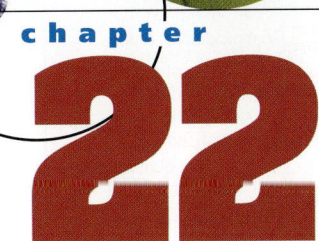

chapter preview

The Industrial Revolution in Britain
- What were the origins of the Industrial Revolution in Britain, and how did it develop between 1780 and 1850?

Industrialization in Continental Europe
- How after 1815 did continental countries respond to the challenge of industrialization?

Relations Between Capital and Labor
- How did the Industrial Revolution affect social classes, the standard of living, and patterns of work? What measures were taken to improve the conditions of workers?

While the revolution in France was opening a new political era, another revolution was beginning to transform economic and social life. This was the Industrial Revolution, which began in Great Britain around the 1780s and started to influence continental Europe after 1815. Because the Industrial Revolution was less dramatic than the French Revolution, some historians see industrial development as basically moderate and evolutionary. But from a longer perspective, it was rapid and brought about numerous radical changes. Quite possibly only the development of agriculture during Neolithic times had a comparable impact and significance.

The Industrial Revolution profoundly modified much of human experience. It changed patterns of work, transformed the social class structure and the way people thought about class, and eventually even altered the international balance of political power. The Industrial Revolution also helped ordinary people gain a higher standard of living as the widespread poverty of the preindustrial world was gradually reduced.

Unfortunately, the improvement in the European standard of living was quite limited until about 1850 for at least two reasons. First, even in Britain, only a few key industries experienced a technological revolution. Many more industries continued to use old methods, especially on the continent, and this held down the increase in total production. Second, the increase in total population, which began in the eighteenth century (see pages 625–628), continued all across Europe as the era of the Industrial Revolution unfolded. As a result, the rapid growth in population threatened to eat up the growth in production and to leave most individuals poorer than ever. As a consequence, rapid population growth provided a somber background for European industrialization and made the wrenching transformation all the more difficult.

Online Study Center

This icon will direct you to interactive activities and study materials on the website **college.hmco.com/pic/mckaywest9e**

The Industrial Revolution in Britain

The Industrial Revolution began in Great Britain, that historic union of Scotland, Wales, and England—the wealthiest and the dominant part of the country. It was something new in history, and it was quite unplanned. With no models to copy and no idea of what to expect, Britain had to pioneer not only in industrial technology but also in social relations and urban living. Between 1793 and 1815, these formidable tasks were complicated by almost constant war with France. As the trailblazer in economic development, as France was in political change, Britain must command special attention.

• **What were the origins of the Industrial Revolution in Britain, and how did it develop between 1780 and 1850?**

Eighteenth-Century Origins

Although many aspects of the British Industrial Revolution are still matters for scholarly debate, it is generally agreed that the industrial changes that did occur grew out of a long process of development. First, the expanding Atlantic economy of the eighteenth century served mercantilist Britain remarkably well. The colonial empire that Britain aggressively built, augmented by a strong position in Latin America and in the African slave trade, provided a growing market for British manufactured goods. So did the domestic market. In an age when it was much cheaper to ship goods by water than by land, no part of England was more than twenty miles from navigable water. Beginning in the 1770s, a canal-building boom greatly enhanced this natural advantage (see Map 22.1). Rivers and canals provided easy movement of England's and Wales's enormous deposits of iron and coal, resources that would be critical raw materials in Europe's early industrial age. Nor were there any tariffs within the country to hinder trade, as there were in France before 1789 and in politically fragmented Germany.

Second, agriculture played a central role in bringing about the Industrial Revolution in Britain. English farmers in particular were second only to the Dutch in productivity in 1700, and they were continually adopting new methods of farming as the century went on. The result, especially before 1760, was a period of bountiful crops and low food prices. The ordinary English family did not have to spend almost everything it earned just to

MAP 22.1 Cottage Industry and Transportation in Eighteenth-Century England England had an unusually good system of navigable rivers. From about 1770 to 1800 a canal-building boom linked these rivers together and greatly improved inland transportation.

Online Study Center Improve Your Grade
Interactive Map: Cottage Industry and Transportation in Eighteenth-Century England

buy bread. It could spend more on, for example, manufactured goods—leather shoes or a razor for the man, a bonnet or a shawl for the woman, toy soldiers for the son, and a doll for the daughter. Thus demand for goods within the country complemented the demand from the colonies.

Third, Britain had other assets that helped give rise to industrial leadership. Unlike eighteenth-century France, Britain had an effective central bank and well-developed credit markets. The monarchy and the aristocratic oligarchy, which had jointly ruled the country since 1688, provided stable and predictable government. At the same time, the government let the domestic economy operate with few controls, encouraging personal initiative, technical change, and a free market. Finally, Britain had long had a large class of hired agricultural laborers, rural proletarians whose numbers were further increased by the second great round of enclosures in the late eighteenth century. These rural wage earners were relatively mobile—compared to village-bound peasants in France and western Germany, for example—and along with cottage workers they formed a potential industrial labor force for capitalist entrepreneurs.

All these factors combined to initiate the **Industrial Revolution,** a term first coined by awed contemporaries in the 1830s to describe the burst of major inventions and technical changes they had witnessed in certain industries. This technical revolution went hand in hand with an impressive quickening in the annual rate of industrial growth in Britain. Whereas industry had grown at only 0.7 percent between 1700 and 1760 (before the Industrial Revolution), it grew at the much higher rate of 3 percent between 1801 and 1831 (when industrial transformation was in full swing).[1] The decisive quickening of growth probably came in the 1780s, after the American War of Independence and just before the French Revolution.

Therefore, the great economic and political revolutions that shaped the modern world occurred almost simultaneously, though they began in different countries. The Industrial Revolution was, however, a longer process than the political upheavals. It was not complete in Britain until 1850 at the earliest, and it had no real impact on continental countries until after 1815.

The First Factories

The pressure to produce more goods for a growing market was directly related to the first decisive breakthrough of the Industrial Revolution—the creation of the world's first large factories in the British cotton textile industry. Technological innovations in the manufacture of cotton cloth led to a new system of production and social relationships. Since no other industry experienced such a rapid or complete transformation before 1830, these trailblazing developments deserve special consideration.

Although the putting-out system of merchant capitalism (see page 629) was expanding all across Europe in the eighteenth century, this pattern of rural industry was most fully developed in Britain. There, under the pressure of growing demand, the system's limitations began to outweigh its advantages for the first time. This was especially true in the British textile industry after about 1760.

Chronology

ca 1765	Hargreaves invents spinning jenny
1769	Watt creates modern steam engine
1775–1783	American Revolution
1780s–1850	Industrial Revolution
1780–1851	Population boom in England
1789–1799	French Revolution
1798	Malthus, *Essay on the Principle of Population*
1799	Combination Acts passed
1810	Strike of Manchester cotton spinners
1824	Combination Acts repealed
1830s	Industrial banks in Belgium
1830	Stephenson's *Rocket*; first important railroad
1833	Factory Act
1841	List, *National System of Political Economy*
1842	Mines Act
1844	Engels, *The Condition of the Working Class in England*
1851	Great Exhibition held at Crystal Palace

A constant shortage of thread in the textile industry focused attention on ways of improving spinning. Many a tinkering worker knew that a better spinning wheel promised rich rewards. It proved hard to spin the traditional raw materials—wool and flax—with improved machines, but cotton was different. Cotton textiles had first been imported into Britain from India by the East India Company, and by 1760 there was a tiny domestic industry in northern England. After many experiments over a generation, a gifted carpenter and jack-of-all-trades, James Hargreaves, invented his cotton-spinning jenny about 1765. At almost the same moment, a barber-turned-manufacturer named Richard Arkwright invented (or possibly pirated) another kind of spinning machine, the water frame. These breakthroughs produced an explosion in the infant cotton textile industry in the 1780s, when it was increasing the value of its output at an unprecedented rate of about 13 percent each year. By 1790 the new machines were producing ten times as much cotton yarn as had been made in 1770.

Woman Working a Hargreaves's Spinning Jenny
The loose cotton strands on the slanted bobbins passed up to the sliding carriage and then on to the spindles in back for fine spinning. The worker, almost always a woman, regulated the sliding carriage with one hand, and with the other she turned the crank on the wheel to supply power. By 1783 one woman could spin by hand a hundred threads at a time on an improved model. *(Mary Evans Picture Library)*

Online Study Center Improve Your Grade
Primary Source: Manchester Becomes a Thriving Industrial City

Hargreaves's **spinning jenny** was simple and inexpensive. In early models, from six to twenty-four spindles were mounted on a sliding carriage, and each spindle spun a fine, slender thread. The woman moved the carriage back and forth with one hand and turned a wheel to supply power with the other. Now it was the male weaver who could not keep up with the vastly more efficient female spinner.

Arkwright's **water frame** employed a different principle. It quickly acquired a capacity of several hundred spindles and demanded much more power—waterpower. The water frame thus required large specialized mills, factories that employed as many as one thousand workers from the very beginning. The water frame could spin only coarse, strong thread, which was then put out for respinning on hand-powered cottage jennies. Around 1790 an alternative technique invented by Samuel Crompton also began to require more power than the human arm could supply. After that time, all cotton spinning was gradually concentrated in factories.

The first consequences of these revolutionary developments were more beneficial than is generally believed.

Cotton goods became much cheaper, and they were bought and treasured by all classes. In the past, only the wealthy could afford the comfort and cleanliness of underwear, which was called **body linen** because it was made from expensive linen cloth. Now millions of poor people, who had earlier worn nothing underneath their coarse, filthy outer garments, could afford to wear cotton slips and underpants as well as cotton dresses and shirts.

Families using cotton in cottage industry were freed from their constant search for adequate yarn from scattered, part-time spinners, since all the thread needed could be spun in the cottage on the jenny or obtained from a nearby factory. The wages of weavers, now hard-pressed to keep up with the spinners, rose markedly until about 1792. Weavers were among the best-paid workers in England. They were known to walk proudly through the streets with 5-pound notes stuck in their hatbands, and they dressed like the middle class. As a result, large numbers of agricultural laborers became hand-loom weavers, while mechanics and capitalists sought to invent a power loom to save on labor costs. This Edmund Cartwright achieved in 1785. But the power looms of the factories worked poorly at first, and hand-loom weavers continued to receive good wages until at least 1800.

Working conditions in the early factories were less satisfactory than those of cottage weavers and spinners, and people were reluctant to work in them. Therefore, factory owners often turned to young children who had been abandoned by their parents and put in the care of local parishes. Parish officers often "apprenticed" such unfortunate foundlings to factory owners. The parish thus saved money, and the factory owners gained workers over whom they exercised almost the authority of slave owners.

Apprenticed as young as five or six years of age, boy and girl workers were forced by law to labor for their "masters" for as many as fourteen years. Housed, fed, and locked up nightly in factory dormitories, the young workers received little or no pay. Hours were appalling—commonly thirteen or fourteen hours a day, six days a week. Harsh physical punishment maintained brutal discipline. To be sure, poor children typically worked long hours and frequently outside the home for brutal masters. But the wholesale coercion of orphans as factory apprentices constituted exploitation on a truly unprecedented scale. This exploitation ultimately piqued the conscience of reformers and reinforced more humanitarian attitudes toward children and their labor in the early nineteenth century.

The creation of the world's first modern factories in the British cotton textile industry in the 1770s and 1780s, which grew out of the putting-out system of cottage production, was a major historical development. Both symbolically and substantially, the big new cotton mills marked the beginning of the Industrial Revolution in Britain. By 1831 the largely mechanized cotton textile industry towered above all others, accounting for fully 22 percent of the country's entire industrial production.

The Problem of Energy

The growth of the cotton textile industry might have been stunted or cut short, however, if water from rivers and streams had remained the primary source of power for the new factories. But this did not occur. Instead, an epoch-making solution was found to the age-old problem of energy and power. This solution permitted continued rapid development in cotton textiles, the gradual generalization of the factory system, and the triumph of the Industrial Revolution in Britain.

Human beings have long used their toolmaking abilities to construct machines that convert one form of energy into another for their own benefit. In the medieval period, people began to develop water mills to grind their grain and windmills to pump water and drain swamps. More efficient use of water and wind in the sixteenth and seventeenth centuries enabled human beings to accomplish more; intercontinental sailing ships were a prime example. Nevertheless, even into the eighteenth century, society continued to rely for energy mainly on plants, and human beings and animals continued to perform most work. This dependence meant that Western civilization remained poor in energy and power.

Lack of power lay at the heart of the poverty that afflicted the large majority of people. The man behind the plow and the woman at the spinning wheel could employ only horsepower and human muscle in their labor. No matter how hard they worked, they could not produce very much.

The shortage of energy had become particularly severe in Britain by the eighteenth century. Because of the growth of population, most of the great forests of medieval Britain had long ago been replaced by fields of grain and hay. Wood was in ever-shorter supply, yet it remained tremendously important. It served as the primary source of heat for all homes and industries and as a basic raw material. Processed wood (charcoal) was the fuel that was mixed with iron ore in the blast furnace to produce pig iron. The iron industry's appetite for wood was enormous, and by 1740 the British iron industry was stagnating. Vast forests enabled Russia to become the world's leading producer of iron, much of which was exported to Britain. But Russia's potential for growth was limited, too, and in a few decades Russia would reach the barrier of inadequate energy that was already holding England back.

The Steam Engine Breakthrough

As this early energy crisis grew worse, Britain looked toward its abundant and widely scattered reserves of coal as an alternative to its vanishing wood. Coal was first used in Britain in the late Middle Ages as a source of heat. By 1640 most homes in London were heated with it, and it also provided heat for making beer, glass, soap, and other products. Coal was not used, however, to produce mechanical energy or to power machinery. It was there that coal's potential was enormous, as a simple example shows.

A hard-working miner can dig out 500 pounds of coal a day using hand tools. Even an extremely inefficient converter, which transforms only 1 percent of the heat energy in coal into mechanical energy, will produce 27 horsepower-hours of work from that 500 pounds of coal. The miner, by contrast, produces only about 1 horsepower-hour in the course of a day. Early steam engines were powerful but still inefficient converters of energy.

As more coal was produced, mines were dug deeper and deeper and were constantly filling with water. Mechanical pumps, usually powered by animals walking in circles at the surface, had to be installed. At one mine, fully five hundred horses were used in pumping. Such power was expensive and bothersome. In an attempt to

Manchester, England, 1851 The development of the steam engine enabled industry to concentrate in towns and cities. Manchester mushroomed from a town of 20,000 in 1750 into "Cottonopolis," cotton city, with 400,000 inhabitants in 1850. In this painting the artist contrasts the smoky city and its awesome power with the idealized beauty of the suburbs, where the new rich settled and built their mansions. *(The Royal Collection, © 2007 Her Majesty Queen Elizabeth II)*

overcome these disadvantages, Thomas Savery in 1698 and Thomas Newcomen in 1705 invented the first primitive **steam engines.** Both engines were extremely inefficient. Both burned coal to produce steam, which was then used to operate a pump. However, by the early 1770s, many of the Savery engines and hundreds of the Newcomen engines were operating successfully, though inefficiently, in English and Scottish mines.

In the early 1760s, a gifted young Scot named James Watt (1736–1819) was drawn to a critical study of the steam engine. Watt was employed at the time by the University of Glasgow as a skilled craftsman making scientific instruments. The Scottish universities were pioneers in practical technical education, and in 1763 Watt was called on to repair a Newcomen engine being used in a physics course. After a series of observations, Watt saw that the Newcomen engine's waste of energy could be reduced by adding a separate condenser. This splendid invention, patented in 1769, greatly increased the efficiency of the steam engine.

To invent something in a laboratory is one thing; to make it a practical success is quite another. Watt needed skilled workers, precision parts, and capital, and the relatively advanced nature of the British economy proved essential. A partnership with a wealthy English toymaker provided risk capital and a manufacturing plant. In the craft tradition of locksmiths, tinsmiths, and millwrights, Watt found skilled mechanics who could install, regulate, and repair his sophisticated engines. From ingenious manufacturers such as the cannonmaker John Wilkinson, Watt was gradually able to purchase precision parts. This support allowed him to create an effective vacuum and regulate a complex engine. In more than twenty years of constant effort, Watt made many further improvements. By the late 1780s, the steam engine had become a practical and commercial success in Britain.

The steam engine of Watt and his followers was the Industrial Revolution's most fundamental advance in technology. For the first time in history, humanity had, at least for a few generations, almost unlimited power at its disposal. For the first time, inventors and engineers could devise and implement all kinds of power equipment to aid people in their work. For the first time, abundance was at least a possibility for ordinary men and women.

The steam engine was quickly put to use in several industries in Britain. It drained mines and made possible the production of ever more coal to feed steam engines elsewhere. The steam-power plant began to replace waterpower in the cotton-spinning mills during the 1780s, contributing greatly to that industry's phenomenal rise. Steam also took the place of waterpower in flour mills, in the malt mills used in breweries, in the flint mills supplying the china industry, and in the mills exported by Britain to the West Indies to crush sugar cane.

Steam power promoted important breakthroughs in other industries. The British iron industry was radically transformed. The use of powerful, steam-driven bellows in blast furnaces helped ironmakers switch over rapidly from limited charcoal to unlimited **coke** (which is made from coal) in the smelting of pig iron after 1770. In the 1780s, Henry Cort developed the puddling furnace, which allowed pig iron to be refined in turn with coke. Strong, skilled ironworkers—the puddlers—"cooked" molten pig iron in a great vat, raking off globs of refined iron for further processing. Cort also developed heavy-duty, steam-powered rolling mills, which were capable of spewing out finished iron in every shape and form.

The economic consequence of these technical innovations was a great boom in the British iron industry. In 1740 annual British iron production was only 17,000 tons. With the spread of coke smelting and the first impact of Cort's inventions, production reached 68,000 tons in 1788, 125,000 tons in 1796, and 260,000 tons in 1806. In 1844 Britain produced 3 million tons of iron. This was a truly amazing expansion. Once scarce and expensive, iron became the cheap, basic, indispensable building block of the economy.

The Coming of the Railroads

The second half of the eighteenth century saw extensive construction of hard and relatively smooth roads, particularly in France before the Revolution. Yet it was passenger traffic that benefited most from this construction. Overland shipment of freight, relying solely on horsepower, was still quite limited and frightfully expensive;

James Nasmyth's Mighty Steam Hammer Nasmyth's invention was the forerunner of the modern pile driver, and its successful introduction in 1832 epitomized the rapid development of steam power technology in Britain. In this painting by the inventor himself, workers manipulate a massive iron shaft being hammered into shape at Nasmyth's foundry near Manchester. *(Science & Society Picture Library, London)*

The Saltash Bridge Railroad construction presented innumerable challenges, such as the building of bridges to span rivers and gorges. Civil engineers responded with impressive feats, and their profession bounded ahead. This painting portrays the inauguration of I. K. Brunel's Saltash Bridge, where the railroad crosses the Tamar River into Cornwall in southwest England. The high spans allow large ships to pass underneath. *(Elton Collection, Ironbridge Gorge Museum Trust)*

shippers used rivers and canals for heavy freight whenever possible. It was logical, therefore, that inventors would try to use steam power.

As early as 1800, an American ran a "steamer on wheels" through city streets. Other experiments followed. In the 1820s, English engineers created steam cars capable of carrying fourteen passengers at ten miles an hour—as fast as the mail coach. But the noisy, heavy steam automobiles frightened passing horses and damaged themselves as well as the roads with their vibrations. For the rest of the century, horses continued to reign on highways and city streets.

The coal industry had long been using plank roads and rails to move coal wagons within mines and at the surface. Rails reduced friction and allowed a horse or a human being to pull a heavier load. Thus once a rail capable of supporting a heavy locomotive was developed in 1816, all sorts of experiments with steam engines on rails went forward. In 1825 after ten years of work, George Stephenson built an effective locomotive. In 1830 his **Rocket** sped down the track of the just-completed Liverpool and Manchester Railway at sixteen miles per hour. This was the world's first important railroad, fittingly steaming in the heart of industrial England. The line from Liverpool to Manchester was a financial as well as a technical success, and many private companies were quickly organized to build more rail lines. Within twenty years, they had completed the main trunk lines of Great Britain. Other countries were quick to follow.

The significance of the railroad was tremendous. The railroad dramatically reduced the cost and uncertainty of shipping freight overland. This advance had many economic consequences. Previously, markets had tended to be small and local; as the barrier of high transportation costs was lowered, markets became larger and even nationwide. Larger markets encouraged larger factories with more sophisticated machinery in a growing number of industries. Such factories could make goods more cheaply and gradually subjected most cottage workers and many urban artisans to severe competitive pressures.

In all countries, the construction of railroads created a strong demand for unskilled labor and contributed to the growth of a class of urban workers. Hard work on construction gangs was done in the open air with animals and hand tools. Many landless farm laborers and poor peasants, long accustomed to leaving their villages for temporary employment, went to build railroads. By the time the work was finished, life back home in the village often seemed dull and unappealing, and many men drifted to towns in search of work. By the time they sent for their wives and sweethearts to join them, they had become urban workers.

The railroad changed the outlook and values of the entire society. The last and culminating invention of the Industrial Revolution, the railroad dramatically revealed the power and increased the speed of the new age. Racing down a track at sixteen miles per hour or, by 1850, at a phenomenal fifty miles per hour was a new and awesome experience. As a French economist put it after a ride on the Liverpool and Manchester in 1833, "There are certain impressions that one cannot put into words!"

Some great painters, notably Joseph M. W. Turner (1775–1851) and Claude Monet (1840–1926), succeeded in expressing this sense of power and awe. So did the massive new train stations, the cathedrals of the industrial age. Leading railway engineers such as Isambard Kingdom Brunel and Thomas Brassey, whose tunnels pierced mountains and whose bridges spanned valleys, became public idols—the astronauts of their day. Everyday speech absorbed the images of railroading. After you got up a "full head of steam," you "highballed" along. And if you didn't "go off the track," you might "toot your own whistle." The railroad fired the imagination.

Industry and Population

In 1851 London was the site of a famous industrial fair. This Great Exhibition was held in the newly built **Crystal Palace,** an architectural masterpiece made entirely of glass and iron, both of which were now cheap and abundant. For the millions who visited, one fact stood out: the little island of Britain was the "workshop of the world." It alone produced two-thirds of the world's coal and more than one-half of its iron and cotton cloth. More generally, it has been carefully estimated that in 1860 Britain produced a truly remarkable 20 percent of the entire world's output of industrial goods, whereas it had produced only about 2 percent of the world total in 1750.[2] Experiencing revolutionary industrial change, Britain became the first industrial nation (see Map 22.2).

MAP 22.2 The Industrial Revolution in England, ca 1850 Industry concentrated in the rapidly growing cities of the north and the Midlands, where rich coal and iron deposits were in close proximity.

Online Study Center Improve Your Grade
Interactive Map: Industrialization in England, ca 1850

As the British economy significantly increased its production of manufactured goods, the gross national product (GNP) rose roughly fourfold at constant prices between 1780 and 1851. In other words, the British people as a whole increased their wealth and their national income dramatically. At the same time, the population of Britain boomed, growing from about 9 million in 1780 to almost 21 million in 1851. Thus growing numbers consumed much of the increase in total production. According to one important study, average consumption per person increased by only 75 percent between 1780 and 1851, as the growth in the total population ate up a large part of the fourfold increase in GNP in those years.[3]

Although the question is still debated, many economic historians now believe that rapid population growth in

The Crystal Palace The Great Exhibition of 1851 attracted more than six million visitors, many of whom journeyed to London on the newly built railroads. Countries and companies from all over the world displayed their products and juries awarded prizes in the strikingly modern Crystal Palace, an architectural marvel built using the cheap iron and glass of the industrial age. In this illustration visitors stroll through the domed hall and peruse the 1500 exhibits. *(Courtesy of the Trustees of the British Museum)*

Great Britain was not harmful because it facilitated industrial expansion. More people meant a more mobile labor force, with a wealth of young workers in need of employment and ready to go where the jobs were. Contemporaries were much less optimistic. In his famous and influential *Essay on the Principle of Population* (1798), Thomas Malthus (1766–1834) argued that population would always tend to grow faster than the food supply. In Malthus's opinion, the only hope of warding off such "positive checks" to population growth as war, famine, and disease was "prudential restraint." That is, young men and women had to limit the growth of population by the old tried-and-true means of marrying late in life. But Malthus was not optimistic about this possibility. The powerful attraction of the sexes would cause most people to marry early and have many children.

Online Study Center Improve Your Grade
Primary Source: Malthus Predicts Gloomy Prospects for the Human Condition

Wealthy English stockbroker and leading economist David Ricardo (1772–1823) coldly spelled out the pessimistic implications of Malthus's thought. Ricardo's depressing **iron law of wages** posited that because of the pressure of population growth, wages would always sink to subsistence level. That is, wages would be just high enough to keep workers from starving. With Malthus and Ricardo setting the tone, economics was soon dubbed "the dismal science."

Malthus, Ricardo, and their many followers were proved wrong—in the long run. However, until the 1820s, or even the 1840s, contemporary observers might reasonably have concluded that the economy and the total population were racing neck and neck, with the outcome very much in doubt. The closeness of the race added to the difficulties inherent in the journey toward industrial civilization.

There was another problem as well. Perhaps workers, farmers, and ordinary people did not get their rightful share of the new wealth. Perhaps only the rich got richer, while the poor got poorer or made no progress. We will turn to this great issue after looking at the process of industrialization in continental countries.

Industrialization in Continental Europe

The new technologies developed in the British Industrial Revolution were adopted rather slowly by businesses in continental Europe. Yet by the end of the nineteenth century, several European countries as well as the United States had also industrialized their economies to a considerable but variable degree. This meant that the process of Western industrialization proceeded gradually, with uneven jerks and national (and regional) variations.

Scholars are still struggling to explain these variations, especially since good answers may offer valuable lessons in our own time for poor countries seeking to improve their material condition through industrialization and economic development. The latest findings on the Western experience are encouraging. They suggest that there were alternative paths to the industrial world in the nineteenth century and that, today as then, there was no need to follow a rigid, predetermined British model.

- **How after 1815 did continental countries respond to the challenge of industrialization?**

National Variations

European industrialization, like most economic developments, requires some statistical analysis as part of the effort to understand it. Comparative data on industrial production in different countries over time help give us an overview of what happened. One set of data, the work of a Swiss scholar, compares the level of industrialization on a per capita basis in several countries from 1750 to 1913. These data are far from perfect because there are gaps in the underlying records. But they reflect basic trends and are presented in Table 22.1 for closer study.

As the heading of Table 22.1 makes clear, this is a per capita comparison of levels of industrialization—a comparison of how much industrial product was produced, on average, for each person in a given country in a given year. Therefore, all the numbers in Table 22.1 are expressed in terms of a single index number of 100, which equals the per capita level of industrial goods in Great Britain (and Ireland) in 1900. Every number in the table is thus a percentage of the 1900 level in Britain and is directly comparable with other numbers. The countries are listed in roughly the order that they began to use large-scale, power-driven technology.

What does this overview of European industrialization tell us? First, and very significantly, one sees in the first column that in 1750 all countries were fairly close together and that Britain was only slightly ahead of its archenemy, France. Second, the column headed 1800 shows that Britain had opened up a noticeable lead over all continental countries by 1800, and that gap progressively widened as the British Industrial Revolution accelerated to 1830 and reached full maturity by 1860. The British level of per capita industrialization was twice the French level in 1830, for example, and more than three times the French level in 1860. All other large countries (except the United States) had fallen even further behind Britain than France had at both dates.

Third, variations in the timing and in the extent of industrialization in the continental powers and the United States are also apparent. Belgium, independent in 1831 and rich in iron and coal, led in adopting Britain's new technology, and it experienced a truly revolutionary surge between 1830 and 1860. France developed factory production more gradually, and most historians now detect no burst in French mechanization and no acceleration in the growth of overall industrial output that may accurately be called revolutionary. They stress instead France's relatively good pattern of early industrial growth, which was unjustly tarnished by the spectacular rise of Germany and the United States after 1860. In general, eastern and southern Europe began the process of modern industrialization later than northwestern and central Europe. Nevertheless, these regions made real progress in the late nineteenth century, as growth after 1880 in Austria-Hungary, Italy, and Russia suggests.

Finally, the late but substantial industrialization in eastern and southern Europe meant that all European states (as well as the United States, Canada, and Japan) managed to raise per capita industrial levels in the nineteenth century. These continent-wide increases stood in stark contrast to the large and tragic decreases that occurred at the same time in many non-Western countries, most notably in China and India, as Table 22.1 clearly shows. European countries industrialized to a greater or lesser extent even as most of the non-Western world *de*-industrialized. Thus differential rates of wealth- and power-creating industrial development, which heightened disparities within Europe,

Table 22.1 Per Capita Levels of Industrialization, 1750–1913

	1750	1800	1830	1860	1880	1900	1913
Great Britain	10	16	25	64	87	100	115
Belgium	9	10	14	28	43	56	88
United States	4	9	14	21	38	69	126
France	9	9	12	20	28	39	59
Germany	8	8	9	15	25	52	85
Austria-Hungary	7	7	8	11	15	23	32
Italy	8	8	8	10	12	17	26
Russia	6	6	7	8	10	15	20
China	8	6	6	4	4	3	3
India	7	6	6	3	2	1	2

Note: All entries are based on an index value of 100, equal to the per capita level of industrialization in Great Britain in 1900. Data for Great Britain are actually for the United Kingdom, thereby including Ireland with England, Wales, and Scotland.

Source: P. Bairoch, "International Industrialization Levels from 1750 to 1980," *Journal of European Economic History* 11 (Spring 1982): 294. Reprinted with permission.

also greatly magnified existing inequalities between Europe and the rest of the world. We shall return to this momentous change in world economic relationships in Chapter 26.

The Challenge of Industrialization

The different patterns of industrial development suggest that the process of industrialization was far from automatic. Indeed, building modern industry was an awesome challenge. To be sure, throughout Europe the eighteenth century was an era of agricultural improvement, population increase, expanding foreign trade, and growing cottage industry. Thus when the pace of British industry began to accelerate in the 1780s, continental businesses began to adopt the new methods as they proved their profitability. British industry enjoyed clear superiority, but at first the continent was close behind.

By 1815, however, the situation was quite different. In spite of wartime difficulties, British industry maintained the momentum of the 1780s and continued to grow and improve between 1789 and 1815. On the continent, the upheavals that began with the French Revolution had another effect: they disrupted trade, created runaway inflation, and fostered social anxiety. War severed normal communications between Britain and the continent, severely handicapping continental efforts to use new British machinery and technology. Moreover, the years from 1789 to 1815 were, even for the privileged French economy receiving special favors from Napoleon, a time of "national catastrophe"—in the graphic words of a famous French scholar.[4] Thus France and the rest of Europe were further behind Britain in 1815 than in 1789.

This widening gap made it more difficult, if not impossible, for other countries to follow the British pattern in energy and industry after peace was restored in 1815. Above all, in the newly mechanized industries, British goods were being produced very economically, and these goods had come to dominate world markets completely while the continental states were absorbed in war between 1792 and 1815. In addition, British technology had become so advanced and complicated that very few engineers or skilled technicians outside England understood it. Moreover, the technology of steam power had grown much more expensive. It involved large investments in the iron and coal industries and, after 1830, required the existence of railroads, which were very costly. Continental business people had great difficulty finding the large sums of money the new methods demanded, and there was a shortage of laborers accustomed to working in factories. All these disadvantages slowed the spread of modern industry (see Map 22.3).

After 1815, however, when continental countries began to face up to the British challenge, they had at least three important advantages. First, most continental countries had a rich tradition of putting-out enterprise, merchant capitalists, and skilled urban artisans. Such a tradition gave continental firms the ability to adapt and survive in the face of new market conditions. Second, continental capitalists did not need to develop their own

Mapping the Past

MAP 22.3 Continental Industrialization, ca 1850 Although continental countries were beginning to make progress by 1850, they still lagged far behind Britain. For example, continental railroad building was still in an early stage, whereas the British rail system was essentially complete (review Map 22.2, page 725). Coal played a critical role in nineteenth-century industrialization both as a power source for steam engines and as a raw material for making iron and steel. ❶ Locate the major exposed (that is, known) coal deposits in 1850. Which countries and areas appear rich in coal resources, and which appear poor? Is there a difference between northern and southern Europe? ❷ What is the relationship between known coal deposits and emerging industrial areas?

advanced technology. Instead, they could simply "borrow" the new methods developed in Great Britain, as well as engineers and some of the financial resources these countries lacked. European countries such as France and Russia also had a third asset that many non-Western areas lacked in the nineteenth century. They had strong independent governments, which did not fall under foreign political control. These governments could fashion economic policies to serve their own interests, as they proceeded to do. They would eventually use the power of the state to promote industry and catch up with Britain.

Agents of Industrialization

The British realized the great value of their technical discoveries and tried to keep their secrets to themselves. Until 1825 it was illegal for artisans and skilled mechanics to leave Britain; until 1843 the export of textile machinery and other equipment was forbidden. Many talented, ambitious workers, however, slipped out of the country illegally and introduced the new methods abroad.

One such man was William Cockerill, a Lancashire carpenter. He and his sons began building cotton-spinning equipment in French-occupied Belgium in 1799. In 1817 the most famous son, John Cockerill, purchased the old summer palace of the deposed bishops of Liège in southern Belgium. Cockerill converted the palace into a large industrial enterprise, which produced machinery, steam engines, and then railway locomotives. He also established modern ironworks and coal mines.

Cockerill's plants in the Liège area became an industrial nerve center, continually gathering new information and transmitting it across Europe. Many skilled British workers came illegally to work for Cockerill, and some went on to found their own companies throughout Europe. Newcomers brought the latest plans and secrets, so Cockerill could boast that ten days after an industrial advance occurred in Britain, he knew all about it in Belgium. Thus British technicians and skilled workers were a powerful force in the spread of early industrialization.

A second agent of industrialization were talented entrepreneurs such as Fritz Harkort, a business pioneer in the German machinery industry. Serving in England as a Prussian army officer during the Napoleonic wars, Harkort was impressed and enchanted with what he saw. He concluded that Germany had to match all these English achievements as quickly as possible. Setting up shop in an abandoned castle in the still-tranquil Ruhr Valley, Harkort felt an almost religious calling to build steam engines and become the "Watt of Germany."

Harkort's basic idea was simple, but it was enormously difficult to carry out. Lacking skilled laborers to do the job, Harkort turned to England for experienced, though expensive, mechanics. Getting materials also posed a great problem. He had to import the thick iron boilers that he needed from England at great cost. In spite of all these problems, Harkort built and sold engines, winning fame and praise. His ambitious efforts over sixteen years also resulted in large financial losses for himself and his partners, and in 1832 he was forced out of his company by his financial backers, who cut back operations to reduce losses. His career illustrates both the great efforts of a few important business leaders to duplicate the British achievement and the difficulty of the task.

Entrepreneurs like Harkort were obviously exceptional. Most continental businesses adopted factory technology slowly, and handicraft methods lived on. Indeed, continental industrialization usually brought substantial but uneven expansion of handicraft industry in both rural and urban areas for a time. Artisan production of luxury items grew in France as the rising income of the international middle class created foreign demand for silk scarfs, embroidered needlework, perfumes, and fine wines.

Government Support and Corporate Banking

Another major force in continental industrialization was government, which often helped business people in continental countries to overcome some of their difficulties. **Tariff protection** was one such support. For example, after Napoleon's wars ended in 1815, France was suddenly flooded with cheaper and better British goods. The French government responded by laying high tariffs on many British imports in order to protect the French economy. After 1815 continental governments bore the cost of building roads and canals to improve transportation.

They also bore to a significant extent the cost of building railroads. Belgium led the way in the 1830s and 1840s. In an effort to tie the newly independent nation together, the Belgian government decided to construct a state-owned system. Built rapidly as a unified network, Belgium's state-owned railroads stimulated the development of heavy industry and made the country an early industrial leader. Several of the smaller German states also built state systems.

The Prussian government provided another kind of invaluable support. It guaranteed that the state treasury would pay the interest and principal on railroad bonds if the closely regulated private companies in Prussia were

A German Ironworks, 1845 This big business enterprise, the Borsig ironworks in Berlin, mastered the new British method of smelting iron ore with coke. Germany, and especially the state of Prussia, was well endowed with both iron and coal, and the rapid exploitation of these resources after 1840 transformed a poor agricultural country into an industrial powerhouse. *(akg-images)*

unable to do so. Thus railroad investors in Prussia ran little risk, and capital was quickly raised. In France the state shouldered all the expense of acquiring and laying roadbed, including bridges and tunnels. Finished roadbed was leased to a carefully supervised private company, which usually benefited from a state guarantee of its debts. In short, governments helped pay for railroads, the all-important leading sector in continental industrialization.

The career of German journalist and thinker Friedrich List (1789–1846) reflects government's greater role in industrialization on the continent than in England. List considered the growth of modern industry of the utmost importance because manufacturing was a primary means of increasing people's well-being and relieving their poverty. Moreover, List was a dedicated nationalist. He wrote that the "wider the gap between the backward and advanced nations becomes, the more dangerous it is to remain behind." An agricultural nation was not only poor but also weak, increasingly unable to defend itself and maintain its political independence. To promote industry was to defend the nation.

The practical policies that List focused on in articles and in his influential *National System of Political Economy* (1841) were railroad building and the tariff. List supported the formation of a customs union, or *Zollverein,* among the separate German states. Such a tariff union came into being in 1834, allowing goods to move between the German member states without tariffs, while erecting a single uniform tariff against other nations. List wanted a high protective tariff, which would encourage infant industries, allowing them to develop and eventually hold their own against their more advanced British counterparts. List denounced the British doctrine of free trade as little more than Britain's attempt "to make the rest of the world, like the Hindus, its serfs in all industrial and commercial relations." By the 1840s List's

economic nationalism had become increasingly popular in Germany and elsewhere.

Finally, banks, like governments, also played a larger and more creative role on the continent than in Britain. Previously, almost all banks in Europe had been private, organized as secretive partnerships. Because of the possibility of unlimited financial loss, the partners of private banks tended to be quite conservative and were content to deal with a few rich clients and a few big merchants. They generally avoided industrial investment as being too risky.

In the 1830s, two important Belgian banks pioneered in a new direction. They received permission from the growth-oriented government to establish themselves as corporations enjoying limited liability. That is, a stockholder could lose only his or her original investment in the bank's common stock and could not be assessed for any additional losses. Publicizing the risk-reducing advantage of limited liability, these Belgian banks were able to attract many shareholders, large and small. They mobilized impressive resources for investment in big companies, became industrial banks, and successfully promoted industrial development.

Similar corporate banks became important in France and Germany in the 1850s and 1860s. Usually working in collaboration with governments, they established and developed many railroads and many companies working in heavy industry, which were increasingly organized as limited liability corporations. The most famous such bank was the Crédit Mobilier of Paris, founded by Isaac and Emile Pereire, two young Jewish journalists from Bordeaux. The Crédit Mobilier advertised extensively. It used the savings of thousands of small investors as well as the resources of big ones. The activities of the bank were far-reaching; it built railroads all over France and Europe. As Emile Pereire had said in 1835, "It is not enough to outline gigantic programs on paper. I must write my ideas on the earth."

The combined efforts of skilled workers, entrepreneurs, governments, and industrial banks meshed successfully between 1850 and the financial crash of 1873. This was a period of unprecedentedly rapid economic growth on the continent. In Belgium, Germany, and France, key indicators of modern industrial development—such as railway mileage, iron and coal production, and steam-engine capacity—increased at average annual rates of 5 to 10 percent. As a result, rail networks were completed in western and much of central Europe, and the leading continental countries mastered the industrial technologies that had first been developed in Great Britain. In the early 1870s, Britain was still Europe's most industrial nation, but a select handful of countries were closing the gap that had been opened up by the Industrial Revolution.

Relations Between Capital and Labor

Industrial development brought new social relations and intensified long-standing problems between capital and labor in both urban workshops and cottage industry (see pages 628–631). A new group of factory owners and industrial capitalists arose. These men and women and their families strengthened the wealth and size of the middle class, which had previously been made up mainly of merchants and professional people. The nineteenth century became the golden age of the middle class. Modern industry also created a much larger group, the factory workers. For the first time, large numbers of men, women, and children came together under one roof to work with complicated machinery for a single owner or a few partners in large companies.

The growth of new occupational groups in industry stimulated new thinking about social relations. Often combined with reflections on the French Revolution, this thinking led to the development of a new overarching interpretation—a new paradigm—regarding social relationships (see Chapter 23). Briefly, this paradigm argued, with considerable success, that individuals were members of economically determined classes, which had conflicting interests. Accordingly, the comfortable, well-educated "public" of the eighteenth century came increasingly to see itself as the backbone of the middle class (or the middle classes), and the "people" gradually transformed themselves into the modern working class (or working classes). And if the new class interpretation was more of a deceptive simplification than a fundamental truth for some critics, it appealed to many because it seemed to explain what was happening. Therefore, conflicting classes existed, in part, because many individuals came to believe they existed and developed an appropriate sense of class feeling—what Marxists call **class-consciousness**.

• How did the Industrial Revolution affect social classes, the standard of living, and patterns of work? What measures were taken to improve the conditions of workers?

The New Class of Factory Owners

Early industrialists operated in a highly competitive economic system. As the careers of Watt and Harkort illus-

Ford Maddox Brown: Work This midcentury painting provides a rich visual representation of the new concepts of social class that became common by 1850. The central figures are the colorful laborers, endowed by the artist with strength and nobility. Close by, a poor girl minds her brother and sister for her working mother. On the right, a middle-class minister and a social critic observe and do intellectual work. What work does the couple on horseback perform? *(Birmingham Museums and Art Gallery/ The Bridgeman Art Library)*

trate, there were countless production problems, and success and large profits were by no means certain. Manufacturers therefore waged a constant battle to cut their production costs and stay afloat. Much of the profit had to go back into the business for new and better machinery. "Dragged on by the frenzy of this terrible life," according to one of the dismayed critics, the struggling manufacturer had "no time for niceties. He must conquer or die, make a fortune or drown himself."[5]

Most early industrialists drew upon their families and friends for labor and capital, but they came from a variety of backgrounds. Many, such as Harkort, were from well-established merchant families, which provided a rich network of contacts and support. Others, such as Watt and Cockerill, were of modest means, especially in the early days. Artisans and skilled workers of exceptional ability had unparalleled opportunities. Members of ethnic and religious groups who had been discriminated against in the traditional occupations controlled by the landed aristocracy jumped at the new chances and often helped each other. Scots, Quakers, and other Protestant dissenters were tremendously important in Britain; Protestants and Jews dominated banking in Catholic France. Many of the industrialists were newly rich, and, not surprisingly, they were very proud and self-satisfied.

As factories and firms grew larger, opportunities declined, at least in well-developed industries. It became considerably harder for a gifted but poor young mechanic to start a small enterprise and end up as a wealthy manufacturer. Formal education (for sons and males) became more important as a means of success and advancement, and formal education at the advanced level was expensive. In Britain by 1830 and in France and Germany by 1860, leading industrialists were more likely to have inherited their well-established enterprises, and they were financially much more secure than their struggling fathers and mothers had been. They also had a greater sense of class-consciousness, fully aware that ongoing industrial development had widened the gap between themselves and their workers.

The wives and daughters of successful businessmen also found fewer opportunities for active participation in Europe's increasingly complex business world. Rather than contributing as vital partners in a family-owned enterprise, as so many middle-class women such as Elizabeth Strutt had done (see the feature "Individuals in Society: The Strutt Family"), these women were increasingly valued for their ladylike gentility. By 1850 some influential women writers and most businessmen assumed that middle-class wives and daughters should steer clear of undignified work in offices and factories. Rather, a middle-class lady should protect and enhance her femininity. She should concentrate on her proper role as wife and mother, preferably in an elegant residential area far removed from ruthless commerce and the volatile working class.

The New Factory Workers

The social consequences of the Industrial Revolution have long been hotly debated. The condition of British workers during the transformation has always generated the most controversy among historians because Britain was the first country to industrialize and because the social consequences seemed harshest there. Before 1850 other countries had not proceeded very far with industrialization, and almost everyone agrees that the economic conditions of European workers improved after 1850. Thus the experience of British workers to about 1850 deserves special attention. (Industrial growth also promoted rapid urbanization, with its own awesome problems, as will be shown in Chapter 24.)

From the beginning, the Industrial Revolution in Britain had its critics. Among the first were the romantic poets. William Blake (1757–1827) called the early factories "satanic mills" and protested against the hard life of the London poor. William Wordsworth (1770–1850) lamented the destruction of the rural way of life and the pollution of the land and water. Some handicraft workers—notably the **Luddites,** who attacked whole factories in northern England in 1812 and after—smashed the new machines, which they believed were putting them out of work. Doctors and reformers wrote eloquently of problems in the factories and new towns, while Malthus and Ricardo concluded that workers would earn only enough to stay alive.

Online Study Center Improve Your Grade
Primary Source: Yorkshire Luddites Threaten the Owner of a Mechanized Factory

This pessimistic view was accepted and reinforced by Friedrich Engels (1820–1895), the future revolutionary and colleague of Karl Marx. After studying conditions in northern England, this young middle-class German published in 1844 *The Condition of the Working Class in England,* a blistering indictment of the middle classes. "At the bar of world opinion," he wrote, "I charge the English middle classes with mass murder, wholesale robbery, and all the other crimes in the calendar." The new poverty of industrial workers was worse than the old poverty of cottage workers and agricultural laborers, according to Engels. The culprit was industrial capitalism, with its relentless competition and constant technical change. Engels's extremely influential charge of middle-class exploitation and increasing worker poverty was embellished by Marx and later socialists.

Meanwhile, other observers believed that conditions were improving for the working people. Andrew Ure wrote in 1835 in his study of the cotton industry that conditions in most factories were not harsh and were even quite good. Edwin Chadwick, a great and conscientious government official well acquainted with the problems of the working population, concluded that the "whole mass of the laboring community" was increasingly able "to buy more of the necessities and minor luxuries of life."[6] Nevertheless, if all the contemporary assessments had been counted up, those who thought conditions were getting worse for working people would probably have been the majority.

In an attempt to go beyond the contradictory judgments of contemporaries, some historians have looked at different kinds of sources. Statistical evidence is one such source. If working people suffered a great economic decline, as Engels and later socialists asserted, then the purchasing power of the working person's wages must have declined drastically.

Scholarly statistical studies have weakened the idea that the condition of the working class got much worse

Individuals in Society

The Strutt Family

For centuries economic life in Europe revolved around hundreds of thousands of small family enterprises. These family enterprises worked farms, crafted products, and traded goods. They built and operated the firms and factories of the early industrial era, with the notable exceptions of the capital-hungry railroads and a few big banks. Indeed, until late in the nineteenth century, close-knit family groups continued to control most successful businesses, including those organized as corporations.

One successful and fairly well-documented family enterprise began with the marriage of Jedediah Strutt (1726–1797) and Elizabeth Woollat (1729–1774) in Derbyshire in northern England in 1755. The son of a farmer, Jedediah fell in love with Elizabeth when he was apprenticed away from home as a wheelwright and lodged with her parents. Both young people grew up in the close-knit dissenting Protestant community, which did not accept the doctrines of the state-sponsored Church of England, and the well-educated Elizabeth worked in a local school for dissenters and then for a dissenter minister in London. Indecisive and self-absorbed, Jedediah inherited in 1754 a small stock of animals from an uncle and finally married Elizabeth the following year.

Aided by Elizabeth, who was "obviously a very capable woman" and who supplied some of the drive her husband had previously lacked, Jedediah embarked on a new career.* He invented a machine to make handsome, neat-fitting ribbed silk stockings, which had previously been made by hand. He secured a patent, despite strong opposition from competitors, and went into production. Elizabeth helped constantly in the enterprise, which was nothing less than an informal partnership between husband and wife.†

In 1757, for example, when Jedediah was fighting to uphold his patent in the local court, Elizabeth left her son of nine months and journeyed to London to seek a badly needed loan from her former employer. She also canvassed her London relatives and dissenter friends for orders for stockings and looked for sales agents and sources of capital. Elizabeth's letters reveal a detailed knowledge of ribbed stockings and the prices and quality of different kinds of thread. The family biographers, old-line economic historians writing without a trace of feminist concerns, conclude that her husband "owed much of his success to her energy and counsel." Elizabeth was always "active in the business—a partner in herself."‡ Historians have often overlooked such invaluable contributions from wives like Elizabeth, partly because the legal rights and consequences of partnership were denied to married women in Britain and Europe in the eighteenth and nineteenth centuries.

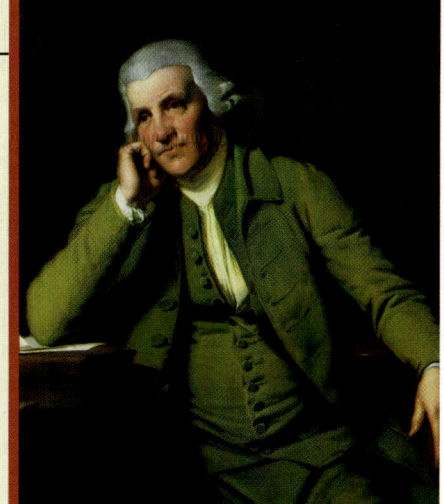

Jedediah Strutt (ca 1790), by Joseph Wright of Derby. (Derby Museum & Art Gallery/The Bridgeman Art Library)

The Strutt enterprise grew and gradually prospered, but it always retained its family character. The firm built a large silk mill and then went into cotton spinning in partnership with Richard Arkwright, the inventor of the water frame (see page 720). The brothers of both Jedediah and Elizabeth worked for the firm, and their eldest daughter worked long hours in the warehouse. Bearing three sons, Elizabeth fulfilled yet another vital task because the typical family firm looked to its own members for managers and continued success. All three sons entered the business and became cotton textile magnates. Elizabeth never saw these triumphs. The loyal and talented wife in the family partnership died suddenly at age forty-five while in London with Jedediah on a business trip.

Questions for Analysis

1. How and why did the Strutts succeed?
2. What does Elizabeth's life tell us about the role of British women in the early Industrial Revolution?

*R. Fitton and A. Wadsworth, *The Strutts and the Arkwrights, 1758–1830: A Study of the Early Factory System* (Manchester, England: Manchester University Press, 1958), p. 23.
†See the excellent discussion by C. Hall, "Strains in the 'Firm of Wife, Children and Friends'? Middle-Class Women and Employment in Early Nineteenth-Century England," in P. Hudson and W. Lee, eds., *Women's Work and the Family Economy in Historical Perspective* (Manchester, England: Manchester University Press, 1990), pp. 106–132.
‡Fitton and Wadsworth, *The Strutts*, pp. 110–111.

Online Study Center Improve Your Grade
Going Beyond Individuals in Society

with industrialization. But the most recent studies also confirm the view that the early years of the Industrial Revolution were hard ones for British workers. There was little or no increase in the purchasing power of the average British worker from about 1780 to about 1820. The years from 1792 to 1815, a period of almost constant warfare with France, were particularly difficult. Food prices rose faster than wages, and the living conditions of the laboring poor declined. Only after 1820, and especially after 1840, did real wages rise substantially, so that the average worker earned and consumed roughly 50 percent more in real terms in 1850 than in 1770.[7] In short, there was considerable economic improvement for workers throughout Great Britain by 1850, but that improvement was hard won and slow in coming.

This important conclusion must be qualified, however. First, the hours in the average workweek increased, as some economic historians now believe it had been increasing in parts of northern Europe since the seventeenth century. Thus, to a large extent, workers earned more simply because they worked more. Indeed, significant recent research shows that in England nonagricultural workers labored about 250 days per year in 1760 as opposed to 300 days per year in 1830, while the normal workday remained an exhausting eleven hours throughout the entire period. In 1760 nonagricultural workers still observed many religious and public holidays by not working, and Monday was popularly known as "Saint Monday" because so many workers took the day off. These days of leisure and relaxation declined rapidly after 1760, and by 1830 nonagricultural workers had joined landless agricultural laborers in toiling six rather than five days a week.[8]

Second, the wartime decline in the average worker's standard of living was very important. The difficult war years were formative years for the new factory labor force, and they colored the early experience of modern industrial life in somber tones.

Another way to consider the workers' standard of living is to look at the goods that they purchased. Again the evidence is somewhat contradictory. Speaking generally, workers ate somewhat more food of higher nutritional quality as the Industrial Revolution progressed, except during wartime. Diets became more varied; people ate more potatoes, dairy products, fruits, and vegetables. Clothing improved, but housing for working people probably deteriorated somewhat. In short, per capita use of specific goods supports the position that the standard of living of the working classes rose, at least moderately, after the long wars with France.

Conditions of Work

What about working conditions? Did workers eventually earn more only at the cost of working longer and harder? Were workers exploited harshly by the new factory owners?

The first factories were cotton mills, which began functioning along rivers and streams in the 1770s. Cottage workers, accustomed to the putting-out system, were reluctant to work in the new factories even when they received relatively good wages because factory work was unappealing. In the factory, workers had to keep up with the machine and follow its tempo. They had to show up every day and work long, monotonous hours. Factory workers had to adjust their daily lives to the shrill call of the factory whistle.

Cottage workers were not used to that kind of life and discipline. All members of the family worked hard and long, but in spurts, setting their own pace. They could interrupt their work when they wanted to. Women and children could break up their long hours of spinning with other tasks. On Saturday afternoon the head of the family delivered the week's work to the merchant manufacturer and got paid. Saturday night was a time of relaxation and drinking, especially for the men. Recovering from his hangover on Tuesday, the weaver bent to his task on Wednesday and then worked frantically to meet his deadline on Saturday. Like some students today, he might "pull an all-nighter" on Thursday or Friday in order to get his work in.

Also, early factories resembled English poorhouses, where totally destitute people went to live at public expense. Some poorhouses were industrial prisons, where the inmates had to work in order to receive their food and lodging. The similarity between large brick factories and large stone poorhouses increased the cottage workers' fear of factories and their hatred of factory discipline.

It was cottage workers' reluctance to work in factories that prompted the early cotton mill owners to turn to abandoned and pauper children for their labor. As we have seen, these owners contracted with local officials to employ large numbers of these children, who had no say in the matter. Pauper children were often badly treated and terribly overworked in the mills, as they were when they were apprenticed as chimney sweeps, market girls, shoemakers, and so forth. In the eighteenth century, semiforced child labor seemed necessary and was socially accepted. From our modern point of view, it was cruel exploitation and a blot on the record of the new industrial system.

Workers at a Large Cotton Mill This 1833 engraving shows adult women operating power looms under the supervision of a male foreman, and it accurately reflects both the decline of family employment and the emergence of a gender-based division of labor in many English factories. The jungle of belts and shafts connecting the noisy looms to the giant steam engine on the ground floor created a constant din. *(Time Life Pictures/Getty Images)*

By 1790 the early pattern was rapidly changing. The use of pauper apprentices was in decline, and in 1802 it was forbidden by Parliament. Many more factories were being built, mainly in urban areas, where they could use steam power rather than waterpower and attract a workforce more easily than in the countryside. The need for workers was great. Indeed, people came from near and far to work in the cities, both as factory workers and as laborers, builders, and domestic servants. Yet as they took these new jobs, working people did not simply give in to a system of labor that had formerly repelled them. Rather, they helped modify the system by carrying over old, familiar working traditions.

For one thing, they often came to the mills and the mines as family units. This was how they had worked on farms and in the putting-out system. The mill or mine owner bargained with the head of the family and paid him or her for the work of the whole family. In the cotton mills, children worked for their mothers or fathers, collecting scraps and "piecing" broken threads together. In the mines, children sorted coal and worked the ventilation equipment. Their mothers hauled coal in the tunnels below the surface, while their fathers hewed with pick and shovel at the face of the seam.

The preservation of the family as an economic unit in the factories from the 1790s on made the new surroundings more tolerable, both in Great Britain and in other countries, during the early stages of industrialization. Parents disciplined their children, making firm measures socially acceptable, and directed their upbringing.

The presence of the whole family meant that children and adults worked the same long hours (twelve-hour shifts were normal in cotton mills in 1800). In the early years, some very young children were employed solely to keep the family together. For example, Jedediah Strutt (see page 735) believed children should be at least ten years old to work in his mills, but he reluctantly employed seven-year-olds to satisfy their parents. Adult workers were not particularly interested in limiting the minimum working age or hours of their children as long as family members worked side by side. Only when technical changes threatened to place control and discipline in the hands of impersonal managers and overseers did adult workers protest against inhuman conditions in the name of their children.

Some enlightened employers and social reformers in Parliament definitely felt otherwise. They argued that more humane standards were necessary, and they used widely circulated parliamentary reports to influence public opinion. For example, Robert Owen (1771–1858), a very successful manufacturer in Scotland, testified in 1816 before an investigating committee on the basis of his experience. He stated that "very strong facts" demonstrated that employing children under ten years of age as factory workers was "injurious to the children, and not beneficial to the proprietors."[9] Workers also provided graphic testimony at such hearings as the reformers pressed Parliament to pass corrective laws. They scored some important successes.

Their most significant early accomplishment was the **Factory Act of 1833.** It limited the factory workday for children between nine and thirteen to eight hours and that of adolescents between fourteen and eighteen to twelve hours, although the act made no effort to regulate the hours of work for children at home or in small businesses. Children under nine were to be enrolled in the elementary schools that factory owners were required to establish. The employment of children declined rapidly. Thus the Factory Act broke the pattern of whole families working together in the factory because efficiency required standardized shifts for all workers.

Ties of blood and kinship were important in other ways in Great Britain in the formative years between about 1790 and 1840. Many manufacturers and builders hired workers through subcontractors. They paid the subcontractors on the basis of what the subcontractors and their crews produced—for smelting so many tons of pig iron or moving so much dirt or gravel for a canal or roadbed. Subcontractors in turn hired and fired their own workers, many of whom were friends and relations. The subcontractor might be as harsh as the greediest capitalist, but the relationship between subcontractor and work crew was close and personal. This kind of personal relationship had traditionally existed in cottage industry and in urban crafts, and it was more acceptable to many workers than impersonal factory discipline. This system also provided people with an easy way to find a job. Even today, a friend or relative who is a supervisor is frequently worth a host of formal application forms.

Ties of kinship were particularly important for newcomers, who often traveled great distances to find work. Many urban workers in Great Britain were from Ireland. Forced out of rural Ireland by population growth and deteriorating economic conditions from 1817 on, Irish in search of jobs could not be choosy; they took what they could get. As early as 1824, most of the workers in the Glasgow cotton mills were Irish; in 1851 one-sixth of the population of Liverpool was Irish. Like many other immigrant groups held together by ethnic and religious ties, the Irish worked together, formed their own neighborhoods, and not only survived but also thrived.

The Sexual Division of Labor

The era of the Industrial Revolution witnessed major changes in the sexual division of labor. In preindustrial Europe most people generally worked in family units. By tradition, certain jobs were defined by gender—women and girls for milking and spinning, men and boys for plowing and weaving—but many tasks might go to either sex. Family employment carried over into early factories and subcontracting, but it collapsed as child labor was restricted and new attitudes emerged. A different sexual division of labor gradually arose to take its place. The man emerged as the family's primary wage earner, while the woman found only limited job opportunities. Generally denied good jobs at good wages in the growing urban economy, women were expected to concentrate on unpaid housework, child care, and craftwork at home.

This new pattern of "separate spheres" had several aspects. First, all studies agree that married women from the working classes were much less likely to work full-time for wages outside the house after the first child arrived, although they often earned small amounts doing putting-out handicrafts at home and taking in boarders. Second, when married women did work for wages outside the house, they usually came from the poorest families, where the husbands were poorly paid, sick, unemployed, or missing. Third, these poor married (or widowed) women were joined by legions of young unmarried women, who worked full-time but only in certain jobs. Fourth, all women were generally confined to low-paying, dead-end jobs. Virtually no occupation open to women paid a wage sufficient for a person to live independently. Men predominated in the better-paying, more promising employments. Evolving gradually, but largely in place by 1850, the new sexual division of labor in Britain constituted a major development in the history of women and of the family.

If the reorganization of paid work along gender lines is widely recognized, there is no agreement on its causes. One school of scholars sees little connection with industrialization and finds the answer in the deeply ingrained sexist attitudes of a "patriarchal tradition," which predated the economic transformation. These scholars stress the role of male-dominated craft unions in denying working women access to good jobs and relegating them to unpaid housework. Other scholars, stressing that the gender roles of women and men can vary enormously with time and culture, look more to a combination of economic and biological factors in order to explain the emergence of a sex-segregated division of labor.

Three ideas stand out in this more recent interpretation. First, the new and unfamiliar discipline of the clock and the machine was especially hard on married women of the laboring classes. Above all, relentless factory discipline conflicted with child care in a way that labor on the farm or in the cottage had not. A woman operating ear-splitting spinning machinery could mind a child of seven or eight working beside her (until such work was outlawed), but she could no longer pace herself through pregnancy or breast-feed her baby on the job. Thus a working-class woman had strong incentives to concentrate on child care within her home if her family could afford it.

Second, running a household in conditions of primitive urban poverty was an extremely demanding job in its own right. There were no supermarkets or public transportation. Everything had to be done on foot. Shopping and feeding the family constituted a never-ending challenge. The woman marched from one tiny shop to another, dragging her tired children (for who was to watch them?) and struggling valiantly with heavy sacks and tricky shopkeepers. Yet another brutal job outside the house—a "second shift"—had limited appeal for the average married woman. Thus women might well have accepted the emerging division of labor as the best available strategy for family survival in the industrializing society.[10]

Third, why were the women who did work for wages outside the home segregated and confined to certain "women's jobs"? No doubt the desire of males to monopolize the best opportunities and hold women down provides part of the answer. Yet as some feminist scholars have argued, sex-segregated employment was also a collective response to the new industrial system. Previously, at least in theory, young people worked under a watchful parental eye. The growth of factories and mines brought unheard-of opportunities for girls and boys to mix on the job, free of familial supervision. Continuing to mix after work, they were "more likely to form liaisons, initiate courtships, and respond to advances."[11] Such intimacy also led to more unplanned pregnancies and fueled the illegitimacy explosion that had begun in the late eighteenth century and that gathered force until at least 1850 (see pages 656–657). Thus segregation of jobs by gender was partly an effort by older people to help control the sexuality of working-class youths.

Investigations into the British coal industry before 1842 provide a graphic example of this concern. (See the feature "Listening to the Past: The Testimony of Young Mine Workers" on pages 744–745.) The middle-class men leading the inquiry, who expected their daughters and wives to pursue ladylike activities, often failed to appreciate the physical effort of the girls and women who dragged with belt and chain the unwheeled carts of coal along narrow underground passages. But they professed horror at the sight of girls and women working without shirts, which was a common practice because of the heat, and they quickly assumed the prevalence of licentious sex with the male miners, who also wore very little clothing. In fact, most girls and married women worked for related males in a family unit that provided considerable protection and restraint. Yet many witnesses from the working class also believed that "blackguardism and debauchery" were common and that "they are best out of the pits, the lasses." Some miners stressed particularly the danger of sexual aggression for girls working past puberty. As one explained: "I consider it a scandal for girls to work in the pits. Till they are 12 or 14 they may work very well but after that it's an abomination. . . . The work of the pit does not hurt them, it is the effect on their morals that I complain of."[12] The **Mines Act of 1842** prohibited underground work for all women as well as for boys under ten.

Some women who had to support themselves protested against being excluded from coal mining, which paid higher wages than most other jobs open to working-class women. But provided they were part of families that could manage economically, the girls and the women who had worked underground were generally pleased with the law. In explaining her satisfaction in 1844, one mother of four provided a real insight into why many women accepted the emerging sexual division of labor:

While working in the pit I was worth to my [miner] husband seven shillings a week, out of which we had to pay 2½ shillings to a woman for looking after the younger children. I used to take them to her house at 4 o'clock in the morning, out of their own beds, to put them into hers. Then there was one shilling a week for washing; besides, there was mending to pay for, and other things. The house was not guided. The other children broke things; they did not go to school when they were sent; they would be playing about, and get ill-used by other children, and their clothes torn. Then when I came home in the evening, everything was to do after the day's labor, and I was so tired I had no heart for it; no fire lit, nothing cooked, no water fetched, the house dirty, and nothing comfortable for my husband. It is all far better now, and I wouldn't go down again.[13]

The Early Labor Movement in Britain

Many kinds of employment changed slowly during and after the Industrial Revolution in Great Britain. In 1850 more British people still worked on farms than in any other occupation. The second-largest occupation was domestic service, with more than one million household servants, 90 percent of whom were women. Thus many old, familiar jobs outside industry lived on and provided alternatives for individual workers. This helped ease the transition to industrial civilization.

Within industry itself, the pattern of artisans working with hand tools in small shops remained unchanged in many trades, even as some others were revolutionized by technological change. For example, as in the case of cotton and coal, the British iron industry was completely dominated by large-scale capitalist firms by 1850. Many large ironworks had more than one thousand people on their payrolls. Yet the firms that fashioned iron into small metal goods, such as tools, tableware, and toys, employed on average fewer than ten wage workers, who used time-honored handicraft skills. Only gradually after 1850 did some owners find ways to reorganize some handicraft industries with new machines and new patterns of work. The survival of small workshops gave many workers an alternative to factory employment.

Working-class solidarity and class-consciousness developed in small workshops as well as in large factories. In the northern factory districts, where thousands of "hired hands" looked across at a tiny minority of managers and owners, anticapitalist sentiments were frequent by the 1820s. Commenting in 1825 on a strike in the woolen center of Bradford and the support it had gathered from other regions, one paper claimed with pride that "it is all the workers of England against a few masters of Bradford."[14] Modern technology had created a few versus a many.

The transformation of some traditional trades by organizational changes, rather than technological innovations, could also create ill will and class feeling. The liberal concept of economic freedom gathered strength in the late eighteenth and early nineteenth centuries. As in France during the French Revolution, the British government attacked monopolies, guilds, and workers combinations in the name of individual liberty. In 1799 Parliament passed the **Combination Acts,** which outlawed unions and strikes. In 1813 and 1814, Parliament repealed the old and often disregarded law of 1563 regulating the wages of artisans and the conditions of apprenticeship. As a result of these and other measures, certain skilled artisan workers, such as bootmakers and high-quality tailors, found aggressive capitalists ignoring traditional work rules and flooding their trades with unorganized women workers and children to beat down wages.

Celebrating Skilled Labor This handsome engraving embellished the membership certificate of the British carpenters union, one of the leading "new model unions" that represented skilled workers effectively after 1850. The upper panel shows carpenters building the scaffolding for a great arch; the lower panel captures the spirit of a busy workshop. *(HIP/Art Resource, NY)*

The liberal capitalist attack on artisan guilds and work rules was bitterly resented by many craftworkers, who subsequently played an important part in Great Britain and in other countries in gradually building a modern labor movement to improve working conditions and to serve worker needs. The Combination Acts were widely disregarded by workers. Printers, papermakers, carpenters, tailors, and other such craftsmen continued to take collective action, and societies of skilled factory workers also organized unions. Unions sought to control the number of skilled workers, limit apprenticeship to members' own children, and bargain with owners over wages. They were not afraid to strike; there was, for example, a general strike of adult cotton spinners in Manchester in 1810. In the face of widespread union activity, Parliament repealed the Combination Acts in 1824, and unions were tolerated, though not fully accepted, after 1825.

The next stage in the development of the British trade-union movement was the attempt to create a single large national union. This effort was led not so much by working people as by social reformers such as Robert Owen. Owen, a self-made cotton manufacturer (see page 738), had pioneered in industrial relations by combining firm discipline with concern for the health, safety, and hours of his workers. After 1815 he experimented with cooperative and socialist communities, including one at New Harmony, Indiana. Then in 1834 Owen organized one of the largest and most visionary of the early national unions, the **Grand National Consolidated Trades Union.** When this and other grandiose schemes collapsed, the British labor movement moved once again after 1851 in the direction of craft unions. The most famous of these "new model unions" was the Amalgamated Society of Engineers, which represented skilled machinists. These unions won real benefits for members by fairly conservative means and thus became an accepted part of the industrial scene.

British workers also engaged in direct political activity in defense of their own interests. After the collapse of Owen's national trade union, many working people went into the Chartist movement, which sought political democracy. The key Chartist demand—that all men be given the right to vote—became the great hope of millions of aroused people. Workers were also active in campaigns to limit the workday in factories to ten hours and to permit duty-free importation of wheat into Great Britain to secure cheap bread. Thus working people developed a sense of their own identity and played an active role in shaping the new industrial system. They were neither helpless victims nor passive beneficiaries.

Chapter Summary

 Online Study Center   ACE the Test

- **What were the origins of the Industrial Revolution in Britain, and how did it develop between 1780 and 1850?**
- **How after 1815 did continental countries respond to the challenge of industrialization?**
- **How did the Industrial Revolution affect social classes, the standard of living, and patterns of work? What measures were taken to improve the conditions of workers?**

Western society's industrial breakthrough grew out of a long process of economic and social change in which the rise of capitalism, overseas expansion, and the growth of rural industry stood out as critical preparatory developments. Eventually taking the lead in all of these developments, and also profiting from stable government, abundant natural resources, and a flexible labor force, Britain experienced between the 1780s and the 1850s an epoch-making transformation, one that is still aptly termed the Industrial Revolution.

Building on technical breakthroughs, power-driven equipment, and large-scale enterprise, the Industrial Revolution in England greatly increased output in certain radically altered industries, stimulated the large handicraft and commercial sectors, and speeded up overall economic growth. Rugged Scotland industrialized at least as fast as England, and Great Britain became the first industrial nation. By 1850 the level of British per capita industrial production was surpassing continental levels by a growing margin, and Britain savored a near monopoly in world markets for mass-produced goods.

Continental countries inevitably took rather different paths to the urban industrial society. They relied more on handicraft production in both towns and villages. Only in the 1840s did railroad construction begin to create the strong demand for iron, coal, and railway equipment that speeded up the process of industrialization in the 1850s and 1860s.

The rise of modern industry had a profound impact on people and their lives. In the early stages, Britain again led the way, experiencing in a striking manner the long-term social changes accompanying the economic transformation. Factory discipline and Britain's stern capitalist economy weighed heavily on working people, who, however, actively fashioned their destinies and refused to be passive victims. Improvements in the standard of living came slowly, but they were substantial by 1850. The era of industrialization fostered new attitudes toward child labor, encouraged protective factory legislation, and called forth a new sense of class feeling and an assertive labor movement. It also promoted a more rigid division of roles and responsibilities within the family that was detrimental to women, another gradual but profound change of revolutionary proportions.

Key Terms

- Industrial Revolution
- spinning jenny
- water frame
- body linen
- steam engines
- coke
- *Rocket*
- Crystal Palace
- iron law of wages
- tariff protection
- economic nationalism
- class-consciousness
- Luddites
- Factory Act of 1833
- Mines Act of 1842
- Combination Acts
- Grand National Consolidated Trades Union

 Online Study Center   Improve Your Grade Flashcards

Suggested Reading

Cameron, Rondo, and Larry Neal. *A Concise Economic History of the World*, 4th ed. 2003. Provides an introduction to key issues related to the Industrial Revolution and has a carefully annotated bibliography.

Clapham, J. H. *Economic Development of France and Germany.* 1963. A classic study.

Davidoff, Leonore, and Catherine Hall. *Family Fortunes: Men and Women of the English Middle Class, 1750–1850,* rev. ed. 2003. Examines both economic activities and cultural beliefs with great skill.

Fuchs, Rachel G. *Gender and Poverty in Nineteenth-Century Europe.* 2005. Provides a broad comparative perspective.

Gaskell, Elizabeth. *Mary Barton.* 1848. Gaskell's novel offers a realistic portrayal of the new industrial society.

Goodman, Jordan, and Katrina Honeyman. *Gainful Pursuits: The Making of Industrial Europe, 1600–1914.* 1988. An excellent general treatment of European industrial growth.

Kemp, Tom. *Industrialization in Europe,* 2d ed. 1985. A useful overview.

Landes, David. *Dynasties: Fortunes and Misfortunes of the World's Great Family Businesses.* 2006. A collection offering fascinating and insightful histories of famous enterprises and leading capitalists.

Pomeranz, Kenneth. *The Great Divergence: China, Europe, and the Making of the Modern World Economy.* 2000. A sophisticated reconsideration of why western Europe underwent industrialization and China did not.

Stearns, Peter N. *The Industrial Revolution in World History,* 3d ed. 2007. A useful brief survey.

Thompson, E. P. *The Making of the English Working Class.* 1963. A fascinating book in the Marxian tradition that is rich in detail and early working-class lore.

Valenze, Deborah. *The First Industrial Woman.* 1995. A gender study that reinvigorates the debate between "optimists" and "pessimists" about the consequences of industrialization in Britain.

Walton, Whitney. *France and the Crystal Palace: Bourgeois Taste and Artisan Manufacture in the 19th Century.* 1992. Examines the gradual transformation of handicraft techniques and their persistent importance in the international economy.

Wrigley, E. A. *Continuity, Chance and Change: The Character of the Industrial Revolution in England.* 1994. An important reconsideration stressing resources and population.

Notes

1. N. F. R. Crafts, *British Economic Growth During the Industrial Revolution* (Oxford: Oxford University Press, 1985), p. 32.
2. P. Bairoch, "International Industrialization Levels from 1750 to

1980," *Journal of European Economic History* 11 (Spring 1982): 269–333.
3. Crafts, *British Economic Growth,* pp. 45, 95–102.
4. M. Lévy-Leboyer, *Les banques européennes et l'industrialisation dans la première moitié du XIXe siècle* (Paris: Presses Universitaires de France, 1964), p. 29.
5. J. Michelet, *The People,* trans. with an introduction by J. P. McKay (Urbana: University of Illinois Press, 1973; original publication, 1846), p. 64.
6. Quoted in W. A. Hayek, ed., *Capitalism and the Historians* (Chicago: University of Chicago Press, 1954), p. 126.
7. Crafts, *British Economic Growth,* p. 95.
8. H-J. Voth, *Time and Work in England, 1750–1830* (Oxford: Oxford University Press, 2000), pp. 268–270; also pp. 118–133.
9. Quoted in E. R. Pike, *"Hard Times": Human Documents of the Industrial Revolution* (New York: Praeger, 1966), p. 109.
10. See especially J. Brenner and M. Rama, "Rethinking Women's Oppression," *New Left Review* 144 (March–April 1984): 33–71, and sources cited there.
11. J. Humphries, ". . . 'The Most Free from Objection' . . . : The Sexual Division of Labor and Women's Work in Nineteenth-Century England," *Journal of Economic History* 47 (December 1987): 948.
12. Ibid., p. 941; Pike, *"Hard Times,"* p. 266.
13. Pike, *"Hard Times,"* p. 208.
14. Quoted in D. Geary, ed., *Labour and Socialist Movements in Europe Before 1914* (Oxford: Berg, 1989), p. 29.

Listening to the Past

The Testimony of Young Mine Workers

The use of child labor in British industrialization quickly attracted the attention of humanitarians and social reformers. This interest led to investigations by parliamentary commissions, which resulted in laws limiting the hours and the ages of children working in large factories. Designed to build a case for remedial legislation, parliamentary inquiries gave large numbers of workers a rare chance to speak directly to contemporaries and to historians.

The moving passages that follow are taken from testimony gathered in 1841 and 1842 by the Ashley Mines Commission. Interviewing employers and many male and female workers, the commissioners focused on the physical condition of the youth and on the sexual behavior of workers far underground. The subsequent Mines Act of 1842 sought to reduce immoral behavior and sexual bullying by prohibiting underground work for all women (and for boys younger than ten).

Mr. Payne, coal master:

That children are employed generally at nine years old in the coal pits and sometimes at eight. In fact, the smaller the vein of coal is in height, the younger and smaller are the children required; the work occupies from six to seven hours per day in the pits; they are not ill-used or worked beyond their strength; a good deal of depravity exists but they are certainly not worse in morals than in other branches of the Sheffield trade, but upon the whole superior; the morals of this district are materially improving; Mr. Bruce, the clergyman, has been zealous and active in endeavoring to ameliorate their moral and religious education. . . .

Ann Eggley, hurrier, 18 years old:

I'm sure I don't know how to spell my name. We go at four in the morning, and sometimes at half-past four. We begin to work as soon as we get down. We get out after four, sometimes at five, in the evening. We work the whole time except an hour for dinner, and sometimes we haven't time to eat. I hurry [move coal wagons underground] by myself, and have done so for long. I know the corves [small coal wagons] are very heavy, they are the biggest corves anywhere about. The work is far too hard for me; the sweat runs off me all over sometimes. I am very tired at night. Sometimes when we get home at night we have not power to wash us, and then we go to bed. Sometimes we fall asleep in the chair. Father said last night it was both a shame and a disgrace for girls to work as we do, but there was naught else for us to do. I began to hurry when I was seven and I have been hurrying ever since. I have been 11 years in the pits. The girls are always tired. I was poorly twice this winter; it was with headache. I hurry for Robert Wiggins; he is not akin to me. . . . We don't always get enough to eat and drink, but we get a good supper. I have known my father go at two in the morning to work . . . and he didn't come out till four. I am quite sure that we work constantly 12 hours except on Saturdays. We wear trousers and our shifts in the pit and great big shoes clinkered and nailed. The girls never work naked to the waist in our pit. The men don't insult us in the pit. The conduct of the girls in the pit is good enough sometimes and sometimes bad enough. I never went to a day-school. I went a little to a Sunday-school, but I soon gave it over. I thought it too bad to be confined both Sundays and week-days. I walk about and get the fresh air on Sundays. I have not learnt to read. I don't know my letters. I never learnt naught. I never go to church or chapel; there is no church or chapel at Gawber, there is none nearer than a mile. . . . I have never heard that a good man came into the world who was God's son to save sinners. I never

This illustration of a girl dragging a coal wagon was one of several that shocked public opinion and contributed to the Mines Act of 1842. *(The British Library)*

heard of Christ at all. Nobody has ever told me about him, nor have my father and mother ever taught me to pray. I know no prayer; I never pray.

Patience Kershaw, aged 17:

My father has been dead about a year; my mother is living and has ten children, five lads and five lasses; the oldest is about thirty, the youngest is four; three lasses go to mill; all the lads are colliers, two getters and three hurriers; one lives at home and does nothing; mother does nought but look after home.

All my sisters have been hurriers, but three went to the mill. Alice went because her legs swelled from hurrying in cold water when she was hot. I never went to day-school; I go to Sunday-school, but I cannot read or write; I go to pit at five o'clock in the morning and come out at five in the evening; I get my breakfast of porridge and milk first; I take my dinner with me, a cake, and eat it as I go; I do not stop or rest any time for the purpose; I get nothing else until I get home, and then have potatoes and meat, not every day meat. I hurry in the clothes I have now got on, trousers and ragged jacket; the bald place upon my head is made by thrusting the corves; my legs have never swelled, but sisters' did when they went to mill; I hurry the corves a mile and more under ground and back; they weigh 300; I hurry 11 a day; I wear a belt and chain at the workings to get the corves out; the putters [miners] that I work for are *naked* except their caps; they pull off all their clothes; I see them at work when I go up; sometimes they beat me, if I am not quick enough, with their hands; they strike me upon my back; the boys take liberties with me, sometimes, they pull me about; I am the only girl in the pit; there are about 20 boys and 15 men; all the men are naked; I would rather work in mill than in coal-pit.

Isabel Wilson, 38 years old, coal putter:

When women have children thick [fast] they are compelled to take them down early. I have been married 19 years and have had 10 bairns [children]; seven are in life. When on Sir John's work was a carrier of coals, which caused me to miscarry five times from the strains, and was gai [very] ill after each. Putting is no so oppressive; last child was born on Saturday morning, and I was at work on the Friday night.

Once met with an accident; a coal brake my cheek-bone, which kept me idle some weeks.

I have wrought below 30 years, and so has the guid man; he is getting touched in the breath now.

None of the children read, as the work is no regular. I did read once, but no able to attend to it now; when I go below lassie 10 years of age keeps house and makes the broth or stir-about.

Questions for Analysis

1. To what extent are the testimonies of Ann Eggley and Patience Kershaw in harmony with that of Payne?
2. Describe the work of Eggley and Kershaw. What do you think of their work? Why?
3. What strikes you most about the lives of these workers?
4. The witnesses were responding to questions from middle-class commissioners. What did the commissioners seem interested in? Why?

Source: J. Bowditch and C. Ramsland, eds., *Voices of the Industrial Revolution.* Copyright © 1961, 1989 by the University of Michigan. Reprinted by permission.

Revolutionaries in Transylvania. Ana Ipatescu, of the first group of revolutionaries in Transylvania against Russia, 1848. *(National Historical Museum, Bucharest/The Art Archive)*

chapter 23
IDEOLOGIES AND UPHEAVALS, 1815–1850

chapter preview

The Peace Settlement
• How did the victorious allies fashion a general peace settlement, and how did Metternich uphold a conservative European order?

Radical Ideas and Early Socialism
• What were the basic tenets of liberalism, nationalism, and socialism, and what groups were most attracted to these ideologies?

The Romantic Movement
• What were the characteristics of the romantic movement, and who were some of the great romantic artists?

Reforms and Revolutions
• How after 1815 did liberal, national, and socialist forces challenge conservatism in Greece, Great Britain, and France?

The Revolutions of 1848
• Why in 1848 did revolution triumph briefly throughout most of Europe, and why did it fail almost completely?

The momentous economic and political transformation of modern times began in the late eighteenth century with the Industrial Revolution in England and then the French Revolution. Until about 1815, these economic and political revolutions were separate, involving different countries and activities and proceeding at very different paces. After peace returned in 1815, the situation changed. Economic and political changes tended to fuse, reinforcing each other and bringing about what historian Eric Hobsbawm has incisively called the **dual revolution.** For instance, the growth of the industrial middle class encouraged the drive for representative government, and the demands of the French sans-culottes in 1793 and 1794 inspired many socialist thinkers. Gathering strength, the dual revolution rushed on to alter completely first Europe and then the rest of the world. Much of world history in the past two centuries can be seen as the progressive unfolding of the dual revolution.

In Europe in the nineteenth century, as in Asia and Africa in more recent times, the interrelated economic and political transformation was built on complicated histories, strong traditions, and highly diverse cultures. Radical change was eventually a constant, but the particular results varied enormously. In central and eastern Europe especially, the traditional elites—the monarchs, noble landowners, and bureaucrats—proved capable of defending their privileges and eventually using nationalism as a way to respond to the dual revolution and to serve their interests, as we shall see in Chapter 25.

The dual revolution also posed a tremendous intellectual challenge. The meanings of the economic, political, and social changes that were occurring, as well as the ways they would be shaped by human action, were anything but clear. These changes fascinated observers and stimulated the growth of new ideas and powerful ideologies. The most important of these ideological forces were revitalized conservatism and three ideologies of change—liberalism, nationalism, and socialism. All played critical roles in the political and social battles of the era and the great popular upheaval that eventually swept across Europe in the revolutions of 1848.

Online Study Center
This icon will direct you to interactive activities and study materials on the website **college.hmco.com/pic/mckaywest9e**

The Peace Settlement

The eventual triumph of revolutionary economic and political forces was by no means certain as the Napoleonic era ended. Quite the contrary. The conservative, aristocratic monarchies of Russia, Prussia, Austria, and Great Britain—the Quadruple Alliance—had finally defeated France and reaffirmed their determination to hold France in line. But many other international questions were outstanding, and the allies agreed to meet at the **Congress of Vienna** to fashion a general peace settlement.

Most people felt a profound longing for peace. The great challenge for political leaders in 1814 was to construct a settlement that would last and not sow the seeds of another war. Their efforts were largely successful and contributed to a century unmarred by destructive, generalized war (see Map 23.1).

- *How did the victorious allies fashion a general peace settlement, and how did Metternich uphold a conservative European order?*

Chronology

1790s–1840s	Romantic movement in literature and the arts
1809–1848	Metternich serves as Austrian foreign minister
1810	Staël, *On Germany*
1815	Holy Alliance formed; revision of Corn Laws in Britain
1819	Carlsbad Decrees issued by German Confederation
1830	Greece wins independence from Turks
1830–1848	Reign of Louis Philippe in France
1832	Reform Bill in Britain
1839	Blanc, *Organization of Work*
1845–1851	Great Famine in Ireland
1847	Ten Hours Act in Britain
1848	Revolutions in France, Austria, and Prussia; Marx and Engels, *The Communist Manifesto*

The European Balance of Power

The allied powers were concerned first and foremost with the defeated enemy, France. Agreeing to the restoration of the Bourbon dynasty (see page 708), the allies were quite lenient toward France after Napoleon's abdication. The first Peace of Paris gave to France the boundaries it possessed in 1792, which were larger than those of 1789, and France did not have to pay any war reparations. Thus the victorious powers did not foment a spirit of injustice and revenge in the defeated country.

When the four allies of the Quadruple Alliance met together at the Congress of Vienna, assisted in a minor way by a host of delegates from the smaller European states, they also agreed to raise a number of formidable barriers against renewed French aggression. The Low Countries—Belgium and Holland—were united under an enlarged Dutch monarchy capable of opposing France more effectively. Above all, Prussia received considerably more territory on France's eastern border so as to stand as the "sentinel on the Rhine" against France. In these ways, the Quadruple Alliance combined leniency toward France with strong defensive measures.

In their moderation toward France, the allies were motivated by self-interest and traditional ideas about the balance of power. To Klemens von Metternich and Robert Castlereagh, the foreign ministers of Austria and Great Britain, respectively, as well as their French counterpart, Charles Talleyrand, the balance of power meant an international equilibrium of political and military forces that would discourage aggression by any combination of states or, worse, the domination of Europe by any single state. The Great Powers—Austria, Britain, Prussia, Russia, and France—used the balance of power to settle their own dangerous disputes at the Congress of Vienna. There was general agreement among the victors that

Mapping the Past

MAP 23.1 Europe in 1815 Europe's leaders re-established a balance of political power after the defeat of Napoleon. Prussia gained territory on the Rhine and in Saxony, consolidating its position as a Great Power. Austria gained the Italian provinces of Lombardy and Venetia as well as Galicia and land along the Adriatic Sea. In 1815 Europe contained many different states, but international politics was dominated by the five Great Powers (or six, if one includes the Ottoman Empire). Trace the political boundaries of each Great Power, and compare their geographical strengths and weaknesses.

❶ In which directions might the different Great Powers seek to expand further and gain more people and territory? **❷** At what points might these states then come into conflict with one another?

Adjusting the Balance The Englishman on the left uses his money to counterbalance the people that the Prussian and the fat Metternich are gaining in Saxony and Italy. Alexander I sits happily on his prize, Poland. This cartoon captures the essence of how most people thought about balance-of-power diplomacy at the Congress of Vienna. *(Bibliothèque nationale de France)*

each of them should receive compensation in the form of territory for their successful struggle against the French. Great Britain had already won colonies and strategic outposts during the long wars. Metternich's Austria gave up territories in Belgium and southern Germany but expanded greatly elsewhere, taking the rich provinces of Venetia and Lombardy in northern Italy as well as former Polish possessions and new lands on the eastern coast of the Adriatic (see Map 23.1).

One ticklish question almost led to renewed war in January 1815, however. The vaguely progressive, impetuous Tsar Alexander I of Russia wanted to restore the ancient kingdom of Poland, on which he expected to bestow the benefits of his rule. The Prussians agreed, provided they could swallow up the large and wealthy kingdom of Saxony, their German neighbor to the south. These demands were too much for Castlereagh and Metternich, who feared an unbalancing of forces in central Europe. In an astonishing about-face, they turned for diplomatic support to the wily Talleyrand and the defeated France he represented, signing a secret alliance directed against Russia and Prussia. War seemed imminent. But the threat of war caused the rulers of Russia and Prussia to moderate their demands. Russia accepted a small Polish kingdom, and Prussia took only part of Saxony (see Map 23.1). This compromise was very much within the framework of balance-of-power ideology.

Unfortunately for France, Napoleon suddenly escaped from his "comic kingdom" on the island of Elba. Yet the second Peace of Paris, concluded after Napoleon's final defeat at Waterloo, was still relatively moderate toward France. Fat old Louis XVIII was restored to his throne for a second time. France lost only a little territory, had to pay an indemnity of 700 million francs, and had to support a large army of occupation for five years.

The rest of the settlement already concluded at the Congress of Vienna was left intact. The members of the Quadruple Alliance, however, did agree to meet periodically to discuss their common interests and to consider appropriate measures for the maintenance of peace in Europe. This agreement marked the beginning of the European "congress system," which lasted long into the nineteenth century and settled many international crises through international conferences and balance-of-power diplomacy.

Intervention and Repression

There was also a domestic political side to the re-establishment of peace. Within their own countries, the leaders of the victorious states were much less flexible. In 1815 under Metternich's leadership, Austria, Prussia, and Russia embarked on a crusade against the ideas and politics of the dual revolution. This crusade lasted until 1848. The first step was the **Holy Alliance,** formed by Austria, Prussia, and Russia in September 1815. First proposed by Russia's Alexander I, the alliance soon became a symbol of the repression of liberal and revolutionary movements all over Europe.

In 1820 revolutionaries succeeded in forcing the monarchs of Spain and the southern Italian kingdom of the Two Sicilies to grant liberal constitutions against their wills. Metternich was horrified: revolution was rising once again. Calling a conference at Troppau in Austria under the provisions of the Quadruple Alliance, he and Alexander I proclaimed the principle of active intervention to maintain all autocratic regimes whenever they were threatened. Austrian forces then marched into Naples in 1821 and restored Ferdinand I to the throne of the Two Sicilies, while French armies likewise restored the Spanish regime.

In the following years, Metternich continued to battle against liberal political change. Sometimes he could do little, as in the case of the new Latin American republics that broke away from Spain. Nor could he undo the dynastic changes of 1830 and 1831 in France and Belgium. Nonetheless, until 1848 Metternich's system proved quite effective in central Europe, where his power was the greatest.

Metternich's policies dominated not only Austria and the Italian peninsula but also the entire German Confederation, which the peace settlement of Vienna had called into being. The confederation was composed of thirty-eight independent German states, including Prussia and Austria (see Map 23.1). These states met in complicated assemblies dominated by Austria, with Prussia a willing junior partner in the execution of repressive measures.

It was through the German Confederation that Metternich had the infamous **Carlsbad Decrees** issued in 1819. These decrees required the thirty-eight German member states to root out subversive ideas in their universities and newspapers. The decrees also established a permanent committee with spies and informers to investigate and punish any liberal or radical organizations.

Metternich and Conservatism

Metternich's determined defense of the status quo made him a villain in the eyes of most progressive, optimistic historians of the nineteenth century. Yet rather than denounce the man, we can try to understand him and the general conservatism he represented.

Born into the middle ranks of the landed nobility of the Rhineland, Prince Klemens von Metternich (1773–1859) was an internationally oriented aristocrat who made a brilliant diplomatic career in Austria. Austrian foreign minister from 1809 to 1848, the cosmopolitan Metternich always remained loyal to his class and jealously defended its rights and privileges. Like most other conservatives of his time, he did so with a clear conscience. The nobility was one of Europe's most ancient institutions, and conservatives regarded tradition as the basic source of human institutions. In their view, the proper state and society remained those of pre-1789 Europe, which rested on a judicious blend of monarchy, bureaucracy, aristocracy, and respectful commoners.

Metternich firmly believed that liberalism, as embodied in revolutionary America and France, had been responsible for a generation of war with untold bloodshed and suffering. Like many other conservatives then and since, Metternich blamed liberal middle-class revolutionaries for stirring up the lower classes, which he believed desired nothing more than peace and quiet.

The threat of liberalism appeared doubly dangerous to Metternich because it generally went with national aspirations. Liberals believed that each people, each national group, had a right to establish its own independent government and seek to fulfill its own destiny. The idea of national self-determination was repellent to Metternich. It not only threatened the primacy of the aristocracy but also threatened to destroy the Austrian Empire and revolutionize central Europe.

The vast Austrian Empire of the Habsburgs was a great dynastic state. Formed over centuries by war, marriage, and luck, it was made up of many peoples (see Map 23.2). The Germans had long dominated the empire, yet they accounted for only one-fourth of the population. The Magyars (Hungarians), a substantially smaller group, dominated the kingdom of Hungary, though they did not account for a majority of the population in that part of the Austrian Empire.

MAP 23.2 Peoples of the Habsburg Monarchy, 1815 The old dynastic state was a patchwork of nationalities. Note the widely scattered pockets of Germans and Hungarians.

Metternich This portrait by Sir Thomas Lawrence reveals much about Metternich the man. Handsome, refined, and intelligent, Metternich was a great aristocrat who was passionately devoted to the defense of his class and its interests. *(The Royal Collection, © 2007 Her Majesty Queen Elizabeth II)*

The Czechs, the third major group, were concentrated in Bohemia and Moravia. There were also large numbers of Italians, Poles, and Ukrainians as well as smaller groups of Slovenes, Croats, Serbs, Ruthenians, and Romanians. The various Slavic peoples, together with the Italians and the Romanians, represented a widely scattered and completely divided majority in an empire dominated by Germans and Hungarians. Different ethnic groups often lived in the same provinces and even in the same villages. Thus the different parts and provinces of the empire differed in languages, customs, and institutions.

The multiethnic state Metternich served was both strong and weak. It was strong because of its large population and vast territories; it was weak because of its many and potentially dissatisfied nationalities. In these circumstances, Metternich virtually had to oppose liberalism and nationalism, for Austria was simply unable to accommodate these ideologies of the dual revolution.

In his efforts to hold back liberalism and nationalism Metternich was supported by the Russian Empire and, to a lesser extent, by the Ottoman Empire. Bitter enemies and often at war with each other, these far-flung empires also shared several basic characteristics. Both were absolutist states with powerful armies and long traditions of expansion and conquest. Both were multinational empires made up of many peoples, languages, and religions, but in each case most of the ruling elite came from the dominant ethnic group—the Orthodox Christian Russians centered in central and northern Russia, and the Muslim Ottoman Turks of Anatolia (much of modern Turkey). After 1815, both multinational, absolutist states worked to preserve their respective traditional, conservative orders. Only in the middle of the nineteenth century did each in turn experience a profound crisis and embark on a program of fundamental reform and modernization, as we shall see in Chapter 25.

Radical Ideas and Early Socialism

In the years following the peace settlement of 1815 intellectuals and social observers sought to understand the revolutionary changes that had occurred and were still taking place. These efforts led to ideas that still motivate the world.

Almost all of these basic ideas were radical. In one way or another, they rejected the old, deeply felt conservatism, with its stress on tradition, a hereditary monarchy, a strong and privileged landowning aristocracy, and an official church. Instead, they developed and refined alternative visions—alternative ideologies—and tried to convince society to act on them. With time, they were very successful.

• *What were the basic tenets of liberalism, nationalism, and socialism, and what groups were most attracted to these ideologies?*

Liberalism

The principal ideas of **liberalism**—liberty and equality—were by no means defeated in 1815. First realized successfully in the American Revolution and then achieved in part in the French Revolution, this political and social philosophy continued to pose a radical challenge to revived conservatism. Liberalism demanded representative government as opposed to autocratic monarchy, equality before the law as opposed to legally separate classes. The idea of liberty also meant specific individual freedoms: freedom of the press, freedom of speech, freedom of assembly, and freedom from arbitrary arrest. In Europe only France with Louis XVIII's Constitutional Charter and Great Britain with its Parliament and historic rights of English men and women had realized much of the liberal program in 1815. Even in those countries, liberalism had not fully succeeded.

Although liberalism retained its cutting edge, it was seen by many as being a somewhat duller tool than it had been. The reasons for this were that liberalism faced more radical ideological competitors in the early nineteenth century. Opponents of liberalism especially criticized its economic principles, which called for unrestricted private enterprise and no government interference in the economy. This philosophy was popularly known as the doctrine of **laissez faire.** (This form of liberalism is often called "classical" liberalism in the United States in order to distinguish it sharply from modern American liberalism, which usually favors more government programs to meet social needs and to regulate the economy.)

The idea of a free economy had first been persuasively formulated by Scottish philosophy professor Adam Smith, whose *Inquiry into the Nature and Causes of the Wealth of Nations* (1776) founded modern economics. Smith was highly critical of eighteenth-century mercantilism and its attempt to regulate trade and economic activity. Far preferable were free competition and the "invisible hand" of the self-regulating market, which would give all citizens a fair and equal opportunity to do what they did best. Smith argued effectively that freely competitive private enterprise would result in greater income for everyone, not just the rich.

Online Study Center **Improve Your Grade**
Primary Source: The Wealth of Nations: A Natural Law of Economy

In early-nineteenth-century Britain this economic liberalism, which promoted continued economic growth in the Industrial Revolution, was embraced most enthusiastically by business groups and became a doctrine associated with business interests. Businessmen used the doctrine to defend their right to do as they wished in their factories. Labor unions were outlawed because they supposedly restricted free competition and the individual's "right to work."

In the early nineteenth century, liberal political ideals also became more closely associated with narrow class interests. Early nineteenth-century liberals favored representative government, but they generally wanted property qualifications attached to the right to vote. In practice, this meant limiting the vote to well-to-do aristocratic landowners, substantial businessmen, and successful members of the professions. Workers and peasants, as well as the lower middle class of shopkeepers, clerks, and artisans, did not own the necessary property and thus could not vote.

As liberalism became increasingly identified with the middle class after 1815, some intellectuals and foes of conservatism felt that liberalism did not go nearly far enough. Inspired by memories of the French Revolution and the example of Jacksonian democracy in the young American republic, they called for universal voting rights, at least for males, and for democracy. These democrats and republicans were more radical than the liberals, and they were more willing than most liberals to endorse violent upheaval to achieve goals. All of this meant that liberals and radical, democratic republicans could join forces against conservatives only up to a point.

Nationalism

Nationalism was a second radical idea in the years after 1815—an idea destined to have an enormous influence in the modern world. Nationalism had its immediate origins in the French Revolution and the Napoleonic wars, and there were already hints of its remarkable ability to spread and develop.

Early advocates of the "national idea" argued that each people had its own genius and its own *cultural* unity. For nationalists this cultural unity was basically self-evident, manifesting itself especially in a common language, history, and territory. In fact, in the early nineteenth century such cultural unity was more a dream than a reality as far as most nationalities were concerned. Within each ethnic grouping only an elite spoke a standardized written language. Local dialects abounded, and peasants from nearby villages often failed to understand each other. As for historical memory, it divided the inhabitants of the different German or Italian states as much as it unified them. Moreover, a variety of ethnic groups shared the territory of most states.

Despite these basic realities, sooner or later European nationalists usually sought to turn the cultural unity that they perceived into a *political* reality. They sought to make the territory of each people coincide with well-defined boundaries in an independent nation-state. It was this political goal that made nationalism so explosive in central and eastern Europe after 1815, when there were either too few states (Austria, Russia, and the Ottoman

Building German Nationalism As popular upheaval in France spread to central Europe in March 1848, Germans from the solid middle classes came together in Frankfurt to draft a constitution for a new united Germany. This woodcut commemorates the solemn procession of delegates entering Saint Paul's Cathedral in Frankfurt, where the delegates would have their deliberations. Festivals, celebrations, and parades helped create a feeling of belonging to a large unseen community, a nation binding millions of strangers together. *(akg-images)*

Empire) or too many (the Italian peninsula and the German Confederation) and when different peoples overlapped and intermingled.

In recent years scholars have been trying to understand how the nationalist vision, often fitting so poorly with existing conditions and promising so much upheaval, was so successful in the long run. Certain interrelated ideas stand out.

Of fundamental importance in the rise of nationalism was the epoch-making development of complex industrial and urban society, which required much better communication between individuals and groups.[1] These communication needs promoted the use of a standardized national language within many countries, creating at least a superficial cultural unity as it eventually encompassed the entire population through mass education. When a minority population was large and concentrated, the nationalist campaign for a standardized language often led to a push for a separate nation-state.

Many scholars also argue that nations are recent creations, the product of the new, self-conscious nationalist ideology. Thus nation-states emerged in the nineteenth century as "imagined communities," communities seeking to bind millions of strangers together around the abstract concept of an all-embracing national identity. This meant bringing citizens together with emotionally charged symbols and ceremonies, such as independence holidays and patriotic parades. On such fleeting occasions the imagined nation of spiritual equals might celebrate its most hallowed traditions, which were often recent inventions.[2]

Historians also stress the dynamic, ever-changing character of nationalism. Industrialism and mass education, so important in the later nineteenth century, played only a minor role before 1850. In those years the faith in nationhood was fresh, idealistic, and progressive.

Between 1815 and 1850 most people who believed in nationalism also believed in either liberalism or radical, democratic republicanism. A common faith in the creativity and nobility of the people was perhaps the single most important reason for the linking of these two concepts. Liberals and especially democrats saw the people as the ultimate source of all government. Yet liberals and nationalists agreed that the benefits of self-government would be possible only if the people were united by common traditions that transcended local interests and even class differences.

Early nationalists usually believed that every nation, like every citizen, had the right to exist in freedom and to develop its character and spirit. They were confident that a symphony of nations would promote the harmony and ultimate unity of all peoples. The great Italian patriot Guiseppe Mazzini (1805–1872) believed that "in laboring according to the true principles of our country we are laboring for Humanity." Thus the liberty of the individual and the love of a free nation overlapped greatly in the early nineteenth century.

Yet early nationalists also stressed the differences among peoples. Even early nationalism developed a strong sense of "we" and "they." To this "we-they" outlook, it was all too easy for nationalists to add two highly volatile ingredients: a sense of national mission and a sense of national superiority. Even the French historian Jules Michelet, so alive to the national aspirations of other peoples, could not help speaking in 1846 of the "superiority of France"; the principles espoused in the French Revolution had made France the "salvation of mankind." (See the feature "Individuals in Society: Jules Michelet" on page 769.)

Russian and German nationalists had a very different opinion of France. In the narratives they constructed, the French often seemed oppressive, as the Russians did to the Poles and as the Germans did to the Czechs. (See the feature "Listening to the Past: Speaking for the Czech Nation" on pages 776–777.) Thus "they" often emerged as the enemy.

Early nationalism was ambiguous. Its main thrust was liberal and democratic. But below the surface lurked ideas of national superiority and national mission that could lead to aggression and conflict.

French Utopian Socialism

Socialism, the new radical doctrine after 1815, began in France, despite the fact that France lagged far behind Great Britain in developing modern industry. Early French socialist thinkers were acutely aware that the political revolution in France, the rise of laissez faire, and the emergence of modern industry in Britain were transforming society. They were disturbed because they saw these developments as fomenting selfish individualism and splitting the community into isolated fragments. There was, they believed, an urgent need for a further reorganization of society to establish cooperation and a new sense of community.

Early French socialists believed in economic planning. Inspired by the emergency measures of 1793 and 1794 in France, they argued that the government should rationally organize the economy and not depend on destructive competition to do the job. Early socialists also shared an intense desire to help the poor, and they preached that the rich and the poor should be more nearly equal economically. Finally, socialists believed that private property should be strictly regulated by the government or that it should be abolished and replaced by state or community ownership. Planning, greater economic equality, and state regulation of property—these were the key ideas of early French socialism and of all socialism since.

One of the most influential early socialist thinkers was a nobleman, Count Henri de Saint-Simon (1760–1825). Saint-Simon optimistically proclaimed the tremendous possibilities of industrial development: "The age of gold is before us!" The key to progress was proper social organization. Such an arrangement of society required the **parasites**—the court, the aristocracy, lawyers, and churchmen—to give way, once and for all, to the **doers**—the leading scientists, engineers, and industrialists. The doers would carefully plan the economy and guide it forward by undertaking vast public works projects and establishing investment banks. Saint-Simon also stressed in highly moralistic terms that every social institution ought to have as its main goal improved conditions for the poor.

After 1830 the socialist critique of capitalism became sharper. Charles Fourier (1772–1837), a lonely, saintly man with a tenuous hold on reality, envisaged a socialist utopia of mathematically precise, self-sufficient communities, each made up of 1,620 people. Fourier was also an early proponent of the total emancipation of women. Extremely critical of middle-class family life, Fourier believed that most marriages were only another kind of prostitution. According to Fourier, young single women were shamelessly "sold" to their future husbands for dowries and other financial considerations. Therefore, Fourier called for the abolition of marriage, free unions based only on love, and sexual freedom. Many middle-class men and women found these ideas, which were shared and even practiced by some followers of Saint-Simon, shocking and immoral. The socialist program for the liberation of women as well as workers appeared to them as doubly dangerous and revolutionary.

Louis Blanc (1811–1882), a sharp-eyed, intelligent journalist, focused on practical improvements. In his *Organization of Work* (1839), he urged workers to agitate for universal voting rights and to take control of the state peacefully. Blanc believed that the state should set up government-backed workshops and factories to guarantee full employment. The right to work had to become as sacred as any other right.

Finally, there was Pierre Joseph Proudhon (1809–1865), a self-educated printer who wrote a pamphlet in 1840 titled *What Is Property?* His answer was that it was nothing but theft. Property was profit that was stolen from the worker, who was the source of all wealth. Unlike most socialists, Proudhon feared the power of the state and was often considered an anarchist.

Of great importance, the message of French utopian socialists interacted with the experiences of French urban workers. Workers cherished the memory of the radical phase of the French Revolution, and they became violently opposed to laissez-faire laws that denied workers the right to organize. Developing a sense of class in the process, workers favored collective action and government intervention in economic life. Thus the aspirations of workers and utopian theorists reinforced each other, and a genuine socialist movement emerged in Paris in the 1830s and 1840s. To Karl Marx was left the task of establishing firm foundations for modern socialism.

The Birth of Marxian Socialism

In 1848 the thirty-year-old Karl Marx (1818–1883) and the twenty-eight-year-old Friedrich Engels (1820–1895) published *The Communist Manifesto,* which became the bible of socialism. The son of a Jewish lawyer who had converted to Christianity, the atheistic young Marx had studied philosophy at the University of Berlin before turning to journalism and economics. He read widely in French socialist thought, and like Fourier he looked forward to the emancipation of women and the abolition of the family. By the time Marx was twenty-five, he was developing his own socialist ideas.

Early French socialists often appealed to the middle class and the state to help the poor. Marx ridiculed such appeals as naive. He argued that the interests of the middle class and those of the industrial working class were inevitably opposed to each other. Indeed, according to the *Manifesto,* the "history of all previously existing society is the history of class struggles." In Marx's view, one class had always exploited the other, and with the advent of modern industry, society was split more clearly than ever before: between the middle class (the **bourgeoisie**) and the modern working class (the **proletariat**).

Just as the bourgeoisie had triumphed over the feudal aristocracy, Marx predicted that the proletariat would conquer the bourgeoisie in a violent revolution. While a tiny minority owned the means of production and grew richer, the ever-poorer proletariat was constantly growing in size and in class-consciousness. In this process, the proletariat was aided, according to Marx, by a portion of the bourgeoisie who had gone over to the proletariat and who (like Marx and Engels) "had raised themselves to the level of comprehending theoretically the historical moment." The critical moment, Marx thought, was very near. "Let the ruling classes tremble at a Communist revolution. The proletarians have nothing to lose but their chains. They have a world to win. WORKING MEN OF ALL COUNTRIES, UNITE!" So ends *The Communist Manifesto.*

Online Study Center Improve Your Grade
Primary Source: "Working Men of All Countries, Unite!"

Marx's ideas united sociology, economics, and all human history in a vast and imposing edifice. He synthesized in his socialism not only French utopian schemes but also English classical economics and German philosophy—the major intellectual currents of his day.

Marx's debt to England was great. He was the last of the classical economists. Following David Ricardo, who

Karl Marx Active in the revolution of 1848, Marx fled from Germany in 1849 and settled in London. There he wrote *Capital,* the weighty exposition of his socialist theories, and worked to organize the working class. Marx earned a modest living as a journalist, supplemented by financial support from his coauthor, Friedrich Engels. *(The Granger Collection, New York)*

had taught that labor was the source of all value, Marx went on to argue that profits were really wages stolen from the workers. Moreover, Marx incorporated Engels's charges of terrible oppression of the new class of factory workers in England; thus Marx's doctrines seemed to be based on hard facts.

Marx's theory of historical evolution was built on the philosophy of the German Georg Hegel (1770–1831). Hegel believed that each age is characterized by a dominant set of ideas, which produces opposing ideas and eventually a new synthesis. The idea of being had been dominant initially, for example, and it had produced its antithesis, the idea of nonbeing. This idea in turn had resulted in the synthesis of becoming. Thus history has pattern and purpose.

Marx retained Hegel's view of history as a dialectic process of change but made economic relationships between classes the driving force. This dialectic explained the decline of agrarian feudalism and the rise of industrial capitalism. Marx stressed repeatedly that the "bourgeoisie, historically, has played a most revolutionary part. . . . During its rule of scarcely one hundred years the bourgeoisie has created more massive and more colossal productive forces than have all preceding generations together." Marx's next idea, that it was now the bourgeoisie's turn to give way to the socialism of revolutionary workers, appeared to many the irrefutable capstone of a brilliant interpretation of humanity's long development. Thus Marx pulled together powerful ideas and insights to create one of the great secular religions out of the intellectual ferment of the early nineteenth century.

The Romantic Movement

Radical concepts of politics and society were accompanied by comparable changes in literature and other arts during the dual revolution. The early nineteenth century marked the acme of the romantic movement, which profoundly influenced the arts and enriched European culture immeasurably.

The romantic movement was in part a revolt against classicism and the Enlightenment. Classicism was essentially a set of artistic rules and standards that went hand in glove with the Enlightenment's belief in rationality, order, and restraint. The classicists believed that the ancient Greeks and Romans had discovered eternally valid aesthetic rules and that playwrights and painters should continue to follow them. Classicists could enforce these rules in the eighteenth century because they dominated the courts and academies for which artists worked.

Forerunners of the romantic movement appeared from about 1750 on. Of these, Rousseau (see page 607)—the passionate advocate of feeling, freedom, and natural goodness—was the most influential. Romanticism then crystallized fully in the 1790s, primarily in England and Germany. The French Revolution kindled the belief that radical reconstruction was also possible in cultural and artistic life (even though many early English and German romantics became disillusioned with events in France and turned from liberalism to conservatism in politics). Romanticism gained strength until the 1840s.

- **What were the characteristics of the romantic movement, and who were some of the great romantic artists?**

Romanticism's Tenets

Romanticism was characterized by a belief in emotional exuberance, unrestrained imagination, and spontaneity in both art and personal life. In Germany early romantics of the 1770s and 1780s called themselves the **Sturm und Drang** ("Storm and Stress"), and many romantic artists of the early nineteenth century lived lives of tremendous emotional intensity. Suicide, duels to the death, madness, and strange illnesses were not uncommon among leading romantics. Romantic artists typically led bohemian lives, wearing their hair long and uncombed in preference to powdered wigs and living in cold garrets rather than frequenting stiff drawing rooms. They rejected materialism and sought to escape to lofty spiritual heights through their art. Great individualists, the romantics believed the full development of one's unique human potential to be the supreme purpose in life.

Nowhere was the break with classicism more apparent than in romanticism's general conception of nature. Classicism was not particularly interested in nature. In the words of the eighteenth-century English author Samuel Johnson, "A blade of grass is always a blade of grass; men and women are my subjects of inquiry." Nature was portrayed by classicists as beautiful and chaste, like an eighteenth-century formal garden. The romantics, in contrast, were enchanted by nature. For some it was awesome and tempestuous, while others saw nature as a source of spiritual inspiration. As the great English landscape artist John Constable declared, "Nature is Spirit visible."

Most romantics saw the growth of modern industry as an ugly, brutal attack on their beloved nature and on the human personality. They sought escape—in the unspoiled Lake District of northern England, in exotic North Africa, in an idealized Middle Ages.

Fascinated by color and diversity, the romantic imagination turned toward history with a passion. Beautiful, exciting, and important, history was the art of change over time—the key to a universe that was now perceived to be organic and dynamic, not mechanical and static as the Enlightenment had believed. Historical studies promoted the growth of national aspirations, fanning the embers of memory and encouraging entire peoples to seek in the past their special destinies.

Literature

Britain was the first country where romanticism flowered fully in poetry and prose, and the British romantic writers were among the most prominent in Europe. Wordsworth,

Nature and the Meaning of Life
Caspar David Friedrich (1774–1840) was Germany's greatest romantic painter, and his *Traveler Looking over a Sea of Fog* (1815) is a representative masterpiece. Friedrich's paintings often focus on dark, silhouetted figures silently contemplating an eerie landscape. Friedrich came to believe that humans were only an insignificant part of an all-embracing higher unity. *(Bildarchiv Preussischer Kulturbesitz/Art Resource, NY)*

Coleridge, and Scott were all active by 1800, to be followed shortly by Byron, Shelley, and Keats. All were poets: romanticism found its distinctive voice in poetry, as the Enlightenment had in prose.

A towering leader of English romanticism, William Wordsworth (1770–1850) traveled in France after his graduation from Cambridge. There he fell passionately in love with a Frenchwoman, who bore him a daughter. Deeply influenced by Rousseau and the spirit of the early French Revolution, Wordsworth returned to England and settled in the countryside with his sister, Dorothy, and Samuel Taylor Coleridge (1772–1834). In 1798 the two poets published their *Lyrical Ballads*, which abandoned flowery classical conventions for the language of ordinary speech and endowed simple subjects with the loftiest majesty.

One of the best examples of Wordsworth's romantic credo and genius is "Daffodils":

I wandered lonely as a cloud
That floats on high o'er vales and hills,
When all at once I saw a crowd,

A host, of golden daffodils;
Beside the lake, beneath the trees,
Fluttering and dancing in the breeze.

. . . .

The waves beside them danced, but they
Out-did the sparkling waves in glee:
A poet could not but be gay,
In such a jocund company:
I gazed—and gazed—but little thought
What wealth the show to me had brought:

For oft, when on my couch I lie
In vacant or in pensive mood,
They flash upon that inward eye
Which is the bliss of solitude;
And then my heart with pleasure fills,
And dances with the daffodils.

Here indeed are simplicity and love of nature in commonplace forms, which could be appreciated by everyone. Wordsworth's conception of poetry as the "spontaneous overflow of powerful feeling recollected in tranquility" is well illustrated by the last stanza.

Born in Edinburgh, Walter Scott (1771–1832) personified the romantic movement's fascination with history. Raised on his grandfather's farm, Scott fell under the spell of the old ballads and tales of the Scottish border. He was also deeply influenced by German romanticism, particularly by the immortal poet and dramatist Johann Wolfgang von Goethe (1749–1832). Scott translated Goethe's famous *Gotz von Berlichingen*, a play about a sixteenth-century knight who revolted against centralized authority and championed individual freedom—at least in Goethe's romantic drama. A natural storyteller, Scott composed long narrative poems and a series of historical novels. Scott excelled in re-creating the spirit of bygone ages and great historical events, especially those of Scotland.

Classicism remained strong in France under Napoleon and inhibited the growth of romanticism there. In 1813 Germaine de Staël (1766–1817), a Franco-Swiss writer living in exile, urged the French to throw away their worn-out classical models. Her study *On Germany* (1810) extolled the spontaneity and enthusiasm of German writers and thinkers, and it had a powerful impact on the post-1815 generation in France. Between 1820 and 1850, the romantic impulse broke through in the poetry and prose of Lamartine, de Vigny, Hugo, Dumas, and Sand. Of these, Victor Hugo (1802–1885) was the greatest in both poetry and prose.

Son of a Napoleonic general, Hugo achieved an amazing range of rhythm, language, and image in his lyric poetry. His powerful novels exemplified the romantic fascination with fantastic characters, exotic historical settings, and human emotions. The hero of Hugo's famous *Hunchback of Notre Dame* (1831) is the great cathedral's deformed bell-ringer, a "human gargoyle" overlooking the teeming life of fifteenth-century Paris. Renouncing his early conservatism, Hugo equated freedom in literature with liberty in politics and society. Hugo's political evolution was thus exactly the opposite of Wordsworth's, in whom youthful radicalism gave way to middle-aged caution. As the contrast between the two artists suggests, romanticism was a cultural movement compatible with many political beliefs.

Amandine Aurore Lucie Dupin (1804–1876), generally known by her pen name, George Sand, defied the narrow conventions of her time in an unending search for self-fulfillment. After eight years of unhappy marriage she abandoned her husband and took her two children to Paris to pursue a career as a writer. There Sand soon achieved fame and wealth, eventually writing over eighty novels on a variety of romantic and social themes. George Sand's striking individualism went far beyond her flamboyant preference for men's clothing and her notorious affairs. Her semi-autobiographical novel *Lélia* was shockingly modern, delving deeply into her tortuous quest for sexual and personal freedom.

In central and eastern Europe, literary romanticism and early nationalism often reinforced each other. Seeking a unique greatness in every people, well-educated romantics plumbed their own histories and cultures. Like modern anthropologists, they turned their attention to peasant life and transcribed the folk songs, tales, and proverbs that the cosmopolitan Enlightenment had disdained. The brothers Jacob and Wilhelm Grimm were particularly successful at rescuing German fairy tales from oblivion. In the Slavic lands, romantics played a decisive role in converting spoken peasant languages into modern written languages. The greatest of all Russian poets, Aleksander Pushkin (1799–1837), rejecting eighteenth-century attempts to force Russian poetry into a classical straitjacket, used his lyric genius to mold the modern literary language.

Art and Music

The greatest and most moving romantic painter in France was Eugène Delacroix (1798–1863), probably the illegitimate son of French foreign minister Talleyrand. Delacroix was a master of dramatic, colorful scenes that stirred the emotions. He was fascinated with remote and exotic subjects, whether lion hunts in Morocco or dreams of languishing, sensuous women in a sultan's harem. Yet he was also a passionate spokesman for freedom.

In England the most notable romantic painters were Joseph M. W. Turner (1775–1851) and John Constable (1776–1837). Both were fascinated by nature, but their interpretations of it contrasted sharply, aptly symbolizing the tremendous emotional range of the romantic movement. Turner depicted nature's power and terror; wild storms and sinking ships were favorite subjects. Constable painted gentle Wordsworthian landscapes in which human beings were at one with their environment, the comforting countryside of unspoiled rural England.

It was in music that romanticism realized most fully and permanently its goals of free expression and emotional intensity. Abandoning well-defined structures, the great romantic composers used a wide range of forms to create a thousand musical landscapes and evoke a host of powerful emotions. Romantic composers also transformed the small classical orchestra, tripling its size by adding wind instruments, percussion, and more brass and strings. The crashing chords evoking the surge of the masses in Chopin's Revolutionary Etude, and the bottomless despair of the funeral march in Beethoven's Third Symphony—such were the modern orchestra's musical paintings that plumbed the depths of human feeling.

This range and intensity gave music and musicians much greater prestige than in the past. Music no longer simply complemented a church service or helped a nobleman digest his dinner. Music became a sublime end in itself, most perfectly realizing the endless yearning of the soul. The unbelievable one-in-a-million performer—the great virtuoso who could transport the listener to ecstasy and hysteria—became a cultural hero. People swooned for Franz Liszt (1811–1886), the greatest pianist of his age, as they scream for rock stars today.

Though romanticism dominated music until late in the nineteenth century, no composer ever surpassed its first great master, Ludwig van Beethoven (1770–1827). Extending and breaking open classical forms, Beethoven used contrasting themes and tones to produce dramatic conflict and inspiring resolutions. As one contemporary admirer wrote, "Beethoven's music sets in motion the lever of fear, of awe, of horror, of suffering, and awakens just that infinite longing which is the essence of Romanticism." Beethoven's range and output were tremendous. At the peak of his fame, he began to lose his hearing. He considered suicide but eventually overcame despair: "I will take fate by the throat; it will not bend me completely to its will."[3] Beethoven continued to pour out immortal music, although his last years were silent, spent in total deafness.

Reforms and Revolutions

While the romantic movement was developing, liberal, national, and socialist forces battered against the conservatism of 1815. In some countries, change occurred gradually and peacefully. Elsewhere, pressure built up like steam in a pressure cooker without a safety valve and eventually caused an explosion in 1848. Three important countries—Greece, Great Britain, and France—experienced variations on this basic theme between 1815 and 1848.

- **How after 1815 did liberal, national, and socialist forces challenge conservatism in Greece, Great Britain, and France?**

National Liberation in Greece

National, liberal revolution, frustrated in Italy and Spain by conservative statesmen, succeeded first after 1815 in Greece. Since the fifteenth century, the Greeks had been living under the domination of the Ottoman Turks. In spite of centuries of foreign rule, the Greeks had survived as a people, united by their language and the Greek Orthodox religion. It was perfectly natural that the general growth of national aspirations and a desire for independence would inspire some Greeks in the early nineteenth century. This rising national movement led to the formation of secret societies and then to revolt in 1821, led by Alexander Ypsilanti, a Greek patriot and a general in the Russian army.

The Great Powers, particularly Metternich, were opposed to all revolution, even revolution against the Islamic Turks. They refused to back Ypsilanti and supported the Ottoman Empire. Yet for many Europeans, the Greek cause became a holy one. Educated Americans and Europeans were in love with the culture of classical Greece; Russians were stirred by the piety of their Orthodox brethren. Writers and artists, moved by the romantic impulse, responded enthusiastically to the Greek national struggle. The famous English romantic poet Lord Byron even joined the Greeks and died fighting "that Greece may yet be free."

Delacroix: Massacre at Chios The Greek struggle for freedom and independence won the enthusiastic support of liberals, nationalists, and romantics. The Ottoman Turks were portrayed as cruel oppressors who were holding back the course of history, as in this moving masterpiece by Delacroix. *(Réunion des Musées Nationaux/Art Resource, NY)*

The Greeks, though often quarreling among themselves, battled on against the Turks and hoped for the eventual support of European governments. In 1827 Great Britain, France, and Russia responded to popular demands at home and directed Turkey to accept an armistice. When the Turks refused, the navies of these three powers trapped the Turkish fleet at Navarino and destroyed it. Russia then declared another of its periodic wars of expansion against the Turks. This led to the establishment of a Russian protectorate over much of present-day Romania, which had also been under Turkish rule. Great Britain, France, and Russia finally declared Greece independent in 1830 and installed a German prince as king of the new country in 1832. In the end, the Greeks had won: a small nation had gained its independence in a heroic war of liberation against a foreign empire.

Liberal Reform in Great Britain

Eighteenth-century British society had been both flexible and remarkably stable. It was dominated by the landowning aristocracy, but that class was neither closed nor rigidly defined. Successful business and professional people could buy land and become gentlefolk, while the common people had more than the usual opportunities of the preindustrial world. Basic civil rights for all were balanced by a tradition of deference to one's social superiors. Parliament was manipulated by the king and was thoroughly undemocratic. Only about 8 percent of the population could vote for representatives to Parliament, and by the 1780s there was growing interest in some kind of political reform.

But the French Revolution threw the British aristocracy into a panic for a generation, making it extremely hostile to any attempts to change the status quo. The Tory Party, completely controlled by the landed aristocracy, was particularly fearful of radical movements at home and abroad. After 1815 the aristocracy defended its ruling position by repressing every kind of popular protest.

The first step in this direction began with revision of the **Corn Laws** in 1815. Corn Laws to regulate the foreign grain trade had long existed, but they were not needed during a generation of war with France because the British had been unable to import cheap grain from eastern Europe, leading to high prices and large profits for the landed aristocracy. Peace meant that grain could be imported again and that the price of wheat and bread would go down, benefiting almost everyone except the aristocracy. The aristocracy, however, rammed far-reaching changes in the Corn Laws through Parliament. The new regulation prohibited the importation of foreign grain unless the price at home rose to improbable levels. Seldom has a class legislated more selfishly for its own narrow economic advantage or done more to promote a class-based view of political action.

The change in the Corn Laws, coming as it did at a time of widespread unemployment and postwar economic distress, resulted in protests and demonstrations by urban laborers, who were supported by radical intellectuals. In 1817 the Tory government responded by temporarily suspending the traditional rights of peaceable assembly and habeas corpus. Two years later, Parliament passed the infamous Six Acts, which, among other things, placed controls on a heavily taxed press and practically eliminated all mass meetings. These acts followed an enormous but orderly protest, at Saint Peter's Fields in Manchester, that had been savagely broken up by armed cavalry. Nicknamed the **Battle of Peterloo,** in scornful reference to the British victory at Waterloo, this incident demonstrated the government's determination to repress and stand fast.

Strengthened by ongoing industrial development, the new manufacturing and commercial groups insisted on a place for their new wealth alongside the landed wealth of the aristocracy in the framework of political power and social prestige. They called for many kinds of liberal reform: reform of town government, organization of a new police force, more rights for Catholics and dissenters, and reform of the Poor Laws that provided aid to some low-paid workers. In the 1820s, a less frightened Tory government moved in the direction of better urban administration, greater economic liberalism, civil equality for Catholics, and limited imports of foreign grain. These actions encouraged the middle classes to press on for reform of Parliament so they could have a larger say in government.

The Whig Party, though led like the Tories by great aristocrats, had by tradition been more responsive to commercial and manufacturing interests. In 1830 a Whig ministry introduced "an act to amend the representation of the people of England and Wales." Defeated, then passed by the House of Commons, this reform bill was rejected by the House of Lords. But when in 1832 the Whigs got the king to promise to create enough new peers to pass the law, the House of Lords reluctantly gave in rather than see its snug little club ruined by upstart manufacturers and plutocrats. A mighty surge of popular protest had helped the king and lords make up their minds.

The Reform Bill of 1832 had profound significance. The House of Commons had emerged as the all-important legislative body. The new industrial areas of the country gained representation in the Commons, and many old "rotten boroughs"—electoral districts that had very few voters and that the landed aristocracy had bought and sold—were eliminated.

The redistribution of seats reflected the shift in population to the northern manufacturing counties and the gradual emergence of an urban society. As a result of the Reform Bill of 1832, the number of voters increased by about 50 percent, giving about 12 percent of adult men in Britain and Ireland the right to vote. Comfortable middle-class groups in the urban population, as well as some substantial farmers who leased their land,

Hayter: The House of Commons, 1833 This collective portrait of the first parliament elected after the Reform Bill of 1832 was painted over several years. The arrangement of the members reflects Britain's historic two-party system, with the majority on one side and the "loyal opposition" on the other. Most European countries developed multiparty systems and coalition politics, with competing groups seated in a large half circle. *(Trustees of the National Portrait Gallery, London)*

received the vote. Thus the pressures building in Great Britain were successfully—though only temporarily—released. A major reform had been achieved peacefully. Continued fundamental reform within the system appeared difficult but not impossible.

The principal radical program was embodied in the "People's Charter" of 1838 and the Chartist movement (see page 741). Partly inspired by the economic distress of the working class in the 1830s and 1840s, the Chartists' core demand was universal male (but not female) suffrage. They saw complete political democracy and rule by the common people as the means to a good and just society. Hundreds of thousands of people signed gigantic petitions calling on Parliament to grant all men the right to vote, first and most seriously in 1839, again in 1842, and yet again in 1848. Parliament rejected all three petitions. In the short run, the working poor failed with their Chartist demands, but they learned a valuable lesson in mass politics.

While calling for universal male suffrage, many working-class people joined with middle-class manufacturers in the Anti–Corn Law League, founded in Manchester in 1839. Mass participation made possible a popular crusade led by fighting liberals, who argued that lower food prices and more jobs in industry depended on repeal of the Corn Laws. Much of the working class agreed. When Ireland's potato crop failed in 1845 and famine prices for food seemed likely in England, Tory prime minister Robert Peel joined with the Whigs and a minority of his own party to repeal the Corn Laws in 1846 and allow free imports of grain. England escaped famine. Thereafter the liberal doctrine of free trade became almost sacred dogma in Great Britain.

Online Study Center Improve Your Grade
Primary Source: A Denunciation of the Corn Laws

The following year, the Tories passed a bill designed to help the working classes, but in a different way. The Ten

The Prelude to 1848

March 1814	Russia, Prussia, Austria, and Britain form the Quadruple Alliance to defeat France.
April 1814	Napoleon abdicates.
May–June 1814	Bourbon monarchy is restored; Louis XVIII issues the Constitutional Charter providing for civil liberties and representative government.
	First Peace of Paris: allies combine leniency with a defensive posture toward France.
October 1814–June 1815	Congress of Vienna peace settlement establishes balance-of-power principle and creates the German Confederation.
February 1815	Napoleon escapes from Elba and marches on Paris.
June 1815	Napoleon defeated at the Battle of Waterloo.
September 1815	Austria, Prussia, and Russia form the Holy Alliance to repress liberal and revolutionary movements.
November 1815	Second Peace of Paris and renewal of Quadruple Alliance punish France and establish the European "congress system."
1819	In Carlsbad Decrees, Metternich imposes harsh measures throughout the German Confederation.
1820	Revolution occurs in Spain and the kingdom of the Two Sicilies.
	At the Congress of Troppau, Metternich and Alexander I of Russia proclaim the principle of intervention to maintain autocratic regimes.
1821	Austria crushes a liberal revolution in Naples and restores the Sicilian autocracy.
	Greeks revolt against the Ottoman Turks.
1823	French armies restore the Spanish regime.
1824	Reactionary Charles X succeeds Louis XVIII in France.
1830	Charles X repudiates the Constitutional Charter; insurrection and collapse of the government follow. Louis Philippe succeeds to the throne and maintains a narrowly liberal regime until 1848.
	Greece wins independence from the Ottoman Empire.
1832	Reform Bill expands British electorate and encourages the middle class.
1839	Louis Blanc publishes *Organization of Work*.
1840	Pierre Joseph Proudhon publishes *What Is Property?*
1846	Jules Michelet publishes *The People*.
1848	Karl Marx and Friedrich Engels publish *The Communist Manifesto*.

Hours Act of 1847 limited the workday for women and young people in factories to ten hours. Tory aristocrats continued to champion legislation regulating factory conditions. They were competing vigorously with the middle class for the support of the working class. This healthy competition between a still-vigorous aristocracy and a strong middle class was a crucial factor in Great Britain's peaceful evolution. The working classes could make temporary alliances with either competitor to better their own conditions.

Ireland and the Great Famine

The people of Ireland did not benefit from the political competition in Britain. The great mass of the population (outside of the northern counties of Ulster, which were partly Presbyterian) were Irish Catholics, who rented their land from a tiny minority of Church of England Protestants. These landlords were content to use their power to grab as much as possible.

The result was that the condition of the Irish peasantry around 1800 was abominable. The typical peasant lived in a wretched cottage and could afford neither shoes nor stockings. Hundreds of shocking accounts describe hopeless poverty. Yet in spite of terrible conditions, population growth sped onward. The 3 million of 1725 reached 4 million in 1780 and doubled to 8 million by 1840. Between 1780 and 1840, 1.75 million people left Ireland for Britain and America.

The population grew so quickly for three reasons: extensive cultivation of the potato, early marriage, and exploitation of peasants by landlords. The cultivation of the potato, introduced into Ireland (and all of Europe) in the late sixteenth century, was originally a response to the pressure of numbers. Once peasants began to cultivate potatoes, many more people could exist. A single acre of land spaded and planted with potatoes could feed an Irish family of six for a year, whereas two to four acres of grain and pasture were needed to feed the same number. The potato also could thrive on boggy wastelands.

Needing only a big potato patch to survive, Irish men and women married early. Setting up housekeeping was easy, for a cabin of mud and stone could be slapped together with the help of friends and relatives in a few days. A mat for a bed, chairs and a table, and an iron pot to boil potatoes were easily acquired. To be sure, the young couple was embracing a life of extreme poverty. They would literally live on potatoes—ten pounds a day for an average male—moistened at best with a cup of milk.

Yet the decision to marry and have large families made sense. Landlords leased land for short periods only. Peasants had no incentive to make permanent improvements because anything beyond what was needed for survival would quickly be taken by higher rent. Rural poverty was inescapable and better shared with a spouse, while a dutiful son or a loving daughter was an old person's best hope of escaping destitution.

Daniel McDonald: The Discovery of the Potato Blight Although the leaves of diseased plants usually shriveled and died, they could also look deceptively healthy. This Irish family has dug up its potato harvest and just discovered to its horror that the blight has rotted the crop. Like thousands of Irish families, this family now faces the starvation and the mass epidemics of the Great Famine. *(Department of Irish Folklore, University College, Dublin)*

As population and potato dependency grew, conditions became more precarious. From 1820 onward deficiencies and diseases in the potato crop became more common. In 1845 and 1846, and again in 1848 and 1851, the potato crop failed in Ireland.

The result was unmitigated disaster—the **Great Famine.** Blight attacked the young plants, the leaves withered, and the tubers rotted. Widespread starvation and mass fever epidemics followed. Yet the British government, committed to rigid laissez-faire ideology, was slow to act. When it did, its relief efforts were tragically inadequate. Moreover, the government continued to collect taxes, and landlords demanded their rents. Tenants who could not pay were evicted and their homes destroyed. Famine or no, Ireland remained the conquered jewel of foreign landowners.

Online Study Center Improve Your Grade
Primary Source: The Misery That Was Ireland: The Potato Famine

The Great Famine shattered the pattern of Irish population growth. Fully 1 million emigrants fled the famine between 1845 and 1851, and at least 1.5 million died or went unborn because of the disaster. Alone among the countries of Europe, Ireland experienced a declining population in the nineteenth century, from about 8 million in 1845 to 4.4 million in 1911. Ireland became a land of continuous out-migration, late marriage, and widespread celibacy.

The Great Famine also intensified anti-British feeling and promoted Irish nationalism, for the bitter memory of starvation, exile, and British inaction was burned deeply into the popular consciousness. Patriots could call on powerful collective emotions in their campaigns for land reform, home rule, and, eventually, Irish independence.

The Revolution of 1830 in France

Louis XVIII's Constitutional Charter of 1814—theoretically a gift from the king but actually a response to political pressures—was basically a liberal constitution (see page 711). The economic and social gains made by sections of the middle class and the peasantry in the French Revolution were fully protected, great intellectual and artistic freedom was permitted, and a parliament with upper and lower houses was created. Immediately after Napoleon's abortive Hundred Days, the moderate, worldly king refused to bow to the wishes of die-hard aristocrats such as his brother Charles, who wished to sweep away all the revolutionary changes and return to a bygone age of royal absolutism and aristocratic pretension. Instead, Louis appointed as his ministers moderate royalists, who sought and obtained the support of a majority of the representatives elected to the lower Chamber of Deputies between 1816 and Louis's death in 1824.

Louis XVIII's charter was anything but democratic. Only about 100,000 of the wealthiest males out of a total population of 30 million had the right to vote for the deputies who, with the king and his ministers, made the laws of the nation. Nonetheless, the "notable people" who did vote came from very different backgrounds. There were wealthy businessmen, war profiteers, successful professionals, ex-revolutionaries, large landowners from the old aristocracy and the middle class, Bourbons, and Bonapartists.

The old aristocracy, with its pre-1789 mentality, was a minority within the voting population. It was this situation that Louis's successor, Charles X (r. 1824–1830), could not abide. Crowned in a lavish, utterly medieval, five-hour ceremony in the cathedral of Reims in 1824, Charles was a true reactionary. He wanted to re-establish the old order in France. Increasingly blocked by the opposition of the deputies, Charles's government turned in 1830 to military adventure in an effort to rally French nationalism and gain popular support. A long-standing economic and diplomatic dispute with Muslim Algeria, a vassal state of the Ottoman Empire, provided the opportunity.

In June 1830, a French force of 37,000 crossed the Mediterranean, landed to the west of Algiers, and took the capital city in three short weeks. Victory seemed complete, but in 1831 tribes in the interior revolted and waged a fearsome war until 1847, when French armies finally subdued the country. Bringing French, Spanish, and Italian settlers to Algeria and leading to the expropriation of large tracts of Muslim land, the conquest of Algeria marked the rebirth of French colonial expansion.

Emboldened by the good news from Algeria, which actually had limited impact in Paris, Charles repudiated the Constitutional Charter in an attempted coup in July 1830. He issued decrees stripping much of the wealthy middle class of its voting rights, and he censored the press. The immediate reaction, encouraged by journalists and lawyers, was an insurrection in the capital by printers, other artisans, and small traders. In "three glorious days," the government collapsed. Paris boiled with revolutionary excitement, and Charles fled. Then the upper middle class, which had fomented the revolt, skillfully seated Charles's cousin, Louis Philippe, duke of Orléans, on the vacant throne.

Louis Philippe (r. 1830–1848) accepted the Constitutional Charter of 1814; adopted the red, white, and blue flag of the French Revolution; and admitted

The Fall of Algiers, July 1830 France assembled more than six hundred ships for its attack on the Ottoman dependency of Algeria, and this contemporary engraving depicts the ferocious naval bombardment that destroyed the capital's last remaining fortifications. However, after the surrender French soldiers rampaged through the city, and news of this brutal behavior encouraged Muslims in the interior to revolt and fight on until 1847. *(Musée de la Ville de Paris, Musée Carnavalet, Paris, France/Lauros/Giraudon/The Bridgeman Art Library)*

that he was merely the "king of the French people." In spite of such symbolic actions, the situation in France remained fundamentally unchanged. The vote was extended only from 100,000 to 170,000 citizens. The wealthy notable elite actually tightened its control as the old aristocracy retreated to the provinces to sulk harmlessly. For the upper middle class, there had been a change in dynasty in order to protect the status quo and the narrowly liberal institutions of 1815. Republicans, democrats, social reformers, and the poor of Paris were bitterly disappointed. They had made a revolution, but it seemed for naught. The social and political divisions that so troubled Jules Michelet in the 1840s were clear for all to see. (See the feature "Individuals in Society: Jules Michelet.")

The Revolutions of 1848

In 1848 revolutionary political and social ideologies combined with severe economic crisis and the romantic impulse to produce a vast upheaval across Europe. Only the most advanced and the most backward major countries—reforming Great Britain and immobile Russia—escaped untouched. Governments toppled; monarchs and ministers bowed or fled. National independence, liberal-democratic constitutions, and social reform: the lofty aspirations of a generation seemed at hand. Yet in the end, the revolutions failed.

- **Why in 1848 did revolution triumph briefly throughout most of Europe, and why did it fail almost completely?**

Individuals in Society

Jules Michelet

Famous proponent of democratic nationalism and generally recognized as France's pre-eminent romantic historian, Jules Michelet (1798–1874) was born and educated in Paris, the only child in a loving family of poor printers. Largely self-taught in the family print shop in his early years, the awkward apprentice-turned-student entered the prestigious Charlemagne College in 1813 and had to repeat his first year. Then he sped forward, winning prizes and building a brilliant academic career. Yet Michelet remained true to his roots in the common people, and he drew from history a vision of a generous France that would embrace all its children and heal their social divisions.

The young Michelet was strongly influenced by the still largely ignored Italian philosopher Giovanni Battista Vico (1668–1744), who viewed history as the development of societies and human institutions, as opposed to the biographies of great men or the work of divine providence. Translating and popularizing Vico's work and quickly writing three general histories, Michelet was rewarded with a professorship in Paris. He then launched an in-depth study of French society in the Middle Ages.

Motivated by the Gothic revival and romantic nationalism, Michelet was also inspired by his appointment as historical director of the National Archives after the revolution of 1830. This enabled him to combine teaching and writing with intense research in still largely unexplored documentary collections and present what he believed to be the first genuine history of his country and its people. Many historians, though not Michelet himself, believe that his history of France in the Middle Ages—published between 1833 and 1844 and becoming the first six volumes in his multivolume *History of France* (1833–1867)—is his most solid, useful, and lasting accomplishment. They single out his vast knowledge of the sources, his uncanny evocation of times and places, and his empathic and balanced understanding of different views and individuals. His treatment of the national revival under Joan of Arc in the fifteenth century is a famous example of his early work.

Finishing his study of the Middle Ages and shaken by his wife's death, Michelet became eager to write the history of the French Revolution as the ultimate achievement, the time the French people reached maturity and began the long-delayed liberation of mankind. Yet, confronted by growing social divisions and seeing

"France sinking hour by hour," he tried first to write a book that would save France. Published in 1846, *The People* drew on personal experience, history, and contemporary debates, painting a vivid picture of French society and the social dislocation that afflicted all classes. Rejecting socialism as an unrealistic fantasy, Michelet pleaded instead for national unity: "One

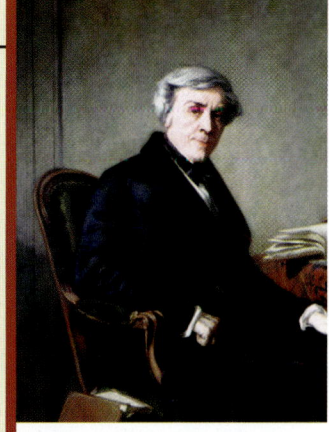

Jules Michelet, in a portrait by Joseph Court. (Photo12.com)

people! one country! one France! Never, never, I beg you, must we become two nations! Without unity, we perish!"* He also called for universal secular education, which would teach the revolution in 1789 and anchor France in a culture of republican democracy. Michelet's book was widely read and discussed.

Sickened by the failure of the revolution of 1848 and refusing to swear allegiance to Louis Napoleon, Michelet lost his government positions and turned to full-time writing. He completed his seven-volume history of the French Revolution, filled in the early modern period history of France with another eleven volumes, and wrote popular impressions of nature and anticlerical polemics. Michelet's later history is often criticized for being overly emotional and biased against the monarchy, the nobility, and the clergy while idealizing popular forces and revolutionary upheaval. A great individualist, Michelet was a gifted writer with a grand, heartfelt historical narrative of compassionate nationhood for a noble people.

Questions for Analysis

1. How would you describe Michelet's conception of history, and how did it evolve over time?
2. Does the study of history help solve contemporary problems? Debate this question, and defend your position.

*Jules Michelet, *The People*, trans. with an introduction by John P. McKay (Urbana: University of Illinois Press, 1973), p. 21.

Online Study Center   Improve Your Grade
Going Beyond Individuals in Society

A Democratic Republic in France

The late 1840s in Europe were hard economically and tense politically. The potato famine in Ireland in 1845 and 1846 had many echoes on the continent. Bad harvests jacked up food prices and caused misery and unemployment in the cities. "Prerevolutionary" outbreaks occurred all across Europe: an abortive Polish revolution in the northern part of Austria in 1846, a civil war between radicals and conservatives in Switzerland in 1847, and an armed uprising in Naples, Italy, in January 1848. Revolution was almost universally expected, but it took revolution in Paris—once again—to turn expectations into realities.

Louis Philippe's "bourgeois monarchy" had been characterized by stubborn inaction and complacency. There was a glaring lack of social legislation, and politics was dominated by corruption and selfish special interests. With only the rich voting for deputies, many of the deputies were docile government bureaucrats.

The government's stubborn refusal to consider electoral reform heightened a sense of class injustice among middle-class shopkeepers, skilled artisans, and unskilled working people, and it eventually touched off a popular revolt in Paris. Barricades went up on the night of February 22, 1848, and by February 24 Louis Philippe had abdicated in favor of his grandson. But the common people in arms would tolerate no more monarchy. This refusal led to the proclamation of a provisional republic, headed by a ten-man executive committee and certified by cries of approval from the revolutionary crowd.

A generation of historians and journalists had praised the First French Republic, and their work had borne fruit: the revolutionaries were firmly committed to a republic (as opposed to any form of constitutional monarchy), and they immediately set about drafting a constitution for France's Second Republic. Moreover, they wanted a truly popular and democratic republic so that the healthy, life-giving forces of the common people—the peasants, the artisans, and the unskilled workers—could reform society

The Triumph of Democratic Republics This French illustration constructs a joyous, optimistic vision of the initial revolutionary breakthrough in 1848. The peoples of Europe, joined together around their respective national banners, are achieving republican freedom, which is symbolized by the statue of liberty and the discarded crowns. The woman wearing pants—very radical attire—represents feminist hopes for liberation. *(Archive of Arnoldo Mondadori Editore, Milan)*

with wise legislation. In practice, building such a republic meant giving the right to vote to every adult male, and this was quickly done. Revolutionary compassion and sympathy for freedom were expressed in the freeing of all slaves in French colonies, the abolition of the death penalty, and the establishment of a ten-hour workday for Paris.

Yet there were profound differences within the revolutionary coalition in Paris. On the one hand, there were the moderate, liberal republicans of the middle class. They viewed universal male suffrage as the ultimate concession to be made to popular forces, and they strongly opposed any further radical social measures. On the other hand, there were radical republicans and hard-pressed artisans. Influenced by a generation of utopian socialists, and appalled by the poverty and misery of the urban poor, the radical republicans were committed to some kind of socialism. So were many artisans, who hated the unrestrained competition of cutthroat capitalism and who advocated a combination of strong craft unions and worker-owned businesses.

Worsening depression and rising unemployment brought these conflicting goals to the fore in 1848. Louis Blanc, who along with a worker named Albert represented the republican socialists in the provisional government, pressed for recognition of a socialist right to work. Blanc asserted that permanent government-sponsored cooperative workshops should be established for workers. Such workshops would be an alternative to capitalist employment and a decisive step toward a new, noncompetitive social order.

The moderate republicans wanted no such thing. They were willing to provide only temporary relief. The resulting compromise set up national workshops—soon to become little more than a vast program of pick-and-shovel public works—and established a special commission under Blanc to "study the question." This satisfied no one. The national workshops were, however, better than nothing. An army of desperate poor from the French provinces and even from foreign countries streamed into Paris to sign up. As the economic crisis worsened, the number enrolled in the workshops soared from 10,000 in March to 120,000 by June, and another 80,000 were trying unsuccessfully to join.

While the workshops in Paris grew, the French masses went to the election polls in late April. Voting in most cases for the first time, the people of France elected to the new Constituent Assembly about five hundred moderate republicans, three hundred monarchists, and one hundred radicals who professed various brands of socialism. One of the moderate republicans was the author of *Democracy in America,* Alexis de Tocqueville (1805–1859), who had predicted the overthrow of Louis Philippe's government. To this brilliant observer, socialism was the most characteristic aspect of the revolution in Paris.

This socialist revolution was evoking a violent reaction not only among the frightened middle and upper classes but also among the bulk of the population—the peasants. The French peasants owned land, and according to Tocqueville, "private property had become with all those who owned it a sort of bond of fraternity."[4] Returning from Normandy to take his seat in the new Constituent Assembly, Tocqueville saw that a majority of the members were firmly committed to the republic and strongly opposed to the socialists and their artisan allies, and he shared their sentiments.

This clash of ideologies—of liberal capitalism and socialism—became a clash of classes and arms after the elections. The new government's executive committee dropped Blanc and thereafter included no representative of the Parisian working class. Fearing that their socialist hopes were about to be dashed, artisans and unskilled workers invaded the Constituent Assembly on May 15 and tried to proclaim a new revolutionary state. But the government was ready and used the middle-class National Guard to squelch this uprising. As the workshops continued to fill and grow more radical, the fearful but powerful propertied classes in the Assembly took the offensive. On June 22, the government dissolved the national workshops in Paris, giving the workers the choice of joining the army or going to workshops in the provinces.

The result was a spontaneous and violent uprising. Frustrated in attempts to create a socialist society, masses of desperate people were now losing even their life-sustaining relief. As a voice from the crowd cried out when the famous astronomer François Arago counseled patience, "Ah, Monsieur Arago, you have never been hungry!"[5] Barricades sprang up in the narrow streets of Paris, and a terrible class war began. Working people fought with the courage of utter desperation, but the government had the army and the support of peasant France. After three terrible "June Days" and the death or injury of more than ten thousand people, the republican army under General Louis Cavaignac stood triumphant in a sea of working-class blood and hatred.

The revolution in France thus ended in spectacular failure. The February coalition of the middle and working classes had in four short months become locked in mortal combat. In place of a generous democratic republic, the Constituent Assembly completed a constitution featuring a strong executive. This allowed Louis Napoleon, nephew of Napoleon Bonaparte, to win a landslide victory in the election of December 1848. The appeal of his great name as well as the desire of the propertied classes for order at any cost had produced a semi-authoritarian regime.

The Austrian Empire in 1848

Throughout central Europe, the first news of the upheaval in France evoked feverish excitement and eventually revolution. Liberals demanded written constitutions, representative government, and greater civil liberties from authoritarian regimes. When governments hesitated, popular revolts followed. Urban workers and students served as the shock troops, but they were allied with middle-class liberals and peasants. In the face of this united front, monarchs collapsed and granted almost everything. The popular revolutionary coalition, having secured great and easy victories, then broke down as it had in France. The traditional forces—the monarchy, the aristocracy, the regular army—recovered their nerve, reasserted their authority, and took back many, though not all, of the concessions. Reaction was everywhere victorious.

The revolution in the Austrian Empire began in Hungary, where nationalistic Hungarians demanded national autonomy, full civil liberties, and universal suffrage. When the monarchy in Vienna hesitated, Viennese students and workers took to the streets, and peasant disorders broke out in parts of the empire. The Habsburg emperor Ferdinand I (r. 1835–1848) capitulated and promised reforms and a liberal constitution. Metternich fled in disguise toward London. The old absolutist order seemed to be collapsing with unbelievable rapidity.

The coalition of revolutionaries was not stable, however. The Austrian Empire was overwhelmingly agricultural, and serfdom still existed. On March 20, as part of its capitulation before upheaval, the monarchy abolished serfdom, with its degrading forced labor and feudal services. Feeling they had won a victory reminiscent of that in France in 1789, newly free men and women of the land then lost interest in the political and social questions agitating the cities. Meanwhile, the coalition of urban revolutionaries also broke down. When artisan workers and the urban poor rose in arms and presented their own demands for socialist workshops and universal voting rights for men, the prosperous middle classes recoiled in alarm.

The coalition of March was also weakened, and ultimately destroyed, by conflicting national aspirations. In March the Hungarian revolutionary leaders pushed through an extremely liberal, almost democratic, constitution. But the Hungarian revolutionaries also sought to transform the mosaic of provinces and peoples that was the kingdom of Hungary into a unified, centralized, Hungarian nation. To the minority groups that formed half of the population—the Croats, Serbs, and Romanians—such unification was completely unacceptable. Each felt entitled to political autonomy and cultural independence. The Habsburg monarchy in Vienna exploited the fears of the minority groups, and they were soon locked in armed combat with the new Hungarian government. In a somewhat similar way, Czech nationalists based in Bohemia and the city of Prague came into conflict with German nationalists. (See the feature "Listening to the Past: Speaking for the Czech Nation" on pages 776–777.) Thus conflicting national aspirations within the Austrian Empire enabled the monarchy to play off one ethnic group against the other.

Finally, the conservative aristocratic forces gathered around Emperor Ferdinand I regained their nerve and reasserted their great strength. The archduchess Sophia, a conservative but intelligent and courageous Bavarian princess married to the emperor's brother, provided a rallying point. Deeply ashamed of the emperor's collapse before a "mess of students," she insisted that Ferdinand, who had no heir, abdicate in favor of her son, Francis Joseph.[6] Powerful nobles who held high positions in the government, the army, and the church agreed completely. They organized around Sophia in a secret conspiracy to reverse and crush the revolution.

Their first breakthrough came when the army bombarded Prague and savagely crushed a working-class revolt there on June 17. Other Austrian officials and nobles began to lead the minority nationalities of Hungary against the revolutionary government proclaimed by the Hungarian patriots. At the end of October, the well-equipped, predominately peasant troops of the regular Austrian army attacked the student and working-class radicals in Vienna and retook the city at the cost of more than four thousand casualties. Thus the determination of the Austrian aristocracy and the loyalty of its army were the final ingredients in the triumph of reaction and the defeat of revolution.

When Francis Joseph (r. 1848–1916) was crowned emperor of Austria immediately after his eighteenth birthday in December 1848, only Hungary had yet to be brought under control. But another determined conservative, Nicholas I of Russia (r. 1825–1855), obligingly lent his iron hand. On June 6, 1849, 130,000 Russian troops poured into Hungary and subdued the country after bitter fighting. For a number of years, the Habsburgs ruled Hungary as a conquered territory.

Prussia and the Frankfurt Assembly

After Austria, Prussia was the largest and most influential German kingdom. Prior to 1848, the goal of middle-class Prussian liberals had been to transform absolutist Prussia into a liberal constitutional monarchy, which would lead the thirty-eight states of the German Confederation into the liberal, unified nation desired by liberals throughout the German states. The agitation following the fall of Louis Philippe encouraged Prussian liberals to press their demands. When the artisans and factory workers in Berlin exploded in March and joined temporarily with the middle-class liberals in the struggle against the monarchy, the autocratic yet paternalistic Frederick William IV (r. 1840–1861) vacillated and finally caved in. On March 21, he promised to grant Prussia a liberal constitution and to merge Prussia into a new national German state that was to be created. But urban workers wanted much more and the Prussian aristocracy wanted much less than the moderate constitutional liberalism

Street Fighting in Frankfurt, 1848 Workers and students could tear up the cobblestones, barricade a street, and make it into a fortress. But urban revolutionaries were untrained and poorly armed. They were no match for professional soldiers led by tough officers who were sent against them after frightened rulers had recovered their nerve. *(The Granger Collection, New York)*

the king conceded. The workers issued a series of democratic and vaguely socialist demands that troubled their middle-class allies, and the conservative clique gathered around the king to urge counter-revolution.

As an elected Prussian Constituent Assembly met in Berlin to write a constitution for the Prussian state, a self-appointed committee of liberals from various German states successfully called for a national assembly to begin writing a federal constitution for a unified German state. Meeting in Frankfurt in May, the National Assembly was a curious revolutionary body. It was a really serious middle-class body of lawyers, professors, doctors, officials, and businessmen.

Convened to write a constitution, the learned body was soon absorbed in a battle with Denmark over the provinces of Schleswig and Holstein, an extremely complicated issue from a legal point of view. The provinces were inhabited primarily by Germans but were ruled by the king of Denmark, although Holstein was a member of the German Confederation. When Frederick VII, the new nationalistic king of Denmark, tried to integrate both provinces into the rest of his state, the Germans in these provinces revolted. Hypnotized by this conflict, the National Assembly at Frankfurt debated ponderously and finally called on the Prussian army to oppose Denmark in the name of the German nation. Prussia responded and began war with Denmark. As the Schleswig-Holstein issue demonstrated, the national ideal was a crucial factor motivating the German middle classes in 1848.

In March 1849, the National Assembly finally completed its drafting of a liberal constitution and elected King Frederick William of Prussia emperor of the new German national state (minus Austria and Schleswig-Holstein). By early 1849, however, reaction had been successful almost everywhere. Frederick William had reasserted his royal authority, disbanded the Prussian Constituent Assembly, and granted his subjects a limited, essentially conservative constitution. Reasserting that he ruled by divine right, Frederick William contemptuously refused to accept the "crown from the gutter." Bogged down by their preoccupation with nationalist issues, the reluctant revolutionaries in Frankfurt had waited too long and acted too timidly.

When Frederick William, who really wanted to be emperor but only on his own authoritarian terms, tried to get the small monarchs of Germany to elect him emperor, Austria balked. Supported by Russia, Austria forced Prussia to renounce all its schemes of unification in late 1850. The German Confederation was re-established. Attempts to unite the Germans—first in a liberal national state and then in a conservative Prussian empire—had failed completely.

Chapter Summary

- How did the victorious allies fashion a general peace settlement, and how did Metternich uphold a conservative European order?
- What were the basic tenets of liberalism, nationalism, and socialism, and what groups were most attracted to these ideologies?
- What were the characteristics of the romantic movement, and who were some of the great romantic artists?
- How after 1815 did liberal, national, and socialist forces challenge conservatism in Greece, Great Britain, and France?
- Why in 1848 did revolution triumph briefly throughout most of Europe, and why did it fail almost completely?

In 1814 the victorious allied powers sought to restore peace and stability in Europe. Dealing moderately with France and wisely settling their own differences, the allies laid the foundations for beneficial international cooperation throughout much of the nineteenth century. Led by Metternich, the conservative powers also sought to prevent the spread of subversive ideas and radical changes in domestic politics. Yet European thought has seldom been more powerfully creative than after 1815, and ideologies of liberalism, nationalism, and socialism all developed to challenge the existing order in this period of early industrialization and rapid population growth. The romantic movement, breaking decisively with the dictates of classicism, reinforced the spirit of change and revolutionary anticipation.

All of these forces shaped European development after 1815, and they culminated in the liberal and nationalistic revolutions of 1848. Political, economic, and social pressures that had been building since 1815 exploded dramatically and rocked the continent. Yet the upheavals of 1848 were abortive, and very few revolutionary goals were realized. The moderate, nationalistic middle classes were unable to consolidate their initial victories in France or elsewhere in Europe. Instead, they drew back when artisans, factory workers, and radical socialists rose up to present their own much more revolutionary demands. This retreat facilitated the efforts of dedicated aristocrats in central Europe to reassert their power. And it made possible the crushing of Parisian workers by a coalition of solid bourgeoisie and landowning peasantry in France. A host of fears, a sea of blood, and a torrent of disillusion had drowned the lofty ideals and utopian visions of a generation. The age of romantic revolution was over. Soon tough-minded realists would take command to confront the challenges of the dual revolution.

Key Terms

dual revolution
Congress of Vienna
Holy Alliance
Carlsbad Decrees
liberalism
laissez faire
nationalism
socialism
parasites
doers
bourgeoisie
proletariat
romanticism
Sturm und Drang
Corn Laws
Battle of Peterloo
Great Famine

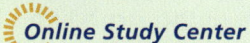 Online Study Center   Improve Your Grade Flashcards

Suggested Reading

Berger, Stefan, ed. *A Companion to Nineteenth-Century Europe, 1789–1914.* 2006. A useful study with an up-to-date bibliography.

Chadwick, Owen. *The Secularization of the European Mind in the Nineteenth Century.* 1976. Considers the important place of religion in nineteenth-century thought.

Gildea, Robert. *Barricades and Borders: Europe, 1800–1914,* 2d ed. 1996. A recommended general study.

Greene, Abigail. *Fatherlands: State-Building and Nationhood in Nineteenth-Century Germany.* 2001. A brilliant discussion of the smaller German states.

Lindemann, Albert S. *A History of European Socialism.* 1983. A stimulating survey of early socialism and Marxism.

Malia, Martin, and Terence Emmons. *History's Locomotives: Revolutions and the Making of the Modern World.* 2006. An ambitious comparative work of high quality.

Mann, Thomas. *Buddenbrooks.* A wonderful historical novel that traces the rise and fall of a prosperous German family over three generations.

Merriman, John. *Police Stories: Building the French State, 1815–1851.* 2006. An outstanding and innovative compendium.

Pilbeam, Pamela. *French Socialists Before Marx: Workers, Women, and the Social Question.* 2000. Shows the significant role of women in utopian socialism.

Price, Roger. *A Social History of Nineteenth-Century France.* 1987. A fine synthesis.

Rubinstein, W. D. *Britain's Century: A Political and Social History, 1815–1905.* 1998. An excellent English history.

Sheehan, James J. *German History, 1770–1866.* 1993. A stimulating general history that skillfully incorporates recent research.

Shelley, Mary. *Frankenstein.* A great nineteenth-century romantic novel that draws an almost lovable picture of the famous monster and is highly recommended.

Sperber, Jonathan. *The European Revolutions, 1848–1851.* 1993. A solid synthesis of the great revolutionary upheaval.

Notes

1. E. Gellner, *Nations and Nationalism* (Oxford: Basil Blackwell, 1983), especially pp. 19–39.
2. This paragraph draws on the influential views of B. Anderson, *Imagined Communities: Reflections on the Origins and Spread of Nationalism,* rev. ed. (London/New York: Verso, 1991), and E. J. Hobsbawm and T. Ranger, eds., *The Invention of Tradition* (Cambridge: Cambridge University Press, 1983).
3. Quoted in F. B. Artz, *From the Renaissance to Romanticism: Trends in Style in Art, Literature, and Music, 1300–1830* (Chicago: University of Chicago Press, 1962), pp. 276, 278.
4. A. de Tocqueville, *Recollections* (New York: Columbia University Press, 1949), p. 94.
5. M. Agulhon, *1848* (Paris: Éditions du Seuil, 1973), pp. 68–69.
6. W. L. Langer, *Political and Social Upheaval, 1832–1852* (New York: Harper & Row, 1969), p. 361.

Listening to the Past

Speaking for the Czech Nation

The creation of national consciousness and nationalism often began with a cultural revival that focused on a people's language and history, which led to calls for cultural autonomy and political independence. In Austria, the influential historian Frantisek Palacky (1798–1876) inspired the Czech cultural and political revival, re-creating the Czechs in his books as progressive and democratic before the Counter-Reformation and the long process of Germanization under Habsburg rule.

In the revolution of 1848, when the German National Assembly in Frankfurt assumed that Austrian provinces that were part of the German Confederation would also join a united Germany, it asked Palacky to represent Czech Bohemia. In the famous letter that follows Palacky rejected this invitation. Asserting the reality of a Czech nation and warning of both Russian and German expansionism, he proposed a "union of equals" in a radically transformed Austria. A version of Palacky's proposal was passed by Austria's constituent assembly in 1849, but the resurgent absolutist government vetoed it.

. . . I am a Czech of Slav descent and with all the little I own and possess I have devoted myself wholly and for ever to the service of my nation. That nation is small, it is true, but from time immemorial it has been an independent nation with its own character; its rulers have participated since old times in the federation of German princes, but the nation never regarded itself nor was it regarded by others throughout all the centuries, as part of the German nation. The whole union of the Czech lands first with the Holy German Empire and then with the German Confederation was always a purely dynastic one of which the Czech nation, the Czech Estates, hardly wished to know and which they hardly noticed. . . . If anyone asks that the Czech nation should now unite with the German nation, beyond this heretofore existing federation between princes, this is then a new demand which has no historical legal basis. . . . The second reason which prevents me from participating in your deliberations is the fact that . . . you . . . are . . . aiming to undermine Austria forever as an independent empire and to make its existence impossible—an empire whose preservation, integrity and consolidation is, and must be, a great and important matter not only for my own nation but for the whole of Europe, indeed for mankind and civilization itself. Allow me kindly to explain myself briefly on this point.

You know, gentlemen, what power it is that holds the whole great eastern part of our continent; you know that this power [Russia] which now already has grown to vast dimensions, increases and expands by its own strength every decade . . . has for a long time been a threat to its neighbours; and . . . that every further step which it will take forward on this path threatens at an ever accelerated pace to produce and found a *universal monarchy,* that is to say, an infinite and inexpressible evil, a misfortune without measure or bound which I, though heart and soul a Slav, would nonetheless deeply regret for the good of mankind even though that monarchy proclaimed itself a Slav one. . . . The bare possibility of a Russian universal monarchy has no more determined opponent or adversary than myself, not because that monarchy would be Russian but because it would be universal.

You know that in south-east Europe, along the frontiers of the Russian empire, there live many nations widely different in origin, language, history and habits—Slavs, Rumanians, Magyars [Hungarians] and Germans, not to speak of Greeks, Turks and Albanians—none of whom is strong enough by itself to be able to resist successfully for all time the superior neighbour to the east; they could do it only if a close and firm tie bound them all together. The vital artery of this necessary union of nations is the Danube; the focus of its power must never be removed far from this river, if the union is to be effective at all and to remain so. Certainly, if the Austrian state had not existed for ages, we would be obliged in the interests of Europe and even of mankind to endeavor to create it as fast as possible.

But why have we seen this state, which by nature and history is destined to be the bulwark and guardian of Europe against Asiatic elements of every kind—why have we seen it in a critical moment helpless and almost unadvised in the face of the advancing storm? It is because in an unhappy blindness which has lasted for very long, Austria has not recognized the real legal and moral foundation of its existence and has denied it: the fundamental rule that all the nationalities united under its scepter should enjoy complete equality of rights and respect. The right of nations is truly a natural right; no nation on earth has the right to demand that its neighbour should sacrifice itself for its benefit, no nation obliged to deny or sacrifice itself for the good of its neighbour. Nature knows neither ruling nor subservient nations. If the union which unites several different nations is to be firm and lasting, no nation must have cause to fear that by that union it will lose any of the goods which it holds most dear; on the contrary each must have the certain hope that it will find in the central authority defense and protection against possible violations of equality by neighbours; then every nation will do its best to strengthen that central authority so that it can successfully provide the aforesaid defense. I am convinced that even now it is not too late for the Austrian empire to proclaim openly and sincerely this fundamental rule of justice, the sacred anchor for a ship in danger of floundering and to carry it out energetically in common and in every respect; but every moment is precious; for God's sake do not let us delay another hour with this! . . .

When I look behind the Bohemian frontiers, then natural and historical reasons make me turn not to Frankfurt but to Vienna to seek there the center which is fitted and destined to ensure and defend the peace, the liberty and the right of my nation. Your efforts, gentlemen, seem to me now to be directed as I have already stated, not only

Frantisek Palacky, in a frontispiece portrait accompanying his most important work on Czech history. *(Visual Connection Archive)*

towards ruinously undermining, but even utterly destroying that center from whose might and strength I expect the salvation not only of the Czech land. . . . For the sake of Europe, Vienna must not sink to the role of a provincial town. If there are in Vienna itself such people who demand to have your Frankfurt as their capital, then we must cry: Lord, forgive them, for they know not what they ask!

Questions for Analysis

1. Why did Palacky refuse to participate in the German National Assembly?

2. What is Palacky's attitude toward Russia? Why?

3. In a famous epigram inspired by Voltaire, Palacky writes, "If the Austrian state had not existed for ages, we would be obliged . . . to create it as fast as possible." What does he mean?

4. How has Austria failed to perform its mission? Why?

Source: Slightly adapted from Hans Kohn, *Pan-Slavism: Its Ideology and History*, pp. 65–69. Copyright © 1953. Reprinted by permission of the University of Notre Dame Press.

John Perry, *A Bill-poster's Fantasy* (1855), explores the endless diversity of big-city entertainment.
(dunhill Museum & Archive, 48 Germyn Street, St. James's, London)

Chapter 24

Life in the Emerging Urban Society in the Nineteenth Century

chapter preview

Taming the City
- What was life like in the cities, and how did urban life change in the nineteenth century?

Rich and Poor and Those in Between
- What did the emergence of urban industrial society mean for rich and poor and those in between?

The Changing Family
- How did families change as they coped with the challenges and the opportunities of the developing urban civilization?

Science and Thought
- What major changes in science and thought reflected and influenced the new urban society?

The era of intellectual and political upheaval that culminated in the revolutions of 1848 was also an era of rapid urbanization. After 1848 Western political development veered off in a novel and uncharted direction, but the growth of towns and cities rushed forward with undiminished force. Thus Western society was urban and industrial in 1900 as surely as it had been rural and agrarian in 1800. The urbanization of society was both a result of the Industrial Revolution and a reflection of its enormous long-term impact.

Taming the City

The growth of industry posed enormous challenges for all elements of Western society, from young factory workers confronting relentless discipline to aristocratic elites maneuvering to retain political power. As we saw in Chapter 22, the early consequences of economic transformation were mixed and far-reaching and by no means wholly negative. By 1850 at the latest, working conditions were improving and real wages were rising for the mass of the population, and they continued to do so until 1914. Thus given the poverty and uncertainty of preindustrial life, some historians maintain that the history of industrialization in the nineteenth century is probably better written in terms of increasing opportunities than in terms of greater hardships.

Critics of this relatively optimistic view of industrialization claim that it neglects the quality of life in urban areas. They stress that the new industrial towns and cities were awful places where people, especially poor people, suffered from bad housing, lack of sanitation, and a sense of hopelessness. They ask if these drawbacks did not more than cancel out higher wages and greater opportunity. An examination of the development of

Online Study Center
This icon will direct you to interactive activities and study materials on the website **college.hmco.com/pic/mckaywest9e**

Mapping the Past

MAP 24.1 European Cities of 100,000 or More, 1800 and 1900 There were more large cities in Great Britain in 1900 than in all of Europe in 1800. A careful comparison of these historical snapshots reveals key aspects of nineteenth-century urbanization. ❶ In 1800, what common characteristics were shared by many large European cities? (For example, how many big cities were capitals and/or leading ports?) ❷ Compare the spatial distribution of cities in 1800 with the distribution in 1900. Where and why in 1900 are many large cities concentrated in two clusters?

cities in the nineteenth century provides some answers to this complex question.

- **What was life like in the cities, and how did urban life change in the nineteenth century?**

Industry and the Growth of Cities

Since the Middle Ages, European cities had been centers of government, culture, and large-scale commerce. They had also been congested, dirty, and unhealthy. People were packed together almost as tightly as possible within the city limits. The typical city was a "walking city": for all but the wealthiest classes, walking was the only available form of transportation.

Infectious disease spread with deadly speed in cities, and people were always more likely to die in the city than in the countryside. In the larger towns, more people died each year than were born, on average, and urban populations were able to maintain their numbers only because newcomers were continually arriving from rural areas. Little could be done to improve these conditions, given the pervasive poverty, absence of urban transportation, lack of medical knowledge, and deadly overcrowding.

Clearly, deplorable urban conditions did not originate with the Industrial Revolution. What the Industrial Revolution did was to reveal those conditions more nakedly than ever before. The steam engine freed industrialists from dependence on the energy of fast-flowing streams and rivers so that by 1800 there was every incentive to build new factories in urban areas. Cities had better shipping facilities than the countryside and thus better supplies of coal and raw materials. There were also many hands wanting work in the cities, for cities drew people like a magnet. And it was a great advantage for a manufacturer to have other factories nearby to supply the business's needs and buy its products. Therefore, as industry grew, there was also a rapid expansion of already overcrowded and unhealthy cities.

The challenge of the urban environment was felt first and most acutely in Great Britain. The number of people living in cities of 20,000 or more in England and Wales jumped from 1.5 million in 1801 to 6.3 million in 1851 and reached 15.6 million in 1891. Such cities accounted for 17 percent of the total English population in 1801, 35 percent as early as 1851, and fully 54 percent in 1891. Other countries duplicated the English pattern as they industrialized (see Map 24.1). An American observer was hardly exaggerating when he wrote in 1899 that "the most remarkable social phenomenon of the present century is the concentration of population in cities."[1]

In the 1820s and 1830s, people in Britain and France began to worry about the condition of their cities. In those years, the populations of a number of British cities were increasing by 40 to 70 percent each decade. With urban areas expanding at such previously undreamed-of rates, people's fatalistic acceptance of overcrowded, unsanitary urban living conditions began to give way to active concern. Something urgently needed to be done.

On one point everyone could agree: except on the outskirts, each town or city was using every scrap of land to the fullest extent. Parks and open areas were almost nonexistent. Buildings were erected on the smallest possible lots in order to pack the maximum number of people into a given space. Narrow houses were built wall to wall in long rows. These row houses had neither front nor back yards, and only a narrow alley in back separated one row from the next. Or buildings were built around tiny courtyards completely enclosed on all four sides. Many people lived in extremely small, often overcrowded cellars or attics. "Six, eight, and even ten occupying one room is anything but uncommon," wrote a doctor from Aberdeen in Scotland for a government investigation in 1842.

These highly concentrated urban populations lived in extremely unsanitary and unhealthy conditions. Open drains and sewers flowed alongside or down the middle of unpaved streets. Toilet facilities were primitive in the extreme. In parts of Manchester, as many as two hundred people shared a single outhouse. Such privies filled up rapidly, and since they were infrequently emptied, sewage often overflowed and seeped into cellar dwellings. Moreover, some courtyards in poorer neighborhoods became dunghills, collecting excrement that was sometimes sold as fertilizer. By the 1840s there was among the better-off classes a growing, shocking "realization that, to put it as mildly as possible, millions of English men, women, and children were living in shit."[2]

Who or what was responsible for these awful conditions? The crucial factors were the tremendous pressure of more people and the *total* absence of public transportation. People simply had to jam themselves together if they were to be able to walk to shops and factories. Another factor was that government in Great Britain, both local and national, was slow to provide sanitary facilities and establish adequate building codes. This slow pace was probably attributable more to a need to explore and identify what precisely should be done than to rigid middle-class opposition to government action. Certainly, Great Britain had no monopoly on overcrowded and unhealthy urban conditions; many continental cities with stronger traditions of municipal regulation were every bit as bad.

Chronology

ca 1850–1870	Modernization of Paris
1850–1914	Condition of working classes improves
1854	Pasteur studies fermentation and develops pasteurization
1854–1870	Development of germ theory
1857	Flaubert, *Madame Bovary*
1859	Darwin, *On the Origin of Species*
1859–1870	Unification of Italy
1861–1865	U.S. Civil War
1866	Austro-Prussian War
1869	Mendeleev creates periodic table
1870–1871	Franco-Prussian War
1880–1881	Dostoevski, *The Brothers Karamazov*
1880–1913	Birthrate steadily declines in Europe
1890s	Electric streetcars introduced in Europe

Most responsible of all was the sad legacy of rural housing conditions in preindustrial society combined with appalling ignorance. As one authority concludes, "the decent cottage was the exception, the hovel the rule."[3] Thus housing was far down on the newcomer's list of priorities, and ordinary people generally took dirt and filth for granted. One English miner told an investigator, "I do not think it usual for the lasses [in the coal mines] to wash their bodies; my sisters never wash themselves." As for the men, "their legs and bodies are as black as your hat."[4]

Public Health and the Bacterial Revolution

Although cleanliness was not next to godliness in most people's eyes, it was becoming so for some reformers. The most famous of these was Edwin Chadwick, one of the commissioners charged with the administration of relief to paupers under Britain's revised Poor Law of 1834. Chadwick was a good **Benthamite**—that is, a follower of radical philosopher Jeremy Bentham (1748–1832). Bentham had taught that public problems ought to be dealt with on a rational, scientific basis and according to the

Filth and Disease This 1852 drawing from *Punch* tells volumes about the unhealthy living conditions of the urban poor. In the foreground children play with a dead rat and a woman scavenges a dung heap. Cheap rooming houses provide shelter for the frightfully overcrowded population. *(The British Library)*

"greatest good for the greatest number." Applying these principles, Chadwick soon became convinced that disease and death actually caused poverty simply because a sick worker was an unemployed worker and orphaned children were poor children. Most important, Chadwick believed that disease could be prevented by cleaning up the urban environment. That was his "sanitary idea."

Chadwick collected detailed reports from local Poor Law officials on the "sanitary conditions of the laboring population" and published his hard-hitting findings in 1842. This mass of widely publicized evidence proved that disease was related to filthy environmental conditions, which were in turn caused largely by lack of drainage, sewers, and garbage collection.

Chadwick correctly believed that the stinking excrement of communal outhouses could be dependably carried off by water through sewers at less than one-twentieth the cost of removing it by hand. The cheap iron pipes and tile drains of the industrial age would provide running water and sewerage for all sections of town, not just the wealthy ones. In 1848, with the cause strengthened by the cholera epidemic of 1846, Chadwick's report became the basis of

Great Britain's first public health law, which created a national health board and gave cities broad authority to build modern sanitary systems.

The public health movement won dedicated supporters in the United States, France, and Germany from the 1840s on. Governments accepted at least limited responsibility for the health of all citizens, and their programs broke decisively with the age-old fatalism of urban populations in the face of shockingly high mortality. By the 1860s and 1870s, European cities were making real progress toward adequate water supplies and sewerage systems, city dwellers were beginning to reap the reward of better health, and death rates began to decline (see Figure 24.1).

Still, effective control of communicable disease required a great leap forward in medical knowledge and biological theory. Early reformers such as Chadwick were seriously handicapped by the prevailing **miasmatic theory** of disease—the belief that people contract disease when they breathe the bad odors of decay and putrefying excrement. Keen observation by doctors and public health officials in the 1840s and 1850s pinpointed the role of bad drinking water in the transmission of disease and suggested that contagion was *spread through* filth and not caused by it, thus weakening the miasmatic idea.

The breakthrough was the development of the **germ theory** of disease by Louis Pasteur (1822–1895), a French chemist who began studying fermentation in 1854 at the request of brewers. Using his microscope to develop a simple test that brewers could use to monitor the fermentation process and avoid spoilage, Pasteur found that fermentation depended on the growth of living organisms and that the activity of these organisms could be suppressed by heating the beverage—by **pasteurization.** The breathtaking implication was that specific diseases were caused by specific living organisms—germs—and that those organisms could be controlled in people as well as in beer, wine, and milk.

By 1870 the work of Pasteur and others had demonstrated the general connection between germs and disease. When, in the middle of the 1870s, German country doctor Robert Koch and his coworkers developed pure cultures of harmful bacteria and described their life cycles, the dam broke. Over the next twenty years, researchers—mainly Germans—identified the organisms responsible for disease after disease. These discoveries led to the development of a number of effective vaccines.

Acceptance of the germ theory brought about dramatic improvements in the deadly environment of hospitals and surgery. In 1865, when Pasteur showed that the air was full of bacteria, English surgeon Joseph Lister (1827–1912) immediately grasped the connection be-

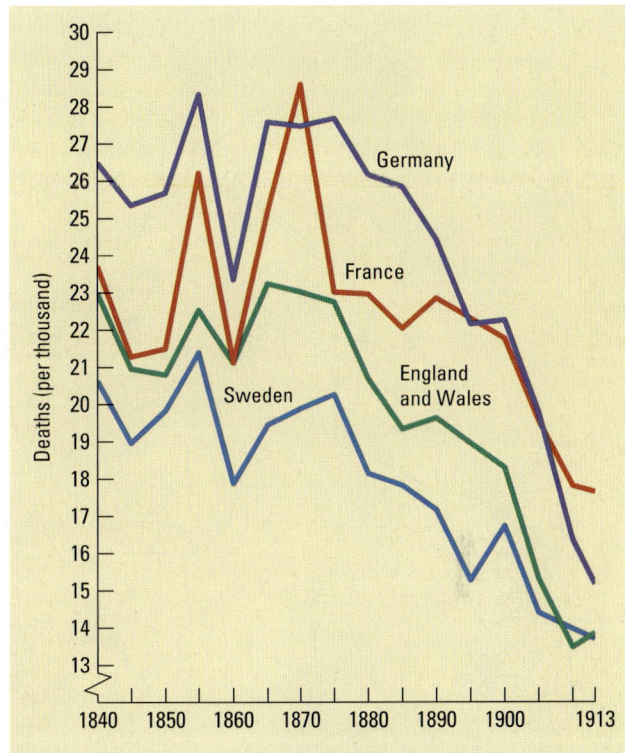

FIGURE 24.1 **The Decline of Death Rates in England and Wales, Germany, France, and Sweden, 1840–1913** A rising standard of living, improvements in public health, and better medical knowledge all contributed to the dramatic decline of death rates in the nineteenth century.

tween aerial bacteria and the problem of wound infection. He reasoned that a chemical disinfectant applied to a wound dressing would "destroy the life of the floating particles." Lister's **antiseptic principle** worked wonders. In the 1880s, German surgeons developed the more sophisticated practice of sterilizing not only the wound but also everything—hands, instruments, clothing—that entered the operating room.

The achievements of the bacterial revolution coupled with the ever more sophisticated public health movement saved millions of lives, particularly after about 1880. Mortality rates began to decline dramatically in European countries (see Figure 24.1) as the awful death sentences of the past—diphtheria, typhoid, typhus, cholera, yellow fever—became vanishing diseases. City dwellers benefited especially from these developments. By 1910 a great silent revolution had occurred: the death rates for people of all ages in urban areas were generally no greater than those for people in rural areas, and sometimes they were less.

MAP 24.2 The Modernization of Paris, ca 1850–1870 Broad boulevards, large parks, and grandiose train stations transformed Paris. The cutting of the new north-south axis—known as the Boulevard Saint-Michel—was one of Haussmann's most controversial projects. It razed much of Paris's medieval core and filled the Île de la Cité with massive government buildings.

Urban Planning and Public Transportation

More effective urban planning was one of the keys to improving the quality of urban life. Urban planning was in decline by the early nineteenth century, but after 1850 its practice was revived and extended. France took the lead during the rule of Napoleon III (r. 1848–1870), who sought to stand above class conflict and promote the welfare of all his subjects through government action. He believed that rebuilding much of Paris would provide employment, improve living conditions, and testify to the power and glory of his empire. In the baron Georges Haussmann (1809–1884), an aggressive, impatient Alsatian whom he placed in charge of Paris, Napoleon III found an authoritarian planner capable of bulldozing both buildings and opposition. In twenty years, Paris was transformed (see Map 24.2).

The Paris of 1850 was a labyrinth of narrow, dark streets, the results of desperate overcrowding. In a central city not twice the size of New York's Central Park lived more than

Apartment Living in Paris This drawing shows how different social classes lived close together in European cities in about 1850. Passing the middle-class family on the first floor (American second floor), the economic condition of the tenants declined until one reached abject poverty in the garret. *(Bibliothèque nationale de France)*

one-third of the city's 1 million inhabitants. Terrible slum conditions and extremely high death rates were facts of life. There were few open spaces and only two public parks for the entire metropolis. Public transportation played a very small role in this enormous walking city.

Haussmann and his fellow planners proceeded on many interrelated fronts. With a bold energy that often shocked their contemporaries, they razed old buildings in order to cut broad, straight, tree-lined boulevards through the center of the city as well as in new quarters on the outskirts (see Map 24.2). These boulevards, designed in part to prevent the easy construction and defense of barricades by revolutionary crowds, permitted traffic to flow freely and afforded impressive vistas. Their creation also demolished some of the worst slums. New streets stimulated the construction of better housing, especially for the middle classes. Small neighborhood parks and open spaces were created throughout the city, and two very large parks suitable for all kinds of holiday activities were developed—one on the wealthy west side and one on the poor east side of the city. The city also improved its sewers, and a system of aqueducts more than doubled the city's supply of good fresh water.

Rebuilding Paris provided a new model for urban planning and stimulated modern urbanism throughout Europe, particularly after 1870. In city after city, public authorities mounted a coordinated attack on many of the interrelated problems of the urban environment. As in Paris, improvements in public health through better water supply and waste disposal often went hand in hand with new boulevard construction. Cities such as Vienna and Cologne followed the Parisian example of tearing down old walled fortifications and replacing them with broad, circular boulevards on which office buildings, town halls, theaters, opera houses, and museums were erected. These ring roads and the new boulevards that radiated out from them toward the outskirts eased movement and encouraged urban expansion (see Map 24.2). Zoning expropriation laws, which allowed a majority of the owners of land in a given quarter of the city to impose major street or sanitation improvements on a reluctant minority, were an important mechanism of the new urbanism.

The development of mass public transportation was also of great importance in the improvement of urban living conditions. In the 1870s, many European cities authorized private companies to operate horse-drawn streetcars, which had been developed in the United States, to carry riders along the growing number of major thoroughfares. Then in the 1890s, the real revolution occurred: European countries adopted another American transit innovation, the electric streetcar.

Electric streetcars were cheaper, faster, more dependable, and more comfortable than their horse-drawn counterparts. Service improved dramatically. Millions of Europeans—workers, shoppers, schoolchildren—hopped on board during the workweek. And on weekends and holidays, streetcars carried millions on happy outings to parks and countryside, racetracks and music halls. In 1886 the horse-drawn streetcars of Austria-Hungary, France, Germany, and Great Britain were carrying about 900 million riders. By 1910 electric streetcar systems in the four countries were carrying 6.7 billion riders.[5] Each man, woman, and child was using public transportation four times as often in 1910 as in 1886.

Good mass transit helped greatly in the struggle for decent housing. The new boulevards and horse-drawn streetcars had facilitated a middle-class move to better housing in the 1860s and 1870s; after 1890 electric streetcars gave people of modest means access to new, improved housing. The still-crowded city was able to expand and become less congested. In England in 1901, only 9 percent of the urban population was "overcrowded" in terms of the official definition of more than two persons per room. On the continent, many city governments in the early twentieth century were building electric streetcar systems that provided transportation to new public and private housing developments in outlying areas of the city for the working classes.

Rich and Poor and Those in Between

General improvements in health and in the urban environment had beneficial consequences for all kinds of people. Yet differences in living conditions among social classes remained gigantic.

- *What did the emergence of urban industrial society mean for rich and poor and those in between?*

Social Structure

How much did the almost-completed journey to an urban, industrialized world change the social framework of rich and poor and those in between? The first great change was a substantial and undeniable increase in the standard of living for the average person. The real wages of British workers, for example, which had already risen by 1850, almost doubled between 1850 and 1906. Similar increases occurred in continental countries as indusgood hard cash. Some of the best bargains were made through marriages to American heiresses. Correspondingly, wealthy aristocrats tended increasingly to exploit their agricultural and mineral resources as if they were business people. Bismarck was not the only proud nobleman to make a fortune distilling brandy on his estates.

Below the wealthy upper middle class were much larger, much less wealthy, and increasingly diversified middle-class groups. Here one found the moderately successful industrialists and merchants as well as professionals in law and medicine. This was the middle middle class, solid and quite comfortable but lacking great wealth. Below it were independent shopkeepers, small traders, and tiny manufacturers—the lower middle class. Both of these traditional elements of the middle class expanded modestly in size with economic development.

Meanwhile, the traditional middle class was gaining two particularly important additions. The expansion of industry and technology created a growing demand for experts with specialized knowledge. The most valuable of the specialties became solid middle-class professions. Engineering, for example, emerged from the world of skilled labor as a full-fledged profession of great importance, considerable prestige, and many branches. Architects, chemists, accountants, and surveyors, to name only a few, first achieved professional standing in this period. They established criteria for advanced training and certification and banded together in organizations to promote and defend their interests.

Management of large public and private institutions also emerged as a kind of profession as governments provided more services and as very large corporations such as railroads came into being. Government officials and many private executives were not capitalists in the sense that they owned business enterprises. But public and private managers did have specialized knowledge and the capacity to earn a good living. And they shared most of the values of the business-owning entrepreneurs and the older professionals.

Industrialization also expanded and diversified the lower middle class. The number of independent, property-owning shopkeepers and small business people grew, and so did the number of white-collar employees—a mixed group of traveling salesmen, bookkeepers, store managers, and clerks who staffed the offices and branch stores of large corporations. White-collar employees were propertyless and often earned no more than the better-paid skilled or semiskilled workers did. Yet white-collar workers were fiercely committed to the middle class and to the ideal of moving up in society. In the Balkans, for example, clerks let their fingernails grow very long to distinguish themselves from people who worked with their hands. The tie, the suit, and soft, clean hands were no-less-subtle marks of class distinction than wages.

Relatively well educated but without complex technical skills, many white-collar groups aimed at achieving professional standing and the accompanying middle-class status. Elementary school teachers largely succeeded in this effort. From being miserably paid part-time workers in the early nineteenth century, teachers rode the wave of mass education to respectable middle-class status and income. Nurses also rose from the lower ranks of unskilled labor to precarious middle-class standing. Dentistry was taken out of the hands of working-class barbers and placed in the hands of highly trained (and middle-class) professionals.

Middle-Class Culture

In spite of growing occupational diversity and conflicting interests, the middle classes were loosely united by a certain style of life and culture. Food was the largest item in the household budget, for middle-class people liked to eat very well. The European middle classes consumed meat in abundance, and a well-off family might spend 10 percent of its substantial earnings on meat and fully 25 percent of its income on food and drink. Spending on food was also great because the dinner party was this class's favored social occasion. A wealthy family might give a lavish party for eight to twelve almost every week, whereas more modest households would settle for once a month.

The middle-class wife could cope with this endless procession of meals, courses, and dishes because she had both servants and money at her disposal. Indeed, the employment of at least one enormously helpful full-time maid to cook and clean was the best single sign that a family had crossed the cultural divide separating the working classes from what some contemporary observers called the "servant-keeping classes." The greater a family's income, the greater the number of servants it employed. Food and servants together absorbed about 50 percent of income at all levels of the middle class.

Well fed and well served, the middle classes were also well housed by 1900. Many quite prosperous families rented, rather than owned, their homes. Apartment living, complete with tiny rooms for servants under the eaves of the top floor, was commonplace, and wealthy investors and speculative builders found good profits in middle-class housing. By 1900 the middle classes were also quite clothes-conscious. The factory, the sewing machine, and the department store had all helped reduce the cost and expand the variety of clothing. Middle-class women were particularly attentive to the fickle dictates of fashion. (See the feature "Images in Society: Class and Gender Boundaries in Women's Fashion, 1850–1914" on pages 792–793.)

Education was another growing expense, as middle-class parents tried to provide their children with ever more crucial advanced education. The keystones of culture and leisure were books, music, and travel. The long realistic novel, the heroics of composers Wagner and Verdi, the diligent striving of the dutiful daughter at the piano, and the packaged tour to a foreign country were all sources of middle-class pleasure.

Finally, the middle classes were loosely united by a shared code of expected behavior and morality. This code was strict and demanding. It laid great stress on hard work, self-discipline, and personal achievement. Men and women who fell into crime or poverty were generally assumed to be responsible for their own circumstances. Traditional Christian morality was reaffirmed by this code and was preached tirelessly by middle-class people. Drunkenness and gambling were denounced as vices; sexual purity and fidelity were celebrated as virtues. In short, the middle-class person was supposed to know right from wrong and was expected to act accordingly.

The Working Classes

About four out of five people belonged to the working classes at the turn of the century. Many members of the working classes—that is, people whose livelihoods depended on physical labor and who did not employ domestic servants—were still small landowning peasants and hired farm hands. This was especially true in eastern Europe. In western and central Europe, however, the typical worker had left the land. In Great Britain, less than 8 percent of the people worked in agriculture, and in rapidly industrializing Germany only 25 percent were employed in agriculture and forestry. Even in less industrialized France, less than 50 percent of the people depended on the land in 1900.

The urban working classes were even less unified and homogeneous than the middle classes. In the first place, economic development and increased specialization expanded the traditional range of working-class skills, earnings, and experiences. Meanwhile, the old sharp distinction between highly skilled artisans and unskilled manual workers gradually broke down. To be sure, highly skilled

"A Corner of the Table"
With photographic precision, the French academic artist Paul-Émile Chabas (1869–1937) idealizes the elegance and intimacy of a sumptuous dinner party. Throughout Europe, such dinners were served in eight or nine separate courses, beginning with appetizers and ending with coffee and liqueurs. *(Archives Charmet/The Bridgeman Art Library)*

printers and masons as well as unskilled dockworkers and common laborers continued to exist. But between these extremes there appeared ever more semiskilled groups, many of which were composed of factory workers and machine tenders (see Figure 24.3).

In the second place, skilled, semiskilled, and unskilled workers developed widely divergent lifestyles and cultural values, and their differences contributed to a keen sense of social status and hierarchy within the working classes. The result was great variety and limited class unity.

Highly skilled workers, who made up about 15 percent of the working classes, became a real **labor aristocracy.** These workers earned only about two-thirds of the income of the bottom ranks of the servant-keeping classes, but that was fully twice as much as the earnings of unskilled workers. The most "aristocratic" of the highly skilled workers were construction bosses and factory foremen, men who had risen from the ranks and were fiercely proud of their achievement. The labor aristocracy also included members of the traditional highly skilled handicraft trades that had not been mechanized or placed in factories, like cabinetmakers, jewelers, and printers.

This group as a whole was under constant long-term pressure. Irregularly but inexorably, factory methods were being extended to more crafts, and many skilled artisans were being replaced by lower-paid semiskilled factory workers. Traditional woodcarvers and watchmakers virtually disappeared, for example, as the making of furniture and timepieces now took place in the factory. At the same time, the labor aristocracy was consistently being enlarged by new kinds of skilled workers such as shipbuilders and railway locomotive engineers. Thus the labor elite remained in a state of flux as individuals and whole crafts moved in and out of it.

To maintain this precarious standing, the upper working class adopted distinctive values and strait-laced, almost puritanical behavior. Like the middle classes, the labor aristocracy was strongly committed to the family and to economic improvement. Families in the upper working class saved money regularly, worried about their children's education, and valued good housing. Despite these similarities, skilled workers viewed themselves not as aspirants to the middle class but as the pacesetters and natural leaders of all the working classes. Well aware of the degradation not so far below them, they practiced self-discipline and stern morality.

The upper working class in general frowned on heavy drinking and sexual permissiveness. An organized temperance movement was strong in the countries of northern Europe. As one German labor aristocrat somberly

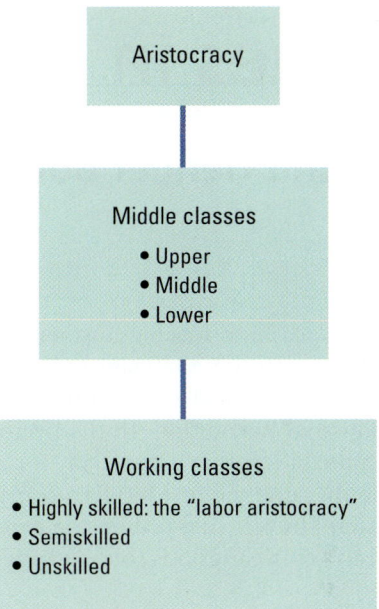

FIGURE 24.3 The Urban Social Hierarchy

warned, "The path to the brothel leads through the tavern" and from there quite possibly to drastic decline or total ruin for person and family.[6] Men and women of the labor aristocracy were also quick to find fault with those below them who failed to meet their standards. Finally, many members of the labor aristocracy had definite political and philosophical beliefs, which further strengthened their firm moral code.

Below the labor aristocracy stood semiskilled and unskilled urban workers. The enormous complexity of this sector of the world of labor is not easily summarized. Workers in the established crafts—carpenters, bricklayers, pipe fitters—stood near the top of the semiskilled hierarchy, often flirting with (or sliding back from) the labor elite. A large number of the semiskilled were factory workers who earned highly variable but relatively good wages and whose relative importance in the labor force was increasing.

Below the semiskilled workers was a larger group of unskilled workers that included day laborers such as longshoremen, wagon-driving teamsters, teenagers, and every kind of "helper." Many of these people had real skills and performed valuable services, but they were unorganized and divided, united only by the common fate of meager earnings. The same lack of unity characterized street vendors and market people—self-employed workers who competed savagely with each other and with the established shopkeepers of the lower middle class.

Images in Society

Class and Gender Boundaries in Women's Fashion, 1850–1914

Women's fashion was big business in the nineteenth century. Long the dominant industrial pursuit in human history, the production of textiles took off with the Industrial Revolution. In the later nineteenth century fashionable clothing, especially for middle-class women, became the first modern consumer industry as careful buyers snapped up the constantly changing ready-to-wear goods sold by large department stores.

In the nineteenth century, before society fragmented into many different groups expressing themselves in many dress styles, clothing patterns focused mainly on perceived differences in class and gender. The four illustrations presented here allow one to analyze the social information communicated through women's clothing. As you study these illustrations, note the principal characteristics and then try to draw out the larger implications. What does the impractical, restrictive clothing in these images reveal about society's view of women during this period? What is the significance of the emergence of alternative styles of well-groomed dress?

Most changes in women's fashion originated in Paris in the nineteenth century. Image 1 shows the attire worn by French aristocratic and wealthy middle-class women in the 1850s and 1860s. Note that these expensive dresses, flawlessly tailored by an army of skilled seamstresses, abound in elaborate embroidery, rich velvety materials, and fancy accessories. The circular spread of these floor-sweeping gowns is due to the crinoline, a slip with metal hoops that holds the skirt out on all sides. These women also are wearing the corset, the century's most characteristic women's undergarment, which was laced up tightly in back and pressed unmercifully from the breasts to the hips. What does this image tell you about the life of these women (their work, leisure activities, and so on)?

The intriguing 1875 painting by Atkinson Grimshaw, *Summer* (Image 2), shows a middle-class interior and the evolution of women's summer fashion two decades later. The corset still binds, but crinoline hoops have given way to the bustle, a cotton fan with steel reinforcement that pushes the dress out in back and exaggerates gender differences. The elaborate costume of the wealthy elite, available in cheaper ready-to-wear versions sold through department stores and mail-order catalogues throughout Europe, had become the standard for middle-class women. Emulating the elite in style, conventional middle-class women shopped carefully, scouting for sales, and drew a boundary separating themselves from working-class women in their simple cotton clothes. What implications, if any, do you see this having on class distinctions?

The young middle-class Englishwoman in an 1893 photo (Image 3) has chosen a woman's tailored suit, the only major English innovation in nineteenth-

Image 1 Crinoline Dresses, Paris, 1859. *(The Illustrated London News Picture Library)*

792

Image 2 Summer Dress with Bustle, England, 1875. *(Roy Miles, Esq./The Bridgeman Art Library)*

Image 3 Alternative Fashion, England, 1893. *(Manchester City Art Galleries)*

Image 4 Loose-fitting Dress, France, 1910. *(© Corbis)*

century women's fashion. This "alternative dress" combines the tie, suit jacket, vest, and straw hat—all initially items of male attire—with typical feminine elements, such as the skirt and gloves. This practical, socially accepted alternative dress appealed to the growing number of women in paid employment in the 1890s. The historian Diana Crane has argued that this departure from the dominant style can be seen as a symbolic, nonverbal assertion of independence and equality with men.* Do you agree with this? If so, what was the significance of the pre-1914 turn from stifling corset to the more flexible brassiere and the mainstream embrace of loose-fitting garments, such as the 1910 dress in Image 4? Did the greater freedom of movement in clothing reflect the emerging emancipation of Western women? Or was the coquettish femininity of these loose, flowing dresses only a repackaging of the dominant culture's sharply defined gender boundaries?

*Diana Crane, *Fashion and Its Social Agendas: Class, Gender, and Identity in Clothing* (Chicago: University of Chicago Press, 2000), pp. 99–114.

The Labor Aristocracy This group of British foremen is attending the International Exhibition in Paris in 1862. Their "Sunday best" includes the silk top hats and long morning coats of the propertied classes, but they definitely remain workers, the proud leaders of laboring people. (© The Board of Trustees of the Victoria & Albert Museum)

One of the largest components of the unskilled group was domestic servants, whose numbers grew steadily in the nineteenth century. In advanced Great Britain, for example, one out of every seven employed persons was a domestic servant in 1911. The great majority were women; indeed, one out of every three girls in Britain between the ages of fifteen and twenty was a domestic servant. Throughout Europe and America, a great many female domestics in the cities were recent migrants from rural areas. As in earlier times, domestic service was still hard work at low pay with limited personal independence and the danger of sexual exploitation. For the full-time general maid in a lower-middle-class family, there was an unending routine of babysitting, shopping, cooking, and cleaning. In the great households, the girl was at the bottom of a rigid hierarchy of status-conscious butlers and housekeepers.

Nonetheless, domestic service had real attractions for "rough country girls" with strong hands and few specialized skills. Marriage prospects were better, or at least more varied, in the city. And though wages were low, they were higher and more regular than in hard agricultural work. Finally, as one London observer noted, young girls and other migrants were drawn to the city by

the contagion of numbers, the sense of something going on, the theaters and the music halls, the brightly lighted streets and busy crowds—all, in short, that makes the difference between the Mile End fair on a Saturday night, and a dark and muddy country lane, with no glimmer of gas and with nothing to do.[7]

Many young domestics from the countryside made a successful transition to working-class wife and mother. Yet with an unskilled or unemployed husband and a growing family, such a woman often had to join the broad ranks of workingwomen in the "sweated industries." These industries flowered after 1850 and resembled the old putting-out and cottage industries of earlier times. The women normally worked at home, paid by the piece and not by the hour. They and their young daughters, for whom organization and collective action were virtually impossible, earned pitiful wages and lacked any job security.

Some women did hand-decorating of every conceivable kind of object; the majority, however, made clothing, especially after the advent of the sewing machine. By 1900 only a few such tailors lingered on in high-priced "tailor-made" shops. An army of poor women accounted for the bulk of the inexpensive "ready-made" clothes displayed on department store racks and in tiny shops.

Working-Class Leisure and Religion

Notwithstanding the rise and fall of groups and individuals, the urban working classes sought fun and recreation, and they found both. Across the face of Europe, drinking remained unquestionably the favorite leisure-time activity of working people. For many middle-class moralists as well as moralizing historians since, love of drink has been a curse of

A School for Servants Although domestic service was poorly paid, there was always plenty of competition for the available jobs. Schools sprang up to teach young women the manners and the household skills that employers in the "servant-keeping classes" demanded. *(Corporation of London: London Metropolitan Archives)*

Big City Nightlife The most famous dance hall and cabaret in Paris was the Moulin Rouge. There La Goulue ("the Glutton"), who is featured on this poster, performed her provocative version of the cancan and reigned as the queen of Parisian sensuality. This is one of many colorful posters done by Henri de Toulouse-Lautrec (1864–1901), who combined stupendous creativity and dedicated debauchery in his short life. *(Bridgeman-Giraudon/Art Resource, NY)*

the modern age—a sign of social dislocation and popular suffering. Certainly, drinking was deadly serious business. One English slum dweller recalled that "drunkenness was by far the commonest cause of dispute and misery in working class homes. On account of it one saw many a decent family drift down through poverty into total want."[8]

Generally, however, heavy "problem" drinking declined in the late nineteenth century as it became less and less socially acceptable. This decline reflected in part the moral leadership of the upper working class. At the same time, drinking became more public and social. Cafés and pubs became increasingly bright, friendly places. Working-class political activities, both moderate and radical, were also concentrated in taverns and pubs. Moreover, social drinking in public places by married couples and sweethearts became an accepted and widespread practice for the first time. This greater participation by women undoubtedly helped civilize the world of drink and hard liquor.

The two other leisure-time passions of the working classes were sports and music halls. A great decline in "cruel sports," such as bullbaiting and cockfighting, had occurred throughout Europe by the late nineteenth century. Their place was filled by modern spectator sports, of which racing and soccer were the most popular. There was a great deal of gambling on sports events, and for many a working person a desire to decipher racing forms provided a powerful incentive toward literacy. Music halls and vaudeville theaters, the working-class counterparts of middle-class opera and classical theater, were enormously popular throughout Europe. In 1900 there were more than fifty such halls and theaters in London alone. Music hall audiences were thoroughly mixed, which may account for the fact that drunkenness, sexual intercourse and pregnancy before marriage, marital difficulties, and problems with mothers-in-law were favorite themes of broad jokes and bittersweet songs.

In more serious moments, religion and Christian churches continued to provide working people with solace and meaning. The eighteenth-century vitality of popular religion in Catholic countries and the Protestant rejuvenation exemplified by German Pietism and English Methodism (see pages 672–673) carried over into the nineteenth century. Indeed, many historians see the early nineteenth century as an age of religious revival. Yet historians also recognize that by the last two or three decades of the nineteenth century, a considerable decline in both church attendance and church donations was occurring in most European countries. And it seems clear that this decline was greater for the urban working classes than for their rural counterparts or for the middle classes.

What did the decline in working-class church attendance really mean? Some have argued that it accurately reflected a general decline in faith and religious belief. Others disagree, noting correctly that most working-class families still baptized their children and considered themselves Christians. Although more research is necessary, it appears that the urban working classes in Europe did become more secular and less religious in the late nineteenth and early twentieth centuries. They rarely repudiated the Christian religion, but it tended to play a diminishing role in their daily lives.

Part of the reason for this change was that the construction of churches failed to keep up with the rapid growth of urban population, especially in new working-class neighborhoods. Thus the vibrant, materialistic urban environment undermined popular religious impulses, which were poorly served in the cities. Equally important, however, was the fact that throughout the nineteenth century both Catholic and Protestant churches were normally seen as they saw themselves—as conservative institutions defending social order and custom. Therefore, as the European working classes became more politically conscious, they tended to see the established (or quasi-established) "territorial church" as defending what they wished to change and as allied with their political opponents. Especially the men of the urban working classes developed vaguely antichurch attitudes, even though they remained neutral or positive toward religion. They tended to regard regular church attendance as "not our kind of thing"—not part of urban working-class culture.

The pattern was different in the United States. There, most churches also preached social conservatism in the nineteenth century. But because church and state had always been separate and because there was always a host of competing denominations and even different religions, working people identified churches much less with the political and social status quo. Instead, individual churches in the United States were often closely identified with an ethnic group rather than with a social class, and churches thrived, in part, as a means of asserting ethnic identity. This same process did occur in Europe if the church or synagogue had never been linked to the state and served as a focus for ethnic cohesion. Irish Catholic churches in Protestant Britain and Jewish synagogues in Russia were outstanding examples.

The Changing Family

Urban life wrought many fundamental changes in the family. Although much is still unknown, it seems clear that in the second half of the nineteenth century the family had stabilized considerably after the disruption of the late eighteenth and early nineteenth centuries. The home became more important for both men and women. The role of women and attitudes toward children underwent substantial change, and adolescence emerged as a distinct stage of life. These are but a few of the transformations that affected all social classes in varying degrees.

- *How did families change as they coped with the challenges and the opportunities of the developing urban civilization?*

Premarital Sex and Marriage

By 1850 the preindustrial pattern of lengthy courtship and mercenary marriage was pretty well dead among the working classes. In its place, the ideal of romantic love had triumphed. Couples were ever more likely to come from different, even distant, towns and to be more nearly the same age, further indicating that romantic sentiment was replacing tradition and financial considerations.

Economic considerations in marriage remained more important to the middle classes than to the working classes after 1850. In France dowries and elaborate legal marriage contracts were common practice among the middle classes in the later nineteenth century, and marriage was for many families one of life's most crucial financial transactions. A popular author advised young Frenchmen that "marriage is in general a means of increasing one's credit and one's fortune and of insuring one's success in the world."[9] This preoccupation with money led many middle-class men in

France and elsewhere to marry late, after they had been established economically, and to choose women considerably younger than themselves. These differences between husband and wife became a source of tension in many middle-class marriages.

A young woman of the middle class found her romantic life carefully supervised by her well-meaning mother, who schemed for a proper marriage and guarded her daughter's virginity like the family's credit. (See the feature "Listening to the Past: Middle-Class Youth and Sexuality" on pages 812–813.) After marriage, middle-class morality sternly demanded fidelity.

Middle-class boys were watched, too, but not as vigilantly. By the time they reached late adolescence, they had usually attained considerable sexual experience with maids or prostitutes.

In the early nineteenth century, sexual experimentation before marriage also triumphed, as did illegitimacy. There was an **illegitimacy explosion** between 1750 and 1850 (see page 656). By the 1840s, one birth in three was occurring outside of wedlock in many large cities of western, northern, and central Europe. In Vienna and Stockholm, one out of every two births was illegitimate. Although poverty and economic uncertainty undoubtedly prevented many lovers from marrying, there were also many among the poor and propertyless who saw little wrong with having illegitimate offspring. Thus the pattern of romantic ideals, premarital sexual activity, and widespread illegitimacy was firmly established by mid-century among the urban working classes.

Some regions, especially those little touched by industrialization and urbanization, did not experience an illegitimacy explosion. Neither did certain churches and religious communities that strictly prohibited premarital sex. "The Catholic Church in Ireland and many southern European regions, Calvinist communities in the Netherlands, Moslems in the Balkans, and Jewish communities throughout Europe seem to have been successful in enforcing this norm."[10] Although these religious groups exercised strict external control, they succeeded in large part because their young people internalized the values they were taught and acted accordingly.

In western, northern, and central Europe, the rising rate of illegitimacy was reversed in the second half of the nineteenth century: more babies were born to married mothers. Some observers have argued that this shift reflected the growth of puritanism and a lessening of sexual permissiveness among the unmarried. This explanation, however, is unconvincing.

The percentage of brides who were pregnant continued to be high and showed little or no tendency to decline after 1850. In many parts of urban Europe around 1900, as many as one woman in three was going to the altar an expectant mother. Moreover, unmarried people almost certainly used the cheap condoms and diaphragms the industrial age had made available to prevent pregnancy, at least in predominately Protestant countries.

Thus unmarried young people were probably engaging in just as much sexual activity as their parents and grandparents who had created the illegitimacy explosion of 1750 to 1850. But in the later nineteenth century, pregnancy for a young single woman led increasingly to marriage and the establishment of a two-parent household. This important development reflected the growing respectability of the working classes as well as their gradual economic improvement. Skipping out was less acceptable, and marriage was less of an economic challenge. Thus the urban working-class couple became more stable, and that stability strengthened the family as an institution.

Prostitution

In Paris alone, 155,000 women were registered as prostitutes between 1871 and 1903, and 750,000 others were suspected of prostitution in the same years. Men of all classes visited prostitutes, but the middle and upper classes supplied much of the motivating cash. Thus, though many middle-class men abided by the publicly professed code of stern puritanical morality, others indulged their appetites for prostitutes and sexual promiscuity.

My Secret Life, the anonymous eleven-volume autobiography of an English sexual adventurer from the servant-keeping classes, provides a remarkable picture of such a man. Beginning at an early age with a maid, the author becomes progressively obsessed with sex and devotes his life to living his sexual fantasies. In almost every one of his innumerable encounters all across Europe, this man of wealth simply buys his pleasure. Usually meetings are arranged in a businesslike manner: regular and part-time prostitutes quote their prices; working-class girls are corrupted by hot meals and baths.

At one point, he offers a young girl a sixpence for a kiss and gets it. Learning that the pretty, unskilled working girl earns nine pence a day, he offers her the equivalent of a week's salary for a few moments of fondling. When she finally agrees, he savagely exults that "*her* want was my opportunity." Later he offers more money for more gratification, and when she refuses, he tries unsuccessfully to rape her in a hackney cab. On another occasion he takes a farm worker by force.[11]

Obviously atypical in its excesses, *My Secret Life* does reveal the dark side of sex and class in urban society. Frequently thinking of their wives largely in terms of money, family, and social position, the men of the comfortable classes often purchased sex and even affection from poor girls both before and after marriage. Moreover, the great continuing differences between rich and poor made for every kind of debauchery and sexual exploitation. Brutal sexist behavior was part of life—a part the sternly moral women (and men) of the upper working class detested and tried to shield their daughters from. For many poor young women, prostitution, like domestic service, was a stage of life and not a permanent employment. Having done it for a while in their twenties, they went on to marry (or live with) men of their own class and establish homes and families.

Kinship Ties

Within working-class homes, ties to relatives after marriage—kinship ties—were in general much stronger than many social observers have recognized. Most newlyweds tried to live near their parents, though not in the same house. Indeed, for many married couples in later-nineteenth-century cities, ties to mothers and fathers, uncles and aunts, were more important than ties to unrelated acquaintances.

People turned to their families for help in coping with sickness, unemployment, death, and old age. Although governments were generally providing more welfare services by 1900, the average couple and its children inevitably faced crises. Funerals, for example, brought sudden demands, requiring a large outlay for special clothes, carriages, and burial services. Unexpected death or desertion could leave the bereaved or abandoned, especially widows and orphans, in need of financial aid or perhaps a foster home. Relatives responded hastily to such cries, knowing full well that their own time of need and repayment would undoubtedly come.

Relatives were also valuable at less tragic moments. If a couple was very poor, an aged relation often moved in to cook and mind the children so that the wife could earn badly needed income outside the home. Sunday dinners were often shared, as were outgrown clothing and useful information. Often the members of a large family group all lived in the same neighborhood.

Gender Roles and Family Life

Industrialization and the growth of modern cities brought great changes to the lives of European women. These changes were particularly consequential for married women, and most women did marry in the nineteenth century.

After 1850 the work of most wives became increasingly distinct and separate from that of their husbands. Husbands became wage earners in factories and offices, while wives tended to stay home and manage households and care for children. The preindustrial pattern among both peasants and cottage workers, in which husbands and wives worked together and divided up household duties and child rearing, declined. Only in a few occupations, such as retail trade, did married couples live where they worked and struggle together to make their mom-and-pop operations a success. Factory employment for married women also declined as the early practice of hiring entire families in the factory disappeared.

As economic conditions improved, most men expected married women to work outside the home only in poor families. One old English worker recalled that "the boy wanted to get into a position that would enable him to keep a wife and family, as it was considered a thoroughly unsatisfactory state of affairs if the wife had to work to help maintain the home."[12] The ideal became a strict division of labor by gender and rigidly constructed **separate spheres:** the wife as mother and homemaker, the husband as wage earner.

This rigid gender division of labor meant that married women faced great injustice when they needed—or wanted—to move into the man's world of employment outside the home. Husbands were unsympathetic or hostile. Well-paying jobs were off-limits to women, and a woman's wage was almost always less than a man's, even for the same work.

Moreover, married women were subordinated to their husbands by law and lacked many basic legal rights. In England the situation in the early nineteenth century was summed up in a famous line from jurist William Blackstone: "In law husband and wife are one person, and the husband is that person." Thus a wife in England had no legal identity and hence no right to own property in her own name. Even the wages she might earn belonged to her husband. In France the Napoleonic Code (see pages 704–705) also enshrined the principle of female subordination and gave the wife few legal rights regarding property, divorce, and custody of the children. Legal inferiority for women permeated Western society.

With all women facing discrimination in education and employment and with middle-class women suffering especially from a lack of legal rights, there is little wonder that some women rebelled and began the long-continuing fight for equality of the sexes and the rights of women. Their struggle proceeded on two main fronts. First, following in the steps of women such as Mary Wollstonecraft (see page 694), organizations founded by middle-class feminists campaigned for equal legal rights for women as well as access to higher education and professional employment. These middle-class feminists argued that unmarried women and middle-class widows with inadequate incomes simply had to have more opportunities to support themselves. Middle-class feminists also recognized that paid (as opposed to unpaid) work could relieve the monotony that some women found in their sheltered middle-class existence and put greater meaning into their lives.

In the later nineteenth century, these organizations scored some significant victories, such as the 1882 law giving English married women full property rights. More women found professional and white-collar employment, especially after about 1880. But progress was slow and hard won. For example, in Germany before 1900, women were not admitted as fully registered students at a single university, and it was virtually impossible for a woman to receive certification and practice as a lawyer or doctor. (See the feature "Individuals in Society: Franziska Tiburtius.") In the years before 1914, middle-class feminists increasingly focused their attention on political action and fought for the right to vote for women.

Women inspired by utopian and especially Marxian socialism blazed a second path. Often scorning the programs of middle-class feminists, socialist women leaders argued that the liberation of working-class women would come only with the liberation of the entire working class through revolution. In the meantime, they championed the cause of workingwomen and won some practical improvements, especially in Germany, where the socialist movement was most effectively organized. In a general way, these different approaches to women's issues reflected the diversity of classes in urban society.

Online Study Center Improve Your Grade
Primary Source: A Socialist Solution to the Question of Women's Rights

If the ideology and practice of rigidly separate spheres undoubtedly narrowed women's horizons and caused some women to rebel, there was a brighter side to the same coin. As home and children became the typical wife's main concerns in the late nineteenth century, her control and influence there apparently became increasingly strong throughout Europe. Among the English working classes, it was the wife who generally determined how the family's money was spent. In many families, the husband gave all his earnings to his wife to manage, whatever the law might read. She returned to him only a small allowance for carfare, beer, tobacco, and union dues. All the major domestic decisions, from the children's schooling and religious instruction to the selection of new furniture or a new apartment, were hers. In France women had even greater power in their assigned domain. One English feminist noted in 1908 that "though legally women occupy a much inferior status than men [in France], in practice they constitute the superior sex. They are the power behind the throne."[13]

Women ruled at home partly because running the urban household was a complicated, demanding, and valuable task. Twice-a-day food shopping, penny-pinching, economizing, and the growing crusade against dirt—not to mention child rearing—were a full-time occupation. Nor were there any laborsaving appliances to help, and even when servants were present, they had to be carefully watched and supervised. Working yet another job for wages outside the home had limited appeal for most married women unless such earnings were essential for family survival. Many married women in the working classes did make a monetary contribution to family income by taking in boarders or doing piecework at home in the sweated industries (see page 794).

The wife also guided the home because a good deal of her effort was directed toward pampering her husband as he expected. In countless humble households, she saw that he had meat while she ate bread, that he relaxed by the fire while she did the dishes.

The woman's guidance of the household went hand in hand with the increased emotional importance of home and family. The home she ran was idealized as a warm shelter in a hard and impersonal urban world. For a child of the English slums in the early 1900s,

home, however poor, was the focus of all love and interests, a sure fortress against a hostile world. Songs about its beauties were ever on people's lips. "Home, sweet home," first heard in the 1870s, had become "almost a second national anthem." Few walls in lower-working-class houses lacked "mottoes"—colored strips of paper, about nine inches wide and eighteen inches in length, attesting to domestic joys: EAST, WEST, HOME'S BEST; BLESS OUR HOME; GOD IS MASTER OF THIS HOUSE; HOME IS THE NEST WHERE ALL IS BEST.[14]

By 1900 home and family were what life was all about for millions of people of all classes.

Married couples also developed stronger emotional ties to each other. Even in the comfortable classes, marriages in the late nineteenth century were based more on sentiment and sexual attraction than they had been earlier in the century, as money and financial calculation declined in importance. Affection and eroticism became more central to the couple after marriage. Gustave Droz, whose bestseller *Mr., Mrs., and Baby* went through 121

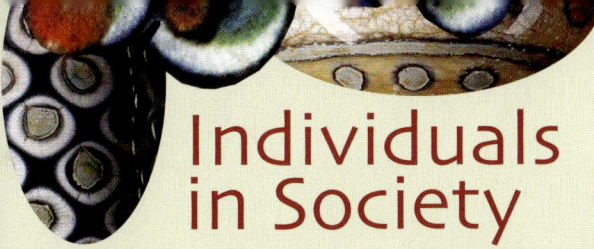

Individuals in Society

Franziska Tiburtius

Why did a small number of women in the late nineteenth century brave great odds and embark on professional careers? And how did a few of those manage to reach their objectives? The career and personal reflections of Franziska Tiburtius, a pioneer in German medicine, suggest that talent, determination, and economic necessity were critical ingredients.*

Like many women of her time who would study and pursue professional careers, Franziska Tiburtius (1843–1927) was born into a property-owning family of modest means. The youngest of nine children on a small estate in northeastern Germany, the sensitive child wilted under a harsh governess but flowered with a caring teacher and became an excellent student.

Graduating at sixteen and needing to support herself, Tiburtius had few opportunities. A young woman from a "proper" background could work as a governess or a teacher without losing her respectability and spoiling her matrimonial prospects, but that was about it. She tried both avenues. Working for six years as a governess in a noble family and no doubt learning that poverty was often one's fate in this genteel profession, she then turned to teaching. Called home from her studies in Britain in 1871 to care for her brother, who had contracted typhus as a field doctor in the Franco-Prussian War, she found her calling. She decided to become a medical doctor.

Supported by her family, Tiburtius's decision was truly audacious. In all Europe, only the University of Zurich in republican Switzerland accepted female students. Moreover, if it became known that she had studied medicine and failed, she would never get a job as a teacher. No parent would entrust a daughter to an "emancipated" radical who had carved up dead bodies!

Although the male students at the university sometimes harassed the women with crude pranks, Tiburtius thrived. The revolution of the microscope and the discovery of microorganisms was rocking Zurich, and she was fascinated by her studies. She became close friends with a fellow female medical student from Germany, Emilie Lehmus, with whom she would form a lifelong partnership in medicine. She did her internship with families of cottage workers around Zurich and loved her work.

Graduating at age thirty-three in 1876, Tiburtius went to stay with her brother the doctor in Berlin. Though well qualified to practice, she ran into pervasive discrimination. She was not even permitted to take the state medical exams and could practice only as an unregulated (and unprofessional) "natural healer." But after persistent fighting with the bureaucrats, she was able to display her diploma and practice as "Franziska Tiburtius, M.D. University of Zurich." She and Lehmus were in business.

Franziska Tiburtius, pioneering woman physician in Berlin. (Ullstein Bilderdienst/The Granger Collection, New York)

Soon the two women realized their dream and opened a clinic, subsidized by a wealthy industrialist, for women factory workers. The clinic filled a great need and was soon treating many patients. A room with beds for extremely sick women was later expanded into a second clinic.

Tiburtius and Lehmus became famous. For fifteen years, they were the only women doctors in all Berlin. An inspiration for a new generation of women, they added the wealthy to their thriving practice. But Tiburtius's clinics always concentrated on the poor, providing them with subsidized and up-to-date treatment. Talented, determined, and working with her partner, Tiburtius experienced the joys of personal achievement and useful service, joys that women and men share in equal measure.

Questions for Analysis

1. How does Franziska Tiburtius's life reflect both the challenges and the changing roles of middle-class women in the later nineteenth century?
2. In what ways was Tiburtius's career related to improvements in health in urban society and to the expansion of the professions?

*This portrait draws on Conradine Lück, *Frauen: Neun Lebensschicksale* (Reutlingen: Ensslin & Laiblin, n.d.), pp. 153–185.

Online Study Center **Improve Your Grade**
Going Beyond Individuals in Society

editions between 1866 and 1884, saw love within marriage as the key to human happiness. He condemned men who made marriage sound dull and practical, men who were exhausted by prostitutes and rheumatism and who wanted their young wives to be little angels. He urged women to follow their hearts and marry men more nearly their own age:

A husband who is stately and a little bald is all right, but a young husband who loves you and who drinks out of your glass without ceremony, is better. Let him, if he ruffles your dress a little and places a kiss on your neck as he passes. Let him, if he undresses you after the ball, laughing like a fool. You have fine spiritual qualities, it is true, but your little body is not bad either and when one loves, one loves completely. Behind these follies lies happiness.[15]

Many French marriage manuals of the late 1800s stressed that women had legitimate sexual needs, such as the "right to orgasm." Perhaps the French were a bit more enlightened in these matters than other nationalities. But the rise of public socializing by couples in cafés and music halls as well as franker affection within the family suggests a more erotic, pleasurable intimate life for women throughout Western society. This, too, helped make the woman's role as mother and homemaker acceptable and even satisfying.

Child Rearing

One striking sign of deepening emotional ties within the family was the growing love and concern that mothers gave their tiny infants. Because so many babies died so early in life, mothers in preindustrial Western society often avoided making a strong emotional commitment to a newborn in order to shield themselves from recurrent heartbreak. Early emotional bonding and a willingness to make real sacrifices for the welfare of the infant were beginning to spread among the comfortable classes by the end of the eighteenth century, but the ordinary mother of modest means adopted new attitudes only as the nineteenth century progressed. The baby became more important, and women became better mothers.

Mothers increasingly breast-fed their infants, for example, rather than paying wet nurses to do so. Breast-feeding involved sacrifice—a temporary loss of freedom, if nothing else. Yet in an age when there was no good alternative to mother's milk, it saved lives. This surge of maternal feeling also gave rise to a wave of specialized books on child rearing and infant hygiene, such as Droz's phenomenally successful book. Droz urged fathers to get into the act and pitied those "who do not know how to

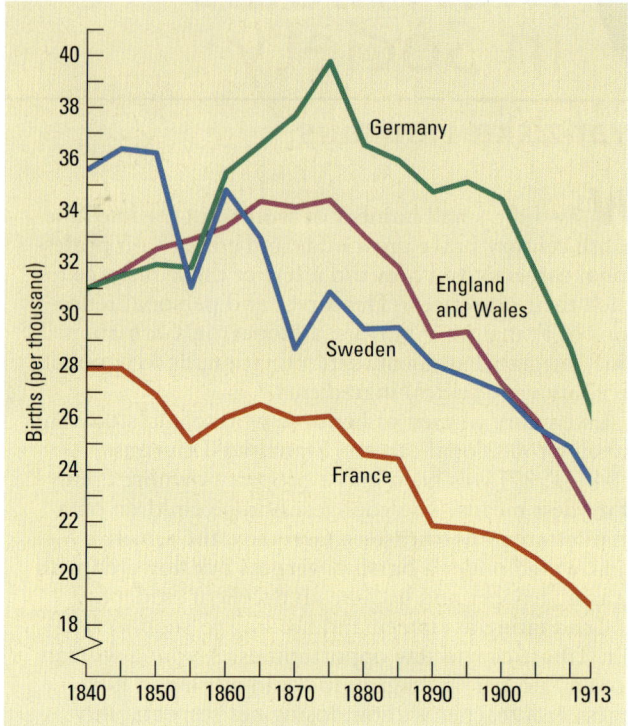

FIGURE 24.4 The Decline of Birthrates in England and Wales, France, Germany, and Sweden, 1840–1913
Women had fewer babies for a variety of reasons, including the fact that their children were increasingly less likely to die before reaching adulthood. Compare with Figure 24.1 on page 783.

roll around on the carpet, play at being a horse and a great wolf, and undress their baby."[16] Another sign, from France, of increased affection is that fewer illegitimate babies were abandoned as foundlings after about 1850. Moreover, the practice of swaddling disappeared completely. Instead, ordinary mothers allowed their babies freedom of movement and delighted in their spontaneity.

The loving care lavished on infants was matched by greater concern for older children and adolescents. They, too, were wrapped in the strong emotional ties of a more intimate and protective family. For one thing, European women began to limit the number of children they bore in order to care adequately for those they had. It was evident by the end of the nineteenth century that the birthrate was declining across Europe, as Figure 24.4 shows, and it continued to do so until after World War II. The Englishwoman who married in the 1860s, for example, had an average of about six children; her daughter marrying in the 1890s had only four; and her granddaughter marrying in the 1920s had only two or possibly three.

A Working-Class Home, 1875 Emotional ties within ordinary families grew stronger in the nineteenth century. Parents gave their children more love and better care. *(Illustrated London News Library)*

The most important reason for this revolutionary reduction in family size, in which the comfortable and well-educated classes took the lead, was parents' desire to improve their economic and social position and that of their children. Children were no longer an economic asset in the later nineteenth century. By having fewer youngsters, parents could give those they had valuable advantages, from music lessons and summer vacations to long, expensive university educations and suitable dowries. A young German skilled worker with only one child spoke for many in his class when he said, "We want to get ahead, and our daughter should have things better than my wife and sisters did."[17] Thus the growing tendency of couples in the late nineteenth century to use a variety of contraceptive methods—rhythm method, withdrawal method, and mechanical devices—certainly reflected increased concern for children.

Indeed, many parents, especially in the middle classes, probably became *too* concerned about their children, unwittingly subjecting them to an emotional pressure cooker of almost unbearable intensity. The result was that many children and especially adolescents came to feel trapped and in need of greater independence.

Prevailing biological and medical theories led parents to believe in the possibility that their own emotional characteristics were passed on to their offspring and that they were thus directly responsible for any abnormality in a child. The moment the child was conceived was thought to be of enormous importance. "Never run the risk of conception when you are sick or over-tired or unhappy," wrote one influential American woman. "For the bodily condition of the child, its vigor and magnetic qualities, are much affected by conditions ruling this great moment."[18] So might the youthful "sexual excess" of the father curse future generations. Although this was true in the case of syphilis, which could be transmitted to unborn children, the rigid determinism of such views left little scope for the child's individual development.

Another area of excessive parental concern was the sexual behavior of the child. Masturbation was viewed with horror, for it represented an act of independence and even defiance. Diet, clothing, games, and sleeping were carefully regulated. Girls were discouraged from riding horses and bicycling because rhythmic friction simulated masturbation. Boys were dressed in trousers with shallow and widely separated pockets. Between 1850 and 1880, there were surgical operations for children who persisted in masturbating. Thereafter until about 1905, various restraining apparatuses were more often used.

These and less blatant attempts to repress the child's sexuality were a source of unhealthy tension, often made worse by the rigid division of gender roles within the family. It was widely believed that mother and child loved each other easily but that relations between father and child were necessarily difficult and often tragic. The father was a stranger; his world of business was far removed from the maternal world of spontaneous affection. Moreover, the father was demanding, often expecting the child to succeed where he himself had failed and making his love conditional on achievement. Little wonder that the imaginative literature of the late nineteenth century came to deal with the emotional and destructive elements of father-son relationships. In the Russian Feodor Dostoevski's great novel *The Brothers Karamazov* (1880–1881), for example, four sons work knowingly or unknowingly to destroy their father. Later at the murder trial, one of the brothers claims to speak for all mankind and screams out, "Who doesn't wish his father dead?"

Sigmund Freud (1856–1939), the Viennese founder of psychoanalysis, formulated the most striking analysis of the explosive dynamics of the family, particularly the middle-class family in the late nineteenth century. A physician by training, Freud began his career treating mentally ill patients. He noted that the hysteria of his patients appeared to originate in bitter early-childhood experiences wherein the child had been obliged to repress strong feelings. When these painful experiences were recalled and reproduced under hypnosis or through the patient's free association of ideas, the patient could be brought to understand his or her unhappiness and eventually deal with it.

One of Freud's most influential ideas concerned the Oedipal tensions resulting from the son's instinctive competition with the father for the mother's love and affection. More generally, Freud postulated that much of human behavior is motivated by unconscious emotional needs whose nature and origins are kept from conscious awareness by various mental devices he called **defense mechanisms.** Freud concluded that much unconscious psychological energy is sexual energy, which is repressed and precariously controlled by rational thinking and moral rules. If Freud exaggerated the sexual and familial roots of adult behavior, that exaggeration was itself a reflection of the tremendous emotional intensity of family life in the late nineteenth century.

The working classes probably had more avenues of escape from such tensions than did the middle classes. Unlike their middle-class counterparts, who remained economically dependent on their families until a long education was finished or a proper marriage secured, working-class boys and girls went to work when they reached adolescence. Earning wages on their own, they could bargain with their parents for greater independence within the household by the time they were sixteen or seventeen. If they were unsuccessful, they could and did leave home to live cheaply as paying lodgers in other working-class homes. Thus the young person from the working classes broke away from the family more easily when emotional ties became oppressive. In the twentieth century, middle-class youths would follow this lead.

Science and Thought

Major changes in Western science and thought accompanied the emergence of urban society. Two aspects of these complex intellectual developments stand out as especially significant. First, scientific knowledge expanded rapidly, influencing the Western worldview even more profoundly than ever before and spurring the creation of new products and whole industries. Second, between about the 1840s and the 1890s, European literature underwent a shift from soaring romanticism to tough-minded realism.

- *What major changes in science and thought reflected and influenced the new urban society?*

The Triumph of Science

As the pace of scientific advance quickened and as theoretical advances resulted in great practical benefits, science exercised growing influence on human thought. The intellectual achievements of the scientific revolution had resulted in few such benefits, and theoretical knowledge had also played a relatively small role in the Industrial Revolution in England. But breakthroughs in industrial technology enormously stimulated basic scientific inquiry, as researchers sought to explain theoretically how such things as steam engines and blast furnaces actually worked. The result was an explosive growth of fundamental scientific discoveries from the 1830s onward. And in contrast to earlier periods, these theoretical discoveries were increasingly transformed into material improvements for the general population.

A perfect example of the translation of better scientific knowledge into practical human benefits was the work of Louis Pasteur and his followers in biology and the medical sciences. Another was the development of the branch of physics known as **thermodynamics.** Building on Isaac Newton's laws of mechanics and on studies of steam engines, thermodynamics investigated the relationship between heat and mechanical energy. By midcentury, physicists had formulated the fundamental laws of thermodynamics, which were then applied to mechanical engineering, chemical processes, and many other fields. The *law of conservation of energy* held that different forms of energy—such as heat, electricity, and magnetism—could be converted but neither created nor destroyed. Nineteenth-century thermodynamics demonstrated that the physical world was governed by firm, unchanging laws.

Chemistry and electricity were two other fields characterized by extremely rapid scientific progress. And in both fields, "science was put in the service of industry," as the influential economist Alfred Marshall (1842–1924) argued at the time.

Chemists devised ways of measuring the atomic weight of different elements, and in 1869 the Russian chemist Dmitri Mendeleev (1834–1907) codified the rules of chemistry in the periodic law and the periodic table. Chemistry was subdivided into many specialized branches, such as **organic chemistry**—the study of the compounds of carbon. Applying theoretical insights gleaned from this new field, researchers in large German chemical companies discovered ways of transforming the dirty, useless coal tar that accumulated in coke ovens into beautiful, expensive synthetic dyes for the world of fashion. The basic discoveries of Michael Faraday (1791–1867) in electromagnetism in the 1830s and 1840s resulted in the first dynamo (generator) and opened the way for the subsequent development of the telegraph, electric motor, electric light, and electric streetcar.

The successful application of scientific research in the fast-growing electrical and organic chemical industries promoted solid economic growth between 1880 and 1913 and provided a model for other industries. Systematic "R & D"—research and development—was born in the late nineteenth century.

The triumph of science and technology had at least three more significant consequences. First, though ordinary citizens continued to lack detailed scientific knowledge, everyday experience and innumerable popularizers impressed the importance of science on the popular mind.

Second, as science became more prominent in popular thinking, the philosophical implications of science formulated in the Enlightenment spread to broad sections of the population. Natural processes appeared to be determined by rigid laws, leaving little room for either divine intervention or human will. Yet scientific and technical advances had also fed the Enlightenment's optimistic faith in human progress, which now appeared endless and automatic to many middle-class minds.

Third, the methods of science acquired unrivaled prestige after 1850. For many, the union of careful experiment and abstract theory was the only reliable route to truth and objective reality. The "unscientific" intuitions of poets and the revelations of saints seemed hopelessly inferior.

Social Science and Evolution

From the 1830s onward, many thinkers tried to apply the objective methods of science to the study of society. In some ways, these efforts simply perpetuated the critical thinking of the philosophes. Yet there were important differences. The new "social scientists" had access to the massive sets of numerical data that governments had begun to collect on everything from children to crime, from population to prostitution. In response, social scientists developed new statistical methods to analyze these facts "scientifically" and supposedly to test their theories. And the systems of the leading nineteenth-century social scientists were more unified, all-encompassing, and dogmatic than those of the philosophes. Marx was a prime example (see pages 757–758).

Another extremely influential system builder was French philosopher Auguste Comte (1798–1857). Initially a disciple of the utopian socialist Saint-Simon (see page 756), Comte wrote the six-volume *System of Positive Philosophy* (1830–1842), which was largely overlooked during the romantic era. But when the political failures of 1848 completed the swing to realism, Comte's philosophy came into its own. Its influence has remained great to this day.

Comte postulated that all intellectual activity progresses through predictable stages:

The great fundamental law ... is this:—that each of our leading conceptions—each branch of our knowledge—passes successively through three different theoretical conditions: the Theological, or fictitious; the Metaphysical, or abstract; and the Scientific, or positive.... The first is the necessary point of departure of human understanding, and the third is the fixed and definitive state. The second is merely a transition.[19]

By way of example, Comte noted that the prevailing explanation of cosmic patterns had shifted, as knowledge of astronomy developed, from the will of God (the

Satirizing Darwin's Ideas The heated controversies over Darwin's theory of evolution also spawned innumerable jokes and cartoons. This cartoon depicts a bearded Charles Darwin and the atheistic materialist Emile Littré performing as monkeys in a circus. *(Musée de la Ville de Paris, Musée Carnavalet/Archives Charmet/The Bridgeman Art Library)*

theological) to the will of an orderly nature (the metaphysical) to the rule of unchanging laws (the scientific). Later, this same intellectual progression took place in increasingly complex fields—physics, chemistry, and, finally, the study of society. Comte believed that by applying the scientific method, also called the **positivist method,** his new discipline of sociology would soon discover the eternal laws of human relations. This colossal achievement would in turn enable expert social scientists to impose a disciplined harmony and well-being on less enlightened citizens. Dismissing the "fictions" of traditional religions, Comte became the chief priest of the religion of science and rule by experts.

Comte's stages of knowledge exemplify the nineteenth-century fascination with the idea of **evolution** and dynamic development. Thinkers in many fields, such as the romantic historians and "scientific" Marxists, shared and applied this basic concept. In geology, Charles Lyell (1797–1875) effectively discredited the long-standing view that the earth's surface had been formed by short-lived cataclysms, such as biblical floods and earthquakes. Instead, according to Lyell's principle of uniformitarianism, the same geological processes that are at work today slowly formed the earth's surface over an immensely long time. The evolutionary view of biological development, first proposed by the Greek Anaximander in the sixth century B.C., re-emerged in a more modern form in the work of Jean Baptiste Lamarck (1744–1829). Lamarck asserted that all forms of life had arisen through a long process of continuous adjustment to the environment.

Lamarck's work was flawed—he believed that the characteristics parents acquired in the course of their lives could be inherited by their children—and was not accepted, but it helped prepare the way for Charles Darwin (1809–1882), the most influential of all nineteenth-century evolutionary thinkers. As the official naturalist on a five-year scientific cruise to Latin America and the South Pacific beginning in 1831, Darwin carefully collected specimens of the different animal species he encountered on the voyage. Back in England, convinced by fossil evidence and by his friend Lyell that the earth and life on it were immensely ancient, Darwin came to doubt the general belief in a special divine creation of each species of animal. Instead, he concluded, all life had gradually evolved from a common ancestral origin in an unending "struggle for survival." After long hesitation, Darwin published his research, which immediately attracted wide attention.

Darwin's great originality lay in suggesting precisely *how* biological evolution might have occurred. His theory is summarized in the title of his work *On the Origin of Species by the Means of Natural Selection* (1859). Decisively influenced by Thomas Malthus's gloomy theory that populations naturally grow faster than their food supplies (see page 726), Darwin argued that chance differences among the members of a given species help some survive while others die. Thus the variations that prove useful in the struggle for survival are selected naturally and gradually spread to the entire species through reproduction. Darwin did not explain why such variations occurred in the first place, and not until the early twentieth century did the study of genetics and the concept of mutation provide some answers.

Online Study Center **Improve Your Grade**
Primary Source: The Theory of Natural Selection and the Evolution of Species

As the capstone of already-widespread evolutionary thinking, Darwin's theory had a powerful and many-sided influence on European thought and the European middle classes. Darwin was hailed as the great scientist par excellence, the "Newton of biology," who had revealed once again the powers of objective science. Darwin's findings also reinforced the teachings of secularists such as Comte and Marx, who scornfully dismissed religious belief in favor of agnostic or atheistic materialism. In the great cities especially, religion was on the defensive. Finally, many writers applied the theory of biological evolution to human affairs. Herbert Spencer (1820–1903), an English disciple of Auguste Comte, saw the human race as driven forward to ever-greater specialization and progress by the brutal economic struggle. According to Spencer, this unending struggle efficiently determined the "survival of the fittest." The poor were the ill-fated weak; the prosperous were the chosen strong. Understandably, Spencer and other **Social Darwinists** were especially popular with the upper middle class.

Online Study Center **Improve Your Grade**
Primary Source: Survival of the Fittest Applied to Human Kind

Realism in Literature

In literature, the key themes of **realism** emerged in the 1840s and continued to dominate Western culture and style until the 1890s. Realist writers believed that literature should depict life exactly as it was. Forsaking poetry for prose and the personal, emotional viewpoint of the romantics for strict, scientific objectivity, the realists simply observed and recorded—content to let the facts speak for themselves.

The major realist writers focused their extraordinary powers of observation on contemporary everyday life. Emphatically rejecting the romantic search for the exotic and the sublime, they energetically pursued the typical and the commonplace. Beginning with a dissection of the middle classes, from which most of them sprang, many realists eventually focused on the working classes, especially the urban working classes, which had been neglected in imaginative literature before this time. The realists put a microscope to many unexplored and taboo subjects—sex, strikes, violence, alcoholism—and hastened to report that slums and factories teemed with savage behavior. Many shocked middle-class critics denounced realism as ugly sensationalism wrapped provocatively in pseudoscientific declarations and crude language.

The realists' claims of objectivity did not prevent the elaboration of a definite worldview. Unlike the romantics, who had gloried in individual freedom and an unlimited universe, realists were strict determinists. Human beings,

Manet: Emile Zola The young novelist's sensitivity and strength of character permeate this famous portrait by the great French painter Edouard Manet. Focusing on nuances and subtle variations, Manet was at first denounced by the critics, and after Zola lost a newspaper job defending Manet they became close friends. Manet was strongly influenced by Japanese prints, seen in the background. *(Erich Lessing/Art Resource, NY)*

like atoms, were components of the physical world, and all human actions were caused by unalterable natural laws. Heredity and environment determined human behavior; good and evil were merely social conventions.

The realist movement began in France, where romanticism had never been completely dominant, and three of its greatest practitioners—Balzac, Flaubert, and Zola—were French. Honoré de Balzac (1799–1850) spent thirty years writing a vastly ambitious panorama of postrevolutionary French life. Known collectively as *The Human Comedy,* this series of nearly one hundred books vividly portrays more than two thousand characters from virtually all sectors of French society. Balzac pictures urban society as grasping, amoral, and brutal, characterized by a Darwinian struggle for wealth and power. In *Le Père Goriot* (1835), the hero, a poor student from the provinces, eventually surrenders his idealistic integrity to feverish ambition and society's pervasive greed.

Madame Bovary (1857), the masterpiece of Gustave Flaubert (1821–1880), is far narrower in scope than Balzac's work but unparalleled in its depth and accuracy of psychological insight. Unsuccessfully prosecuted as an outrage against public morality and religion, Flaubert's carefully crafted novel tells the ordinary, even banal, story of a frustrated middle-class housewife who has an adulterous love affair and is betrayed by her lover. Without moralizing, Flaubert portrays the provincial middle class as petty, smug, and hypocritical.

Emile Zola (1840–1902) was most famous for his seamy, animalistic view of working-class life. But he also wrote gripping, carefully researched stories featuring the stock exchange, the big department store, and the army, as well as urban slums and bloody coal strikes. Like many later realists, Zola sympathized with socialism, a sympathy evident in his overpowering novel *Germinal* (1885).

Realism quickly spread beyond France. In England, Mary Ann Evans (1819–1880), who wrote under the pen name George Eliot, brilliantly achieved a more deeply felt, less sensational kind of realism. "It is the habit of my imagination," George Eliot wrote, "to strive after as full a vision of the medium in which a character moves as one of the character itself." Her great novel *Middlemarch: A Study of Provincial Life* (1871–1872) examines masterfully the ways in which people are shaped by their social medium as well as their own inner strivings, conflicts, and moral choices. Thomas Hardy (1840–1928) was more in the Zola tradition. His novels, such as *Tess of the D'Urbervilles* (1891) and *The Return of the Native* (1878), depict men and women frustrated and crushed by fate and bad luck.

The greatest Russian realist, Count Leo Tolstoy (1828–1910), combined realism in description and character development with an atypical moralizing, which came to dominate his later work. Tolstoy's greatest work is *War and Peace* (1864–1869), a monumental novel set against the historical background of Napoleon's invasion of Russia in 1812. Tolstoy probed deeply into the lives of a multitude of unforgettable characters, such as the ill-fated Prince Andrei; the shy, fumbling Pierre; and the enchanting, level-headed Natasha. Tolstoy went to great pains to develop his fatalistic theory of history, which regards free will as an illusion and the achievements of even the greatest leaders as only the channeling of historical necessity. Yet Tolstoy's central message is one that most of the people discussed in this chapter would have readily accepted: human love, trust, and everyday family ties are life's enduring values.

Thoroughgoing realism (or "naturalism," as it was often called) arrived late in the United States, most arrestingly in the work of Theodore Dreiser (1871–1945). His first novel, *Sister Carrie* (1900), a story of an ordinary farm girl who does well going wrong in Chicago, so outraged conventional morality that the publisher withdrew the book. The United States subsequently became a bastion of literary realism in the twentieth century after the movement had faded away in Europe.

"Life Is Everywhere" The simple but profound joys of everyday life infuse this outstanding example of Russia's powerful realist tradition. Painted in 1888 by N. A. Yaroshenko, this representation of the mother and child and adoring men also draws on the classic theme of the infant Jesus and the holy family. *(Sovfoto)*

Chapter Summary

- What was life like in the cities, and how did urban life change in the nineteenth century?
- What did the emergence of urban industrial society mean for rich and poor and those in between?
- How did families change as they coped with the challenges and the opportunities of the developing urban civilization?
- What major changes in science and thought reflected and influenced the new urban society?

The revolution in industry had a decisive influence on the urban environment. The populations of towns and cities grew rapidly because it was economically advantageous to locate factories and offices in urban areas. This rapid growth worsened long-standing overcrowding and unhealthy living conditions and posed a frightening challenge for society. Eventually government leaders, city planners, reformers, scientists, and ordinary citizens responded. They took effective action in public health and provided themselves with other badly needed urban services. Gradually they tamed the ferocious savagery of the traditional city.

As the quality of urban life improved, the class structure became more complex and diversified than before. Urban society featured many distinct social groups, which existed in a state of constant flux and competition. The gap between rich and poor remained enormous and really quite traditional in mature urban society, although there were countless gradations between the extremes. Large numbers of poor women in particular continued to labor as workers in sweated industries, as domestic servants, and as prostitutes in order to satisfy the demands of their masters in the servant-keeping classes.

Major changes in family life accompanied the more complex and diversified class system. Especially among the working classes, family life became more stable, more loving, and less mercenary. These improvements had a price, however. Gender roles for men and women became sharply defined and rigidly separate. Women especially tended to be locked into a subordinate and stereotypical role. Nonetheless, on balance, the quality of family life improved for all family members. Better, more stable family relations reinforced the benefits for the masses of higher real wages, increased social security, political participation, and education. Urban society in the late nineteenth century represented a long step forward for humanity, but it remained very unequal.

Inequality was a favorite theme of realist novelists such as Balzac and Zola. More generally, literary realism reflected Western society's growing faith in science, material progress, and evolutionary thinking. The emergence of urban, industrial civilization accelerated the secularization of the Western worldview.

Key Terms

Benthamite
miasmatic theory
germ theory
pasteurization
antiseptic principle
labor aristocracy
illegitimacy explosion
separate spheres
defense mechanisms
thermodynamics
organic chemistry
positivist method
evolution
Social Darwinists
realism

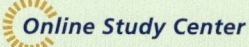

Suggested Reading

Anderson, Bonnie S., and Judith P. Zinsser. *A History of Their Own: Women in Europe from Prehistory to the Present*, vol. 2, rev. ed. 2000. An excellent, wide-ranging survey.

Barnes, David S. *The Great Stink of Paris and the Nineteenth-Century Struggle Against Filth and Germs.* 2006. An excellent introduction to sanitary developments and attitudes toward public health.

Coontz, Stephanie. *Marriage, a History: From Obedience to Intimacy, or How Love Conquered Marriage.* 2005. A lively investigation of the historical background to current practice.

Crane, Diana. *Fashion and Its Social Agendas: Class, Gender, and Identity.* 2001. An innovative and extremely helpful historical investigation.

Gottlieb, Beatrice. *The Family in the Western World*. 1993. A wide-ranging synthesis.

Hunt, Tristram. *Building Jerusalem: The Rise and Fall of the Victorian City*. 2006. Considers British urban life and civic pride.

Maynes, Mary Jo. *Taking the Hard Road: Life Course in French and German Workers' Biographies in the Era of Industrialization*. 1995. Includes fascinating stories that provide insight into how workers saw themselves.

Olsen, Donald J. *The City as a Work of Art: London, Paris, and Vienna*. 1988. An architectural feast.

Perrot, Michelle, ed. *A History of Private Life*. 1990. A fascinating multivolume work.

Pilbeam, Pamela. *The Middle Classes in Europe, 1789–1914: France, Germany, Italy, and Russia*. 1990. A stimulating introduction to middle-class life.

Schmiechen, James, and Kenneth Carls. *The British Market Hall: A Social and Architectural History*. 1999. A pathbreaking and beautiful study of Britain's enclosed markets and how they revolutionized the sale of food.

Thompson, F. M. L. *The Rise of Respectable Society: A Social History of Victorian Britain, 1830–1900*. 1986. A laudable survey.

Weiner, Jonathan. *The Beak of the Finch: The Story of Evolution in Our Time*. 1994. A prize-winning, highly readable account of Darwin and evolution.

Zeldin, Theodore. *France, 1848–1945*, 2 vols. 1973, 1977. A pioneering social history that opened many new lines of inquiry.

Notes

1. A. Weber, *The Growth of Cities in the Nineteenth Century* (New York: Columbia University Press, 1899), p. 1.
2. S. Marcus, "Reading the Illegible," in *The Victorian City: Images and Realities*, ed. H. J. Dyos and Michael Wolff, vol. 1 (London: Routledge & Kegan Paul, 1973), p. 266.
3. E. Gauldie, *Cruel Habitations: A History of Working-Class Housing, 1780–1918* (London: George Allen & Unwin, 1974), p. 21.
4. Quoted in E. Chadwick, *Report on the Sanitary Condition of the Labouring Population of Great Britain*, ed. M. W. Flinn (Edinburgh: University of Edinburgh Press, 1965; original publication, 1842), pp. 315–316.
5. J. P. McKay, *Tramways and Trolleys: The Rise of Urban Mass Transport in Europe* (Princeton, N.J.: Princeton University Press, 1976), p. 81.
6. Quoted in R. P. Neuman, "The Sexual Question and Social Democracy in Imperial Germany," *Journal of Social History* 7 (Winter 1974): 276.
7. Quoted in J. A. Banks, "The Contagion of Numbers," in *The Victorian City: Images and Realities*, ed. H. J. Dyos and Michael Wolff, vol. 1 (London: Routledge & Kegan Paul, 1973), p. 112.
8. Quoted in R. Roberts, *The Classic Slum: Salford Life in the First Quarter of the Century* (Manchester, England: University of Manchester Press, 1971), p. 95.
9. Quoted in T. Zeldin, *France, 1848–1945,* vol. 1 (Oxford: Clarendon Press, 1973), p. 288.
10. J. Ehmer, "Marriage," in *The History of the European Family*, ed. D. Kertzer and M. Barbagli, vol. 2 (New Haven: Yale University Press, 2002), p. 319.
11. S. Marcus, *The Other Victorians: A Study of Sexuality and Pornography in Mid-Nineteenth-Century England* (New York: Basic Books, 1966), p. 142.
12. Quoted in G. S. Jones, "Working-Class Culture and Working-Class Politics in London, 1870–1900: Notes on the Remaking of a Working Class," *Journal of Social History* 7 (Summer 1974): 486.
13. Quoted in Zeldin, *France*, p. 346.
14. Roberts, *The Classic Slum*, p. 35.
15. Quoted in Zeldin, *France*, p. 295.
16. Quoted ibid., p. 328.
17. Quoted in Neuman, "The Sexual Question," p. 281.
18. Quoted in S. Kern, "Explosive Intimacy: Psychodynamics of the Victorian Family," *History of Childhood Quarterly* 1 (Winter 1974): 439.
19. A. Comte, *The Positive Philosophy of Auguste Comte,* trans. H. Martineau, vol. 1 (London: J. Chapman, 1853), pp. 1–2.

Listening to the Past

Middle-Class Youth and Sexuality

Growing up in Vienna in a prosperous Jewish family, Stephan Zweig (1881–1942) became an influential voice calling for humanitarian values and international culture in early-twentieth-century Europe. Passionately opposed to the First World War, Zweig wrote poetry, plays, and novels. But he was most famous for many outstanding biographies, which featured shrewd psychological portraits of intriguing historical figures such as Magellan and Marie Antoinette. After Hitler came to power in Germany in 1933, Zweig lived in exile until his death in 1942.

Zweig's last work was The World of Yesterday (1943), one of the truly fascinating autobiographies of the twentieth century. In the following passage taken from that work, Zweig recalls and also interprets the romantic experiences and the sexual separation of middle-class youth before the First World War.

During the eight years of our higher schooling [beyond grade school], something had occurred which was of great importance to each one of us: we ten-year-olds had grown into virile young men of sixteen, seventeen, and eighteen, and Nature began to assert its rights. . . . It did not take us long to discover that those authorities in whom we had previously confided—school, family, and public morals—manifested an astonishing insincerity in this matter of sex. But what is more, they also demanded secrecy and reserve from us in this connection. . . .

This "social morality," which on the one hand privately presupposed the existence of sexuality and its natural course, but on the other would not recognize it openly at any price, was doubly deceitful. While it winked one eye at a young man and even encouraged him with the other "to sow his wild oats," as the kindly language of the home put it, in the case of a woman it studiously shut both eyes and acted as if it were blind. That a man could experience desires, and was permitted to experience them, was silently admitted by custom. But to admit frankly that a woman could be subject to similar desires, or that creation for its eternal purposes also required a female polarity, would have transgressed the conception of the "sanctity of womanhood." In the pre-Freudian era, therefore, the axiom was agreed upon that a female person could have no physical desires as long as they had not been awakened by man, and that, obviously, was officially permitted only in marriage. But even in those moral times, in Vienna in particular, the air was full of dangerous erotic infection, and a girl of good family had to live in a completely sterilized atmosphere, from the day of her birth until the day when she left the altar on her husband's arm. In order to protect young girls, they were not left alone for a single moment. . . . Every book which they read was inspected, and above all else, young girls were constantly kept busy to divert their attention from any possible dangerous thoughts. They had to practise the piano, learn singing and drawing, foreign languages, and the history of literature and art. They were educated and overeducated. But while the aim was to make them as educated and as socially correct as possible, at the same time society anxiously took great pains that they should remain innocent of all natural things to a degree unthinkable today. A young girl of good family was not allowed to have any idea of how the male body was formed, or to know how children came into the world, for the angel was to enter into matrimony not only physically untouched, but completely "pure" spiritually as well. "Good breeding," for a young girl of that time, was identical with ignorance of life; and this ignorance ofttimes lasted for the rest of their lives. . . .

What possibilities actually existed for a young man of the middle-class world? In all the others, in the so-called lower classes, the problem was no problem at all. . . . In most of our Alpine villages the number of natural children greatly exceeded the legitimate ones. Among the proletariat, the worker, before he could get married, lived with another worker in free love. . . . It was only in our middle-class society that such a remedy as an early marriage was scorned. . . . And so there was an artificial interval of six, eight, or ten years between actual manhood and manhood as society accepted it; and in this interval the young man had to take care of his own "affairs" or adventures.

Those days did not give him too many opportunities. Only a very few particularly rich young men could afford the luxury of keeping a mistress, that is, taking an apartment and paying her expenses. And only a very few fortunate young men achieved the literary ideal of love of the times—the only one which it was permitted to describe in novels—an affair with a married woman. The others helped themselves for the most part with shopgirls and waitresses, and this offered little inner satisfaction. . . . But, generally speaking, prostitution was still the foundation of the erotic life outside of marriage; in a certain sense it constituted a dark underground vault over which rose the gorgeous structure of middle-class society with its faultless, radiant façade.

The present generation has hardly any idea of the gigantic extent of prostitution in Europe before the [First] World War. Whereas today it is as rare to meet a prostitute on the streets of a big city as it is to meet a wagon in the road, then the sidewalks were so sprinkled with women for sale that it was more difficult to avoid than to find them. To this was added the countless number of "closed houses," the night clubs, the cabarets, the dance parlours with their dancers and singers, and the bars with their "come-on" girls. At that time female wares were offered for sale at every hour and at every price. . . . And this was the same city, the same society, the same morality, that was indignant when young girls rode bicycles, and declared it a disgrace to the dignity of science when Freud in his calm, clear, and penetrating manner established truths that they did not wish to be true. The same world that so pathetically defended the purity of womanhood allowed this cruel sale of women, organized it, and even profited thereby.

We should not permit ourselves to be misled by sentimental novels or stories of that epoch. It was a bad time for youth. The young girls were

An elegant ball for upper-class youth, with debutantes, junior officers, and vigilant chaperons watching in the background. *(State Russian Museum, St. Petersburg, Russia/The Bridgeman Art Library)*

hermetically locked up under the control of the family, hindered in their free bodily as well as intellectual development. The young men were forced to secrecy and reticence by a morality which fundamentally no one believed or obeyed. Unhampered, honest relationships—in other words, all that could have made youth happy and joyous according to the laws of Nature—were permitted only to the very few.

Questions for Analysis

1. According to Zweig, how did the sex lives of young middle-class women and young middle-class men differ? What accounted for these differences?

2. Was there nonetheless a basic underlying unity in the way society treated both the young men and the young women of the comfortable middle class? If so, what was that unity?

3. Zweig ends this passage with a value judgment: "It was a bad time for youth." Do you agree or disagree? Why?

Source: The World of Yesterday by Stephan Zweig, translated by Helmut Ripperger. Translation copyright 1943 by the Viking Press, Inc. Used with permission of Viking Penguin, a division of Penguin Group (USA) Inc.

France's Napoleon III and Empress Eugénie greet Britain's Queen Victoria and Prince Albert in a dazzling ceremony in Paris in 1855. *(The Royal Collection, © 2007 Her Majesty Queen Elizabeth II)*

chapter 25

THE AGE OF NATIONALISM, 1850–1914

chapter preview

Napoleon III in France
- How in France did Napoleon III seek to reconcile popular and conservative forces in an authoritarian nation-state?

Nation Building in Italy and Germany
- How did the process of unification in Italy and Germany create conservative nation-states?

Nation Building in the United States
- In what ways did the United States experience the full drama of nation building?

The Modernization of Russia and the Ottoman Empire
- What steps did Russia and the Ottoman Turks take toward modernization, and how successful were they?

The Responsive National State, 1871–1914
- Why after 1871 did ordinary citizens feel a growing loyalty to their governments?

Marxism and the Socialist Movement
- Why did the socialist movement grow, and how revolutionary was it?

The revolutions of 1848 closed one era and opened another. Urban industrial society began to take a strong hold on the continent and in the young United States, as it already had in Great Britain. Internationally, the repressive peace and diplomatic stability of Metternich's time were replaced by a period of war and rapid change. In thought and culture, exuberant romanticism gave way to hardheaded realism. In the Atlantic economy, the hard years of the 1840s were followed by good times and prosperity throughout most of the 1850s and 1860s. Perhaps most important of all, Western society progressively developed, for better or worse, a new and effective organizing principle capable of coping with the many-sided challenge of the dual revolution and the emerging urban civilization. That principle was nationalism—dedication to an identification with the nation-state.

The triumph of nationalism is an enormously significant historical development that was by no means completely predictable. After all, nationalism had been a powerful force since at least 1789, but it had repeatedly failed to realize its goals, most spectacularly so in 1848. Yet by 1914 nationalism had become in one way or another an almost universal faith in Europe and in the United States, a faith that had evolved to appeal not only to predominately middle-class liberals but also to the broad masses of society. To understand this fateful evolution is the task of this chapter.

Napoleon III in France

Early nationalism was generally liberal and idealistic and often democratic and radical as well. The ideas of nationhood and popular sovereignty posed a fearful revolutionary threat to conservatives like Metternich. Yet from the vantage point of the twenty-first century, it is clear that nationalism wears many masks: it may be narrowly liberal or democratic and radical, as it was for Mazzini and Michelet, but it can also flourish in dictatorial states, which may be conservative, fascist, or communist. Napoleon I's France had already combined national feeling with authoritarian rule. Significantly, it

Online Study Center
This icon will direct you to interactive activities and study materials on the website **college.hmco.com/pic/mckaywest9e**

was Napoleon's nephew, Louis Napoleon, who revived and extended this merger. In doing so, he provided a model for political leaders elsewhere.

- **How in France did Napoleon III seek to reconcile popular and conservative forces in an authoritarian nation-state?**

The Second Republic and Louis Napoleon

Although Louis Napoleon Bonaparte had played no part in French politics before 1848, universal male suffrage gave him three times as many votes as the four other presidential candidates combined in the French presidential election of December 1848. This outcome occurred for several reasons. First, Louis Napoleon had the great name of his uncle, whom romantics had transformed from a dictator into a demigod as they created a Napoleonic legend after 1820. Second, as Karl Marx stressed at the time, middle-class and peasant property owners feared the socialist challenge of urban workers, and they wanted a tough ruler to provide protection. Third, in late 1848 Louis Napoleon had a positive "program" for France, which had been elaborated in widely circulated pamphlets before the election and which guided him through his long reign.

Above all, Louis Napoleon believed that the government should represent the people and that it should try hard to help them economically. But how were these tasks to be done? Parliaments and political parties were not the answer, according to Louis Napoleon. French politicians represented special-interest groups, particularly middle-class ones. The answer was a strong, even authoritarian, national leader, like the first Napoleon, who would serve all the people, rich and poor. This leader would be linked

Paris in the Second Empire The flash and glitter of unprecedented prosperity in the Second Empire come alive in this vibrant contemporary painting. Writers and intellectuals chat with elegant women and trade witticisms with financiers and government officials at the Café Tortoni, a favorite rendezvous for fashionable society. Horse-drawn omnibuses with open top decks mingle with cabs and private carriages on the broad new boulevard. *(Lauros/Giraudon/ The Bridgeman Art Library)*

to each citizen by direct democracy, his sovereignty uncorrupted by politicians and legislative bodies. These political ideas went hand in hand with Louis Napoleon's vision of national unity and social progress. The state and its leader had a sacred duty to provide jobs and stimulate the economy. All classes would benefit by such action.

Louis Napoleon's political and social ideas were at least vaguely understood by large numbers of French peasants and workers in December 1848. To many common people, he appeared to be a strong man *and* a forward-looking champion of their interests, and that is why they voted for him.

Online Study Center Improve Your Grade
Primary Source: The French Elect Another Bonaparte: Louis Napoleon Bonaparte

Elected to a four-year term, President Louis Napoleon had to share power with a conservative National Assembly. But in 1851, after the Assembly failed to change the constitution so he could run for a second term, Louis Napoleon began to conspire with key army officers. On December 2, 1851, he illegally dismissed the Assembly and seized power in a coup d'état. There was some armed resistance in Paris and widespread insurrection in the countryside in southern France, but these protests were crushed by the army. Restoring universal male suffrage, Louis Napoleon called on the French people, as his uncle had done, to legalize his actions. They did: 92 percent voted to make him president for ten years. A year later, 97 percent in a plebiscite made him hereditary emperor; for the third time, and by the greatest margin yet, the authoritarian Louis Napoleon was overwhelmingly elected to lead the French nation.

Napoleon III's Second Empire

Louis Napoleon—now proclaimed Emperor Napoleon III—experienced both success and failure between 1852 and 1870. His greatest success was with the economy, particularly in the 1850s. His government encouraged the new investment banks and massive railroad construction that were at the heart of the Industrial Revolution on the continent. The government also fostered general economic expansion through an ambitious program of public works, which included the rebuilding of Paris to improve the urban environment (see page 784). The profits of business people soared with prosperity, and unemployment declined greatly.

Louis Napoleon always hoped that economic progress would reduce social and political tensions. This hope was

Chronology

1852–1871	Reign of Napoleon III in France
1859–1870	Unification of Italy
1860–1900	Industrialization of Russia
1861	Freeing of Russian serfs
1861–1865	U.S. Civil War
1866	Austro-Prussian War
1870–1871	Franco-Prussian War
1870–1878	Kulturkampf, Bismarck's attack on Catholic Church
1880s	Educational reforms affect Catholic schools in France
1883	First social security laws to help workers in Germany
1905	Bloody Sunday in Russia
1908	Young Turks in power

at least partially realized. Until the mid-1860s there was considerable support from France's most dissatisfied group, the urban workers. Napoleon III's regulation of pawnshops and his support of credit unions and better housing for the working classes were evidence of positive concern in the 1850s. In the 1860s, he granted workers the right to form unions and the right to strike—important economic rights denied by earlier governments.

At first, political power remained in the hands of the emperor. He alone chose his ministers, and they had great freedom of action. At the same time, Napoleon III restricted but did not abolish the Assembly. Members were elected by universal male suffrage every six years, and Louis Napoleon and his government took the parliamentary elections very seriously. They tried to entice notable people, even those who had opposed the regime, to stand as government candidates in order to expand the base of support. Moreover, the government used its officials and appointed mayors to spread the word that the election of the government's candidates—and the defeat of the opposition—was the key to roads, tax rebates, and a thousand other local concerns.

In 1857 and again in 1863, Louis Napoleon's system worked brilliantly and produced overwhelming electoral victories. Yet in the 1860s, Napoleon III's electoral system gradually disintegrated. A sincere nationalist, Napoleon had wanted to reorganize Europe on the principle of nationality and gain influence and territory for France and himself in the process. Instead, problems in Italy and the rising power of Prussia led to increasing criticism at home from his Catholic and nationalist supporters. With increasing effectiveness, the middle-class liberals who had always wanted a less authoritarian regime continued to denounce his rule.

Napoleon was always sensitive to the public mood. Public opinion, he once said, always wins the last victory. Thus in the 1860s, he progressively liberalized his empire. He gave the Assembly greater powers and the opposition candidates greater freedom, which they used to good advantage. In 1869 the opposition, consisting of republicans, monarchists, and liberals, polled almost 45 percent of the vote.

The next year, a sick and weary Louis Napoleon again granted France a new constitution, which combined a basically parliamentary regime with a hereditary emperor as chief of state. In a final great plebiscite on the eve of the disastrous war with Prussia, 7.5 million Frenchmen voted in favor of the new constitution, and only 1.5 million opposed it. Napoleon III's attempt to reconcile a strong national state with universal male suffrage was still evolving and was doing so in a democratic direction.

Nation Building in Italy and Germany

Louis Napoleon's triumph in 1848 and his authoritarian rule in the 1850s provided the old ruling classes of Europe with a new model in politics. To what extent might the expanding urban middle classes and even portions of the growing working classes rally to a strong and essentially conservative national state? This was one of the great political questions in the 1850s and 1860s. In central Europe, a resounding answer came with the national unification of Italy and Germany.

- **How did the process of unification in Italy and Germany create conservative nation-states?**

Italy to 1850

Italy had never been united prior to 1850. Part of Rome's great empire in ancient times, the Italian peninsula was divided in the Middle Ages into competing city-states that led the commercial and cultural revival of the West with amazing creativity. A battleground for Great Powers after 1494, Italy was reorganized in 1815 at the Congress of Vienna. The rich northern provinces of Lombardy and Venetia were taken by Metternich's Austria. Sardinia and Piedmont were under the rule of an Italian monarch, and Tuscany, with its famous capital Florence, shared north-central Italy with several smaller states. Central Italy and Rome were ruled by the papacy, which had always considered an independent political existence necessary to fulfill its spiritual mission. Naples and Sicily were ruled, as they had been for almost a hundred years, by a branch of the Bourbons. Metternich was not wrong in dismissing Italy as "a geographical expression" (see Map 25.1).

Between 1815 and 1848, the goal of a unified Italian nation captured the imaginations of many Italians. There were three basic approaches. The first was the radical program of the idealistic patriot Giuseppe Mazzini, who preached a centralized democratic republic based on universal male suffrage and the will of the people (see page 755). The second was that of Vincenzo Gioberti, a Catholic priest who called for a federation of existing states under the presidency of a progressive pope. The third was the program of those who looked for leadership to the autocratic kingdom of Sardinia-Piedmont, much as many Germans looked to Prussia.

The third alternative was strengthened by the failures of 1848, when Austria smashed Mazzini's republicanism. Almost by accident, Sardinia's monarch, Victor Emmanuel, retained the liberal constitution granted under duress in March 1848. This constitution provided for a fair degree of civil liberties and real parliamentary government, with deputies elected by a limited franchise based on income. To the Italian middle classes, Sardinia appeared to be a liberal, progressive state ideally suited to achieve the goal of national unification. By contrast, Mazzini's brand of democratic republicanism seemed quixotic and too radical.

As for the papacy, the initial cautious support by Pius IX (r. 1846–1878) for unification had given way to fear and hostility after he was temporarily driven from Rome during the upheavals of 1848. For a long generation, the papacy would stand resolutely opposed not only to national unification but also to most modern trends. In 1864 in the *Syllabus of Errors,* Pius IX strongly denounced rationalism, socialism, separation of church and state, and religious liberty, denying that "the Roman pontiff can and ought to reconcile and align himself with progress, liberalism, and modern civilization."

Cavour and Garibaldi in Italy

Sardinia had the good fortune of being led by a brilliant statesman, Count Camillo Benso di Cavour, the dominant figure in the Sardinian government from 1850 until his death in 1861. Indicative of the coming tacit alliance

Nation Building in Italy and Germany

MAP 25.1 The Unification of Italy, 1859–1870 The leadership of Sardinia-Piedmont, nationalist fervor, and Garibaldi's attack on the kingdom of the Two Sicilies were decisive factors in the unification of Italy.

between the aristocracy and the solid middle class under the banner of the strong nation-state, Cavour came from a noble family, and he made a substantial fortune in business before entering politics. Cavour's national goals were limited and realistic. Until 1859 he sought unity only for the states of northern and perhaps central Italy in a greatly expanded kingdom of Sardinia.

In the 1850s, Cavour worked to consolidate Sardinia as a liberal constitutional state capable of leading northern Italy. His program of highways and railroads, of civil liberties and opposition to clerical privilege, increased support for Sardinia throughout northern Italy. Yet Cavour realized that Sardinia could not drive Austria out of Lombardy and Venetia and unify northern Italy under Victor Emmanuel without the help of a powerful ally. Accordingly, he worked for a secret diplomatic alliance with Napoleon III against Austria.

Finally, in July 1858 Cavour succeeded and goaded Austria into attacking Sardinia in 1859. Napoleon III came to Sardinia's defense. Then after the victory of the combined Franco-Sardinian forces, Napoleon III did a sudden about-face. Deciding it was not in his interest to have too strong a state on his southern border and criticized by French Catholics for supporting the pope's declared enemy, Napoleon III abandoned Cavour. He made a compromise peace with the Austrians at Villafranca in July 1859. Sardinia would receive only Lombardy, the area around Milan. The rest of the map of Italy would remain essentially unchanged. Cavour resigned in a rage.

Yet Cavour's plans were salvaged by the skillful maneuvers of his allies in the moderate nationalist movement. While the war against Austria had raged in the north, pro-Sardinian nationalists in central Italy had fanned popular revolts and driven out their easily toppled princes. Using and controlling the popular enthusiasm, the middle-class nationalist leaders in central Italy called for fusion with Sardinia. This was not at all what France and the other Great Powers wanted, but the nationalists held firm. Cavour returned to power in early 1860 and gained Napoleon III's support by ceding Savoy and Nice to France. The people of central Italy then voted overwhelmingly to join a greatly enlarged kingdom of Sardinia. Cavour had achieved his original goal of a northern Italian state (see Map 25.1).

Garibaldi and Victor Emmanuel The historic meeting in Naples between the leader of Italy's revolutionary nationalists and the king of Sardinia sealed the unification of northern and southern Italy in a unitary state. With only the sleeve of his red shirt showing, Garibaldi offers his hand—and his conquests—to the uniformed king and his moderate monarchical government. *(Scala/Art Resource, NY)*

For superpatriots such as Giuseppe Garibaldi (1807–1882), the job of unification was still only half done. The son of a poor sailor, Garibaldi personified the romantic, revolutionary nationalism and republicanism of Mazzini and 1848. Leading a corps of volunteers against Austria in 1859, Garibaldi emerged in 1860 as an independent force in Italian politics.

Partly to use him and partly to get rid of him, Cavour secretly supported Garibaldi's bold plan to "liberate" the kingdom of the Two Sicilies. Landing on the shores of Sicily in May 1860, Garibaldi's guerrilla band of a thousand **Red Shirts** captured the imagination of the Sicilian peasantry. Outwitting the twenty-thousand-man royal army, the guerrilla leader won battles, gained volunteers, and took Palermo. Then he and his men crossed to the mainland, marched triumphantly toward Naples, and prepared to attack Rome and the pope. But the wily Cavour quickly sent Sardinian forces to occupy most of the Papal States (but not Rome) and to intercept Garibaldi.

Cavour realized that an attack on Rome would bring about war with France, and he also feared Garibaldi's radicalism and popular appeal. Thus he immediately organized a plebiscite in the conquered territories. Despite the urging of some radical supporters, the patriotic Garibaldi did not oppose Cavour, and the people of the south voted to join Sardinia. When Garibaldi and Victor Emmanuel rode through Naples to cheering crowds, they symbolically sealed the union of north and south, of monarch and nation-state.

Cavour had succeeded. He had controlled Garibaldi and had turned popular nationalism in a conservative direction. The new kingdom of Italy, which expanded to include Venice in 1866 and Rome in 1870, was a parliamentary monarchy under Victor Emmanuel, neither radical nor democratic. Despite political unity, only a small minority of Italian males had the right to vote. The propertied classes and the common people were divided. A great and growing social and cultural gap separated the progressive, industrializing north from the stagnant, agrarian south. The new Italy was united on paper, but profound divisions remained.

Germany Before Bismarck

In the aftermath of 1848, the German states were locked in a political stalemate. After Austria and Russia blocked Frederick William's attempt to unify Germany "from above," tension grew between Austria and Prussia as each power sought to block the other within the German Confederation (see pages 751 and 773–774). Stalemate also prevailed in the domestic politics of the individual states in the 1850s.

At the same time, powerful economic forces were undermining the political status quo. Modern industry grew rapidly within the German customs union, or **Zollverein**, founded in 1834 to stimulate trade and increase the revenues of member states. The Zollverein had not included Austria, and after 1848 this exclusion became a crucial factor in the Austro-Prussian rivalry.

The Zollverein's tariff duties were substantially reduced so that Austria's highly protected industry could not bear to join. In retaliation, Austria tried to destroy the Zollverein, but without success. Indeed, by the end of 1853 all the German states except Austria had joined the customs union. A new Germany excluding Austria was becoming an economic reality. Middle-class and business groups in the Zollverein were enriching themselves and finding solid economic reasons to bolster their idealistic support of national unification. Prussia's leading role within the Zollverein gave it a valuable advantage in its struggle against Austria's supremacy in German political affairs.

The national uprising in Italy in 1859 made a profound impression in the German states. In Prussia great political change and war—perhaps with Austria, perhaps with France—seemed quite possible. Along with his top military advisers, the tough-minded William I of Prussia (r. 1861–1888), who had replaced the unstable Frederick William IV as regent in 1858 and become king himself in 1861, was convinced of the need for major army reforms. William I wanted to double the size of the highly disciplined regular army. Army reforms meant a bigger defense budget and higher taxes.

Prussia had emerged from 1848 with a parliament of sorts, which was in the hands of the liberal middle class by 1859. The wealthy middle class wanted society to be less, not more, militaristic. Above all, middle-class representatives wanted to establish once and for all that the parliament, not the king, had the ultimate political power and that the army was responsible to Prussia's elected representatives. These demands were popular. The parliament rejected the military budget in 1862, and the liberals triumphed completely in new elections. King William then called on Count Otto von Bismarck to head a new ministry and defy the parliament. This was a momentous choice.

Bismarck and the Austro-Prussian War, 1866

The most important figure in German history between Luther and Hitler, Otto von Bismarck (1815–1898) has been the object of enormous interest and debate. A great hero to some, a great villain to others, Bismarck was above all a master of politics. Born into the Prussian landowning aristocracy, the young Bismarck was a wild and tempestuous student given to duels and drinking. Proud of his Junker heritage and always devoted to his Prussian sovereign, Bismarck had a strong personality and an unbounded desire for power. Yet in his drive to secure power for himself and for Prussia, Bismarck was extraordinarily flexible and pragmatic. "One must always have two irons in the fire," he once said. He kept his options open, pursuing one policy and then another as he moved with skill and cunning toward his goal.

Bismarck first honed his political skills as a high-ranking diplomat for the Prussian government. When he took office as chief minister in 1862, he made a strong but unfavorable impression. His speeches were a sensation and a scandal. Declaring that the government would rule without parliamentary consent, Bismarck lashed out at the middle-class opposition: "The great questions of the day will not be decided by speeches and resolutions—that was the blunder of 1848 and 1849—but by blood and iron." Denounced for this view that "might makes right," Bismarck had the Prussian bureaucracy go right on collecting taxes, even though the parliament refused to approve the budget. Bismarck reorganized the army. And for four years, from 1862 to 1866, the voters of Prussia continued to express their opposition by sending large liberal majorities to the parliament.

Opposition at home spurred the search for success abroad. The ever-knotty question of Schleswig-Holstein provided a welcome opportunity. In 1864, when the Danish king tried again, as in 1848, to bring the provinces into a more centralized Danish state against the will of the German Confederation, Prussia joined Austria in a short and successful war against Denmark. However, Bismarck was convinced that Prussia had to control completely the northern, predominately Protestant part of the German Confederation, which meant expelling Austria from German affairs. After the victory over Denmark, Bismarck's skillful maneuvering had Prussia in a position to force Austria out by war, if necessary. Bismarck knew that a war with Austria would have to be a localized one that would not provoke a mighty alliance against Prussia. By skillfully neutralizing Russia and France, he was in a position to engage in a war of his own making.

The Austro-Prussian War of 1866 lasted only seven weeks. Utilizing railroads to mass troops and the new breechloading needle gun to achieve maximum firepower, the reorganized Prussian army overran northern Germany and defeated Austria decisively at the Battle of Sadowa in Bohemia. Anticipating Prussia's future needs, Bismarck offered Austria realistic, even generous, peace terms. Austria paid no reparations and lost no territory to Prussia, although Venetia was ceded to Italy. But the German Confederation was dissolved, and Austria agreed to withdraw from German affairs. The states north of the Main River were grouped in the new North German Confederation, led by an expanded Prussia. The mainly Catholic states of the south remained independent while forming alliances with Prussia. Bismarck's fundamental goal of Prussian expansion was being realized (see Map 25.2).

The Taming of the Parliament

Bismarck had long been convinced that the old order he so ardently defended should make peace, on its own terms, with the liberal middle class and the nationalist movement. He realized that nationalism was not necessarily hostile to conservative, authoritarian government. Moreover, Bismarck believed that because of the events of 1848, the German middle class could be led to prefer the reality of national unity under conservative leadership to a long, uncertain battle for truly liberal institutions. During the constitutional struggle over army reform and parliamentary authority, he had delayed but not abandoned this goal. Thus during the attack on Austria in 1866, he increasingly identified Prussia's fate with the "national development of Germany."

In the aftermath of victory, Bismarck fashioned a federal constitution for the new North German Confederation. Each state retained its own local government, but the king of Prussia became president of the confederation, and the chancellor—Bismarck—was responsible only to the president. The federal government—William I and Bismarck—controlled the army and foreign affairs. There was also a legislature with members of the lower house elected by universal, single-class, male suffrage. With this radical innovation, Bismarck opened the door to popular participation and the possibility of going over the head of the middle class directly to the people, much as Napoleon III had done in France. All the while, however, ultimate power rested in the hands of Prussia and its king and army.

In Prussia itself, Bismarck held out an olive branch to the parliamentary opposition. Marshaling all his diplomatic skill, Bismarck asked the parliament to pass a special indemnity bill to approve after the fact all the government's spending between 1862 and 1866. Most of the liberals jumped at the chance to cooperate. With German unity in sight, they repented their "sins." The constitutional struggle was over, and the German middle class was accepting respectfully the monarchical authority and the aristocratic superiority that Bismarck represented. In the

Nation Building in Italy and Germany • 823

Mapping the Past

MAP 25.2 The Unification of Germany, 1866–1871 This map shows how Prussia expanded and a new German empire was created through two wars, the Austro-Prussian War of 1866 and the Franco-Prussian War of 1870–1871. It deserves careful study because it highlights how central Europe was remade and the power of Prussia-Germany was greatly increased. ❶ What were the results of the Austro-Prussian War? Specifically, how did Prussia treat its neighbors in the north, such as Hanover and Saxony? ❷ What losses did Austria experience in 1866? ❸ What were the results of the Franco-Prussian War for France and for the predominately Catholic states of southern Germany, such as Bavaria and Württemberg?

Online Study Center Improve Your Grade
Interactive Map: Unification of Germany, 1866–1871

Proclaiming the German Empire, January 1871 This commemorative painting by Anton von Werner testifies to the nationalistic intoxication in Germany after the victory over France. William I of Prussia stands on a platform surrounded by princes and generals in the famous Hall of Mirrors in the palace of Versailles, while officers from all the units around a besieged Paris cheer and salute him with uplifted swords as emperor of a unified Germany. Bismarck, like a heroic white knight, stands between king and army. *(akg-images)*

years before 1914, the values of the aristocratic Prussian army officer increasingly replaced those of the middle-class liberal in public esteem and set the social standard.[1]

The Franco-Prussian War, 1870–1871

The final act in the drama of German unification followed quickly. Bismarck realized that a patriotic war with France would drive the south German states into his arms. The French obligingly played their part. The apparent issue—whether a distant relative of Prussia's William I (and France's Napoleon III) might become king of Spain—was only a diplomatic pretext. By 1870 the French leaders of the Second Empire, goaded by Bismarck and alarmed by their powerful new neighbor on the Rhine, had decided on a war to teach Prussia a lesson.

As soon as war against France began in 1870, Bismarck had the wholehearted support of the south German states. With other governments standing still—Bismarck's generosity to Austria in 1866 was paying big dividends—German forces under Prussian leadership decisively defeated the main French army at Sedan on September 1, 1870. Louis Napoleon himself was captured and humiliated. Three days later, French patriots in Paris proclaimed yet another French republic and vowed to continue fighting. But after five months, in January 1871, a starving Paris surrendered, and France went on to accept Bismarck's harsh peace terms. By this time, the south German states had agreed to join a new German Empire. The victorious William I was proclaimed emperor of Germany in the Hall of Mirrors in the palace of Versailles. Europe had a nineteenth-century German "sun king." As in the 1866 constitution, the king of Prussia and his ministers had ultimate power in the new German Empire, and the lower house of the legislature was elected by universal male suffrage.

Bismarck and the German Empire imposed a harsh peace on France. France was forced to pay a colossal indemnity of 5 billion francs and to cede the rich eastern province of Alsace and part of Lorraine to Germany. The German general staff asserted that this annexation would enhance military security, and German nationalists claimed that the Alsacians, who spoke a German dialect as well as French, wanted to rejoin the fatherland after more than two hundred years. But both cases were weak, and revenge for France's real and imagined aggression in the past was probably the decisive factor. In any event, French men and women of all classes viewed the seizure of Alsace and Lorraine as a terrible crime. They could never forget and never forgive, and thus relations between France and Germany after 1871 were tragically poisoned.

The Franco-Prussian War, which Europeans generally saw as a test of nations in a pitiless Darwinian struggle for existence, released an enormous surge of patriotic feeling in Germany. Bismarck's genius, the invincible Prussian army, the solidarity of king and people in a unified nation—these and similar themes were trumpeted endlessly during and after the war. The weakest of the Great Powers in 1862 (after Austria, Britain, France, and Russia), Prussia had become, with fortification by the other German states, the most powerful state in Europe in less than a decade. Most Germans were enormously proud, blissfully imagining themselves the fittest and best of the European species. Semi-authoritarian nationalism and a "new conservatism," which was based on an alliance of the propertied classes and sought the active support of the working classes, had triumphed in Germany.

Nation Building in the United States

- **In what ways did the United States experience the full drama of nation building?**

Closely linked to European developments in the nineteenth century, the United States experienced the full drama of bloody nation building. The "United" States was divided by slavery from its birth, as economic development in the young republic carried free and slaveholding states in very different directions. Northerners extended family farms westward and began building English-model factories in the Northeast. By 1850 an industrializing, urbanizing North was also building a system of canals and railroads and attracting most of the European immigrants. In sharp contrast, industry and cities did not develop in the South, and newcomers avoided the region. And even though three-quarters of all Southern white families were small farmers and owned no slaves in 1850, plantation owners holding twenty or more slaves dominated the economy and society. These profit-minded slave owners used gangs of black slaves to claim a vast new kingdom across the Deep South where cotton was king (see Map 25.3). By 1850, this kingdom produced 5 million bales a year and satisfied an apparently insatiable demand from textile mills in Europe and New England.

The rise of the cotton empire revitalized slave-based agriculture, spurred exports, and played a key role in igniting rapid U.S. economic growth. The large profits flowing from cotton also led influential Southerners to defend slavery. In doing so, Southern whites developed a strong cultural identity and came to see themselves as a closely knit "we" distinct from the Northern "they." Northern whites viewed their free-labor system as being no less economically and morally superior. Thus regional antagonisms intensified.

These antagonisms came to a climax after 1848 when a defeated Mexico ceded to the United States a vast area stretching from west Texas to the Pacific Ocean. Debate over the extension of slavery in this new territory caused attitudes to harden on both sides. In Abraham Lincoln's famous words, the United States was a "house divided" by slavery, contradictory economic systems, conflicting values, and regional loyalties.

Lincoln's election as president in 1860 gave Southern "fire-eaters" the chance they had been waiting for. Eventually eleven states left the Union, determined to win their own independence, and formed the Confederate States of America. When Southern troops fired on a Union fort in South Carolina's Charleston harbor, war began.

The long Civil War (1861–1865) was the bloodiest conflict in all of American history, but in the end the South was decisively defeated and the Union preserved. The vastly superior population, industry, and transportation of the North placed the South at a great, probably fatal, disadvantage. Yet less obvious factors tied to morale and national purpose were also extremely important. The enormous gap between the slave-owning elite and the poor whites also made it impossible for the South to build effectively on the

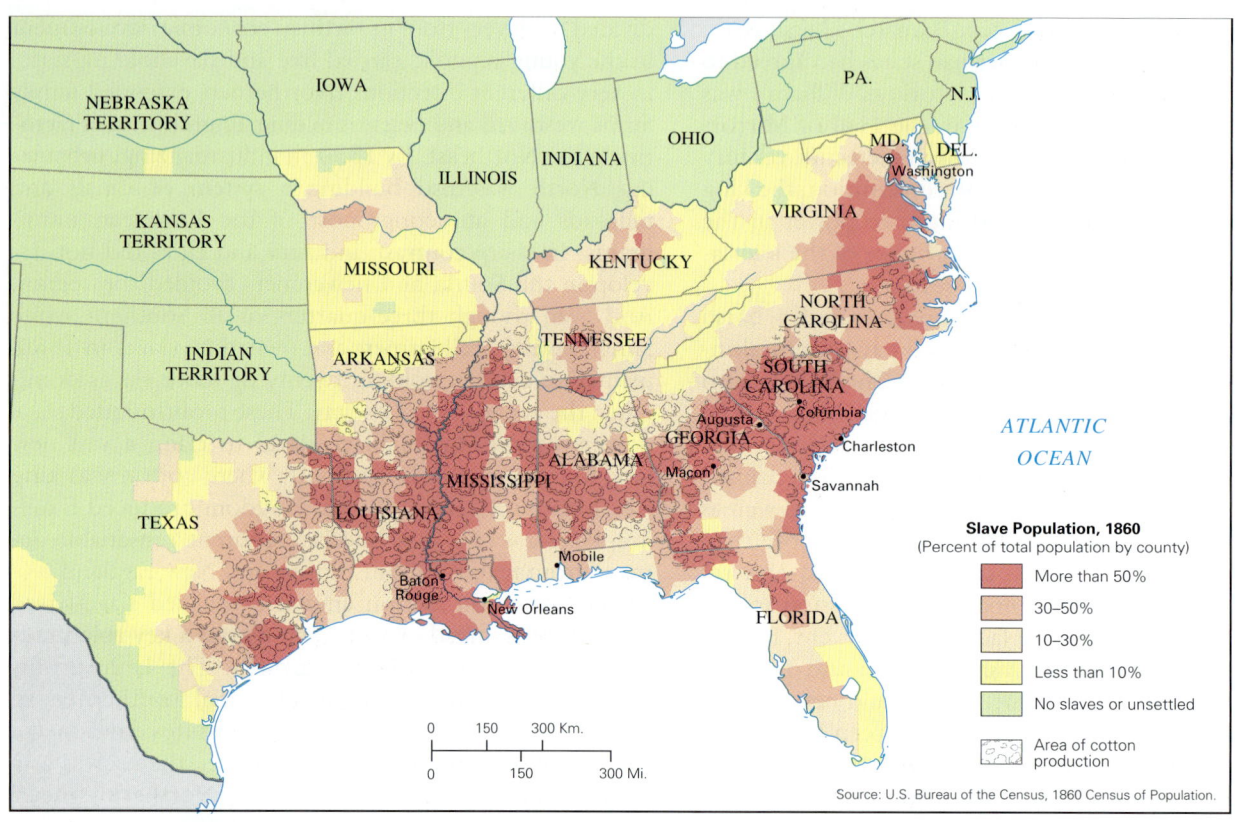

MAP 25.3 Slavery in the United States, 1860 This map illustrates the nation on the eve of the Civil War. Although many issues contributed to the developing opposition between North and South, slavery was the fundamental, enduring force that underlay all others. Lincoln's prediction, "I believe this government cannot endure permanently half slave and half free," tragically proved correct. (*Source: Carol Berkin et al.,* Making America: A History of the United States, *2d ed., p. 322. Copyright © 1999 by Houghton Mifflin Company. Reprinted with permission.*)

patriotism of 1861. As the war ground on, many ordinary whites felt that the burden was falling mainly on their shoulders as big planters resisted taxation and used loopholes to avoid the draft. Desertions from Southern armies mounted rapidly from 1863 on as soldiers became disillusioned.

In the North, by contrast, many people prospered during the war years. Enthusiasm remained high, and certain dominant characteristics of American life and national culture took shape. Powerful business corporations emerged, steadfastly supported by the Republican Party during and after the war. The **Homestead Act** of 1862, which gave western land to settlers, and the Thirteenth Amendment of 1865, which ended slavery, reinforced the concept of free labor taking its chances in a market economy. Finally, the success of Lincoln and the North in holding the Union together seemed to confirm that the "manifest destiny" of the United States was indeed to straddle a continent as a great world power. Thus a new American nationalism grew out of the war to prevent the realization of Southern nationhood.

Online Study Center Improve Your Grade
Primary Source: "Four Score and Seven Years Ago . . ."

The Modernization of Russia and the Ottoman Empire

The Russian and the Ottoman empires also experienced profound political crises in the mid-nineteenth century. These crises were unlike those occurring in Italy and Germany, for neither Russia nor the Ottoman Empire aspired to build a single powerful state out of a jumble of principalities. Both empires were already vast multinational states, built on long traditions of military conquest and absolutist rule by elites from the dominant ethnic groups—the Russians and the Ottoman Turks. In the early nineteenth century these governing elites in both states were strongly opposed to representative government and national self-determination, and they continued to concentrate on absolutist rule and competition with other Great Powers.

For both states relentless power politics led to serious trouble. It became clear to the leaders of both empires that they had to embrace the process of **modernization,** defined narrowly and usefully as the changes that enable a country to compete effectively with the leading countries at a given time. This limited conception of modernization fits Russia after the Crimean War particularly well, and it helps explain developments in the Ottoman Empire.

- *What steps did Russia and the Ottoman Turks take toward modernization, and how successful were they?*

The "Great Reforms"

In the 1850s, Russia was a poor agrarian society with a rapidly growing population. Industry was little developed, and almost 90 percent of the population lived off the land. Agricultural techniques were backward, and serfdom was still the basic social institution. Bound to the lord on a hereditary basis, the peasant serf was little more than a slave. Serfs were obliged to furnish labor services or money payments as the lord saw fit. Moreover, the lord could choose freely among the serfs for army recruits, who had to serve for twenty-five years, and he could punish a serf with deportation to Siberia. Sexual exploitation of female serfs by their lords was common.

Serfdom had become the great moral and political issue for the government by the 1840s. Then the Crimean War of 1853 to 1856, arising out of a dispute with France over who should protect certain Christian shrines in the Ottoman Empire, brought crisis. Because the fighting was concentrated in the Crimean peninsula on the Black Sea, Russia's transportation network of rivers and wagons failed to supply the distant Russian armies adequately. France and Great Britain, aided by Sardinia and the Ottoman Empire, inflicted a humiliating defeat on Russia.

This military defeat marked a turning point in Russian history because it demonstrated that Russia had fallen behind the rapidly industrializing nations of western Europe in many areas. At the very least, Russia needed railroads, better armaments, and reorganization of the army if it was to maintain its international position. Moreover, the disastrous war had caused hardship and raised the specter of massive peasant rebellion. Reform of serfdom was imperative. Military disaster thus forced Alexander II (r. 1855–1881) and his ministers along the path of rapid social change and general modernization.

The first and greatest of the reforms was the freeing of the serfs in 1861. Human bondage was abolished forever, and the emancipated peasants received, on average, about half of the land. Yet they had to pay fairly high prices for their land, and because the land was owned collectively, each peasant village was jointly responsible for the payments of all the families in the village. Collective ownership and responsibility made it very difficult for individual peasants to improve agricultural methods or leave their villages. Thus old patterns of behavior predominated, and the effects of reform were limited.

Most of the later reforms were also halfway measures. In 1864 the government established a new institution of local government, the **zemstvo.** Members of this local assembly were elected by a three-class system of towns, peasant villages, and noble landowners. A zemstvo executive council dealt with local problems. Russian liberals hoped that this reform would lead to an elected national parliament, but they were soon disappointed. The local zemstvo remained subordinate to the traditional bureaucracy and the local nobility. More successful was reform of the legal system, which established independent courts and equality before the law. Education and policies toward Russian Jews were also liberalized somewhat, and censorship was relaxed but not removed.

Until the twentieth century, Russia's greatest strides toward modernization were economic rather than political. Industry and transport, both so vital to the military, were transformed in two industrial surges. The first of these came after 1860. The government encouraged and subsidized private railway companies, and construction boomed. In 1860 the empire had only about 1,250 miles of railroads; by 1880 it had about 15,500 miles. The railroads enabled agricultural Russia to export grain and thus earn money for further industrialization. Industrial suburbs grew up around Moscow and St. Petersburg, and a class of modern factory workers began to take shape.

Industrial development strengthened Russia's military forces and gave rise to territorial expansion to the south and east. Imperial expansion greatly excited many ardent Russian nationalists and superpatriots, who became some of the government's most enthusiastic supporters. Industrial development also contributed mightily to the spread of Marxian thought and the transformation of the Russian revolutionary movement after 1890.

In 1881 Alexander II was assassinated by a small group of terrorists. The era of reform came to an abrupt end, for the new tsar, Alexander III (r. 1881–1894), was a determined reactionary. Nevertheless, economic modernization

The Fruits of Terrorism, 1881 In the late 1870s a small group of revolutionaries believed that killing the tsar could destroy the Russian state. Succeeding in blowing up the reforming Alexander II after several near misses, the five assassins, including one woman, were quickly caught and hanged. Russia entered an era of reaction and harsh authoritarian rule. *(Visual Connection Archive)*

sped forward in the massive industrial surge of the 1890s. Nationalism played a decisive role, as it had after the Crimean War. The key leader was Sergei Witte, the tough, competent minister of finance from 1892 to 1903. Inspired by the writings of Friedrich List (see pages 731–732), Witte believed that the harsh reality of industrial backwardness was threatening Russia's power and greatness.

Therefore, under Witte's leadership the government built state-owned railroads rapidly, doubling the network to thirty-five thousand miles by the end of the century. Witte established high protective tariffs to build Russian industry, and he put the country on the gold standard of the "civilized world" in order to strengthen Russian finances.

Witte's greatest innovation was to use the West to catch up with the West. He aggressively encouraged foreigners to build great factories in backward Russia, and this policy was brilliantly successful, especially in southern Russia. There, in eastern Ukraine, foreign capitalists and their engineers built an enormous and very modern steel and coal industry.[2] In 1900 peasants still constituted the great majority of the population, but a fiercely autocratic and independent Russia was industrializing and catching up with the advanced nations of the West.

The Revolution of 1905

Catching up partly meant vigorous territorial expansion, for this was the age of Western imperialism. By 1903 Russia had established a sphere of influence in Chinese Manchuria and was casting greedy eyes on northern Korea. When the diplomatic protests of equally imperialistic Japan were ignored, the Japanese launched a surprise attack in February 1904. To the amazement of self-confident Europeans, Japan scored repeated victories, and Russia was forced in September 1905 to accept a humiliating defeat.

As is often the case, military disaster abroad brought political upheaval at home. The business and professional classes had long wanted to match economic with political modernization. Their minimal goal was to turn the last of Europe's absolutist monarchies into a liberal, representative regime. Factory workers, strategically concentrated in the large cities, had all the grievances of early industrialization and were organized in a radical and still illegal labor movement. Peasants had gained little from the era of reforms and were suffering from poverty and overpopulation. At the same time, nationalist sentiment was emerging among the empire's minorities. The politically and culturally dominant ethnic Russians were only about 45 percent of the population, and by 1900 some intellectuals among the subject nationalities were calling for self-rule and autonomy. Separatist nationalism was strongest among the Poles and Ukrainians. With the army pinned down in Manchuria, all these currents of discontent converged in the **revolution of 1905.**

The beginning of the revolution pointed up the incompetence of the government. On a Sunday in January 1905, a massive crowd of workers and their families converged peacefully on the Winter Palace in St. Petersburg to present a petition to the tsar. Suddenly troops opened fire, killing and wounding hundreds. The **Bloody Sunday** massacre turned ordinary workers against the tsar and produced a wave of general indignation.

Outlawed political parties came out into the open, and by the summer of 1905 strikes, peasant uprisings, revolts among minority nationalities, and troop mutinies were sweeping the country. The revolutionary surge culminated in October 1905 in a great paralyzing general strike, which forced the government to capitulate. The tsar issued the **October Manifesto,** which granted full civil rights and promised a popularly elected Duma (parliament) with real legislative power. The manifesto split the opposition. Frightened middle-class leaders helped the government repress the uprising and survive as a constitutional monarchy.

On the eve of the opening of the first **Duma** in May 1906, the government issued the new constitution, the Fundamental Laws. The tsar retained great powers. The Duma, elected indirectly by universal male suffrage, and a largely appointive upper house could debate and pass laws, but the tsar had an absolute veto. As in Bismarck's Germany, the emperor appointed his ministers, who did not need to command a majority in the Duma.

The disappointed, predominantly middle-class liberals, the largest group in the newly elected Duma, saw the Fundamental Laws as a step backward. Efforts to cooperate with the tsar's ministers soon broke down. After months of deadlock, the tsar dismissed the Duma. Thereupon he and his reactionary advisers unilaterally rewrote the electoral law so as to increase greatly the weight of the propertied classes at the expense of workers, peasants, and national minorities.

The new law had the intended effect. With landowners assured half the seats in the Duma, the government secured a loyal majority in 1907 and again in 1912. Thus armed, the tough, energetic chief minister, Peter Stolypin, pushed through important agrarian reforms designed to break down collective village ownership of land and encourage the more enterprising peasants—his "wager on the strong." In 1914, Russia was partially modernized, a conservative constitutional monarchy with a peasant-based but industrializing economy.

Decline and Reform in the Ottoman Empire

Although the Ottoman Empire began to decline slowly after reaching its high point of development under Suleiman the Magnificent in the sixteenth century, the Ottomans began in the eighteenth century to fall rapidly behind western Europe in science, industrial skill, and military technology. At the same time, Russia's powerful westernized army pushed southward, overrunning and occupying Ottoman provinces on the Danube River. The danger that the Great Powers of Europe would gradually conquer the Ottoman Empire and divide up its vast territories was real.

Caught up in the Napoleonic wars and losing more territory to Russia, the Ottomans were forced in 1816 to grant Serbia local autonomy. In 1830, the Greeks won their national independence, while French armies began their long and bloody conquest of the Arabic-speaking province of Algeria (see pages 776–777). French efforts to strip Algerians of their culture and identity were brutal and persistent, eventually resulting in one of Africa's most bitter anticolonial struggles after 1945.

Ottoman weakness reflected the decline of the sultan's "slave army," the so-called **janissary corps.** In the sixteenth century the Ottoman sultans levied an annual slave tax of one thousand to three thousand male children on the conquered Christian provinces in the Balkans. The boys and other slaves were raised in Turkey as Muslims, were trained to fight and administer, and joined the elite corps of the Ottoman infantry. With time, however, the janissaries became a corrupt and privileged hereditary caste. A transformation of the army was absolutely necessary to battle the Europeans more effectively, as well as to enhance the sultanate's authority within the empire.

The reform-minded Mahmud III (r. 1808–1839) proceeded cautiously, picking loyal officers and building up his dependable artillery corps. In 1826 his council ordered the janissaries to drill in the European manner. As expected, the janissaries revolted and charged the palace, where they were mowed down by the waiting artillery corps.

The destruction of the janissaries cleared the way for building a new army, but it came too late to stop the rise of Muhammad Ali, the Ottoman governor in Egypt (see pages 853–854). In 1831, and again in 1839, his French-trained forces occupied the Ottoman provinces of Syria and then Iraq and appeared ready to depose Mahmud II. The Ottoman sultan survived, but only because the European powers forced Muhammad Ali to withdraw. The European powers, minus France, preferred a weak and dependent Ottoman state to a strong and revitalized Muslim entity under a dynamic leader such as Muhammad Ali.

Realizing their precarious position, liberal Ottoman statesmen launched in 1839 an era of radical reforms, which lasted with fits and starts until 1876 and culminated in a constitution and a short-lived parliament. Known as the **Tanzimat** (literally, regulations or orders), these reforms were designed to remake the empire on a

Pasha Halim Receiving Archduke Maximilian of Austria As this painting suggests, Ottoman leaders became well versed in European languages and culture. They also mastered the game of power politics, playing one European state off against another and securing the Ottoman Empire's survival. The black servants on the right may be slaves from Sudan. *(Miramare Palace Trieste/Dagli Orti/The Art Archive)*

western European model. New decrees called for the equality of Muslims, Christians, and Jews before the law and a modernized administration and military. New commercial laws allowed free importation of foreign goods and permitted foreign merchants to operate freely throughout the empire. Of great importance for later developments, growing numbers among the elite and the upwardly mobile embraced Western education and accepted secular values to some extent.

Intended to bring revolutionary modernization such as that experienced by Japan in the Meiji era (see pages 870–872), the Tanzimat permitted partial recovery but fell short of its goals for several reasons. First, the liberal reforms failed to halt the growth of nationalism among Christian subjects in the Balkans (see Chapter 29), which resulted in crises and defeats that undermined all reform efforts. Second, the Ottoman initiatives did not curtail the appetite of Western imperialism, which secured a stranglehold on the Ottoman economy.

Finally, equality before the law for all citizens and religious communities actually increased religious disputes, which were in turn exacerbated by the relentless interference of the European powers. This development embittered relations between the religious communities, distracted the government from its reform mission, and split Muslims into secularists and religious conservatives. These Islamic conservatives became the most dependable support of Sultan Abdülhamid (r. 1876–1909), who abandoned the model of European liberalism in his long and repressive reign.

The combination of declining international power and conservative tyranny eventually led to a powerful resurgence of the modernizing impulse among idealistic Turkish exiles in Europe and young army officers in Istanbul. These fervent patriots, the so-called **Young Turks,** seized power in the revolution of 1908, and they forced the sultan to implement reforms. Failing to stop the rising tide of anti-Ottoman nationalism in the Balkans, the Young Turks helped prepare the way for the birth of modern secular Turkey after the defeat and collapse of the Ottoman Empire in World War I (see pages 889–890).

The Responsive National State, 1871–1914

For central and western Europe, the unification of Italy and Germany by "blood and iron" marked the end of a dramatic period of nation building. After 1871 the heartland of Europe was organized into strong national states. Only on the borders of Europe—in Ireland and Russia, in Austria-Hungary and the Ottoman Empire—did subject peoples still strive for political unity and independence.

- *Why after 1871 did ordinary citizens feel a growing loyalty to their governments?*

General Trends

Despite some major differences between countries, European domestic politics after 1871 had a common framework, the firmly established national state. The common themes within that framework were the emergence of mass politics and growing mass loyalty toward the national state.

For good reason, ordinary people—the masses of an industrializing, urbanizing society—felt increasing loyalty to their governments. More people could vote. By 1914 universal male suffrage had become the rule rather than the exception. This development had as much psychological as political significance. Ordinary men were no longer denied the right to vote because they lacked wealth or education. They felt that they counted; they could influence the government to some extent. They were becoming "part of the system."

Women also began to demand the right to vote. The women's suffrage movement achieved its first success in the western United States, and by 1913 women could vote in twelve states. Europe, too, moved slowly in this direction. In 1914 Norway gave the vote to most women. Elsewhere, women such as the English Emmeline Pankhurst were very militant in their demands. They heckled politicians and held public demonstrations. These efforts generally failed before 1914, but they prepared the way for the triumph of the women's suffrage movement immediately after World War I.

As the right to vote spread, politicians and parties in national parliaments represented the people more responsively. The multiparty system prevailing in most countries meant that parliamentary majorities were built on shifting coalitions of different parties, and this gave individual parties leverage to obtain benefits for their supporters. Governments also passed laws to alleviate general problems, thereby acquiring greater legitimacy and appearing more worthy of support.

There was a less positive side to building support for strong nation-states after 1871. Governments found that they could manipulate national feeling to create a sense of unity and to divert attention away from underlying class conflicts. Conservative and moderate leaders found that workers who voted socialist would rally around the flag in a diplomatic crisis or cheer when distant territory of

"Votes for Women!" The long-simmering campaign for women's suffrage in England came to a rapid boil after 1903, as militants took to the streets, disrupted political meetings, and tried to storm Parliament. Manhandled by the police and often jailed, some activists responded by damaging public property and going on hunger strikes in prison. This 1908 illustration shows demonstrators giving a hero's welcome to Mary Leigh, the first suffragette imprisoned for property damage after she threw rocks through the windows of the prime minister's house. *(The Art Archive)*

doubtful value was seized in Africa or Asia (see Chapter 26). Therefore, after 1871 governing elites frequently used antiliberal and militaristic policies to help manage domestic conflicts, but at the expense of increasing the international tensions that erupted in 1914 in cataclysmic war and revolution (see Chapter 27).

In these same years some fanatics and demagogic political leaders also sought to build extreme nationalist movements by whipping up popular animosity toward imaginary enemies, especially the Jews. The growth of modern anti-Semitism after 1880 epitomized the most negative aspects of European nationalism before the First World War.

The German Empire

Politics in Germany after 1871 reflected many of the general developments. The new German Empire was a federal union of Prussia and twenty-four smaller states. Much of the everyday business of government was conducted by the separate states, but there was a strong national government with a chancellor—until 1890, Bismarck—and a popularly elected lower house, called the **Reichstag.** Although Bismarck refused to be bound by a parliamentary majority, he tried nonetheless to maintain one. This situation gave the political parties opportunities. Until 1878 Bismarck relied mainly on the National Liberals, who had rallied to him after 1866. They supported legislation useful for further economic and legal unification of the country.

Less wisely, they backed Bismarck's attack on the Catholic Church, the so-called **Kulturkampf,** or "struggle for civilization." Like Bismarck, the middle-class National Liberals were particularly alarmed by Pius IX's declaration of papal infallibility in 1870. That dogma seemed to ask German Catholics to put loyalty to their church above loyalty to their nation. Only in Protestant Prussia did the Kulturkampf have even limited success. Catholics throughout the country generally voted for the Catholic Center Party, which blocked passage of national laws hostile to the church. Finally, in 1878 Bismarck abandoned his attack. Indeed, he and the Catholic Center Party entered into an uneasy but mutually advantageous alliance. Their reasons for doing so were largely economic.

Bismarck moved to enact high tariffs on cheap grain from the United States, Canada, and Russia, against which less efficient European producers could not compete. This won over not only the Catholic Center, whose supporters were small farmers in western and southern Germany, but also the Protestant Junkers, who had large landholdings in the east. With the tariffs, then, Bismarck won Catholic and conservative support.

Bismarck had been looking for a way to increase taxes, and the solution he chose was higher tariffs. Many other governments acted similarly. The 1880s and 1890s saw a widespread return to protectionism. France, in particular, established very high tariffs to protect agriculture and industry, peasants and manufacturers, from foreign competition. Thus the German government and other governments responded effectively to a major economic problem and won greater loyalty. The general rise of protectionism in this period was also an outstanding example of the dangers of self-centered nationalism: new tariffs led to international name-calling and nasty trade wars.

As for socialism, Bismarck tried to stop its growth in Germany because he genuinely feared its revolutionary language and allegiance to a movement transcending the nation-state. In 1878, after two attempts on the life of William I by radicals (though not socialists), Bismarck used a carefully orchestrated national outcry to ram through the Reichstag a law that strictly controlled socialist meetings and publications and outlawed the Social Democratic Party, which was thereby driven underground. However, German socialists displayed a discipline and organization worthy of the Prussian army itself. Bismarck decided to try another tack.

Thus Bismarck's essentially conservative nation-state pioneered with social measures designed to win the support of working-class people. In 1883 he pushed through the Reichstag the first of several modern social security laws to help wage earners. The laws of 1883 and 1884 established national sickness and accident insurance; the law of 1889 established old-age pensions and retirement benefits. Henceforth sick, injured, and retired workers could look forward to some regular benefits from the state. This national social security system, paid for through compulsory contributions by wage earners and employers as well as grants from the state, was the first of its kind anywhere. Bismarck's social security system did not wean workers from voting socialist, but it did give them a small stake in the system and protect them from some of the uncertainties of the complex urban industrial world. This enormously significant development was a product of political competition and government efforts to win popular support.

Online Study Center Improve Your Grade
Primary Source: The Welfare State Is Born

Increasingly, the great issues in German domestic politics were socialism and the Marxian Social Democratic Party. In 1890 the new emperor, the young, idealistic, and unstable William II (r. 1888–1918), opposed Bismarck's attempt to renew the law outlawing the Social Democratic Party. Eager to rule in his own right and to earn the support of the workers, William II forced Bismarck to resign. After the "dropping of the pilot," German foreign policy changed profoundly and mostly for the worse, but the government did pass new laws to aid workers and to legalize socialist political activity.

Yet William II was no more successful than Bismarck in getting workers to renounce socialism. Indeed, socialist ideas spread rapidly, and more and more Social Democrats were elected to the Reichstag in the 1890s. After opposing a colonial war in German Southwest Africa in 1906 that led to important losses in the general elections of 1907, the German Social Democratic Party broadened its base and adopted a more patriotic tone. In 1912 the party scored a great electoral victory, becoming the largest single party in the Reichstag. This victory shocked aristocrats and their wealthy conservative middle-class allies, heightening the fears of an impending socialist upheaval in both groups. Yet the "revolutionary" socialists were actually becoming less radical in Germany. In the years before World War I, the strength of socialist opposition to greater military spending and imperialist expansion declined substantially, for example. German socialists identified increasingly with the German state, and they concentrated on gradual social and political reform.

Republican France

Although Napoleon III's reign made some progress in reducing antagonisms between classes, the war with Prussia undid these efforts, and in 1871 France seemed hopelessly divided once again. The patriotic republicans who proclaimed the Third Republic in Paris after the military disaster at Sedan refused to admit defeat. They defended Paris with great heroism for weeks, living off rats and zoo animals until they were starved into submission by German armies in January 1871. When national elections then sent a large majority of conservatives and monarchists to the National Assembly and France's new leaders decided they had no choice but to surrender Alsace and Lorraine to Germany, the traumatized Parisians exploded in patriotic frustration and proclaimed the Paris Commune in March 1871. Vaguely radical, the leaders of the Commune wanted to govern Paris without interference from the conservative French countryside. The National Assembly, led by aging politician Adolphe Thiers, would hear none of it. The Assembly ordered the French army into Paris and brutally crushed the Commune. Twenty thousand people died in the fighting. As in June 1848, it was Paris against the provinces, French against French.

Out of this tragedy, France slowly formed a new national unity, achieving considerable stability before 1914.

How is one to account for this? Luck played a part. Until 1875 the monarchists in the "republican" National Assembly had a majority but could not agree who should be king. The compromise Bourbon candidate refused to rule except under the white flag of his ancestors—a completely unacceptable condition. In the meantime, Thiers's destruction of the radical Commune and his other firm measures showed the fearful provinces and the middle class that the Third Republic might be moderate and socially conservative. France therefore retained the republic, though reluctantly. As President Thiers cautiously said, this was "the government which divides us least."

Another stabilizing factor was the skill and determination of the moderate republican leaders in the early years. The most famous of these was Léon Gambetta, the son of an Italian grocer, a warm, easygoing, unsuccessful lawyer who had turned professional politician. By 1879 the great majority of members of both the upper and the lower houses of the National Assembly were republicans, and the Third Republic had firm foundations after almost a decade.

The moderate republicans sought to preserve their creation by winning the hearts and minds of the next generation. Trade unions were fully legalized, and France acquired a colonial empire. More important, a series of laws between 1879 and 1886 established free compulsory elementary education for both girls and boys. At the same time, they greatly expanded the state system of public tax-supported schools. In France and elsewhere the general expansion of public education served as a critical nation-building tool throughout the Western world in the late nineteenth century. In France most elementary and much secondary education had traditionally been in the parochial schools of the Catholic Church, which had long been hostile to republics and to much of secular life. Free compulsory elementary education in France became secular republican education.

Although the educational reforms of the 1880s disturbed French Catholics, many of them rallied to the republic in the 1890s. The limited acceptance of the modern world by the more liberal Pope Leo XIII (1878–1903) eased tensions between church and state. Unfortunately, the **Dreyfus affair** changed all that.

Captain Alfred Dreyfus Leaving an 1899 reconsideration of his original court martial, Dreyfus receives an insulting "guard of dishonor" from soldiers whose backs are turned. Top army leaders were determined to brand Dreyfus a traitor. *(Roger-Viollet/Getty Images)*

Alfred Dreyfus, a Jewish captain in the French army, was falsely accused and convicted of treason. His family never doubted his innocence and fought to reopen the case, enlisting the support of prominent republicans and intellectuals such as novelist Emile Zola. In 1898 and 1899, the case split France apart. On one side was the army, which had manufactured evidence against Dreyfus, joined by anti-Semites and most of the Catholic establishment. On the other side stood the civil libertarians and most of the more radical republicans.

Online Study Center Improve Your Grade
Primary Source: "J'Accuse" the French Army

This battle, which eventually led to Dreyfus's being declared innocent, revived republican feeling against the church. Between 1901 and 1905, the government severed all ties between the state and the Catholic Church after centuries of close relations. The salaries of priests and bishops were no longer paid by the government, and all churches were given to local committees of lay Catholics. Catholic schools were put on their own financially and soon lost a third of their students. The state school system's power of indoctrination was greatly strengthened. In France only the growing socialist movement, with its very different and thoroughly secular ideology, stood in opposition to patriotic, republican nationalism.

Great Britain and Ireland

Britain in the late nineteenth century has often been seen as a shining example of peaceful and successful political evolution, where an effective two-party parliament skillfully guided the country from classical liberalism to full-fledged democracy with hardly a misstep. This view of Great Britain is not so much wrong as it is incomplete. After the right to vote was granted to males of the solid middle class in 1832, opinion leaders and politicians wrestled with the uncertainties of a further expansion of the franchise. In 1867 Benjamin Disraeli and the Conservatives extended the vote to all middle-class males and the best-paid workers in the Second Reform Bill, in order to broaden the Conservative Party's traditional base of aristocratic and landed support. After 1867 English political parties and electoral campaigns became more modern, and the "lower orders" appeared to vote as responsibly as their "betters." Hence the Third Reform Bill of 1884 gave the vote to almost every adult male.

While the House of Commons was drifting toward democracy, the House of Lords was content to slumber nobly. Between 1901 and 1910, however, that bastion of aristocratic conservatism tried to reassert itself. Acting as supreme court of the land, it ruled against labor unions in two important decisions. And after the Liberal Party came to power in 1906, the Lords vetoed several measures passed by the Commons, including the so-called **People's Budget,** which was designed to increase spending on social welfare services. The Lords finally capitulated, as they had done in 1832, when the king threatened to create enough new peers to pass the bill.

Aristocratic conservatism yielded to popular democracy once and for all. The result was that extensive social welfare measures, slow to come to Great Britain, were passed in a spectacular rush between 1906 and 1914. During those years, the Liberal Party, inspired by the fiery Welshman David Lloyd George (1863–1945), substantially raised taxes on the rich as part of the People's Budget. This income helped the government pay for national health insurance, unemployment benefits, old-age pensions, and a host of other social measures. The state was integrating the urban masses socially as well as politically.

This record of accomplishment was only part of the story, however. On the eve of World War I, the unanswered question of Ireland brought Great Britain to the brink of civil war. The terrible Irish famine fueled an Irish revolutionary movement. Thereafter, the English slowly granted concessions, such as the abolition of the privileges of the Anglican Church and rights for Irish peasants. Liberal prime minister William Gladstone (1809–1898), who had proclaimed twenty years earlier that "my mission is to pacify Ireland," introduced bills to give Ireland self-government in 1886 and in 1893. They failed to pass. After two decades of relative quiet, Irish nationalists in the British Parliament saw their chance. They supported the Liberals in their battle for the People's Budget and received a home-rule bill for Ireland in return.

Thus Ireland, the emerald isle, was on the brink of achieving self-government. Yet Ireland was composed of two peoples. As much as the Irish Catholic majority in the southern counties wanted home rule, precisely that much did the Irish Protestants of the northern counties of Ulster come to oppose it. Motivated by the accumulated fears and hostilities of generations, the Protestants of Ulster refused to submerge themselves in a Catholic Ireland, just as Irish Catholics had refused to submit to a Protestant Britain.

The Ulsterites vowed to resist home rule in northern Ireland. By December 1913 they had raised 100,000 armed volunteers, and they were supported by much of English public opinion. Thus in 1914 the Liberals in the House of Lords introduced a compromise home-rule bill that did not apply to the northern counties. This bill, feeling. Though Great Britain had much going for it—power, Parliament, prosperity—none of these availed in the face of the conflicting nationalisms created by Catholics and Protestants in northern Ireland. Similarly, progressive Sweden was powerless to stop the growth of the Norwegian national movement, which culminated in Norway's breaking away from Sweden and becoming a fully independent nation in 1905. In this light, one can also see how hopeless was the case of the Ottoman Empire in Europe in the later nineteenth century. It was only a matter of time before the Serbs, Bulgarians, and Romanians would break away, and they did.

The Austro-Hungarian Empire

The dilemma of conflicting nationalisms in Ireland also helps one appreciate how desperate the situation in the Austro-Hungarian Empire had become by the early twentieth century. In 1849 Magyar nationalism had driven Hungarian patriots to declare an independent Hungarian republic, which was savagely crushed by Russian and Austrian armies (see page 772). Throughout the 1850s, Hungary was ruled as a conquered territory, and Emperor Francis Joseph and his bureaucracy tried hard to centralize the state and Germanize the language and culture of the different nationalities.

Then in the wake of defeat by Prussia in 1866, a weakened Austria was forced to strike a compromise and establish the so-called dual monarchy. The empire was divided in two, and the nationalistic Magyars gained virtual independence for Hungary. Henceforth each half of the empire agreed to deal with its own "barbarians"—its own minorities—as it saw fit. The two states were joined only by a shared monarch and common ministries for finance, defense, and foreign affairs.

In Austria ethnic Germans were only one-third of the population, and in 1895 many Germans saw their traditional dominance threatened by Czechs, Poles, and other Slavs. A particularly emotional issue in the Austrian parliament was the language used in government and elementary education at the local level. From 1900 to 1914 the parliament was so divided that ministries generally could not obtain a majority and ruled instead by decree. Efforts by both conservatives and socialists to defuse national antagonisms by stressing economic issues that cut across ethnic lines were largely unsuccessful.

In Hungary the Magyar nobility in 1867 restored the constitution of 1848 and used it to dominate both the Magyar peasantry and the minority populations until 1914. Only the wealthiest one-fourth of adult males had the right to vote, making the parliament the creature of

"No Home Rule" Posters like this one helped to foment pro-British, anti-Catholic sentiment in the northern Irish counties of Ulster before the First World War. The rifle raised defiantly and the accompanying rhyme are a thinly veiled threat of armed rebellion and civil war. *(Reproduced with the kind permission of the Trustees of the National Museums & Galleries of Northern Ireland. Photograph © Ulster Museum, Belfast)*

which openly betrayed promises made to Irish nationalists, was rejected, and in September the original home-rule bill was passed but simultaneously suspended for the duration of the hostilities—the momentous Irish question had been overtaken by an earth-shattering world war in August 1914.

Irish developments illustrated once again the power of national feeling and national movements in the nineteenth century. Moreover, they were proof that governments could not elicit greater loyalty unless they could capture and control that elemental current of national the Magyar elite. Laws promoting the use of the Magyar (Hungarian) language in schools and government were rammed through and bitterly resented, especially by the Croatians and Romanians. While Magyar extremists campaigned loudly for total separation from Austria, the radical leaders of the subject nationalities dreamed in turn of independence from Hungary. Unlike most major countries, which harnessed nationalism to strengthen the state after 1871, the Austro-Hungarian Empire was progressively weakened and destroyed by it.

Jewish Emancipation and Modern Anti-Semitism

Revolutionary changes in political principles and the triumph of the nation-state brought equally revolutionary changes in Jewish life in western and central Europe. Beginning in France in 1791, Jews gradually gained their civil rights, although the process was slow and uneven. The decisive turning point came in 1848, when Jews formed part of the revolutionary vanguard in Vienna and Berlin and the Frankfurt Assembly endorsed full rights for German Jews. Important gains in 1848 survived the conservative reaction, and throughout the 1850s and 1860s liberals in Austria, Italy, and Prussia pressed successfully for legal equality. In 1871 the constitution of the new German Empire consolidated the process of Jewish emancipation in central Europe. It abolished all restrictions on Jewish marriage, choice of occupation, place of residence, and property ownership. Exclusion from government employment and discrimination in social relations remained. However, according to one leading historian, by 1871 "it was widely accepted in Central Europe that the gradual disappearance of anti-Jewish prejudice was inevitable."[3]

The process of emancipation presented Jews with challenges and opportunities. Traditional Jewish occupations, such as court financial agent, village moneylender, and peddler, were undermined by free-market reforms, but careers in business, the professions, and the arts were opening to Jewish talent. Many Jews responded energetically and successfully. Active in finance and railroad building, European Jews excelled in wholesale and retail trade, consumer industries, journalism, medicine, and law. By 1871 a majority of Jewish people in western and central Europe had improved their economic situation and entered the middle classes. Most Jewish people also identified strongly with their respective nation-states and with good reason saw themselves as patriotic citizens.

Vicious anti-Semitism reappeared after the stock market crash of 1873, beginning in central Europe. Drawing on long traditions of religious intolerance, ghetto exclusion, and periodic anti-Jewish riots and expulsions, this anti-Semitism was also a modern development. It built on the general reaction against liberalism and its economic and political policies. Modern anti-Semitism whipped up resentment against Jewish achievement and Jewish "financial control," while fanatics claimed that the Jewish race (rather than the Jewish religion) posed a biological threat to the German people. Anti-Semitic beliefs were particularly popular among conservatives, extremist nationalists, and people who felt threatened by Jewish competition, such as small shopkeepers, officeworkers, and professionals.

Anti-Semites also created modern political parties to attack and degrade Jews. In 1893, the prewar electoral high

Edmond de Rothschild Visits Palestine Born into the French branch of modern Europe's most famous banking family, Baron Edmond de Rothschild played an important role in early Jewish settlements in the Ottoman province of Palestine. Beginning in the 1880s, Rothschild purchased large tracts of land from Arab landowners, and on several occasions he visited the Jewish colonists that he continued to support. Seen here in a long coat on a Turkish train, he is flanked by Ottoman officials. *(Courtesy, Central Zionist Archive, Jerusalem)*

point in Germany, small anti-Semitic parties secured 2.9 percent of the votes cast. However, in Austrian Vienna in the early 1890s, Karl Lueger and his "Christian socialists" won striking electoral victories, spurring Theodor Herzl to turn from German nationalism and advocate political **Zionism** and the creation of a Jewish state. (See the feature "Individuals in Society: Theodor Herzl.") Lueger, the popular mayor of Vienna from 1897 to 1910, combined fierce anti-Semitic rhetoric with municipal ownership of basic services, and he appealed especially to the German-speaking lower middle class—and an unsuccessful young artist named Adolf Hitler.

Before 1914 anti-Semitism was most oppressive in eastern Europe, where Jews also suffered from terrible poverty. In the Russian empire, where there was no Jewish emancipation and 4 million of Europe's 7 million Jewish people lived in 1880, officials used anti-Semitism to channel popular discontent away from the government and onto the Jewish minority. Russian Jews were denounced as foreign exploiters who corrupted national traditions, and in 1881–1882 a wave of violent pogroms commenced in southern Russia. The police and the army stood aside for days while peasants looted and destroyed Jewish property. Official harassment continued in the following decades, and quotas were placed on Jewish residency, education, and participation in the professions. As a result, some Russian Jews turned toward self-emancipation and the vision of a Zionist settlement in Palestine. Large numbers also emigrated to western Europe and the United States. About 2.75 million Jews left eastern Europe between 1881 and 1914.

Online Study Center **Improve Your Grade**
Primary Source: A Russian Zionist Makes the Case for a Jewish Homeland

Marxism and the Socialist Movement

Nationalism served, for better or worse, as a new unifying principle. But what about socialism? Socialist parties, which were generally Marxian parties dedicated to an international proletarian revolution, grew rapidly in these years. Did this mean that national states had failed to gain the support of workers? Certainly, many prosperous and conservative citizens were greatly troubled by the socialist movement. And numerous historians have portrayed the years before 1914 as a time of increasing conflict between revolutionary socialism, on the one hand, and a nationalist alliance of the conservative aristocracy and the prosperous middle class, on the other.

- *Why did the socialist movement grow, and how revolutionary was it?*

The Socialist International

Socialism appealed to large numbers of workingmen and workingwomen in the late nineteenth century, and the growth of socialist parties after 1871 was phenomenal. (See the feature "Listening to the Past: The Making of a Socialist" on pages 844–845.) Neither Bismarck's antisocialist laws nor his extensive social security system checked the growth of the German Social Democratic Party, which espoused the Marxian ideology. By 1912 it had millions of followers and was the largest party in the Reichstag. Socialist parties also grew in other countries, though nowhere else with such success. In 1883 Russian exiles in Switzerland founded the Russian Social Democratic Party, which grew rapidly after 1890 despite internal disputes. In France various socialist parties re-emerged in the 1880s after the carnage of the Paris Commune. They were finally unified in 1905 in an increasingly powerful Marxian party called the French Section of the Workers International. Belgium and Austria-Hungary also had strong socialist parties.

As the name of the French party suggests, Marxian socialist parties were eventually linked together in an international organization. As early as 1848, Marx had laid out his intellectual system in *The Communist Manifesto* (see pages 757–758). He had declared that "the working men have no country," and he had urged proletarians of all nations to unite against their governments. Joining the flood of radicals and republicans who fled continental Europe for England and America after the unsuccessful revolutions of 1848, Marx settled in London. Poor and depressed, he lived on his meager earnings as a journalist and on the gifts of his friend Friedrich Engels. Marx never stopped thinking of revolution. Digging deeply into economics and history, he concluded that revolution follows economic crisis and tried to prove this in his greatest theoretical work, *Capital* (1867).

The bookish Marx also excelled as a practical organizer. In 1864 he played an important role in founding the First International of socialists—the International Working Men's Association. In the following years, he battled successfully to control the organization and used its annual meetings as a means of spreading his realistic, "scientific" doctrines of inevitable socialist revolution. Then Marx enthusiastically embraced the passionate, vaguely radical patriotism of the Paris Commune and its terrible conflict with the French National Assembly as a

Individuals in Society

Theodor Herzl

Theodor Herzl. (Library of Congress)

In September 1897, only days after his vision and energy had called into being the First Zionist Congress in Basel, Switzerland, Theodor Herzl (1860–1904) assessed the results in his diary: "If I were to sum up the Congress in a word—which I shall take care not to publish—it would be this: At Basel I founded the Jewish state. If I said this out loud today I would be greeted by universal laughter. In five years perhaps, and certainly in fifty years, everyone will perceive it."* Herzl's buoyant optimism, which so often carried him forward, was prophetic. Leading the Zionist movement until his death at age forty-four in 1904, Herzl guided the first historic steps toward modern Jewish political nationhood and the creation of Israel in 1948.

Theodor Herzl was born in Budapest, Hungary, into an upper-middle-class, German-speaking Jewish family. When Herzl was eighteen, his family moved to Vienna, where he studied law. As a university student, he soaked up the liberal beliefs of most well-to-do Viennese Jews, who also championed the assimilation of German culture. Wrestling with his nonreligious Jewishness and his strong pro-German feeling, Herzl embraced German nationalism and joined a German dueling fraternity. There he discovered that full acceptance required openly anti-Semitic attitudes and a repudiation of all things Jewish. This Herzl could not tolerate, and he resigned. After receiving his law degree, he embarked on a literary career. In 1889 Herzl married into a wealthy Viennese Jewish family, but he and his socialite wife were mismatched and never happy together.

Herzl achieved considerable success as both a journalist and a playwright. His witty comedies focused on the bourgeoisie, including Jewish millionaires trying to live like aristocrats. Accepting many German stereotypes, Herzl sometimes depicted eastern Jews as uneducated and grasping. But as a dedicated, highly educated liberal, he mainly believed that the Jewish shortcomings he perceived were the results of age-old persecution and would disappear through education and assimilation. Herzl also took a growing pride in Jewish steadfastness in the face of victimization and suffering. He savored memories of his early Jewish education and going with his father to the synagogue.

The emergence of modern anti-Semitism shocked Herzl, as it did many acculturated Jewish Germans. Moving to Paris in 1891 as the correspondent for Vienna's leading liberal newspaper, Herzl studied politics and pondered recent historical developments. He then came to a bold conclusion, published in 1896 as *The Jewish State: An Attempt at a Modern Solution to the Jewish Question.* According to Herzl, Jewish assimilation had failed, and attempts to combat anti-Semitism would never succeed. Only by building an independent Jewish state could the Jewish people achieve dignity and renewal. As recent scholarship shows, Herzl developed his political nationalism, or Zionism, before the anti-Jewish agitation accompanying the Dreyfus affair, which only strengthened his faith in his analysis.

Generally rebuffed by skeptical Jewish elites in western and central Europe, Herzl turned for support to youthful idealists and the poor Jewish masses. He became an inspiring man of action, rallying the delegates to the annual Zionist congresses, directing the growth of the worldwide Zionist organization, and working himself to death. Herzl also understood that national consciousness required powerful emotions and symbols, such as a Jewish flag. Flags build nations, he said, because people "live and die for a flag."

Putting the Zionist vision before non-Jews and world public opinion, Herzl believed in international diplomacy and political agreements. He traveled constantly to negotiate with European rulers and top officials, seeking their support in securing territory for a Jewish state, usually in the Ottoman Empire. Aptly described by an admiring contemporary as "the first Jewish statesman since the destruction of Jerusalem," Herzl proved most successful in Britain. He paved the way for the 1917 Balfour Declaration, which solemnly pledged British support for a "Jewish homeland" in Palestine.

Questions for Analysis

1. Describe Theodor Herzl's background and early beliefs. Do you see a link between Herzl's early German nationalism and his later Zionism?
2. How did Herzl work as a leader to turn his Zionist vision into a reality?

*Quotes are from Theodor Herzl, *The Diaries of Theodor Herzl*, trans. and ed. with an introduction by Marvin Lowenthal (New York: Grosset & Dunlap, 1962), pp. 224, 22, xxi.

Online Study Center **Improve Your Grade**
Going Beyond Individuals in Society

giant step toward socialist revolution. This impetuous action frightened many of his early supporters, especially the more moderate British labor leaders. The First International collapsed.

Yet international proletarian solidarity remained an important objective for Marxists. In 1889, as the individual parties in different countries grew stronger, socialist leaders came together to form the Second International, which lasted until 1914. The International was only a federation of national socialist parties, but it had a great psychological impact. Every three years, delegates from the different parties met to interpret Marxian doctrines and plan coordinated action. May 1 (May Day) was declared an annual international one-day strike, a day of marches and demonstrations. A permanent executive for the International was established. Many feared and many others rejoiced in the growing power of socialism and the Second International.

Unions and Revisionism

Was socialism really radical and revolutionary in these years? On the whole, it was not. Indeed, as socialist parties grew and attracted large numbers of members, they looked more and more toward gradual change and steady improvement for the working class and less and less toward revolution. The mainstream of European socialism became militantly moderate; that is, socialists increasingly combined radical rhetoric with sober action.

Workers themselves were progressively less inclined to follow radical programs. There were several reasons for this. As workers gained the right to vote and to partici-

"Greetings from the May Day Festival" Workers participated enthusiastically in the annual one-day strike on May 1 to honor internationalist socialist solidarity, as this postcard from a happy woman visitor to her cousin suggests. Speeches, picnics, and parades were the order of the day, and workers celebrated their respectability and independent culture. Picture postcards developed with railroads and mass travel. *(akg-images)*

pate politically in the nation-state, they focused their attention more on elections than on revolutions. And as workers won real, tangible benefits, this furthered the process. Workers were also not immune to patriotic education and indoctrination during military service, and many responded positively to drum-beating parades and aggressive foreign policy as they loyally voted for socialists. Nor were workers a unified social group.

Perhaps most important of all, workers' standard of living rose gradually but substantially after 1850 as the promise of the Industrial Revolution was at least partially realized. In Great Britain, for example, workers could buy almost twice as much with their wages in 1906 as in 1850, and most of the increase came after 1870. Workers experienced similar gradual increases in most continental countries after 1850, though much less strikingly in late-developing Russia. Improvement in the standard of living was much more than merely a matter of higher wages. The quality of life improved dramatically in urban areas. For all these reasons, workers tended more and more to become militantly moderate: they demanded gains, but they were less likely to take to the barricades in pursuit of them.

The growth of labor unions reinforced this trend toward moderation. In the early stages of industrialization, modern unions were generally prohibited by law. A famous law of the French Revolution had declared all guilds and unions illegal in the name of "liberty" in 1791. In Great Britain, attempts by workers to unite were considered criminal conspiracies after 1799. Other countries had similar laws, and these obviously hampered union development. In France, for example, about two hundred workers were imprisoned each year between 1825 and 1847 for taking part in illegal combinations. Unions were considered subversive bodies, only to be hounded and crushed.

From this sad position workers struggled to escape. Great Britain led the way in 1824 and 1825 when unions won the right to exist but (generally) not the right to strike. After the collapse of Robert Owen's attempt to form one big union in the 1830s (see page 741), new and more practical kinds of unions appeared. Limited primarily to highly skilled workers such as machinists and carpenters, the "new model unions" avoided both radical politics and costly strikes. Instead, their sober, respectable leaders concentrated on winning better wages and hours for their members through collective bargaining and compromise. This approach helped pave the way to full acceptance in Britain in the 1870s, when unions won the right to strike without being held legally liable for the financial damage inflicted on employers. After 1890 unions for unskilled workers developed, and between 1901 and 1906 the legal position of British unions was further strengthened.

Germany was the most industrialized, socialized, and unionized continental country by 1914. German unions were not granted important rights until 1869, and until the antisocialist law was repealed in 1890, they were frequently harassed by the government as socialist fronts. Nor were socialist leaders particularly interested in union activity, believing as they did in the iron law of low wages and the need for political revolution. The result was that as late as 1895, there were only about 270,000 union members in a male industrial workforce of nearly 8 million. Then, with German industrialization still storming ahead and almost all legal harassment eliminated, union membership skyrocketed, reaching roughly 3 million in 1912.

This great expansion both reflected and influenced the changing character of German unions. Increasingly, unions in Germany focused on bread-and-butter issues—wages, hours, working conditions—rather than on the dissemination of pure socialist doctrine. Genuine collective bargaining, long opposed by socialist intellectuals as a "sellout," was officially recognized as desirable by the German Trade Union Congress in 1899. When employers proved unwilling to bargain, a series of strikes forced them to change their minds.

Between 1906 and 1913, successful collective bargaining gained a prominent place in German industrial relations. In 1913 alone, over ten thousand collective bargaining agreements affecting 1.25 million workers were signed. Gradual improvement, not revolution, was becoming the primary goal of the German trade-union movement.

The German trade unions and their leaders were in fact, if not in name, thoroughgoing revisionists. **Revisionism**—that most awful of sins in the eyes of militant Marxists in the twentieth century—was an effort by various socialists to update Marxian doctrines to reflect the realities of the time. Thus the socialist Edward Bernstein (1850–1932) argued in 1899 in his *Evolutionary Socialism* that Marx's predictions of ever-greater poverty for workers and ever-greater concentration of wealth in ever-fewer hands had been proved false. Therefore, Bernstein suggested, socialists should reform their doctrines and tactics. They should combine with other progressive forces to win gradual evolutionary gains for workers through legislation, unions, and further economic development. These views were denounced as heresy by the German Social Democratic Party and later by the entire Second International. Yet the revisionist, gradualist approach continued to gain the tacit acceptance of many German socialists, particularly in the trade unions.

Moderation found followers elsewhere. In France the great socialist leader Jean Jaurès (1859–1914) formally repudiated revisionist doctrines in order to establish a unified socialist party, but he remained at heart a gradualist and optimistic secular humanist. Questions of revolution split Russian Marxists.

Socialist parties before 1914 had clear-cut national characteristics. Russians and socialists in the Austro-Hungarian Empire tended to be the most radical. The German party talked revolution and practiced reformism, greatly influenced by its enormous trade-union movement. The French party talked revolution and tried to practice it, unrestrained by a trade-union movement that was both very weak and very radical. In England the socialist but non-Marxian Labour Party, reflecting the well-established union movement, was formally committed to gradual reform. In Spain and Italy, Marxian socialism was very weak. There anarchism, seeking to smash the state rather than the bourgeoisie, dominated radical thought and action.

In short, socialist policies and doctrines varied from country to country. Socialism itself was to a large extent "nationalized" behind the imposing façade of international unity. This helps explain why when war came in 1914, almost all socialist leaders supported their governments.

Chapter Summary

- How in France did Napoleon III seek to reconcile popular and conservative forces in an authoritarian nation-state?
- How did the process of unification in Italy and Germany create conservative nation-states?
- In what ways did the United States experience the full drama of nation building?
- What steps did Russia and the Ottoman Turks take toward modernization, and how successful were they?
- Why after 1871 did ordinary citizens feel a growing loyalty to their governments?
- Why did the socialist movement grow, and how revolutionary was it?

After 1850, Western society became nationalistic as well as urban and industrial. Conservative monarchical governments, recovering from the revolutionary trauma of 1848, learned to remodel early so as to build stronger states with greater popular support. Napoleon III in France led the way, combining authoritarian rule with economic prosperity and positive measures for the poor. In Italy, Cavour joined traditional diplomacy with national revolt in the north and Garibaldi's revolutionary patriotism in the south, expanding the liberal Sardinian monarchy into a conservative nation-state. Bismarck also combined traditional statecraft with national feeling to expand the power of Prussia and its king in a new German Empire.

In the midcentury years, the United States, Russia, and the Ottoman Empire also experienced crises of nation building. The United States overcame sectionalism in a war that prevented an independent South and seemed to confirm America's destiny as a great world power. In autocratic Russia, defeat in the Crimean War led to the emancipation of the serfs, economic modernization with railroad building and industrialization, and limited political reform. The Ottoman Empire also sought to modernize to protect the state, but it was considerably less successful.

Nation-states gradually enlisted widespread popular support, providing men and women with a greater sense of belonging and giving them specific political, social, and economic improvements. Even the growing socialist movement became increasingly national in orientation, gathering strength as a champion of working-class interests in domestic politics. Yet even though nationalism served to unite peoples, it also drove them apart—obvious not only in the United States before the Civil War and in Austria-Hungary and Ireland, but also throughout Europe. There the universal national faith, which usually reduced social tensions within states, promoted a bitter, almost Darwinian, competition between states and thus threatened the progress and unity it had helped to build, as we shall see in Chapters 26 and 27.

Key Terms

- Red Shirts
- Zollverein
- Homestead Act
- modernization
- zemstvo
- revolution of 1905
- Bloody Sunday
- October Manifesto
- Duma
- janissary corps
- Tanzimat
- Young Turks
- Reichstag
- Kulturkampf
- Dreyfus affair
- People's Budget
- Zionism
- revisionism

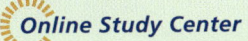 **Improve Your Grade** Flashcards

Suggested Reading

Berend, Ivan T. *History Derailed: Central and Eastern Europe in the Long Nineteenth Century.* 2003. Focuses on industrialization and its consequences.

Blanning, T. C. W. *Oxford Illustrated History of Modern Europe.* 1996. A heavily illustrated text that provides useful surveys of the entire nineteenth century.

Boyce, D. George. *Nationalism in Ireland,* 2d ed. 1991. Provides an excellent account of the Irish struggle for nationhood.

Clyman, Toby W., and Judith Vowles, eds. *Russia Through Women's Eyes: Autobiographies from Tsarist Russia.* 1999. An eye-opening collection detailing women's experiences in Russia.

Fink, Carole. *Defending the Rights of Others: The Great Powers, the Jews, and the International Protection, 1878–1938.* 2004. Skilled consideration of the cruelty and tragedy of ethnic conflict and minority oppression.

Geary, Dick, ed. *Labour and Socialist Movements in Europe Before 1914.* 1989. An excellent collection that examines labor movements in several different countries.

Hobsbawm, Eric. *The Age of Empire, 1875–1914.* 1987. An outstanding interpretative work.

Kitchen, Martin. *The Cambridge Illustrated History of Germany.* 1996. Features handsome pictures and a readable text.

Quataert, Donald. *The Ottoman Empire, 1700–1900,* 2d ed. 2005. An excellent introduction.

Ridley, Jasper. *Phoenix: Garibaldi.* 2001. A thorough study of the world-renowned revolutionary nationalist.

Rogger, Hans. *Russia in the Age of Modernisation and Revolution, 1881–1917.* 1983. A fine study on Russian development that includes an excellent bibliography.

Schulze, Hagen, and William E. Yuill. *States, Nations and Nationalism: From the Middle Ages to the Present.* 1996. An important study that explores the resurgence of European nationalism since the fall of communism.

Slezkine, Yuri. *The Jewish Century.* 2004. A brilliant interpretation of Jewish achievement in the modern era.

Tombs, Robert. *France, 1814–1914.* 1996. An impressive survey with a useful bibliography.

Vital, David. *A People Apart: The Jews in Europe, 1789–1939.* 1999. An engaging and judicious survey.

Notes

1. H. Schulze, *States, Nations and Nationalism: From the Middle Ages to the Present* (Oxford: Blackwell, 1994), pp. 222–223, 246–247.
2. J. McKay, *Pioneers for Profit: Foreign Entrepreneurship and Russian Industrialization, 1885–1913* (Chicago: University of Chicago Press, 1970), pp. 112–157.
3. R. Seltzer, *Jewish People, Jewish Thought: The Jewish Experience in History* (New York: Macmillan, 1980), p. 533.

Listening to the Past

The Making of a Socialist

Nationalism and socialism appeared locked in bitter competition in Europe before 1914, but they actually complemented each other in many ways. Both faiths were secular as opposed to religious, and both fostered political awareness. A working person who became interested in politics and developed nationalist beliefs might well convert to socialism at a later date.

This was the case for Adelheid Popp (1869–1939), a self-taught workingwoman who became an influential socialist leader. Born into a desperately poor working-class family in Vienna and remembering only a "hard and gloomy childhood," she was forced by her parents to quit school at age ten to begin full-time work. She struggled with low-paying piecework for years before she landed a solid factory job, as she recounts in the following selection from her widely read autobiography.

Always an avid reader, Popp became the editor of a major socialist newspaper for German working-women. She then told her life story so that all workingwomen might share her truth: "Socialism could change and strengthen others, as it did me."

[Finally] I found work again; I took everything that was offered me in order to show my willingness to work, and I passed through much. But at last things became better. [At age fifteen] I was recommended to a great factory which stood in the best repute. Three hundred girls and about fifty men were employed. I was put in a big room where sixty women and girls were at work. Against the windows stood twelve tables, and at each sat four girls. We had to sort the goods which had been manufactured, others had to count them, and a third set had to brand on them the mark of the firm. We worked from 7 A.M. to 7 P.M. We had an hour's rest at noon, half-an-hour in the afternoon. . . . I had never yet been paid so much. . . .

I seemed to myself to be almost rich. . . . [Yet] from the women of this factory one can judge how sad and full of deprivation is the lot of a factory worker. In none of the neighbouring factories were the wages so high; we were envied everywhere. Parents considered themselves fortunate if they could get their daughters of fourteen in there on leaving school. . . . And even here, in this paradise, all were badly nourished. Those who stayed at the factory for the dinner hour would buy themselves for a few pennies a sausage or the leavings of a cheese shop. . . . In spite of all the diligence and economy, every one was poor, and trembled at the thought of losing her work. All humbled themselves, and suffered the worst injustice from the foremen, not to risk losing this good work, not to be without food. . . .

I did not only read novels and tales; I had begun . . . to read the classics and other good books. I also began to take an interest in public events. . . . I was not democratically inclined. I was full of enthusiasm then for emperors, and kings and highly placed personages played no small part in my fancies. . . . I bought myself a strict Catholic paper, that criticised very adversely the workers' movement, which was attracting notice. Its aim was to educate in a patriotic and religious direction. . . . I took the warmest interest in the events that occurred in the royal families, and I took the death of the Crown Prince of Austria so much to heart that I wept a whole day. . . . Political events [also] held me in suspense. The possibility of a war with Russia roused my patriotic enthusiasm. I saw my brother already returning from the battlefield covered with glory. . . .

When a particularly strong anti-Semitic feeling was noticeable in political life, I sympathised with it for a time. A broad sheet, "How Israel Attained

Power and Sovereignty over all the Nations of the Earth," fascinated me. . . .

About this time an Anarchist group was active. Some mysterious murders which had taken place were ascribed to the Anarchists, and the police made use of them to oppress the rising workmen's movement. . . . I followed the trial of the Anarchists with passionate sympathy. I read all the speeches, and because, as always happens, Social Democrats, whom the authorities really wanted to attack, were among the accused, I learned their views. I became full of enthusiasm. Every single Social Democrat . . . seemed to me a hero. . . .

There was unrest among the workers . . . and demonstrations of protest followed. When these were repeated the military entered the "threatened" streets. . . . In the evenings I rushed in the greatest excitement from the factory to the scene of the disturbance. The military did not frighten me; I only left the place when it was "cleared."

Later on my mother and I lived with one of my brothers who had married. Friends came to him, among them some intelligent workmen. One of these workmen was particularly intelligent, and . . . could talk on many subjects. He was the first Social Democrat I knew. He brought me many books, and explained to me the difference between Anarchism and Socialism. I heard from him, also for the first time, what a republic was, and in spite of my former enthusiasm for royal dynasties, I also declared myself in favour of a republican form of government. I saw everything so near and so clearly, that I actually counted the weeks which must still elapse before the revolution of state and society would take place.

From this workman I received the first Social Democratic party organ. . . . I first learned from it to understand and judge of my own lot. I learned to see that all I had suffered was the result not of a divine ordinance, but of an unjust organization of society. . . .

In the factory I became another woman. . . . I told my [female] comrades all that I had read of the workers' movement. Formerly I had often told stories when they had begged me for them. But instead of narrating . . . the fate of some queen, I now held forth on oppression and exploitation. I told of accumulated wealth in the

1890 engraving of a meeting of workers in Berlin. *(Bildarchiv Preussischer Kulturbesitz/Art Resource, NY)*

hands of a few, and introduced as a contrast the shoemakers who had no shoes and the tailors who had no clothes. On breaks I read aloud the articles in the Social Democratic paper and explained what Socialism was as far as I understood it. . . . [While I was reading] it often happened that one of the clerks passing by shook his head and said to another clerk: "The girl speaks like a man."

Questions for Analysis

1. How did Popp describe and interpret work in the factory?
2. To what extent did her socialist interpretation of factory life fit the facts she described?
3. What were Popp's political interests before she became a socialist?
4. How and why did she become a Social Democrat?
5. Was this account likely to lead other workingwomen to socialism? Why or why not?

Source: Slightly adapted from A. Popp, *The Autobiography of a Working Woman,* trans. E. C. Harvey (Chicago: F. G. Browne, 1913), pp. 29, 34–35, 39, 66–69, 71, 74, 82–90.

Africans in Madagascar transport a French diplomat in 1894, shortly before France annexed the island. *(Snark/Art Resource, NY)*

chapter 26
THE WEST AND THE WORLD, 1815–1914

chapter preview

Industrialization and the World Economy
- *What were some of the global consequences of European industrialization between 1815 and 1914?*

The Great Migration
- *How was massive migration an integral part of Western expansion?*

Western Imperialism, 1880–1914
- *How and why after 1875 did European nations rush to build political empires in Africa and Asia?*

Responding to Western Imperialism
- *What was the general pattern of non-Western responses to Western expansion, and how did India, Japan, and China meet the imperialist challenge?*

While industrialization and nationalism were transforming urban life and Western society, Western society itself was reshaping the world. At the peak of its power and pride, the West entered the third and most dynamic phase of the aggressive expansion that had begun with the Crusades and continued with the great discoveries and the rise of seaborne colonial empires. An ever-growing stream of products, people, and ideas flowed out of Europe in the nineteenth century. Hardly any corner of the globe was left untouched. The most spectacular manifestations of Western expansion came in the late nineteenth century when the leading European nations established or enlarged their far-flung political empires. The political annexation of territory in the 1880s—the "new imperialism," as it is often called by historians—was the capstone of a profound underlying economic and technological process.

Industrialization and the World Economy

The Industrial Revolution created, first in Great Britain and then in continental Europe and North America, a growing and tremendously dynamic economic system. In the course of the nineteenth century, that system was extended across the face of the earth. Some of this extension into non-Western areas was peaceful and beneficial for all concerned, for the West had many products and techniques the rest of the world desired. If peaceful methods failed, however, Europeans did not stand on ceremony. They used their superior military power to force non-Western nations to open their doors to Western economic interests. In general, Westerners fashioned the global economic system so that the largest share of the ever-increasing gains from trade, technology, and migration flowed to the West and its propertied classes.

- *What were some of the global consequences of European industrialization between 1815 and 1914?*

Online Study Center
This icon will direct you to interactive activities and study materials on the website **college.hmco.com/pic/mckaywest9e**

The Rise of Global Inequality

The Industrial Revolution in Europe marked a momentous turning point in human history. Indeed, only by placing Europe's economic breakthrough in a global perspective can one truly appreciate its revolutionary implications and consequences.

From such a global perspective, the ultimate significance of the Industrial Revolution was that it allowed those regions of the world that industrialized in the nineteenth century to increase their wealth and power enormously in comparison to those that did not. As a result, a gap between the industrializing regions (mainly Europe and North America) and the nonindustrializing ones (mainly Africa, Asia, and Latin America) opened up and grew steadily throughout the nineteenth century. Moreover, this pattern of uneven global development became institutionalized, or built into the structure of the world economy. Thus we evolved a "lopsided world," a world of rich lands and poor.

In recent years historical economists have begun to chart the long-term evolution of this gap with some precision. Figure 26.1 summarizes the important findings of one such study. It compares the long-term evolution of average income per person in today's "developed" (or industrialized) regions—defined as Europe, North America, and Japan—with that found in Africa, Asia, and Latin America, also often known as the **Third World**. To get these individual income figures, researchers estimate a country's gross national product (GNP) at different points in time, convert those estimates to some common currency, and divide by the total population.

Figure 26.1 highlights three main points. First, in 1750 the average standard of living was no higher in Europe as a whole than in the rest of the world. In 1750 Europe was still a poor agricultural society. By 1970, however, the average person in the wealthiest countries had an income fully twenty-five times as great as that received by the average person in the poorest countries of Africa and Asia.

Second, it was industrialization that opened the gaps in average wealth and well-being among countries and regions. One sees that Great Britain had jumped well above the European average by 1830, when the first industrial nation was well in advance of its continental competitors. One also sees how Great Britain's lead gradually narrowed as other European countries and the United States successfully industrialized in the course of the nineteenth century.

Third, income per person stagnated in the Third World before 1913, in striking contrast to the industrializing regions. Only after 1945, in the era of political independence

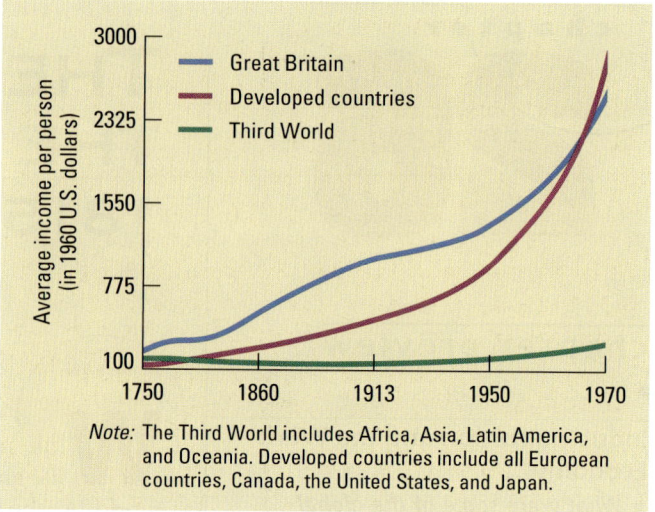

FIGURE 26.1 The Growth of Average Income per Person in the Third World, Developed Countries, and Great Britain, 1750–1970 Growth is given in 1960 U.S. dollars and prices. (Source: P. Bairoch and M. Lévy-Leboyer, eds., Disparities in Economic Development Since the Industrial Revolution. Copyright © 1981. Reprinted by permission of Palgrave Macmillan, UK.)

dence and decolonization, did Third World countries finally make some real economic progress, beginning in their turn the critical process of industrialization.

The rise of these enormous income disparities, which are poignant indicators of equal disparities in food and clothing, health and education, life expectancy and general material well-being, has generated a great deal of debate. One school of interpretation stresses that the West used science, technology, capitalist organization, and even its critical worldview to create its wealth and greater physical well-being. Another school argues that the West used its political and economic power to steal much of its riches, continuing in the nineteenth (and twentieth) century the rapacious colonialism born of the era of expansion.

These issues are complex, and there are few simple answers. As noted in Chapter 22, the wealth-creating potential of technological improvement and more intensive capitalist organization was indeed great. At the same time, those breakthroughs rested, in part, on Great Britain's having already used political force to dominate part of the world economy by the late eighteenth century. In the nineteenth century other industrializing countries joined with Britain to extend Western domination over the entire world economy. Wealth—unprecedented wealth—was indeed created, but the lion's share of that new wealth flowed to the West and its propertied classes.

The World Market

Commerce between nations has always been a powerful stimulus to economic development. Never was this more true than in the nineteenth century, when world trade grew prodigiously. In 1913 the value of world trade was roughly $38 billion, or about *twenty-five* times what it had been in 1800, even though prices of both manufactured goods and raw materials were lower in 1913 than in 1800. In a general way, the enormous increase in international commerce summed up the growth of an interlocking world economy centered in and directed by Europe.

Great Britain played a key role in using trade to tie the world together economically. In 1815 Britain already had a colonial empire, for India, Canada, Australia, and other scattered areas remained British possessions after American independence. The technological breakthroughs of the Industrial Revolution allowed Britain to manufacture cotton textiles, iron, and other goods more cheaply and to far outstrip domestic demand for such products. Thus British manufacturers sought export markets first in Europe and then around the world.

Take the case of cotton textiles. By 1820 Britain was exporting 50 percent of its production. Europe bought 50 percent of these cotton textile exports, while India bought only 6 percent. Then as European nations and the United States erected protective tariff barriers and promoted domestic industry, British cotton textile manufacturers aggressively sought and found other foreign markets in non-Western areas. By 1850 India was buying 25 percent and Europe only 16 percent of a much larger total. As a British colony, India could not raise tariffs to protect its ancient cotton textile industry, and thousands of Indian weavers lost their livelihoods.

After the repeal of the Corn Laws in 1846 (see page 764), Britain became the world's single best market. Until 1914 Britain remained the world's emporium, where not only agricultural products and raw materials but also manufactured goods entered freely. Free access to Britain's market stimulated the development of mines and plantations in many non-Western areas.

The growth of trade was facilitated by the conquest of distance. The earliest railroad construction occurred in Europe (including Russia) and in America north of the Rio Grande; other parts of the globe saw the building of rail lines after 1860. By 1920 more than one-quarter of the world's railroads were in Latin America, Asia, Africa, and Australia. Wherever railroads were built, they drastically reduced transportation costs, opened new economic opportunities, and called forth new skills and attitudes. Much of the railroad construction undertaken in Latin America, Asia, and Africa connected seaports with inland cities and regions, as opposed to linking and developing cities and regions within a given country. Thus railroads dovetailed admirably with Western economic interests, facilitating the inflow and sale of Western manufactured goods and the export and the development of local raw materials.

Chronology

1853	Perry "opens" Japan for trade
1863–1879	Reign of Ismail in Egypt
1865–1909	Reign of Leopold II in Belgium
1867	Meiji Restoration in Japan
1869	Completion of Suez Canal
1898	United States takes over Philippines; hundred days of reform in China
1899	Kipling, "The White Man's Burden"
1902	Conrad, *Heart of Darkness*; Hobson, *Imperialism*

The power of steam revolutionized transportation by sea as well as by land. Steam power, long used to drive paddle wheelers on rivers, particularly in Russia and North America, finally began to supplant sails on the oceans of the world in the late 1860s. Lighter, stronger, cheaper steel replaced iron, which had replaced wood. Screw propellers superseded paddle wheels, while mighty compound steam engines cut fuel consumption by half. Passenger and freight rates tumbled, and the intercontinental shipment of low-priced raw materials became feasible.

An account of an actual voyage by a typical tramp freighter highlights nineteenth-century developments in global trade. The ship left England in 1910 carrying rails and general freight to western Australia. From there it carried lumber to Melbourne in southeastern Australia, where it took on harvester combines for Argentina. In Buenos Aires it loaded wheat for Calcutta, and in Calcutta it took on jute for New York. From New York it carried a variety of industrial products to Australia before returning to England with lead, wool, and wheat after a voyage of approximately seventy-two thousand miles to six continents in seventeen months.

The revolution in land and sea transportation helped European pioneers open up vast new territories and produce agricultural products and raw materials there for sale in Europe. Improved transportation enabled Asia, Africa, and Latin America to ship not only the traditional tropical products—

cargo to Australia. World commodity prices were also instantaneously conveyed by the same network of communications.

The growth of trade and the conquest of distance encouraged the expanding European economy to make massive foreign investments beginning about 1840. By the outbreak of World War I in 1914, Europeans had invested more than $40 billion abroad. Great Britain, France, and Germany were the principal investing countries (see Map 26.1). The great gap between rich and poor within Europe meant that the wealthy and moderately well-to-do could and did send great sums abroad in search of interest and dividends.

Most of the capital exported did not go to European colonies or protectorates in Asia and Africa. About three-quarters of total European investment went to other European countries, the United States and Canada, Australia and New Zealand, and Latin America. Europe found its most profitable opportunities for investment in construction of the railroads, ports, and utilities that were necessary to settle and develop the almost-vacant lands in such places as Australia and the Americas. By lending money for a foreign railroad, Europeans also enabled white settlers to buy European rails and locomotives and developed sources of cheap food and raw materials. Much of this investment was peaceful and mutually beneficial for lenders and borrowers. The victims were Native American Indians and Australian aborigines, who were decimated by the diseases, liquor, and weapons of an aggressively expanding Western society.

The Opening of China and Japan

Europe's relatively peaceful development of robust offshoots in sparsely populated North America, Australia, and much of Latin America absorbed huge quantities of goods, investments, and migrants. From a Western point of view, that was the most important aspect of Europe's global thrust. Yet Europe's economic and cultural penetration of old, densely populated civilizations was also profoundly significant, especially for the non-European peoples affected by it. With such civilizations Europeans also increased their trade and profit, and they were prepared to use force, if necessary, to attain their desires. This was what happened in China and Japan, two crucial examples of the general pattern of intrusion into non-Western lands.

Traditional Chinese civilization was self-sufficient. For centuries China had sent more goods and inventions to Europe than it had received, and this was still the case in the early nineteenth century. Trade with Europe was care-

British Ships and Shipbuilders The British continued to dominate international trade before the First World War. This handsome membership certificate of the British shipbuilders union features the vessels that drew the world together and were Britain's pride. Britain's thriving shipbuilding industry was concentrated in southern Scotland along the Clyde. *(Trade Union Congress, London/The Bridgeman Art Library)*

spices, tea, sugar, coffee—but also new raw materials for industry, such as jute, rubber, cotton, and coconut oil.

Intercontinental trade was enormously facilitated by the Suez and Panama Canals. Of great importance, too, was large and continual investment in modern port facilities, which made loading and unloading cheaper, faster, and more dependable. Finally, transoceanic telegraph cables inaugurated rapid communications among the financial centers of the world. While a British tramp freighter steamed from Calcutta to New York, a broker in London was arranging by telegram for it to carry an American

MAP 26.1 European Investment to 1914 Foreign investment grew rapidly after 1850, and Britain, France, and Germany were the major investing nations. As this map suggests, most European investment was not directed to the African and Asian areas seized by the "new imperialism" after 1880.

fully regulated by the Chinese imperial government—the Qing (or Manchu) Dynasty—which required all foreign merchants to live in the southern city of Canton and to buy from and sell to only the local merchant monopoly. Practices considered harmful to Chinese interests, such as the sale of opium, were strictly forbidden.

For years the little community of foreign merchants in Canton had to accept the Chinese system. By the 1820s, however, the dominant group, the British, were flexing their muscles. Moreover, in the smoking of opium—that "destructive and ensnaring vice" denounced by Chinese decrees—they had found something the Chinese really wanted. Grown legally in British-occupied India, opium was smuggled into China by means of fast ships and bribed officials. By 1836 the aggressive goal of the British merchants in Canton was an independent British colony in China and "safe and unrestricted liberty" in trade. Spurred on by economic motives, they pressured the British government to take decisive action and enlisted the support of British manufacturers with visions of vast Chinese markets to be opened.

At the same time, the Qing government decided that the **opium trade** had to be stamped out. It was ruining the people and stripping the empire of its silver, which was going to British merchants to pay for the opium. The government began to prosecute Chinese drug dealers vigorously and in 1839 it ordered the foreign merchants to obey China's laws. The British merchants refused and were expelled, whereupon war soon broke out.

Using troops from India and being in control of the seas, the British occupied several coastal cities and forced China to surrender. In the Treaty of Nanking in 1842,

Britain and China at War, 1841 Britain capitalized on its overwhelming naval superiority, and this British aquatint celebrates a dramatic moment in a crucial battle near Guangzhou. Having received a direct hit from a steam-powered British ironclad, a Chinese sailing ship explodes into a wall of flame. The Chinese lost eleven ships and five hundred men in the two-hour engagement; the British suffered only minor damage. *(National Maritime Museum, London)*

the imperial government was forced to cede the island of Hong Kong to Britain forever, pay an indemnity of $100 million, and open up four large cities to foreign trade with low tariffs.

Thereafter the opium trade flourished, and Hong Kong developed rapidly as an Anglo-Chinese enclave. China continued to accept foreign diplomats in Beijing (Peking), the imperial capital. Finally, there was a second round of foreign attack between 1856 and 1860, culminating in the occupation of Beijing by seventeen thousand British and French troops and the intentional burning of the emperor's summer palace. Another round of harsh treaties gave European merchants and missionaries greater privileges and protection and forced the Chinese to accept trade and investment on unfavorable terms for several more cities. Thus did Europeans use military aggression to blow a hole in the wall of Chinese seclusion and open the country to foreign trade and foreign ideas.

China's neighbor Japan had its own highly distinctive civilization and even less use for Westerners. European traders and missionaries first arrived in Japan in the sixteenth century. By 1640 Japan had reacted quite negatively to their presence. The government decided to seal off the country from all European influences in order to preserve traditional Japanese culture and society. When American and British whaling ships began to appear off Japanese coasts almost two hundred years later, the policy of exclusion was still in effect. An order of 1825 commanded Japanese officials to "drive away foreign vessels without second thought."[1]

Japan's unbending isolation seemed hostile and barbaric to the West, particularly to the United States. It complicated the practical problems of shipwrecked American sailors and the provisioning of whaling ships and China traders sailing in the eastern Pacific. It also thwarted the hope of trade and profit. Moreover, Americans shared the self-confidence and dynamism of expanding Western society, and they felt destined to play a great role in the

Pacific. To Americans it seemed the duty of the United States to force the Japanese to share their ports and behave as a "civilized" nation.

After several unsuccessful American attempts to establish commercial relations with Japan, Commodore Matthew Perry steamed into Edo (now Tokyo) Bay in 1853 and demanded diplomatic negotiations with the emperor. Japan entered a grave crisis. Some Japanese warriors urged resistance, but senior officials realized how defenseless their cities were against naval bombardment. Shocked and humiliated, they reluctantly signed a treaty with the United States that opened two ports and permitted trade. Over the next five years, more treaties spelled out the rights and privileges of the Western nations and their merchants in Japan. Japan was "opened." What the British had done in China with war, the Americans had done in Japan with only the threat of war.

Western Penetration of Egypt

Egypt's experience illustrates not only the explosive power of the expanding European economy and society but also their seductive appeal in non-Western lands. European involvement in Egypt also led to a new model of formal political control, which European powers applied widely in Africa and Asia after 1882.

Of great importance in African and Middle Eastern history, the ancient land of the pharaohs had since 525 B.C. been ruled by a succession of foreigners, most recently by the Ottoman Turks. In 1798 French armies under young General Napoleon Bonaparte invaded the Egyptian part of the Ottoman Empire and occupied the territory for three years. Into the power vacuum left by the French withdrawal stepped an extraordinary Albanian-born Turkish general, Muhammad Ali (1769–1849).

First appointed governor of Egypt by the Turkish sultan, Muhammad Ali set out to build his own state on the strength of a large, powerful army organized along European lines. He drafted for the first time the illiterate, despised peasant masses of Egypt, and he hired French and Italian army officers to train these raw recruits and their Turkish officers. The government was also reformed, new lands were cultivated, and communications were improved. By the time of his death in 1849, Muhammad Ali had established a strong and virtually independent Egyptian state, to be ruled by his family on a hereditary basis within the Turkish empire.

Muhammad Ali's policies of modernization attracted large numbers of Europeans to the banks of the Nile. The port city of Alexandria had more than fifty thousand Europeans by 1864. Europeans served not only as army officers but also as engineers, doctors, government officials, and police officers. Others turned to trade, finance, and shipping.

To pay for his ambitious plans, Muhammad Ali encouraged the development of commercial agriculture. This development had profound implications. Egyptian peasants were poor but largely self-sufficient, growing food for their own consumption on state-owned lands allotted to them by tradition. Faced with the possibility of export agriculture, high-ranking officials and members of Muhammad Ali's family began carving large private landholdings out of the state domain. The new landlords made the peasants their tenants and forced them to grow cash crops geared to European markets. Thus Egyptian landowners "modernized" agriculture, but to the detriment of peasant well-being.

These trends continued under Muhammad Ali's grandson Ismail, who in 1863 began his sixteen-year rule as Egypt's **khedive,** or prince. Educated at France's leading military academy, Ismail was a westernizing autocrat. The large irrigation networks he promoted caused cotton production and exports to Europe to boom, and with his support the Suez Canal was completed by a French company in 1869. The Arabic of the masses replaced the Turkish of the conquerors as the official language. Young Egyptians educated in Europe spread new skills, and Cairo acquired modern boulevards and Western hotels. As Ismail proudly declared, "My country is no longer in Africa, we now form part of Europe."[2]

Yet Ismail was too impatient and reckless. His projects were enormously expensive, and by 1876 Egypt owed foreign bondholders a colossal debt that it could not pay. Rather than let Egypt go bankrupt and repudiate its loans, the governments of France and Great Britain intervened politically to protect the European bondholders. They forced Ismail to appoint French and British commissioners to oversee Egyptian finances so that the Egyptian debt would be paid in full. This momentous decision implied direct European political control and was a sharp break with the previous pattern of trade and investment. Throughout most of the nineteenth century, Europeans had used military might and political force primarily to make sure that non-Western lands would accept European trade and investment. Now Europeans were going to determine the state budget and effectively rule Egypt.

Foreign financial control evoked a violent nationalistic reaction among Egyptian religious leaders, young intellectuals, and army officers. In 1879, under the leadership of Colonel Ahmed Arabi, they formed the Egyptian

The Opening of the Suez Canal A long procession of eighty ships passed through the Suez Canal when it was opened in November 1869, and thousands of spectators lined the shores and joined in the celebrations. The building of the hundred-mile canal was a momentous event, cutting in half the length of the journey between Europe and Asia. *(Archives Charmet/The Bridgeman Art Library)*

Nationalist Party. Continuing diplomatic pressure, which forced Ismail to abdicate in favor of his weak son, Tewfiq (r. 1879–1892), resulted in bloody anti-European riots in Alexandria in 1882. A number of Europeans were killed, and Tewfiq and his court had to flee to British ships for safety. When the British fleet bombarded Alexandria, more riots swept the country, and Colonel Arabi led a revolt. But a British expeditionary force put down the rebellion and occupied all of Egypt.

The British said their occupation was temporary, but British armies remained in Egypt until 1956. They maintained the façade of the khedive's government as an autonomous province of the Ottoman Empire, but the khedive was a mere puppet. British rule did result in tax reforms and somewhat better conditions for peasants, while foreign bondholders received their interest and Egyptian nationalists nursed their injured pride.

British rule in Egypt provided a new model for European expansion in densely populated lands. Such expansion was based on military force, political domination, and a self-justifying ideology of beneficial reform. This model was to predominate until 1914. Thus did Europe's Industrial Revolution lead to tremendous political as well as economic expansion throughout the world after 1880.

The Great Migration

A poignant human drama was interwoven with economic expansion: millions of people pulled up stakes and left their ancestral lands in the course of history's greatest migration. To millions of ordinary people, for whom the opening of China and the interest on the Egyptian debt had not the slightest significance, this great movement was the central experience in the saga of Western expansion. It was, in part, because of this **great migration** that the West's impact on the world in the nineteenth century was so powerful and many-sided.

- How was massive migration an integral part of Western expansion?

The Pressure of Population

In the early eighteenth century, the growth of European population entered its third and decisive stage, which continued unabated until the early twentieth century (see Figure 26.2). Birthrates eventually declined in the nineteenth century, but so did death rates, mainly because of the rising standard of living and secondarily because of the medical revolution. Thus the population of Europe (including Asiatic Russia) more than doubled, from approximately 188 million in 1800 to roughly 432 million in 1900.

These figures actually understate Europe's population explosion, for between 1815 and 1932 more than 60 million people left Europe. These migrants went primarily to the "areas of European settlement"—North and South America, Australia, New Zealand, and Siberia—where they contributed to a rapid growth in numbers. Since population grew more slowly in Africa and Asia than in Europe and the Americas, as Figure 26.2 shows, Europeans and people of predominately European origin jumped from about 22 percent of the world's total to about 38 percent on the eve of World War I.

The growing number of Europeans provided further impetus for Western expansion. It was a driving force behind emigration. As in the eighteenth century, the rapid increase in numbers put pressure on the land and led to land hunger and relative overpopulation in area after area. In most countries, migration increased twenty years after a rapid growth in population, as many children of the baby boom grew up, saw little available land and few opportunities, and migrated. This pattern was especially prevalent when rapid population increase predated extensive industrial development, which offered the best long-term hope of creating jobs within the country and reducing poverty. Thus millions of country folk went abroad as well as to nearby cities in search of work and economic opportunity.

Before looking at the people who migrated, let us consider three facts. First, the number of men and women who left Europe increased rapidly before World War I. As Figure 26.3 shows, more than 11 million left in the first decade of the twentieth century, over five times the number departing in the 1850s. The outflow of migrants was clearly an enduring characteristic of European society for the entire period.

Second, different countries had very different patterns of movement. As Figure 26.3 also shows, people left Britain and Ireland (which are not distinguished in the British figures) in large numbers from the 1840s on. This

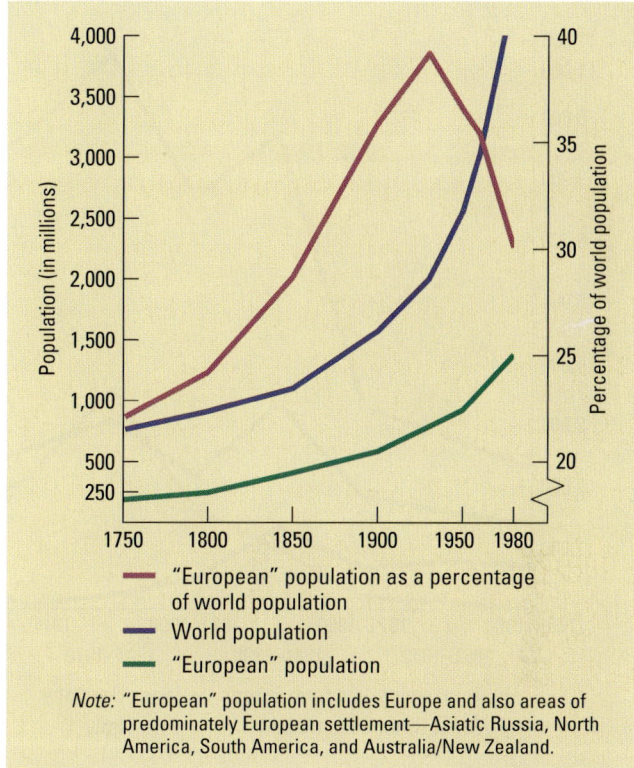

FIGURE 26.2 The Increase of European and World Populations, 1750–1980 (Sources: W. Woodruff, Impact of Western Man: A Study of Europe's Role in the World Economy. St. Martin's Press, New York, 1967, p. 103; United Nations, Statistical Yearbook, 1982, 1985, pp. 2–3.)

emigration reflected not only rural poverty but also the movement of skilled, industrial technicians and the preferences shown to British migrants in the British Empire. Ultimately, about one-third of all European migrants between 1840 and 1920 came from the British Isles. German migration was quite different. It grew irregularly after about 1830, reaching a first peak in the early 1850s and another in the early 1880s. Thereafter it declined rapidly, for Germany's rapid industrialization was providing adequate jobs at home. This pattern contrasted sharply with that of Italy. More and more Italians left the country right up to 1914, reflecting severe problems in Italian villages and relatively slow industrial growth. Thus migration patterns mirrored social and economic conditions in the various European countries and provinces.

Third, although the United States absorbed the largest number of European migrants, less than half of all migrants went to the United States. Asiatic Russia, Canada, Argentina, Brazil, Australia, and New Zealand also attracted

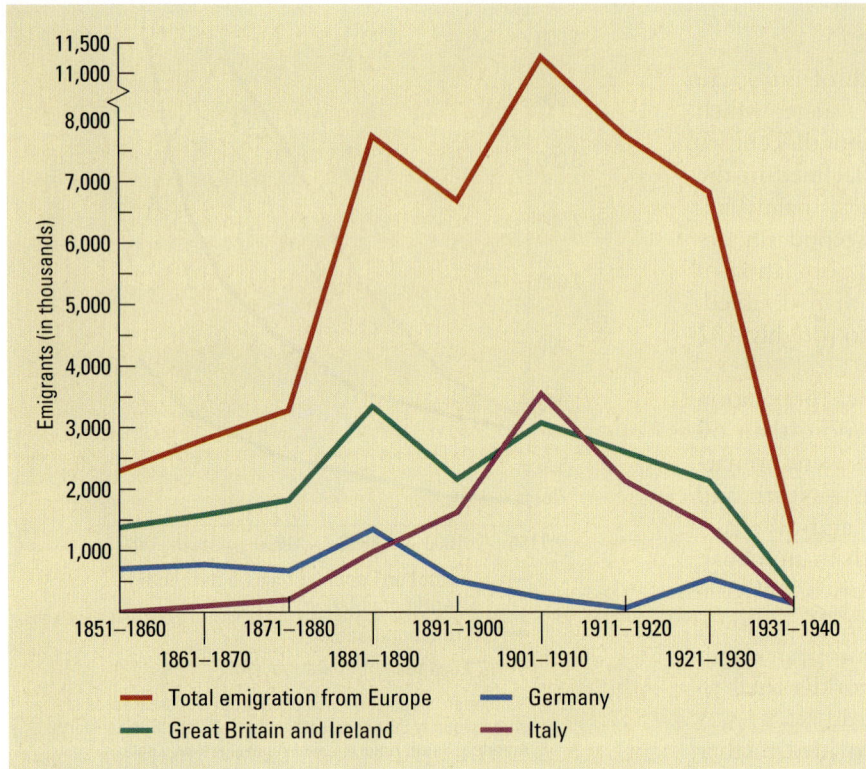

FIGURE 26.3 Emigration from Europe by Decades, 1851–1940 (*Source:* Copyright © W. Woodruff, from *Impact of Western Man*, by W. Woodruff, 1982. Reprinted with permission of University Press of America.)

large numbers, as Figure 26.4 shows. Moreover, migrants accounted for a larger proportion of the total population in Argentina, Brazil, and Canada than in the United States. The common American assumption that European migration meant migration to the United States is quite inaccurate.

European Migrants

What kind of people left Europe, and what were their reasons for doing so? The European migrant was most often a small peasant landowner or a village craftsman whose traditional way of life was threatened by too little land, estate agriculture, and cheap, factory-made goods. German peasants who left the Rhineland and southwestern Germany between 1830 and 1854, for example, felt trapped by what Friedrich List called the "dwarf economy," with its tiny landholdings and declining craft industries. Selling out and moving to buy much cheaper land in the American Midwest became a common response. Thus the European migrant was generally an energetic small farmer or skilled artisan trying hard to stay ahead of poverty, not a desperately impoverished landless peasant or urban proletarian.

Determined to maintain or improve their status, migrants were a great asset to the countries that received them. This was doubly so because the vast majority were young and very often unmarried. They came in the prime of life and were ready to work hard in the new land, at least for a time. Many Europeans moved but remained within Europe, settling temporarily or permanently in another European country. Jews from eastern Europe and peasants from Ireland migrated to Great Britain, Russians and Poles sought work in Germany, and Latin peoples from Spain, Portugal, and Italy entered France. Many Europeans were truly migrants as opposed to immigrants—that is, they returned home after some time abroad. One in two migrants to Argentina and probably one in three to the United States eventually returned to their native land.

The likelihood of repatriation varied greatly by nationality. People who migrated from the Balkans, for instance, were much more likely to return to their countries than people from Ireland and eastern European Jews. Once again, the possibility of buying land in the old country was of central importance. In Ireland (as well as in England and Scotland) land was tightly held by large, often absentee landowners, and little land was available for purchase. In Russia most land was held by non-Jews. Therefore, when Russian Jewish artisans began in the 1880s to escape both factory competition and oppression by mi-

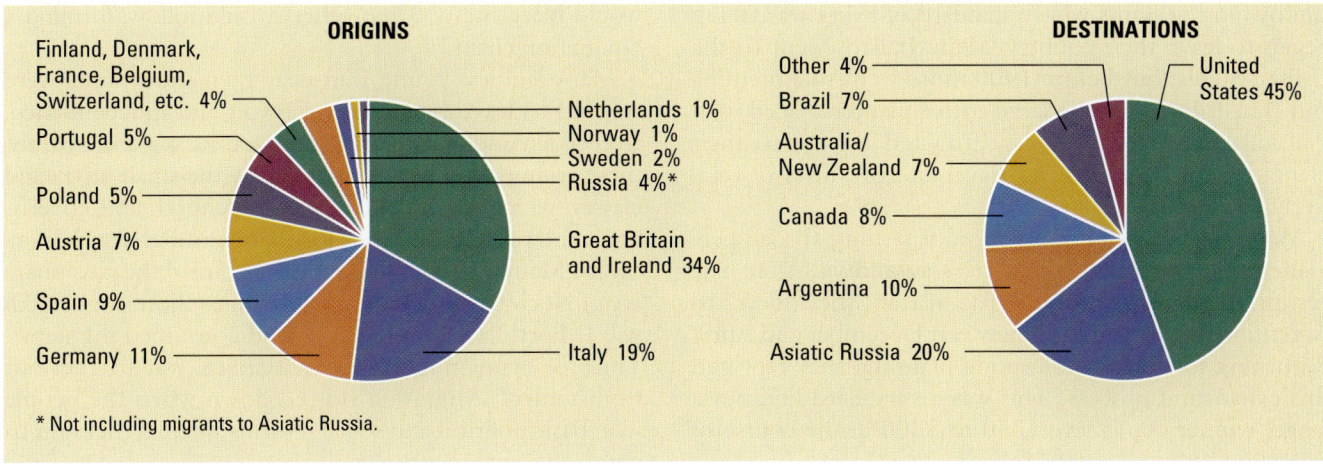

FIGURE 26.4 Origins and Destinations of European Emigrants, 1851–1960 (Source: Copyright © W. Woodruff, from Impact of Western Man, by W. Woodruff, 1982. Reprinted with permission of University Press of America.)

grating, it was basically a once-and-for-all departure. Non-Jewish migrants from Russia had access to land and returned much more frequently to their peasant villages in central Russia, Poland, and Ukraine.

The mass movement of Italians illustrates many of the characteristics of European migration. As late as the 1880s, three of every four Italians depended on agriculture. With the influx of cheap North American wheat, many small

An Italian Custom in Argentina Italian immigrants introduced the game of boccia to Argentina, where it took hold and became a popular recreation for men. Dressed up in their Sunday best, these Argentinian laborers are totally focused on the game, which is somewhat like horseshoes or shuffleboard. (Hulton Archive/Getty Images)

landowning peasants whose standard of living was falling began to leave their country. Many Italians went to the United States, but before 1900 more went to Argentina and Brazil. In Brazil the large coffee planters, faced with the collapse of black slavery, attracted Italians to their plantations with subsidized travel and promises of relatively high wages.

Many Italians had no intention of settling abroad permanently. Some called themselves **swallows.** After harvesting their own wheat and flax in Italy, they "flew" to Argentina to harvest wheat between December and April. Returning to Italy for the spring planting, they repeated this exhausting process. This was a very hard life, but a frugal worker could save $250 to $300 in the course of a season.

Ties of family and friendship played a crucial role in the movement of peoples. Many people from a given province or village settled together in rural enclaves or tightly knit urban neighborhoods thousands of miles away. Very often a strong individual—a businessman, a religious leader— would blaze the way and others would follow, forming a "migration chain."

Many landless young European men and women were spurred to leave by a spirit of revolt and independence. In Sweden and in Norway, in Jewish Russia and in Italy, these young people felt frustrated by the small privileged classes, which often controlled both church and government and resisted demands for change and greater opportunity. Many a young Norwegian seconded the passionate cry of Norway's national poet, Martinius Bjørnson: "Forth will I! Forth! I will be crushed and consumed if I stay."[3] Thus for many, migration was a radical way to "get out from under." Migration slowed down when the people won basic political and social reforms, such as the right to vote and social security.

Asian Migrants

Not all migration was from Europe. A substantial number of Chinese, Japanese, Indians, and Filipinos—to name

Vaccinating Migrants Bound for Hawaii, 1904 First Chinese, then Japanese, and finally Koreans and Filipinos went in large numbers across the Pacific to labor in Hawaii on American-owned sugar plantations in the late nineteenth century. The native Hawaiians had been decimated by disease, preparing the way for the annexation of Hawaii by the United States in 1898. *(Corbis)*

only four key groups—responded to rural hardship with temporary or permanent migration. At least 3 million Asians (as opposed to more than 60 million Europeans) moved abroad before 1920. Most went as indentured laborers to work under incredibly difficult conditions on the plantations or in the gold mines of Latin America, southern Asia, Africa, California, Hawaii, and Australia. White estate owners very often used Asians to replace or supplement blacks after the suppression of the slave trade.

In the 1840s, for example, there was a strong demand for field hands in Cuba, and the Spanish government actively recruited Chinese laborers. Between 1853 and 1873, when such migration was stopped, more than 130,000 Chinese laborers went to Cuba. The majority spent their lives as virtual slaves. The great landlords of Peru also brought in more than 100,000 workers from China in the nineteenth century, and there were similar movements of Asians elsewhere.

Such migration from Asia would undoubtedly have grown to much greater proportions if planters and mine owners in search of cheap labor had been able to hire as many Asian workers as they wished. But they could not. Asians fled the plantations and gold mines as soon as possible, seeking greater opportunities in trade and towns. There they came into conflict with local populations, whether in Malaya, East Africa, or areas settled by Europeans. These European settlers demanded a halt to Asian migration. By the 1880s, Americans and Australians were building **great white walls**—discriminatory laws designed to keep Asians out.

A crucial factor in the migrations before 1914 was, therefore, the general policy of "whites only" in the open lands of possible permanent settlement. This, too, was part of Western dominance in the increasingly lopsided world. Largely successful in monopolizing the best overseas opportunities, Europeans and people of European ancestry reaped the main benefits from the great migration. By 1913 people in Australia, Canada, and the United States all had higher average incomes than people in Great Britain, still Europe's wealthiest nation.

Western Imperialism, 1880–1914

The expansion of Western society reached its apex between about 1880 and 1914. In those years, the leading European nations not only continued to send massive streams of migrants, money, and manufactured goods around the world, but also rushed to create or enlarge vast *political* empires abroad. This political empire building contrasted sharply with the economic penetration of non-Western territories between 1816 and 1880, which had left a China or a Japan "opened" but politically independent. By contrast, the empires of the late nineteenth century recalled the old European colonial empires of the seventeenth and eighteenth centuries and led contemporaries to speak of the **new imperialism.**

Characterized by a frantic rush to plant the flag over as many people and as much territory as possible, the new imperialism had momentous consequences. It resulted in new tensions among competing European states, and it led to wars and rumors of war with non-European powers. The new imperialism was aimed primarily at Africa and Asia. It put millions of black, brown, and yellow peoples directly under the rule of whites.

- *How and why after 1875 did European nations rush to build political empires in Africa and Asia?*

The Scramble for Africa

The most spectacular manifestation of the new imperialism was the seizure of Africa, which broke sharply with previous patterns and fascinated contemporary Europeans and Americans. As late as 1880, European nations controlled only 10 percent of the African continent, and their possessions were hardly increasing. The French had begun conquering Algeria in 1830, and by 1880 substantial numbers of French, Italian, and Spanish colonists had settled among the overwhelming Arab majority.

At the other end of the continent, in South Africa, the British had taken possession of the Dutch settlements at Cape Town during the wars with Napoleon I. This takeover had led disgruntled Dutch cattle ranchers and farmers in 1835 to make their so-called Great Trek into the interior, where they fought the Zulu and Xhosa peoples for land. After 1853, while British colonies such as Canada and Australia were beginning to evolve toward self-government, the Boers, or **Afrikaners** (as the descendants of the Dutch in the Cape Colony were beginning to call themselves), proclaimed their political independence and defended it against British armies. By 1880 Afrikaner and British settlers, who detested each other, had wrested control of much of South Africa from the Zulu, Xhosa, and other African peoples.

European trading posts and forts dating back to the Age of Discovery and the slave trade dotted the coast of West Africa. The Portuguese proudly but ineffectively held their old possessions in Angola and Mozambique. Elsewhere over the great mass of the continent, Europeans did not rule.

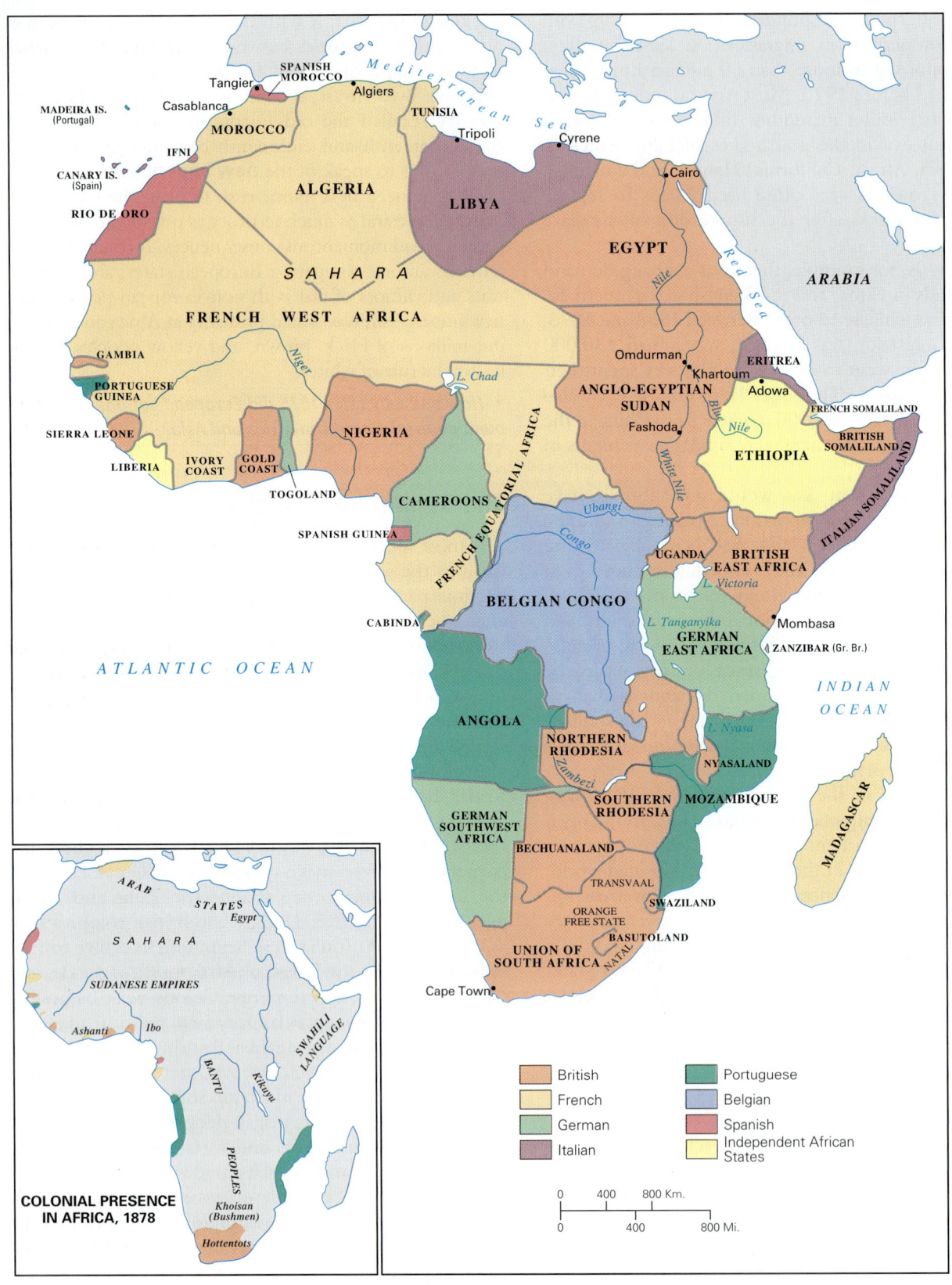

Between 1880 and 1900, the situation changed drastically. Britain, France, Germany, and Italy scrambled for African possessions as if their national livelihoods depended on it (see Map 26.2). By 1900 nearly the whole continent had been carved up and placed under European rule: only Ethiopia in northeast Africa, which repulsed Italian invaders, and Liberia on the West African coast, which had been settled by freed slaves from the United States, remained independent. In the years before 1914, the European powers tightened their control and established colonial governments to rule their gigantic empires.

Online Study Center Improve Your Grade
Primary Source: European Imperialism in Africa: A Veteran Explains the Rules of the Game

The Dutch settler republics also succumbed to imperialism, but the final outcome was quite different. The British, led by Cecil Rhodes in the Cape Colony, leapfrogged over the Afrikaner states in the early 1890s and established protectorates over Bechuanaland (now Botswana) and Rhodesia (now Zimbabwe and Zambia), named in honor of its freelance imperial founder. Trying unsuccessfully to undermine the stubborn Afrikaners in the Transvaal, where English-speaking capitalists like Rhodes were developing fabulously rich gold mines, the British conquered their white rivals in the bloody South African War (1899–1902). In 1910 their territories were united with the old Cape Colony and the eastern province of Natal in a new Union of South Africa, established—unlike any other territory in Africa—as a largely "self-governing" colony. This enabled the defeated Afrikaners to use their numerical superiority over the British settlers to gradually take political power, as even the most educated nonwhites lost the right to vote outside the Cape Colony. (See the feature "Individuals in Society: Cecil Rhodes.")

In the complexity of the European seizure of Africa, certain events and individuals stand out. Of enormous importance was the British occupation of Egypt in 1882, which established the new model of formal political control. There was also the role of Leopold II of Belgium (r. 1865–1909), an energetic, strong-willed monarch with a lust for distant territory. "The sea bathes our coast, the world lies before us," he had exclaimed in 1861. "Steam and electricity have annihilated distance, and all the non-appropriated lands on the surface of the globe can become the field of our operations and of our success."[4] By 1876 Leopold was focusing on central Africa. Subsequently, he formed a financial syndicate under his personal control to send Henry M. Stanley, a sensation-seeking journalist and part-time explorer, to the Congo basin. Stanley was able to establish trading stations, sign "treaties" with African chiefs, and plant Leopold's flag. Leopold's actions alarmed the French, who quickly sent out an expedition under Pierre de Brazza. In 1880 de Brazza signed a treaty of protection with the chief of the large Teke tribe and began to establish a French protectorate on the north bank of the Congo River.

Leopold's buccaneering intrusion into the Congo area raised the question of the political fate of Africa. By 1882 Europe had caught "African fever." There was a gold rush mentality, and the race for territory was on.

To lay down some basic rules for this new and dangerous game of imperialist competition in sub-Saharan Africa, Jules Ferry of France and Otto von Bismarck of Germany arranged an international conference on Africa in Berlin in 1884 and 1885. The conference established the principle that European claims to African territory had to rest on "effective occupation" in order to be recognized by other states. This meant that Europeans would push relentlessly into interior regions from all sides and that no single European power would be able to claim the entire continent. The conference recognized Leopold's personal rule over a neutral Congo free state and agreed to work to stop slavery and the slave trade in Africa.

The **Berlin conference** coincided with Germany's sudden emergence as an imperial power. Prior to about 1880, Bismarck, like many other European leaders at the time, had seen little value in colonies. Colonies reminded him, he said, of a poor but proud nobleman who wore a fur coat when he could not afford a shirt underneath. Then in 1884 and 1885, as political agitation for expansion increased, Bismarck did an abrupt about-face, and Germany established protectorates over a number of

Mapping the Past

MAP 26.2 The Partition of Africa The European powers carved up Africa after 1880 and built vast political empires. European states also seized territory in Asia in the nineteenth century, although some Asian states and peoples managed to maintain their political independence, as may be seen on Map 26.3, page 864. The late nineteenth century was the high point of European imperialism. Compare the patterns of European imperialism in Africa and Asia, using this map and Map 26.3. ❶ What European countries were leading imperialist states in both Africa and Asia, and what lands did they hold? ❷ What countries in Africa and Asia maintained their political independence? ❸ From an imperialist perspective, what in 1914 did the United States and Japan, two very different countries, have in common in Africa and Asia?

Online Study Center Improve Your Grade
Interactive Map: Africa in 1914

European Imperialism at Its Worst This 1908 English cartoon, "Leopold, King of the Congo, in his national dress," focuses on the barbaric practice of cutting off the hands and feet of Africans who refused to gather as much rubber as Leopold's company demanded. In 1908 an international human rights campaign forced the Belgian king to cede his personal fief to the Belgian state. *(The Granger Collection, New York)*

small African kingdoms and tribes in Togo, Cameroons, southwest Africa, and, later, East Africa. In acquiring colonies, Bismarck cooperated against the British with France's Ferry, who was as ardent for empire as he was for education. With Bismarck's tacit approval, the French pressed southward from Algeria, eastward from their old forts on the Senegal coast, and northward from their protectorate on the Congo River.

Meanwhile, the British began enlarging their West African enclaves and impatiently pushing northward from the Cape Colony and westward from Zanzibar. Their thrust southward from Egypt was blocked in Sudan by fiercely independent Muslims who massacred a British force at Khartoum in 1885.

A decade later, another British force, under General Horatio H. Kitchener, moved cautiously and more successfully up the Nile River, building a railroad to supply arms and reinforcements as it went. Finally, in 1898 these British troops met their foe at Omdurman (see Map 26.2), where Muslim tribesmen armed with spears charged time and time again, only to be cut down by the recently invented machine gun. For one smug participant, the young British officer Winston Churchill, it was "like a pantomime scene" in a play. "These extraordinary foreign figures . . . march up one by one from the darkness of Barbarism to the footlights of civilization . . . and their conquerors, taking their possessions, forget even their names." For another, more somber English observer, "It was not a battle but an execution. The bodies were not in heaps . . . but they spread evenly over acres and acres."[5] In the end, eleven thousand brave Muslim tribesmen lay dead, while only twenty-eight Britons had been killed.

Continuing up the Nile after the Battle of Omdurman, Kitchener's armies found that a small French force had already occupied the village of Fashoda. Locked in imperial competition with Britain ever since the British occupation of Egypt, France had tried to beat the British to one of Africa's last unclaimed areas—the upper reaches of the Nile. The result was a serious diplomatic crisis and even the threat of war. Eventually, wracked by the Dreyfus affair (see page 834) and unwilling to fight, France backed down and withdrew its forces, allowing the British to take over.

The British conquest of Sudan exemplifies the general process of empire building in Africa. The fate of the Muslim force at Omdurman was eventually inflicted on all native peoples who resisted European rule: they were blown away by vastly superior military force. But however much the European powers squabbled for territory and privilege around the world, they always had the sense

Individuals in Society

Cecil Rhodes

Cecil Rhodes (1853–1902) epitomized the dynamism and the ruthlessness of the new imperialism. He built a corporate monopoly, claimed vast tracts in Africa, and established the famous Rhodes scholarships to develop colonial (and American) leaders who would love and strengthen the British Empire. But to Africans, he left a bitter legacy.

Rhodes came from a large middle-class family and at seventeen went to southern Africa to seek his fortune. He soon turned to diamonds, newly discovered at Kimberley, picked good partners, and was wealthy by 1876. But Rhodes, often called a dreamer, wanted more. He entered Oxford University, while returning periodically to Africa, and his musings crystallized in a belief in progress through racial competition and territorial expansion. "I contend," he wrote, "that we [English] are the finest race in the world and the more of the world we inhabit the better it is for the human race."*

Rhodes's belief in British expansion never wavered. In 1880 he formed the De Beers Mining Company, and by 1888 his firm monopolized southern Africa's diamond production and earned fabulous profits. Rhodes also entered the Cape Colony's legislature and became the all-powerful prime minister from 1890 to 1896. His main objective was to dominate the Afrikaner republics and to impose British rule on as much land as possible beyond their northern borders. Working through a state-approved private company financed in part by De Beers, Rhodes's agents forced and cajoled African kings to accept British "protection," then put down rebellions with Maxim machine guns. Britain thus obtained a great swath of empire on the cheap.

But Rhodes, like many high achievers obsessed with power and personal aggrandizement, went too far. He backed, and then in 1896 declined to call back, a failed invasion of the Transvaal, which was designed to topple the Dutch-speaking republic. Repudiated by top British leaders who had encouraged his plan, Rhodes had to resign as prime minister. In declining health, he continued to agitate against the Afrikaner republics. He died at age forty-nine as the South African War (1899–1902) ended.

In accounting for Rhodes's remarkable but flawed achievements, both sympathetic and critical biographers stress his imposing size, enormous energy, and powerful personality. His ideas were commonplace, but he believed in them passionately, and he could persuade and inspire others to follow his lead. Rhodes the idealist was nonetheless a born negotiator, a crafty

Cecil Rhodes, after crushing the last African revolt in Rhodesia in 1896.
(Brown Brothers)

dealmaker who believed that everyone could be had for a price. According to his best biographer, Rhodes's homosexuality—discreet, partially repressed, and undeniable—was also "a major component of his magnetism and his success."† Never comfortable with women, he loved male companionship. He drew together a "band of brothers," both gay and straight, to share in the pursuit of power.

Rhodes cared nothing for the rights of blacks. Ever a combination of visionary and opportunist, he looked forward to an eventual reconciliation of Afrikaners and British in a united white front. Therefore, as prime minister of the Cape Colony, he broke with the colony's liberal tradition and supported Afrikaner demands to reduce drastically the number of black voters and limit black freedoms. This helped lay the foundation for the Union of South Africa's brutal policy of racial segregation known as *apartheid* after 1948.

Questions for Analysis

1. How did Rhodes relate to Afrikaners and to black Africans? How do you account for the differences and the similarities?
2. In what ways does Rhodes's career throw additional light on the debate over the causes of the new imperialism?

*Robert Rotberg, *The Founder: Cecil Rhodes and the Pursuit of Power* (New York: Oxford University Press, 1988), p. 150.
†Ibid., p. 408.

Online Study Center Improve Your Grade
Going Beyond Individuals in Society

MAP 26.3 Asia in 1914 India remained under British rule, while China precariously preserved its political independence. The Dutch empire in modern-day Indonesia was old, but French control of Indochina was a product of the new imperialism.

to stop short of actually fighting each other. Imperial ambitions were not worth a great European war.

Imperialism in Asia

Although the sudden division of Africa was more spectacular, Europeans also extended their political control in Asia. In 1815 the Dutch ruled little more than the island of Java in the East Indies. Thereafter they gradually brought almost all of the three-thousand-mile archipelago under their political authority, though—in good imperialist fashion—they had to share some of the spoils with Britain and Germany. In the critical decade of the 1880s, the French under the leadership of Ferry took Indochina. India, Japan, and China also experienced a profound imperialist impact (see Map 26.3).

Two other great imperialist powers, Russia and the United States, also acquired rich territories in Asia. Russia moved steadily forward on two fronts throughout the nineteenth century. Russians conquered Muslim areas to the south in the Caucasus and in Central Asia and also proceeded to nibble greedily on China's outlying provinces in the Far East, especially in the 1890s.

The United States's great conquest was the Philippines, taken from Spain in 1898 after the Spanish-American War. When it quickly became clear that the United States had no intention of granting independence, Philippine patriots rose in revolt and were suppressed only after long, bitter fighting. Some Americans protested the taking of the Philippines, but to no avail. Thus another great Western power joined the imperialist ranks in Asia.

Causes of the New Imperialism

Many factors contributed to the late-nineteenth-century rush for territory and empire, which was in turn one aspect of Western society's generalized expansion in the age of industry and nationalism. It is little wonder that controversies have raged over interpretation of the new imperialism, especially since authors of every persuasion have often exaggerated particular aspects in an attempt to prove their own theories. Yet despite complexity and controversy, basic causes are clearly identifiable.

Economic motives played an important role in the extension of political empires, especially the British Empire. By the late 1870s, France, Germany, and the United States were industrializing rapidly behind rising tariff barriers. Great Britain was losing its early lead and facing increasingly tough competition in foreign markets. In this new economic situation, Britain came to value old possessions, especially its vast colony of India, which it had exploited most profitably for more than a century. When continental powers began to grab territory in the 1880s, the British followed suit immediately. They feared that France and Germany would seal off their empires with high tariffs and restrictions and that future economic opportunities would be lost forever.

Actually, the overall economic gains of the new imperialism proved quite limited before 1914. The new colonies were simply too poor to buy much, and they offered few immediately profitable investments. Nonetheless, even the poorest, most barren desert was jealously prized, and no territory was ever abandoned. Colonies became important for political and diplomatic reasons. Each leading country saw colonies as crucial to national security, military power, and international prestige. For instance, safeguarding the Suez Canal played a key role in the British occupation of Egypt, and protecting Egypt in turn led to the bloody conquest of Sudan. Far-flung possessions guaranteed ever-growing navies the safe havens and the dependable coaling stations they needed in time of crisis or war.

Many people were convinced that colonies were essential to great nations. "There has never been a great power without great colonies," wrote one French publicist in 1877. "Every virile people has established colonial power," echoed the famous nationalist historian of Germany, Heinrich von Treitschke. "All great nations in the fullness of their strength have desired to set their mark upon barbarian lands and those who fail to participate in this great rivalry will play a pitiable role in time to come."[6]

Treitschke's harsh statement reflects not only the increasing aggressiveness of European nationalism after Bismarck's wars of German unification but also Social Darwinian theories of brutal competition among races. As one prominent English economist argued, the "strongest nation has always been conquering the weaker . . . and the strongest tend to be best." Thus European nations, which were seen as racially distinct parts of the dominant white race, had to seize colonies to show they were strong and virile. Moreover, since racial struggle was nature's inescapable law, the conquest of "inferior" peoples was just. "The path of progress is strewn with the wreck . . . of inferior races," wrote one professor in 1900. "Yet these dead peoples are, in very truth, the stepping stones on which mankind has risen to the higher intellectual and deeper emotional life of today."[7] Social Darwinism and harsh racial doctrines fostered imperialist expansion.

So did the industrial world's unprecedented technological and military superiority. Three aspects were crucial. First, the rapidly firing machine gun, so lethal at Omdurman in Sudan, was an ultimate weapon in many another unequal battle. Second, newly discovered quinine proved no less effective in controlling attacks of malaria, which had previously decimated whites in the tropics whenever they left breezy coastal enclaves and dared to venture into mosquito-infested interiors. Third, the combination of the steamship and the international telegraph permitted Western powers to quickly concentrate their firepower in a given area when it was needed. Never before—and never again after 1914—would the technological gap between the West and non-Western regions of the world be so great.

Social tensions and domestic political conflicts also contributed mightily to overseas expansion. In Germany, in Russia, and in other countries to a lesser extent, contemporary critics of imperialism charged conservative political leaders with manipulating colonial issues in order to divert popular attention from the class struggle at home and to create a false sense of national unity. Thus imperial propagandists relentlessly stressed that colonies benefited workers as well as capitalists, providing jobs and cheap raw materials that raised workers' standard of living. Government leaders and their allies in the tabloid press successfully encouraged the masses to savor foreign triumphs and glory in the supposed increase in national prestige. In short, conservative leaders defined imperialist development as a national necessity, which they used to justify the status quo and their hold on power.

Finally, certain special-interest groups in each country were powerful agents of expansion. Shipping companies wanted lucrative subsidies. White settlers demanded more land and greater protection. Missionaries and humanitarians wanted to spread religion and stop the slave trade. Military men and colonial officials, whose role has often been overlooked, foresaw rapid advancement and high-paid positions in growing empires. The actions of such groups pushed the course of empire forward.

A Missionary School A Swahili schoolboy leads his classmates in a reading lesson in Dar es Salaam in German East Africa before 1914, as portraits of Emperor William II and his wife look down on the classroom. Europeans argued that they were spreading the benefits of a superior civilization with schools like this one, which is unusually solid because of its strategic location in the capital city. *(Ullstein Bilderdienst/The Granger Collection, New York)*

A "Civilizing Mission"

Western society did not rest the case for empire solely on naked conquest and a Darwinian racial struggle or on power politics and the need for naval bases on every ocean. Imperialists developed additional arguments in order to satisfy their consciences and answer their critics.

A favorite idea was that Europeans could and should "civilize" more primitive, nonwhite peoples. According to this view, nonwhites would eventually receive the benefits of modern economies, cities, advanced medicine, and higher standards of living. In time, they might be ready for self-government and Western democracy. Thus the French spoke of their sacred "civilizing mission." In 1899 Rudyard Kipling (1865–1936), who wrote masterfully of Anglo-Indian life and was perhaps the most influential British writer of the 1890s, exhorted Europeans (and Americans in the United States) to unselfish service in distant lands:

Take up the White Man's Burden—
    Send forth the best ye breed—
Go bind your sons to exile
    To serve your captives' need,
To wait in heavy harness,
    On fluttered folk and wild—
Your new-caught, sullen peoples
    Half-devil and half-child.[8]

Many Americans accepted the ideology of the **white man's burden.** It was an important factor in the decision to rule, rather than liberate, the Philippines after the Spanish-American War. Like their European counterparts, these Americans sincerely believed that their civilization had reached unprecedented heights and that they had unique benefits to bestow on all "less advanced" peoples. Another argument was that imperial government protected natives from tribal warfare as well as cruder forms of exploitation by white settlers and business people.

Peace and stability under European control also facilitated the spread of Christianity. In Africa Catholic and Protestant missionaries competed with Islam south of the Sahara, seeking converts and building schools to spread the Gospel. Many Africans' first real contact with whites was in mission schools. Some peoples, such as the Ibo in Nigeria, became highly Christianized.

Such occasional successes in black Africa contrasted with the general failure of missionary efforts in India, China, and the Islamic world. There Christians often preached in vain to peoples with ancient, complex religious beliefs. Yet the number of Christian believers around the world did increase substantially in the nineteenth century, and missionary groups kept trying. Unfortunately, "many missionaries had drunk at the well of European racism," and this probably prevented them from doing better.[9]

Critics of Imperialism

The expansion of empire aroused sharp, even bitter, critics. A forceful attack was delivered in 1902, after the unpopular South African War, by radical English economist J. A. Hobson (1858–1940) in his *Imperialism,* a work that influenced Lenin and others. Hobson contended that the rush to acquire colonies was due to the economic needs of unregulated capitalism, particularly the need of the rich to find outlets for their surplus capital. Yet, Hobson argued, imperial possessions did not pay off economically for the country as a whole. Only unscrupulous special-interest groups profited from them, at the expense of both the European taxpayer and the natives. Moreover, Hobson argued that the quest for empire diverted popular attention away from domestic reform and the need to reduce the great gap between rich and poor. These and similar arguments were not very persuasive, however. Most people then (and now) were sold on the idea that imperialism was economically profitable for the homeland, and a broad and genuine enthusiasm for empire developed among the masses.

Hobson and many other critics struck home, however, with their moral condemnation of whites imperiously ruling nonwhites. They rebelled against crude Social Darwinian thought. "O Evolution, what crimes are committed in thy name!" cried one foe. Another sardonically coined a new beatitude: "Blessed are the strong, for they shall prey on the weak."[10] Kipling and his kind were lampooned as racist bullies whose rule rested on brutality, racial contempt, and the Maxim machine gun. Henry Labouchère, a member of Parliament and prominent spokesman for this position, mocked Kipling's famous poem:

Pile on the Brown Man's burden!
And if ye rouse his hate,
Meet his old-fashioned reasons
With Maxims up to date,
With shells and Dum-Dum bullets
A hundred times plain
The Brown Man's loss must never
Imply the White Man's gain.[11]

Similarly, in 1902 in *Heart of Darkness* Polish-born novelist Joseph Conrad (1857–1924) castigated the "pure selfishness" of Europeans in "civilizing" Africa; the main character, once a liberal scholar, turns into a savage brute.

Critics charged Europeans with applying a degrading double standard and failing to live up to their own noble ideals. At home Europeans had won or were winning representative government, individual liberties, and a certain equality of opportunity. In their empires, Europeans imposed military dictatorships on Africans and Asians; forced them to work involuntarily, almost like slaves; and discriminated against them shamelessly. Only by renouncing imperialism, its critics insisted, and giving captive peoples the freedoms Western society had struggled for since the French Revolution would Europeans be worthy of their traditions. Europeans who denounced the imperialist tide provided colonial peoples with a Western ideology of liberation.

Responding to Western Imperialism

To peoples in Africa and Asia, Western expansion represented a profoundly disruptive assault. Everywhere it threatened traditional ruling classes, traditional economies, and traditional ways of life. Christian missionaries and European secular ideologies challenged established beliefs and values. Non-Western peoples experienced a crisis of identity, one made all the more painful by the power and arrogance of the white intruders.

- *What was the general pattern of non-Western responses to Western expansion, and how did India, Japan, and China meet the imperialist challenge?*

The Pattern of Response

Generally, the initial response of African and Asian rulers to aggressive Western expansion was to try to drive the unwelcome foreigners away. This was the case in China, Japan, and upper Sudan, as we have seen. Violent anti-foreign reactions exploded elsewhere again and again, but the superior military technology of the industrialized West almost invariably prevailed. Beaten in battle, many Africans and Asians concentrated on preserving their cultural traditions at all costs. Others found themselves forced to reconsider their initial hostility. Some (such as Ismail of Egypt) concluded that the West was indeed superior in some ways and that it was therefore necessary to reform their societies and copy some European achievements, especially if they wished to escape full-blown Western political rule. Thus it is possible to think of responses to the Western impact as a spectrum, with "traditionalists" at one end, "westernizers" or "modernizers" at the other, and many shades of opinion in between. Both before and after European domination, the struggle among these groups was often intense. With time, however, the modernizers tended to gain the upper hand.

When the power of both the traditionalists and the modernizers was thoroughly shattered by superior force, the great majority of Asians and Africans accepted imperial rule. Political participation in non-Western lands was historically limited to small elites, and the masses were used to doing what their rulers told them. In these circumstances Europeans, clothed in power and convinced of their righteousness, governed smoothly and effectively. They received considerable support from both traditionalists (local chiefs, landowners, religious leaders) and modernizers (Western-educated professional classes and civil servants).

Nevertheless, imperial rule was in many ways an imposing edifice built on sand. Support for European rule among the conforming and accepting millions was shallow and weak. Thus the conforming masses followed with greater or lesser enthusiasm a few determined personalities who came to oppose the Europeans. Such leaders always arose, both when Europeans ruled directly and when they manipulated native governments, for at least two basic reasons.

First, the nonconformists—the eventual anti-imperialist leaders—developed a burning desire for human dignity. They came to feel that such dignity was incompatible with foreign rule. Second, potential leaders found in the Western world the ideologies and justification for their protest. They discovered liberalism, with its credo of civil liberty and political self-determination. They echoed the demands of anti-imperialists in Europe and America that the West live up to its own ideals. Above all, they found themselves attracted to modern nationalism, which asserted that every people had the right to control its own destiny. After 1917 anti-imperialist revolt would find another weapon in Lenin's version of Marxian socialism. Thus the anti-imperialist search for dignity drew strength from Western thought and culture, as is apparent in the development of three major Asian countries—India, Japan, and China.

Empire in India

India was the jewel of the British Empire, and no colonial area experienced a more profound British impact. Unlike Japan and China, which maintained a real or precarious independence, and unlike African territories, which were annexed by Europeans only at the end of the nineteenth century, India was ruled more or less absolutely by Britain for a very long time.

Arriving in India on the heels of the Portuguese in the seventeenth century, the British East India Company had conquered the last independent native state by 1848. The

Imperial Complexities in India Britain permitted many native princes to continue their rule, if they accepted British domination. This photo shows a road-building project designed to facilitate famine relief in a southern native state. Officials of the local Muslim prince and their British "advisers" watch over workers drawn from the Hindu majority. (*Nizam's Good Works Project—Famine Relief: Road Building, Aurangabad 1895–1902, from Judith Mara Gutman, Through Indian Eyes. Courtesy, Private Collection*)

last "traditional" response to European rule—the attempt by the established ruling classes to drive the white man out by military force—was broken in India in 1857 and 1858. Those were the years of the **Great Rebellion** (which the British called a "mutiny"), when an insurrection by Muslim and Hindu mercenaries in the British army spread throughout northern and central India before it was finally crushed, primarily by loyal native troops from southern India. Thereafter Britain ruled India directly.

After 1858 India was ruled by the British Parliament in London and administered by a tiny, all-white civil service in India. In 1900 this elite consisted of fewer than 3,500 top officials, for a population of 300 million. The white elite, backed by white officers and native troops, was competent and generally well-disposed toward the welfare of the Indian peasant masses. Yet it practiced strict job discrimination and social segregation, and most of its members quite frankly considered the jumble of Indian peoples and castes to be racially inferior. As Lord Kitchener, one of the most distinguished top military commanders in India, stated:

It is this consciousness of the inherent superiority of the European which has won for us India. However well educated and clever a native may be, and however brave he may prove himself, I believe that no rank we can bestow on him would cause him to be considered an equal of the British officer.[12]

British women played an important part in the imperial enterprise, especially after the opening of the Suez Canal in 1869 made it much easier for civil servants and businessmen to bring their wives and children with them to India. These British families tended to live in their own separate communities, where they occupied large houses with well-shaded porches, handsome lawns, and a multitude of servants. It was the wife's responsibility to manage this complex household. Many officials' wives learned to relish their duties, and they directed their households and servants with the same self-confident authoritarianism that characterized British political rule in India. (See the feature "Listening to the Past: A British Woman in India" on pages 876–877.)

A small minority of British women—many of them feminists, social reformers, or missionaries, both married and single—sought to go further and shoulder the "white women's burden" in India, as one historian has described it.[13] These women tried especially to improve the lives of Indian women, both Hindu and Muslim, and to move them closer through education and legislation to the better conditions that they believed Western women had attained. Their greatest success was educating some elite Hindu women who took up the cause of reform.

With British men and women sharing a sense of mission as well as strong feelings of racial and cultural superiority, the British acted energetically and introduced many desirable changes to India. Realizing that they needed well-educated Indians to serve as skilled subordinates in the government and army, the British established a modern system of progressive secondary education in which all instruction was in English. Thus through education and government service, the British offered some Indians excellent opportunities for both economic and social advancement. High-caste Hindus, particularly quick to respond, emerged as skillful intermediaries between the British rulers and the Indian people, and soon they formed a new elite profoundly influenced by Western thought and culture.

This new bureaucratic elite played a crucial role in modern economic development, which was a second result of British rule. Irrigation projects for agriculture, the world's third-largest railroad network for good communications, and large tea and jute plantations geared to the world economy were all developed. Unfortunately, the lot of the Indian masses improved little, for the increase in production was eaten up by population increase.

Finally, with a well-educated, English-speaking Indian bureaucracy and modern communications, the British created a unified, powerful state. They placed under the same general system of law and administration the different Hindu and Muslim peoples and the vanquished kingdoms of the entire subcontinent—groups that had fought each other for centuries and had been repeatedly conquered by Muslim and Mongol invaders. It was as if Europe, with its many states and varieties of Christianity, had been conquered and united in a single great empire.

In spite of these achievements, the decisive reaction to European rule was the rise of nationalism among the Indian elite. No matter how anglicized and necessary a member of the educated classes became, he or she could never become the white ruler's equal. The top jobs, the best clubs, the modern hotels, and even certain railroad compartments were sealed off to brown-skinned Indians. The peasant masses might accept such inequality as the latest version of age-old oppression, but the well-educated, English-speaking elite eventually could not. For the elite, racial discrimination meant injured pride and bitter injustice. It flagrantly contradicted those cherished Western concepts of human rights and equality. Moreover, it was based on dictatorship, no matter how benign.

By 1885, when educated Indians came together to found the predominately Hindu Indian National Congress, demands were increasing for the equality and self-government that Britain had already granted white-settler colonies, such as Canada and Australia. By 1907, emboldened in part by Japan's success (see the next section), the radicals in the Indian National Congress were calling for complete independence. Even the moderates were demanding home rule for India through an elected parliament. Although there were sharp divisions between Hindus and Muslims, Indians were finding an answer to the foreign challenge. The common heritage of British rule and Western ideals, along with the reform and revitalization of the Hindu religion, had created a genuine movement for national independence.

The Example of Japan

When Commodore Matthew Perry arrived in Japan in 1853 with his crude but effective gunboat diplomacy,

Japan was a complex feudal society. At the top stood a figurehead emperor, but real power was in the hands of a hereditary military governor, the **shogun.** With the help of a warrior nobility known as **samurai,** the shogun governed a country of hard-working, productive peasants and city dwellers. Often poor and restless, the intensely proud samurai were humiliated by the sudden American intrusion and the unequal treaties with Western countries.

When foreign diplomats and merchants began to settle in Yokohama, radical samurai reacted with a wave of antiforeign terrorism and antigovernment assassinations between 1858 and 1863. The imperialist response was swift and unambiguous. An allied fleet of American, British, Dutch, and French warships demolished key forts, further weakening the power and prestige of the shogun's government. Then in 1867, a coalition led by patriotic samurai seized control of the government with hardly any bloodshed and restored the political power of the emperor. This was the Meiji Restoration, a great turning point in Japanese development.

The immediate, all-important goal of the new government was to meet the foreign threat. The battle cry of the Meiji reformers was "Enrich the state and strengthen the armed forces." Yet how were these tasks to be done? In an about-face that was one of history's most remarkable chapters, the young but well-trained, idealistic but flexible leaders of Meiji Japan dropped their antiforeign attacks. Convinced that Western civilization was indeed superior in its military and industrial aspects, they initiated from above a series of measures to reform Japan along modern lines. In the broadest sense, the Meiji leaders tried to harness the power inherent in Europe's dual revolution in order to protect their country and catch up with the West.

In 1871 the new leaders abolished the old feudal structure of aristocratic, decentralized government and formed a strong unified state. Following the example of the French Revolution, they dismantled the four-class legal system and declared social equality. They decreed freedom of movement in a country where traveling abroad had been a most serious crime. They created a free, competitive, government-stimulated economy. Japan began to build railroads and modern factories. Thus the new generation adopted many principles of a free, liberal society, and, as in Europe, such freedom resulted in a tremendously creative release of human energy.

Yet the overriding concern of Japan's political leadership was always a powerful state, and to achieve this, more than liberalism was borrowed from the West. A powerful modern navy was created, and the army was completely reorganized along European lines, with three-year military service for all males and a professional officer corps.

The Rapid Modernization of the Japanese Army This woodcut from about 1870 shows Japanese soldiers outfitted in Western uniforms and marching in Western formation. Japanese reformers, impressed by Prussian discipline and success on the battlefield, looked to Germany for their military models. *(Ryogoku Tsuneo Tamba Collection/Laurie Platt Winfrey)*

This army of draftees effectively put down disturbances in the countryside, and in 1877 it was used to crush a major rebellion by feudal elements protesting the loss of their privileges. Japan also borrowed rapidly and adapted skillfully the West's science and modern technology, particularly in industry, medicine, and education. Many Japanese were encouraged to study abroad, and the government paid large salaries to attract foreign experts. These experts were always carefully controlled, however, and replaced by trained Japanese as soon as possible.

By 1890, when the new state was firmly established, the

wholesale borrowing of the early restoration had given way to more selective emphasis on those things foreign that were in keeping with Japanese tradition. Following the model of the German Empire, Japan established an authoritarian constitution and rejected democracy. The power of the emperor and his ministers was vast, that of the legislature limited.

Japan successfully copied the imperialism of Western society. Expansion not only proved that Japan was strong; it also cemented the nation together in a great mission. Having "opened" Korea with the gunboat diplomacy of imperialism in 1876, Japan decisively defeated China in a war over Korea in 1894 and 1895 and took Formosa (modern-day Taiwan). In the next years, Japan competed aggressively with the leading European powers for influence and territory in China, particularly Manchuria. There Japanese and Russian imperialism met and collided. In 1904 Japan attacked Russia without warning, and after a bloody war, Japan emerged with a valuable foothold in China, Russia's former protectorate over Port Arthur (see Map 26.3). By 1910, with the annexation of Korea, Japan had become a major imperialist power.

Japan became the first non-Western country to use an ancient love of country to transform itself and thereby meet the many-sided challenge of Western expansion. Moreover, Japan demonstrated convincingly that a modern Asian nation could defeat and humble a great Western power. Many Chinese nationalists were fascinated by Japan's achievement. A group of patriots in French-ruled southern Vietnam sent Vietnamese students to Japan to learn the island empire's secret of success. Japan provided patriots throughout Asia and Africa with an inspiring example of national recovery and liberation.

Toward Revolution in China

In 1860 the two-hundred-year-old Qing Dynasty in China appeared on the verge of collapse. Efforts to repel foreigners had failed, and rebellion and chaos wracked the country. Yet the government drew on its traditional strengths and made a surprising comeback that lasted more than thirty years.

Two factors were crucial in this reversal. First, the traditional ruling groups temporarily produced new and effective leadership. Loyal scholar-statesmen and generals quelled disturbances such as the great Tai Ping rebellion. The empress dowager Tzu Hsi, a truly remarkable woman, governed in the name of her young son and combined shrewd insight with vigorous action to revitalize the bureaucracy.

Second, destructive foreign aggression lessened, for the Europeans had obtained their primary goal of commercial and diplomatic relations. Indeed, some Europeans contributed to the dynasty's recovery. A talented Irishman effectively reorganized China's customs office and increased the government tax receipts, while a sympathetic American diplomat represented China in foreign lands and helped strengthen the central government. Such efforts dovetailed with the dynasty's efforts to adopt some aspects of Western government and technology while maintaining traditional Chinese values and beliefs.

The parallel movement toward domestic reform and limited cooperation with the West collapsed under the blows of Japanese imperialism. The Sino-Japanese War of 1894 to 1895 and the subsequent harsh peace treaty revealed China's helplessness in the face of aggression, triggering a rush for foreign concessions and protectorates in China. At the high point of this rush in 1898, it appeared that the European powers might actually divide China among themselves, as they had recently divided Africa. Probably only the jealousy each nation felt toward its imperialist competitors saved China from partition, although the U.S. Open Door policy, which opposed formal annexation of Chinese territory, may have helped tip the balance. In any event, the tempo of foreign encroachment greatly accelerated after 1894.

So, too, did the intensity and radicalism of the Chinese reaction. Like the leaders of the Meiji Restoration, some modernizers saw salvation in Western institutions. In 1898 the government launched a desperate **hundred days of reform** in an attempt to meet the foreign challenge. More radical reformers, such as the revolutionary Sun Yat-sen (1866–1925), who came from the peasantry and was educated in Hawaii by Christian missionaries, sought to overthrow the dynasty altogether and establish a republic.

On the other side, some traditionalists turned back toward ancient practices, political conservatism, and fanatical hatred of the "foreign devils." "Protect the country, destroy the foreigner" was their simple motto. Such conservative, antiforeign patriots had often clashed with foreign missionaries, whom they charged with undermining reverence for ancestors and thereby threatening the Chinese family and the entire society. In the agony of defeat and unwanted reforms, secret societies such as the Boxers rebelled. In northeastern China, more than two hundred foreign missionaries and several thousand Chinese Christians were killed. Once again the imperialist response was swift and harsh. Peking was occupied and plundered by foreign armies. A heavy indemnity was imposed.

The years after the Boxer Rebellion (1900–1903) were

The Empress Dowager Tzu Hsi (1835–1908) Tzu Hsi drew on conservative forces, like the court eunuchs surrounding her here, to maintain her power. Three years after her death in 1908, a revolution broke out and forced the last Chinese emperor, a boy of six, to abdicate. *(Freer Gallery of Art and Arthur M. Sackler Gallery Archives, Smithsonian Institution. Photographer: Hsun-ling. Negative no. 261)*

ever more troubled. Anarchy and foreign influence spread as the power and prestige of the Qing Dynasty declined still further. Antiforeign, antigovernment revolutionary groups agitated and plotted. Finally in 1912, a spontaneous uprising toppled the Qing Dynasty. After thousands of years of emperors and empires, a loose coalition of revolutionaries proclaimed a Western-style republic and called for an elected parliament. The transformation of China under the impact of expanding Western society entered a new phase, and the end was not in sight.

Chapter Summary

- What were some of the global consequences of European industrialization between 1815 and 1914?
- How was massive migration an integral part of Western expansion?
- How and why after 1875 did European nations rush to build political empires in Africa and Asia?
- What was the general pattern of non-Western responses to Western expansion, and how did India, Japan, and China meet the imperialist challenge?

Key Terms

Third World
opium trade
khedive
great migration
swallows
great white walls
new imperialism

Afrikaners
Berlin conference
white man's burden
Great Rebellion
shogun
samurai
hundred days of reform

In the nineteenth century, the industrializing West entered the third and most dynamic phase of its centuries-old expansion into non-Western lands. In so doing, Western nations promoted a prodigious growth of world trade, forced reluctant countries such as China and Japan into the globalizing economy, and profitably subordinated many lands to their economic interests. Western nations also sent forth millions of emigrants to the sparsely populated areas of European settlement, which generally limited migration from Asia.

After 1875, Western countries grabbed vast political empires in Africa and rushed to establish political influence in Asia. The reasons for this culminating surge were many, but the economic thrust of robust industrial capitalism, an ever-growing lead in technology, and the competitive pressures of European nationalism were particularly important.

Western expansion had far-reaching consequences. For the first time in human history, the world became in many ways a single unit. Moreover, European expansion diffused the ideas and techniques of a highly developed civilization. Yet the West relied on force to conquer and rule, and it treated non-Western peoples as racial inferiors. Thus non-Western elites, often armed with Western doctrines, gradually responded to the Western challenge. As the histories of India, Japan, and China show, non-Western elites launched a national, anti-imperialist struggle for dignity, genuine independence, and modernization. This struggle would emerge as a central drama of world history after the great European civil war of 1914 to 1918, which reduced the West's technological advantage and shattered its self-confidence and complacent moral superiority.

Suggested Reading

Aldrich, Robert. *Greater France: A History of French Overseas Expansion.* 1996. A well-balanced study.

Bagchi, Amiya Kumar. *Perilous Passage: Mankind and the Ascendancy of Capital.* 2005. A spirited radical critique of the "rise of the West."

Conklin, Alice. *A Mission to Civilize: The French Republican Ideal and West Africa, 1895–1930.* 1997. An outstanding examination of French imperialism.

Conrad, Joseph. *Heart of Darkness.* A novel that unforgettably probes European imperial motives.

Cook, Scott B. *Colonial Encounters in the Age of High Imperialism.* 1996. A stimulating overview with a very readable account of the explorer Stanley and central Africa.

Crews, Robert. *For Prophet and Tsar: Islam and Empire in Russia and Central Asia.* 2006. Considers neglected aspects of Russian imperialism.

Curtin, P., et al. *African History: From Earliest Times to Independence,* 2d ed. 1995. An excellent brief introduction to Africa in the age of imperialism.

Ebrey, Patricia Buckley. *The Cambridge Illustrated History of China.* 1999. A lively and beautiful work by a leading specialist.

Fage, J. D. *A History of Africa,* 3d ed. 1995. A highly recommended account.

Goodlad, Graham. *British Foreign and Imperial Policy, 1865–1919.* 2000. A lively examination of Britain's leading position in European imperialism.

Hochshild, Adam. *King Leopold's Ghost: A Story of Greed, Terror, and Heroism in Colonial Africa, 1895–1930.* 1997. A chilling account of Belgian imperialism in the Congo.

Maier, Charles S. *Among Empires: American Ascendancy and Its Predecessors.* 2006. Examines imperial power in history and how well America measures up.

Marshall, P. J., ed. *Cambridge Illustrated History of the British Empire.* 1996. A stunning pictorial history.

Midgley, Clare, ed. *Gender and Imperialism.* 1998. Examines the complex questions related to European women and imperialism.

Rotberg, Robert I. *The Founder: Cecil Rhodes and the Pursuit of Power.* 1988. Examines the imperialist's mind and times with great acuity.

Said, Edward. *Orientalism.* 1978. An exceedingly influential cultural study of imperialism and non-Europeans.

Notes

1. Quoted in J. W. Hall, *Japan, from Prehistory to Modern Times* (New York: Delacorte Press, 1970), p. 250.
2. Quoted in Earl of Cromer, *Modern Egypt* (London, 1911), p. 48.
3. Quoted in T. Blegen, *Norwegian Migration to America,* vol. 2 (Northfield, Minn.: Norwegian-American Historical Association, 1940), p. 468.
4. Quoted in W. L. Langer, *European Alliances and Alignments, 1871–1890* (New York: Vintage Books, 1931), p. 290.
5. Quoted in J. Ellis, *The Social History of the Machine Gun* (New York: Pantheon Books, 1975), pp. 86, 101.
6. Quoted in G. H. Nadel and P. Curtis, eds., *Imperialism and Colonialism* (New York: Macmillan, 1964), p. 94.
7. Quoted in W. L. Langer, *The Diplomacy of Imperialism,* 2d ed. (New York: Alfred A. Knopf, 1951), pp. 86, 88.
8. Rudyard Kipling, *The Five Nations* (London, 1903).
9. E. H. Berman, "African Responses to Christian Mission Education," *African Studies Review* 17 (1974): 530.
10. Quoted in Langer, *The Diplomacy of Imperialism,* p. 88.
11. Quoted in Ellis, *The Social History of the Machine Gun,* pp. 99–100.
12. Quoted in K. M. Panikkar, *Asia and Western Dominance: A Survey of the Vasco da Gama Epoch of Asian History* (London: George Allen & Unwin, 1959), p. 116.
13. A. Burton, "The White Women's Burden: British Feminists and 'The Indian Women,' 1865–1915," in *Western Women and Imperialism: Complicity and Resistance,* ed. N. Chauduri and M. Strobel (Bloomington: Indiana University Press, 1992), pp. 137–157.

Listening to the Past

A British Woman in India

Guides for housekeeping became popular in Europe in the nineteenth century as middle-class women funneled great energy into their homes. A British woman in India probably consulted The Complete Indian Housekeeper and Cook by Flora Annie Steel and Grace Gardiner, a bestseller published in 1888 and frequently updated.

Steel (1847–1929) moved to India in 1867 with her husband, a civil engineer, and lived there until the family returned to England in 1889. Accustomed to directing a large household with several Indian servants, Steel believed herself well qualified to offer advice "to English girls to whom fate may assign the task of being house-mothers in our Eastern empire." The following passage focuses on how the British mistress should manage her Indian servants, and along with practical suggestions it lays bare some basic attitudes and assumptions of Europeans in colonial settings. Steel subsequently wrote books on India, education, and women's issues.

Housekeeping in India, when once the first strangeness has worn off, is a far easier task in many ways than it is in England, though it none the less requires time, and, in this present transitional period, an almost phenomenal patience. . . .

And, first it must be distinctly understood that it is not necessary, or in the least degree desirable, that an educated woman should waste the best years of her life in scolding and petty supervision. Life holds higher duties, and it is indubitable that friction and over-zeal is a sure sign of a bad housekeeper. . . .

Easy, however, as the actual housekeeping is in India, the personal attention of the mistress is quite as much needed here as at home. The Indian servant, it is true, learns more readily, and is guiltless of the sniffiness with which Mary Jane [the servant in England] receives suggestions, but a few days of absence or neglect on the part of the mistress, results in the servants falling into their old habits with the inherited conservatism of dirt. This is, of course, disheartening, but it has to be faced as a necessary condition of life, until a few generations of training shall have started the Indian servant on a new inheritance of habit. It must never be forgotten that at present those mistresses who aim at anything beyond keeping a good table are in the minority, and that pioneering is always arduous work.

The first duty of a mistress is, of course, to be able to give intelligible orders to her servants; therefore it is necessary she should learn to speak Hindustani. No sane Englishwomen would dream of living, say, for twenty years, in Germany, Italy, or France, without making the *attempt,* at any rate, to learn the language. . . .

The next duty is obviously to insist on her orders being carried out. And here we come to the burning question: "How is this to be done?" Certainly, there is at present very little to which we can appeal in the average Indian servant, but then, until it is implanted by training, there is very little sense of duty in a child; yet in some well-regulated nurseries obedience is a foregone conclusion. The secret lies in making rules, and *keeping to them.* The Indian servant is a child in everything save age, and should be treated as a child; that is to say, kindly, but with the greatest firmness. The laws of the household should be those of the Medes and Persians, and first faults should never go unpunished. By overlooking a first offence, we lose the only opportunity we have of preventing it becoming a habit.

But it will be asked, How are we to punish our servants when we have no hold either on their minds or bodies? . . .

In their own experience the authors have found a system of rewards and punishments perfectly easy of attainment. One of them has for years adopted the plan of engaging her servants at so much a month—the lowest rate at which such servant is obtainable—and so much extra as *buksheesh* [a bonus], conditional on good service. For instance, a *khitmutgâr* [male table servant] is engaged permanently on Rs. 9 a month, but the additional rupee which makes the wage up to that usually demanded by good servants is a fluctuating assessment! . . . That plan has never been objected to, and . . . the household quite enters into the spirit of the idea, infinitely preferring it to volcanic eruptions of fault-finding. . . .

In regard to actual housekeeping, the authors emphatically deny the common assertion that it must necessarily run on different lines to what it does in England. Economy, prudence, efficiency are the same all over the world, and because butcher meat is cheap, that is no excuse for its being wasted. Some modification, of course, there must be, *but as little as possible*. . . .

A good mistress in India will try to set a good example to her servants in routine, method, and tidiness. Half-an-hour after breakfast should be sufficient for the whole arrangements for the day; but that half-hour should be given as punctually as possible. An untidy mistress invariably has *untidy,* a weak one, *idle* servants. It should never be forgotten that—though it is true in both hemispheres that if you want a thing done you should do it yourself—still, having to do it is a distinct confession of failure in your original intention. Anxious housewifes are too apt to accept defeat in this way; the result being that the lives of educated women are wasted in doing the work of lazy servants.

The authors' advice is therefore—

"Never do work which an ordinarily good servant ought to be able to do. If the one you have will not or cannot do it, get another who can." . . .

Having thus gone generally into the duties of the mistress, we may detail what in our opinion should be the daily routine.

The great object is to secure three things—smooth working, quick ordering, and subsequent peace and leisure to the mistress. It is as well, therefore, with a view to the preservation of temper, to eat your breakfast in peace before venturing into the pantry and cookroom; it is besides a mistake to be constantly on the worry.

Inspection parade should begin, then, immediately after breakfast, or as near ten o'clock as circumstances will allow. The cook should be waiting—in clean raiment—with a pile of plates, and his viands for the day spread out on a table. With everything *en evidence,* it will not take five minutes to decide on what is best, while a very constant occurrence at Indian tables—the serving up of stale, sour, and unwholesome food—will be avoided. It is perhaps *not* pleasant to go into such details, but a good mistress will remember the breadwinner who requires blood-forming nourishment, and the children whose constitutions are

An English lady attended by her Indian servants. *(Stapleton Collection, UK/The Bridgeman Art Library)*

being built up day by day, sickly or healthy, according to the food given them; and bear in mind the fact that, in India especially, half the comfort of life depends on clean, wholesome, digestible food. . . .

We do not wish to advocate an unholy haughtiness; but an Indian household can no more be governed peacefully, without dignity and prestige, than an Indian Empire. For instance, if the mistress wishes to teach the cook a new dish, let her give the order for everything, down to charcoal, to be ready at a given time, and the cook in attendance; and let her do nothing herself that the servants can do, if only for this reason, that the only way of teaching is to *see* things done, not to let others see *you* do them.

Questions for Analysis

1. What challenges does the British housekeeper face in India? How, according to Steel, should she meet them?

2. In what ways do Steel's comments and housekeeping policies reflect the attitudes of European imperialism?

Source: F. A. Steel and G. Gardiner, *The Complete Indian Housekeeper and Cook* (London: William Heinemann, 1902), chap. 1. Reprinted in L. DiCaprio and M. Wiesner, eds., *Lives and Voices: Sources in European Women's History* (Boston: Houghton Mifflin, 2001), pp. 323–328.

French soldiers in the trenches man a machine gun, the weapon that killed so many, in this chilling work by Christopher Nevinson. *(© Tate, London 2007/Art Resource, NY)*

chapter 27

THE GREAT BREAK: WAR AND REVOLUTION, 1914–1919

chapter preview

The First World War
- *What caused the Great War, and why did it have such revolutionary consequences?*

The Home Front
- *What was the impact of total war on civilian populations?*

The Russian Revolution
- *Why did World War I bring socialist revolution in Russia?*

The Peace Settlement
- *How did the Allies fashion a peace settlement, and why was it unsuccessful?*

In the summer of 1914, the nations of Europe went willingly to war. They believed they had no other choice. Moreover, both peoples and governments confidently expected a short war leading to a decisive victory. Such a war, they believed, would "clear the air," and European society would be able to go on as before.

These expectations were almost totally mistaken. The First World War was long, indecisive, and tremendously destructive. To the shell-shocked generation of survivors, it was known simply as the Great War: the war of unprecedented scope and intensity. From today's perspective, it is clear that the First World War marked a great break in the course of Western historical development since the French and Industrial Revolutions. A noted British political scientist has gone so far as to say that even in victorious and relatively fortunate Great Britain, the First World War was *the* great turning point in government and society, "as in everything else in modern British history.... There's a much greater difference between the Britain of 1914 and, say, 1920, than between the Britain of 1920 and today."[1] This strong statement contains a great amount of truth, for all of Europe as well as for Britain. World War I was a revolutionary conflict of gigantic proportions.

The First World War

The First World War was extremely long and destructive because it involved all the Great Powers and because it quickly degenerated into a senseless military stalemate. Like evenly matched boxers in a championship bout, the two sides tried to wear each other down. But there was no referee to call a draw, only the blind hammering of a life-or-death struggle.

- *What caused the Great War, and why did it have such revolutionary consequences?*

Online Study Center

This icon will direct you to interactive activities and study materials on the website **college.hmco.com/pic/mckaywest9e**

879

The Bismarckian System of Alliances

The Franco-Prussian War and the founding of the German Empire opened a new era in international relations. France was decisively defeated in 1871 and forced to pay a large war indemnity and give up Alsace-Lorraine. In ten short years, from 1862 to 1871, Bismarck had made Prussia-Germany—traditionally the weakest of the Great Powers—the most powerful nation in Europe (see pages 821–825).

Yet, as Bismarck never tired of repeating after 1871, Germany was a "satisfied" power. Within Europe, Germany had no territorial ambitions and wanted only peace.

But how was peace to be preserved? Bismarck's first concern was to keep an embittered France diplomatically isolated and without military allies. His second concern was the threat to peace posed from the east, from Austria-Hungary and from Russia. Those two enormous multinational empires had many conflicting interests, particularly

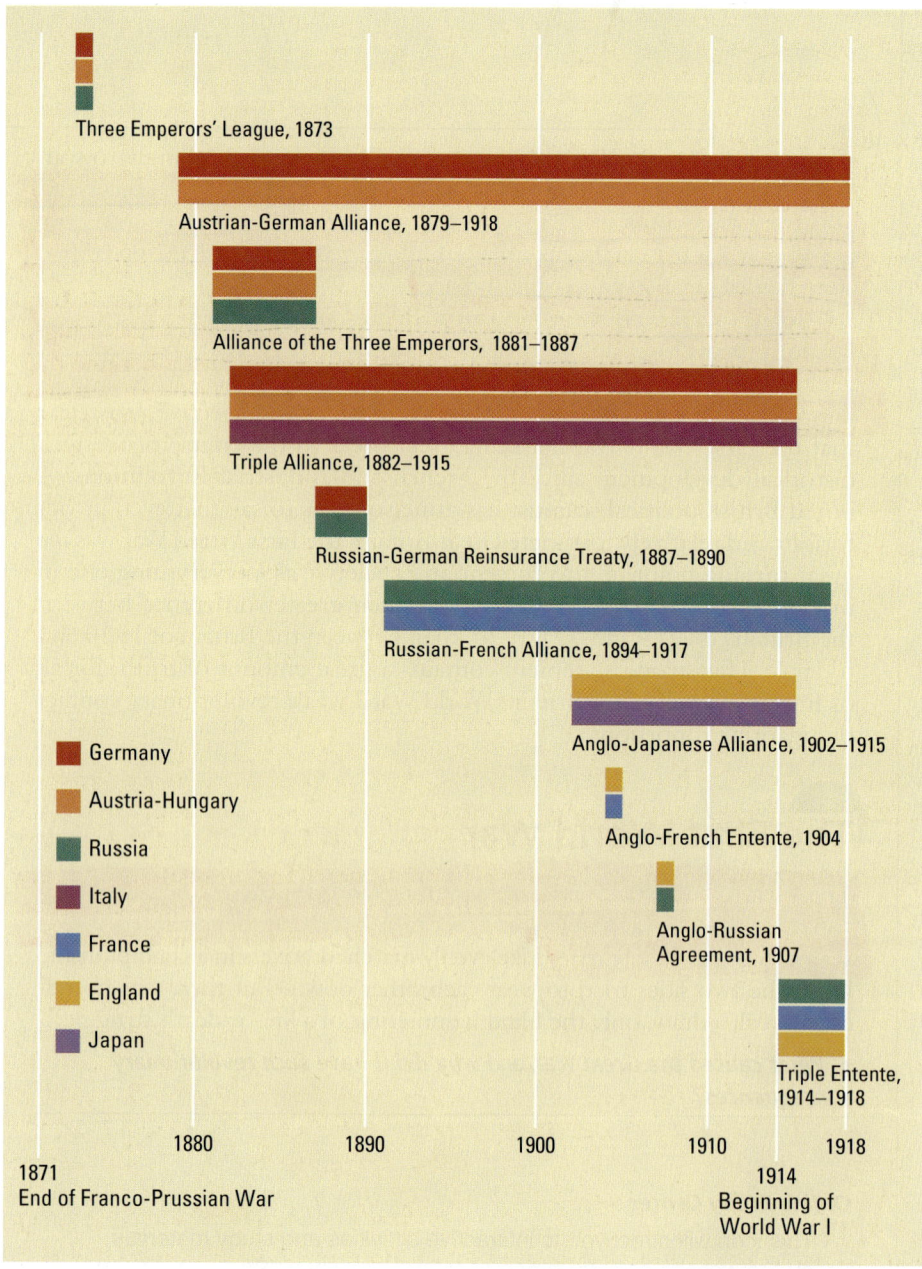

FIGURE 27.1 The Alliance System After 1871 Bismarck's subtle diplomacy maintained reasonably good relations among the eastern monarchies—Germany, Russia, and Austria-Hungary—and kept France isolated. The situation changed dramatically in 1891, when the Russian-French Alliance divided the Great Powers into two fairly equal military blocs.

in southeastern Europe, where the strength of the Ottoman Empire was ebbing fast. There was a real threat that Germany might be dragged into a great war between the two rival empires. Bismarck's solution was a system of alliances (see Figure 27.1) to restrain both Russia and Austria-Hungary, to prevent conflict between them, and to isolate a hostile France, which could never forget the loss of Alsace-Lorraine.

A first step was the creation in 1873 of the conservative Three Emperors' League, which linked the monarchs of Austria-Hungary, Germany, and Russia in an alliance against radical movements. In 1877 and 1878, when Russia's victories in a war with the Ottoman Empire threatened the balance of Austrian and Russian interests in the Balkans and the balance of British and Russian interests in the entire Middle East, Bismarck played the role of sincere peacemaker. But his balancing efforts at the Congress of Berlin in 1878 infuriated Russian nationalists, and this led Bismarck to conclude a defensive military alliance with Austria against Russia in 1879. This alliance lasted until 1918 and the end of World War I. Motivated by tensions with France, Italy joined Germany and Austria in 1882, thereby forming what became known as the Triple Alliance.

Bismarck continued to work for peace in eastern Europe, seeking to neutralize tensions between Austria-Hungary and Russia. In 1881 he capitalized on their mutual fears and cajoled them both into a secret alliance with Germany. This Alliance of the Three Emperors lasted until 1887.

Bismarck also maintained good relations with Britain and Italy, while encouraging France in Africa but keeping France isolated in Europe. In 1887 Russia declined to renew the Alliance of the Three Emperors because of new tensions in the Balkans. Bismarck craftily substituted the Russian-German Reinsurance Treaty, by which both states promised neutrality if the other was attacked.

Bismarck's accomplishments in foreign policy after 1871 were great. For almost a generation, he maintained German leadership in international affairs, and he worked successfully for peace by managing conflicts and by restraining Austria-Hungary and Russia with defensive alliances.

The Rival Blocs

In 1890 the young, impetuous Emperor William II dismissed Bismarck, in part because of the chancellor's friendly policy toward Russia since the 1870s. William then adamantly refused to renew the Russian-German Reinsurance Treaty, in spite of Russian willingness to do so. This fateful departure in foreign affairs prompted long-

Chronology

1912	First Balkan War
1914	Assassination of Archduke Francis Ferdinand
1914–1918	World War I
1915	Italy and Bulgaria enter World War I; Ministry of Munitions established in Britain
1916	German males between seventeen and sixty required to work only for war effort; Rasputin murdered
1916–1918	Growth of antiwar movement throughout Europe
1917	Russian Revolution
1919	Treaty of Versailles

isolated republican France to court absolutist Russia, offering loans, arms, and friendship. In both countries, there were enthusiastic public demonstrations of friendship in 1891, and in early 1894 France and Russia became military allies. This alliance (see Figure 27.1) was to remain in effect as long as the Triple Alliance of Austria, Germany, and Italy existed. As a result, continental Europe was dangerously divided into two rival blocs.

Online Study Center Improve Your Grade
Primary Source: Bismarck's Worst Nightmare: A Franco-Russian Rapprochement

Great Britain's foreign policy became increasingly crucial. Long content with "splendid isolation" and no permanent alliances, Britain after 1891 was the only uncommitted Great Power. Could Britain afford to remain isolated, or would it feel compelled to take sides? Many Germans and some Britons felt that a "natural alliance" united the advanced, racially related Germanic and Anglo-Saxon peoples. However, the generally good relations that had prevailed between Prussia and Great Britain ever since the mid-eighteenth century gave way to a bitter Anglo-German rivalry.

There were several reasons for this tragic development. Commercial rivalry in world markets between Germany and Great Britain increased sharply in the 1890s, and Germany's pursuit of world power unsettled the British. Above all, Germany's decision in 1900 to expand greatly its battle fleet posed a challenge to Britain's long-standing naval supremacy. This decision coincided with the hard-fought South African War (1899–1902) between the British and the tiny Dutch republics of southern Africa,

German Warships Under Full Steam As these impressive ships engaged in battle exercises in 1907 suggest, Germany did succeed in building a large modern navy. But Britain was equally determined to maintain its naval superiority, and the spiraling arms race helped poison relations between the two countries. *(Archives Charmet/Bibliothèque des Arts Décoratifs/Archives Charmet/The Bridgeman Art Library)*

which brought into the open widespread anti-British feeling, as editorial writers in many nations denounced this latest manifestation of British imperialism. Thus British leaders prudently set about shoring up their exposed position with alliances and agreements.

Britain improved its often-strained relations with the United States and in 1902 concluded a formal alliance with Japan (see Figure 27.1). Britain then responded favorably to the advances of France's skillful foreign minister, Théophile Delcassé, who wanted better relations with Britain and was willing to accept British rule in Egypt in return for British support of French plans to dominate Morocco. The resulting Anglo-French Entente of 1904 settled all outstanding colonial disputes between Britain and France.

Frustrated by Britain's turn toward France in 1904, Germany's leaders decided to test the strength of the entente. They foolishly rattled their swords by insisting in 1905 on an international conference on the whole Moroccan question. But Germany's crude bullying forced France and Britain closer together, and the conference left Germany empty-handed and isolated (except for Austria-Hungary).

The result of the Moroccan crisis was something of a diplomatic revolution. Britain, France, Russia, and even the United States began to see Germany as a potential threat, a would-be intimidator that might seek to dominate all Europe. At the same time, German leaders began to see sinister plots to "encircle" Germany and block its development as a world power. In 1907 Russia, battered by its disastrous war with Japan and the revolution of 1905, agreed to settle its quarrels with Great Britain in

Persia and Central Asia with the Anglo-Russian Agreement (see Figure 27.1).

Germany's decision to add a large, enormously expensive fleet of big-gun battleships to its already expanding navy also heightened tensions after 1907. German nationalists, led by the extremely persuasive Admiral Alfred von Tirpitz, saw a large navy as the legitimate mark of a great world power and as a source of pride and patriotic unity. But British leaders such as David Lloyd George saw it as a detestable military challenge, which forced them to spend the "People's Budget" (see page 835) on battleships rather than social welfare. Unscrupulous journalists and special-interest groups in both countries also portrayed healthy competition in foreign trade and investment as a form of economic warfare. In 1909 the mass-circulation London *Daily Mail* hysterically informed its readers in a series of reports that "Germany is deliberately preparing to destroy the British Empire."[2] By then Britain was psychologically, if not officially, in the Franco-Russian camp. The leading nations of Europe were divided into two hostile blocs, both ill-prepared to deal with upheaval on Europe's southeastern frontier.

The Outbreak of War

In the early years of the twentieth century, war in the Balkans was as inevitable as anything can be in human history. The reason was simple: nationalism was destroying the Ottoman Empire in Europe and threatening to break up the Austro-Hungarian Empire. The only questions were what kinds of wars would occur and where they would lead.

Greece had long before led the struggle for national liberation, winning its independence in 1832. In 1875 widespread nationalist rebellion in the European provinces of the sprawling Ottoman Empire had resulted in Turkish repression, Russian intervention, and Great Power tensions. Bismarck had helped resolve this crisis at the 1878 Congress of Berlin, which worked out the partial division of Turkish possessions in Europe. Austria-Hungary obtained the right to "occupy and administer" Bosnia and Herzegovina. Serbia and Romania won independence, and a part of Bulgaria won local autonomy. The Ottoman Empire retained important Balkan holdings, for Austria-Hungary and Russia each feared the other's domination of totally independent states in the area (see Map 27.1).

By 1903, however, nationalism in southeastern Europe was on the rise once again. Serbia led the way, becoming openly hostile toward both Austria-Hungary and the Ottoman Empire. The Serbs, a Slavic people, looked to Slavic Russia for support of their national aspirations. To block Serbian expansion and to take advantage of Russia's weakness after the revolution of 1905, Austria in 1908 formally annexed Bosnia and Herzegovina, with their large Serbian, Croatian, and Muslim populations. The kingdom of Serbia erupted in rage but could do nothing without Russian support.

Then, in 1912, in the First Balkan War, Serbia joined Greece and Bulgaria to attack the Ottoman Empire and then quarreled with Bulgaria over the spoils of victory—a dispute that led in 1913 to the Second Balkan War. Austria intervened in 1913 and forced Serbia to give up Albania. After centuries, nationalism had finally destroyed the Ottoman Empire in Europe (see Map 27.2). This sudden but long-awaited event elated the Balkan nationalists and dismayed the leaders of multinational Austria-Hungary. The former hoped and the latter feared that Austria might be next to be broken apart.

Within this tense context, Archduke Francis Ferdinand, heir to the Austrian and Hungarian thrones, and his wife, Sophie, were assassinated by Serbian revolutionaries living in Bosnia on June 28, 1914, during a state visit to the Bosnian capital of Sarajevo. After some hesitation, the leaders of Austria-Hungary concluded that Serbia was implicated and had to be severely punished once and for all. On July 23 Austria-Hungary finally presented Serbia with an unconditional ultimatum. The Serbian government had forty-eight hours in which to agree to demands that would amount to ceding control of the Serbian state. When Serbia replied moderately but evasively, Austria began to mobilize and then declared war on Serbia on July 28. Thus a desperate multinational Austria-Hungary deliberately chose war in a last-ditch attempt to stem the rising tide of hostile nationalism within its borders and save the existing state. The "Third Balkan War" had begun.

Of prime importance in Austria-Hungary's fateful decision was Germany's unconditional support. Emperor William II and his chancellor, Theobald von Bethmann-Hollweg, realized that war between Austria and Russia was the most probable result, for a resurgent Russia could not stand by, as in the Bosnian crisis, and simply watch the Serbs be crushed. Yet Bethmann-Hollweg apparently hoped that while Russia (and therefore France) would go to war, Great Britain would remain neutral, unwilling to fight for "Russian aggression" in the distant Balkans.

In fact, the diplomatic situation was already out of control. Military plans and timetables began to dictate policy. Russia, a vast country, would require much longer to mobilize its armies than Germany and Austria-Hungary. All the complicated mobilization plans of the Russian general staff had assumed a war with both Austria and Germany: Russia could not mobilize against one without

MAP 27.1 The Balkans After the Congress of Berlin, 1878 The Ottoman Empire suffered large territorial losses but remained a power in the Balkans.

MAP 27.2 The Balkans in 1914 Ethnic boundaries did not follow political boundaries, and Serbian national aspirations threatened Austria-Hungary.

mobilizing against the other. Therefore, on July 29 Tsar Nicholas II ordered full mobilization and in effect declared general war.

The German general staff had also thought only in terms of a two-front war. The staff's plan for war called for knocking out France first with a lightning attack through neutral Belgium before turning on Russia. So German armies attacked Belgium, whose neutrality had been solemnly guaranteed in 1839 by all the great states including Prussia. Thus Germany's terrible, politically disastrous response to a war in the Balkans was an all-out invasion of France by way of the plains of neutral Belgium on August 3. In the face of this act of aggression, Great Britain joined France and declared war on Germany the following day. The First World War had begun.

Online Study Center Improve Your Grade
Primary Source: The British Rationale for Entering World War I

Reflections on the Origins of the War

In reflecting on the origins of the First World War, it seems clear that Austria-Hungary deliberately started the Third Balkan War. A war for the right to survive was Austria-Hungary's desperate, though understandable, response to the aggressive, yet understandable, revolutionary drive of Serbian nationalists to unify their people in a single state. Moreover, in spite of Russian intervention in the quarrel, it is clear that from the beginning of the crisis, Germany not only pushed and goaded Austria-Hungary but also was re-

Nationalist Opposition in the Balkans This band of well-armed and determined guerrillas from northern Albania was typical of groups fighting against Ottoman rule in the Balkans. Balkan nationalists succeeded in driving the Ottoman Turks out of most of Europe, but their victory increased tensions with Austria-Hungary and among the Great Powers. *(Roger-Viollet/Getty Images)*

sponsible for turning a little war into the Great War by means of a sledgehammer attack on Belgium and France. Why Germany was so aggressive in 1914 is less certain.

Diplomatic historians stress that German leaders lost control of the international system after Bismarck's resignation in 1890. They felt increasingly that Germany's status as a world power was declining, while that of Britain, France, Russia, and the United States was growing. Indeed, the powers of what officially became in August 1914 the **Triple Entente**—Great Britain, France, and Russia—were checking Germany's vague but real aspirations as well as working to strangle Austria-Hungary, Germany's only real ally. Germany's aggression in 1914 reflected the failure of all European leaders, not just those in Germany, to incorporate Bismarck's mighty empire permanently and peacefully into the international system.

A more controversial interpretation argues that domestic conflicts and social tensions lay at the root of German aggression. Determined to hold on to power and frightened by the rising socialist movement, the German ruling class was willing to gamble on diplomatic victory and even on war as the means of rallying the masses to its side and preserving its privileged position. Historians have also discerned similar, if less clear-cut, behavior in Great Britain, where leaders faced civil war in northern Ireland, and in Russia, where the revolution of 1905 had brought tsardom to its knees.

This debate over social tensions and domestic political factors correctly suggests that the triumph of nationalism was a crucial underlying precondition of the Great War. Nationalism was at the heart of the Balkan wars, in the form of Serbian aspirations and the grandiose pan-German versus pan-Slavic racism of some fanatics. Nationalism also drove the spiraling arms race. Broad popular commitment

MAP 27.3 The First World War in Europe Trench warfare on the western front was concentrated in Belgium and northern France, while the war in the east encompassed an enormous territory.

"Never Forget!" This 1915 French poster with its passionate headline dramatizes Germany's brutal invasion of Belgium in 1914. Neutral Belgium is personified as a traumatized mother, assaulted and ravished by savage outlaws. The "rape of Belgium" featured prominently—and effectively—in anti-German propaganda. *(Mary Evans Picture Library)*

Stalemate and Slaughter

When the Germans invaded Belgium in August 1914, they and everyone else believed that the war would be short, for urban society rested on the food and raw materials of the world economy: "The boys will be home by Christmas." The Belgian army heroically defended its homeland, however, and fell back in good order to join a rapidly landed British army corps near the Franco-Belgian border. Instead of quickly capturing Paris in a vast encircling movement, by the end of August dead-tired German soldiers were advancing along an enormous front in the scorching summer heat.

On September 6 the French attacked a gap in the German line at the Battle of the Marne. For three days, France threw everything into the attack. At one point, the French government desperately requisitioned all the taxis of Paris to rush reserves to the troops at the front. Finally, the Germans fell back. Paris and France had been miraculously saved (see Map 27.3).

Soon, with the armies stalled, both sides began to dig trenches to protect themselves from machine-gun fire. By November 1914, an unbroken line of trenches extended from the Belgian ports through northern France, past the fortress of Verdun, and on to the Swiss frontier. In the face of this unexpected stalemate, slaughter on the western front began in earnest. The defenders on both sides dug in behind rows of trenches, mines, and barbed wire. For days and even weeks, ceaseless shelling by heavy artillery supposedly "softened up" the enemy in a given area (and also signaled the coming attack). Then young draftees and their junior officers went "over the top" of the trenches in frontal attacks on the enemy's line.

The cost in lives of this **trench warfare** was staggering, the gains in territory minuscule. The massive French and British offensives during 1915 never gained more than 3 miles of blood-soaked earth from the enemy. In the Battle of the Somme in the summer of 1916, the British and French gained an insignificant 125 square miles at the cost of 600,000 dead or wounded, while the Germans lost 500,000 men. In that same year the unsuccessful German campaign against Verdun cost 700,000 lives on both sides. British poet Siegfried Sassoon (1886–1967) wrote of the Somme offensive, "I am staring at a sunlit picture of Hell."

The year 1917 was equally terrible. The hero of Erich Remarque's great novel *All Quiet on the Western Front* (1929) describes one attack:

We see men living with their skulls blown open; we see soldiers run with their two feet cut off. . . . Still the little piece of convulsed earth in which we lie is held. We have yielded no

to "my country right or wrong" weakened groups that thought in terms of international communities and consequences. In each country, the great majority of the population enthusiastically embraced the outbreak of war in August 1914. In each country, people believed that their country had been wronged, and they rallied to defend it. Patriotic nationalism brought unity in the short run.

In all of this, the wealthy governing classes certainly underestimated the risk of war to themselves in 1914. They had forgotten that great wars and great social revolutions very often go hand in hand. Metternich's alliance of conservative forces in support of international peace and the social status quo had become only a distant memory.

The Tragic Absurdity of Trench Warfare Soldiers charge across a scarred battlefield and overrun an enemy trench. The dead defender on the right will fire no more. But this is only another futile charge that will yield much blood and little land. A whole generation is being decimated by the slaughter. *(By courtesy of the Trustees of the Imperial War Museum)*

more than a few hundred yards of it as a prize to the enemy. But on every yard there lies a dead man.

Such was war on the western front.

Trench warfare shattered an entire generation of young men. Millions who could have provided political creativity and leadership after the war were forever missing. Moreover, those who lived through the slaughter were maimed, shell-shocked, embittered, and profoundly disillusioned. The young soldiers went to war believing in the world of their leaders and elders—the pre-1914 world of order, progress, and patriotism. Then, in Remarque's words, the "first bombardment showed us our mistake, and under it the world as they had taught it to us broke in pieces."

The Widening War

On the eastern front, slaughter did not degenerate into suicidal trench warfare. With the outbreak of the war, the "Russian steamroller" immediately moved into eastern Germany. Very badly damaged by the Germans under Generals Paul von Hindenburg and Erich Ludendorff at the Battles of Tannenberg and the Masurian Lakes in August and September 1914, Russia never threatened

The Armenian Atrocities When in 1915 some Armenians welcomed Russian armies as liberators after years of persecution, the Ottoman government ordered a genocidal mass deportation of its Armenian citizens from their homeland in the empire's eastern provinces. This photo, taken in Kharpert in 1915 by a German businessman from his hotel window, shows Turkish guards marching Armenian men off to a prison, where they will be tortured to death. A million Armenians died from murder, starvation, and disease during World War I. *(Courtesy of the Armenian Library, Watertown, Mass.)*

Germany again. On the Austrian front, enormous armies seesawed back and forth, suffering enormous losses. Austro-Hungarian armies were repulsed twice by Serbia in bitter fighting. But with the help of German forces, they reversed the Russian advances of 1914 and forced the Russians to retreat deep into their own territory in the eastern campaign of 1915. A staggering 2.5 million Russians were killed, wounded, or taken prisoner that year.

These changing tides of victory and hopes for territorial gains brought neutral countries into the war (see Map 27.3). Italy, a member of the Triple Alliance since 1882, had declared its neutrality in 1914 on the grounds that Austria had launched a war of aggression. Then in May 1915, Italy joined the Triple Entente of Great Britain, France, and Russia in return for promises of Austrian territory. In October 1914 the Ottoman Empire joined with Austria and Germany, by then known as the Central Powers. The following September Bulgaria decided to follow the Ottoman Empire's lead in order to settle old scores with Serbia. The Balkans, with the exception of Greece, came to be occupied by the Central Powers.

The entry of the Ottoman Turks carried the war into the Middle East. Heavy fighting between the Ottomans and the Russians saw battle lines seesawing back and forth and enveloping the Armenians, who lived on both sides of the border and had experienced brutal repression by the Turks in 1909 (see Map 27.5 on page 906). When in 1915 some Armenians welcomed Russian armies as liberators, the Ottoman government ordered a genocidal mass deportation of its Armenian citizens from their homeland. A million Armenians died from murder, starvation, and disease during World War I. In 1915 British forces tried to take the Dardanelles and Constantinople from the Ottomans but were badly defeated.

The British were more successful at inciting the Arabs to revolt against their Turkish overlords. They bargained with the foremost Arab leader, Hussein ibn-Ali (1856–1931), who was a direct descendant of the prophet Muhammad and the chief magistrate (*sharif*) of Mecca, the holiest city in the Muslim world. Controlling much of the Ottoman Empire's territory along the Red Sea, an area known as the Hejaz (see Map 27.5), Hussein managed in 1915 to win vague British commitments for an independent Arab kingdom. Thus in 1916 Hussein revolted against the Turks, proclaiming himself king of the Arabs. He joined forces with the British under T. E. Lawrence, who in 1917 led Arab tribesmen and Indian soldiers in a highly successful guerrilla war against the Turks on the Arabian peninsula.

Similar victories were eventually scored in the Ottoman province of Iraq. Britain occupied the southern Iraqi city of Basra in 1914 and captured Baghdad in 1917. In September 1918 British armies and their Arab allies rolled into Syria. This offensive culminated in the triumphal entry of Hussein's son Faisal into Damascus. Throughout Syria and Iraq there was wild Arab rejoicing. Many patriots expected a large, unified Arab nation-state to rise from the dust of the Ottoman collapse.

As world war engulfed and revolutionized the Middle East, it also spread to some parts of East Asia and Africa. Instead of revolting as the Germans hoped, the colonial subjects of the British and French generally supported their foreign masters, providing crucial supplies and fighting in Europe and the Ottoman Empire. They also helped local British and French commanders seize Germany's colonies around the globe. The Japanese, allied in Asia with the British since 1902, similarly used the war to grab German outposts in the Pacific Ocean and on the Chinese mainland, infuriating Chinese patriots and heightening long-standing tensions between China and Japan. More than a million Africans and Asians served in the various armies of the warring powers; more than double that number served as porters to carry equipment. The French, facing a shortage of young men, made especially heavy use of colonial troops.

In April 1917 the United States declared war on Germany, another crucial development in the expanding conflict. American intervention grew out of the war at sea, sympathy for the Triple Entente, and the increasing desperation of total war. At the beginning of the war, Britain and France had established a total naval blockade to strangle the Central Powers. No neutral ship was permitted to sail to Germany with any cargo. In early 1915 Germany retaliated with a counter-blockade using the murderously effective submarine, a new weapon that violated traditional niceties of fair warning under international law. In May 1915 a German submarine sank the British passenger liner **Lusitania,** claiming more than 1,000 lives, among them 139 Americans. President Woodrow Wilson protested vigorously. Germany was forced to relax its submarine warfare for almost two years; the alternative was almost certain war with the United States.

Early in 1917, the German military command—confident that improved submarines could starve Britain into submission before the United States could come to its rescue—resumed unrestricted submarine warfare. Like the invasion of Belgium, this was a reckless gamble. "German submarine warfare against commerce," President Wilson had told a sympathetic Congress and people, "is a warfare against mankind." Thus the last uncommitted great nation, as fresh and enthusiastic as Europe had been in 1914, entered the world war in April 1917, almost three years after it began. Eventually the United States was to tip the balance in favor of the Triple Entente and its allies.

The Home Front

Before looking at the last year of the Great War, let us turn our attention to the people on the home front. They were tremendously involved in the titanic struggle. War's impact on them was no less massive than on the men crouched in the trenches.

- *What was the impact of total war on civilian populations?*

Mobilizing for Total War

In August 1914, most people greeted the outbreak of hostilities enthusiastically. In every country, the masses believed that their nation was in the right and defending itself from aggression. With the exception of a few extreme left-wingers, even socialists supported the war. Everywhere the support of the masses and working class contributed to national unity and an energetic war effort.

By mid-October generals and politicians had begun to realize that more than patriotism would be needed to win the war, whose end was not in sight. Each country experienced a relentless, desperate demand for men and weapons. In each country, economic life and organization had to change and change fast to keep the war machine from sputtering to a stop. And change they did.

In each country, a government of national unity began to plan and control economic and social life in order to wage **total war.** Free-market capitalism was abandoned, at least "for the duration." Instead, government planning boards established priorities and decided what was to be produced and consumed. Rationing, price and wage controls, and even restrictions on workers' freedom of movement were imposed by government. Only through such regimentation could a country make the greatest possible military effort. Thus, though there were national variations, the great nations all moved toward planned economies commanded by the established political leadership.

The economy of total war blurred the old distinction between soldiers on the battlefield and civilians at home. The war was a war of whole peoples and entire populations. Based on tremendously productive industrial economies not confined to a single nation, total war yielded an effective— and therefore destructive—war effort on all sides.

However awful the war was, the ability of governments to manage and control highly complicated economies strengthened the cause of socialism. With the First World War, state socialism became for the first time a realistic economic blueprint rather than a utopian program. Germany illustrates the general trend. It also went furthest in developing a planned economy to wage total war.

As soon as war began, Walter Rathenau, the talented, foresighted Jewish industrialist in charge of Germany's largest electric company, convinced the government to set up the **War Raw Materials Board** to ration and distribute raw materials. Under Rathenau's direction, every useful material from foreign oil to barnyard manure was inventoried and rationed. Moreover, the board launched successful attempts to produce substitutes such as synthetic rubber and synthetic nitrates, needed to make explosives and essential to the blockaded German war machine. An aggressive recycling campaign, including everything from fruit peels to women's hair, augmented these efforts.

Food was also rationed in accordance with physical need. Men and women doing hard manual work were given extra rations. During the last two years of the war, only children and expectant mothers received milk rations. At the same time, Germany failed to tax the war profits of private firms heavily enough. This failure contributed to massive deficit financing, inflation, the growth of a black market, and the eventual re-emergence of class conflict.

Following the terrible Battles of Verdun and the Somme in 1916, Chancellor Bethmann-Hollweg was driven from office in 1917 by military leaders Hindenburg and Ludendorff, who became the real rulers of Germany. They

Hair for the War Effort Blockaded and cut off from overseas supplies, Germany mobilized effectively to find substitutes at home. This poster calls on German women—especially young women with long flowing tresses—to donate their hair, which was used to make rope. Children were organized by their teachers into garbage brigades to collect every scrap of useful material. *(akg-images)*

decreed the ultimate mobilization for total war. Germany, said Hindenburg, could win only "if all the treasures of our soil that agriculture and industry can produce are used exclusively for the conduct of War. . . . All other considerations must come second."[3] Thus in December 1916, military leaders rammed through the Reichstag the Auxiliary Service Law, which required all males between seventeen and sixty to work only at jobs considered critical to the war effort.

Although women and children were not specifically mentioned, this forced-labor law was also aimed at them. Many women already worked in war factories, mines, and steel mills, where they labored, like men, at the heaviest and most dangerous jobs. With the passage of the Auxiliary Service Law, many more women followed. People averaged little more than one thousand calories a day. Thus in Germany total war led to the establishment of history's first "totalitarian" society, and war production increased while some people starved to death.

Great Britain mobilized for total war less rapidly and less completely than Germany, for it could import materials from its empire and from the United States. By 1915, however, a serious shortage of shells had led to the establishment of the Ministry of Munitions under David Lloyd George. The ministry organized private industry to produce for the war, controlled profits, allocated labor, fixed wage rates, and settled labor disputes. By December 1916, when Lloyd George became prime minister, the British economy was largely planned and regulated. Great Britain had followed successfully in Germany's footsteps.

The Social Impact

The social impact of total war was no less profound than the economic impact, though again there were important national variations. The millions of men at the front and the insatiable needs of the military created a tremendous demand for workers. Jobs were available for everyone. This situation—seldom, if ever, seen before 1914, when unemployment and poverty had been facts of urban life—brought about momentous changes.

One such change was greater power and prestige for labor unions. Having proved their loyalty in August 1914, labor unions cooperated with war governments on work rules, wages, and production schedules in return for real participation in important decisions. This entry of labor leaders and unions into policymaking councils paralleled the entry of socialist leaders into the war governments.

The role of women changed dramatically. In every country, large numbers of women left home and domestic service to work in industry, transportation, and offices. Moreover, women became highly visible—not only as munitions workers but as bank tellers, mail carriers, even police officers. Women also served as nurses and doctors at the front. (See the feature "Individuals in Society: Vera Brittain.") In general, the war greatly expanded the range of women's activities and changed attitudes toward women. As a direct result of women's many-sided war ef-

Waging Total War A British war plant strains to meet the insatiable demand for trench-smashing heavy artillery shells. Quite typically, many of these defense workers are women. *(By courtesy of the Trustees of the Imperial War Museum)*

Individuals in Society

Vera Brittain

Although the Great War upended millions of lives, it struck Europe's young people with the greatest force. For Vera Brittain (1893–1970), as for so many in her generation, the war became life's defining experience, which she captured forever in her famous autobiography, *Testament of Youth* (1933).

Brittain grew up in a wealthy business family in northern England, bristling at small-town conventions and discrimination against women. Very close to her brother Edward, two years her junior, Brittain read voraciously and dreamed of being a successful writer. Finishing boarding school and beating down her father's objections, she prepared for Oxford's rigorous entry exams and won a scholarship to its women's college. Brittain also fell in love with Roland Leighton, an equally brilliant student from a literary family and her brother's best friend. All three, along with two more close friends, Victor Richardson and Geoffrey Thurlow, confidently prepared to enter Oxford in late 1914.

When war suddenly approached in July 1914, Brittain shared with millions of Europeans a thrilling surge of patriotic support for her government, a pro-war enthusiasm she later played down in her published writings. She wrote in her diary that her "great fear" was that England would declare its neutrality and commit the "grossest treachery" toward France.* She seconded Roland's decision to enlist, agreeing with her sweetheart's glamorous view of war as "very ennobling and very beautiful." Later, exchanging anxious letters in 1915 with Roland in France, Vera began to see the conflict in personal, human terms. She wondered if any victory or defeat could be worth Roland's life.

Struggling to quell her doubts, Brittain redoubled her commitment to England's cause and volunteered as an army nurse. For the next three years she served with distinction in military hospitals in London, Malta, and northern France, repeatedly torn between the vision of noble sacrifice and the reality of human tragedy. She lost her sexual inhibitions caring for mangled male bodies, and she longed to consummate her love with Roland. Awaiting his return on leave on Christmas Day in 1915, she was greeted instead with a telegram: Roland had been killed two days before.

Roland's death was the first of the devastating blows that eventually overwhelmed Brittain's idealistic patriotism. In 1917, first Geoffrey and then Victor died from gruesome wounds. In early 1918, as the last great German offensive covered the floors of her war-zone hospital with maimed and dying German prisoners, the bone-weary Vera felt a common humanity and saw only more victims. A few weeks later brother Edward—her last hope—died in action. When the war ended, she was, she said, a "complete automaton," with "my deepest emotions paralyzed if not dead."

Returning to Oxford and finishing her studies, Brittain gradually recovered. She formed a deep, restorative friendship with another talented woman writer, Winifred Holtby, published novels and articles, and became a leader in the feminist campaign for gender equality. She also married and had children. But her wartime memories were always there. Finally, Brittain succeeded in coming to grips with them in *Testament of Youth*, her powerful antiwar autobiography. The unflinching narrative spoke to the experiences of an entire generation and became a runaway bestseller. Above all perhaps, Brittain captured the ambivalent, contradictory character of the war, when millions of young people found excitement, courage, and common purpose but succeeded only in destroying their lives with their superhuman efforts and futile sacrifices. Becoming ever more committed to pacifism, Brittain opposed England's entry into World War II.

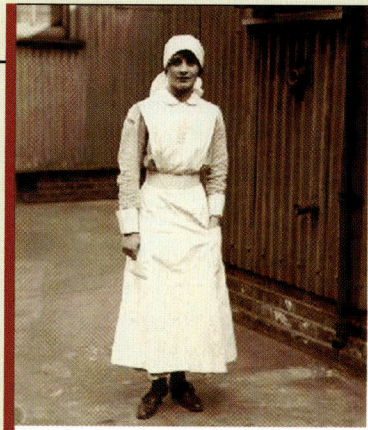

Vera Brittain, marked forever by her wartime experiences. (Vera Brittain Archive, William Ready Division of Archives and Research Collections, McMaster University Library)

Questions for Analysis

1. What were Brittain's initial feelings toward the war? How did they change as the conflict continued? Why did they change?
2. Why did Brittain volunteer as a nurse, as many women did? Judging from her account, how might wartime nursing have influenced women of her generation?
3. In portraying the ambivalent, contradictory character of World War I for Europe's youth, was Brittain describing the contradictory character of all modern warfare?

*Quoted in the excellent study by P. Berry and M. Bostridge, *Vera Brittain: A Life* (London: Virago Press, 2001), p. 59; additional quotes are from pp. 80 and 136. This work is highly recommended.

Online Study Center Improve Your Grade
Going Beyond Individuals in Society

fort, Britain, Germany, and Austria granted women the right to vote immediately after the war. Women also showed a growing spirit of independence during the war, as they started to bob their hair, shorten their skirts, and smoke in public.

Online Study Center **Improve Your Grade**
Primary Source: A British Feminist Analyzes the Impact of the War on Women

War promoted greater social equality, blurring class distinctions and lessening the gap between rich and poor. This blurring was most apparent in Great Britain, where wartime hardship was never extreme. In fact, the bottom third of the population generally lived *better* than they ever had, for the poorest gained most from the severe shortage of labor. In continental countries, greater equality was reflected in full employment, rationing according to physical needs, and a sharing of hardships. There, too, society became more uniform and more egalitarian, in spite of some war profiteering.

Finally, death itself had no respect for traditional social distinctions. It savagely decimated the young aristocratic officers who led the charge, and it fell heavily on the mass of drafted peasants and unskilled workers who followed. Yet death often spared the aristocrats of labor, the skilled workers and foremen. Their lives were too valuable to squander at the front, for they were needed to train the newly recruited women and older unskilled men laboring valiantly in war plants at home.

Growing Political Tensions

During the first two years of war, most soldiers and civilians supported their governments. Belief in a just cause, patriotic nationalism, the planned economy, and a sharing of burdens united peoples behind their various national leaders.

Each government employed rigorous censorship to control public opinion, and each used both crude and subtle propaganda to maintain popular support. German propaganda hysterically pictured black soldiers from France's African empire raping German women, while German atrocities in Belgium and elsewhere were ceaselessly recounted and exaggerated by the French and British. Patriotic posters and slogans, slanted news, and biased editorials inflamed national hatreds and helped sustain superhuman efforts.

By the spring of 1916, however, people were beginning to crack under the strain of total war. In April 1916, Irish nationalists in Dublin tried to take advantage of this situation and rose up against British rule in their great Easter Rebellion. A week of bitter fighting passed before the rebels were crushed and their leaders executed. On May 1, 1916, several thousand demonstrators in Berlin heard the radical socialist leader Karl Liebknecht (1871–1919) shout, "Down with the government! Down with the war!" Liebknecht was immediately arrested and imprisoned, but his daring action electrified Europe's far left. Strikes and protest marches over inadequate food began to flare up on every home front.

Soldiers' morale also began to decline. Italian troops mutinied. Numerous French units refused to fight after the disastrous French offensive of May 1917. Only tough military justice for leaders and a tacit agreement with the troops that there would be no more grand offensives enabled the new general in chief, Henri Philippe Pétain, to restore order. A rising tide of war-weariness and defeatism also swept France's civilian population before Georges Clemenceau emerged as a ruthless and effective wartime leader in November 1917. Clemenceau (1841–1929) established a virtual dictatorship, pouncing on strikers and jailing without trial journalists and politicians who dared to suggest a compromise peace with Germany.

The strains were worse for the Central Powers. In October 1916, the chief minister of Austria was assassinated by a young socialist crying, "Down with Absolutism! We want peace!"[4] The following month, when feeble old Emperor Francis Joseph died, a symbol of unity disappeared. In spite of absolute censorship, political dissatisfaction and conflicts among nationalities grew. In April 1917, Austria's chief minister summed up the situation in the gloomiest possible terms. The country and army were exhausted. Another winter of war would bring revolution and disintegration. Both Czech and Yugoslav leaders demanded autonomous democratic states for their peoples. The British blockade kept tightening; people were starving.

The strain of total war and of the Auxiliary Service Law was also evident in Germany. In the winter of 1916 to 1917, Germany's military position appeared increasingly desperate. Stalemates and losses in the west were matched by temporary Russian advances in the east: hence the military's insistence on an all-or-nothing gamble of unrestricted submarine warfare when the Triple Entente refused in December 1916 to consider peace on terms favorable to the Central Powers.

Also, the national political unity of the first two years of war was collapsing as the social conflict of prewar Germany re-emerged. A growing minority of moderate socialists in the Reichstag called for a compromise "peace without annexations or reparations." Such a peace was unthinkable for conservatives and military leaders. So also was the surge in revolutionary agitation and strikes by war-weary workers that occurred in early 1917. When the bread ration was further reduced in April, more than 200,000 workers struck and demonstrated for a week in Berlin, returning to work only under the threat of prison and military discipline. Thus militaristic Germany, like its ally Austria-Hungary (and its enemy France), was beginning to crack in 1917. Yet it was Russia that collapsed first and saved the Central Powers—for a time.

The Russian Revolution

The Russian Revolution of 1917 was one of modern history's most momentous events. Directly related to the growing tensions of World War I, it had a significance far beyond the wartime agonies of a single European nation. The Russian Revolution opened a new era. For some, it was Marx's socialist vision come true; for others, it was the triumph of dictatorship. To all, it presented a radically new prototype of state and society.

- **Why did World War I bring socialist revolution in Russia?**

The Fall of Imperial Russia

Like its allies and its enemies, Russia embraced war with patriotic enthusiasm in 1914. At the Winter Palace, while throngs of people knelt and sang, "God save the tsar," Tsar Nicholas II (r. 1894–1917) repeated the oath Alexander I had sworn in 1812 and vowed never to make peace as long as the enemy stood on Russian soil. Russia's lower house, the Duma, voted war credits. Conservatives anticipated expansion in the Balkans, while liberals and most socialists believed alliance with Britain and France would bring democratic reforms. For a moment, Russia was united.

Unprecedented artillery barrages used up Russia's supplies of shells and ammunition, and better-equipped German armies inflicted terrible losses. In 1915 substantial numbers of Russian soldiers were sent to the front without rifles; they were told to find their arms among the dead. There were 2 million Russian casualties in 1915 alone. Nevertheless, Russia's battered peasant army did not collapse but continued to fight courageously, and Russia moved toward full mobilization on the home front. The Duma and organs of local government took the lead, setting up special committees to coordinate defense, industry, transportation, and agriculture. These efforts improved the military situation. Yet there were many failures, and Russia mobilized less effectively for total war than the other warring nations.

The great problem was leadership. Under the constitution resulting from the revolution of 1905 (see pages 828–829), the tsar had retained complete control over the bureaucracy and the army. Legislation proposed by the Duma, which was weighted in favor of the wealthy and conservative classes, was subject to the tsar's veto. Moreover, Nicholas II fervently wished to maintain the sacred inheritance of supreme royal power. A kindly, slightly stupid man, Nicholas failed to form a close partnership with his citizens in order to fight the war more effectively. He came to rely instead on the old bureaucratic apparatus, distrusting the moderate Duma, rejecting popular involvement, and resisting calls to share power.

As a result, the Duma, the educated middle classes, and the masses became increasingly critical of the tsar's leadership. In September 1915 parties ranging from conservative to moderate socialist formed the Progressive bloc, which called for a completely new government responsible to the Duma instead of the tsar. In answer, Nicholas temporarily adjourned the Duma and announced that he was traveling to the front in order to lead and rally Russia's armies.

His departure was a fatal turning point. With the tsar in the field with the troops, control of the government was taken over by the hysterical empress, Tsarina Alexandra, and a debauched adventurer and self-proclaimed holy man, Rasputin. Nicholas's wife was a strong-willed woman with a hatred of parliaments. Having constantly urged her husband to rule absolutely, Alexandra tried to do so herself in his absence. She seated and unseated the top ministers. Her most trusted adviser was "our Friend Grigori," an uneducated Siberian preacher who was appropriately nicknamed "Rasputin"—the "Degenerate."

Rasputin's influence rested on mysterious healing powers. Alexis, Alexandra's fifth child and heir to the throne, suffered from the rare blood disease hemophilia, and only Rasputin could miraculously stop the bleeding, perhaps through hypnosis.

In a desperate attempt to right the situation and end unfounded rumors that Rasputin was the empress's lover, three members of the high aristocracy murdered Rasputin in December 1916. The empress went into semipermanent shock. Food shortages in the cities worsened; morale declined. On March 8, women calling for bread in Petrograd (formerly St. Petersburg) started riots, which spontaneously spread to the factories and then elsewhere throughout the city. From the front, the tsar ordered troops to restore order, but discipline broke down, and the soldiers joined the revolutionary crowd. The Duma responded by declaring a provisional government on March 12, 1917. Three days later, Nicholas abdicated.

"The Russian Ruling House" This wartime cartoon captures the ominous, spellbinding power of Rasputin over Tsar Nicholas II and his wife, Alexandra. Rasputin's manipulations disgusted Russian public opinion and contributed to the monarchy's collapse. *(Stock Montage)*

The Provisional Government

The March revolution was the result of an unplanned uprising of hungry, angry people in the capital, but it was joyfully accepted throughout the country. The patriotic upper and middle classes rejoiced at the prospect of a more determined and effective war effort, while workers happily anticipated better wages and more food. All classes and political parties called for liberty and democracy. They were not disappointed. As Vladimir Lenin said, Russia became the freest country in the world. After generations of arbitrary authoritarianism, the provisional government quickly established equality before the law; freedom of religion, speech, and assembly; the right of unions to organize and strike; and the rest of the classic liberal program.

Yet both liberal and moderate socialist leaders of the provisional government rejected social revolution. The reorganized government formed in May 1917 included the fiery agrarian socialist Alexander Kerensky, who became prime minister in July. He refused to confiscate large landholdings and give them to peasants, fearing that such drastic action in the countryside would only complete the disintegration of Russia's peasant army. For the patriotic Kerensky, as for other moderate socialists, the continuation of war was still the all-important national duty. Human suffering and war-weariness grew, sapping the limited strength of the provisional government.

From its first day, the provisional government had to share power with a formidable rival—the **Petrograd Soviet** (or council) of Workers' and Soldiers' Deputies. Modeled on the revolutionary soviets of 1905, the Petrograd Soviet was a huge, fluctuating mass meeting of two thousand to three thousand workers, soldiers, and socialist intellectuals. Seeing itself as a true grassroots revolutionary democracy, this counter- or half-government suspiciously watched the provisional government and issued its own radical orders, further weakening the provisional government. Most famous of these was **Army Order No. 1,** issued to all Russian military forces as the provisional government was forming.

Army Order No. 1 stripped officers of their authority and placed power in the hands of elected committees of common soldiers. Designed primarily to protect the revolution from some counter-revolutionary Bonaparte on horseback, the order instead led to a total collapse of army discipline. Many an officer was hanged for his sins. Meanwhile, following the foolhardy summer offensive, masses of peasant soldiers began "voting with their feet," to use Lenin's graphic phrase. That is, they began returning to their villages to help their families get a share of the land, which peasants were simply seizing as they settled old scores in a great agrarian upheaval. All across the country, liberty was turning into anarchy in the summer of 1917. It was an unparalleled opportunity for the most radical and most talented of Russia's many socialist leaders, Vladimir Ilyich Lenin (1870–1924).

Lenin and the Bolshevik Revolution

From his youth, Lenin's whole life had been dedicated to the cause of revolution. Born into the middle class, Lenin became an implacable enemy of imperial Russia when his older brother was executed for plotting to kill the tsar in

The Russian Revolution

1914	Russia enthusiastically enters the First World War.
1915	Russia suffers 2 million casualties.
	Progressive bloc calls for a new government responsible to the Duma rather than to the tsar.
	Tsar Nicholas adjourns the Duma and departs for the front; Alexandra and Rasputin exert a strong influence on the government.
December 1916	Rasputin is murdered.
March 8, 1917	Bread riots take place in Petrograd (St. Petersburg).
March 12, 1917	Duma declares a provisional government.
March 15, 1917	Tsar Nicholas abdicates without protest.
April 3, 1917	Lenin returns from exile and denounces the provisional government.
May 1917	Reorganized provisional government, including Kerensky, continues the war.
	Petrograd Soviet issues Army Order No. 1, granting military power to committees of common soldiers.
Summer 1917	Agrarian upheavals: peasants seize estates; peasant soldiers desert the army to participate.
October 1917	Bolsheviks gain a majority in the Petrograd Soviet.
November 6, 1917	Bolsheviks seize power; Lenin heads the new "provisional workers' and peasants' government."
November 1917	Lenin accepts peasant seizure of land and worker control of factories; all banks are nationalized.
January 1918	Lenin permanently disbands the Constituent Assembly.
February 1918	Lenin convinces the Bolshevik Central Committee to accept a humiliating peace with Germany in order to safeguard the revolution.
March 1918	Treaty of Brest-Litovsk: Russia loses one-third of its population.
	Trotsky as war commissar begins to rebuild the Russian army.
	Government moves from Petrograd to Moscow.
1918–1920	Great civil war takes place.
Summer 1918	Eighteen regional governments compete for power.
	White armies oppose the Bolshevik Revolution.
1919	White armies are on the offensive but divided politically; they receive little benefit from Allied intervention.
1920	Lenin and the Red Army are victorious, retaking Belorussia and Ukraine.

1887. As a law student, Lenin found a revolutionary faith in Marxian socialism, which began to win converts among radical intellectuals as industrialization surged forward in Russia in the 1890s. Exiled to Siberia for three years, Lenin studied Marxian doctrines with religious intensity. After his release, this young priest of socialism then joined fellow socialists in western Europe and developed his own revolutionary interpretations of the body of Marxian thought.

Three interrelated ideas were central for Lenin. First, like other eastern European radical socialists after 1900, he turned to the early fire-breathing Marx of 1848 and *The Communist Manifesto* for inspiration. Thus Lenin stressed that capitalism could be destroyed only by violent revolution. He tirelessly denounced all revisionist theories of a peaceful evolution to socialism as betraying Marx's message of unending class conflict. Lenin's second, more original idea was that under certain conditions a socialist revolution was possible even in a relatively backward country like Russia. There the industrial working class was small, but peasants were poor and thus potential revolutionaries.

Lenin believed that at a given moment revolution was determined more by human leadership than by vast historical laws. Thus was born his third basic idea: the necessity of a highly disciplined workers' party, strictly controlled by a dedicated elite of intellectuals and full-time revolutionaries like Lenin himself. Unlike ordinary workers and trade-union officials, this elite would never be seduced by short-term gains. It would not stop until revolution brought it to power.

Lenin's theories and methods did not go unchallenged by other Russian Marxists. At meetings of the Russian Social Democratic Labor Party in London in 1903, matters came to a head. Lenin demanded a small, disciplined, elitist party, while his opponents wanted a more democratic party with mass membership. The Russian party of Marxian socialism promptly split into two rival factions. Lenin's camp was called **Bolsheviks,** or "majority group"; his opponents were *Mensheviks,* or "minority group." Lenin's majority did not last, but Lenin did not care. He kept the fine-sounding name Bolshevik and developed the party he wanted: tough, disciplined, revolutionary.

Online Study Center **Improve Your Grade**
Primary Source: What Is to Be Done with Russia?

Unlike most other socialists, Lenin did not rally round the national flag in 1914. Observing events from neutral Switzerland, he saw the war as a product of imperialistic rivalries and as a marvelous opportunity for class war and socialist upheaval. After the March revolution the German government provided the impatient Lenin, his wife, and about twenty trusted colleagues with safe passage across Germany and back into Russia in April 1917. The Germans hoped that Lenin would undermine the sagging war effort of the world's freest society. They were not disappointed.

Arriving triumphantly at Petrograd's Finland Station on April 3, Lenin attacked at once. To the great astonishment of the local Bolsheviks, he rejected all cooperation with the "bourgeois" provisional government of the liberals and moderate socialists. His slogans were radical in the extreme: "All power to the soviets"; "All land to the peasants"; "Stop the war now." Never a slave to Marxian determinism, the brilliant but not unduly intellectual Lenin was a superb tactician. The moment was now.

Yet Lenin almost overplayed his hand. An attempt by the Bolsheviks to seize power in July collapsed, and Lenin fled and went into hiding. He was charged with being a German agent, and indeed he and the Bolsheviks were getting money from Germany.[5] But no matter. Intrigue between Kerensky, who became prime minister in July, and his commander in chief, General Lavr Kornilov, resulted in Kornilov's leading a feeble attack against the provisional government in September. In the face of this rightist "counter-revolutionary" threat, the Bolsheviks were rearmed and redeemed. Kornilov's forces disintegrated, but Kerensky lost all credit with the army, the only force that might have saved him and democratic government in Russia.

Trotsky and the Seizure of Power

Throughout the summer, the Bolsheviks had appealed very effectively to the workers and soldiers of Petrograd, markedly increasing their popular support. Party membership had soared from 50,000 to 240,000, and in October the Bolsheviks gained a fragile majority in the Petrograd Soviet. It was now Lenin's supporter Leon Trotsky (1879–1940), a spellbinding revolutionary orator and independent radical Marxist, who brilliantly executed the Bolshevik seizure of power.

Painting a vivid but untruthful picture of German and counter-revolutionary plots, Trotsky first convinced the Petrograd Soviet to form a special military-revolutionary committee in October and make him its leader. Military power in the capital passed into Bolshevik hands. Then, on the night of November 6, militants from Trotsky's committee joined with trusty Bolshevik soldiers to seize government buildings and pounce on members of the provisional government. Then they went on to the congress of soviets. There a Bolshevik majority—roughly 390 of 650 turbulent delegates—declared that all power had passed to the soviets and named Lenin head of the new government.

The Bolsheviks came to power for three key reasons. First, by late 1917 democracy had given way to anarchy: power was there for those who would take it. Second, in Lenin and Trotsky the Bolsheviks had an utterly determined and truly superior leadership, which both the tsarist government and the provisional government lacked. Third, in 1917 the Bolsheviks succeeded in appealing to many soldiers and urban workers, people who were exhausted by war and eager for socialism. With time, many workers would become bitterly disappointed, but for the moment they had good reason to believe that they had won what they wanted.

Dictatorship and Civil War

History is full of short-lived coups and unsuccessful revolutions. The truly monumental accomplishment of Lenin, Trotsky, and the rest of the Bolsheviks was not taking power but keeping it. In the next four years, the Bolsheviks went on to conquer the chaos they had helped create, and they began to build their kind of dictatorial socialist society. The conspirators became conquerors. How was this done?

Lenin had the genius to profit from developments over which he and the Bolsheviks had no control. Since summer, a peasant revolution had been sweeping across Russia as the tillers of the soil invaded and divided among themselves the estates of the landlords and the church. Peasant seizure of the land—a Russian 1789—was not very Marxian, but it was quite unstoppable in 1917. Thus Lenin's first law, which supposedly gave land to the peasants, actually merely approved what peasants were already doing. Urban workers' great demand in November was direct control of individual factories by local workers committees. This, too, Lenin ratified with a decree in November.

Unlike many of his colleagues, Lenin acknowledged that Russia had lost the war with Germany and that the only realistic goal was peace at any price. That price was very high. Germany demanded in December 1917 that the Soviet government give up all its western territories. These areas were inhabited by Poles, Finns, Lithuanians, and other non-Russians—all those people who had been conquered by the tsars over three centuries and put into the "prisonhouse of nationalities," as Lenin had earlier called the Russian empire.

At first, Lenin's fellow Bolsheviks would not accept such great territorial losses. But when German armies resumed their unopposed march into Russia in February 1918, Lenin had his way in a very close vote in the Central Committee of the party. "Not even his greatest enemy can deny that at this moment Lenin towered like a giant over his Bolshevik colleagues."[6] A third of old Russia's population was sliced away by the German meat ax in the Treaty of Brest-Litovsk in March 1918. With peace, Lenin had escaped the certain disaster of continued war and could pursue his goal of absolute political power for the Bolsheviks—now renamed Communists—within Russia.

In November 1917, the Bolsheviks had cleverly proclaimed their regime only a "provisional workers' and peasants' government," promising that a freely elected

Lenin Rallies Worker and Soldier Delegates At a midnight meeting of the Petrograd Soviet, the Bolsheviks rise up and seize power on November 6, 1917. This painting from the 1940s idealizes Lenin, but his great talents as a revolutionary leader are undeniable. In this re-creation Stalin, who actually played only a small role in the uprising, is standing behind Lenin, already his trusty right-hand man. *(Sovfoto)*

Constituent Assembly would draw up a new constitution. But free elections produced a stunning setback for the Bolsheviks, who won less than one-fourth of the elected delegates. The Socialist Revolutionaries—the peasants' party—had a clear majority. The Constituent Assembly met for only one day, on January 18, 1918. It was then permanently disbanded by Bolshevik soldiers acting under Lenin's orders. Thus even before the peace with Germany, Lenin was forming a one-party government.

The destruction of the democratically elected Constituent Assembly helped feed the flames of civil war. People who had risen up for self-rule in November saw that once again they were getting dictatorship from the capital. For the next three years, "Long live the [democratic] soviets; down with the Bolsheviks" was to be a popular slogan. The officers of the old army took the lead in organizing the so-called White opposition to the Bolsheviks in southern Russia, Ukraine, Siberia, and west of Petrograd. The

"You! Have You Volunteered?" A Red Army soldier makes a compelling direct appeal to the ordinary citizen and demands all-out support for the Bolshevik cause in this 1920 poster by Dmitri Moor, a popular Soviet artist. Lenin recognized the importance of visual propaganda in a vast country with limited literacy, and mass-produced posters like this one were everywhere during the civil war of 1918–1920. *(Stephen White, University of Glasgow)*

Whites came from many social groups and were united only by their hatred of the Bolsheviks—the Reds.

By the summer of 1918, fully eighteen self-proclaimed regional governments—several of which represented minority nationalities—were competing with Lenin's Bolsheviks in Moscow. By the end of the year, White armies were on the attack. In October 1919, it appeared they might triumph, as they closed in on Lenin's government from three sides. Yet they did not. By the spring of 1920, the White armies had been almost completely defeated, and the Bolshevik Red Army had retaken Belorussia and Ukraine. The following year, the Communists also reconquered the independent nationalist governments of the Caucasus. The civil war was over; Lenin had won.

Lenin and the Bolsheviks won for several reasons. Strategically, they controlled the center, while the Whites were always on the fringes and disunited. Moreover, the poorly defined political program of the Whites was vaguely conservative, and it did not unite all the foes of the Bolsheviks under a progressive, democratic banner. Most important, the Communists quickly developed a better army, an army for which the divided Whites were no match.

Once again, Trotsky's leadership was decisive. The Bolsheviks had preached democracy in the army and elected officers in 1917. But beginning in March 1918, Trotsky as war commissar re-established the draft and the most drastic discipline for the newly formed Red Army. Soldiers deserting or disobeying an order were summarily shot. Moreover, Trotsky made effective use of former tsarist army officers, who were actively recruited and given unprecedented powers of discipline over their troops. In short, Trotsky formed a disciplined and effective fighting force.

The Bolsheviks also mobilized the home front. Establishing **war communism**—the application of the total war concept to a civil conflict—they seized grain from peasants, introduced rationing, nationalized all banks and industry, and required everyone to work. Although these measures contributed to a breakdown of normal economic activity, they also served to maintain labor discipline and to keep the Red Army supplied.

"Revolutionary terror" also contributed to the Communist victory. The old tsarist secret police was re-established as the **Cheka,** which hunted down and executed thousands of real or supposed foes, such as the tsar and his family and other "class enemies." Moreover, people were shot or threatened with being shot for minor nonpolitical failures. The terror caused by the secret police became a tool of the government. The Cheka sowed fear, and fear silenced opposition.

Finally, foreign military intervention in the civil war ended up helping the Communists. After Lenin made peace with Germany, the Allies (United States, Britain, Japan) sent troops to Archangel and Vladivostok to prevent war materiel they had sent the provisional government from being captured by the Germans. After the Soviet government nationalized all foreign-owned factories without compensation and refused to pay all of Russia's foreign debts, Western governments, particularly France, began to support White armies in the south and west. Yet these efforts were small and halfhearted. In 1919 Western peoples were sick of war, and few Western politicians believed in a military crusade against the Bolsheviks. Thus Allied intervention in the civil war did not aid the Whites effectively, though it did permit the Communists to appeal to the patriotic nationalism of ethnic Russians, in particular former tsarist army officers. Allied intervention was both too little and too much.

Together, the Russian Revolution and the Bolshevik triumph were one of the reasons the First World War was such a great turning point in modern history. A radically new government, based on socialism and one-party dictatorship, came to power in a great European state, maintained power, and eagerly encouraged worldwide revolution. Although halfhearted constitutional monarchy in Russia was undoubtedly headed for some kind of political crisis before 1914, it is hard to imagine the triumph of the most radical proponents of change and reform except in a situation of total collapse. That was precisely what happened to Russia in the First World War.

The Peace Settlement

Victory over revolutionary Russia boosted sagging German morale, and in the spring of 1918 the Germans launched their last major attack against France. Yet this offensive failed, just as those before it had. With breathtaking rapidity, the United States, Great Britain, and France decisively defeated Germany militarily. The guns of world war finally fell silent. Then as civil war spread in Russia and as chaos engulfed much of eastern Europe, the victorious Western Allies came together in Paris to establish a lasting peace.

Expectations were high; optimism was almost unlimited. The Allies labored intensively and soon worked out terms for peace with Germany and for the creation of the peacekeeping League of Nations. Nevertheless, the hopes of peoples and politicians were soon disappointed, for the peace settlement of 1919 turned out to be a failure. Rather than creating conditions for peace, it sowed the seeds of another war. Surely this was the ultimate tragedy of the Great War, a war that directly and indirectly cost $332 billion and left 10 million dead and another 20 million wounded.

- *How did the Allies fashion a peace settlement, and why was it unsuccessful?*

The End of the War

In early 1917, the strain of total war was showing everywhere. After the Russian Revolution in March, there were major strikes in Germany. In July a coalition of moderates passed a "peace resolution" in the Reichstag, calling for peace without territorial annexations. To counter this moderation born of war-weariness, the German military established a virtual dictatorship. The military also aggressively exploited the collapse of Russian armies, winning great concessions in the Treaty of Brest-Litovsk in March 1918.

With victory in the east quieting German moderates, General Ludendorff and company fell on France once more in the great spring offensive of 1918. For a time, German armies pushed forward, coming within thirty-five miles of Paris. But Ludendorff's exhausted, overextended forces never broke through. They were decisively stopped in July at the second Battle of the Marne, where 140,000 fresh American soldiers saw action. Adding 2 million men in arms to the war effort by August, the late but massive American intervention decisively tipped the scales in favor of Allied victory.

By September British, French, and American armies were advancing steadily on all fronts, and a panicky General Ludendorff realized that Germany had lost the war. Yet he insolently insisted that moderate politicians shoulder the shame of defeat, and on October 4 the emperor formed a new, more liberal German government to sue for peace. As negotiations over an armistice dragged on, an angry and frustrated German people finally rose up. On November 3, sailors in Kiel mutinied, and throughout northern Germany soldiers and workers began to establish revolutionary councils on the Russian soviet model. The same day, Austria-Hungary surrendered to the Allies and began breaking apart. Revolution broke out in Germany, and masses of workers demonstrated for peace in Berlin. With army discipline collapsing, the emperor abdicated and fled to Holland. Socialist leaders in Berlin proclaimed a German republic on November 9 and simultaneously agreed to tough Allied terms of surrender. The armistice went into effect on November 11, 1918. The war was over.

Revolution in Germany

Military defeat brought political revolution to Germany and Austria-Hungary, as it had to Russia. In Austria-Hungary the revolution was primarily nationalistic and republican in character. Having started the war to preserve an antinationalistic dynastic state, the Habsburg empire had perished in the attempt. In its place, independent Austrian, Hungarian, and Czechoslovakian republics were proclaimed, while a greatly expanded Serbian monarchy united the South Slavs and took the name Yugoslavia. The prospect of firmly establishing the new national states overrode class considerations for most people in east-central Europe.

The German Revolution of November 1918 resembled the Russian Revolution of March 1917. In both cases, a genuine popular uprising welled up from below, toppled an authoritarian monarchy, and brought the establishment of a liberal provisional republic. In both countries, liberals and moderate socialists took control of the central government, while workers' and soldiers' councils formed a counter-government. In Germany, however, the moderate socialists and their liberal allies won, and the Lenin-like radical revolutionaries in the councils lost. In communist terms, the liberal, republican revolution in Germany in 1918 was only half a revolution: a bourgeois political revolution without a communist second installment. It was Russia without Lenin's Bolshevik triumph.

There were several reasons for the German outcome. The great majority of Marxian socialist leaders in the Social Democratic Party were, as before the war, really pink and not red. They wanted to establish real political democracy and civil liberties, and they favored the gradual elimination of capitalism. They were also German nationalists, appalled by the prospect of civil war and revolutionary terror. Moreover, there was less popular support among workers, soldiers, and peasants.

Of crucial importance was the fact that the moderate German Social Democrats, unlike Kerensky and company, accepted defeat and ended the war the day they took power. This act ended the decline in morale among soldiers and prevented the regular army, with its conservative officer corps, from disintegrating. When radicals headed by Karl Liebknecht and Rosa Luxemburg and their supporters in the councils tried to seize control of the government in Berlin in January, the moderate socialists called on the army to crush the uprising. Liebknecht and Luxemburg were arrested and then brutally murdered by army leaders. Their murders, widely believed to have had government support, caused many working-class activists in the Social Democratic Party to break away in anger and join the pro-Lenin German Communist Party that Liebknecht's group had just founded. Finally, even if the moderate socialists had followed Liebknecht and Luxemburg on the Leninist path, it is very unlikely they would have succeeded. Civil war in Germany would certainly have followed. And the Allies, who were already occupying western Germany according to the terms of the armistice, would have marched on to Berlin and ruled Germany directly.

The Treaty of Versailles

The peace conference opened in Paris in January 1919 with seventy delegates representing twenty-seven victorious nations. There were great expectations. A young British diplomat later wrote that the victors "were convinced that they would never commit the blunders and iniquities of the Congress of Vienna [of 1815]." Then the "misguided, reactionary, pathetic aristocrats" had cynically shuffled populations; now "we believed in nationalism, we believed in the self-determination of peoples." Indeed, "we were journeying to Paris . . . to found a new order in Europe. We were preparing not Peace only, but Eternal Peace."[7] This general optimism and idealism had been greatly strengthened by President Wilson's January 1918 peace proposal, the Fourteen Points, which stressed national self-determination and the rights of small countries.

Online Study Center Improve Your Grade
Primary Source: A New Diplomacy: The Fourteen Points

The real powers at the conference were the United States, Great Britain, and France, for Germany was not allowed to participate and Russia was locked in civil war and did not attend. Italy was considered part of the Big Four, but its role was quite limited. Almost immediately the three great Allies began to quarrel. President Wilson, who was wildly cheered by European crowds as the spokesman for a new idealistic and democratic international cooperation, was almost obsessed with creating the **League of Nations.** Wilson insisted that this question come first, for he passionately believed that only a permanent international organization could protect member states from aggression and avert future wars. Wilson had his way, although Lloyd George of Great Britain and especially Clemenceau of France were unenthusiastic. They were primarily concerned with punishing Germany.

Playing on British nationalism, Lloyd George had already won a smashing electoral victory in December on the popular platform of making Germany pay for the war. "We shall," he promised, "squeeze the orange until the pips squeak." Personally inclined to make a somewhat moderate peace with Germany, Lloyd George was to a considerable extent a captive of demands for a total victory worthy of the sacrifices of total war against a totally depraved enemy. As Kipling summed up the general British feeling at the end of the war, the Germans were "a people with the heart of beasts."[8]

France's Georges Clemenceau, "the Tiger" who had broken wartime defeatism and led his country to victory, wholeheartedly agreed. Like most French people, Clemenceau wanted old-fashioned revenge. He also wanted lasting security for France. This, he believed, required the creation of a buffer state between France and Germany, the permanent demilitarization of Germany, and vast German reparations. He feared that sooner or later Germany with its 60 million people would attack France with its 40 million unless the Germans were permanently weakened. Moreover, France had no English Channel (or Atlantic Ocean) as a reassuring barrier against German aggression. Wilson, supported by Lloyd George, would hear none of this. Clemenceau's demands seemed vindictive, violating morality and the principle of national self-determination. By April the countries attending the conference were deadlocked on the German question, and Wilson packed his bags to go home.

In the end, convinced that France could not afford to face Germany alone in the future, Clemenceau agreed to a compromise. He gave up the French demand for a Rhineland buffer state in return for a formal defensive alliance with the United States and Great Britain. Under the terms of this alliance, both Wilson and Lloyd George promised that their countries would come to France's aid in the event of a German attack. Thus Clemenceau appeared to win his goal of French security, as Wilson had won his of a permanent international organization. The Allies moved quickly to finish the settlement, believing that any adjustments would later be possible within the dual framework of a strong Western alliance and the League of Nations (see Map 27.4).

The **Treaty of Versailles** between the Allies and Germany was the key to the settlement, and the terms were not unreasonable as a first step toward re-establishing international order. Had Germany won, it seems certain that France and Belgium would have been treated with greater severity, as Russia had been at Brest-Litovsk. Germany's colonies were given to France, Britain, and Japan as League of Nations mandates. Germany's territorial losses within Europe were minor, thanks to Wilson. Alsace-Lorraine was returned to France. Parts of Germany inhabited primarily by Poles were ceded to the new Polish state, in keeping with the principle of national self-determination. Predominately German Danzig was also placed within the Polish tariff lines, but as a self-governing city under League of Nations protection. Germany had to limit its army to 100,000 men and agree to build no military fortifications in the Rhineland.

More harshly, the Allies declared that Germany (with Austria) was responsible for the war and had therefore to pay reparations equal to all civilian damages caused by the war. This unfortunate and much-criticized clause expressed inescapable popular demands for German blood, but the actual figure was not set, and there was the clear possibility that reparations might be set at a reasonable level in the future when tempers had cooled.

When presented with the treaty, the German government protested vigorously. But there was no alternative, especially considering that Germany was still starving because the Allies had not yet lifted their naval blockade. On June 28, 1919, German representatives of the ruling moderate Social Democrats and the Catholic Party signed the treaty in the Sun King's Hall of Mirrors at Versailles, where Bismarck's empire had been joyously proclaimed almost fifty years before.

Online Study Center Improve Your Grade
Primary Source: A Defeated Germany Contemplates the Peace Treaty

Separate peace treaties were concluded with the other defeated European powers—Austria, Hungary, and Bulgaria. For the most part, these treaties merely ratified the existing situation in east-central Europe following the breakup of the Austro-Hungarian Empire. Like Austria, Hungary was a particularly big loser, as its "captive" nationalities (and some interspersed Hungarians) were ceded to Romania, Czechoslovakia, Poland, and Yugoslavia. Italy got some Austrian territory.

The Peace Settlement in the Middle East

Although Allied leaders at Versailles focused mainly on European questions, they also imposed a political settlement on what had been the Ottoman Empire. This settlement brought radical changes to the Middle East, and it became very controversial. Basically, the Ottoman Empire was broken up, Britain and France expanded their power and influence in the Middle East, and Arab nationalists felt cheated and betrayed.

The British government had encouraged the wartime Arab revolt against the Ottoman Turks (see page 890) and had even made vague promises of an independent Arab kingdom. However, when the fighting stopped, the British and the French chose instead to honor secret wartime agreements to divide and rule the Ottoman lands. Most important, in 1916 Britain and France had agreed that France would receive modern-day Lebanon and Syria, and much of southern Turkey, and Britain would receive Palestine, Transjordan, and Iraq. This agreement contradicted British (and later Wilsonian) promises concerning Arab independence after the war. When Britain and France set about implementing their secret plans after the armistice, Arab nationalists felt they were being double-crossed.

British plans for the old Ottoman province of Palestine also angered Arab nationalists. The **Balfour Declaration** of November 1917, made by the British foreign secretary Arthur Balfour, had declared that Britain favored a "National Home for the Jewish People" in Palestine, but without prejudicing the civil and religious rights of the non-Jewish communities already living in Palestine.

904 CHAPTER 27 • THE GREAT BREAK: WAR AND REVOLUTION, 1914–1919

Mapping the Past

MAP 27.4 Shattered Empires and Territorial Changes After World War I The Great War brought tremendous changes in eastern Europe. New nations and new boundaries were established, generally on the principle of national self-determination. A dangerous power vacuum was created by the new, usually small states established between Germany and Soviet Russia. ❶ Identify the boundaries of Germany, Austria-Hungary, and Russia in 1914, and note carefully the changes caused by the war. ❷ What territory did Germany lose, and why did France, Poland, and even Denmark receive it? Why was Austria sometimes called a head without a body in the 1920s? ❸ What new independent states (excluding disputed Bessarabia) were formed from the old Russian empire, and what nationalities lived in these states?

Some members of the British cabinet believed the declaration would appeal to German, Austrian, and American Jews and thus help the British war effort. Others sincerely supported the Zionist vision of a Jewish homeland (pages 838–839), which they hoped would also help Britain maintain control of the Suez Canal. In any event, Palestinian Arabs were dismayed.

In 1914 Jews accounted for about 11 percent of the predominantly Arab population in the three Ottoman administrative units that would subsequently be lumped together by the British to form Palestine. The "National Home for the Jewish People" mentioned in the Balfour Declaration implied to the Arabs—and to the Zionist Jews as well—the establishment of some kind of Jewish state that would be incompatible with majority rule. Moreover, a state founded on religious and ethnic exclusivity was out of keeping with both Islamic and Ottoman tradition, which had historically been more tolerant of religious diversity and minorities than had the Christian monarchs or nation-states in Europe.

Despite strong French objections, Hussein of the Hejaz (see page 890) was allowed to send his son Faisal (1885–1933) as his representative to the Versailles Peace Conference. Yet Hussein's efforts to secure Arab independence came to nothing. President Wilson wanted to give the Arab case serious consideration, but the British and the French were determined to rule Syria, Iraq, Transjordan, and Palestine as League of Nations mandates, and they confirmed only the independence of Hussein's kingdom of Hejaz (see Map 27.5). In response Arab nationalists came together in Damascus as the General Syrian Congress in 1919 and unsuccessfully called again for political independence. (See the feature "Listening to the Past: Arab Political Aspirations in 1919" on pages 910–911.) Brushing aside Arab opposition, the British mandate in Palestine formally incorporated the Balfour Declaration and its commitment to a Jewish national home. When Faisal returned to Syria, his followers repudiated the agreement he had reluctantly accepted. In March 1920 they met as the Syrian National Congress and proclaimed Syria independent, with Faisal as king. A similar congress declared Iraq an independent kingdom.

Prince Faisal at the Versailles Peace Conference, 1919 Standing in front, Faisal is supported by his allies and black slave. Nur-as-Said, an officer in the Ottoman army who joined the Arab revolt, is second from the left, and the British officer T. E. Lawrence—popularly known as Lawrence of Arabia—is fourth from the left in back. Faisal failed to win political independence for the Arabs, as the British backed away from the vague promises they had made during the war. *(Courtesy of the Trustees of the Imperial War Museum)*

MAP 27.5 The Partition of the Ottoman Empire, 1914–1923 By 1914 the Ottoman Turks had been pushed out of the Balkans, and their Arab provinces were on the edge of revolt. That revolt, in alliance with the British, erupted in the First World War and contributed greatly to the Ottomans' defeat. Refusing to grant independence to the Arabs, the Allies established League of Nations mandates and replaced Ottoman rulers in Syria, Iraq, Transjordan, and Palestine.

Western reaction to events in Syria and Iraq was swift and decisive. A French army stationed in Lebanon attacked Syria, taking Damascus in July 1920. Faisal fled, and the French took over. Meanwhile, the British put down an uprising in Iraq with bloody fighting and established effective control there. Western imperialism, in the form of League of Nations mandates, appeared to have replaced Ottoman rule in the Arab Middle East (see Map 27.5).

The Allies sought to impose even harsher terms on the defeated Turks than on the "liberated" Arabs. A treaty forced on the helpless Ottoman sultan dismembered the Turkish heartland. Great Britain and France occupied parts of modern-day Turkey, and Italy and Greece also claimed shares. There was a sizable Greek minority in western Turkey, and Greek nationalists wanted to build a modern Greek empire modeled on long-dead Christian Byzantium. In 1919 Greek armies carried by British ships landed on the Turkish coast at Smyrna and advanced unopposed into the interior. Turkey seemed finished.

But Turkey produced a great leader and revived to become an inspiration for many modernizing reformers. Mustafa Kemal (1881–1938), later known as **Atatürk,** which means "father of the Turks," was a military man who had directed the successful defense of the Dardanelles against British attack. Watching the Allies' aggression and the sultan's cowardice after the armistice, in early 1919 he moved to central Turkey and gradually unified the Turkish resistance. Refusing to acknowledge the Allied dismemberment of their country, the Turks battled on through 1920 despite staggering defeats. The

Mustafa Kemal Surnamed Atatürk, meaning "father of the Turks," Mustafa Kemal and his supporters imposed revolutionary changes aimed at modernizing and westernizing Turkish society and the new Turkish government. Dancing here with his adopted daughter at her high-society wedding, Atatürk often appeared in public in elegant European dress—a vivid symbol for the Turkish people of his radical break with traditional Islamic teaching and custom. *(Hulton Archive/Getty Images)*

next year they won a great victory in central Turkey, and the Greeks and their British allies sued for peace. After long negotiations, the resulting Treaty of Lausanne (1923) solemnly abolished the hated Capitulations, which the European powers had imposed over the centuries to give their citizens special privileges in the Ottoman Empire, and recognized the territorial integrity of a truly independent Turkey. Turkey lost only its former Arab provinces.

Mustafa Kemal, a nationalist without religious faith, believed that Turkey should modernize and secularize along Western lines. He established a republic, had himself elected president, and created a one-party system—partly inspired by the Bolshevik example—in order to transform his country. The most radical reforms pertained to religion and culture. For centuries most of the intellectual and social activities of believers had been regulated by Islamic religious authorities. Profoundly influenced by the example of western Europe, Mustafa Kemal set out to limit the place of religion and religious leaders in daily affairs. He decreed a revolutionary separation of church and state, promulgated law codes inspired by European models, and established a secular public school system. Women received rights that they never had before. By the time of his death in 1938, Mustafa Kemal had implemented successfully much of his revolutionary program. He had moved Turkey much closer to Europe, foretelling current efforts by Turkey to join the European Union as full-fledged member.

American Rejection of the Versailles Treaty

The rapidly concluded Versailles treaty of early 1919 was not perfect, but within the context of war-shattered Europe it was an acceptable beginning. The principle of national self-determination, which had played such a large role in starting the war, was accepted for Europe and served as an organizing framework. Germany had been punished but not dismembered. A new world organization complemented a traditional defensive alliance of satisfied powers. The serious remaining problems could be worked out in the future. Moreover, Allied leaders had seen speed as essential for another reason: they detested Lenin and feared that his Bolshevik Revolution might spread. They realized that their best answer to Lenin's unending calls for worldwide upheaval was peace and tranquillity for war-weary peoples.

There were, however, two great interrelated obstacles to such peace: Germany and the United States. Plagued by communist uprisings, reactionary plots, and popular disillusionment with losing the war at the last minute, Germany's moderate socialists and their liberal and Catholic supporters faced an enormous challenge. Like French republicans after 1871, they needed time (and luck) if they were to establish firmly a peaceful and democratic republic. Progress in this direction required understanding but firm treatment of Germany by the victorious Western Allies, particularly by the United States.

However, the U.S. Senate and, to a lesser extent, the American people rejected Wilson's handiwork. Republican senators led by Henry Cabot Lodge refused to ratify the

...y of Versailles without changes in the articles creating the League of Nations. The key issue was the League's power—more apparent than real—to require member states to take collective action against aggression. Lodge and others believed that this requirement gave away Congress's constitutional right to declare war. In failing health, Wilson, with narrow-minded self-righteousness, rejected all attempts at compromise. In doing so, he ensured that the treaty would never be ratified by the United States in any form and that the United States would never join the League of Nations. Moreover, the Senate refused to ratify Wilson's treaties forming a defensive alliance with France and Great Britain. America turned its back on Europe.

The Wilson-Lodge fiasco and the newfound gospel of isolationism represented a tragic and cowardly renunciation of America's responsibility. Using America's action as an excuse, Great Britain, too, refused to ratify its defensive alliance with France. Bitterly betrayed by its allies, France stood alone. Very shortly France was to take actions against Germany that would feed the fires of German resentment and seriously undermine democratic forces in the new republic. The great hopes of early 1919 had turned to ashes by the end of the year. The Western alliance had collapsed, and a grandiose plan for permanent peace had given way to a fragile truce. For this and for what came later, the United States must share a large part of the guilt.

Chapter Summary

- What caused the Great War, and why did it have such revolutionary consequences?
- What was the impact of total war on civilian populations?
- Why did World War I bring socialist revolution in Russia?
- How did the Allies fashion a peace settlement, and why was it unsuccessful?

World War I had truly revolutionary consequences because, first and foremost, it was a war of committed peoples. In France, Britain, and Germany in particular, governments drew on genuine popular support. This support reflected in part the diplomatic origins of the war, which citizens saw as growing out of an unwanted crisis in the Balkans and an inflexible alliance system of opposing blocs. More importantly, popular support reflected the way western European society had been unified under the nationalist banner in the later nineteenth century, despite the fears that the growing socialist movement aroused in conservatives.

The relentlessness of total war helps explain why so many died, why so many were crippled physically and psychologically, and why Western civilization would in so many ways never be the same again. More concretely, the war swept away monarchs and multinational empires. National self-determination apparently triumphed across Europe, not only in Austria-Hungary but also in many of Russia's western borderlands. Except in Ireland and parts of Soviet Russia (and the Arab Middle East), the revolutionary dream of national unity, born of the French Revolution, had finally come true.

Two other revolutions were products of the war. In Russia the Bolsheviks established a radical regime, smashed existing capitalist institutions, and stayed in power with a new kind of authoritarian rule. Whether the new Russian regime was truly Marxian or socialist was questionable, but it indisputably posed a powerful, ongoing revolutionary challenge to Europe and its colonial empires.

More subtle but quite universal in its impact was an administrative revolution. This revolution, born of the need to mobilize entire societies and economies for total war, greatly increased the power of government. Freewheeling market capitalism and a well-integrated world economy were among the many casualties of the administrative revolution, and greater social equality was everywhere one of its results. Thus even in European countries where a communist takeover never came close to occurring, society still experienced a great revolution.

Finally, the "war to end war" did not bring peace—only a fragile truce. In the West, the Allies failed to maintain their wartime solidarity. Germany remained unrepentant and would soon have more grievances to nurse. Moreover, the victory of national self-determination in eastern Europe created small, weak states and thus a power vacuum between a still-powerful Germany and a potentially mighty communist Russia. A vast area lay open to military aggression from two sides.

Key Terms

Three Emperors' League
Triple Entente
trench warfare
Lusitania
total war
War Raw Materials Board
Petrograd Soviet
Army Order No. 1
Bolsheviks
Constituent Assembly
war communism
Cheka
League of Nations
Treaty of Versailles
Balfour Declaration
Atatürk

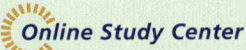 **Improve Your Grade** Flashcards

Suggested Reading

Davis, Belinda J. *Home Fires Burning: Food, Politics, and Everyday Life in Berlin in World War I*. 2000. A moving account of women struggling to feed their families.

Eksteins, Modris. *Rites of Spring: The Great War and the Birth of the Modern Age*. 1989. An imaginative cultural investigation that has won critical acclaim.

Fromkin, David. *A Peace to End All Peace*. 2001. A brilliant reconsideration of the collapse of the Ottoman Empire and its division by the Allies.

Gatrell, Peter. *Russia's First World War: A Social and Economic History*. 2005. An excellent resource for students and specialists.

Herwig, Holger H. *The First World War: Germany and Austria, 1914–1918*. 1997. Ably follows the hard road to defeat and collapse.

Higonnet, Margaret R., Jane Jenson, Sonya Michel, and Margaret Collins Weitz, eds. *Behind the Lines: Gender and the Two World Wars*. 1989. Examines the changes that the war brought for women and for relations between the sexes.

Hobsbawm, Eric. *The Age of Extremes: A History of the World, 1914–1991*. 1996. A provocative interpretation by a famous historian, with a good discussion of war and revolution.

Howard, Michael. *The First World War: A Very Short Introduction*. 2007. A fine brief introduction.

Macmillan, Margaret. *Paris, 1919: Six Months That Changed the World*. 2001. A comprehensive, exciting account of all aspects of the peace conference.

Neiberg, Michael S. *Fighting the Great War: A Global History*. 2006. A lively and up-to-date account.

Read, Christopher. *From Tsar to Soviets: The Russian People and Their Revolution, 1917–1921*. 1996. A highly recommended account of the Russian Revolution.

Remarque, Erich Maria. *All Quiet on the Western Front*. Originally published in 1928, this novel remains one of the most moving fictional treatments of World War I.

Tucker, Jonathan. *War of Nerves: Chemical Warfare from World War I to Al-Qaeda*. 2007. A comprehensive and informative survey of chemical warfare.

Winter, J. M. *The Experience of World War I*. 1988. A striking illustrated history of the war.

Zuckerman, Larry. *The Rape of Belgium: The Untold Story of World War I*. 2004. A poignant examination of German atrocities.

Notes

1. M. Beloff, quoted in *U.S. News & World Report*, March 8, 1976, p. 53.
2. Quoted in J. Remak, *The Origins of World War I* (New York: Holt, Rinehart & Winston, 1967), p. 84.
3. Quoted in F. P. Chambers, *The War Behind the War, 1914–1918* (London: Faber & Faber, 1939), p. 168.
4. Quoted in R. O. Paxton, *Europe in the Twentieth Century* (New York: Harcourt Brace Jovanovich, 1975), p. 109.
5. A. B. Ulam, *The Bolsheviks* (New York: Collier Books, 1968), p. 349.
6. Ibid., p. 405.
7. H. Nicolson, *Peacemaking 1919* (New York: Grosset & Dunlap Universal Library, 1965), pp. 8, 31–32.
8. Quoted ibid., p. 24.

Listening to the Past

Arab Political Aspirations in 1919

Great Britain and France had agreed to divide up the Arab lands, and the British also had made conflicting promises to Arab and Jewish nationalists. However, President Wilson insisted at Versailles that the right of self-determination should be applied to the conquered Ottoman territories, and he sent an American commission of inquiry to Syria, even though the British and French refused to participate. The commission canvassed political views throughout greater Syria, and its long report with many documents reflected public opinion in the region in 1919.

To present their view to the Americans, Arab nationalists from present-day Syria, Lebanon, Israel, and Jordan came together in Damascus as the General Syrian Congress, and they passed the following resolution on July 2, 1919. In addition to the Arab call for political independence, the delegates addressed the possibility of French rule under a League of Nations mandate and the establishment of a Jewish national home.

We the undersigned members of the General Syrian Congress, meeting in Damascus on Wednesday, July 2nd, 1919, . . . provided with credentials and authorizations by the inhabitants of our various districts, Moslems, Christians, and Jews, have agreed upon the following statement of the desires of the people of the country who have elected us to present them to the American Section of the International Commission; the fifth article was passed by a very large majority; all the other articles were accepted unanimously.

1. We ask absolutely complete political independence for Syria within these boundaries. [Describes the area including the present-day states of Syria, Lebanon, Israel, and Jordan.]

2. We ask that the Government of this Syrian country should be a democratic civil constitutional Monarchy on broad decentralization principles, safeguarding the rights of minorities, and that the King be the Emir Faisal, who carried on a glorious struggle in the cause of our liberation and merited our full confidence and entire reliance.

3. Considering the fact that the Arabs inhabiting the Syrian area are not naturally less gifted than other more advanced races and that they are by no means less developed than the Bulgarians, Serbians, Greeks, and Roumanians at the beginning of their independence, we protest against Article 22 of the Covenant of the League of Nations, placing us among the nations in their middle stage of development which stand in need of a mandatory power.

4. In the event of the rejection by the Peace Conference of this just protest for certain considerations that we may not understand, we, relying on the declarations of President Wilson that his object in waging war was to put an end to the ambition of conquest and colonization, can only regard the mandate mentioned in the Covenant of the League of Nations as equivalent to the rendering of economical and technical assistance that does not prejudice our complete independence. And desiring that our country should not fall a prey to colonization and believing that the American Nation is farthest from any thought of colonization and has no political ambition in our country, we will seek the technical and economical assistance from the United States of America, provided that such assistance does not exceed 20 years.

5. In the event of America not finding herself in a position to accept our desire for assistance, we will seek this assistance from Great Britain, also provided that such assistance does not infringe the complete independence and unity of our country and that the duration of such assistance does not exceed that mentioned in the previous article.

Palestinian Arabs protest against large-scale Jewish migration into Palestine. *(Roger-Viollet/Getty Images)*

6. We do not acknowledge any right claimed by the French Government in any part whatever of our Syrian country and refuse that she should assist us or have a hand in our country under any circumstances and in any place.

7. We oppose the pretensions of the Zionists to create a Jewish commonwealth in the southern part of Syria, known as Palestine, and oppose Zionist migration to any part of our country; for we do not acknowledge their title but consider them a grave peril to our people from the national, economical, and political points of view. Our Jewish compatriots shall enjoy our common rights and assume the common responsibilities.

8. We ask that there should be no separation of the southern part of Syria, known as Palestine, nor of the littoral western zone, which includes Lebanon, from the Syrian country. We desire that the unity of the country should be guaranteed against partition under whatever circumstances.

9. We ask complete independence for emancipated Mesopotamia [today's Iraq] and that there should be no economical barriers between the two countries.

10. The fundamental principles laid down by President Wilson in condemnation of secret treaties impel us to protest most emphatically against any treaty that stipulates the partition of our Syria country and against any private engagement aiming at the establishment of Zionism in the southern part of Syria; therefore we ask the complete annulment of these conventions and agreements.

The noble principles enunciated by President Wilson strengthen our confidence that our desires emanating from the depths of our hearts, shall be the decisive factor in determining our future; and that President Wilson and the free American people will be our supporters for the realization of our hopes, thereby proving their sincerity and noble sympathy with the aspiration of the weaker nations in general and our Arab people in particular.

We also have the fullest confidence that the Peace Conference will realize that we would not have risen against the Turks, with whom we had participated in all civil, political, and representative privileges, but for their violation of our national rights, and so will grant us our desires in full in order that our political rights may not be less after the war than they were before, since we have shed so much blood in the cause of our liberty and independence.

We request to be allowed to send a delegation to represent us at the Peace Conference to defend our rights and secure the realization of our aspirations.

Questions for Analysis

1. What kind of state did the delegates want?
2. How did the delegates want to modify an unwanted League of Nations mandate to make it less objectionable?
3. Did the delegates view their "Jewish compatriots" and the Zionists in different ways? Why?

Source: "Resolution of the General Syrian Congress at Damascus, 2 July 1919," from the King-Crane Commission Report, in *Foreign Relations of the United States: Paris Peace Conference,* 1919, 12: 780–781.

This detail of George Grosz's *Draussen und Drinnen* (Outside and Inside) captures the uncertainty and anxiety of the 1920s. *(akg-images)*

chapter

The Age of Anxiety,
ca 1900–1940

chapter preview

Uncertainty in Modern Thought
• *In what ways did new and disturbing ideas in philosophy, physics, psychology, and literature reflect the general crisis in Western thought?*

Modern Art and Music
• *How did modernism revolutionize architecture, painting, and music?*

Movies and Radio
• *In what ways did movies and radio become mainstays of popular culture?*

The Search for Peace and Political Stability
• *How did the democratic leaders of the 1920s deal with deep-seated instability and try to establish real peace and prosperity?*

The Great Depression, 1929–1939
• *What caused the Great Depression, and how did the Western democracies respond to this challenge?*

When Allied diplomats met in Paris in early 1919 with their optimistic plans for building a lasting peace, most people looked forward to happier times. They hoped that life would return to normal after the terrible trauma of total war. They hoped that once again life would make sense in the familiar prewar terms of peace, prosperity, and progress. These hopes were in vain. The Great Break—the First World War and the Russian Revolution—had mangled too many things beyond repair. Life would no longer fit neatly into the old molds.

Instead, great numbers of men and women felt themselves increasingly adrift in a strange, uncertain, and uncontrollable world. They saw themselves living in an age of anxiety, an age of continual crisis (this age lasted until at least the early 1950s). In almost every area of human experience, people went searching for ways to put meaning back into life.

Uncertainty in Modern Thought

A complex revolution in thought and ideas was under way before the First World War, but only small, unusual groups were aware of it. After the war, these new and upsetting ideas began to spread through the entire population. Western society as a whole began to question and even abandon many cherished values and beliefs that had guided it since the eighteenth-century Enlightenment and the nineteenth-century triumph of industrial development, scientific advances, and evolutionary thought.

• *In what ways did new and disturbing ideas in philosophy, physics, psychology, and literature reflect the general crisis in Western thought?*

The "Cruelly Injured Mind"

Before 1914 most people still believed in progress, reason, and the rights of the individual. Progress was a daily reality, apparent in the rising standard of living, the taming of the city, and the steady increase in popular

Online Study Center
This icon will direct you to interactive activities and study materials on the website **college.hmco.com/pic/mckaywest9e**

education. Such developments also encouraged the comforting belief in the logical universe of Newtonian physics as well as faith in the ability of a rational human mind to understand that universe through intellectual investigation. And just as there were laws of science, so were there laws of society that rational human beings could discover and then wisely act on. At the same time, the rights of the individual were not just taken for granted; they were actually increasing. Well-established political rights were gradually spreading to women and workers, and new "social rights," such as old-age pensions, were emerging. In short, before World War I most Europeans had a moderately optimistic view of the world, and with good reason.

Nevertheless, since the 1880s, a small band of serious thinkers and creative writers had been attacking these well-worn optimistic ideas. These critics rejected the general faith in progress and the power of the rational human mind. An expanding chorus of thinkers echoed and enlarged their views after the experience of history's most destructive war—a war that suggested to many that human beings were a pack of violent, irrational animals quite capable of tearing the individual and his or her rights to shreds. Disorientation and pessimism were particularly acute in the 1930s, when the rapid rise of harsh dictatorships and the Great Depression transformed old certainties into bitter illusions, as we shall see in Chapter 29.

No one expressed this state of uncertainty better than French poet and critic Paul Valéry (1871–1945) in the early 1920s. Speaking of the "crisis of the mind," Valéry noted that Europe was looking at its future with dark foreboding:

The storm has died away, and still we are restless, uneasy, as if the storm were about to break. Almost all the affairs of men remain in a terrible uncertainty. We think of what has disappeared, and we are almost destroyed by what has been destroyed; we do not know what will be born, and we fear the future, not without reason. . . . Doubt and disorder are in us and with us. There is no thinking man, however shrewd or learned he may be, who can hope to dominate this anxiety, to escape from this impression of darkness.[1]

In the midst of economic, political, and social disruptions, Valéry saw the "cruelly injured mind," besieged by doubts and suffering from anxieties. This was the general intellectual crisis of the twentieth century, which touched almost every field of thought. The implications of new

Kollwitz: The Grieving Parents After the renowned German artist Kathe Kollwitz learned in October 1914 that her son Peter had died in battle, the heartbroken mother conceived of a sculpture to honor his memory. Yet her efforts were repeatedly overwhelmed by sorrow. Only in 1931 could she complete this graveside memorial in a military cemetery, a telling indication of the war's ongoing devastation for millions. The grieving father and mother are finally reunited with their son, and they beg forgiveness for the mad war their generation inflicted on its children. *(John Parker, photographer, © 2007 Artists Rights Society [ARS], New York/VG Bild-Kunst, Bonn)*

ideas and discoveries in philosophy, physics, psychology, and literature played a central role in this crisis, disturbing "thinking people" everywhere.

Modern Philosophy

Among the small band of thinkers in the late nineteenth century who challenged the belief in progress and the general faith in the rational human mind, German philosopher Friedrich Nietzsche (1844–1900) was particularly influential. The son of a Lutheran minister, Nietzsche rejected Christianity and became a professor of classical languages until ill health forced him to retire at an early age. Never a systematic philosopher, Nietzsche wrote as a prophet in a provocative and poetic style. His first great work in 1872 argued that ever since classical Athens, the West had overemphasized rationality and stifled the passion and animal instinct that drive human activity and true creativity. Nietzsche went on to question all values. He claimed that Christianity embodied a "slave morality" that glorified weakness, envy, and mediocrity. In Nietzsche's most famous line, a wise fool proclaims that "God is dead," dead because he has been murdered by lackadaisical modern Christians who no longer really believe in him. Nietzsche viewed the pillars of conventional morality—reason, democracy, progress, respectability—as outworn social and psychological constructs whose influence was suffocating self-realization and excellence.

Online Study Center **Improve Your Grade**
Primary Source: God Is Dead, the Victim of Science

Nietzsche painted a dark world, foreshadowing perhaps his loss of sanity in 1889. The West was in decline; false values had triumphed. The death of God left people disoriented and depressed. The only hope for the individual was to accept the meaninglessness of human existence and then make that very meaninglessness a source of self-defined personal integrity and hence liberation. This would at least be possible for a few superior individuals who could free themselves from the humdrum thinking of the masses and become true heroes. Little read during his active years, Nietzsche attracted growing attention in the early twentieth century, especially from German radicals who found inspiration in Nietzsche's ferocious assault on the conventions of pre-1914 imperial Germany. Subsequent generations have each discovered new Nietzsches, and his influence remains enormous to this day.

This growing dissatisfaction with established ideas before 1914 was apparent in other important thinkers. In the 1890s, French philosophy professor Henri Bergson

Chronology

1919	Treaty of Versailles; Freudian psychology gains popular attention; Keynes, *Economic Consequences of the Peace*; Rutherford splits the atom
1920s	Existentialism gains prominence
1920s–1930s	Dadaism and surrealism (artistic movements)
1922	Eliot, *The Waste Land*; Joyce, *Ulysses*; Woolf, *Jacob's Room*; Wittgenstein writes on logical empiricism
1923	French and Belgian armies occupy the Ruhr
1924	Dawes Plan
1925	Berg's opera *Wozzeck* first performed; Kafka, *The Trial*
1926	Germany joins League of Nations
1927	Heisenberg's principle of uncertainty
1928	Kellogg-Briand Pact
1929	Faulkner, *The Sound and the Fury*
1929–1939	Great Depression
1930	Van der Rohe becomes director of Bauhaus
1932	Franklin Roosevelt elected U.S. president
1934	Riefenstahl's documentary film *The Triumph of the Will*
1935	Creation of WPA as part of New Deal
1936	Formation of Popular Front in France

(1859–1941) convinced many young people through his writing that immediate experience and intuition were as important as rational and scientific thinking for understanding reality. Indeed, according to Bergson, a religious experience or a mystical poem was often more accessible to human comprehension than a scientific law or a mathematical equation.

Another thinker who agreed about the limits of rational thinking was French socialist Georges Sorel (1847–1922). Sorel frankly characterized Marxian socialism as an inspiring but unprovable religion rather than a rational scientific truth. Socialism would come to power, he believed, through a great, general strike of all working people, which would shatter capitalist society. Sorel rejected democracy and believed that the masses of the new socialist society

Friedrich Nietzsche This colored photograph of the German philosopher was taken in 1882, when he was at the height of his creative powers. A brilliant iconoclast, Nietzsche debunked European values and challenged the optimistic faith in human rationality before World War I. *(akg-images)*

would have to be tightly controlled by a small revolutionary elite.

The First World War accelerated the revolt against established certainties in philosophy, but that revolt went in two very different directions. In English-speaking countries, the main development was the acceptance of logical empiricism (or logical positivism) in university circles. In continental countries, the primary development in philosophy was existentialism.

Logical empiricism was truly revolutionary. It quite simply rejected most of the concerns of traditional philosophy, from the existence of God to the meaning of happiness, as nonsense and hot air. This outlook began primarily with Austrian philosopher Ludwig Wittgenstein (1889–1951), who later immigrated to England, where he trained numerous disciples.

Wittgenstein argued in his pugnacious *Tractatus Logico-Philosophicus* (Essay on Logical Philosophy) in 1922 that philosophy is only the logical clarification of thoughts, and therefore it becomes the study of language, which expresses thoughts. The great philosophical issues of the ages—God, freedom, morality, and so on—are quite literally senseless, a great waste of time, for statements about them can be neither tested by scientific experiments nor demonstrated by the logic of mathematics. Statements about such matters reflect only the personal preferences of a given individual. As Wittgenstein put it in the famous last sentence of his work, "Of what one cannot speak, of that one must keep silent." Logical empiricism, which has remained dominant in England and the United States to this day, drastically reduced the scope of philosophical inquiry. Anxious people could find few, if any, answers in this direction.

Some looked for answers in **existentialism.** Highly diverse and even contradictory, existential thinkers were loosely united in a courageous search for moral values in a world of terror and uncertainty. Theirs were true voices of the age of anxiety.

Most existential thinkers in the twentieth century were atheists. Often inspired by Nietzsche, who had already proclaimed the death of God and called for new values, they did not believe a supreme being had established humanity's fundamental nature and given life its meaning. In the words of the famous French existentialist Jean-Paul Sartre (1905–1980), human beings simply exist: "They turn up, appear on the scene." Only after they "turn up" do they seek to define themselves. Honest human beings are terribly alone, for there is no God to help them. They are hounded by despair and the meaninglessness of life. The crisis of the existential thinker epitomized the modern intellectual crisis—the shattering of beliefs in God, reason, and progress.

Existentialists did recognize that human beings, unless they kill themselves, must act. Indeed, in the words of Sartre, "man is condemned to be free." There is therefore the possibility—indeed, the necessity—of giving meaning to life through actions, of defining oneself through choices. To do so, individuals must become "engaged" and choose their own actions courageously and consistently and in full awareness of their inescapable responsibility for their own behavior. In the end, existentialists argued, human beings can overcome life's absurdity.

Modern existentialism first attained prominence in Germany in the 1920s when philosophers Martin Heidegger and Karl Jaspers found a sympathetic audience among disillusioned postwar university students. But it was in France during and immediately after World War II that existentialism came of age. The terrible conditions of the war (see Chapter 29) reinforced the existential view of and approach to life. On the one hand, the armies of the German dictator Hitler had conquered most of Europe and unleashed a hideous reign of barbarism. On the other, men and women had more than ever to define themselves by their actions. Specifically, each individual had to choose whether to join the resistance against Hitler or accept and even abet tyranny. The writings of Sartre, who along with Albert Camus (1913–1960) was the leading French existentialist, became enormously influential. Himself active in the French resistance, Sartre and his colleagues offered a powerful answer to profound moral issues and the contemporary crisis.

The Revival of Christianity

The loss of faith in human reason and in continual progress also led to a renewed interest in the Christian view of the world. Christianity and religion in general had been on the defensive in intellectual circles since the Enlightenment. In the years before 1914, some theologians, especially Protestant ones, had felt the need to interpret Christian doctrine and the Bible so that they did not seem to contradict science, evolution, and common sense. Christ was therefore seen primarily as the greatest moral teacher, and the "supernatural" aspects of his divinity were strenuously played down. Indeed, some modern theologians were embarrassed by the miraculous, unscientific aspects of Christianity and turned away from them.

Especially after World War I, a number of thinkers and theologians began to revitalize the fundamentals of Christianity. Sometimes described as Christian existentialists because they shared the loneliness and despair of atheistic existentialists, they stressed human beings' sinful nature, the need for faith, and the mystery of God's forgiveness. The revival of fundamental Christian belief after World War I was fed by rediscovery of the work of nineteenth-century Danish religious philosopher Søren Kierkegaard (1813–1855), whose ideas became extremely influential. Having rejected formalistic religion, Kierkegaard had eventually resolved his personal anguish over his imperfect nature by making a total religious commitment to a remote and majestic God.

Similar ideas were brilliantly developed by Swiss Protestant theologian Karl Barth (1886–1968), whose many influential writings after 1920 sought to re-create the religious intensity of the Reformation. For Barth, the basic fact about human beings is that they are imperfect, sinful creatures whose reason and will are hopelessly flawed. Religious truth is therefore made known to human beings only through God's grace. People have to accept God's word and the supernatural revelation of Jesus Christ with awe, trust, and obedience. Lowly mortals should not expect to "reason out" God and his ways.

Among Catholics, the leading existential Christian thinker was Gabriel Marcel (1887–1973). Born into a cultivated French family, where his atheistic father was "gratefully aware of all that . . . art owed to Catholicism but regarded Catholic thought itself as obsolete and tainted with absurd superstitions,"[2] Marcel found in the Catholic Church an answer to what he called the postwar "broken world." Catholicism and religious belief provided the hope, humanity, honesty, and piety for which he hungered. Flexible and gentle, Marcel and his countryman Jacques Maritain (1882–1973) denounced anti-Semitism and supported closer ties with non-Catholics.

After 1914 religion became much more relevant and meaningful to thinking people than it had been before the war. In addition to Marcel and Maritain, many other illustrious individuals turned to religion between about 1920 and 1950. Poets T. S. Eliot and W. H. Auden, novelists Evelyn Waugh and Aldous Huxley, historian Arnold Toynbee, Oxford professor C. S. Lewis, psychoanalyst Karl Stern, physicist Max Planck, and philosopher Cyril Joad were all either converted to religion or attracted to it for the first time. Religion, often of a despairing, existential variety, was one meaningful answer to terror and anxiety. In the words of a famous Roman Catholic convert, English novelist Graham Greene, "One began to believe in heaven because one believed in hell."[3]

The New Physics

Ever since the scientific revolution of the seventeenth century, scientific advances and their implications had greatly influenced the beliefs of thinking people. By the late nineteenth century, science was one of the main pillars supporting Western society's optimistic and rationalistic view of the world. The Darwinian concept of evolution had been accepted and assimilated in most intellectual circles. Progressive minds believed that science, unlike religion and philosophical speculation, was based on hard facts and controlled experiments. Science seemed to have achieved an unerring and almost complete picture of reality. Unchanging natural laws seemed to determine physical processes and permit useful solutions to more and more problems. All this was comforting, especially to people who were no longer committed to traditional religious beliefs. And all this was challenged by the new physics.

An important first step toward the new physics was the discovery at the end of the nineteenth century that atoms were not like hard, permanent little billiard balls. They were actually composed of many far-smaller, fast-moving particles, such as electrons and protons. Polish-born physicist Marie Curie (1867–1934) and her French husband, Pierre, discovered that radium constantly emits subatomic particles and thus does not have a constant atomic weight. Building on this and other work in radiation, German physicist Max Planck (1858–1947) showed in 1900 that subatomic energy is emitted in uneven little spurts, which Planck called "quanta," and not in a steady stream, as previously believed. Planck's discovery called into question the old sharp distinction between matter and energy; the implication was that matter and energy might be different forms of the same thing. The old view of atoms as the stable, basic building blocks of nature, with a different kind of unbreakable atom for each of the ninety-two chemical elements, was badly shaken.

In 1905 the German-Jewish genius Albert Einstein (1879–1955) went further than the Curies and Planck in undermining Newtonian physics. His famous theory of special relativity postulated that time and space are relative to the viewpoint of the observer and that only the speed of light is constant for all frames of reference in the universe. In order to make his revolutionary and paradoxical idea somewhat comprehensible to the nonmathematical layperson, Einstein later used analogies involving moving trains. For example, if a woman in the middle of a moving car got up and walked forward to the door, she had gone, relative to the train, a half car length. But relative to an observer on the embankment, she had gone farther. The closed framework of Newtonian physics was quite limited compared to that of Einsteinian physics, which unified an apparently infinite universe with the incredibly small, fast-moving subatomic world. Moreover, Einstein's theory stated clearly that matter and energy are interchangeable and that even a particle of matter contains enormous levels of potential energy.

The 1920s opened the "heroic age of physics," in the apt words of one of its leading pioneers, Ernest Rutherford (1871–1937). Breakthrough followed breakthrough. In 1919 Rutherford showed that the atom could be split. By 1944 seven subatomic particles had been identified, of which the most important

Unlocking the Power of the Atom Many of the fanciful visions of science fiction came true in the twentieth century, although not exactly as first imagined. This 1927 cartoon satirizes a professor who has split the atom and unwittingly destroyed his building and neighborhood in the process. In the Second World War the professors harnessed the atom in bombs and decimated faraway cities and foreign civilians. (*Mary Evans Picture Library*)

was the **neutron.** The neutron's capacity to pass through other atoms allowed for even more intense experimental bombardment of matter, leading to chain reactions of unbelievable force. This was the road to the atomic bomb.

Although few nonscientists understood this revolution in physics, the implications of the new theories and discoveries, as presented by newspapers and popular writers, were disturbing to millions of men and women in the 1920s and 1930s. The new universe was strange and troubling. It lacked any absolute objective reality. Everything was "relative," that is, dependent on the observer's frame of reference. Moreover, the universe was uncertain and undetermined, without stable building blocks. In 1927 German physicist Werner Heisenberg (1901–1976) formulated the "principle of uncertainty," which postulates that because it is impossible to know the position and speed of an individual electron, it is therefore impossible to predict its behavior. Instead of Newton's dependable, rational laws, there seemed to be only tendencies and probabilities in an extraordinarily complex and uncertain universe.

Moreover, a universe described by abstract mathematical symbols seemed to have little to do with human experience and human problems. When, for example, Planck was asked what science could contribute to resolving conflicts of values, his response was simple: "Science is not qualified to speak to this question." Physics, the queen of the sciences, no longer provided people easy, optimistic answers—for that matter, it did not provide any answers at all.

Giorgio de Chirico: The Song of Love De Chirico strongly influenced the surrealist painters of the 1920s and 1930s, who saw civilization in crisis and found inspiration in Freudian theories of human thought and action. In this 1914 painting De Chirico tightly groups unrelated images—a classical head, a glove, a ball, a building—in a fantastic, dreamlike combination that fascinates and puzzles. What mysterious significance, if any, lies behind this reordering of everyday reality? *(Digital image © The Museum of Modern Art/Licensed by Scala/Art Resource, NY/© 2007 Artists Rights Society [ARS], New York/SIAE, Rome)*

Freudian Psychology

With physics presenting an uncertain universe so unrelated to ordinary human experience, questions regarding the power and potential of the human mind assumed special significance. The findings and speculations of leading psychologist Sigmund Freud (see page 804) were particularly disturbing.

Before Freud, poets and mystics had probed the unconscious and irrational aspects of human behavior. But most professional, "scientific" psychologists assumed that a single, unified conscious mind processed sense experiences in a rational and logical way. Human behavior in turn was the result of rational calculation—of "thinking"—by the conscious mind. Basing his insights on the analysis of dreams and of hysteria, Freud developed a very different view of the human psyche beginning in the late 1880s.

According to Freud, human behavior is basically irrational. The key to understanding the mind is the primitive, irrational unconscious, which he called the **id.** The unconscious is driven by sexual, aggressive, and pleasure-seeking desires and is locked in a constant battle with the other parts of the mind: the rationalizing conscious (the **ego**), which mediates what a person *can* do, and ingrained moral values (the **superego**), which specify what a person *should* do. Human behavior is a product of a fragile compromise between instinctual drives and the controls of rational thinking and moral values. Since the instinctual drives are extremely powerful, the ever-present danger for individuals and whole societies is that unacknowledged drives will overwhelm the control mechanisms in a violent, distorted way. Yet Freud also agreed with Nietzsche that the mechanisms of rational thinking and traditional moral values can be too strong. They can repress sexual desires too effectively, crippling individuals and entire peoples with guilt and neurotic fears.

Freudian psychology and clinical psychiatry had become an international movement by 1910, but only after 1918 did they receive popular attention, especially in the Protestant countries of northern Europe and in the United States. Many opponents and even some enthusiasts interpreted Freud as saying that the first requirement for mental health is an uninhibited sex life. Thus after the First World War, the popular interpretation of Freud reflected and encouraged growing sexual experimentation, particularly among middle-class women. For more serious students, the psychology of Freud and his followers drastically undermined the old, easy optimism about the rational and progressive nature of the human mind.

Twentieth-Century Literature

The general intellectual climate of pessimism, relativism, and alienation was also articulated in literature. Novelists developed new techniques to express new realities. The great nineteenth-century novelists had typically written as all-knowing narrators, describing realistic characters and their relationship to an understandable, if sometimes harsh, society. In the twentieth century, most major writers adopted the limited, often confused viewpoint of a single individual. Like Freud, these novelists focused their attention on the complexity and irrationality of the human mind, where feelings, memories, and desires are forever scrambled. The great French novelist Marcel Proust (1871–1922), in his semi-autobiographical *Remembrance of Things Past* (1913–1927), recalled bittersweet memories of childhood and youthful love and tried to discover their innermost meaning. To do so, Proust lived like a hermit in a soundproof Paris apartment for ten years, withdrawing from the present to dwell on the past.

Serious novelists also used the **stream-of-consciousness technique** to explore the psyche. In *Jacob's Room* (1922), Virginia Woolf (1882–1941) created a novel made up of a series of internal monologues, in which ideas and emotions from different periods of time bubble up as randomly as from a patient on a psychoanalyst's couch. William Faulkner (1897–1962), perhaps America's greatest twentieth-century novelist, used the same technique in *The Sound and the Fury* (1929), much of whose intense drama is confusedly seen through the eyes of an idiot. The most famous stream-of-consciousness novel—and surely the most disturbing novel of its generation—is *Ulysses,* which Irish novelist James Joyce (1882–1941) published in 1922. Into an account of an ordinary day in the life of an ordinary man, Joyce weaves an extended ironic parallel between his hero's aimless wanderings through the streets and pubs of Dublin and the adventures of Homer's hero Ulysses on his way home from Troy. Abandoning conventional grammar and blending foreign words, puns, bits of knowledge, and scraps of memory together in bewildering confusion, the language of *Ulysses* is intended to mirror modern life itself: a gigantic riddle waiting to be unraveled.

As creative writers turned their attention from society to the individual and from realism to psychological relativity, they rejected the idea of progress. Some even described "anti-utopias," nightmare visions of things to come. In 1918 an obscure German high school teacher named Oswald Spengler (1880–1936) published *The Decline of the West,* which quickly became an international sensation. According to Spengler, every culture experiences a life cycle of growth and decline. Western civilization, in Spengler's opinion, was in its old age, and death was approaching in the form of conquest by the yellow race. T. S. Eliot (1888–1965), in his famous poem *The Waste Land* (1922), depicts a world of growing desolation, although after his conversion to Anglo-Catholicism in 1927, Eliot came to hope cautiously for humanity's salvation. No such hope appears in the work of Franz Kafka (1883–1924), whose novels *The Trial* (1925) and *The Castle* (1926), as well as several of his greatest short stories, portray helpless individuals crushed by inexplicably hostile forces. The German-Jewish Kafka died young, at forty-one, and so did not see the world of his nightmares materialize in the Nazi state.

Englishman George Orwell (1903–1950), however, had seen both that reality and its Stalinist counterpart by 1949, when he wrote perhaps the ultimate in anti-utopian literature: *1984.* Orwell set the action in the future, in 1984. Big Brother—the dictator—and his totalitarian state use a new kind of language, sophisticated technology, and psychological terror to strip a weak individual of his last shred of human dignity. The supremely self-confident chief of the Thought Police tells the tortured, broken, and framed Winston Smith, "If you want a picture of the future, imagine a boot stamping on a human face—forever."[4] A phenomenal bestseller, *1984* spoke to millions of people in the closing years of the age of anxiety.

1984 This intriguing cover for an early edition of Orwell's brilliant novel hints at the tragic love affair between Winston and Julia. Considered a crime in Orwell's totalitarian dictatorship of the future, the love affair leads to the couple's arrest, torture, and betrayal. No one can escape the scrutiny of Big Brother and the Thought Police. *(Signet Books/New American Library photo)*

Modern Art and Music

Throughout the twentieth century, there was considerable unity in the arts. Even today the "modernism" of the immediate prewar years and the 1920s still seems strikingly modern. Like the scientists and creative artists who were partaking of the same culture, creative artists rejected old forms and old values. Modernism in art and music meant constant experimentation and a search for new kinds of expression. And though many people find the numerous and varied modern visions of the arts strange, disturbing, and even ugly, the first half of the twentieth century, so dismal in many respects, will probably stand as one of Western civilization's great artistic eras.

- *How did modernism revolutionize architecture, painting, and music?*

Architecture and Design

Modernism in the arts was loosely unified by a revolution in architecture. This revolution intended nothing less than a transformation of the physical framework of urban society according to a new principle: **functionalism.** Buildings, like industrial products, should be useful and "functional"—that is, they should serve, as well as possible, the purpose for which they were made. Thus architects and designers had to work with engineers, town planners, and even sanitation experts. Moreover, they had to throw away useless ornamentation and find beauty and aesthetic pleasure in the clean lines of practical constructions and efficient machinery. Franco-Swiss genius Le Corbusier (1887–1965) insisted that "a house is a machine for living in."[5]

The United States, with its rapid urban growth and lack of rigid building traditions, pioneered in the new architecture. In the 1890s, the Chicago school of architects, led by Louis H. Sullivan (1856–1924), used cheap steel, reinforced concrete, and electric elevators to build skyscrapers and office buildings lacking almost any exterior ornamentation. In the first decade of the twentieth century, Sullivan's student Frank Lloyd Wright (1869–1959) built a series of radically new and truly modern houses featuring low lines, open interiors, and mass-produced building materials. Europeans were inspired by these and other American examples of functional construction, like the massive, unadorned grain elevators of the Midwest.

In Europe architectural leadership centered in German-speaking countries until Hitler took power in 1933. In 1911 twenty-eight-year-old Walter Gropius (1883–1969) broke sharply with the past in his design of the Fagus shoe factory at Alfeld, Germany—a clean, light, elegant building of glass and iron. After the First World War, Gropius merged the schools of fine and applied arts at Weimar into a single, interdisciplinary school, the **Bauhaus.** The Bauhaus brought together many leading modern architects, designers, and theatrical innovators. Working as

Walter Gropius: The Fagus Shoe Factory, 1911 The factory's sleek exterior is inspired by the revolutionary principles of functionalism. The striking glass façade creates a feeling of lightness and eliminates the traditional separation between interior and exterior. The glass façade also provides workers with healthy natural light—a practical, "functional" concern. (Vanni/Art Resource, NY)

an effective, inspired team, they combined the study of fine art, such as painting and sculpture, with the study of applied art in the crafts of printing, weaving, and furniture making. Throughout the 1920s, the Bauhaus, with its stress on functionalism and good design for everyday life, attracted enthusiastic students from all over the world. It had a great and continuing impact.

Another leader in the "international" style, Ludwig Mies van der Rohe (1886–1969), followed Gropius as director of the Bauhaus in 1930 and immigrated to the United States in 1937. His classic Lake Shore Apartments in Chicago, built between 1948 and 1951, symbolized the triumph of steel-frame and glass-wall modern architecture in the great building boom after the Second World War.

Modern Painting

Modern painting grew out of a revolt against French impressionism. The *impressionism* of such French painters as Claude Monet (1840–1926), Pierre Auguste Renoir (1841–1919), and Camille Pissarro (1830–1903) was, in part, a kind of "superrealism." Leaving exact copying of objects to photography, these artists sought to capture the momentary overall feeling, or impression, of light falling on a real-life scene before their eyes. By 1890, when impressionism was finally established, a few artists known as *postimpressionists,* or sometimes as *expressionists,* were already striking out in new directions. After 1905 art increasingly took on a nonrepresentational, abstract character, a development that reached its high point after World War II.

Though individualistic in their styles, postimpressionists were united in their desire to know and depict worlds other than the visible world of fact. Like the early-nineteenth-century romantics, they wanted to portray unseen, inner worlds of emotion and imagination. Like modern novelists, they wanted to express a complicated psychological view of reality as well as an overwhelming emotional intensity. In

The Starry Night (1889), for example, the great Dutch expressionist Vincent van Gogh (1853–1890) painted the moving vision of his mind's eye (see the illustration below). Paul Gauguin (1848–1903), the French stockbroker-turned-painter, pioneered in expressionist techniques, though he used them to infuse his work with tranquillity and mysticism. In 1891 he fled to the South Pacific in search of unspoiled beauty and a primitive way of life. Gauguin believed that the form and design of a picture were important in themselves and that the painter need not try to represent objects on canvas as the eye actually saw them.

Fascination with form, as opposed to light, was characteristic of postimpressionism and expressionism. Paul Cézanne (1839–1906), who had a profound influence on twentieth-century painting, was particularly committed to form and ordered design. He told a young painter, "You must see in nature the cylinder, the sphere, and the cone."[6] As Cézanne's later work became increasingly abstract and nonrepresentational, it also moved away from the traditional three-dimensional perspective toward the two-dimensional plane, which has characterized so much of modern art. The expressionism of a group of painters led by Henri Matisse (1869–1954) was so extreme that an exhibition of their work in Paris in 1905 prompted

Van Gogh: The Starry Night Van Gogh absorbed impressionism in Paris, but under the burning sun of southern France he went beyond the portrayal of external reality. In *The Starry Night* (1889) flaming cypress trees, exploding stars, and a comet-like Milky Way swirl together in one great cosmic rhythm. Painting an inner world of intense emotion and wild imagination, van Gogh contributed greatly to the rise of expressionism in modern art. *(Digital image © The Museum of Modern Art/Licensed by Scala/Art Resource, NY)*

Images in Society

Pablo Picasso and Modern Art

Pablo Picasso (1881–1973) was probably the most significant artist of the early twentieth century. For more than seventy years, he personified the individuality, freedom, and revolutionary creativity of the modern artist.

Born at Málaga in southern Spain, Picasso quickly demonstrated a precocious talent. At nineteen he headed for Paris, Europe's art capital. Suffering from poverty and falling into depression, he painted the weak and the poor in somber blue and purple tones. These pessimistic paintings of Picasso's "Blue Period" (1901–1904) are masterpieces in the tradition of Spanish realism.

Yet the young Picasso soon sought a new visual reality. In 1907 his arduous struggle to create a new style resulted in *Les Demoiselles d'Avignon* (Image 1), a painting originating in memories of a brothel scene in Barcelona. This work was considered a revolutionary upheaval in art. Since the Renaissance, artists had been expected to follow established rules, seeing objects in an orderly perspective from a single viewpoint and creating "beauty" and unified human forms. Do the faces of the central figures in this work conform to these rules? Regard the figures on either side, who were painted later. Notice how the light fails to combine with the shadow to create bodies with continuous, three-dimensional contours. The figures appear broken into large, flat planes with heads that are twisted, fractured dislocations. Do you see the magical violence of a pictorial breakthrough or a grotesque, ugly departure?

Picasso extended his revolutionary experiments, and after 1910 he was joined by others. A critic called the new school cubism because these artists used many geometric forms in intersecting planes. Objects, viewed from many shifting viewpoints, often emerged as purely abstract designs.

Three Musicians (Image 2), painted in 1921, represents mature cubism. Many people believe that it marks the culmination of Picasso's cubist style. What similarities and differences do you see between this picture and Image 1? Notice the limited number of viewpoints, with the white clown, the harlequin, the monk, their

Image 1 Les Demoiselles d'Avignon (1907). *(Digital image © The Museum of Modern Art/Licensed by Scala/Art Resource, NY/© 2004 Estate of Pablo Picasso/Artists Rights Society [ARS], New York)*

instruments, and the table in front cut up into rectangular shapes and reassembled in recognizable form on a shallow series of planes. What is the effect of the bright primary colors and the harmonious, decorative order? Picasso had been making the sets for Sergei Diaghilev's famous Russian dance company in Paris, and these three jagged figures from traditional Italian comedy seem to convey the atmosphere of the theater and the dissonant, syncopated rhythm of modern music. Picasso always drew back from pure abstraction because he began with real objects and used models.

Picasso's passionate involvement in his times infuses his immense painting *Guernica* (Image 3), often considered his greatest work. Painted for the Spanish pavilion at the Paris International Exhibition in 1937, this mural, with its mournful white, black, and blue colors, was inspired by the Spanish civil war and the deadly terror bombing of Guernica by fascist planes in a single night. In this complex work, a shrieking woman falls from a burning house on the far right. On the left, a woman holds a dead child, while toward the center are fragments of a warrior and a screaming horse pierced by a spear. Do cubist techniques heighten the effect? Picasso also draws on other aspects of the modernist revolution here. Compare *Guernica* with the expressionist work on page 923. Surrealists were fascinated with grotesque subject matter and apparently unrelated objects in surprising situations. Are these elements also

Image 2 **Three Musicians** (1921). *(Digital image © The Museum of Modern Art/Licensed by Scala/Art Resource, NY/© 2004 Estate of Pablo Picasso/Artists Rights Society [ARS], New York)*

present here? Picasso wanted his painting to be an unforgettable attack on "brutality and darkness." Did he succeed? How do the works presented here enhance your understanding of modern art?

Image 3 **Guernica** (1937). *(Bridgeman-Giraudon/Art Resource, NY/© 2004 Estate of Pablo Picasso/Artists Rights Society [ARS], New York)*

Online Study Center **Improve Your Grade**
Going Beyond Images in Society

shocked critics to call them *les fauves*—"the wild beasts." Matisse and his followers still painted real objects, but their primary concern was the arrangement of color, line, and form as an end in itself.

In 1907 a young Spaniard in Paris, Pablo Picasso (1881–1973), founded another movement—*cubism*. (See the feature "Images in Society: Pablo Picasso and Modern Art" on pages 924–925.) Cubism concentrated on a complex geometry of zigzagging lines and sharply angled, overlapping planes. About three years later came the ultimate stage in the development of abstract, nonrepresentational art. Artists such as the Russian-born Wassily Kandinsky (1866–1944) turned away from nature completely. "The observer," said Kandinsky, "must learn to look at [my] pictures . . . as form and color combinations . . . as a representation of mood and not as a representation of *objects*."[7] On the eve of the First World War, extreme expressionism and abstract painting were developing rapidly not only in Paris but also in Russia and Germany. Modern art had become international.

In the 1920s and 1930s, the artistic movements of the prewar years were extended and consolidated. The most notable new developments were *dadaism* and *surrealism*. **Dadaism** attacked all accepted standards of art and behavior, delighting in outrageous conduct. Its name, from the French word *dada*, meaning "hobbyhorse," is deliberately nonsensical. A famous example of dadaism is a reproduction of Leonardo da Vinci's *Mona Lisa* in which the famous woman with the mysterious smile sports a mustache and is ridiculed with an obscene inscription. After 1924 many dadaists were attracted to surrealism, which became very influential in art in the late 1920s and 1930s. Surrealists painted a fantastic world of wild dreams and complex symbols, where watches melted and giant metronomes beat time in precisely drawn but impossible alien landscapes. Refusing to depict ordinary visual reality, surrealist painters made powerful statements about the age of anxiety.

Modern Music

Developments in modern music were strikingly parallel to those in painting. Composers, too, were attracted by the emotional intensity of expressionism. The ballet *The Rite of Spring* by composer Igor Stravinsky (1882–1971) practically caused a riot when it was first performed in Paris in 1913 by Sergei Diaghilev's famous Russian dance company. The combination of pulsating, dissonant rhythms from the orchestra pit and an earthy representation of lovemaking by the dancers on the stage seemed a shocking, almost pornographic enactment of a primitive fertility rite.

After the experience of the First World War, when irrationality and violence seemed to pervade the human experience, expressionism in opera and ballet flourished. One of the most famous and powerful examples was the opera *Wozzeck*, by Alban Berg (1885–1935), first performed in Berlin in 1925. Blending a half-sung, half-spoken kind of dialogue with harsh, atonal music, *Wozzeck* is a gruesome tale of a soldier driven by Kafka-like inner terrors and vague suspicions of unfaithfulness to murder his mistress.

Some composers turned their backs on long-established musical conventions. As abstract painters arranged lines and color but did not draw identifiable objects, so modern composers arranged sounds without creating recognizable harmonies. Led by Viennese composer Arnold Schönberg (1874–1951), they abandoned traditional harmony and tonality. The musical notes in a given piece were no longer united and organized by a key; instead they were independent and unrelated. Schönberg's twelve-tone music of the 1920s arranged all twelve notes of the scale in an abstract, mathematical pattern, or "tone row." This pattern sounded like no pattern at all to the ordinary listener and could be detected only by a highly trained eye studying the musical score. Accustomed to the harmonies of classical and romantic music, audiences generally resisted modern atonal music. Only after the Second World War did it begin to win acceptance.

Movies and Radio

- **In what ways did movies and radio become mainstays of popular culture?**

Until after World War II at the earliest, these revolutionary changes in art and music appealed mainly to a minority of "highbrows" and not to the general public. That public was primarily and enthusiastically wrapped up in movies and radio. The long-declining traditional arts and amusements of people in villages and small towns almost vanished, replaced by standardized, commercial entertainment.

Moving pictures were first shown as a popular novelty in naughty peepshows—"What the Butler Saw"—and penny arcades in the 1890s, especially in Paris. The first movie houses date from an experiment in Los Angeles in 1902. They quickly attracted large audiences and led to the production of short, silent action films such as the eight-minute *Great Train Robbery* of 1903. American directors and business people then set up "movie factories," at first in the New York area and then after 1910 in Los

Angeles. These factories churned out two short films each week. On the eve of the First World War, full-length feature films such as the Italian *Quo Vadis* and the American *Birth of a Nation,* coupled with improvements in the quality of pictures, suggested the screen's vast possibilities.

During the First World War, the United States became the dominant force in the rapidly expanding silent-film industry. In the 1920s, Mack Sennett (1884–1960) and his zany Keystone Kops specialized in short, slapstick comedies noted for frantic automobile chases, custard-pie battles, and gorgeous bathing beauties. Screen stars such as Mary Pickford and Lillian Gish, Douglas Fairbanks and Rudolf Valentino, became household names, with their own "fan clubs." Yet Charlie Chaplin (1889–1978), a funny little Englishman working in Hollywood, was unquestionably the king of the "silver screen" in the 1920s. In his enormously popular role as the lonely Little Tramp, complete with baggy trousers, battered derby, and an awkward, shuffling walk, Chaplin symbolized the "gay spirit of laughter in a cruel, crazy world."[8] Chaplin also demonstrated that in the hands of a genius, the new medium could combine mass entertainment and artistic accomplishment.

The early 1920s were also the great age of German films. Protected and developed during the war, the large German studios excelled in bizarre expressionist dramas, beginning with *The Cabinet of Dr. Caligari* in 1919. Unfortunately, their period of creativity was short-lived. By 1926 American money was drawing the leading German talents to Hollywood and consolidating America's international domination. Film making was big business, and European theater owners were forced to book whole blocks of American films to get the few pictures they really wanted. This system put European producers at a great disadvantage until "talkies" permitted a revival of national film industries in the 1930s, particularly in France.

Whether foreign or domestic, motion pictures became the main entertainment of the masses until after the Second World War. In Great Britain one in every four adults went to the movies twice a week in the late 1930s, and two in five went at least once a week. Continental countries had similar figures. The greatest appeal of motion pictures was that they offered ordinary people a temporary escape from the hard realities of everyday life. The appeal of escapist entertainment was especially strong during the Great Depression. Millions flocked to musical comedies featuring glittering stars such as Ginger Rogers and Fred Astaire and to the fanciful cartoons of Mickey Mouse and his friends.

Radio became possible with the transatlantic "wireless" communication of Guglielmo Marconi (1874–1937) in 1901 and the development of the vacuum tube in 1904, which permitted the transmission of speech and music.

The Great Dictator In 1940 the renowned actor and director Charlie Chaplin abandoned the Little Tramp role to satirize the "great dictator," Adolf Hitler. Chaplin had strong political views and made a number of films with political themes as the escapist fare of the Great Depression gave way to the reality of the Second World War. *(The Museum of Modern Art/Still Film Archives)*

But only in 1920 were the first major public broadcasts of special events made in Great Britain and the United States. Lord Northcliffe, who had pioneered in journalism with the inexpensive, mass-circulation *Daily Mail,* sponsored a broadcast of "only one artist . . . the world's very best, the soprano Nellie Melba."[9] Singing from London in English, Italian, and French, Melba was heard simultaneously all over Europe on June 16, 1920. This historic event captured the public's imagination. The meteoric career of radio was launched.

Every major country quickly established national broadcasting networks. In the United States such networks were privately owned and financed by advertising. In Great Britain Parliament set up an independent, public corporation, the British Broadcasting Corporation (BBC), supported by licensing fees. Elsewhere in Europe the typical pattern was direct control by the government.

Whatever the institutional framework, radio became popular and influential. By the late 1930s, more than three out of every four households in both democratic Great Britain and dictatorial Germany had at least one cheap, mass-produced radio.

Radio in unscrupulous hands was particularly well suited for political propaganda. Dictators such as Mussolini and Hitler controlled the airwaves and could reach enormous national audiences with their frequent, dramatic speeches. In democratic countries, politicians such as President Franklin Roosevelt and Prime Minister Stanley Baldwin effectively used informal "fireside chats" to bolster their support.

Motion pictures also became powerful tools of indoctrination, especially in countries with dictatorial regimes. Lenin himself encouraged the development of Soviet film making, believing that the new medium was essential to the social and ideological transformation of the country. Beginning in the mid-1920s, a series of epic films, the most famous of which were directed by Sergei Eisenstein (1898–1948), brilliantly dramatized the communist view of Russian history.

In Germany Hitler turned to a young and immensely talented woman film maker, Leni Riefenstahl (1902–2003), for a masterpiece of documentary propaganda, *The Triumph of the Will,* based on the Nazi Party rally at Nuremberg in 1934. Riefenstahl combined stunning aerial photography, joyful crowds welcoming Hitler, and mass processions of young Nazi fanatics. Her film was a brilliant and all-too-powerful documentary of Germany's "Nazi rebirth." The new media of mass culture were potentially dangerous instruments of political manipulation.

The Search for Peace and Political Stability

As established patterns of thought and culture were challenged and mangled by the ferocious impact of World War I, so also was the political fabric stretched and torn by the consequences of the great conflict. The Versailles settlement had established a shaky truce, not a solid peace. Thus national leaders faced a gigantic task as they struggled with uncertainty and sought to create a stable international order within the general context of intellectual crisis and revolutionary artistic experimentation.

The pursuit of real and lasting peace proved difficult for many reasons. Germany hated the Treaty of Versailles. France was fearful and isolated. Britain was undependable, and the United States had turned its back on European problems. Eastern Europe was in ferment, and no one could predict the future of communist Russia. Moreover, the international economic situation was poor and greatly complicated by war debts and disrupted patterns of trade. Yet for a time, from 1925 to late 1929, it appeared that peace and stability were within reach. When the subsequent collapse of the 1930s mocked these hopes and brought the rise of brutal dictators, the disillusionment of liberals in the democracies was intensified.

- *How did the democratic leaders of the 1920s deal with deep-seated instability and try to establish real peace and prosperity?*

Germany and the Western Powers

Germany was the key to lasting peace. Yet to Germans of all political parties, the Treaty of Versailles represented a harsh, dictated peace, to be revised or repudiated as soon as possible. The treaty had neither broken nor reduced Germany, which was potentially still the strongest country in Europe. Thus the treaty had fallen between two stools: too harsh for a peace of reconciliation, too soft for a peace of conquest.

Moreover, with ominous implications for the future, France and Great Britain did not see eye to eye on Germany. By the end of 1919, France wanted to stress the harsh elements in the Treaty of Versailles. Most of the war in the west had been fought on French soil, and the expected costs of reconstruction, as well as repaying war debts to the United States, were staggering. Thus French politicians believed that massive reparations from Germany were a vital economic necessity. Also, having compromised with President Wilson only to be betrayed by America's failure to ratify the treaty, many French leaders saw strict implementation of all provisions of the Treaty of Versailles as France's last best hope. Large reparation payments could hold Germany down indefinitely, and France would realize its goal of security.

The British soon felt differently. Prewar Germany had been Great Britain's second-best market in the entire world, and after the war a healthy, prosperous Germany appeared to be essential to the British economy. Indeed, many English people agreed with the analysis of the young English economist John Maynard Keynes (1883–1946), who eloquently denounced the Treaty of Versailles in his famous *Economic Consequences of the Peace* (1919). According to

Keynes's interpretation, astronomical reparations and harsh economic measures would impoverish Germany and also increase economic hardship in all countries. Only a complete revision of the foolish treaty could save Germany—and Europe. Keynes's attack exploded like a bombshell and became very influential. It stirred deep guilt feelings about Germany in the English-speaking world, feelings that often paralyzed English and American leaders in their relations with Germany and its leaders between the First and Second World Wars.

Online Study Center Improve Your Grade
Primary Source: An Economist Analyzes the Versailles Treaty and Finds It Lacking

The British were also suspicious of France's army—the largest in Europe, and authorized at Versailles to occupy the German Rhineland until 1935—and France's foreign policy. Ever since 1890, France had looked to Russia as a powerful ally against Germany. But with Russia hostile and communist, and with Britain and the United States unwilling to make any firm commitments, France turned to the newly formed states of eastern Europe for diplomatic support. In 1921 France signed a mutual defense pact with Poland and associated itself closely with the so-called Little Entente, an alliance that joined Czechoslovakia, Romania, and Yugoslavia against defeated and bitter Hungary.

While French and British leaders drifted in different directions, the Allied reparations commission completed its work. In April 1921, it announced that Germany had to pay the enormous sum of 132 billion gold marks ($33 billion) in annual installments of 2.5 billion gold marks. Facing possible occupation of more of its territory, the young German republic—generally known as the Weimar Republic—made its first payment in 1921. Then in 1922, wracked by rapid inflation and political assassinations and motivated by hostility and arrogance as well, the Weimar Republic announced its inability to pay more. It proposed a moratorium on reparations for three years, with the clear implication that thereafter reparations would be either drastically reduced or eliminated entirely.

The British were willing to accept a moratorium on reparations, but the French were not. Led by their tough-minded prime minister, Raymond Poincaré (1860–1934), they decided they had to either call Germany's bluff or see the entire peace settlement dissolve to France's great disadvantage. So, despite strong British protests, in early January 1923, armies of France and its ally Belgium moved out of the Rhineland and began to occupy the Ruhr district, the heartland of industrial Germany, creating the most serious international crisis of the 1920s. If forcible collection proved impossible, France would use occupation to paralyze Germany and force it to accept the Treaty of Versailles.

Strengthened by a wave of patriotism, the German government ordered the people of the Ruhr to stop working and start passively resisting the French occupation. The coal mines and steel mills of the Ruhr grew silent, leaving 10 percent of Germany's total population in need of relief. The French answer to passive resistance was to seal off the Ruhr and the entire Rhineland from the rest of Germany, letting in only enough food to prevent starvation.

By the summer of 1923, France and Germany were engaged in a great test of wills. French armies could not collect reparations from striking workers at gunpoint. But French occupation was indeed paralyzing Germany and its economy and had turned rapid German inflation

"Hands Off the Ruhr" The French occupation of the Ruhr to collect reparations payments raised a storm of patriotic protest in Germany. This anti-French poster of 1923 turns Marianne, the personification of French republican virtue, into a vicious harpy. *(International Instituut voor Sociale Geschiedenis)*

into runaway inflation. Faced with the need to support the striking Ruhr workers and their employers, the German government began to print money to pay its bills. Prices soared. People went to the store with a big bag of paper money; they returned home with a handful of groceries. German money rapidly lost all value.

Runaway inflation brought about a social revolution. The accumulated savings of many retired and middle-class people were wiped out. Catastrophic inflation cruelly mocked the old middle-class virtues of thrift, caution, and self-reliance. Many Germans felt betrayed. They hated and blamed the Western governments, their own government, big business, the Jews, the workers, and the communists for their misfortune. They were psychologically prepared to follow radical leaders in a crisis.

In August 1923, as the mark fell and political unrest grew throughout Germany, Gustav Stresemann (1878–1929) assumed leadership of the government. Stresemann adopted a compromising attitude. He called off passive resistance in the Ruhr and in October agreed in principle to pay reparations but asked for a re-examination of Germany's ability to pay. Poincaré accepted. His hard line was becoming increasingly unpopular with French citizens, and it was hated in Britain and the United States. (See the feature "Individuals in Society: Gustav Stresemann.")

More generally, in both Germany and France, power was finally passing to the moderates, who realized that continued confrontation was a destructive, no-win situation. Thus after five long years of hostility and tension, culminating in a kind of undeclared war in the Ruhr in 1923, Germany and France decided to give compromise and cooperation a try. The British, and even the Americans, were willing to help. The first step was a reasonable agreement on the reparations question.

Hope in Foreign Affairs, 1924–1929

The reparations commission appointed an international committee of financial experts headed by American banker Charles G. Dawes to re-examine reparations from a broad perspective. The resulting **Dawes Plan** (1924) was accepted by France, Germany, and Britain. Germany's yearly reparations were reduced and depended on the level of German economic prosperity. Germany would also receive large loans from the United States to promote German recovery. In short, Germany would get private loans from the United States and pay reparations to France and Britain, thus enabling those countries to repay the large sums they owed the United States.

This circular flow of international payments was complicated and risky, but for a while it worked. The German republic experienced a spectacular economic recovery. With prosperity and large, continual inflows of American capital, Germany easily paid about $1.3 billion in reparations in 1927 and 1928, enabling France and Britain to pay the United States. In this way the Americans belatedly played a part in the general economic settlement that, though far from ideal, facilitated the worldwide recovery of the late 1920s.

This economic settlement was matched by a political settlement. In 1925 the leaders of Europe signed a number of agreements at Locarno, Switzerland. Germany and France solemnly pledged to accept their common border, and both Britain and Italy agreed to fight either France or Germany if one invaded the other. Stresemann also agreed to settle boundary disputes with Poland and Czechoslovakia by peaceful means, and France promised those countries military aid if Germany attacked them. For years, a "spirit of Locarno" gave Europeans a sense of growing security and stability in international affairs.

Other developments also strengthened hopes. In 1926 Germany joined the League of Nations, where Stresemann continued his "peace offensive." In 1928 fifteen countries signed the Kellogg-Briand Pact, initiated by French prime minister Aristide Briand and U.S. secretary of state Frank B. Kellogg. This multinational pact "condemned and renounced war as an instrument of national policy." The signing states agreed to settle international disputes peacefully. Often seen as idealistic nonsense because it made no provisions for action in case war actually occurred, the pact was still a positive step. It fostered the cautious optimism of the late 1920s and also encouraged the hope that the United States would accept its responsibilities as a great world power and contribute to European stability.

Hope in Democratic Government

Domestic politics also offered reason to hope. During the occupation of the Ruhr and the great inflation, republican government in Germany had appeared on the verge of collapse. In 1923 communists momentarily entered provincial governments, and in November an obscure nobody named Adolf Hitler leaped onto a table in a beer hall in Munich and proclaimed a "national socialist revolution." But Hitler's plot to seize control of the government was poorly organized and easily crushed, and Hitler was sentenced to prison, where he outlined his theories and program in his book **Mein Kampf** (My Strug-

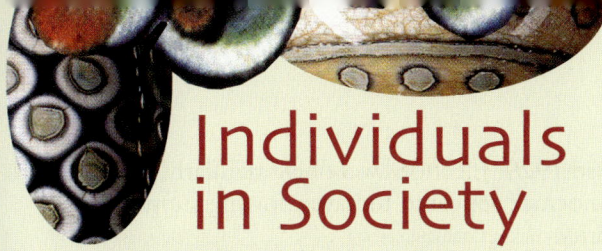

Individuals in Society

Gustav Stresemann

The German foreign minister Gustav Stresemann (1878–1929) is a controversial historical figure. Hailed by many as a hero of peace, he was denounced as a traitor by radical German nationalists and then by Hitler's Nazis. After World War II, revisionist historians stressed Stresemann's persistent nationalism and cast doubt on his peaceful intentions. Weimar Germany's most renowned leader is a fascinating example of the restless quest for convincing historical interpretation.

Stresemann's origins were modest. His parents were Berlin innkeepers and retailers of bottled beer, and only Gustav of their five children was able to attend high school. Attracted first to literature and history, Stresemann later turned to economics, earned a doctoral degree, and quickly reached the top as a manager and director of German trade associations. A highly intelligent extrovert with a knack for negotiation, Stresemann entered the Reichstag in 1907 as a business-oriented liberal and nationalist. When World War I erupted, he believed, like most Germans, that Germany had acted defensively and was not at fault. He emerged as a strident nationalist and urged German annexation of conquered foreign territories. Germany's collapse in defeat and revolution devastated Stresemann. He seemed a prime candidate for the hateful extremism of the far right.

Yet although Stresemann opposed the Treaty of Versailles as an unjust and unrealistic imposition, he turned back toward the center. He accepted the new Weimar Republic and played a growing role in the Reichstag as the leader of his own small probusiness party. His hour came in the Ruhr crisis, when French and Belgian troops occupied the district. Named chancellor in August 1923, he called off passive resistance and began talks with the French. His government also quelled communist uprisings; put down rebellions in Bavaria, including Hitler's attempted coup; and ended runaway inflation with a new currency. Stresemann fought to preserve German unity, and he succeeded.

Voted out as chancellor in November 1923, Stresemann remained as foreign minister in every government until his death in 1929. Proclaiming a policy of peace and agreeing to pay reparations, he achieved his greatest triumph in the Locarno agreements of 1925 (see page 930). But the interlocking guarantees of existing French and German borders (and the related agreements to resolve peacefully all disputes with Poland and Czechoslovakia) did not lead the French to make any further concessions that might have disarmed Stresemann's extremist foes. Working himself to death, he made little additional progress in achieving international reconciliation and sovereign equality for Germany.

Foreign Minister Gustav Stresemann of Germany (right) *leaves a meeting with Aristide Briand, his French counterpart.* (Corbis)

Stresemann was no fuzzy pacifist. Historians debunking his "legend" are right in seeing an enduring love of nation in his defense of German interests. But Stresemann, like his French counterpart Aristide Briand, was a statesman of goodwill who wanted peace through mutually advantageous compromise. A realist trained by business and politics in the art of the possible, Stresemann also reasoned that Germany had to be a satisfied and equal partner if peace was to be secure. His unwillingness to guarantee Germany's eastern borders (see Map 27.4 on page 904), which is often criticized, reflects his conviction that keeping some Germans under Polish and Czechoslovak rule created a ticking time bomb in Europe. Stresemann was no less convinced that war on Poland would almost certainly re-create the Allied coalition that had crushed Germany in 1918.* His insistence on the necessity of peace in the east as well as the west was prophetic. Hitler's 1939 invasion of Poland resulted in an even mightier coalition that almost annihilated Germany in 1945.

Questions for Analysis

1. What did Gustav Stresemann do to promote reconciliation in Europe? How did his policy toward France differ from that toward Poland and Czechoslovakia?
2. What is your interpretation of Stresemann? Does he arouse your sympathy or your suspicion and hostility? Why?

*Robert Grathwol, "Stresemann: Reflections on His Foreign Policy," *Journal of Modern History* 45 (March 1973): 52–70.

Online Study Center Improve Your Grade
Going Beyond Individuals in Society

gle). Throughout the 1920s, Hitler's National Socialist Party attracted support only from a few fanatical anti-Semites, ultranationalists, and disgruntled ex-servicemen. In 1928 his party had an insignificant twelve seats in the Reichstag. Indeed, after 1923 democracy seemed to take root in Weimar Germany. A new currency was established, and the economy boomed.

The moderate businessmen who tended to dominate the various German coalition governments were convinced that economic prosperity demanded good relations with the Western Powers, and they supported parliamentary government at home. Stresemann himself was a man of this class, and he was the key figure in every government until his death in 1929. Elections were held regularly, and republican democracy appeared to have growing support among a majority of Germans.

There were, however, sharp political divisions in the country. Many unrepentant nationalists and monarchists populated the right and the army. Members of Germany's recently formed Communist Party were noisy and active on the left. The Communists, directed from Moscow, reserved their greatest hatred and sharpest barbs for their cousins the Social Democrats, whom they endlessly accused of betraying the revolution. The working classes were divided politically, but a majority supported the nonrevolutionary but socialist Social Democrats.

The situation in France had numerous similarities to that in Germany. Communists and Socialists battled for the support of the workers. After 1924 the democratically elected government rested mainly in the hands of coalitions of moderates, and business interests were well represented. France's great accomplishment was rapid rebuilding of its war-torn northern region. The expense of this undertaking led, however, to a large deficit and substantial inflation. By early 1926, the franc had fallen to 10 percent of its prewar value, causing a severe crisis. Poincaré was recalled to office, while Briand remained minister for foreign affairs. The Poincaré government proceeded to slash spending and raise taxes, restoring confidence in the economy. The franc was "saved," stabilized at about one-fifth of its prewar value. Good times prevailed until 1930.

Despite political shortcomings, France attracted artists and writers from all over the world in the 1920s. Much of the intellectual and artistic ferment of the times flourished in Paris. As writer Gertrude Stein (1874–1946), a leader of the large colony of American expatriates living in Paris, later recalled, "Paris was where the twentieth century was."[10] More generally, France appealed to foreigners and the French as a harmonious combination of small businesses and family farms, of bold innovation and solid traditions.

Britain, too, faced challenges after 1920. The wartime trend toward greater social equality continued, however, helping maintain social harmony. The great problem was unemployment. Many of Britain's best markets had been lost during the war. In June 1921, almost 2.2 million people—23 percent of the labor force—were out of work, and throughout the 1920s unemployment hovered around 12 percent. Yet the state provided unemployment benefits of equal size to all those without jobs and supplemented those payments with subsidized housing, medical aid, and increased old-age pensions. These and other measures kept living standards from seriously declining, defused

American Jazz in Paris This woodcut from a 1928 French book on cafés and nightclubs suggests how black musicians took Europe by storm, although the blacks are represented stereotypically. One French critic concluded that American blacks had attained a "pre-eminent" place in music since the war, "for they have impressed the entire world with their vibrating or melancholy rhythms." *(akg-images)*

class tensions, and pointed the way toward the welfare state Britain established after World War II.

Relative social harmony was accompanied by the rise of the Labour Party as a determined champion of the working classes and of greater social equality. Committed to the kind of moderate, "revisionist" socialism that had emerged before World War I (see pages 840–842), the Labour Party replaced the Liberal Party as the main opposition to the Conservatives. The new prominence of the Labour Party reflected the decline of old liberal ideals of competitive capitalism, limited government control, and individual responsibility. In 1924 and 1929, the Labour Party under Ramsay MacDonald (1866–1937) governed the country with the support of the smaller Liberal Party. Yet Labour moved toward socialism gradually and democratically, so that the middle classes were not overly frightened as the working classes won new benefits.

The Conservatives under Stanley Baldwin (1867–1947) showed the same compromising spirit on social issues. The last line of Baldwin's greatest speech in March 1925 summarized his international and domestic programs: "Give us peace in our time, O Lord." In spite of such conflicts as the 1926 strike by hard-pressed coal miners, which ended in an unsuccessful general strike, social unrest in Britain was limited in the 1920s and in the 1930s as well. In 1922 Britain granted southern, Catholic Ireland full autonomy after a bitter guerrilla war, thereby removing another source of prewar friction. Thus developments in both international relations and the domestic politics of the leading democracies gave cause for optimism in the late 1920s.

The Great Depression, 1929–1939

Like the Great War, the **Great Depression** must be spelled with capital letters. Economic depression was nothing new. Depressions occurred throughout the nineteenth century with predictable regularity, as they recur in the form of recessions and slumps to this day. What was new about this depression was its severity and duration. It struck the entire world with ever-greater intensity from 1929 to 1933, and recovery was uneven and slow. Only with the Second World War did the depression disappear in much of the world.

The social and political consequences of prolonged economic collapse were enormous. The depression shattered the fragile optimism of political leaders in the late 1920s. Mass unemployment and failing farms made insecurity a reality for millions of ordinary people, who had paid little attention to the intellectual crisis or to new directions in art and ideas (see Map 28.1). In desperation, people looked for leaders who would "do something."

- *What caused the Great Depression, and how did the Western democracies respond to this challenge?*

The Economic Crisis

There is no agreement among historians and economists about why the Great Depression was so deep and lasted so long. Thus it is best to trace the course of the great collapse before trying to identify what caused it.

Though economic activity was already declining moderately in many countries by early 1929, the crash of the stock market in the United States in October of that year triggered the collapse into the Great Depression. The American economy had prospered in the late 1920s, but there were large inequalities in income and a serious imbalance between "real" investment and stock market speculation. Thus net investment—in factories, farms, equipment, and the like—actually fell from $3.5 billion in 1925 to $3.2 billion in 1929. In the same years, as money flooded into stocks, the value of shares traded on the exchanges soared from $27 billion to $87 billion. As a financial historian concluded in an important study, "It should have been clear to everybody concerned that a crash was inevitable under such conditions."[11] Of course it was not. Irving Fisher, one of America's most brilliant economists, was highly optimistic in 1929 and fully invested in stocks. He then lost his entire fortune and would have been forced from his house if his university had not bought it and rented it to him.

The American stock market boom was built on borrowed money. Many wealthy investors, speculators, and people of modest means had bought stocks by paying only a small fraction of the total purchase price and borrowing the remainder from their stockbrokers. Such buying "on margin" was extremely dangerous. When prices started falling, the hard-pressed margin buyers either had to put up more money, which was often impossible, or sell their shares to pay off their brokers. Thus thousands of people started selling all at once. The result was a financial panic. Countless investors and speculators were wiped out in a matter of days or weeks.

The general economic consequences were swift and severe. Stripped of wealth and confidence, battered investors and their fellow citizens started buying fewer goods. Prices fell, production began to slow down, and unemployment began to rise. Soon the entire American economy was caught in a spiraling decline.

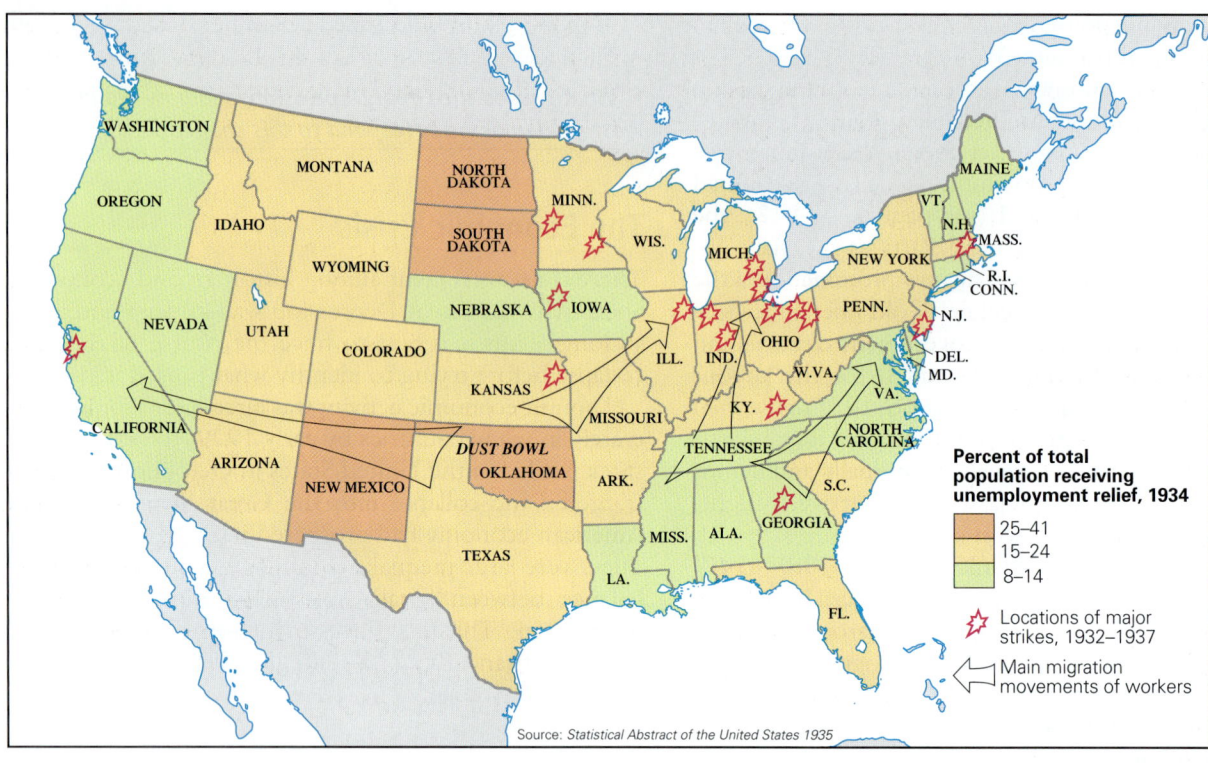

Percent of total population receiving unemployment relief, 1934
- 25–41
- 15–24
- 8–14

☆ Locations of major strikes, 1932–1937

⇐ Main migration movements of workers

Source: *Statistical Abstract of the United States 1935*

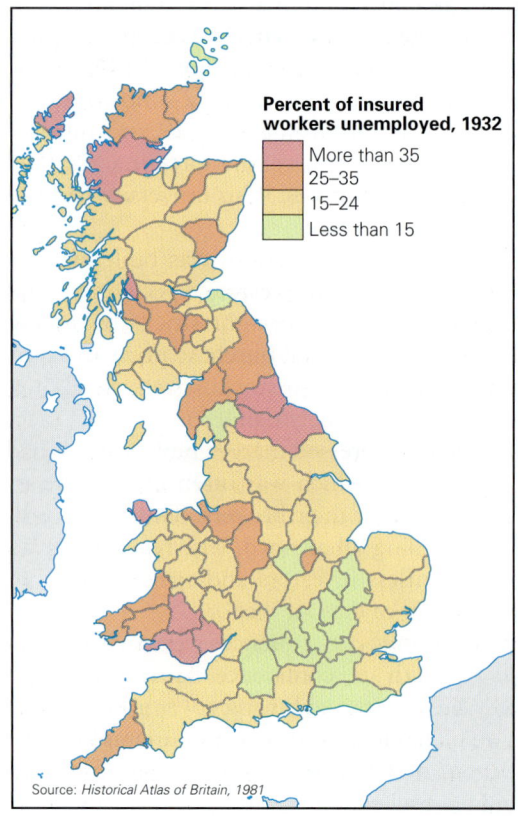

Percent of insured workers unemployed, 1932
- More than 35
- 25–35
- 15–24
- Less than 15

Source: *Historical Atlas of Britain, 1981*

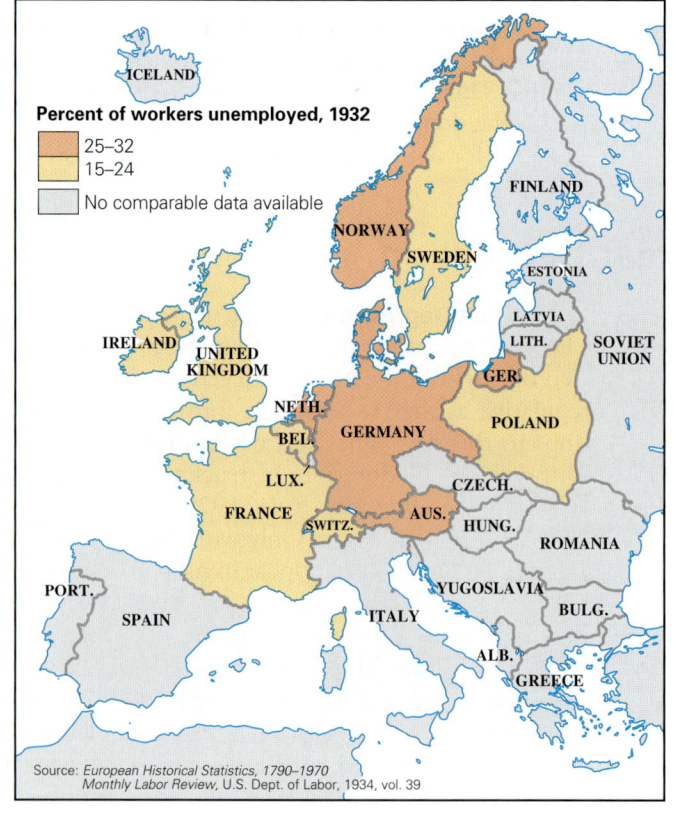

Percent of workers unemployed, 1932
- 25–32
- 15–24
- No comparable data available

Source: *European Historical Statistics, 1790–1970*
Monthly Labor Review, U.S. Dept. of Labor, 1934, vol. 39

The financial panic in the United States triggered a worldwide financial crisis. Throughout the 1920s, American bankers and investors had lent large amounts of capital to many countries. Many of these loans were short-term, and once panic broke, New York bankers began recalling them. Gold reserves thus began to flow out of European countries, particularly Germany and Austria, toward the United States. It became very hard for European business people to borrow money, and the panicky public began to withdraw its savings from the banks. These banking problems eventually led to the crash of the largest bank in Austria in 1931 and then to general financial chaos. The recall of private loans by American bankers also accelerated the collapse in world prices, as business people around the world dumped industrial goods and agricultural commodities in a frantic attempt to get cash to pay what they owed.

The financial crisis led to a general crisis of production: between 1929 and 1933, world output of goods fell by an estimated 38 percent. As this happened, each country turned inward and tried to go it alone. In 1931, for example, Britain went off the gold standard, refusing to convert bank notes into gold, and reduced the value of its money. Britain's goal was to make its goods cheaper and therefore more salable in the world market. But because more than twenty nations, including the United States in 1934, also went off the gold standard, few countries gained a real advantage. Similarly, country after country followed the example of the United States when in 1930 it raised protective tariffs to their highest levels ever and tried to seal off shrinking national markets for American producers only. Within this context of fragmented and destructive economic nationalism, recovery finally began in 1933.

Although opinions differ, two factors probably best explain the relentless slide to the bottom from 1929 to early 1933. First, the international economy lacked a leadership able to maintain stability when the crisis came. Specifically, as a noted American economic historian concluded, the seriously weakened British, the traditional leaders of the world economy, "couldn't and the United States wouldn't" stabilize the international economic system in 1929.[12] The United States, which had momentarily played a positive role after the occupation of the Ruhr, cut back its international lending and erected high tariffs.

The second factor was poor national economic policy in almost every country. Governments generally cut their budgets and reduced spending when they should have run large deficits in an attempt to stimulate their economies. After World War II, such a "counter-cyclical policy," advocated by John Maynard Keynes, became a well-established weapon against downturn and depression. But in the 1930s, Keynes's prescription was generally regarded with horror by orthodox economists.

Mass Unemployment

The need for large-scale government spending was tied to mass unemployment. As the financial crisis led to cuts in production, workers lost their jobs and had little money to buy goods. In Britain unemployment had averaged 12 percent in the 1920s; between 1930 and 1935, it averaged more than 18 percent. Far worse was the case of the United States, where unemployment had averaged only 5 percent in the 1920s. In 1932 unemployment soared to about 33 percent of the entire labor force: 14 million people were out of work (see Map 28.1). Only by pumping new money into the economy could the government increase demand and break the vicious cycle of decline.

Along with economic effects, mass unemployment posed a great social problem. Poverty increased dramatically, although in most countries unemployed workers generally received some kind of meager unemployment benefits or public aid that prevented starvation. (See the feature "Listening to the Past: Life on the Dole in Great Britain" on pages 942–943.) Millions of people lost their spirit, condemned to an apparently hopeless search for work or to idle boredom. Homes and ways of life were disrupted in millions of personal tragedies. Young people postponed marriages, and birthrates fell sharply. There was an increase in suicide and mental illness. Poverty or the threat of

> ### Mapping the Past
>
> **MAP 28.1 The Great Depression in the United States, Britain, and Europe** These maps show that unemployment was high almost everywhere, but that national and regional differences were also substantial. With this in mind: ❶ In the United States, what in 1934 were the main channels of migration for workers? ❷ In Britain, why do you think unemployment was higher in south Wales than in the greater London area? (*Hints*: First locate both regions on Map 22.1 on page 718; assume that Map 22.2 on page 725 provides clues regarding the kinds of work that might be available in 1932; and integrate this information with the discussion in the text on Britain's changing economy in the 1920s and 1930s.) ❸ Which European countries in 1932 had the highest rate of unemployment (usually considered a good indicator of the level of economic hardship)?

Isaac Soyer: Employment Agency (1937) The frustration and agony of looking for work against long odds are painfully evident in this American masterpiece. The time-killing, pensive resignation and dejection seen in the three figures are only aspects of the larger problem. One of three talented brothers born in Russia and trained as artists in New York, Isaac Soyer worked in the tradition of American realism and concentrated on people and the influence of their environment. *(Oil on canvas, 34¼ × 45 in. Whitney Museum of American Art, New York; Purchase 37.44. Courtesy, Estate of artist, Isaac Soyer)*

poverty became a grinding reality. In 1932 the workers of Manchester, England, appealed to their city officials—a typical plea echoed throughout the Western world:

We tell you that thousands of people . . . are in desperate straits. We tell you that men, women, and children are going hungry. . . . We tell you that great numbers are being rendered distraught through the stress and worry of trying to exist without work. . . .

If you do not do this—if you do not provide useful work for the unemployed—what, we ask, is your alternative? Do not imagine that this colossal tragedy of unemployment is going on endlessly without some fateful catastrophe. Hungry men are angry men.[13]

Only strong government action could deal with mass unemployment, a social powder keg preparing to explode.

The New Deal in the United States

Of all the major industrial countries, only Germany was harder hit by the Great Depression, or reacted more radically to it, than the United States (see Chapter 29). The depression was so traumatic in the United States because the 1920s had been a period of complacent optimism. The Great Depression and the response to it marked a major turning point in American history.

President Herbert Hoover (1895–1972) and his administration initially reacted to the stock market crash and economic decline with dogged optimism and limited action. But when the full force of the financial crisis struck Europe in the summer of 1931 and boomeranged back to the United States, people's worst fears became reality. Banks failed; unemployment soared. Between 1929 and 1932, industrial production fell by about 50 percent.

In these tragic circumstances, Franklin Delano Roosevelt (1882–1945), an inspiring wheelchair-bound aristocrat previously crippled by polio, won a landslide electoral victory in 1932 with grand but vague promises of a "**New Deal** for the forgotten man."

Roosevelt's basic goal was to reform capitalism in order to preserve it. Roosevelt rejected socialism and government ownership of industry in 1933. To right the situation, he chose forceful government intervention in the economy. In this choice, Roosevelt was flexible, pragmatic, and willing to experiment. He and his "brain trust" of advisers adopted policies echoing the American experience in World War I, when the American economy had been thoroughly planned and regulated.

Innovative programs promoted agricultural recovery, a top priority. Almost half of the American population still lived in rural areas, and American farmers were hard hit by the depression. Roosevelt's decision to leave the gold standard and devalue the dollar was designed to raise American prices and rescue farmers. The Agricultural Adjustment Act of 1933 also aimed at raising prices and farm income by limiting production. These planning measures worked for a while, and farmers repaid Roosevelt in 1936 with overwhelming support.

The most ambitious attempt to control and plan the economy was the National Recovery Administration (NRA). Intended to reduce competition and fix prices and wages for everyone's benefit, the NRA broke with the cherished American tradition of free competition and aroused conflicts among business people, consumers, and bureaucrats. It did not work well and was declared unconstitutional in 1935.

Roosevelt and his advisers then attacked the key problem of mass unemployment directly. The federal government accepted the responsibility of employing directly as many people as financially possible. New agencies were created to undertake a vast range of projects. The most famous of these was the Works Progress Administration (**WPA**), set up in 1935. One-fifth of the entire labor force worked for the WPA at some point in the 1930s, constructing public buildings, bridges, and highways. The WPA was enormously popular, and the hope of a government job helped check the threat of social revolution in the United States.

Relief programs like the WPA were part of the New Deal's most fundamental commitment, the commitment to use the federal government to provide for the welfare of all Americans. This commitment marked a profound shift from the traditional stress on family support and community responsibility. Embraced by a large majority in the 1930s, this shift in attitudes proved to be one of the New Deal's most enduring legacies.

Other social measures aimed in the same direction. Following the path blazed by Germany's Bismarck in the 1880s, the U.S. government in 1935 established a national social security system, with old-age pensions and unemployment benefits, to protect many workers against some of life's uncertainties. The National Labor Relations Act of 1935 gave union organizers the green light by declaring collective bargaining to be the policy of the United States. Union membership more than doubled, from 4 million in 1935 to 9 million in 1940. In general, between 1935 and 1938 government rulings and social reforms chipped away at the privileges of the wealthy and tried to help ordinary people.

Yet despite undeniable accomplishments in social reform, the New Deal was only partly successful as a response to the Great Depression. At the height of the recovery in May 1937, 7 million workers were still unemployed, as opposed to a high of 15 million in 1933. The economic situation then worsened seriously in the recession of 1937 and 1938, and unemployment was still a staggering 10 million when war broke out in Europe in September 1939. The New Deal never did pull the United States out of the depression.

The Scandinavian Response to the Depression

Of all the Western democracies, the Scandinavian countries under Social Democratic leadership responded most successfully to the challenge of the Great Depression. Having grown steadily in number in the late nineteenth century, the **Social Democrats** became the largest political party in Sweden and then in Norway after the First World War. In the 1920s, they passed important social reform legislation for both peasants and workers, gained practical administrative experience, and developed a unique kind of socialism. Flexible and nonrevolutionary, Scandinavian socialism grew out of a strong tradition of cooperative community action. Even before 1900, Scandinavian agricultural cooperatives had shown how individual peasant families could join together for everyone's benefit. Labor leaders and capitalists were also inclined to work together.

When the economic crisis struck in 1929, socialist governments in Scandinavia built on this pattern of cooperative social action. Sweden in particular pioneered in the use of large-scale deficits to finance public works and thereby maintain production and employment. Scandinavian governments also increased social welfare benefits, from old-age pensions and unemployment insurance to subsidized housing and maternity allowances. All this spending required a large bureaucracy and high taxes, first on the rich and then on practically everyone. Yet both private and cooperative enterprise thrived, as did democracy. Some observers saw Scandinavia's welfare socialism as an appealing "middle way" between sick capitalism and cruel communism or fascism.

Recovery and Reform in Britain and France

In Britain MacDonald's Labour government and then, after 1931, the Conservative-dominated coalition government followed orthodox economic theory. The budget was balanced, but unemployed workers received barely enough welfare to live. Despite government lethargy, the economy recovered considerably after 1932. By 1937 total production was about 20 percent higher than in 1929. In fact, for Britain the years after 1932 were actually somewhat better than the 1920s had been, quite the opposite of the situation in the United States and France.

This good but by no means brilliant performance reflected the gradual reorientation of the British economy. After going off the gold standard in 1931 and establishing protective tariffs in 1932, Britain concentrated increasingly on the national, rather than the international, market. The old export industries of the Industrial Revolution, such as textiles and coal, continued to decline, but new industries, such as automobiles and electrical appli-

Oslo Breakfast Scandinavian socialism championed cooperation and practical welfare measures, playing down strident rhetoric and theories of class conflict. The Oslo Breakfast exemplified the Scandinavian approach. It provided every schoolchild in the Norwegian capital with a good breakfast free of charge. *(Courtesy, Directorate for Health and Social Affairs, Oslo)*

ances, grew in response to British home demand. Moreover, low interest rates encouraged a housing boom. By the end of the decade, there were highly visible differences between the old, depressed industrial areas of the north and the new, growing areas of the south. These developments encouraged Britain to look inward and avoid unpleasant foreign questions.

Online Study Center Improve Your Grade
Primary Source: The Great Depression in Britain: The "Special Areas"

Because France was relatively less industrialized and more isolated from the world economy, the Great Depression came late. But once the depression hit France, it stayed and stayed. Decline was steady until 1935, and a short-lived recovery never brought production or employment back up to predepression levels. Economic stagnation both reflected and heightened an ongoing political crisis. There was no stability in government. As before 1914, the French parliament was made up of many political parties, which could never cooperate for very long. In 1933, for example, five coalition cabinets formed and fell in rapid succession.

The French lost the underlying unity that had made government instability bearable before 1914. Fascist-type organizations agitated against parliamentary democracy and looked to Mussolini's Italy and Hitler's Germany for inspiration (see Chapter 29). In February 1934, French fascists and semifascists rioted and threatened to overturn the republic. At the same time, the Communist Party and many workers opposed to the existing system were looking to Stalin's Russia for guidance. The vital center of moderate republicanism was sapped from both sides.

Frightened by the growing strength of the fascists at home and abroad, the Communists, the Socialists, and the Radicals formed an alliance—the **Popular Front**—for the national elections of May 1936. Their clear victory reflected the trend toward polarization. The number of Communists in the parliament jumped dramatically from 10 to 72, while the Socialists, led by Léon Blum, became the strongest party in France, with 146 seats. The really quite moderate Radicals slipped badly, and the conservatives lost ground to the semifascists.

In the next few months, Blum's Popular Front government made the first and only real attempt to deal with the social and economic problems of the 1930s in France. Inspired by Roosevelt's New Deal, the Popular Front encouraged the union movement and launched a far-reaching program of social reform, complete with paid vacations and a forty-hour workweek. Popular with workers and the lower middle class, these measures were quickly sabotaged by rapid inflation and cries of revolution from fascists and frightened conservatives. Wealthy people sneaked their money out of the country, labor unrest grew, and France entered a severe financial crisis. Blum was forced to announce a "breathing spell" in social reform.

The fires of political dissension were also fanned by civil war in Spain. Communists demanded that France support the Spanish republicans, while many French conservatives would gladly have joined Hitler and Mussolini in aiding the attack of Spanish fascists. Extremism grew, and France itself was within sight of civil war. Blum was forced to resign in June 1937, and the Popular Front quickly collapsed. An anxious and divided France drifted aimlessly once again, preoccupied by Hitler and German rearmament.

Chapter Summary

- In what ways did new and disturbing ideas in philosophy, physics, psychology, and literature reflect the general crisis in Western thought?
- How did modernism revolutionize architecture, painting, and music?
- In what ways did movies and radio become mainstays of popular culture?
- How did the democratic leaders of the 1920s deal with deep-seated instability and try to establish real peace and prosperity?
- What caused the Great Depression, and how did the Western democracies respond to this challenge?

After the First World War, Western society entered a complex and difficult era—truly an age of anxiety. Intellectual life underwent a crisis marked by pessimism, uncertainty, and fascination with irrational forces. Ceaseless experimentation and rejection of old forms characterized art and music, while motion pictures and radio provided new, standardized entertainment for the masses. Intellectual and artistic developments that had been confined to small avant-garde groups before 1914, along with the insecure state of mind they expressed, gained wider currency.

Politics and economics were similarly disrupted. In the 1920s, political leaders groped to create an enduring peace and rebuild the prewar prosperity, and for a brief period late in the decade, they even seemed to have succeeded. Then the Great Depression, growing out of the complicated international financial system and the speculative boom and bust in the U.S. stock market, shattered that fragile stability. Uncertainty returned with redoubled force in the 1930s. The international economy collapsed, and unemployment struck millions worldwide. The democracies turned inward as they sought to cope with massive domestic problems and widespread disillusionment. Generally speaking, they were not very successful, although relief measures and social concern eased distress and prevented revolutions in the leading Western nations. The old liberal ideals of individual rights and responsibilities, elected government, and economic freedom declined and seemed outmoded to many. And in many countries of central and eastern Europe, these ideas were abandoned completely, as we shall see in the next chapter.

Key Terms

- logical empiricism
- existentialism
- neutron
- id, ego, and superego
- stream-of-consciousness technique
- functionalism
- Bauhaus
- dadaism
- Dawes Plan
- *Mein Kampf*
- Great Depression
- New Deal
- WPA
- Social Democrats
- Popular Front

Suggested Reading

Berend, Ivan T. *Decades of Crisis: Central and Eastern Europe Before World War II*. 2001. An up-to-date study of this complex region.

Berghahn, Volker R. *Europe in the Era of Two World Wars: From Militarism and Genocide to Civil Society*. 2006. A short and stimulating account.

Bullock, Alan, ed. *The Twentieth Century: A Promethean Age*. 1971. Particularly noteworthy because it is a lavish visual feast combined with penetrating essays on major developments.

Burrow, J. W. *The Crisis of Reason: European Thought, 1848–1914*. 2002. A rewarding intellectual history.

Cawood, Ian. *Britain in the Twentieth Century*. 2003. A useful national survey.

Crossman, Richard, ed. *The God That Failed*. 1950. Features famous Western writers telling why they were attracted to and later repelled by communism.

Jules-Rossette, Bennetta. *Josephine Baker in Art and Life: The Icon and the Image*. 2007. Tells the fascinating story of the African American dancer who won fame and fortune in Paris.

Kertzer, David I., and Marzio Barbagli, eds. *The History of the European Family,* Vol. 3: *Family Life in the Twentieth Century.* 2003. A distinguished collection of essays by experts.

McMillan, James F. *Twentieth-Century France: Politics and Society, 1898–1991.* 1992. A recommended national survey.

Paxton, Robert O. *Europe in the Twentieth Century.* 2004. An excellent account of contemporary history with a liberal viewpoint.

Winders, James A. *European Culture Since 1848: From Modernism to Postmodern and Beyond.* 1998. A lively and accessible account.

Notes

1. P. Valéry, *Variety,* trans. M. Cowley (New York: Harcourt Brace, 1927), pp. 27–28.
2. Quoted in S. Hughes, *The Obstructed Path: French Social Thought in the Years of Desperation, 1930–1960* (New York: Harper & Row, 1967), p. 82.
3. G. Greene, *Another Mexico* (New York: Viking Press, 1939), p. 3.
4. G. Orwell, *1984* (New York: New American Library, 1950), p. 220.
5. C. E. Jeanneret-Gris (Le Corbusier), *Towards a New Architecture* (London: J. Rodker, 1931), p. 15.
6. Quoted in A. H. Barr Jr., *What Is Modern Painting?* 9th ed. (New York: Museum of Modern Art, 1966), p. 27.
7. Quoted ibid., p. 25.
8. R. Graves and A. Hodge, *The Long Week End: A Social History of Great Britain, 1918–1939* (New York: Macmillan, 1941), p. 131.
9. Quoted in A. Briggs, *The Birth of Broadcasting,* vol. 1 (London: Oxford University Press, 1961), p. 47.
10. Quoted in R. J. Sontag, *A Broken World, 1919–1939* (New York: Harper & Row, 1971), p. 129.
11. Dietmar Rothermund, *The Global Impact of the Great Depression, 1929–1939* (London: Routledge, 1996), p. 50.
12. C. P. Kindleberger, *The World in Depression, 1929–1939* (Berkeley: University of California Press, 1973), p. 292.
13. Quoted in S. B. Clough et al., eds., *Economic History of Europe: Twentieth Century* (New York: Harper & Row, 1968), pp. 243–245.

Listening to the Past

Life on the Dole in Great Britain

Periodic surges in unemployment were an old story in capitalist economies, but the long-term joblessness of millions in the Great Depression was something new and unexpected. In Britain especially, where the depression followed a weak postwar recovery, large numbers suffered involuntary idleness for years at a time. Whole families lived "on the dole," the weekly welfare benefits paid by the government.

One of the most insightful accounts of unemployed workers was written by the British journalist and novelist George Orwell (1903–1950), who studied the conditions in northern England and wrote The Road to Wigan Pier *(1937), an excerpt of which follows. An independent socialist who distrusted rigid Marxism, Orwell believed that socialism could triumph in Britain if it came to mean "justice and liberty" for a commonsense majority. Orwell's disillusionment with authoritarian socialism and communism pervades his most famous work,* 1984 *(1949).*

When you see the unemployment figures quoted at two millions, it is fatally easy to take this as meaning that two million people are out of work and the rest of the population is comparatively comfortable. . . . [Adding in the destitute,] you might take the number of underfed people in England (for *everyone* on the dole or thereabouts is underfed) as being, at the very most, five millions.

This is an enormous under-estimate, because, in the first place, the only people shown on unemployment figures are those actually drawing the dole—that is, in general, heads of families. An unemployed man's dependants do not figure on the list unless they too are drawing a separate allowance. . . . In addition there are great numbers of people who are in work but who, from a financial point of view, might equally be unemployed, because they are not drawing anything that can be described as a living wage. Allow for these and their dependants, throw in as before the old-age pensioners, the destitute and other nondescripts, and you get an *underfed* population of well over ten millions. . . .

Take the figures for Wigan, which is typical enough of the industrial and mining districts. . . . The total population of Wigan is a little under 87,000; so that at any moment more than one person in three out of the whole population—not merely the registered workers—is either drawing or living on the dole. . . .

Nevertheless, in spite of the frightful extent of unemployment, it is a fact that poverty—extreme poverty—is less in evidence in the industrial North than it is in London. Everything is poorer and shabbier, there are fewer motor-cars and fewer well-dressed people; but also there are fewer people who are obviously destitute. . . . In the industrial towns the old communal way of life has not yet broken up, tradition is still strong and almost everyone has a family—potentially, therefore, a home. In a town of 50,000 or 100,000 inhabitants there is no casual and as it were unaccounted-for population; nobody sleeping in the streets, for instance. Moreover, there is just this to be said for the unemployment regulations, that they do not discourage people from marrying. A man and wife on twenty-three shillings a week are not far from the starvation line, but they can make a home of sorts; they are vastly better off than a single man on fifteen shillings. . . .

But there is no doubt about the deadening, debilitating effect of unemployment upon everybody, married or single, and upon men more than upon women. . . . Everyone who saw Greenwood's play *Love on the Dole* must remember that dreadful moment when the poor, good, stupid working man beats on the table and cries out, "O God, send me some work!" This was not dramatic exaggeration, it was a touch from life. That cry must have been uttered, in almost those words, in tens of thousands, perhaps hundreds of thousands of English homes, during the past fifteen years.

But, I think not again—or at least, not so often. . . . When people live on the dole for years at a time they grow used to it, and drawing the dole, though it remains unpleasant, ceases to be shameful. Thus the old, independent, workhouse-fearing tradition is undermined. . . .

So you have whole populations settling down, as it were, to a lifetime of the P.A.C. . . . Take, for instance, the fact that the working class think nothing of getting married on the dole. . . . Life is still fairly normal, more normal than one really has the right to expect. Families are impoverished, but the family-system has not broken up. The people are in effect living a reduced version of their former lives. Instead of raging against their destiny they have made things tolerable by lowering their standards.

But they don't necessarily lower their standards by cutting out luxuries and concentrating on necessities; more often it is the other way about—the more natural way, if you come to think of it. Hence the fact that in a decade of unparalleled depression, the consumption of all cheap luxuries has increased. The two things that have probably made the greatest difference of all are the movies and the mass-production of cheap smart clothes since the war. The youth who leaves school at fourteen and gets a blind-alley job is out of work at twenty, probably for life; but for two pounds ten on the hire-purchase system he can buy himself a suit which, for a little while and at a little distance, looks as though it had been tailored in Savile Row. The girl can look like a fashion plate at an even lower price. . . . You can stand on the street corner, indulging in a private daydream of yourself as Clark Gable or Greta Garbo, which compensates you for a great deal. . . .

Trade since the war has had to adjust itself to meet the demands of underpaid, underfed people, with the result that a luxury is nowadays almost always cheaper than a necessity. One pair of plain solid shoes costs as much as two ultra-smart pairs. . . . And above all there is gambling, the cheapest of all luxuries. Even people on the verge of starvation can buy a few days' hope ("Something to live for," as they call it) by having a penny on a sweepstake. . . . Twenty million people are underfed but literally everyone in England has access to a radio. What we have lost in food we have gained in electricity. Whole sections of the working class who have been plundered of all they really need are being compensated, in part, by cheap luxuries which mitigate the surface of life.

Do you consider all this desirable? No, I don't. But it may be that the psychological adjustment

Poster used in the election campaign of 1931, when unemployment rose to a new record high. *(Conservative Research Department/The Bridgeman Art Library)*

which the working class are visibly making is the best they could make in the circumstances. They have neither turned revolutionary nor lost their self-respect; merely they have kept their tempers and settled down to make the best of things on a fish-and-chip standard. The alternative would be God knows what continued agonies of despair; or it might be attempted insurrections which, in a strongly governed country like England, could only lead to futile massacres and a régime of savage repression.

Questions for Analysis

1. According to Orwell, "extreme poverty" was less visible in the northern industrial towns than in London. Were family relations important in this regard?

2. What were the consequences of long-term unemployment for English workers? Were some of the consequences surprising?

3. Judging from Orwell's description, did radical revolution seem likely in England in the Great Depression? Why?

Source: Excerpts from Chapter V in *The Road to Wigan Pier* by George Orwell, copyright © 1958 and renewed 1986 by the Estate of Sonia B. Orwell. Reprinted by permission of Harcourt, Inc.

Hugo Jager's photograph of a crowd of enthusiastic Hitler supporters. *(Time Life Pictures/Getty Images)*

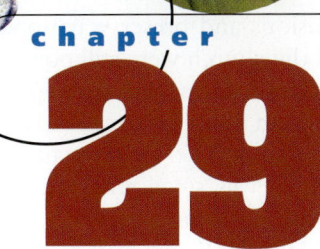

chapter 29

Dictatorships and the Second World War, 1919–1945

chapter preview

Authoritarian States
• What was the nature of radical totalitarian dictatorship, and how did it differ from conservative authoritarianism?

Stalin's Soviet Union
• How did Stalin and the Communist Party build a modern totalitarian state in the Soviet Union?

Mussolini and Fascism in Italy
• How did Mussolini's dictatorship come to power and govern in Italy?

Hitler and Nazism in Germany
• How did Hitler gain power, what policies did totalitarian Nazi Germany pursue, and why did they lead to World War II?

The Second World War
• How did Germany and Japan create enormous empires that were defeated by the Allies—Britain, the Soviet Union, and the United States?

The era of anxiety and economic depression was also a time of growing strength for political dictatorship. Popularly elected governments and basic civil liberties declined drastically in Europe. On the eve of the Second World War, liberal democratic governments were surviving only in Great Britain, France, the Low Countries, the Scandinavian nations, and Switzerland. Elsewhere in Europe, various kinds of "strongmen" ruled. Dictatorship seemed the wave of the future. Thus the intellectual and economic crisis discussed in Chapter 28 and the decline in liberal political institutions and rise of dictatorship to be considered in this chapter were interrelated elements in the general crisis of European civilization.

The era of dictatorship is a highly disturbing chapter in the history of Western civilization. The key development was not only the resurgence of authoritarian rule but also the rise of a particularly ruthless and dynamic tyranny. This new kind of tyranny reached its full realization in the Soviet Union and Nazi Germany in the 1930s. Stalin and Hitler mobilized their peoples for enormous undertakings and ruled with unprecedented severity. Hitler's mobilization was ultimately directed toward racial aggression and territorial expansion, and his sudden attack on Poland in 1939 started World War II.

Nazi armies were defeated by a great coalition, and today we want to believe that the era of totalitarian dictatorship was a terrible accident, that Stalin's slave-labor camps and Hitler's gas chambers "can't happen again." Yet the cruel truth is that horrible atrocities continue to plague the world in our time. The Khmer Rouge inflicted genocide on its people in Kampuchea, and civil war in Bosnia and in Rwanda led to racially motivated atrocities recalling the horrors of World War II. And there are other examples. Thus it is all the more vital that we understand Europe's era of brutal and aggressive dictatorship in order to guard against the possibility of its recurrence in the future.

Online Study Center
This icon will direct you to interactive activities and study materials on the website **college.hmco.com/pic/mckaywest9e**

945

Authoritarian States

Both conservative and radical dictatorships swept through Europe in the 1920s and 1930s. Although these two types of dictatorship shared some characteristics and sometimes overlapped in practice, they were in essence profoundly different. Conservative authoritarian regimes were an old story in Europe. Radical, totalitarian dictatorships were a new and frightening development.

- **What was the nature of radical totalitarian dictatorship, and how did it differ from conservative authoritarianism?**

Conservative Authoritarianism

The traditional form of antidemocratic government in European history was conservative authoritarianism. Like Catherine the Great in Russia and Metternich in Austria, the leaders of such governments tried to prevent major changes that would undermine the existing social order. To do so, they relied on obedient bureaucracies, vigilant police departments, and trustworthy armies. Popular participation in government was forbidden or limited to such natural allies as landlords, bureaucrats, and high church officials. Liberals, democrats, and socialists were persecuted as subversive radicals, often finding themselves in jail or exile.

Yet old-fashioned authoritarian governments were limited in their power and in their objectives. They had neither the ability nor the desire to control many aspects of their subjects' lives. Nor did they wish to do so. Preoccupied with the goal of mere survival, these governments largely limited their demands to taxes, army recruits, and passive acceptance. As long as the people did not try to change the system, they often had considerable personal independence.

After the First World War, this kind of authoritarian government revived, especially in the less-developed eastern part of Europe. There the parliamentary regimes that had been founded on the wreckage of empires in 1918 fell one by one. By early 1938, only economically and socially advanced Czechoslovakia remained true to liberal political ideals. Conservative dictators also took over in Spain and Portugal.

There were several reasons for this development. These lands lacked a strong tradition of self-government, with its necessary restraint and compromise. Moreover, many of these new states, such as Yugoslavia, were torn by ethnic conflicts that threatened their very existence. Dictatorship appealed to nationalists and military leaders as a way to repress such tensions and preserve national unity. Large landowners and the church were still powerful forces in these largely agrarian areas, and they often looked to dictators to save them from progressive land reform or communist agrarian upheaval. So did some members of the middle class, which was small and weak in eastern Europe. Finally, though some kind of democracy managed to stagger through the 1920s in Austria, Bulgaria, Romania, Greece, Estonia, and Latvia, the Great Depression delivered the final blow to those countries by 1936.

Although some of the conservative authoritarian regimes adopted certain Hitlerian and fascist characteristics in the 1930s, their general aims were limited. They were concerned more with maintaining the status quo than with forcing society into rapid change or war. This tradition continued into the twenty-first century, especially in some of the military dictatorships that ruled in Latin America until the late 1980s.

Radical Totalitarian Dictatorships

Conservative authoritarianism predominated in the smaller states of central and eastern Europe by the mid-1930s, but a new kind of radical dictatorship emerged in the Soviet Union, Germany, and, to a lesser extent, Italy. Almost all scholars agree that the leaders of these radical dictatorships violently rejected parliamentary restraint and liberal values. Scholars also agree that these dictatorships exercised unprecedented control over the masses and sought to mobilize them for action. However, there has always been controversy over the interpretation of these regimes.

One extremely useful approach relates the radical dictatorships to the rise of modern totalitarianism. The concept of **totalitarianism** emerged in the 1920s and 1930s, although it is frequently and mistakenly seen as developing only after 1945 as part of anti-Soviet propaganda during the cold war. In 1924 Benito Mussolini spoke of the "fierce totalitarian will" of his movement in Italy. In the 1930s more and more British, American, and German exiled writers used the concept of totalitarianism to describe what they saw happening before their eyes. They linked Italian and especially German fascism with Soviet communism in "a 'new kind of state' that could be called totalitarian." With the alliance between Hitler and Stalin in 1939, "all doubts" about the totalitarian nature of both dictatorships "were swept away for most Americans."[1]

Early writers believed that modern totalitarian dictatorship burst on the scene with the revolutionary total war effort of 1914–1918. The war called forth a tendency to subordinate all institutions and all classes to the state in order to achieve one supreme objective: victory. As the French thinker Elie Halévy put it in 1936 in his influential *The Era of Tyrannies,* the varieties of modern totalitarian tyranny—fascism, Nazism, and communism—could be thought of as "feuding brothers" with a common father: the nature of modern war.[2]

Writers such as Halévy believed that the crucial experience of World War I was carried further by Lenin and the Bolsheviks during the Russian civil war. Lenin showed how a dedicated minority could achieve victory over a less determined majority and subordinate institutions and human rights to the needs of a single group—the Communist Party—and its leader. Providing a model for single-party dictatorship, Lenin inspired imitators, including Adolf Hitler. The modern totalitarian state reached maturity in the 1930s in the Stalinist U.S.S.R. and Nazi Germany.

Embellishing on early insights, numerous Western political scientists and historians argued in the 1950s and 1960s that the totalitarian state used modern technology and communications to exercise complete political power. But it did not stop there. Increasingly, the state took over and tried to control just as completely the economic, social, intellectual, and cultural aspects of people's lives. Deviation from the norm, even in art or family behavior, could become a crime.

This vision of total state represented a radical revolt against liberalism. Classical liberalism (see page 753) sought to limit the power of the state and protect the rights of the individual. Moreover, liberals stood for rationality, peaceful progress, economic freedom, and a strong middle class. All of that disgusted totalitarians as sentimental slop. They believed in willpower, preached conflict, and worshiped violence. The individual was infinitely less valuable than the state.

Unlike old-fashioned authoritarianism, modern totalitarianism was based not on an elite but on people who had already become engaged in the political process, most notably through commitment to nationalism and socialism. Thus totalitarian societies were fully mobilized societies moving toward some goal and possessing boundless dynamism. As soon as one goal was achieved at the cost of enormous sacrifice, another arose at the leader's command to take its place. Thus totalitarianism was a *permanent* revolution, an *unfinished* revolution, in which rapid, profound change imposed from on high went on forever.

In developing the concept of totalitarianism, scholars recognized that there were major differences between Stalin's communist U.S.S.R. and Hitler's Nazi Germany. Soviet communism, growing out of Marxian socialism, seized all private property (except personal property) for

Chronology

1921	New Economic Policy (NEP) in U.S.S.R.
1922	Mussolini seizes power in Italy
1924–1929	Buildup of Nazi Party in Germany
1927	Stalin comes to power in U.S.S.R.
1928	Stalin's first five-year plan
1929	Lateran Agreement; start of collectivization in Soviet Union
1929–1939	Great Depression
1932–1933	Famine in Ukraine
1933	Hitler appointed chancellor in Germany; Nazis begin to control intellectual life and blacklist authors
1934	Sergei Kirov, Stalin's number-two man, murdered
1935	Mussolini invades Ethiopia
1936	Start of great purges under Stalin; Halévy, *The Era of Tyrannies,* analyzes totalitarianism
1939	Germany occupies Czech lands; Germany invades Poland; Britain and France declare war on Germany
1941	SS stops Jewish emigration from Europe; Germany invades Soviet Union; bombing of Pearl Harbor; U.S. enters war
1941–1945	Six million Jews killed in death camps
1944	Allied invasion at Normandy
1945	Atomic bombs dropped on Japan; end of war

the state and crushed the middle classes. Nazi Germany, growing out of extreme nationalism and racism, criticized big landowners and industrialists, but both private property and the middle classes survived. This difference in property and class relations led some scholars to speak of "totalitarianism of the left"—Stalinist Russia—and "totalitarianism of the right"—Nazi Germany.

A second group of writers in the 1930s approached radical dictatorships outside the Soviet Union through the concept of **fascism.** A term of pride for Mussolini and Hitler, who used it to describe the supposedly "total" and revolutionary character of their movements, fascism was severely criticized by these writers and linked to decaying capitalism and domestic class conflict. Orthodox Marxists, generally sympathetic to the Soviet Union and

Nazi Mass Rally, 1936 This picture captures the essence of the totalitarian interpretation of dynamic modern dictatorship. The uniformed members of the Nazi Party have willingly merged themselves into a single force and await the command of the godlike leader. *(AP/Wide World Photos)*

the socialism it established, argued that fascism was the way powerful capitalists sought to create a mass movement capable of destroying the revolutionary working class and thus protect their enormous profits.

Scholarly interest in fascism declined in the 1950s but revived thereafter. Comparative studies of fascist movements all across Europe showed that they shared many characteristics, including extreme, often expansionist nationalism; an antisocialism aimed at destroying working-class movements; alliances with powerful capitalists and landowners; a dynamic and violent leader; and glorification of war and the military. Yet these studies also highlighted how fascist movements generally failed to gain political power.

In recent years, many historians have tended to adopt a third approach, emphasizing the uniqueness of developments in each country. This is especially true for Hitler's Germany, where some elements of the totalitarian interpretation have been nuanced and revised, as we shall see. A similar revaluation of Stalin's U.S.S.R. began after the fall of communism opened the former Soviet Union's archives to new research. For many of today's historians, the differences within broad historical patterns often seem more important than the similarities.

In summary, these conclusions seem appropriate. First, although the concept of totalitarianism has been questioned, it remains a valuable tool for historical understanding. It correctly highlights that both Hitler's Germany and Stalin's Soviet Union made an unprecedented "total claim" on the belief and behavior of their respective citizens, as a noted scholar has recently concluded.³ Second, antidemocratic, antisocialist fascist movements sprang up all over Europe, but only in Italy and Germany (and some would say Spain) were they able to take power. Studies of fascist movements seeking to gain power locate important common elements, but they do not explain what fascist governments in Italy and Germany actually did. Finally, it is important to remember that the problem of Europe's radical dictatorships is complex and that there are few easy answers.

Stalin's Soviet Union

Lenin's harshest critics claim that he established the basic outlines of a modern totalitarian dictatorship after the Bolshevik Revolution and during the Russian civil war. If this is so, then Joseph Stalin (1879–1953) certainly finished the job. A master of political infighting, Stalin cautiously consolidated his power and eliminated his enemies in the mid-1920s. Then in 1928, as undisputed leader of the ruling Communist Party, he launched the first **five-year plan**—the "revolution from above," as he so aptly termed it.

The five-year plans were extremely ambitious. Often incorrectly considered a mere set of economic measures to speed up the Soviet Union's industrial development, the five-year plans actually marked the beginning of a renewed attempt to mobilize and transform Soviet society along socialist lines. The ultimate goal of the plans was to generate new attitudes, new loyalties, and a new socialist humanity. The means Stalin and the small Communist Party elite chose in order to do so were constant propaganda, enormous sacrifice by the people, and the concentration of all power in party hands. Thus the Soviet Union in the 1930s became a dynamic, modern totalitarian state.

- **How did Stalin and the Communist Party build a modern totalitarian state in the Soviet Union?**

From Lenin to Stalin

By spring 1921, Lenin and the Bolsheviks had won the civil war, but they ruled a shattered and devastated land. Many farms were in ruins, and food supplies were exhausted. In southern Russia, drought combined with the ravages of war to produce the worst famine in generations. Industrial production also broke down completely. The Bolsheviks had destroyed the economy as well as their foes.

In the face of economic disintegration, riots by peasants and workers, and an open rebellion by previously pro-Bolshevik sailors at Kronstadt, the tough but ever-flexible Lenin changed course. In March 1921, he announced the **New Economic Policy (NEP),** which re-established limited economic freedom in an attempt to rebuild agriculture and industry. During the civil war, the Bolsheviks had simply seized grain without payment. Now peasant producers were permitted to sell their surpluses in free markets, and private traders and small handicraft manufacturers were allowed to reappear. Heavy industry, railroads, and banks, however, remained wholly nationalized.

The NEP was shrewd and successful both politically and economically. Politically, it was a necessary but temporary compromise with the Soviet Union's overwhelming peasant majority. Realizing that his government was not strong enough to take land from the peasants and turn them into state workers, Lenin made a deal with the only force capable of overturning his government. Economically, the NEP brought rapid recovery. In 1926 industrial output surpassed the level of 1913, and Soviet peasants were producing almost as much grain as before the war.

As the economy recovered and the government partially relaxed its censorship and repression, an intense struggle for power began in the inner circles of the Communist Party, for Lenin had left no chosen successor when he died in 1924. The principal contenders were the stolid Stalin and the flamboyant Trotsky.

The son of a shoemaker, Joseph Dzhugashvili—later known as Stalin—studied for the priesthood but was expelled from his theological seminary, probably for rude rebelliousness. By 1903 he was a Bolshevik revolutionary in southern Russia.

Stalin was a good organizer but a poor speaker and writer, with no experience outside of Russia. Trotsky, a great and inspiring leader who had planned the 1917 takeover (see page 898) and then created the victorious Red Army, appeared to have all the advantages. Yet it was Stalin who succeeded Lenin. Stalin won because he was more effective at gaining the all-important support of the party, the only genuine source of power in the one-party state. Rising to general secretary of the party's Central Committee just before Lenin's first stroke in 1922, Stalin used his office to win friends and allies with jobs and promises.

The practical Stalin also won because he appeared better able than the brilliant Trotsky to relate Marxian teaching to Soviet realities in the 1920s. Stalin developed a theory of "socialism in one country" that was more appealing to the majority of communists than Trotsky's doctrine of "permanent revolution." Stalin argued that the Russian-dominated Soviet Union had the ability to build socialism on its own. Trotsky maintained that

Kazimir Malevich: Suprematism, ca 1917 Russian artists occupied a prominent position in the international avant-garde in the early twentieth century, and the Ukrainian-born Malevich is widely recognized as a leading figure in the development of modern abstract art. Malevich originated the theory of suprematism, whereby he abandoned images from nature and painted pure forms that were beautiful in themselves, as in this outstanding example. When the Bolsheviks condemned abstraction and demanded "socialist realism," Malevich returned to more recognizable forms and taught design. *(Erich Lessing/Art Resource, NY)*

socialism in the Soviet Union could succeed only if revolution occurred quickly throughout Europe. To many Russian communists, Trotsky's views seemed to sell their country short and to promise risky conflicts with capitalist countries by recklessly encouraging revolutionary movements around the world. Stalin's willingness to break with the NEP and "build socialism" at home appealed to young militants in the party, who detested the capitalist-appearing NEP.

With cunning skill, Stalin gradually achieved supreme power between 1922 and 1927. First, he allied with Trotsky's personal enemies to crush Trotsky, and then he aligned with the moderates to suppress Trotsky's radical followers. Third, having defeated all the radicals, he turned against his allies, the moderates, and destroyed them as well. Stalin's final triumph came at the party congress of December 1927, which condemned all "deviation from the general party line" formulated by Stalin. The dictator and his followers were then ready to launch the revolution from above—the real revolution for millions of ordinary citizens.

The Five-Year Plans

The party congress of 1927, which ratified Stalin's consolidation of power, marked the end of the NEP and the beginning of the era of socialist five-year plans. Building on planning models developed by Soviet economists in the 1920s, the first five-year plan had staggering economic objectives. In just five years, total industrial output was to increase by 250 percent. Heavy industry, the preferred sector, was to grow even faster. Agricultural production was slated to increase by 150 percent, and one-fifth of the peasants in the Soviet Union were scheduled to give up their private plots and join socialist collective farms. By 1930 economic and social change was sweeping the country.

Stalin unleashed his "second revolution" for a variety of interrelated reasons. There were, first of all, ideological considerations. Like Lenin, Stalin and his militant supporters were deeply committed to socialism as they understood it. They feared a gradual restoration of capitalism, and they burned to stamp out the NEP's private traders, independent artisans, and property-owning peasants. Purely economic motivations were also important. Although the economy had recovered, it seemed to have stalled in 1927 and 1928. A new socialist offensive seemed necessary if industry and agriculture were to grow rapidly.

Political considerations were most important. Internationally, there was the old problem, remaining from pre-revolutionary times, of catching up with the advanced and presumably hostile capitalist nations of the West. Stalin said in 1931, when he pressed for ever-greater speed and sacrifice, "We are fifty or a hundred years behind the advanced countries. We must make good this distance in ten years. Either we do it, or we shall go under." (See the feature "Listening to the Past: Stalin Justifies the Five-Year Plan" on pages 978–979.)

Domestically, there was the problem of the peasants. For centuries the peasants had wanted to own the land, and finally they had it. Sooner or later, the communists reasoned, the peasants would become conservative little capitalists and pose a threat to the regime. At the same time, the mainly urban communists believed that the feared and despised "class enemy" in the villages could be squeezed to provide the enormous sums needed for all-out industrialization. Thus Stalin decided on a war against the peasantry in order to bring it under the control of the state and to make it pay the costs of the new socialist offensive.

That war was **collectivization**—the forcible consolidation of individual peasant farms into large, state-controlled enterprises. Beginning in 1929, peasants all over the Soviet Union were ordered to give up their land and animals and become members of collective farms, although they continued to live in their own homes. As for the **kulaks,** the better-off peasants, Stalin instructed party workers to "liquidate them as a class." Stripped of land and livestock, the kulaks were generally not even permitted to join the collective farms. Many starved or were deported to forced-labor camps for "re-education."

Since almost all peasants were in fact poor, the term *kulak* soon meant any peasant who opposed the new system. Whole villages were often attacked. One conscience-stricken colonel in the secret police confessed to a foreign journalist,

I am an old Bolshevik. I worked in the underground against the Tsar and then I fought in the Civil War. Did I do all that

Life in a Forced-Labor Camp This rare photo from about 1933 shows the reality of deported peasants and other political prisoners building the Stalin–White Sea Canal in far northern Russia, with their bare hands and under the most dehumanizing conditions. In books and plays Stalin's followers praised the project as a model for the regeneration of "reactionaries" and "kulak exploiters" through the joys of socialist work. *(David King Collection)*

in order that I should now surround villages with machine guns and order my men to fire indiscriminately into crowds of peasants? Oh, no, no![4]

Forced collectivization of the peasants led to economic and human disaster. Large numbers of peasants slaughtered their animals and burned their crops in sullen, hopeless protest. Between 1929 and 1933, the number of horses, cattle, sheep, and goats in the Soviet Union fell by at least half. Nor were the state-controlled collective farms more productive. The output of grain barely increased between 1928 and 1938. Collectivized agriculture was unable to make any substantial financial contribution to Soviet industrial development in the first five-year plan.

The human dimension of the tragedy was absolutely staggering. As one leading historian writes in outrage, "The number dying in Stalin's war against the peasants was higher than the total deaths of all the countries in World War I." Yet, he notes, in Stalin's war only one side was armed and the other side bore almost all the casualties, many of whom were women, children, and the old.[5]

Online Study Center **Improve Your Grade**
Primary Source: Stalinist Interrogation Techniques Revealed

In Ukraine the drive against peasants snowballed into a general assault on Ukrainians as reactionary nationalists and enemies of socialism. Thus in 1932, as collectivization and deportations continued, Stalin and his associates set levels of grain deliveries for the Ukrainian collective at excessively high levels, and they refused to relax those quotas or even allow food relief when Ukrainian communist leaders reported that starvation was occurring. The result was a terrible man-made famine in Ukraine in 1932 and 1933, which probably claimed 6 million lives.

Collectivization, justly called the "second serfdom," was a cruel but real victory for communist ideologues. By the end of 1932, fully 60 percent of peasant families had been herded onto collective farms; by 1938, 93 percent. Regimented as employees of the state and dependent on the state-owned tractor stations, the collectivized peasants were no longer even a potential political threat to Stalin and the Communist Party.

Peasants fought back with indirect daily opposition and forced the supposedly all-powerful state to make modest compromises. Peasants secured the right to limit a family's labor on the state-run farms and to cultivate tiny family plots, which provided them with much of their food. In 1938 these family plots produced 22 percent of all Soviet agricultural produce on only 4 percent of all cultivated land.

The industrial side of the five-year plans was more successful—indeed, quite spectacular. Soviet industry produced about four times as much in 1937 as it had in 1928. No other major country had ever achieved such rapid industrial growth. Heavy industry led the way; consumer industry grew quite slowly. A new heavy industrial complex was built almost from scratch in western Siberia. Industrial growth also went hand in hand with urban development, and more than 25 million people migrated to cities during the 1930s.

The great industrialization drive, concentrated between 1928 and 1937, was an awe-inspiring achievement purchased at enormous sacrifice. The sudden creation of dozens of new factories required a great increase in total investment. The money for investment was collected from the people by means of heavy, hidden sales taxes.

Two other factors contributed importantly to rapid industrialization: firm labor discipline and foreign engineers. Between 1930 and 1932, trade unions lost most of their power. The government could assign workers to any job anywhere in the country, and individuals could not move without the permission of the police. When factory managers needed more hands, they called on their counterparts on the collective farms, who sent them millions of "unneeded" peasants over the years.

Foreign engineers were hired to plan and construct many of the new factories. Highly skilled American engineers, hungry for work in the depression years, were particularly important until newly trained Soviet experts began to replace them after 1932. The gigantic mills of the new Siberian steel industry were modeled on America's best. Thus Stalin's planners harnessed even the skill and technology of capitalist countries to promote the surge of socialist industry.

Life and Culture in Soviet Society

The aim of Stalin's five-year plans was to create a new kind of society and human personality as well as a strong industrial economy and a powerful army. Stalin and his helpers were good Marxian economic determinists. Once everything was owned by the state, they believed, a socialist society and a new kind of human being would inevitably emerge. Their utopian vision of a new humanity floundered, but they did build a new society, whose broad outlines existed into the mid-1980s. Life in this society had both good and bad aspects.

Because consumption was reduced to pay for investment, there was no improvement in the average standard of living. Indeed, the most careful studies show that the average nonfarm wage apparently purchased only about half as many goods in 1932 as in 1928. After 1932 real wages rose slowly, so that in 1937 workers could buy about 60 percent of what they had bought in 1928 and less than in 1913. Collectivized peasants experienced greater declines.

Life was hard in Stalin's Soviet Union. The masses of people lived primarily on black bread and wore old, shabby clothing. There were constant shortages in the stores, although very heavily taxed vodka was always readily available. A shortage of housing was a particularly serious problem. Millions were moving into the cities, but the government built few new apartments. A relatively lucky family received one room for all its members and shared both a kitchen and a toilet with others on the floor.

Life was hard but by no means hopeless. Idealism and ideology had real appeal for many communists, who saw themselves heroically building the world's first socialist society while capitalism crumbled in a worldwide depression and degenerated into fascism in the West. This optimistic belief in the future of the Soviet Union also attracted many disillusioned Westerners to communism in the 1930s.

On a more practical level, Soviet workers did receive some important social benefits, such as old-age pensions, free medical services, free education, and day-care centers for children. Unemployment was almost unknown. Finally, there was the possibility of personal advancement.

The keys to improving one's position were specialized skills and technical education. Rapid industrialization required massive numbers of trained experts, such as skilled workers, engineers, and plant managers. Thus the Stalinist state broke with the egalitarian policies of the 1920s and provided tremendous incentives to those who could serve its needs. It paid the mass of unskilled workers and collective farmers very low wages, but it dangled high salaries and many special privileges before its growing technical and managerial elite. This elite joined with the political and artistic elites in a new upper class, whose members were rich, powerful, and insecure. Thus millions struggled for an education.

The radical transformation of Soviet society had a profound impact on women's lives. Marxists had traditionally believed that both capitalism and the middle-class husband exploited women. The Russian Revolution of 1917 immediately proclaimed complete equality of rights for women. In the 1920s, divorce and abortion were made easily available, and women were urged to work outside the home and

"Let's All Get to Work, Comrades!" Art in the Stalinist era generally followed the official doctrine of socialist realism, representing objects in a literal style and celebrating Soviet achievements. Characteristically, this poster glorifies the working class, women's equality (in hard labor at least), mammoth factories, and the Communist Party (represented by the hammer and sickle by the woman's foot). Assailed by propaganda, Soviet citizens often found refuge in personal relations and deep friendships. (*From* Art of the October Revolution, *Mikhail Guerman [Aurora Publishers, Leningrad]. Reproduced by permission of Mikhail Guerman*)

liberate themselves sexually. The most prominent Bolshevik feminist, Alexandra Kollontai, went so far as to declare that the sex act had no more significance than "drinking a glass of water."[6] After Stalin came to power, sexual and familial liberation was played down, and the most lasting changes for women involved work and education.

Young women were constantly told that they had to be fully equal to men. Peasant women continued to work on farms, and millions of women now toiled in factories and in heavy construction, building dams, roads, and steel mills in summer heat and winter frost. Determined women pursued their studies and entered the ranks of the better-paid specialists in industry and science. Medicine practically became a woman's profession. By 1950, 75 percent of all doctors in the Soviet Union were women.

Soviet society also demanded great sacrifices from women. The vast majority of women simply *had* to work outside the home. Wages were so low that it was almost impossible for a family or couple to live only on the husband's earnings. Men continued to dominate the very best jobs. Finally, rapid change and economic hardship led to many broken families, creating further physical and emotional strains for women. In any event, the massive mobilization of women was a striking characteristic of the Soviet state.

Culture lost its autonomy in the 1930s and became thoroughly politicized through constant propaganda and indoctrination. Party activists lectured workers in factories and peasants on collective farms, while newspapers, films, and radio broadcasts endlessly recounted socialist achievements and capitalist plots. Whereas the 1920s had seen considerable experimentation in modern art and theater, intellectuals were ordered by Stalin to become "engineers of human minds." Writers and artists who could effectively combine genuine creativity and political propaganda became the darlings of the regime. It became increasingly important for the successful writer and artist to glorify Russian nationalism. Russian history was rewritten so that early tsars such as Ivan the Terrible and Peter the Great became worthy forerunners of the greatest Russian leader of all—Stalin.

Stalin seldom appeared in public, but his presence was everywhere—in portraits, statues, books, and quotations from his "sacred" writings. Although the government persecuted religion and turned churches into "museums of atheism," the state had both an earthly religion and a high priest—Marxism-Leninism and Joseph Stalin.

Stalinist Terror and the Great Purges

In the mid-1930s, the great offensive to build socialism and a new socialist personality culminated in ruthless police terror and a massive purging of the Communist Party. First used by the Bolsheviks in the civil war to maintain their power, terror as state policy was revived in the collectivization drive against the peasants. The top members of the party and government publicly supported Stalin's initiatives, but there was some grumbling in the party. At a small gathering in November 1932, even Stalin's wife complained bitterly about the misery of the people and the horrible famine in Ukraine. Stalin showered her with insults, and she died that same night, apparently by her own hand. In late 1934, Stalin's number-two man, Sergei Kirov, was suddenly and mysteriously murdered. Although Stalin himself probably ordered Kirov's murder, he used the incident to launch a reign of terror.

In August 1936, sixteen prominent Old Bolsheviks confessed to all manner of plots against Stalin in spectacular public trials in Moscow. Then in 1937 the secret police arrested a mass of lesser party officials and newer members, also torturing them and extracting more confessions for more show trials. In addition to the party faithful, union officials, managers, intellectuals, army officers, and countless ordinary citizens were struck down. In all, at least 8 million people were probably arrested, and millions of these were executed or never returned from prisons and forced-labor camps.

Stalin and the remaining party leadership recruited 1.5 million new members to take the place of those purged. Thus more than half of all Communist Party members in 1941 had joined since the purges. "These new men were 'thirty-something' products of the Second Revolution of the 1930s, Stalin's upwardly mobile yuppies, so to speak."[7] Often sons (and daughters) of workers, they had usually studied in the new technical schools, and they soon proved capable of managing the government and large-scale production. A product of the great purges, this new generation of Stalin-formed communists would serve the leader effectively until his death in 1953, and they would govern the Soviet Union until the early 1980s.

Stalin's mass purges remain baffling, for almost all historians believe that those purged posed no threat and confessed to crimes they had not committed. Certainly the highly publicized purges sent a warning to the people: no one was secure; everyone had to serve the party and its leader with redoubled devotion. Some Western scholars have also argued that the terror reflected a fully developed totalitarian state, which must always be fighting real or imaginary enemies.

The long-standing Western interpretation that puts the blame for the great purges on Stalin, which became very popular in Russia after the fall of communism, has nevertheless been challenged. Some historians argue that Stalin's fears were exaggerated but real. Moreover, these fears and suspicions were shared by many in the party and in the general population. Bombarded with ideology and political slogans, the population responded energetically to Stalin's directives. Investigations and trials snowballed into a mass hysteria, a new witch-hunt that claimed millions of victims.⁸ In short, in this view of the 1930s, a deluded Stalin found large numbers of willing collaborators for crime as well as for achievement.

Mussolini and Fascism in Italy

Mussolini's movement and his seizure of power in 1922 were important steps in the rise of dictatorships in Europe between the two world wars. Like all the future dictators, the young Mussolini hated liberalism and wanted to destroy it in Italy. But although Mussolini began as a revolutionary socialist, like Stalin, he turned against the working class and successfully sought the support of conservatives. At the same time, Mussolini and his supporters were the first to call themselves "fascists"—revolutionaries determined to create a certain kind of totalitarian state. Yet few scholars today would argue that Mussolini succeeded. His dictatorship was brutal and theatrical, but it remained a halfway house between conservative authoritarianism and dynamic totalitarianism.

- *How did Mussolini's dictatorship come to power and govern in Italy?*

The Seizure of Power

In the early twentieth century, Italy was a liberal state with civil rights and a constitutional monarchy. On the eve of the First World War, the parliamentary regime finally granted universal male suffrage, and Italy appeared to be moving toward democracy. But there were serious problems. Much of the Italian population was still poor, and many peasants were more attached to their villages and local interests than to the national state. Moreover, the papacy, many devout Catholics, conservatives, and landowners remained strongly opposed to liberal institutions and to the heirs of Cavour and Garibaldi—the middle-class lawyers and politicians who ran the country largely for their own benefit. Relations between church and state were often tense. Class differences were also extreme, and a powerful revolutionary socialist movement had developed. Only in Italy among the main European countries did the radical left wing of the Socialist Party gain the leadership as early as 1912, and only in Italy did the Socialist Party unanimously oppose the war from the very beginning.⁹

The war worsened the political situation. Having fought on the side of the Allies almost exclusively for purposes of territorial expansion, the parliamentary government bitterly disappointed Italian nationalists with Italy's modest gains at Versailles. Workers and peasants also felt cheated: to win their support during the war, the government had promised social and land reform, which it did not deliver after the war.

The Russian Revolution inspired and energized Italy's revolutionary socialist movement. The Socialist Party quickly lined up with the Bolsheviks, and radical workers and peasants began occupying factories and seizing land in 1920. These actions scared and mobilized the property-owning classes. Moreover, after the war the pope lifted his ban on participation by Catholics in Italian politics, and a strong Catholic party quickly emerged. Thus by 1921 revolutionary socialists, antiliberal conservatives, and frightened property owners were all opposed—though for different reasons—to the liberal parliamentary government.

Into these crosscurrents of unrest and fear stepped the blustering, bullying Benito Mussolini (1883–1945). Son of a village schoolteacher and a poor blacksmith, Mussolini began his political career as a Socialist Party leader and radical newspaper editor before World War I. In 1914, powerfully influenced by antidemocratic cults of violent action, the young Mussolini urged that Italy join the Allies, a stand for which he was expelled from the Italian Socialist Party. Later Mussolini fought at the front and was wounded in 1917. Returning home, he began organizing bitter war veterans like himself into a band of fascists—from the Italian word for "a union of forces."

At first Mussolini's program was a radical combination of nationalist and socialist demands, including territorial expansion, benefits for workers, and land reform for peasants. As such, it competed directly with the well-organized Socialist Party and failed to get off the ground. When Mussolini saw that his violent verbal assaults on rival Socialists won him growing support from conservatives and the frightened middle classes, he shifted gears in 1920. In thought and action, Mussolini was a striking example of the turbulent uncertainty of the age of anxiety.

Mussolini and his growing private army of **Black Shirts** began to grow violent. Typically, a band of fascist toughs would roar off in trucks at night and swoop down on a few isolated Socialist organizers, beating them up and force-feeding them almost deadly doses of castor oil. Few people were killed, but socialist newspapers, union halls, and local Socialist Party headquarters were destroyed. Mussolini's toughs pushed Socialists out of the city governments of northern Italy.

A skillful politician, Mussolini allowed his followers to convince themselves that they were not just opposing the

"Reds" but also making a real revolution of their own, forging a strong, dynamic movement that would help the little people against the established interests. With the government breaking down in 1922, largely because of the chaos created by his direct-action bands, Mussolini stepped forward as the savior of order and property. Striking a conservative note in his speeches and gaining the sympathetic neutrality of army leaders, Mussolini demanded the resignation of the existing government and his own appointment by the king. In October 1922, to force matters, a large group of fascists marched on Rome to threaten the king and force him to call on Mussolini. The threat worked. Victor Emmanuel III (r. 1900–1946), who had no love for the old liberal politicians, asked Mussolini to form a new cabinet. Thus, after widespread violence and a threat of armed uprising, Mussolini seized power "legally." He was immediately granted dictatorial authority for one year by the king and the parliament.

The Regime in Action

Mussolini became dictator on the strength of Italians' rejection of parliamentary government coupled with fears of Soviet-style revolution. Yet what he intended to do with his power was by no means clear until 1924. Some of his dedicated supporters pressed for a "second revolution." Mussolini's ministers, however, included old conservatives, moderates, and even two reform-minded Socialists. A new electoral law was passed giving two-thirds of the representatives in the parliament to the party that won the most votes, a change that allowed the Fascist Party and its allies to win an overwhelming majority in 1924. Shortly thereafter, five of Mussolini's thugs kidnapped and murdered Giacomo Matteotti, the leader of the Socialists in the parliament. In the face of this outrage, the opposition demanded that Mussolini's armed squads be dissolved and all violence be banned.

Hitler and Mussolini in Italy, May 1938 At first Mussolini distrusted Hitler, but Mussolini's conquest of Ethiopia in 1936 and Hitler's occupation of the Rhineland brought the two dictators together in a close alliance. State visits by Mussolini to Berlin in 1937 and by Hitler to Rome in 1938 included gigantic military reviews, which were filmed to impress the whole world. Uniformed Italian fascists accompany this motorcade. *(Time Life Pictures/Getty Images)*

Although Mussolini may or may not have ordered Matteotti's murder, he stood at the crossroads of a severe political crisis. After some hesitation, he charged forward. Declaring his desire to "make the nation Fascist," he imposed a series of repressive measures. Freedom of the press was abolished, elections were fixed, and the government ruled by decree. Mussolini arrested his political opponents, disbanded all independent labor unions, and put dedicated Fascists in control of Italy's schools. Moreover, he created a fascist youth movement, fascist labor unions, and many other fascist organizations. Mussolini trumpeted his goal in a famous slogan of 1926: "Everything in the state, nothing outside the state, nothing against the state." By the end of that year, Italy was a one-party dictatorship under Mussolini's unquestioned leadership.

Mussolini, however, did not complete the establishment of a modern totalitarian state. His Fascist Party never became all-powerful. It never destroyed the old power structure, as the Communists did in the Soviet Union, or succeeded in dominating it, as the Nazis did in Germany. Membership in the Fascist Party was more a sign of an Italian's respectability than a commitment to radical change. Interested primarily in personal power, Mussolini was content to compromise with the old conservative classes that controlled the army, the economy, and the state. He never tried to purge these classes or even move very vigorously against them. He controlled and propagandized labor but left big business to regulate itself, profitably and securely. There was no land reform.

Mussolini also drew increasing support from the Catholic Church. In the **Lateran Agreement** of 1929, he recognized the Vatican as a tiny independent state, and he agreed to give the church heavy financial support. The pope expressed his satisfaction and urged Italians to support Mussolini's government.

Nothing better illustrates Mussolini's unwillingness to harness everyone and everything for dynamic action than his treatment of women. He abolished divorce and told women to stay at home and produce children. To promote that goal, he decreed a special tax on bachelors in 1934. In 1938 women were limited by law to a maximum of 10 percent of the better-paying jobs in industry and government. Italian women appear not to have changed their attitudes or behavior in any important way under fascist rule.

Mussolini's government did not pass racial laws until 1938 and did not persecute Jews savagely until late in the Second World War, when Italy was under Nazi control. Nor did Mussolini establish a truly ruthless police state. Only twenty-three political prisoners were condemned to death between 1926 and 1944. In spite of much pompous posing by the chauvinist leader and in spite of mass meetings, salutes, and a certain copying of Hitler's aggression in foreign policy after 1933, Mussolini's fascist Italy, though repressive and undemocratic, was never really totalitarian.

Hitler and Nazism in Germany

The most frightening dictatorship developed in Nazi Germany. A product of Hitler's evil genius as well as of Germany's social and political situation and the general attack on liberalism and rationality in the age of anxiety, the Nazi movement shared some of the characteristics of Mussolini's Italian model and was a form of fascism. But Nazi dictatorship smashed or took over most independent organizations, mobilized the economy, and violently persecuted the Jewish population. Thus Nazism asserted an unlimited claim over German society and proclaimed the ultimate power of its endlessly aggressive leader—Adolf Hitler. Truly totalitarian in its aspirations, the dynamism of Hitler and the Nazi elite was ultimately directed to war, territorial expansion, and racial aggression.

- *How did Hitler gain power, what policies did totalitarian Nazi Germany pursue, and why did they lead to World War II?*

The Roots of Nazism

Nazism grew out of many complex developments, of which the most influential were extreme nationalism and racism. These two ideas captured the mind of the young Hitler, and it was he who dominated Nazism for as long as it lasted.

Born the fourth child of a successful Austrian customs official and an indulgent mother, Adolf Hitler (1889–1945) spent his childhood in small towns in Austria. A good student in grade school, Hitler did poorly on reaching high school and dropped out at age fourteen following the death of his father. After four years of unfocused loafing, Hitler finally left for Vienna, where he lived a comfortable, lazy life on his generous orphan's pension and found most of the perverted beliefs that guided his life.

In Vienna Hitler soaked up extreme German nationalism, which was particularly strong there. Austro-German nationalists believed Germans to be a superior people and the natural rulers of central Europe. They often advocated union with Germany and violent expulsion of "inferior" peoples as the means of maintaining German domination of the Austro-Hungarian Empire.

Hitler was deeply impressed by Vienna's mayor, Karl Lueger (1844–1910). With the help of the Catholic trade unions, Lueger had succeeded in winning the support of the little people of Vienna, and he showed Hitler the enormous potential of anticapitalist and antiliberal propaganda. From Lueger and others, Hitler eagerly absorbed virulent anti-Semitism, racism, and hatred of Slavs. He developed an unshakable belief in the crudest, most exaggerated distortions of the Darwinian theory of survival, the superiority of Germanic races, and the inevitability of racial conflict. Thus anti-Semitism and racism became Hitler's most passionate convictions, his explanation for everything. The Jews, he claimed, directed an international conspiracy of finance capitalism and Marxian socialism against German culture, German unity, and the German race. Hitler's belief was totally irrational, but he never doubted it.

Although he moved to Munich in 1913 to avoid being drafted in the Austrian army, the lonely Hitler greeted the outbreak of the First World War as a salvation. He later wrote in his autobiography, *Mein Kampf*, that, "overcome by passionate enthusiasm, I fell to my knees and thanked heaven out of an overflowing heart." The struggle and discipline of war gave life meaning, and Hitler served bravely as a dispatch carrier on the western front.

When Germany was suddenly defeated in 1918, Hitler's world was shattered. Not only was he a fanatical nationalist, but war was also his reason for living. Convinced that Jews and Marxists had "stabbed Germany in the back," he vowed to fight on.

In late 1919, Hitler joined a tiny extremist group in Munich called the German Workers' Party. In addition to denouncing Jews, Marxists, and democrats, the German Workers' Party promised unity under a uniquely German "national socialism" that would abolish the injustices of capitalism and create a mighty "people's community." By 1921 Hitler had gained absolute control of this small but growing party. He was already a master of mass propaganda and political showmanship. His most effective tool was the mass rally, where he often worked his audience into a frenzy with wild, demagogic attacks on the Versailles treaty, the Jews, the war profiteers, and Germany's Weimar Republic.

Party membership multiplied tenfold after early 1922. In late 1923, the Weimar Republic seemed on the verge of collapse, and Hitler, inspired by Mussolini's recent easy victory, decided on an armed uprising in Munich. Despite the failure of the poorly organized plot and Hitler's arrest, Nazism had been born.

Hitler's Road to Power

At his trial, Hitler violently denounced the Weimar Republic, and he gained enormous publicity and attention. Moreover, he learned from his unsuccessful revolt. Hitler concluded that he had to undermine, rather than overthrow, the government and come to power legally through electoral competition. He forced his more violent supporters to accept his new strategy. He also used his brief prison term to dictate *Mein Kampf*. There he expounded on his basic themes: "race," with a stress on anti-Semitism; "living space," with a sweeping vision of war and conquered territory; and the leader-dictator (**Führer**), with unlimited, arbitrary power.

In the years of prosperity and relative stability between 1924 and 1929, Hitler concentrated on building his National Socialist German Workers' Party, or Nazi Party. By 1928 the party had 100,000 highly disciplined members under Hitler's absolute control. To appeal to the middle-class voters, Hitler de-emphasized the anticapitalist elements of national socialism and vowed to fight Bolshevism. Yet the Nazis remained a small splinter group in 1928, when they received only 2.6 percent of the vote in the general elections and twelve seats in the Reichstag. There the Nazi deputies pursued the legal strategy of using democracy to destroy democracy.

The Great Depression, shattering economic prosperity from 1929 on, presented Hitler with a fabulous opportunity. Unemployment jumped from 1.3 million in 1929 to 5 million in 1930. By the end of 1932, an incredible 43 percent of the labor force was unemployed. Industrial production fell by one-half between 1929 and 1932. No factor contributed more to Hitler's success than the economic crisis. Never very interested in economics before, Hitler began promising German voters economic as well as political and international salvation.

Above all, Hitler rejected free-market capitalism and advocated government programs to bring recovery. Hitler pitched his speeches especially to middle- and lower-middle-class groups—small business people, officeworkers, artisans, and peasants—as well as to skilled workers striving for middle-class status. Seized by panic as bankruptcies increased, unemployment soared, and the Communists made dramatic election gains, great numbers of middle- and lower-middle-class people "voted their pocketbooks"[10] and deserted the conservative and moderate parties for the Nazis. In the election of 1930, the Nazis won 6.5 million votes and 107 seats, and in July 1932 they gained 14.5 million votes—38 percent of the total—and became the largest party in the Reichstag.

The appeal to pocketbook interests was particularly

The Great Depression in Germany As unemployment increased almost fourfold from 1929 to 1930, millions of Germans felt the lash of poverty and hunger. This soup kitchen, operated by the Salvation Army in Berlin in 1930, is serving up free meals to a broad cross section of society—young and old, weak and able-bodied. *(Ullstein Bilderdienst/The Granger Collection, New York)*

effective in the early 1930s because Hitler appeared more mainstream, playing down his anti-Jewish hatred and racist nationalism. A master of mass propaganda and psychology, he had written in *Mein Kampf* that the masses were the "driving force of the most important changes in this world" and were themselves driven by fanaticism and not by knowledge. To arouse such hysterical fanaticism, he believed that all propaganda had to be limited to a few simple, endlessly repeated slogans. But now when he harangued vast audiences with wild oratory and simple slogans, he featured "national rebirth" and the "crimes" of the Versailles treaty. And many uncertain individuals, surrounded by thousands of enthralled listeners, found a sense of belonging as well as hope for better times.

Online Study Center Improve Your Grade
Primary Source: The Art of Propaganda: A Master Reveals His Secrets (Hitler, 1924)

Hitler and the Nazis also appealed strongly to German youth. Indeed, in some ways the Nazi movement was a mass movement of young Germans. Hitler himself was only forty in 1929, and he and most of his top aides were much younger than other leading German politicians. "National Socialism is the organized will of the youth," proclaimed the official Nazi slogan, and the battle cry of Gregor Strasser, a leading Nazi organizer, was "Make way, you old ones."[11] In 1931 almost 40 percent of Nazi party members were under thirty, compared with 20 percent of Social Democrats. National recovery, exciting and rapid change, and personal advancement were the appeals of Nazism to millions of German youths.

Another reason Hitler came to power was that normal democratic government broke down as early as May 1930. Unable to gain the support of a majority in the Reichstag, Chancellor (chief minister) Heinrich Brüning convinced the president, the aging war hero General Hindenburg, to authorize rule by decree. Intending to use this emergency measure indefinitely, Brüning was determined to overcome the economic crisis by cutting back government spending and ruthlessly forcing down prices and wages. Brüning's ultra-orthodox policies not only intensified the economic collapse in Germany but also convinced many voters that the country's republican leaders were stupid and corrupt, thereby adding to Hitler's appeal.

The continuation of the struggle between the Social Democrats and the Communists, right up until the moment Hitler took power, was another aspect of the breakdown of democratic government. The Communists refused to cooperate with the Social Democrats, even though the two parties together outnumbered the Nazis in the Reichstag, even after the elections of 1932. German Communists (and the still complacent Stalin) were blinded by hatred of socialists and by ideology: the Communists believed that Hitler's fascism represented the last agonies of monopoly capitalism and that a communist revolution would soon follow his taking power. Disunity on the left was undoubtedly another nail in the republic's coffin.

Finally, Hitler excelled in the dirty, backroom politics of the decaying Weimar Republic. That, in fact, brought him to power. In complicated infighting in 1932, he cleverly succeeded in gaining additional support from key people in the army and big business. These people thought they could use Hitler for their own advantage to get increased military spending, fat contracts, and tough measures against workers. Many conservative and nationalistic politicians thought similarly. They thus accepted Hitler's demand to join the government only if he became chancellor. There would be only two other National Socialists and nine solid conservatives as ministers, and in such a coalition government, they reasoned, Hitler could be used and controlled. On January 30, 1933, Adolf Hitler, leader of the largest party in Germany, was legally appointed chancellor by Hindenburg.

The Nazi State and Society

Hitler moved rapidly and skillfully to establish an unshakable dictatorship. Continuing to maintain legal appearances, he immediately called for new elections. In the midst of a violent electoral campaign, the Reichstag building was partly destroyed by fire. Hitler screamed that the Communist Party was responsible, and he convinced President Hindenburg to sign dictatorial emergency acts that practically abolished freedom of speech and assembly as well as most personal liberties.

When the Nazis won only 44 percent of the vote in the elections, Hitler immediately outlawed the Communist Party and arrested its parliamentary representatives. Then on March 23, 1933, the Nazis pushed through the Reichstag the so-called **Enabling Act,** which gave Hitler absolute dictatorial power for four years. Armed with the Enabling Act, Hitler and the Nazis moved to smash or control all independent organizations. Their deceitful stress on legality, coupled with divide-and-conquer techniques, disarmed the opposition until it was too late for effective resistance.

Germany soon became a one-party state. Only the Nazi Party was legal. Elections were farces. The Reichstag was jokingly referred to as the most expensive glee club in the country, for its only function was to sing hymns of praise to the Führer. Hitler and the Nazis took over the government bureaucracy intact, installing many Nazis in top positions. At the same time, they created a series of overlapping Nazi Party organizations responsible solely to Hitler.

As research in recent years shows, the resulting system of dual government was riddled with rivalries, contradic-

Reaching a National Audience This poster ad promotes the VE-301 receiver, "the world's cheapest radio," and claims that "All Germany listens to the Führer on the people's receiver." Constantly broadcasting official views and attitudes, the state-controlled media also put the Nazis' favorite entertainment—gigantic mass meetings that climaxed with Hitler's violent theatrical speeches—on an invisible stage for millions. *(Bundesarchiv Koblenz Plak 003-022-025)*

tions, and inefficiencies. Thus the Nazi state was sloppy and often disorganized, lacking the all-encompassing unity that its propagandists claimed. Yet this fractured system suited Hitler and his purposes. He could play the established bureaucracy against his private, personal "party government" and maintain his freedom of action. Hitler could concentrate on general principles and the big decisions, which he always made.

In the economic sphere, one big decision outlawed strikes and abolished independent labor unions, which were replaced by the Nazi Labor Front. Professional people—doctors and lawyers, teachers and engineers—also saw their previously independent organizations swallowed up by Nazi associations. Publishing houses were put under Nazi control, and universities and writers were quickly brought into line. Democratic, socialist, and Jewish literature was put on ever-growing blacklists. Passionate students and pitiful professors burned forbidden books in public squares. Modern art and architecture were ruthlessly prohibited. Life became violently anti-intellectual. By 1934 a brutal dictatorship characterized by frightening dynamism and obedience to Hitler was already largely in place.

Only the army retained independence, and Hitler moved brutally and skillfully to establish his control there, too. The Nazi storm troopers (the SA), the quasi-military band of 3 million toughs in brown shirts who had fought communists and beaten up Jews before the Nazis took power, expected top positions in the army and even talked of a "second revolution" against capitalism. Hitler decided that the SA leaders had to be eliminated. Needing to preserve good relations with the army as well as with big business, he struck on the night of June 30, 1934. Hitler's elite personal guard—the SS—arrested and shot without trial roughly a thousand SA leaders and assorted political enemies. Shortly thereafter army leaders swore a binding oath of "unquestioning obedience . . . to the Leader of the German State and People, Adolf Hitler." The SS grew rapidly. Under its methodical, inhuman leader, Heinrich Himmler (1900–1945), the SS joined with the political police, the Gestapo, to expand its network of special courts and concentration camps. Nobody was safe.

From the beginning, Jews were a special object of Nazi persecution. By the end of 1934, most Jewish lawyers, doctors, professors, civil servants, and musicians had lost their jobs and the right to practice their professions. In 1935 the infamous Nuremberg Laws classified as Jewish anyone having one or more Jewish grandparents and deprived Jews of all rights of citizenship. By 1938 roughly 150,000 of Germany's half a million Jews had emigrated, sacrificing almost all their property in order to leave Germany.

Online Study Center Improve Your Grade
Primary Source: The Centerpiece of Nazi Racial Legislation: The Nuremberg Laws

In late 1938, the attack on the Jews accelerated. A well-organized wave of violence, known to history as "Kristallnacht," smashed windows, looted shops, and destroyed homes and synagogues. German Jews were then rounded up and made to pay for the damage. Another 150,000 Jews fled Germany. Some Germans privately opposed these outrages, but most went along or looked the other way. This lack of opposition reflected anti-Semitism to a degree still being debated by historians, but it certainly reflected the strong popular support Hitler's government enjoyed.

Hitler's Popularity

Hitler had promised the masses economic recovery—"work and bread"—and he delivered. Breaking with Brüning's do-nothing policies, Hitler launched a large public works program to help pull Germany out of the depression. Work began on superhighways, offices, gigantic sports stadiums, and public housing. Hitler also appointed as Germany's central banker a well-known conservative named Hjalmar Schacht, who skillfully restored credit and business. In 1936 an openly aggressive Hitler broke with Schacht, and Germany turned decisively toward rearmament and preparation for war. As a result of these policies (and plain good luck), unemployment dropped steadily, from 6 million in January 1933 to about 1 million in late 1936. By 1938 there was a shortage of workers, as unemployment fell to 2 percent, and women began to take jobs previously denied them by the antifeminist Nazis. Thus between 1932 and 1938, the standard of living for the average employed worker increased moderately. The profits of business rose sharply. For millions of people, economic recovery was tangible evidence that Nazi promises were more than show and propaganda.

For the masses of ordinary German citizens who were not Jews, Slavs, Gypsies, Jehovah's Witnesses, communists, or homosexuals, Hitler's government meant greater equality and more opportunities. In 1933 the position of the traditional German elites—the landed aristocracy, the wealthy capitalists, and the well-educated professional classes—was still very strong. Barriers between classes were generally high. Hitler's rule introduced changes that lowered these barriers. For example, stiff educational requirements, which favored the well-to-do, were relaxed. The new Nazi elite included many young and poorly educated dropouts, rootless lower-middle-class people like Hitler who rose to the top with breathtaking speed. More generally, the Nazis tolerated privilege and wealth only as long as they served the needs of the party. Even big business was constantly ordered around.

Yet few historians today believe that Hitler and the Nazis brought about a real social revolution, as an earlier generation of scholars often argued. Millions of modest middle-class and lower-middle-class people *felt* that Germany was becoming more open and equal, as Nazi propagandists constantly claimed. But quantitative studies show that the well-educated classes held on to most of their advantages and that only a modest social leveling occurred in the Nazi years. It is significant that the Nazis shared with the Italian fascists the stereotypic view of women as housewives and mothers. Only under the relentless pressure of war did they reluctantly mobilize large numbers of German women for work in offices and factories.

Hitler's rabid nationalism, which had helped him gain power, continued to appeal to Germans after 1933. Ever since the wars against Napoleon, many Germans had believed in a special mission for a superior German nation. The successes of Bismarck had furthered such feelings, and near-victory in World War I made nationalists eager for renewed expansion in the 1920s. Thus when Hitler went from one foreign triumph to another and a great German Empire seemed within reach, as we shall see, the majority of the population was delighted and kept praising the Führer's actions well into World War II.

Not all Germans supported Hitler, however, and a number of German groups actively resisted him after 1933. Tens of thousands of political enemies were imprisoned, and thousands were executed. But opponents of the Nazis pursued various goals, and they were never unified, a fact that helps account for their ultimate lack of success. In the first years of Hitler's rule, the principal resisters were the communists and the socialists in the trade unions. But the expansion of the SS system of terror after 1935 smashed most of these leftists. A second group of opponents arose in the Catholic and Protestant churches. However, their efforts were directed primarily at preserving genuine religious life, not at overthrowing Hitler. Finally in 1938 (and again in 1942–1944), some high-ranking army officers, who feared the consequences of Hitler's reckless aggression, plotted against him, unsuccessfully.

Aggression and Appeasement, 1933–1939

Although economic recovery and somewhat greater opportunity for social advancement won Hitler support, they were only byproducts of the Nazi regime. The guiding and unique concepts of Nazism remained space and race—the territorial expansion of the superior German race. As we shall see, German expansion was facilitated by the uncertain and divided Western democracies, which tried to buy off Hitler to avoid war.

Hitler realized that his aggressive policies had to be carefully camouflaged at first, for Germany's army was limited by the Treaty of Versailles to only one hundred thousand men. As he told a group of army commanders in February 1933, the early stages of his policy of "conquest of new living space in the East and its ruthless Germanization" had serious dangers. If France had real leaders, Hitler said, it would "not give us time but attack us, presumably with its eastern satellites."[12] Thus, although Hitler loudly proclaimed his peaceful intentions, Germany's withdrawal from the League of Nations in October 1933 indicated that Gustav Stresemann's policy of peaceful cooperation (see pages 930–932) was dead.

Following this action, Hitler sought to incorporate independent Austria into a greater Germany. But a worried Mussolini threatened to fight, and Hitler backed down. When in March 1935 Hitler established a general military draft and declared the "unequal" disarmament clauses of the Treaty of Versailles null and void, other countries appeared to understand the danger. With France taking the lead, Italy and Great Britain protested strongly and warned against future aggressive actions.

Yet the emerging united front against Hitler quickly collapsed. Of crucial importance, Britain adopted a policy of **appeasement,** granting Hitler everything he could reasonably want (and more) in order to avoid war. The first step was an Anglo-German naval agreement in June 1935 that broke Germany's isolation. The second step came in March 1936 when Hitler suddenly marched his armies into the demilitarized Rhineland, brazenly violating the Treaties of Versailles and Locarno. This was the last good chance to stop the Nazis, but an uncertain France would not move without British support, and Britain refused to act (Map 29.1).

British appeasement, which practically dictated French policy, lasted far into 1939. It was motivated by British feelings of guilt toward Germany and the pacifism of a population still horrified by the memory of the First World War. As in Germany, many powerful conservatives in Britain underestimated Hitler. They believed that Soviet communism was the real danger and that Hitler could be used to stop it. Such strong anticommunist feelings made an alliance between the Western Powers and Stalin unlikely.

As Britain and France opted for appeasement and the Soviet Union watched all developments suspiciously, Hitler found powerful allies. In 1935 the bombastic

MAP 29.1 The Growth of Nazi Germany, 1933–1939 Until March 1939, Hitler brought ethnic Germans into the Nazi state; then he turned on the Slavic peoples he had always hated. He stripped Czechoslovakia of its independence and prepared for an attack on Poland in September 1939.

Mussolini attacked the independent African kingdom of Ethiopia. The Western Powers and the League of Nations piously condemned Italian aggression, but Hitler supported Italy energetically and overcame Mussolini's lingering doubts about the Nazis. The result in late 1936 was an agreement on close cooperation between Italy and Germany, the so-called Rome-Berlin Axis. Japan, which had been expanding into Manchuria since 1931, soon joined the Axis alliance.

At the same time, Germany and Italy intervened in the Spanish civil war (1936–1939), which broke out in July 1936. Their support eventually helped General Francisco Franco's fascist movement defeat republican Spain. Spain's only official aid came from the Soviet Union, for public opinion in Britain and especially in France was hopelessly divided on the Spanish question.

In late 1937 Hitler moved forward with plans to crush Austria and Czechoslovakia at the earliest possible moment

Events Leading to World War II

1919	Treaty of Versailles is signed; J. M. Keynes publishes *Economic Consequences of the Peace.*
1919–1920	U.S. Senate rejects the Treaty of Versailles.
1921	Germany is billed $33 billion in reparations.
1922	Mussolini seizes power in Italy; Germany proposes a moratorium on reparations.
January 1923	France and Belgium occupy the Ruhr; Germany orders passive resistance to the occupation.
October 1923	Stresemann agrees to reparations based on Germany's ability to pay.
1924	Dawes Plan: German reparations are reduced and put on a sliding scale. Large U.S. loans to Germany are recommended to promote German recovery; Adolf Hitler dictates *Mein Kampf.*
1924–1929	Spectacular German economic recovery occurs; circular flow of international funds enables sizable reparations payments.
1925	Treaties of Locarno promote European security and stability.
1926	Germany joins the League of Nations.
1928	Kellogg-Briand Pact renounces war as an instrument of international affairs.
1929	U.S. stock market crashes and triggers worldwide financial crisis.
1929–1939	Great Depression rages.
1931	Japan invades Manchuria.
1932	Nazis become the largest party in the Reichstag.
January 1933	Hitler is appointed chancellor of Germany.
March 1933	Reichstag passes the Enabling Act, granting Hitler absolute dictatorial power.
October 1933	Germany withdraws from the League of Nations.
1935	Nuremberg Laws deprive Jews of all rights of citizenship.
March 1935	Hitler announces German rearmament.
June 1935	Anglo-German naval agreement is signed.
October 1935	Mussolini invades Ethiopia and receives Hitler's support.
March 1936	German armies move unopposed into the demilitarized Rhineland.
July 1936	Civil war breaks out in Spain.
1937	Japan invades China; Rome-Berlin Axis in effect.
March 1938	Germany annexes Austria.
September 1938	Munich Conference: Britain and France agree to German seizure of the Sudetenland from Czechoslovakia.
March 1939	Germany occupies the rest of Czechoslovakia; appeasement ends in Britain.
August 1939	Nazi-Soviet nonaggression pact is signed.
September 1, 1939	Germany invades Poland.
September 3, 1939	Britain and France declare war on Germany.

Hitler's Success with Aggression
This biting criticism of appeasing leaders by the cartoonist David Low appeared shortly after Hitler remilitarized the Rhineland. Appeasement also appealed to millions of ordinary citizens in Britain and France, who wanted to avoid at any cost another great war. *(Solo Syndication/Associated Newspapers)*

as the first step in his long-contemplated drive to the east for living space. By threatening Austria with invasion, Hitler forced the Austrian chancellor in March 1938 to put local Nazis in control of the government. The next day, German armies moved in unopposed, and Austria became two more provinces of Greater Germany (see Map 29.1).

Simultaneously, Hitler began demanding that the pro-Nazi, German-speaking minority of western Czechoslovakia—the Sudetenland—be turned over to Germany. Yet democratic Czechoslovakia was prepared to defend itself. Moreover, France had been Czechoslovakia's ally since 1924; and if France fought, the Soviet Union was pledged to help. War appeared inevitable, but appeasement triumphed again. In September 1938, Chamberlain flew to Germany three times in fourteen days. In these negotiations, to which the U.S.S.R. was deliberately not invited, Chamberlain and the French agreed with Hitler that the Sudetenland should be ceded to Germany immediately. Returning to London from the Munich Conference, Chamberlain told cheering crowds that he had secured "peace with honor . . . peace for our time." Sold out by the Western Powers, Czechoslovakia gave in.

Confirmed once again in his opinion of the Western democracies as weak and racially degenerate, Hitler accelerated his aggression. His armies occupied the Czech lands in March 1939. The effect on Western public opinion was electrifying. For the first time, there was no possible rationale of self-determination for Nazi aggression since Hitler was seizing Czechs and Slovaks as captive peoples. Thus when Hitler used the question of German minorities in Danzig as a pretext to confront Poland, a suddenly militant Chamberlain declared that Britain and France would fight if Hitler attacked his eastern neighbor. Hitler did not take these warnings seriously and decided to press on.

In an about-face that stunned the world, Hitler offered and Stalin signed a ten-year Nazi-Soviet nonaggression pact in August 1939. Each dictator promised to remain neutral if the other became involved in war. An attached secret protocol, which became known only after the war, ruthlessly divided eastern Europe into German and Soviet zones, "in the event of a political territorial reorganization." The nonaggression pact itself was enough to make Britain and France cry treachery, for they, too, had been negotiating with Stalin. But Stalin had remained distrustful of Western intentions, and Hitler had offered immediate territorial gain.

For Hitler, everything was set. He told his generals on the day of the nonaggression pact, "My only fear is that at the last moment some dirty dog will come up with a mediation plan." On September 1, 1939, German armies and warplanes smashed into Poland from three sides.

Two days later, Britain and France, finally true to their word, declared war on Germany. The Second World War had begun.

The Second World War

War broke out in both western and eastern Europe because Hitler's ambitions were essentially unlimited. On both war fronts, Nazi soldiers scored enormous successes until late 1942, establishing a vast empire of death and destruction. Hitler's victories increased tensions in Asia between Japan and the United States and prompted Japan to attack the United States and overrun much of Southeast Asia. Yet reckless aggression by Germany and Japan also raised a mighty coalition determined to smash the aggressors. Led by Britain, the United States, and the Soviet Union, the Grand Alliance—to use Winston Churchill's favorite name for it—functioned quite effectively in military terms. Thus the Nazi and Japanese empires proved short-lived.

- How did Germany and Japan create enormous empires that were defeated by the Allies—Britain, the Soviet Union, and the United States?

Hitler's Empire, 1939–1942

Using planes, tanks, and trucks in the first example of a **blitzkrieg,** or "lightning war," Hitler's armies crushed Poland in four weeks. While the Soviet Union quickly took its part of the booty—the eastern half of Poland and the independent Baltic states of Lithuania, Estonia, and Latvia—French and British armies dug in in the west. They expected another war of attrition and economic blockade.

In spring 1940, the lightning war struck again. After occupying Denmark, Norway, and Holland, German motorized columns broke through southern Belgium, split the Franco-British forces, and trapped the entire British army on the beaches of Dunkirk. By heroic efforts, the British withdrew their troops but not their equipment.

France was taken by the Nazis. Aging Marshal Henri-Philippe Pétain formed a new French government—the so-called Vichy government—to accept defeat, and German armies occupied most of France. By July 1940, Hitler ruled practically all of western continental Europe; Italy was an ally, and the Soviet Union and Spain were friendly neutrals. Only Britain, led by the uncompromising Winston Churchill (1874–1965), remained unconquered.

London, 1940 Hitler believed that his relentless terror bombing of London—the "blitz"—could break the will of the British people. He was wrong. The blitz caused enormous destruction, but Londoners went about their business with courage and calm determination, as this unforgettable image of a milkman in the rubble suggests. *(Corbis)*

Online Study Center Improve Your Grade
Primary Source: "This Was Their Finest Hour"

Germany sought to gain control of the air, the necessary first step toward an amphibious invasion of Britain. In the Battle of Britain, up to a thousand German planes attacked British airfields and key factories in a single day, dueling with British defenders high in the skies. Losses were heavy on both sides. Then in September Hitler angrily turned from military objectives to indiscriminate bombing of British cities in an attempt to break British morale. British aircraft factories increased production, and the heavily bombed people of London defiantly dug in. In September and October 1940, Britain was beating Germany three to one in the air war. There was no possibility of an immediate German invasion of Britain.

Turning from Britain and moving into the Balkans by April 1941, Hitler now allowed his lifetime obsession with a vast eastern European empire for the "master race" to dictate policy. In June 1941, German armies suddenly attacked the Soviet Union along a vast front (see Map 29.2). By October Leningrad was practically surrounded, Moscow was besieged, and most of Ukraine had been conquered. But the Soviets did not collapse, and when a severe winter struck German armies outfitted in summer uniforms, the invaders were stopped.

Stalled in Russia, Hitler ruled over a vast European empire stretching from the outskirts of Moscow to the English Channel. Hitler, the Nazi leadership, and the loyal German army were positioned to greatly accelerate construction of their "New Order" in Europe, and they continued their efforts until their final collapse in 1945. In doing so, they showed what Nazi victory would have meant.

Hitler's **New Order** was based firmly on the guiding principle of Nazi totalitarianism: racial imperialism. Within this New Order, the Nordic peoples—the Dutch, Norwegians, and Danes—received preferential treatment, for they were racially related to the master race, the Germans. The French, an "inferior" Latin people, occupied a middle position. All the occupied territories of western and northern Europe were exploited with increasing intensity. Material shortages and both mental and physical suffering afflicted millions of people.

Slavs in the conquered territories to the east were treated with harsh hatred as "subhumans." At the height of his success in 1941 and 1942, Hitler set the tone. He painted for his intimate circle the fantastic vision of a vast eastern colonial empire where Poles, Ukrainians, and Russians would be enslaved and forced to die out, while Germanic peasants resettled the resulting abandoned lands. But he needed countless helpers and many ambitious initiators to turn his dreams into reality. These accomplices came forth. Himmler and the elite corps of SS volunteers shared Hitler's ideology of barbarous racial imperialism, and they rarely wavered in their efforts to realize his goals.[13] Supported (or condoned) by military commanders and German policemen in the occupied territories, the SS corps pressed relentlessly to implement the program of destruction and to create a "mass settlement space" for Germans. Many Poles, captured communists, Gypsies, and Jehovah's Witnesses were murdered in cold blood.

The Holocaust

The ultimate abomination of Nazi racism was the condemnation of all European Jews to extermination in the Holocaust. After the fall of Warsaw, the Nazis stepped up their expulsion campaign and began deporting all German Jews to occupied Poland. There they and Jews from all over Europe were concentrated in ghettos, compelled to wear the Jewish star, and turned into slave laborers.

Online Study Center Improve Your Grade
Primary Source: The Ghettoization of the Jews: Prelude to the Final Solution

In 1941, as part of the "war of annihilation" in the Soviet Union, expulsion spiraled into extermination. On the Russian front, Himmler's special SS killing squads and also regular army units forced Soviet Jews to dig giant pits, which became mass graves as the victims were lined up on the edge and cut down by machine guns. Then in late 1941, Hitler and the Nazi leadership, in some still-debated combination, ordered the SS to stop all Jewish emigration from Europe and speeded up planning for mass murder. As one German diplomat put it, "The Jewish Question must be resolved in the course of the war, for only so can it be solved without a worldwide outcry."[14] The "final solution of the Jewish question"—the murder of every single Jew—had begun. Jews were systematically arrested, packed like cattle onto freight trains, and dispatched to extermination camps. Many Jews could hardly imagine the enormity of the crime that lay before them.

Arriving at their destination, small numbers of Jews were sent to nearby slave labor camps, where they were starved and systematically worked to death. But most of the victims were moved immediately to the death camps, where they were taken by force or deception to "shower rooms" that were actually gas chambers. These gas chambers, first perfected in the quiet, efficient execution

Prelude to Murder This photo captures the terrible inhumanity of Nazi racism and the Holocaust. Frightened and bewildered families from the soon-to-be-destroyed Warsaw Ghetto are being forced out of their homes by German soldiers for deportation to concentration camps. There they face murder in the gas chambers. *(Hulton Archive/Getty Images)*

of seventy thousand mentally ill Germans between 1938 and 1941, permitted rapid, hideous, and thoroughly bureaucratized mass murder. For fifteen to twenty minutes came the terrible screams and gasping sobs of men, women, and children choking to death on poison gas. Then, only silence. Special camp workers quickly yanked the victims' gold teeth from their jaws, and the bodies were then cremated or sometimes boiled for oil to make soap. At Auschwitz-Birkenau, the most infamous of the Nazi death factories, as many as twelve thousand human beings were slaughtered each day. The extermination of European Jews was the ultimate monstrosity of Nazi racism and racial imperialism. By 1945, 6 million Jews had been murdered. (See the feature "Individuals in Society: Primo Levi.")

Who was responsible for this terrible crime? An older generation of historians usually laid most of the guilt on Hitler and the Nazi leadership. Ordinary Germans had little knowledge of the extermination camps, it was argued, and those who cooperated had no alternative given the brutality of Nazi terror and totalitarian control. But in recent years, many studies have revealed a much broader participation of German people in the Holocaust and popular indifference (or worse) to the fate of the Jews. Yet exactly why so many perpetrated or condoned Nazi crimes has remained unclear.

In a controversial work, the American historian Daniel

Mapping the Past

MAP 29.2 World War II in Europe The map shows the extent of Hitler's empire before the Battle of Stalingrad in late 1942 and the subsequent advances of the Allies until Germany surrendered on May 7, 1945. This map, combined with Map 29.1 on page 963, can be used to trace the rise and fall of the Nazi empire over time. ❶ First, using Map 29.1, what was the first country to be conquered by Hitler (and divided with the Soviet Union)? ❷ Second, locate Germany's advance and retreat on the Russian front at different dates: December 1941, November 1942, Spring 1944, and February 1945. Locate the position of British and American forces on the battlefield at similar points in time, and then compare the respective Russian and British-American positions. What implications might the battle lines on February 1945 have for the postwar settlement in Europe?

Online Study Center **Improve Your Grade** Interactive Map: WWII in Europe

Goldhagen reignited discussion of Nazi crimes by arguing that, above all, the extreme anti-Semitism of "ordinary Germans" led them to respond to Hitler and to become his "willing executioners" in World War II.[15] Yet in most occupied countries, local non-German officials also cooperated in the arrest and deportation of Jews to a large extent. As in Germany, only a few exceptional bystanders did not turn a blind eye. Thus some scholars have concluded that the key for most Germans (and most people in occupied countries) was that they felt no personal responsibility for Jews and therefore were not prepared to help them. This meant that many individuals, conditioned by Nazi racist propaganda but also influenced by peer pressure and brutalizing wartime violence, were psychologically prepared to join the SS ideologues and perpetrate ever-greater crimes. They were ready to plumb the depths of evil and to spiral downward from mistreatment to arrest to mass murder.

Japan's Empire in Asia

By late 1938, 1.5 million Japanese troops were bogged down in China, holding a great swath of territory but unable to defeat the Nationalists and the Communists (see Map 29.3). Nor had Japan succeeded in building a large, self-sufficient Asian economic zone, for it still depended on oil and scrap metal from the Netherlands East Indies and the United States. Thus Japanese leaders followed events in Europe closely, looking for alliances and actions that might improve their position in Asia. At home they gave free rein to the anti-Western ultranationalism that had risen in the 1920s and 1930s. In speeches, schools, and newspapers ultranationalists proclaimed Japan's liberating mission in Asia, glorified the warrior virtues of honor and sacrifice, and demanded absolute devotion to the semidivine emperor.

The outbreak of war in Europe in 1939 and Hitler's early victories opened up opportunities for the Japanese in Southeast Asia, where European empires appeared vulnerable. Expanding the war in China, the Japanese also pressured the Dutch to surrender control of the Netherlands East Indies and its rich oil fields, but Dutch colonial officials, backed by the British and the Americans, refused. The United States had repeatedly condemned Japanese aggression in China, and it now feared that embattled Britain would collapse if it lost the support of its Asian colonies.

Japan's invasion of southern Indochina in July 1941 further worsened relations with the United States. President Franklin Roosevelt demanded that Japan withdraw from China, which was completely unacceptable to the Japanese, and they refused. The United States responded with strong action, cutting off the sale of U.S. oil to Japan and thereby reducing Japan's oil supplies by 90 percent. Japanese leaders believed increasingly that war with the United States was inevitable, for Japan's battle fleet would run out of fuel in eighteen months, and its industry would be crippled. After much debate and almost in desperation, Japanese leaders decided to launch a surprise attack on the United States. They hoped to cripple their Pacific rival, gain time to build a defensible Asian empire, and eventually win an ill-defined compromise peace.

The Japanese attack on the U.S. naval base at Pearl Harbor in the Hawaiian Islands was a complete surprise but a limited success. On December 7, 1941, the Japanese sank or crippled every American battleship, but by chance all the all-important American aircraft carriers were at sea and escaped unharmed. More important, Pearl Harbor humiliated Americans and brought them together in a spirit of anger and revenge.

Hitler immediately declared war on the United States. Simultaneously, Japanese armies successfully attacked European and American colonies in Southeast Asia. Japanese armies were small (because most soldiers remained in China), but they were well trained, highly motivated, and very successful. By May 1942 Japan held a vast empire in Southeast Asia and the western Pacific (see Map 29.3).

The Japanese claimed that they were freeing Asians from Western imperialism, and they called their empire the Greater East Asian Co-prosperity Sphere. Some—perhaps many—Japanese army officers and officials sincerely believed that they were creating a mutually advantageous union for the long-term development of Asia. Initially they tapped currents of nationalist sentiment, and most local populations were glad to see the Western Powers go. But Asian faith in "co-prosperity" and support for Japan steadily declined as the war went on. Why was this so?

First of all, although the Japanese set up anticolonial governments and promised genuine independence, real power always rested with Japanese military commanders and their superiors in Tokyo. The "independent" governments were basically shams. Second, the Japanese never really delivered on their promises because they were constantly improvising a frantic defense of their far-flung conquests from relentless attack by a determined foe with vastly superior resources. Thus, as living standards plummeted in Japan and heavy industry sputtered, the Japanese occupiers exploited local peoples for Japan's wartime needs. Finally, the Japanese often exhibited

Individuals in Society

Primo Levi

Most Jews deported to Auschwitz were murdered as soon as they arrived, but the Nazis made some prisoners into slave laborers and a few of these survived. Primo Levi (1919–1987), an Italian Jew, became one of the most influential witnesses to the Holocaust and its death camps.

Like much of Italy's small Jewish community, Levi's family belonged to the urban professional classes. The young Primo graduated in 1941 from the University of Turin with highest honors in chemistry. But since 1938, when Italy introduced racial laws, he had faced growing discrimination, and two years after graduation he joined the antifascist resistance movement. Quickly captured, he was deported to Auschwitz with 650 Italian Jews in February 1944. Stone-faced SS men picked only ninety-six men and twenty-nine women to work in their respective labor camps. Primo was one of them.

Nothing prepared Levi for what he encountered. The Jewish prisoners were kicked, punched, stripped, branded with tattoos, crammed into huts, and worked unmercifully. Hoping for some sign of prisoner solidarity in this terrible environment, Levi found only a desperate struggle of each against all and enormous status differences among prisoners. Many stunned and bewildered newcomers, beaten and demoralized by their bosses—the most privileged prisoners—simply collapsed and died. Others struggled to secure their own privileges, however small, because food rations and working conditions were so abominable that ordinary Jewish prisoners perished in two to three months.

Sensitive and noncombative, Levi found himself sinking into oblivion. But instead of joining the mass of the "drowned," he became one of the "saved"—a complicated surprise with moral implications that he would ponder all his life. As Levi explained in *Survival in Auschwitz* (1947), the usual road to salvation in the camps was some kind of collaboration with German power.* Savage German criminals were released from prison to become brutal camp guards; non-Jewish political prisoners competed for jobs entitling them to better conditions, and, especially troubling for Levi, a small number of Jewish men plotted and struggled for the power of life and death over other Jewish prisoners. Though not one of these Jewish bosses, Levi believed that he himself, like almost all survivors, had entered the "gray zone" of moral compromise. Only a very few superior individuals, "the stuff of saints and martyrs," survived the death camps without shifting their moral stance.

For Levi, compromise and salvation came from his profession. Interviewed by a German technocrat for the camp's synthetic rubber program, Levi performed brilliantly in scientific German and savored his triumph as a Jew over Nazi racism. Work in the warm camp laboratory offered Levi opportunities to pilfer equipment that could then be traded for food and necessities with other prisoners. Levi also gained critical support from three saintly prisoners, who refused to do wicked and hateful acts. And he counted "luck" as essential for his survival: in the camp infirmary with scarlet fever in February 1945 as advancing Russian armies prepared to liberate the camp, Levi was not evacuated by the Nazis and shot to death like most Jewish prisoners.

After the war Primo Levi was forever haunted by the nightmare that the Holocaust would be ignored or forgotten. Always ashamed that so many people whom he considered better than himself had perished, he wrote and lectured tirelessly to preserve the memory of Jewish victims and guilty Nazis. Wanting the world to understand the Jewish genocide in all its complexity so that never again would people tolerate such atrocities, he grappled tirelessly with his vision of individual choice and moral compromise in a hell designed to make the victims collaborate and persecute each other.

Primo Levi, who never stopped thinking, writing, and speaking about the Holocaust. (Giansanti/Corbis Sygma)

Questions for Analysis

1. Describe Levi's experience at Auschwitz. How did camp prisoners treat each other? Why?
2. What does Levi mean by the "gray zone"? How is this concept central to his thinking?
3. Will a vivid historical memory of the Holocaust help to prevent future genocide?

*Primo Levi, *Survival in Auschwitz: The Nazi Assault on Humanity*, rev. ed. 1958 (London: Collier Books, 1961), pp. 79–84, and *The Drowned and the Saved* (New York: Summit Books, 1988). These powerful testimonies are highly recommended.

Online Study Center   Improve Your Grade
Going Beyond Individuals in Society

MAP 29.3 World War II in the Pacific Japanese forces overran an enormous amount of territory in 1942, which the Allies slowly recaptured in a long, bitter struggle. As this map shows, Japan still held a large Asian empire in August 1945, when the unprecedented devastation of atomic warfare suddenly forced it to surrender.

Online Study Center **Improve Your Grade** Interactive Map: WWII in the Pacific

great cruelty toward prisoners of war and civilians, as they had toward the Chinese since 1937. Recurring cruel behavior aroused local populations against the invaders.

The Grand Alliance

While the Nazis and the Japanese built their savage empires, the Allies faced the hard fact that chance, rather than choice, had brought them together. Stalin had been cooperating fully with Hitler between August 1939 and June 1941, and only the Japanese attack on Pearl Harbor in December 1941 had overwhelmed powerful isolationism in the United States.

As a first step toward building an unshakable alliance, U.S. president Franklin D. Roosevelt accepted the contention of British prime minister Winston Churchill that the United States should agree on a policy of **Europe first**. Only after Hitler was defeated would the Allies turn toward the Pacific for an all-out attack on Japan, the lesser threat. The Allies also put immediate military needs first, postponing until after the war tough political questions relating to the eventual peace settlement that might have split the alliance.

To further encourage mutual trust, the Allies adopted the principle of the "unconditional surrender" of Germany and Japan. This policy cemented the Grand Alliance because it denied Hitler any hope of dividing his foes. It also meant that victorious Soviet and Anglo-American armies would almost certainly come together to divide all of Germany, and that Japan would fight to the bitter end.

The military resources of the Grand Alliance were awesome. The strengths of the United States were its mighty industry, its large population, and its national unity. Gearing up rapidly for all-out war in 1942, the United States acquired a unique capacity to wage global war. In 1943 it outproduced not only Germany, Italy, and Japan but also all of the rest of the world combined.

Britain continued to make a great contribution as well. The British economy was totally and effectively mobilized, and the sharing of burdens through rationing and heavy taxes on war profits maintained social harmony. By early 1943 the Americans and the British were combining small aircraft carriers with radar-guided bombers to rid the Atlantic of German submarines. Britain, the impregnable floating fortress, became a gigantic frontline staging area for the decisive blow to the heart of Germany.

As for the Soviet Union, so great was its strength that it might well have defeated Germany without Western help. In the face of the German advance, whole factories and populations were successfully evacuated to eastern Russia and Siberia. There war production was reorganized and expanded, and the Red Army was increasingly well supplied and well led. Above all, Stalin drew on the massive support and heroic determination of the Soviet people, especially those in the central Russian heartland. Broad-based Russian nationalism, as opposed to narrow communist ideology, became the powerful unifying force in what the Soviet people appropriately called the "Great Patriotic War of the Fatherland."

Finally, the United States, Britain, and the Soviet Union had the resources of much of the world at their command. They were also aided by a growing resistance movement against the Nazis throughout Europe, even in Germany. After the Soviet Union was invaded in June 1941, communists throughout Europe took the lead in the underground resistance, joined by a growing number of patriots, Christians, and agents sent by governments-in-exile in London.

The War in Europe, 1942–1945

Barely halted at the gates of Moscow and Leningrad in 1941, the Germans renewed their offensive against the Soviet Union in July 1942, driving toward the southern city of Stalingrad and occupying most of the city in a month of incredibly savage house-to-house fighting.

Then, in November 1942, Soviet armies counterattacked. They rolled over Romanian and Italian troops to the north and south of Stalingrad, quickly closing the trap and surrounding the entire German Sixth Army of 300,000 men. The surrounded Germans were systematically destroyed, until by the end of January 1943 only 123,000 soldiers were left to surrender. Hitler, who had refused to allow a retreat, had suffered a catastrophic defeat. In summer 1943, the larger, better-equipped Soviet armies took the offensive and began moving forward (see Map 29.2).

Not yet prepared to attack Germany directly through France, the Western Allies saw heavy fighting in North Africa from 1940 onward (see Map 29.2). In May 1942, combined German and Italian armies were finally defeated by British forces only seventy miles from Alexandria at the Battle of El Alamein. Almost immediately thereafter, an Anglo-American force landed in Morocco and Algeria. These French possessions, which were under the control of Pétain's Vichy government, quickly went over to the side of the Allies.

Having driven the Axis powers from North Africa by spring 1943, Allied forces maintained the initiative by invading Sicily and then mainland Italy. Mussolini was deposed by a war-weary people, and the new Italian government publicly accepted unconditional surrender in September 1943. Italy, it seemed, was liberated. Yet German commandos rescued Mussolini in a daring raid and put him at the head of a puppet government. German armies seized Rome and all of northern Italy. Fighting continued in Italy.

Indeed, bitter fighting continued in Europe for almost two years. Germany, less fully mobilized for war than Britain in 1941, applied itself to total war in 1942 and enlisted millions of German women and millions of prisoners of war and slave laborers from all across occupied Europe in that effort. Between early 1942 and July 1944, German war production actually tripled in spite of heavy bombing by the British and American air forces. German resistance against Hitler also failed. After an unsuccessful attempt on Hitler's life in July 1944, SS fanatics brutally liquidated thousands of Germans. Terrorized at home and frightened by the prospect of unconditional surrender, the Germans fought on with suicidal stoicism.

On June 6, 1944, American and British forces under General Dwight Eisenhower landed on the beaches of Normandy, France, in history's greatest naval invasion. In a hundred dramatic days, more than 2 million men and almost half a million vehicles pushed inland and broke through German lines. Rejecting proposals to strike straight at Berlin in a massive attack, Eisenhower moved forward cautiously on a broad front. Not until March 1945 did American troops cross the Rhine and enter Germany.

The Soviets, who had been advancing steadily since July 1943, reached the outskirts of Warsaw by August 1944. For the next six months, they moved southward into Romania, Hungary, and Yugoslavia. In January 1945, the Red Army again moved westward through Poland, and on April 26 it met American forces on the Elbe River. The Allies had closed their vise on Nazi Germany and overrun Europe. As Soviet forces fought their way into Berlin, Hitler committed suicide in his bunker, and on May 7 the remaining German commanders capitulated.

The War in the Pacific, 1942–1945

In Asia, as gigantic armies clashed in Europe, the greatest naval battles in history decided the fate of warring nations. First, in the Battle of the Coral Sea in May 1942, an American carrier force fought its Japanese counterpart to a draw, thereby stopping the Japanese advance on Port Moresby and relieving Australia from the threat of invasion. This engagement was followed in June 1942 by the Battle of Midway, in which American carrier-based pilots sank all four of the attacking Japanese aircraft carriers and established overall naval equality with Japan in the Pacific. In August 1942 American marines attacked and took Guadalcanal in the Solomon Islands in heavy fighting.

Hampered by the policy of "Europe first," the United States gradually won control of the sea and air as it geared up massive production of aircraft carriers, submarines, and fighter planes. By 1943 the United States was producing one hundred thousand aircraft a year, almost twice as many as Japan produced in the entire war. In July 1943 the Americans and their Australian allies opened an "island hopping" campaign toward Japan. Pounding Japanese forces on a given island with satura-

"Follow Me!" This painting by Charles McBarron, Jr., shows the action at Red Beach on October 20, 1944, in the Battle of Leyte Gulf in the Philippine Islands. It captures the danger and courage of U.S. troops, which had to storm well-fortified Japanese positions again and again in their long island-hopping campaign. The officer exhorts his men, and death is all around. *(The Granger Collection, New York)*

tion bombing, American army and marine units would then hit the beaches with rifles and flame throwers and secure victory in hand-to-hand combat. Many islands were bypassed, and their Japanese defenders were blockaded and left to starve.

The war in the Pacific was extremely brutal—a "war without mercy," in the words of a leading American scholar—and atrocities were committed on both sides.[16] Knowing of Japanese atrocities in China and the Philippines, the U.S. Marines and Army troops seldom took Japanese prisoners after the Battle of Guadalcanal, killing even those rare Japanese soldiers who offered to surrender. A product of spiraling violence, mutual hatred, and dehumanizing racial stereotypes, the war without mercy intensified as it moved toward Japan.

In June 1944 giant U.S. bombers began a relentless bombing campaign that intensified steadily until the end of the war. In October 1944, as Allied advances in the Pacific paralleled those in Europe, American forces won a great victory in the four-day Battle of Leyte Gulf, the greatest battle in naval history, with 282 ships involved. The Japanese navy was practically finished.

In spite of all their defeats, Japanese troops continued to fight with enormous courage and determination. Indeed, the bloodiest battles of the Pacific war took place on Iwo Jima in February 1945 and on Okinawa in June 1945. American commanders believed the conquest of Japan might cost a million American casualties and claim 10 to 20 million Japanese lives. In fact, Japan was almost helpless, its industry and dense, fragile wooden cities largely destroyed by incendiary bombing and uncontrollable hurricanes of fire. Yet the Japanese seemed determined to fight on, ever ready to die for a hopeless cause.

On August 6 and 9, 1945, the United States dropped atomic bombs on Hiroshima and Nagasaki in Japan. Mass bombing of cities and civilians, one of the terrible new practices of World War II, had ended in the final nightmare—unprecedented human destruction in a single blinding flash. On August 14, 1945, the Japanese announced their surrender. The Second World War, which had claimed the lives of more than 50 million soldiers and civilians, was over.

Chapter Summary

- What was the nature of radical totalitarian dictatorship, and how did it differ from conservative authoritarianism?
- How did Stalin and the Communist Party build a modern totalitarian state in the Soviet Union?
- How did Mussolini's dictatorship come to power and govern in Italy?
- How did Hitler gain power, what policies did totalitarian Nazi Germany pursue, and why did they lead to World War II?
- How did Germany and Japan create enormous empires that were defeated by the Allies—Britain, the Soviet Union, and the United States?

The Second World War marked the climax of the tremendous practical and spiritual maladies of the age of anxiety, which led in many lands to the rise of dictatorships. Many of these dictatorships were variations on conservative authoritarianism, but there was also a fateful innovation—a new kind of totalitarian dictatorship that was dynamic and theoretically unlimited in its actions. Liberals especially have fastened on the violent, profoundly antiliberal, and apparently totalitarian character of these brutal new dictatorships, linking the one-party socialism of Lenin and Stalin with the one-party fascism of Mussolini and Hitler.

Surely Stalin's Soviet Union asserted a total claim on the lives of its citizens. It posed ambitious goals in the form of rapid state-directed industrialization and savage collectivization of agriculture. And it found enthusiastic supporters who believed that Stalin and the Communist Party were building their kind of socialism and a new socialist personality at home. As for Mussolini's Italy, it also proclaimed its revolutionary, "totalitarian" character, but it retained many elements of conservative authoritarianism, such as compromising with the Catholic Church and keeping women in traditional roles.

Coming to power legally with cunning skill, Hitler also quickly established a one-party totalitarian regime with ambitious goals and widespread popular support. But whereas Stalin concentrated on building socialism at home, Hitler and the Nazi elite aimed at unlimited territorial and racial aggression on behalf of a master race. Economic recovery was only a means to that heinous end.

Nazi racism and unlimited aggression made war inevitable, first with the western European democracies, then with hated eastern neighbors, and finally with the United States. Joined by Japan after Pearl Harbor, Hitler's forces overran much of western and eastern Europe, annihilated millions of Jews, and plunged Europe into the ultimate nightmare. But unlimited aggression unwittingly forged a mighty coalition led by Britain, the Soviet Union, and the United States. This Grand Alliance held together and smashed the racist Nazi empire and its leader. The United States also destroyed Japan's vast, overextended empire in the Pacific, thus bringing to a close history's most destructive war.

Key Terms

- totalitarianism
- fascism
- five-year plan
- New Economic Policy (NEP)
- collectivization
- kulaks
- Black Shirts
- Lateran Agreement
- Nazism
- Führer
- Enabling Act
- appeasement
- blitzkrieg
- New Order
- Europe first

Online Study Center **Improve Your Grade** Flashcards

Suggested Reading

Applebaum, Anne. *Gulag: A History*. 2004. An excellent study of Soviet police terror.

Bosworth, R. J. B. *Mussolini's Italy: Life Under the Fascist Dictatorship, 1915–1945*. 2007. An outstanding study of Italy under Mussolini.

Browning, Christopher R. *Ordinary Men: Reserve Police Battalion 101 and the Final Solution in Poland,* 2d ed. 2001. A carefully researched, unnerving account of Polish police atrocities during World War II.

Bullock, Alan. *Hitler and Stalin: Parallel Lives*. 1998. A fascinating comparison by a master biographer.

Burleigh, Michael. *The Third Reich: A New History*. 2001. A splendid accomplishment that includes a refurbishing of the concept of totalitarianism.

Conquest, Robert. *The Great Terror: A Reassessment*. 1991. An excellent account of Stalin's purges of the 1930s.

Frank, Anne. *The Diary of Anne Frank*. A remarkable first-person account by a Jewish girl in hiding during the Nazi occupation of Holland.

Friedrich, Jorg. *The Fire: The Bombing of Germany, 1940–1945*. 2006. Presents the Allied fire bombing in harrowing detail.

Marrus, Michael R. *The Holocaust in History*. 1989. An excellent interpretive survey.

Merridale, Catherine. *Ivan's War: Life and Death in the Red Army, 1939–1945*. 2007. A moving account of ordinary Soviet soldiers.

Ransel, David L. *Village Mothers: Three Generations of Change in Russia and Tataria*. 2005. A pathbreaking study based on oral histories made in the 1990s.

Service, Robert. *Lenin: A Biography*. 2002. A major work using recently available sources.

Weinberg, Gerhard L. *World at Arms: A Global History of World War II,* new ed. 2005. A masterful interconnected overview.

Notes

1. A. Gleason, *Totalitarianism: The Inner History of the World War* (New York: Oxford University Press, 1995), p. 50.
2. E. Halévy, *The Era of Tyrannies* (Garden City, N.Y.: Doubleday, 1965), pp. 265–316, esp. p. 300.
3. I. Kershaw, *The Nazi Dictatorship: Problems and Perspectives of Interpretation*, 2d ed. (London: Edward Arnold, 1989), p. 34.
4. Quoted in I. Deutscher, *Stalin: A Political Biography*, 2d ed. (New York: Oxford University Press, 1967), p. 325.
5. R. Conquest, *The Harvest of Sorrow: Soviet Collectivization and the Terror-Famine* (New York: Oxford University Press, 1986), pp. 4, 303.
6. Quoted in B. Rosenthal, "Women in the Russian Revolution and After," in *Becoming Visible: Women in European History*, ed. R. Bridenthal and C. Koonz (Boston: Houghton Mifflin, 1976), p. 383.
7. M. Malia, *The Soviet Tragedy: A History of Socialism in Russia* (New York: Free Press, 1994), p. 248.
8. R. Thurston, *Life and Terror in Stalin's Russia, 1934–1941* (New Haven, Conn.: Yale University Press, 1996), esp. pp. 16–106; also Malia, *The Soviet Tragedy*, pp. 227–270.
9. R. Vivarelli, "Interpretations on the Origins of Fascism," *Journal of Modern History* 63 (March 1991): 41.
10. W. Brustein, *The Logic of Evil: The Social Origins of the Nazi Party, 1925–1933* (New Haven, Conn.: Yale University Press, 1996), pp. 52, 182.
11. Quoted in K. D. Bracher, *The German Dictatorship: The Origins, Structure and Effects of National Socialism* (New York: Praeger, 1970), pp. 146–147.
12. Quoted ibid., p. 289.
13. R. Allen, *The Business of Genocide: The SS, Slave Labor, and the Concentration Camps* (Chapel Hill: University of North Carolina Press, 2002), pp. 270–285.
14. Quoted in M. Marrus, *The Holocaust in History* (Hanover, N.H.: University Press of New England, 1987), p. 28.
15. D. Goldhagen, *Hitler's Willing Executioners: Ordinary Germans and the Holocaust* (New York: Vintage Books, 1997).
16. J. Dower, *War Without Mercy: Race and Power in the Pacific War* (New York: Pantheon, 1986).

Listening to the Past

Stalin Justifies the Five-Year Plan

On February 4, 1931, Joseph Stalin delivered the following address, entitled "No Slowdown in Tempo!" to the First Conference of Soviet Industrial Managers. Published the following day in *Pravda*, the newspaper of the Communist Party, and widely publicized at home and abroad, Stalin's speech reaffirmed the leader's commitment to the breakneck pace of industrialization and collectivization set forth in the first five-year plan. Arguing that more sacrifices were necessary, Stalin sought to rally the people and generate support for the party's program. His address captures the spirit of Soviet public discourse in the early 1930s.

Stalin's concluding idea, that Bolsheviks needed to master technology and industrial management, reflected another major development. The Soviet Union was training a new class of communist engineers and technicians, who were beginning to replace foreign engineers and "bourgeois specialists," Russian engineers trained in tsarist times who were grudgingly tolerated after the revolution.

It is sometimes asked whether it is not possible to slow down the tempo somewhat, to put a check on the movement. No, comrades, it is not possible! The tempo must not be reduced! On the contrary, we must increase it as much as is within our powers and possibilities. This is dictated to us by our obligations to the workers and peasants of the U.S.S.R. This is dictated to us by our obligations to the working class of the whole world.

To slacken the tempo would mean falling behind. And those who fall behind get beaten. But we do not want to be beaten. No, we refuse to be beaten! One feature of the history of old Russia was the continual beatings she suffered because of her backwardness. She was beaten by the Mongol khans, . . . the Turkish beys, . . . and the Japanese barons. All beat her—because of her backwardness, cultural backwardness, political backwardness, industrial backwardness, agricultural backwardness. They beat her because to do so was profitable and could be done with impunity. . . . Such is the law of the exploiters—to beat the backward and the weak. It is the jungle law of capitalism. You are backward, you are weak—therefore you are wrong; hence you can be beaten and enslaved. You are mighty—therefore you are right; hence we must be wary of you.

That is why we must no longer lag behind.

In the past we had no fatherland, nor could we have had one. But now that we have overthrown capitalism and power is in our hands, in the hands of the people, we have a fatherland, and we will uphold its independence. Do you want our socialist fatherland to be beaten and to lose its independence? If you do not want this, you must put an end to its backwardness in the shortest possible time and develop a genuine Bolshevik tempo in building up its socialist economy. There is no other way. That is why Lenin said on the eve of the October Revolution: "Either perish, or overtake and outstrip the advanced capitalist countries."

We are fifty or a hundred years behind the advanced countries. We must make good this distance in ten years. Either we do it, or we shall go under.

That is what our obligations to the workers and peasants of the U.S.S.R. dictate to us.

But we have yet other, more serious and more important, obligations. They are our obligations to the world proletariat. . . . We achieved victory not solely through the efforts of the working class of the U.S.S.R., but also thanks to the support of the working class of the world. Without this support we would have been torn to pieces long ago. . . . Why does the international proletariat support us? How did we merit this support? By the fact that we were the first to hurl ourselves into the battle against capitalism, we were the first to establish working-class state power, we were the first to begin building socialism. By the fact that we are engaged on a cause which, if successful, will transform the whole world and free the entire working class. But what is needed for success? The elimination of our backwardness, the development of a high Bolshevik tempo of construction. We must march forward in such a way that the working class of the whole world, looking at us, may say: There you have my advanced detachment, my shock brigade, my working-class state power, my fatherland; they are engaged on their cause, *our* cause, and they are working well; let us support them against the capitalists and promote the cause of the world revolution. Must we not justify the hopes of the world's working class, must we not fulfill our obligations to them? Yes, we must if we do not want to utterly disgrace ourselves.

Such are our obligations, internal and international.

As you see, they dictate to us a Bolshevik tempo of development.

I will not say that we have accomplished nothing in regard to management of production during these years. In fact, we have accomplished a good deal. . . . But we could have accomplished still more if we had tried during this period really to master production, the technique of production, the financial and economic side of it.

In ten years at most we must make good the distance that separates us from the advanced capitalist countries. We have all the "objective" possibilities for this. The only thing lacking is the ability to make proper use of these possibilities. And that depends on us. *Only* on us! . . . If you are a factory manager—interfere in all the affairs of the factory, look into everything, let nothing escape you, learn and learn again. Bolsheviks must master technique. It is time Bolsheviks themselves became experts. . . .

It is said that it is hard to master technique. That is not true! There are no fortresses that Bolsheviks cannot capture. We have solved a number of most difficult problems. We have overthrown capitalism. We have assumed power. We have built up a huge socialist industry. We have transferred the middle peasants on the path of socialism. We have already accomplished what is most important from the point of view of construction. What remains to be done is not so

"Our program is realistic," Stalin proclaims on this poster, "because it is you and me working together."
(David King Collection)

much: to study technique, to master science. And when we have done that we shall develop a tempo of which we dare not even dream at present.

And we shall do it if we really want to.

Questions for Analysis

1. What reasons does Stalin give to justify an unrelenting "Bolshevik" tempo of industrial and social change? In the light of history, which reason seems most convincing? Why?

2. Imagine that the year is 1931 and you are a Soviet student reading Stalin's speech. Would Stalin's determination inspire you, frighten you, or leave you cold? Why?

3. Some historians argue that Soviet socialism was a kind of utopianism—that zealots believed that the economy, the society, and even human beings could be completely remade and perfected. What utopian elements do you see in Stalin's declaration?

Source: Joseph Stalin, "No Slowdown in Tempo!," *Pravda,* February 5, 1931.

The youth revolution. London, ca 1980. *(Wellcome Photo Library/Anthea Seiveking)*

chapter 30

Cold War Conflicts and Social Transformations, 1945–1985

chapter preview

The Division of Europe
- What were the causes of the cold war?

The Western Renaissance, 1945–1968
- Why did western Europe recover so successfully? How did colonial peoples win political independence and American blacks triumph in the civil rights movement?

Soviet Eastern Europe, 1945–1968
- What was the pattern of postwar rebuilding and development in the Soviet Union and Communist eastern Europe?

Postwar Social Transformations, 1945–1968
- How did changing patterns in technology, class relations, women's work, and youth culture bring major social transformations?

Conflict and Challenge in the Late Cold War, 1968–1985
- What were the key aspects of political conflict, economic stagnation, and the feminist movement in the late cold war?

The total defeat of the Nazis and their allies in 1945 laid the basis for one of Western civilization's most remarkable recoveries. A battered western Europe dug itself out from under the rubble and fashioned a great renaissance, building strong democracies, vibrant economies, and new societies. The United States also made solid progress, and the Soviet Union became more humane and less dictatorial. Yet there was also a tragic setback. The Grand Alliance against Hitler gave way to an apparently endless cold war in which tension between East and West threatened world peace.

In the late 1960s and early 1970s, the postwar Western renaissance came to an end. First, as cold war competition again turned very hot in Vietnam, postwar certainties such as domestic political stability and social harmony evaporated, and several countries experienced major crises. Second, the astonishing postwar economic advance came to a halt, and this had serious social consequences. Third, new roles for women after World War II led to a powerful "second wave" of feminist thought and action in the 1970s, resulting in major changes for women and gender relations. Thus the long cold war created an underlying unity for the years 1945–1985, but the first half of the cold war era was quite different from the second.

The Division of Europe

In 1945 triumphant American and Russian soldiers came together and embraced on the banks of the Elbe River in the heart of vanquished Germany. At home, in the United States and in the Soviet Union, the soldiers' loved ones erupted in joyous celebration. Yet victory was flawed.

Online Study Center
This icon will direct you to interactive activities and study materials on the website **college.hmco.com/pic/mckaywest9e**

The Allies could not cooperate politically in peacemaking. Motivated by different goals and hounded by misunderstandings, the United States and the Soviet Union soon found themselves at loggerheads. By the end of 1947, Europe was rigidly divided. It was West versus East in a cold war that was waged around the world for forty years.

- *What were the causes of the cold war?*

The Origins of the Cold War

The most powerful allies in the wartime coalition—the Soviet Union and the United States—began to quarrel almost as soon as the unifying threat of Nazi Germany disappeared. A tragic disappointment for millions of people, the hostility between the Eastern and Western superpowers was the sad but logical outgrowth of military developments, wartime agreements, and long-standing political and ideological differences.

In the early phases of the Second World War, the Americans and the British made military victory their highest priority. They consistently avoided discussion of Stalin's war aims and the shape of the eventual peace settlement. Stalin received only a military alliance and no postwar commitments. Yet the United States and Britain did not try to take advantage of the Soviet Union's precarious position in 1942, because they feared that hard bargaining would encourage Stalin to consider making a separate peace with Hitler. They focused instead on the policy of unconditional surrender to solidify the alliance.

By late 1943, discussion about the shape of the postwar world could no longer be postponed. The conference that Stalin, Roosevelt, and Churchill held in the Iranian capital of Teheran in November 1943 thus proved of crucial importance in determining subsequent events. There, the **Big Three** jovially reaffirmed their determination to crush Germany and searched for the appropriate military strategy. Churchill, fearful of the military dangers of a direct attack, argued that American and British forces should follow up their Italian campaign with an indirect attack on Germany through the Balkans. Roosevelt, however, agreed with Stalin that an American-British frontal assault through France would be better. This agreement was part of Roosevelt's general effort to

The Big Three In 1945 a triumphant Winston Churchill, an ailing Franklin Roosevelt, and a determined Joseph Stalin met at Yalta in southern Russia to plan for peace. Cooperation soon gave way to bitter hostility. *(Franklin D. Roosevelt Presidential Library)*

meet Stalin's wartime demands whenever possible, and it had momentous political implications. It meant that the Soviet and the American-British armies would come together in defeated Germany along a north-south line and that only Soviet troops would liberate eastern Europe. Thus the basic shape of postwar Europe was emerging even as the fighting continued.

When the Big Three met again in February 1945 at Yalta on the Black Sea in southern Russia, advancing Soviet armies were within a hundred miles of Berlin. The Red Army had occupied not only Poland but also Bulgaria, Romania, Hungary, part of Yugoslavia, and much of Czechoslovakia. The temporarily stalled American-British forces had yet to cross the Rhine into Germany. Moreover, the United States was far from defeating Japan. In short, the Soviet Union's position was strong and America's weak.

There was little the increasingly sick and apprehensive Roosevelt could do but double his bet on Stalin's peaceful intentions. It was agreed at Yalta that Germany would be divided into zones of occupation and would pay heavy reparations to the Soviet Union. At American insistence, Stalin agreed to declare war on Japan after Germany was defeated. As for Poland and eastern Europe—"that Pandora's Box of infinite troubles," according to American secretary of state Cordell Hull—the Big Three struggled to reach an ambiguous compromise at Yalta: eastern European governments were to be freely elected but pro-Russian.

The Yalta compromise over eastern Europe broke down almost immediately. Even before the Yalta Conference, Bulgaria and Poland were controlled by communists who arrived home with the Red Army. Elsewhere in eastern Europe, pro-Soviet "coalition" governments of several parties were formed, but the key ministerial posts were reserved for Moscow-trained communists.

At the postwar Potsdam Conference of July 1945, the long-avoided differences over eastern Europe finally surged to the fore. The compromising Roosevelt had died and been succeeded by the more determined President Harry Truman, who demanded immediate free elections throughout eastern Europe. Stalin refused point-blank. "A freely elected government in any of these East European countries would be anti-Soviet," he admitted simply, "and that we cannot allow."[1]

Here, then, is the key to the much-debated origins of the cold war. American ideals, pumped up by the crusade against Hitler, and American politics, heavily influenced by millions of voters from eastern Europe, demanded free elections in Soviet-occupied eastern Europe. Stalin, who

Chronology

1945–1962	U.S. takes lead in Big Science
1945–1960s	Decolonization of Asia and Africa
1947	Truman Doctrine; Marshall Plan
1949	Formation of NATO; Stalin launches verbal attack on Soviet Jews; Beauvoir, *The Second Sex*
1950–1953	Korean War
1953–1964	De-Stalinization of Soviet Union
1956	Pasternak, *Doctor Zhivago*
1957	Formation of Common Market
1961	Building of Berlin Wall
1962	Cuban missile crisis; Solzhenitsyn, *One Day in the Life of Ivan Denisovich*
1964	Civil Rights Act in the United States
1964–1973	U.S. involvement in Vietnam War
1966	Formation of National Organization for Women (NOW)
1968	Soviet invasion of Czechoslovakia; student protests in Paris
1969	First Apollo moon landing
1972	Watergate break-in
1973	OPEC oil embargo
1979	Margaret Thatcher becomes British prime minister

had lived through two enormously destructive German invasions, wanted absolute military security from Germany and its potential Eastern allies. Suspicious by nature, he believed that only communist states could be truly dependable allies, and he realized that free elections would result in independent and possibly hostile governments on his western border. Moreover, by the middle of 1945, there was no way short of war that the United States could determine political developments in eastern Europe, and war was out of the question. Stalin was bound to have his way.

West Versus East

The American response to Stalin's exaggerated conception of security was to "get tough." In May 1945, Truman abruptly cut off all aid to the U.S.S.R. In October he declared that the United States would never recognize any government established by force against the free will of its people. In March 1946, former British prime minister Churchill ominously informed an American audience that an "iron curtain" had fallen across the continent, dividing Germany and all of Europe into two antagonistic camps. Emotional, moralistic denunciations of Stalin and communist Russia emerged as part of American political life. Yet the United States also responded to the popular desire to "bring the boys home" and demobilized its troops with great speed. Some historians have argued that American leaders believed that the atomic bomb gave the United States all the power it needed, but "getting tough" really meant "talking tough."

Stalin's agents quickly reheated what they viewed as the "ideological struggle against capitalist imperialism." The large, well-organized Communist Parties of France and Italy obediently started to uncover "American plots" to take over Europe and challenged their own governments with violent criticisms and large strikes. The Soviet Union also put pressure on Iran, Turkey, and Greece, while a bitter civil war raged in China. By the spring of 1947, it appeared to many Americans that Stalin was determined to export communism by subversion throughout Europe and around the world.

The United States responded to this challenge with the Truman Doctrine, which was aimed at "containing" communism to areas already occupied by the Red Army. Truman told Congress in March 1947, "I believe it must be the policy of the United States to support free people who are resisting attempted subjugation by armed minorities or by outside pressure." To begin, Truman asked Congress for military aid to Greece and Turkey, countries that Britain, weakened by war and financially overextended, could no longer protect. Then, in June, Secretary of State George C. Marshall offered Europe economic aid—the **Marshall Plan**—to help it rebuild.

Online Study Center **Improve Your Grade**
Primary Source: An American Plan to Rebuild a Shattered Europe

Stalin refused Marshall Plan assistance for all of eastern Europe. He purged the last remaining noncommunist elements from the coalition governments of eastern Europe and established Soviet-style, one-party communist dictatorships. The seizure of power in Czechoslovakia in February 1948 was particularly antidemocratic, and it greatly strengthened Western fears of limitless communist expansion. Thus, when Stalin blocked all traffic through the Soviet zone of Germany to Berlin, the former capital, which the occupying powers had also divided into sectors at the end of the war, the Western allies acted firmly but not provocatively. Hundreds of planes began flying over the Soviet roadblocks around the clock, supplying provisions to the people of West Berlin and thwarting Soviet efforts to swallow up the West Berliners. After 324 days, the Soviets backed down: containment seemed to work. In 1949, therefore, the United States formed an anti-Soviet military alliance of Western governments: the North Atlantic Treaty Organization (**NATO**). Stalin countered by tightening his hold on his satellites, later united in the Warsaw Pact. Europe was divided into two hostile blocs.

In late 1949, the communists triumphed in China, frightening and angering many Americans, who saw new evidence of a powerful worldwide communist conspiracy. When the Russian-backed communist army of North Korea invaded South Korea in 1950, President Truman acted swiftly. American-led United Nations forces under General Douglas MacArthur intervened. Initially, the North Koreans almost conquered the entire peninsula, but the South Koreans and the Americans rallied and advanced until China suddenly entered the war. The bitter, bloody contest then seesawed back and forth near where it had begun, as President Truman rejected General MacArthur's call to attack China and fired him instead. In 1953 a fragile truce was negotiated, and the fighting stopped. Thus the United States extended its policy of containment to Asia but drew back from an attack on communist China and possible nuclear war.

The rapid descent from victorious Grand Alliance to bitter **cold war** was directly connected to the tragic fate of eastern Europe. After 1933, when the eastern European power vacuum invited Nazi racist imperialism, the appeasing Western democracies mistakenly did nothing. They did, however, have one telling insight: how, they asked themselves, could they unite with Stalin to stop Hitler without giving Stalin great gains on his western borders? After Hitler's invasion of the Soviet Union, the Western Powers preferred to ignore this question and hope for the best. But when Stalin later began to claim the spoils of victory, the United States began to protest and professed outrage. This belated opposition quite possibly encouraged even more aggressive measures by the always-suspicious Stalin, and it helped explode the quarrel over eastern Europe into a global confrontation. Thus the Soviet-American confrontation became institutionalized and formed the bedrock of the long cold war

The Berlin Airlift Standing in the rubble of their bombed-out city, a German crowd in the American sector awaits the arrival of a U.S. transport plane flying in over the Soviet blockade in 1948. The crisis over Berlin was a dramatic indication of growing tensions among the Allies, which resulted in the division of Europe into two hostile camps. *(Time Life Pictures/Getty Images)*

era, which lasted until the mid-1980s despite intermittent periods of relaxation.

The Western Renaissance, 1945–1968

As the cold war divided Europe into two blocs, the future appeared bleak on both sides of the iron curtain. European economic conditions were the worst in generations, and Europe was weak and divided, a battleground for cold war ambitions. Moreover, western European empires were crumbling in the face of nationalism in Asia and Africa. Yet Europe recovered, and the nations of western Europe led the way. In less than a generation, western Europe achieved unprecedented economic prosperity and peaceful social transformation, while the United States boomed and eventually experienced a wholesome social revolution. It was an amazing rebirth—a true renaissance.

- Why did western Europe recover so successfully? How did colonial peoples win political independence and American blacks triumph in the civil rights movement?

The Postwar Challenge

After the war, economic conditions in western Europe were terrible. Runaway inflation and black markets testified to severe shortages and hardships. Many people believed that Europe was quite simply finished.

Suffering was most intense in defeated Germany. The major territorial change of the war had moved the Soviet Union's border far to the west. Poland was in turn compensated for this loss to the Soviets with land taken from Germany (see Map 30.1). To solidify these changes in boundaries, 13 million Germans were driven from their homes and forced to resettle in a greatly reduced Germany. The Russians were also seizing factories and equipment as reparations in their zone, even tearing up railroad tracks and sending the rails to the Soviet Union.

In 1945 and 1946, conditions were not much better in the Western zones, for the Western allies also treated the German population with severity at first. Countless Germans sold prized possessions to American soldiers to buy food. By the spring of 1947, refugee-clogged, hungry, prostrate Germany was on the verge of total collapse and threatening to drag down the rest of Europe. Yet western

MAP 30.1 The Results of World War II in Europe Millions of refugees fled westward because of war and territorial changes. The Soviet Union and Poland took land from Germany, which the Allies partitioned into occupation zones. Those zones subsequently formed the basis of the East and West German states, as the iron curtain fell to divide both Germany and Europe. Austria was detached from Germany, but the Soviets subsequently permitted Austria to reunify as a neutral state.

Europe was not finished. The Nazi occupation and the war had discredited old ideas and old leaders. All over Europe, many people were willing to change and experiment, and new groups and new leaders were coming to the fore to guide these aspirations. Progressive Catholics and revitalized Catholic political parties—the **Christian Democrats**—were particularly influential.

In Italy the Christian Democrats emerged as the leading party in the first postwar elections in 1946, and in early 1948 they won an absolute majority in the parliament in a landslide victory. Their very able leader was Alcide De Gasperi, a courageous antifascist firmly committed to political democracy, economic reconstruction, and moderate social reform. In France, too, the Catholic Party also provided some of the best postwar leaders after January 1946, when General Charles de Gaulle, the inspiring wartime leader of the Free French, resigned after having re-established the free and democratic Fourth Republic. As Germany was partitioned by the cold war, a purified Federal Republic of Germany (as West Germany was officially known) found new and able leadership among its Catholics. In 1949 Konrad Adenauer, the former mayor of Cologne and a long-time anti-Nazi, began his long, highly successful democratic rule; the Christian Democrats became West Germany's majority party for a generation. In providing effective leadership for their respective countries, the Christian Democrats were inspired and united by a common Christian and European heritage. They steadfastly rejected authoritarianism and narrow nationalism and placed their faith in democracy and cooperation.

The socialists and the communists, active in the resistance against Hitler, also emerged from the war with increased power and prestige, especially in France and Italy. They, too, provided fresh leadership and pushed for social change and economic reform. In the immediate postwar years, welfare measures such as family allowances, health insurance, and increased public housing were enacted throughout continental Europe. Britain followed the same trend, as the newly elected socialist Labour Party established a "welfare state." Many British industries were nationalized, and the government provided free medical service. Thus all across Europe, social reform complemented political transformation, creating solid foundations for a great European renaissance.

The United States also supplied strong and creative leadership, providing western Europe with both massive economic aid and ongoing military protection. Economic aid was channeled through the Marshall Plan, and military security was provided through NATO, which featured American troops stationed permanently in Europe and the American nuclear umbrella. Thus the United States assumed the international responsibilities it had shunned after 1919.

As Marshall Plan aid poured in, the battered economies of western Europe began to turn the corner in 1948. The outbreak of the Korean War in 1950 further stimulated economic activity, and Europe entered a period of rapid economic progress that lasted into the late 1960s. Never before had the European economy grown so fast. There were many reasons for western Europe's brilliant economic performance. American aid helped the process get off to a fast start. Moreover, economic growth became a basic objective of all western European governments, for leaders and voters were determined to avoid a return to the dangerous and demoralizing stagnation of the 1930s. Thus governments generally accepted Keynesian economics (see pages 928 and 935) and sought to stimulate their economies. They also adopted a variety of imaginative and successful strategies.

In postwar West Germany, Minister of Economy Ludwig Erhard, a roly-poly, cigar-smoking former professor, broke decisively with the straitjacketed Nazi economy. Erhard bet on the free-market economy while maintaining the extensive social welfare network inherited from the Hitler era. He and his teachers believed not only that capitalism was more efficient but also that political and social freedom could thrive only if there were real economic freedom. Erhard's first step was to reform the currency and abolish rationing and price controls in 1948. He boldly declared, "The only ration coupon is the Mark."[2] West Germany's success renewed respect for free-market capitalism.

The French innovation was a new kind of planning. Under the guidance of Jean Monnet, an economic pragmatist and apostle of European unity, a planning commission set ambitious but flexible goals for the French economy and used the nationalized banks to funnel money into key industries. Thus France combined flexible planning and a "mixed" state and private economy to achieve the most rapid economic development in its long history.

In most countries, there were many people ready to work hard for low wages and the hope of a better future. Moreover, although many consumer products had been invented or perfected since the late 1920s, few Europeans had been able to buy them. In 1945 the electric refrigerator, the washing machine, and the automobile were rare luxuries. There was a great potential demand, which the economic system moved to satisfy. Finally, western European nations abandoned protectionism and gradually created a large unified market known as the "Common Market." This historic action, which certainly

stimulated the economy, was part of a larger search for European unity.

Toward European Unity

Western Europe's political recovery was spectacular in the generation after 1945. Republics were re-established in France, West Germany, and Italy. Constitutional monarchs were restored in Belgium, Holland, and Norway. Democratic governments, often within the framework of multiparty politics and shifting parliamentary coalitions, took root again and thrived. National self-determination was accompanied by civil liberties and individual freedom.

A similarly extraordinary achievement was the march toward a united Europe. The Christian Democrats, with their shared Catholic heritage, were particularly committed to "building Europe," and other groups shared their dedication. Many Europeans believed that only unity in a new "European nation" could reassert western Europe's influence in world affairs.

The close cooperation among European states required by the Americans for Marshall Plan aid led to the creation of both the Organization of European Economic Cooperation (OEEC) and the Council of Europe in 1948. European federalists hoped that the Council of Europe would quickly evolve into a true European parliament with sovereign rights, but this did not happen. Britain, with its empire and its "special relationship" with the United States, consistently opposed giving any real political power—any sovereignty—to the council. Many continental nationalists and communists felt similarly.

Frustrated in the direct political approach, European federalists turned toward economics as a way of working toward genuine unity. Two far-seeing French statesmen, the planner Jean Monnet and Foreign Minister Robert Schuman, took the lead in 1950 and called for a special international organization to control and integrate all European steel and coal production. West Germany, Italy, Belgium, the Netherlands, and Luxembourg accepted the French idea in 1952; the British would have none of it. The immediate economic goal—a single steel and coal market without national tariffs or quotas—was rapidly realized. The more far-reaching political goal was to bind the six member nations so closely together economically that war among them would eventually become unthinkable and virtually impossible.

In 1957 the six nations of the Coal and Steel Community signed the Treaty of Rome, which created the European Economic Community, generally known as the **Common Market** (see Map 30.2). The first goal of the treaty was a gradual reduction of all tariffs among the six in order to create a single market almost as large as that of the United States. Other goals included the free movement of capital and labor and common economic policies and institutions. The Common Market was a great success, encouraging companies and regions to specialize in what they did best.

The development of the Common Market fired imaginations and encouraged hopes of rapid progress toward political as well as economic union. In the 1960s, however, these hopes were frustrated by a resurgence of more traditional nationalism. France took the lead. Mired in a bitter colonial war in Algeria, the French turned in 1958 to General de Gaulle, who established the Fifth Republic and ruled as its president until 1969. De Gaulle was at heart a romantic nationalist, and he viewed the United States as the main threat to genuine French (and European) independence. He withdrew all French military forces from the "American-controlled" NATO, developed France's own nuclear weapons, and vetoed the scheduled advent of majority rule within the Common Market. Thus throughout the 1960s, the Common Market thrived economically but remained a union of sovereign states.

Decolonization in East Asia

In the postwar era, Europe's long-standing overseas expansion was dramatically reversed. Future generations will almost certainly see this rolling back of Western expansion as one of world history's great turning points (see Map 30.3).

The most basic cause of imperial collapse—what Europeans called **decolonization**—was the rising demand of Asian and African peoples for national self-determination, racial equality, and personal dignity. This demand spread from intellectuals to the masses in nearly every colonial territory after the First World War. As a result, colonial empires had already been shaken by 1939, and the way

Mapping the Past

MAP 30.2 European Alliance Systems, 1949–1989
After the cold war divided Europe into two hostile military alliances, six western European countries formed the Common Market in 1957. The Common Market grew later to include most of western Europe. The communist states organized their own economic association—COMECON. ❶ Identify the countries that were the original members of the Common Market. What do they have in common? ❷ Identify the members of COMECON. What communist country or countries did not join COMECON? Why? ❸ Which non-allied nations had joined the Common Market by 1989?

MAP 30.3 The New States in Africa and Asia Divided primarily along religious lines into two states, British India led the way to political independence in 1947. Most African territories achieved statehood by the mid-1960s, as European empires passed away, unlamented.

was prepared for the eventual triumph of independence movements.

European empires had been based on an enormous power differential between the rulers and the ruled, a difference that had greatly declined by 1945. Not only was western Europe poor and battered immediately after the war, but imperial rulers had been driven from large parts of South Asia by the Japanese, and in these areas Europeans now faced strong nationalist movements that had developed under the Japanese occupation.

Many Europeans also regarded their empires very differently after 1945 than before 1914, or even before 1939. Empire had rested on self-confidence and self-righteousness; Europeans had believed their superiority to be not only technical and military but also spiritual and moral. The horrors of the Second World War destroyed such complacent arrogance and gave opponents of imperialism much greater influence in Europe. With their political power and moral authority in tatters in 1945, many Europeans had little taste for bloody colonial wars and wanted to concentrate on rebuilding at home.

India, Britain's oldest, largest, and most lucrative nonwhite possession, played a key role in decolonization. Nationalist opposition to British rule coalesced after the First World War under the leadership of British-educated lawyer Mohandas "Mahatma" Gandhi (1869–1948), one of the twentieth century's most significant and influential figures. In the 1920s and 1930s Gandhi built a mass movement preaching nonviolent "noncooperation" with the British. In 1935 Gandhi wrested from the frustrated and unnerved British a new constitution that was practically a blueprint for independence. When the Labour Party came to power in Great Britain in 1945, it was ready to relinquish sovereignty. British socialists had always been critical of imperialism, and the heavy cost of governing India had become a large financial burden. The obstacle to India's independence posed by conflict between India's Hindu and Muslim populations was

Gandhi Arrives in Delhi, October 1939 A small frail man, Gandhi possessed enormous courage and determination. His campaign of nonviolent resistance to British rule inspired the Indian masses and nurtured national identity and self-confidence. Here he arrives for talks with the British viceroy after the outbreak of World War II. *(Corbis)*

resolved in 1947 through the creation of two states, predominately Hindu India and Muslim Pakistan.

If Indian nationalism drew on Western parliamentary liberalism, Chinese nationalism developed and triumphed in the framework of Marxist-Leninist ideology. In the turbulent early 1920s, a broad alliance of nationalist forces within the Soviet-supported Guomindang (Kuomintang, or National People's Party) was dedicated to unifying China and abolishing European concessions. But in 1927 Chiang Kai-shek (1887–1975), successor to Sun Yat-sen (see page 872) and leader of the Guomindang, broke with his more radical communist allies, headed by Mao Zedong (Mao Tse-tung), and tried to destroy them.

In 1931, to escape Guomindang armies closing in for the kill, Mao (1893–1976) led his followers on an incredible 5,000-mile march to remote northern China and built up an independent power base there. Even war could not force Mao and Chiang to cooperate. By late 1945 their long-standing quarrel had erupted in civil war. Stalin gave Mao some aid, and the Americans gave Chiang much more. Winning the support of the peasantry by promising to expropriate the big landowners, the tougher, better-organized communists forced the Nationalists to withdraw to the island of Taiwan in 1949.

Mao and the communists united China's 550 million inhabitants in a strong centralized state, expelled foreigners, and began building a new society along Soviet lines, with mass arrests, forced-labor camps, and ceaseless propaganda. The peasantry was collectivized, and the inevitable five-year plans concentrated successfully on the expansion of heavy industry.

Most Asian countries followed the pattern of either India or China. In 1946 the Philippines achieved independence peacefully from the United States. Britain quickly granted Sri Lanka (Ceylon) and Burma independence in 1948. However, Indonesian nationalists had to beat off attempts by the Dutch to reconquer the Dutch East Indies before Indonesia emerged in 1949 as a sovereign state.

The French also tried their best to re-establish colonial rule in Indochina, but despite American aid, they were defeated in 1954 by forces under the communist and nationalist guerrilla leader Ho Chi Minh (1890–1969), who was supported by the Soviet Union and China. But Indochina was not unified, and two independent Vietnamese states came into being, which led to civil war and subsequent intervention by the United States (see page 1006).

Decolonization in the Middle East and Africa

In the Middle East, the movement toward political independence continued after World War II (see Map 30.3). In 1944 the French gave up their League of Nations mandates in Syria and Lebanon. In British-mandated Palestine, where after 1918 the British government established a Jewish homeland alongside the Arab population, violence and terrorism mounted on both sides. In 1947 the frustrated British decided to leave Palestine, and the United Nations then voted in a nonbinding resolution to divide Palestine into two states—one Arab and one Jewish, which became Israel. The Jews accepted the plan but the Arabs did not, and in 1948 they attacked the Jewish state as soon as it was proclaimed. The Israelis drove off the invaders and conquered more territory, as roughly 900,000 Arabs fled or were expelled. Holocaust survivors from Europe streamed into Israel, as Theodor Herzl's Zionist dream came true (see page 839). The next fifty years saw four more wars between the Israelis and the Arab states and innumerable clashes between the Israelis and the Palestinians.

The Arab defeat in 1948 triggered a powerful nationalist revolution in Egypt in 1952, where a young army officer named Gamal Abdel Nasser (1918–1970) drove out the pro-Western king. In 1956 Nasser abruptly nationalized the foreign-owned Suez Canal Company, the last symbol and substance of Western power in the Middle East. Infuriated, the British and the French, along with the Israelis, invaded Egypt. This was, however, the dying gasp of traditional imperial power: the Americans joined with the Soviets to force the British, French, and Israelis to withdraw. Nasser and anti-Western Egyptian nationalism triumphed.

The failure of Britain and France to unseat Nasser in 1956 encouraged Arab nationalists in Algeria. The country's large French population considered colonial Algeria an integral part of France and was determined to stay in Algeria and continue dominating the Arab majority. This settler determination made the Algerian war for independence long, bloody, and dirty, with systematic torture and numerous atrocities on both sides. In the end, General de Gaulle, who had returned to power as part of the movement to keep Algeria French, accepted the principle of Algerian self-determination. In 1962, after more than a century of French rule, Algeria became independent and its European population quickly fled to France.

In much of Africa south of the Sahara, decolonization proceeded much more smoothly. Beginning in 1957, Britain's colonies achieved independence with little or no bloodshed and then entered a very loose association with Britain as members of the British Commonwealth of Nations. In 1958 the clever de Gaulle offered the leaders of French black Africa the choice of a total break with France or immediate independence within a kind of

Nationalizing the Suez Canal Nasser's 1956 takeover of the Suez Canal, cheered here by a huge crowd in Cairo, was wildly popular throughout Egypt and the Arab world. Jubilation quickly turned to humiliation as invading forces from Israel, Britain, and France crushed the Egyptian army, and a shell-shocked Nasser offered to resign. But the Egyptian masses demanded he stay, enabling the charismatic Nasser to emerge triumphant with American support. *(Hulton-Deutsch Collection/Corbis)*

French commonwealth. All but one of the new states chose association with France. African leaders did so because they identified with French culture and because they wanted aid from France. The French were eager to help—provided their former colonies would accept close ties with France on French terms. As in the past, the French and their Common Market partners, who helped foot the bill, saw themselves as continuing their civilizing mission in sub-Saharan Africa. More important, they saw in Africa untapped markets for their industrial goods, raw materials for their factories, outlets for profitable investment, and good temporary jobs for their engineers and teachers. The British acted somewhat similarly.

As a result, western European countries actually managed to increase their economic and cultural ties with their former African colonies in the 1960s and 1970s. Above all, they used the lure of special trading privileges and heavy investment in French- and English-language education to enhance a powerful Western presence in the new African states. This situation led a variety of leaders and scholars to charge that western Europe (and the United States) had imposed a system of neocolonialism on the former colonies. According to this view, **neocolonialism** was a system designed to perpetuate Western economic domination and undermine the promise of political independence, thereby extending to Africa (and much of Asia) the economic subordination that the United States had established in Latin America in the nineteenth century. At the very least, enduring influence in sub-Saharan Africa testified to western Europe's resurgent economic and political power in international relations.

The March on Washington, August 1963 The march marked a dramatic climax in the civil rights struggle. More than 200,000 people gathered at the Lincoln Memorial to hear the young Martin Luther King, Jr., deliver his greatest address, the "I have a dream" speech. *(Time Life Pictures/Getty Images)*

America's Civil Rights Revolution

The Second World War cured the depression in the United States and brought about an economic boom. Despite fears that peace would bring renewed depression, conversion to a peacetime economy went smoothly. As in western Europe, the U.S. economy proceeded to advance fairly steadily for a long generation.

Belatedly and reluctantly, postwar America did experience a genuine social revolution. After a long struggle, African Americans (and their white supporters) threw off a deeply entrenched system of segregation, discrimination, and repression. Eloquent lawyers challenged school segregation and in 1954 won a landmark decision in the Supreme Court, which ruled in *Brown v. Board of Education* that "separate educational facilities are inherently unequal." Blacks effectively challenged institutionalized inequality with bus boycotts, sit-ins, and demonstrations. As civil rights leader Martin Luther King, Jr. (1929–1968), told the white power structure, "We will not hate you, but we will not obey your evil laws."[3]

In key northern states, African Americans used their growing political power to gain the support of the liberal wing of the Democratic Party. A liberal landslide elected Lyndon Johnson (1908–1973) president in 1964. The Civil Rights Act of 1964 prohibited discrimination in public services and on the job; the Voting Rights Act of 1965 guaranteed all blacks the right to vote. By the 1970s, substantial numbers of blacks had been elected to public and private office throughout the southern states, proof positive that dramatic changes had occurred in American race relations.

President Johnson also declared "unconditional war on poverty," and Congress and the administration created a host of antipoverty programs intended to aid all poor Americans and bring greater economic equality. Thus the United States promoted in the mid-1960s the kind of fundamental social reform that western Europe had embraced immediately after the Second World War. The United States became more of a welfare state, as government spending for social benefits rose dramatically and approached European levels.

Soviet Eastern Europe, 1945–1968

While western Europe surged ahead economically after the Second World War and increased its political power as American influence gradually waned, eastern Europe followed a different path. The Soviet Union first tightened its grip on the "liberated" nations of eastern Europe under Stalin and then refused to let go. Thus postwar economic recovery in eastern Europe proceeded along Soviet lines, and political and social developments were strongly influenced by changes in the Soviet Union.

- **What was the pattern of postwar rebuilding and development in the Soviet Union and Communist eastern Europe?**

Stalin's Last Years, 1945–1953

Americans were not the only ones who felt betrayed by Stalin's postwar actions. The "Great Patriotic War of the Fatherland" had fostered Russian nationalism and a relaxation of dictatorial terror. It also had produced a rare but real unity between Soviet rulers and most Russian people. Having made a heroic war effort, the vast majority of the Soviet people hoped in 1945 that a grateful party and government would grant greater freedom and democracy. Such hopes were soon crushed.

Even before the war ended, Stalin was moving his country back toward rigid dictatorship. As early as 1944, the leading members of the Communist Party were being given a new motivating slogan: "The war on Fascism ends, the war on capitalism begins."[4] By early 1946, Stalin was publicly singing the old tune that war was inevitable as long as capitalism existed. Stalin's new foreign foe in the West provided an excuse for re-establishing a harsh dictatorship. Many returning soldiers and ordinary citizens were purged in 1945 and 1946, as Stalin revived the terrible forced-labor camps of the 1930s.

Culture and art were also purged in violent campaigns that reimposed rigid anti-Western ideological conformity. Many artists were denounced, including the composers Sergei Prokofiev and Dimitri Shostakovich and the film director Sergei Eisenstein. In 1949 Stalin launched a savage verbal attack on Soviet Jews, accusing them of being pro-Western and antisocialist.

In the political realm, Stalin reasserted the Communist Party's complete control of the government and his absolute mastery of the party. Five-year plans were reintroduced to cope with the enormous task of economic reconstruction. Once again, heavy industry and the military were given top priority, and consumer goods, housing, and collectivized agriculture were neglected. Everyday life was very hard. In short, it was the 1930s all over

Sergei Eisenstein: Ivan the Terrible Eisenstein's final masterpiece—one of the greatest films ever—was filmed during the Second World War and released in two parts in 1946. In this chilling scene, the crafty paranoid tyrant, who has saved Russia from foreign invaders, invites the unsuspecting Prince Vladimir to a midnight revel that will lead to his murder. The increasingly demonic Ivan seemed to resemble Stalin, and Eisenstein was censored and purged. *(David King Collection)*

again in the Soviet Union, although police terror was less intense.

Stalin's prime postwar innovation was to export the Stalinist system to the countries of eastern Europe. The Communist Parties of eastern Europe had established one-party states by 1948, thanks to the help of the Red Army and the Russian secret police. Rigid ideological indoctrination, attacks on religion, and a lack of civil liberties were soon facts of life. Industry was nationalized, and the middle class was stripped of its possessions. Economic life was then faithfully recast in the Stalinist mold. Forced industrialization lurched forward without regard for human costs. The collectivization of agriculture began.

Only Josip Broz Tito (1892–1980), the resistance leader and Communist chief of Yugoslavia, was able to resist Soviet domination successfully. Tito stood up to Stalin in 1948, and since there was no Russian army in Yugoslavia, he got away with it. Yugoslavia prospered as a multiethnic state until it began to break apart in the 1980s. Tito's proclamation of independence infuriated Stalin. Popular Communist leaders who, like Tito, had led the resistance against Germany were purged as Stalin sought to create absolutely obedient instruments of domination in eastern Europe.

Reform and De-Stalinization, 1953–1964

In 1953 the aging Stalin finally died, and the dictatorship that he had built began to change. Even as Stalin's heirs struggled for power, they realized that reforms were necessary because of the widespread fear and hatred of Stalin's political terrorism. The power of the secret police was curbed, and many of the forced-labor camps were gradually closed. Change was also necessary for economic reasons. Moreover, Stalin's belligerent foreign policy had led directly to a strong Western alliance, which isolated the Soviet Union.

On the question of just how much change should be permitted in order to preserve the system, the Communist leadership was badly split. Conservatives wanted to make as few changes as possible. Reformers, who were led by Nikita Khrushchev, argued for major innovations. Khrushchev (1894–1971), who had joined the party as an uneducated coal miner in 1918 and risen to a high-level position in the 1930s, emerged as the new ruler in 1955.

To strengthen his position and that of his fellow reformers within the party, Khrushchev launched an all-out attack on Stalin and his crimes at a closed session of the Twentieth Party Congress in 1956. In gory detail, he described to the startled Communist delegates how Stalin had tortured and murdered thousands of loyal Communists, how he had trusted Hitler completely and bungled the country's defense, and how he had "supported the glorification of his own person with all conceivable methods." Khrushchev's "secret speech" was read at Communist Party meetings held throughout the country, and it strengthened the reform movement.

The liberalization—or **de-Stalinization,** as it was called in the West—of the Soviet Union was genuine. The Communist Party jealously maintained its monopoly on political power, but Khrushchev shook up the party and brought in new members. Some resources were shifted from heavy industry and the military toward consumer goods and agriculture, and Stalinist controls over workers were relaxed. The Soviet Union's very low standard of living finally began to improve and continued to rise substantially throughout the booming 1960s.

De-Stalinization created great ferment among writers and intellectuals who hungered for cultural freedom. The poet Boris Pasternak (1890–1960) finished his great novel *Doctor Zhivago* in 1956. Published in the West but not in Russia, *Doctor Zhivago* is both a literary masterpiece and a powerful challenge to communism. It tells the story of a prerevolutionary intellectual who rejects the violence and brutality of the revolution of 1917 and the Stalinist years. Even as he is destroyed, he triumphs because of his humanity and Christian spirit. Pasternak was denounced—but he was not shot. Other talented writers followed Pasternak's lead, and courageous editors let the sparks fly.

The writer Aleksandr Solzhenitsyn (b. 1918) created a sensation when his *One Day in the Life of Ivan Denisovich* was published in the Soviet Union in 1962. Solzhenitsyn's novel portrays in grim detail life in a Stalinist concentration camp—a life to which Solzhenitsyn himself had been unjustly condemned—and is a damning indictment of the Stalinist past.

Online Study Center Improve Your Grade
Primary Source: *One Day in the Life of Ivan Denisovich* Describes the Stalinist Gulag

Khrushchev also de-Stalinized Soviet foreign policy. "Peaceful coexistence" with capitalism was possible, he argued, and great wars were not inevitable. Khrushchev even made concessions, agreeing in 1955 to real independence for a neutral Austria after ten long years of Allied occupation. Thus there was considerable relaxation of cold war tensions between 1955 and 1957. At the same time, Khrushchev began wooing the new nations of Asia and Africa—even if they were not communist—with promises and aid.

De-Stalinization stimulated rebelliousness in the eastern European satellites. Having suffered in silence under Stalin, communist reformers and the masses were quickly emboldened to seek much greater liberty and national independence. Poland took the lead in 1956, when extensive rioting brought a new government that managed to win greater autonomy.

Hungary experienced a real and tragic revolution. Led by students and workers—the classic urban revolutionaries—the people of Budapest installed a liberal communist reformer as their new chief in October 1956. Soviet troops were forced to leave the country. But after the new government promised free elections and renounced Hungary's military alliance with Moscow, the Russian leaders ordered an invasion and crushed the national and democratic revolution. Fighting was bitter until the end, for the Hungarians hoped that the United States would come to their aid. When this did not occur, most people in eastern Europe concluded that their only hope was to strive for small domestic gains while following Russia obediently in foreign affairs.

The End of Reform

By late 1962, opposition in party circles to Khrushchev's policies was strong, and in 1964 Khrushchev fell in a bloodless palace revolution. Under Leonid Brezhnev (1906–1982), the Soviet Union began a period of stagnation and limited "re-Stalinization." The basic reason for this development was that Khrushchev's Communist colleagues saw de-Stalinization as a dangerous threat to the dictatorial authority of the party. The party had to tighten up considerably while there was still time. Khrushchev had to go.

Another reason for conservative opposition was that Khrushchev's policy toward the West was erratic and ultimately unsuccessful. In 1958 he ordered the Western allies to evacuate West Berlin within six months. In response, the allies reaffirmed their unity in West Berlin, and Khrushchev backed down. Then in 1961, as relations with communist China deteriorated dramatically, Khrushchev ordered the East Germans to build a wall between East and West Berlin, thereby sealing off West Berlin in clear violation of existing access agreements between the Great Powers. The recently elected U.S. president, John F. Kennedy, acquiesced to the construction of the Berlin Wall. Emboldened and seeing a chance to change the balance of military power decisively, Khrushchev ordered missiles with nuclear warheads installed in Fidel Castro's communist Cuba in 1962. President Kennedy countered with a naval blockade of Cuba. After a tense diplomatic crisis, Khrushchev agreed to remove the Soviet missiles in return for American pledges not to disturb Castro's regime. Khrushchev looked like a bumbling buffoon; his influence, already slipping, declined rapidly after the Cuban fiasco.

In 1964, Brezhnev and his supporters took over. Almost immediately they started talking quietly of Stalin's "good points" and ignoring his crimes. This change informed Soviet citizens that further liberalization could not be expected at home. Soviet leaders, determined never to suffer Khrushchev's humiliation in the face of American nuclear superiority, also launched a massive arms buildup. Yet Brezhnev and company proceeded cautiously in the mid-1960s and avoided direct confrontation with the United States.

In the wake of Khrushchev's reforms, the 1960s brought modest liberalization and more consumer goods to eastern Europe, as well as somewhat greater national autonomy, especially in Poland and Romania. In January 1968, the reform elements in the Czechoslovak Communist Party gained a majority and voted out the long-time Stalinist leader in favor of Alexander Dubček (1921–1992), whose new government launched dramatic reforms.

Educated in Moscow, Dubček was a dedicated Communist. But he and his allies believed that they could reconcile genuine socialism with personal freedom and internal party democracy. Thus local decision making by trade unions, managers, and consumers replaced rigid bureaucratic planning, and censorship was relaxed. The reform program proved enormously popular.

Although Dubček remembered the lesson of the Hungarian revolution and constantly proclaimed his loyalty to the Warsaw Pact, the determination of the Czechoslovak reformers to build what they called "socialism with a human face" frightened hard-line Communists. These fears were particularly strong in Poland and East Germany, where leaders knew full well that they lacked popular support. Moreover, the Soviet Union feared that a liberalized Czechoslovakia would eventually be drawn to neutrality or even to the democratic West. Thus the Eastern bloc countries launched a concerted campaign of intimidation against the Czechoslovak leaders, and in August 1968, 500,000 Russian and allied eastern European troops suddenly occupied Czechoslovakia. The Czechoslovaks made no attempt to resist militarily, and the arrested leaders surrendered to Soviet demands. The reform program was abandoned, and the Czechoslovak experiment in humanizing communism came to an end. Shortly after the invasion of Czechoslovakia, Brezhnev declared the so-called **Brezhnev Doctrine,** according to which the Soviet Union and its allies had the right to intervene in any socialist country whenever they saw the need.

The Invasion of Czechoslovakia Armed with Czechoslovakian flags, courageous Czechs in downtown Prague try to stop a Soviet tank and repel the invasion and occupation of their country by the Soviet Union and its eastern European allies. This dramatic confrontation marked a high point, because the Czechs and the Slovaks realized that military resistance would be suicidal. *(AP/Wide World Photos)*

The 1968 invasion of Czechoslovakia was the crucial event of the Brezhnev era, which really lasted beyond the aging leader's death in 1982 until the emergence in 1985 of Mikhail Gorbachev. The invasion demonstrated the determination of the ruling elite to maintain the status quo throughout the Soviet bloc. Only in the 1980s, with Poland taking the lead, would a strong current of reform and opposition develop again to challenge Communist rule.

The Soviet Union to 1985

Determined to maintain firm control of eastern Europe, Soviet leaders set the example at home. There was a certain **re-Stalinization** of the U.S.S.R., but now dictatorship was collective rather than personal, and coercion replaced terror. This compromise seemed to suit the leaders and a majority of the people.

A slowly rising standard of living for ordinary people contributed to the apparent stability in the Soviet Union, although long lines and innumerable shortages persisted. Ambitious individuals had a tremendous incentive to do as the state wished in order to gain access to special, well-stocked stores, to attend special schools, and to travel abroad.

Another source of stability was the enduring nationalism of ordinary Great Russians. Party leaders successfully identified themselves with Russian patriotism, stressing their role in saving the country during the Second World War and protecting it now from foreign foes, including eastern European "counter-revolutionaries." Moreover, the politically dominant Great Russians, who were concentrated in the central Russian heartland, generally feared that greater freedom might result in demands for autonomy and even independence not only by eastern European nationalities but also by the non-Russian nationalities within the Soviet Union itself.

The strength of the government was expressed in the re-Stalinization of culture and art. Critical free expression disappeared. Acts of open nonconformity and public protest were severely punished, but by sophisticated, cunning methods. Most frequently, dissidents were blacklisted and thus rendered unable to find decent jobs since the government was the only employer. This fate was enough to keep most in line. More determined protesters were quietly imprisoned, while celebrated nonconformists such as Aleksandr Solzhenitsyn were permanently expelled from the country. Eliminating the worst aspects of Stalin's dictatorship strengthened the regime, and almost all Western experts concluded that rule by a self-perpetuating Communist Party elite in the Soviet Union appeared to be quite solid in the 1970s and early 1980s.

Yet beneath the dreary immobility of political life in the Brezhnev era, the Soviet Union was actually experiencing profound changes. Three of these changes, which were seldom appreciated by Western observers at the time, were particularly significant.

First, the growth of the urban population, which had raced forward at breakneck speed in the Stalin years, continued rapidly in the 1960s and 1970s. In 1985 two-thirds of all Soviet citizens lived in cities, and one-quarter lived in big cities. Of great significance, this expanding urban population lost its old peasant ways, exchanging them for more education, better job skills, and greater sophistication.

Second, the number of highly trained scientists, managers, and specialists expanded prodigiously, increasing fourfold between 1960 and 1985. Thus the class of well-educated, pragmatic, and self-confident experts, which played such an important role in restructuring industrial societies after World War II (see the discussion in the next section), continued to develop rapidly in the Soviet Union after 1968.

Third, education and freedom for experts in their special areas helped foster the gradual growth of Soviet public opinion. Educated people read, discussed, and formed definite ideas on important issues, many of which could be approached and debated in "nonpolitical" terms. Developing ideas on such questions as environmental pollution and urban transportation, educated urban people increasingly saw themselves as worthy of having a voice in society's decisions, even its political decisions. While Brezhnev and his aging colleagues slept, a revolution was in the making.

Postwar Social Transformations, 1945–1968

While Europe staged its astonishing political and economic recovery from the Nazi nightmare, the patterns of everyday life and the structure of Western society were changing no less rapidly and remarkably. Epoch-making inventions and new technologies profoundly affected human existence. Important groups in society formulated new attitudes and demands, which were closely related to the changing class structure and social reforms. The structure of women's lives changed dramatically. An international youth culture took shape and rose to challenge established lifestyles and even governments.

- *How did changing patterns in technology, class relations, women's work, and youth culture bring major social transformations?*

Science and Technology

Ever since the scientific revolution of the seventeenth century and the Industrial Revolution at the end of the eighteenth century, scientific and technical developments had powerfully influenced attitudes, society, and everyday life. Never was this influence stronger than after about 1940. Science and technology proved so productive and influential because, for the first time in history, "pure theoretical" science and "practical" technology (or "applied" science) were effectively joined together on a massive scale.

With the advent of the Second World War, pure science lost its impractical innocence. Most leading university scientists went to work on top-secret projects to help their governments fight the war. The development by British scientists of radar to detect enemy aircraft was a particularly important outcome of this new kind of sharply focused research. A radically improved radar system played a key role in Britain's victory in the battle for air supremacy in 1940. The air war also greatly stimulated the development of jet aircraft and spurred further research on electronic computers, which calculated the complex mathematical relationships between fast-moving planes and anti-aircraft shells to increase the likelihood of a hit.

The most spectacular result of directed scientific research during the war was the atomic bomb. In August 1939, physicist Albert Einstein wrote to President Franklin Roosevelt that recent work in physics suggested that "it may become possible to set up a nuclear chain reaction in a large mass of uranium" and to construct "extremely powerful bombs of a new type."[5] This letter and ongoing experiments by nuclear physicists led to the top-secret Manhattan Project, which ballooned into a mammoth crash program. After three years of intensive effort, the first atomic bomb was successfully tested in July 1945. In August 1945, two bombs were dropped on Hiroshima and Nagasaki, thereby ending the war with Japan.

Online Study Center **Improve Your Grade**
Primary Source: Witness to the Birth of the Atomic Age

The atomic bomb showed the world both the awesome power and the heavy moral responsibilities of modern science and its high priests. As one Los Alamos scientist exclaimed as he watched the first mushroom cloud rise over the American desert, "We are all sons-of-bitches now!"[6]

The spectacular results of directed research during World War II inspired a new model for science—**Big Science**. By combining theoretical work with sophisticated engineering in a large organization, Big Science could attack extremely difficult problems, from better products for consumers to new and improved weapons for the military. Big Science was extremely expensive, requiring large-scale financing from governments and large corporations.

Populous, victorious, and wealthy, the United States took the lead in Big Science after World War II. Between 1945 and 1965, spending on scientific research and development in the United States grew five times as fast as the national income, and by 1965 such spending took 3 percent of all U.S. income. It was generally accepted that government should finance science heavily in both the "capitalist" United States and the "socialist" Soviet Union.

One reason for the parallel between the two countries was that science was not demobilized in either country after the war. Scientists remained a critical part of every major military establishment, and a large portion of all postwar scientific research went for "defense." New weapons such as rockets, nuclear submarines, and spy satellites demanded breakthroughs no less remarkable than those of radar and the first atomic bomb. After 1945 roughly one-quarter of all men and women trained in science and engineering in the West—and perhaps more in the Soviet Union—were employed full-time in the production of weapons to kill other humans.

Sophisticated science, lavish government spending, and military needs all came together in the space race of the 1960s. In 1957 the Soviets used long-range rockets developed in their nuclear weapons program to put a satellite in orbit. In 1961 they sent the world's first cosmonaut circling the globe. Embarrassed by Soviet triumphs, the United States made an all-out U.S. commitment to catch up with the Soviets and landed a crewed spacecraft on the moon in 1969. Four more moon landings followed by 1972.

The rapid expansion of government-financed research in the United States attracted many of Europe's best scientists during the 1950s and 1960s. Thoughtful Europeans lamented this "brain drain" and feared that Europe was falling hopelessly behind the United States in science and technology. In fact, a revitalized Europe was already responding to the American challenge, with countries pooling their efforts on such Big Science projects as the Concorde supersonic passenger airliner and the peaceful uses of atomic energy.

The rise of Big Science and of close ties between science and technology greatly altered the lives of scientists. The scientific community grew much larger than ever before. There were about four times as many scientists in Europe and North America in 1975 as in 1945. Scientists, technologists, engineers, and medical specialists were counted after 1945, in part because there were so many of them.

One consequence of the growth of science was its high degree of specialization, for no one could possibly master a broad field such as physics or medicine. Intense specialization in new disciplines and subdisciplines increased the rates at which both basic knowledge was acquired and practical applications were made.

Highly specialized modern scientists and technologists normally had to work as members of a team, which completely changed the work and lifestyle of modern scientists. A great deal of work therefore went on in large bureaucratic organizations, where the individual was very often a small cog in a great machine. The growth of large scientific bureaucracies in government and private enterprise suggested how scientists and technologists permeated the entire society and many aspects of life.

Modern science became highly, even brutally, competitive. This competitiveness is well depicted in Nobel Prize winner James Watson's fascinating book *The Double Helix*, which tells how in 1953 Watson and an Englishman, Francis Crick, discovered the structure of DNA, the molecule of heredity. A brash young American Ph.D. in his twenties, Watson seemed almost obsessed by the idea that some other research team would find the solution first and thereby deprive him of the fame and fortune he desperately wanted. With so many thousands of like-minded researchers in the wealthy countries of the world, scientific and technical knowledge rushed forward in the postwar era.

The Changing Class Structure

Rapid economic growth went a long way toward creating a new society in Europe after the Second World War. European society became more mobile and more democratic. Old class barriers relaxed, and class distinctions became fuzzier.

Changes in the structure of the middle class were particularly influential in the general drift toward a less rigid class structure. In the nineteenth and early twentieth centuries, the model for the middle class had been the independent, self-employed individual who owned a business or practiced a liberal profession such as law or medicine. Ownership of property—very often inherited property—and strong family ties had often been the keys to wealth and standing within the middle class. After 1945 this pattern declined drastically in western Europe. A new breed of managers and experts replaced traditional property owners as the leaders of the middle class. Ability to serve the needs of a big organization largely replaced inherited property and family connections in determining an individual's social position in the middle and upper middle classes. At the same time, the middle class grew massively and became harder to define.

There were several reasons for these developments. Rapid industrial and technological expansion created in large corporations and government agencies a powerful demand for technologists and managers. Moreover, the old propertied middle class lost control of many family-owned businesses, and many small businesses (including family farms) simply passed out of existence as their former owners joined the ranks of salaried employees.

Top managers and ranking civil servants therefore represented the model for a new middle class of salaried specialists. Well paid and highly trained, often with backgrounds in engineering or accounting, these experts increasingly came from all social classes, even the working class. Pragmatic and realistic, they were primarily concerned with efficiency and practical solutions to concrete problems. This new middle class was more open, democratic, and insecure than the old propertied middle class.

The structure of the lower classes also became more flexible and open. There was a mass exodus from farms and the countryside, as one of the most traditional and least mobile groups in European society drastically declined. Meanwhile, the industrial working class ceased to expand and began to decline, while job opportunities for white-collar and service employees grew rapidly. Such employees bore a greater resemblance to the new middle class of salaried specialists than to industrial workers, who were also better educated and more specialized.

European governments were reducing class tensions with a series of social security reforms. Many of these reforms—such as increased unemployment benefits and more extensive old-age pensions—simply strengthened social security measures first pioneered in Bismarck's Germany before the First World War (see page 833). Other programs were new, like comprehensive national health systems directed by the state. Most countries introduced family allowances—direct government grants to parents to help them raise their children. These allowances helped many poor families make ends meet. Most European governments also gave maternity grants and built inexpensive public housing for low-income families and individuals. These and other social reforms provided a humane floor of well-being. Reforms also promoted greater equality because they were expensive and were paid for in part by higher taxes on the rich.

Consumers on the Move In the early postwar years the Italians had their motor scooters and the French their motorbikes. This ad promises young people that "sooner or later" they will have a "Velo," and it subtly assures housewives that the bike is safe. In small towns and villages the slow-moving motorbike could be a godsend for errands and daily shopping. *(Roger Perrin/The Bridgeman Art Library)*

The rising standard of living and the spread of standardized consumer goods also worked to level Western society, as the percentage of income spent on food and drink declined substantially. For example, the European automobile industry expanded phenomenally after lagging far behind the United States since the 1920s. In 1948 there were only 5 million cars in western Europe, but in 1965 there were 44 million. Car ownership was democratized and came within the range of better-paid workers.

Europeans took great pleasure in the products of the "gadget revolution" as well. Like Americans, Europeans filled their houses and apartments with washing machines, vacuum cleaners, refrigerators, dishwashers, radios, TVs, and stereos. The purchase of consumer goods was greatly facilitated by installment purchasing, which allowed people to buy on credit. With the expansion of social security safeguards, reducing the need to accumulate savings for hard times and old age, ordinary people were increasingly willing to take on debt. This change had far-reaching consequences.

Leisure and recreation occupied an important place in consumer societies. The most astonishing leisure-time development was the blossoming of mass travel and tourism. With month-long paid vacations required by law in most European countries and widespread automobile ownership, beaches and ski resorts came within the reach of the middle class and much of the working class. By the late 1960s, packaged tours with cheap group flights and bargain hotel accommodations had made even distant lands easily accessible. A French company grew rich building imitation Tahitian paradises around the world. At Swedish nudist colonies on secluded West African beaches, officeworkers from Stockholm fleetingly worshiped the sun in the middle of the long northern winter. Truly, consumerism had come of age.

New Roles for Women

A growing emancipation of women in Europe and North America was unquestionably one of the most significant transformations of the cold war era. This historic development grew out of long-term changes in the basic patterns of motherhood and paid work outside the home. These changing patterns altered women's experiences and expectations, preparing the way for the success of a new generation of feminist thinkers and a militant women's movement in the 1970s and 1980s (see pages 1009–1010).

Before the Industrial Revolution, most Europeans married late. Once a woman was married, however, she usually had children as long as she was fertile. By the late nineteenth century, improved diet, higher incomes, and the use of contraception within marriage were producing the demographic transition from high birthrates and death rates to low birthrates and death rates.

These trends continued in the twentieth century. In the 1950s and 1960s, the typical woman in the West married early and bore her children quickly. The postwar baby boom did make for larger families and a fairly rapid population growth of 1 to 1.5 percent per year in many European countries. However, in the 1960s the long-term decline in birthrates resumed, and from the mid-1970s on in many European countries, the total population practically stopped growing from natural increase, with limited subsequent growth coming mainly from immigration.

The postwar culmination of the trends toward early marriage, early childbearing, and small family size in wealthy urban societies had revolutionary implications for women. Above all, pregnancy and child care occupied a much smaller portion of a woman's life than in earlier times. By the early 1970s, about half of Western women were having their last baby by the age of twenty-six or twenty-seven. When the youngest child trooped off to kindergarten, the average mother had more than forty years of life in front of her.

This was a momentous change. Throughout history male-dominated society insisted on defining most women as mothers or potential mothers, and motherhood was very demanding. In the postwar years, however, motherhood no longer absorbed the energies of a lifetime, and more and more married women looked for new roles in the world of work outside the family.

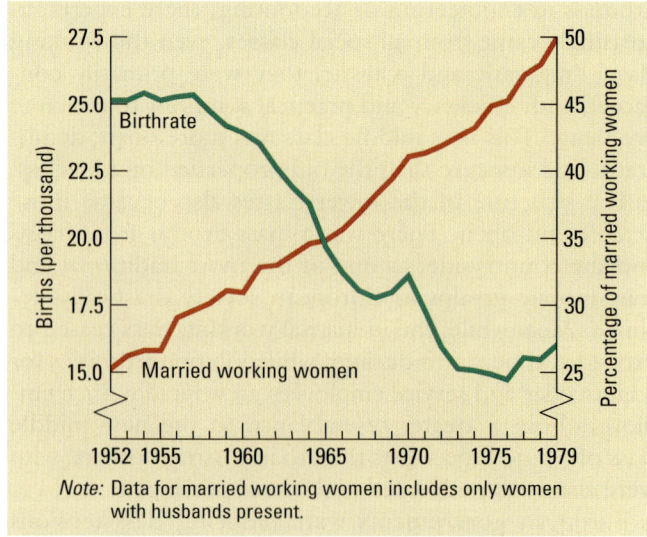

FIGURE 30.1 **The Decline of the Birthrate and the Increase of Married Working Women in the United States, 1952–1979** The challenge of working away from home encouraged American wives to prefer fewer children and helped lower the birthrate.

For centuries before the Industrial Revolution, ordinary women worked hard and long on farms and in home industries while caring for their large families. With the growth of modern industry and much more rigid gender roles, few middle-class women worked outside the home for wages, although charity work was socially acceptable. Young unmarried women continued to work as wage earners, but poor married women typically earned their money at home in low-paid crafts as they looked after their children.

In the twentieth century and especially after World War II, the ever-greater complexity of the modern economy meant that almost all women had to go outside the home to find cash income. Three major forces helped women searching for jobs. First, the economy boomed from about 1950 to 1973 and created a strong demand for labor. Second, the economy continued its gradual shift away from the old, male-dominated heavy industries, such as coal, steel, and shipbuilding, to the more dynamic, "white-collar" service industries, such as government, education, trade, and health care. Some women had always worked in these service fields. Third, young Western women shared fully in the postwar education revolution and could take advantage of the growing need for officeworkers and well-trained professionals. Thus more and more married women became full-time and part-time wage earners.

The trend went the furthest in communist eastern Europe, where women accounted for almost half of all employed persons. In noncommunist western Europe and North America, there was a good deal of variation, with the percentage of married women in the workforce rising from a range of roughly 20 to 25 percent in 1950 to a range of 40 to 70 percent in the early 1980s.

Rising employment for married women went hand in hand with the decline of the birthrate (see Figure 30.1). Women who worked outside the home had significantly fewer children than women of the same age who did not. Raising a family while holding down a full-time job was a tremendous challenge and often resulted in a woman's being grossly overworked. The multiple demands of job, motherhood, and marriage became more manageable with fewer children.

Married women entering (or re-entering) the labor force faced widespread, long-established discrimination in pay,

Celebrating Women's History Judy Chicago's multimedia creation *The Dinner Party* features thirty-nine handcrafted placemats and ceramic plates, each embellished with a painted motif associated with the woman being honored. Begun in 1974 and completed in 1978 with the participation of more than one hundred women, *The Dinner Party* was intended to represent the "historic struggle of women to participate in all the aspects of society." It attracted enormous crowds. *(© 2007 Judy Chicago/Artists Rights Society [ARS], New York)*

advancement, and occupational choice in comparison to men. Moreover, many women could find only part-time work. As the divorce rate rose in the 1960s, part-time work, with its low pay and scanty benefits, meant poverty for many women with teenage children. Finally, in the best of circumstances, married working women still carried most of the child-raising and housekeeping responsibilities. A reason for many to accept part-time employment, this gendered imbalance meant an exhausting "double day"—on the job and at home—for the full-time worker.

The injustices that married women encountered as wage earners contributed greatly to the subsequent movement for women's equality and emancipation. A young unmarried woman of a hundred years ago was more likely to accept such problems as temporary nuisances because she looked forward to marriage and motherhood for fulfillment. In the postwar era, a married wage earner in her thirties gradually developed a very different perspective. She saw employment as a permanent condition within which she, like her male counterpart, sought not only income but also psychological satisfaction. Sexism and discrimination in the workplace—and in the home—grew loathsome and evoked the sense of injustice that drives revolutions and reforms. When powerful voices arose to challenge the system, they found widespread support among working women.

Youth and the Counterculture

Economic prosperity and a more democratic class structure had a powerful impact on youth throughout the Western world. The bulging cohort of youth born after World War II developed a distinctive and very international youth culture, which eventually became a "counterculture" that rebelled against parents, authority figures, and the status quo.

Young people in the United States took the lead. American college students in the 1950s were often dismissed as the "Silent Generation," but by the late 1950s the "beat" movement was stoking the fires of revolt in selected urban enclaves, such as the Near North Side of Chicago. There the young (and the not-so-young) fashioned a highly publicized subculture that blended radical politics, unbridled personal experimentation (with drugs and communal living, for example), and new artistic styles. This subculture quickly spread to major American and western European cities. The young folksinger Bob Dylan summed up the increasingly radical political and cultural aspirations of the "younger generation" in lyrics that became a rallying cry, "the times they are a'changing."[7]

Certainly the sexual behavior of young people appeared to change dramatically in the 1960s and into the 1970s. More young people engaged in sexual intercourse, and they did so at an earlier age, in part because the discovery of safe and effective contraceptive pills could eliminate the risk of unwanted pregnancy. A 1973 study reported that only 4.5 percent of West German youths born in 1945 and 1946 had experienced sexual relations before their seventeenth birthday but that 32 percent of those born in 1953 and 1954 had done so.[8] Perhaps even more significant was the growing tendency of young unmarried people to live together in a separate

Woodstock, 1969 The brainchild of four young entrepreneurs, Woodstock snowballed into the world's biggest rock concert, a three-day bash in upstate New York that drew 450,000 guests and caused twenty-mile traffic jams. Standout performers included the guitarist Jimi Hendrix, Janis Joplin, and Joe Cocker. A high point for the youth culture, with antiwar and free love overtones, Woodstock spawned many myths and conflicting interpretations. (© Lisa Law)

Student Rebellion in Paris These rock-throwing students in the Latin Quarter of Paris are trying to force education reforms and even to topple de Gaulle's government. Throughout May 1968 students clashed repeatedly with France's tough riot police in bloody street fighting. De Gaulle remained in power, but a major reform of French education did follow. *(Bruno Barbey/Magnum Photos)*

household on a semipermanent basis, with little thought of getting married or having children. Thus many youths, especially middle-class youths, defied social custom, claiming in effect that the long-standing monopoly of married couples on legitimate sexual unions was dead.

Several factors contributed to the emergence of the international youth culture in the 1960s. First, mass communications and youth travel linked countries and continents together. Second, the postwar baby boom meant that young people became an unusually large part of the population and could therefore exercise exceptional influence on society as a whole. Third, postwar prosperity and greater equality gave young people more purchasing power than ever before. This enabled them to set their own trends and patterns of consumption, which fostered generational loyalty. Finally, prosperity meant that good jobs were readily available. Students and young job seekers had little need to fear punishment from strait-laced employers for unconventional behavior.

The youth culture practically fused with the counterculture in opposition to the established order in the late 1960s. Student protesters embraced romanticism and revolutionary idealism, dreaming of complete freedom and simpler, purer societies. The materialistic West was hopelessly rotten, but better societies were being built in the newly independent countries of Asia and Africa, or so many young radicals believed. Thus the Vietnam War took on special significance. Many politically active students believed that the older generation was fighting an immoral and imperialistic war against a small and heroic people. As the war in Vietnam intensified, so did worldwide student opposition to it.

Student protests in western Europe also highlighted more general problems of youth, education, and a society of specialists. In contrast to the United States, high school and university educations in Europe had been limited for centuries to a small elite. Whereas 22 percent of the American population was going on to some form of higher education in 1950, only 3 to 4 percent of western European youths were doing so. Then enrollments skyrocketed. By 1960 at least three times as many students were going to some kind of university as had attended before the war, and the number continued to rise sharply until the 1970s. Reflecting the development of a more democratic class structure and a growing awareness that higher education was the key to success, European universities gave more scholarships and opened their doors to more students from the lower middle and lower classes.

The rapid expansion of higher education meant that classes were badly overcrowded. Competition for grades became intense. Moreover, although more practical areas of study were gradually added, many students felt that they were not getting the kind of education they needed for jobs in the modern world. At the same time, some reflective students feared that universities would soon do nothing but turn out docile technocrats both to stock and to serve "the establishment."

The many tensions within the exploding university population came to a head in the late 1960s and early 1970s. As in the United States, European university students rose to challenge their university administrations and even their governments. The most far-reaching of these revolts occurred in France in 1968. Students occupied buildings and took over the University of Paris, which led to violent clashes with police. Rank-and-file workers ignored the advice of their cautious union officials, and a more or less spontaneous general strike spread across France in May 1968. It seemed certain that President de Gaulle's Fifth Republic would collapse.

In fact, de Gaulle stiffened, like an old-fashioned irate father. He moved troops toward Paris and called for new elections. Thoroughly frightened by the student-sparked upheaval and fearing an eventual communist takeover, the masses of France voted overwhelmingly for de Gaulle's party and a return to law and order. Workers went back to work, and the mini-revolution collapsed. Yet the proud de Gaulle and the postwar European renaissance that he represented had been shaken, and within a year he resigned. Growing out of the counterculture and youthful idealism, the student rebellion of 1968 signaled the end of an era and the return of unrest and uncertainty in the 1970s and early 1980s.

Conflict and Challenge in the Late Cold War, 1968–1985

Similar to but more important than the student upheaval in France and the crushing of socialist reform in Czechoslovakia, the Vietnam War marked the beginning of a new era of challenges and uncertainties in the late 1960s. The Vietnam War and its aftermath divided the people of the United States, shook the ideology of containment, and weakened the Western alliance. A second challenge affecting the whole world appeared when the great postwar economic boom came to a close in 1973, opening a long period of economic stagnation, widespread unemployment, and social dislocation.

- *What were the key aspects of political conflict, economic stagnation, and the feminist movement in the late cold war?*

The United States and Vietnam

President Johnson wanted to go down in history as a master reformer and a healer of old wounds. Instead, he opened new ones with the Vietnam War.

Although many student radicals believed that imperialism was the main cause, American involvement in Vietnam was more clearly a product of the cold war and the policy of containment (see page 984). From the late 1940s on, most Americans and their leaders viewed the world in terms of a constant struggle to stop the spread of communism. As western Europe began to revive and China established a communist government in 1949, efforts to contain communism shifted to Asia. The bloody Korean War (1950–1953) ended in stalemate, but the United States did succeed in preventing a communist victory in South Korea. After the defeat of the French in Vietnam in 1954, the Eisenhower administration refused to sign the Geneva Accords that temporarily divided the country into two zones pending national unification by means of free elections. President Eisenhower then acquiesced in the refusal of the anticommunist South Vietnamese government to accept the verdict of elections and provided it with military aid. President Kennedy greatly increased the number of American "military advisers" to sixteen thousand.

After winning the 1964 election on a peace platform, President Johnson greatly expanded the American role in the Vietnam conflict. American strategy was to "escalate" the war sufficiently to break the will of the North Vietnamese and their southern allies without resorting to "overkill," which might risk war with the entire Communist bloc. Thus South Vietnam received massive military aid, American forces in the South gradually grew to half a million men, and the United States bombed North Vietnam with ever-greater intensity. But there was no invasion of the North or naval blockade. In the end, the American strategy of limited warfare backfired. It was the American people who grew weary and the American leadership that cracked.

The undeclared war in Vietnam, fought nightly on American television, eventually divided the nation. Initial support was strong. The politicians, the media, and the population as a whole saw the war as part of a legitimate defense against communist totalitarianism in all poor countries. But an antiwar movement quickly emerged on college campuses, where the prospect of being drafted to fight savage battles in Asian jungles made male stomachs churn. In October 1965, student protesters joined forces with old-line socialists, New Left intellectuals, and pacifists in antiwar demonstrations in fifty American cities. By 1967 a growing number of critics denounced the war as a criminal intrusion into a complex and distant civil war.

Criticism reached a crescendo after the Vietcong Tet Offensive in January 1968. This, the communists' first comprehensive attack with conventional weapons on major cities in South Vietnam, failed militarily: the Vietcong suffered heavy losses, and the attack did not spark a mass uprising. But Washington had been claiming that victory in South Vietnam was in sight, and U.S. critics of the Vietnam War quickly interpreted the bloody combat as a decisive American defeat. America's leaders lost heart. In 1968, after a narrow victory in the New Hampshire primary, President Johnson called for negotiations with North Vietnam and announced that he would not stand for re-election.

Elected by a razor-slim margin in 1968, President Richard Nixon (1913–1994) sought to gradually disengage America from Vietnam and the accompanying national crisis. Intensifying the continuous bombardment of the enemy while simultaneously pursuing peace talks with the North Vietnamese, Nixon suspended the draft, so hated on college campuses, and cut American forces in Vietnam from 550,000 to 24,000 in four years. The cost of the war dropped dramatically. Moreover, President Nixon launched a flank attack in diplomacy. He journeyed to China in 1972 and reached a spectacular if limited reconciliation with the People's Republic of China. In doing so, Nixon took advantage of China's growing fears of the Soviet Union and undermined North Vietnam's position.

Fortified by the overwhelming endorsement of the voters in his 1972 electoral triumph, President Nixon and Secretary of State Henry Kissinger finally reached a peace agreement with North Vietnam. The agreement allowed remaining American forces to complete their withdrawal, and the United States reserved the right to resume bombing if the accords were broken. Fighting declined markedly in South Vietnam, where the South Vietnamese army appeared to hold its own against the Vietcong. The storm of crisis in the United States seemed to have passed.

On the contrary, the country reaped the **Watergate** whirlwind. Like some other recent American presidents, Nixon authorized spying activities that went beyond the law. Going further than his predecessors, he allowed special units to use various illegal means to stop the leaking of government documents to the press. One such group broke into the Democratic Party headquarters in Washington's Watergate complex in June 1972 and was promptly arrested. Nixon and many of his assistants then tried to hush up the bungled job, but the media and the machinery of congressional investigation eventually exposed the administration's web of lies and lawbreak-

Seymour Chwast: End Bad Breath Antiwar messages came in every shape and form as opposition to the Vietnam War heated up. This vibrant poster assumes, quite reasonably, that the American viewer is steeped in the popular culture of the mass media. It ridicules American military involvement with a sarcastic parody of familiar television commercials. *(Courtesy, Seymour Chwast/Push Pin Group)*

ing. In 1974 a beleaguered Nixon was forced to resign in disgrace.

The consequences of renewed political crisis flowing from the Watergate affair were profound. First, Watergate resulted in a major shift of power away from the presidency and toward Congress, especially in foreign affairs. Therefore, as American aid to South Vietnam diminished in 1973 and as an emboldened North Vietnam launched a general invasion against South Vietnamese armies in early 1974, Congress refused to permit any American military response. A second consequence of the U.S. crisis was that after more than thirty-five years of battle, the Vietnamese communists unified their country in 1975 as a harsh dictatorial state. Third, the belated fall of South Vietnam in the wake of Watergate shook America's postwar confidence and left the country divided and uncertain about its proper role in world affairs.

Détente or Cold War?

One alternative to the badly damaged policy of containing communism was the policy of **détente,** or the progressive piecemeal relaxation of cold war tensions. Thus while the cold war continued to rage outside Europe and generally defined superpower relations between the Soviet Union and the United States, West Germany took a major step toward genuine peace in Europe.

West German chancellor Willy Brandt (1913–1992) took the lead when in December 1970 he flew to Poland for the signing of a historic treaty of reconciliation. In a dramatic moment rich in symbolism, Brandt laid a wreath at the tomb of the Polish unknown soldier and another at the monument commemorating the armed uprising of Warsaw's Jewish ghetto against occupying Nazi armies. Standing before the ghetto memorial, a somber Brandt fell to his knees and knelt as if in prayer. "I wanted," Brandt said later, "to ask pardon in the name of our people for a million-fold crime which was committed in the misused name of the Germans."⁹

Brandt's gesture at the Warsaw Ghetto memorial and the treaty with Poland were part of his policy of reconciliation with eastern Europe. Indeed, Brandt aimed at nothing less than a comprehensive peace settlement for central Europe and the two German states established after 1945. The Federal Republic of Germany (West Germany) had long claimed that the communist German Democratic Republic (East Germany) lacked free elections and hence any legal or moral basis. West Germany also refused to accept the loss of German territory taken by Poland and the Soviet Union after 1945. But Brandt, the popular socialist mayor of West Berlin when the Berlin Wall was built in 1961, believed that the wall showed the painful limitations of West Germany's official hard line toward communist eastern Europe. A new foreign policy was needed.

Winning the chancellorship in 1969, Brandt negotiated treaties with the Soviet Union, Poland, and Czechoslovakia that formally accepted existing state boundaries in return for a mutual renunciation of force or the threat of force. Using the imaginative formula of "two German states within one German nation," Brandt's government also broke decisively with the past and entered into direct relations with East Germany. He aimed for modest practical improvements rather than reunification, which at that point was completely impractical.

The policy of détente reached its high point when all European nations (except isolationist Albania), the United States, and Canada signed the Final Act of the Helsinki Conference in 1975. The thirty-five nations participating agreed that Europe's existing political frontiers could not be changed by force. They also solemnly accepted numerous provisions guaranteeing the human rights and political freedoms of their citizens.

Online Study Center Improve Your Grade
Primary Source: The Helsinki Final Act: Human Rights and Fundamental Freedoms Enunciated

Optimistic hopes for détente in international relations gradually faded in the later 1970s. Brezhnev's Soviet Union ignored the human rights provisions of the Helsinki agreement, and East-West political competition remained very much alive outside Europe. Many Americans became convinced that the Soviet Union was taking advantage of détente, steadily building up its military might and pushing for political gains and revolutions in Africa, Asia, and Latin America. The Soviet invasion of Afghanistan in December 1979, which was designed to save an increasingly unpopular Marxist regime, was especially alarming. Many Americans feared that the oil-rich states of the Persian Gulf would be next, and once again they looked to the Atlantic alliance and military might to thwart communist expansion.

President Jimmy Carter (b. 1924), elected in 1976, tried to lead the Atlantic alliance beyond verbal condemnation and urged economic sanctions against the Soviet Union. Yet only Great Britain among the European allies supported the American initiative. The alliance showed the same lack of concerted action when the Solidarity movement rose in Poland. Some observers concluded that the alliance had lost the will to think and act decisively in dealing with the Soviet bloc.

The Atlantic alliance endured, however. The U.S. military buildup launched by Carter in his last years in office was greatly accelerated by President Ronald Reagan (1911–2004), who was swept into office in 1980 by a wave of patriotism and economic discontent. The new American leadership acted as if the military balance had tipped in favor of the Soviet Union, which Reagan anathematized as the "evil empire." Increasing defense spending enormously, the Reagan administration concentrated on nuclear arms and an expanded navy as keys to American power in the post-Vietnam age.

A broad swing in the historical pendulum toward greater conservatism in the 1980s gave Reagan invaluable allies in western Europe. In Great Britain a strong-willed Margaret Thatcher worked well with Reagan and was a forceful advocate for a revitalized Atlantic alliance. After a strongly pro-American Helmut Kohl (b. 1930) came to power with the conservative Christian Democrats in 1982, West Germany and the United States once again effectively coordinated military and political policy toward the Soviet bloc.

Passing in the 1970s and early 1980s from détente to confusion to regeneration, the Atlantic alliance bent, but it did not break. In maintaining the alliance, the Western nations gave indirect support to ongoing efforts to liberalize authoritarian communist eastern Europe and probably helped convince the Soviet Union's Mikhail Gorbachev that endless cold war conflict was foolish and dangerous.

The Women's Movement

The 1970s marked the birth of a broad-based feminist movement devoted to securing genuine gender equality and promoting the general interests of women. Three basic reasons accounted for this major development. First, ongoing changes in underlying patterns of motherhood and paid work created novel conditions and new demands (see pages 1002–1004). Second, a vanguard of feminist intellectuals articulated a powerful critique of gender relations, which stimulated many women to rethink their assumptions and challenge the status quo. Third, taking a lesson from the civil rights movement in the United States and worldwide student protest against the Vietnam War, dissatisfied individuals recognized that they had to band together if they were to influence politics and secure fundamental reforms.

One of the most influential works produced by this new feminist wave was *The Second Sex* (1949) by the French writer and philosopher Simone de Beauvoir (1908–1986). Characterizing herself as a "dutiful daughter" of the bourgeoisie in childhood, the adolescent Beauvoir came to see her pious and submissive mother as foolishly renouncing any self-expression outside of home and marriage and showing Beauvoir the dangers of a life she did not want. A brilliant university student, Beauvoir began at the Sorbonne a complex relationship with Jean-Paul Sartre, the future philosopher who became her lifelong intellectual companion and sometime lover.

Beauvoir analyzed the position of women within the framework of existential thought (see pages 916–917). She argued that women—like all human beings—were in essence free but that they had almost always been trapped by particularly inflexible and limiting conditions. (See the feature "Listening to the Past: A Feminist Critique of Marriage" on pages 1016–1017.) Only by means of courageous action and self-assertive creativity could a woman become a completely free person and escape the role of the inferior "other" that men had constructed for her gender. Drawing on history, philosophy, psychology, biology, and literature, Beauvoir's massive investigation inspired a generation of women intellectuals.

Online Study Center Improve Your Grade
Primary Source: *The Second Sex*: Existential Feminism

One such woman was Betty Friedan (b. 1924), who played a key role in reopening a serious discussion of women's issues in the United States. As a working wife and the mother of three small children in the 1950s, Friedan became acutely aware of the conflicting pressures of career and family. Conducting an in-depth survey of her classmates at Smith College fifteen years after their graduation, she concluded that many well-educated women shared her growing dissatisfaction. In her pathbreaking study *The Feminine Mystique* (1963), Friedan identified this dissatisfaction as the "problem that has no name." According to Friedan, the cause of this nameless problem was a crisis of identity. Women were not permitted to become mature adults and genuine human beings. Instead, they were expected to conform to a false, infantile pattern of femininity and live (like Beauvoir's mother) for their husbands and children. In short, women faced what feminists would soon call *sexism*, a pervasive social problem that required drastic reforms.

When long-standing proposals to treat sex discrimination as seriously as race discrimination fell again on deaf ears, Friedan took the lead in 1966 in founding the National Organization for Women (NOW) to press for women's rights. NOW flourished, growing from seven hundred members in 1967 to forty thousand in 1974. Many other women's organizations of varying persuasions rose to follow NOW in Europe and the United States. Throughout the 1970s, a proliferation of publications, conferences, and institutions devoted to women's issues reinforced the emerging international movement.

Although national peculiarities abounded, this movement generally shared the common strategy of entering the political arena and changing laws regarding women. First, advocates of women's rights pushed for new statutes in the workplace: laws against discrimination, "equal pay for equal work," and measures such as maternal leave and affordable day care designed to help women combine careers and family responsibilities. Second, the movement concentrated on gender and family questions, including the right to divorce (in some Catholic countries), legalized abortion, the needs of single mothers, and protection from rape and physical violence. In almost every country, the effort to decriminalize abortion served as a catalyst in mobilizing an effective, self-conscious women's movement (and in creating an opposition to it, as in the United States).

In countries that had long placed women in a subordinate position, the legal changes were little less than revolutionary. In Italy, for example, new laws abolished restrictions on divorce and abortion, which had been strengthened by Mussolini and defended energetically by the Catholic Church in the postwar era. By 1988 divorce

Italian Feminists These women demonstrate in Rome in 1981 for the passage of legislation legalizing abortion, which the pope and the Catholic Church have steadfastly opposed. This woman's provocative sign says that she does not want the pope in her bed. *(Giansanti/Corbis Sygma)*

and abortion were common in Italy, which had the lowest birthrate in Europe. More generally, the sharply focused women's movement of the 1970s won new rights for women. Subsequently, the movement became more diffuse, a victim of both its successes and the resurgence of an antifeminist opposition.

The accomplishments of the women's movement encouraged mobilization by many other groups. Gay men and lesbian women pressed their own demands, organizing politically and calling for an end to legal discrimination and social harassment. People with physical disabilities joined together to promote their interests. Thus many subordinate groups challenged the dominant majorities,

and the expansion and redefinition of human liberty—one of the great themes of modern Western and world history—continued.

The Troubled Economy

For twenty years after 1945, most Europeans were preoccupied with the possibilities of economic progress and consumerism. The more democratic class structure also helped to reduce social tension, and ideological conflict went out of style. In the late 1960s, sharp criticism and social conflict re-emerged, however, marking the passing of postwar stability.

Yet it was the reappearance of economic crisis in the early 1970s that brought the most serious challenges for the average person. The postwar international monetary system was based on the American dollar, valued in gold at $35 an ounce. Giving foreign aid and fighting foreign wars, the United States sent billions abroad. By early 1971, it had only $11 billion in gold left, and Europe had accumulated U.S. $50 billion. Foreigners then panicked and raced to exchange their dollars for gold. President Richard Nixon responded by stopping the sale of American gold. The value of the dollar fell sharply, and inflation accelerated worldwide. Fixed rates of exchange were abandoned, and great uncertainty replaced postwar predictability in international trade and finance.

Even more damaging was the dramatic reversal in the price and availability of energy. The great postwar boom was fueled by cheap oil from the Middle East, which permitted energy-intensive industries—automobiles, chemicals, and electric power—to expand rapidly and lead other sectors of the economy forward. By 1971 the Arab-led Organization of Petroleum Exporting Countries (**OPEC**) had watched the price of crude oil decline consistently compared with the rising price of manufactured goods and had decided to reverse that trend by presenting a united front against the oil companies. The stage was set for a revolution in energy prices during the fourth Arab-Israeli war in October 1973, when Egypt and Syria launched a surprise attack on Israel. OPEC then declared an embargo on oil shipments to the United States, Israel's ally, and within a year crude oil prices quadrupled. Western nations realized that the rapid price rise was economically destructive, but they did nothing. Thus governments, industry, and individuals had no other choice than to deal piecemeal with the so-called oil shock—a "shock" that turned out to be an earthquake.

Coming on the heels of upheaval in the international monetary system, the revolution in energy prices plunged the world into its worst economic decline since the 1930s.

The energy-intensive industries that had driven the economy up in the 1950s and 1960s now dragged it down. Unemployment rose; productivity and living standards declined. By 1976 a modest recovery was in progress. But when a fundamentalist Islamic revolution struck Iran and oil production collapsed in that country, the price of crude oil doubled in 1979 and the world economy succumbed to its second oil shock. Unemployment and inflation rose dramatically before another uneven recovery began in 1982. In 1985 the unemployment rate in western Europe rose to its highest level since the Great Depression. Nineteen million people were unemployed.

One telling measure of the troubled economy was the **misery index,** which combined rates of inflation and unemployment in a single, powerfully emotional number. Figure 30.2 shows a comparison of misery indexes for the United States, Japan, and the Common Market countries between 1970 and 1986. "Misery" increased on both sides of the Atlantic, but the increase was substantially greater in western Europe, where these hard times were often referred to simply as "the crisis." Japan did better than both Europe and the United States in this period.

Throughout the 1970s and 1980s, anxious observers, recalling the disastrous consequences of the Great Depression, worried that the Common Market would disintegrate in the face of severe economic dislocation and that economic nationalism would halt steps toward European unity. Yet the Common Market—now officially known as the European Economic Community—continued to attract new members. In 1973 Denmark and Iceland, in addition to Britain, finally joined. Greece joined in 1981, and Portugal and Spain entered in 1986. The nations of the European Economic Community also cooperated more closely in international undertakings, and the movement toward unity for western Europe stayed alive.

Society in a Time of Economic Uncertainty

The most pervasive consequences of economic stagnation in the 1970s and early 1980s were probably psychological and attitudinal. Optimism gave way to pessimism; romantic utopianism yielded to sober realism. This drastic change in mood—a complete surprise only to those who had never studied history—affected states, institutions, and individuals in countless ways.

To be sure, there were heartbreaking human tragedies—lost jobs, bankruptcies, homelessness, and mental breakdowns. But on the whole, the welfare system fashioned in the postwar era prevented mass suffering and degradation

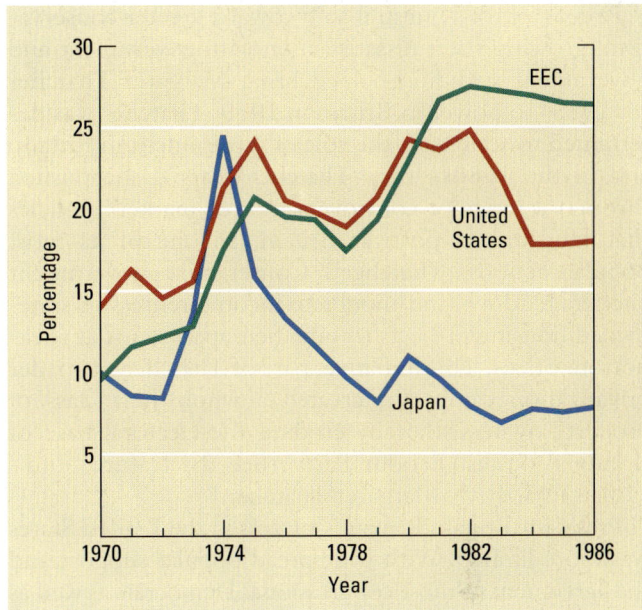

FIGURE 30.2 The Misery Index, 1970–1986 Combining rates of unemployment and inflation provided a simple but effective measure of economic hardship. This particular index represents the sum of two times the unemployment rate plus the inflation rate, reflecting the widespread belief that joblessness causes more suffering than higher prices. EEC = European Economic Community, or Common Market countries. (Source: OECD data, as given in *The Economist*, June 15, 1985, p. 69.)

through extended benefits for the unemployed, pensions for the aged, free medical care and special allowances for the needy, and a host of lesser supports. The responsive, socially concerned national state undoubtedly contributed to the preservation of political stability and democracy in the face of economic difficulties that might have brought revolution and dictatorship in earlier times.

The energetic response of governments to social needs helps explain the sharp increase in total government spending in most countries during the 1970s and early 1980s. In 1982 western European governments spent an average of more than 50 percent of all national income, as compared to only 37 percent fifteen years earlier. In all countries, people were much more willing to see their governments increase spending than raise taxes. This imbalance contributed to the rapid growth of budget deficits, national debts, and inflation. By the late 1970s, a powerful reaction against government's ever-increasing role had set in, however, and Western governments were gradually forced to introduce austerity measures to slow the growth of public spending and the welfare state.

Part of a broad cultural shift toward greater conservatism, growing voter dissatisfaction with government and government spending helped bring Margaret Thatcher (b. 1925) to power in Britain in 1979. Thatcher was determined to scale back the role of government in Britain, and in the 1980s—the "Thatcher years"—she pushed through a series of controversial "free-market" policies that transformed postwar Britain. In one of its most popular actions, Thatcher's Conservative government encouraged low- and moderate-income renters in state-owned housing projects to buy their apartments at rock-bottom prices. This initiative, part of Thatcher's broader privatization campaign, created a whole new class of property owners, thereby eroding the electoral base of Britain's socialist Labour Party. (See the feature "Individuals in Society: Margaret Thatcher.")

President Ronald Reagan's success in the United States was more limited. With widespread popular support and the agreement of most congressional Democrats as well as Republicans, Reagan in 1981 pushed through major cuts in income taxes all across the board. But Reagan and Congress failed to cut government spending, which increased as a percentage of national income in the course of his presidency. Reagan's massive military buildup was partly responsible, but spending on social programs also grew rapidly. The harsh recession of the early 1980s required that the government spend more on unemployment benefits, welfare benefits, and medical treatment for the poor. Moreover, Reagan's antiwelfare rhetoric mobilized the liberal opposition and eventually turned many moderates against him. Thus the budget deficit soared and the U.S. government debt tripled in a decade.

The most striking temporary exception to the general trend toward greater frugality was François Mitterrand (1916–1996) of France. After his election as president in 1981, Mitterrand led his Socialist Party on a lurch to the left, launching a vast program of nationalization and public investment designed to spend France out of economic stagnation. By 1983 this attempt had clearly failed. Mitterrand's Socialist government was then compelled to impose a wide variety of austerity measures and to maintain those policies for the rest of the decade.

When governments were forced to restrain spending, large scientific projects were often singled out for cuts. These reductions reinforced the ongoing computer revolution, which increased the efficiency of small businesses and stimulated new ventures by young innovative entrepreneurs. Big organizations lost some of their advantages over small firms.

Individuals felt the impact of austerity at an early date, for unlike governments, they could not pay their bills by printing money and going ever further into debt. The energy crisis of the 1970s forced them to re-examine not only their fuel bills but also the whole pattern of self-indulgent materialism in the postwar years. A growing number of experts and citizens concluded that the world was running out of resources and decried wasteful industrial practices and environmental pollution. In West Germany young activists known as the Greens in 1979 founded a political party to fight for environmental causes. The German Green movement elected some national and local representatives, and similar parties developed throughout Europe as environmentalism became a leading societal concern.

Another consequence of austerity in both Europe and North America was a leaner, tougher lifestyle in the 1970s and early 1980s, featuring more attention to nutrition and a passion for exercise. Correspondingly, there was less blind reliance on medical science for good health and a growing awareness that individuals had to accept a large portion of the responsibility for illness and disease. More people began to realize that they could substantially increase their life spans simply by eating regular meals, sleeping seven or eight hours each night, exercising two or three times a week, maintaining moderate weight, forgoing smoking, and using alcohol only in moderation.

Economic troubles also strengthened the new trends within the family. Men and women were encouraged to postpone marriage until they had put their careers on a firm foundation, so the age of marriage rose sharply for both sexes in many Western countries. Indeed, the very real threat of unemployment—or "underemployment" in a dead-end job—seemed to shape the outlook of a whole generation. College students of the 1980s were serious, practical, and often conservative. As one young woman at a French university told a reporter in 1985, "Jobs are the big worry now, so everyone wants to learn something practical."[10] In France as elsewhere, the shift away from the romantic visions and the political activism of the late 1960s was astonishing.

Harder times also help explain why ever more women entered or remained in the workforce after they did marry. Although attitudes related to personal fulfillment were one reason for the continuing increase—especially for well-educated, upper-middle-class women—many wives in poor and middle-class families simply had to work outside the home because of economic necessity. As in preindustrial Europe, the wife's earnings provided the margin of survival for millions of hard-pressed families.

Individuals in Society

Margaret Thatcher

Margaret Thatcher (b. 1925), the first woman elected to lead a major European state, stands as one of the most significant leaders of the late twentieth century. The controversial "Iron Lady" attacked socialism, promoted capitalism, and changed the face of modern Britain.

Born Margaret Roberts in a small city in southeastern England, her father was a small shopkeeper who instilled in his daughter the classic lower-middle-class virtues—hard work, personal responsibility, and practical education. A scholarship student at a local girls school, she entered Oxford in 1943 to study chemistry but soon found that politics was her passion. Elected president of student Conservatives, she ran in 1950 for Parliament in a solidly Labour district to gain experience. Articulate and attractive, she also gained the attention of Denis Thatcher, a wealthy businessman who drove her to campaign appearances in his Jaguar. Married a year later, the new Mrs. Thatcher abandoned chemistry, went to law school, gave birth to twins, and practiced as a tax attorney. In 1959, she returned to politics and won a seat in the Conservative triumph.

For the next fifteen years Mrs. Thatcher served in Parliament and held various ministerial posts when the Conservatives governed. In 1974, as the economy soured and the Conservatives lost two close elections, a rebellious Margaret Thatcher adroitly ran for the leadership position of the Conservative Party and won. In the 1979 election, as the Labour government faced rampant inflation and crippling strikes, Mrs. Thatcher promised to reduce union power, lower taxes, and promote free markets. Attracting swing votes from skilled workers, she won and became prime minister.

A self-described "conviction politician," Thatcher rejected postwar Keynesian efforts to manage the economy, arguing that governments had created inflation by printing too much money. Thus her government reduced the supply of money and credit, and it refused to retreat as interest rates and unemployment soared. Her popularity plummeted. But Thatcher was saved by good luck—and courage. In 1982, the generals ruling Argentina suddenly seized the Falkland Islands off the Argentine coast, the home of 1,800 British citizens. Ever a staunch nationalist, Thatcher detached a naval armada that recaptured the Falklands without a hitch. Britain loved Thatcher's determination, and the "Iron Lady" was re-elected in 1983.

Thatcher's second term was the high point of her success and influence. Her whole-hearted commitment to privatization changed the face of British industry. More than fifty state-owned companies, ranging from the state tele-phone monopoly to the nationalized steel trust, were sold to private investors. Small investors were offered shares at bargain prices to promote "people's capitalism." Thatcher also curbed the power of British labor unions with various laws and actions. Most spectacularly, when in 1984 the once-mighty coal miners rejected more mine closings and doggedly struck for a year, Thatcher stood firm and beat them. This outcome had a profound psychological impact on the public.

Margaret Thatcher as prime minister.
(AP Images/Staff-Caulkin)

Elected again in 1987, Thatcher became increasingly stubborn, overconfident, and uncaring. Working well with her ideological soul mate, U.S. president Ronald Reagan, she opposed greater political and economic unity within the European Community. This, coupled with an unpopular effort to assert financial control over city governments, proved her undoing. In 1990, as in 1974, party stalwarts suddenly revolted and elected a new Conservative leader. Raised to the peerage by Queen Elizabeth II, the new Lady Thatcher then sat in the largely ceremonial House of Lords. The transformational changes of the Thatcher years endured, consolidated by her Conservative successor and largely accepted by the "New Labour" prime minister, the moderate Tony Blair.

Questions for Analysis

1. Why did Margaret Thatcher want to change Britain, and how did she do it?
2. Historians have often debated whether great leaders determine the course of history, or whether they only ride successfully the major forces of their time. Which view of history is supported by Thatcher's achievements? Why?

Online Study Center **Improve Your Grade**
Going Beyond Individuals in Society

German Greens Supporting Poland's Solidarity Best known for its passionate commitment to the environment, the German Green Party has also supported many progressive causes and campaigned against militarism and communism. These Greens are protesting in 1982 against the crackdown on Solidarity, the trade union movement that challenged Communist rule in Poland in the 1980s. The Greens are now Germany's third-largest political party, and they exercise real influence. *(Time Life Pictures/Getty Images)*

Chapter Summary

- What were the causes of the cold war?
- Why did western Europe recover so successfully? How did colonial peoples win political independence and American blacks triumph in the civil rights movement?
- What was the pattern of postwar rebuilding and development in the Soviet Union and Communist eastern Europe?
- How did changing patterns in technology, class relations, women's work, and youth culture bring major social transformations?
- What were the key aspects of political conflict, economic stagnation, and the feminist movement in the late cold war?

Online Study Center ACE the Test

The recovery of western Europe after World War II was one of the most striking chapters in the long, uneven course of Western civilization. Although the dangerous tensions of the cold war frustrated hopes for a truly peaceful international order, the transition from imperialism to decolonization proceeded rapidly, surprisingly smoothly, and without serious damage to western Europe. Genuine political democracy gained unprecedented strength in western Europe, and rapid economic progress marked a generation.

Fundamental social changes accompanied the political recovery and economic expansion after World War II. Pure science combined with applied technology to achieve remarkable success. The triumphs of applied science contributed not only to economic expansion but also to a more fluid, less antagonistic class structure, in which specialized education was the high road to advancement for men and women. Married women entered the labor force in growing numbers.

Postwar developments in eastern Europe displayed both similarities to and differences from developments in western Europe and North America. Perhaps the biggest difference was that Stalin imposed harsh one-party rule in the lands occupied by his armies, which led to the bitter cold war. Nevertheless, the Soviet Union became less dictatorial under Khrushchev, and the standard of living in the Soviet Union improved markedly in the 1950s and 1960s.

In the late 1960s and early 1970s, Europe and North America entered a time of crisis. Many nations, from France to Czechoslovakia to the United States, experienced major political difficulties, as cold war conflicts and ideological battles divided peoples and shook governments. Beginning with the oil shocks of the 1970s, severe economic problems added to the turmoil and brought real hardship to millions of people. Yet in western Europe and North America, the welfare system held firm, and both democracy and the movement toward European unity successfully passed through the storm. The women's movement also mobilized effectively and won expanded rights in the best tradition of Western civilization. Finally, efforts to achieve détente in central Europe while still maintaining a strong Atlantic alliance met some success. This modest progress helped lay the foundations for the sudden end of the cold war and the opening of a new era.

Key Terms

Big Three
Marshall Plan
NATO
cold war
Christian Democrats
Common Market
decolonization
neocolonialism
de-Stalinization
Brezhnev Doctrine
re-Stalinization
Big Science
Watergate
détente
OPEC
misery index

 Improve Your Grade Flashcards

Suggested Reading

Bernstein, Serge. *The Republic of de Gaulle, 1958–1969.* 2006. An outstanding work on France.

Caute, David. *The Year of the Barricades: A Journey Through 1968.* 1990. A high-energy examination that brings the 1968 upheavals to life.

Chamberlain, M. E. *Decolonization: The Fall of European Empires,* 2d ed. 1999. A clear, up-to-date account.

de Grazia, Victoria. *Irresistible Empire: America's Advance Through Twentieth-Century Europe.* 2005. Lively, provocative account of Europe's "Americanization."

de Senarclens, Pierre. *From Yalta to the Iron Curtain: The Great Powers and the Origins of the Cold War.* 1995. A valuable work on the cold war.

Eksteins, Modris. *Walking Since Daybreak: A Story of Eastern Europe, World War II, and the Heart of Our Century.* 2000. A powerful, partly autobiographical account that is highly recommended.

Gillingham, John. *European Integration, 1950–2003: Superstate or New Market Economy?* 2003. A brilliant interpretive history.

Hitchcock, William I. *The Struggle for Europe: The Turbulent History of a Divided Continent, 1945 to the Present.* 2004. A valuable general study with extensive bibliographies.

Jaraush, Konrad. *After Hitler: Recivilizing Germans, 1945–1995.* 2006. A stimulating survey by a distinguished historian.

Judt, Tony. *Postwar: A History of Europe Since 1945.* 2005. A masterful reconsideration, especially strong on smaller countries.

Reitan, Earl. *Tory Radicalism: Margaret Thatcher, John Major, and the Transformation of Modern Britain, 1979–1997.* 1997. Clear, concise, and very useful.

Scott, Joan W. *Only Paradoxes to Offer: French Feminists and the Rights of Man.* 1997. An important study of French feminism.

Tipton, Frank B., and Robert Aldrich. *An Economic and Social History of Europe from 1939 to the Present.* 1987. An interesting, wide-ranging account.

Westad, Odd Arne. *The Global Cold War: Third World Interventions and the Making of Our Times.* 2007. Up-to-date study of the cold war's global impact.

Notes

1. Quoted in N. Graebner, *Cold War Diplomacy, 1945–1960* (Princeton, N.J.: Van Nostrand, 1962), p. 17.
2. Quoted in J. Hennessy, *Economic "Miracles"* (London: Andre Deutsch, 1964), p. 5.
3. Quoted in S. E. Morison et al., *A Concise History of the American Republic* (New York: Oxford University Press, 1977), p. 697.
4. Quoted in D. Treadgold, *Twentieth Century Russia,* 5th ed. (Boston: Houghton Mifflin, 1981), p. 442.
5. Quoted in J. Ziman, *The Force of Knowledge: The Scientific Dimension of Society* (Cambridge: Cambridge University Press, 1976), p. 128.
6. Quoted in S. Toulmin, *The Twentieth Century: A Promethean Age,* ed. A. Bullock (London: Thames & Hudson, 1971), p. 294.
7. Quoted in N. Cantor, *Twentieth-Century Culture: Modernism to Deconstruction* (New York: Peter Lang, 1988), p. 252.
8. M. Mitterauer, *The History of Youth* (Oxford: Basil Blackwell, 1992), p. 40.
9. Quoted in Kessing's Research Report, *Germany and East Europe Since 1945: From the Potsdam Agreement to Chancellor Brandt's "Ostpolitik"* (New York: Charles Scribner's Sons, 1973), pp. 284–285.
10. *Wall Street Journal,* June 28, 1985, p. 1.

Listening to the Past

A Feminist Critique of Marriage

Having grown up in Paris in a middle-class family and become a teacher, novelist, and intellectual, Simone de Beauvoir (1908–1986) turned increasingly to feminist concerns after World War II. Her most influential work was The Second Sex (1949), a massive declaration of independence for contemporary women.

As an existentialist, Beauvoir believed that all individuals must accept responsibility for their lives and strive to overcome the tragic dilemmas they face. Studying the experience of women since antiquity, Beauvoir argued that men had generally used education and social conditioning to create a dependent "other," a negative nonman who was not permitted to grow and strive for freedom.

Marriage—on men's terms—was part of this unjust and undesirable process. Beauvoir's conclusion that some couples could establish free and equal unions was based in part on her experience with philosopher Jean-Paul Sartre, Beauvoir's encouraging companion and sometime lover.

Every human existence involves transcendence and immanence at the same time; to go forward, each existence must be maintained, for it to expand toward the future it must integrate the past, and while intercommunicating with others it should find self-confirmation. These two elements—maintenance and progression—are implied in any living activity, and for *man* marriage permits precisely a happy synthesis of the two. In his occupation and his political life he encounters change and progress, he senses his extension through time and the universe; and when he is tired of such roaming, he gets himself a home, a fixed location, and an anchorage in the world. At evening he restores his soul in the home, where his wife takes care of his furnishings and children and guards the things of the past that she keeps in store. But she has no other job than to maintain and provide for life in pure and unvarying generality; she perpetuates the species without change, she ensures the even rhythm of the days and the continuity of the home, seeing to it that the doors are locked. But she is allowed no direct influence upon the future nor upon the world; she reaches out beyond herself toward the social group only through her husband as intermediary.

Marriage today still retains, for the most part, this traditional form. . . . The male is called upon for action, his vocation is to produce, fight, create, progress, to transcend himself toward the totality of the universe and the infinity of the future; but traditional marriage does not invite woman to transcend herself with him; it confines her in immanence, shuts her up within the circle of herself. She can thus propose to do nothing more than construct a life of stable equilibrium in which the present as a continuance of the past avoids the menaces of tomorrow—that is, construct precisely a life of happiness. . . .

In domestic work, with or without the aid of servants, woman makes her home her own, finds social justification, and provides herself with an occupation, an activity, that deals usefully and satisfyingly with material objects—shining stoves, fresh, clean clothes, bright copper, polished furniture—but provides no escape from immanence and little affirmation of individuality. . . . Few tasks are more like the torture of Sisyphus than housework, with its endless repetition: the clean becomes soiled, the soiled is made clean, over and over, day after day. The housewife wears herself out marking time: she makes nothing, simply perpetuates the present. She never senses conquest of a positive Good, but rather indefinite struggle against negative Evil. . . . Washing, ironing, sweeping, ferreting out rolls of lint from under wardrobes—all this halting of decay is also the denial of life;

for time simultaneously creates and destroys, and only its negative aspect concerns the housekeeper....

Thus woman's work within the home gives her no autonomy; it is not directly useful to society, it does not open out on the future, it produces nothing. It takes on meaning and dignity only as it is linked with existent beings who reach out beyond themselves, transcend themselves, toward society in production and action. That is, far from freeing the matron, her occupation makes her dependent upon husband and children; she is justified through them; but in their lives she is only an inessential intermediary....

The tragedy of marriage is not that it fails to assure woman the promised happiness—there is no such thing as assurance in regard to happiness—but that it mutilates her; it dooms her to repetition and routine. The first twenty years of woman's life are extraordinarily rich, as we have seen; she discovers the world and her destiny. At twenty or thereabouts mistress of a home, bound permanently to a man, a child in her arms, she stands with her life virtually finished forever. Real activities, real work, are the prerogative of her man: she has mere things to occupy her which are sometimes tiring but never fully satisfying....

Marriage should be a combining of two whole, independent existences, not a retreat, an annexation, a flight, a remedy.... The couple should not be regarded as a unit, a close cell; rather each individual should be integrated as such in society at large, where each (whether male or female) could flourish without aid; then attachments could be formed in pure generosity with another individual equally adapted to the group, attachments that would be founded upon the acknowledgment that both are free.

This balanced couple is not a utopian fancy: such couples do exist, sometimes even within the frame of marriage, most often outside it. Some mates are united by a strong sexual love that leaves them free in their friendships and in their work; others are held together by a friendship that does not preclude sexual liberty; more rare are those who are at once lovers and friends but do not seek in each other their sole reasons for living. Many nuances are possible in the relations between a man and a woman: in comradeship, pleasure, trust, fondness, co-operation, and love, they can be for each other the most abundant

Simone de Beauvoir as a teacher in 1947, when she was writing *The Second Sex*. *(Hulton-Deutsch Collection/Corbis)*

source of joy, richness, and power available to human beings.

Questions for Analysis

1. How did Beauvoir analyze marriage and marriage partners in terms of existential philosophy?

2. To what extent does a married woman benefit from a "traditional" marriage, according to Beauvoir? Why?

3. What was Beauvoir's solution to the situation she described? Was her solution desirable? Realistic?

4. What have you learned about the history of women that supports or challenges Beauvoir's analysis? Include developments since World War II and your own reflections.

Source: Simone de Beauvoir, *The Second Sex,* trans. H. M. Parshley. Copyright © 1952 and renewed 1980 by Alfred A. Knopf, a division of Random House, Inc. Used by permission of Alfred A. Knopf, a division of Random House, Inc.

Italians protesting government economic policies gather in front of the Roman Coliseum during a nationwide strike in October 2003. *(Philippe Desmazes/AFP/Getty Images)*

chapter 31

Revolution, Rebuilding, and New Challenges: 1985 to the Present

chapter preview

The Decline of Communism in Eastern Europe
- In what ways did Solidarity confront the communist system in Poland, and how did Mikhail Gorbachev try to reverse the decline of communism in the Soviet Union?

The Revolutions of 1989
- How did anticommunist revolutions sweep through eastern Europe in 1989, and what were the immediate consequences?

Building a New Europe in the 1990s
- How, in the 1990s, did the different parts of a reunifying Europe meet the challenges of postcommunist reconstruction, resurgent nationalism, and economic union?

New Challenges in the Twenty-first Century
- Why did the prospect of population decline, the reality of large-scale immigration, and concern for human rights emerge as critical issues in contemporary Europe?

The West and the Islamic World
- How and why did relations between the West and the Islamic world deteriorate dramatically in the early twenty-first century?

The Future in Perspective
- What does the study of history have to tell us about the future?

In the late twentieth century, massive changes swept through eastern Europe and opened a new era in human history. In the 1980s a broad movement to transform the communist system took root in Poland, and efforts to reform and revitalize the communist system in the Soviet Union snowballed out of control. In 1989 revolutions swept away communist rule throughout the entire Soviet bloc. The cold war came to a spectacular end, West Germany absorbed East Germany, and the Soviet Union broke into fifteen independent countries. Thus after forty years of cold war division, Europe regained an underlying unity, as faith in democratic government and some kind of market economy became the common European creed. In 1991 hopes for peaceful democratic progress throughout Europe were almost universal.

The post–cold war years saw the realization of some of these hopes, but the new era brought its own problems and tragedies. The cold war division of Europe had kept a lid on ethnic conflicts and nationalism, which suddenly burst into the open and led to a disastrous civil war in the former Yugoslavia. Moreover, most western European economies were plagued by high unemployment and struggling to adapt to the wide-open global economy, which undermined cherished social benefits and complicated the task of working together with the former communist states. Thus in eastern Europe, the process of rebuilding shattered societies was more difficult than optimists had envisioned in 1991, and in western Europe, the road toward greater unity and eastward expansion proved bumpy. Nevertheless, the will to undo the cold war division prevailed, and in 2004 eight former communist countries as well as the islands of Cyprus and Malta joined the European Union—a historic achievement.

Online Study Center
This icon will direct you to interactive activities and study materials on the website **college.hmco.com/pic/mckaywest9e**

The new century brought a growing awareness of a new set of fundamental challenges, which were related to the prospect of population decline, the reality of large-scale immigration, and the promotion of human rights. These challenges promised to preoccupy Western society for years to come.

More dramatically, the old, often contentious question of relations with the Islamic world suddenly re-emerged as a critical issue after the attack on New York's World Trade Center and the Pentagon in 2001. After the West united in a quick response against the Taliban in Afghanistan, the subsequent war in Iraq divided western Europe and threatened the future of Western cooperation in world affairs. The war in Iraq also complicated the ongoing integration of Europe's rapidly growing Muslim population.

The Decline of Communism in Eastern Europe

Following the 1968 invasion of Czechoslovakia, the crucial event of the Brezhnev era (pages 997–999), the Soviet Union repeatedly demonstrated that it remained a harsh and aggressive dictatorship. It paid only lip service to egalitarian ideology at home and was determined to uphold its rule throughout eastern Europe. Thus the Soviet Union eventually crushed the Solidarity movement in Poland, the powerful, peaceful challenge to Communist rule in Poland in the early 1980s. Periodic efforts to achieve fundamental political change were doomed to failure sooner or later—or so it seemed to most Western experts into the mid-1980s.

And then Mikhail Gorbachev burst on the scene. The new Soviet leader opened an era of reform that was as sweeping as it was unexpected. Although many believed that Gorbachev would soon fall from power, his reforms rapidly transformed Soviet culture and politics, and they drastically reduced cold war tensions. But communism, which Gorbachev wanted so desperately to revitalize in order to save it, continued to decline as a functioning system throughout the Soviet bloc.

- *In what ways did Solidarity confront the communist system in Poland, and how did Mikhail Gorbachev try to reverse the decline of communism in the Soviet Union?*

Solidarity in Poland

Gorbachev's reforms interacted with a resurgence of popular protest in the Soviet Union's satellite empire. Developments in Poland were most striking and significant.

Poland had been an unruly satellite from the beginning. Stalin said that introducing communism to Poland was like putting a saddle on a cow. Efforts to saddle the cow—really a spirited stallion—led to widespread riots in 1956 (see page 997). As a result, Polish Communists dropped their efforts to impose Soviet-style collectivization on the peasants and to break the Roman Catholic Church. Most agricultural land remained in private hands, and the Catholic Church thrived. Thus the Communists failed to monopolize society.

They also failed to manage the economy effectively. Even the booming 1960s saw little economic improvement. In 1970 Poland's working class rose again in angry protest. A new Communist leader came to power, and he wagered that massive inflows of Western capital and technology, especially from rich and now-friendly West Germany (see page 1008), could produce a Polish "economic miracle." Instead, bureaucratic incompetence and the first oil shock in 1973 put the economy into a nosedive. Workers, intellectuals, and the church became increasingly restive. Then the real Polish miracle occurred: Cardinal Karol Wojtyla, archbishop of Cracow, was elected pope in 1978. In June 1979, he returned from Rome, preaching love of Christ and country and the "inalienable rights of man." Pope John Paul II drew enormous crowds and electrified the Polish nation. The economic crisis became a moral and spiritual crisis as well.

In August 1980, the sixteen thousand workers at the gigantic Lenin Shipyards in Gdansk (formerly known as Danzig) laid down their tools and occupied the plant. As other workers joined "in solidarity," the strikers advanced revolutionary demands, including the right to form free-trade unions, freedom of speech, release of political prisoners, and economic reforms. After eighteen days of shipyard occupation, the government gave in and accepted the workers' demands in the **Gdansk Agreement.** In a state where the Communist Party claimed to rule on behalf of the proletariat, a working-class revolt had won an unprecedented victory.

Online Study Center Improve Your Grade
Primary Source: The "Twenty-one Demands": A Call for Workers' Rights and Freedom in a Socialist State

Led by feisty Lenin Shipyards electrician and devout Catholic Lech Walesa (b. 1943), the workers proceeded to organize their free and democratic trade union. They called it **Solidarity.** Joined by intellectuals and supported by the Catholic Church, Solidarity became the union of a nation. By March 1981, a full-time staff of 40,000 linked 9.5 million union members together as Solidarity published its own newspapers and cultural and intellectual freedom blossomed in Poland. Solidarity's leaders had tremendous support, and the ever-present threat of calling a nationwide strike gave them real power in ongoing negotiations with the Communist bosses.

But if Solidarity had power, it did not try to take the reins of government in 1981. History, the Brezhnev Doctrine, and virulent attacks from communist neighbors all seemed to guarantee the intervention of the Red Army and a terrible bloodbath if Polish Communists "lost control." Thus the Solidarity revolution remained a "self-limiting revolution" aimed at defending the cultural and trade-union freedoms won in the Gdansk Agreement, and it refused to use force to challenge directly the Communist monopoly of political power.

Solidarity's combination of strength and moderation postponed a showdown, as the Soviet Union played a waiting game of threats and pressure. After a confrontation in March 1981, Walesa settled for minor government concessions, and Solidarity dropped plans for a massive general strike. Criticism of Walesa's moderate leadership grew, and Solidarity lost its cohesiveness. The worsening economic crisis also encouraged grassroots radicalism, as the Polish Communist leadership shrewdly denounced Solidarity for promoting economic collapse and provoking Soviet invasion. In December 1981, Communist leader General Wojciech Jaruzelski suddenly struck, proclaiming martial law, arresting Solidarity's leaders, and "saving" the nation.

Outlawed and driven underground, Solidarity fought successfully to maintain its organization and to voice the aspirations of the Polish masses after 1981. Part of the reason for the union's survival was the government's unwillingness (and probably its inability) to impose full-scale terror. Moreover, millions of Poles decided to continue acting as if they were free, even though they were not. Cultural and intellectual life remained extremely vigorous as the faltering Polish economy continued to deteriorate. Thus popular support for outlawed Solidarity remained strong under martial law in the 1980s, preparing the way for the union's political rebirth toward the end of the decade.

The rise and survival of Solidarity showed the desire of millions of eastern Europeans for greater political liberty and the enduring appeal of cultural freedom, trade-union rights, patriotic nationalism, and religious feeling. Not least, Solidarity's challenge encouraged fresh thinking in the Soviet Union, ever the key to lasting change in the Eastern bloc.

Chronology

1985	Glasnost leads to greater freedom of speech and expression in the Soviet Union
1985–	Decline in birthrate in industrialized nations continues
1986	Single European Act lays groundwork for single currency
August 1989	Solidarity gains power in Poland
November 1989	Collapse of the Berlin Wall
November–December 1989	Velvet Revolution ends communism in Czechoslovakia
October 1990	Reunification of Germany
1990–1991	First war with Iraq
July 1991	Failed coup against Gorbachev in Russia
December 1991	Dissolution of the Soviet Union
1991	Maastricht treaty sets financial criteria for European monetary union
1991–2000	Resurgence of nationalism and ethnic conflict in eastern Europe
1991–2001	Civil war in Yugoslavia
1992–1997	"Shock therapy" in Russia causes decline of the economy
1993	Creation of the European Union; growth of illegal immigration in Europe
1996	Cronin, *The World the Cold War Made*
1998–	Growing support for global human rights in Europe
1999	Russian economy booms
September 2001	Terrorist attack on the United States
2001	War in Afghanistan
January 2002	New euro currency goes into effect in the European Union
2003	Second war in Iraq begins
2004	Ten new states join European Union
November 2005	Young Muslims riot in France
2006	Murderous sectarian conflict in Iraq increases

Lech Walesa and Solidarity An inspiration for fellow workers at the Lenin Shipyards in the dramatic and successful strike against the Communist bosses in August 1980, Walesa played a key role in Solidarity before and after it was outlawed. Speaking here to old comrades at the Lenin Shipyards after Solidarity was again legalized in 1988, Walesa personified an enduring opposition to Communist rule in eastern Europe. *(G. Merrillon/Gamma Presse/EYEDEA)*

Gorbachev's Reforms in the Soviet Union

Fundamental change in Russian history has often come in short, intensive spurts, which contrast vividly with long periods of immobility. The era of reform launched by Mikhail Gorbachev in 1985 was one such decisive transformation. Gorbachev's initiatives brought political and cultural liberalization to the Soviet Union, and they then permitted democracy and national self-determination to triumph spectacularly in the old satellite empire and eventually in the Soviet Union itself, although this was certainly not Gorbachev's original intention.

As we have seen (page 998), the Soviet Union's Communist Party elite seemed secure in the early 1980s as far as any challenge from below was concerned. The long-established system of administrative controls continued to stretch downward from the central ministries and state committees to provincial cities, and from there to factories, neighborhoods, and villages. At each level of this massive state bureaucracy, the overlapping hierarchy of the Communist Party, with its 17.5 million members, continued to watch over all decisions and manipulate every aspect of national life. Organized opposition was impossible, and average people simply left politics to the bosses.

Yet the massive state and party bureaucracy was a mixed blessing. It safeguarded the elite, but it promoted apathy in the masses. Therefore, when the ailing Brezhnev finally died in 1982, his successor, the long-time chief of the secret police, Yuri Andropov (1914–1984), tried to invigorate the system. Relatively little came of these efforts, but they combined with a sharply worsening economic situation to set the stage for the emergence in 1985 of Mikhail Gorbachev (b. 1931), the most vigorous Soviet leader in a generation.

Trained as a lawyer and working his way up as a Communist Party official in the northern Caucasus, Gorbachev was smart, charming, and tough. Gorbachev believed in communism, but he realized it was failing to keep up with Western capitalism and technology. This was eroding the Soviet Union's status as a superpower. Thus Gorbachev (and his intelligent, influential wife, Raisa, a dedicated professor of Marxist-Leninist thought) wanted to save the Soviet system by revitalizing it with fundamental reforms. Gorbachev was also an idealist. He wanted to improve conditions for ordinary citizens. Understanding that the endless waste and expense of the cold war arms race had had a disastrous impact on living conditions in the Soviet Union, he realized that improvement at home required better relations with the West.

In his first year in office, Gorbachev attacked corruption and incompetence in the bureaucracy, and he consolidated his power. He attacked alcoholism and drunkenness, which were deadly scourges of Soviet society, and elaborated his ambitious reform program.

The first set of reform policies was designed to transform and restructure the economy, in order to provide for the real needs of the Soviet population. To accomplish this economic "restructuring," or **perestroika,** Gorbachev and his supporters permitted an easing of government price controls on some goods, more independence for state enterprises, and the setting up of profit-seeking private cooperatives to provide personal services for consumers. These timid economic reforms initially produced a few improvements, but shortages then grew as the economy stalled at an intermediate point between central planning and free-market mechanisms. By late 1988, widespread consumer dissatisfaction posed a serious threat to Gorbachev's leadership and the entire reform program.

Online Study Center **Improve Your Grade**
Primary Source: The Last Heir of Lenin Explains His Reform Plans: Perestroika and Glasnost

Gorbachev's bold and far-reaching campaign "to tell it like it is" was much more successful. Very popular in a country where censorship, dull uniformity, and outright lies had long characterized public discourse, the newfound "openness," or **glasnost,** of the government and the media marked an astonishing break with the past. Long-banned and vilified émigré writers sold millions of copies of their works in new editions, while denunciations of Stalin and his terror became standard fare in plays and movies. Thus initial openness in government pronouncements quickly went much further than Gorbachev intended and led to something approaching free speech and free expression, a veritable cultural revolution.

Democratization was the third element of reform. Beginning as an attack on corruption in the Communist Party, it led to the first free elections in the Soviet Union

Mikhail Gorbachev In his acceptance speech before the Supreme Soviet (the U.S.S.R.'s parliament), newly elected president Mikhail Gorbachev vowed to assume "all responsibility" for the success or failure of perestroika. Previous parliaments were no more than tools of the Communist Party, but this one actively debated and even opposed government programs. *(Vlastimir Shone/Gamma Presse/EYEDEA)*

since 1917. Gorbachev and the party remained in control, but a minority of critical independents was elected in April 1989 to a revitalized Congress of People's Deputies. Millions of Soviets then watched the new congress for hours on television as Gorbachev and his ministers saw their proposals debated and even rejected. Thus

MAP 31.1 Democratic Movements in Eastern Europe, 1989 With Gorbachev's repudiation of the Brezhnev Doctrine, the revolutionary drive for freedom and democracy spread throughout eastern Europe. Countries that had been satellites in the orbit of the Soviet Union began to set themselves free to establish their own place in the universe of free nations.

millions of Soviet citizens took practical lessons in open discussion, critical thinking, and representative government. The result was a new political culture at odds with the Communist Party's monopoly of power and control.

Democratization ignited demands for greater autonomy and even for national independence by non-Russian minorities, especially in the Baltic region and in the Caucasus. In April 1989, troops with sharpened shovels charged into a rally of Georgian separatists in Tbilisi and left twenty dead. But whereas China's Communist leaders brutally massacred similar prodemocracy demonstrators in Beijing in June 1989 and reimposed rigid authoritarian rule, Gorbachev drew back from repres-

sion. Thus nationalist demands continued to grow in the non-Russian Soviet republics.

Finally, the Soviet leader brought "new political thinking" to the field of foreign affairs and acted on it. He withdrew Soviet troops from Afghanistan and sought to reduce East-West tensions. Of enormous importance, he sought to halt the arms race with the United States and convinced President Ronald Reagan of his sincerity. In December 1987, the two leaders agreed in a Washington summit to eliminate all land-based intermediate-range missiles in Europe, setting the stage for more arms reductions. Gorbachev also encouraged reform movements in Poland and Hungary and pledged to respect the political choices of the peoples of eastern Europe, repudiating the Brezhnev Doctrine. By early 1989, it seemed that if Gorbachev held to his word, the tragic Soviet occupation of eastern Europe might well wither away, taking the long cold war with it once and for all.

The Revolutions of 1989

Instead, history accelerated. In 1989 Gorbachev's plan to reform communism in order to save it snowballed out of control. A series of largely peaceful revolutions swept across eastern Europe (see Map 31.1), overturning existing communist regimes and ending the communists' monopoly of power. Watched on television in the Soviet Union and around the world, these stirring events marked the triumph and the transformation of long-standing opposition to communist rule and foreign domination in eastern Europe.

The revolutions of 1989 had momentous consequences. First, the peoples of eastern Europe joyfully re-entered the mainstream of contemporary European life and culture, after having been conquered and brutalized by Nazis and communists for almost sixty years. Second, Gorbachev's reforms boomeranged, and a complicated anticommunist revolution swept through the Soviet Union, as the multinational empire broke into a large Russia and fourteen other independent states. Third, West Germany quickly absorbed its East German rival and emerged as the most influential country in Europe. Finally, the long cold war came to an abrupt end, and the United States suddenly stood as the world's only superpower.

- *How did anticommunist revolutions sweep through eastern Europe in 1989, and what were the immediate consequences?*

The Collapse of Communism in Eastern Europe

Solidarity and the Polish people led the way to revolution in eastern Europe. In 1988 widespread labor unrest, raging inflation, and the outlawed Solidarity's refusal to cooperate with the military government had brought Poland to the brink of economic collapse. Thus Solidarity skillfully pressured Poland's frustrated Communist leaders into another round of negotiations that might work out a sharing of power to resolve the political stalemate and the economic crisis. The subsequent agreement in early 1989 legalized Solidarity and declared that a large minority of representatives to the Polish parliament would be chosen by free elections in June 1989. Still guaranteed a parliamentary majority and expecting to win many of the contested seats, the Communists believed that their rule was guaranteed for four years and that Solidarity would keep the workers in line.

Lacking access to the state-run media, Solidarity succeeded nonetheless in mobilizing the country and winning most of the contested seats in an overwhelming victory. Moreover, many angry voters crossed off the names of unopposed party candidates, so that the Communist Party failed to win the majority its leaders had anticipated. Solidarity members jubilantly entered the Polish parliament, and a dangerous stalemate quickly developed. But Solidarity leader Lech Walesa, a gifted politician who always repudiated violence, adroitly obtained a majority by securing the allegiance of two minor procommunist parties that had been part of the coalition government after World War II. In August 1989, the editor of Solidarity's weekly newspaper was sworn in as Poland's new noncommunist leader.

In its first year and a half, the new Solidarity government cautiously introduced revolutionary political changes. It eliminated the hated secret police, the Communist ministers in the government, and finally Jaruzelski himself, but it did so step by step in order to avoid confrontation with the army or the Soviet Union. However, in economic affairs, the Solidarity-led government was radical from the beginning. It applied **shock therapy** designed to make a clean break with state planning and move quickly to market mechanisms and private property. Thus the Solidarity government abolished controls on many prices on January 1, 1990, and reformed the monetary system with a "big bang."

Hungary followed Poland. Hungary's Communist Party boss, János Kádár, had permitted liberalization of the rigid planned economy after the 1956 uprising in exchange for political obedience and continued Communist control. In May 1988, in an effort to retain power by granting modest political concessions, the party replaced Kádár with a reform communist. But opposition groups rejected piecemeal progress, and in the summer of 1989 the Hungarian Communist Party agreed to hold free elections in early 1990. Welcoming Western investment and moving rapidly toward multiparty democracy, Hungary's Communists now enjoyed considerable popular support, and they believed, quite mistakenly it turned out, that they could defeat the opposition in the upcoming elections. In an effort to strengthen their support at home and also put pressure on East Germany's hard-line Communist regime, the Hungarians opened their border to East Germans and tore down the barbed-wire "iron curtain" with Austria. Thus tens of thousands of dissatisfied East German "vacationers" began pouring into Hungary, crossed into Austria as refugees, and continued on to immediate resettlement in thriving West Germany.

The flight of East Germans led to the rapid growth of a homegrown protest movement in East Germany. Intellectuals, environmentalists, and Protestant ministers took the lead, organizing huge candlelight demonstrations and arguing that a democratic but still socialist East Germany was both possible and desirable. These "stayers" failed to convince the "leavers," however, who continued to flee the country en masse. In a desperate attempt to stabilize the situation, the East German government opened the Berlin Wall in November 1989, and people danced for joy atop that grim symbol of the prison state. East Germany's aging Communist leaders were swept aside, and a reform government took power and scheduled free elections.

In Czechoslovakia, communism died quickly in November–December 1989 in an almost good-humored ousting of Communist bosses. This so-called **Velvet Revolution** grew out of popular demonstrations led by students, intellectuals, and a dissident playwright turned moral revolutionary named Václav Havel. The protesters practically took control of the streets and forced the Communists into a power-sharing arrangement, which quickly resulted in the resignation of the Communist

Demonstrators During the Velvet Revolution Hundreds of thousands of Czechoslovakian citizens flooded the streets of Prague in peaceful, daily protests after the police savagely beat student demonstrators in mid-November 1989. On the night of November 24, three hundred thousand people roared "Dubček-Havel" when Alexander Dubček, the aging reformer ousted in 1968 by the Soviets, stood on a balcony with Václav Havel, the leading opponent of communism. That night the communists agreed to share power, and a few days later they resigned from the government. *(Corbis)*

government. As 1989 ended, the Czechoslovakian assembly elected Havel president.

Only in Romania was revolution violent and bloody. There ironfisted Communist dictator Nicolae Ceauşescu (1918–1989) had long combined Stalinist brutality with stubborn independence from Moscow. Faced with mass protests in December, Ceauşescu, alone among eastern European bosses, ordered his ruthless security forces to slaughter thousands, thereby sparking a classic armed uprising. After Ceauşescu's forces were defeated, the tyrant and his wife were captured and executed by a military court. A coalition government emerged from the fighting, although the legacy of Ceauşescu's oppression left a very troubled country.

The Disintegration of the Soviet Union

As 1990 began, revolutionary changes had triumphed in all but two eastern European states—tiny Albania and the vast Soviet Union. The great question now became whether the Soviet Union would follow its former satellites and whether reform communism would give way to a popular anticommunist revolution.

In February 1990, as competing Russian politicians noisily presented their programs, and nationalists in the non-Russian republics demanded autonomy or independence from the Soviet Union, the Communist Party suffered a stunning defeat in local elections throughout the country. As in the eastern European satellites, democrats and anticommunists won clear majorities in the leading cities of the Russian Federation. Moreover, in Lithuania the people elected an uncompromising nationalist as president, and the newly chosen parliament declared Lithuania an independent state. Gorbachev responded by placing an economic embargo on Lithuania, but he refused to use the army to crush the separatist government. The result was a tense political stalemate, which undermined popular support for Gorbachev. Separating himself further from Communist hardliners, Gorbachev asked Soviet citizens to ratify a new constitution, which formally abolished the Communist Party's monopoly of political power and expanded the power of the Congress of People's Deputies. Retaining his post as party secretary, Gorbachev convinced a majority of deputies to elect him president of the Soviet Union.

Gorbachev's eroding power and his unwillingness to risk a universal suffrage election for the presidency strengthened his great rival, Boris Yeltsin (1931–2007). A radical reform communist who had been purged by party conservatives in 1987, Yeltsin embraced the democratic movement, and in May 1990 he was elected leader of the Russian Federation's parliament. He boldly announced that Russia would put its interests first and declare its independence from the Soviet Union, thereby broadening the base of the anticommunist movement as he joined the patriotism of ordinary Russians with the democratic aspirations of big-city intellectuals. Gorbachev tried to save the Soviet Union with a new treaty that would link the member republics in a looser, freely accepted confederation, but six of the fifteen Soviet republics rejected Gorbachev's pleas.

The Fall of the Berlin Wall The sudden opening of the Berlin Wall in November 1989 dramatized the spectacular collapse of communism throughout eastern Europe. Built by the Soviet leader Nikita Khrushchev in 1961, the hated barrier had stopped the flow of refugees from East Germany to West Germany. *(Patrick Piel/Gamma Presse/EYEDEA)*

Celebrating Victory, August 1991 A Russian soldier flashes the victory sign in front of the Russian parliament, as the last-gasp coup attempt of Communist hardliners is defeated by Boris Yeltsin and an enthusiastic public. The soldier has cut the hammer and sickle out of the Soviet flag, consigning those famous symbols of proletarian revolution to what Trotsky once called the "garbage can of history." *(Filip Horvat/Corbis Saba)*

Opposed by democrats and nationalists, Gorbachev was also challenged again by the Communist old guard. Defeated at the Communist Party congress in July 1990, a gang of hardliners kidnapped a vacationing Gorbachev and his family in the Caucasus and tried to seize the Soviet government in August 1991. But the attempted coup collapsed in the face of massive popular resistance, which rallied around Yeltsin, recently elected president of the Russian Federation by universal suffrage. As the world watched spellbound on television, Yeltsin defiantly denounced the rebels from atop a stalled tank in central Moscow and declared the "rebirth of Russia." The army supported Yeltsin, and Gorbachev was rescued and returned to power as head of the Soviet Union.

The leaders of the coup wanted to preserve Communist power, state ownership, and the multinational Soviet Union, but they succeeded only in destroying all three. An anticommunist revolution swept the Russian Federation as Yeltsin and his supporters outlawed the Communist Party and confiscated its property. Locked in a personal and political duel with Gorbachev, Yeltsin and his democratic allies declared Russia independent and withdrew from the Soviet Union. All the other Soviet republics also left. The Soviet Union—and Gorbachev's job—ceased to exist on December 25, 1991 (see Map 31.2). The independent republics of the old Soviet Union then established a loose confederation, the Commonwealth of Independent States, which played only a minor role in the 1990s.

German Unification and the End of the Cold War

The sudden death of communism in East Germany in 1989 reopened the "German question" and raised the

MAP 31.2 Russia and the Successor States After the attempt in August 1991 to depose Gorbachev failed, an anticommunist revolution swept the Soviet Union. Led by Russia and Boris Yeltsin, the republics that formed the Soviet Union declared their sovereignty and independence. Eleven of the fifteen republics then formed a loose confederation called the Commonwealth of Independent States, but the integrated economy of the Soviet Union dissolved into separate national economies, each with its own goals and policies.

threat of renewed cold war conflict over Germany. Taking power in October 1989, East German reform communists, enthusiastically supported by leading East German intellectuals and former dissidents, wanted to preserve socialism by making it genuinely democratic and responsive to the needs of the people. They argued for a **third way,** which would go beyond the failed Stalinism they had experienced and the ruthless capitalism they saw in the West. These reformers supported closer ties with West Germany, but they feared unification and wanted to preserve a distinct East German identity.

These efforts failed, and within a few months East Germany was absorbed into an enlarged West Germany, much like a faltering company is merged into a stronger rival and ceases to exist. Three factors were particularly important in this sudden absorption. First, in the first week after the Berlin Wall was opened, almost 9 million East Germans—roughly one-half of the total population—poured across the border into West Germany. Almost all returned to their homes in the East, but the joy of warm welcomes from long-lost friends and loved ones and the exhilarating experience of shopping in the well-stocked stores of the much wealthier West aroused long-dormant hopes of unity among ordinary citizens.

Second, West German chancellor Helmut Kohl and his closest advisers skillfully exploited the historic opportunity on their doorstep. Sure of support from the United States, whose leadership he had steadfastly followed, in November 1989 Kohl presented a ten-point plan for a step-by-step unification in cooperation with both East Germany and the international community. Kohl then promised the struggling citizens of East Germany an immediate economic bonanza—a one-for-one exchange of all East German marks in savings accounts and pensions into much more valuable West German marks. This generous offer helped a well-financed conservative-liberal **Alliance for**

Germany, which was set up in East Germany and was closely tied to Kohl's West German Christian Democrats, to overwhelm those who argued for the preservation of some kind of independent socialist society in East Germany. In March 1990, the Alliance outdistanced the Socialist Party and won almost 50 percent of the votes in an East German parliamentary election. (The Communists ignominiously fell to fringe-party status.) The Alliance for Germany quickly negotiated an economic union on favorable terms with Chancellor Kohl.

Finally, in the summer of 1990, the crucial international aspect of German unification was successfully resolved. Unification would once again make Germany the strongest state in central Europe and would directly affect the security of the Soviet Union. But Gorbachev swallowed hard—Western cartoonists showed Stalin turning over in his grave—and negotiated the best deal he could. In a historic agreement signed by Gorbachev and Kohl in July 1990, a uniting Germany solemnly affirmed its peaceful intentions and pledged never to develop nuclear, biological, or chemical weapons. Germany also sweetened the deal by promising to make enormous loans to the hard-pressed Soviet Union. In October 1990, East Germany merged into West Germany, forming henceforth a single nation under the West German laws and constitution.

The peaceful reunification of Germany accelerated the pace of agreements to liquidate the cold war. In November 1990, delegates from twenty-two European countries joined those from the United States and the Soviet Union in Paris and agreed to a scaling down of all their armed forces. The delegates also solemnly affirmed that all existing borders in Europe—from unified Germany to the newly independent Baltic republics—were legal and valid. The **Paris Accord** was for all practical purposes a general peace treaty, bringing an end to World War II and the cold war that followed.

Peace in Europe encouraged the United States and the Soviet Union to scrap a significant portion of their nuclear weapons in a series of agreements. In September 1991, a confident President George H. W. Bush also canceled the around-the-clock alert status for American bombers outfitted with atomic bombs, and a floundering Gorbachev quickly followed suit. For the first time in four decades, Soviet and American nuclear weapons were no longer standing ready to destroy capitalism, communism, and life itself.

The Gulf War of 1991

As anticommunist revolutions swept eastern Europe and East-West tensions rapidly disappeared, the Soviet Union lost both the will and the means to be a global superpower. Yet the United States retained the strength and the desire to influence political and economic developments on a global scale. Thus the United States, still flanked by many allies, emerged rather suddenly as the world's only surviving superpower.

In 1991 the United States used its military superiority on a grand scale in a quick war with Iraq in western Asia. Emerging in 1988 from an eight-year war with neighboring Iran with a big, tough army equipped by the Soviet bloc, western Europe, and the United States, Iraq's strongman Saddam Hussein (1937–2006) set out to make himself the leader of the entire Arab world. Eyeing the great oil wealth of his tiny southern neighbor, Saddam Hussein's forces suddenly invaded Kuwait in August 1990 and proclaimed the annexation of Kuwait.

Reacting vigorously to free Kuwait, the United States mobilized the U.N. Security Council, which in August 1990 imposed a strict naval blockade on Iraq. Receiving the support of some Arab states, as well as of Great Britain and France, the United States also landed 500,000 American soldiers in Saudi Arabia near the border of Kuwait. When a defiant Saddam Hussein refused to withdraw from Kuwait, the Security Council authorized the U.S.-led military coalition to attack Iraq. The American army and air force then smashed Iraqi forces in a lightning-quick desert campaign, although the United States stopped short of toppling Saddam because it feared a sudden disintegration of Iraq more than Saddam's hanging on to power.

The defeat of Iraqi armies in the Gulf War demonstrated the awesome power of the U.S. military, rebuilt and revitalized by the spending and patriotism of the 1980s. Little wonder that in the flush of yet another victory, the first President Bush spoke of a **"new world order,"** an order that would apparently feature the United States and a cooperative United Nations working together to impose stability throughout the world.

Building a New Europe in the 1990s

The fall of communism, the end of the cold war, and the collapse of the Soviet Union opened a new era in European and world history. The dimensions and significance of this new era, opening suddenly and unexpectedly, are subject to debate. We are so close to what is going on that we lack vital perspective. Yet the historian must take a stand.

First, it seems clear that Europe took giant strides toward a loose unification of fundamental institutions and beliefs and that many broad economic, social, and political trends operated all across the continent in the 1990s. We shall focus on three of the most important trends: the pressure on national economies increasingly caught up in global capitalism; the defense of social achievements under attack; and a resurgence of nationalism and ethnic conflict. Second, with these common themes providing an organizational framework, we shall examine the course of development in the three overlapping but still distinct regions of contemporary Europe. These are Russia and the western states of the old Soviet Union, previously communist eastern Europe, and western Europe.

- *How, in the 1990s, did the different parts of a reunifying Europe meet the challenges of postcommunist reconstruction, resurgent nationalism, and economic union?*

Common Patterns and Problems

The end of the cold war and the disintegration of the Soviet Union ended the division of Europe into two opposing camps with two different political and economic systems. Thus, although Europe in the 1990s was a collage of diverse peoples with their own politics, cultures, and histories, the entire continent shared an underlying network of common developments and challenges.

Of critical importance, in economic affairs European leaders embraced, or at least accepted, a large part of the neoliberal, free-market vision of capitalist development. This was most strikingly the case in eastern Europe, where states such as Poland and Hungary implemented market reforms and sought to create vibrant capitalist economies. Thus postcommunist governments in eastern Europe freed prices, turned state enterprises over to private owners, and sought to move toward strong currencies and balanced budgets. Milder doses of this same free-market medicine were administered by politicians and big business to the lackluster economies of western Europe. These initiatives and proposals for further changes marked a considerable modification in western Europe's still-dominant welfare capitalism, which featured government intervention, high taxes, and high levels of social benefits.

Two factors were particularly important in accounting for this ongoing shift from welfare state activism to tough-minded capitalism. First, Europeans were only following practices and ideologies revived and enshrined in the 1980s in the United States and Great Britain (see page 1012). Western Europeans especially took American prescriptions more seriously because U.S. prestige and power were so high after the United States "won the cold war" and because the U.S. economy continued to outperform its western European counterparts in the Clinton years. Second, the deregulation of markets and the privatization of state-controlled enterprises were an integral part of the powerful trend toward a wide-open, wheeler-dealer global economy. The rules of the global economy, which were laid down by Western governments, multinational corporations, and international financial organizations such as the International Monetary Fund (IMF), called for the free movement of capital and goods and services, as well as low inflation and limited government deficits. Accepting these rules and attempting to follow them was the price of full participation in the global economy.

The ongoing computer and electronics revolution strengthened the move toward a global economy. That revolution thrived on the diffusion of ever-cheaper computational and informational capacity to small research groups and private businesses, which were both cause and effect of the revolution itself. By the 1990s, an inexpensive personal computer had the power of a 1950s mainframe that filled a room and cost hundreds of thousands of dollars. The computer revolution reduced the costs of distance, speeding up communications and helping businesses tap cheaper labor overseas. Reducing the friction of distance made threats of moving factories abroad ring true and helped hold down wages at home.

Globalization, the emergence of a freer global economy, probably did speed up world economic growth as enthusiasts invariably claimed, but it also had powerful and quite negative social consequences. Millions of ordinary citizens in western Europe believed that global capitalism and freer markets were undermining hard-won social achievements. As in the United States and Great Britain in the 1980s, the public in other countries generally associated globalization with the increased unemployment that accompanied corporate downsizing, the efforts to reduce the power of labor unions, and, above all, government plans to reduce social benefits. The reaction was particularly intense in France and Germany, where unions remained strong and socialists championed a minimum of change in social policies.

Indeed, the broad movement toward neoliberal global development sparked a powerful counterattack as the 1990s ended. Financial crises, which devastated many of Asia's smaller economies and threatened to spread, triggered this reaction. Many critics and protesters argued increasingly that globalization damaged poor countries as much as wealthy ones. Above all, critics insisted that globalization hurt the world's poor, because multinational corporations destroyed local industries and paid pitiful wages, and because international financial organizations

Santiago Calatrava: Tenerife Concert Hall, 2003 One of the most celebrated of the "postmodern" architects, who go beyond the modernism that dominated from the 1920s to the 1970s, Calatrava is known for swooping shapes and unusual spaces that convey a sense of motion to his buildings. The enormous, free-standing "roof" of this concert hall rises on a waterfront property like a cresting, crashing wave, linking the ocean with the city and beckoning tourists to Tenerife and Portugal's Canary Islands. Postmodern architects rely heavily on three-dimensional computer modeling to fashion complex forms and translate them into construction blueprints. *(Barbara Burg and Oliver Schuh/Palladium Photodesign, Cologne, Germany)*

demanded harsh balanced budgets and deep cuts in government social programs. These attacks shook global neoliberalism, but it remained dominant.

Political developments across Europe also were loosely unified by common patterns and problems. The demise of European communism brought the apparent triumph of liberal democracy everywhere. All countries embraced genuine electoral competition, with elected presidents and legislatures and the outward manifestations of representative liberal governments. With some notable exceptions, such as discrimination against Gypsies, countries also guaranteed basic civil liberties. Thus, for the first time since before the French Revolution, almost all of Europe followed the same general political model, although the variations were endless.

The triumph of the liberal democratic program led the American scholar Francis Fukuyama to discern in 1992 the "end of history" in his influential book by that title. According to Fukuyama, first fascism and Nazism and then communism had been definitively bested by liberal democratic politics and market economics. Conversely, as James Cronin perceptively noted in 1996 in *The World the Cold War Made*, the fall of communism also marked the return of nationalism and national history.[1] The cold war and the superpowers generally kept their allies and clients in line, either by force or by granting them conditional aid. As soon as the cold war was over, nationalism and ethnic conflict re-emerged, and history, as the story of different peoples, began again.

The resurgence of nationalism in the 1990s led to terrible tragedy and bloodshed in parts of eastern Europe, as it did in several hot spots in Africa and Asia. During the civil wars in Yugoslavia, many observers feared that national and ethnic hatreds would spread throughout eastern Europe and infect western Europe in the form of racial hostility toward minorities and immigrants. Yet if nationalist and racist incidents were a recurring European theme, they remained limited in the extent of their damage. Of critical importance in this regard was the fact that all European states wished to become or remain full-fledged members of the European society of nations and to join eventually an ever-expanding European Community, renamed the **European Union** in 1993. States that embraced national hatred and ethnic warfare, most notably Serbia, were branded as outlaws and boycotted and isolated by the European Union and the international community. The process of limiting resurgent nationalism in Europe was almost as significant as the resurgence itself.

Recasting Russia

Politics and economics were closely intertwined in Russia after the attempted Communist coup in 1991 and the dissolution of the Soviet Union. President Boris Yeltsin, his democratic supporters, and his economic ministers wanted to create conditions that would prevent forever a return to communism and would also right the faltering economy. Following the example of some postcommunist governments in eastern Europe and agreeing with those Western advisers who argued that private economies were always best, the Russian reformers opted in January 1992 for breakneck liberalization. Their "shock therapy" freed prices on 90 percent of all Russian goods, with the exception of bread, vodka, oil, and public transportation. The government also launched a rapid privatization of industry and turned thousands of factories and mines over to new private companies. Each citizen received a voucher worth 10,000 rubles (about $22) to buy stock in private companies, but control of the privatized companies usually remained in the hands of the old bosses, the managers and government officials from the communist era.

President Yeltsin and his economic reformers believed that shock therapy would revive production and bring prosperity after a brief period of hardship. The results of the reforms were in fact quite different. Prices increased 250 percent on the very first day, and they kept on soaring, increasing twenty-six times in the course of 1992. At the same time, Russian production fell a staggering 20 percent. Nor did the situation stabilize quickly. Throughout 1995 rapid but gradually slowing inflation raged, and output continued to fall. According to most estimates, in 1996 the Russian economy produced at least one-third and possibly as much as one-half less than in 1991. Only in 1997 did the economy stop declining, before crashing yet again in 1998 in the wake of Asia's financial crisis.

Rapid economic liberalization worked poorly in Russia for several reasons. Soviet industry had been highly monopolized and strongly tilted toward military goods. Production of many items had been concentrated in one or two gigantic factories or in interconnected combines that supplied the entire economy. With privatization these powerful state monopolies became powerful private monopolies, which cut production and raised prices in order to maximize their financial returns. Moreover, powerful managers and bureaucrats forced Yeltsin's government to hand out enormous subsidies and credits to reinforce the positions of big firms and to avoid bankruptcies and the discipline of a free market. The managerial elite also combined with criminal elements to intimidate would-be rivals and prevent the formation of new businesses. Not that most ordinary Soviet citizens were eager to start businesses. In the end, enterprise directors and politicians succeeded in eliminating worker ownership and converted large portions of previously state-owned industry into their own private property.

Runaway inflation and poorly executed privatization brought a profound social revolution to Russia. A new capitalist elite acquired great wealth and power, while large numbers of people fell into abject poverty, and the majority struggled in the midst of decline to make ends meet.

Managers, former officials, and financiers who came out of the privatization process with large shares of the old state monopolies stood at the top of the reorganized elite. The richest plums were found in Russia's enormous oil and natural resources industries, where unscrupulous enterprise directors pocketed enormous dishonest gains. The new elite was more highly concentrated than ever before. By 1996 Moscow, with 5 percent of Russia's population, accounted for 35 percent of the country's national income and controlled 80 percent of its capital resources.

At the other extreme, the vast majority saw their savings become practically worthless. Pensions lost much of their value, and whole markets were devoted to people selling off their personal goods to survive. Perhaps the most telling statistic, summing up millions of hardships and tragedies, was the truly catastrophic decline in the life expectancy of the average Russian male from sixty-nine years in 1991 to only fifty-eight years in 1996.

Rapid economic decline in 1992 and 1993 and rising popular dissatisfaction encouraged a majority of communists, nationalists, and populists in the Russian parliament to oppose Yeltsin and his coalition of democratic reformers and big-business interests. The erratic, increasingly hard-drinking Yeltsin would accept no compromise and insisted on a strong presidential system. Winning in April 1993 the support of 58 percent of the population in a referendum on his proposed constitution, Yeltsin then brought in tanks to crush a parliamentary mutiny in October 1993 and literally blew away the opposition. Subsequently, Yeltsin consolidated his power, and in 1996 he used his big-business cronies in the media to win an impressive come-from-behind victory. But effective representative government failed to develop, and many Russians came to equate "democracy" with the corruption, poverty, and national decline they experienced throughout the 1990s.

This widespread disillusionment set the stage for the "managed democracy" of Vladimir Putin, first elected president as Yeltsin's chosen successor in 2000 and re-elected in a landslide in March 2004. An officer in the secret police in the communist era, Putin maintained relatively free markets in the economic sphere but re-established semi-authoritarian political rule. Aided greatly by high oil prices for Russia's most important export, this combination worked well and seemed to suit most Russians. In 2007, the Russian economy had been growing rapidly for eight years, the Russian middle class was expanding, and the elected parliament supported Putin overwhelmingly. Proponents of liberal democracy were in retreat, while conservative Russian intellectuals were on the offensive, arguing

Russia's Leading Capitalist on Trial, 2004 Mikhail Khodorkovsky emerged from the privatization of Russian industry as the progressive chief and largest shareholder of Yukos, Russia's most successful oil company. But after he supported liberal opposition parties in 2002, an increasingly authoritarian President Putin jailed the billionaire, charged him with tax fraud, and confiscated his wealth before the trial even began. Putin's behavior was widely criticized in the West, but most ordinary Russians applauded because they believed the super rich had plundered the Russian state. *(Alexander Natruskin/Reuters/Corbis)*

that free markets and capitalism required strong political rule to control corruption and prevent chaos. Historians saw a reassertion of Russia's long authoritarian tradition.

Putin's forceful, competent image in world affairs also soothed the country's injured pride and symbolized its national resurgence. Nor did the government permit any negative television reports on the civil war in Chechnya, the tiny republic of 1 million Muslims on Russia's southern border, which in 1991 had declared its independence from the Russian Federation (see Map 31.2). The savage conflict in Chechnya continued, largely unreported, with numerous atrocities on both sides.

Progress in Eastern Europe

Developments in eastern Europe shared important similarities with those in Russia, as many of the problems were the same. Thus the postcommunist states of the former satellite empire worked to replace state planning and socialism with market mechanisms and private property. Western-style electoral politics also took hold, and as in Russia, these politics were marked by intense battles between presidents and parliaments and by weak political parties. The social consequences of these revolutionary changes were similar to those in Russia. Ordinary citizens and the elderly were once again the big losers, while the young and the ex-Communists were the big winners. Inequalities between richer and poorer regions also increased. Capital cities such as Warsaw, Prague, and Budapest concentrated wealth, power, and opportunity as never before, while provincial centers stagnated and old industrial areas declined. Crime and gangsterism increased in the streets and in the executive suites.

Yet the 1990s saw more than a difficult transition, with high social costs, to market economies and freely elected governments in eastern Europe. Many citizens had never fully accepted communism, which they equated with Russian imperialism and the loss of national independence. The joyous crowds that toppled communist regimes in 1989 believed that they were liberating the nation as well as the individual. Thus communism died and nationalism was reborn.

The surge of nationalism in eastern Europe recalled a similar surge of state creation after World War I. Then, too, authoritarian multinational empires had come crashing down in defeat and revolution. Then, too, nationalities with long histories and rich cultures had drawn upon ideologies of popular sovereignty and national self-determination to throw off foreign rule and found new democratic states.

The response to this opportunity in the former communist countries was quite varied in the 1990s, but most observers agreed that Poland, the Czech Republic, and Hungary were the most successful (see Map 31.3). Each of these three countries met the critical challenge of economic reconstruction more successfully than Russia, and each could claim to be the economic leader in eastern Europe, depending on the criteria selected. The reasons for these successes included considerable experience with limited market reforms before 1989, flexibility and lack of dogmatism in government policy, and an enthusiastic embrace of capitalism by a new entrepreneurial class. In the first five years of reform, Poland created twice as many new businesses as Russia, with a total population only one-fourth as large.

The three northern countries in the former Soviet bloc also did far better than Russia in creating new civic institutions, legal systems, and independent broadcasting networks that reinforced political freedom and national revival. Lech Walesa in Poland and Václav Havel in Czechoslovakia were elected presidents of their countries and proved as remarkable in power as in opposition. After Czechoslovakia's "Velvet Revolution" in 1989, Havel and the Czech parliament accepted a "velvet divorce" in 1993 when Slovakian nationalists wanted to break off and form their own state. All three northern countries managed to control national and ethnic tensions that might have destroyed their postcommunist reconstruction.

Above all, and in sharp contrast to Russia, the popular goal of "rejoining the West" reinforced political moderation and compromise. Seeing themselves as heirs to medieval Christendom and liberal democratic values in the 1920s, Poles, Hungarians, and Czechs hoped to find security in NATO membership and economic prosperity in western Europe's ever-tighter union. Membership required many proofs of character and stability, however. Providing these proofs and endorsed by the Clinton administration, Poland, Hungary, and the Czech Republic were accepted into the NATO alliance in 1997. Gaining admission to the European Union (EU) proved more difficult, because candidates also had to accept and be ready to apply all the rules and regulations that the EU had developed since 1956—an awesome task.

Romania and Bulgaria were the eastern European laggards in the postcommunist transition. Western traditions were much weaker there, and both countries were much poorer than neighbors to the north. In 1993 Bulgaria and Romania had per capita national incomes of $1,140, in contrast to Hungary ($3,830) and the Czech Republic ($2,710). Although Romania and Bulgaria eventually made progress in the late 1990s, full membership for both countries in either NATO or the EU still lay far in the future.

Escape from Srebrenica A Bosnian Muslim refugee arrives at the United Nations base in Tuzla and with her anguished screams tells the world of the Serbian atrocities. Several thousand civilians were murdered at Srebrenica, and Western public opinion finally demanded decisive action. Efforts continue to arrest those Serbs believed responsible and to try them for crimes against humanity. *(J. Jones/Corbis Sygma)*

Mapping the Past

MAP 31.3 Contemporary Europe No longer divided by ideological competition and the cold war, today's Europe features a large number of independent states. Several of these states were previously part of the Soviet Union and Yugoslavia, both of which broke into many different countries. Czechoslovakia also divided on ethnic lines, while a reunited Germany emerged, once again, as the dominant nation in central Europe. ❶ Which countries shown here were previously part of the Soviet Union? ❷ Which countries were part of Yugoslavia? ❸ Where did the old "iron curtain" run? (See Map 30.2, page 988, if necessary.)

Tragedy in Yugoslavia

The great postcommunist tragedy was Yugoslavia, which under Josip Tito had been a federation of republics and regions under strict communist rule (see page 996). After Tito's death in 1980, power passed increasingly to the sister republics, which encouraged a revival of regional and ethnic conflicts that were exacerbated by charges of ethnically inspired massacres during World War II and a dramatic economic decline in the mid-1980s.

The revolutions of 1989 accelerated the breakup of Yugoslavia. Serbian president Slobodan Milosevic intended to grab land from other republics and unite all Serbs, regardless of where they lived, in a "greater Serbia." In 1989 Milosevic arbitrarily abolished self-rule in the Serbian province of Kosovo, where Albanian-speaking people

MAP 31.4 The Ethnic Composition of Yugoslavia, 1991
Yugoslavia had the most ethnically diverse population in eastern Europe. The Republic of Croatia had substantial Serbian and Muslim minorities. Bosnia-Herzegovina had large Muslim, Serbian, and Croatian populations, none of which had a majority. In June 1991, Serbia's brutal effort to seize territory and unite all Serbs in a single state brought a tragic civil war.

constituted the overwhelming majority. Milosevic's moves strengthened the cause of separatism, and in June 1991 Slovenia and Croatia declared their independence. Slovenia repulsed a Serbian attack, but Milosevic's armies managed to take about 30 percent of Croatia. In 1992 the civil war spread to Bosnia-Herzegovina, which had declared its independence. Serbs—about 30 percent of that region's population—refused to live under the more numerous Bosnian Muslims (see Map 31.4). Yugoslavia had once been a tolerant and largely successful multiethnic state, with different groups living side by side and often intermarrying. The Bosnian civil war unleashed ruthless brutality, with murder, rape, destruction, and the herding of refugees into concentration camps.

While scenes of horror shocked the world, the Western nations had difficulty formulating an effective response. The turning point came in July 1995, when Bosnian Serbs overran Srebrenica—a Muslim city previously declared a United Nations "safe area"—and killed several thousand civilians. World outrage prompted NATO to bomb Bosnian Serb military targets intensively, and the Croatian army drove all the Serbs from Croatia. In November 1995, President Bill Clinton helped the warring sides hammer out a complicated accord that gave the Bosnian Serbs about 49 percent of Bosnia and the Muslim-Croatian peoples the rest. Troops from NATO countries patrolled Bosnia to try to keep the peace.

The Albanian Muslims of Kosovo had been hoping for a restoration of self-rule, but they gained nothing from the Bosnian agreement. In early 1998, frustrated Kosovar militants formed the **Kosovo Liberation Army (KLA)** and began to fight for independence. Serbian repression of the Kosovars increased, and in 1998 Serbian forces attacked both KLA guerrillas and unarmed villagers, displacing 250,000 people within Kosovo. By January 1999, the Western Powers, led by the United States, were threatening Milosevic with heavy air raids if he did not withdraw Serbian armies from Kosovo and accept self-government (but not independence) for Kosovo. Milosevic refused, and in March 1999 NATO began bombing Yugoslavia. Serbian paramilitary forces responded by driving about 780,000 Kosovars into exile. NATO redoubled its highly destructive bombing campaign, which eventually forced Milosevic to withdraw and allowed the joyous Kosovars to regain their homeland. The impoverished Serbs eventually voted the still-defiant Milosevic out of office, and in July 2001 a new pro-Western Serbian government turned him over to the war crimes tribunal in the Netherlands, to stand trial for crimes against humanity. The civil wars in the former Yugoslavia were a monument to human cruelty and evil in the worst tradition of the twentieth century. But ongoing efforts to preserve peace, repatriate refugees, and try war criminals also testified to the regenerative power of liberal values and human rights as the twenty-first century unfolded.

Unity and Identity in Western Europe

The movement toward western European unity, which since the late 1940s had inspired practical politicians seeking economic recovery and idealistic visionaries imagining a European identity that transcended destructive national rivalries, received a powerful second wind in the mid-1980s. The Single European Act of 1986 laid down a detailed legal framework for establishing a single market, which would add the free movement of labor, capital, and services to the existing free trade in goods. With work proceeding vigorously toward the single market, which went into effect in 1993 as the European Community proudly rechristened itself the European Union (EU), French president François Mitterrand and German chancellor Helmut Kohl took the lead in pushing for a monetary union of EU members. After long negotiations and compromises, designed especially to overcome Britain's long-standing reluctance to cede aspects of sovereignty, in December 1991 the member states reached an agreement in the Dutch town of Maastricht. The **Maastricht treaty** set strict financial criteria for joining the proposed monetary union, with its single currency, and set 1999 as the target date for its establishment. The treaty also anticipated the development of common policies on defense and foreign affairs after achieving monetary union.

Western European elites and opinion makers generally supported the decisive step toward economic integration embodied in the Maastricht treaty. They saw monetary union as a means of coping with Europe's ongoing economic problems, imposing financial discipline, cutting costs, and reducing high unemployment. European elites also viewed monetary union as a historic, irreversible step toward a basic political unity. This unity would allow western Europe as a whole to regain its rightful place in world politics and to deal with the United States as an equal.

The Maastricht plan for monetary union encountered widespread skepticism and considerable opposition from ordinary people, leftist political parties, and patriotic nationalists. Ratification votes were close, especially when the public rather than the politicians could vote yes or no on the question.

There were several interrelated reasons for this widespread popular opposition. Many people resented the unending flow of rules handed down by the EU's ever-growing bureaucracy in Brussels, which sought to impose common standards on everything from cheese to day care and undermined national practices and local traditions. Moreover, increased unity meant yielding still more power to distant "Eureaucrats" and political insiders, thereby undermining popular sovereignty and democratic control through national politics and electoral competition. Above all, many ordinary citizens feared that the new Europe was being made at their expense. Joining the monetary union required national governments to meet stringent fiscal standards and impose budget cuts. The resulting reductions in health care and social benefits hit ordinary citizens and did nothing to reduce western Europe's high unemployment rate.

Events in France dramatically illustrated these developments. Mitterrand's Socialist government had been forced to adopt conservative financial policies in the 1980s (see page 1012), and in early 1993 a coalition of conservatives and moderates won an overwhelming victory by promising a vigorous attack on unemployment. However, the Maastricht criteria soon forced the new government to resume deficit-reducing cuts in health benefits and transportation services. France's powerful unions and railroad workers responded with a crippling national strike that shut down rail traffic throughout France for almost a month. Yet despite the enormous inconvenience and economic damage, many people felt that the transport workers were also fighting for them. The government had to back down, and soon the Socialists returned to power. The Socialists quickly passed a controversial new law to reduce the legal workweek to thirty-five hours in an attempt to reduce France's stubborn 12 percent unemployment rate without budget-busting spending. More generally, much of the western European public increasingly saw laws to cut the workweek and share the work as a way to reconcile desires for social welfare and a humane market economy with financial discipline and global competition.

Battles over budgets and high unemployment throughout the European Union in the 1990s raised profound questions about the meaning of European unity and identity. Would the European Union expand as promised to include the postcommunist nations of eastern Europe, and if it did, how could Muslim Turkey's long-standing application be ignored? How could a European Union of twenty-five to thirty countries have any real cohesion and common identity? Conversely, would a large, cohesive Europe remain closely linked with the United States in the NATO alliance and with an evolving Western tradition?

The merging of East Germany into the German Federal Republic suggested the enormous difficulties of full East-West integration under the best conditions. After 1991 Helmut Kohl's Germany pumped massive investments into its new eastern provinces, but Germans in the east still saw factories closed and social dislocation. Unemployment in Germany reached a postwar high of 12.8 percent in late 1997, and it soared to 20 percent in the eastern region. Germany's generous social benefits cushioned the economic difficulties, but many ordinary citizens felt hurt and humiliated.

Eastern German women suffered in particular. Before unification, the overwhelming majority had worked outside the home, effectively supported by cheap child care, flexible hours, and the prevailing socialist ideology. Now they faced expensive child care and a variety of pressures to stay at home and let men take the hard-to-find jobs. Many of these women, who had found autonomy and self-esteem in paid work, felt a keen sense of loss. They helped vote Kohl out of office in 1998.

Instructed by the serious difficulties of unification in Germany, western Europeans proceeded cautiously in considering new requests for EU membership. Sweden, Finland, and Austria were admitted because they had strong capitalist economies and because they no longer needed to maintain the legal neutrality that the Soviet Union had required during the cold war.

Turkey's Struggle for EU Membership Turkish elites and the general population want to "join Europe," but the road to EU membership is proving long and difficult. The EU has required Turkey to make many constitutional reforms and give greater autonomy to Turkish Kurds. Yet the Turks face ever more demands, and many now believe that the real roadblock is Europe's anti-Muslim feeling. *(CartoonStock Limited)*

At the same time the former communist states pressed toward meeting the EU's detailed criteria for membership. In December 2000, the EU's fifteen members agreed to begin final negotiations with the eight leading eastern candidates in the near future. The very smooth establishment of the euro on January 1, 2002, when brand-new euros entered the billfolds of all euro-zone citizens as their unified common currency, built confidence and brought an acceleration of arduous but triumphant negotiations. Thus on May 1, 2004, the European Union added 70 million people and expanded to include 455 million citizens in twenty-five different countries. The largest newcomer by far was Poland, followed in descending size by the Czech Republic, Hungary, Slovenia, Slovakia, Estonia, Lithuania, Latvia, Malta, and Cyprus.

In June 2004, more than two years after charging a special commission to write "a new constitution for European citizens," the leaders of the European Union reached agreement on the final document. Above all, the new constitution, with almost 350 articles, established a single rulebook to replace the complex network of treaties concluded by the member states since the 1957 creation of the European Economic Community. The EU constitution created a president, a foreign minister, and a voting system weighted to reflect the number of people in the different states. The result of intense debate and many compromises, the constitution moved toward a more centralized federal system in several fields, but each state retained veto power in the most sensitive areas, such as taxation, social policy, and foreign affairs. In order for the constitution to take effect, each and every EU country needed to ratify it.

Nine countries, led by Germany, Italy, and seven eastern European members, soon ratified the constitution by parliamentary action, while seven states planned to go beyond the political elites and let the voters decide. The referendum campaigns were noisy and contentious, as generally well-informed citizens debated whether the new constitution surrendered too much national sovereignty to an emerging central European government in Brussels. British voters were considered most likely to vote no, but both the French and the Dutch beat them to it, rejecting the new constitution by clear majorities. Nationalist fears about losing sovereignty were matched by fears that an unwieldy European Union would grow to include Ukraine, Georgia, and Muslim Turkey—countries with cultures and histories that were very different from those in western Europe. Thus the long postwar march toward ever greater European unity stopped, or at least stalled, and the European Union concentrated on fully integrating the new eastern European members.

New Challenges in the Twenty-first Century

As the twenty-first century opened and the historic movement toward European unity began to include post-communist eastern Europe, European society faced new uncertainties. Of great significance, Europe continued to experience a remarkable **baby bust,** as birthrates fell to levels that seemed to promise a shrinking and aging population in the future. At the same time, the peaceful, wealthy European Union attracted rapidly growing numbers of refugees and illegal immigrants from the former Soviet Union, the Middle East, Africa, and Asia. The unexpected arrival of so many newcomers raised many perplexing questions and prompted serious thinking about European identity, Europe's humanitarian mission, and Europe's place in the world.

- *Why did the prospect of population decline, the reality of large-scale immigration, and concern for human rights emerge as critical issues in contemporary Europe?*

The Prospect of Population Decline

Population is still growing rapidly in many poor countries, but this is not the case in the world's industrialized nations. In 2000, women in developed countries had only 1.6 children on average; only in the United States did women have, almost exactly, the 2.1 children necessary to maintain a stable population. In European countries, where women have been steadily having fewer babies since the 1950s, national fertility rates ranged from 1.2 to 1.8 children per woman. Italy, once renowned for big Catholic families, had achieved the world's lowest birthrate—a mere 1.2 babies per woman. In 2006, the European fertility rate was little changed at about 1.4 children per woman.

If the current baby bust continues, the long-term consequences could be dramatic, though hardly predictable. At the least, Europe's population would decline and age. Projections for Germany are illustrative. Total German population, barring much greater immigration, would gradually decline from 82 million in 2001 to only 62 million around 2050. The number of people of working age would drop by a third, and almost half of the population would be over sixty. Social security taxes paid by the shrinking labor force would need to soar for the skyrocketing costs of pensions and health care for seniors to be met—a recipe for generational tension and conflict. As the premier of Bavaria, Germany's biggest state, has warned, the prospect of demographic decline was a "ticking time bomb under our social welfare system and entire economy."[2]

Why, in times of peace, were Europeans failing to reproduce themselves? Certainly the uneven, uninspiring European economic conditions of the 1980s and much of the 1990s played some role. High unemployment fell heavily on young people and often frustrated their plans to settle down and have children. Some observers also argued that a partial rejection of motherhood and parenting was critical. They noted that many women chose to have no children or only one child. By 2000, 30 percent of German women born in 1965 were childless, whereas 90 percent would have had children in earlier generations. In the Catholic countries of southern Europe, where strong pressures to have children still exist, a quarter of the couples were fulfilling their "social duty" with a single child.

In our view, the ongoing impact of careers for married women and the related drive for gender equality remained the decisive factors in the long-term decline of postwar birthrates. After World War II, Western women married early, had their children early, and then turned increasingly to full-time employment, where they suffered from the discrimination that drove the women's movement (see pages 1009–1010). As the twenty-first century opened, women had attained many (but not all) of their objectives. They did as well as or better than men in school, and educated young women earned almost as much as their male counterparts.

Research showed that European women (and men) in their twenties, thirties, and early forties still wanted to have two or even three children—about the same number as their parents had wanted. But unlike their parents, young couples did not realize their ideal family size. Many women postponed the birth of their first child into their thirties in order to finish their education and establish themselves in their careers. Then, finding that raising even one child was more difficult and time-consuming than anticipated, new mothers tended to postpone and eventually forgo a second child. This was especially true of professional women. The better educated and the more economically successful a woman was, the more likely she was to stop with a single child or to have no children at all.

By 2005 some population experts believed that European women were no longer postponing having children. At the least, birthrates appeared to have stabilized. Moreover, the frightening implications of dramatic population decline had emerged as a major public issue. Opinion leaders, politicians, and the media started to press the case for more babies and more support for families with children. Europeans may respond with enough vigor to limit the extent of their population decline and avoid societal disaster.

The Growth of Immigration

As European demographic vitality waned in the 1990s, a surge of migrants from Africa, Asia, and eastern Europe headed for western Europe. Some migrants entered the European Union legally, but increasing numbers were smuggled in past beefed-up border patrols. Large-scale immigration emerged as a contentious and critical challenge.

Historically a source rather than a destination of immigrants, booming western Europe drew heavily on North Africa and Turkey for manual laborers from about 1960 until about 1973, when unemployment started to rise and governments abruptly stopped the inflow. Many foreign workers stayed on, however, eventually bringing their families to western Europe and establishing permanent immigrant communities there.

A new and different surge of migration into western Europe began in the 1990s. The collapse of communism in the East and savage civil wars in Yugoslavia sent hundreds of thousands of refugees fleeing westward. Equally brutal conflicts in Afghanistan, Iraq, Somalia, and Rwanda—to name only four countries—brought thousands more from Asia and Africa. Illegal immigration into the European Union also exploded, rising from an estimated 50,000 people in 1993 to perhaps 500,000 a decade later. This movement exceeded the estimated 300,000 unauthorized foreigners entering the United States each year.

In the early twenty-first century, many migrants still applied for political asylum and refugee status, but most were eventually rejected and classified as illegal job seekers. Certainly, greater economic opportunities exerted a powerful pull. Germans earned on average five times more than neighboring Poles, who in turn earned much more than people farther east and in North Africa.

Illegal immigration also soared because powerful criminal gangs turned to "people smuggling" for big, low-risk profits. Ruthless Russian-speaking gangs played an important role in the trade, passing their human cargo across Russia and through the Balkans to western Europe. A favorite final leg involved Albanian smugglers with speedy motorboats, who slipped across the narrow Adriatic Sea past Italian coastal patrols and landed their high-paying passengers on the beaches of southern Italy. From there new arrivals could head off unimpeded in al-

Illegal Immigrants from Eritrea Italian police have just rescued these young immigrants from an overloaded boat off the coast of Italy. Fleeing civil war and desperate for work, the immigrants are weary because of the long and dangerous voyage from Libya. Every year thousands of illegal immigrants try to reach Italy and Spain from North Africa. Many are found dead on the shoreline. *(Mimi Mollica/Corbis)*

most any direction, because in 1998 the European Union abolished all border controls between member states. After 2000, growing numbers from Africa and the Middle East tried similar entries across the Strait of Gibraltar into southern Spain.

A large portion of the illegal immigrants were young women from eastern Europe, especially Russia and Ukraine. Often lured by criminals promising jobs as maids or waitresses and sometimes simply kidnapped and sold like slaves from hand to hand for a few thousand dollars, these women were smuggled into the most prosperous parts of central Europe and into the European Union and forced into prostitution or worse.

Illegal immigration generated intense discussion and controversy in western Europe. A majority opposed the newcomers, who were accused of taking jobs from the unemployed and somehow undermining national unity. The idea that cultural and ethnic diversity could be a force for vitality and creativity ran counter to deep-seated beliefs. Concern about illegal migration in general often fused with fears of Muslim immigrants and Muslim residents who had grown up in Europe. As busy mosques came to outnumber dying churches in parts of some European cities, rightist politicians especially tried to exploit widespread doubts that immigrant populations from Muslim countries would ever assimilate to the different national cultures. These doubts increased after the attack on New York's World Trade Center, as we shall see later in the chapter.

An articulate minority challenged the anti-immigrant campaign and its racist overtones. They argued that Europe badly needed newcomers—preferably talented newcomers—to limit the impending population decline and provide valuable technical skills. European leaders also focused on improved policing of EU borders and tougher common procedures to combat people smuggling and punish international crime. Above all, growing illegal immigration pushed Europeans to examine the whys of this dramatic human movement and to consider how it related to Europe's proper role in world affairs.

Promoting Human Rights

The tide of refugees and illegal job seekers made thinking people in western Europe acutely aware of their current good fortune, the sweet fruit of more than fifty years of peace, security, and rising standards of living. The nearby agonies of barbarism and war in the former Yugoslavia vividly recalled the horrors of World War II, and they cast in bold relief the ever-present reality of collective violence in today's world. At the same time, western European countries were generally doing their best to limit or expel the foreigners arriving at their gates, as we have seen. This ongoing rejection gave some Europeans a guilty conscience and a feeling that they needed to do more when they had so much and so many others had so little. As a result, European intellectuals and opinion makers began to envision a new historic mission for Europe—the promotion of domestic peace and human rights in those lands plagued by instability, violence, and oppression.

European leaders and humanitarians believed that Europe's mission required more global agreements and new international institutions to set moral standards and to regulate countries, political leaders, armies, corporations, and individuals. In practice, this meant more curbs on the sovereign rights of the world's states, just as the states of the European Union had imposed increasingly strict standards of behavior on themselves in order to secure the rights and welfare of EU citizens. As Nicole Gnesotto, the director of the European Union's institute, concluded, the EU has a "historical responsibility" to make morality "a basis of policy," because "human rights are more important than states' rights."[3] In general, the United States reacted coolly to the idea of preferring human rights to states' rights. American leaders stressed the preservation of U.S. freedom of action in world affairs, particularly after George W. Bush was elected president in 2000.

In practical terms, western Europe's evolving human rights mission meant, first of all, humanitarian interventions to stop civil wars and to prevent tyrannical governments from slaughtering their own people. Thus the European Union joined with the United States to inter-

Fighting the AIDS Epidemic These women, financed in part by the European Union, are treating an AIDS patient at his home in Mozambique. In 2004 the United Nations estimated that about 42 million persons were infected with HIV, the virus that causes AIDS. AIDS is the fourth-leading cause of death in the world. *(Black Star/stockphoto.com)*

vene militarily to stop the killing in Bosnia, Kosovo, and Macedonia and to protect the rights of embattled minorities (see pages 1037–1039). The states of the EU also vigorously supported UN-sponsored conferences and treaties that sought to verify the compliance of anti–germ warfare conventions, outlawed the use of hideously destructive land mines, and established a new international court to prosecute war criminals.

Europeans also pushed for broader definitions of individual rights. Abolishing the death penalty in the European Union, for example, they condemned its continued use in China, the United States, Saudi Arabia, and some other countries as inhumane and uncivilized. Rights for Europeans in their personal relations also continued to expand. In the pacesetting Netherlands, for example, a growing network of laws gave prostitutes (legally recognized since 1917) pensions and full workers' rights and legalized gay and lesbian marriages, the smoking of pot in licensed coffee shops, and assisted suicide (euthanasia) for the terminally ill.

As the twenty-first century opened, western Europeans also pushed as best they could to extend their broad-based concept of social and economic rights to the world's poor countries. These efforts were related to sharp criticism of globalization and unrestrained capitalism (see pages 1031–1032), criticism that helped socialists regain power in several countries in the European Union. Quite typically, Europe's moderate social democrats combined with human rights campaigners in 2001 to help African governments secure drastic price cuts from the big international drug companies on the drug cocktails needed to combat Africa's AIDS crisis. Strong advocates of greater social equality and state-funded health care, European socialists embraced morality as a basis for action and the global expansion of human rights as a primary goal.

The West and the Islamic World

A hundred years from now, when historians assess developments in the early twenty-first century, they will almost certainly highlight the dramatic deterioration in the long, rich, up-and-down relationship between the West and the Islamic world. They will examine the reasons that the peaceful conclusion of the cold war and the joyful reunification of a divided continent gave way to spectacular terrorist attacks, Western invasions of Muslim countries, and new concern about Muslims living in the West. Unfortunately, we lack the perspective and the full range of source materials that future historians will have at their disposal.

Yet we are deeply involved in this momentous historical drama, and we must try to find insight and understanding.

• *How and why did relations between the West and the Islamic world deteriorate dramatically in the early twenty-first century?*

The al-Qaeda Attack of September 11, 2001

On the morning of September 11, 2001, two hijacked passenger planes from Boston crashed into and destroyed the World Trade Center towers in New York City. Shortly thereafter a third plane crashed into the Pentagon, and a fourth, believed to be headed for the White House or the U.S. Capitol, crashed into a field in rural Pennsylvania. These terrorist attacks took the lives of more than three thousand people from many countries and put the personal safety of ordinary citizens at the top of the West's agenda. Stunned and horrified, the peoples and governments of the world joined Americans in heartfelt solidarity.

The United States, led by President George W. Bush, launched a military campaign to destroy the perpetrators of the crime—Saudi-born millionaire Osama bin Laden's al-Qaeda network of terrorists and Afghanistan's reactionary Muslim government, the Taliban. Drawing on the world's sympathy and building a broad international coalition that included western Europe, Russia, and Pakistan, the United States joined its tremendous airpower with the faltering Northern Alliance in Afghanistan, which had been fighting the Taliban for years. By mid-October 2001 American special forces on the ground were directing precision air strikes that devastated Taliban and al-Qaeda troops, and a rejuvenated Northern Alliance took the offensive. In mid-November the Taliban collapsed, and jubilant crowds in the capital of Kabul welcomed Northern Alliance soldiers as liberators. Afghan opposition leaders and United Nations mediators worked out plans for a new broad-based government, while American planes, ground troops, and tribal fighters searched for bin Laden and his die-hard supporters in their mountain hideaways. In 2002 foreign governments, aid organizations, and the United Nations turned to the arduous task of helping the Afghans get themselves back on their feet after a generation of conflict and civil war following the 1979 Soviet invasion of their country.

In trying to make some sense out of the heinous attack of September 11, 2001, and the current wave of terrorist action in general, it is helpful to realize that civil war and terrorism often went hand in hand in the twentieth century. Beginning in the 1920s and peaking in the 1960s, many nationalist movements used terrorism in their battles to achieve political independence and decolonization. This was the case in several new states, including Algeria, Cyprus, Ireland, Israel, and Yemen.[4] Those fighting for independence and political power often targeted police forces for assassination campaigns, thereby breaking down confidence in the colonial government and provoking counter-atrocities that generated increased support for the independence movement.

In the Vietnam War era, a second wave of terrorism saw some far-left supporters of the communist Vietcong, such as the American Weathermen, the German Red Army Faction, and the Italian Red Brigade, practicing "revolutionary terror" in an effort to cripple the Western heartland. These groups engineered a series of deadly bombings, assassinations, and kidnappings. These terrorists also hijacked airplanes—more than one hundred each year in the 1970s—in order to take hostages and blackmail governments into meeting some demand, such as the release of convicted fellow terrorists. Some terrorists trained in the facilities of the PLO (the Palestine Liberation Organization) operated international networks and targeted Israel and U.S. installations abroad. This second wave receded in the 1980s as painstaking police work and international cooperation defeated these "revolutionaries" in country after country.

In recent years a third wave has been building, leading toward al-Qaeda's attack on the World Trade Center and the Pentagon on September 11, 2001. In analyzing this third wave, many commentators were quick to stress the role of extreme Islamic fundamentalism as a motivating factor. But the most perceptive scholars noted that recent deadly attacks had been committed by terrorists inspired by several religious faiths and religious sects and were by no means limited to Islamic extremists.[5] These scholars noted that the different terrorist movements in today's

New York, September 11, 2001 Pedestrians race for safety as the World Trade Center towers collapse after being hit by jet airliners. Al-Qaeda terrorists with box cutters hijacked four aircraft and used three of them as suicide missiles to perpetrate their unthinkable crime. Heroic passengers on the fourth plane realized what was happening and forced their hijackers to crash in a field. *(AP Images/Suzanne Plunkett)*

world need to be linked to underlying political conflicts and civil wars for meaningful understanding.

When this perspective is applied to Osama bin Laden and al-Qaeda members, two stages stand out. First, in the long bitter fighting against the Soviet Union and the local communists in Afghanistan, bin Laden and like-minded "holy warriors" developed terrorist skills and a narrow-minded, fanatical Islamic puritanism. They also developed a hatred of most existing Arab governments, which they viewed as corrupt, un-Islamic, and unresponsive to the needs of ordinary Muslims. The objects of their hostility included the absolute monarchy of oil-rich Saudi Arabia (bin Laden's own country), pro-Western but undemocratic Egypt, and the secular, one-party dictatorship of Saddam Hussein.

Second, when these Islamic extremists returned home from Afghanistan and began to organize, they usually met the fate of many earlier Islamic extremists and were jailed or forced into exile, often in tolerant Europe. There they blamed the United States for being the supporter and corrupter of existing Arab governments, and they organized murderous plots against the United States—a despised proxy for the Arab rulers they could not reach. This development set the stage for the 1998 bombing of the U.S. embassy in Nairobi, Kenya, which claimed nearly 200 lives, the World Trade Center atrocity, and the U.S.-led counterattack on al-Qaeda in Afghanistan.

The War in Iraq

Unfortunately, Western unity in Afghanistan soon turned into bitter quarreling and international crisis over the prospect of war with Iraq. As soon as he was elected in 2000, President Bush and his most influential advisers, led by Vice President Dick Cheney and Secretary of Defense Donald Rumsfeld, began to consider how to overthrow Iraq's Saddam Hussein and remake the Middle East. Paul O'Neill, Bush's secretary of the treasury, summed up discussions on Iraq by the president and his cabinet this way: "From the start, they were building the case against Hussein and looking at how we could take him out and change Iraq into a new country. And, if we did that, it would solve everything."[6] And indeed, many in the administration believed that the United States could create a democratic, pro-American Iraq, an Iraq that would transform the Middle East, make peace with Israel, provide easy access to the world's second-largest oil reserves, and show small states the folly of opposing the United States. The most effective prowar argument, however, played on American fears of renewed terrorism and charged that Saddam Hussein was still developing weapons of mass destruction in flagrant disregard of his promise to end all such programs following the first war with Iraq, in 1991 (see page 1030). Saddam had used chemical weapons in his war with Iran in the 1980s and against the Kurdish population of northern Iraq, and the Bush administration argued that sooner or later he would probably use these terrible weapons against the United States and its allies or would give them to anti-American fanatics like those who struck New York on September 11, 2001.

In August 2002, Vice President Cheney promised Iraqi exiles that the United States would depose Saddam, although according to the United Nations charter, the Security Council has the sole authority to use armed force, except in self-defense, and Iraq, impoverished by a decade of tough United Nations sanctions, gave no indication of attacking any of its neighbors, much less the United States. Moreover, large numbers of Americans shared widespread doubts in Europe about the legality—and wisdom—of an American attack on Iraq and argued for a peaceful settlement of the Iraqi weapons crisis. So the Bush administration reluctantly agreed to new Security Council resolutions requiring Iraq to accept the return of United Nations weapons inspectors and destroy any remaining prohibited weapons. Iraq accepted the inspectors, declaring it had destroyed all prohibited weapons.

As 2003 opened, the inspectors operated freely in Iraq and found no weapons of mass destruction. However, the United States and Britain said Iraq was hiding prohibited weapons, moved armies to the Middle East, and lobbied for a new United Nations resolution authorizing immediate military action against Iraq. The world followed the debates in the Security Council with unprecedented interest and generally opposed an attack on Iraq. France, Russia, China, Germany, and a majority of the smaller states argued for continued weapons inspections. Western governments became bitterly divided, and the Security Council deadlocked and failed to act.

In March 2003 the United States and Britain invaded Iraq from bases in Kuwait and quickly overwhelmed the Iraqi army. Yet even as Saddam's dictatorship collapsed, the confident expectation of a long and peaceful occupation in a pro-American Iraq was impaired by serious errors of American judgment. As chaos spread and looters stripped government buildings and hospitals of everything from computers to faucets, American and British troops simply turned a blind eye and took no action. Disbanding the Iraqi army also alienated the population, worsened security, and created mass unemployment, while the failure to seize huge stocks of weapons left Iraqi

The Golden Mosque of Samarra: Before and After Built to commemorate two of Shi'ite Islam's most revered saints, the Golden Mosque drew countless Shi'ite pilgrims. Then, on June 13, 2006, insurgents dressed as Iraqi policemen entered the mosque, overwhelmed the guards, and detonated two bombs that collapsed the golden dome and destroyed the mosque. Sectarian conflict exploded. (A second terrorist bombing in June 2007 levelled the two minarets seen on the right.) *(AP Images/Khalid Mohammed, Hameed Rasheed)*

insurgents with guns and explosives for subsequent counterattacks. The allies found no weapons of mass destruction, which raised many questions about a prewar manipulation of intelligence data.

American efforts to establish a stable, pro-American Iraq proved difficult if not impossible. Poor postwar planning and management by President Bush and his top aides was one factor, but there were others. Modern Iraq, a creation of Western imperialism after World War I (see page 906), is a fragile state with three distinct groups: non-Arab Kurds, and Sunnis and Shi'ites—Arab Muslims who were forever divided by a great schism in the seventh century. Saddam's dictatorship preached Arab and Iraqi nationalism, but it relied heavily on the Sunni minority—20 percent of the population—and repressed the Shi'ites, who made up 60 percent of the population. Jailed or ousted from their positions by American forces, top Sunnis quickly turned against the occupation, rallied their supporters, and launched an armed insurgency. By late 2004, radical Sunnis and al-Qaeda converts were slipping into Iraq, where they directed horrendous suicide bombings at American soldiers, Iraqi security forces, and defenseless Shi'ite civilians.

Believing in democracy and representative institutions, the Americans restored Iraqi sovereignty in July 2004, formed a provisional government, and held relatively free national elections in January 2005. Boycotted by the Sunnis, these elections brought the Shi'ite majority to power and marked the high point of Iraqi and American hopes for security and a gradual reconciliation with the Sunni population. Instead, Sunni fighters and jihadist extremists stepped up their deadly campaign. Then, in February 2005 in a carefully planned operation, they blew up the beautiful Golden Mosque of Samarra, one of the most sacred shrines of Shi'ite Islam. This outrage touched off violent retaliation. Shi'ite militias became death squads, killing Sunnis and driving them from their homes. By 2006 a deadly sectarian conflict had taken hold of Baghdad. American soldiers, continuing loyally to do their duty, were increasingly caught in the crossfire. In 2007, as President Bush faced widespread opposition at home, it seemed unlikely that yet another intensification of American efforts to create stability in Iraq would succeed.

The West and Its Muslim Citizens

The attack on the World Trade Center and the long war in Iraq, signaling a dramatic worsening of relations between the West and the Islamic world, had major repercussions in Western countries. In the United States there were great fears of more terrorist attacks, but to almost everyone's surprise Europe received the extremists' next blows. In May 2004 Moroccan Muslims living in Spain exploded bombs planted on morning trains bound for Madrid and killed 252 commuters. A year later a similar attack was carried out in London by British citizens of Pakistani descent, young men who had grown up in Britain and seemed to be ordinary fellows.

Even more traumatic for the tolerant Dutch and many other Europeans was the repeated stabbing and brutal murder of Theo van Gogh by a young Dutch Muslim. Van Gogh, a provocative filmmaker, had joined an anti-Islamic feminist and refugee from East Africa in making a vulgar ten-minute film that mocked the prophet Muhammad and denounced Islam's treatment of women. For his "blasphemy," van Gogh was "executed" by the son of Moroccan immigrants, who proudly explained his action to the court in colloquial Dutch.

These spectacular attacks and lesser actions by Islamic militants sharpened the European debate on immigration (see pages 1042–1044). A shrill chorus warned that, in addition to the security danger, Europe's rapidly growing Muslim population posed a dire threat to the West's entire Enlightenment tradition, which embraced freedom of thought, representative government, toleration, separation of church and state, and, more recently, equal rights for women and gays. Islamic extremists and radical clerics settled in Europe were, the critics claimed, rejecting these fundamental Western values and preaching instead the supremacy of Islamic laws for Muslims living in Europe, and even for non-Muslim Europeans on some issues. Moreover, the critics claimed, many "moderate" Islamic teachers were really anti-Western radicals playing for time. (See the feature "Individuals in Society: Tariq Ramadan.") And time was on the side of Euro-Islam. Europe's Muslim population, estimated at 15 million in 2006, appeared likely to double to 30 million by 2025, and it would increase rapidly thereafter as the number of non-Europeans plummeted (see pages 1041–1042).

Admitting that Islamic extremism could pose a serious challenge, many mainstream observers focused instead on the problem of immigrant integration. Whereas the first generation of Muslim immigrants—predominately Turks in Germany, Algerians in France, Pakistanis in Britain, and Moroccans in the Netherlands—had found jobs as unskilled workers in Europe's great postwar boom, they and their children had been hard hit after 1973 by the general economic downturn. Immigrants also suffered from the ongoing decline of European manufacturing due to globalization. Provided for modestly by the welfare state and housed minimally in ugly housing projects, many Muslims of the second and third generations were finding themselves locked out in their adopted countries. In short, economics, inadequate job training, and discrimination trumped religion and extremist teachings.

This argument was strengthened by widespread rioting in France in November 2005 that saw hundreds of young second- and third-generation Muslim immigrants go on a rampage. Almost always French by birth, language, and education, marauding groups of "Arabs" torched hundreds of automobiles night after night in Paris suburbs and large cities. (See the feature "Listening to the Past: The French Riots: Will They Change Anything?" on pages 1054–1055.) The rioters complained bitterly of very high unemployment, systematic discrimination, and exclusion. Religious ideology appeared almost nonexistent in their thinking. Studies sparked by the rioting in France found poor, alienated Muslims in unwholesome ghettos throughout western Europe.

Although Muslim immigrants in the United States certainly experienced increased hostility after the September 11 attack, it was generally recognized that they were integrating more successfully with their adopted homeland than were their European counterparts. This is partly because the United States believes that it has always been a nation of immigrants, whereas the European ideal remains the homogeneous national state. Equally important, Muslim immigrants to the United States have often been well educated, have come from several countries speaking different languages, and have spread out within cities and across the country. Muslim immigrants to western Europe, usually a larger percentage of the host country's population than in America, have generally been poor rural people with limited education who came to do manual labor. In each of the leading host countries, they came mainly from a single Muslim country and then lived together on the fringes of the largest cities. Muslim immigrants to the United States brought more "human capital," and this facilitated more successful integration.

Finally, the fact that Americans and western Europeans have gone their separate ways on religion probably impacts their relations with their Muslim citizens. A large though declining number of Americans still take religion seriously, whereas western Europeans have largely abandoned Christianity, with less than 5 percent of the population attending church on most Sundays. Thus many Americans still can—or should—understand and even appreciate the power of Islam for devout Muslims, whereas western Europeans tend to find all traditional religious belief irrational and out-of-date. This is why, in addition to determined efforts to root out anti-Muslim discrimination, the renowned French scholar Olivier Roy argues, Europe must recognize that Islam is now a European religion and a vital part of European life. This recognition, he argues, will open the way to eventual full acceptance of European Muslims in both political and cultural terms. It will head off the resentment that can drive Europe's Muslim believers to separatism and acts of terror.

The Future in Perspective

- **What does the study of history have to tell us about the future?**

For centuries astrologers and scientists, experts and ordinary people, have sought to peek into the future. And although it may seem that the study of the past has little to say about the future, the study of history over a long period is actually very useful in this regard. It helps put the future in perspective.

Certainly, history is full of erroneous predictions, a few of which we have mentioned in this book. Yet lack of success has not diminished the age-old desire to look into the future. Self-proclaimed experts even pretend that they have created a new science of futurology. With great pomposity, they often act as if their hunches and guesses about future human development are inescapable realities. Yet the study of history teaches healthy skepticism regarding such predictions, however scientific and learned they may appear. Past results suggest that most such predictions will simply not come true, or at least not in the anticipated ways. Thus history provides some psychological protection from the visions of modern prognosticators.

This protection is particularly valuable when we realize that views of the future tend to swing between pessimistic and optimistic extremes from one generation, or even from one decade, to the next. These swings back and forth between optimism and pessimism, which one historian has aptly called "the great seesaw" in the development of the Western world, reflect above all the current situation of the observers.[7] Thus in the economic stagnation and revived cold war of the 1970s and 1980s, many projections into the future were quite pessimistic, just as they were very optimistic in the 1950s and 1960s. Many people in the Western world feared that conditions were going to get worse rather than better. For example, there were fears that pollution would destroy the environment and that the traditional family would disappear. Some gloomy experts predicted that twenty to thirty states might well have nuclear weapons by the end of the twentieth century. Many forecasters and politicians predicted that the energy crisis—in the form of skyrocketing oil prices—meant disaster in the form of lower standards of living at best and the collapse of civilization at worst. In fact, oil prices collapsed in the early 1980s and generally stayed low until the second Iraq war in 2003. It was heartening in that time of pessimism to know that most dire predictions do not prove true, just as the same knowledge of likely error is sobering in times of optimistic expectations.

Optimistic visions of the future were certainly in the air after the end of the cold war. The pendulum had definitely swung, most notably in the United States. Untroubled in the late 1990s by the high unemployment and the early stages of corporate downsizing that soured the mood in western Europe, the United States celebrated its dynamic economy and its booming stock market. U.S. military power, leadership in world affairs, and excellence in advanced technologies also encouraged optimism and rosy projections.

In 2000 the American mood shifted. The dot-com bubble burst, and in 2001 the U.S. economy slid into a recession. The al-Qaeda attack on New York and the tragic war in Iraq, with its endless carnage and suicide bombings, led to many pessimistic forecasts of a long uphill struggle against global extremism, especially Islamic extremism. Most frightening of all were grim warnings by some self-described experts who predicted that terrorist groups were likely to succeed in developing or buying biological and nuclear weapons of mass destruction, which they would then turn on millions of innocent people with unspeakable cruelty. Such nightmare scenarios are not impossible, but we should remember that modern governments possess tremendous resources that they can mobilize to control individuals and opposition groups, especially when the leading states decide to work together, as they did immediately after September 11, 2001. Once again, just as it is sobering to know that the rosiest predictions in optimistic times usually do not prove true, so is it heartening to know that the direst projections in pessimistic times normally do not come to pass.

Whatever does or does not happen, the study of history puts the future in perspective in other ways. We have seen that every age has its problems and challenges. Others before us have trodden the paths of uncertainty and crisis. This knowledge helps save us from exaggerated self-pity in the face of our own predicaments.

Perhaps our Western heritage may rightly inspire us with pride and measured self-confidence. We stand, momentarily, at the head of the long procession of Western civilization. Sometimes the procession has wandered, or backtracked, or done terrible things. But it has also

Individuals in Society

Tariq Ramadan

Religious teacher, activist professor, and media star, Tariq Ramadan (b. 1962) is Europe's most famous Muslim intellectual. He is also a controversial figure, praised by many as a moderate bridge-builder and denounced by others as an Islamic militant in clever disguise.

Born in Switzerland of Egyptian ancestry, Ramadan is the grandson of Hassan al-Banna, the charismatic founder of the powerful Muslim Brotherhood. Al-Banna fought to reshape Arab nationalism within a framework of Islamic religious orthodoxy and anti-British terrorism until he himself was assassinated in 1949. Growing up in Geneva, where his father sought refuge in 1954 after Nasser's anti-Islamic crackdown in Egypt, the young Tariq attended mainstream public schools, played soccer, and absorbed a wide-ranging Islamic heritage. For example, growing up fluent in French and Arabic, he learned English mainly from listening to Pakistani Muslims discuss issues with his father, who represented the Muslim Brotherhood and its ideology in Europe.

Ramadan studied philosophy and French literature as an undergraduate at the University of Geneva, and he then earned a doctorate in Arabic and Islamic studies. Marrying a Swiss woman who converted to Islam, Ramadan moved his family to Cairo in 1991 to study Islamic law and philosophy. It proved to be a pivotal experience. Eagerly anticipating the return to his Muslim roots, Ramadan gradually realized that only in Europe did he feel truly "at home." In his personal experience he found his message: that Western Muslims should feel equally "at home" and that they should participate fully as active citizens in their adopted countries.

In developing his message, Ramadan left the classroom and focused on creating non-scholarly books, audio cassettes that sell in the tens of thousands, and media events. Slim and elegant in well-tailored suits and open collars, Ramadan is a brilliant speaker. His public lectures in French and English draw hundreds of Muslims (and curious non-Muslims).

Ramadan argues that Western Muslims basically live in security, have fundamental legal rights, and can freely practice their religion. He notes that Muslims in the West are often more secure than are believers in the Muslim world, where governments are frequently repressive and arbitrary. According to Ramadan, Islamic teaching requires Western Muslims to obey Western laws, although in rare cases they may need to plead "conscientious objection" and disobey on religious grounds. Becoming full citizens and refusing to live in parallel as the foreign Other, Muslims should work with non-Muslims on matters of common concern, such as mutual respect, better schools, and economic justice.* Ramadan is most effective with second- or third-generation college graduates. He urges them to think for themselves and distinguish the sacred revelation of Islam from the nonessential cultural aspects that their parents brought from African and Asian villages.

With growing fame has come growing controversy. In 2004, preparing to take up a professorship in the United States, he was denied an entry visa on the grounds that he had contributed to a Palestinian charity with ties to terrorists. Defenders disputed the facts and charged that his criticism of Israeli policies and the invasion of Iraq were the real reasons. Ramadan's critics also claim that he says different things to different groups: hard-edged criticism of the West found on tapes for Muslims belies the reasoned moderation of his books. Some critics also argue that his recent condemnation of Western capitalism and globalization is an opportunistic attempt to win favor with European leftists and does not reflect a self-proclaimed Islamic passion for justice. Yet, on balance, Ramadan's reputation remains intact.† An innovative bridge-builder, he symbolizes the growing importance of Europe's Muslim citizens.

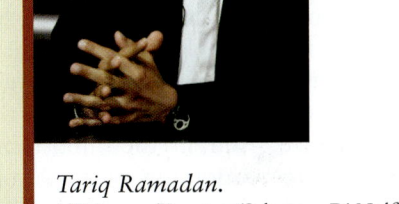

Tariq Ramadan.
(AP Images/Keystone/Salvatore Di Nolfi)

Questions for Analysis

1. What is Ramadan's message to Western Muslims? How did he reach his conclusions?
2. Do you think Ramadan's ideas are realistic? Why?

*See, especially, Tariq Ramadan, *Western Muslims and the Future of Islam* (Oxford: Oxford University Press, 2004).
†See Ian Buruma, *The New York Times Magazine*, February 4, 2007.

Online Study Center **Improve Your Grade**
Going Beyond Individuals in Society

carried the efforts and sacrifices of generations of toiling, struggling ancestors. Through no effort of our own, we are the beneficiaries of those sacrifices and achievements. Now that it is our turn to carry the torch onward, we may remember these ties with our forebears.

To change the metaphor, we in the West are like a card player who has been dealt many good cards. Some of them are obvious, such as our technical and scientific heritage or our commitment to human rights, religious freedom, and the individual. Others are not so obvious, sometimes half-forgotten or even hidden up the sleeve. Think, for example, of the Christian Democrats, the moderate Catholic party that emerged after World War II to play such an important role in the western European renaissance. And in the almost miraculous victory of peaceful revolution in eastern Europe in 1989—in what Czech playwright-turned-president Václav Havel called "the power of the powerless"—we see again the regenerative strength of the Western ideals of individual rights, representative government, and nationhood in the European homeland. We hold a good hand.

Our study of history, of mighty struggles and fearsome challenges, of shining achievements and tragic failures, gives a sense of the essence of life itself: the process of change over time. Again and again we have seen how peoples and societies evolve, influenced by ideas, human passions, and material conditions. As surely as anything is sure, this process of change over time will continue as the future becomes the present and then the past. And students of history are better prepared to make sense of this unfolding process because they have already observed it. They know how change is rooted in existing historical forces, and their projections will probably be better than many of the trendy speculations of futurologists. Students of history are also prepared for the new and unexpected in human development, for they have already seen great breakthroughs and revolutions. They have an understanding of how things really happen.

Demonstrating for Peace Millions long for peace, but history and current events suggest that bloody conflicts will continue. Yet there is cause for some cautious optimism: since 1945 wars have been localized and cataclysmic catastrophes like World Wars I and II have been averted. Holding torches, some 3,500 people form the sign of peace in an antiwar, antiviolence rally in Heroes Square in central Budapest. The rally marked the third anniversary of the U.S.-led invasion of Iraq. *(Peter Kollanyi/epa/Corbis)*

Chapter Summary

- In what ways did Solidarity confront the communist system in Poland, and how did Mikhail Gorbachev try to reverse the decline of communism in the Soviet Union?
- How did anticommunist revolutions sweep through eastern Europe in 1989, and what were the immediate consequences?
- How, in the 1990s, did the different parts of a reunifying Europe meet the challenges of postcommunist reconstruction, resurgent nationalism, and economic union?
- Why did the prospect of population decline, the reality of large-scale immigration, and concern for human rights emerge as critical issues in contemporary Europe?
- How and why did relations between the West and the Islamic world deteriorate dramatically in the early twenty-first century?
- What does the study of history have to tell us about the future?

The rise of Solidarity in Poland showed again that the communist system in eastern Europe depended ultimately on Soviet armies. Therefore, when the Russian leader Mikhail Gorbachev refused to use force abroad and his ambitious reforms at home spiraled out of control, the peoples of eastern Europe rose and overturned communist rule in the spectacular, peaceful revolutions of 1989. In a dramatic finale, the democratic movement triumphed in the Soviet Union, the two Germanies joined in a single state, the cold war ended, and the United States remained the only superpower.

In the 1990s, post–cold war Europe grappled with neoliberal market economies, welfare systems under continuing attack, and globalization. Social and economic reconstruction in Russia was less successful than it was in eastern Europe, with the glaring exception of the former Yugoslavia, which was destroyed by resurgent ethnic nationalism. Eastern Europe's rebuilding and its determination to "rejoin Europe" stimulated the long postwar movement toward European unity, and the newly named European Union expanded to include almost all of Europe west of Russia, Ukraine, and the Caucasus. This triumph was the shining achievement of the post–cold war era.

The twenty-first century highlighted critical issues, and we have seen how the European baby bust, the growth of illegal immigration, and the increased commitment to human rights were all interrelated. The most disturbed development was the renewed hostility between the West and the Islamic world, which was marked indelibly by the al-Qaeda attack of 2001, the campaign to punish Afghanistan, and the American and British invasion of Iraq. Essentially an effort to remake Iraq (and the Arab world) along Western lines, the war in Iraq saw American soldiers run up against a potent combination of Arab nationalism, Islamic extremism, and sectarian conflict. War in the Middle East encouraged shrill cries about an ominous Muslim threat from immigrants living in western Europe, but a study of history would suggest that these fears were greatly exaggerated.

Key Terms

Gdansk Agreement
Solidarity
perestroika
glasnost
shock therapy
Velvet Revolution
third way
Alliance for Germany
Paris Accord
"new world order"
globalization
European Union
Kosovo Liberation Army (KLA)
Maastricht treaty
baby bust

Suggested Reading

Bernstein, Richard B. *Out of the Blue: A Narrative of September 11, 2001.* 2003. A gripping account by a talented journalist.

Brubaker, Rogers. *Nationalism Reframed: Nationhood and the National Question.* 1996. An excellent analysis of the contemporary resurgence of nationalism.

(continued on page 1056)

Listening to the Past

The French Riots: Will They Change Anything?

In late November 2005, young Muslim males rioted for several nights in the suburbs of Paris and other French cities. Receiving saturation coverage from the media, this explosion of car-burning and arson ignited controversy and debate throughout France and across Europe. What caused the riots? What could and should be done? How did the conditions of second- and third-generation Muslims in France compare with conditions of Muslims in other Western countries?

One penetrating commentary, aimed at an American audience and reprinted here, came from William Pfaff, a noted author and political columnist with many years of European experience. As you read Pfaff's analysis, note in particular the contrast he draws between the French government's policy toward Muslims and the policy pursued in Britain and the Netherlands.

The rioting in France's ghetto suburbs is a phenomenon of futility—but a revelation nonetheless. It has no ideology and no purpose other than to make a statement of distress and anger. It is beyond politics. It broke out spontaneously and spread in the same way, communicated by televised example, ratified by the huge attention it won from the press and television and the politicians, none of whom had any idea what to do.

It has been an immensely pathetic spectacle, whose primary meaning has been that it happened. It has been the most important popular social phenomenon in France since the student uprisings of 1968. But those uprisings . . . had consequences for power. The new riots have nothing to do with power.

They started with the accidental electrocutions of two boys hiding from the police, who they thought were after them. The police say there was no pursuit and they had no interest in the boys. However, under the policies of the minister of interior—the presidential candidate Nicolas Sarkozy—there had been a general police crackdown in these ugly suburban clusters of deteriorating high-rise apartments built years ago to house immigrant workers. They were meant to be machines for living. The police attention meant random identity checks, police suspicion, and harassment of young men hanging about—maybe dealing in drugs, maybe simply doing nothing because there is nothing for them to do. (In the past, they at least had to do national military service, which was a strong integrative force, but now France has a professional army.)

Their grandfathers came to France, mostly from North Africa, to do the hard labor in France's industrial reconstruction after the Second World War. Their fathers saw the work gradually dry up as Europe's economies slowed, following the first oil shock in the early 1970s. After that came unemployment. The unemployment rate in the zones where there has been the most violence is nearly 40 percent and among young people it is higher. Many of the young men in these places have never been offered a job. When they applied, their names often excluded them.

Their grandfathers were hard-working men. Their fathers saw their manhood undermined by unemployment. These young men are doomed to be boys. They often take their frustration out on their sisters and girlfriends, who are more likely to have done well in school and found jobs—and frequently a new life—outside the ghetto. . . .

The Muslim mothers and wives of the French ghetto are often confined in the home. Drugs are big business in the American ghetto; they are not that big in France. The crimes of the French ghetto are robbery and shoplifting, stealing mobile phones, stealing cars for joyrides, burning them afterward to eliminate fingerprints, or burning cars just for the hell of it, as well as robbing middle-class students in the city and making trouble on suburban trains, looking for excitement.

Religion is important . . . in the French ghetto, it provides the [shell] that protects against the France that excludes Muslims. To the European Muslim, it seems that all of the powerful in the world are in collusion to exclude Muslims—or are at war with them. The war in Iraq, on television, is the constant backdrop to Muslim life in Europe. There are itinerant imams who can put the young ghetto Muslim on the road to danger and adventure in Afghanistan, Pakistan, Iraq—or elsewhere. There are plenty more who preach a still deeper ghettoization: a retreat inside Islamic fundamentalism, totally shutting out a diabolized secular world.

One would think there would be a revolutionary potential in these ghettos, vulnerability to a mobilizing ideology. This seems not to be so. We may be living in a religious age, but it is not one of political ideology. In any case, it is difficult to imagine how the marginalized, thirteen- to twenty-three-year-old children of the Muslim immigration could change France other than by what they are doing, which is to demonstrate that the French model of assimilating immigrants as citizens, and not as members of religious or ethnic groups, has failed for them. It has failed because it has not seriously been tried.

The ghettoization of immigrant youth in France is the consequence of negligence. It has been as bad as the ghettoization through political correctness of Muslims in Britain and the Netherlands, where many people who thought of themselves as enlightened said that assimilation efforts were acts of cultural aggression. The immigrant in France is told that he or she is a citizen just like everyone else, with all the rights and privileges of citizenship—including the right to be unemployed.

Nicolas Sarkozy's zero tolerance of crime and of the petty mafias in the ghetto contributed to touching off these riots, but until recently he was the only French politician to say there has to be affirmative action to get an immigrant elite out of the ghettos and into important roles in French life, where they can pull their communities after them. Some affirmative action has been attempted in recruiting candidates for the elite *grandes écoles* [state schools] that train the French administrative and political class, where the cultural hurdles are immense for candidates. Virtually no children of the Muslim immigration are prominent in mainstream electoral politics; the political parties have yet to make a serious effort to include them. The present government has one junior minister of Algerian origin. I am not aware of any Muslims of immigrant origin in French diplomacy or the top ranks of police and military.

President Jacques Chirac has announced a civilian national service agency to give training and employment to 50,000 young people from the troubled zones by 2007. The age of apprenticeship has been lowered to fourteen, with a corresponding drop in the age of compulsory academic schooling and new measures to support apprenticeships. There will be more money for schools, local associations, and housing construction and renovation. This is change. Whether it is enough, and in time, is another matter.

French police face off with young rioters, silhouetted against the flames of burning automobiles. *(Reuters/Corbis)*

Questions for Analysis

1. Describe the situation of young Muslims in France. What elements of their situation strike you most forcefully? Why?

2. France has maintained that, since all citizens are equal, they should all be treated the same way. Why has this policy failed for French Muslims? What alternatives would you suggest? Why?

Source: William Pfaff, "The French Riots: Will They Change Anything?" *The New York Review of Books,* December 15, 2005, pp. 88–89. Reprinted with permission from The New York Review of Books. Copyright © 2005 NYREV, Inc.

Buruma, Ian. *Murder in Amsterdam: The Death of Theo van Gogh and the Limits of Toleration*. 2006. A masterful, very readable investigation of the crime that electrified Europe.

Dobbs, Michael. *Down with Big Brother: The Fall of the Soviet Empire*. 1998. A superb firsthand study by an inspired journalist.

Johnson, Lonnie R. *Central Europe: Enemies, Neighbors, Friends*. 2001. A book that ably interprets developments in eastern Europe before and after the revolutions of 1989.

Lampe, John R. *Yugoslavia as History: Twice There Was a Country*, 2d ed. 2003. An excellent, judicious work on the tragedy in Yugoslavia.

Lucassen, Leo. *The Immigrant Threat: The Integration of Old and New Immigrants in Western Europe Since 1850*. 2005. Argues effectively that Muslims are assimilating as rapidly as previous immigrants.

Reid, T. R. *The United States of Europe: The New Superpower and the End of American Supremacy*. 2005. A lively, informative examination by a perceptive American.

Ross, George. *Jacques Delors and European Integration*. 1995. Analyzes the controversies surrounding the European Union in the 1990s.

Sakwa, Richard. *Putin: Russia's Choice*. 2003. Puts the Russian leader in social and historical context.

Shore, Zachary. *Breeding Bin Ladens: America, Islam, and the Future of Europe*. 2006. A comprehensive overview of the Muslim question in Europe.

Stiglitz, Joseph E. *Making Globalization Work*. 2006. An excellent overview of the successes and failures of globalization by a distinguished economist.

Suny, Ronald Grigor. *The Soviet Experiment: Russia, the USSR, and the Successor States*. 1998. An outstanding history of Russia in the 1990s.

Viorst, Milton. *Storm from the East: The Struggle Between the Arab World and the Christian West*. 2007. Recommended short study of twentieth-century developments within a broad historical perspective.

Woodward, Bob. *State of Denial: Bush at War, Part III*. 2006. Best-selling account based on extensive interviews.

Notes

1. F. Fukuyama, *The End of History and the Last Man* (New York: Free Press, 1992); and J. Cronin, *The World the Cold War Made: Order, Chaos, and Return of History* (New York: Routledge, 1996), pp. 267–281.
2. Quoted in *The Economist,* January 6, 2001, p. 6.
3. Quoted by Flora Lewis, *International Herald Tribune,* June 15, 2001, p. 6.
4. D. Rappaport, "The Fourth Wave: September 11 in the History of Terrorism," *Current History,* December 2001, pp. 419–424.
5. Ibid.
6. R. Suskind, *The Price of Loyalty: George W. Bush, the White House, and the Education of Paul O'Neill* (New York: Simon and Schuster, 2004), p. 86.
7. G. Blainey, *The Great Seesaw: A New View of the Western World* (London: Macmillan, 1988).

Index

Abandoned children, 660, 736
Abbas I (Safavid), 489, 490
Abdülhamid II (Sultan, Ottomans), 831
Abolition of slavery: slave trade and, 643; in France and French territories, 702, 711
Aborigines: Western society and, 850
Abortion, 1009–1010, 1010(illus.)
Absenteeism: clerical, 446
Absolute monarchy and absolutism, 523, 525, 528–542; in France, 526, 528–534, 600, 686, 689; army size and, 527; in Spain, 534–538; culture of, 539–542; in England, 543–544; Puritanical, 546–547; Ottoman, 559; in central and eastern Europe, 559–584; in Prussia, 565, 571–572; religion and, 566; Hohenzollern, 567; in Brandenburg-Prussia, 570–571; enlightened, 609–616
Abstract art, 924–925, 950(illus.)
Academy (Athens): humanists and, 414
Act in Restraint of Appeals (England), 461
Act of Union (England, 1707), 603
Address to the Christian Nobility of the German Nation (Luther), 451
Aden, 488
Adenauer, Konrad, 987
Administration: of France, 529; of Spanish colonies, 538–539; Ottoman, 582. *See also* Government
Admonition to Peace, An (Luther), 455
Adolescence: work during, 655
Adoration of the Magi (Mantegna), 423(illus.)
Adultery: punishment of, 656
Afghanistan: Soviets in, 1008, 1024, 1045; war against Taliban in, 1020, 1045; refugees from, 1042
Africa: blacks from, 429–431; culture of, 430–431; trade with, 484, 485–488; Ottomans and, 489; Portugal and, 497; slavery and, 508, 513–514, 641–643; Dutch and, 553; English exports to, 640(map); France and, 846(illus.); imperialism in, 860(map); partition of, 860(map); Christianization of, 867; First World War in, 890; decolonization in, 990(map), 992–993; neocolonialism and, 992–993; nationalism and violence in, 1033; AIDS epidemic in, 1044(illus.). *See also* North Africa
African Americans: in Europe, 932(illus.); civil rights movement and, 994–995, 994(illus.)
Africans: as slaves, 513–514
Afrikaners, 859, 861
Against the Murderous, Thieving Hordes of the Peasants (Luther), 455
Age of Anxiety, 913–940
Age of Discovery, 483–516
Age of Louis XIV (Voltaire), 602

Agincourt, battle at, 385
Agricultural revolution, 622–623
Agriculture: crisis in 14th century, 372–373; serfdom and, 561; after Thirty Years' War, 563–565; in Holy Roman Empire, 567; in Prussia, 610; in 18th century, 622–625; in England, 623, 624–625; in Low Countries, 624–625, 624(illus.); Industrial Revolution and, 718; in Egypt, 853; migration and, 857–858; Scandinavian cooperatives, 938; collectivization in, 951–952, 992, 995, 996. *See also* Farms and farming; Manors and manorialism; Peasant(s)
Ahasuerus, 428, 428(illus.)
Ahmed Arabi, 853–854
AIDS epidemic, 1044(illus.)
Aiguillon, duke of, 691
Aircraft: jet, 999
Air force: in Second World War, 967, 974–975
Albania, 883, 1026, 1042–1043; guerilas in, 885(illus.)
Albanian Muslims: of Kosovo, 1037–1038
Albert (England), 814(illus.)
Alberti, Leon Battista, 413, 414
Albert of Mainz, 447, 448
Albert of Wallenstein, 562
Albi, 394
Albuquerque, Alfonso de, 498
Alcohol and alcoholism: of working class, 795–796; Soviet, 1023
Alcuin, 415
Alembert, Jean le Rond, 602, 605
Alexander I (Russia), 706, 707, 708, 750, 751
Alexander II (Russia), 827, 828(illus.)
Alexander III (Russia), 827
Alexander VI (Pope), 410, 436, 500
Alexandra (Russia), 895, 896(illus.)
Alexandria: riots in, 854
Alexis (Russia), 895
Alfonso I (Aragon): Muslims and, 397
Algebra, 595
Algeciras Conference, 882
Algeria, 859, 973, 1046; fall of Algiers, 767, 768(illus.); France and, 767, 829, 992
Allan, David, 657(illus.)
Alliance(s): Russian, 576; in Seven Years' War, 610; after First World War, 903, 908, 929. *See also* specific alliances
Alliance for Germany, 1029–1030
Alliance of the Three Emperors, 880(illus.)
Alliance systems: of Bismarck, 880–881, 880(illus.), 885; in cold war, 988(map)
Allies (First World War): in Russian civil war, 900–901; Treaty of Versailles and, 903, 907; Middle East and, 906
Allies (Second World War), *see* Grand Alliance

All Quiet on the Western Front (Remarque), 887–888
Al-Qaeda, 1045, 1046, 1047
Alsace: France and, 534; Germany and, 825; surrender to Germany, 834. *See also* Alsace-Lorraine
Alsace-Lorraine, 880, 881
Alva, duke of, 474
Alvarado, 502
Amalgamated Society of Engineers, 741
American Indians, 635; Columbus and, 498; enslavement of, 505–508; in Latin America, 644; Western society and, 850
American Revolution, 687–688
Americas: exploration of, 493; naming of, 500; European conquest of, 501–504; decline of indigenous population in, 504–505; European colonies in, 504–508, 634–644; economic exploitation of, 505–508; silver bullion from, 509–510; colonial wars over, 634–637; labor in, 640–641; English exports to, 640(map). *See also* New World; specific countries
Amiens: insurrection at, 528; Treaty of, 705
Anabaptists, 451–454
Analytic geometry, 595
Anarchism: in Spain and Italy, 842
Anastasia Romanov (wife of Ivan IV), 574–575
Anatolia, 580; Ottomans and, 489
Anaximander (Greece), 807
Andes region, 503
Anglican Church, 462–463, 548; Puritans and, 544–545; Methodists and, 673; Ireland and, 835
Anglo-French Entente, 892
Anglo-Japanese Alliance, 880(illus.)
Anglo-Russian Agreement, 880(illus.)
Angola, 859
Animals: in Columbian Exchange, 509; on farms, 623
Anjou: house of, 435
Anna of Austria, 512, 530
Anne of Brittany, 435
Annexation: of Hawaii, 858(illus.)
Anticlericalism, 446, 458
Anticommunists: in Soviet Union, 1028, 1029(map)
Anti-Corn Law League, 764
Antigua, 642(illus.)
Anti-immigrant campaign, 1043–1044; challenges to, 1049–1050
Anti-Semitism: in Spain, 437–439; before First World War, 832; Dreyfus affair and, 834–835; modern, 837–838; Zionism and, 838, 839; in Nazi Germany, 961, 970. *See also* Jews and Judaism

I-1

Antiseptic principle, 783
Antiwar movement, 1006–1007, 1052(illus.)
Antwerp, 474
Apartheid policy, 863
Apothecaries, 667
Appeasement: of Hitler, 962, 965(illus.), 984
Apprenticeships, 654–655, 740
Aquinas, *see* Thomas Aquinas
Aquitaine, 381, 382, 385
Arabian Peninsula: Ottomans and, 581
Arabian Sea, 484
Arab-Israeli wars, 992, 1010
Arabs and Arab world: Indian Ocean trade and, 485; slave trade and, 513–514; after First World War, 903, 905–907, 905(illus.); Ottomans and, 903; Palestine and, 992; nationalism in, 992–993; OPEC and, 1010; terrorism and, 1046. *See also* Islam
Arago, François, 771
Aragon, 436; kingdom of Naples and, 410
Archers, 383
Architecture: in Renaissance, 424–425; of St. Petersburg, 579; functionalism in, 921; postmodern, 1032(illus.)
Aretino, Pietro, 425
Argentina: migration to, 856, 858; Italian immigrants in, 857(illus.); Falkland Islands and, 1013
Arguim, 497
Aristocracy, 788–789; in England, 763; in France, 767; in Austrian Empire, 772; labor, 791. *See also* Nobility
Aristotelian worldview, 599
Aristotle, 590–591; on universe, 590(illus.)
Arkwright, Richard, 719, 735
Armada (Spain), 474–475, 512–513
Armed forces: French, 434, 527, 541, 690; size of, 526–527; Habsburg, 567; in Russia, 576, 577; Ottoman, 829–830, 831; in Japan, 871, 871(illus.). *See also* Military; Soldiers
Armenians: genocide against, 889–890, 889(illus.)
Armistice: for First World War, 901
Arms race, 1024
Army Order No. 1 (Russia), 896
Arouet, François Marie, *see* Voltaire
Art(s): in Renaissance, 421–428; subject matter of, 423; of northern Renaissance, 424; creativity of artists and, 425–428; in Reformation, 452–453, 452(illus.), 453(illus.); Protestantism and, 473; baroque, 539–540; romanticism in, 758–761; impressionism and, 922; postimpressionism (expressionism) in, 922–926; modern, 924; abstract, 924–925, 950(illus.); cubism in, 924–925; surrealism in, 925; dadaism in, 926; social realism in, 950(illus.); Soviet, 950(illus.), 954, 995, 999; suprematism and, 950(illus.); women's history and, 1003(illus.). *See also* Architecture; Literature; specific types
Arthur (England), 435, 461
Artisans, 740; in Russia, 575; in guilds, 633. *See also* Labor; Workers
Ashley Mines Commission (England), 744
Asia: trade with, 484, 499, 644–647; European empires and, 644–647; European trade with, 646–647; migration from, 858–859, 858(illus.); in 1914, 864(map); Second World War in, 970, 972, 972(map), 974–975; containment policy and, 984; decolonization in, 990(map); financial crises in, 1031, 1033; nationalism and violence in, 1033. *See also* specific countries
Asiento, 635
Assemblies: after Hundred Years' War, 386; organized by class (estate), 431; in France, 688–689. *See also* National assembly (France)
Assembly of Notables (France), 688–689
Astaire, Fred, 927
Astell, Mary, 597
Astrolabe, 482(illus.), 495
Astrology, 591
Astronomy: Aristotle and, 590–591, 590(illus.); Copernicus and, 591–592; Galileo and, 592–594; Newton and, 594. *See also* Scientific revolution; Universe
Atatürk (Mustafa Kemal), 906, 907(illus.)
Atauhualpa (Inca), 503–504
Athletics, *see* Sports
Atlantic alliance, 1008
Atlantic Ocean region: slave trade in, 508, 641–643; powers of, 621; economy in, 634–640, 636(map)
Atomic power: discoveries in, 917–919, 918(illus.); Hiroshima, Nagasaki, and, 975, 1000; Einstein and, 999
Aubry, Madame, 715(illus.)
Auden, W. H., 917
Audiencia, 538
Auerstädt, battle at, 707
Augsburg: Peace of (1555), 459, 563
Augsburg Confession, 458
Augustine (Hippo, Saint), 415
Augustinian friars, 446–447
Auschwitz-Birkenau, 969
Austerlitz, Battle of, 706
Australia: in Second World War, 974
Austria, 1040; Black Death in, 377; Habsburgs and, 457–458, 565–567, 613–615; Burgundy and, 458; in Grand Alliance (1701), 534; Hungary and, 566–567, 1025; growth to 1748, 570(map); Prussia and, 610; marriage in, 654; church control in, 672; Napoleon and, 705, 706, 708; Holy Alliance and, 751; revolt in, 770; Italy and, 818, 820, 821; Zollverein and, 821; Germany and, 822, 824, 963(map), 964–965; republic of, 901; peace treaty with, 903; Great Depression in, 935; Hitler and, 962. *See also* Austro-Hungarian Empire
Austrian Empire: under Habsburgs, 751–753, 752(map); in 1848, 772
Austrian Netherlands: France and, 696, 697; Napoleon and, 705
Austro-Hungarian Empire (Austria-Hungary), 836–837; industrialization in, 727, 728(illus.); Alliance System and, 880–881, 880(illus.); Balkan nationalism and, 883; end of, 903. *See also* First World War
Austro-Prussian War, 821–822, 823(map)
Authoritarianism, 945, 946–949; in Russia, 1034–1035

Authority, *see* Power (authority)
Authorized Bible, 516
Autobiography (Cellini), 413
Autocracy: in Russia, 579–580
Autocrats: in Moscow, 574
Automobiles: in postwar era, 1002
Auxiliary Service Law, 891–892, 894
Avignon: pope in, 387
Axis alliance, 963
Azores, 505
Aztec Empire: Spanish in, 501–502

Baby boom, 1002
Baby bust, 1041
Babylonian Captivity: of Catholic Church, 387
Bach, Johann Sebastian, 540
Bacon, Francis, 595, 596–597
Bacteria, *see* Disease
Bahamas, 499
Balance of power: among Italian city-states, 410–412, 411(map); industrialization and, 717
Baldwin, Stanley, 928, 933
Balfour, Arthur, 903
Balfour Declaration (1917), 839, 903–904, 905
Balkan region, 559; Ottomans and, 489, 580, 829; Enlightenment and, 603; nationalism and, 831, 883; Alliance System and, 881; in 1878 and 1914, 884(map); in First World War, 889; in Second World War, 967
Ballet, 925
Baltic region: Black Death and, 377; Lutheranism in, 466; after Thirty Years' War, 563; Poland and, 571; Sweden and, 571, 576; Russia and, 573, 576, 578(illus.); Second World War and, 966; nationalism in, 1023
Balzac, Honoré de, 808
Banking: in Florence, 408, 408(illus.); in England, 718; in continental industrialization, 732
Bank of Amsterdam, 550
Bankruptcy: in France, 688, 689
Banten: port of, 487(illus.)
Baptism: infant, 451
Baptistery (Florence): doors of, 421, 425
Baptists, 454
Barbarians: race and, 608
Barcelona, 437, 437(map)
Barons: English, 373; French, 381, 382
Baroque period, 539; arts of, 539–540
Barth, Karl, 917
Basel, Council of, 388
Basilicas, 416
Bastille (Paris): surrender of, 690
Battle of San Romano (Uccello), 412(illus.)
Battles, *see* specific battles and wars
Bauhaus, 921
Bavaria, 565
Bayle, Pierre, 599–600
Beards: in Russia, 578
"Beat" movement, 1004
Beattie, James, 609
Beaumont, Henry, 397
Beauvoir, Simone de, 1009, 1015(illus.), 1016–1017

Beethoven, Ludwig van, 761
Beijing (Peking), China, 484, 852
Belgium, 696, 749, 966; Charles V and, 474; industrialization in, 727, 728(illus.), 730; banks in, 732; Africa and, 861; invasion of, 884, 887, 887(illus.); in First World War, 886(map); Treaty of Versailles and, 903; European unity and, 989. *See also* Netherlands
Bellini, Gentile and Giovanni, 426(illus.)
Belorussia, 900
Benefices (offices), 446
Bentham, Jeremy, 781–782
Benthamite, 781
Berbers: as slaves, 492
Berg, Alban, 926
Bergson, Henri, 915
Berlin, 567, 974; airlift to, 984, 985(illus.); blockade of, 984
Berlin conference (1884, 1885), 861
Berlin Wall, 997, 1008; fall of, 1025, 1027(illus.)
Bernstein, Edward, 841
Bethmann-Hollweg, Theobald von, 883, 891
Beverages, 665
Bible: Erasmus and, 417–418; Authorized Version of, 516. *See also* New Testament
Bigarny, Felipe, 438(illus.)
Big Four, 902
Big Science, 1000
Big Three: wartime conferences of, 982–985, 982(illus.)
Bill-poster's Fantasy, A (Perry), 778(illus.)
Bin Laden, Osama, 1045, 1047
Biology, 805; race and, 608
Birth control, 656, 798, 803
Birth of a Nation (film), 926
Birthrate: in 17th century, 626; illegitimacy and, 656–657, 798; decline of, 802, 802(illus.), 855, 1041–1042; in Great Depression, 935; in postwar era, 1002, 1002(illus.); in western Europe, 1041
Bismarck, Otto von, 821–822, 824(illus.); Prussian parliament and, 822–824; Franco-Prussian War and, 824–825; as chancellor, 832, 833; Berlin conference and, 861–862; African territory and, 862; Alliance System of, 880–881, 880(illus.)
Black Code: in Saint-Domingue, 693
Black Death, 374–381, 386; spread of, 375–377; course of, 376(map); treatment of, 377–378; hospitals and, 378, 379(illus.); consequences of, 378–381; pessimism after, 380–381; colleges founded after, 381; pilgrimages and, 381. *See also* Plague
Blacks, 429–431, 430(illus.); as slaves, 492, 513–514; Linné on, 608. *See also* African Americans; Slaves and slavery
Black Sea region: slave trade and, 492; Constantinople and, 580
Black Shirts, 955
Blackstone, William, 799
Blair, Tony, 1013
Blake, William, 734
Blanc, Louis, 756, 771
Blitzkrieg, 966(illus.), 967

Blockade(s): in First World War, 890, 903; of Berlin, 984, 985(illus.); of Cuba, 997; of Iraq, 1030
Block-book, 418, 419
Blood sports, 675–676, 676(illus.)
Bloody Sunday massacre (Russia), 829
Blum, Léon, 939
Blumenbach, Johann Friedrich, 429
Boats, *see* Ships and shipping
Boccaccio, Giovanni, 378, 416, 432–433
Body linen, 720
Boers, 859
Boer War, *see* South African War
Bohemia, 391, 753, 776; Reformation in, 465–466; Protestantism in, 562, 565; Thirty Years' War and, 562; Habsburgs in, 565–566; absolutism in, 566
Bohemian Estates, 565
Boleyn, Anne, 461
Bologna, 409
Bolotnikov, Ivan, 576
Bolshevik Revolution, 949; Lenin and, 896–898, 899(illus.)
Bolsheviks, 898, 947; Five-Year Plan and, 978–979. *See also* Communists and communism; Russia; Soviet Union
Bombs and bombings: blitzkrieg and, 966(illus.), 967; in Pacific islands, 974–975; of cities, 975; of Hiroshima and Nagasaki, 975; in Vietnam War, 1006; in Yugoslavia, 1038–1039. *See also* Terrorism
Bonhomme, Jacques, 390
Book of Common Order (Knox), 465
Book of Common Prayer (England), 463, 545
Book of Revelation, 371
Books: printing of, 418–421, 604(illus.); *Index of Prohibited Books* and, 467; in Enlightenment, 603–607. *See also* Literature
Bordeaux, 383(illus.); insurrection at, 528; illegitimacy in, 656–657
Borders: Locarno agreements and, 930, 931; of Hungary, 1025. *See also* Boundaries; Frontiers
Borgia, Cesare, 410
Borodino, Battle of, 708
Bosnia, 883, 1045
Bosnia-Herzegovina: civil war in, 1038; ethnic groups in, 1038, 1038(map)
Bosnian Muslims, 1037(illus.), 1038
Bosnian Serbs, 1038
Boston Tea Party, 687, 687(illus.)
Botticelli, Sandro, 422(illus.), 425
Boucher, François, 654(illus.)
Boundaries: after Second World War, 985; Final Act and, 1008. *See also* Borders; Frontiers
Bourbon dynasty, 528; in Spain, 536(map); restoration of, 708–710, 749; in Naples and Sicily, 818
Bourgeoisie, 431, 684, 685; in France, 685; Marx on, 757
Boxer Rebellion, 872
Boyars, 574
Brahe, Tycho, 592
Brain drain, 1000
Brandenburg: elector of, 457, 567–571
Brandenburg-Prussia, 563, 570–571, 570(map)

Brandt, Willy, 1008
Brassey, Thomas, 725
Brazil: Portugal and, 497, 539; sugar in, 508(illus.), 510; slaves in, 640, 642; Italians in, 858
Brazza, Pierre de, 861
Bread: in peasant diet, 524–525; in France, 690, 697
Breast-feeding, 658, 661, 802
Breitenfeld, battle at, 562
Brest-Litovsk: Treaty of, 899, 901
Brezhnev, Leonid, 997, 1020
Brezhnev Doctrine, 997, 1021, 1024
Briand, Aristide, 930, 931, 932
Bride wealth, 484
Bridget (Sweden), 389–390
Britain: Battle of, 967. *See also* England (Britain)
British Broadcasting Corporation, 928
British Commonwealth of Nations, 992
British East India Company, 647, 687, 719, 868
British Empire: in 19th century, 849. *See also* Colonies and colonization
Brittain, Vera, 893
Brittany, 435
Broadcasting networks, 927–928
Brothels, 394, 456–457
Brothers Karamazov, The (Dostoevski), 804
Brown, Ford Maddox, 733(illus.)
Brown v. Board of Education, 994
Brunel, I. K., 724(illus.), 725
Brunelleschi, Filippo, 421, 424
Bruni, Leonardo, 413
Brüning, Heinrich, 959–960
Brussels, 474, 632(illus.)
Bubo, 374
Bubonic plague, 374, 627–628, 627(illus.). *See also* Black Death
Buchuanaland (Botswana), 861
Budget deficits, 1012
Bulgaria: peace treaty with, 903; Second World War and, 983; postcommunist, 1035
Bureaucracy: in England, 463; in absolutist state, 526; in France, 530–531, 705; in Spain, 537; in Prussia, 571–572, 822; Ottoman, 582; Russia, 827; in India, 869–870; Soviet, 1022, 1023; of European Union, 1039
Burgos, 437
Burgundians (France), 385
Burgundy: Austria and, 458
Burials: medieval, 372(illus.)
Burke, Edmund, 694
Burma: independence for, 992
Bush, George H. W., 1030
Bush, George W., 1044, 1045, 1047, 1048
Business: women and, 735; in U.S., 826. *See also* Commerce
Bussy, William, 396
Byron, George Gordon, Lord, 759, 761
Byzantine Empire: Russia and, 575(illus.); Ottomans and, 580

"Cabal": in England, 547
Cabinet of Dr. Caligari, The (film), 927
Cabinet system: in England, 547
Cabot, John, 501

Cabral, Pedro Alvares, 497–498, 500
Cairo, 487, 582
Calais: England and, 385
Calatrava, Santiago, 1032(illus.)
Calicut, India, 498
Caliph, 584
Calling of Saint Matthew, The (Pareja), 540(illus.)
Calvin, John, and Calvinism, 452, 461, 463–465, 464(illus.); in Poland, 466; France and, 473; in Netherlands, 474, 550; England and, 544
Cambodia, *see* Kampuchea (Cambodia)
Camel: caravans and, 487
Cameroons, 862
Camus, Albert, 917
Canada: France and, 501, 532, 635; Loyalist migrants to, 687
Canals, 850; in England, 718, 718(map)
Canary Islands, 499
Candide (Voltaire), 618
Cannon, 383, 494
Canonization: of Joan of Arc, 385
Canon law: marriage and, 456
Canterbury Tales (Chaucer), 399–400
Canton: foreign merchants in, 851
Cape Colony, 859, 861, 863
Cape of Good Hope, 497, 501, 511, 553, 646
Capetian dynasty (France), 381
Cape Town, 553
Cape Verde Islands, 505
Capital (financial): industry and, 732; free movement of, 1031
Capital (Marx), 838
Capitalism, 393; labor and, 631; Smith and, 647–648; industrial, 732; socialists on, 756; imperialism and, 867; neoliberal, free-market version of, 1031–1032; criticism of, 1045
Capito, Wolfgang, 442–443
Capture of Louis XVI, The, June 1791, 695(illus.)
Caraffa, Gian Pietro, 467
Caravans, 487–488
Caravel, 494
Caribbean region: Columbus in, 498; slaves in, 640, 643; French Revolution and, 693; slavery in French colonies, 707. *See also* West Indies
Carlsbad Decrees, 751
Carmelite nuns, 471
Carnival, 675, 676
Carpaccio, 430(illus.)
Carter, Jimmy, 1008
Cartesian dualism, 596, 598
Cartier, Jacques, 501
Cartography, 495
Cartoons, 927
Cartwright, Edmund, 720
Casta paintings: in Mexico, 644(illus.)
Castiglione, Baldassare, 414, 415(illus.), 433
Castile, 436, 534. *See also* Ferdinand and Isabella (Spain); Spain
Castle, The (Kafka), 920
Castlereagh, Robert, 749, 750
Castles: of Mortagne, 383(illus.)
Castro, Fidel, 997
Catalan Atlas, 488
Catalonia, 437(map), 537

Cateau-Cambrésis, Treaty of, 472
Catechisms: of Luther, 451
Cathedrals: in Florence, 424
Catherine de' Medici, 473
Catherine of Aragon, 435, 461, 463
Catherine the Great (Russia), 578, 610–613, 612(illus.), 688, 946
Catholic Center Party (Germany), 833
Catholic Church: Babylonian Captivity of, 387; Great Schism in, 387–388; Conciliar movement in, 388; lay piety and, 389–390; mysticism and, 389–390; in Renaissance, 416; in France, 435, 472–473, 529, 834, 835; Spain and, 436; conversos in, 437–438; reformation of, 445–457, 466; indulgences in, 448; Protestantism and, 449; on marriage, 456; in England, 461–463, 544, 547; in Hungary, 466; baroque art and, 539; in Ireland, 545, 835, 836; Catholic League and, 562; in northern German states, 563; Copernican hypothesis and, 592; science and, 596; in Austria, 615; church regulation by, 671–672; contributions to social and religious life, 672; Pietism and, 674; French Revolution and, 693, 703; Napoleon and, 705; papal infallibility and, 832; Christian existentialism in, 917; in fascist Italy, 957; in Poland, 1020. *See also* Christianity; Counter-Reformation; Protestantism
Catholic League, 562
Catholic Party: of Italy, 955; of France, 987
Catholic Reformation, 466–472
Caucasian: use of term, 429
Caucasus region, 900
Cavaignac, Louis, 771
Cavendish, Margaret, 597
Cavour, Camillo Benso di, 818–820, 821
Ceausescu, Nicolae, 1026
Cederstrom, Gustaf, 577(illus.)
Celibacy: Luther on, 449; vs. marriage, 455
Cellini, Benvenuto, 413, 491(illus.)
Censorship: in Russia, 827; in First World War, 894; in Soviet Union, 995(illus.)
Central Committee (Soviet Union), 949
Central Europe: absolutism in, 559, 609–610, 615–616; warfare and social change in, 559; serfdom in, 560–561; Thirty Years' War and, 562, 563–565, 564(map)
Central Middle Ages, *see* High Middle Ages; Middle Ages
Central Powers, 889, 890, 894
Ceremonies: religious, 450
Cervantes, Miguel de, 537–538
Ceuta, 497
Ceylon, 501, 553, 647, 992
Cézanne, Paul, 923
Chabas, Paul-Émile, 790(illus.)
Chadwick, Edwin, 734, 781–782
Chamberlain, Neville, 965
Chamber of Deputies (France), 711, 767
Chaplin, Charlie, 927, 927(illus.)
Charcoal, 721
Charity schools, 662
Charles I (England), 544–546; Parliament and, 543, 545–546
Charles I (Van Dyck), 544(illus.)

Charles II (England), 547–548, 635
Charles II (Spain), 534, 537
Charles III (Spain), 538–539
Charles IV (France), 381
Charles V (Holy Roman Empire), 439, 457, 500(illus.); Luther and, 449; empire of, 458, 460(maps), 511; Protestantism and, 458–459, 461; abdication by, 459; papacy and, 467; Netherlands under, 473–475, 474(map); Indians and, 505
Charles VI (Austria), 567, 610
Charles VI (France), 386
Charles VII (France), 385, 434
Charles VIII (France), 411–412
Charles X (France), 767
Charles XI (Sweden), 568, 576
Charles XII (Sweden), 576
Charles the Bold (Burgundy), 435
Charles University (Prague), 381
Charpentier, Marc-Antoine, 542
Chartist movement, 741, 764
Châtelet, marquise de, 601, 602(illus.)
Chaucer, Geoffrey, 399, 400
Chaumont, Treaty of, 708
Chechnya, 1035
Cheka, 900
Chemistry, 805
Cheney, Dick: Iraq war and, 1047
Chiang Kai-shek, 992
Chicago: architecture in, 922; counterculture in, 1004
Chicago, Judy, 1003(illus.)
Childbirth: deaths from, 658
Child care, 739
Child labor, 721, 736, 737–738, 740; in mines, 739, 744–745, 745(illus.)
Child rearing, 802–804
Children, 658–661, 800; as Ottoman tax, 582; infanticide and, 659–660; abandonment of, 660; 18th-century attitudes toward, 660–661; in Enlightenment, 661; Rousseau on, 661; workdays for, 738, 765; women factory workers and, 739; illegitimate, 798; in 19th century, 802–804; sexual behavior of, 803–804; in First World War, 891–892; in postwar era, 1002. *See also* Abandoned children; Illegitimacy
Chile, 509
China: trade with, 484, 510, 511(illus.); industrialization and, 727, 728(illus.); Western impact on, 850–852; British war with, 851–852, 852(illus.); migration from, 858–859, 864(map); in 1914, 864(map); imperialism and, 865, 872; Japan and, 872, 970; rebellion in, 873(illus.); First World War in, 890; civil war in, 984, 992; communists in, 984, 992; Korean War and, 984; Nixon in, 1007
Chinggis Khan, 572–573
Chirac, Jacques, 1055
Chivalry, 383
Chopin, Frédéric, 761
Christening Feast (Steen), 549(illus.)
Christian III (Denmark), 451
Christian IV (Denmark), 562
Christian church: reforms of, 445; in early 16th century, 446

Christian Democrats: in Europe, 987, 989, 1052; in West Germany, 987, 1008, 1030
Christian existentialism, 917
Christian humanism, 416–418
Christianity: in Renaissance, 416; Erasmus on, 417–418; skin color and, 431; Columbus and, 499; slave trade and, 513–514; Ottomans and, 580, 584; Aristotelianism and, 590; of working class, 797; spread of, 867; revival of, 917. *See also* Cathedrals; Reformation
Christian socialists (Austria), 838
Christine de Pizan, 393, 404–405, 405(illus.), 432, 433
Church(es): in Scotland, 545; parish, 671; institutional, 671–676; national, 672; Hogarth on, 673(illus.); in French Revolution, 693; working class and, 797. *See also* Religion
Church councils, *see* Councils
Churchill, Winston, 862; leadership of, 966; Grand Alliance and, 972–973; at wartime conferences, 982–983, 982(illus.); "iron curtain" speech of, 984
Church of England, *see* Anglican Church
Church of Ireland, 462
Church of Scotland, *see* Presbyterian Church
Chwast, Seymour, 1007(illus.)
Ciompi revolts (Florence), 392–393, 408
Cistercians, 398
Cities and towns: Black Death and, 378; prostitution in, 394; in Italian Renaissance, 409–410, 432(illus.); third estate in, 431; hierarchies of orders and class in, 431–432; in Poland-Lithuania, 466; landlords and, 561; guilds in, 632; illegitimacy in, 657; foundlings in, 660; in 19th century, 779–780; sanitation in, 780, 781; population of, 780(map); transportation in, 786; servants in, 794; bombing of, 975; Soviet, 999. *See also* City-states; Urban planning; specific locations
Citizens and citizenship: in Italian cities, 409
City of Ladies, The (Christine de Pizan), 404–405
City-states: in Italy, 409–412, 411(map), 818
Civil Code (France, 1804), 704, 705
Civilization(s): spread of European, 867. *See also* Culture(s)
Civil Rights Act (1964), 994
Civil rights movement (U.S.), 994–995
Civil service, *see* Bureaucracy
Civil war(s): in France, 382; in Netherlands, 474; in Switzerland, 770; in United States, 825–826; in Russia, 899–901; in Spain, 963; in Yugoslavia, 1033, 1038; humanitarian intervention in, 1044–1045
Clandestine unions, 469
Class-consciousness, 732, 734, 740
Classes, 732, 733(illus.); wealth-based, 431; categorizing people by, 431–432; in England, 436; in London, 638; in France, 705; factory owners as, 732–734; liberal politics and, 754; city living by, 785(illus.); in urban areas, 786–797; First World War and, 894; Marxian concept of, 898; Soviet, 953; in Italy, 955; in Nazi Germany, 961; in postwar era, 1000–1002. *See also* Estates (classes); Hierarchy; Orders; specific classes
Classical liberalism, 754; totalitarianism and, 947
Classical music, 542
Classicism, 758; French, 541–542
Classics: Renaissance humanists and, 412–414
Class war: in Paris (1848), 771
Claustration, 469
Clemenceau, Georges, 894, 902, 903
Clement VII (Pope), 387, 461
Clergy: wealth of, 378–379; plague and, 379; hypocrisy of, 389(illus.); literacy of, 401; absenteeism by, 446; reforms of, 446, 467–468; Protestant, 450; education of, 469; local, 671; Pietism and, 672; in France, 684, 689; in French Revolution, 693. *See also* Friars; Pope(s); Priests and priestesses
Climate: change in 14th century, 371–373; in 17th century, 523, 525
Clinton, Bill, 1031, 1038
Clive, Robert, 647
Cloth, *see* Textile industry
Clothing: consumerism and, 666; body linen, 720; of workers, 736; of middle class, 789–790; ready-made, 795. *See also* Fashion
Cloves, 492
Coal and Steel Community, 989
Coal industry: in England, 721–722, 739; industrialization and, 729(map); child labor in, 739, 744–745
Cockerill, William, 730, 733
Cockfighting in England (Hogarth), 676(illus.)
Code Napoleon, *see* Civil Code (France, 1804)
Code noir (Black Code): in Saint-Domingue, 693
Codes of law, *see* Law codes
Coercive Acts, 687
Coffee: trade in, 640
Coitus interruptus, 656
Coke, 723
Colbert, Jean-Baptiste, 532–533, 632, 634
Cold war, 981, 1015; origins of, 982–985; Truman Doctrine and, 983; Korean War and, 984; eastern Europe and, 984–985; Khrushchev and, 996; from 1968–1985, 1006–1007; détente and, 1008–1009; end of, 1019; Reagan and, 1024–1025, 1030; German reunification and, 1028–1030; nationalism and, 1032–1033. *See also* Soviet Union
Coleridge, Samuel Taylor, 759
Colet, John, 417
Collective bargaining: in Germany, 841
Collectivization: in Russia, 827; in Soviet Union, 951, 952, 978–979; in China, 992
College of cardinals: in Great Schism, 388
Colleges, *see* Universities
Colloquy of Marburg, 450
Colonies and colonization: Spanish, 501–504, 535; in Americas, 504–510, 635–644; English, 548–549; mercantilism and, 635–637; European rivalry over, 635–640; trade and, 637–640; in Latin America, 643–644; in Asia, 644–647; European consumer society and, 666; French, 693, 707, 834; Industrial Revolution and, 718; by West, 848; in Africa, 859–865; new imperialism and, 865; Anglo-French Entente and, 882; Japan and, 970; Second World War and, 970, 989–993; neocolonialism and, 992–993. *See also* Decolonization; Imperialism; New Imperialism
Color: in Saint-Domingue, 693
Colseby, John de, 396
Columbian Exchange, 508–509
Columbus, Christopher, 493, 498–499; religiosity of, 499; first voyage of, 518–519
Combination Acts (England), 740, 741
COMECON, 988(map)
Comedy: French, 542
Commerce: in Renaissance, 408; women in, 484; in Indian Ocean, 484–485; boom in, 510; mercantilism and, 532; Dutch, 550–553, 552(illus.). *See also* Trade
Committee of Public Safety (France), 697, 698, 702
Commodities: markets for, 850
Commoners: in Enlightenment, 607; as French estate, 684
Common lands, 622, 623
Common Market, 987–988, 988(map), 989, 1011; misery index for, 1010. *See also* European Economic Community
Commons: knights and wealthy urban residents as, 386
Common Sense (Paine), 663
Commonwealth: in England, 547
Commonwealth of Independent States, 1028, 1029(map)
Communes: in France, 386; in northern Italian cities, 409. *See also* Paris Commune (1871)
Communication(s): nationalism and, 755; telegraph and, 850; broadcasting networks and, 927–928
Communion, *see* Eucharist
Communist Manifesto, The (Marx), 757, 838, 898
Communist Party: in Germany, 932, 960; in France, 939; Soviet, 996, 1022, 1027, 1028
Communists and communism: totalitarianism and, 947; Soviet, 947–949; Nazis and, 967; after Second World War, 987; Tito and, 996; decline in Europe, 1020–1024
Community controls, 656
Company of the East Indies (France), 532
Compass, 482(illus.), 495
Competition: in modern science, 999
Complete Indian Housekeeper and Cook, The (Steel and Gardiner), 876
Computer and electronics revolution, 1031
Comte, Auguste, 805–806, 807
Concentration camps: Nazi, 961, 967, 969; Soviet, 996
Conciliarists, 388
Concordat of Bologna, 435, 472–473
Concubines: Ottoman, 583
Condition of the Working Class in England, The (Engels), 734
Condottieri, 409
Confraternities, 389
Congo, 643, 861

Congregationalists, 454
Congress of Berlin (1878), 881, 883
Congress of People's Deputies (Soviet Union), 1023, 1027
Congress of Vienna, 749, 818
Congress system: in Europe, 751
Conrad, Joseph, 867
Conscription, *see* Draft (military)
Conservation of energy, law of, 805
Conservatism: Metternich and, 751; in 1970s and 1980s, 1012; Thatcher and, 1013
Conservative Party: in England, 835, 933
Consistory (Geneva), 464–465
Constable, John, 758, 761
Constance, Council of, 388, 449
Constantinople, 488, 890; fall to Turks, 489; sacks of, 489(illus.), 490; Ottoman siege of, 580. *See also* Byzantine Empire
Constituent Assembly: in France, 771; in Russia, 899
Constitution: Montesquieu's theories and, 601; in United States, 601, 688; in France, 694, 702, 818; in Haiti, 707; in Prussia, 774; in North German Confederation, 822; in Russia, 829, 1034; Ottoman, 830; in Hungary, 836–837; in India, 991; in Soviet Union, 1027; in Turkey, 1040(illus.); in European Union, 1041
Constitutional Charter (France), 711, 754, 767
Constitutionalism, 542–553
Constitutional monarchies, 525; in England, 548–549; in France, 689, 692; in Russia, 829
Consumer goods: in Soviet Union, 952–953, 1023; after Second World War, 987–988, 1001(illus.), 1002; in eastern Europe, 997
Consumer society: 18th-century roots of, 665–667
Consumption: in Renaissance Italy, 421; in 18th century, 663–664; of food, 664
Containment policy (U.S.), 984, 1006–1007
Continental Europe: rural industry in, 630; industrialization in, 727–732, 729(map)
Continental system: of Napoleon, 708
Contraception, *see* Birth control
Convents: Teresa of Ávila and, 471; Jansenists and, 674(illus.). *See also* Nuns
Conversations on the Plurality of Worlds (Fontenelle), 598, 599(illus.)
Conversion: of Spanish Jews, 437–439; of Protestants in France, 531; to Methodism, 673
Conversos, 437–439
Conway, Anne, 597
Copernican hypothesis, 591–592, 596
Copernicus, Nicolaus, 591–592
Coral Sea, Battle of, 974
Corner of the Table, A (Chabas), 790(illus.)
Corn Laws (England, 1815), 763, 764, 849
Coromandel Coast, 485, 510
Coronation: of Napoleon, 706(illus.)
Corporations: industrialization and, 732. *See also* Guilds
Corregidores, 539
Corruption: in Soviet bureaucracy, 1023; in Russia, 1033, 1034
Cort, Henry, 723

Cortes (Spain), 436
Cortés, Hernando, 493, 501–502, 503(illus.)
Cortés, Martín, 503(illus.)
Cossacks (Russia), 575, 576
Cottage industry, 628–631, 736; putting-out system in, 629–630; workers in, 657; in England, 718(map); cotton yarn in, 720; workweek in, 736
Cotton industry: Britain and, 719–721, 849; in Industrial Revolution, 719–721; in Manchester, 722(illus.); Ure on, 734; factory conditions in, 736; workers in, 737(illus.); in United States, 825; in Egypt, 853. *See also* Textile industry
Coudray, Madame du, 669, 669(illus.)
"Council of Blood" (Netherlands), 474
Council of Europe, 989
Council of Trent (School of Titian), 470
Councils: at Basel, 388; of Constance, 388, 449; at Ferrara-Florence, 388; at Pisa, 388; in England, 435; of Trent, 452–453, 467–469
Counterculture, 1004–1006
Counter-Reformation, 466, 675
Coup d'état: by Napoleon III, 817; in Soviet Union, 1028, 1028(illus.), 1033
Couperin, François, 542
Court (legal): French parlements as, 601, 685–686
Court (royal): culture of, 540–541; of Louis XIV (France), 541, 542
Court, Joseph, 769(illus.)
Courtier, The (Castiglione), 414, 433
Courtiers, *see* Nobility
Courtly culture: in Italy, 410
Court of High Commission (England), 545
Court of Star Chamber, 435, 436
Courtrai, battle at, 390
Courtship: sex and, 657–658
Cracow: University of, 381
Cradock, Fanny, 666
Craft guilds, 393
Crafts, *see* Art(s)
Craft unions, 741
Cranach, Lucas, the Elder, 450(illus.), 452, 456(illus.)
Cranach, Lucas, the Younger, 452, 452(illus.)
Crane, Diana, 793
Cranmer, Thomas, 463
Crash, *see* Financial crash
Creativity: of Renaissance artists, 425–428
Crécy, battle at, 383
Crédit Mobilier, 732
Creoles, 643
Crick, Francis, 1000
Crime: fur-collar, 396–397; in eastern Europe, 1035. *See also* Justice; Law(s)
Crimea: Tatars and, 571, 613
Crimean War, 827
Criminal gangs: people smuggling by, 1042–1043
Croatia, 466, 1038, 1038(map)
Croats, 772, 883
Crompton, Samuel, 720
Cromwell, Oliver, 546–547, 546(illus.); Jews and, 547; science and, 596–597; Navigation Acts and, 635

Cromwell, Thomas, 461
Cronin, James, 1032
Crop rotation, 623
Crops: climate change and, 372; in Columbian Exchange, 509. *See also* Agriculture
"Cruel sports," 796
Crusader kingdoms, 490
Cryptograms, 377
Crystal Palace exhibition, 725, 726(illus.)
Cuba: Columbus in, 499; Chinese labor in, 859; blockade of, 997
Cuban missile crisis, 997
Cubells y Ruiz, Enrique Martinez, 787(illus.)
Cubism, 924–925
Culture(s): courtly, 410; trade and, 484; spread of Chinese, 485; of Brazil, 539; of absolutism, 539–542; of royal courts, 540–541; classicism in, 541–542; scientific revolution and, 595–597; in Enlightenment, 598–609, 606(illus.); urban, 603–607; popular, 671–676; national unity and, 754; middle-class, 789–790; imperialism and, 868
Curie, Marie, 597, 918
Custom: by country, 600
Customs union: German Zollverein as, 731, 821
Cyprus, 1019, 1041, 1046
Czech nation: Palacky on, 776–777
Czechoslovakia, 901, 903, 946, 1036(map); Little Entente and, 929; Nazis in, 963(illus.), 965; Second World War and, 983; communism in, 984; liberalization in, 997; Soviets in, 997–998, 998(illus.), 1020; Velvet Revolution in, 1025–1026, 1035; Slovakia and, 1035
Czech people, 465, 753, 836; Germans and, 398; Habsburgs and, 565
Czech Republic, 1041; Hus and, 391; in postcommunist era, 1035

Dadaism, 926
"Daffodils" (Wordsworth), 759–760
Da Gama, Vasco, 495, 497
Dahomey, 643
Daily life, *see* Lifestyle
Dalimil Chronicle, 398, 399(illus.)
Dancing: modern, 926
Danish phase: of Thirty Years' War, 562
Dante Alighieri, 399–400
Danton, Georges Jacques, 696, 702
Danzig, 398, 903
Dardanelles, 890
Dar es Salaam, 866(illus.)
Dark Ages (Europe), 412
Darwin, Charles, 806(illus.), 807
David (Michelangelo), 421
David, Jacques-Louis, 706(illus.)
Dawes, Charles G., and Dawes Plan, 930
Death: from famine, 372(illus.)
Death camps, 967, 969–970
Death penalty: abolishing, 1045
Death rate, *see* Mortality; Mortality rate
"Debate about women," 432–433
De Beers Mining Company, 863
Debt: in France, 688
Debt peonage: in Latin America, 644
Decameron, The (Boccaccio), 378, 416

De Chirico, Georgio, 919(illus.)
Declaration of Independence (U.S.), 687
Declaration of Pillnitz, 695
Declaration of the Rights of Man and of the Citizen (France), 691, 714–715
Declaration of the Rights of Man and of the Citizen (Vallain), 682(illus.)
"Declaration of the Rights of Woman" (de Gouges), 714–715
Decline of the West, The (Spengler), 920
Decolonization: after Second World War, 989–993, 990(map)
Defenestration of Prague, 562
Defense mechanisms, 804
Defensor Pacis (Marsiglio of Padua), 388
Deficits: Keynes and, 935; in Sweden, 938; global economy and, 1031
Defoe, Daniel, 660
De Gasperi, Alcide, 987
De Gaulle, Charles, 987, 989, 1006
Delacroix, Eugène, 760–761, 782(illus.)
Delcassé, Théophile, 882
Democracy, 542; in England, 549, 835; in Germany, 932; in Europe, 987, 989; in West Germany, 987
Democracy in America (Tocqueville), 771
Democratic republics: in France, 770–772
Democratization: in Soviet Union, 1023–1024; in eastern Europe, 1024(map)
Demography: plague and, 379–380; in 17th century, 524–525; population and, 626. *See also* Population
Denmark, 966, 1011; Russia and, 576; Enlightenment in, 609; Prussian war with, 774; Schleswig-Holstein and, 774, 822; distribution of income in, 788(illus.). *See also* Scandinavia
Denmark-Norway: Protestantism in, 451
Depression(s): in France, 690. *See also* Great Depression
Deregulation: of markets, 1031
Desacralization: of French monarchy, 686
Descartes, René, 595–596, 598
Dessalines, Jean Jacques, 707
De-Stalinization, 996–997
Détente, 1008–1009
Developed countries: income in, 848, 848(illus.)
Devil: witches and, 475, 476, 477
Diaghilev, Sergei, 925, 926
Dialectic: history as, 758
Dialogue on the Two Chief Systems of the World (Galileo), 594
Diamonds: in Africa, 863
Diaspora: Chinese, 485
Diaz, Bartholomew, 497
Dictators and dictatorship: military (England), 546–547; Directory as, 703; in Europe, 945; conservative authoritarianism and, 946; radical totalitarianism and, 946–949; Mussolini and, 957; Enabling Act and, 960; in Soviet Union, 995
Dictionary (Bayle), 599–600
Dictionary (Voltaire), 618–619
Diderot, Denis, 602–603, 604(illus.)
Diet (food): of peasants, 524–525; regional differences in, 664; in 18th century, 664–665;
of workers, 736; potato and, 766–767; on middle class, 789
Diet (political): Diet of Worms (1521), 449, 511; Imperial Diet (1530) and, 458; of 1555, 466; in Hungary, 466
Dijon: insurrection at, 528
Dinner Party, The (Judy Chicago), 1003
Dioceses: Christian, 467–469
Diplomacy: Spanish, 439; Algeciras Conference and, 882; Nixon and, 1007. *See also* Balance of power
Directory (France), 703; Napoleon and, 703–704
"Disasters of the War, The" (Goya), 711(illus.)
Discovery, *see* Age of Discovery; Expansion; Voyages
Discovery of the Potato Blight, The (McDonald), 766(illus.)
Discrimination: against Irish, 397; against Asians, 859; against women workers, 1003–1004; sex-based, 1009–1010; against Gypsies, 1032
Disease: in 14th century, 372; Black Death as, 374–381; in Columbian Exchange, 504; in 17th century, 525; 18th-century medicine and, 627; in urban areas, 780, 781; germ theory of, 783; miasmatic theory of, 783; AIDS and, 1044(illus.), 1045. *See also* Black Death
"Dismal science": economics as, 726
Disraeli, Benjamin, 835
Dissent: Calvin on, 465
Districts: in France, 529
Diversity, 1043; in Spain, 436, 437; Ottoman, 584
Divine Comedy (Dante), 399–400
Divine right of kings: of Louis XIV, 530; of Louis XVI, 690
Division of labor: gender, 738–740, 799
Divorce, 1009–1010; in fascist Italy, 957; in postwar era, 1003
Doctors, *see* Physicians
Doctor Zhivago (Pasternak), 996
Doers: Saint-Simon on, 756
Domestic servants, 740, 794, 795(illus.)
Dominicans, 389, 398, 505
Donatello, 423
Donation of Constantine, 416
Don Quixote (Cervantes), 537–538
Dostoevski, Feodor, 804
Dot-com bubble, 1050
Downsizing (corporate), 1031
Draft (military): in Vietnam War, 1007
Drainage: Dutch and English, 624–625
Drama: of Shakespeare, 515–516; French, 542
Draussen und Drinnen (Grosz), 912(illus.)
Dreiser, Theodore, 809
Dreyfus, Alfred, 834(illus.), 835
Dreyfus affair, 834–835, 862
Drinking, *see* Alcohol and alcoholism
Drogheda: rebellion at, 547
Droz, Gustave, 800–802
Dualism: ethnicity and, 397, 398; Cartesian, 596
Dual monarchy, *see* Austro-Hungarian Empire (Austria-Hungary)
Dual revolution, 747, 751
Dubcek, Alexander, 997, 1026(illus.)
Dubrovnik, 381
Duma (Russia), 829, 895
Dumas, Alexandre, 760
Dunkirk: battle at, 966
Dutch, 881; trading empire of, 510–511; France and, 533; in Grand Alliance, 534; commerce of, 550–553, 552(illus.); in Thirty Years' War, 562; Peter the Great and, 576; farming by, 624–625, 624(illus.); England and, 635; Indonesian trade by, 646–647; in Africa, 859; in Java, 865. *See also* Dutch Republic; Holland; Netherlands
Dutch East India Company, 501, 511, 552–553, 646
Dutch East Indies, 646–647, 992
Dutch Empire, 510–511
Dutch Republic, 474; independence of, 475, 513; in 17th century, 549–553. *See also* Dutch
Dutch War: French army in, 527
Dutch West India Company, 508, 553
Dylan, Bob, 1004
Dynamics, law of, 594
Dynamo, 805
Dynasties: female rulers of, 433; Thirty Years' War and, 562
Dzhugashvili, Joseph, *see* Stalin, Joseph

Early Middle Ages, *see* Middle Ages
Earth, *see* Astronomy; Universe
East: technology borrowed from, 495. *See also* Asia; Middle East
East Africa, 862, 866(illus.)
East Anglia, 373
East Asia: First World War in, 890
Eastern Christian church, *see* Orthodox Christianity
Eastern Europe, 1052; Reformation in, 465–466; absolutism in, 559, 610–613, 615–616; warfare and social changes in, 559–565; serfdom in, 560–561; Slavs in, 572; peasants in, 622; Jews and, 838; after First World War, 929; wartime conferences and, 982–984; Marshall Plan and, 983; COMECON in, 988(map); communism in, 996, 1025–1026; women in, 1003; after cold war, 1019; revolutions of 1989 in, 1024–1030, 1024(map); capitalism in, 1031; postcommunist, 1035; refugees from, 1042–1043
Eastern front: in First World War, 889
Eastern Orthodoxy, *see* Orthodox Christianity
Eastern Slavs, 572
Easter Rebellion, 894
East Germany: West Germany and, 1008, 1019, 1040; Berlin Wall and, 1025, 1027(illus.); reform and, 1029; women in, 1040. *See also* Germany
East Indies, 865; Portugal and, 501, 646; Dutch in, 646–647; Second World War in, 970
Eck, Johann, 449
Economic Consequences of the Peace (Keynes), 928–929
Economic determination, 732

Economic interests: of West, 847, 874; railroads and, 849; new imperialism and, 865
Economic liberalism, 647–648
Economic nationalism, 732
Economic planning, *see* Planned economies
Economics: Malthus and, 726; Ricardo and, 726, 757; laissez faire, 754; Marx and, 757
Economy: plague and, 379; Hundred Years' War and, 382; in 14th century, 390–392; urban, 393; in Renaissance, 408; exploration and, 493; Spain and, 509–510; global, 510–511, 634–648, 1031; in 17th century, 524–525; moral, 525; in France, 532, 686, 688, 690, 697, 703, 704, 771, 817; mercantilism and, 532, 640–641; in England, 547, 718–719; Dutch, 550–553; after Thirty Years' War, 565; scientific revolution and, 598; in Atlantic region, 635–640, 636(map); slaves in Americas and, 642–643; Industrial Revolution and, 718–719; dual revolution and, 747; scientific research and, 805; in Russia, 827; crash in 1873, 837; worldwide, 847–854, 935, 940; imperialism and, 865; in First World War, 891; Germany and, 928; reparations and, 930; Great Depression and, 933, 935; in Soviet Union, 949, 950, 1023; after Second World War, 981, 985; Marshall Plan and, 984, 987; Keynesian, 987; neocolonialism and, 992–993; women and, 1003; in early 1970s, 1010–1011, 1015; eastern European, 1031; birthrates and, 1041–1042; after September 11, 2001, 1050. *See also* Capitalism; Commerce; Communists and communism; Finances; Great Depression; Inflation; Trade
Ecumenical council: of Trent, 467
Edict of Nantes, 473, 529, 531, 548
Edict on Idle Institutions (Austria), 672
Edo (Tokyo, Japan), 853
Education, 661(illus.); in Renaissance, 414–415; Erasmus on, 418; art and, 421; of priests, 446; of clergy, 469; public, 603; reading revolution and, 604–605; of children, 658; Rousseau on, 661; popular, 662; literacy and, 662–663; of physicians, 667; industrialization and, 734; for middle class, 790; in Russia, 827; Ottoman, 831; in France, 834; in India, 870; in Soviet Union, 953, 999; student protests and, 1005–1006. *See also* Schools; Universities
Education of a Christian Prince, The (Erasmus), 418
Edward (Black Prince, England), 383–385
Edward I (England), 373
Edward II (England), 373, 381
Edward III (England), 381, 382, 383, 408
Edward IV (England), 435
Edward VI (England), 461, 462(illus.), 463
Ego, 919
Egypt, 853–854, 993(illus.), 1047; Mameluke, 485–486, 581; trade with, 487; Ottomans and, 489; modernization of, 853; British rule in, 854, 861; Suez Canal and, 854, 865; nationalist revolution in, 992
Egyptian Nationalist Party, 854
Einstein, Albert, 918

Eisenhower, Dwight, 974, 1006
Eisenstein, Sergei, 995, 995(illus.)
El Alamein: Battle of, 973
Elba: Napoleon at, 708, 711, 750
Elbe River region, 565, 981
"Elect": Calvin on, 464
Elections: in France, 689; in Napoleonic France, 705; in eastern Europe, 1025–1026; after communism, 1032
Electors: of Saxony, 451; of Brandenburg, 457, 567; in Germany, 457
Electricity, 805
Electric streetcars, 786
Electromagnetism, 805
Elementary education, 661–662
Elements, 590–591
Eleonore of Portugal, 457
Eliot, George (Mary Ann Evans), 809
Eliot, T. S., 917, 920
Elites: in Habsburg lands, 567; in Brandenburg-Prussia, 571; popular literature and, 663; in Saint-Domingue, 693–694; in Haiti, 707; in central and eastern Europe, 747; in colonies, 868; in India, 869–870; of Lenin, 898; in Soviet Union, 953, 999, 1022; in Nazi Germany, 961; in Russia, 1033; of western Europe, 1039. *See also* Aristocracy; Nobility
Elizabeth (Bohemia), 598
Elizabeth (Russia), 580, 612
Elizabeth I (England), 396, 433, 456, 461, 462(illus.), 463; Netherlands and, 471–472; Mary, Queen of Scots, and, 512; absolutism and, 543
Elizabethan literature, 514–516
Elizabethan Settlement, 463
Elizabeth II (England), 1013
Emancipation: of Russian serfs, 827; of Jews, 837
Emigration: during Black Death, 377; from Ireland, 766, 767; by Jews, 838; from Europe, 856(illus.)
Émigré writers: Soviet, 1023
Emile (Rousseau), 661, 692
Empires: Islamic, 488–490; Portuguese, 495–498, 511; Dutch, 510–511; Spanish, 511–513; colonial, 634–647; rivalries over, 635–640; in Asia, 644–647; French Napoleonic, 708, 710(map); political, 859; after First World War, 903, 904(map); decolonization and, 989, 990(map), 991. *See also* Colonies and colonization; Imperialism; New imperialism; specific locations
Empiricism, 595
Employers: workers and, 631
Employment: in cities, 657; Blanc on, 756; for Jews, 837
Employment Agency (Soyer), 936(illus.)
Enabling Act (Germany), 960
Enclosure, 623, 625, 625(illus.)
Encomienda system, 504, 505
Encyclopedia (Diderot and Alembert), 602–603, 604(illus.), 613
Encyclopedists, 603
End Bad Breath (Chwast), 1007(illus.)
"End of history": Fukuyama on, 1032

Energy (power), 721–723; oil embargo and, 1010
Engels, Friedrich, 734, 757
Engineers, 789; railroad construction by, 724(illus.), 725
Engines, *see* Steam power
England (Britain): population in, 373, 626(illus.); Black Death in, 377; Hundred Years' War and, 381–387, 384(maps); Wyclif in, 388; lay piety in, 389; Peasants' Revolts in (1381), 390–392; serfs in, 392; taxation in, 392; Ireland and, 397, 398, 436, 513, 545, 547; More in, 416–418; in Renaissance in, 435–436; Catholic Church in, 461–463; Protestantism in, 461–463, 544–547, 548; marriage in, 469, 654; Armada (Spain) and, 474, 512–513; Spanish Armada and, 474–475, 512–513; witchcraft executions in, 476; exploration by, 501; mercantilism and, 511, 640–641; food riot in, 524(illus.); in Grand Alliance, 534; absolutism in, 543–544, 546–547; cabinet system in, 547; Jews in, 547; Restoration in, 547–548; Glorious Revolution in, 548–549; women's rights in, 549; Peter the Great and, 576; Voltaire on, 602; Act of Union in, 603; Enlightenment in, 603; agriculture in, 623, 624–625; enclosure in, 623, 625, 625(illus.); textile industry in, 633; Great Britain and, 634; North America and, 635–640, 637(maps); trade and, 637–640, 849–850; slave trade and, 643; India and, 646(illus.), 647, 865, 868–870, 877(illus.); Asian trade by, 647; infant mortality in, 658; Methodism in, 673–674; American Revolution and, 687–688; Napoleon and, 705, 706, 708; railroads in, 716(illus.), 723–725; energy in, 721; steam engine in, 721–723; Crystal Palace exhibit in, 725, 726(illus.); industrialization in, 727, 728, 728(illus.); workers in, 734, 736, 738, 841; labor movement in, 740–741; liberalism in, 754, 763–765; romanticism in, 758–760; Great Famine (Ireland) and, 767; cities in, 780–781; distribution of income in, 788(illus.); fashion in, 792–793, 793(illus.); domestic servants in, 794; realist literature in, 809; women's suffrage in, 832(illus.); before First World War, 835–836; unions in, 841; Industrial Revolution and, 847; income per person in, 848(illus.); foreign investment by, 850; shipbuilding in, 850(illus.); Opium War and, 851–852, 852(illus.); Egypt and, 854; emigration from, 856, 856(illus.); Nile River and, 862; empire of, 865; British women in India and, 876–877, 877(illus.); pre-First World War alliances of, 880(illus.); isolationism of, 881–882; mobilization by (First World War), 892; Treaty of Versailles and, 902–903, 928–930; Middle East and, 903, 905–906, 910–911; in 1920s, 932–933; unemployment in, 932–933, 935–936, 942–943, 943(illus.); Great Depression in, 934(map), 935; Hitler and, 962; Dunkirk and, 966; in Second World War, 973; European unity and, 989; Africa and, 992; Palestine, Israel, and, 992; privatization in,

1012, 1013; Thatcher in, 1012; Falkland Islands and, 1013; Gulf War (1991) and, 1030; European Union and, 1039. *See also* Britain; British East India Company; First World War; London; Second World War

English Channel: Spanish Armada in, 474, 512–513

Enlightened absolutism, 609–616

Enlightenment, 588(illus.), 589, 598–609; in France, 598–603; race and, 608–609; Frederick the Great (Prussia) and, 610; Jewish, 610, 611; childhood and, 661; among ordinary people, 663; French reforms and, 693

Entertainment: urban, 778(illus.); films as, 926–928

Entrepôt, 484

Environment: urban, 780–781

Environmentalism, 1012

Epidemics: of typhoid fever, 372. *See also* Disease

Equality: Voltaire on, 602; race and, 609; Ottoman, 831

Equiano, Olaudah, 641(illus.), 643, 645, 645(illus.)

Era of Tyrannies, The (Halévy), 947

Erasmus (Holbein), 443(illus.)

Erasmus, Desiderius, 417–418, 442–443, 446; Zwingli and, 449

Erhard, Ludwig, 987

Eritrea, 1043(illus.)

Erlach, Joseph Bernhard Fischer von, 568

Essay Concerning Human Understanding (Locke), 600

Essay on Logical Philosophy (Wittgenstein), 916

Essay on the Principle of Population (Malthus), 726

Essays (Montaigne), 514

Essen, 565

Established church, 454

Estates (assemblies): in France, 532–533; Dutch, 549; in Bohemia, 565

Estates (classes), 431; in France, 431, 684, 684(illus.); in Prussia, 570

Estates General (France), 531, 689–690

Este, Isabella of, 430

Esther Before Ahasuerus (Gentileschi), 428

Estonia, 561(illus.), 576, 578, 966, 1041

Ethiopia, 861; Portuguese voyage to, 488; Italian conquest of, 956(illus.)

Ethnic groups: in Middle Ages, 397–399; marriage between, 398; purity of, 398; Ottoman, 580(map); church membership and, 797; racism and, 1033; of Yugoslavia, 1038(map). *See also* Diversity; Minorities

EU, *see* European Union (EU)

Eucharist, 449–450; Zwingli on, 450

Eugene of Savoy, 568

Eugénie (France), 814(illus.)

Eulogies of Scientists (Fontenelle), 599

Euro, 1041

Eurocrats, 1039

Europe: climate in 14th century, 371–373; Great Famine in, 372; printing and, 418–421, 420(map); religion in, 468(map), 1049–1050; exploration and conquest by, 483–516; expansion of, 492, 621–648; voyages of discovery from, 492–504; racism in, 513–514; in 1715, 536(map); after Thirty Years' War, 563–565, 564(map); Enlightened monarchs in, 609–616; population growth in, 626; African slaves in, 643; French Revolution and, 694; French expansion in, 705–707; in 1810, 710(map); in 1815, 748(map); balance of power in, 749–751; large cities in, 780(map); Industrial Revolution and, 847, 848; in 1750, 848; foreign investment by, 850; Japan and, 850, 852–853; China and, 850–852; Egypt and, 853; population in, 855, 1041–1042, 1053; migration from, 855(illus.), 856–858; Africa partitioned by, 860(map); imperialism of, 862(illus.), 867–868; "civilizing" by, 866(illus.), 867; First World War and, 890–892; after First World War, 903, 904(map); jazz in, 932(illus.); Great Depression in, 934(map); dictators in, 945; Second World War and, 966–970, 968(map), 973–974; division of, 981–985; Marshall Plan and 983, 989; after Second World War, 985–989, 986(map); in 1990s, 1030–1041; contemporary, 1036(map); in 21st century, 1042; terrorist attacks on, 1048–1049; Muslims and, 1049

European Community, 1033, 1039

European Economic Community, 989, 1011, 1041. *See also* Common Market

European Union (EU), 1019, 1033, 1039, 1040(illus.); admission to, 1035; standards of, 1039, 1044–1045; identity of, 1039–1040; membership in, 1040–1041; constitution of, 1041; borders and, 1043

"Europe first" policy, 972–973

Euthanasia, 1045

Evangelicalism: in Reformation, 452; Methodist, 673

Evans, Mary Ann, *see* Eliot, George (Mary Ann Evans)

Evolution, 806–807, 806(illus.); Anaximander and, 807

Evolutionary Socialism (Bernstein), 841

Existentialism, 916, 917, 1009

Expansion: Ottoman, 489; European, 492–493; French, 533, 705–707; by Russia, 573(map), 576, 613, 827, 828–829; maritime, 620(illus.); in 18th century, 621–648; of United States, 825; in late 19th century, 847; great migration and, 855–859; of Western society, 859; of Nazi Germany, 962–963, 965; by Japan, 963. *See also* Exploration

Expatriates: American, 932

Experimental method, 592, 593

Exploration: European, 483; before Columbus, 483–493; reasons for, 492–493; technology and, 493–495; by Portugal, 495–498; overseas, 496(map); by Spain, 501–504

Exports: English, 640(illus.). *See also* Trade

Expressionism: in art, 922–926, 923(illus.)

Factories, 734–738, 791; in England, 719–721

Factory Act (1833, England), 738

Faerie Queen (Spenser), 515

Fagus shoe factory (Gropius), 921, 922(illus.)

Fairbanks, Douglas, 927

Fairfax, Thomas, 546

Fairy tales, 662, 760

Faisal (Hejaz, Syria), 890, 905–906, 905(illus.); General Syrian Congress and, 910–911

Faith: salvation by, 447. *See also* Religion(s)

Faith healers, 667

Fall of Algiers, The, 768(illus.)

Fallow: elimination of, 623

Families: planning of, 656; marriage and, 657; Napoleon and, 705; as mill workers, 736–737; in mines, 739–740; in Ireland, 766; in upper working class, 791; in 19th century, 797–804; gender and, 799–802, 804; sizes of, 802, 1042; migration and, 858; in 1970s–early 1980s, 1012. *See also* Marriage

Famine, 372–373, 372(illus.), 622; in 17th century, 525; in Ireland, 767, 835; in Ukraine, 952

Faraday, Michael, 805

Farms and farming: open-field system of, 622; enclosure and, 623, 625; improvements in, 623. *See also* Agriculture; Manors and manorialism; Peasant(s)

Farnese, Alexander (Cardinal), *see* Paul III (Pope)

Fascism: in France, 939; in Spain, 939; totalitarianism and, 946, 947–948; radical dictatorships and, 947. *See also* Italy; Nazi Germany

Fascist Party (Italy), 955, 956, 957

Fashion: of middle class, 789–790; for women (1850–1914), 792–793

Fashoda, 862

Fathers, 804

Faulkner, William, 920

Federal Republic of Germany, *see* West Germany

Felonies: by nobles, 396–397

Feminine Mystique, The (Friedan), 1009

Feminism, 799–800, 953; Second World War and, 981; in Italy, 1010(illus.); marriage and, 1016–1017. *See also* Women

Ferdinand I (Austrian Empire), 772

Ferdinand I (Holy Roman Empire), 459, 474, 489, 565

Ferdinand I (Two Sicilies), 751

Ferdinand II (Holy Roman Empire), 562

Ferdinand and Isabella (Spain), 436, 437(map), 438(illus.), 458; Inquisition and, 438–439; Jews and, 438–439; expansionism and, 492; Columbus and, 498–499

Fernández de Oviedo, Gonzalo, 493

Ferrara-Florence, council at, 388

Ferry, Jules, 861, 862, 865

Fertility, 626

Fertilizers, 622

Fields: enclosure of, 623

Fifth Republic (France), 989, 1006

Films, *see* Movies

Final Act (Helsinki Conference), 1008

"Final solution": of Hitler, 967, 969–970

Finances: women and, 484; absolutist monarchs and, 526; in France, 532–533, 688–689; for industry, 730–731; of Suez Canal, 853

Financial crash: of 1873, 837; of 1929, 933

Finland, 1040; Sweden and, 576
Finland Station: Lenin at, 898
Fireside chats: of Roosevelt, 928
First Balkan War, 883
First Coalition, 696, 697
First Continental Congress, 687
First estate (France): clergy as, 684
First French Republic, 770
First International, 838, 840
First World War: national state before, 831–838; impact of, 879, 908; as turning point, 879; origins of, 880–881, 884–885, 887; outbreak of, 883–884; invasion of Belgium in, 884, 887, 887(illus.); in Europe, 886(map); casualties of, 887, 889, 895, 901; trench warfare in, 887–888; fronts in, 887–889; support for, 890, 894; United States in, 890; home front in, 891–892; experiences of, 894; Lenin and, 898; cost of, 901; Russian revolution and, 901; changes after, 904(map)
Fisher, Irving, 933
Fisher, John, 461
Fishing industry: Dutch economy and, 552
Five-year plans: in Soviet Union, 949, 950–952, 978–979, 995; in China, 992
Flagellants, 380(illus.), 381
Flanders: disease in, 372; famine in, 373; English merchants and, 382, 382(illus.); peasant revolt in, 390; France and, 533. *See also* Holland; Low Countries
Flaubert, Gustave, 808
Flemish language and people, *see* Flanders
Florence, 410, 412(illus.); Black Death and, 377; University of, 381; ciompi revolts in, 392–393, 408; homosexuality in, 395–396; banks in, 408, 408(illus.); Renaissance in, 408; government of, 409; Medicis in, 410; France and, 410–412; arts in, 421; cathedral in, 424
Flying shuttle, 631
"Follow Me" (McBarron), 974(illus.)
Fontenelle, Bernard de, 598–599, 599(illus.), 605, 606
Food: in Columbian Exchange, 508; riots over, 524(illus.); introduction of, 628; in 18th century, 663–665; of middle class, 789. *See also* Agriculture; Diet (food)
Forced labor: in Russia, 580; in First World War Germany, 891; in Soviet Union, 945, 951(illus.), 954; in China, 992. *See also* Slaves and slavery
Foreign affairs: from 1924–1929, 930; Soviet, 1024
Foreigners: in Russia, 586–587, 587(illus.)
Foreign policy: in England, 435; in France, 529–530; Bismarck's Alliance System and, 880(illus.)
Forests: for energy, 721
Formosa (Taiwan), 872
Fouché, Joseph, 705
Foundlings, 659–660, 802
Fourier, Charles, 756
Fourteen Points: of Wilson, 902
Fourth Republic (France), 987
France: Great Famine in, 372; Black Death and, 377; Salic Law in, 381–382; Hundred Years' War and, 381–387, 384(maps); Joan of Arc and, 385; Jacquerie in, 390; Italy and, 410; Habsburg-Valois Wars and, 411–412, 459; Italian invasion by, 411–412; in Renaissance, 434–435; Burgundy and, 458; Catholic Reformation and, 467; religious wars in, 472–473; exploration by, 501; mercantilist empire of, 511; absolutism in, 526, 528, 530–534, 600; army in, 527, 541; urban disorders in, 528; administration of, 529; nobility in, 529; Fronde in, 530; Canada and, 532; North America and, 532, 635–637, 637(maps); social hierarchy in, 534; Spain and, 537; classicism in, 541–542; Enlightenment in, 598–603; Montesquieu's theories and, 601; parlements in, 601; books in, 603–604; population in, 626; guilds in, 632–633; England and, 635; India and, 647; marriage in, 654, 797–798; birth control in, 656; illegitimacy in, 657–658; wet-nursing in, 658–659, 659(illus.); Jesuit expulsion from, 672; Jansenism in, 674–675; estates in, 684; bourgeoisie in, 684–685; American Revolution and, 687–688; houses of government in, 689; limited monarchy in, 691–693; constitution of (1795), 702; Napoleon I in, 703–711; industrialization in, 727, 728, 728(illus.), 730; corporate banking in, 732; boundaries of, 749; liberalism in, 754; utopian socialism in, 756; Algeria and, 767, 829, 992; revolution of 1830 in, 767–768; First Republic in, 770; Second Republic in, 770–771, 816–817; democratic republic in, 770–772; cities in, 781; literature in, 808–809; Napoleon III in, 815–818; Second Empire in, 817–818; Third Republic in, 824, 833–835; Germany and, 825; colonial empire of, 834; Dreyfus affair in, 834–835; unions in, 841; Madagascar and, 846(illus.); foreign investment by, 850; Egypt and, 853; Suez Canal and, 854; Africa and, 861; Nile River and, 862; in Indochina, 865, 992; Alliance System and, 880, 880(illus.), 881; Russian alliance with, 881; First World War and, 886(map), 887, 890; Treaty of Versailles and, 902–903, 928–930; Middle East and, 903, 905, 906, 910–911; after First World War, 908; existentialism in, 916–917; Little Entente and, 929; Ruhr crisis and, 929(illus.); in 1920s, 932; Popular Front in, 939; Rhineland and, 962; Nazi occupation of, 966; Vichy government in, 966, 973; Catholic Party in, 987; economy in, 989; Fifth Republic in, 989, 1006; after Second World War, 989; neocolonialism and, 992–993; general strike in, 1006; government spending in, 1012; Gulf War (1991) and, 1030; globalization and, 1031; European Union and, 1039, 1041; protests and strike in, 1039; Muslim head scarves in, 1049; Muslim riots in, 1054–1055. *See also* First World War; French Revolution; Second World War
Franche-Comté, 458, 533
Franchise (vote), *see* Voting and voting rights
Francis I (France), 435, 472

Francis II (Austria), 696, 706
Franciscans, 389, 398, 505
Francis Ferdinand (Austria-Hungary), 883
Francis Joseph (Austria-Hungary), 772, 836, 894
Franco, Francisco, 963
Franco-Prussian War, 823(map), 824–825, 833–834, 880
Frankfurt, 773(illus.)
Frankfurt Assembly, 774, 837
Franklin, Benjamin, 688
Frederick (elector of Palatinate), 562
Frederick I (Prussia), 571
Frederick II (Holy Roman Empire), 563
Frederick II the Great (Prussia): palace of, 541, 568; Voltaire and, 588(illus.), 602; Enlightenment and, 609–610; Russia and, 613; War of the Austrian Succession and, 635; potato and, 665(illus.)
Frederick III ("the Ostentatious") (Elector of Brandenburg), *see* Frederick I (Prussia)
Frederick III (Holy Roman Empire), 457
Frederick VII (Denmark), 774
Frederick William (Great Elector, Brandenburg), 567, 570–571
Frederick William I (the "Soldiers' King") (Prussia), 571–572, 609
Frederick William III (Prussia), 707
Frederick William IV (Prussia), 773, 774, 821
Freedom(s): Rousseau and, 607; Napoleon and, 705; liberalism and, 754
Free French government, 987
Free-market economy, 987
Free-market reforms, 1031
Free people of color: in Saint-Domingue, 693, 694
Free trade: in England, 764
French Academy, 541
French Academy of Science, 597
French Canada, 532
French Guiana, 707
French Indochina, *see* Indochina
French language, 542
French phase: of Thirty Years' War, 562
French Revolution, 747; background to, 683–689; second revolution in, 696–697; Reign of Terror in, 698–700; Thermidorian Reaction and Directory in, 702–703. *See also* Guillotine (France)
French Section of the Workers International, 838
Frescoes: in Renaissance, 428
Freud, Sigmund, 804, 919–920
Friars: Luther as, 446–447
Friedan, Betty, 1009
Friedrich, Caspar David, 759(illus.)
Froissart, Jean, 383
Fronde (France), 530
Frontiers: ethnic groups along, 397. *See also* Borders; Boundaries
Fugger family, 447
Führer, 958
Fukuyama, Francis, 1032
Functionalism: in architecture, 921, 922(illus.)
Fundamental Laws (Russia), 829

Fur-collar crime, 396–397
Future: study of history and, 1050, 1052

Gabelle (tax), 434
Galilei, Galileo, 592–594
Galleys, 494
Gambetta, Léon, 834
Gandhi, Mohandas "Mahatma," 991, 991(illus.)
Gangsterism: in eastern Europe, 1035
Gardens: of palaces, 569
Gardiner, Grace, 876
Garibaldi, Giuseppe, 819(map), 820(illus.), 821
Gas chambers: in Holocaust, 945, 967, 969–970
Gauguin, Paul, 923
Gays, *see* Homosexuality
Gdansk Agreement, 1020
Gender: categorizing people by, 432–434; division of labor, 738–740, 799; family life and, 799–802, 804. *See also* Men; Sex and sexuality; Voting and voting rights; Women
General History of the Indies (Oviedo), 493
General strike: in France, 1006; in Italy, 1018(illus.)
General Syrian Congress, 910–911
General will, 608
Genesis (Bible), 455
Geneva, 463, 464–465
Geneva Accords (1954), 1006
Genevan Catechism (Calvin), 464
Genius: in Renaissance, 425–426
Genoa, 408, 409, 490, 491
Genocide: against Armenians, 889(illus.)
Gentileschi, Artemesia, 428(illus.)
Gentry: beverages of, 665
Geoffrin, Marie-Thérèse: salon of, 606
Geography: in Age of Discovery, 494
Geography (Ptolemy), 494, 494(illus.)
Geometry, 595
George III (England), 687
Georgia, 1041
German Confederation, 751, 773, 774, 821, 822
German Confederation of the Rhine, 706
German Empire, 824(illus.), 825, 832–833, 880; Black Death in, 377; Protestantism in, 451; religious divisions in, 467; Jewish rights in, 837. *See also* Germany; Holy Roman Empire
German people, 751, 836
German Southwest Africa: colonial war in, 833
German Trade Union Congress, 841
German Workers' Party, 958
Germany, 1036(map); Black Death in, 377; migrations from, 398; printing in, 418; Lutheranism and, 446–451, 458–459; Peasants' War (1525) in, 454–455; Reformation and politics in, 457–459; Habsburgs and, 458–459, 635; Estonia and, 561(illus.); Thirty Years' War and, 562, 563–565; Sweden and, 576; books in, 603; Enlightenment in, 603; population decline in, 626; guilds in, 633; Prussia and, 635; marriage in, 654; compulsory education in, 662; Pietism in, 672; Napoleon and, 705, 706–707; industrialization in, 727, 728(illus.), 730–732; iron industry in, 731(illus.); nationalism in, 755(illus.); unification of, 755(illus.), 774, 821–825, 823(map) 824(illus.); national state of, 774; before Bismarck, 821; Bismarck in, 832–833; Social Democrats in, 833; anti-Semitic political parties in, 837–838; trade unions in, 841; foreign investment by, 850; emigration from, 856(illus.); Africa and, 861–862; Alliance System and, 880(illus.), 881; before First World War, 881–883; mobilization in (First World War), 883–884, 891–892; home front in (First World War), 891–892; totalitarian society in, 892; in First World War, 894–895; peace settlement with Russia, 899; political parties in, 901–902; Treaty of Versailles and, 902–903, 928–930, 962; films from, 927; reparations and, 928, 929, 930; Western powers and, 928–930; Ruhr crisis and, 929, 930, 931; Dawes Plan and, 930; Weimar Republic in, 930; Great Depression in, 958, 959(illus.); Hitler in, 958–960; in Second World War, 966–967, 969, 973–974; Holocaust and, 967, 969; after Second World War, 985–987; reunification of, 1028–1030, 1040, 1053; globalization and, 1031; European Union and, 1039, 1040, 1041; women in, 1040; birthrate in, 1041. *See also* First World War; German Empire; Holy Roman Empire; Nazi Germany; Second World War
Germinal (Zola), 809
Germ theory of disease, 783
Gerritz, Decker Cornelis, 629(illus.)
Gesù: ceiling of, 453, 539
Ghent, 474
Ghent Altarpiece (van Eyck), 424
Ghettos: in France, 1054–1055
Ghiberti, Lorenzo, 421, 425
Gibbon, Edward, 660
Gioberti, Vincenzo, 818
Giotto, 422
Giovanni Arnolfini and His Bride (van Eyck), 424
Girls: as servants, 655; education for, 661. *See also* Women
Girondists, 696, 697
Gish, Lillian, 927
Gladstone, William, 835
Glasnost, 1023
Global economy, 510–511, 634–648, 1031–1032
Globalization, 511, 1031, 1045
Glorious Revolution (England, 1688–1689), 548–549
Glückel of Hameln, 551
Gnesotto, Nicole, 1044
GNP, *see* Gross national product (GNP)
Goa, 498
Goethe, Johann Wolfgang von, 760
Gold: from Africa, 487; Columbus and, 499; from Americas, 539; mercantilism and, 634–635; in France, 688; in South Africa, 861; dollar exchange for, 1010
Golden age: in Netherlands, 549–553
Golden Bull (1356), 457
Golden Horde, 572–573
Golden Mosque of Samara, 1048(illus.)
Goldhagen, Daniel, 970
Gold standard: Great Depression and, 935, 937; England and, 938
Goods and services: free movement of, 1031
Gorbachev, Mikhail, 1009, 1020, 1023(illus.); reforms of, 1022–1024, 1024–1025; disintegration of Soviet Union and, 1026–1028; Lithuania and, 1027; German unification and, 1030
Gorbachev, Raisa, 1023
Gouges, Olympe de, 695, 714–715, 715(illus.)
Government: in 14th century, 373–374; of England, 382–383, 386, 435–436; of France, 382–383, 386–387, 434–435, 530–531; in Italian cities, 409; in Renaissance, 434–439; of Spain, 436–439, 537; of Poland-Lithuania, 466; absolutism in, 523–542; of Spanish colonies, 538–539; constitutional, 542–553; by English Puritans, 546–547; Dutch, 550; of Prussia, 571–572, 610; Ottoman, 582; Montesquieu on, 601; Smith, Adam, on, 647; industrialization and, 730–732; First World War and, 831–832, 890, 945; in India, 870; in Japan, 871; in Russia, 896; in Turkey, 907; in Germany, 932; authoritarian, 946–949; after Second World War, 989; funding research, 1000; dissatisfaction with, 1011–1012; in Britain, 1012. *See also* Law(s)
Goya, Francisco, 711(illus.)
Gozzoli, Bennozzo, 417(illus.), 430
Grain: lack of, 373–374; distribution of, 377; price of, 380; in France, 534
Granada, 439, 499
Grand Alliance: against Louis XIV, 534; in Second World War, 966, 972, 976, 981
Grand Duchy of Lithuania, 466
Grand Empire (Napoleon), 708–711
Grand National Consolidated Trades Union, 741
Graneri, Michele, 652(illus.)
Gravitation, 594–595
Great Army (France), 708
Great Break, *see* First World War; Russian Revolution (1917)
Great Britain: formation of, 634. *See also* England (Britain)
"Great chain of being," 591
Great Depression, 914, 940; financial crisis and, 933, 935; unemployment in, 934(map), 935–936; in Scandinavia, 937–938; in France, 939; in England, 939–940; democracy and, 946; in Germany, 958, 959(illus.); Hitler and, 958
Great Elector, *see* Frederick William (Great Elector, Brandenburg)
Greater East Asian Co-prosperity Sphere, 970
Greater Germany, 965
Greater Serbia, 1037
Great Exhibition (London), 725, 726(illus.)
Great Famine: in northern Europe, 372–373; in Ireland, 766–767
Great Fear (France), 691
Great Fire of 1666 (London), 638, 638(illus.)
Great Lakes region, 635

Great migration, 855–859; Europeans in, 859
Great Northern War, 576, 578
"Great Patriotic War of the Fatherland," 995
Great Powers, 879–880; Prussia as, 610; at Congress of Vienna, 749–750; on revolutions, 761
Great Rebellion (India), 869
Great Russians, 998–999
Great Schism (Russia), 387–388
Great Train Robbery (film), 926
Great Trek, 859
Great War, *see* First World War
Great white walls, 859
Greece, 883, 1011; Enlightenment and, 603; national liberation in, 761–763, 829; after First World War, 906; aid to, 984
Greek Orthodox Church: in Hungary, 466. *See also* Orthodox Christianity
Greenland, 372
Green movement (West Germany), 1012, 1014(illus.)
Gregory I (Pope), 375(illus.)
Gregory XI (Pope), 387
Grien, Hans Baldung, 477(illus.)
Grieving Parents, The (Kollwitz), 914(illus.)
Grimm, Jacob and Wilhelm, 760
Grimshaw, Atkinson, 792, 793(illus.)
Gropius, Walter, 921, 922(illus.)
Gross national product (GNP), 725, 848
Grosz, George, 912(illus.)
Growth: of income, 848(illus.)
Guadalcanal: Battle of, 974, 975
Guadeloupe, 640, 702, 707
Guanajuato, 509
Guanche people: as slaves, 492
Guangzhou, China: battle near, 852(illus.)
Guernica (Picasso), 925, 925(illus.)
Guerrillas: in Balkans, 885(illus.)
Guilds, 628, 631–633, 632(illus.), 651(illus.); plague and, 380; women and, 393, 633; groups excluded from, 628; urban, 631–633; debate over, 650–651
Guillotine (France): Louis XVI and, 696
Gujarat, 510
Gulf War (1991), 1030
Gunboat diplomacy, 871
Gunpowder, 495
Guns, *see* Weapons
Guomindang, 992
Gustavus Adolphus (Sweden), 530, 562
Gustavus Vasa (Sweden), 451
Gutenberg, Johan, 418, 419
Gypsies, 969, 1032

Habsburg dynasty, 457–458, 635; France and, 529–530; in Spain, 537; in Thirty Years' War, 562; in Hungary, 566–567; Ottomans and, 582; in Austria, 613–615, 772; peoples under, 752(map)
Habsburg-Valois Wars, 411–412, 459
Hague, The, 550
Haiti: independence of, 701(map), 707–708. *See also* L'Ouverture, Toussaint; Saint-Domingue
Halévy, Elie, 947
Halim, Pasha (Ottomans), 830(illus.)

Hall of Mirrors (Versailles), 541, 568, 824(illus.), 825
Hamburg, 565
Hameln, 551
Hamlet (Shakespeare), 516
Hanseatic League, 435
Hardwicke Act (England), 469
Hardy, Thomas, 809
Harem, 583, 583(illus.); of Ottoman sultan, 582, 582(illus.)
Hargreaves, James, 719, 720(illus.)
Harkort, Fritz, 730, 732–733
Harvests: declines in, 372, 373
Hassan al-Banna, 1051
Haussmann, Georges, 784, 786
Havel, Václav, 1025–1026, 1026(illus.), 1035, 1052
Hawaii: migration to, 858(illus.)
Hayter, George, 764(illus.)
Health: public, 781–783; urban, 782(illus.); in 1970s and early 1980s, 1012. *See also* Disease; Medicine; Nutrition
Heart of Darkness (Conrad), 867
Hébert, Jacques, 702
Hegel, Georg, 757–758
Heidegger, Martin, 916
Heidelberg: University of, 381
Heine, Heinrich, 707
Heisenberg, Werner, 919
Hejaz, 890, 905
Helsinki Conference (1975): Final Act of, 1008
Henrietta Marie (England), 544, 547
Henry III (France), 473
Henry IV (France), 473, 528–529, 531(illus.), 686
Henry IV and The Proclamation of the Regency (1622–1625) (Rubens), 531(illus.)
Henry V (England), 385
Henry VI (England), 435
Henry VII (England), 435, 436, 501
Henry VIII (England), 462(illus.); Protestant Reformation and, 461–462
Henry the Navigator (Portugal), 493, 495–496
Hereditary subjugation, 560
Heresy: of Joan of Arc, 385; Philip II (Spain) and, 512
Hermandades, 436
Hermitage Museum (St. Petersburg), 580
Herzegovina, 883. *See also* Bosnia-Herzegovina
Herzl, Theodor, 838, 839, 992
Hierarchy: in Renaissance society, 428–434; of wealth, 431; in French society, 533. *See also* Classes
Higher education, *see* Education; Schools; Universities
High Middle Ages: political institutions in, 434; state in, 434. *See also* Middle Ages
Hijackings, 1046
Hildebrandt, Johann Lukas von, 569
Himmler, Heinrich, 961
Hindenburg, Paul von, 888, 891, 959, 960
Hindus: in India, 870, 991–992
Hiroshima: atomic bombing of, 975, 1000
Hispaniola, 499, 501, 637(map)
Historians: Ibn Khaldun, 513; on French Revolution, 685, 712; on factory workers,

734–736; on nationalism, 755; Michelet, Jules, 769; Palacky, Frantisek, 776–777; on Holocaust and anti-Semitism, 970
Historical and Critical Dictionary (Bayle), 599–600
Historical evolution: Marx and, 757–758
History: as dialectic, 758; future and, 1050, 1052
History of France (Michelet), 769
Hitler, Adolf, 838, 917, 927(illus.), 957, 976; radio and movie use by, 928, 960; emergence of, 930, 931; Mussolini and, 956(illus.); rise to power, 958–960; aggression by, 962–965, 965(illus.); empire of, 966–967; New Order of, 967; resistance to, 973; suicide of, 974. *See also* Nazi Germany; Second World War
HIV, 1044(illus.)
Hobsbawm, Eric, 747
Hobson, J. A., 867
Hoche (General), 700
Ho Chi Minh, 992
Hogarth, William, 673(illus.), 676(illus.)
Hohenzollern dynasty, 536(map), 567, 571–572
Holbein, Ambrosius, 400(illus.)
Holbein, Hans, the Younger, 443(illus.)
Holland, 749, 966; lay piety in, 389; Spanish attacks on, 474; seaborne empire of, 511; France and, 533; Napoleon and, 705; after Second World War, 989; Dutch East Indies and, 992. *See also* Netherlands
Holocaust, 967, 969–970, 969(illus.), 971
Holstein, 774
Holy Alliance, 751
Holy League: Christian, 581
Holy Office, 467
Holy Roman Empire: Protestantism and, 457; under Charles V, 458, 511; witchcraft executions in, 476; Dutch war and, 533; Thirty Years' War and, 562, 563–565; elector of Brandenburg and, 567. *See also* Germany; Habsburg dynasty
Home front: in Russia, 895
Home rule: for Ireland, 835–836, 836(illus.)
Homestead Act (United States, 1862), 826
Homosexuality: in Middle Ages, 395–396, 396(illus.); women's movement and, 1010; legalized marriage for, 1045
Hong Kong: cession of, 851–852
Honor: classes organized by, 431
Hoover, Herbert, 937
Hormuz, 488, 490
Hosius, Stanislaus, 466
Hospitals, 670(illus.); medieval, 378; plague and, 378, 379(illus.); foundling, 660; germ theory and, 783
Hôtel-Dieu (Paris), 379(illus.)
Houdon, 619(illus.)
Households: in Renaissance, 421–422; workers in, 654–656; of urban poverty, 739; income of, 787; women in, 799, 800
House of Commons (England), 543–544, 763, 835; English Reformation and, 461
House of Commons, The, 1833 (Hayter), 764(illus.)
House of Lords (England), 544, 763, 835

House of Orange, 549–550
Houses of government: in France, 689
Housing: medieval, 376; Dutch, 550(illus.); in London, 638–639, 639(illus.); in 18th century, 666–667; of workers, 736; urban, 781; in Paris, 785(illus.), 786; of middle class, 789; Soviet, 953; for low-income families, 1001
Huascar (Inca), 503
Huayna Capac (Inca), 503
Hudson Bay region, 635
Hugo, Victor, 760
Huguenots (France), 473, 529–530; Edict of Nantes and, 473, 529, 531; expulsion of, 599
Huitzilopochtli (god), 501
Hull, Cordell, 983
Human Comedy, The (Balzac), 808
Humanism: in Renaissance, 412–414; Christian, 416–418; in northern Europe, 416–418; of Montaigne, 514
Human rights: promotion of, 1044–1045, 1049–1050; terrorism and, 1049; of immigrants, 1055
Hume, David, 603, 608, 609
Hunchback of Notre Dame (Hugo), 760
Hundred Days: of Napoleon, 711, 767
Hundred days of reform (China), 872
Hundred Years' War, 381–387, 384(maps); Joan of Arc and, 385; England and France after, 386–387
Hungary, 1024, 1031, 1041; Reformation in, 466; Habsburgs in, 565, 582; in Austrian Empire, 566–567, 751; Ottoman defeat of, 581; Enlightenment and, 603; revolt in, 772, 836; Magyar nobility in, 836–837; republic of, 901; peace treaty with, 903; Second World War and, 974, 983; revolutions in, 997, 1025; in postcommunist era, 1035. *See also* Austro-Hungarian Empire (Austria-Hungary); Magyars
Hürrem (Ottomans), 582(illus.), 583, 583(illus.)
Hus, Jan, 388, 391, 391(illus.), 449, 465
Husbands, 800, 802
Hussein ibn-Ali (Hejaz, Syria), 890, 905
Hussites, 465
Huxley, Aldous, 917
Hygiene: plague and, 376–377
Hymns: by Luther, 451; by Charpentier, 542

Iberian Peninsula: blacks in, 429–430; uniting of, 439. *See also* Portugal; Spain
Ibn Battuta, 488
Ibn Khaldun, 513
Ice age: little ice age as, 371–372
Iceland, 1011; Protestantism in, 451
Iconoclasm, 473, 474, 475(illus.)
Id, 919
Identity: European, 1039–1040
Ideologies: liberalism as, 753–754; nationalism as, 754–756; socialism as, 756; Marxian Socialism as, 757–758; romanticism as, 758; in Paris revolution of 1848, 771; of separate spheres, 799, 800; Marxist-Leninist, 992
"I have a dream" speech (Martin Luther King, Jr.), 994(illus.)

Illegitimacy: explosion of, 656–657, 739, 798; marriage patterns and, 656–658
Illness: care for, 377, 667. *See also* Disease; Health; Medicine
Illustration: scientific, 597, 597(illus.)
Imams, 1055
Imitation of Christ, The (Thomas à Kempis), 389
Immigrants and immigration: Chinese, 485; racism and, 1033; illegal, into European Union, 1042–1043; growth of, 1042–1044; from Eritrea, 1043(illus.); Muslim, 1049, 1054; ghettoization of, 1055. *See also* Migration
Imperial Diet (Augsburg, 1530), 458
Imperialism: Russian, 828–829; Ottoman and Western, 831; political, 859; inhumane practices of, 862(illus.); in Asia, 864(map), 865; critics of, 867–869; response to, 868; in India, 869(illus.); by Japan, 872; of West, 874; after First World War, 903; League of Nations and, 906; racial, 967; after Second World War, 991. *See also* Empires; New imperialism
Imperialism (Hobson), 867
Imports: English, 635
Impressionism, 922
Inca Empire: Spanish conquest of, 502–504, 509
Income: gap in, 787–788; women's contributions to, 800; in Great Britain, 848; in Third World, 848; wealth gap and, 848; per person, 848(illus.)
Income taxes, 787
Independence: of Haiti, 701(map), 707–708
Independence movements: after Second World War, 989, 991; in Middle East, 992–993
Index of Prohibited Books, 467, 603
India: trade with, 484, 485, 640; spices from, 490; sailing routes to, 495, 497; Anglo-French conflicts in, 635, 647; Britain and, 646(illus.), 647, 865, 868–870, 877(illus.); France and, 647; industrialization and, 727, 728(illus.); opium and, 851; migration from, 858–859; in 1914, 864(map); imperialism in, 865, 869(illus.); decolonization and independence in, 991–992, 991(illus.)
Indian National Congress, 870
Indians, *see* American Indians
Indies: search for water route to, 497–498, 497(illus.), 499–501
Individualism: in Renaissance, 413
Individual rights, 1044–1045
Indochina, 970, 992
Indonesia, 490, 511, 992; Dutch trade with, 646–647; in 1914, 864(map)
Indulgences, 442, 447–448, 448(illus.); in England, 548
Industrialization, 722(illus.), 728(illus.); steam engine and, 721–723; population and, 725–727; in continental Europe, 727–732, 729(map); factory owners and, 732–734; nationalism and, 755; urbanization and, 779–780; middle class and, 789; science and, 805; in Russia, 827, 828; world economy and, 847–854; uneven development of, 848;

imperialism and, 865; in Soviet Union, 951, 952, 978–979, 995; in eastern Europe, 996
Industrial Revolution, 717, 747; labor patterns and, 633–634; in England, 718–727, 725(map), 849; urban areas and, 780–781; global inequality and, 847; as turning point, 848
"Industrious revolution," 633–634, 634(illus.)
Industry: in 17th century, 525; colonial, 535; in Brazil, 539; in Russia, 578, 1033; in Prussia, 610; in 18th century, 629–631, 630(map); cities and, 780–781; workers in, 791; in England, 938–939. *See also* Cottage industry; specific types
Infant baptism, 451
Infanticide, 659–660
Infant mortality: wet-nursing and, 658
Inflation: from Black Death, 380; in Spain, 509–510; in Europe, 510; after Thirty Years' War, 565; in Germany, 929, 930; in France, 932; in 1970s, 1010; global economy and, 1031; in Russia, 1033
Influenza, 504
Inner light: of Baptists, 454
Inoculation: against smallpox, 670–671
Inquiry into the Nature and Causes of the Wealth of Nations (Smith), 647, 754
Inquisition: Spain and, 438–439, 512, 534; Holy Office and, 467; Netherlands and, 474; witchcraft and, 476; Galileo at, 594
Institutes of the Christian Religion, The (Calvin), 463–464, 473
Instruction, *see* Teaching
Insurance: in Germany, 833
Intellectual thought: in Renaissance, 407–408, 412–421; about race, 513–514; Montaigne and, 514; Enlightenment and, 589, 598–609; scientific revolution and, 595–597; science and, 597–598, 804–807; Comte on, 805; uncertainty in, 913–921; on totalitarianism, 947; de-Stalinization and, 996; feminist, 1009–1010. *See also* Art(s); Enlightenment; Ideologies; Literature; Philosophy; Religion(s); Renaissance
Intendants (royal officials), 529, 538–539
Interesting Narrative . . . (Equiano), 645
Interest rates (financial), 373
Intermarriage: between Old and New Spanish Christians, 438–439
International Monetary Fund (IMF), 1031
International phase: of Thirty Years' War, 562
International system: pre-First World War, 894
International Working Men's Association, 838
International youth culture, 1004–1006
Inuit people, 372
Inventions: of scientific instruments, 595. *See also* Industrial Revolution; specific inventions and inventors
Investments: in Prussian industry, 731–732; in Russian industry, 828; European, 850, 851(map)
Invisible hand, 754
Ipatescu, Ana, 746(illus.)
Iraq, 830, 903; independence of, 905; Gulf War (1991) and, 1030; refugees from, 1042
Iraq war, 1020, 1047–1049, 1052(illus.)

I-14 • Index

Ireland, 1046; England and, 397, 398, 436, 513, 545, 547; Protestant Reformation in, 462–463; Act of Union and, 603; linen industry in, 634(illus.); trade with, 640; factory workers from, 738; potato and, 764, 766; Great Famine in, 766–767, 835; nationalism in, 767, 835–836; home rule for, 835–836; Easter Rebellion in, 894; autonomy for southern, 933
Iron and iron industry: in England, 721, 723, 740; German, 731(illus.)
"Iron curtain" speech (Churchill), 984
Iron law of wages, 726
Isabella (Castile), 436, 438. *See also* Ferdinand and Isabella (Spain)
Isabella (England), 381
Isabella (Este), 430
Islam: empires of, 488–490; slave trade and, 513–514; Ottoman, 580; as a European religion, 1050; West and, 1053. *See also* Arabs and Arab world; Muslims
Islamic conservatism: Ottoman, 831
Islands: in Atlantic, 492
Ismail (Egypt), 853
Isolationism: of Great Britain, 881–882; of United States, 908, 972
Israel, 1046; General Syrian Congress and, 910–911; establishment of, 992. *See also* Arab-Israeli wars; Jews and Judaism; Palestine
Istanbul: Constantinople as, 488, 580–581, 582
Italy: Black Death and, 374, 377; communes in, 409; city-states in, 409–412, 411(map); arts in, 421–428; Habsburgs and, 458; trade in, 490–492; baroque art in, 539; female scientists in, 597; Enlightenment and, 603; Napoleon and, 705, 706; industrialization in, 727, 728(illus.); kingdom of the Two Sicilies in, 751; unification of, 818–821, 819(map); immigration from, 856, 856(illus.), 857–858, 857(illus.); in Ethiopia, 861; Alliance System and, 881; in First World War, 889; Treaty of Versailles and, 902; after First World War, 903, 906; Mussolini and fascism in, 955–957; Rome-Berlin Axis and, 963; Second World War and, 966, 989; Jews in, 971; Allied invasion of, 973; Christian Democrats in, 987; European unity and, 989; women's movement in, 1009, 1010(illus.); general strike in, 1018(illus.); birthrate in, 1041; European Union and, 1041; illegal immigration in, 1042, 1043(illus.)
Ivan III (Russia), 573–574
Ivan IV the Terrible (Russia), 574–575, 574(illus.)
Ivan the Terrible (Eisenstein), 995(illus.)
Iwo Jima, 975

Jacobean literature, 516
Jacobin club (France), 695, 696
Jacob's Room (Woolf), 920
Jacquerie, 390
Jager, Hugo, 944(illus.)
Jakarta, 647
James I (England), 515, 543, 544; literature under, 516
James V (Scotland), 465

Janissary corps, 582, 829–830
Jansen, Cornelius, 674–675
Jansenism, 674–675, 674(illus.)
Japan: trade with, 510; Russo-Japanese War and, 828–829; West and, 850, 852–853, 865; Europeans in, 852; isolation of, 852; opening of, 853; Perry in, 853; migration from, 858–859; imperialism and, 870–872; Meiji Restoration in, 871; military in, 871(illus.); Anglo-Japanese Alliance and, 881(illus.), 882; First World War in, 890; Rome-Berlin Axis and, 963; empire of, 970, 972, 991; in Second World War, 970, 972, 972(map), 974–975; atomic bombing of, 975, 1000; oil embargo and, 1011
Jaruzelski, Wojciech, 1021, 1025
Jaspers, Karl, 916
Jaurès, Jean, 842
Java, 647, 965
Jazz, 932(illus.)
Jefferson, Thomas, 687
Jehovah's Witnesses: Nazis and, 967
Jena, battle at, 707
Jenner, Edward, 670–671
Jesuits, 466, 469–472, 472(illus.), 505; schools of, 661; nobility and, 672
Jewish Bride, The (Rembrandt), 551(illus.)
Jewish Question, 967
Jewish State, The: . . . (Herzl), 839
Jews and Judaism: attacks on, 373, 378; in Spain, 436–437; conversion in Spain, 437–438; expulsion from Spain, 439; as slaves, 492; in England, 547; Dutch, 550, 551; Ottoman, 580, 584; in Prussia, 610; in Russia, 827; emancipation of, 837; migration of, 856–857; homeland for, 903, 905, 992; in fascist Italy, 957, 971; Nazis and, 961, 967, 969–970, 969(illus.); Soviet, 995. *See also* Anti-Semitism; Israel
Joad, Cyril, 917
Joanna of Castile: Philip of Burgundy and, 439
Joan of Arc, 385
John (England), 397
John II (Portugal), 497
John IV (Portugal), 537
John of Cracow, 398
John of Spoleto, 387–388
John Paul II (pope), 1020
Johnson, Lyndon, 994, 1006–1007
Johnson, Samuel, 758
Joliet, Louis, 532
Jonson, Ben: on death of son, 660
Jordan: General Syrian Congress and, 910–911
Joseph II (Austria), 613, 615, 615(illus.); church and, 672
Josephine (France), 706(illus.)
Journal (Columbus), 498
Journal (Wesley), 673
Journeymen's guilds, 393
Joyce, James, 920
Judaism, *see* Jews and Judaism
Julius II (Pope), 416, 424, 470(illus.)
"June Days" (Paris), 771
Junkers, 570, 571, 822

Justice: in England, 435; witchcraft trials and, 475–476
Justices of the peace (England), 435–436
Just price, 664

Kádár, János, 1025
Kafka, Franz, 920
Kampuchea (Cambodia), 945
Kandinsky, Wassily, 926
Kant, Immanuel, 608–609
Kay, John, 631
Keats, 759
Kellogg, Frank B., 930
Kellogg-Briand Pact (1928), 930
Kelly, Joan, 414
Kemal, Mustafa (Atatürk), 906, 907(illus.)
Kennedy, John F.: Berlin Wall and, 997; Cuban missile crisis and, 997; Vietnam War and, 1006
Kepler, Johannes, 592
Kerensky, Alexander, 896, 898
Keynes, John Maynard, 928–929, 935
Keynesian economics, 987
Khartoum: massacre at, 862
Khedive (Egypt), 853
Khmer Rouge, 945
Khodorkovsky, Mikhail, 1034(illus.)
Khrushchev, Nikita, 1027(illus.); de-Stalinization and reform by, 996–997; Cuban missile crisis and, 997; fall of, 997
Kidnapping, 1046
Kiel: mutiny at, 901
Kierkegaard, Søren, 917
Kievan principality, 572
Kilwa, 487
King, Martin Luther, Jr., 994
Kingdom of Naples, 410
Kingdom of the Two Sicilies, 819(map), 820
King James Bible, 516
Kings and kingdoms, *see* Empires; specific locations and rulers
Kinship: in 19th century, 738, 799
Kipling, Rudyard, 867, 902
Kirov, Sergei, 954
Kissinger, Henry, 1007
Kitchener, Horatio H., 862, 870
Knights: crime by, 396–397
Knox, John, 465
Koch, Robert, 783
Kohl, Helmut, 1008, 1029, 1030, 1039, 1040
Kollontai, Alexandra, 953
Kollwitz, Kathe, 914(illus.)
Königsberg, 571
Korea, 872; migration from, 858–859
Korean War, 984, 987, 1007
Kornilov, Lavr, 898
Kosovo, 1037–1038, 1045
Kosovo Liberation Army (KLA), 1038–1039
Kristallnacht, 961
Kronstadt: sailors' rebellion in, 949
Kulaks: in Soviet Union, 951
Kulturkampf, 832–833
Kuomintang, *see* Guomindang
Kurds, 1047, 1048
Kuwait: Iraq invasion of, 1030

Index • I-15

Labor: Black Death and, 380; of women, 393, 434, 532; black, 430(illus.); Dutch, 553; in Russia, 580; in cottage industries, 629–630; guilds and, 631–633; patterns of, 633–634; in British America, 640–641; in North America, 640–641; slave, 640–643; away from home, 654–655; in England, 719; on railroads, 725; sexual division of, 738–740, 799; migrants and, 858, 858(illus.); in First World War, 891–892; for Nazi Germany, 967, 971. *See also* Gender; Slaves and slavery; Strikes; Workers

Labor aristocracy, 791, 794(illus.)

Labor movement: in England, 740–741

Labor strikes, *see* Strikes

Labor unions: outlawing of, 740, 841; in England, 740–741, 740(illus.), 841; in France, 817; in Germany, 841, 961; First World War and, 892; in Great Depression, 937; in Poland, 1020–1021; globalization and, 1031

Labouchère, Henry, 867

Labour Party (England), 842, 933, 938

Lady with an Ermine (Leonardo da Vinci), 427(illus.)

Lafayette, marquis de, 688, 690, 691

Laissez faire, 754

Lake Texcoco, 502

Lamarck, Jean Baptiste, 807

Lamartine, Alphonse de, 760

Lancaster, house of, 435

Land: common, 622; in 18th century, 622–625; in British America, 640–641; in Latin America, 643–644; migration and, 856, 857; in Russia, 896, 899. *See also* Agriculture

Landlords: plague and, 379; in central and eastern Europe, 561; agricultural revolution and, 622–623; in England, 625; in Ireland, 766, 767

Landowners: in England, 435–436

Landscapes, 761

Langport, battle at, 546

Language(s): of Luther, 451; in 17th century, 526; in France, 542; in Austrian parliament, 836; in Hungarian parliament, 837

Languedoc, 373, 394

La Plata, 538

Larger Catechism (Luther), 451

La Rochelle: siege of, 529

La Salle, Robert, 532

Las Casas, Bartolomé de, 504–505

Last Judgment, The: of Michelangelo, 425

Last Supper, The (Leonardo da Vinci), 423, 427

Lateen sail, 494

Lateran Agreement, 957

Later Middle Ages, 371–401. *See also* Middle Ages

Latin America: Dutch and, 553; trade and, 640; colonial, 643–644; railroads in, 849; authoritarianism in, 946

Latvia, 578, 966, 1041

Laud, William, 544–545

Lausanne: Treaty of, 907

Law(s): for prostitution, 395; marital, 456; in England, 548; Ottoman, 584. *See also* Canon law; Law codes; Natural law; specific laws

Law (scientific): of dynamics, 594; of universal gravitation, 594–595

Law codes: in Russia, 613; Napoleonic, 799

Law of conservation of energy, 805

Law of inertia: of Galileo, 593

Law of universal gravitation, 594–595

Lawrence of Arabia, 890, 905(illus.)

Laypeople: sacraments and, 379; literacy of, 400–401; Protestant, 450; instruction of, 469

Lay piety, 389–390

League of Armed Neutrality, 688

League of Nations, 901, 902; Middle East and, 905; mandates of, 906, 906(map), 910–911; Germany and, 930, 962, 963

Learning, *see* Education; Intellectual thought; Schools; Universities

Lebanon, 903; General Syrian Congress and, 910–911; decolonization and, 992

Leclerc, Charles-Victor-Emmanuel, 707

Le Corbusier, 921

Leeuwenhoek, Anton van, 552

Legal system: in Russia, 827; in Japan, 871. *See also* Law(s)

Legends: of Robin Hood, 397

Legislative Assembly (France), 695–696

Lehmus, Emilie, 801

Leigh, Mary, 832(illus.)

Leisure: religion and, 675–676; working-class, 795–797; in postwar era, 1002

Lélia (Sand), 760

Lenin, Vladimir: Hobson and, 867; Bolshevik Revolution and, 896–898, 899(illus.); government formed by, 898; Marxian thought and, 898; Soviet film industry and, 928; single-party dictatorship and, 947; New Economic Policy of, 949; Soviet economy and, 949

Leningrad: siege of, 967

Lenin Shipyards (Gdansk), 1020, 1022(illus.)

Le Nôtre, André (architect), 540

Leo X (Pope), 435, 442, 447

Leo XIII (Pope), 834

León, 436, 437(map)

Leonardo da Vinci, 423, 425, 427, 427(illus.), 926

Leopold I (Holy Roman Empire), 567, 568

Leopold II (Belgium), 861, 862(illus.)

Leopold II (Holy Roman Empire), 615

Lepanto, Battle of, 581(illus.)

Le Peletier, Claude, 534

Lesbians, *see* Homosexuality

Les Demoiselles d'Avignon (Picasso), 924, 924(illus.)

Lespinasse, Julie de, 606

Le Tellier, Michel, 541

Le Vau (architect), 540, 568

Levi, Primo, 971, 971(illus.)

Lewis, C. S., 917

Leyte Gulf, Battle of, 974(illus.)

Liberal capitalism: vs. socialism, 771

Liberal democracy: communism and, 1032

Liberal Party (England), 835

Liberals and liberalism: economic, 647–648, 754; Metternich on, 751; ideology of, 753–754; in England, 754, 763–765; nationalism and, 755; in Prussia, 773; in Germany, 822, 824; totalitarianism vs. classical, 947

Liberia, 861

Liberty: Gallican (French), 434; of conscience, 531; liberalism and, 753, 754

Liebknecht, Karl, 894, 902

Liège: industrialization in, 730

Life expectancy: in Russia (1991), 1033

"Life Is Everywhere" (Yaroshenko), 809(illus.)

Lifestyle: Dutch trade and, 553; changes in, 621, 653–677; of rural workers, 631; consumerism in, 665–667; urban, 779; of middle class, 789–790; Soviet, 952–954; in Nazi slave-labor camp, 971; in 1970s and early 1980s, 1012. *See also* Children; Families; Marriage

Lille, 533, 534

Lima: Spanish in, 509

Limited liability, 732

Limited monarchy: in France, 691–693

Lincoln, Abraham: Civil War and, 825, 826

Linen industry: in Ireland, 634(illus.)

Linné, Carl von, 608

List, Friedrich, 731–732, 828, 856

Lister, Joseph, 783

Literacy, 662–663, 662(map); in Middle Ages, 399–400; of laypeople, 400–401; printing and, 418–420; reading revolution and, 604–607

Literature: in northern Renaissance, 416–421; Elizabethan, 514–516; Jacobean, 516; popular, 662–663; romanticism in, 758–760; on child rearing, 802; realism in, 804, 807–809; imperialism and, 867; of First World War, 887–888; in Age of Anxiety, 919–920; stream of consciousness in, 920; Soviet, 954, 1023; de-Stalinization and, 996; of women's movement, 1009. *See also* Poets and poetry

Lithuania, 966, 1041; Grand Duchy of, 466; in Poland-Lithuania, 466; independence, 1027

Little Entente, 929

"Little ice age," 371–372

Littré, Emile, 806(illus.)

Liturgy: Protestantism and, 450

Liverpool and Manchester Railway, 724

Lloyd George, David, 835, 883, 892, 902–903

Locarno agreements, 930, 931, 962

Locke, John, 548, 600, 603

Lodge, Henry Cabot, 907–908

Logical empiricism, 916

Lollards, 388

Lombardy, 750, 818, 820

London, 620(illus.), 637, 638–639, 639(illus.), 640(illus.); runaway slaves in, 643; blitzkrieg in, 966(illus.), 967

Long-distance trade, 510–511

Long Parliament (England), 545

Lopez de Legazpi, Miguel, 510

Lord protector (England): Cromwell as, 546–547

Lords: in eastern Europe, 560–561; peasant lands and, 560–561. *See also* Nobility

Lord's Supper: Zwingli on, 450

Lorraine: French seizure of, 533; Germany and, 825; surrender to Germany, 834. *See also* Alsace-Lorraine
Lotto, Lorenzo, 432(illus.)
Louis XI "Spider King" (France), 435
Louis XII (France), 435
Louis XIII (France), 562, 568
Louis XIV (France), 522(illus.), 685; absolutism of, 526, 528, 530–534; army of, 527; wars of, 533–534, 635; acquisitions of, 533(illus.); baroque arts and, 540–541; Versailles and, 541, 557(illus.), 568; classicism and, 542; Charles II (England) and, 547–548; Saint-Simon on, 556–557
Louis XV (France), 685, 686, 688
Louis XVI (France), 686; French Revolution and, 689–694; capture of, 691–692, 695, 695(illus.); guillotining of, 696
Louis XVIII (France), 711, 750, 767
Louisiana, 532, 643
Louis Philippe (France), 767–768, 770
L'Ouverture, Toussaint, 701–702, 707, 709(illus.)
Louvois, marquis de (François le Tellier), 533, 541
Low, David, 965(illus.)
Low Countries: population decline in, 373; Hundred Years' War in, 383; Habsburgs and, 458, 474; Spain and, 474, 512; agriculture in, 623, 624–625; at Congress of Vienna, 749. *See also* Belgium; Holland; Netherlands
Lower classes: in postwar era, 1001
Loyalists: in American Revolution, 687
Loyola, Ignatius, 469–470, 472(illus.)
Lübeck, 565
Luddites, 734
Ludendorff, Erich, 888, 891, 901
Lueger, Karl, 838
Lully, Jean-Baptiste, 542
Lunéville, Treaty of, 705
Lusitania (ship), 890
Luther, Martin, 446–451, 452, 481(illus.), 511, 671; music and, 451, 452; German patriotism and, 458; *On Christian Liberty,* 480–481; on Copernicus, 592. *See also* Lutheranism; Protestantism
Lutheranism, 449; German recognition of, 459; in Bohemia, 465
Lützen, battle at, 562
Luxembourg: European unity and, 989
Luxemburg, Rosa, 902
Luxury goods, 665; in Renaissance, 421–422; trade and, 483, 511(illus.)
Lyell, Charles, 806–807
Lyons, France: insurrection at, 528
Lyrical Ballads (Wordsworth and Coleridge), 759

Maastricht treaty, 1039
Macao, 510
MacArthur, Douglas, 984
Macbeth (Shakespeare), 515–516
MacDonald, Ramsay, 933, 938
Macedonia, 1045
Machiavelli, Niccolò, 410, 415
Machine gun, 862, 865–866, 878(illus.), 887

Machines, 721
Madagascar: French in, 846(illus.)
Madame Bovary (Flaubert), 808
Madeira, 497, 505
Madrid, 437; urban living in, 787(illus.). *See also* Spain
Magellan, Ferdinand, 500–501
Magistrates: in France, 686
Magnetic compass, 495
Magyar language, 837
Magyars, 466, 751, 836. *See also* Hungary
Mahmud III (Ottomans), 830
Maintenon, Madame de, 531, 541
Maize (corn), 509
Malacca, 484, 498, 553
Malaria, 866
Malay Archipelago, 500
Malevich, Kazimir, 950(illus.)
Mali, 487, 488
Malinche, La, 503(illus.)
Malta, 1019, 1041
Malthus, Thomas, 726, 734, 807
Mameluke Egyptian empire, 485–486, 581
"Managed democracy": of Putin, 1034
Management: as profession, 789
Manchester, England: industry in, 722(illus.)
Manchu dynasty (China), *see* Qing (Manchu) Dynasty (China)
Manchuria, 828, 829, 872, 963
Mandates: of League of Nations, 906, 906(map), 910–911, 992
Manet, Edouard, 808(illus.)
Manhattan Project, 999–1000
Manifest destiny: of U. S., 826
Mannerism: as art style, 425
Manors and manorialism: manorial rights of French nobility, 684. *See also* Serfs and serfdom
Mansa Musa, *see* Musa (Mansa)
Mantegna, Andrea, 422, 423(illus.)
Manual on the Art of Childbirth (Coudray), 669, 669(illus.)
Manuel (Portugal), 497
Manufacturing: cottage industry and, 628, 629–630; English, 640(illus.). *See also* Industrialization; Industry
Mao Zedong (Mao Tse-Tung), 992
Maps, 482(illus.), 494–495, 494(illus.); by Ribeiro, 500(illus.)
Marcel, Gabriel, 917
March on Washington (1963), 994(illus.)
Marconi, Guglielmo, 927
Margaret (Valois), 473
Marginal people, 507
Maria Theresa (Austria), 613–615, 615(illus.), 635; Frederick the Great and, 610; church control and, 672
Maria-Theresa (France), 534
Marie Antoinette (France), 691, 695
Marie de' Medici, 529, 531(illus.), 540
Marijuana, 1045
Marina (Doña), 503(illus.)
Maritain, Jacques, 917
Maritime trade, 620(illus.); European, 510–511
Market(s): in 19th century, 849–850; worldwide, 849–850; in Europe, 989

Market agriculture: in Holy Roman Empire, 567
Market economies: in eastern Europe, 1035
Marlowe, Christopher, 515
Marne: Battle of (first), 887; Battle of (second), 901
Marquette, Jacques, 532
Marriage: age at, 393–394, 653–654; between ethnic groups in Ireland, 398; gender roles and, 434; Luther on, 449; Protestantism and, 450, 454(illus.), 455–457; church consent for, 469; in Southeast Asia, 484; patterns of, 656–658; Fourier on, 756; in Ireland, 766; in 19th century, 797–798, 800–802; women and, 798, 799–800; youth counterculture and, 1004–1005; in 1970s and early 1980s, 1012; feminist critique of, 1016–1017; legalized gay and lesbian, 1045. *See also* Intermarriage
"Marseillaise," 696
Marseilles: Black Death and, 377; plague and, 377, 627, 627(illus.)
Marshall, Alfred, 805
Marshall, George C., 983
Marshall Plan, 984, 987, 989
Marsiglio of Padua, 388, 415
Martial law: in England, 547
Martin V (Pope), 388
Martin, Pierre-Denis, 568(illus.)
Martinique, 640, 702, 707
Marx, Karl, and Marxism, 757, 757(illus.), 816, 838–842, 898; class consciousness and, 732; social sciences and, 805; Social Democrats and, 833; revisionism and, 841
Marxian socialism, 838–842, 947–948; Lenin and, 897; Bolsheviks, Mensheviks, and, 898
Mary I Tudor (England), 461, 462(illus.), 463
Mary II (England), 548
Mary, Queen of Scots, 465, 512
Mary of Burgundy, 457–458
Masaccio, 423
Massacre at Chios (Delacroix), 762(illus.)
Massacre of Coligny and the Huguenots (Vasari), 444(illus.)
Massacres: in Second World War, 1037; in Yugoslavia, 1037
Mass transit, 786
Master race: Nordic people as, 967
Masturbation, 803–804
Masurian Lakes: Battle of, 888
Materialism, 1012
Mathematical Principles of Natural Philosophy (Newton), *see Principia* (Newton)
Mathematics, 595; of Newton, 594; Descartes and, 595
Matisse, Henri, 923–924
Matrimony, *see* Marriage
Matteotti, Giacomo, 956
Matter: Descartes on, 595–596
Maupeou, René de, 686
Maupeou parlements, 686
Maurice (House of Orange), 549
Mauritania, 498
Maximilian (archduke, Austria), 830(illus.)
Maximilian I (Holy Roman Empire), 457–458
May Day, 840, 840(illus.)
Mazarin, Jules, 530

Mazzini, Giuseppe, 755, 818
McBarron, Charles, Jr., 974(illus.)
McDonald, Daniel, 766(illus.)
Meat: in diet of common people, 664
Medici family, 410; Cosimo de', 410, 417(illus.), 430; Lorenzo de', 410, 421, 424, 442; Piero de', 417(illus.); chapel of, 422; Leo X in, 447; Catherine de', 473; Marie de', 529, 531(illus.), 540
Medicine, 805; Black Death and, 377–378; spices as, 492; plague and, 627–628; quack doctors and, 652(illus.); in 18th century, 663; treatments in, 667; practice of, 667–671; advances in, 670; women in, 801, 801(illus.), 954. *See also* Health
Mediterranean region: trade in, 484, 488, 491–492; Constantinople and, 580
Meiji Restoration (Japan), 871, 872
Mein Kampf (Hitler), 930, 958, 959
Melba, Nellie, 927
Memmingen, 455
Memoirs, The (Saint-Simon), 556–557
Men: marriage age of, 394; homosexuality and, 395–396; gender roles and, 433–434. *See also* Families; Fathers; Gender; Husbands
Mendeleev, Dmitri, 805
Mendelssohn family: Moses, 610, 611, 611(illus.); Dorothea, 611; Felix, 611
Mendicant friars, 389, 398; Augustinian, 446
Ménétra, Jacques-Louis, 607
Mensheviks, 898
Mental illness: Nazis and, 967
Mercantile families, 408
Mercantilism, 532, 634–640; in England, 511, 640–641; in France, 511, 532
Mercenaries: in Thirty Years' War, 562
Merchant marine: in France, 532; Dutch, 552
Merchants: hospitals founded by, 378; English, in Flanders, 382(illus.); as class of wealthy, 431; in third estate, 431; in Venice, 490–491; in Russia, 580; workers and, 631; fashion boutiques and, 666(illus.)
Mercier, Louis-Sébastien, 678–679
Merian, Maria Sibylla, 597(illus.)
Merici, Angela, 469
Mestizos: in Latin America, 644; in Mexico, 644(illus.)
Metals, *see* Gold; Mines and mining; Silver
Methodists, 673–674
Metric system: in France, 692–693
Metternich, Klemens von, 708, 749, 750, 753(illus.), 946; Carlsbad Decrees and, 751; revolutions of 1848 and, 772; Italy and, 818
Mexico: Spanish conquest of, 501; crops in, 509; trade with, 510; industry in, 535; casta paintings in, 644(illus.); people of, 644(illus.)
Mexico City, 501
Meytens, Martin, 615(illus.)
Miasmatic theory, 783
Michael Romanov, 576
Michelangelo, 406(illus.), 416, 421, 424–425, 447
Michelet, Jules, 755, 768, 769, 769(illus.)
Microscope, 552
Middle Ages: later period in, 371–401; sex and sexuality in, 393–396; prostitution in, 394; rape in, 395; homosexuality in, 395–396; ethnic groups in, 397–399; Renaissance and, 407. *See also* High Middle Ages
Middle class, 431, 747; in England, 436; in Spain, 535–536; in Thermidorian Reaction, 703; in 19th century, 732, 787, 788–790; liberalism and, 754; in France, 767; marriage in, 797–798; feminists in, 799–800; child rearing in, 802–804; youth and sexuality in, 812–813; in Germany, 821, 822, 961; Jews in, 837; in postwar era, 1001; in Russia, 1034
Middle colonies: slavery in, 641
Middle East: trade with, 484; Alliance System and, 881; First World War and, 890, 903, 905–906; Ottomans and, 906(map); decolonization in, 992–993; oil embargo and, 1010
Middlemarch: A Study of Provincial Life (Eliot), 809
Middleton, Gilbert de, 397
Midway: Battle of, 974
Midwives, 668–670; Coudray, Madame du, 669, 669(illus.)
Mies van der Rohe, Ludwig, 922
"Mighty Fortress Is Our God, A" (Luther), 451
Migration: Germanic, 209–210, 288; Black Death and, 377; ethnicity and, 397; from England, 640–641; slave trade and, 641–643; from Ireland, 766; from Asia, 858(illus.); to Soviet cities, 952; from Nazi Germany, 961; after Second World War, 985, 986(map); of Holocaust survivors, 992; to cities (postwar), 1001; in 1990s, 1042. *See also* Immigrants and immigration
Milan, 408, 410, 820
Military: in Hundred Years' War, 386; size of, 526–527; in Prussia, 571; Russian, 827; in United States, 1008. *See also* Armed forces; Soldiers
Military dictatorship: in England, 546–547
Millet system (nations): Ottoman, 584
Mills: children in, 736, 737–738. *See also* Factories; Textile industry
Milosevic, Slobodan, 1037, 1039
Mind-body split: Cartesian dualism and, 596, 598
Mines Act (1842, England), 739
Mines and mining: in Americas, 643; in England, 721–722; child labor in, 737; women in, 737, 739–740; worker testimonies about, 744–745
Ming Dynasty (China), 484, 499
Ministry of Munitions, 892
Minorities: in Austrian Empire, 772; in Russia, 829; in Austro-Hungarian Empire, 836–837; rights of, 1045
Misery index, 1011, 1011(illus.)
Misogyny, 476
Missions and missionaries: in Americas, 499, 505, 643; in New World, 499, 505; in Japan, 852; schools and, 866(illus.); in China, 872
Mitterand, François, 1012, 1039
Mobility, *see* Social mobility
Mobilization: in French Revolution, 700; for First World War, 883–884; in Russia (First World War), 895; of totalitarian societies, 947; in Germany, 973
Modernism: in art, 924
Modernity: in Saint Paintersburg, 579
Modernization: of Ottoman Empire, 826, 829–831; of Russia, 826–829; definition of, 827; of Egypt, 853; of colonies, 868; of Japanese army, 871(illus.)
Mogadishu, 487
Mohács, Battle of, 466, 566, 566(illus.), 581
Molière (Jean-Baptiste Poquelin), 542
Moluccas, 484, 500
Mombasa, 487
Mona Lisa (Leonardo da Vinci), 427, 926
Monarchy: nobility and, 317; in France, 386–387, 473, 686, 696; female rulers and, 433; in England, 435; in Poland, 466; constitutional, 525, 548–549; in 17th century, 526; in Spain, 537; serfdom and, 561; Enlightened, 609–616; in French family, 705. *See also* specific rulers
Monet, Claude, 725, 922
Monetary union: in Europe, 1039
Money: lending of, 437. *See also* Economy
Mongols: trade and, 484, 485, 492; in Russia, 572–574
Mongol Yoke, 573
Monks and monasteries, *see* Friars; Missions and missionaries; Religious orders; specific orders
Monnet, Jean, 987, 989
Monopolies: in Chinese trade, 851
Monsoons: trade and, 484
Montagu, Mary Wortley, 670
Montaigne, Michel de, 514, 660
Montcalm, marquis de (Louis-Joseph de), 635
Montesquieu, baron de (Charles-Louis de Secondat), 600–601, 606
Montezuma II (Aztec), 501–502, 503(illus.)
Montpellier, 394; insurrection at, 528
Moon: Galileo on, 593, 593(illus.)
Moor, Dimitri, 900(illus.)
Moors, 439
Moral economy, 525
Morality: in Renaissance, 414; middle-class, 790; of upper working class, 791; European Union and, 1045
Moravia, 753
More, Thomas, 416–417, 461
Moriscos, 534
Morison, Samuel Eliot: on Columbus, 498
Morocco, 882, 973; Black Death in, 378
Mortagne, Castle of: siege of, 383(illus.)
Mortality: from plague, 377; in 17th century, 626; infant, 660–661; public health and, 783. *See also* Death; Infant mortality
Mortality rate: in 17th century, 626; decline in, 783, 783(illus.), 854
Mortimer (England), 381
Moscow, 967; princes of, 573; Saint Basil's Cathedral in, 575(illus.); Napoleon at, 708
Mothers, 802, 804; unwed, 656
Motion: Aristotle on, 591; Kepler's laws of, 592; Galileo on, 592–593
Motion pictures, *see* Movies
Moulin Rouge, 796(illus.)
Mountain, the, 696, 697

Movable type, 418, 419
Movement of peoples, *see* Immigrants and immigration; Migration
Movies, 926–928; stars of early, 926–927; indoctrination and, 928
Mozambique, 859
Mr., Mrs., and Baby (Droz), 800–802
Muftis, 584
Mughals (India), 647
Muhammad Ali (Egypt), 830, 853
Multiethnic state: Austrian Empire as, 751–753; Ottoman Empire as, 753, 826–827; Russian Empire as, 753, 826–827
Multiparty system: before First World War, 831
Mundus Novus, 500
Munich: Hitler's uprising in, 930, 958
Musa (Mansa), 487–488
Muscovite princes, 573
Music: Luther and, 451, 452; baroque, 540; classical, 542; romantic, 761; atonal, 926; modern, 926; jazz, 932(illus.)
Music halls, 796–797
Muslim Brotherhood, 1051
Muslims, 883; in Spain, 397, 436, 439, 534; trade by, 484, 486(map), 487(illus.); locations of, 490; as slaves, 492; Portuguese exploration and, 498; Ottomans as, 584, 831; in Algeria, 767; at Omdurman, 862; in India, 870, 991–992; in Chechnya, 1035; in former Yugoslavia, 1038(map); as immigrants, 1043, 1049; Tariq Ramadan and, 1051; as threat, 1053. *See also* Arabs and Arab world; Islam
Mussolini, Benito, 946, 962, 973; propaganda and, 928; dictatorship of, 955–957; Hitler and, 956(illus.)
Mustafa Kemal (Atatürk), *see* Kemal, Mustafa (Atatürk)
Mutiny, *see* Great Rebellion (India)
Myconius, 400(illus.)
My Secret Life, 798–799
Mysticism: of Bridget of Sweden, 389–390

Nagasaki: atomic bombing of, 975, 1000
Nahuatl language, 503
Nanking, Treaty of (1851), 851
Naples, 770, 818; kingdom of, 410
Napoleon I (Napoleon Bonaparte), 703–711; coronation of, 706(illus.); Europe in 1810 and, 708, 710(map); at Waterloo, 711; Congress of Vienna after, 749–751; Egypt and, 853
Napoleon III (Louis Napoleon), 771–772, 814(illus.), 815–818, 824, 833; urban planning and, 784; Second Empire of, 817–818; Italian unification and, 820
Napoleonic Code (France), 704, 705, 799
Narva, battle at, 576, 577(illus.)
Naseby, battle at, 546
Nasmyth, James, 723(illus.)
Nasser, Gamal Abdul, 992, 993(illus.)
Nation, *see* State (nation)
National Assembly (France), 386–387, 532–533, 834, 838; free blacks and, 386–387, 532–533, 690, 692, 694, 701; disbanding of, 695; Napoleon III and, 817, 818

National Assembly (Germany), 774
National church: Catholic, 672
National Convention (France), 696, 697, 702–703
National debt, 1012; in Spain, 535
National Guard (France), 771
Nationalism, 698–700, 754–756, 1031; after Hundred Years' War, 387; economic, 732; in Ireland, 767, 835–836; in Austrian Empire, 772; age of, 815–842; Napoleon III and, 817–818; in Italy, 818–821; in Germany, 821–825, 902, 959, 962; in United States, 825–826; in Russia, 828, 829; Ottoman, 831; First World War and, 832, 884–885, 887, 894; tariffs and, 833; in France, 833–835; Magyar, 836; in Austro-Hungarian Empire, 836–837; among socialists, 842; in Egypt, 854, 992; in colonies, 868; in India, 870; in Japan, 872; European unity and, 989; in Soviet Union, 995; after cold war, 1033; in eastern Europe, 1035
Nationalist Chinese, 992
Nationality, 398
Nationalization: by Soviets, 900; in Britain, 987; in Egypt, 992, 993(illus.)
National Labor Relations Act (1935), 937
National Liberals (Germany), 832
National Organization for Women (NOW), 1009
National People's Party, *see* Guomindang
National Recovery Administration (NRA), 937
National self-determination, *see* Self-determination
National socialism: German, 957, 958
National Socialist German Workers' (Nazi) Party, 932, 958
National state: before First World War, 831–838
National System of Political Economy (List), 731
Native Americans, *see* American Indians
Native peoples, 397–398; European exploration and, 495
NATO (North Atlantic Treaty Organization), 984, 988(map); French withdrawal from, 989; Poland, Hungary, and Czech Republic in, 1035; Bosnian Serb military targets and, 1038; bombing of Yugoslavia, 1038–1039; Kosovo and, 1038–1039
Natural History, A (Linné), 608
Naturalism: in United States, 809
Natural law: Rousseau on, 607
Natural philosophy, 589, 590, 595
Natural rights, 687
Nature: scientific revolution and, 597; representation as female, 598
Navarino, battle at, 762
Navarre, 436
Navigation: exploration and, 495–496; scientific revolution and, 595, 598. *See also* Maritime trade
Navigation Acts (England), 547, 635, 637
Navy: Chinese, 485; Portuguese, 510; Spanish Armada as, 512–513; French, 532; Russian, 579; English, 635, 881; in Japan, 872; German, 881, 882(illus.), 883, 890; in First World War, 890; in Second World War, 974

Nazi Germany, 944(illus.), 976; tyranny in, 945; mass rally in, 948(illus.); Hitler and, 958–960; expansionism of, 962–963, 965; Rome-Berlin Axis and, 963; growth of, 963(map); empire of, 966–967; Holocaust in, 967, 969–970, 969(illus.). *See also* Germany; Second World War
Nazi Labor Front, 961
Nazism, 947; defined, 957; racial imperialism and, 967
Nazi-Soviet nonaggression pact, 965
Near East, *see* Middle East
Nelson, Horatio: at Trafalgar, 706
Neocolonialism, 993
NEP, *see* New Economic Policy
Netherlands: Protestantism in, 452; under Charles V, 473–475, 474(map); iconoclasm in, 475(illus.); revolt against Spain, 527–528; Flanders and, 533; golden age in, 549–553; European unity and, 989; European Union and, 1041; human rights in, 1045; Muslims in, 1049. *See also* Austrian Netherlands; Holland; Low Countries
Neutron, 919
Nevinson, Christopher, 878(illus.)
Nevsky, Alexander, 573
New Amsterdam, 635
New Christians: Jews as, 437–439; Muslims as, 439; Teresa of Ávila as, 471
Newcomen, Thomas, 722
New Deal (U.S.), 936–937
New Economic Policy (NEP), 949, 950
New England: slavery in, 641
Newfoundland, 635
New France, 635
New Granada, 509, 538
New imperialism, 847, 851(map), 859; in Africa, 859–865; causes of, 865–866; spread of Christianity and, 867; Japan and, 870–872
New Model Army, 546
New Order (Germany), 967
New physics, 917–919
New Spain, 538–539
New Testament, 371; Erasmus on, 418; Luther and, 451
Newton, Isaac, 594–595, 594(illus.), 599, 601–602, 805
New World: European "discovery" of, 492–504; Spanish conquests in, 501–504; plantation agriculture in, 505–508. *See also* Americas
New world order: of Bush, George H. W., 1030
New York (city): World Trade Center destruction in, 1045
New York (colony): New Amsterdam as, 635
Niani, 487
Nice, 696, 820
Nicholas I (Russia), 772
Nicholas II (Russia), 884, 895, 896(illus.)
Nietzsche, Friedrich, 915, 916(illus.), 920
Nijmegen, Treaty of, 533
Nikon (patriarch), 576
Nile River region, 862
1984 (Orwell), 920, 921(illus.), 942
"Ninety-five Theses on the Power of Indulgences" (Luther), 448
Nixon, Richard, 1007, 1010

Nobility, 527(illus.); in England, 386; in France, 386, 529, 685, 689, 705; crime among, 396–397; in Italy, 409; class organization and, 431; in Spain, 438–439; in Poland, 466; vs. monarchy, 526; at Versailles, 541; Czech, 565; in Bohemia, 565–566; Hungarian, 566–567; in Prussia, 571; in Russia, 574, 580, 613; as French estate, 684; in French Revolution, 691. *See also* Aristocracy
Noblesse d'épée, 530
Noblesse de robe, 529
Nocturnal, 495(illus.)
Nonviolent resistance: by Gandhi, 991
Nordic peoples, 967
Nördlingen, Battle of, 562
Normandy: France and, 385; invasion of, 974
North (United States), 825–826
North Africa: Ottomans and, 489, 581; Second World War in, 973; workers from, 1042, 1054
North America: European conflicts over, 635–640, 637(maps); migration to, 640–641; Industrial Revolution and, 847; steam power in, 849. *See also* Americas
North Atlantic Treaty Organization (NATO), *see* NATO
Northcliffe, Lord, 927
Northern Alliance (Afghanistan), 1045
Northern Europe: great Famine in, 372; Renaissance in, 416–421, 424
Northern Ireland, *see* Ulster
North German Confederation, 822
North Korea, *see* Korean War
Norway, 966; Protestantism in, 451; independence from Sweden, 836; Great Depression in, 937–938; after Second World War, 989. *See also* Scandinavia
Notables: in France, 688–689
Nova Scotia, 635
Novels, *see* Literature
Novgorod, 573
NOW, *see* National Organization for Women
Nuclear family, 654
Nuclear weapons, 1030; U.S. and, 987; French, 989
Nuns: Protestantism and, 450; marriage and, 457; Jansenism and, 674(illus.)
Nur-as-Said (Ottoman officer), 905(illus.)
Nuremberg: observatory at, 596(illus.)
Nuremberg Laws, 961
Nurses, 789
Nursing, *see* Breast-feeding
Nutrition: in 18th century, 664–665. *See also* Diet (food); Food; Health

Oath of the Tennis Court, 690
Observatory: at Nuremberg, 596(illus.)
Occupation zones: after Second World War, 986(map)
October Manifesto (Russia), 829
Oedipal tensions: Freud on, 804
Of Natural Characters (Hume), 608
Ogé, Vincent, 694
Oil and oil industry: in Russia, 1034(illus.)
Oil embargo, 1010–1011
Oil shock, 1010, 1011, 1020
Okinawa, 975

Old-age pensions: in Germany, 833; in England, 835
Old Believers (Russia), 576
Olearius, Adam: in Russia, 586–587, 587(illus.)
Oligarchy: in Italian cities, 409
Olivares, count-duke of (Gaspar de Guzmán), 537
Omdurman: battle at, 862
"On Cannibals" (Montaigne), 514
On Christian Liberty (Luther), 480–481
One Day in the Life of Ivan Denisovich (Solzhenitsyn), 996
O'Neill, Paul, 1047
On Germany (Staël), 760
On Pleasure (Valla), 416
On Secular Government (Luther), 451
On the Different Races of Man (Kant), 609
On the Dignity of Man (Pico della Mirandola), 413
On the False Donation of Constantine (Valla), 416
On the Family (Alberti), 414
"On the Immortality of the Soul" (Mendelssohn), 610
On the Origin of Species by the Means of Natural Selection (Darwin), 807
On the Revolutions of the Heavenly Spheres (Copernicus), 591
OPEC, *see* Organization of Petroleum Exporting Countries
Open Door policy: in China, 872
Open-field system, 622; enclosure and, 623
Opium trade, 851
Oppenheim, Moritz, 610(illus.)
Optimism: about the future, 1050
Orders: social classes as, 431; religious, 469–472. *See also* Clergy; Nobility; Peasant(s)
Organic chemistry, 805
Organization of European Economic Cooperation (OEEC), 989
Organization of Petroleum Exporting Countries (OPEC), 1010–1011
Organization of Work (Blanc), 756
Origin: categorizing people by, 429
Original sin: Jansen and, 675
Orléans: Joan of Arc at, 385; duke of, 685–686
Orlov, Grigory, 612, 612(illus.)
Ormuz, 498
Orphans: in factories, 721
Orthodox Christianity: in Russia, 574
Orwell, George, 920, 921(illus.), 942–943
Oslo Breakfast, 938(illus.)
Ottoman Empire, 580–584, 836; Hungary and, 466; trade and, 488–489; absolutism in, 559; Habsburgs and, 566, 567; in 1566, 581(map); conservatism in, 753; Greece nationalism and, 761; decline of, 829–830; reform in, 830–831; Tanzimat in, 830–831; Jewish settlement in, 837(illus.); Egypt and, 853, 854; Alliance System and, 881; Balkan nationalism and, 885(illus.); First World War and, 889–890, 903; end of, 890; partition of, 906(map). *See also* Ottoman Turks
Ottoman-Safavid war, 489
Ottoman Turks, 761; Spain and, 512. *See also* Ottoman Empire
Otumba, battle at, 502

Overland trade, *see* Caravans; Trade
Owen, Robert, 738, 741, 841
Oxford University, 381

Pacific Ocean region: Magellan in, 500–501, 510; Spanish empire in, 510; Second World War in, 972(map), 974–975
Pacifism: of Anabaptists, 454
Paine, Thomas, 663
Painting: in Italian Renaissance, 422–424; of northern Renaissance, 424; by women, 426–428; in Mexico, 644(illus.); romantic, 759(illus.), 760–761; realism in, 809(illus.); modern, 924
Pakistan, 992
Palaces: Stockholm Royal Palace and, 568; of absolute monarchs, 568–569, 568(illus.), 569(illus.)
Palacky, Frantisek, 777(illus.); on Czech nation, 776–777
Palestine: Ottomans and, 489; Jews in, 837(illus.), 838, 839; Balfour Declaration and, 903, 905; division of, 992. *See also* Israel
Panama Canal, 850
Papacy, 416; Conciliar movement and, 388; France and, 435, 472–473; Inquisition and, 438; reform of, 446, 467; Reformation and, 458; in Austria, 614; central Italy, Rome, and, 818. *See also* Catholic Church; specific popes
Papal infallibility doctrine, 832
Papal States, 410, 467, 821
Paper, 418
Parasites: Saint-Simon on, 756
Pareja, Juan de, 507, 507(illus.), 540(illus.)
Paris, 678–679; religious violence in, 473; Peace of, 749, 750; revolution of 1848 in, 770, 771; revolt in, 770–771; modernization of, 784–786, 784(map); lifestyle in, 785(illus.), 792, 792(illus.); in Second Empire, 816(illus.); in Franco-Prussian War, 833–834; First World War peace conference in, 902; American expatriates in, 932. *See also* France
Paris, Treaty of: of 1259, 381; of 1763, 635–637, 647; of 1783, 683
Paris Accord (1990), 1030
Paris Commune (1871), 834, 838
Parishes: churches in, 671
Paris International Exhibition, 925
Parlement of Paris: finances and, 530, 688; taxation and, 686
Parlements (France), 601, 685–686; Maupeou and, 686
Parliament: in Prussia, 821, 822–824; in Austria, 836
Parliament (England), 754; after Hundred Years' War, 386; monarchy and, 435; Charles I and, 543, 545–546; under Puritans, 546–547; Charles II and, 547–548; constitutional monarchy and, 548–549; enclosure and, 625; voting for, 763–764. *See also* House of Commons (England); House of Lords (England)
Parliamentary government: in Italy, 955, 956
Parma, 409
Parma, duke of, 512

Partitions: of Poland, 613, 614(map); of Africa, 860(map); of Palestine, 992
Passarowitz, Treaty of, 582
Passive resistance: in Ruhr crisis, 929
Pasternak, Boris, 996
Pasteur, Louis, 783, 805
Pasteurization, 783
Patriarch: Nikon as, 576
Patriarchal tradition: among workers, 739
Patriotism: in Germany, 458, 824; in First World War, 890–891
Patronage: at Versailles, 541
Patrons: of Renaissance arts, 421, 425–428
Paul III (Pope), 467, 472(illus.)
Paulette (tax), 528
Paupers, 781; children as, 736
Peace: search for, 928–933; demonstrations for, 1052(illus.)
Peace agreement: for Vietnam War, 1007
Peaceful coexistence policy, 996
Peace of Augsburg, 459
Peace of Paris, 749, 750
Peace of Utrecht, 534, 536(map), 635
Peace of Westphalia, 549, 563–566
Pearl Harbor, Hawaii, 972; Japanese attack on, 970
Peasant(s), 527(illus.); Luther and, 455; lifestyle in 17th century, 524–525; in France, 528, 767; in central and eastern Europe, 560–561; Thirty Years' War and, 563(illus.); in Prussia, 567, 572; in Russia, 577, 580, 827, 829; in Austria, 614, 615; in 18th century, 622; agricultural revolution and, 622–623; marriage by, 657; popular literature and, 663; religion of, 675; in French Revolution, 690–691; in Ireland, 766, 835; in Egypt, 853; in Soviet Union, 949, 951, 951(illus.); in Ukraine, 952. See also Manors and manorialism; Serfs and serfdom
Peasant revolts, 390–392, 392(map); in England (1381), 370(illus.), 390–392; in Flanders, 390
Peasants' War (Germany, 1525), 454–455
Peel, Robert, 764
Penance: Christian, 448
Pennsylvania: as colony, 635; terrorist plane crash in, 1045
Penny Wedding, The (Allan), 657(illus.)
Pentagon: terrorist attack on, 1020, 1045
People, the: categorizations of, 429–434
People, The (Michelet), 769
People of color: free, 693, 694
People's Budget (England), 835, 883
People's Charter (England), 764
Peoples of the book, 584
People's Republic of China, see China
Pepper, 490
Père Goriot, Le (Flaubert), 808
Pereire, Isaac and Emile, 732
Perestroika, 1023
Periodic law and periodic table, 805
Perry, John, 778(illus.)
Perry, Matthew, 853, 870–871
Persian Gulf, 1008
Persian Letters, The (Montesquieu), 600–601
Perspective: in painting, 422

Peru, 509, 510, 538; Inca in, 502–504; industry in, 535; Chinese labor in, 859
Pétain, Henri-Philippe, 894, 966
Peter III (Russia), 610, 612(illus.)
Peterloo, Battle of, 763
Peter the Great (Russia), 576–578, 578(illus.); Peterhof of, 541; coronation crown of, 558(illus.); St. Petersburg and, 578
Petrarch, Francesco, 412
Petrograd (St. Petersburg), see St. Petersburg
Petrograd Soviet, 896, 898
Petroleum, see Oil and oil industry
Petty, William, 547
Pfaff, William, 1054–1055
Pharmacy: in 18th century, 668(illus.). See also Apothecaries
Philip II (Spain), 439, 459, 474, 510, 512(illus.); Mary Tudor and, 462(illus.), 463; empire of, 511–513; Armada and, 512–513
Philip III (Spain), 513, 534, 537
Philip IV the Fair (France), 373
Philip IV (Spain), 527–528, 537
Philip V (Spain), 534, 643
Philip VI (France), 382
Philip of Burgundy: Joanna of Castile and, 439
Philippines, 484, 500, 501; trade with, 510; migration from, 858–859; U.S. conquest of, 865, 867; Battle of Leyte Gulf and, 974(illus.); independence of, 992
Philosophes, 600, 607, 686
Philosophical Dictionary (Voltaire), 618–619
Philosophy: "natural," 589, 590; of Descartes, 595–596; in Age of Anxiety, 915. See also Intellectual thought
Physicians, 667–671; women as, 801, 801(illus.). See also Medicine
Physics, 595, 805; of Aristotle, 591; Newtonian, 594–595, 914, 918, 919; new, 919
Picasso, Pablo, 924–925
Pickford, Mary, 927
Pico della Mirandola, Giovanni, 413
Piero della Francesca, 422
Pietism, 672
Pigafetta, Antonio, 493
Pile driver, 723(illus.)
Pilgrimage of Grace (England), 462
Pilgrimages: Black Death and, 381
Pisa: council at, 388
Pissarro, Camille, 922
Pitt, William, 635
Pius VII (Pope), 705, 706(illus.)
Pius IX (Pope), 818, 832
Pizarro, Francisco, 503–504
Plague: in Marseilles, 377, 627, 627(illus.). See also Black Death
Planck, Max, 917, 918, 919
Planetary motion: Kepler's laws of, 592
Planned economies, 987; in France, 697; socialists on, 756; First World War and, 890; New Deal and, 937; in Europe, 989
Plantations: slaves for, 430, 505–508, 640–641, 642(illus.); Portuguese, 497; sugar and, 505–508; French trade and, 640
Platonic Academy: humanists and, 414
Plays, see Drama
PLO (Palestine Liberation Organization), 1046

Pluralism, 398; in church, 446, 447
Pneumonic plague, see Black Death
Poets and poetry: romantic, 759–760. See also Literature
Pogroms: in Russia, 838
Poincaré, Raymond, 929, 930, 932
Poison gas, 969
Poland, 985, 1024, 1031, 1041, 1046(map); Black Death and, 377; Prussian peasants and, 567; Baltic region and, 571; Russia and, 576, 613, 750; Ottomans and, 583; Enlightenment and, 603; partitions of, 613, 614(illus.); revolt by, 770; migration from, 856, 857; after First World War, 903; Treaty of Versailles and, 903; Little Entente and, 929; Nazis and, 945, 963(illus.), 965–966, 967; blitzkrieg in, 966; Second World War and, 974, 983; de-Stalinization and, 997; riots in, 997; Solidarity movement in, 1008, 1020–1021, 1025; West Germany and, 1008; Communism in, 1020; Gdansk Agreement in, 1020; economy of, 1025; in postcommunist era, 1035
Poland-Lithuania, 466; Russia and, 466, 574–575
Polish people: in Austro-Hungarian Empire, 836
Political asylum, 1042
Political parties, 831; in Germany, 832–833, 932; anti-Semitic, 837–838; socialist, 838, 840, 841–842; in Russia, 895; in England, 933; in France, 939. See also specific parties
Politics: in Renaissance, 415, 434–439; and German Reformation, 457–459; revolution in (1775–1815), 683–711; dual revolution and, 747; liberal, 754; nationalism and, 754–755; Ottoman, 830(illus.); after First World War, 928–933; Hitler and, 960; women's movement and, 1009–1010
Politiques (France), 473
Polo, Marco, 484, 499, 518
Poltava, battle at, 578, 579
Pomerania, 562
Pompadour, Madame de, 686
Poorhouses, 736
Poor Laws (England), 763, 781, 782
Poor people: in 17th century, 525; diet of, 664, 697; French Revolution and, 690–691, 703; globalization and, 1031. See also Poverty
Pope(s): in Great Schism, 387; in Renaissance, 416; as artistic patrons, 424. See also Papacy; specific popes
Popolo, 409
Popp, Adelheid, 844–845
Popular culture: religion and, 671–676; Protestant attack on, 676
Popular Front, 939
Popular literature, 662–663
Popular revolts: in 17th century, 527–528
Population: in 14th century, 373; plague and, 379–380; of Venice, 490; decline of indigenous American, 504–505; in Spain, 509; growth of, 625–628, 717, 855; limits on, 626; in 18th century, 628, 630(map); of London, 638; of Paris, 638; of African slaves, 642; of Britain, 725–726; industry and, 725–727; Malthus on, 726, 807; in Ireland,

766; urban, 780; Darwin and, 807; of Russia, 899; Soviet, 999; decline in Europe, 1041–1042; of Muslims, 1049
Poquelin, Jean-Baptiste, *see* Molière
Porcelain: from China, 511(illus.)
Pornography: in France, 604
Port Arthur: Japan and, 872
Port-au-Prince, Haiti, 701(map)
Port Moresby, 974
Portolans, 498
Portraiture: Renaissance, 422; by Van Dyck, 544(illus.)
Port-Royal: convent of, 674(illus.)
Portugal, 1011; Spain and, 439, 537; expansion of Christianity and, 492–493; caravel of, 494; voyages of exploration by, 495; exploration by, 495–498; overseas empire of, 495–498; Africa and, 497, 859; Brazil and, 497, 539; sugar plantations and, 505; trade by, 510; seaborne empire of, 511; Dutch and, 553, 647; slave trade and, 643; Asian trade of, 644–646
Positivist method, 806
Postimpressionist art, 922–926
Postmodernism, 1032(illus.)
Potatoes, 509, 665(illus.); introduction into Europe, 628; in Ireland, 766–767
Potosí, 509
Potsdam Conference, 983
Poverty: as reason for exploration, 493; lack of power (energy) and, 721; in Ireland, 766; in France, 771; in Great Depression, 935–936. *See also* Poor people
Power (authority): in male-female relationships, 434; Christian, 449; of lords in eastern Europe, 561; in Atlantic Ocean region, 621; Industrial Revolution and, 848; in Germany, 885; in conservative authoritarianism, 946; in radical totalitarianism, 946, 947; European Union and, 1039. *See also* Absolute monarchy and absolutism; Constitutionalism
Power (energy), *see* Energy (power)
Power looms, 720
Prado: portraits of Spanish monarchs in, 537
Pragmatic Sanction (1713), 567, 610
Pragmatic Sanction of Bourges (1438), 434, 435
Prague, 391; defenestration of, 562
Praise of Folly, The (Erasmus), 418, 446
Prato, 393, 394
Predestination: Calvin on, 464; Jansen and, 675
Pregnancy: marriage and, 656, 798; in postwar era, 1002. *See also* Illegitimacy
Premarital sex, 656, 798
Presbyterian Church: in Scotland, 465
Presses: War of the Austrian Succession and, 635
Prester John, 480, 497
Pretty Cook, The (Bouchere), 654
Price: "just," 664
Price and wage controls: in First World War, 891
Price revolution, 509–510
Priests and priestesses: education and, 446. *See also* Clergy
Primavera (Botticelli), 422(illus.)
Prince, The (Machiavelli), 410, 415, 416
Principia (Newton), 594, 601–602

Printing: in Renaissance, 418–421, 419(illus.); growth in Europe, 420(map); in Enlightenment, 604(illus.). *See also* Books
"Print Shop, The," 604(illus.)
Privatization: in Britain, 1012, 1013; global economy and, 1031; in Russia, 1033, 1034(illus.)
Procession in the Piazza San Marco (Bellini), 491(illus.)
Procession of the Magi (Gozzoli), 417(illus.)
Production: in England, 625; by cottage industries, 629–630; industrial, 727
Professions: middle class, 789
Profit: Utopians on, 417
Progress: concept of, 598–599; race and, 609
Prokofiev, Sergei, 995
Proletarianization, 625
Proletariat, 757
Propaganda: of imperialists, 866; in First World War, 894; of Lenin, 900(illus.); radio and, 928, 960(illus.); of Stalin, 954, 979(illus.); of Hitler, 959, 960(illus.)
Property: women's rights to, 800; rights to, 1001
Prophet, *see* Muhammad
Prostitution: laws regulating, 394, 395(illus.); Protestant condemnation of, 456; in 16th and 17th centuries, 655; in 19th century, 798–799; illegal immigrants and, 1043; in Netherlands, 1045
Protectionism, 833
Protectorate: in England, 546–547
Protectorates: German, 861–862; French, 862
Protest(s): against forced collectivization, 951–952; student, 1005–1006; in Italy, 1018(illus.); in France, 1039. *See also* Revolts and rebellions
Protestant ethic, 544
Protestantism, 449–454, 455–458; Luther and, 446–451; salvation in, 449; appeal of, 450–451; Calvin and, 452; marriage and, 455–457; political impact of, 458–459; in England, 461–463, 544–547, 548; in Hungary, 466; Catholic reconciliation and, 469; in France, 473, 529–530; in northern Netherlands, 474–475; Thirty Years' War and, 562; in northern German states, 563; Bohemia and, 565; Habsburgs in, 565; scientific revolution and, 596–597; church regulation by, 671; revival of, 672–673; in Germany, 832–833; in Ireland, 835, 836; Christian existentialism in, 917. *See also* Christianity; Edict of Nantes; Lutheranism
Protestant Reformation, 449–454, 455–459; Wyclif and, 388; in England and Ireland, 462–463; in eastern Europe, 465–466
Protestant Union, 562
Proudhon, Pierre Joseph, 756
Proust, Marcel, 920
Provinces: in France, 692. *See also* Colonies and colonization
Provisional government: in Russia, 896–898
Prussia: in Grand Alliance (1701), 534; after Thirty Years' War, 563; absolutism in, 565, 571–572; duke of, 567; in 17th century, 567–571; Frederick William in, 567–571;

military in, 571–572; Austria and, 610; Jews in, 610; compulsory education in, 662; Napoleon and, 706–707, 708; iron industry in, 731(illus.); at Congress of Vienna, 749, 750; Holy Alliance and, 751; Frankfurt Assembly and, 773–774; distribution of income in, 788(illus.); Bismarck and, 821–824. *See also* Brandenburg-Prussia; Germany
Prussian Constituent Assembly, 774
Psalter, 463
Psychology and psychoanalysis: Freud and, 804, 919–920
Ptolemy, Claudius (scientist), 494, 494(illus.), 591
Public education: in Enlightenment, 603. *See also* Education
Public health, 628, 781–783
Public opinion: in Hundred Years' War, 382–383; Napoleon III on, 818; before First World War, 883
Public sphere, 607
Public transportation, 786, 787(illus.)
Public works programs: of Hitler, 961. *See also* New Deal (U.S.)
Puddling furnace, 723
Pugachev, Emelian, 613
Purgatory, 448
Purges: in Soviet Union, 954–955
Purging, 667
Puritans, 463, 465, 544, 545(illus.); occupations of, 545(illus.); English absolutism of, 546–547
Pushkin, Aleksander, 760
Putin, Vladimir, 1034, 1034(illus.)
Putting-out system, 629–630, 650–651, 719, 721, 729
Pyrenees, Treaty of the, 537

Qing (Manchu) Dynasty (China), 851, 872, 873
Quadruple Alliance: at Congress of Vienna, 749–750
Quakers, 454
Quanta, 918
Quarantines, 381, 627
Quebec, 501, 532, 635
Queens, *see* Monarchy; specific rulers
Quinine, 866
Quinto, 539
Quo Vadis (film), 927

Race and racism: categorizing people by, 399, 429–431; meanings of, 429–431; anti-Semitism and, 439; ideas about, 513–514; Enlightenment and, 608–609; imperialism and, 865, 967; nationalism and, 885; Nazis and, 957–958, 969(illus.); in 1990s, 1033. *See also* Ethnic groups; Holocaust; Slaves and slavery
Racial difference, 608
Racine, Jean, 542
Racing, 796
Radar, 999
Radical Reformation, 451–454
Radicals (France), 939
Radicals and radicalism, 753–758, 915–916

Radio, 927, 960(illus.)
Railroads, 849; in England, 716(illus.), 723–725; continental, 730–731, 732; in Russia, 827; investment in, 850; in India, 870
Raison d'état, 530
Rákóczy, Francis, 567
Ralph (bishop of Bath and Wells), 379
Ramadan, 1051
R&D, *see* Research, and development (R&D)
Raoux, 663(illus.)
Rape, 1009; in Middle Ages, 394–395
Raphael, 415(illus.), 425
Rasputin, Grigori, 895, 896(illus.)
Rastrelli, Bartolomeo, 580
Ratification: of EU constitution, 1041
Rationalism, 598, 603, 607
Rationing: in First World War, 891, 894–895
Ravaillac, François, 529
Raw materials: transportation of, 849–850; rationing of (First World War), 891
Razin, Stenka, 576
Reading: in Enlightenment, 603–607; revolution in, 604–605; popular literature and, 662–663
Reagan, Ronald, 1008, 1012, 1024
Realism: in Renaissance painting, 422, 423; in literature, 804, 807–809; Comte and, 805; in painting, 809(illus.); in art, 924
Rearmament: by Nazi Germany, 961
Reason: use of term, 589; Descartes and, 595–596, 598; in Enlightenment, 598, 603; race and, 609. *See also* Enlightenment
Rebellions, *see* Revolts and rebellions
Recession: of early 1980s, 1012
Reconciliation treaty (West Germany), 1008
Reconquista (Spain), 436
Recreation: postwar, 1002
Red Army (Soviet Union), 900(illus.), 949, 973, 974, 983
Red Army Faction (Germany), 1046
Red Brigade (Italy), 1046
Reds: in Russian civil war, 899–900, 900(illus.)
Red Sea region, 484, 487
Red Shirts, 821
Reflections on the Revolution in France (Burke), 694
Reform(s): of Christian Church, 391, 445; Erasmus on, 418; of papacy, 467; by Peter the Great (Russia), 576–578; in Prussia, 609–610; in Russia, 612–613, 827; in Austria, 614–615; central and eastern European, 615–616; in churches, 672; in France, 688, 692–693; in 19th century, 761–768; in England, 763–765, 835; Ottoman, 830–831; after Second World War, 987; in West Germany, 987; in United States, 994–995; in Soviet Union, 996–997; in Czechoslovakia, 997; by Gorbachev, 1020, 1022–1024, 1024–1025. *See also* Protestant Reformation; Reformation
Reformation: of Christian church, 445–457; Protestant, 449–454, 455–459; radical, 451–454; arts in, 452–453, 452(illus.), 453(illus.); marriage and, 455–457; women and, 457; German politics and, 457–459; in eastern Europe, 465–466; Catholic, 466–472; witchcraft trials and, 475; church regulation and, 671–672. *See also* Counter-Reformation; Protestant Reformation
Reform Bill (England, 1832), 763
Reformed church: of Calvin, 465
Refugees: religious, in Geneva, 465; after Second World War, 985, 986(map); in 1990s, 1042–1043
Regents: Dutch, 549
Reichstag (Germany), 832, 833, 891, 901, 932; Hitler and, 958
Reign of Terror: in French Revolution, 698–700, 702–703
Reinhart, Anna, 455
Relativity theory, 918
Relief programs: in Great Depression, 935, 937, 959(illus.); Orwell on, 942–943
Religion(s): Black Death and, 381; established, 454; divisions in Europe, 468(map); in Netherlands, 474, 550; witches and, 475–477; European expansion and, 492–493; Spanish imposition of, 513; Montaigne on, 514; in France, 529, 531–532; after Thirty Years' War, 563; in Bohemia, 565; absolutism and, 566; in Ottoman Empire, 584, 831; science and, 596–597; Voltaire on, 602, 618–619; popular culture and, 671–676; of peasants, 675; French Revolution and, 693, 703; working-class, 797; illegitimacy and, 798; revival of, 917; in India, 991–992; attitudes about, 1049–1050. *See also* specific groups
Religious festivals, 675–676
Religious orders: in Catholic Reformation, 467, 469–472
Religious toleration: Edict of Nantes and, 473; in France, 473; Ottoman, 490, 580; in Puritan England, 547; in England, 548; Dutch, 550; in Russia, 613
Religious truth: science, Enlightenment, and, 599
Religious wars: in Europe, 458–459, 472–477
Remarque, Erich, 887
Rembrandt von Rijn, 551(illus.)
Remembrance of Things Past (Proust), 920
Renaissance, 407–440; economy in, 408; humanism in, 412–414; intellectual thought in, 412–421; education in, 414–415; political thought in, 415; secularism in, 416; in North, 416–421, 424; printing in, 418–421; arts in, 421–428; Italian, 421–428; social hierarchy in, 428–434; gender in, 432–433; wedding chest in, 433(illus.); state (nation) in, 434–439; science and, 595
Renoir, Pierre Auguste, 922
Reparations: Germany and, 928, 929, 929(illus.), 930; after Second World War, 985
Repatriation: of migrants, 856
Representative assemblies: after Hundred Years' War, 375; organization by orders, 431; in France, 533
Representative government, 747, 753–754
Republic, 410; in Italian cities, 409, 410; in France, 696, 770–772, 824, 833–835. *See also* Dutch Republic; England (Britain)
Republicanism: in France, 835
Research: and development (R&D), 805; during and after Second World War, 1000
Resistance: to Nazis, 962; in Second World War, 971
Re-Stalinization, 997, 998
Restoration: in England, 547–548, 635
Retirement benefits: in Germany, 833
Return of the Native, The (Hardy), 809
Reunification: of Germany, 1028–1030
Revisionism, 841
Revolts and rebellions: by peasants, 390–392, 392(map), 454–455; ciompi revolts and, 392–393, 408; urban, 392–393; popular, 527–528; in Ottoman Empire, 582; by Pugachev, 613; by Saint-Domingue slaves, 700–702, 700(illus.), 701(map); against Napoleon, 708; in India, 869; in Japan, 871; in First World War, 894; of Arabs, 903; Kronstadt sailors' rebellion, 949; nonviolent, 989; in eastern Europe, 997–998; students in, 1005–1006
Revolution(s): in politics (1775–1815), 683–711; American, 687–688; dual, 747; of 1830, 767–768; of 1848, 768–774, 837; of 1905, 829; of 1908 (Ottoman Empire), 831; in transportation, 849–850; in Germany, 901–902; totalitarianism as, 947; permanent, 949; youth, 980(illus.); in 1989, 1019, 1024–1030, 1024(map), 1053; in computers and electronics, 1031; in eastern Europe, 1052
Revolutionaries in Transylvania (Ipatescu), 746(illus.)
Revolutionary War in America, *see* American Revolution
Rhineland, 962; France and, 696
Rhodes, Cecil, 861, 863, 863(illus.)
Rhodesia, 861
Ribeiro, Diogo: world map by, 500(illus.)
Ricardo, David, 726, 734, 757
Richard II (England): wife of, 388; Peasants' Revolt and, 390–392
Richard III (England), 435
Richelieu, Cardinal (Armand Jean du Plessis), 529, 541; foreign policy of, 530; Thirty Years' War and, 530, 562
Riefenstahl, Leni, 928
Rigaud, André, 707
Rigaud, Hyacinthe, 522(illus.)
Rights: of French Protestants, 531–532; in France, 692; in Saint-Domingue, 694; of married women, 799; of Jews, 837; in revolutionary Russia, 896; before First World War, 914; for Soviet women, 953; in Europe, 1032
Riots: food, 524(illus.); in France, 530, 1054–1055; in Russia, 895; in Soviet Union, 949; in Poland, 997, 1020
Rite of Spring, The (Stravinsky), 926
Rituals: at Versailles, 541
Rivers: transportation on, 718
Roads and highways: in England, 723
Road to Wigan Pier, The (Orwell), 942
Robe nobility (France), 529, 530, 686. *See also* Estates (classes)

Robespierre, Maximilien, 694, 696, 697; Reign of Terror and, 698–700; execution of, 702, 702(illus.)
Robin Hood, 397
Robot (days of unpaid labor), 565
Rocket (locomotive), 724
Rococo style, 605–606
Rocroi, battle at, 537
Rogers, Ginger, 927
Rolling mills, 723
Roman Catholic Church, *see* Catholic Church
Romania, 762, 883, 903, 997; Little Entente and, 929; in Second World War, 974; 1989 revolution in, 1026; in postcommunist era, 1035
Romanians, 772
Roman Inquisition, 467
Romanov family: Anastasia (wife of Ivan IV), 574–575; Michael, 576. *See also* specific rulers
Romantic movement, 758–761; Rousseau and, 607
Rome: baroque art in, 539; papacy in, 818; Treaty of (1957), 989
Rome-Berlin Axis, 963
Roosevelt, Franklin Delano: fireside chats of, 928; New Deal of, 937; Grand Alliance and, 972; at wartime conferences, 982–983, 982(illus.); Manhattan Project and, 999–1000
Rothschild, Edmond de, 837(illus.)
Rotten boroughs, 763
Rousseau, Jean-Jacques, 607–608, 609, 692, 759; on education, 661
Roy, Olivier, 1050
Royal council: in England, 435; in Spain, 436
"Royall Oake of Brittayne, The," 546(illus.)
Royal Palace (Stockholm), 568
Royal Society of London, 596
Rubens, Peter Paul, 531(illus.), 539–540
Rudder, 495
Ruhr region: after Thirty Years' War, 565; crisis in, 929–930, 929(illus.), 931
Rump Parliament (England), 546
Rumsfeld, Donald, 1047
Runaway slaves: in London, 643
Rural areas: wet-nursing in, 658. *See also* Agriculture; Farms and farming; Peasant(s); Serfs and serfdom
Russia, 572–580; Black Death and, 377; absolutism in, 559; Estonia and, 561(illus.); Mongols in, 572–574; expansion of, 573(map), 613, 614; alliances of, 576; peasants in, 577, 580; navy in, 579; foreign traveler in, 586–587, 587(illus.); Enlightenment and, 603, 610–613; Napoleon and, 706, 707, 708; industrialization in, 727, 728(illus.), 730; at Congress of Vienna, 750; Holy Alliance and, 751; Turks and, 762; aid to Austria, 772; modernization of, 826–829; Crimean War and, 827; foreign investment in, 828; anti-Semitism in, 838; Marxists in, 842; steam power in, 849; migration from, 856–857; imperialism by, 865; Alliance System and, 880–881, 880(illus.); pre-First World War alliances of, 881, 882–883; Balkan wars and, 883; First World War impact on, 895; peace settlement with Germany, 899; independence of, 1028; successor states and, 1029(map); social revolution in, 1033. *See also* First World War; Razin, Stenka; Russian Revolution (1905); Russian Revolution (1917); Soviet Union
Russian civil war, 949
Russian Empire: conservatism in, 753
Russian Federation, 1027, 1028, 1035
Russian-French Alliance, 880(illus.), 881
Russian-German Reinsurance Treaty, 881
Russian Orthodox Church, 574, 576. *See also* Orthodox Christianity
Russian Revolution (1905), 829
Russian Revolution (1917), 579(illus.), 895–899, 897(illus.), 953; Italian socialists and, 955
Russo-Japanese War, 872
Rutherford, Ernest, 918
Rwanda, 945, 1042

SA, *see* Storm troopers (SA)
Sacks: of Constantinople (1453), 489(illus.), 580; of Constantinople (1204), 490
Sacraments: administration of, 379; Luther on, 449; marriage as, 456
Saddam Hussein, 1030, 1047
Sadowa, Battle of, 822
Safavid Empire: trade and, 489–490
Sahara: trade and, 487
Sailors: hospitals for, 378; lifestyle of, 493; Atlantic passage and, 508
Sails: lateen, 494
Saint(s): veneration of images of, 452–453
Saint Bartholomew's Day massacre, 473
Saint Basil's Cathedral (Moscow), 575(illus.)
Saint Bavo, Church of, 453(illus.)
Saint-Domingue, 637(map), 640, 693; slave revolt on, 700–702, 700(illus.), 701(map)
St. Helena: Napoleon at, 711
St. Lawrence River region, 501, 635
Saint Mark Preaching in Alexandria (Gentile and Giovanni Bellini), 426
Saint Peter's Basilica, 416, 447
St. Petersburg, 578–580, 579(illus.)
Saint Peter's Fields, Manchester: protests in, 763
Saint-Simon, Duc de, 540–541, 556–557
Saint-Simon, Henri de, 756, 805
Salic Law: women under, 381; in France, 381–382
Salons, 605–606
Salt: tax on, 434
Saltash Bridge, The (Brunel), 724(illus.)
Salvation: by faith, 447; Luther on, 447; Protestants on, 449; education and, 662; society and, 671–672; in Methodism, 673
Salvation Army, 959(illus.)
Same-sex relationships: in Middle Ages, 395–396, 396(illus.). *See also* Homosexuality
Samurai, 871
Sand, George, 760
Sanitation: plague and, 375–376; urban, 780, 781; Chadwick and, 782–783
San Salvador, 499
Sans-culottes (France), 697, 698(illus.)
Santa Fe capitulations, 499

Sarajevo: Francis Ferdinand assassination in, 883
Sardinia, 818–820
Sardinia-Piedmont: Italian unification and, 818, 819(map), 820
Sarkozy, Nicolas, 1054, 1055
Sartre, Jean-Paul, 916, 917
Sassoon, Siegfried, 887
Saudi Arabia, 1030, 1047
Savages: Africans seen as, 513
Savonarola, Girolamo, 410–411
Savoy, 696, 820
Saxony, 465, 565, 750; Elector of, 451, 457; Napoleon and, 706
Scandinavia: Great Depression in, 937–938
Schacht, Hjalmar, 961
Schleswig, 774
Schleswig-Holstein, 774, 822
Scholarship, *see* Intellectual thought
Schönberg, Arnold, 926
Schönbrunn palace, 541, 567, 569(illus.), 615(illus.)
Schools, 400(illus.), 658, 661–662; medieval, 400(illus.); humanist, 414; Jesuit, 470–472; missions and, 866(illus.). *See also* Education; Universities
Schuman, Robert, 989
Science: religion and, 596–597; society and, 597–598; popularization of, 599(illus.); racism and, 609; in 19th century, 804–807; pure theoretical vs. applied, 999; in postwar era, 999–1000; reduced spending in, 1012. *See also* Scientific revolution
Scientific community, 597–598
Scientific farming, 623
Scientific method, 597, 806
Scientific revolution, 590–598
Scientists, 1000
Scotland: population decline in, 373; England and, 436; Presbyterian Church in, 465; Stuart dynasty from, 543; church in, 545; Enlightenment in, 603; in Great Britain, 634
Scott, Samuel, 620(illus.)
Scott, Walter, 759, 760
Scriptures: Luther on, 447, 450
Sculpture: by Donatello, 423; Kollwitz and, 914(illus.)
Seaborne trade, 484; routes to East and, 497; trading empires and, 506(map), 510–511
Seaport cities: medieval, 381
Second Balkan War, 883
Second Coalition, 705
Second Continental Congress, 687
Second Empire (France), 816(illus.), 817–818, 824
Second estate (France): nobility as, 684
Second International, 840, 841
Second Reform Bill (England, 1867), 835
Second Republic (France), 770–771, 816–817
Second revolution: in French Revolution, 696–697
Second Sex, The (Beauvoir), 1009, 1015(illus.)
Second Treatise of Civil Government (Locke), 548
Second World War: origins of, 931, 964(illus.); opening of, 966–967; in Europe, 966–970, 968(map); in Africa, 968(map); casualties of, 970, 975; in Pacific Ocean region, 970, 972,

Second World War *(cont.)* 972(map), 974–975; Normandy invasion in, 974; in Asia, 974–975; atomic bombings in, 975, 1000; recovery after, 981, 1014; end of, 981–982; results in Europe, 985–989, 986(map); decolonization after, 989–993, 990(map); science, technology, and, 999–1000
Secret police: in Soviet Union, 900, 954; in eastern Europe, 996; in Poland, 1025
Secularism: in Renaissance, 416; in art subject matter, 423; in Enlightenment, 598; Ottoman, 831
Secularization: of society, 454
Security Council (United Nations): Iraq and, 1047
Sedan, battle at, 824, 833
Segovia, 437
Segregation: apartheid as, 863; in British India, 870
Self-determination: Metternich on, 751; Treaty of Versailles and, 907; in Middle East, 910–911; after Second World War, 989
Self-interest: Smith on, 647
Selim I (Ottoman), 581
Selim II (Ottomans), 583
Semiskilled workers, 791
Seneca, 514
Senegal, 862
Sennett, Mack, 927
Separate spheres, 738–739, 799, 800
Separation of church and state, 454
Separation of powers, 601
September 11, 2001 terrorist attacks, 1020, 1045–1046, 1046(illus.), 1047, 1050
September Massacres (France), 696, 697
Serbia, 883; local autonomy for, 829; boycott of, 1033; Milosevic and, 1037–1039, 1038(map)
Serbian people, 772, 883, 1038(map)
Serfs and serfdom: in England, 392; in Spain, 393; in central and eastern Europe, 559–560; after Thirty Years' War, 565; in Russia, 577–578, 580, 613, 827; in Prussia, 610; in Austria, 614, 615, 772. *See also* Peasant(s)
Sermon on the Mount: Erasmus and, 418
Servants: blacks as, 429–430; women as, 655; of middle class, 789; domestic, 794, 795(illus.)
Servetus, Michael, 465
Service nobility: in Russia, 574, 578
Seven Years' War, 635; alliances in, 610; European claims and, 637(maps); India and, 647; France and, 686, 687–688
Seville, 437
Sewage systems, 628, 782–783
Sewing machine, 795
Sex and sexuality: in urban areas, 393–396; gender and, 432; Protestants on, 456–457; servant girls and, 655; premarital sex, 656, 798; gender segregation of jobs and, 739; in 19th century, 797–798; in marriage, 800, 802; women and, 802; sexual behavior of children, 803–804; Freud on, 804; middle-class youth and, 812–813; after First World War, 920; in youth counterculture, 1004–1005; discrimination and, 1009. *See also* Homosexuality; Prostitution
Sex discrimination, 1009–1010
Sexism, 1009
Sexual division of labor, *see* Gender
Seymour, Jane, 461
Sforza family, 410; Francesco, 427; Ludovico, 427; Gian Galazzo, 430
Shah: Abbas I as, 489, 490
Shakespeare, William, 515–516
Sheep, 373
Shelley, Percy Bysshe, 759
Shi'ite (Shi'a) Muslims, 1048, 1048(illus.)
Shipbuilding: British, 850(illus.)
"Ship money," 545
Ships and shipping, 881, 882(illus.); Venetian, 490; types of, 494; Dutch, 552; steam power in, 849; port facilities for, 850; British dominance of, 850(illus.). *See also* Maritime trade; Navy
Shock therapy: in Polish economy, 1025; in Russian economy, 1033
Shogun, 871
Shopping: as pastime, 666(illus.)
Shorter Catechism (Luther), 451
Shostakovich, Dimitri, 995
Siberia, 827, 899; Russia and, 576
Sicily, 818, 820, 973; Spanish-occupied, 527–528. *See also* Kingdom of the Two Sicilies
Sidney, Philip, 515
Sieges: of Castle of Mortagne, 383(illus.). *See also* Sacks
Siena, 409, 410; Florence and, 412(illus.)
Sieyès, Emmanuel Joseph, 689–690, 703–704
Sigismund (Holy Roman Empire), 391
Sigismund I (Poland), 466
Sigismund Augustus (Poland), 583
Signori (rulers), 409
Silent Generation, 1004
Silesia, 562; Prussian control of, 610, 614, 635
Silk Road, 488
Silks: trade in, 510
Silver: from Americas, 509–510, 539, 643; Spanish income from, 510, 513
Sin: Luther on, 447; forgiveness through indulgences, 447–448; Jansen on, 675
Single European Act (1986), 1039
Sino-Japanese War, 872
Sister Carrie (Dreiser), 809
Sistine Chapel: Michelangelo and, 406(illus.), 424, 425
Six Acts (England), 763
Sixtus IV (Pope), 438
Sixtus V (Pope), 512
Skepticism, 514, 599–600
Skilled workers, 740(illus.), 791
Skin color: categorizing people by, 429
Skyscrapers, 922
Slave labor: for Nazi Germany, 967. *See also* Forced labor
Slaves and slavery: from Africa, 429, 430, 488; sugar plantations and, 505–508, 508(illus.); Ottoman, 582, 830; science used to defend, 609; in American colonies, 640–641; abolition of slave trade, 643; in Saint Domingue, 693; Saint-Domingue revolt and, 700–702, 700(illus.), 701(map); in France and French colonies, 702, 707, 771; in United States, 825–826, 826(map). *See also* Race and racism
Slave trade, 499, 506(map); Genoa and, 492; Portugal and, 510; asiento and, 635; Atlantic, 640–643; Equiano on, 641(illus.), 645; abolition of, 643; slave ships and, 651(illus.); African, 861
Slavs, 572–573, 967; in Russia, 572; in Austro-Hungarian Empire, 836. *See also* Russia
Slovakia, 1035, 1041
Slovenia, 1038, 1041
Smallpox, 504; inoculation against, 670–671
Smith, Adam, 647–648, 754
Smolensk, 708
Smyrna, 906
Snayers, Peeter, 538(illus.)
Soccer, 796
Social classes, *see* Classes
Social Contract, The (Rousseau), 608
Social Darwinism, 807, 865, 867
Social Democrats: in Germany, 833, 838, 841, 932, 959, 960; in Russia, 838; in Scandinavia, 937–938
Social equality: First World War and, 892, 894
Socialist Party, 841, 842; in France, 842, 1039; in Germany, 932, 1030; in Italy, 955
Socialists and socialism, 838–842; in French Revolution, 697; utopian, 755; in France, 756, 835, 939; Marxian, 757–758; vs. liberal capitalism, 771; women and, 800; in Germany, 833; non-revolutionary nature of, 840; of Adelheid Popp, 844–845; First World War and, 890; Sorel and, 915–916; in Scandinavia, 937–938, 938(illus.); in 2001, 1045
Social mobility: in England, 543
Social revolution: in Russia, 1033
Social rights: before First World War, 914
Social science: in 19th century, 805–807
Social security: in Germany, 833; in United States, 937; reforms in postwar era, 1001; in 1970s, 1011
Social welfare, *see* Welfare
Society: in 14th century, 390–401; Machiavelli on, 415; utopia and, 417; in Renaissance, 428–434; Calvinist, 463; in France, 534, 684–685; Dutch, 550; in central and eastern Europe, 559–565; in Russia, 576; science and, 597–598; in Prussia, 610; lifestyle changes and, 621; 18th-century changes in, 621–648; consumer, 665–667; economic determination in, 732; urban, 786–797, 791(illus.); postwar (1945–1968), 999–1006; in 1970s and 1980s, 1011–1012. *See also* Estates (classes); Orders; Social mobility
Society of Friends, *see* Quakers
Society of Jesus, *see* Jesuits
Sodomy, 395, 396
Soil: fertility of, 622
Solar system, 590; Copernicus on, 591–592; Brahe on, 592; Kepler on, 592. *See also* Astronomy; Universe

Soldiers: in Thirty Years' War, 563(illus.); in Prussia, 572(illus.); of First World War, 894. *See also* Armed forces; Military
Solidarity movement, 1008, 1014(illus.), 1020–1021, 1022(illus.), 1025
Solzhenitsyn, Aleksandr, 996, 999
Somalia: refugees from, 1042
Somme: Battle of, 887, 891
Song of Love, The (De Chirico), 919(illus.)
Sophia (Austria), 772
Sorel, Georges, 915–916
Sorgh, Hendrick, 624(illus.)
Sound and the Fury, The (Faulkner), 920
South (U.S.), 825–826; slavery in, 641
South Africa: England and, 859
South African War (1899–1902), 863, 867, 881
South America, 509; silver from, 509, 539; gold from, 539
Southeast Asia: trade with, 484; Chinese immigration to, 485
South Korea, *see* Korean War
Sovereignty, 526; of American states, 687
Soviets, 896
Soviet Union: forced-labor camps in, 945, 951(illus.), 954; tyranny in, 945; five-year plans in, 949, 950–952, 978–979; totalitarianism in, 949; life and culture in, 952–954; terror and purges in, 954; German attack on, 967, 968(map); Second World War and, 967, 973; Stalin and, 975–976; eastern Europe and, 996; de-Stalinization in, 996–997; Brezhnev Doctrine and, 997; disintegration of, 1019, 1026–1028; from 1970s to 1985, 1020–1024; Russia and successor states of, 1029(map); end of cold war and, 1030. *See also* Cold war; Russia; Russian Revolution (1917); Second World War
Soyer, Isaac, 936(illus.)
Space programs: in U.S. and Soviet Union, 1000
Spain, 946, 1011, 1043; serfdom and, 393; Jews in, 436–437; in Renaissance, 436–439; New Christians in, 437–439; in 1492, 437(map); Inquisition in, 438–439, 534; Muslims in, 439; in Holy Roman Empire, 474; Armada and, 474–475, 512–513; expansion of Christianity and, 492–493; exploration by, 498–499, 501–504; New World and, 501–504; colonial settlement by, 504–508, 643–644; seaborne empire of, 506(map), 511; silver in, 509–510; trading empire of, 510–511; Dutch war and, 533; War of the Spanish Succession and, 534, 553, 571, 635, 643; absolutism in, 534–538; commerce in, 535–537; Bourbon dynasty in, 536(map); decline of, 537; France and, 537; monarchy in, 537; colonies of, 538–539; in Thirty Years' War, 562; churches in, 672; at Battle of Trafalgar, 706; Napoleon and, 708, 711(illus.); revolt in, 751; civil war in, 925(illus.), 963; fascism in, 939; terrorist attack on, 1049. *See also* Silver
Spanish America: slaves in, 642
Spanish-American War, 865, 867
Spanish Armada, 474–475, 512–513
Spanish civil war, 963
Spanish Empire, 511–513

Spanish Netherlands, 533
Spanish Troops (Snayers), 538(illus.)
Special-interest groups, 866
Spectator sports, 796
Speculation: in England, 373
Spencer, Herbert, 807
Spengler, Oswald, 920
Spenser, Edmund, 515
Spice Islands, *see* Moluccas
Spices and spice trade, 490, 492, 497, 510–511
Spies and spying: in France, 531, 705
Spinning jenny, 719, 720
Spinsters: origins of term, 631
Spirit of the Laws, The (Montesquieu), 601
Spiritual Exercises (Loyola), 469
Sports: blood sports, 675, 676(illus.); of working class, 796
Spurs, Battle of the, 390
Srebrenica: massacre at, 1037(illus.), 1038
Sri Lanka, *see* Ceylon
SS squads (Nazi Germany), 961, 962, 967, 973–974
Stadholder (Dutch), 549–550
Staël, Germaine de, 760
Stalin, Joseph, 979(illus.); rise to power of, 949–950; Trotsky and, 950; propaganda and, 954; wife of, 954; Hitler pact with, 965; Five-Year Plan of, 978–979; at wartime conferences, 982–983, 982(illus.)
Stalingrad: Battle of, 968(map), 973
Stalin-White Sea Canal, 951(illus.)
Standard of living: industrialization and, 717, 786–787; of workers, 736; in 1750, 848; in Soviet Union, 953, 996, 998; in postwar era, 1002. *See also* Lifestyle
Standards and standardization: European Union and, 1039
Stanley, Henry M., 861
Star Chamber (England), 435, 436
Starry Night, The (Van Gogh), 923(illus.)
Starvation, *see* Famine
State (nation): in Renaissance, 415, 434–439; in 17th century, 525–526; absolutist, 528–542; Habsburgs and, 567; in Russia, 576, 577; creation of, 755; before First World War, 831–838; authoritarian, 947. *See also* Government
States General (Netherlands), 549
Status: in France, 689. *See also* Classes
Statute of Kilkenny, 399–400
Statute of Laborers (England, 1351), 380, 390
Staupitz, John, 447
Steam power, 849; steam engine and, 721–723, 728–729; steamship and, 866
Steele, Flora Annie, 876
Steen, Jan, 549(illus.)
Stein, Gertrude, 932
Stephenson, George, 724
Sterilization: in operating room, 783
Stern, Karl, 917
Sternpost rudder, 495
Stockholders: in banks, 732
Stockholm: Royal Palace in, 568
Stock market crash (1929), 933
Stolypin, Peter, 829
Storm troopers (SA), 961

Strasbourg: Jews killed in, 378; France and, 534
Strasser, Gregor, 959
Stravinsky, Igor, 926
Stream-of-consciousness technique, 920
Streetcars, 786
Streptomycin, 377
Stresemann, Gustav, 930, 931, 932
Strikes, 841; in Britain, 740, 933; in Manchester (1810), 741; in France, 817, 1006, 1039; in First World War, 894–895; in Germany, 902; in Poland, 1020–1021, 1022(illus.)
Strutt family, 735; Elizabeth, 734, 735; Jedediah, 735, 735(illus.)
Stuart dynasty. *See also* specific rulers
Stuart dynasty (England), 543, 544
Student protests, 1004–1005, 1012; in United States, 1006–1007
Sturm und Drang, 758
Styria, 565
Subcontractors: industrialization and, 738
Submarines, 890
Sub-Saharan Africa, 513
Succession, *see* War of the Austrian Succession; War of the Spanish Succession
Sudan, 862, 865
Sudetenland, 965
Suez Canal, 850, 865, 905, 993(illus.); opening of, 854(illus.)
Suez Canal Company, 992
Suffrage, *see* Universal suffrage; Voting and voting rights; Women's suffrage movement
Sugar and sugar industry: trade in, 484, 491–492, 640; slavery and, 505–508, 642(illus.); refinery for, 508(illus.); in Brazil, 539; consumption of, 665; migrant labor for, 858(illus.)
Suleiman I the Magnificent (Ottoman), 489, 512, 580, 581, 582, 583, 829; Hungary defeated by, 466
Sullivan, Louis H., 921
Sully, duke of (Maximilien de Béthune), 529, 532
Sultan, 581; Ottoman, 584
Summer (Grimshaw), 792, 793(illus.)
Summer Palace (Vienna), 569, 569(illus.)
Sumptuary laws, 431–432
Sundiata Keita, 487
Sun King: Louis XIV (France) as, 530
Sunni Islam, 582, 1048
Sun Yat-sen, 872, 992
Superego, 919
Superpowers, 1008, 1025, 1030, 1032–1033
Supremacy Act (England), 461
Suprematism (Malevich), 950(illus.)
Surgeons and surgery, 783; in 18th century, 667–668
Surrealism, 919(illus.), 925
Survival in Auschwitz (Levi), 971
Survival of the fittest, 807
Swabia, 455
Swallows: Italian migrants as, 858
Sweated industries, 794–795
Sweden, 1040; Lutheranism in, 451; Baltic region and, 571; Russia and, 576; Napoleon and, 706; Norwegian nationalism and, 836; Great Depression in, 937–938. *See also* Scandinavia

Swedish phase: of Thirty Years' War, 530, 562
Swedish Victory at Narva, The, 1701 (Cederstrom), 577(illus.)
Swinka, Jakub, 398
Switzerland: Protestantism in, 451; civil war in, 770
Sword nobility (France), 530
Syllabus of Errors (Pius IX), 818
Syphilis, 504, 803
Syria, 903, 910–911; Ottomans and, 489, 830; independence of, 905; decolonization and, 992
Syrian National Congress, 905–906
System of Nature, The (Linné), 608
System of Positive Philosophy (Comte), 805
Szlachta (Polish nobility), 466

Tableau de Paris (Mercier), 678–679
Tabula rasa, 600
Taille, 533
Tai Ping Rebellion, 872
Taiwan, 992
Taliban, 1020, 1045
Talleyrand, Charles, 749, 750
Tamerlane, 495
Tametsi decree, 469
Tannenberg: Battle of, 888
Tanzimat, 830–831
Tariff protection: industrialization and, 718, 730; in Germany, 833; in Great Depression, 935; Common Market and, 989
Tatars, 571, 613. *See also* Mongols
Taxation: in England, 392, 544, 835; in France, 434, 528–529, 532–533, 686, 688–689; of prostitutes, 457; papal, 458; in Russia, 577–578; by Ottomans, 582, 829; income taxes, 787
Taxonomies: race and, 608
Tea: consumption of, 665
Teaching, 789
Technology: Chinese, 485; exploration and, 493–495; agricultural, 622–623; British, 728; wealth and, 848; imperialism and, 865, 866; Soviet Union and, 978–979; in postwar era, 999–1000. *See also* Industrial Revolution
Teheran Conference, 982–983
Teke people, 861
Telegraph, 866
Telescope, 593(illus.), 595
Tempest, The (Shakespeare), 516
Tencin, Madame de, 605
Ten Commandments, The (Cranach the Elder), 450(illus.), 452
Tenerife Concert Hall, 1032(illus.)
Ten Hours Act (England, 1847), 764–765
Tenochtitlán, 501, 502(illus.)
Teresa of Ávila (Saint), 471, 471(illus.)
Territorial expansion, *see* Expansion
Terror, the: in French Revolution, 698–700
Terrorism: in Russia, 828(illus.), 954; in Japan, 871; attacks on United States, 1045–1046; Islamic fundamentalism and, 1045–1046; al-Qaeda and, 1046–1047; U. S. embassy bombing and, 1047; attacks on Europe, 1048–1049; in Spain, 1049; predictions about, 1050

Tess of the D'Urbervilles (Hardy), 809
Test Act (England), 548
Tet Offensive, 1007
Tetzel, John, 447–448
Tewfiq (Egypt), 854
Textile industry, 631; foreign trade and, 510; in England, 630, 633, 719–721; in Low Countries, 630; improvements in, 719–720; energy in, 721; children in, 737–738; families in, 737–738. *See also* Woolen industry
Thatcher, Denis, 1013
Thatcher, Margaret, 1008, 1012, 1013
Theater, *see* Drama
Theodore (Russia), 575
Theology: on subjugation of women to men, 455–456; of Calvin, 463–464; Voltaire on, 602
Thermidorian Reaction, 702–703
Thermodynamics, 805
Thiers, Adolphe, 834
Third Balkan War, 883. *See also* First World War
Third Coalition, 706
Third estate, 431
Third estate (France): commoners as, 684; Estates General and, 689
Third Reform Bill (England, 1884), 835
Third Republic (France), 824, 833–835
Third Rome, 574
Third way: in East Germany, 1029
Third World: income per person in, 848, 848(illus.)
Thirteenth Amendment (U.S.), 826
Thirty Years' War, 549, 562; French army in, 527; phases of, 530, 562; Spain in, 537, 562; Europe after, 563–565, 564(map); elector of Brandenburg in, 567
Thomas à Kempis, 389
Thomas Aquinas, 590
Three Emperors' League, 880(illus.), 881
Three Musicians (Picasso), 924, 925(illus.)
Tiburtius, Franziska, 801, 801(illus.)
Tiepolo, Giovanni, 535(illus.)
Tilsit, Treaty of, 707
Timbuktu, 487, 488
Time of Troubles (Russia), 575–576
Tirpitz, Alfred von, 883
Titian, 425, 512(illus.)
Tito, Josip Broz, 996, 1037
Titus Andronicus (Shakespeare), 515(illus.)
Tocqueville, Alexis de, 771
Tofts, Mary, 673(illus.)
Togo, 862
Tokyo (Edo), Japan, 853
Toledo: Jews in, 437; conversos in, 438
Toleration, *see* Religious toleration
Tolstoy, Leo, 809
Topkapi Palace, 582, 582(illus.)
Tordesillas, Treaty of, 500
Tories (England), 763, 764
Torture: in Inquisition, 439
Totalitarianism, 945, 976; in First World War Germany, 892; racial imperialism and, 967. *See also* Communists and communism; Nazi Germany; Soviet Union
Total state, 947–948

Total war: in French Revolution, 697–698; First World War as, 890–892; social impact of, 892, 894; Russia and, 895; Second World War as, 973
Toulouse, 394
Toulouse-Lautrec, Henri de, 796(illus.)
Tourism: in postwar era, 1002
Tournai, 533
Toussaint L'Ouverture, *see* L'Ouverture, Toussaint
Towns, *see* Cities and towns
Toynbee, Arnold, 917
Tractatus Logico-Philosophicus (Wittgenstein), 916
Trade: in Italian cities, 409; European exploration and, 483; in Indian Ocean, 484–485; Afro-Asian, 486(map); Muslim, 486(map), 487(illus.); overland, 488; Ottoman, 489; by Venice, 490–491; by Genoa, 491–492; transatlantic, 510; long-distance, 510–511; with Spanish colonies, 535; English, 547, 635, 637–640; Dutch, 552–553; after Thirty Years' War, 563–565; in Atlantic region, 636(map), 637–640; colonial, 637–640; with Asia, 644–647; in 19th century, 849–850; transportation and, 849–850; world market and, 849–850; China and, 850–852; Japan and, 852. *See also* Business; Commerce; Maritime trade; Slave trade
Trade corporations, *see* Guilds
Trade routes: Silk Road as, 488
Trade unions, 741, 834; in Soviet Union, 952. *See also* Labor unions
Trading companies, *See* British East India Company; Dutch East India Company; Dutch West India Company
Trading empires: seaborne, 506(map)
Traditions: of colonies, 868
Trafalgar, Battle of, 706
Tragedy: Shakespearean, 515–516; French, 542
Training, *see* Education
Tramp freighter: voyage of, 849
Transatlantic trade, 510
Transjordan, 903
Transportation: in England, 718, 718(map); railroads and, 724–725; public, 786, 787(illus.); revolution in, 849–850; trade and, 849–850. *See also* Railroads; Roads and highways
Trans-Saharan trade, 487
Transubstantiation, 449–450
Transvaal, 861, 863
Transylvania, 466, 746(illus.); Habsburgs and, 466, 566, 582
Travel: dangers of, 397; in postwar era, 1002. *See also* Expansion; Exploration
Traveler Looking over a Sea of Fog (Friedrich), 759(illus.)
Travels (Marco Polo), 518
Travels in Muscovy (Olearius), 586–587, 587(illus.)
Treaties, *see* specific treaties
Treitschke, Heinrich von, 865
Trench warfare, 886(map), 887, 888, 888(illus.)
Trent, Council of, 452–453, 467–469

Trial, The (Kafka), 920
Trials: for sodomy, 396; for witchcraft, 475–476
Tridentine decrees, 467, 469
Triennial Act (England), 545
Trinity: Servetus and, 465
Triple Alliance, 880(illus.), 881, 889
Triple Entente, 880(illus.), 885, 889, 890, 894
Triumph of Democratic Republics, The (French illustration), 770(illus.)
Triumph of Spain, The (Tiepolo), 535
Triumph of the Will, The (Riefenstahl), 928
Trotsky, Leon, 898, 900, 949, 950
Truce: ending Korean War, 984
True and False Churches, The (Cranach the Younger), 452(illus.)
Truman, Harry S: at Potsdam Conference, 983; Korean War and, 984
Truman Doctrine, 983
Truth: religious, 599
Tsars (Russia), 574–576; use of title, 574. *See also* specific rulers
Tudor dynasty (England), 435, 436, 461–463, 462(illus.). *See also* specific rulers
Tuileries palace, 696
Tull, Jethro, 625
Turgot, Jacques, 650, 686
Turkey: Ottomans and, 580; Russia, Prussia, and, 613; Greek independence and, 762; Young Turks and, 831; after First World War, 903, 906; independence of, 907; aid to, 984; European Union and, 1040, 1040(illus.), 1041; workers from, 1042. *See also* Anatolia; Ottoman Empire
Turks: Russia and, 613; Young Turks and, 831; Atatürk and, 906–907. *See also* Ottoman Empire; Turkey
Turner, Joseph M. W., 725, 761
Tuscany, 818
Twelve Articles, 455
Twentieth Party Congress, 996
Two New Sciences (Galileo), 592–593
Two Sicilies, kingdom of, *see* Kingdom of the Two Sicilies
Tyler, Wat, 370(illus.), 392
Typhoid fever, 372, 783
Typhus, 504
Tyrants and tyranny: in authoritarian rule, 945
Tyrol, 565
Tzu Hsi (China), 872, 873(illus.)

Ubertinus of Carrara, 414
Uccello, Paolo, 412(illus.)
Ukraine, 828, 899, 900, 952, 967, 1041; Russia and, 576; serfdom in, 613
Ulster, 766; opposition to home rule in, 835–836, 836(illus.)
Ulysses (Joyce), 920
Uncertainty principle, 919
Unconditional surrender policy: of Grand Alliance (Allies), 973, 982
Unconscious: Freud on, 804
Underemployment, 1012
Unemployment: in Great Depression, 934(map), 935–936, 936(illus.), 937; in England, 935–936, 942–943, 943(illus.); in United States, 937; Orwell on, 942–943; in Soviet Union, 953; in Germany, 958, 961, 1040; in 1970s, 1010; globalization and, 1031; European Union and, 1039; in western Europe, 1039, 1040, 1042; in Europe, 1054
Unification: of Russia, 573; of Germany, 755(illus.), 774, 821–825, 823(map) 824(illus.); of Italy, 818–821, 819(map)
Uniformitarianism principle (Lyell), 807
Union of South Africa, 861, 863
Union of Utrecht (1581), 474, 475
Unions, *see* Labor unions
United Kingdom, *see* England (Britain)
United Nations: Korean War and, 984; Palestine division by, 992; Iraq and, 1030, 1047; in Afghanistan, 1045
United Provinces of the Netherlands, *see* Dutch Republic
United States: Montesquieu's theories and, 601; industrialization in, 727, 728(illus.); urban transportation in, 786; naturalism in, 809; nation building in, 825–826; slavery in, 826(map); Japan and, 852, 972; migration to, 856; annexation of Hawaii by, 858(illus.); imperialism by, 865; Philippines and, 867; in First World War, 890, 901; Treaty of Versailles and, 902–903, 907–908, 928–930; Middle East and, 910–911; modern architecture in, 922; films from, 926–927; stock market crash in, 933; Great Depression in, 934(map), 936–937; New Deal in, 936–937; Soviet industrialization and, 952; Pearl Harbor attack and, 970, 972; in Second World War, 970, 973, 974–975; isolationism of, 972; atomic bombing of Japan by, 975, 1000; containment policy of, 984; Korean War and, 984, 1006; Marshall Plan and, 984, 987; military protection by, 987; civil rights movement in, 994–995, 994(illus.); science and technology in, 1000; student protests in, 1005; Vietnam War and, 1006–1007; Atlantic alliance and, 1008; international monetary system and, 1010; oil embargo and, 1010; misery index for, 1011; military buildup in, 1012; as superpower, 1025, 1030; end of cold war and, 1030; Gulf War (1991) and, 1030; economic practices of, 1031; NATO admissions and, 1035; Kosovo and, 1038; birthrate in, 1041; human rights vs. states' rights and, 1044; terrorist attacks on, 1045–1046, 1048; attacks on embassies of, 1047; Iraq War (2003–), 1047–1049. *See also* Cold war; First World War; Second World War
Unity movement: in western Europe, 987, 988(map), 989
Universal suffrage: male, 754, 764, 818, 955; in Russian Federation, 1028
Universe: Aristotle on, 590; Copernicus on, 591–592; Newton on, 595
Universities: colleges founded in, 381; student protests and, 1005–1006
Unskilled workers, 791, 794
Unwed mothers, 656
Upper classes, 787; sexual exploitation of girls by, 655; diet of, 664. *See also* Aristocracy; Nobility

Upper middle class, 788–789
Upper working class, 791
Urban VI (Pope), 387
Urban VIII (Pope): Galileo and, 594
Urban areas: plague and, 379–380; discontent, 392; in 14th century, 392–393; in Russia, 575; culture in, 603–607; illegitimacy in, 657; lifestyle in, 779, 780–786; classes in, 786–797, 791(illus.); standard of living in, 841. *See also* Cities and towns
Urban guilds, 631–633
Urbanization: Industrial Revolution and, 779
Urban planning, 784–786, 784(map)
Ure, Andrew, 734
Ursuline order, 469
Utopia (More), 417
Utopian socialism, 756
Utrecht: Union of, 474, 475; Peace of, 534, 536(map), 635

Vaccine, 783; for plague, 377
Vaclav IV (Bohemia, Holy Roman Empire), 391
Valdes Leal, Juan de, 472(illus.)
Valencia, 437
Valentino, Rudolph, 927
Valla, Lorenzo, 416
Vallain, Nanine, 682(illus.)
Valmy, Battle of, 696
Valois dynasty: Habsburg-Valois Wars and, 411–412, 459
Values: of upper working class, 791
Van den Vondel, Joost, 550–553
Van der Weyden, Rogier, 424, 424(illus.)
Van Dyck, Anthony, 544(illus.)
Van Eyck, Jan, 424
Van Gogh, Theo, 1049
Van Gogh, Vincent, 923
Vasa family, *see* Gustavus Vasa (Sweden)
Vasari, Giorgio, 407, 426, 444(illus.)
Vassals: English king as, 381
Vatican: Sistine Chapel in, 406(illus.); Lateran Agreement and, 957. *See also* Catholic Church; Papacy
Vaudeville theater, 796–797
Vegetable Market, 1662 (Sorgh), 624(illus.)
Velázquez, Diego, 507, 507(illus.)
Velvet Revolution, 1025–1026, 1026(illus.)
Venetia, 750, 818, 822
Venice, 409, 410; trade in, 408, 490–491; arts in, 425
Verdun, 887; Battle of, 891
Vergerio, Peter Paul, 414
Vermuyden, Cornelius, 625
Vernacular languages: literature in, 399–400
Verrocchio, Andrea del, 427
Versailles, Treaty of, 902, 903, 905(illus.), 928, 962; U.S. rejection of, 907–908
Versailles palace, 540–541, 568, 568(illus.); court at, 541; gardens of, 569, 569(illus.); Estates General in, 690; women's march on, 691–692, 692(illus.). *See also* Hall of Mirrors (Versailles)
Vespucci, Amerigo, 500
Viceroyalties: in Spanish New World, 538–539
Vichy government, 966, 973
Vico, Giovanni Battista, 769

Victor Emmanuel II (Italy), 818, 820, 820(illus.), 821
Victor Emmanuel III (Italy), 956
Victoria (England), 814(illus.)
Vienna, 567, 581; University of, 381; Ottoman siege of, 489, 582; anti-Semitism in, 838
Vietcong, 1007, 1046
Vietnam, 872, 981, 992
Vietnam War, 1006–1007, 1007(illus.)
Villafranca, treaty at, 820
Villages, *see* Cities and towns
Vindication of the Rights of Man, A (Wollstonecraft), 694
Vindication of the Rights of Woman, A (Wollstonecraft), 694
Violence: religious, 472–477; against indigenous Americans, 504–505; against imperialists, 869; against women, 1009
Virocha (god), 503
Vitry, Jacques de, 390
Vocations (callings): for clergy, 469
Voltaire, 588(illus.), 601–602, 613, 619(illus.); on religion, 618–619
Von Bora, Katherina, 450, 455, 456
Voting and voting rights, 831; for women, 549, 831, 832(illus.), 894; Chartists and, 741, 764; liberalism and, 754; in England, 763–764, 835; in France, 767, 768, 771, 818; in Austria-Hungary, 836; for workers, 840–841; for African Americans, 994. *See also* Universal suffrage
Voting Rights Act (1965), 994
Voyages: Chinese, 485; European voyages of discovery, 492–504, 496(map); of Columbus, 518–519

Wage earners: peasant farmers as, 625
Wages: for men vs. women, 631, 1003–1004; Ricardo on, 726; for workers, 736, 786–787
Waksman, Selman, 377
Wales, 781
Walesa, Lech, 1020, 1021, 1022(illus.), 1025, 1035
Wallenstein, *see* Albert of Wallenstein
Walsingham (chronicler), 386
War and Peace (Tolstoy), 809
War communism, 900
War crime tribunal (Netherlands): Milosevic at, 1039
War of Independence, *see* American Revolution
War of the Austrian Succession, 610, 614, 635, 686
War of the League of Augsburg: French army in, 527
War of the Spanish Succession, 534, 553, 571, 635, 643
War Raw Materials Board, 891
Warriors: kings perceived as, 433
Wars and warfare: religious, 458–459, 472–477; army size and, 526–527; in France, 533–534; in central and eastern Europe, 559–565; in Russia, 576, 578; imperial, 635–637; industrialization and, 728; trench warfare and, 887–888, 888(illus.); submarine warfare, 890; blitzkrieg, 966; saturation bombing in, 974–975; bombing and, 975. *See also* Civil war(s); specific battles and wars
Warsaw, 974
Warsaw Ghetto, 969(illus.), 1008
Warsaw Pact, 984
Wars of the Roses, 435
Warthmüller, R., 665(illus.)
Washington, George, 688
Waste Land, The (Eliot), 920
Water frame, 719, 720
Watergate scandal, 1007
Waterloo, battle at, 711, 750
Watson, James, 1000
Watt, James, 722, 732–733
Waugh, Evelyn, 917
Wealth: clerical, 378–379; decline from plague, 380; hierarchy of classes by, 431; nobility and, 431; of Catholic Church, 450–451; in England, 727; of aristocracy, 788–789; of upper middle class, 788–789; of American heiresses, 789; disparities in, 848; Industrial Revolution and, 848; technology and, 848; in Russia, 1034(illus.); in eastern Europe, 1035
Wealth of Nations (Smith), *see Inquiry into the Nature and Causes of the Wealth of Nations* (Smith)
Weapons: in Hundred Years' War, 383; on ships, 494; after Second World War, 1000
Weapons of mass destruction, 1050; war with Iraq and, 1047
Weather, *see* Climate
Weathermen, 1046
Weavers and weaving, 720. *See also* Textile industry
Weaver's Repose, The (Gerritz), 629(illus.)
Wedding chest: in Renaissance, 433(illus.)
Weimar Republic, 929, 958
Welfare: in England, 835; after Second World War, 987; 1970s monetary crisis and, 1011–1012
Welfare state: in Britain, 987; shift to capitalism, 1031
Werner, Anton von, 824(illus.)
Wesley, John, 660, 673–674
Wesley, Susannah, 660–661
West, the, *see* Western world
West Africa: Muslim world and, 487–488; trade and, 640; imperialism in, 862
West Berlin, 997. *See also* Berlin
Western Europe: grain distribution in, 377; Peter the Great and, 576, 578; in 18th century, 622; postwar period in, 985–989; Common Market in, 987; unity movements in, 987–989, 1039–1041; decolonization by, 989–993; student protests in, 1005; after cold war, 1019; shift from welfare state to capitalism, 1031; migration to, 1042–1044
Western front: in First World War, 887
Westernization: of colonies, 868
Western powers: Germany and, 928–930
Western world: expansion of, 847; China and Japan and, 850–853; new imperialism of, 859–865; values in, 915
West Germany: economic recovery in, 987; after Second World War, 987, 989; European unity and, 989; East Germany and, 1008, 1019, 1040; Poland and, 1008; Berlin Wall and, 1025, 1027(illus.). *See also* Germany
West Indies, 501, 640
Wet-nursing, 658, 659(illus.), 802
What Is Enlightenment? (Kant), 608
What Is Property? (Proudhon), 756
What Is the Third Estate? (Sieyès), 689–690
Wheat, 380, 509; in France, 534
Whigs: in England, 763
White-collar groups, 789
White man's burden, 867
White Mountain, Battle of, 562, 565
White people: Enlightenment thinkers on, 609
Whites: in Russian civil war, 899–900
Widows: in High Middle Ages, 393. *See also* Women
Wilkinson, John, 722
William I (Germany), 821, 822, 824(illus.), 825, 833
William II (Germany), 833, 881, 883
William and Mary (England), 548
William Louis (House of Orange), 550
William of Orange (king of England), 548, 553
William of Orange ("the Silent"), 474, 550
Wilson, Woodrow, 890; Fourteen Points of, 902; League of Nations and, 902
Winter Palace (St. Petersburg), 579(illus.), 580
Winter (Town) Palace (Vienna), 569
Witches and witchcraft: European persecution of, 472, 475–477
Witches' Sabbat (Grien), 477(illus.)
Witte, Sergei, 828
Wittenberg, 451; Luther at, 447
Wittgenstein, Ludwig, 916
Wojtyla, Karol, *see* John Paul II (pope)
Wollstonecraft, Mary, 694–695, 799
Women: in France, 381–382, 532; as Lollards, 388; in High Middle Ages, 393; marriage age of, 394; homosexuality among, 396; in schools, 400(illus.); Christine de Pizan and, 404–405; humanists and, 414; as Renaissance painters, 426–428; Renaissance debate about, 432–433; as rulers, 433; gender roles and, 433–434, 799–802; in Protestant churches, 450; religious status of, 455–456; Reformation and, 457; as witches, 475–477; in Southeast Asia, 484; in sciences, 597, 597(illus.); in Enlightenment, 601; elite, 605–606; Rousseau on role of, 607, 609; in textile manufacturing, 631; in guilds, 633; in workforce, 634, 794–795, 891–892, 894, 953–954, 1002–1004, 1012, 1040; prostitution and, 655, 798–799; work by, 655; education for, 661; fashion for, 666, 789–790, 792–793, 792(illus.), 793(illus.); as midwives, 668–670; in French Revolution, 691–692, 692(illus.); Napoleonic Code and, 705; middle class, 734, 789–790; in factories, 737(illus.); sexual division of labor and, 738–740; in coal industry, 739–740; workdays for, 765; in working class, 794–795; rights of, 799; voting rights for, 831,

832(illus.); British Empire and, 870, 876–877; in First World War, 891–892, 891(illus.), 892, 893, 894; in Turkey, 907; in literature, 920; in Soviet Union, 953–954; in fascist Italy, 957; in Nazi Germany, 961, 962; after Second World War, 981; in postwar era, 1002–1004; Beauvoir on, 1016–1017; after German reunification, 1040; birthrate declines and, 1042; as illegal immigrants, 1043; Muslim girls in France, 1049. *See also* Marriage; Nuns

Women's movement, 1003–1004, 1009–1010

Women's rights: married women and, 799–800; in Soviet Union, 953; in workplace, 1010

Women's suffrage movement, 831, 832(illus.)

Wood: as energy source, 721

Woodstock, 1004(illus.)

Woolen industry: sheep and, 373; in England, 382(illus.), 386. *See also* Textile industry

Woolf, Virginia, 920

Wordsworth, William, 734, 758, 759–760

Work: increased pace of, 633–634. *See also* Labor; Workers

Work (Brown), 733(illus.)

Workday, 738, 765, 771

Workers: Dutch, 553; employers and, 631; rural, 631; in French Revolution, 697; in factories, 734–736; conditions of, 736–738; in cotton mill, 737(illus.); in England, 738; on mining, 744–745; socialism and, 756, 844–845; Marx on, 757; in France, 817; in Russia, 829; in Germany, 833; on May Day, 840(illus.); living standards of, 841; in Berlin, 845(illus.); migrants as, 858; women as, 892, 894, 953–954, 1003–1004, 1012, 1040; Soviet, 952, 953. *See also* Labor; Peasant(s); Working class

Workers International, *see* International Working Men's Association

Workforce: women in, 532, 634, 794–795

Working class, 732, 787, 790–797; marriage in, 657–658; condition of, 736; labor movement and, 740–741; in England, 764, 765; leisure and religion of, 795–797; home of, 803(illus.). *See also* Workers

Workplace: conditions in, 631, 720–721, 736–738; women's rights in, 631

Workshops: in Paris, 771

Works Progress Administration (WPA), 937

Workweek: hours in, 736

World of Yesterday, The (Zweig), 812–813

World the Cold War Made, The (Cronin), 1032

World Trade Center: terrorist attacks on, 1020, 1045, 1046, 1046(illus.)

Worldview: science and, 593–594, 804; of Enlightenment, 598

World War I, *see* First World War

World War II, *see* Second World War

Worms: Diet of (1521), 449

Worship, *see* Freedom; Religion(s)

Wozzeck (Berg), 926

WPA, *see* Works Progress Administration (WPA)

Wright, Frank Lloyd, 921

Wright, Joseph, 661(illus.), 735(illus.)

Writing, *see* Literature

Wyclif, John, 388

Xhosa people, 859

Yalta Conference, 982(illus.), 983

Yaroshenko, N. A., 809(illus.)

Yeltsin, Boris, 1027, 1028, 1028(illus.), 1033, 1034

Yemen, 1046

Yokohama: Westerners in, 871

Yongle (China), 485

York: house of, 435; duke of (James II), 548

Young Turks, 831

Young Woman Reading a Letter (Raoux), 663

Youth culture: middle class, 812–813; international, 1004–1006

Youth movement, 980(illus.); of Italian fascism, 957; of Nazis, 959

Ypres: deaths in, 372–373

Ypsilanti, Alexander, 761

Yucatec Mayan language, 503

Yugoslavia, 901, 903, 1046(map); Little Entente and, 929; ethnic groups in, 946, 1038(map); Second World War and, 974, 983; Tito in, 996; civil war in, 1019, 1033; disintegration of, 1037–1039; NATO and, 1038–1039

Yukos, 1034(illus.)

Zacatecas, 509

Zambia, 861

Zapolya, Janos, 466

Zeeland, 474

Zemstvo, 827

Zheng He, 485, 486(map)

Zimbabwe, 861

Zionism, 838, 905, 992; Herzl and, 838, 839

Zola, Emile, 808–809, 808(illus.), 835

Zollverein, 731, 821

Zones of occupation, *see* Occupation zones

Zoning, 786

Zulu people, 859

Zurich, 451

Zweig, Stephan, 812–813

Zwingli, Ulrich, 449, 450, 451, 452, 458

Timeline   A History of Western Society: A Brief Overview

	Government	**Society and Economy**
3200 B.C.	Dominance of Sumerian cities in Mesopotamia, ca 3200–2340 Unification of Egypt; Archaic Period, ca 3100–2660 Old Kingdom of Egypt, ca 2660–2180 Dominance of Akkadian empire in Mesopotamia, ca 2331–2200 Middle Kingdom in Egypt, ca 2080–1640	Neolithic peoples rely on settled agriculture, while others pursue nomadic life, ca 7000–ca 3000 Development of wheeled transport in Mesopotamia, by ca 3200 Expansion of Mesopotamian trade and culture into modern Turkey, the Middle East, and Iran, ca 2600
2000 B.C.	Babylonian empire, ca 2000–1595 Hyksos invade Egypt, ca 1640–1570 Hittite Empire, ca 1600–1200 New Kingdom in Egypt, ca 1570–1075	First wave of Indo-European migrants, by 2000 Extended commerce in Egypt, by ca 2000 Horses introduced into western Asia, by ca 2000
1500 B.C.	Third Intermediate Period in Egypt, ca 1100–700 Unified Hebrew Kingdom under Saul, David, and Solomon, ca 1025–925	Use of iron increases in western Asia, by ca 1300–1100 Second wave of Indo-European migrants, by ca 1200
1000 B.C.	Hebrew Kingdom divided into Israel and Judah, 925 Assyrian Empire, ca 900–612 Phoenicians found Carthage, 813 Kingdom of Kush conquers and reunifies Egypt, 8th c. Medes conquers Persia, 710 Babylon wins independence from Assyria, 626 Dracon issues law code at Athens, 621 Cyrus the Great conquers Medes, founds Persian Empire, 550 Solon's reforms at Athens, ca 549 Persians complete conquest of ancient Near East, 521–464 Reforms of Cleisthenes in Athens, 508	Concentration of landed wealth in Greece, ca 750–600 Greek overseas expansion, ca 750–550 Beginning of coinage in western Asia, ca 640
500 B.C.	Battle of Marathon, 490 Xerxes' invasion of Greece, 480–479 Delian Confederacy, 478/7 Twelve Tables in Rome, 451/0 Valerio-Horatian laws in Rome, 449 Peloponnesian War, 431–404 Rome captures Veii, 396 Gauls sack Rome, 390 Roman expansion in Italy, 390–290 Conquests of Alexander the Great, 334–323 Punic Wars, 264–146 Reforms of the Gracchi, 133–121	Building of the Via Appia begins, 312 Growth of Hellenistic trade and cities, ca 300–100 Beginning of Roman silver coinage, 269 Growth of slavery, decline of small farmers in Rome, ca 250–100 Agrarian reforms of the Gracchi, 133–121

Religion and Philosophy	Science and Technology	Arts and Letters
Growth of anthropomorphic religion in Mesopotamia, ca 3000–2000 Emergence of Egyptian polytheism and belief in personal immortality, ca 2660 Spread of Mesopotamian and Egyptian religious ideas as far north as modern Anatolia and as far south as central Africa, ca 2600	Development of wheeled transport in Mesopotamia, by ca 3200 Use of widespread irrigation in Mesopotamia and Egypt, ca 3000 Construction of the first pyramid in Egypt, ca 2600	Sumerian cuneiform writing, ca 3200 Egyptian hieroglyphic writing, ca 3100
Emergence of Hebrew monotheism, ca 1700 Mixture of Hittite and Near Eastern religious beliefs, ca 1595	Construction of the first ziggurats in Mesopotamia, ca 2000 Widespread use of bronze in the ancient Near East, ca 1900 Babylonian mathematical advances, ca 1800	*Epic of Gilgamesh,* ca 1900 Code of Hammurabi, ca 1790
Exodus of the Hebrews from Egypt into Palestine, 13th c. Religious beliefs of Akhenaten, ca 1367	Hittites introduce iron technology, ca 1400	Phoenicians develop alphabet, ca 1400 Naturalistic art in Egypt under Akhenaten, ca 1367 Egyptian Book of the Dead, ca 1300
Era of the prophets in Israel, ca 1100–500 Intermixture of Etruscan and Roman religious cults, ca 753–509 Growing popularity of local Greek religious cults, ca 700 B.C.–A.D. 337 Babylonian Captivity of the Hebrews, 586–539	Babylonian astronomical advances, ca 750–400	Beginning of the Hebrew Bible, ca 9th c. First Olympic Games, 776 Babylonian astronomical advances, ca 750–400 Homer, traditional author of the *Iliad* and *Odyssey,* ca 700 Hesiod, author of the *Theogony* and *Works and Days,* ca 700 Archilochos, lyric poet, 648 Aeschylus, first significant Athenian tragedian, 525/4–456
Pre-Socratic philosophers, 5th c. Socrates, 469–399 Plato, 429–347 Diogenes, leading proponent of cynicism, ca 412–323 Aristotle, 384–322 Epicurus, 340–270 Zeno, founder of Stoic philosophy, 335–262 Emergence of Mithraism, ca 300 Spread of Hellenistic mystery religions, 2nd c. Greek cults brought to Rome, ca 200	Hippocrates, formal founder of medicine ca 430 Theophrastus, founder of botany, ca 372–288 Aristarchos of Samos, advances in astronomy, ca 310–230 Euclid codifies geometry, ca 300 Herophilus, discoveries in medicine, ca 300–250 Archimedes, works on physics and hydrologics, ca 287–212	Sophocles, tragedian who used his plays to explore moral and political problems, ca 496–406 Euripides, the most personal of the Athenian tragedians, ca 480–406 Thucydides, historian of the Peloponnesian War, ca 460–400 Aristophanes, the greatest writer of Old Comedy, ca 457–ca 385 Herodotus, the father of history, ca 450

	Government	**Society and Economy**
100 B.C.	Dictatorship of Sulla, 88–79 Civil war in Rome, 78–27 Dictatorship of Caesar, 45–44 Principate of Augustus, 31 B.C.–A.D. 14	Reform of the Roman calendar, 46
A.D. 300	Constantine removes capital of Roman Empire to Constantinople, ca 315 Visigoths defeat Roman army at Adrianople (378), signaling massive German invasions into the empire Bishop Ambrose asserts church's independence from the state, 380 Death of emperor Romulus Augustus marks end of Roman Empire in the West, 476 Clovis issues Salic law of the Franks, ca 490	Growth of serfdom in Roman Empire, ca 200–500 Economic contraction in Roman Empire, 3rd c.
500	Law Code of Justinian, 529 Dooms of Ethelbert, king of Kent, ca 604 Spread of Islam across Arabia, the Mediterranean region, Spain, North Africa, and Asia as far as India, ca 630–733	Gallo-Roman aristocracy intermarries with Germanic chieftains Decline of towns and trade, ca 500–700 Agrarian economy predominates in the West, ca 500–1800
700	Charles Martel defeats Muslims at Tours, 732 Pippin III anointed king of the Franks, 754 Charlemagne secures Frankish crown, r. 768–814	Height of Muslim commercial activity, ca 700–1300, with western Europe
800	Imperial coronation of Charlemagne, Christmas 800 Treaty of Verdun, 843 Viking, Magyar, and Muslim invasions, ca 845–900	Byzantine commerce and industry, ca 800–1000 Invasions and unstable conditions lead to increase of serfdom
1000	Seljuk Turks conquer Muslim Baghdad, 1055 Norman conquest of England, 1066 Penance of Henry IV at Canossa, 1077	Decline of Byzantine free peasantry, ca 1025–1100 Growth of towns and trade in the West, ca 1050–1300 Domesday Book, 1086
1100	Henry I of England, r. 1100–1135 Louis VI of France, r. 1108–1137 Frederick I of Germany, r. 1152–1190 Henry II of England, r. 1154–1189 Thomas Becket murdered, 1170 Philip Augustus of France, r. 1180–1223	Henry I of England establishes the Exchequer, 1130 Beginnings of the Hanseatic League, 1159

Religion and Philosophy	Science and Technology	Arts and Letters
Mithraism spreads to Rome, 27 B.C.–A.D. 270 Dedication of the Ara Pacis Augustae, 9 Traditional birth of Jesus, ca 3	Pliny the Elder, student of natural history, 23 B.C.–A.D. 79 Frontinus, engineering advances in Rome, 30 B.C.–A.D. 104	Virgil, 70–19 B.C. Livy, ca 59 B.C.–A.D. 17 Ovid, 43 B.C.–A.D. 17
Constantine legalizes Christianity, 312 Theodosius declares Christianity the official state religion, 380 Donatist heretical movement at its height, ca 400 St. Augustine, *The City of God,* ca 425 Clovis adopts Roman Christianity, 496		St. Jerome publishes the Latin *Vulgate,* late 4th c. St. Augustine, *Confessions,* ca 390 Byzantines preserve Greco-Roman culture, ca 400–1000
Rule of St. Benedict, 529 Monasteries established in Anglo-Saxon England, 7th c. Muhammad preaches reform, ca 610 Publication of the Qu'ran, 651 Synod of Whitby, 664	Using watermills, Benedictine monks exploit energy of fast-flowing rivers and streams Heavy plow and improved harness facilitate use of multiple-ox teams; harrow widely used in northern Europe	Boethius, *The Consolation of Philosophy,* ca 520 Justinian constructs church of Santa Sophia, 532–537 Pope Gregory the Great publishes *Dialogues, Pastoral Care, Moralia,* 590–604
Missionary work of St. Boniface in Germany, ca 710–750 Iconoclastic controversy in Byzantine Empire, 726–843 Pippin III donates Papal States to the papacy, 756	Byzantines successfully use "Greek fire" in naval combat against Arab fleets attacking Constantinople, 673, 717	Lindisfarne Gospel Book, ca 700 Bede, *Ecclesiastical History of the English Nation,* ca 700 *Beowulf,* ca 700 Carolingian Renaissance, ca 780–850
Foundation of abbey of Cluny, 909 Byzantine conversion of Russia, late 10th c.	Stirrup and nailed horseshoes become widespread in shock combat Paper, invented in China ca 2d c., enters Europe through Muslim Spain in 10th c.	Byzantines develop the Cyrillic script, late 10th c.
Beginning of reformed papacy, 1046 Schism between Roman and Greek Orthodox churches, 1054 Pope Gregory VII, 1073–1085 Peter Abelard, 1079–1142 St. Bernard of Clairvaux, 1090–1153 First Crusade, 1095–1099	Arab conquests bring new irrigation methods, cotton cultivation, and manufacture to Spain, Sicily, southern Italy Avicenna, Arab scientist, d. 1037	Romanesque style in architecture and art, ca 1000–1200 *Song of Roland,* ca 1095 Muslim musicians introduce lute, rebec—stringed instruments and ancestors of violin
Universities begin, ca 1100–1300 Concordat of Worms ends investiture controversy, 1122 Height of Cistercian monasticism, 1125–1175 Aristotle's works translated into Latin, ca 1140–1260 Third Crusade, 1189–1192 Pope Innocent III, 1198–1216	In castle construction Europeans, copying Muslim and Byzantine models, erect rounded towers and crenelated walls Windmill invented, ca 1180 Some monasteries, such as Clairvaux and Canterbury Cathedral Priory, supplied by underground pipes with running water and indoor latrines, elsewhere rare until 19th c.	*Rubaiyat of Umar Khayyam,* ca 1120 Dedication of abbey church of Saint-Denis launches Gothic style, 1144 Hildegard of Bingen, 1098–1179 Court of troubador poetry, especially that of Chrétien de Troyes, circulates widely

	Government	**Society and Economy**
1200	Spanish victory over Muslims at Las Navas de Tolosa, 1212 Frederick II of Germany and Sicily, r. 1212–1250 Magna Carta, 1215 Louis IX of France, r. 1226–1270 Mongols end Abbasid caliphate, 1258 Edward I of England, r. 1272–1307 Philip IV (the Fair) of France, r. 1285–1314 England and France at war, 1296	Economic revival, growth of towns, clearing of wasteland contribute to growth of personal freedom, 13th c. Crusaders capture Constantinople (Fourth Crusade) and spur Venetian economy, 1204 Agricultural expansion leads to population growth, ca 1225–1300
1300	Philip IV orders arrest of Pope Boniface at Anagni, 1303 Hundred Years' War, 1337–1453 Political disorder in Germany, ca 1350–1450 Merchant oligarchies or despots rule Italian city-states	European economic depression, ca 1300–1450 Black Death appears ca 1347; returns intermittently until 18th c. Height of the Hanseatic League, 1350–1450 Peasant and working-class revolts: Flanders, 1302; France, 1358; Florence, 1378; England, 1381
1400	Joan of Arc rallies French monarchy, 1429–1431 Medici domination of Florence begins, 1434 Princes in Germany consolidate power, ca 1450–1500 Ottoman Turks under Mahomet II capture Constantinople, May 1453 Wars of the Roses in England, 1453–1471 Ferdinand and Isabella complete reconquista in Spain, 1492 French invasion of Italy, 1494	Population decline, peasants' revolts, high labor costs contribute to decline of serfdom in western Europe Christopher Columbus reaches the Americas, October 1492 Portuguese gain control of East Indian spice trade, 1498–1511 Flow of Balkan slaves into eastern Mediterranean; of African slaves into Iberia and Italy, ca 1400–1500
1500	Charles V, Holy Roman emperor, 1519–1556 Imperial sack of Rome, 1527 Philip II of Spain, r. 1556–1598 Revolt of the Netherlands, 1566–1609 St. Bartholomew's Day massacre, August 24, 1572 Defeat of the Spanish Armada, 1588 Henry IV of France issues Edict of Nantes, 1598	Balboa discovers the Pacific, 1513 Magellan's crew circumnavigates the earth, 1519–1522 Spain and Portugal gain control of regions of Central and South America, ca 1520–1550 Peasants' Revolt in Germany, 1524–1525 "Time of Troubles" in Russia, 1598–1613
1600	Thirty Years' War, 1618–1648 Richelieu dominates French government, 1624–1643 Frederick William, Elector of Brandenburg, r. 1640–1688 English Civil War, 1642–1649	Chartering of British East India Company, 1600 Famine and taxation lead to widespread revolts, decline of serfdom in western Europe, ca 1600–1650 English Poor Law, 1601

Religion and Philosophy	Science and Technology	Arts and Letters
Maimonides, d. 1204 Founding of Franciscan order, 1210 Fourth Lateran Council, 1215 Founding of Dominican order, 1216 Thomas Aquinas (1225–1274) marks height of Scholasticism Pope Boniface VIII, 1294–1303	*Notebooks* of Villard de Honnecourt, a master mason (architect), a major source for Gothic engineering, ca 1250 Development of double-entry bookkeeping in Florence and Genoa, ca 1250–1340 Venetians purchase secrets of glass manufacture from Syria, 1277 Mechanical clock invented, ca 1290	*Parzifal, Roman de la Rose, King Arthur and the Round Table* celebrate virtues of knighthood Height of Gothic style, ca 1225–1300
Babylonian Captivity of the papacy, 1307–1377 John Wyclif, ca 1330–1384 Great Schism in the papacy, 1377–1418	Edward III of England uses cannon in siege of Calais, 1346	Petrarch, 1304–1374 Paintings of Giotto, ca 1305–1337 Dante, *Divine Comedy*, ca 1310 Boccaccio, *The Decameron,* ca 1350 Jan van Eyck, 1366–1441 Brunelleschi, 1377–1446 Chaucer, *Canterbury Tales,* ca 1385–1400
Council of Constance, 1414–1418 Pragmatic Sanction of Bourges, 1438 Expulsion of Jews from Spain, 1492	Water-powered blast furnaces operative in Sweden, Austria, the Rhine Valley, Liège, ca 1400 Leonardo Fibonacci's *Liber Abaci* (1202) popularizes use of Hindu-Arabic numerals, "a major factor in the rise of science in the Western world" Paris and largest Italian cities pave streets, making street cleaning possible Printing and movable type, ca 1450	Masaccio, 1401–1428 Botticelli, 1444–1510 Leonardo da Vinci, 1452–1519 Albrecht Dürer, 1471–1528 Michelangelo, 1475–1564 Raphael, 1483–1520 Rabelais, ca 1490–1553
Lateran Council attempts reforms of church abuses, 1512–1517 Machiavelli, *The Prince,* 1513 Concordat of Bologna, 1516 More, *Utopia,* 1516 Luther, *Ninety-five Theses,* 1517 Henry VIII of England breaks with Rome, 1532–1534 Loyola establishes Society of Jesus, 1540 Calvin establishes theocracy in Geneva, 1541 Merici establishes Ursuline order for education of women, 1544 Council of Trent, 1545–1563 Peace of Augsburg, 1555 Hobbes, 1588–1679 Descartes, 1596–1650	Copernicus, *On the Revolutions of the Heavenly Bodies,* 1543 Galileo, 1564–1642 Kepler, 1571–1630 Harvey, 1578–1657	Erasmus, *The Praise of Folly,* 1509 Castiglione, *The Courtier,* 1528 Cervantes, 1547–1616 Baroque movement in the arts, ca 1550–1725 Shakespeare, 1564–1616 Rubens, 1577–1640 Montaigne, *Essays,* 1598 Velazquez, 1599–1660
Huguenot revolt in France, 1625	Bacon, *The Advancement of Learning,* 1605 Boyle, 1627–1691 Leeuwenhoek, 1632–1723	Rembrandt van Rijn, 1606–1669 Golden Age of Dutch culture, 1625–1675 Vermeer, 1632–1675 Racine, 1639–1699

	Government	**Society and Economy**
1600 (cont.)	Louis XIV, r. 1643–1715 Peace of Westphalia, 1648 The Fronde in France, 1648–1660	Chartering of Dutch East India Company, 1602 Height of Dutch commercial activity, ca 1630–1665
1650	Protectorate in England, 1653–1658 Leopold I, Habsburg emperor, r. 1658–1705 Treaty of the Pyrenees, 1659 English monarchy restored, 1660 Ottoman Siege of Vienna, 1683 Glorious Revolution in England, 1688–1689 Peter the Great of Russia, r. 1689–1725	Height of mercantilism in Europe, ca 1650–1750 Principle of peasants' "hereditary subjugation" to their lords affirmed in Prussia, 1653 Colbert's economic reforms in France, ca 1663–1683 Cossack revolt in Russia, 1670–1671
1700	War of the Spanish Succession, 1701–1713 Peace of Utrecht, 1713 Frederick William I of Prussia, r. 1713–1740 Louis XV of France, r. 1715–1774 Maria Theresa of Austria, r. 1740–1780 Frederick the Great of Prussia, r. 1740–1786	Foundation of St. Petersburg, 1701 Last appearance of bubonic plague in western Europe, ca 1720 Enclosure movement in England, ca 1730–1830 Jeremy Bentham, 1748–1823
1750	Seven Years' War, 1756–1763 Catherine the Great of Russia, r. 1762–1796 Partition of Poland, 1772–1795 Louis XVI of France, r. 1774–1792 American Revolution, 1776–1783 Beginning of the French Revolution, 1789	Start of general European population increase, ca 1750 Growth of illegitimate births, ca 1750–1850 Adam Smith, *The Wealth of Nations*, 1776 Thomas Malthus, *Essay of the Principle of Population*, 1798
1800	Napoleonic era, 1799–1815 Congress of Vienna, 1814–1815 "Battle of Peterloo," Great Britain, 1819	European economic imperialism, ca 1816–1880
1825	Greece wins independence, 1830 French conquest of Algeria, 1830 Revolution in France, 1830 Great Britain: Reform Bill of 1832; Poor Law reform, 1834; Chartists, repeal of Corn Laws, 1838–1848 British complete occupation of India, 1848 Revolutions in Europe, 1848	Height of French utopian socialism, 1830s–1840s German Zollverein founded, 1834 European capitalists begin large-scale foreign investment, 1840s Great Famine in Ireland, 1845–1851 Marx, *Communist Manifesto*, 1848
1850	Second Empire in France, 1852–1870 Crimean War, 1853–1856 Unification of Italy, 1859–1870 Civil War, United States, 1861–1865 Bismarck leads Germany, 1862–1890 Unification of Germany, 1864–1871 Britain's Second Reform Bill, 1867 Third Republic in France, 1870–1940	Crédit Mobilier founded in France, 1852 Japan opened to European influence, 1853 Mill, *On Liberty*, 1859 Russian serfs emancipated, 1861 First Socialist International, 1864–1871 Marx, *Das Capital*, 1867

Religion and Philosophy	Science and Technology	Arts and Letters
Patriarch Nikon's reforms split Russian Orthodox church, 1652 Test Act in England excludes Roman Catholics from public office, 1673 Revocation of Edict of Nantes, 1685 James II tries to restore Catholicism as state religion, 1685–1688 Montesquieu, 1689–1755 Locke, *Second Treatise on Civil Government,* 1690 Pierre Bayle, *Historical and Critical Dictionary,* 1697	Tull (1674–1741) encourages innovation in English agriculture Newton, *Principia Mathematica,* 1687 Newcomen develops steam engine, 1705	Construction of baroque palaces and remodeling of capital cities throughout central and eastern Europe, ca 1650–1725 J. S. Bach, 1685–1750 Fontenelle, *Conversations on the Plurality of Worlds,* 1686 The Enlightenment, ca 1690–1790 Voltaire, 1694–1778
Wesley, 1703–1791 Hume, 1711–1776 Diderot, 1713–1784 Condorcet, 1743–1794	Charles Townsend introduces four-year crop rotation, 1730	Montesquieu, *The Spirit of Laws,* 1748
Ricardo, 1772–1823 Fourier, 1772–1837 Papacy dissolves the Jesuits, 1773 Church reforms of Joseph II in Austria, 1780s Reorganization of the church in France, 1790s	Hargreaves's spinning jenny, ca 1765 Arkwright's water frame, ca 1765 Watt's steam engine promotes industrial breakthroughs, 1780s War widens the gap in technology between Britain and the continent, 1792–1815 Jenner's smallpox vaccine, 1796	*Encyclopedia,* edited by Diderot and d'Alembert, published, 1751–1765 Mozart, 1756–1791 Rousseau, *The Social Contract,* 1762 Beethoven, 1770–1827 Wordsworth, 1770–1850 Romanticism, ca 1790–1850 Wollstonecraft, *A Vindication of the Rights of Women,* 1792
Napoleon signs Concordat with Pope Pius VII regulating Catholic church in France, 1801 Spencer, 1820–1903		Staël, *On Germany,* 1810 Liszt, 1811–1886
Comte, *System of Positive Philosophy,* 1830–1842 List, *National System of Political Economy,* 1841 Nietzsche, 1844–1900 Sorel, 1847–1922	First railroad, Great Britain, 1825 Faraday studies electromagnetism, 1830–1840s	Balzac, *The Human Comedy,* 1829–1841 Delacroix, *Liberty Leading the People,* 1830 Hugo, *Hunchback of Notre Dame,* 1831
Decline in church attendance among working classes, ca 1850–1914 Pope Pius IX, *Syllabus of Errors,* denounces modern thoughts, 1864 Doctrine of papal infallibility, 1870	Modernization of Paris, ca 1850–1870 Great Exhibition, London, 1851 Darwin, *Origin of Species,* 1859 Pasteur develops germ theory of disease, 1860s Suez Canal opened, 1869 Mendeleev develops the periodic table, 1869	Realism, ca 1850–1870 Freud, 1856–1939 Flaubert, *Madame Bovary,* 1857 Tolstoy, *War and Peace,* 1869 Impressionism in art, ca 1870–1900 Eliot (Mary Ann Evans), *Middlemarch,* 1872

	Government	**Society and Economy**
1875	Congress of Berlin, 1878 European "scramble for Africa," 1880–1900 Britain's Third Reform Bill, 1884 Dreyfus affair in France, 1894–1899 Spanish-American War, 1898 Boer War, 1899–1902	Full property rights for women, Great Britain, 1882 Social welfare legislation, Germany, 1883–1889 Second Socialist International, 1889–1914 Witte directs modernization of Russian economy, 1892–1899
1900	Russo-Japanese War, 1904–1905 Revolution in Russia, 1905 Balkan wars, 1912–1913	Women's suffrage movement, England, ca 1900–1914 Social welfare legislation, France, 1904, 1910; England, 1906–1914 Agrarian reforms in Russia, 1907–1912
1914	World War I, 1914–1918 Armenian genocide, 1915 Easter Rebellion, 1916 U.S. declares war on Germany, 1917 Bolshevik Revolution, 1917–1918 Treaty of Versailles, 1919	Planned economics in Europe, 1914 Auxiliary Service Law in Germany, 1916 Bread riots in Russia, March 1917
1920	Mussolini seizes power, 1922 Stalin uses forced collectivization, police terror, ca 1929–1939 Hitler gains power, 1933 Rome-Berlin Axis, 1936 Nazi-Soviet Non-Aggression Pact, 1939 World War II, 1939–1945	New Economic Policy in the Soviet Union, 1921 Dawes Plan for reparations and recovery, 1924 The Great Depression, 1929–1939 Rapid industrialization in Soviet Union, 1930s Roosevelt's "New Deal," 1933
1940	United Nations, 1945 Cold war begins, 1947 Fall of colonial empires, 1947–1962 Communist government in China, 1949 Korean War, 1950–1953 "De-Stalinization," 1955–1962	The Holocaust, 1941–1945 Marshall Plan, 1947 European economic progress, ca 1950–1969 European Coal and Steel Community, 1952 European Economic Community, 1957
1960	The Berlin Wall goes up, 1961 United States in Vietnam, ca 1961–1973 Student rebellion in France, 1968 Soviet tanks end Prague Spring, 1968 Détente, 1970s Soviets in Afghanistan, 1979	Civil rights movement in United States, 1960s Collapse of postwar monetary system, 1971 OPEC oil price increases, 1973 and 1979 Stagflation, 1970s Women's movement, 1970s
1980	U.S. military buildup, 1980s Solidarity in Poland, 1980 Unification of Germany, 1989 Revolutions in eastern Europe, 1989–1990 End of Soviet Union, 1991 War in former Yugoslavia, 1991–1995 War in Chechnya, 1991–present	Growth of debt, 1980s Economic crisis in Poland, 1988 Maastricht Treaty proposes monetary union, 1990 European Community becomes European Union, 1993 Migration to western Europe grows, 1990s
2000	Terrorist attack on U.S., Sept. 11, 2001 War in Afghanistan, 2001 War in Iraq, 2003–present	Euro note enters circulation, 2002 Voters reject new constitution for the European Union, 2005 Immigrant riots in France, 2005

Religion and Philosophy	Science and Technology	Arts and Letters
Growth of public education in France, ca 1880–1900 Growth of mission schools in Africa, 1890–1914	Emergence of modern immunology, ca 1875–1900 Trans-Siberian Railroad, 1890s Marie Curie, discovery of radium, 1898 Electrical industry: lighting and streetcars, 1880–1900	Zola, *Germinal,* 1885 Kipling, "The White Man's Burden," 1899
Separation of church and state, France, 1901–1905 Jean-Paul Sartre, 1905–1980	Planck develops quantum theory, ca 1900 First airplane flight, 1903 Einstein develops relativity theory, 1905–1910	"Modernism," ca 1900–1929 Conrad, *Heart of Darkness,* 1902 Cubism in art, ca 1905–1930 Proust, *Remembrance of Things Past,* 1913–1927
Schweitzer, *Quest of the Historical Jesus,* 1906	Submarine warfare, 1915 Ernest Rutherford splits the atom, 1919	Spengler, *The Decline of the West,* 1918
Emergence of modern existentialism, 1920s Wittgenstein, *Essay on Logical Philosophy,* 1922 Revival of Christianity, 1920s and 1930s	"Heroic age of physics," 1920s First major public radio broadcasts in Great Britain and the United States, 1920 Heisenberg, "principle of uncertainty," 1927 Talking movies, 1930 Radar system in England, 1939	Gropius, the Bauhaus, 1920s Dadaism and surrealism, 1920s Woolf, *Jacob's Room,* 1922 Joyce, *Ulysses,* 1922 Eliot, *The Waste Land,* 1922 Remarque, *All Quiet on the Western Front,* 1929 Picasso, *Guernica,* 1937
De Beauvoir, *The Second Sex,* 1949 Communists fail to break Catholic church in Poland, 1950s	Oppenheimer, 1904–1967 "Big Science" in United States, ca 1940–1970 U.S. drops atomic bombs on Japan, 1945 Watson and Crick discover structure of DNA molecule, 1953 Russian satellite in orbit, 1957	Cultural purge in Soviet Union, 1946–1952 Van der Rohe, Lake Shore Apartments, 1948–1951 Orwell, *1984,* 1949 Pasternak, *Doctor Zhivago,* 1956 The "beat" movement in the U.S., late 1950s
Catholic church opposes the legalization of divorce and abortion, 1970 to present Pope John Paul II electrifies Poland, 1979	European Council for Nuclear Research (CERN), 1960 Space race, 1960s Russian cosmonaut first to orbit globe, 1961 American astronaut first person on the moon, 1969	The Beatles, 1960s Solzhenitsyn, *One Day in the Life of Ivan Denisovitch,* 1962 Friedan, *The Feminine Mystique,* 1963 Servan-Schreiber, *The American Challenge,* 1967
Revival of religion in Soviet Union, 1985 to present Fukuyama proclaims "end of history," 1991 Growth of Islam in Europe, 1990s	Reduced spending on Big Science, 1980s Computer revolution continues, 1980s and 1990s U.S. Genome Project begins, 1990 First WWW server/browser, 1991 Pentium processor invented, 1993 "Dolly," first genetically cloned sheep, 1996	Solzhenitsyn returns to Russia, 1994 Author Salman Rushdie is exiled from Iran, 1989 Gehry, Guggenheim Museum, Bilbao, 1997
Ramadan, *Western Muslims and the Future of Islam,* 2004 Conservative elected as Pope Benedict XVI, 2005	Growing concern about global warming, 2000s First hybrid car, 2003	Calatrava, Tenerife Concert Hall, 2003